STATUTORY HISTORY
OF THE
UNITED STATES

CIVIL RIGHTS

STATUTORY HISTORY
OF THE
UNITED STATES

CIVIL RIGHTS
PART I

Editor

Bernard Schwartz

New York University School of Law

CHELSEA HOUSE PUBLISHERS

In Association with

McGRAW-HILL BOOK CO.

New York   Toronto   London   Sydney

Library of Congress Catalog Card Number: 79-78410
ISBN 07–055681–4

PREFACE

Man-made legislation is far older than most people realize. As I write this, I have before me a commemorative cone in which Lipit-Ishtar, King of Isin in ancient Sumeria (twenty-third century B.C.), refers to his promulgation of a law code for Sumer and Akkad. And we know of codes issued even centuries earlier in the ancient world. For all we know, indeed, man the legislator may appear virtually as soon as he displays the characteristics that distinguish him from other species.

At the same time, it is fair to say that not until modern times did legislation begin to play the positive role in ordering the society to which we have become accustomed. The change in this respect is usually associated with the name of Jeremy Bentham. Prodded by his *Philippics* (which make our current diatribes seem bland and amiable), Parliament consciously used its legislative power to regulate the economic, social, and political systems. Statute-law was the main weapon in the Benthamite armory; for the first time, legislation became the great instrument of advance.

During the past century, Benthamism came to the United States—and with a vengeance. And in this country, as in Benthamite Britain, the essential governmental instrument has been statute-law enacted by the national legislature. More and more, acts of Congress have been asserting control over matters formerly deemed outside the range of governmental concern.

The primary place of legislation in the governmental system has made it appropriate to publish the *Statutory History of the United States*. The series will include the principal subjects dealt with by federal legislation. Each volume will contain in historical order the important statutes on the subject covered, as well as their legislative history, including detailed extracts from the congressional debates and other pertinent materials, such as committee reports and Presidential messages. In addition, major Supreme Court decisions which bear upon the history of the statutes will be given. All of these materials will be carefully compiled by the editors of the respective volumes, who will also explain the statutes and their legislative history in commentaries interspersed throughout the volumes.

The *Statutory History* will make available legislative materials that are missing in most libraries. This series will also enable the reader to trace, in workable compass, the legislative history of all important statutes in the fields covered. As such, it should serve as a useful tool which is at present wholly lacking to those interested in law and legislation in this country.

Bernard Schwartz
Edwin D. Webb Professor of Law
New York University
June 1969

CONTENTS

THE ANTI-PEONAGE ACT

THE FOURTEENTH AMENDMENT

THE FIFTEENTH AMENDMENT

THE CIVIL RIGHTS ACT OF 1875

THE 1894 REPEAL OF VOTING RIGHTS LEGISLATION

THE CIVIL RIGHTS ACT OF 1957

THE ORIGINS

THE DEBATE

THE CIVIL RIGHTS ACT OF 1960

THE ORIGINS

THE DEBATE

THE CIVIL RIGHTS ACT OF 1964

THE ORIGINS

INTRODUCTION

EQUALITY AND THE CONSTITUTION

On June 26, 1857, Abraham Lincoln replied to the contention of Stephen A. Douglas that the signers of the Declaration of Independence, in declaring "that all men are created equal," were only "speaking of British subjects on this continent being equal to British subjects born and residing in Great Britain." Lincoln emphatically rejected such contention, saying that "the authors of that notable instrument intended to include *all* men. . . . They meant to set up a standard maxim for free society, which should be familiar to all, and revered by all; constantly looked to, constantly labored for, and even though never perfectly attained, constantly approximated, and thereby constantly spreading and deepening its influence, and augmenting the happiness and value of life to all people of all colors everywhere." The assertion of equality "was placed in the Declaration for future use. . . . I had thought the Declaration contemplated the progressive improvement in the condition of all men everywhere."

In emphasizing the concept of equality as a central theme of the Declaration of Independence—in another address, he referred to it as "the electric cord in that Declaration that links the hearts of patriotic and liberty-loving men together"—Lincoln demonstrated acute perception of the ultimate consequences of the establishment of the United States as an independent political entity. The effort to emphasize the Declaration's great theme of the equality of man has been a dominant driving force in American history since the founding of the Republic itself.

It is true that the framers of the federal Constitution did not repeat the unqualified assertion of the Declaration of Independence in the instrument which they wrote. Nowhere in the organic document drafted in 1787, indeed, is there any guaranty of equality or even any mention of that concept as an essential element of the new polity.

One may go further and say that, to the men who drew up the American Constitution, the notion of equality was one scarcely to be fostered in the organic framework they were creating. A society characterized by equality among men was, in many ways, the opposite of that in which they desired to live. In their thought and action, they sharply distinguished between a democracy and a republic. To them, equality was an extreme democratic concept, inconsistent with and even destructive of the republican institutions they sought to establish.

The eighteenth-century republicans who founded the nation understood equality in terms of equality among those having equal status. Like the constitutionalists of antiquity, they were, in the main, not democrats in the sense of extending the rights and privileges of citizenship to *all* persons. In the early Republic, "slavery still exists; and a large part even of those who are not in economic bondage remains outside the pale of citizenship, disqualified by accidents of birth such as race or sex, and by the lack of sufficient wealth or property which makes it necessary for them to labor in order to live. It is not only an ancient oligarch like Aristotle who thinks that the ruling class should be the owners of property, for they are citizens, and the citizens of a state should be in good circumstances; whereas mechanics should have 'no share in the state.' In the eighteenth century, as well as in ancient Greece, extending the privileges of citizenship to indentured apprentices, day laborers, or journeymen, is a form of radicalism known as 'extreme democracy.' " [Adler, *The Great Ideas; A Syntopicon* 221 (1952).]

Yet, whatever may have been the actual intent of the Founding Fathers, there can be little doubt that their work has served as a catalyst in diffusing the ideals of both liberty and equality throughout the world during the past two centuries. "What Archimedes said of the mechanical powers," wrote Tom Paine in his *Rights of Man*, "may be applied to Reason and Liberty. 'Had we,' said he, 'a place to stand upon, we might raise the world.' The revolution of America presented in politics what was only theory in mechanics."

More than the men who made the Revolution and wrote the Constitution could possibly have foreseen, the twin levers which they furnished to their posterity were precisely those of liberty and equality, which have accomplished in the field of political science virtually what Archimedes posited in that of mechanics.

From the very founding of the nation, as already intimated, the theme of equality has proved a dominant one in American development. If, at the time the framers wrote, the political and economic systems were permeated with inequalities, only a century later James Bryce could declare, "The United States are deemed all the world over to be preeminently the land of equality."

The triumphant march of the concept of equality that has characterized our history as an independent nation is one that became all but inevitable when the framers set up what some of them were already calling a "representative democracy." Real equality is, in Montesquieu's phrase, "the very soul of democracy." The dominant theme in any democratic polity must be the movement to provide equality, as well as liberty, for *all*. In no other form of government is a comparable movement as inevitable, for no other calls *all* men to the privileges as well as the duties of citizenship. Democratic communities, concluded de Tocqueville after his observation of the American democracy, may "have a natural taste for freedom . . . . But for equality their passion is ardent, insatiable, incessant, invincible."

De Tocqueville's conclusion is amply borne out by the course of American development, both before and after his visit to this country. If we look at the early history of American politics from an economic point of view, we may say that, of the two great parties that began to form during Washington's second term, one party might be said to represent wealth, the other numbers.

One party would fear, the other would seek majority rule. From almost the beginning of party history, however, the thrust of political development has been in the direction advocated by the party of numbers. The basic movement in our early political history involved the diffusion of political equality, with the spread of the notion of universal suffrage (at least for free males) and the elimination of property qualifications for the exercise of political rights as its principal concrete accomplishments.

It was under the Jacksonian Democracy that the early movement for political equality reached its climax. But Jackson and his followers did not limit their concern to equality in the political field. Instead, they extended such concern to other fields as well. In particular, they recognized that political democracy itself might be rendered more theoretical than real in the face of gross economic inequality. "It is one of the serious evils of our present system, . . ." asserted Jackson in his 1837 Farewell Address, "that it enables one class of society, and that by no means a numerous one, . . . to act injuriously upon the interests of all the others and to exercise more than its just proportion of influence in political affairs."

To deal with the problem thus posed, the Jacksonian program called for legislation designed to curb corporations, monopolies, and special privileges. For, as Jackson warned, "unless you become more watchful . . . and check this spirit of monopoly and thirst for exclusive privileges, you will, in the end, find that the most important powers of Government have been given or bartered away, and the control over your dearest interests has passed into the hands of these corporations."

However far-reaching the Jacksonian notion of equality might have seemed to its contemporary opponents, it was (by present-day conceptions) actually quite limited. The Jacksonian Democracy might have gone much further than the Founding Fathers in the direction of both political and economic equality; but it, too, in emphasizing the democratic ideal as providing both liberty and equality for all, must be sharply distinguished from the twentieth-century conception of the meaning of the word *all*.

The Jacksonians, like the framers before them, did not carry their concept of equality to the point of extending the rights and privileges of citizenship to *all* members of the community. Like most of their contemporaries, they did not understand the ideal of liberty and equality *for all men* to require the abolition of slavery, the emancipation of women from legal and political subjection, or the eradication of all constitutional discriminations based on wealth, race, or condition of servitude.

Yet, though the Jacksonian concept of equality was, by present-day standards, most limited, one should not underestimate its significance. It was under the Jacksonian aegis that there was achieved the first great egalitarian revolution, without which the subsequent progress made in that field would hardly have been possible. Even if we realize that the Jacksonian Democracy was scarcely intended to be as radically democratic as its contemporaries feared, we must still recognize that it made substantial contributions to both the theory and practice of equality.

When the occasion demanded it, indeed, the Jacksonians could eloquently articulate the concept of equality and the premises upon which it was based. "In the full enjoyment of the gifts of Heaven and the fruits of superior industry, economy, and virtue," declared Jackson in his famous 1832 veto of the bill rechartering the Bank of the United States, "every man is equally entitled to protection by law; but when the laws undertake to add to these natural and just advantages artificial distinctions, to grant titles, gratuities, and exclusive privileges, to make the rich richer, and the potent more powerful, the humble members of society—the farmers, mechanics, and laborers—who have neither the time nor the means of securing like favors to themselves, have a right to complain of the injustice of their Government. . . .

"If it would confine itself to equal protection, and, as Heaven does its rains, shower its favors alike on the high and the low, the rich and the poor, it would be an unqualified blessing."

In the Jackson message there is a statement, in positive terms, of the equal right of all persons to the equal protection of equal laws in terms that are comparable to the negative version in the Fourteenth Amendment which was adopted over thirty-five years later.

Post-Civil War Amendments

It was the Fourteenth Amendment's equal protection clause that, for the first time on a national level, elevated the concept of equality to the constitutional plane. As Justice Arthur Goldberg has pointed out, it may seem strange that, prior to the ratification of that amendment, the Constitution did not expressly mention equality. It was, however, scarcely feasible for the organic document to seek to guarantee something that was so contrary to the reality of the society in which it was written. This was true even with the diffusion of the concept of equality that was the great achievement of the Jacksonian Democracy. Even the Jacksonian conception of equality, we saw, was most restricted; it did not include Negroes or women and was consequently not really contrary to the Aristotelian notion of the inherent inequality of the person.

It was the institution of slavery in particular that rendered a constitutional guaranty of equality inappropriate. Slavery was the great gap in the principles upon which the Republic had been based. "In sum, then," Justice Goldberg tells us, "the Constitution . . . while heralding liberty, in effect declared all men to be free and equal—except black men, who were to be neither free nor equal. This inconsistency reflected a fundamental departure from the American creed, a departure which it took a civil war to set right." [39 *New York University Law Review* 205 (1964).]

With the Emancipation Proclamation (January 1, 1863) and the post-Civil War amendments, the situation in this respect was completely altered. To quote Justice Goldberg again, "With adoption of the Thirteenth, Fourteenth, and Fifteenth Amendments to the Constitution freedom and equality were expressly guaranteed to all—regardless of 'race, color, or previous condition of servitude.' These amendments cleared the way for our 'new kind of society—fresh, equal, just, open, free, and forever respectful of conscience.' "

With slavery and lesser forms of involuntary servitude abolished, the American system had repudiated the heresy that (as Lincoln once expressed it) "all men are created equal, except Negroes." It was no longer inconsistent with reality for the Constitution to contain an express guaranty of equality. Such guaranty was added to the organic document in the Fourteenth Amendment's categorical provision: "nor shall any State . . . deny to any person within its jurisdiction the equal protection of the laws."

To one interested in civil rights, the legislative history of the subject really starts with the post-Civil War amendments. As just stated, it was those amendments that expressly made the concept of equality a constitutional one. That in turn made it possible for the Congress to enact civil rights legislation, under the power vested in it by the amendments to enforce their provisions "by appropriate legislation." The subject of the present volume thus has its direct genesis in the Thirteenth, Fourteenth, and Fifteenth Amendments.

The post-Civil War amendments (ratified in 1865, 1868, and 1870) constituted the first changes in the constitutional text in over sixty years. The Thirteenth Amendment was plainly necessary to resolve the unsatisfactory status of slavery. But mere abolition of slavery was scarcely enough to vest the Negro with anything like the civil status of others in the community. The Fourteenth Amendment was needed to provide for equality of the races in the possession of fundamental civil rights. The Fifteenth Amendment completed the picture by giving the Negro the right of suffrage, which is the primary attribute of effective citizenship.

It is the first section of the Fourteenth Amendment that deals specifically with the question of civil rights. It was intended to have two principal effects. The first was to sweep away the *Dred Scott* decision [*Scott* v. *Sandford,* 19 How. 393 (1857)] barring citizenship for the Negro. "All persons born or naturalized in the United States . . . ," it reads, "are citizens [both] of the United States and of the State wherein they reside."

In addition, the intent was to make it illegal for the states to deny equal civil rights to those thus made citizens. The Negro was to be given the protection of due process and equality before the law. Hence, the provision that no state was to "deprive any person of life, liberty, or property without due process of law" or to "deny any person within its jurisdiction the equal protection of the laws." These two clauses—the due process clause and the equal protection clause—of the Fourteenth Amendment were to transform the American constitutional system completely. Much of the stuff of our constitutional law in the century that has followed has, in truth, been in the nature of mere gloss upon those two pregnant provisions.

It should not be forgotten that in our early history the Bill of Rights itself was of little practical effect as a restraint upon governmental power. It should be noted, in the first place, that the first amendments were applicable only as restrictions upon the federal government. So the Supreme Court had held in one of John Marshall's last important opinions—delivered in the 1833 case of *Barron* v. *Mayor of Baltimore,* 7 Pet. 243—and its decision to that effect was never questioned. This meant that the federal Constitution was, prior to the Civil War, of small moment as a curb against state infringements upon individual rights, except for the limitations upon state power (notably the contract clause) contained in Article I, section 10.

In the actual operation of the constitutional system, during the early years of the Republic, there was little occasion for application of the guaranties contained in the Bill of Rights against the federal government. That was the case because there were then relatively few interferences from Washington with the personal and property rights of the individual. It is true that the danger of abridgment of such rights has always existed at the state and local levels. Until the Civil War, nevertheless, it was felt that such danger could be dealt with adequately through enforcement by the states of their own organic guaranties.

It was after the Civil War that demand arose for national protection against alleged abuses of state power. The Civil War itself clearly marked a crucial turning point in American development, the true import of which we are only now beginning to comprehend. "The Civil War," says Bruce Catton, "is the thing that makes America different. It was our most tremendous experience." As such, it was bound to have significant constitutional, as well as other, effects. By far the most important of these was the inclusion in the Constitution of the guaranties contained in the post-Civil War amendments, particularly the Fourteenth Amendment. It was those amendments which made the protection of life, liberty, and property a national responsibility— federalizing, as it were, the vindication of individual rights throughout the land.

The adoption of the postbellum amendments plainly marks an epoch in the constitutional history of the nation. Like the victory of the North during the war itself, they constituted the culmination of the nationalistic theory that had first taken root eighty years earlier in Philadelphia.

From the founding of the Republic to the end of the Civil War, it was the states which were the primary guardians of the rights and liberties of their citizens, and they alone could determine the character and extent of such rights and liberties. That was true because the federal Bill of Rights, as has been emphasized, was binding upon the federal government alone—not the states. As far as the federal Constitution was concerned, the states were free to encroach upon individual rights as they chose, except for the comparatively minor restrictions contained in the contract and ex post facto clauses.

With the adoption of the postbellum amendments, all this was changed. Those amendments called upon the national government to protect the citizens of a state against the state itself. Thenceforth, the safeguarding of personal and property rights was to become primarily a federal function.

Before the firing on Fort Sumter (April 12, 1861), the great theme in American constitutional history was the nation-state problem. Nation and states all too often appeared to confront each other as equals, and all was overshadowed by the danger that centrifugal forces would tear the nation apart.

Appomattox put an end to such danger. From then on, the Union was, as the Supreme Court itself put it, in *Texas* v. *White*, 7 Wall. 700 (1869), "indestructible" and the supremacy of federal power was ensured. The law could now turn from the federal-state problem to the constitutional issues posed by the new amendments. The focus of constitutional concern could be transferred from the protection of federal power to the safe-guarding of individual rights against governmental power.

Reconstruction Legislation

From a legal point of view, the post-Civil War amendments have two aspects. In the first place, they contain self-executing prohibitions protecting civil rights which lay down rules of decision to be enforced by the courts. Thus, the Thirteenth Amendment of its own force outlaws all forms of slavery and involuntary servitude; the Fourteenth Amendment similarly strikes down all "state action" which denies due process or equal protection; the Fifteenth Amendment, in like manner, automatically puts an end to all state attempts to restrict the franchise on racial grounds. It is the self-executing aspect of the amendments that have made possible the many cases that have been brought directly under them, particularly to secure judicial enforcement of the Fourteenth Amendment's guaranties.

But the framers of the postbellum amendments recognized that direct judicial enforcement of their prohibitions alone might not be enough to secure the goal of civil equality for the emancipated race. Hence, they provided specifically for legislative, as well as judicial, enforcement. Each of the amendments contains an express grant to the Congress of authority to enforce its provisions "by appropriate legislation." These enforcement clauses have been the constitutional source of the civil rights statutes enacted by Congress, which form the subject matter of most of the present volumes.

Chronologically, the civil rights laws enacted by Congress fall into two groups. First of all, there were the statutes enacted during the Reconstruction period as part of the Radical Republican program. These Reconstruction statutes (from the Civil Rights Act of 1866 to that of 1875) were, like the amendments upon which they were based, intended to ensure the possession by the emancipated Negro of all the civil rights vested in other citizens.

The civil rights laws of the Reconstruction period were, as we shall see, far-reaching (though we can adopt a much more tolerant attitude toward them today, in view of the recent spate of comparable federal legislation, than might have been the case not too long ago). The Reconstruction laws had two main goals. The first was to ensure enforcement of the Fifteenth Amendment, for it was seen that protection of the right to vote was the key to the securing of civil rights for the Negro. The statutes enacted sought to secure Negro voting, both by express criminal prohibitions and by setting up independent federal enforcement machinery to ensure affirmative vindication of the right to vote. In addition, the Reconstruction laws sought to protect other civil rights, by providing sanctions to deter infringements upon the civil rights guaranteed by the Constitution or federal law, and by providing affirmatively for equality in public accommodations. The latter purpose motivated the passage of the Civil Rights Act of 1875, which constituted the culmination of the Reconstruction laws in the field of civil rights.

It has become all but constitutional cliché that the Reconstruction statutes did not succeed in their goal of securing equality in civil rights for the Negro. In part that was true because of the decisions of the Supreme Court in the *Slaughter–House Cases* (*infra* p. 335) and the *Civil Rights Cases* (*infra* p. 780). It can scarcely be denied that the high-bench decisions did nullify some of the key measures of the Reconstruction Congress, notably the 1875 Civil Rights Act provisions. Yet, as will be seen, the decisions themselves were far from the usurpations of judicial power that critics have contended.

More important, the Supreme Court decisions were but an indication of the general disenchantment with the Reconstruction program. A decade after Appomattox, most of the nation was all too willing to forgive and forget; the civil rights laws that were not invalidated by the Court were either repealed by Congress itself or remained a dead letter on the statute book.

By the turn of the century, "equal protection" had become reduced to the status of a mere slogan for the Negro. It is true that the Thirteenth Amendment had abolished slavery itself, and the Fifteenth Amendment had stricken from state laws all provisions overtly limiting suffrage to whites. But the incidents of slavery remained in the system of discrimination against the former slave that developed, and devices were speedily resorted to (such as the "white primary") to defeat the intent of the Fifteenth Amendment. The situation became that described to James Bryce by a leading Southern politician: "We like the Negro, and we treat him well. We mean to continue doing so. But we vote him."

With regard to the Fourteenth Amendment, the situation was even worse.

The failure of the Reconstruction statutes to implement effectively the amendment's guaranty of equality led directly to "the familiar system of racial segregation in both public and private institutions which cuts across the daily lives of southern citizens from the cradle to the grave." [*Report of the President's Committee on Civil Rights*, 79 (1947).] Jim Crow replaced equal protection and legally enforced segregation became the dominant fact in southern life.

The paradoxical result was that, though the post-Civil War amendments did work a veritable constitutional revolution, until recently they had little effect upon civil rights. Instead, when the amendments began to be given effect as restraints upon state power, their impact was almost entirely confined to the economic sphere. When the Supreme Court came over to the view that the Fourteenth Amendment (and especially its due process clause) was intended to work an essential change in the organic framework, its decisions on the matter all but limited the change effected to the area of property rights. Such limitation may have been understandable in an era of explosive industrial expansion, which so drastically altered the whole social and economic fabric. In such an era, it was not unnatural for the dominant emphasis to be placed upon the proper relationship between government and business. To the law, as to the society which it mirrored, the danger that state sovereignty would impair the power of the nation was replaced by the danger that government would unduly impede industry in its destined economic conquest of a continent. The result was that the Fourteenth Amendment was converted into a Magna Carta for business, in place of the Great Charter for civil rights which its framers had intended.

Recent Civil Rights Laws

The situation just described remained unchanged for the better part of a century. From 1875 to 1957, the federal legislator was silent in the field of civil rights. It was not until our own day, indeed, that civil rights again became an important part of the congressional program. Yet it must be admitted that, if the Congress remained inactive in the field of civil rights for so long, it has done much to restore the balance by its recent spate of activity. From 1957 to 1968, five civil rights statutes were passed, including two (those of 1964 and 1965) as far-reaching as those enacted in the Reconstruction period, and a third (that of 1968) dealing with an area which even the Reconstruction laws had not dared to enter.

What makes the recent governmental activity in civil rights of particular interest is the fact that it was stimulated by that branch which is normally the least noted for transforming innovation. It is not unfair to say that the mid-twentieth century revolution in the field of civil rights has been that rarest of all political animals—a judge-led revolution. For it can scarcely be denied that the great catalyst in the contemporary effort to secure civil rights has been the Supreme Court decisions, starting with *Brown* v. *Board of Education* (*infra* p. 361), the landmark 1954 decision outlawing school segregation. The *Brown* decision was as consequential as any ever handed down by a court, for it will ultimately have an impact as drastic as that of any political revolution or war itself.

But it took more than the Supreme Court alone to prod the other branches into action. What was necessary was a rousing of the national conscience in a manner that would lead to an overwhelming demand for legislation to fulfill the promise of over a century.

The needed appeal to the nation's conscience was made by the civil rights movement, which had come to life in response to the hope generated in Negroes themselves by the Supreme Court decisions. Using the techniques of nonviolent protest, the civil rights demonstrators soon dramatized the moral issues involved and focused the attention of the country on the illegal resistance of the South to vindication of the rights so plainly decreed in the Constitution itself. The result was a massive demand for correction, growing in intensity as racial incidents multiplied, which all but forced the legislative and executive branches into action.

The present-day governmental concern with civil rights has differed from that of the post-Civil War period because, apart from the Supreme Court, it is not unfair to say that the government has not led, but followed, the nation. As a consequence, the governmental efforts were, at first at least, unsure and ineffective. This was particularly true of the steps taken by Congress. As will be seen, the first civil rights laws passed since 1875—those of 1957 and 1960—were, despite all the oratory and exaggerated hopes and fears engendered by them, relatively innocuous measures. But the increasing militancy of the Negro protest movement, and the intransigence which it continued to meet, soon convinced both the executive and legislative branches that much more was necessary. Presidential blandness on the civil rights issue gave way in 1963 to leadership which induced the Congress to enact the most far-reaching civil rights laws (those of 1964, 1965, and 1968) since Reconstruction days.

Three of the recent civil rights statutes (those of 1957, 1960, and 1965) deal almost entirely with voting rights. They seek to secure to the Negro the practical implementation of the Fifteenth Amendment's guaranty, which had for too long been but a word of promise to the ear only to be broken to the hope. The 1964 act also has a title on voting rights. But the most important provisions of that law cover subjects other than voting. The key sections of the 1964 statute are aimed at discrimination in public accommodations, employment, and federally assisted programs. As such, they constitute a veritable Great Charter in the field of civil rights—one which, for the first time, lays a suitable legal foundation for the edifice of full racial equality that must ultimately be constructed.

Retrospect And Prospect

"Popular governments," once wrote John Jay, the first Chief Justice of the United States, "must be influenced by popular opinion, and popular opinion must be *created* not commanded. It is a kind of *creation* too which can proceed but slowly, because often opposed by Prejudices, Ignorances, clashing Interests, and . . . illfounded Jealousies." [Unpublished letter to Reverend D. Price, August 24, 1775.]

The history of the Reconstruction attempts to secure civil rights well supports the validity of the Jay observation. So far as we can tell a century later, the 1866-75 civil rights laws were not a result of popular demand. Instead, they were all but forced through Congress by the Radical Republican leadership in the face of, at first, public apathy, and then a widespread desire to forgive and forget vis-à-vis the defeated South. Without real public understanding and support, it was almost inevitable that the congressional momentum would soon lose force. As it turned out, within a decade the country began to repudiate the Republican leadership, and not long after the whole postbellum civil rights program was laid in legislative limbo.

The situation has been entirely different in connection with the recent outburst of congressional civil rights activity. With regard to the 1957–68 statutes, as has been emphasized, the Congress has not led, so much as followed, the nation. The recent laws have been induced by popular opinion, which has been (in Jay's terms) created from below, not commanded from above. As such, they have had the popular support which was lacking in the Reconstruction period.

In addition, there is the vital factor of judicial support. Whether rightly or wrongly, much of the Reconstruction legislation (notably the 1875 Civil Rights Act) was frustrated by the decisions of the Supreme Court. Here, too, the situation today is entirely different. As already indicated, the Supreme Court has been in the very forefront of the current civil rights activity. From the first cases under the recent civil rights statutes, it has indicated that it would look at such laws with anything but a hostile eye. The Court has not only upheld even the most far-reaching of the recent statutes (such as the 1964 and 1965 Acts), it has given clear indication that it would similarly support congressional action which went even further (as by the opinions in *United States* v. *Guest, infra.* p. 791).

Yet, with all that has been said, the 1969 observer cannot help but note a malaise in the civil rights field, both in the Congress and the nation, which makes one wonder whether we are not, in fact, currently living through a second Reconstruction period. Already there are signs, on and off Capitol Hill, that the nation has begun to lose its pressing concern with civil rights. In this field particularly, the loss of momentum may well foreshadow a demise of governmental activity comparable to that which occurred after 1875.

The post-1965 hiatus in congressional activity is most disturbing to one familiar with the fate of the Reconstruction civil rights laws. At the same time, we must not make the mistake of concluding that the fate of the earlier civil rights program must necessarily be duplicated in our own day. All we can say with assurance is to repeat what Camus said, "As the wheel turns, history changes." To assume, however, that history not only changes but that it must necessarily repeat itself, is to make an error as stifling as it is shortsighted.

In assessing the impact of the recent governmental interest in the civil rights field, particularly the 1957–68 statutes and the Supreme Court decisions, we must never forget the crucial role of the law in a system such as ours. Discrimination against the Negro could never have had the effect it did without the condonation of the legal order. The consent of the courts was necessary for the subordinate status of the Negro to be of more than extralegal consequence.

But now, with the recent Supreme Court decisions and civil rights statutes, the legal prop has been removed. To be sure, such removal may not reach the heart of the problem—the feelings of racial prejudice which have roots deeper than the actions of legislatures and courts. Yet, though the removal of legal condonation will not necessarily abate predilections and prejudices, it cannot be denied that there is a vast difference between restrictions imposed upon Negroes by the State and the refusal of individuals to act in a nondiscriminatory manner. It was the fact that Jim Crow had behind it the force of the law that made it of such moment to the southern Negro. It is because they eliminate the legal sanction that the recent decisions and laws in the field of civil rights have been so important. Outside the legal pale, racial discrimination itself can hardly continue indefinitely to be of such widespread consequence.

Materials Used

Finally, a word about the materials used in these volumes. The intent has been to present, in chronological order, the federal legislation in the field of civil rights—from the Thirteenth Amendment through the Civil Rights Act of 1968. For that purpose, the primary source materials are, of course, the congressional debates themselves. Hence, most of these volumes consist of extracts from the Senate and House debates on the different enactments covered, as they were reported in the *Congressional Globe* and the *Congressional Record*. In addition, materials have been inserted from relevant committee reports and presidential messages, as well as Supreme Court decisions which explain or illustrate the application of the different legislative measures.

It should be emphasized that the materials used have been carefully edited. A literal mass of congressional and other materials have been digested to the size of two workable volumes. Of course, there is danger of arbitrary inclusion and exclusion in such a process, and not all will agree with the editor's choice of what to use and what to leave out of the volumes. At the least, however, the reader can be assured that the selections are the nondelegated choices of the editor himself, who conscientiously addressed himself personally to all the legislative debates and other materials used.

Insofar as the congressional extracts themselves are concerned, it will be noted that, in the earlier enactments, use is made almost entirely of the debates on the floors of the two houses, while in the more recent laws, committee reports have been given greater emphasis. That is true for two main reasons. In the first place, there is the ever increasing resort by the courts to legislative history as a necessary aid in interpreting the meaning of laws. That, in turn, has led congressional committees to prepare reports which seek to explain in detail the provisions of bills reported on by them. Such reports often contain the best indication of legislative intent behind statutes enacted by Congress.

Even more important perhaps to explain the shift from debates to committee reports is the drastic decline in the caliber of the congressional debate during the present century. Such decline is certainly the outstanding impression of one who has had to plow through the mass of materials involved in preparing these volumes. A century ago, the speeches in the Senate and House were real contributions to an understanding of the issues underlying the legislation debated. There were then orators in both chambers whose addresses it is a pleasure to read even now. If there are some disappointments (thus, Charles Sumner's speeches scarcely support his oratorical reputation, making one wonder if he was only the Everett Dirksen of his day), by and large the level of debate was surprisingly high—though no higher perhaps than the country had a right to expect from the heirs of Madison and Webster.

This has all changed during the present century. The most important role of the Congress, declared Woodrow Wilson in his now-classical study *Congressional Government*, is to provide "the instruction and guidance . . . which the people might receive from a body which kept all national concerns suffused in a broad daylight of discussion." In the Wilson conception, the legislative assembly is even more vital as a molder than as a receptacle of public opinion. Its job in this respect is to enlighten and educate by insuring adequate discussion of the significant issues before the nation.

One who has the dreary task of reading the contemporary *Congressional Record* cannot help but conclude that the Congress in recent years has fallen far short of the Wilson conception of its role. The level of debate on the civil rights laws enacted during the past decade has been egregiously low. Intellectually speaking, indeed, instead of the center of enlightenment envisaged by Wilson, Capitol Hill has presented the sorry spectacle of a "seat of desolation, void of light." [1 Milton, *Paradise Lost* 181.] The congressional mode of operation today is scarcely one to give confidence to those who believe in representative government and seek to preserve it as a flourishing institution even in a nuclear age. An observer of the contemporary Congress may well wonder whether it alone will avoid the history of similar assemblies which have brought ruin upon the State or sunk under the burden of its own imbecility.

THE THIRTEENTH AMENDMENT

Commentary

The very notion of civil rights itself can scarcely have practical meaning when there is no constitutional guaranty of freedom in its most elementary sense—freedom from slavery and involuntary servitude. Present-day discussions of constitutional right tend to ignore such guaranty as one which is all but inherent in the very nature of things: to us, the indefensible nature of slavery as a moral and historical anachronism is self-evident.

To all too many men a century ago, the situation was altogether different. Even Lord Acton, though he did later become an apostle of liberty, could write soon after the firing on Fort Sumter (April 12, 1861), "It is as impossible to sympathize on religious grounds with the categorical prohibition of slavery as, on political grounds, with the opinions of the abolitionists."

The situation with regard to slavery was, of course, completely changed by the Civil War, the Emancipation Proclamation (January 1, 1863), and the Thirteenth Amendment (December 18, 1865). Nor should we make the mistake of minimizing what was accomplished in this respect.

From a constitutional point of view, the freeing of the slaves was a measure that must be considered revolutionary in nature. It converted the War between the States into a second American Revolution. Slavery had been the great lacuna in the rule of freedom and equality upon which the Republic had been based—the living lie in the American heritage. While the institution continued, the gulf between ideals and reality remained so wide as to smack of hypocrisy. A constitutional ideal divided against itself also could not stand.

Now, with Lincoln's Proclamation and the Thirteenth Amendment, the picture was completely transformed. From this point of view there can scarcely be any question about the immediate purpose of the Thirteenth Amendment. It was added to the basic document to place the constitutional seal upon the Emancipation Proclamation and, by so doing, to consign any dispute over its legality to the realm of purely academic controversy. The Emancipation Proclamation itself had been issued by Lincoln as a war measure. If it had a constitutional basis, it was in the war powers of the President as Commander-in-chief. This was the basis articulated in the proclamation, which declared that it was issued "by virtue of the power in me vested as Commander-in-chief of the Army and Navy. . . and as a fit and necessary war measure."

If emancipation was to be more than a war measure, lasting only as long as the military necessity that called it forth, it had to be elevated to the constitutional plane. Such elevation was accomplished by the Thirteenth Amendment. With its adoption, the notion that a human being could be relegated to the legal status of mere property was repudiated as constitutional heresy. Thenceforth, the principles embodied in the Declaration of Inde-

19

pendence and the Bill of Rights could be translated into actuality. The nation could, in Lincoln's phrase, "return to the fountain whose waters spring close by the blood of the Revolution."

It is true that mere emancipation could not of itself invest the former slave with complete equality. The Civil War gave the Negro constitutional status similar to that of his former master, but it could not and did not give him the moral status in the sight of the white community that was needed to make his freedom workable. For a century thereafter, indeed, the Negro race was placed in the position of second-class citizens. But a second-class citizen, as the experience in our own day is showing, may hope to become something better. The same can scarcely be true of one considered by society and the law to have only the attributes of a chattel.

AMENDMENT XIII

Proposed: February 1, 1865
Ratified: December 18, 1865

SEC. 1. Neither slavery nor involuntary servitude, except as a punishment for crime whereof the party shall have been duly convicted, shall exist within the United States, or any place subject to their jurisdiction.

SEC. 2. Congress shall have power to enforce this article by appropriate legislation.

THE ORIGINS

THE EMANCIPATION PROCLAMATION
January 1, 1863

Whereas on the 22d day of September, A.D. 1862, a proclamation was issued by the President of the United States, containing, among other things, the following, to wit:

"That on the 1st day of January, A.D. 1863, all persons held as slaves within any State or designated part of a State the people whereof shall then be in rebellion against the United States shall be then, thenceforward, and forever free; and the executive government of the United States, including the military and naval authority thereof, will recognize and maintain the freedom of such persons and will do no act or acts to repress such persons, or any of them, in any efforts they may make for their actual freedom.

"That the executive will on the 1st day of January aforesaid, by proclamation, designate the States and parts of States, if any, in which the people thereof, respectively, shall then be in rebellion against the United States; and the fact that any State or the people thereof shall on that day be in good faith represented in the Congress of the United States by members chosen thereto at elections wherein a majority of the qualified voters of such States shall have participated shall, in the absence of strong countervailing testimony, be deemed conclusive evidence that such State and the people thereof are not then in rebellion against the United States."

Now, therefore, I, Abraham Lincoln, President of the United States, by virtue of the power in me vested as Commander-in-Chief of the Army and Navy of the United States in time of actual armed rebellion against the authority and government of the United States, and as a fit and necessary war measure for suppressing said rebellion, do, on this 1st day of January, A.D. 1863, and in accordance with my purpose so to do, publicly proclaimed for the full period of one hundred days from the first day above mentioned, order and designate as the States and parts of States wherein the people thereof, respectively, are this day in rebellion against the United States the following, to wit:

Arkansas, Texas, Louisiana (except the parishes of St. Bernard, Plaquemines, Jefferson, St. John, St. Charles, St. James, Ascension, Assumption, Terrebonne, Lafourche, St. Mary, St. Martin, and Orleans, including the city of New Orleans), Mississippi, Alabama, Florida, Georgia, South Carolina, North Carolina, and Virginia (except the forty-eight counties designated as West Virginia, and also the counties of Berkeley, Accomac, Northhampton, Elizabeth City, York, Princess Anne, and Norfolk, including the cities of Norfolk and Portsmouth), and which excepted parts are for the present left precisely as if this proclamation were not issued.

And by virtue of the power and for the purpose aforesaid, I do order and declare that all persons held as slaves within said designated States and parts of States are, and henceforward shall be, free; and that the Executive Government of the United States, including the military and naval authorities thereof, will recognize and maintain the freedom of said persons.

And I hereby enjoin upon the people so declared to be free to abstain from all violence, unless in necessary self-defense; and I recommend to them that, in all cases when allowed, they labor faithfully for reasonable wages.

And I further declare and make known that such persons of suitable condition will be received into the armed service of the United States to garrison forts, positions, stations, and other places, and to man vessels of all sorts in said service.

And upon this act, sincerely believed to be an act of justice, warranted by the Constitution upon military necessity, I invoke the considerate judgment of mankind and the gracious favor of Almighty God.

Commentary

The congressional debates bear out what has been said above about the overriding purpose of the Thirteenth Amendment—to "obliterate the last lingering vestiges of the slave system." (Representative James Wilson [R., Iowa]) It was then recognized, as Senator Lyman Trumbull [R., Ill.], the sponsor of the amendment in the Senate, points out, that even opponents of slavery doubted the authority of the government to interfere with it. The amendment was intended to resolve all such doubts, for none could deny the power to amend the Constitution in the mode prescribed or to proscribe slavery through the amending process. The debate extracts which follow show plainly that the amendment was intended as the constitutional confirmation of the Emancipation Proclamation. Though slavery was dead in all areas controlled by Union troops, it was necessary to provide for its permanent disappearance from the American scene—something which could be completely accomplished by the proposed amendment.

It should, however, be pointed out that there are indications in the congressional debates that more than the abolition of slavery alone may have been intended by the men who wrote the Thirteenth Amendment. As is seen in the speech of Senator James Harlan [R., Iowa], they may have intended to abolish, not only the institution of slavery itself, but also "the necessary incidents of slavery." From this point of view, the amendment was intended not only to emancipate but also to secure to the former slave his full civil rights and especially (as is best indicated in the address of Senator Charles Sumner [R., Mass.]) his right to equality before the law.

Yet if the framers of the Thirteenth Amendment had really intended to do more than merely do away with slavery, the language which they used was plainly inadequate to accomplish such broader purpose. The amendment speaks only of "slavery" and "involuntary servitude" as outlawed—words taken directly from the Northwest Ordinance of 1787, and which by themselves are hardly enough to guarantee equality before the law and other civil rights to all persons in this country. In fact (as will be seen in the material on the Civil Rights Act of 1866, *infra* p. 97), the notion that the Thirteenth Amendment did more than abolish slavery was rejected by many of the congressional leaders themselves. Certainly, the very adoption of the Fourteenth Amendment (June 16, 1866, *infra* p. 184) was based upon just such a rejection. Further constitutional change was deemed necessary to eliminate specific appendages of slavery, such as lack of legal personality or protection, and to extend civil rights to the enfranchised race, as well as to all other persons in the community.

The debates on the Thirteenth Amendment took place in the House and Senate in the spring of 1864 and in the House in January, 1865. The amendment was voted overwhelmingly by the Senate (38 to 6) on April 8, 1864, but failed to secure the necessary two-thirds majority in the House, which voted (93 to 65) on June 15. After the 1864 presidential election, Lincoln came out in full support of the amendment, and the House reconsidered its vote and, on January 31, 1865, voted its concurrence, 112 to 57. Ratification by the states was completed on December 6, 1865, and the Thirteenth Amendment was certified as part of the Constitution on December 18, 1865.

The debates themselves opened with the speech of Representative Wilson in the House and Senator Trumbull in the Senate. Their addresses well illustrate the views expressed by supporters of the amendment, though the speeches of other supporters (notably Senators Wilson and Harlan) are also of interest. Apart from extreme opponents like Congressman Fernando Wood [Dem., N.Y.], who still defended the slavery institution, those who resisted the proposed amendment did so on states' rights grounds. They opposed the expansion of federal power and diminution of state authority involved in a national prohibition. Looking back, however, we can see that the Thirteenth Amendment was only the beginning of the movement to federalize civil rights which has been a dominant theme of post-Civil War constitutional development. Still to come were the other postbellum amendments, as well as their implementation by Congress and courts—a process that is still going on at the present time.

THE DEBATE

House of Representatives-38th Congress, 1st Session
March 19-June 15, 1864

JAMES WILSON [R., IOWA]. Mr. Chairman, on the first day of the present session of Congress I gave notice of my intention to introduce a joint resolution submitting to the Legislatures of the several States a proposition to amend the Constitution of the United States. On a subsequent day, in pursuance of the notice thus given, I introduced and had referred to the Committee on the Judiciary the following joint resolution:

Be it resolved by the Senate and House of Representatives of the United States of America in Congress assembled (two thirds of both Houses concurring,) That the following article be proposed to the Legislatures of the several States as an amendment to the Constitution of the United States, which, when ratified by three fourths of said Legislatures, shall be valid, to all intents and purposes, as a part of said Constitution, namely:

ARTICLE XIII

SEC. 1. Slavery, being incompatible with a free Government, is forever prohibited in the United States; and involuntary servitude shall be permitted only as a punishment for crime.

SEC. 2. Congress shall have power to enforce the foregoing section of this article by appropriate legislation.

I am well aware, sir, that a proposition in the Congress of the United States to so amend the Constitution of the Republic as to weaken or destroy slavery is a novel thing. With bills, resolutions, and propositions to amend the Constitution to more firmly establish, extend, and perpetuate slavery the country has been perfectly familiar. It was long the custom in this body, whenever slavery became excited and angry, to try to appease its wrath by offering it some new hold on the life of the nation, some greater advantage over free government and human liberty. When slavery cried "Give, give," by force of habit and loss of conscience we always responded by offering more than it demanded of us. We were the slaves of the slave power.

When slavery became a political power, and held in its hands the rewards which ambition covets, the nation became its most cringing, fawning, stupidly debased slave; and a most cruel task-master it proved. Its political career was an incessant, unrelenting, aggressive warfare upon the principles of the Government, the objects for which the Constitution was ordained, the rights of the people, the development of national resources, the advancement of education, the establishment of public morals, and the purity of religion. It touched everything, defiled everything. And we submitted quietly, tamely, cowardly, while the work of destruction and death was carried on by this insatiable enemy of all that is lovely, desirable, just, and sacred. No political

25

power, whether found in republics or despotisms, ever wielded so baneful an influence on the affairs of nations or men as the one to which we so passively submitted, and under whose shadow we so fearfully dwarfed. Its progress was a constant, crushing dead march over everything which stood in the way of its own aggrandizement; and everything desirable to a free people stood in its way. The nation grew stupid under the manipulations of slavery, and seemed to know but little, and to care less, of the danger which threatened the free institutions of the country with destruction.

The public opinion now existing in this country in opposition to this power is the result of slavery overleaping itself, rather than of the determination of freemen to form it. But, however formed, thank God it is formed, and is our priceless possession of real, active, national life, never to be surrendered. We must hold all we have gained, and add to the strength of public opinion by daring to do our duty as if in the immediate presence of Him who directs the destinies of nations. We may now talk of freedom, act for it, legislate for it, and above all other acts we may place one which shall stamp universal freedom on our national Constitution, never to be erased, never to die while the Republic lives. To accomplish this great end I introduced the joint resolution to which I have alluded, and I believe its passage is desired by the truly loyal people of the country almost without an exception.

In preparing the resolution I was careful to present but one issue, the incompatibility of slavery with a free Government. This issue is no reflection on the wise and good men who laid the firm foundations and fashioned the sublime architecture of our Constitution. They entertained not the remotest idea that they were tolerating a tenant in the grand structure which would, when warmed into life and developed into the form of a political power, endeavor to tear down the altars of liberty, and erect in their stead a throne of absolutism and death. The oft-expressed and universally understood views of the fathers fully attest that they regarded this tenant as the thing to be tolerated only because it promised speedy dissolution. They found it in the house they were erecting for the protection of themselves and their children, looked upon it with horror, and left it to die, never suspecting the dreadful power it embodied. Surrounded by the grand teachings of a successful war, based upon principles utterly destructive of slavery if enforced, they looked forward to the death of the latter by the mere development and power of the former. They believed in the incompatibility of slavery with a free Government; but they regarded the latter to be the stronger, not yet having had experience with slavery as a political power. These reasons will account in great part for the absence from the Constitution of a section prohibiting slavery. It is impossible to believe that the master-workmen who gave to us this best of human Governments in the least degree suspected that they were transmitting with it the seeds of dissolution. They believed their work secure from molestation by this tolerated thing which all good men loathed and expected to see pass speedily away. In this they were mistaken, as we have discovered to our deepest sorrow and infinite cost. But their wisdom provided the means for overruling the disastrous consequences of their mistake. The Constitution which they formed, and which the people ordained and established, contains ample provisions for accomplishing the destruction of that power which so long disturbed the tranquility of the nation, and finally enveloped us in the whirling, leaping, encircling red flame of war. The fifth article of the Constitution of the United States reads as follows:

Congress, whenever two thirds of both Houses shall deem it necessary, shall propose amendments to this Constitution, or, on the application of the Legislatures of two thirds of the several States, shall call a convention for proposing amendments, which, in either case, shall be valid to all intents and purposes, as part of this Constitution, when ratified by the Legislatures of three fourths of the several States, or by conventions in three fourths thereof, as the one or the other mode of ratification may be proposed by Congress: *Provided,* That no amendment which may be made prior to the year 1808 shall in any manner affect the first and fourth clauses in the ninth section of the first article; and that no State, without its consent, shall be deprived of its equal suffrage in the Senate.

This highly practical section of the Constitution, free from all conditions and limitations since the year 1808, with regard to the subjects concerning which amendments may be adopted, with the single exception of the suffrage of the States in the Senate, was provided as a means for adapting the fundamental law of the Republic to the changes incident to the development of the nation. It is the safety-valve of the Constitution, so constructed and guarded as to prevent hasty and inconsiderate action, and utterly destructive of every pretense for forcible revolution. It is impossible to justify a resort to force as a remedy for wrongs imaginary or real, while this recognition of the great doctrine that "Governments derive their just powers from the consent of the governed" remains a part of our organic law; and it would be equally difficult to justify the existence of anything in the Government destructive of the inalienable rights of "life, liberty, and the pursuit of happiness," without at least, an earnest and determined effort to remove it. When the people established the Constitution, embracing the section which I have quoted, they agreed upon the means whereby the consent of the governed should be determined, and by the same act placed upon themselves and upon us the responsibility attached to those things which interfere with the inalienable rights of man, or which tend to the destruction of free government. Amendments proposed by Congress, or by a convention called for that purpose, and adopted or rejected by the Legislatures of the several States are the mediums through which the consent of the governed is to be determined concerning all things not now provided for in the Constitution. It was a fair agreement, placing upon each and every citizen, and upon the several States, all of the risks and responsibilities incident thereto, for "we, the people of the United States," made it. It was expected that the nation would develop into grander proportions, its interests become more varied, its wants and necessities increase, and that it might be beset by dangers not occurring to the minds which molded the form of the organic law. It was agreed and expressly provided that the Constitution should grow to meet all of these new demands, keeping with the bounds of its ordination "to form a more perfect Union, establish justice, insure domestic tranquility, provide for the common defense, promote the general welfare, and secure the blessings of liberty to ourselves and our posterity."

This section of the Constitution is my authority for introducing the joint resolution which I have read; and it also imposes upon this House the responsibility of meeting the question fairly and with a view to the promotion of the best interests of the nation, by releasing it from the thralldoms of a hostile power which has entwined itself around the heart and life of the Republic. The proposition introduces no intricate question of constitutional law for discussion. It simply submits a question of fact for our determination, upon which the past and present throw such a flood of light that not even willfulness can lead us astray. Is slavery incompatible with a free Government? This is the true question involved; and no artful summonings of cunningly devised side issues, or of the ghosts of dead expediencies, can release any member of this body from passing upon the single issue. It is all there is in the case. The contest is squarely between slavery and free government, and in this light it is to be conducted to the end. Let us follow it, and see how it will end.

Slavery is defined to be "the state of entire subjection of one person to the will of another." This is despotism, pure and simple. It is true that this definition concerns more the relations existing between master and slave than it does those between the system of slavery and the Government. But we need not hope to find a system purely despotic acting in harmony with a Government wholly, or even partially, republican. An antagonism exists between the two which can never be reconciled. This our experiences with the principles involved have taught us is a truism from which indifference will not enable us to escape, nor dissimulation release us. But when we connect with the despotism of the slave system of this country the immense land and money power embraced in it, and reflect how thoroughly it had become interwoven with the entire social fabric of nearly one half of the States, we can more readily understand and fully comprehend how and why this antagonism took upon itself the form of political organization through which for many years it controlled the nation, and through which it insisted on the death of the Republic when it could control no longer. We can also understand why the system of which this antagonism is the active life took possession of every department of the local governments of the States where it existed, and hedged itself about with laws which were not only violations of the fundamental principles of our national Constitution but disgraceful to civilization and destructive of free Government. No man, whose conscience has vitality sufficient to make him honest, can read the slave codes of the southern States without admitting that they are utterly repugnant to the genius of our free institutions and irreconcilably opposed to the theory of our Government. And yet every one knows that these tyrannical, hostile, and barbarous codes were absolutely necessary for the preservation of the slave system, even in those dark days of slavery's rule which existed before the present war awakened to its true and real life the moral sense of the nation, and forced its ever-enduring light into the beclouded minds of the bondmen of this land, quickening their perception into that keen appreciation of every man's right to "life, liberty, and the pursuit of happiness," which bids defiance to slave codes, and effectively asserts and maintains the right of every man to own himself. The system, being a pure despotism, was forced to resort to despotic laws for support, defense, and perpetuation.

It was perfectly natural for the comparatively few men who held four million human beings in a bondage which puts to shame all other kindred systems which ever cursed man for their mildness, not only to resort to cruel and despotic laws for aid in their diabolical act, but also to seek refuge in the anti-republican dogma that "the right to govern resides in a very small minority; the duty to obey is inherent in the great mass of mankind." Domestic slavery, backed by immense capital and political power, knitted its lethargic web closely and firmly around statesmen and parties, and soon forged fetters for holding the mass of the people in governmental slavery. The minority commanded, and flew to arms to destory the Government when the mass of the people refused to obey; and the war which is now so severely taxing the energies of our people, and drawing so exhaustively on the resources of the country, is the legitimate offspring of the attempt of a reckless, insolent, and depraved slaveholding oligarchy to mold this Government into a political counterpart of that barbaric domestic despotism which asserts the right of property in man. "The state of entire subjection of one person to the will of another" struck hands with "the right to govern resides in a very small minority; the duty to obey is inherent in the great mass of mankind." Domestic slavery and political slavery were joined in unholy wedlock in the temple of the Republic, and their infernal progeny are now trying to demolish the grand edifice in which their incestuous parents plighted their criminal vows. The entire combination, from minutest nefarious particle to its aggregated atrocity, is an anti-republican, despotic whole, the sworn enemy of all that is good, the bane of all that is just.

Mr. Chairman, we can cast our eyes upon no page of this nation's history whereon it is not written, "Slavery is incompatible with a free Government." We have tried to close our eyes against this constantly repeated and self-evident truth. We have tried to reason it away, to practice arts which should carry us around it, or over it, or under it. We have failed to accomplish the desired result. As immutable as the laws of God stands the declaration, "Slavery is incompatible with a free Government." Decked with the habiliments of death, surrounded by all the dread scenes of war, this incompatibility is thundering at the gates of the citadel of the Republic, demanding recognition. The loyal inmates command us to obey the summons. But we have not yet had enough of sorrow, desolation, and death. We must stop and reason, while the national treasure pours out in streams of increasing volume, while the life-blood flows from other hearts, while graves in untold numbers are preparing, and the ashes of desolation are cast upon unnumbered hearthstones. We must not act rashly. We must be calm, discreet, dignified. We must inquire why this great thunderer is thus disturbing our old traditions and confusing our conservative ideas. Well, let us examine this demand, and ascertain upon what facts it is supported.

In order to understand perfectly the objects which the people had in view when they ordained the Constitution of the United States, we must turn to the preamble which introduces us to that instrument. When we give it our attention we find it a very plain-spoken guide, void of guile or dissimulation. It discloses to us, first, that the Constitution is the work of the people; and this at once develops the thoroughly republico-democratic character of the Government established. It was a grand creation of the people for their own security in the possession of the great objects expressed in the preamble. All of the powers embraced in the Constitution were placed there for the sole purpose of putting these objects above interference from any source and beyond the hazard of loss. These objects are not only compatible with, but absolutely necessary to, the existence and enjoyment of a free Government. No one of them can be destroyed without detriment to the whole; and anything which by its nature is incompatible with either stands in the same relation to all the rest, and must, if permitted to acquire supremacy, ultimately subvert the free principles of the Government itself. How does the account stand between slavery and these great objects? Let us give our attention to this question for a few minutes, for it is one of transcendent importance.

The first object of the people was "to form a more perfect Union." What has been and is now the attitude of slavery toward this primary object of the Constitution? When slavery, in the natural threatening and disturbing course of its development, assumed the character and form of a political power, its first act was a denial that the *people* had formed a "more perfect Union," coupled with the assertion that the Union was a mere compact between the several *States*, which might be dissolved at the pleasure of any party thereto. This position was selected as most likely to terrify the people into submission while their power was being transferred to the hands of the few, and as affording a plausible pretext for the destruction of the Union in the event freedom should prove too strong for slavery and the people should refuse to surrender their power into the hands of those who would destroy their liberties. Shrewd calculators were the men who selected and intrenched this position. For many years the terrors which they exhibited to the people from this cunningly masked battery of error held the mass in check. But, when it was almost too late, the people discovered their danger, regained their power, resolved to enforce the grand principles and traditions of justice and liberty, and stood up in their majesty masters of the situation. Slavery flew to its last resort, sought to enforce by strife and battle its doctrine of a compact of States, and the right to dissolve the same at pleasure, and for three long and bloody years has been by the dread power and fearful enginery of war seeking the destruction of the Union of the people.

The second object of the people was "to establish justice." How could slavery stand otherwise than opposed to this? Slavery is injustice. The establishment of justice would destroy slavery. Both cannot live together in peace. In the very nature of things a state of strife, contention, war, will and must exist unceasingly between these two irreconcilable enemies until one shall succumb to the other. Justice is "the virtue which consists in giving to every one what is his due; practical conformity to the laws and to the principles of rectitude in the dealings of men with each other." Slavery is the direct, perfect, absolute opposite of this. Must not the house in which these two antagonisms exist be divided against itself? Can such a house stand? Is it possible to establish justice and maintain slavery? The long, dark, terrible record written on the pages of an incessant strife, first in unhealthy, feverish, exhausting political excitements, and finally in the best, truest, and bravest blood of the nation, and now culminating amid the awful scenes of a war unprecedented in proportions and unequaled in the matchless glory of its promised results, furnishes to us and to the world an unquestionable negative to the queries I have submitted. Slavery challenged the people in their endeavors to establish justice, and resorted to the ordeal of battle against them in their efforts to maintain a Government founded upon this divine attribute. The ordeal of battle is not yet closed. The contest is in the full tide of its power. All around the combatants the nations of the world as spectators press with an eagerness and intensity of interest never before prepared for the pages of history, while the spirits of the fathers of our republican system look down from their bright and blest abode, hoping for the triumph of justice, and appeal to God who has gathered them to Himself to strengthen the arms which strike for the right. We know, the peoples of the earth know, the spirits of the fathers know, that this grand struggle for victory can be terminated only by the triumph of justice and the death of slavery, or by the success of slavery and the death of the Republic. No compromise can be made, no truce can be adjusted, no silver-tongued appeals for peace can be heard amid the din of this fierce conflict. We must establish justice upon the tomb of slavery, or have it not at all. We must establish it or acknowledge the Republic a failure. We will establish it by destroying, in the manner and form prescribed by our Constitution, that which stands in our way—slavery.

Another object to be accomplished by the adoption of the Constitution was to "insure domestic tranquillity." This was the voice of the people. How stands the account between the Republic and slavery concerning his grand purpose of the people? When, since slavery assumed political proportions, has it subserved the great end of domestic tranquillity? It has been powerful, but what are the fruits of its power? The long line of political, legislative, judicial history of this nation presents not a page which is not disfigured by some blot placed upon it by the aggressive, intolerant, exacting, and despotic spirit of slavery. From school-book to statute-book, from hearthstone opinions to decisions of the Supreme Court of the United States, from political hustings to the sacred desk, from town meetings to Congress, no bright spot appears without a blemish from the hands of the restless, meddling, disturbing genius of slavery. Everywhere its footprints appear, always tending toward a disturbance of our domestic tranquillity. We had no national repose, for constant pro-slavery agitation kept a continual fever in the national system, consuming its energies and its life. This was the condition of the nation in the so-called times of peace, and before the good guns of Sumter answered the war summons of slavery. Since that time our domestic tranquillity, always disturbed, has been enveloped in the dark, dense, impenetrable cloud of war thrown over it and around it by the spirit which discharged the first shot against the flag of the Union, and commenced the present deplorable trial by battle. Instead of insuring domestic tranquillity slavery has been an irrepressible disturber of the nation's repose. It accorded to us no rest in our miscalled day of peace. Steadily it pressed us toward despotism of war. We declined to advance further upon either of these dread alternatives, and turned our faces back to the position which the fathers had occupied. No sooner was our gaze turned in that direction then slavery's shrill bugle-blast aroused the people to the fearful realities of the most gigantic, wicked, and causeless civil war that ever cursed the earth or disturbed the repose of nations. Summoning to its standard panoplied hosts of deceived, misguided, ignorant men, keeping step under the flag of death to the music of disunion, it has forced from the shops and offices and stores and fields of the loyal and freedom-loving North hundreds of thousands of the brave, true, intelligent, patriotic sons of the Republic to sterner work than the enjoyment of domestic tranquility—to the battle field, to death, and the grave. Mourning households, broken hearth-circles, bleeding hearts, everywhere bear witness that slavery is the destroyer and not a promoter of domestic tranquillity.

"To provide for the common defense" was another declared purpose of the people when they ordained the Constitution. The common defense of a republic can never be insured by nurturing within it its implacable enemy. The elements on which a republic relies for that concentration of resources and strength necessary to effective common defense must be homogeneous. Anything which prevents this is inimical to the prosperity and success of the Government. Doctrines of government, systems of labor, social organizations, commercial and manufacturing interests, religious, moral, and educational purposes, all must be so connectedly harmonious "as to create a chain of mutual dependencies," each relying on its fellows for support, while all work in unison for the accomplishment of a common end. Interrupt this harmony and the rule which enforces the resulting discord is arbitrary, and consequently at war with free government. And we must remember that the common defense which the people declared for, and which our security demands, is not merely that which shall meet and overcome the assaults of foreign Powers, but has quite as direct reference to the preservation of the equipoise of our republican system in opposition to all hostile efforts and influences originating among ourselves. Very little good would result from a mere maintenance of our territorial proportions in opposition to outward assailants, if we should fail to preserve our republican forms, our Christian principles, our true moral and social characteristics, from internal efforts to destroy them. We have long had, and now have, a wily, aggressive, restless domestic enemy, which has to a greater extent imperiled the nation than have all other foes combined. It has interfered with every element of national strength, by aggressing upon our doctrines of government, forcing collision between systems of labor, distracting our social organizations, disturbing our commercial relations, injuring our manufacturing interests, dividing our religious communities, debauching the public morals, preventing universality of education, and forcing discord into every fiber of the Republic. Slavery has done this, and now wages war for the purpose of completing the destruction of the nation. These are the contributions of slavery to the common defense.

Following naturally and logically in the chain of objects declared by the people we find the next is to "promote the general welfare." In opposition to this slavery has stood as a wall of brass. For the aggrandizement of a privileged class, the upbuilding of an aristocracy, and the debasement of the masses, slavery has been the chief instrument. But all these ends are opposed to the general welfare. That must rest upon things quite different—upon equality, democracy, and the elevation of the masses. There can be no true development of those qualities which make a nation great and prosperous unless its energies are so diffused as to reach all classes, all interests, all sources of power, and embrace them all in its grand march of progress. Who ever measured the mighty resources of this nation before the present war broke the spell which slavery had cast over the people, and set the national mind and conscience free? Three years, marked by the bloody footprints of war, surcharged with the griefs of a hundred battle-fields, have done more for the development of the powers and resources of this nation than half a century accomplished when slavery controlled the national mind. When slavery ruled, the energies of the people were comparatively dormant. What little of vigor worked its way up to and through the incrusted surface was made captive by the interminable political agitations with which slavery disturbed the country and checked the progress of the Republic. Underlying these agitations were false principles of political economy, unsound doctrines of government, erroneous theories of trade and commerce, ruinous systems of public policy, unjust systems of labor—everything which was calculated to retard the true advancement of the nation. These agitations dominated over everything. The brain-force of the country was subject to them. They everywhere overshadowed the material interests of the country, directed its legislation, overawed its executive agents, controlled its courts, corrupted its religion, debased its morals, vitiated its literature, beclouded and benumbed everything upon which a people must rely for greatness, prosperity, happiness, and the promotion of the general welfare. They kept the public mind in a constant state of unhealthy excitement, and infused their poison into every vein and artery of the body-politic.

Sir, this is the past as molded by slavery. Shall the future be its harmonious counterpart? Shall we pass through this horrid political nightmare again to be awakened therefrom by the bugle-blast and cannon-roar of another war, or shall we secure a permanent peace to ourselves and our children by firmly establishing the general welfare upon the tomb of slavery? We cannot postpone these grave questions for posterity to answer. With us they abide, and we are to answer them. We must answer them, and do it faithfully for freedom, if we would have this war pass into the history of past events, and not "drag its slow length along" the pages of the future. No avenue is presented for our escape except that which leads over the dead body of slavery. This great fact is recognized by the nation. Its immense proportions have attracted the attention of the civilized world. Shall we alone close our eyes to it and attempt to avoid its grave responsibilities? We cannot succeed in this if we should try. We ought not to try, for the general welfare of the nation forbids it.

The last, the grandest, the most sublime of the objects declared by the people in the ordination of the Constitution is, "to secure the blessings of liberty to ourselves and our posterity." Of this great object of the people, Story, in his Commentaries on the Constitution, says:

> Surely no object could be more worthy of the wisdom and ambition of the best men in any age. If there be anything which may justly challenge the admiration of all mankind, it is that sublime patriotism which, looking beyond its own times and its own fleeting pursuits, aims to secure the permanent happiness of posterity by laying the broad foundations of Government upon immovable principles of justice. Our affections, indeed, may naturally be presumed to outlive the brief limits of our own lives, and to repose with deep sensibility upon our own immediate descendants. But there is a noble disinterestedness in that forecast which disregards present objects for the sake of *all mankind* and erects structures to protect, support, and bless the most distant generations.

Let us not overlook that portion of his well-expressed and better-bestowed praise which rests upon the fact that the glorious work of the people was for "the sake of all mankind." Let it bring afresh to our minds that important question propounded by Jefferson:

> Can the liberties of a nation be thought secure when we have removed their only firm basis, a conviction in the minds of the people that these liberties are the gift of God; that they are not to be violated but with His wrath?

Has not slavery denied that this great work of the people was intended for the "safety of all mankind," and brought upon us the just chastisement of God, who intended "these liberties" for all of His creatures? What are the thunders of this war but the voice of God calling upon this nation to return from the evil paths, made rough by errors and misfortunes, blunders and crimes, made slippery by the warm, smoking blood of our brothers and friends, to the grand highway of national thrift, prosperity, happiness, glory, and peace, in which He planted the feet of the fathers? Cannot we hear amid the wild rushing roar of this war storm the voice of Him who rides upon the winds and rules the tempest saying unto us, "You cannot have peace until you secure liberty to all who are subject to your laws?" Sir, this declaration must be heeded. It has been whispered into the ears of this nation since first we pronounced life, liberty, and the pursuit of happiness to be the inalienable rights of all men, and now it rolls in upon us like the voice of the ocean, rendering peace or war to our election. Which shall we elect? Shall it be peace? How can it be peace while liberty and slavery dwell together in our midst? These are enemies. These are ideas which cannot dwell together in harmony. How can we have peace? Let slavery die. Let its death be written in our Constitution. Let the Constitution "proclaim liberty throughout the land to all the inhabitants thereof." This is the way to peace—firm, enduring peace, embracing all mankind, and reaching to the most distant generations. In this way only can we secure liberty to ourselves and our posterity.

But, sir, slavery has not contended itself with manifesting its incompatibility with our free Government by opposing the great objects for securing which the people ordained and established the constitution. It has confronted the Constitution itself, and prevented the enforcement of its most vital provisions. Section two of article six of the Constitution says:

This Constitution, and the laws of the United States which shall be made in pursuance thereof, and all treaties made, or which shall be made, under the authority of the United States, shall be the supreme law of the land; and the judges in every State shall be bound thereby, anything in the Constitution or laws of any state to the contrary notwithstanding.

Of the many provisions of the Constitution devised for the protection of the unity of the nation, this one stands first in importance. Without it the bond of union would be as weak as an invalid between whom and the grave but a breath intervenes. The supremacy of the Constitution, the laws and treaties of the United States, are necessary to our existence as a nation. Our unity can be preserved in no other way. This was the belief of those who ordained the Constitution, and our experience accords therewith. But, sir, slavery planted itself in opposition to this provision of the Constitution, and declared that it should not be enforced. Do you ask for proof? We need not go far to find it. Turn to the Constitution and take as a guide the words:

The citizens of each State shall be entitled to all the privileges and immunities of citizens of the several States.

To what extent has this been regarded as the supreme law of the land in States where slavery controlled legislation, presided in the courts, directed the Executives, and commanded the mob? It is a provision of most vital importance to every citizen. We could not be a nation of equals without it. It is the peerage title of our people. How has it been observed? What has been the conduct of slavery toward it? Let us turn again to the Constitution for practical aid in the solution of these questions. In the first article of the Amendments to the Constitution we find this language:

Congress shall make no law respecting an establishment of religion, or prohibiting the free exercise thereof; or abridging the freedom of speech, or of the press; or the right of the people peaceably to assemble, and to petition the Government for a redress of grievances.

The great rights here enumerated were regarded by the people as too sacred and too essential to the preservation of their liberties to be trusted with no firmer defense than the rule that "Congress can exercise no power which is not delegated to it." Around this negative protection was erected the positive barrier of absolute prohibition. Freedom of religious opinion, freedom of speech and press, and the right of assemblage for the purpose of petition belong to every American citizen, high or low, rich or poor, wherever he may be within the jurisdiction of the United States. With these rights no State may interfere without breach of the bond which holds the Union together. How have these rights essential to liberty been respected in those sections of the Union where slavery held the reins of local authority and directed the thoughts, prejudices, and passions of the people? The bitter, cruel, relentless persecutions of the Methodists in the South, almost as void of pity as those which were visited upon the Huguenots in France, tell how utterly slavery disregards the right to a free exercise of religion. No religion which recognizes God's eternal attribute of justice and breathes that spirit of love which applies to all men the sublime commandment, "Whatsoever ye would that men should do unto you, do ye even so to them," can ever be allowed free exercise where slavery curses men and defies God. No religious denomination can flourish or even be tolerated where slavery rules without surrendering the choicest jewels of its faith into keeping of that infidel power which withholds the Bible from the poor. Religion, "consisting in the performance of all known duties to God and our fellow-men," never has been and never will be allowed free exercise in any community where slavery dwarfs the consciences of men. The Constitution may declare the right, but slavery ever will, as it ever has, trample upon the Constitution and prevent the enjoyment of the right.

How much better has free discussion fared at the hands of the black censor who guards the interests of slavery against the expression of the thoughts of freemen? On what rood of this Republic cursed by slavery have men been free to declare their approval of the divine doctrines of the

Declaration of Independence? Where, except in the free States of this Union, have the nation's toiling millions been permitted to assert their great protective doctrine, "The laborer is worthy of his hire?" What member of our great free labor force, North or South, could stand up in the presence of the despotism which owns men and combat the atrocious assertion that "Slavery is the natural and normal condition of the laboring man, whether white or black," with the noble declaration that "Labor being the sure foundation of the nation's prosperity should be performed by free men, for they alone have an interest in the preservation of free government," with any assurance that his life would not be exacted as the price of his temerity? In all this broad land not one could be found. The press has been padlocked, and men's lips have been sealed. Constitutional defense of free discussion by speech or press has been a rope of sand south of the line which marked the limit of dignified free labor in this country. South of that line an organized element of death was surely sapping the foundations of our free institutions, reversing the theory of our Government, dwarfing our civilization, contracting the national conscience, compassing the destruction of everything calculated to preserve the republican character of our Constitution; and no man in the immediate presence of this rapidly accumulating ruin dared to raise a voice of warning. Submission and silence were inexorably exacted. Such, sir, is the free discussion which slavery tolerates. Such is its observance of the high constitutional rights of the citizen. Its past wll be repeated in its future if the people permit it to curse the world with a continued existence.

"The right of the people peaceably to assemble and to petition the Government for a redress of grievances," has been as completely disregarded as the other rights I have mentioned by the terrorism which guards the citadel of slavery. If slavery persecuted religionists, denied the privilege of free discussion, prevented free elections, trampled upon all of the constitutional guarantees belonging to the citizen, peaceable assemblages of the people to consider these grievances with a view to petition the Government for redress could not be held. If non-slaveholding whites became alarmed at the bold announcement that "slavery is the natural and normal condition of the laboring man, whether white or black," seeing therein the commencement of an effort intended to result in the enslavement of labor instead of the mere enslavement of the African race, they were not privileged to peaceably assemble and petition the Government in regard thereto, or to discuss the barbarism and to arouse the people in opposition to it. Slavery held political and social power sufficient to crush all such attempts on the part of the injured people. Slavery could hold its assemblages, discuss, resolve, petition, threaten, disregard its constitutional obligations, trample upon the rights of labor, do anything its despotic disposition might direct; but freedom and freemen must be deaf, dumb, and blind. Throughout all the dominions of slavery republican government, constitutional liberty, the blessings of our free institutions were mere fables. An aristocracy enjoyed unlimited power, while the people were pressed to the earth and denied the inestimable privileges which by right they should have enjoyed in all the fullness designed by the Constitution.

Sir, I might enumerate many other constitutional rights of the citizen which slavery has disregarded and practically destroyed, but I have enough to illustrate my proposition: that slavery disregards the supremacy of the Constitution and denies to the citizens of each State the privileges and immunities of citizens in the several States.

The proposition needs no argument. We all know that for many years before the commencement of the gigantic rebellion now in progress the supporters of slavery enforced this disregard of the supremacy of the Constitution and of the privileges and immunities of the citizen by every power and influence known to the communities cursed by the presence of a slave. Legislatures, courts, Executives, almost every person holding political or social power and position in the sourthern States, were all arrayed on the side of slavery, and what they could not accomplish was turned over to the mob, which, without law, with abuse, indignities, cruelties, and hempen halters, did its work with fearful accuracy and terrible exactness. Twenty million free men in the free States were practically reduced to the condition of semi-citizens of the United States: for the enjoyment of their rights, privileges, and immunities as citizens depended upon a perpetual residence north of Mason and Dixon's line. South of that line the rights which I have mentioned, and many more which I might mention, could be enjoyed only when debased to the uses of slavery. Slave-holders and their supporters alone were free to think and print, to do and say what seemed to them best on both sides of that line. They could think, read, talk, discuss with perfect freedom in each and every State, and fearfully they used this advantage to destroy the liberties of this country. It is quite time; sir, for the people of the free States to look these facts squarely in the face and provide a remedy which shall make the future safe for the rights of each and every citizen. Had slavery not possessed this advantage, civil war, freighted with sorrow, desolation, and death, would not have visited this nation. But since it has come, the people of the free States should insist on ample protection to their rights, privileges, and immunities, which are none other than those which the Constitution was designed to secure to all citizens alike, and see to it that the power which caused the war shall cease to exist, to the end that the curse of civil war may never be visited upon us again, and that the citizen whose home is in the North shall be as free to assert his opinions and enjoy all of his constitutional rights in the sunny South as he whose roof-tree is the magnolia shall to the same ends be free amid the mountains of New England and the sparkling lakes of the North and the West. An equal and exact observance of the constitutional rights of each and every citizen, in each and every State, is the end to which we should cause the lessons of this war to carry us. Whatever stands between us and the accomplishment of this great end should be removed. Can we reach this end and save slavery? Can we reconcile the antagonisms which have produced this war? Can we mix the oil and water of despotism and republicanism? Can we harmonize the contending elements of absolutism and free government? No, sir; it is not given to human power to accomplish these results. What, then, shall we do? Abolish slavery. How? By amending our national Constitution. Why? Because slavery is incompatible with free government. Peace, prosperity, national harmony, progress, civilization, Christianity, all admonish us that our only safety lies in universal freedom.

Sir, I have endeavored to show that slavery stands arrayed against every object for the attainment of which the people ordained and established the Constitution; that it is seeking the destruction of the Union, is opposed to the establishment of justice, has disturbed our domestic tranquility, makes war upon us instead of providing for the common defense, promotes wide-spread desolation and ruin instead of advancing the general welfare, and seeks to withhold from us and our posterity the blessings of liberty. I have endeavored to show that it has disregarded the Constitution and trampled upon the most sacred rights of the citizen. But the case is so nearly self-evident that it is difficult to argue it. The antagonism is so marked, and the incompatibility so glaringly apparent, that they overshadow proof and argument. The conscience of the nation is so sensitively active concerning the questions to which I have spoken that it arrives at conclusions with the rapidity by which thought measures distance. Argument cannot travel so fast. At best it is but the baggage-train of the grand army of ideas and aspirations which is now leading this nation to that higher and purer civilization that forms the silver lining of the dark war cloud which overhangs the Republic.

Mr. Chairman, the position which this nation maintains to-day in relation to the true character of slavery is more perfect than that which the founders of the Government occupied. They believed that slavery was so directly opposed to justice, so distinctly arrayed against divine law, so utterly depraved and desperately wicked, that its own aggregation of enormities would speedily accomplish its dissolution. We recognize their faith as most correct, except in its conclusion. We see that the death can only be accomplished by an executioner. Slavery will not kill itself. The decree of death has been enrolled. The death-warrant was sealed by the first shot which struck Fort Sumter. But condemned culprits do not execute themselves, and slavery is no exception to the rule.

I admit that the progress of the war has accomplished much toward giving effect to the decree. In our harvest of blood we have gathered great compensatory results. The spirit of patriotism has returned to us clothed with a resurrectional brightness like unto that which shall light the heirs of glory to the abode of the eternal Father. Manhood, as it stood proudly erect in the grand, colossal, symmetrical proportions known to the early days of the Republic, again gives sublimity to American character. An acknowledged dependence on Him who guides the planets and notices the fall of a sparrow is once more the sure defense of our people. An awakened, invigorated, concentrated national conscience revivifies our observance of justice. Fear of God and love of country blend and course from heart to extremities of the earnest masses who struggle amid the awful terrors and black woes of war for that sublime end, a true peace. These happy results have effected many of the preliminaries to the final death of the condemned disturber of our repose. Already the glowing fruits of ultimate victory gather around and about us. Thousands of human beings who were slaves at the commencement of this accursed rebellion are now enjoying the freedom which God designed for all of His creatures. The limits of slavery have been contracted by State action, and other States are directing their efforts to the further compression of the dominion of the black power which wars upon all that is good. Congress has not failed to provide a way through which men may march from bondage to freedom. The President has nobly performed his duty by striking the chains of slavery from millions of men. Public opinion, the conqueror of men and parties, the maker of Presidents and Congresses, has flung its banner to the breeze, inscribed with the glorious words, "Liberty and Union." Providence has opened up the way to that higher civilization and purer Christianity which the Republic is to attain. The very atmosphere which surrounds us is filled with the spirit of emancipation. Every throb of the popular heart sends coursing to the very extremities of national life the warm blood of freedom. These things all cheer the hearts of the true sons of the Republic. Our Red Sea passage promises to be as propitious as was that of God's chosen people when the waters parted and presented the sea-bed for their escape from the hosts upon whom these waters closed and effected the burial appointed by Him who had declared, "Let my people go." The bow of promise now arches the heavens, but the end is not yet. We have advanced, but promise signifies future. We hope for the end, but it is not yet abiding with us; for hope pertains to that which we do not possess. We feel that we have gained much during the terrible trial to which the Republic has been subjected, and we know that at far too great price have the people purchased the position of which they are now the masters to permit it to pass again into the possession of the enemies of free government. The position must be fortified and the lines advanced. What freedom has gained must be intrenched by the strong arm of the Constitution. The life and treasure which the loyal citizens of the Union have expended, in amount unprecedented and with cheerfulness almost incomprehensible, must be made to secure something more durable than a lull of the storm, a delusive hope, and a deceitful peace. Security for the future must be the result of the great demands to which our people have so nobly responded. The price paid is ample, and its returns must be worthy of the grand patriotism which rose, as if by the command of God, all panoplied for war, and equal to all of the exactions of the awful conflict whose birth was announced by the rear of rebel cannon over the bay of Charleston.

Sir, let us not be misled by delusive hopes, nor deceived by artful words. Let no siren song divert us from the path which the events of our fancied days of peace and the lessons of this war have marked out for us with more unerring exactness than that with which the magnetic needle points the course of the mariner on the trackless ocean. There was a lurking devil in the words of the gentleman from New York [Mr. Brooks] when he told us that he accepted "the abolition of slavery as a fact accomplished." He knows, the world knows, that none of the acts hostile to slavery which I have mentioned have gone beyond the fact of making men affected by them free; that no one of them has reached the root of slavery and prepared for the destruction of the system. We have made some men free, but the system yet lives, and has its thousands of active tongues all over this land, hissing its defense and seeking to benumb the public conscience by covering it over with the slime of death. One of these tongues, forked and slimy, speaks from the mouth of the man who holds in his hands the reigns of the executive power of the Empire State the words—

If it is true that slavery must be abolished to save this Union, then the people of the South should be allowed to withdraw themselves from that Government which cannot give them the protection guarantied by its terms.

This man does not believe that the abolition of slavery is a "fact accomplished;" and he has a numerous, active, crafty, unscrupulous party at his back, every member of which accepts the teachings of this master. In this Hall busy tongues paraphrase this guilty declaration, and cry aloud for the "Union as it was," with the great, black crime of slavery "as it was," or "peace on any terms."

From the other end of this Capitol a senatorial tongue has hissed upon the records of the country these defiant words in behalf of slavery:

By your acts you attempt to free slaves. You will not have them among you. You leave them where they are. Then what is to be the result? I presume that local State governments will be preserved. If they are, if the people have a right to make their own laws and to govern themselves, they will not only reënslave every person you attempt to set free, but they will reënslave the whole race.

And a tongue in this body answers, "If you destroy slavery, you destroy our free institutions." These are the tongues which are to be the oracles of the convention that is to meet at Chicago on the 4th day of next July to organize the elements of a powerful party in the interests of slavery.

Sir, is it not madness to act upon the idea that slavery is dead? We hold it as a condemned, unexecuted culprit, and know that it is not dead. Why shall we not recognize the fact and provide for the execution? We must do so, or go on digging graves and pouring sorrow into the loyal homes of the people; for the systems and ideas which flash their lightning among the clouds of this war will never cease from strife until from hill-top to mountain-top, from valley to plain, from ocean to ocean, from the lakes to the Gulf, the swelling tide of the nation's acclaim announces to the people of the earth that American slavery is to be known to the future only through the history of the past. To us is this great work intrusted. How shall we perform it? There lies no difficulty in our way if we will but do our duty.

The Committee on the Judiciary have authorized me to report to the House the proposed amendment of the Constitution of the United States, with a recommendation that it be passed by this body, and submitted to the Legislatures of the several States for their acceptance. A concurrence in this recommendation is the plain road over which we may escape from the difficulties which now beset us. A submission of this proposition to the several States will at once remove from Congress the question of slavery. No further agitation of this vexatious question need disturb our deliberations if we concur in this recommendation, and we shall be far advanced toward a lasting, ever-enduring peace. Send this proposition to the States, trust it to the people, fix it as a center around which public opinion may gather its potent agencies, and we shall have accomplished more for the future tranquillity of the Republic than ever was effected by Congress before. The people are now convinced of the incompatibility of slavery with free government. Let us impart to them an opportunity to give effect to their conviction. If we refuse, our successors will be more obedient; for the people have decreed that slavery shall die, and that its death shall be recorded in the Constitution. We are to construct the machinery which shall execute the decree, or give place to those who will perform the bidding of the people. We cannot evade the responsibility which rests upon us by declaring that we "accept the abolition of slavery as a fact accomplished." The nation knows that this enunciation is a mere lachrymose, diplomatic intrigue employed by slavery to arrest the grand volcanic action that is upheaving the great moral ideas which underlie the Republic. The nation demands more, its faith embraces more; its acute appreciation of the true nature of the disease which preys upon its heart-strings assures it that the work of death cannot be arrested until the fact of slavery's dissolution is accomplished; and that this may not be until, by amendment of the Constitution, we assert the ultimate triumph of liberty over slavery, democracy over aristocracy, free government over absolutism. . . .

FERNANDO WOOD [DEM., N.Y.]. Mr. Speaker, this is a proposition to provide by an amendment to the Constitution for the abolition of slavery without compensation in all of the States in the Union. It will be, if adopted, a change in the fundamental law—a material alteration in the Constitution of the United States as formed by the founders of the Government. It is, therefore, a proposition which involves considerations and reflections such as belong to the gravest questions which can come before the American people for determination. It is whether we shall alter the whole structure and theory of government by changing the basis upon which it rests. My first difficulty in assenting to the resolution is that this is no time for any alteration in the organic law. We are now in the midst of a fearful civil war. The horrid din of this conflict, the groans of the wounded and dying, the sad evidences of death and destruction are all around us. Until recently, even at the very doors of this capital, the armed enemy has presented his threatening hostility. The whole people of America are involved directly or indirectly in this dreadful conflict. Reason, judgment, and that cautious investigation and comparison of interests, opinions, and prejudices necessary to a proper adjustment of a nation's welfare have been banished by the graver realities of war. This is no time to make or alter constitutions. Those who are enveloped in the elemental strifes of the tempest or the earthquake, and involved in the ruin thus created, cannot judge of the cause or measure the extent of the calamity. So it is with the historical convulsions which have desolated vast regions and swept myriads to the grave. The spectator who is himself in the midst of the horrors of war has seldom the coolness to discriminate and decide, with any reasonable degree of accuracy, as to the impelling cause of the struggle. The passions of men, the excitements of the contest, the temptations of ambition, avarice, and fear, all tend to blind the vision and warp the judgments of the actors in the terrible drama now being performed on this continent before the civilized world as spectators. Therefore, in my opinion, this is no time to act upon the proposition, no time to change the fundamental law. Nations do not alter their forms of government amid revolutions. We are now surrounded by dangers from without and from within. The people are in an unnatural excitement, unsuited to that calm deliberation which an alteration of the Constitution requires. All our statesmanship, love of country, efforts at union, consolidation, and good-fellowship, should be devoted to a restoration of our fraternity and prosperity as a people.

But if a change *can* be made, is this such a one as *should* be made? It is sought through this amendment to abolish at once and summarily the system of domestic servitude existing in one third of the States which came into the Union with the Government and which have remained with it until now. The effects of such a revulsion in such an interest will be of the most wide-spread and radical character. It will, of course, add to the existing sectional hostilities, and if possible make the pending conflict yet more intense and deadly.

Mr. Speaker, I see many objections to this amendment, while I fail to find one reason in its favor. I am opposed to it because it aims at the introduction of a new element over which Government shall operate. It proposes to make the social interests subjects for governmental action. This is the introduction of a principle antagonist to that which underlies all republican systems. Our Union was made for the *political* government of the parties to it, for certain specified objects of a very general character, all of them *political,* and none of them relating to or affecting in any manner individual or personal interests in those things which touch the domestic concerns. There is no feature or principle of it giving to the Federal power authority over them. These were reserved and left exclusively to the jurisdiction of the States and "the people thereof." Of this character are the marital relations, the religious beliefs, the right of eminent domain within the territorial limits of the States, other private property, and all matters purely social. Slavery where it exists is a system of domestic labor; it is not the creature of law. It existed without law before this Government was established. It is incorporated into the organization of society as part of the existing domestic regulations. It cannot be brought within constitutional jurisdiction any more than can any or either of the other private and personal interests referred to.

Again, Sir, the proposed amendment to abolish slavery in the States of the Union is unjust in itself, a breach of good faith, and utterly irreconcilable with expediency. It is unjust because it involves a tyrannical destruction of individual property under the plea of a legitimate exercise of the functions of Government. It is in theory the idea which has been derived from despotism and the notions of feudal powers that Governments are omnipotent, and draw within their sphere all that belongs to the individual, even the liberty of thought, speech, and conscience. This is an impious dogma of the past which should be repudiated, as opposed to the fundamental aims and ends of the Constitution of our Government. The essence of a constitution is *protection* of individual rights, and in popular Governments to restrain the power of majorities and secure the rights of minorities. Hence it has been truthfully said that the best Government is that which governs least. I characterize all pure, unmixed, and unconditional Governments, whether dependent on the will of one, few, or many, as alike repugnant to sound reason, to justice, and to the interests and happiness of mankind. Modern Turkey, medieval Venice, and ancient Athens, are examples alike of error in theory and injustice in practice, and wanting in the necessary conditions to secure permanent success and prosperity. I should be sorry to see our system degenerate into either the despotism of monarchy or the despotism of majorities, and I therefore oppose the very first step toward removing the wholesome checks imposed by the constitutional compact. I am well aware in stating this that constitutions are limitations self-imposed by the popular will, and that the sovereign power is competent to change them so as to make them better subserve the great ends of evil order and the welfare of the general mass. Like all other institutions, Governments are made for man, and contrived for his benefit; they conform to the errors and frailties of his nature, and are affected by the ignorances and vices of the times to which they belong. In this enlightened era, and in a land like ours, separated from the influence of ages of barbarism and wars, I shudder at the prospect of going back to any of the exploded forms of arbitrary power. I desire to stand by the traditions of our fathers, and above all to the legacy of that sound and beneficent form of Government which they have given us in the Constitution.

I hold that a good Government is bound to protect the individual in the enjoyment of life and liberty, and in the exercise of his faculties for labor, physical and mental, in the acquisition and preservation of property. It may be destructive, but it should be conservative in these respects. This proposition strikes at property, and it is justified on the doctrine of the wild and erratic though subtle and powerful thinker who proclaimed that all property is founded on robbery. Property, Mr. Speaker, is the stimulus to industry and the foundation of improvement and civilization. All that is valuable or valued belongs to the grand total of public or private wealth, the material products of nature, the field, the mine, and the water, with all their teeming variety of what is useful or necessary; the powers of mind, the stores of knowledge, the genius of the inventor, the harmony of the poet, and last the greatest, virtue itself, the priceless treasure of the soul, all that can be wished and hoped for, are embraced in the idea of property. The social and domestic relations are equally matters of individual ownership with flocks and herds, houses and lands. The affections of man's wife and children are among the dearest of his possessions, and as such are under the protection of the law. The domestic institution of slavery is one of these relations, and was recognized in the States of this Confederation as a species of proprietary interest. The Constitution describes slaves, and I suppose children and apprentices might come under the same class as persons bound to service.

I insist that no vindictory laws can be passed either depriving individuals of anything which can be denominated as property or infringing existing social relations as the punishment of the offenses either of men or communities. Neither Congress nor the assent of the States requisite to incorporate a new article or amendment into the Constitution can do so justly, under any pretense, when the object is to appropriate private property without due compensation, or confiscate it without the formality of trial and condemnation. Within the scope and reason of the Constitution any amendment to it would be legitimate when ratified by the required three fourths of the States; but for those three fourths to attempt a revolution in social or religious rights by seizing on what was never intended to be delegated by any of the parties to the compact, would be a prodigy of injustice carried out under the forms of law, a wrong more fatally so because made by the very highest authority. If an amendment were now proposed to the Constitution declaring an establishment of religion or prohibiting the free exercise of it by the citizen, it would be parallel with the present and no more obnoxious than this is to merited condemnation. The States, sovereign as I claim that they are and continue to be, could not have delegated what they did not themselves possess, that is, to destroy or appropriate individual rights without compensation. In all the acts of emancipation heretofore passed the tacit consent of the citizens affected accompanied the passage of the statute. A species of property which has ceased to be profitable is usually surrendered without protest or opposition. Men are not disposed to cavil at the exercise of a power abstractly arbitrary, which rids them of a relation which is onerous or inconvenient.

Such was slavery in the States where it has been abolished. But where it is one of the main sources of the prosperity of the community it will be regarded very differently.

This proposed alteration of the Constitution is therefore beyond the power of the Government, but the necessary consequences of it are revoltingly so. It involves the extermination of the white men of the southern States, and the forfeiture of all the land and other property belonging to them. Negroes and military colonists will take the place of the race thus blotted out of existence. Is this intended as the last scene of the bloody drama of carnage and civil war now being prosecuted? The world looks on with horror, and it will leave to future ages a fearful warning to avoid similar acts of perfidious atrocity. . . .

The control over slavery, and the domestic and social relations of the people of the respective States, was not and never was intended to be delegated to the United States, and cannot now be delegated except by the consent of all the States. Articles nine and ten of the Amendments to the Constitution are conclusive on this point. These articles are the general rules for the construction and interpretation of the entire instrument. Powers already granted may be modified, enlarged, or taken away by an amendment, but those which are retained by the people, or reserved to them or to the States, cannot be delegated to the United States, except by the unanimous consent of all the States. This is the only reasonable construction of those articles, in accordance with the plain sense and meaning of the words. The entire subject of slavery in the States has been reserved by them, and the right been retained by the people. No power has been delegated to the United States over this relation thus reserved to the legislative power of the State, and which is thus retained by the people, subject to such State power alone. It stands precisely on the same footing as that of eminent domain in the respective States, a prerogative of their inherent sovereignty, which cannot be taken away by an act of other States. How would an agreement between private parties be construed and interpreted which should declare that the articles of association might be modified and altered by three fourths of the number, and then should declare that certain rights were reserved to them individually? Would not, manifestly, the matters not delegated but reserved be considered as excepted from the subjects which were within the scope of the authority to alter or modify? Take the right of the States respectively of eminent domain within their territorial limits, could this be taken away from the States and delegated to the United States by the consent of the Legislatures of three fourths of the States, after a proposal made by two thirds of both Houses of Congress? I maintain that article ten of the Amendments is point-blank against such a supposition, and is equally repugnant to an invasion of the right of the State alone to legislate on the subject of slavery. I insist further, that, as the States themselves could not justly take away property or destroy social relations without giving just compensation, this is not only delegated by the States, but is among the rights retained by the people of the States where it exists, and that if all the States should delegate this power, it must, according to the rules of natural equity, be connected with the condition of allowing the masters a proper equivalent for the property taken or destroyed. . . .

Where now will be the right of each State to order and control its domestic institutions if the institutions of one fourth of the States are to be subjected to the will of the people of three fourths by amending the Constitution so as to make them belong to and under the control of a majority in Congress, or to wipe them out altogether?

About the time of the peace conferences an amendment which was substantially the converse of the present was proposed, declaring explicitly that no amendment affecting slavery should be valid that did not obtain the consent of all the States in which that institution existed. I believe if it had been adopted the present war would have been averted; and I consider that the suggestion made by the present Secretary of State, in one of his speeches during the last presidential canvass, that slavery could be constitutionally abolished when the number of free States had increased so as to allow the passage of this very amendment now under consideration, was one of the impelling causes that precipitated the struggle now convulsing the States and converted the "irrepressible conflict" of that political leader into the fearful strife of contending armies and warring States. This, the crowning act of the agitation of years against slavery, from the Missouri restriction to the invasion of Virginia by John Brown, whose chorus has become the music for the loyal hosts, comes at length to give a show of legality to the destruction of the institution of slavery. The very proposal of this amendment demonstrates the utter bad faith of the long series of acts which, illegally and in defiance of the Constitution, "the pledge of mutual friendship and the instrument of mutual happiness," sought to break down this domestic institution of the States of the South.

The proposal of this amendment arraigns the President as having violated the Constitution in his emancipation proclamation, and stamps it as a nullity and void. It is an implied confession that the Administration, carrying on an aggressive war on States and State institutions, had this design in view from the commencement—that the war was not for the purpose of sustaining the Government, preserving the Union, and maintaining the supremacy of the Constitution, but was directed against the sovereignties of the States, and to destroy such of their domestic institutions as were obnoxious to the views of the party controlling the Government for the time. The aggressor is always in the wrong in case of hostilities among States united under a federal system like ours, no matter on which side the General Government may array itself. This is the spirit embodied in the Crittenden resolutions, but it is not in accordance with the policy now avowed by the Administration in prosecuting the war, nor by the party which supports the President for reelection, and least of all by the proposed amendment to the Constitution. The Administration party have proclaimed "that the utter and complete extirpation of slavery from the soil of the Republic" is its present object, and support the adoption of an amendment to the Constitution to this effect. Impartial history, in dealing with these events, will pronounce a verdict that this attitude, and, above all, the attempt to change the Constitution to make that illegal which was not so before, shows that the moving cause of the war was from the commencement the prohibition of slavery. That design, suspected with such ample ground, is now rendered transparently clear. No candid mind can avoid the inevitable conclusion which will brand northern sectionalism as the primary cause of the war, and that the apprehensions of the southern people were fully justified by the events now taking place and by the previous acts and proclamations of the Government. The pretext that those acts were done in its defense will be regarded as a falsehood, only intended to deceive the people and conceal the real character of the war. . . .

The sentiment of opposition to slavery is so powerful that I could hardly expect to offer any reason which would awaken sympathy in behalf of its continuance, even if I showed that it was the best possible condition to insure the happiness of the negro race, or that its abolition was an invasion of the rights of the masters and the well-being of the communities where it existed. I have abstained from doing any more than to assert that the relation was one having a legal existence in the southern States and fully recognized by the Constitution. This is uncontrovertible, a fact not to be denied, and virtually admitted by the amendment now proposed. The theory that the States never parted with their sovereignty is likewise not acceptable to the opposite side of the House, and the notion that the General Government is paramount and can set aside all State authority is now popular. We are told, "Preserve the nation, though you tear the Constitution to a thousand pieces; hold the Union fast and let the Constitution slide as long as the nation remains; this generation, wiser and more patriotic than any that has gone before, is competent to devise a constitution better and nobler than that of Washington." I fear that I have no eloquence so persuasive, can make no appeals so winning as to convince the friends of the Administration that the Constitution cannot be improved by their wisdom, but I do insist that no cunning of man can frame a system of morality more perfect than that which demands that contracts between States and individuals should be observed inviolate, that mutual promises should be kept, and that faith should be preserved sacred and unbroken. If this is a nation, let not its national character be based on perfidy and falsehood. This would be worse than boldly proclaiming that it is founded on force, and that "might makes right.". . .

WILLIAM KELLEY [R., PA.]. The assertion of power or right in a majority of the States, either through the legislation of the Federal Government or through amendments of the Constitution, to interfere with or control the domestic institutions of a State, such, for example, as slavery, essentially repudiates the principle upon which the Union was formed, namely, the political equality of the States. Such a right or power conceded places the minority of States at the mercy of the majority. A Federal State to which the Constitution affords no guarantee that its domestic institutions shall not be changed by other States nor by the Federal Government, loses the very essence of its freedom, independence, and sovereignty.

The arguments against the proposed joint resolution arise, first, from the character of the proposition itself; and, secondly, from the time and circumstances or the condition of public affairs in which it is presented.

I do not propose, Mr. Speaker, to consider in detail all the objectionable features which this proposed amendment to the Constitution presents. I am, sir, at a loss for words wherein to express my sense of its true character. It assumes the name and form of liberty and the functions and power of free government to perpetrate and cover up a great public wrong. It is not the only instance in history of an attempt to prostitute liberty to unholy purpose and malignant passions. "O liberty, what crimes are committed in thy name!" was the last exclamation of Madam Roland—herself a true lover of liberty—as she stood upon the scaffold, amid the demoniac yells of a Parisian mob, the zealots of "liberty, equality, fraternity."

I shall notice in general terms some of the cardinal objections to the joint resolution:

1. It proposes a revolutionary change in the Government. It seeks to draw within the authority of the Federal Constitution and the Federal Congress a question of local or internal policy belonging exclusively to the slaveholding States, and is in conflict with the principles on which the Union was originally formed, and with the whole theory and spirit of the Constitution as to the rights of the States. It means that three fourths of the States may dictate to the other one fourth what shall be their domestic institutions, and how they shall govern their internal affairs may be taken away. It means that three fourths of the States may at pleasure, by a constitutional amendment, appropriate without compensation or confiscate the property of the other one fourth. In its present form the resolution is aimed at slavery; but it might, with equal propriety, be aimed at any other local law or institution of a State. It might as well propose that freedom of religious opinion should be abolished, and one form of religious worship only prevail in all the States; or that marriage should not take place except between certain classes and at certain ages and otherwise define marital rights, or be extended to regulate the relations of parent and child, or the canons of property, or the elective franchise. The principle of the proposed amendment is the principle of consolidation, and cannot be drawn into precedent without a final subversion of our constitutional Government. It is absurd to call a Federal Union wherein such a principle of consolidation has been introduced into its fundamental law a Union of free and equal States. The minority would be ever the subjects, not the coequals, of the majority of the States.

2. The amendment proposes to change the constitutional basis of representation and taxation. By the Constitution as it is five slaves count as three free persons only in the apportionment of Federal Representatives and direct taxes. The effect of the amendment, therefore, will be to increase southern representation, based upon the negro population, to the extent of two fifths at least of that population; and no man who knows the motives and policy of the party in power questions but that their object in part, by the proposed amendment, is to make the negro population not merely a passive but an active basis of representation in the Federal Government. First, the negro a citizen of the United States; secondly, the negro a free citizen of the United States, protected everywhere, in defiance of existing State constitutions and laws, as such citizen; and thirdly, the negro a voting citizen of the United States, are all propositions logically involved in the proposed amendment. The same revolutionary power which enfranchises negroes by presidential edicts of emancipation, or by constitutional amendments, carried, as this would be, in the southern States, if it receives the two-thirds vote of this Congress, so as to be submitted to the State Legislatures, by fraudulent elections and by duress of arms, would soon admit negroes to the elective franchise in all the States, and negro representatives in Congress would speak the voice of southern if not of the northern States. This is the designed effect of the proposed amendment in its change of the constitutional basis of representation.

In its operation upon the basis of taxation in the southern States, the effect of the proposed amendment would be to increase their quota of direct taxation while it diminished their wealth and ability of payment: first, in the direct loss of the value, equal perhaps to $2,000,000,000, of all slave property, by the act of abolition without compensation; second, in the diminished value of all southern agricultural lands, consequent upon the destruction of the organized system of labor that has made them productive and valuable; third, in the diminution, resulting from the same cause, of the products of all farm or plantation property. Whatever might be the remote and ultimate effects of abolition upon the wealth of the southern States, no man can doubt that its immediate effect would be to immensely reduce their aggregate wealth and to overburden with taxation and impoverish the present owners of property in those States.

3. The effect of this amendment would be to turn loose at once, without preparation or education for freedom, without property or the means whereby to live, and without the guidance, restraint, and protection of the superior intelligence and forethought of their masters or owners, the whole slave population of the southern States, numbering from three and a half to four million persons. A change so sudden and so radical in the industrial and social system of States, and especially in the condition of such a class of persons as the negro population of the southern States, is without precedent or justification in history; and we have no warrant for believing that it would

be a benign and healthful change. On the contrary, we have the testimony of one who, although an instrument, and an active instrument, in bringing about this great social revolution, has declared—but in this as in many other instances proved false to his own opinions—that "gradual, not sudden emancipation is better for all." All who know anything of the negro character know this to be true. Sudden freedom to the negro, without the capacity to appreciate and improve it, has proved not a blessing but a curse. On this point let tens of thousands of homeless, diseased, demoralized, starving, naked, helpless "contrabands" bear testimony.

4. This proposed amendment is designed to be the coadjutor and crowning effort of that stupendous system of confiscation or legalized plunder by which the party in power propose to restore the Union. They have already gone as far as they could do by acts of legislation and executive edicts of emancipation to seize and appropriate the property and free the slaves of those in arms against the Federal Government and to partition the southern lands among negroes, and now the final act of confiscation in the shape of this amendment is proposed to operate upon friend and foe, Union man and rebel alike; in the appropriation to public use without compensation of the entire slave property of the United States.

We have hitherto considered it a fundamental principle of civil polity, as it is a provision of our Constitution, that private property cannot be taken for public use without just compensation. This proposed amendment ignores and tramples upon that principle. If the public good really demands that the slave-owners of the South should surrender their slave property, is there any principle of constitutional freedom or of public justice that justifies the demand for that surrender without making adequate compensation? None, sir; and it is the plunder of despotism, not justice nor constitutional liberty, to take the property without making the compensation. There was a time, sir, when the President of the United States, now in office, and many of his friends in the Thirty-Seventh Congress, thought that slaves were property, and that if they were emancipated for the public good the United States should cooperate and help to pay for them. I refer for evidence on this point to the various messages and resolutions comprising his compensated emancipation scheme sent to the Thirty-Seventh Congress by President Lincoln, and to the action of that Congress on the subject. In this, as in most other cases, the President and his party have been false to their professions. What they once thought should not be taken without being paid for he, by his emancipation proclamation, and they by their proposed amendment to the Constitution—which he no doubt will approve if it passes this Congress—propose to take by the strong hand of a despotic majority without payment or compensation.

Again: if the proposed amendment be based upon the idea of punishment to slaveholders for their rebellion, then is it evidence of an attempt to punish a whole class for the crime of a part, the innocent for the guilty. If the slaveholders of South Carolina, for example, have rebelled and forfeited their slaves to the vengeance or justice of the law, they, and they alone, should be punished according to the law; but, sir, should the slaveholders of Kentucky, who have not rebelled nor forfeited any constitutional right, be swept into the same great revenge which it is proposed to visit upon the slaveholders of South Carolina? . . .

Mr. Speaker, I have no desire to discuss the right or policy of slavery at this time. It may be a sin; it may be impolite; it may be unprofitable. Arguments on both sides have been and can be made, and radical differences of opinion exist on the subject, and neither the power of a political majority nor the power of war can determine the abstract right or wrong of the opposing opinions. I am not the apologist nor friend of slavery, but no abstract or theoretical opinions about slavery determine my vote on the question before the House. If so be that slavery is dead, as the result of civil war, as many say, not of the emancipation proclamation, which the author of it has himself aptly termed *brutum fulmen*, I have no regrets for it; no tears to shed over its grave; its own advocates have done their part to slay it; let them reap as they have sown; I have no desire to revive or restore it. If, however, slavery be wounded high unto death, but not slain, I for one will not, for the sake of giving it its death-blow, either swear to or admit the right to abolish it by executive edict, or introduce into the Constitution of my country, by way of amendment, a principle and a precedent that may in an evil hour of excited passion like the present put the dagger to the heart of the freedom and independence of my own State, and make me the serf of a despotism. Better, sir, for our country, better for man, that negro slavery exist a thousand years than that American white men lose their constitutional liberty in the extinction of the constitutional sovereignty of the Federal States of this Union. Slavery is the creature of the States alone, not of the Federal Union; they made it, let them unmake it. If the States wherein slavery still lives, a mangled, bleeding, prostrate form, see fit to give it the final blow that shall make it a thing of the past, let them do it their own time and way. If, however, they see fit to nurse it into a further brief vitality, let them do it; it is their ward, not yours nor mine. . . .

EBON INGERSOLL [R., ILL.]. Mr. Speaker, having very recently taken a seat in this body, it was my intention to have contented myself with voting for all such measures as I believed to be just and expedient, and against such as I believed to be unjust or inexpedient without taking part in the discussion of such measures. But in justice to the liberty-loving and Union-loving men who sent me here, and in justice to myself I ask the indulgence of the House for the few minutes which have been generously given me by my friend, the honorable gentleman from California, [Mr. Shannon,] out of his hour, in which to discuss the joint resolution under consideration.

I have the proud honor to represent a district in which a very great majority of the people are thoroughly and unalterably anti-slavery. They are in favor of justice and against oppression and wrong everywhere and in every form. There are two grand objects for the accomplishment of which they have already freely given of their best blood and treasure, and stand ready to-day to give much more of both, if necessary, for the absolute and unconditional crushing out of this most wicked and devastating rebellion, and for the complete and utter extinction of human slavery, the sole and fearful cause of the rebellion. . . .

Sir, I hope this resolution may pass by the necessary majority to give it validity. All truly honest and philanthropic men throughout the world will have reason to rejoice and will rejoice if it so passes. It will be heralded over the world as another grand step upward and onward in the irresistible march of a christianized civilization. The old starry banner of our country, as it "floats over the sea and over the land," will be grander and more glorious than ever before. Its stars will be brighter; it will be holier; it will mean more than a mere nationality; it will mean universal liberty; it will mean that the rights of mankind, without regard to color or race, are respected and protected. The oppressed and downtrodden of all the world will take new courage; hope will spring afresh in their struggle and weary hearts; and when they look upon that banner in distant lands they will yearn to be here, where they can enjoy the inestimable blessings which are denied them forever on their native shores. . . .

Sir, I am in favor in the fullest sense of personal liberty. I am in favor of the freedom of speech. The freedom of speech that I am in favor of is the freedom which guaranties to the citizen of Illinois, in common with the citizen of Massachusetts, the right to proclaim the eternal principles of liberty, truth, and justice in Mobile, Savannah, or Charleston with the same freedom and security as though he were standing at the foot of Bunker Hill monument; and if this proposed amendment to the Constitution is adopted and ratified, the day is not far distant when this glorious privilege will be accorded to every citizen of the Republic. I am in favor of the adoption of this amendment because it will secure to the oppressed slave his natural and God-given rights. I believe that the black man has certain inalienable rights, which are as sacred in the sight of Heaven as those of any other race. I believe he has a right to live, and live in a state of freedom. He has a right to breathe the free air and enjoy God's free sunshine. He has a right to till the soil, to earn his bread by the sweat of his brow, and enjoy the rewards of his own labor. He has a right to the endearments and enjoyment of family ties; and no white man has any right to rob him of or infringe upon any of these blessings.

I am in favor of the adoption of this amendment to the Constitution for the sake of the seven millions of poor white people who live in the slave States but who have ever been deprived of the blessings of manhood by reason of this thrice-accused institution of slavery. Slavery has kept them in ignorance, in poverty, and in degradation. Abolish slavery, and school-houses will rise upon the ruins of the slave mart, intelligence will take the place of ignorance, wealth of poverty, and honor of degradation; industry will go hand in hand with virtue, and prosperity with happiness, and a disinthralled and regenerated people will rise up and bless you and be an honor to the American Republic. . . .

Senate-38th Congress, 1st Session
March 28-April 8, 1864

LYMAN TRUMBULL [R., ILL.]. Mr. President, as the organ of the Committee on the Judiciary which has reported this resolution to the Senate, I desire to present briefly some of the considerations which induced me, at least, to give it my support. It is a proposition so to amend the Constitution of the United States as forever to prohibit slavery within its jurisdiction, and authorize the Congress of the United States to pass such laws as may be necessary to carry this provision into effect.

Without stopping to inquire into all the causes of our troubles, and of the distress, desolation, and death which have grown out of this atrocious rebellion, I suppose it will be generally admitted that they sprung from slavery. If a large political party in the North attribute these troubles to the impertinent interference of nothern philanthropists and fanatics with an institution in the southern States with which they had no right to interfere, I reply, if there had been no such alleged impertinent interference; if there had been no slavery in the South, there could have been no abolitionists in the North to interfere with it. If, upon the other hand, it be said that this rebellion grows out of the attempt on the part of those in the interest of slavery to govern this country so as to perpetuate and increase the slaveholding power, and failing in this that they have endeavored to overthrow the Government and set up an empire of their own, founded upon slavery as its chief corner-stone, I reply, if there had been no slavery there could have been no such foundation on which to build. If the freedom of speech and of the press, so dear to the freeman everywhere, especially cherished in this time of war by a large party in the North who are nor opposed to interfering with slavery, has been denied us all our lives in one half the States of the Union, it was by reason of slavery.

If these Halls have resounded from our earliest recollections with the strifes and contests of sections ending sometimes in blood, it was slavery which almost always occasioned them. No superficial observer, even, of our history North or South, or of any party, can doubt that slavery lies at the bottom of our present troubles. Our fathers who made the Constitution regarded it as an evil, and looked forward to its early extinction. They felt the inconsistency of their position, while proclaiming the equal rights of all to life, liberty, and happiness, they denied liberty, happiness, and life itself to a whole race, except in subordination to them. It was impossible, in the nature of things, that a Government based on such antagonistic principles could permanently and peacefully endure, nor did its founders expect it would. They looked forward to the not distant, nor as they supposed uncertain period when slavery should be abolished, and the Government become in fact, what they made it in name, one securing the blessings of liberty to all. The history of the last seventy years has proved that the founders of the Republic were mistaken in their expectations; and slavery, so far from gradually disappearing as they had anticipated, had so strengthened itself that in 1860 its advocates demanded the control of the nation in its interests, failing in which they attempted its overthrow. This attempt brought into hostile collision the slaveholding aristocracy, who made the right to live by the toil of others the chief article of their faith, and the free laboring masses of the North, who believed in the right of every man to eat the bread his own hands had earned.

In the earlier stages of the war there was an indisposition on the part of the executive authority to interfere with slavery at all. For a long time slaves who escaped from their rebel owners and came within our lines were driven back. Congress, however, at an early day took action upon this subject, and at the very first session which met after the rebellion broke out, the special session of July, 1861, a law was passed declaring free all slaves who were permitted by their masters to take any part in the rebellion. Under the provisions of that act, had it been efficiently executed, a great many slaves must necessarily have obtained their freedom. The constitutionality of the act would seem to be clear. I do not suppose that even my honorable friend from Kentucky [Mr. Davis] would deny the proposition that if we captured a slave engaged, by consent of his master, in constructing rebel works and fortifications, we might set him free.

That act, however, has not been executed. So far as I am advised not a single slave has been set at liberty under it. Subsequently, at the regular session of Congress which convened in December, 1861, an act of a more comprehensive character was passed—a law providing for the freedom of all slaves who should come within the lines of our armies, who should be deserted by their masters, or who should be found in regions of country which had been occupied by rebel troops and afterwards came within our possession, and who belonged to rebel masters. It is under the provisions of this law that most of the slaves made free have been emancipated. This act also authorized the President of the United States to organize and employ as many persons of African descent as he should think proper to aid in the suppression of the rebellion. But it was a long time before this law was put in operation. Although it was an act called for by the public sentiment of the country, and although it was the duty of those charged with the execution of the laws to see that it was faithfully executed, it was more than a year after its enactment before any considerable number of persons of African descent were organized and armed; and even at this day a much smaller number are in the service than would have been by an efficient execution of the law. It was not until after the passage of this act that our officers, especially in the West, ceased to expel slaves who came within the lines of our Army; and so persistently was this practice persevered in that Congress had to interfere by positive enactment, and declare that any officer of the Army or Navy who aided in restoring a slave to his master should be dismissed from the public service, before it could be stopped.

But, sir, had these laws, all of them, been efficiently executed they would not wholly have extirpated slavery. They were only aimed at the slaves of rebels. Congress never undertook to free the slaves of loyal men; no act has ever passed for that purpose.

At a later period, the President by proclamation undertook to free the slaves in certain localities. Notice of this proclamation was given in September, 1862, and it was to become effective in January, 1863. Unlike the acts of Congress, which undertook to free the slaves of rebels only, and of such as came under our control, the President's proclamation excepted from its provisions the regions of country subject to our authority, and declared free the slaves only who were in regions of country from which the authority of the United States was expelled, enjoining upon the persons proposed to be made free to abstain from all violence unless in necessary self-defense, and recommending them in all cases, when allowed, to labor faithfully for reasonable wages.

The force and effect of this proclamation are understood very differently by its advocates and opponents. The former insist that it is and was within the constitutional power of the President, as Commander-in-Chief, to issue such a proclamation; that it is the noblest act of his life or the age; and that by virtue of its provisions all slaves within the localities designated become *ipso facto* free; while others declare that it was issued without competent authority, and has not and cannot effect the emancipation of a single slave. These latter insist that the most the President could do, as commander of the armies of the United States, would be, in the absence of legislation, to seize and free the slaves which came within the control of the Army; that the power exercised by a commander-in-chief, as such, must be a power exercised in fact, and that beyond his lines where his armies cannot go his orders are mere *brutum fulmen*, and can neither work a forfeiture of property nor freedom of slaves; that the power of Fremont and Hunter, commanders-in-chief for a certain time in their departments, who assumed to free the slaves within their respective commands, was just as effective within the boundaries of their commands as that of the Commander-in-Chief of all the departments, who as commander could not draw to himself any of his presidential powers; and that neither had or could have any force except within the lines and where the Army actually had the power to execute the order; that to that extent the previous acts of Congress would free the slaves of rebels, and if the President's proclamation had any effect it would only be to free the slaves of loyal men, for which the laws of the land did not provide. I will not undertake to say which of these opinions is correct, nor is it necessary for my purposes to decide. It is enough for me to show that any and all these laws and proclamations, giving to each the largest effect claimed by its friends, are ineffectual to the destruction of slavery. The laws of Congress if faithfully executed would leave remaining the slaves belonging to loyal masters, which, considering how many are held by children and females not engaged in the rebellion, would be no inconsiderable number, and the President's proclamation excepts from its provisions all of Delaware, Maryland, Kentucky, Tennessee, Missouri, and a good portion of Louisiana and Virginia—almost half the slave States.

If then we are to get rid of the institution, we must have some more efficient way of doing it than by the proclamations that have been issued or the acts of Congress which have been passed.

Some, however, say that we may pass an act of Congress to abolish slavery altogether, and petitions are sent to Congress asking it to pass such a law. I am as anxious to get rid of slavery as any person; but has Congress authority to pass a law abolishing slavery everywhere, freeing the slaves of the loyal, the slaves of the friends of the Government as well as the slaves of the disloyal and of the enemies of the Government? Why, sir, it has been an admitted axiom from the foundation of this Government, among all parties, that Congress had no authority to interfere with slavery in the States where it existed. But it is said this was in a time of peace, and we are now at war, and Congress has authority to carry on war, and in carrying on war we may free the slaves. Why so? Because it is necessary; for no other reason. If we can do it by act of Congress it must be because it is a necessity to the prosecution of the war. We have authority to put down the enemies of the country; we have the right to slay them in battle; we have authority to confiscate their property; but, mark you, does that give any authority to slay the friends of the country, to confiscate the property of the friends of the country, or to free the slaves of the friends of the country?

But it is said that freeing slaves would aid us in raising troops; that slaves are unwilling to volunteer and enter the public service unless other slaves are made free, and that we could raise troops better, sooner, and have a more efficient army if slavery were declared abolished. Suppose that were so, is it a necessity? Can we not raise an army without doing this? Has not the Congress of the United States unlimited authority to provide for the raising of armies by draft, by force to put any and every man capable of bearing arms into its service? Have we not already passed a law compelling men to enter the service of the Government in its defense and for the putting down this rebellion? Then there is no necessity to free the slaves in order to raise an army.

But it is a convenience, perhaps some will say; Sir, it is not because a measure would be convenient that Congress has authority to adopt it. The measure must be appropriate and needful to carry into effect some granted power, or we have no authority to adopt it. I can imagine a thousand things that would aid us to raise troops which no one would contend Congress had authority to do. We now find that it is costing us a large sum of money to carry on this war. There are apprehensions in some quarters that the finances of the country will not be sufficient to prosecute it to the end. A measure that would enable us to carry on the war cheaper would certainly be one in aid of this war power. In consequence of the prosperity which prevails in the country, wages at this time are very high. Men are unwilling to enlist without large bounties and large pay, because they get high wages at home. Suppose we introduce a bill that no man shall be paid in any manufacturing establishment, at any mechanic art, or for his daily labor, more than ten cents a day, and we visit with penalities and punishment any man who shall give to his employe more than that sum; do you not think that would hold out an additional inducement to volunteer? But who would contend that Congress had any such authority? Manifestly it has not. Nor can I find the constitutional authority to abolish slavery everywhere by act of Congress as a necessity to prosecuting the war.

Then, sir, in my judgment, the only effectual way of ridding the country of slavery, and so that it cannot be resuscitated, is by an amendment of the Constitution forever prohibiting it within the jurisdiction of the United States. The amendment adopted, not only does slavery cease, but it can never be reestablished by State authority, or in any other way than by again amending the Constitution. Whereas, if slavery should now be abolished by act of Congress or proclamation of the President, assuming that either has the power to do it, there is nothing in the Constitution to prevent any State from reestablishing it. This change of the Constitution will also relieve us of all difficulty in the restoration to the Union of the rebel States when our brave soldiers shall have reduced them to obedience to the laws.

To secure its passage requires, in the first instance, a vote of two thirds in its favor in each branch of Congress, and its ratification subsequently by three fourths of the States of the Union. Can these majorities be obtained? It is very generally conceded, I believe, by men of all political parties, that slavery is gone; that the value of slavery is destroyed by the rebellion. What objection, then, can there be on the part of any one, in the present state of public feeling in the country, to giving the people an opportunity to pass upon this question? I would appeal to Senators upon the opposite side of the Chamber, and ask them—for I expect some of them to support this measure, and I trust all of them will—what objection they have to submitting this question to the people and letting them pass upon it? Do any of you deny that slavery lies at the bottom of this rebellion? Do you believe that we should have had this terrible war upon us had there been no slavery in the land? I repeat, then, why not afford an opportunity to the people to pass upon this amendment? I trust I do not assume too much when I assume that it will receive the requisite vote of two thirds of each branch of Congress.

Having obtained that, the question then arises, is it probable that it can have the ratification of three fourths of the States? We have now thirty-five States, and bills have passed both branches of Congress and been approved by the President for the creation of two more, Colorado and Nevada, which will make thirty-seven. When these States are admitted it will require the concurring vote of twenty-eight States in order to adopt this amendment.

If Nebraska should be admitted, for the admission of which a bill is now pending, that would make the number of States thirty-eight, and the votes of twenty-nine States would then be requisite to adopt the amendment. But the admission of Nebraska would not probably affect the result, as, if admitted, she would most probably vote for the amendment.

Of the thirty-seven States, twenty-one are free States, including Colorado and Nevada, and I assume that all those States would vote for this constitutional amendment. There are, then, the States of Maryland, West Virginia, Missouri, Arkansas, Tennessee, and Louisiana, all of which have taken initiatory steps for the abolition of slavery within their borders; and I think we might confidently count that they would unite with the free States to pass this amendment. Those six added to the twenty-one free States would make twenty-seven. Then there is the State of Delaware, with hardly slaves enough in it to count, which would be left standing alone with free States all around her. Although she has not yet, so far as I am aware, taken any legislative steps for the abolition of slavery, though the question is agitated among her people, I cannot think she would stand alone in such a locality, resisting a constitutional amendment which would forever give us peace on this question.

I have assumed that all the free States will adopt the amendment. It is now very generally conceded that slavery is not a divine institution. The few in the northern or free States who attempt to uphold it do so on constitutional grounds, denying the authority of the Government to interfere with it; but none of these persons deny or can deny the power of the people to amend the Constitution in the mode prescribed by the instrument itself. If, then, they shall oppose an amendment for the abolition of slavery, it will not be because to abolish it in that form is unconstitutional, but because it is not right, or, if right, not expedient.

I think, then, it is reasonable to suppose that if this proposed amendment passes Congress, it will within a year receive the ratification of the requisite number of States to make it a part of the Constitution. That accomplished, and we are forever freed of this troublesome question. We accomplish then what the statesmen of this country have been struggling to accomplish for years. We take this question entirely away from the politics of the country. We relieve Congress of sectional strifes, and, what is better than all, we restore to a whole race that freedom which is theirs by the gift of God, but which we for generations have wickedly denied them.

I know that the passage of this measure will not end this rebellion. I do not claim that for it. There is but one way to do that; and that is by the power of our brave soldiers. We can never have the Union restored, the authority of the Constitution recognized, and its laws obeyed and respected, until our armies shall overcome and vanquish the rebel armies. We must look to our soldiers, to our patriotic Army, to put down the rebellion. But, sir, when they shall have accomplished that, this measure will secure to us future peace. That is what I claim for it. I trust that within a year, in less time than it will take to make this constitutional amendment effective, our armies will have put to flight the rebel armies. I think it ought long ago to have been done; and I think but for the indecision, the irresolution, the want of plan, and the scattering of our forces, it would have been done long ago. Hundreds of millions of treasure and a hundred thousand lives would have been saved had the power of this Republic been concentrated under one mind and hurled in masses upon the main rebel armies. This is what our patriotic soldiers have wanted, and what I trust is now soon to be done.

But instead of looking back and mourning over the errors of the past, let us remember them only for the lessons they teach for the future. Forgetting the things which are past, let us press forward to the accomplishment of what is before. We have at last placed at the head of our armies a man in whom the country has confidence, a man who has won victories wherever he has been, and I trust that his mind is to be permitted uninterfered with to unite our forces, never before so formidable as to-day, in one or two grand armies and hurl them upon the rebel force. Let him put to flight the main rebel army which has threatened the capital for the last three years, and the small rebel armies will quickly succumb. I look for that result during the coming campaign, and with that result, if we civilians do our duty, we shall have the authority of the Constitution vindicated, constitutional liberty reestablished, the Union restored, and freedom everywhere proclaimed. . . .

HENRY WILSON [R., MASS.]. Mr. President, "our country," said that illustrious statesman, John Quincy Adams, "began its existence by the universal emancipation of man from the thralldom of man." Amidst the darkling storms of revolution it proclaimed as its living faith the sublime creed of human equality. From out the rolling clouds of battle the new republic, as it took its position in the family of nations, proclaimed in the ear of all humanity that the poor, the humble, the sons of toil, whose hands were hardened by honest labor, whose limbs were chilled by the blasts of winter, whose cheeks were scorched by the suns of summer, were the peers, the equals, before the law, of kings and princes and nobles, of the most favored of the sons of men. When its splendid edifice of constitutional government rose in grandeur and beauty upon the vision of mankind, the champions of popular rights in the Old World, and the people, in whose hearts still lingered the dimly-remembered accents of liberty, as they turned their gaze hitherward, hailed and welcomed the advent of the new-born Republic. In after years, amid the throes of revolutions, they turned ever to the rising

Republic beyond the seas for the inspiration of faith and hope in the final triumph of struggling humanity. And the republics of the New World, as they emerged from colonial dependence, through the fire and blood of revolutions, to national life, turned toward united America as the great exemplar whose steady lights would illume their darkened pathway to national unity and power, and liberty regulated by law.

We of America have been accustomed, Mr. President, to contemplate with something of gratified and patriotic pride the strength of our democratic institutions and the stability of our republican Government. As we have watched the fraternal strifes, the bloody and desolating wars of factions that, in the republics of the New World, have followed each other like the fleeting shadows of summer clouds, as we have watched, too, the revolutionary throes and struggles, the falling and rising thrones and dynasties of the Old World, we have often turned fondly and proudly to our own country in the undoubting faith that the Republic was immortal, that, sustained by the vital and animating patriotism of a Christian people, it was ever instinct with the freshness and bloom of youth and the vigor of matured manhood. Gazing with beaming eye and the throbbing heart upon the grandeur and beauty of this splendid edifice of constitutional government in America, we came to believe that it was as imperishable as the memory of its illustrious builders.

But the Republic of the United States, the land of so much of affection, of pride, and of hopes, now presents to the startled and astonished gaze of mankind a humiliating and saddening spectacle. The treasonable menaces of other days have now ripened into treasonable deeds. Civil war now holds its carnival and reaps its bloody harvests. The nation is grappling with a gigantic conspiracy, struggling for existence, for the preservation of its menaced life, against a rebellion that finds no parallel in the annals of the world.

When the echoes of the cannon treason trained upon Sumter smote upon the startled ear of the nation, patriotism summoned the people to assume the responsibilities of consummated power, and by the red hand of war shield the life and protect the liberties of the nation, menaced by this foul revolt against law and order, liberty and civilization. That patriotism which garners the hallowed memories of the past, which comprehends the vital issues of the present, which is instinct with the aspirations of the future that looms up grand and great, bade wealth open its coffers to meet the needs of the imperiled nation, and the citizen bare his bosom to the blows aimed at the nation's life; it bade the mother offer upon the altar of her endangered country her fair-haired boy in the bloom and pride of youth; it bade the wife send forth the husband of her love and hope to the harvest of death; and manhood.

— offer youth and beauty
On the wasting shrine
Of a stern and lofty duty.

Mindful of a country to serve and to save, hundreds of thousands of the young men of loyal America have left their blooming fields, their forests and mines, their ringing workshops and mills, their ships that "help to wind the silken chain of commerce round the world," their homes hallowed by associations and memories, their parents, brothers, sisters, wives, children, friends, the dear and the loved, to follow the old flag of united America to the battle-field, there to bear soldiers' burdens, do soldiers' duties, and fill, if it might be, soldiers' graves. We saw them as they thronged at the summons of duty around the unrolled banners of the Republic; we heard the glad music of their march; we gazed upon the glittering steel and upon the gleaming banners as they fluttered away from our straining sight; and with throbbing heart, quickened pulse, quivering lip, and tearful eye, we commended them to the guardian care of that Being who notes even the sparrow's fall.

Through nearly three years of alternate successes and disasters, of weary toils, wasting marches, and decimating battles, they have borne bravely the banners of our unity and power. Many, who went from us in the pride of lusty life, now sleep in their bloody shrouds in the crowded and shallow trenches of the fields made immortal by their constancy and valor. Many, wasted by disease or falling by the hand of war, rest beneath lonely mounds on battle-fields, along the lines of marches, around the encampments and the hospitals, or in the graveyards beneath their own northern skies. Many broken by disease, or maimed by shot shell, lie in the hospitals, or linger among us, reminding us of the appalling sacrifices of this revolt of barbarism. Worn out and wasted by the storms of war, regiments that marched away with crowded ranks are standing sternly front to the armed foes of the Republic wherever they menace the authority of the nation, ready to follow their torn and faded flags into fresh battle-fields. The wasting battalions that opened the Mississippi, so that its waters, from their sources to the Gulf, reflect back the stars of our national flag; the war-smitten regiments of the army of the Potomac, that on the immortal field of Gettysburg rolled back the advancing legions of the rebellion, broke its power, and blasted its hopes forever, must yet be renewed by the fresh vigor and blood of the people. The needs of the imperiled country still demand that the decimated ranks of our veteran heroes that now bear upon their bayonets the unity and existence of the nation should be crowded with the manhood of the Republic.

Why is it, Mr. President, that this magnificent continental Republic is now rent, torn, dissevered, by civil war? Why is it that the land resounds with the measured tread of a million of armed men? Why is it that our bright waters are stained and our green fields reddened with fraternal blood? Why is it that the young men of America, in the pride and bloom of early manhood, are summoned from homes, from the mothers who bore them, from the wives and sisters who love them, to the fields of bloody strife? Why is it that millions of the men and women of Christian America are sorrowing with aching hearts and tearful eyes for the absent, the loved, and the lost? Why is it that the heart of loyal America throbs heavily oppressed with anxiety and gloom for the future of the country?

Sir, this gigantic crime against the peace, the unity, and the life of the nation is to make eternal the hateful dominion of man over the souls and bodies of his fellow-men. These sacrifices of property, of health, and of life, these appalling sorrows and agonies now upon us, are all the merciless inflictions of slavery in its gigantic effort to found its empire and make its hateful power forever dominant in Christian America. Yes, slavery is the conspirator that conceived and organized this mighty conspiracy against the unity and existence of the Republic. Slavery is the traitor that madly plunged the nation into the fire and blood and darkness of civil war. Slavery is the criminal whose hands are dripping with the blood of our murdered sons. Yes, sir, slavery is the conspirator, the traitor, the criminal that is reddening the sods of Christian America with the blood of fathers and husbands, sons and brothers, and bathing them with the bitter tears of mothers, wives, and sisters.

Sir, slavery—bold, proud, domineering, with hate in its heart, scorn in its eye, defiance in its mien—has pronounced against the existence of republican institutions in America, against the supremacy of the Government, the unity and life of the nation. Slavery, hating the cherished institutions that tend to secure the rights and enlarge the privileges of mankind; despising the toiling masses as mudsills and white slaves; defying the Government, its Constitution and its laws, has openly pronounced itself the mortal and unappeasable enemy of the Republic. Slavery stands to-day the only clearly pronounced foe our country has on the globe. Therefore every word spoken, every line written, every act performed, that keeps the breath of life in slavery for a moment, is against the existence of democratic institutions, against the dignity of the toiling millions, against the liberty, the peace, the honor, the renown, and the life of the nation. In the lights of to-day that flash upon us from camp and battle-field, the loyal eye, heart, and brain of America sees and feels and realizes that the death of slavery is the life of the nation! The loyal voice of patriotism pronounces, in clear accents, that American slavery must die that the American Republic may live! . . .

The Thirty-Seventh Congress enacted by decisive majorities a new article of war for the government of all our armies, that persons claimed as fugitive slaves shall not be surrendered by persons engaged in the military or naval service on pain of being dismissed from that service.

Sir, the Thirty-Seventh Congress declared in the confiscation act that no slave escaping into any State, Territory, or the District of Columbia, should be delivered up or deprived of his liberty in any way except for some offense against the laws, unless the person claiming said fugitive shall make oath that he has not been in arms against the United States, nor given aid and comfort to the rebellion in any way; and that no persons in the military or naval service shall assume to decide upon the validity of any claim to fugitive slaves, nor surrender any such persons to the claimant, on pain of being dismissed from the service. By the ninth section of that act, the Thirty-Seventh Congress provided that all slaves of persons in rebellion against the Government of the United States escaping and taking refuge within the lines of the Army, or captured from such persons or deserted by them, should be deemed captures of war and should be forever free. By this sweeping net the Thirty-Seventh Congress decreed that freedom should follow the advancing flag of the Republic wherever our armies should march in the rebel States.

The President was authorized by the Thirty-Seventh Congress to receive into the military service of the United States the slaves of rebel masters, and the slaves so accepted for military purposes, their mothers, their wives, and their children if held in servitude by rebel masters were made free forever. This series of acts of the Thirty-Seventh Congress "loosing," in the words of John C. Breckinridge, "all bonds," though resisted, misrepresented, and maligned will be sanctioned by the approval of the present and of coming ages, by that patriotism that embraces the permanent and lasting interests of United America, by that humanity that cares for the poor and lowly, by that religion that recognizes in the humblest of the children of men a being made in the image of God for whom Christ mounted the cross. The act giving a gratuity of $1,000,000 to the loyal slave-masters of the District of Columbia, and the vote pledging the nation to aid emancipation in the loyal States, will stand forever as evidences of the moderation, the justice, and the self-sacrificing spirit of the statesmen who carried through Congress this series of humane, Christian, and patriotic measures.

Sir, on the 22d of September, 1862, the President of the United States called the attention of all persons engaged in the military and naval service to these humane, wise, and comprehensive provisions of the laws of Congress, and he "enjoined and ordered" them to "observe, obey, and enforce them," and those title-deeds to freedom were thereafter to be enforced in the land of the rebellion by the glittering bayonets of a million men.

But the President of the United States, on the 22d of September, 1862, startled and thrilled the nations by that immortal proclamation that announced "that on the 1st day of January, in the year of our Lord 1863, all persons held as slaves within any State, or in any designated part of a State, the people whereof shall be in rebellion against the United States, shall be then, thenceforward, and forever free; and the Executive Government of the United States, including the military and naval authority thereof, will recognize and maintain the freedom of such persons, and will do no act or acts to repress such persons, or any of them, in any efforts they may make for their actual freedom." On the 1st day of January, 1863, the President of the United States, "invoking the considerate judgment of mankind and the gracious favor of Almighty God," redeemed this solemn pledge of the 22d of September, which the recording angel had registered. On that day the irreversible decree was sent forth to master and slave, to earth and heaven. By this exercise of the war powers of the Government all persons held as slaves in any State or part thereof in rebellion were declared to be "then, thenceforward, and forever free," and the Executive, the military and naval authorities were pledged to recognize and maintain the freedom of such persons. This complete, absolute, and final decree of emancipation in rebel States, born of military necessity, proclaimed by the Commander-in-Chief of the Army and Navy, is the settled and irrepealable law of the Republic, to be observed, obeyed, and enforced, by Army and Navy, and by the irreversible voice of the nation.

The enforcement of this proclamation will give peace and order, freedom and unity, to a now distracted country; the failure to enforce it will bring with it discord and anarchy, a dissevered Union and a broken nation. The issues are clearly and distinctly drawn by this proclamation between law and order and freedom and a united nation on the one hand, and anarchy and discord and slavery and a shivered and dishonored Union on the other. Freedom, humanity, and religion, the unerring voice of patriotism, pronounces all attempts to defeat the enforcement of this proclamation decreeing the freedom of all slaves in rebel States as unpatriotic, as criminal, ay, as treasonable, too, as were the efforts to defeat the final establishment of the Declaration of the 4th of July, 1776. The men who sought to defeat the consummation of that "proclamation of the universal emancipation of man from the thralldom of man" sank into obscure and dishonored graves under the blasting and withering fires of outraged patriotism. The fires of patriotism burn as brightly now as in earlier days, and the men "who," in the words of a gallant soldier, "emerge from their gloom as the shadows fall upon their country," the men who prate of the constitutional rights of slavery, treason, and crime, should remember the fate of the "skulking neutrals" and the sticklers for "rightful authority" in 1776 ere joining in giving aid and comfort to the traitor chiefs. Patriotism instinctively indorses this proclamation of emancipation; treason in every fiber of its being strives with bloody hands to throttle it. In the fiery and bloody struggles through which this proclamation has passed, struggles that have stirred this nation to its profoundest depths, patriotism will mark and brand the men who care more for the safety of the slaves of rebel masters than for the blood of brave men fighting the battles of to the endangered country, more for the perpetuity of slavery in rebellion than for the unity and the perpetuity of the Republic.

Sir, eighteen eventful months have passed since the policy of emancipation in the rebel States was announced to the doubting nations. Met on its announcement by the vehement resistance of mighty interests, assailed by passion and prejudice, misunderstood by timidity and ignorance, that transcendent measure, sanctioned alike by liberty, humanity, and patriotism, has fought its way till it has won for our country doubting friends, conquered the country's enemies in the Old World, and laid low the vaunted power of its assailants in the New. It has lifted up the bloody civil war in America from what European statesmen were went to characterize as "a mere struggle for power on the one hand, and independence on the other," to a holy war for liberty, humanity, and civilization against the rebel slavemongers, fighting to perpetuate in Christian America a vulgar, brutal, and loathsome barbarism. This proclamation of emancipation, sent forth by the President in the name of the menaced nation, by elevating the struggle in which we are engaged, is fast winning for our country the active sympathies of humanity the wide world over.

Since emancipation in the rebel States was proclaimed as the settled policy of the Republic, the huge, horrid, and ghastly system of human slavery in republican and Christian America, that in the pride and arrogance of its power mocked and jeered at the claims of toiling millions, scoffed at and derided the higher law, and defied the authority of the country, is hastening to its unglorious end, to the grave of dishonor that knows no resurrection. Its worshipers, who were swift to come to its support before they were called, and to run on its errands before they were sent, are slinking away from it in this its hour of bitter humiliation, or hastening to announce, in accents of anguish, that the idol of their worship is dethroned, fallen, dead forevermore.

Sir, slavery in the loyal States is hastening to its fall. Delaware sends to the House of Representatives an immediate emancipationist as the exponent of her sentiments and opinions that ere long will be embodied in a decree of liberty. Maryland has summoned a convention to smite the fetters from the limbs of her bondmen, and to place her in the list of free Commonwealths. West Virginia, carved out of the ancient dominion, begins her career by a deed of gradual emancipation. Missouri proclaims a system of gradual emancipation, which her interests and advancing public sentiment alike demand shall be transformed into a system of immediate and unconditional abolition. Kentucky alone, among the loyal States, bears the banners of slavery proudly and defiantly. Spared by the tender mercy of the President of the United States, slavery there vauntingly proclaims its power, and assumes to control the destinies of that Commonwealth. But the inexorable logic of events, the advancing sentiments of her people, the efforts of many of her noblest sons, will rescue "the dark and bloody ground" from the domination of slavemasters, and the opprobrium of continuing to be what she now is, the slave-pen of loyal America, into which slavemongers run slaves from the States where slavery is perishing, and where men made free by the President's proclamation in rebel States are often arrested and imprisoned in shameless defiance of Federal authority. Tennessee, excepted by the President in his proclamation of emancipation, is, under the lead of Andrew Johnson, ripening for immediate and unconditional emancipation. Arkansas accepts the proclamation and prohibits slavery forever in her organic law. Louisiana elects a State administration pledged by her Governor in his inaugural address to the "universal and immediate extinction of slavery as a public and private blessing," to base the regenerated State on a "devotion to the Union, on a love of liberty to all men, and on a spirit of justice and humanity"—to put her constitution in harmony with the proclamation of freedom. The government of Virginia recognized by the Congress of the United States, by an amendment to her organic law decrees immediate emancipation, and Federal bayonets will enforce that decree in that ancient Commonwealth, where repose the ashes of Washington and Henry, Jefferson and Madison, Mason and Marshall, and other champions of emancipation in her better days. Congress, not by the consent of the loyal States or loyal masters, but by the will and power of the nation, makes free at once and forever every slave who enlists into the military service. The Attorney General pronounces the black man, who was said to have no rights that white men were bound to respect, a citizen of the United States. The Secretary of State gives the black man the passport of citizenship, which in every quarter of the globe is evidence that the bearer is a citizen of the North American Republic. The Secretary of War commissions a black man to be a surgeon in the military service of the United States, and the President organizes a hundred and twenty regiments, of eighty thousand black men, who are bearing upon their flashing bayonets the unity of the Republic, and the destinies of their race.

Sir, slavery in America, though upheld by interests, customs, and usages, trenched about by inhuman statutes, and hedged around by passionate, vehement, and unreasoning prejudices, is fast crumbling to atoms beneath the blows rained upon it by a liberty-loving and patriotic people. But let anti-slavery men listen to no truce, to no compromise, to no cry for mercy. Let them now be as inflexible as justice, as inexorable as destiny. Whenever and wherever a blow can be dealt at the vitals of the retreating fiend, let that blow be struck in the name of the bleeding nation, and of the "dumb, toiling millions bound and sold." A truce with slavery is a defeat for the nation. A compromise with slavery is a present of disaster and dishonor and a future of anarchy and blood. Mercy to slavery is a crime against liberty. The death of slavery is the annihilation of the rebellion, the unity of the Republic, the life of the nation, the harmonious development of republican institutions, the repose, culture, and renown of the people.

Though riven and shattered by the storms of the stupendous civil war it inaugurated, slavery still battles for existence with the reckless audacity of that desperation which sees with clear vision its impending doom. Though waning in power, slavery still retains in its grasp vast masses of men in the loyal States, ready to do its bidding, and presents in its defense a rampart of three hundred thousand gleaming bayonets. These masses must be won over to the gathering hosts of freedom, or utterly routed, and that rampart of glittering steel must go down before the advancing legions of the Republic, ere slavery sinks into the grave that knows no resurrection.

Sir, let not the anti-slavery men of this age forget that the founders of the

Republic believed slavery would wither and die beneath the blended rays of
the Christian and democratic institutions they founded. Let them not forget
that slavery was then a mendicant, pleading for forbearance and mercy, for
a little time to hide itself from the gaze of that humanity it outraged and
dishonored. Let them remember how it eluded and deceived our fathers, and
from a feeble mendicant became the master of the Government and the
people, and it consummated its crimes by the inauguration of the revolution
to blot the North American Republic from the master-roll of nations. Let
them remember that masses of our countrymen have been, and still are, its
pliant instruments, ever swift to execute its decrees: at its bidding to trample
upon the sacred right of petition; to arraign John Quincy Adams before the
bar of the representatives the people; to expel Joshna R. Giddings; to annex
slaveholding Texas for the extension and perpetuation of its power; to
open the free territory won from Mexico to its blistering footsteps; to enact an
inhumane fugitive slave law; to repeal the Missouri prohibition of slavery north
and west of 36° 30'; to invade the territory of Kansas, seize the ballot-boxes,
elect a Legislature, enact black codes, murder free State men for no offense,
frame a Lecompton constitution, and attempt to force it upon an unwilling
people by executive power and corruption; to promulgate the Dred Scott
decision; to demand the incorporation into the Constitution of the recognition
and protection of slavery south of 36° 30'; the right to carry slaves to transit
into, through, and over free States; the denial of the right to make the
national capital free without the consent of slaveholding Virginia—the denial of the right of citizenship and of suffrage to colored men in the free States,
and a pledge to expend the treasures of the nation in colonizing free colored
men at the will of slavemasters. Let them remember, too, that hundreds of
thousands of our countrymen in loyal States, since slavery raised the banners
of insurrection, and sent death, wounds, sickness and sorrow into the homes
of the people, have resisted, and still continue to resist, any measure for the
defense of the nation, if that measure tended to impair the vital and
animating powers of slavery. They resisted the act making free the slaves
used by rebels for military purposes; the confiscation of rebel property and
the freedom of the slaves of rebel masters; the abolition of slavery in the
capital of the nation, and the consecration of the Territories to free labor and
free laboring men; the proclamation of emancipation; the enlistment of
colored men to fight the battles of the country; the freedom of the black
soldier, who is fighting, bleeding, dying for the country, and the freedom of
his wife and children. And, now, when war has for nearly three years
menaced the life of the nation, bathed the land in blood, and filled two
hundred thousand graves with our slain sons, these men of the loyal States
still cling to the falling fortunes of the relentless and unappeasable enemy of
their country and its democratic institutions. They mourn, and will not be
comforted, over the expiring system, in the border slave States, and in tones
of indignation or of anguish they utter lamentations over the proclamation of

emancipation and the policy that is bringing rebel States back again, radiant with freedom.

The past with its crowded memories of the development and power, corruptions and crimes of slavery, the present with its lessons to be read by every eye, all demand that the anti-slavery men of united America should seize the first, the last, and every occasion to trample down and stamp out every vestige of slavery. Let them swear it, write it upon the lids of their Bibles, engrave it upon their door-posts, and proclaim it in the face of earth and of heaven, that the barbarous, treasonable, man-dishonoring, and God-defying system of human slavery in America shall perish utterly from the face of the Republic; that its supporters, apologists, and sympathizers shall never more guide the councils or wear the honors of the emancipated, disinthralled, and regenerated nation.

Engraving on every rood of the vast territories of the Republic, on the magnificent forests and prairies, valleys and mountains in the central regions of the continent in letters of light, "Slavery shall be forever prohibited " obliterating slavery and annulling the slave code in the capital of the nation, decreeing under the war powers more than three millions bondmen in the rebel States "thenceforward and forever free," proclaiming the emancipation of the slave by the fiat of the nation the instant he writes his name on the muster-roll of the defenders of the Republic, has riven and shivered the slave system into broken and dismembered fragments; and that huge and ghastly system now lies prostrate in the convulsive throes of dissolution. National legislation, executive action, judicial decision may still further wound and weaken, degrade and humiliate the now impotent system that once in the pride of power gave law to republican America. The hideous fugitive slave act still blackens the statutes of this Christian land, reminding us of the degradation and humiliation of our country when the heel of that master was on its neck. Justice and humanity, self-respect and decency, all demand that the lingering infamy shall be obliterated from the page it blackens. The decree of emancipation, too, should be enforced and sanctioned by measures of legislation; the colored soldiers who are fighting our battles with unsurpassed devotion and heroic courage should be entitled by law to receive the pay and emoluments of other soldiers of the Republic, and their wives and children should be made free by act of Congress, and placed under the protective care of the country for which their husbands and fathers are periling liberty and life on battle-fields in spite of that merciless ban of the rebel leaders which denies to them the rights and usages of civilized warfare.

But, sir, the crowning act in this series of acts for the restriction and extinction of slavery in America is this proposed amendment to the Constitution prohibiting the existence of slavery forevermore in the Republic of the United States. If this amendment shall be incorporated by the will of the nation into the Constitution of the United States, it will obliterate the last lingering vestiges of the slave system; its chattelizing, degrading, and bloody codes; its dark, malignant, barbarizing spirit; all it was and is, everything connected with it or pertaining to it, from the face of the nation it has scarred with more desolation, from the bosom of the country it has reddened with the blood and strewn with the graves of patriotism. The incorporation of this amendment into the organic law of the nation will make impossible forevermore the reappearing of the discarded slave system, and the returning of the despotism of the slavemasters' domination.

Then, sir, when this amendment to the Constitution shall be consummated the shackle will fall from the limits of the hapless bondman, and the lash drop from the weary hand of the taskmaster. Then the sharp cry of the agonizing hearts of severed families will cease to vex the weary ear of the nation, and to pierce the ear of Him whose judgments are now avenging the wrongs of centuries. Then the slave mart, pen, and auctionblock, with their clanking fetters for human limbs, will disappear from the land they have brutalized, and the school-house will rise to enlighten the darkened intellect of a race imbruted by long years of enforced ignorance. Then the sacred rights of human nature, the hallowed family relations of husband and wife, parent and child, will be protected by the guardian spirit of that law which makes sacred alike the proud homes and lowly cabins of freedom. Then the scarred earth, blighted by the sweat and tears of bondage, will bloom again under the quickening culture of rewarded toil. Then the wronged victim of the slave system, the poor white man, the sand-hiller, the clay-eater of the wasted fields of Carolina, impoverished, debased, dishonored by the system that makes toil a badge of disgrace, and the instruction of the brain and soul of man a crime, will lift his abashed forehead to the skies and begin to run the race of improvement, progress, and elevation. Then the nation, "regenerated and disinthralled by the genius of universal emancipation," will run the career of development, power, and glory, quickened, animated, and guided by the spirit of the Christian democracy that "pulls not the highest down, but lifts the lowest up."

Our country is now floating on the stormy waves of civil war. Darkness lowers and tempests threaten. The waves are rising and foaming and breaking around us and over us with ingulfing fury. But amid the thick gloom, the star of duty casts its clear radiance over the dark and troubled waters, making luminous our pathway. Our duty is as plain to the clear vision of intelligent patriotism as though it were written in letters of light on the bending arches of the skies. That duty is, with every conception of the brain, every throb of the heart, every aspiration of the soul, by thought, by word, and by deed to feel, to think, to speak, to act so as to obliterate the last vestiges of slavery in America subjugate rebel slavemasters to the authority of the nation, hold up the weary arm of our struggling Government, crowd with heroic manhood the ranks of our armies that are bearing the destinies of the country on the points of their glittering bayonets, and thus forever blast the last hope of the rebel chiefs. Then the waning star of the rebellion will go down in eternal night, and the star of peace ascend the heavens, casting its mild radiance over fields now darkened by the storm of this fratricidal war. Then, when "the war drums throb no longer and the battle-flags are furled," our absent sons, with the laurels of victory on their brows, will come back to gladden our households and fill the vacant chairs around our hearthstones. Then the star of United America, now obscured, will reappear, radiant with splendor on the forehead of the skies, to illume the pathway and gladden the heart of struggling humanity. . . .

JAMES HARLAN [R., IOWA]. Mr. President, the measure now pending proposes an amendment to the Constitution of the United States. Before this joint resolution can become effective it must be passed by a two-thirds vote of each branch of Congress and receive the approval of the Legislatures of three fourths of the States. It cannot then be objected to on constitutional grounds, for the Constitution itself provides for this mode of amendment. Nor can an objection be well taken to the section of the Senate at this time on account of the rebellious condition of a majority of the people of some of the States of the Union, as has been urged from the other side of the Chamber, for it is not contemplated to exclude those States from account in estimating the majority of votes of the Legislatures of the States. There are thirty-five States now in the Union, counting those that have rebelled. It is expected that three more may be introduced during the coming year, making thirty-eight in all. Three fourths of those, omitting fractions, would be twenty-nine. There are now twenty-five States represented in Congress. Including the three new States that probably will be introduced we should have twenty-eight, and we learn that the State of Arkansas, the State of Louisiana, and also the State of Tennessee are preparing to resume the seats that their Senators and Representatives vacated two or three years since, giving us thirty-one States in all, two more than would be necessary to secure a constitutional majority of all the States, counting those that have rebelled. Others may also resume their accustomed places in time to vote on this proposition; in fact, all may do so if they so decide. But if any should not they would have no just right to complain; for such as might dissent agreed in entering the Union to abide by such amendments as three fourths of the States should desire, notwithstanding the objections of a minority not greater than one fourth. Nor could they plead exemption on account of disability to act occasioned by their own rebellion, for it is a settled principle of law that no one has a right to plead or take advantage of his own wrong. And if not, he may not plead a disability growing out of his own wrong. And it is contemplated that all shall be counted as opposing the amendment who do not vote for it. If any of the disabled States would, if the disability did not exist, support the measure, they could not complain of its adoption, and if they would in that case vote against it, and are counted against it, they would have no cause of complaint. Then, as it seems to me an argument on the constitutionality of this measure would be misapplied, the simple question is presented to the Senate of the propriety of the policy sugguested by the amendment contained in the joint resolution, and it is on that question that I propose briefly to address the Senate.

Ought this policy to be adopted by the United States? Ought the Constitution of the United States to be so amended as to abolish slavery or to prevent the existence of slavery in all the States of the Union? . . .

If it cannot be thus justified, is it a desirable institution? If the supposed owner has no title, is it the duty of the nation to maintain the usurped claim of the master to the services of his slaves? Are the incidents of slavery sufficiently desirable to justify such policy? Some of the incidents of slavery may be stated as follows: it necessarily abolishes the conjugal relation. This, I take it, needs no argument for its support on the floor of the Senate. We have the result of the fruits of the accumulated experience and wisdom of the people of the slave States for a period of three fourths of a century before us in the character of their laws. Here may be found the culmination of their wisdom, the fruits of their ripened judgment. The honorable Senator from Maryland, [Mr. Johnson,] a few days since, when discussing this subject, stated that in none of the slave States was this relation tolerated in opposition to the will of the slave-owner; and that in many of them, I think he said a majority of them, it was prohibited absolutely by their statute laws. This, I take it then, is the matured, ripened opinion of the people of those States. In their opinion the prohibition of the conjugal relation is a necessary incident of slavery, and that slavery cannot or would not be maintained in the absence of such a regulation.

The existence of this institution therefore requires the existence of a law that annuls the law of God establishing the relation of man and wife, which is taught by the churches to be a sacrament as holy in its nature and its designs as the eucharist itself. If informed that in these Christian States of the Union men were prohibited by positive statute law from partaking of the emblems of the broken body and shed blood of the Saviour, what Senator could hesitate to vote for their repeal and future inhibition? And yet here one of these holy sacraments that we are taught to regard with the most sacred feelings, equally holy, instituted by the Author of our being, deemed to be necessary for the preservation of virtue in civil society, is absolutely inhibited by the statute laws of the States where slavery exists. The conjugal relation is abrogated among four million human beings, who are thus driven to heterogeneous intercourse like the beasts of the field, the most of whom are natives of these Christian States. If you continue slavery you must continue this necessary incident of its existence.

Another incident is the abolition practically of the parental relation, robbing the offspring of the care and attention of his parents, severing a relation which is universally cited as the emblem of the relation sustained by the Creator to the human family. And yet, according to the matured judgment of these slave States, this guardianship of the parent over his own children must be abrogated to secure the perpetuity of slavery.

But again, it abolishes necessarily, the relation of person to property. It declares the slave to be incapable of acquiring and holding property, and that this disability shall extend to his offspring from generation to generation throughout the coming ages. We sometimes shed tears over the misfortunes of men, and when by flood or storm or fire they are robbed of their earthly possessions contributions are made to enable them to start again in their accustomed business pursuits; but the Senator who votes to perpetuate slavery votes not only to sweep away every shred of property that four million people can possibly hold, but he votes to destroy their capacity to acquire and hold it to impose this disability on their posterity forever. If successful in perpetuating it he becomes more disastrous to this multitude of people than storm and flood and fire; more disastrous than the sirocco or monsoon of the desert or the unchained pestilence.

But it also necessarily, as an incident of its continuance, deprives all those held to be slaves of a status in court. Having no rights to maintain and no legal wrongs to redress, they are held to be incapable of bringing a suit in the courts of the United States; a disability as it seems to me that ought to shock the moral sensibilities of any Christian statesman. Robbed of all their rights, and then robbed of their capacity to complain of wrong; robbed of the power to appear before impartial tribunals for the redress of any grievances, however severe!

As an incident of this condition, they are robbed of the right to testify; and, as if to put the cap on this climax of gigantic iniquity, they are denied the right to human sympathy. Yes, sir, denied the right to receive the common sympathies of the human race! How frequently have some of us who have occupied seats on this floor for several years been jeered by brother Senators representing slave States for an expression of sympathy for the oppressed, as if it were a crime to feel for another's degradation; and even yesterday the learned and able Senator from Maryland coupled a citation of sympathy in the North for a downtrodden race with the conduct of rebels in the South, as if philanthropy manifested for the African were equally guilty with treason. How does this accord with our ideas of the character of those emotions when manifested towards any other helpless class of our fellow men? You find children in the community without parents, without natural guardians of person or property. You at once provide by law for their protection. You secure the appointment of guardians and the establishment of orphan asylums. You find those who are idiotic and insane, or deaf and dumb and blind, and immediately the treasure and the wisdom of the State are taxed for the establishment of schools for their instruction and hospitals for their treatment. You find a feeble people along your frontier, and at once you take them under your guardianship as a nation, and pour out the public treasure by the million to provide for their welfare. And the churches take up collections all over this land to enable them to send teachers and books and apparatus for schools and churches in all heathen lands in every quarter of the globe, including the ancestors and brothers of the Africans held here as slaves. Their fathers and brothers on the shores of Africa are fit objects for human sympathy, for human commiseration, and Christian and philanthropic effort. How is it then a crime to express for them the same compassion in this country in the bosom of Christian States?

And then another incident of this institution is the suppression of the freedom of speech and of the press, not only among these down-trodden people themselves but among the white race. Slavery cannot exist where it merits can be fairly discussed; hence in the slave States it becomes a crime to discuss its claims for protection or the wisdom of its continuance. Its continuance also requires the perpetuity of the ignorance of its victims. It is therefore made a felony to teach slaves to read and write.

It also precludes the practical possibility of maintaining schools for the education of many of the white race who have not the means to provide for their own mental culture. It consequently degrades the white as well as African race. It also impoverishes the State, as is manifest by a comparison of the relative wealth, population, and prosperity of the free and slave States of the Union.

If, then, none of these necessary incidents of slavery are desirable, how can an American Senator cast a vote to justify its continuance for a single hour, or withhold a vote necessary for its prohibition? The passage of the joint resolution, its adoption by the States of the Union, would not be injurious to slaveholders themselves. A careful examination of this subject as it seems to me proves beyond all reasonable doubt that the wealth and prosperity of slaveholders would be augmented by a change of their system of labor from compulsory to voluntary.

Its adoption will also increase the military strength of the Nation, securing harmony and unity of purpose here at home and furnishing the means to fill up our wasting armies and the crews of our ships of war.

It will also secure the sympathy and support of the nations of the Old World that seem now to be waiting for a favorable opportunity to intervene against our future unity. No one, I think, conversant with our diplomatic history for the last three years can doubt that when in the most imminent peril interposition was prevented by the President's proclamation of freedom.

If, therefore, by the adoption of this amendment to the Constitution of the United States you prohibit slavery and the possibility of its existence hereafter forever, you will secure the sympathy of the masses of the people of the Old World, and thus place it out of the power of despots to endanger the restoration of the Union.

If I am right in my conclusions that slavery as it exists in this country cannot be justified by human reason, has no foundation at common law, and is not supported by the positive municipal laws of the States, nor by the divine law, and that none of its incidents are desirable, and that its abolition would injure no one, and will do no wrong, but will secure unity of purpose, unity of action, and military strength here at home, and the support of the strong nations of the world, as it seems to me, the Senate of the United States ought not to hesitate to take the action necessary to enable the people of the States to terminate its existence forever, and I shall thus vote. . . .

CHARLES SUMNER [R., MASS.]. Mr. President, if an angel from the skies or a stranger from another planet were permitted to visit this earth, and to examine its surface, who can doubt that his eyes would rest with astonishment upon the outstretched extent and exhaustless resources of this Republic of the New World, young in years but already rooted beyond any dynasty in history? In proportion as he considered and understood all those things among us which enter into and constitute the national life, his astonishment would increase, for he would find a numerous people, powerful beyond precedent, without a king or a noble, but with the schoolmaster instead. And yet the astonishment which he confessed, as all these things appeared before him, would swell into marvel as he learned that in this Republic, which had arrested his admiration, where there was neither king nor noble, but the schoolmaster instead, there were four million human beings in abject bondage, degraded to be chattels, under the pretense of property in man, driven by the lash like beasts, despoiled of all rights, even the right to knowledge and the sacred right of family; so that the relation of husband and wife was impossible and no parent could claim his own child; while all were condemned to brutish ignorance. Startled by what he beheld, the stranger would naturally inquire by what authority, under what sanction, and through what terms of law or Constitution, this fearful inconsistency, so shocking to human nature itself, continued to be upheld. But his growing astonishment would know no bounds, when he was pointed to the Constitution of the United States, as the final guardian and conservator of this peculiar and many-headed wickedness.

"And is it true," the stranger would exclaim, "that, in laying the foundations of this Republic, dedicated to human rights, all these wrongs have been positively established?" He would ask to see that Constitution and to know the fatal words by which the sacrifice was commanded. The trembling with which he began its perusal would be succeeded by joy as he finished it; for he would find nothing in that golden text, not a single sentence, phrase, or word, even, to serve as origin, authority, or apology for the outrage. And then his astonishment, already knowing no bounds, would break forth a new, as he exclaimed, "Shameful and irrational as is slavery, it is not more shameful or irrational than that unsupported interpretation which undertakes to make your Constitution the final guardian and conservator of this terrible and unpardonable denial of human rights."

Such a stranger as I have described, coming from afar, with eyes which no local bias had distorted, and with understanding which no local custom had disturbed, would naturally see the Constitution precisely as it is in its actual text, and he would interpret it in its true sense, without prepossession or prejudice. Of course he would know, what all jurisprudence teaches and all reason confirms, that human rights cannot be taken away by any indirection or by any vain imagining of something that was intended but was not said, and, as a natural consequence, that slavery can exist—if exist it can at all—only by virtue of a *positive text*, and that what is true of slavery is true also of all its incidents; and the enlightened stranger would insist that, in all interpretation of the Constitution, that cardinal principle must never for a moment be out of mind, but must be kept ever forward as guide and master, that *slavery cannot stand on inference*, nor can any support of slavery stand on inference. Thus informed, and in the light of a pervasive principle—

How far that little candle throws his beams!

he would peruse the Constitution from beginning to end, from its opening preamble to its final amendment, and then the joyful opinion would be given.

There are three things which he would observe: first and foremost, that the dismal words "slave" and "slavery" do not appear in the Constitution; so that if the unnatural pretension of property in man lurk anywhere in the text, it is under a feigned name or an *alias*, which of itself is cause of suspicion, while an imperative rule renders its recognition impossible. Next, he would consider the preamble, which is the key to open the whole succeeding instrument; but here no single word can be found which does not open the Constitution to freedom and close it to slavery. The object of the Constitution is announced to be "in order to form a more perfect union, establish justice, insure domestic tranquillity, provide for the common defense, promote the general welfare, and secure the blessings of *liberty* to ourselves and our posterity;" all of which in every particular, is absolutely inconsistent with slavery. And thirdly, he would observe these time-honored, most efficacious, chain-breaking words in the Amendments: "*No person shall be deprived* of life, *liberty*, or property, *without due process of law.*" Scorning all false interpretations and glosses which may have been fastened upon the Constitution as a support of slavery, and with these three things before him, he would naturally declare that there was nothing in the original text on which the hideous wrong could be founded anywhere within the sphere of its operation. With astonishment he would ask again by what strange delusion or hallucination the reason had been so far overcome as to recognize slavery in the Constitution, when plainly it is not there, and cannot be there? The answer is humiliating, but it is easy.

People naturally find in texts of Scripture the support of their own religious opinions or prejudices; and, in the same way, they naturally find in texts of the Constitution the support of their own political opinions or prejudices. And this may not be in either case because Scripture or Constitution, when truly interpreted, supports these opinions or prejudices; but because people are apt to find in texts simply a reflection of themselves. Most clearly and indubitably, whoever finds any support of slavery in the Constitution of the United States has first found such support in himself; not that he will hesitate, perhaps, to condemn slavery in words of approved gentleness, but because from unhappy education or more unhappy insensibility to this wrong he has already conceded to it a certain traditional foothold of immunity, which he straightway transfers from himself to the Constitution. In dealing with this subject, it has not been the Constitution, so much as human nature itself, which has been at fault. Let the people change, and the Constitution will change also; for the Constitution is but the shadow, while the people are the substance.

But under the influences of the present struggle for national life, and in obedience to its incessant exigencies, the people have already changed, and in nothing so much as slavery. Old opinions and prejudices have dissolved, and that traditional foothold which slavery once possessed has been gradually weakened until now it scarcely exists. Naturally this change must sooner or later show itself in the interpretation of the Constitution. But it is already visible even there, in the concession of powers over slavery which were formerly denied. The time, then, has come when the Constitution, which has been so long interpreted for slavery, may be interpreted for freedom. This is one stage of triumph. Universal emancipation, which is at hand, can be won only by complete emancipation of the Constitution itself, which has been degraded to wear chains so long that its real character is scarcely known.

Sometimes the concession is made on the ground of *military necessity.* The capacious war powers of the Constitution are invoked, and it is said that in their legitimate exercise slavery may be destroyed. There is much in this concession; more even than in imagined by many from whom it proceeds. It is war, say they, which puts these powers in motion; but they forget that wherever slavery exists there is perpetual war—that slavery itself is a *state of war* between two races, where one is for the moment victor—pictured accurately by Jefferson when he described it as "permitting one half of the citizens to trample on the rights of the other, transforming those into enemies, and these into despots." Therefore, wherever slavery exists, even in seeming peace, the war power may be invoked to put an end to a condition which is internecine, and to overthrow pretensions which are hostile to every attribute of the Almighty.

But it is not on military necessity alone that the concession is made. There are many who, as they read the Constitution now, see its powers over slavery more clearly than before. The old superstition is abandoned; and they join with Patrick Henry when in the Virginia convention, he declared that the power of manumission was given to Congress. He did not hesitate to argue against the adoption of the Constitution because it gave this power. And shall we be less perspicacious for freedom than this Virginia statesman was for slavery? Discerning this power he confessed his dismay; but let us confess our joy.

We have already seen that slavery can find no support in the Constitution. Glance now at the positive provisions by which it is brought completely under the control of Congress.

1. First among the powers of Congress, and associated with the power to lay and collect taxes, is that "to provide for the common defense and general welfare." It has been questioned whether this is a substantive power, or simply incident to that with which it is associated. But it seems difficult, if not absurd, to insist that Congress should not have this substantive power. Shall it not provide for the common defense? Shall it not provide for the general welfare? If it cannot do these things it had better abdicate. In the discussions on the Constitution in the Virginia convention, Mr. George Mason, one of its most decided opponents, said, "That Congress should have power to provide for the general welfare of the Union, *I grant.*" [2 Elliot's *Debates* 327] But the language of Patrick Henry, to which allusion has been already made, was still more explicit. He foresaw that this power would be naturally directed against slavery, and he said:

Slavery is detested. We feel its fatal effects. We deplore it with all the pity of humanity. Let all these considerations, at some future period, press with full force on the minds of Congress. Let that urbanity which, I trust, will distinguish Americans, and the necessity of national defense—let all these things operate on their minds; they will search that paper [the Constitution] and see if they have the power of manumission. And have they not, sir? Have they not the power *to provide for the general defense and welfare?* May they not think that they call for the abolition of slavery. May they not pronounce all slaves free? And will they not be warranted by that power? This is no ambiguous implication or logical deduction. *The paper speaks to the point. They have the power in clear and unequivocal terms, and will clearly and certainly exercise it.* [3 Elliot's *Debates,* 590]

Language could not be more positive. To all who ask for the power of Congress over slavery, here is a sufficient answer; and remember that this is not my speech, but the speech of Patrick Henry, who says that the Constitution "speaks to the point."

2. Next comes the clause, "Congress shall have power to declare war; to raise and support armies; to provide and maintain a navy." A power like this is from its very nature unlimited. In raising and supporting an army, in providing and maintaining a navy, Congress is not restrained to any particular class or color. It may call upon all and authorize that *contract* which the Government makes with an enlisted soldier. But such a contract would be in itself an act of manumission; for a slave cannot make a contract. And if the contract be followed by actual service, who can deny its completest efficacy in enfranchising the soldier-slave and his whole family? Shakespeare, immortal teacher, gives expression to an instinctive sentiment when he makes Henry V, on the eve of the battle of Agincourt, encourage his men by promising,

For he to-day that sheds his blood with me,
Shall be my brother; *be he ne'er so vile.*
This day shall gentle his condition.

3. There is still another clause: "The United States shall guaranty to every State in this Union a *republican form of government."* There again is a plain duty. But the question recurs, what is a republican form of government? John Adams, in the correspondence of his old age, says:

The customary meanings of the words *republic* and *commonwealth* have been infinite. They have been applied to every Government under heaven; that of Turkey and that of Spain, as well as that of Athens and of Rome, of Geneva and San Marino. [John Adams's *Works*, 378]

But the guarantee of a republican form of government must have a meaning congenial with the purposes of the Constitution. If a Government like that of Turkey, or even like that of Venice, could come within the scope of this guarantee, it would be a little value. It would be words and nothing more. Evidently it must be construed so as to uphold the Constitution according to all the promises of its preamble, and Mr. Madison has left a record, first published to the Senate by the distinguished Senator from Vermont [Mr. Collamer] the chairman of the Committee on the Library, showing that this clause was originally suggested in part by the fear of slavery. The record is important, disclosing the real intention of this guarantee. But no American need be at a loss to designate some of the distinctive elements of a republic according to the idea of American institutions. These will be found, first, in the Declaration of Independence, by which it is solemnly announced "that all men are endowed by their Creator with certain unalienable rights; that among these are life, liberty, and the pursuit of happiness." And they will be found, secondly, in that other guarantee and prohibition of the Constitution, in harmony with the Declaration of Independence; *"no person* shall be deprived of life, *liberty,* or property *without due process of law."* Such are some of the essential elements of a "republican form of government," which cannot be disowned by us without disowning the very muniments of our liberties; and it is these which the United States are bound to guaranty. But all these make slavery impossible. It is idle to say that this result was not anticipated. It would be, then, only another illustration that our fathers "builded wiser than they knew."

4. But, independent of the clause of guarantee, there is the clause just quoted, which in itself is a source of power: *"no person* shall be deprived of life, *liberty,* or property *without due process of law."* This was a part of the amendments to the Constitution proposed by the First Congress under the popular demand for a Bill of Rights. Brief as it is, it is in itself alone a whole Bill of Rights. Liberty can be lost only by "due process of law," words borrowed from the old liberty-loving common law, illustrated by our master

in law, Lord Coke, but best explained by the late Mr. Justice Bronson, of New York, in a judicial opinion where he says:

> The meaning of the section then seems to be, that no *member of the State shall be disfranchised or deprived of any of his rights or privileges* unless the matter shall be adjudged against him upon trial had according to the course of common law. The words 'due process of law' in this place cannot mean less than a prosecution or suit instituted and conducted according to the prescribed forms and solemnities for ascertaining guilt or determining the title of property. [4 *Hill's Reports*, 146]

Such is the protection which is thrown by the Constitution over every "person," without distinction of race or color, class or condition. There can be no doubt about the universality of this protection. All, without exception, come within its scope. Its natural meaning is plain; but there is an incident of history which makes its plainer still, excluding all possibility of misconception. A clause of this character was originally recommended as an amendment by two slave States, North Carolina and Virginia, but it was restrained by them to *freemen* thus: "No *freeman* ought to be deprived of his life, *liberty,* or property but by the *law of the land."* But when the recommendation came before Congress the word "person" was substituted for "freeman" and the more searching phrase "due process of law" was substituted for "the law of the land." In making this change, rejecting the recommendation of two slave States, the authors of this amendment revealed their purpose, that *no person* wearing the human form should be deprived of *liberty* without due process of law; and the proposition was adopted by the votes of Congress and then of the States as a part of the Constitution. Clearly on its face it is an express guarantee of personal liberty and an express prohibition against its invasion anywhere.

In the face of this guarantee and prohibition—for it is both—how can any "person" be held as a slave? . . .

Mr. President, thus stands the case. There is nothing in the Constitution on which slavery can rest, or find any the least support. Even on the face of that instrument it is an *outlaw;* but if we look further at its provisions we find at least four distinct sources of power, which, if executed, must render slavery impossible, while the preamble make them all vital for freedom: first, the power to provide for the common defense and general welfare; secondly, the power to raise armies and maintain navies; thirdly, the power to guaranty to every State a republican form of government; and fourthly, the power to secure *liberty* to every person restrained without due process of law. But all these provisions are something more than powers; *they are duties also.* And yet we are constantly and painfully reminded in this Chamber that pending measures against slavery are unconstitutional. Sir, this is an immense mistake. *Nothing against slavery can be unconstitutional.* It is only hesitation which is unconstitutional. . . .

Putting aside, then, all objections that have been interposed, whether proceeding from open opposition or from lukewarm support, the great question recurs, that question which dominates this whole debate, How shall slavery be overthrown? The answer is threefold: first, by the courts, declaring and applying the true principles of the Constitution; secondly, by Congress, in the exercise of the powers which belong to it; and, thirdly, by the people, through an amendment to the Constitution. Courts, Congress, people, all may be invoked, and the occasion will justify the appeal.

1. Let the appeal be made to the courts. But alas! one of the saddest chapters in our history has been the conduct of judges, who have lent themselves to the support of slavery. Injunctions of the Constitution, guarantees of personal liberty, and prohibitions against its invasion, have all been forgotten. Courts which should have been asylums of liberty have been changed into *barracoons*, and the Supreme Court of the United States, by a final decision of surpassing infamy, became the greatest *barracoon* of all. It has been part of the calamity of the times, that, under the influence of slavery, justice, like Astraea of old, had fled. But now at last, in a regenerated Republic, with the power of slavery waning, and the people rising in judgment against it, let us hope that the judgments of courts may be reconsidered, and that the powers of the Constitution in behalf of liberty may be fully exercised, so that the blessed condition shall be fulfilled when—

Ancient frauds shall fail,
Returning justice lift aloft her scale.

Sir, no court can afford to do an act of wrong. Its business is justice; and when under any apology it ceases to do justice, it loses those titles to reverence which otherwise are so willingly bestowed. There are instances of great magistrates who have openly declared their disobedience to laws "against common right and reason," and their names are mentioned with gratitude in the history of jurisprudence. There are other instances of men holding the balance and the sword, whose names have been gathered into a volume, as "atrocious judges." If our judges, who have cruelly interpreted the Constitution in favor of slavery do not come into the latter class, they clearly can claim no place among those others who have stood for justice, like the rock on which the sea breaks in idle spray. Doubtless the model decision of the American bench, destined to be quoted hereafter with the most honor, because the boldest in its conformity with the great principles of humanity and social order, was that of the Vermont judge, who refused to surrender a fugitive slave *until his pretended master should show a title-deed from the Almighty.* . . .

If courts were thus inspired, it is easy to see that slavery would disappear under their righteous judgments.

2. But unhappily the courts will not perform the duty of the hour, and we must look elsewhere. An appeal must be made to Congress; and here, as has been fully developed, the powers are ample, unless in their interpretation you surrender in advance to slavery. By a single brief statute, Congress may

sweep slavery out of existence. Patrick Henry saw that in the maintenance of "the general welfare" and under the influence of a growing detestation of slavery this could be done, even without resort to those capacious war powers which proclaim trumpet-tongued that it can be done.

Of course we encounter here again the "execrable" pretension of property in man, and the claim of "just compensation" for the renunciation of Heaven-defying wrongs. But this pretension is no more applicable to abolition by act of Congress than to abolition by an amendment of the Constitution; so that if the pretension of "just compensation" can be discarded in one case it can be in the other. But the votes that have already been taken in the Senate on the latter proposition testify that it is discarded. Sir, let the "execrable" pretension never again be named, except for condemnation, no matter how or when it appears or what the form it may take.

But even if Congress be not prepared for that single decisive measure which shall promptly put an end to this whole question and strike slavery to death, there are other measures by which this end may be hastened. The towering Upas may be girdled, even if it may not be felled at once to the earth.

The fugitive slave bill, conceived in iniquity and imposed upon the North as a badge of subjugation, may be repealed.

The coastwise slave trade may be deprived of all support in the statute-book.

The traffic in human beings, as an article of "commerce among States," may be extirpated.

And, above all, that odious rule of evidence, so injurious to justice and discreditable to the country, excluding the testimony of colored persons in national courts, may be abolished.

Let these things be done. In themselves they will be much. But they will be more as the assurance of the overthrow sure to follow.

3. But all these will not be enough. The people must be summoned to confirm the whole work. It is for them to put the cap-stone upon the sublime structure. An amendment of the Constitution may do what courts and Congress decline to do, or, even should they act, it may cover their action with its panoply. Such an amendment in any event will give completeness and permanence to emancipation, and bring the Constitution into avowed harmony with the Declaration of Independence. Happy day, long wished for, destined to gladden those beautified spirits who have labored on earth to this end, but died without the sight.

And yet let us not indiscreetly take counsel of our hopes. From the nature of the case such an amendment cannot be consummated at once. Time must intervene, with opportunities of opposition. It can pass Congress only by a vote of two thirds of both branches. And when it has passed both branches of Congress it must be adopted by the Legislatures of three quarters of the States. Even under the most favorable circumstances it is impossible to say when it can become a part of the Constitution. Too tardily, I fear, for all the good that is sought. Therefore I am not content with this measure alone. It postpones till to-morrow what ought to be done to-day; and I much fear that it may be made an apology for indifference to other measures.

> To-morrow, and to-morrow, and to-morrow,
> Creeps in this petty pace from day to day,
> To the last syllable of recorded time;
> And all our yesterdays have lighted fools
> The way to dusty death.

For myself let me confess that, in presence of the mighty events of the day, I feel how insignificant is any individual, whether citizen or Senator; and yet, humbly longing to do my part, I cannot consent to put off till to-morrow what ought to be done to-day. Beyond my general desire to see an act of universal emancipation that shall at once and forever settle this great question, so that it may no longer be the occasion of strife between us, there are two other ideas which are ever present to my mind as a practical legislator; first, to strike at slavery wherever I can hit it; and secondly, to clean the statute-book of all existing supports of slavery, so that it may find nothing there to which it may cling for life. To do less than this at the present moment, when slavery is still menacing, would be an abandonment of duty.

So long as a single slave continues anywhere beneath the flag of the Republic I am unwilling to rest. Too well I know the vitality of slavery with its infinite capacity of propagation, and how little slavery it takes to make a slave State with all the cruel pretensions of slavery. The down of a single thistle is full of all possible thistles, and a single fish its said to contain two hundred million of ova, so that the whole sea might be stocked from its womb. . . .

But the immediate question now before us is on the proposition to prohibit slavery by constitutional amendment; and here I hope to be indulged for a moment with regard to the form which it should take. A new text of the Constitution cannot be considered too carefully even in this respect, especially when it embodies a new article of freedom. Here for a moment we are performing something of that duty which belongs to the *conditores imperii*, placed foremost by Lord Bacon among the actors in human affairs. From the magnitude of the task we may naturally borrow circumspection, and I approach this part of the question with suggestion rather than argument.

Let me say frankly that I should prefer a form of expression different from that which has the sanction of the committee. They have selected what was intended for the old Jeffersonian ordinance, sacred in our history,

although, let me add, they have not imitated it closely. But I must be
pardoned if I venture to doubt the expediency of perpetuating in the Constitution language which, if it have any signification, seems to imply that
"slavery or involuntary servitude" may be provided "for the punishment of
crime." There was a reason for that language when it was first employed, but
that reason no longer exists. If my desires could prevail, I would put aside
the ordinance on this occasion, and find another form.

I know nothing better than these words:

All persons are equal before the law, so that no person can hold another as a slave;
and the Congress shall have power to make all laws necessary and proper to carry this
declaration into effect everywhere within the United States and the jurisdiction thereof.

The words in the latter part supersede all questions as to the applicability
of the declaration to States. But the distinctive words in this clause assert the
equality of all persons before the law. The language may be new in our
country, but it is already well known in history. . . .

It will be felt at once that this expression, *"equality before the law,"* gives
precision to that idea of human rights which is enunciated in our Declaration
of Independence. The sophistries of Calhoun, founded on the obvious inequalities of body and mind, are all overthrown by this simple statement,
which, though borrowed latterly from France, is older than French history.
The curious student will find in the ancient Greek of Herodotus a single
word which supplies the place of this phrase, when he tells us that "the
government of the many has the most beautiful name of ινονομια ," or
equality before the law. [Book 3, p. 80] The father of history was right.
The name is most beautiful; but it is not a little singular that, in an age when
equality before the law was practically unknown, the Greek language, so
remarkable for its flexibility and comprehensiveness, supplied a single word,
not to be found in modern tongues, to express an idea which has been
authoritatively recognized only in modern times. Such a word in our own
language to express that equality of rights which is claimed for all mankind
might have superseded some of the criticism to which this Declaration has
been exposed.

Enough has been said to explain the origin of the words which are now
proposed. It will be for the Senate to determine if it will adopt them. . . .

But while desirous of seeing the great rule of freedom which we are about
to ordain embodied in a text which shall be like the precious casket to the
more precious treasure, yet I confess that I feel humbled by my own
endeavors. And whatever may be the judgment of the Senate, I am consoled
by the thought that the most homely text containing such a rule will be more
beautiful far than any words of poetry or eloquence, and that it will endure
to be read with gratitude when the rising dome of this Capitol, with the
statue of Liberty which surmounts it, has crumbled to dust. . . .

House of Representatives-38th Congress, 2d Session
January 6-10, 1865

JAMES ASHLEY [R., OHIO]. I desire to call up this morning, pursuant to notice previously given, the motion to reconsider the vote by which the joint resolution proposing an amendment to the Constitution in reference to slavery was rejected.

WILLIAM HOLMAN [DEM., IND.]. Does the gentleman call it up for action to-day?

MR. ASHLEY. No, sir; but for discussion, intending to allow that discussion to run on until the House sees fit to order the main question to be put.

THE SPEAKER [SCHUYLER COLFAX, R., IND.]. This being private bill day, it requires a majority vote to set aside the consideration of private bills.

The consideration of private bills was set aside by a majority vote, and the motion to reconsider was taken up.

MR. ASHLEY. Mr. Speaker, *"If slavery is not wrong, nothing is wrong."* Thus simply and truthfully has spoken our worthy Chief Magistrate.

The proposition before us is, whether this universally acknowledged wrong shall be continued or abolished. Shall it receive the sanction of the American Congress by the rejection of this proposition, or shall it be condemned as an intolerable wrong by its adoption?

If slavery had never been known in the United States, and the proposition should be made in Congress to-day to authorize the people of the several States to enslave any portion of our own people or the people of any other country, it would be universally denounced as an infamous and criminal proposition, and its author would be execrated, and justly, by all right-thinking men, and held to be an enemy of the human race.

I do not believe such a proposition could secure a single vote in this House; and yet we all know that a number of gentlemen who could not be induced to enslave a single free man will nevertheless vote to keep millions of men in slavery, who are by nature and the laws of God as much entitled to their freedom as we are. I will not attempt to explain this strange inconsistency or make an argument to show its fallacy. I content myself with simply stating the fact.

It would seem as if no man favorable to peace, concord, and a restored Union could hesitate for a moment as to how he could vote on this proposition. Certainly, whatever of strife, sectional bitterness, and personal animosity these Halls have witnessed since my appearance in Congress, or, indeed, I may say, since the organization of parties in 1836, slavery has usually been the sole cause. No observer of our history, or of the political parties which have been organized and disbanded, now hesitates to declare that slavery is the cause of this terrible civil war. All who understand anything of our troubles, either in this country or Europe, now know that but for slavery there would have been no rebellion in this country to-day. . . .

For more than thirty years past there is no crime known among men which it has not committed under the sanction of law. It has bound men and women in chains, and even the children of the slave-master, and sold them in the public shambles like beasts. Under the plea of Christianizing them it has enslaved, beaten, maimed, and robbed millions of men for whose salvation the Man of sorrows died. It so constituted its courts that the complaints and appeals of these people could not be heard by reason of the decision "that black men had no rights which white men were bound to respect." It has for many years defied the Government and trampled upon the national Constitution, by kidnapping, imprisoning, mobbing, and murdering white citizens of the United States guilty of no offense except protesting against its terrible crimes. It has silenced every free pulpit within its control, and debauched thousands which ought to have been independent. It has denied the masses of poor white children within its power the privilege of free schools, and made free speech and a free press impossible within its domain; while ignorance, poverty, and vice are almost universal wherever it dominates. Such is slavery, our mortal enemy, and these are but a tithe of its crimes. No nation could adopt a code of laws which would sanction such enormities, and live. No man deserves the name of statesman who would consent that such a monster should live in the Republic for a single hour.

Mr. Speaker, if slavery is wrong and criminal, as the great body of enlightened and Christian men admit, it is certainly our duty to abolish it, if we have the power. . . .

In my judgment, Congress may propose, and three fourths of the States may adopt, any amendment, republican in its character and consistent with the continued existence of the nation, save in the two particulars just named.

If they cannot, then is the clause of the Constitution just quoted a dead letter; the States sovereign, the Government a confederation, and the United States not a nation.

The extent to which this question of State rights and State sovereignty has aided this terrible rebellion and manacled and weakened the arm of the national Government can hardly be estimated. Certainly doctrines so at war with the fundamental principles of the Constitution could not be accepted and acted upon by any considerable number of our citizens without eventually culminating in rebellion and civil war.

This fatal heresy doubtless carried many men of character and culture into the rebellion who were sincerely attached to the Union. If we may credit the recently published private letters of General Lee, written in the spring of 1861, to his sister and friends, and never intended for publication, he was induced to unite his fortunes with the insurgents by the so-called secession of Virginia, under the belief that his first and highest allegiance was due to his State. Sir, I know how hard it is for loyal men to credit this. To thinking men nothing seems more absurd than the political heresy called States rights in the sense which makes each State sovereign and the national Government the mere agent and creature of the States. Why, sir, the unity of the people of the United States antedates the Revolution. The original thirteen colonies were never in fact *disunited.* The man who had the right of citizenship in Virginia had the same right in New York. As one people they declared their independence, and as one people, after a seven years' war, conquered it. But the unity and citizenship of the people existed before the Revolution, and before the national Constitution. In fact this unity gave birth to the Constitution. Without this unity and preexisting nationality—if I may so express myself—the Constitution would never have been formed. The men who carried us through the revolutionary struggle never intended, when establishing this Government, to destroy that unity or lose their national citizenship. Least of all did they intend that we should become aliens to each other, and citizens of petty, independent, sovereign States. In order to make fruitful the blessings which they had promised themselves from independence, and to secure the unity and national citizenship for which they periled life, fortune, and honor, they made the national Constitution. They had tried a confederation. It did not secure them such a Union as they had fought for, and they determined to "form a more perfect Union." For this purpose they met in national convention, and formed a national Constitution. They then submitted it to the electors of the States for their adoption or rejection. They did not submit it to the States as States, nor to the governments of the several States, but to the citizens of the United States residing in all the States. This was the only way in which they could have submitted it and been consistent with the declaration made in the preamble, which says that "we, the people of the United States, in order to form a more perfect Union, &c., do ordain and establish this Constitution." The whole people were represented in this convention. Through their representatives they pledged each other that whenever the people of *nine* States should ratify and approve the Constitution submitted to them, it should be the Constitution of the nation.

In the light of these facts, to claim that our Government is a confederation and the States sovereign seems an absurdity too transparent for serious argument. Not only is the letter of the Constitution against such a doctrine, but history also. Since the adoption of the national Constitution *twenty-two* States have been admitted into the Union and clothed with part of the national sovereignty. The territory out of which twenty-one of these States were formed was the common territory of the nation. It had been acquired by cession, conquest, or purchase. The sovereignty of the national Government over it was undisputed. The people who settled upon it were citizens of the United States. These twenty-one States were organized by the concurrent action of the citizens of the United States and the national Government. Without the consent of Congress they would have remained Territories. What an absurdity, to claim that the citizens of the New England States, or of all the States, or of any section of the Union may settle upon the territory of the United States, form State governments, with barely inhabitants enough to secure one Representative in this House under the apportionment, secure admission as a State, and then assume to be sovereign and master of the national Government, with power to secede and unite with another and hostile Government at pleasure, and to treat all citizens of the United States as alien enemies who do not think it their duty to unite with them. This is the doctrine which deluded many men into this rebellion, and which seems to delude some men here with the idea that the national Constitution cannot be amended so as to abolish slavery, even if all the States *in* the Union demanded it save Delaware. Under this theory of State sovereignty, States like Florida and Arkansas, erected on the national domain, may, as soon as they secure admission into the Union, secede and embezzle all the property of the nation, including the public lands and forts and arsenals, declare all citizens of the United States who do not unite with them alien enemies, confiscate their property, rob them of their liberty, by impressing them into their army to fight against their own country and Government, and, if they refuse, to punish them by imprisonment and death. After doing this, if the authority to commit such wholesale robbery, impressments, and murders is denied them by the national Government they set up the claim that they are sovereign and independent, and are only defending their homes, their firesides and household gods, and we have men all over the North who to-day defend this monstrous assumption and villainy.

Mr. Speaker, I presume no man, not even my colleague, will deny that when the thirteen colonies or States assembled by their representatives in convention to make the present national Constitution they might have abolished slavery at once. Or, if the theory of the old parties is true, that a republican Government may authorize or permit the enslavement of men, which I deny, they could have provided for the emancipation of all slaves in twenty or fifty years, if they had seen fit; and if the people of nine States had voted to ratify such a constitution slavery could not, after the period named, have existed by State law and in defiance of the national Constitution, either in one of the old thirteen States or in any one of the States admitted into the Union since its adoption. If it was competent for the men who made the national Constitution to prohibit slavery at that time, or to provide for its future prohibition, why is it not just as competent for us now? The framers of the Constitution provided for its amendment in the section which I have already quoted. This was a wise provision. They provided that when an amendment was proposed and adopted in the manner and form prescribed it should become a part of the national Constitution, and be as valid and binding as though originally a part of that instrument.

Had the framers of the Constitution desired the protection and continuance of slavery they could easily have provided against an amendment of the character of the one now before us by guarding this interest as they did the right of the States to an equal representation in the Senate. They did not do it, because, as the history of the convention abundantly proves, the great majority of the framers of the Constitution desired the speedy abolition of slavery, and I contend that, so far from the Constitution prohibiting such an amendment, it has expressly provided for it.

Mr. Speaker, there is not a single section or clause in the national Constitution which clothes the political organizations which we call States with any of the attributes of a sovereign Power, but, on the other hand, prohibits in positive and unmistakable language any State from doing any act which a sovereign might do without the consent of Congress. . . .

It is past comprehension how any man with the Constitution before him, and the history of the convention which formed that Constitution within his reach, together with the repeated decisions of the Supreme Court against the assumption of the State rights pretensions, can be found at this late day defending the State sovereignty dogmas, and claiming that the national constitution cannot be so amended as to prohibit slavery, even though all the States of the Union save one give it their approval.

That provision of the national Constitution which imposes upon Congress the duty of guarantying to the several States of the Union a republican form of government is one which impresses me as forcibly as any other with the idea of the utter indefensibility of the State sovereignty dogmas, and of the supreme power intended by the framers of the Constitution to be lodged in the national Government.

In this connection we ought not to overlook that provision of the Constitution which secures nationality of citizenship. The Constitution guaranties that the citizens of each State shall enjoy all the rights and privileges of citizens of the several States. It is a universal franchise which cannot be confined to States, but belongs to the citizens of the Republic. We are fighting to maintain this national franchise and prevent its passing under the control of a foreign Power, where this great privilege would be denied us or so changed as to destroy its value. The nationality of our citizenship makes our Army a unit, although from distant States, and makes them also invincible. It is objected that if we pass this proposition the requisite number of States cannot now be secured for its adoption. In answer to this objection I have to say that Congress has not, in submitting the proposed amendment, limited the time in which the States shall adopt it; nor has Congress attempted authoritatively to declare that it will require the ratification of twenty-seven States to adopt this amendment.

I hold that whenever three fourths of the States *now* represented in Congress give their consent to this proposition it will legally become a part of the national Constitution, unless other States, now without civil governments known to the Constitution, establish governments such as Congress shall recognize, and such States, together with any new States which may be admitted, shall be represented in Congress *before* three fourths of the States *now* represented adopt the proposed amendment; in which event the States thus recognized or admitted must be added to the number of States *now* represented in Congress, and the ratification of three fourths of the States thus recognized, and none others, is all that will be required to adopt this amendment. . . .

Mr. Speaker, the year which has just closed has been a year of anxiety and also a year of joy. The ordeal through which as a nation we have passed has been a terrible one. I speak of the ordeal on the battle-field and at the ballot-box. We have presented to the world a sublime spectacle. We have tested our strength and know the constancy and courage of our men. Such disinterestedness, such heroism, and devotion to country, the world has never witnessed. Consecrated by a dispensation of fire and blood, the children of the Republic have grown to the full stature of manhood. Standing here in the nation's Council Halls, in the beginning of a new year, on the threshold of a new era, and in the presence of such events, let us comprehend the duty of true statesmen, and while legislating for the present legislate also for the generations of men which are to succeed us. The eyes of the wise and good in all civilized nations are upon us. The men who embrace and defend the democratic idea in Europe are patiently and anxiously waiting to have us authoritatively proclaim to the world that liberty is the sign in which we conquer; that henceforth freedom is to be the animating principle of our Government and the life of our Constitution.

Mr. Speaker, while the Union soldier fights to vanquish the enemies of the Government, the duty of the true statesman is to provide that the enemy once vanquished shall never again be permitted for the same cause to reorganize and make war upon the nation. Pass this joint resolution submitting to the people for their ratification or rejection this proposed amendment to the national Constitution, and I am sure the nation will adopt it with shouts of acclamation, and when once adopted you know, sir, and I know, and the enemies of this Government know, that we shall have peace, and that no such rebellion will ever be possible again. Pass this amendment and the gloomy shadow of slavery will never again darken the fair fame of our country or tarnish the glory of democratic institutions in the land of Washington. Pass this amendment and the brightest page in the history of the Thirty-Eighth Congress, now so soon to close, will be the one on which is recorded the names of the requisite number of members voting in its favor. Refuse to pass it, and the *saddest* page in the history of the Thirty-Eighth Congress will be the one on which is recorded its defeat. Sir, I feel as if no member of this House will ever live to witness an hour more memorable in our history than the one in which each for himself shall make a record on the question now before us. I implore gentlemen to forget party and remember that we are making a record, not only for ourselves individually, but for the nation and the cause of free government throughout the world. While members of the Thirty-Eighth Congress we cannot change the record which each must now make, and those who do not return to the next Congress can never reverse their votes of to-day, but must forever stand recorded, if voting against this amendment, among those voting to justify the rebellion and perpetuate its cause.

The genius of history with iron pen is waiting to record our verdict where it will remain forever for all the coming generations of men to approve or condemn. God grant that the verdict may be one over which the friends of liberty, impartial and universal in this country and Europe and in every land beneath the sun, may rejoice; a verdict which shall declare that America is free; a verdict which shall add another day of jubilee, and the brightest of all, to our national calendar, if this verdict is not given by the present Congress, I know, and you all know, it will be given by the next Congress; and that, too, with alacrity. The decree has gone forth; the people have pronounced it; and now is the golden hour in which we may all unite, if we will, and inaugurate a new era in our history. Let no man put forth his puny hand to stay the certain approach of the hour in which this act shall pass, or of the grand jubilee which shall follow its enactment into law. Let no member of this House attempt to postpone this great measure with the hope of being able to circumvent, by some petty scheme of compromise, the plainly written decree of Omnipotence. Let no loyal man, in such an hour as this, record his vote against this just proposition, and thus vote to prolong the rebellion and perpetuate the despotism of American slavery in this Republic. . . .

JOHN FARNSWORTH [R., ILL.]. Mr. Speaker, "property," "vested rights," "robbery," are the dying cries from the agonized hearts of the men who defend man-stealing and women-whipping, and who apologize for treason. I do not rise here for the purpose of making a constitutional argument, but only for the purpose of briefly answering those charges. It seems to me that they come from the wrong side of this question when used by the men who oppose this constitutional amendment.

"Property!" What is property? That is property which the Almighty made property. When at the creation He gave man dominion over things animate and inanimate, He established property. Nowhere do you read that He gave man dominion over another man.

"Vested rights!" What vested rights so high or so sacred as a man's right to himself, to his wife and children, to his liberty, and to the fruits of his own industry? Did not our fathers declare those rights were inalienable? And if a man cannot himself alienate those rights, how can another man alienate them without being himself a robber of the vested rights of his brother man?

"Vested rights" and "robbery," forsooth, from the slaveholder! Why, sir, it is passing strange that men, from usage and familiarity with a crime, will even get to using the very words and phrases in defense of that crime which legitimately and property describe the crime itself. There never was a highwayman who had pursued this course of crime for a series of years who did not regard the execution of the law upon him for his crimes as most unjust to him. The poet has well said that—

No man e'er felt the halter draw,
With good opinion of the law.

It has been truly said by the gentleman who preceded me, [Mr. Grinnell,] that in the statutes of no slave State in the Union can you find the origin of slavery. There is not a statute in any one of those States that ever established property in slaves; not one. It is a carbuncle; it is an ulcer; it is a cancer which has grown up by stealth upon the body-politic, and which has only from usage become familiarized to men, and they have surrounded it with the statutes protecting the relation that we find in any of the codes of the slave States. You cannot find in any statutes of any civilized nation on the face of the earth where property in things animate or inanimate is established. Nowhere is that property defined; nowhere is it declared in any statute in the world that man shall have property in this or that thing. Because, as I have said before, the Almighty having given property in these things it is only necessary that civilized society should surround it with laws to protect men in the possession and enjoyment of it.

I trust we will hear no more of robbery, of vested rights. Slavery commenced in robbery and theft, and has been carried on by a trespass, and no usage in the lapse of time can make that just or legal or right which in its origin and inception was a crime.

What is that we now propose to do? We propose to say in the organic law of the land that there shall be no more involuntary servitude except as a punishment for crime. And there is another thing; we are now dealing with a class. While there may be now and then a loyal slaveholder in the rebellious States, as a class the slaveholders are traitors, as a class they brought on this rebellion, as a class they are fighting our soldiers in the field, starving our prisoners in their dungeons, and by every high-handed and ruthless outrage conducting this war of treason. That is the character of slaveholders as a class. . . .

Sir, it is said, I believe, that every man looks upon and appreciates character from his own stand-point. I suppose that a man who stands upon the gallows and feels the halter drawn about his neck would regard a very disreputable person, if exempt from the doom of that punishment, as very respectable; and I suppose that, if a man has escaped the penitentiary by the statute of limitations or any other device, he would regard as very respectable a character which others might consider very ignoble. Men of a low class regard the character of others from their own low stand-point, and by a comparison with their own position in the moral scale. But it is left for the member from New York [Mr. Fernando Wood] to justify and support this barbarous institution of slavery, and to declare that the slaveholders engaged in this rebellion are, *par excellence*, the noble, gallant, and generous people of the United States. Mr. Speaker, I do not so regard them. From the stand-point which I occupy I look upon them in a very different light. I think that they are neither just, generous, nor noble; and, sir, you shall find that wherever slavery has existed for a series of years, it makes the slaveholder ignoble, unjust, ungenerous, and tyrannical. Such is the natural effect of the institution everywhere. . . .

Mr. Speaker, I thank God that by the votes of my constituents, who sent me here by over thirteen thousand majority, I have the privilege to-day of standing up here and advocating this amendment; and I know that when the light of the past and the present and the future shall with their concentrated rays throw a focal blaze upon the page of history that we are making to-day, it will be a source of the highest pride for my children to point to the record which I make and the vote which I give to-day; while I know equally well that as to the men who may vote against this amendment, and particularly those who apologize for the institution of slavery, their action will be an everlasting disgrace to themselves and their children and their children's children. Sir, we are making history, and we are making it fast. These things will not be looked upon fifty years hence as they are now. When this usage of slavery is abolished and when we have ceased to be familiarized with the clank of chains, then we shall look upon this thing with the horror it deserves.

JOHN MCBRIDE [R., ORE.]. Mr. Speaker, by the vote on the motion of the gentleman from Ohio [Mr. Ashley] this House will decide whether the proposed amendment to the Constitution, by which slavery shall be prohibited within the limits of the United States, shall be submitted to the several States for their action or not. No one authorized to speak for the people of the State whose interests I represent upon this floor has yet spoken upon this question in either branch of Congress, and I avail myself of the privilege of giving expression to my views with greater pleasure because my State has been hitherto unheard; and secondly, that they are in emphatic harmony with the clearly-expressed sentiments of my constituents.

I shall ask the indulgence of the House for but a brief time, while I present in concise form the reasons which govern my vote on this grave question. I have no wish to enter the broad field which has been swept by this debate for the purpose of gleaning after the myriad reapers who have entered the harvest before me, but I will traverse the United scope which I have prescribed to myself with as much rapidity as is consistent with the perspicuous presentation of the positions which I shall endeavor to establish by the way, promising to be (for I know how anxious most members are to close this debate) neither elaborate nor diffuse.

The first question that presents itself in the consideration of this proposition is whether we have the power to take the proposed action of initiating the abolition of slavery by a prohibition of it in our fundamental law; if we have not the power to do it, the rightful authority as an American Congress, then all discussion as to the propriety, the expediency, or even the necessity of the act is of course idle folly.

But, sir, I have listened carefully and attentively to the arguments of gentlemen upon the pro-slavery side of this question, who deny our authority to amend the Constitution as proposed, without being able to perceive the justice or soundness of their assumption. I perused with patience the ingenious argument of the distinguished gentleman from Ohio, [Mr. Pendleton,] made at the last session of Congress, and reiterated Saturday last by his colleague, [Mr. Bliss,] the gentleman from New York, [Mr. Pruyn,] and a member from New Jersey whom I do not choose to name. The gist of that argument being that slavery is a State institution, never submitted by them to Federal control, that it is an indefeasible right of property conferred by State laws, and not to be divested by any other sanction, is a fallacy which can, I think, be most easily and conclusively met and answered.

You assert that slavery is a local institution, deriving all its right to exist from the municipal laws of each State where it is acknowledged. I admit the assertion. You assert that it was a subject left by the framers of the Constitution to the States, to be by them controlled, legislated upon, encouraged, fostered, or abolished in the States, as to them seemed most expedient. That I also admit.

You assert that, owing its existence to State laws and State authority, and being a subject left by the framers of our fundamental law to the exclusive control of the State authority, therefore we have no right to so amend the Constitution as to take Federal control of and abolish it. This assertion I deny. The conclusion does not follow from your premises, as I now propose to demonstrate. This is a proposition to amend the Constitution of the United States and to establish in that Constitution a power hitherto not possessed. That Constitution is the existing fundamental law of all the States, having been assented to and ratified by them. It contains among its provisions one by which it prescribes the methods by which the instrument may be altered, changed, and amended. Those methods are, that the two Houses may, by a two-thirds vote, propose amendments; or Congress may, on application of the Legislatures of two thirds of the several States, call a convention to propose amendments to the Constitution; and in either case, whenever the proposed amendment or amendments shall be ratified by three fourths of the States, they shall become valid and binding provisions of the Constitution; and upon this power of amendment there is one and only one limitation, and that is that "no State without its consent shall be deprived of its equal suffrage in the Senate." The full and complete power to amend the Constitution in any and every particular is given and confirmed by the fifth article of the Constitution, curtailed by the single existing limitation as to equal State representation in the Senate. If the Staters had intended, when the Constitution was originally formed, to forever keep the institutions of slavery beyond Federal control, they should and would have excepted that also, with the right of equal suffrage in the senate, from among the subjects of rightful amendment.

I grant that the right to abolish slavery was not given to the Federal authority as a legislative power, but the means by which the national

Government might obtain that power through an amendment to the Constitution were given, and those we now propose to apply.

If domestic slavery was beyond our control originally, the Constitution points out the way by which we may legitimately take it under cognizance, and we are following strictly the methods it prescribes.

Sir, we are told that by this amendment, if it succeeds, we are encroaching upon the rights of the States, and that we are taking a step toward consolidation. Certainly we are; and if the States, in the mode prescribed by the Constitution, choose to yield not only the right which they have hitherto enjoyed of controlling and perpetuating the system of slavery, but every other political right exercised by them, they can unquestionably do so. It maybe very unwise policy for them to do so; but it can nevertheless be done constitutionally; and that is the question I am now considering.

I think, then, that I have established the proposition that, as all the States have agreed by their ratification of the Constitution to abide all amendments which shall be made to that instrument which receives the sanction of three fourths of their number, having first passed the preliminary ordeal of a two-thirds majority of both Houses of Congress, or of a national convention, our proposed amendment is perfectly within our province and power.

And now, Mr. Speaker, I pass from the question of our power to amend, and come to the equally important practical question, the expediency of the proposed amendment. Ought slavery in these United States to be abolished? Is it our duty as statesmen seeking the good of the country and of posterity to put an end to this institution? Is it our duty as citizens, loving our country and seeking her glory and prosperity, and withal having her good name among nations committed to our care, to rid her of this institution?

Sir, it seems to me that but one patriotic answer can be given to these questions, and that is an affirmative one. View it in whatever light you may, the answer must still be the same. Look at it as a question of mere political economy, and the argument of material prosperity alone would say abolish it forever. The argument of statistics and facts, so triumphantly conclusive as to defy all attempts at refutation, which my friend from Maryland [Mr. Creswell] presented the other day, ought of itself to determine every man who seeks for the proper development of this fair western continent, to vote for the abolition of slavery on every proper occasion.

When an American citizen enters a foreign land and sees the degradation to which the downtrodden masses are subjected by their kingly rulers, his soul revolts at the injustice, but his mouth is closed against remonstrance. If he talks of the beneficence of free institutions and the glory of republican government he is told to learn to practice what he preaches before he seeks to proselyte abroad. If the American, indignant at the wrongs he sees done to unhappy Ireland by the proud rulers of England, expresses his hope to see her emancipated from their rigorous rule, he is asked to think of the millions pining in chains beneath the starry flag of the country he so proudly praises. If, burning with that instinctive hatred of tyranny which finds new fuel in the dark history that records the endurance of noble Hungary, and the oppression of despotic Austria, he ventures an utterance of the feelings of his heart, he is shamed into silence by the sneering suggestion that a more galling tyranny and a more degrading slavery stain the prosperity and dim the glory of his own fair land. If then, sir, it were only to make our Government consistent with itself, to make her an example of freedom, to which all the nations of the world might turn and be instructed, free her from every stain, and wipe off every reproach based upon the existence of human bondage; if it were only to vindicate our good name with mankind, I would vote to abolish slavery. . . .

But we are met with another objection, that if we emancipate we must enfranchise also. I deny the conclusion; but I should not be deterred from the move, even if it were correct. A recognition of natural rights is one thing, a grant of political franchises is quite another. We extend to all white men the protection of law when they land upon our shores. We grant them political rights when they comply with the conditions which those laws prescribe. If political rights must necessarily follow the possession of personal liberty, then all but male citizens in our country are slaves. This illustration alone reduces the conclusion to an absurdity. Sir, let the rights and status of the negro settle themselves as they will and must upon their own just basis. If, as a race, they shall prove themselves worthy the elective franchise, I tell gentlemen they will enjoy the right; they will demand and they will win it, and they ought to have it. If, on the contrary, as a race, they are so far inferior to those with whom they must compete as to be unequal to the high and responsible position of free electors, and attempt to elevate them to that standard will be a signal failure. I have no faith in their ability to contend in the race before them successfully, and no fear of degrading my own race by contact with them, for, sir, there is an antagonism between the races which will prevent anything like a complete blending of them, and I leave all questions of the consequences of emancipation to be settled by justice and expediency as experience shall dictate. "Sufficient unto the day is the evil thereof," and I will do what right and expediency require now, and leave the consequences to be provided for as they may arise. Conscious as I am that the best interests of the country and posterity require a mitigation of the evils with which slavery has afflicted this war-desolated and strife-torn land, I will not suffer myself to be prevented from giving my aid to this beneficent proposition by any imaginary evils that it may not provide for. If the abolition of slavery shall still leave us the dregs of this pestiferous question to be dealt with at a future time, I am willing to trust the future for their settlement, well convinced that all others are more subordinate difficulties which time and statesmanship will enable us to wisely overcome. . . .

THE CIVIL RIGHTS ACT OF 1866

Commentary

The Civil Rights Act of 1866 was the first federal statute to provide broad protection in the field of civil rights. Its purpose was to give to the newly emancipated Negro equality with whites before the law. This purpose was fully explained by Senator Lyman Trumbull [R., Ill.], Chairman of the Senate Judiciary Committee, in his address on January 29, 1866, introducing the proposed legislation. According to him, the purpose of the bill was to carry into effect the Thirteenth Amendment by destroying the discrimination against the Negro that existed in the laws of the southern states. In this way, the new statute would (as Trumbull had expressed it a month earlier in a speech not reprinted here) "provide for the real freedom of their former slaves."

Trumbull tells us that "the basis of the whole bill" was in its first section, which, as introduced by him, provided (1) that there should be no discrimination in civil rights on account of race; and (2) that inhabitants of every race shall have the same right to contract, sue, take and dispose of property, bring actions and give evidence, and to equal benefit of all laws for the security of the person and property. This provision, the senator went on, was intended to "secure to all persons within the United States practical freedom." Of particular interest to one concerned with civil rights was Trumbull's answer to the query of Senator James McDougall [Dem., Cal.], with regard to what was meant by "civil rights." Trumbull replied that the term was defined by the bill's first section and it did not include political rights—an approach that is certainly narrower than that used at the present day.

The speech by Senator Willard Saulsbury [Dem., Del.], illustrates the views of those who opposed all congressional action in the civil rights field. More important to the student of legislative history was the opposition based upon a claim of unconstitutionality, which found voice in members of the Republican party who plainly favored federal protection of civil rights. Foremost among these was Representative John Bingham [R., Ohio], whose views are of particular interest to us because of the role he played in the drafting of the Fourteenth Amendment. When the Civil Rights Bill came before the House in March, Bingham made a strong speech in opposition. On March 9, he asserted that Congress had no power to enact such law, on the ground that the constitutional power to protect individual rights then rested only in the states, not the federal government. He said that the evils which the bill sought to remedy should be dealt with by constitutional amendment—thus indicating that his drafts of Section 1 of the Fourteenth Amendment (*infra* p. 187) were intended to give constitutional validity to the principles laid down in the 1866 Civil Rights Act. Interestingly, he took a much broader view of the term "civil rights" than Trumbull, stating that it did embrace political rights.

Trumbull himself had recognized the existence of strong constitutional doubts about his bill. He asserted that the bill was valid under the Thirteenth Amendment—since any encroachment upon a citizen's liberty was "a badge of servitude" and hence within the prohibition of the Thirteenth Amendment, which Congress had the express authority to enforce. The opponents of the bill remained unconvinced. Their detailed attacks on constitutional grounds are not reprinted, with the exception of the addresses by Bingham and Senator Reverdy Johnson [Dem., Md.] whose objections are illustrative of others who expressed similar views.

Two important changes were made in section 1 of the 1866 bill during the congressional debates. The first was the addition of a citizenship clause, making persons born in this country United States citizens. Its purpose was to remove the doubts about the Negro's citizenship status that persisted because of the decision in *Dred Scott* v. *Sandford,* 19 How. 393 (1857). The second change was the dropping in the House of the clause in the original bill containing a general prohibition against discrimination in civil rights on account of race. This had been done to meet Bingham's objections, but did not go far enough to secure his vote and that of those who felt as he did.

Despite the objections of Republicans like Bingham, the Civil Rights Bill passed the Senate on February 2, and the House on March 13, 1866. It was, however, vetoed by President Andrew Johnson on March 27. The veto message was based, in large part, upon the lack of constitutional power in Congress to confer citizenship and abrogate discriminatory state laws. It contains a good summary of the constitutional opposition to the 1866 bill. The Senate debate occasioned by Johnson's veto is not reprinted, for it only repeated what was said earlier. On April 6 and 9, respectively, the Senate and House voted (the latter without debate), by 33 to 15 and 122 to 41, to override the veto, and the bill became law.

The doubts raised by congressional opponents of the 1866 Civil Rights Act had great effect. It is true that the relatively few cases on the matter ultimately divided about evenly (though Justice Arthur Goldberg recently stated that a majority upheld the constitutionality of the Act, he apparently considered only the cases appearing in official reports [*Bell* v. *Maryland,* 378 U.S. 226, 292 (1964)]. But the doubts persisted and led the congressional advocates of federal enforcement of civil rights to resolve such doubts by constitutional amendment. The ultimate solution was to recast section 1 of the Civil Rights Act as section 1 of the Fourteenth Amendment. This, we shall see, was the purpose avowed by most participants in the debates on the Fourteenth Amendment.

The adoption of the Fourteenth Amendment was to make the Civil Rights Act of 1866 largely academic. That is the case because section 1 of the new amendment contained a general prohibition against discrimination in its equal protection clause that was even broader than the original ban against racial discrimination that had been contained in the original version of the 1866 Act. In section 18 of the Enforcement Act of 1870 (*infra* p. 451), Congress expressly reenacted the Civil Rights Act of 1866. By 1870 there was no doubt of the legislative power to legislate in the field of civil rights because of the specific authority given Congress to enforce the Fourteenth Amendment by the latter's last section.

THE CIVIL RIGHTS ACT
April 9, 1866

Be it enacted by the Senate and House of Representatives of the United States of America in Congress assembled, That all persons born in the United States and not subject to any foreign power, excluding Indians not taxed, are hereby declared to be citizens of the United States; and such citizens, of every race and color, without regard to any previous condition of slavery or involuntary servitude, except as a punishment for crime whereof the party shall have been duly convicted, shall have the same right, in every State and Territory in the United States, to make and enforce contracts, to sue, be parties, and give evidence, to inherit, purchase, lease, sell, hold, and convey real and personal property, and to full and equal benefit of all laws and proceedings for the security of person and property, as is enjoyed by white citizens, and shall be subject to like punishment, pains, and penalties, and to none other, any law, statute, ordinance, regulation, or custom, to the contrary notwithstanding.

SEC. 2. *And be it further enacted,* That any person who, under color of any law, statute, ordinance, regulation, or custom, shall subject, or cause to be subjected, any inhabitant of any State or Territory to the deprivation of any right secured or protected by this act, or to different punishment, pains, or penalties on account of such person having at any time been held in a condition of slavery or involuntary servitude, except as a punishment for crime whereof the party shall have been duly convicted, or by reason of his color or race, than is prescribed for the punishment of white persons, shall be deemed guilty of a misdemeanor, and, on conviction, shall be punished by fine not exceeding one thousand dollars, or imprisonment not exceeding one year, or both, in the discretion of the court.

SEC. 3. *And be it further enacted,* That the district courts of the United States, within their respective districts, shall have, exclusively of the courts of the several States, cognizance of all crimes and offences committed against the provisions of this act, and also, concurrently with the circuit courts of the United States, of all causes, civil and criminal, affecting persons who are denied or cannot enforce in the courts or judicial tribunals of the State or locality where they may be any of the rights secured to them by the first section of this act; and if any suit or prosecution, civil or criminal, has been or shall be commenced in any State court, against any such person, for any cause whatsoever, or against any officer, civil or military, or other person, for any arrest or imprisonment, trespasses, or wrongs done or committed by virtue or under color of authority derived from this act or the act establishing a Bureau for the relief of Freedmen and Refugees, and all acts amendatory thereof, or for refusing to do any act upon the ground that it would be inconsistent with this act, such defendants shall have the right to remove such cause for trial to the proper district or circuit court in the manner prescribed by the "Act relating to habeas corpus and regulating judicial proceedings in certain cases," approved March three, eighteen hundred and sixty-three, and all acts amendatory thereof. The jurisdiction in civil and criminal matters hereby conferred on the district and circuit courts of the United States shall be exercised and enforced in conformity with the laws of the United States, so far as such laws are suitable to carry the same into effect; but in all cases where such laws are not adapted to the object, or are deficient in the provisions necessary to furnish suitable remedies and punish offences against law, the common law, as modified and changed by the constitution and statutes of the State wherein the court having jurisdiction of the cause, civil or criminal, is held, so far as the same is not inconsistent with the Constitution and laws of the United States, shall be extended to and govern said courts in the trial and disposition of such cause, and, if of a criminal nature, in the infliction of punishment on the party found guilty.

SEC. 4. *And be it further enacted,* That the district attorneys, marshals, and deputy marshals of the United States, the commissioners appointed by the circuit and territorial courts of the United States, with powers of arresting, imprisoning, or bailing offenders against the laws of the United States, the officers and agents of the Freedmen's Bureau, and every other officer who may be specially empowered by the President of the United States, shall be, and they are hereby, specially authorized and required, at the expense of the United States, to institute proceedings against all and every person who shall violate the provisions of this act, and cause him or them to be arrested and imprisoned, or bailed, as the case may be, for trial before such court of the United States or territorial court as by this act has cognizance of the offence. And with a view to affording reasonable protection to all persons in their constitutional rights of equality before the law, without distinction of race or color, or previous condition of slavery or involuntary servitude, except as a punishment for crime, whereof the party shall have been duly convicted, and to the prompt discharge of the duties of this act, it shall be the duty of the circuit courts of the United States and the superior courts of the Territories of the United States, from time to time, to increase the number of commissioners, so as to afford a speedy and convenient means for the arrest and examination of persons charged with a violation of this act; and such commissioners are hereby authorized and required to exercise and discharge all the powers and duties conferred on them by this act, and the same duties with regard to offences created by this act, as they are authorized by law to exercise with regard to other offences against the laws of the United States.

SEC. 5. *And be it further enacted,* That it shall be the duty of all marshals and deputy marshals to obey and execute all warrants and precepts issued under the provisions of this act, when to them directed; and should any marshal or deputy marshal refuse to receive such warrant or other process when tendered, or to use all proper means diligently to execute the same, he shall, on conviction thereof, be fined in the sum of one thousand dollars, to the use of the person upon whom the accused is alleged to have committed the offence. And the better to enable the said commissioners to execute their duties faithfully and efficiently, in conformity with the Constitution of the United States and the requirements of this act, they are hereby authorized and empowered, within their counties respectively, to appoint, in writing, under their hands, any one or more suitable persons, from time to time, to execute all such warrants and other process as may be issued by them in the lawful performance of their respective duties; and the persons so appointed to execute any warrant or process as aforesaid shall have authority to summon and call to their aid the bystanders or posse comitatus of the proper county, or such portion of the land or naval forces of the United States, or of the militia, as may be necessary to the performance of the duty with which they are charged, and to insure a faithful observance of the clause of the Constitution which prohibits slavery, in conformity with the provisions of this act; and said warrants shall run and be executed by said officers anywhere in the State or Territory within which they are issued.

SEC. 6. *And be it further enacted,* That any person who shall knowingly and wilfully obstruct, hinder, or prevent any officer, or other person charged with the execution of any warrant or process issued under the provisions of this act, or any person or persons lawfully assisting him or them, from arresting any person for whose apprehension such warrant or process may have been issued, or shall rescue or attempt to rescue such person from the custody of the officer, other person or persons, or those lawfully assisting as aforesaid, when so arrested pursuant to the authority herein given and declared, or shall aid, abet, or assist any person so arrested as aforesaid, directly or indirectly, to escape from the custody of the officer or other person legally authorized as aforesaid, or shall harbor or conceal any person for whose arrest a warrant or process shall have been issued as aforesaid, so as to prevent his discovery and arrest after notice or knowledge of the fact that a warrant has been issued for the apprehension of such person, shall, for either of said offences, be subject to a fine not exceeding one thousand dollars, and imprisonment not exceeding six months, by indictment and conviction before the district court of the United States for the district in which said offence may have been committed, or before the proper court of criminal jurisdiction, if committed within any one of the organized Territories of the United States.

SEC. 7. *And be it further enacted,* That the district attorneys, the marshals, their deputies, and the clerks of the said district and territorial courts shall be paid for their services the like fees as may be allowed to them for similar services in other cases; and in all cases where the proceedings are before a commissioner, he shall be entitled to a fee of ten dollars in full for his services in each case, inclusive of all services incident to such arrest and examination. The person or persons authorized to execute the process to be issued by such commissioners for the arrest of offenders against the provisions of this act shall be entitled to a fee of five dollars for each person he or they may arrest and take before any such commissioner as aforesaid, with such other fees as may be deemed reasonable by such commissioner for such other additional services as may be necessarily performed by him or them, such as attending at the examination, keeping the prisoner in custody, and providing him with food and lodging during his detention, and until the final determination of such commissioner, and in general for performing such other duties as may be required in the premises; such fees to be made up in conformity with the fees usually charged by the officers of the courts of justice within the proper district or county, as near as may be practicable, and paid out of the Treasury of the United States on the certificate of the judge of the district within which the arrest is made, and to be recoverable from the defendant as part of the judgment in case of conviction.

SEC. 8. *And be it further enacted,* That whenever the President of the United States shall have reason to believe that offences have been or are likely to be committed against the provisions of this act within any judicial district, it shall be lawful for him, in his discretion, to direct the judge, marshal, and district attorney of such district to attend at such place within the district, and for such time as he may designate, for the purpose of the most speedy arrest and trial of persons charged with a violation of this act; and it shall be the duty of every judge or other officer, when any such requisition shall be received by him, to attend at the place and for the time therein designated.

SEC. 9. *And be it further enacted,* That it shall be lawful for the President of the United States, or such person as he may empower for that purpose, to employ such part of the land or naval forces of the United States, or of the militia, as shall be necessary to prevent the violation and enforce the due execution of this act.

SEC. 10. *And be it further enacted,* That upon all questions of law arising in any cause under the provisions of this act a final appeal may be taken to the Supreme Court of the United States.

Schuyler Colfax,
Speaker of the House of Representatives
La Fayette S. Foster,
President of the Senate, *pro tempore*

In the Senate of the United States, April 6, 1866

The President of the United States having returned to the Senate, in which it originated, the bill entitled "An act to protect all persons in the United States in their civil rights, and furnish the means of their vindication," with his objections thereto, the Senate proceeded, in pursuance of the Constitution, to reconsider the same; and,

Resolved, That the said bill do pass, two-thirds of the Senate agreeing to pass the same.

Attest: *J. W. Forney,*
                                                     Secretary of the Senate

In the United States House of Representatives. April 9, 1866

The House of Representatives having proceeded, in pursuance of the Constitution, to reconsider the bill entitled "An act to protect all persons in the United States in their civil rights, and furnish the means of their vindication," returned to the Senate by the President of the United States, with his objections, and sent by the Senate to the House of Representatives, with the message of the President returning the bill:

Resolved, That the bill do pass, two-thirds of the House of Representatives agreeing to pass the same.

Attest: *Edward McPherson,* Clerk,
                                                     by *Clinton Lloyd,* Chief Clerk

THE DEBATE

Senate-39th Congress, 1st Session
January 29-February 2, 1866

LYMAN TRUMBULL [R., ILL.]. Before proceeding with the bill under consideration, I desire to offer an amendment, to insert after the word "that," in the third line of the first section, the words, "all persons of African descent born in the United States are hereby declared to be citizens of the United States and;" so that the section will read:

That all persons of African descent born in the United States are hereby declared to be citizens of the United States, and there shall be no discrimination in civil rights or immunities among the inhabitants of any State or Territory of the United States on account of race, color, or previous condition of slavery, &c.

Mr. President, I regard the bill to which the attention of the Senate is now called as the most important measure that has been under its consideration since the adoption of the constitutional amendment abolishing slavery. That amendment declared that all persons in the United States should be free. This measure is intended to give effect to that declaration and secure to all persons within the United States practical freedom. There is very little importance in the general declaration of abstract truths and principles unless they can be carried into effect, unless the persons who are to be affected by them have some means of availing themselves of their benefits. Of what avail was the immortal declaration "that all men are created equal; that they are endowed by their Creator with certain inalienable rights; that among these are life, liberty, and the pursuit of happiness," and "that to secure these rights Governments are instituted among men," to the millions of the African race in this country who were ground down and degraded and subjected to a slavery more intolerable and cruel than the world ever before knew? Of what avail was it to the citizen of Massachusetts, who, a few years ago, went to South Carolina to enforce a constitutional right in court, that the Constitution of the United States declared that the citizens of each State shall be entitled to all the privileges and immunities of citizens in the several States? And of what avail will it now be that the Constitution of the United States has declared that slavery shall not exist, if in the late slaveholding States laws are to be enacted and enforced depriving persons of African descent of privileges which are essential to freemen?

It is the intention of this bill to secure those rights. The laws in the slaveholding States have made a distinction against persons of African descent on account of their color, whether free or slave. I have before me the statutes of Mississippi. They provide that if any colored person, any free negro or mulatto, shall come into that State for the purpose of residing there, he shall be sold into slavery for life. If any person of African descent residing in

106

that State travels from one county to another without having a pass or a certificate of his freedom, he is liable to be committed to jail and to be dealt with as a person who is in the State without authority. Other provisions of the statute prohibit any negro or mulatto from having fire-arms; and one provision of the statute declares that for "exercising the functions of a minister of the Gospel free negroes and mulattoes, on conviction, may be punished by any number of lashes not exceeding thirty-nine on the bare back, and shall pay the costs." Other provisions of the statute of Mississippi prohibit a free negro or mulatto from keeping a house of entertainment, and subject him to trial before two justices of the peace and five slaveholders for violating the provisions of this law. The statutes of South Carolina make it a highly penal offense for any person, white or colored, to teach slaves; and similar provisions are to be found running through all the statutes of the late slaveholding States.

When the constitutional amendment was adopted and slavery abolished, all these statutes became null and void, because they were all passed in aid of slavery, for the purpose of maintaining and supporting it. Since the abolition of slavery, the Legislatures which have assembled in the insurrectionary States have passed laws relating to the freedmen, and in nearly all the States they have discriminated against them. They deny them certain rights, subject them to severe penalties, and still impose upon them the very restrictions which were imposed upon them in consequence of the existence of slavery, and before it was abolished. The purpose of the bill under consideration is to destroy all these discriminations, and to carry into effect the constitutional amendment. The first section of the bill, as it is now proposed to be amended, declares that all persons of African descent shall be citizens of the United States, and—

That there shall be no discrimination in civil rights or immunities among the inhabitants of any State or Territory of the United States on account of race, color, or previous condition of slavery; but the inhabitants of every race and color, without regard to any previous condition of slavery or involuntary servitude, except as a punishment for crime whereof the party shall have been duly convicted, shall have the same right to make and enforce contracts, to sue, be parties, and give evidence, to inherit, purchase, lease, sell, hold, and convey real and personal property, and to full and equal benefit of all laws and proceedings for the security of person and property, and shall be subject to like punishment, pains, and penalties, and to none other, any law, statute, ordinance, regulation, or custom to the contrary notwithstanding.

This section is the basis of the whole bill. The other provisions of the bill contain the necessary machinery to give effect to what are declared to be the rights of all persons in the first section, and the question will arise, has Congress authority to pass such a bill? Has Congress authority to give practical effect to the great declaration that slavery shall not exist in the United States? If it has not, then nothing has been accomplished by the adoption of the constitutional amendment. In my judgment, Congress has this authority. It is difficult, perhaps, to define accurately what slavery is and what liberty is. Liberty and slavery are opposite terms; one is opposed to the other. We know that in a civil government, in organized society, no such thing can exist as natural or absolute liberty. Natural liberty is defined to be the—

Power of acting as one thinks fit, without any restraint or control, unless by the law of nature, being a right inherent in us by birth, and one of the gifts of God to man in his creation, when he imbued him with the faculty of will.

But every man who enters society gives up a part of this natural liberty, which is the liberty of the savage, the liberty which the wild beast has, for the advantages he obtains in the protection which civil government gives him. Civil liberty, or the liberty which a person enjoys in society, is thus defined by Blackstone:

Civil liberty is no other than natural liberty, so far restrained by human laws and no further, as is necessary and expedient for the general advantage of the public.

That is the liberty to which every citizen is entitled; that is the liberty which was intended to be secured by the Declaration of Independence and the Constitution of the United States originally, and more especially by the amendment which has recently been adopted; and in a note to Blackstone's *Commentaries* it is stated that—

In this definition of civil liberty it ought to be understood, or rather expressed, that the restraints introduced by the law should be equal to all, or as much so as the nature of things will admit.

Then, sir, I take it that any statute which is not equal to all, and which deprives any citizen of civil rights which are secured to other citizens, is an unjust encroachment upon his liberty; and is, in fact, a badge of servitude which, by the Constitution, is prohibited. We may, perhaps, arrive at a more correct definition of the term "citizen of the United States" by referring to that clause of the Constitution which I have already quoted, and which declares that "the citizens of each State shall be entitled to all privileges and immunities of citizens in the several States." What rights are secured to the citizens of each State under that provision? Such fundamental rights as belong to every free person. Story, in his Commentaries, in commenting upon this clause of the Constitution of the United States, says:

The intention of this clause was to confer on citizens, if one may so say, a general citizenship, and to communicate all the privileges and immunities which the citizens of the same State would be entitled to under the like circumstances.

There have been several decisions of courts upon this clause of the Constitution. It was decided by the general court of the State of Maryland

(Chase and Duval, justices) that this section meant that the citizens of all the States should have the peculiar advantage of acquiring and holding real as well as personal property, and that such property should be protected and secured by the laws of the State in the same manner as the property of the citizens of the State is protected. It meant that such property shall not be liable to any tax or burdens which the property of the citizen is not subject to. It may also mean that, as creditors, they shall be on the same footing with the State creditor in the payment of the debts of a decreased debtor. It secures and protects personal rights. [Campbell v. Morris, 3 Harris and McHenry, 535]

This clause of the Constitution, according to the decision of the Indiana court made in 1797, "secures and protects personal rights" and gives to every person who is a citizen of one State the same rights to hold property, the same personal rights, that the citizen of that State has.

A decision by the supreme court of Massachusetts upon this clause of the Constitution declares that—

The privileges and immunities secured to the people of each State in every other State can be applied only in case of removal from one State into another. By such removal they become citizens of the adopted State without naturalization, and have a right to sue and be sued as citizens; and yet this privilege is qualified and not absolute, for they cannot enjoy the right of suffrage or of eligibility to office, without such term of residence as shall be prescribed by the constitution and laws of the State into which they shall remove. They shall have the privileges and immunities of citizens; that is, they shall not be deemed aliens, but may take and hold real estate; and may, according to the laws of such State, eventually enjoy the full rights of citizenship without the necessity of being naturalized. [6 Pickering 92, Abbott v. Bayley]

But, sir, the decision most elaborate upon this clause of the Constitution is to be found in Washington's Circuit Court Reports, in a case which was reserved for consideration after argument. I will read several sentences from the opinion of the circuit judge, because it will be seen that he enumerates the very rights belonging to a citizen of the United States which are set forth in the first section of this bill. He says:

The next question is, whether this act infringes that section of the Constitution which declares that "the citizens of each State shall be entitled to all privileges and immunities of citizens in the several States?"

The inquiry is, what are the privileges and immunities of citizens in the several States? We feel no hesitation in confining these expressions to those privileges and immunities which are in their nature fundamental; which belong of right to the citizens of all free Governments; and which have at all times been enjoyed by the citizens of the several States which compose this Union, from the time of their becoming free, independent, and sovereign. What these fundamental principles are it would perhaps be more tedious than difficult to enumerate. They may, however, be all comprehended under the following general heads: protection by the Government; the enjoyment of life and liberty, with the right to acquire and possess property of every kind; and to pursue and obtain happiness and safety, subject, nevertheless, to such restraints as the Government may justly prescribe for the general good of the whole. The right of a citizen of one State to pass through, or to reside in any other State, for purposes of trade, agriculture, professional pursuits, or otherwise; to claim the benefit of the writ of *habeas corpus;* to institute and maintain actions of any kind in the courts of the State; to take, hold, and dispose of property, either real or personal, and an exemption from higher taxes or impositions than are paid by the other citizens of the State, may be mentioned as some of the particular privileges and immunities of citizens, which are clearly embraced by the general description of privileges deemed to be fundamental; to which may be added the elective franchise, as regulated and established by the laws or constitution of the State in which it is to be exercised. [Corfield *v.* Coryell, 4 *Washington's Circuit Court Reports,* 380]

This judge goes further than the bill under consideration, and he lays it down as his opinion that under this clause of the Constitution, securing to the citizen of each State all the privileges and immunities of citizens of the several States of the United States, a person who is a citizen in one State and goes to another is even entitled to the elective franchise; but at all events he is entitled to the great fundamental rights of life, liberty, and the pursuit of happiness, and the right to travel, to go where he pleases. This is a right which belongs to the citizen of each State.

Now, sir, if that be so, this being the construction as settled by judicial decisions to be put upon the clause of the Constitution to which I have adverted, how much more are the native-born citizens of the State itself entitled to these rights! In my judgment, persons of African descent, born in the United States, are as much citizens as white persons who are born in the country. I know that in the slaveholding States a different opinion has obtained. The people of those States have not regarded the colored race as citizens, and on that principle many of their laws making discriminations between the whites and the colored people are based; but it is competent for Congress to declare, under the Constitution of the United States, who are citizens. If there were any question about it, it would be settled by the passage of a law declaring all persons born in the United States to be citizens thereof. That this bill proposes to do. Then they will be entitled to the rights of citizens. And what are they? The great fundamental rights set forth in this bill: the right to acquire property, the right to go and come at pleasure, the right to enforce rights in the courts, to make contracts, and to inherit and dispose of property. These are the very rights that are set forth in this bill as appertaining to every freeman.

PETER VAN WINKLE [R., W. VA.]. If the gentleman will permit me, before he passes from this subject I should like him to explain, if these Africans are not now citizens of the United States, where is the authority by law of Congress to make them citizens?

MR. TRUMBULL. The Constitution of the United States confers upon Congress the right to provide uniform rules of naturalization.

MR. VAN WINKLE. For the admission of foreigners.

MR. TRUMBULL. Not necessarily of foreigners.

MR. VAN WINKLE. For the naturalization of foreigners, if I recollect the language.

MR. TRUMBULL. If the Senator from West Virginia will look into the statutes, he will find that it has happened in the history of the Government more than once that Congress by general act has naturalized a whole people. I think there was an act of that kind in reference to the Stockbridge Indians, an act of that character making citizens of the United States of the people of Texas and the people of Florida I think. There have been several general laws of that character; and the authority under the Constitution of the United States to declare who shall be citizens of the United States is, as I understand, vested in Congress and nowhere else. My friend from Massachusetts [Mr. Sumner] has handed me the constitutional clause on this subject, which declares that Congress shall have power "to establish a uniform rule of naturalization." Nothing is said about foreigners.

MR. VAN WINKLE. I perceived my mistake before the gentleman read the clause.

MR. TRUMBULL. So, sir, I take it that it is competent for Congress to declare these persons to be citizens. They being now free and citizens of the United States, as citizens they are entitled, as I have undertaken to show, to the great fundamental rights belonging to free citizens, and we have a right to protect them in the enjoyment of them.

Now, sir, referring again to that other clause of the Constitution upon which there have been judicial constructions, is it not manifest that it was competent for the Congress of the United States to have passed a law that would have protected Mr. Hoar, who went from Massachusetts to South Carolina for the purpose of testing a question in the courts? Would it not have been competent, under these decisions, for Congress to have passed a law punishing any person who should have undertaken to deprive him of this right, and to have vested the proper authorities with power if necessary to call upon the Army and Navy of the United States to protect him in this right? I apprehend it would.

Then, under the constitutional amendment which we have now adopted, and which declares that slavery shall no longer exist, and which authorizes Congress by appropriate legislation to carry this provision into effect, I hold that we have a right to pass any law which, in our judgment, is deemed to appropriate, and which will accomplish the end in view, secure freedom to all people in the United States. The various State laws to which I have referred—and there are many others—although they do not make a man an absolute slave, yet deprive him of the rights of a freeman; and it is perhaps difficult to draw the precise line, to say where freedom ceases and slavery begins, but a law that does not allow a colored person to go from one county to another is certainly a law in derogation of the rights of a freeman. A law that does not allow a colored person to hold property, does not allow him to teach, does not allow him to preach, is certainly a law in violation of the rights of a freeman, and being so may properly be declared void.

Without going elaborately into this question, as my design was to state rather than argue the grounds upon which I place this bill, I will only add on this branch of subject that the clause of the Constitution under which we are called to act in my judgment vests Congress with the discretion of selecting that "appropriate legislation" which it is believed will best accomplish the end and prevent slavery.

Then, sir, the only question is, will this bill be effective to accomplish the object, for the first section will amount to nothing more than the declaration in the Constitution itself unless we have the machinery to carry it into effect. A law is good for nothing without a penalty, without a sanction to it, and that is to be found in the other sections of the bill. The second section provides:

That any person who under color of any law, statute, ordinance, regulation, or custom, shall subject or cause to be subjected any inhabitant of any State or Territory to the deprivation of any right secured or protected by this act, or to different punishment, pains, or penalties on account of such person having at any time been held in a condition of slavery or involuntary servitude, except as a punishment for crime whereof the party shall have been duly convicted, or by reason of his color or race, than is prescribed for the punishment of white persons, shall be deemed guilty of a misdemeanor, and on conviction shall be punished by fine not exceeding $1,000, or imprisonment not exceeding one year, or both, in the discretion of the court.

This is the valuable section of the bill so far as protecting the rights of freedmen is concerned. That they are entitled to be free we know. Being entitled to be free under the Constitution, that we have a right to enact such legislation as will make them free, we believe; and that can only be done by punishing those who undertake to deny them their freedom. When it comes to be understood in all parts of the United States that any person who shall deprive another of any right or subject him to any punishment in consequence of his color or race will expose himself to fine and imprisonment, I think such acts will soon cease.

I think it will only be necessary to go into the late slaveholding States and subject to fine and imprisonment one or two in a State, and the most prominent ones I should hope at that, to break up this whole business.

The third section of the bill provides for giving to the courts of the United States jurisdiction over all persons committing offenses against the provisions of this act, and also over the cases of persons who are discriminated against by State laws or customs. It provides further that no person whose equal civil rights are denied him in the State courts shall be tried by those courts for any offense, but that he shall have a right to remove his cause into the courts of the United States, and be there tried if it be for an offense against the laws of the United States, according to those laws, and if it be for an offense which is not provided for by the laws of the United States, then according to the common law as modified by the statutes and constitution of the State where the offense is committed, so far as they are not inconsistent with the Constitution and laws of the United States.

The other provisions of this bill I shall not go over in detail. Most of them are copied from the late fugitive slave act, adopted in 1850 for the purpose of returning fugitives from slavery into slavery again. The act that was passed at that time for the purpose of punishing persons who should aid negroes to escape to freedom is now to be applied by the provisions of this bill to the punishment of those who shall undertake to keep them in slavery. Surely we have the authority to enact a law as efficient in the interests of freedom, now that freedom prevails throughout the country, as we had in the interest of slavery when it prevailed in a portion of the country. . . .

JAMES MCDOUGALL [DEM., CAL.]. I beg leave to ask the Senator how, he interprets the term "civil rights" in the bill.

MR. TRUMBULL. The first section of the bill defines what I understand to be civil rights: the right to make and enforce contracts, to sue and be sued, and to give evidence, to inherit, purchase, sell, lease, hold, and convey real and personal property, and to full and equal benefit to all laws and proceedings for the security of person and property. These I understand to be civil rights, fundamental rights belonging to every man as a free man, and which under the Constitution as it now exists we have a right to protect every man in.

MR. MCDOUGALL. Allow me to remark that I think all those rights should be conceded. Do I understand that this bill does not go further than to give protection to the enjoyment of life and liberty and the pursuit of happiness and the protection of the courts, and to have justice administered to all? Do I understand that it is not designed to involve the question of political rights?

MR. TRUMBULL. This bill has nothing to do with the political rights or *status* of parties. It is confined exclusively to their civil rights, such rights as should appertain to every free man.

Having stated this much in regard to the object of the bill and its main features, I submit it to the Senate, and shall not further occupy its attention at the present time, and perhaps not at all unless it should be to reply to suggestions which may be made by others.

WILLARD SAULSBURY [DEM., DEL.]. Mr. President, I regard this bill as one of the most dangerous that was ever introduced into the Senate of the United States, or to which the attention of the American people was ever invited. During the last four or five years I have sat in this Chamber and witnessed the introduction of bills into this body which I thought obnoxious to many very grave and serious constitutional objections; but I have never since I have been a member of the body seen a bill so fraught with danger, so full of mischief, as the bill now under consideration. Deeming it to be of this character, duty to my country, duty to my State, duty to myself as a man, as a citizen, and as a legislator, duty to my children, and duty to my fellow-citizens everywhere, demands that I should utter my protest against its enactment into a law. . . .

Whether I have satisfied the mind of any Senator or any person in reference to this point, I at least have satisfied my own mind that my proposition is as clear as the sun at noonday. Then, sir, that being the basis upon which the honorable Senator from Illinois founds his argument, the sole authority which he claims for his bill, I might content myself with dismissing the subject here. I shall not follow the honorable Senator into a consideration of the manner in which slaves were treated in the southern States, nor the privileges that have been denied to them by the laws of the States. I think the time for shedding tears over the poor slave has well nigh passed in this country. The tears which the honest white people of this country have been made to shed from the oppressive acts of this Government in its various departments during the last four years call more loudly for my sympathies than those tears which have been shedding and dropping and dropping for the last twenty years in reference to the poor, oppressed slave—dropping from the eyes of strong-minded women and weak-minded men, until, becoming a mighty flood, they have swept away, in their resistless force, every trace of constitutional liberty in this country.

Mr. President, this bill is founded, in my judgment, in an utter misconception of the true theory, nature, and character of our system of government. Can any man believe that the founders of this Republic, the intellectual giants of the world, in the possession of freedom and self-government under their State governments, enjoying all the rights of free government before they entered into this Union, would have ever entered into the Union, which was intended simply as a contract and agreement of union and government between them for common purposes, if they had supposed that in the short term of eighty years their children would be subjected to the absolute control and the omnipotent will of the Federal Congress? I do not believe it. Let us see whether this bill in its provisions is not a total subversion of the true theory and character of our Federal system. . . .

REVERDY JOHNSON [DEM., MD.]. Mr. President, if this bill is to pass into a law, it is of course advisable and I am sure no one will admit that with more readiness than the honorable member of the committee who reported it— that it should be as free from objections as it can be made. What I am about to suggest is not, therefore, for the purpose of defeating the bill, though I shall not be able to vote for it with the opinion I entertain on the question of power, but for the purpose of improving the bill, or at least relieving it from objections to which it seems to me to be now subject.

The particular question before the Senate is the amendment suggested by the honorable chairman of the Judiciary Committee, as now amended by the honorable member from Kansas. By that amendment he proposes to define citizenship. Nobody is more willing to admit that it is very desirable that such a definition should be given. Since the decision in the case of Dred Scott, as the Senate are aware, a person of African descent, whether born free or not, whether free by birth or free by after events, is not, within the meaning of the Constitution of the United States, a citizen.

Whatever objections may be made to that decision, with reference to the great question which was decided and the question which agitated the country far and wide, cannot be made to that part of the decision which relates to the particular point which I have just stated. The objection to the decision upon the great question was that that was not before the court for adjudication. The suit was instituted in a State court of Missouri, and afterward went into the circuit court of the United States, and was brought, by writ of error, from the decision of the circuit court to the Supreme Court of the United States. There were two questions. The first was whether Scott was a citizen of the United States within the meaning of the third article of the Constitution, which creates and defines the extent of the judicial power. The act of 1789 could not go further, perhaps, than the Constitution provided. The Senate will remember that by that third article the judicial power of the United States was made to extend to, among other cases, controversies existing between citizens of different States. It was very clear, therefore, that no one could be considered as embraced by that power except a person who should be a citizen of the United States. The point was made in the court below, and upon the writ of error to the Supreme Court six judges out of eight, I think, decided that Scott was not a citizen; and not being a citizen, that the court below had no jurisdiction to try the cause.

The Supreme Court, however, went on afterward, for reasons satisfactory to the majority, to decide the questions which arose upon the merits, as they must have decided them if they had sustained the point of jurisdiction.

As far as the decision upon the merits was concerned, it was held to be obnoxious to very serious objection, and perhaps a large majority of the people of the United States, including a great many of the members of the profession throughout the United States, were of opinion that when the court came to the conclusion that they had no jurisdiction because of the incapacity of the party to sue, all that they should have done was to affirm the judgment of the court below upon the ground of want of jurisdiction. But as the Senate will see, the very point whether an African, free or not free born, free or becoming free afterward by State manumission or by manumission given him by his owner, was a citizen of the United States, was before that court and was adjudicated.

Now, without saying where the question has presented itself to my mind, it is sufficient for my purpose to say that I have been exceedingly anxious individually that there should be some definition which will rid this class of our people from that objection. If the Supreme Court decision is a binding one and will be followed in the future, this law which we are now about to pass will be held of course to be of no avail, as far as it professes to define what citizenship is, because it gives the rights of citizenship to all persons without distinction of color, and of course embraces Africans or descendants of Africans.

My own opinion, therefore, is that the object can only be safely and surely attained by an amendment of the Constitution, and I have tried in vain to form such a provision as would be free from objection. Whether I or those who may be associated with me in the future will be able to adopt a definition free from all objection is perhaps doubtful; but at any rate the effort can be made, and will be made in good faith; but I am very much afraid that, so far from settling the question by this legislation, we shall find that if the legislation is adopted the matter will be just as open to controversy as it was before.

There is another observation with which I beg leave to trouble the Senate, for the reason that, as I have just stated, I individually have found very great difficulty in saying who is a citizen. It is a question about which there is as much doubt as upon any other question in relation to which there is any doubt. How those doubts are to be solved, how the definition shall be made so plain as to be apparent to the comprehension of everybody, is with me now a problem. I am afraid, even supposing that we have the authority to do it by legislation, that the manner in which it is proposed to accomplish it by my friend from Illinois will not effect the purpose.

A word now upon the bill only in one particular. Nobody I am sure with whom it has been my happiness to associate during this war and who knows how anxious I have been from the first that the institution of slavery should be abolished, will doubt that from the same motives (whether they be of humanity or of some policy founded on other considerations than mere considerations of humanity) I should be equally anxious that the colored race should be protected in all their rights; that is to say in all proper rights.

The honorable member from Illinois yesterday—I have not the book by me—referred to a decision of Mr. Justice Washington as reported I think in 4 Washington's Circuit Court Reports; but if I heard him distinctly he did not read the whole of that decision. He read that portion of it alone which he supposed bore upon the particular question before the Senate; but I think it will be found that another portion of it which succeeds the particular part that he did read, will not justify him in finding a warrant for this bill in the opinion of Mr. Justice Washington. The case, if I remember it, arose upon an objection to the constitutionality of some of the State laws of New Jersey in relation to their fishing and their oysters. It was insisted that under the clause of the Constitution which secures to the citizens of each State the rights and privileges of citizens of the several States where ever they shall go, a citizen of New York had the right to go into New Jersey and catch fish and dredge for oysters. New Jersey denied it. The decision in that case was that New Jersey's title to the oysters and to the fish was exclusive, that she could legislate on the subject as she thought proper, and that she could therefore deny to the citizens of New York the privilege of catching fish or of dredging for oysters. He goes on to give the reasons why the particular rights which were involved in that case were not in the judgment of the court "fundamental rights." He first states what, in the view of the court, were rights of the latter description, and then goes on to say that this right of property is not one of those fundamental rights which is secured by the clause of the Constitution the interpretation of which was before the court in that case.

Now, Mr. President, the right of a State to its fisheries and to its oyster beds within its territorial limits is no greater than the right of the State to its real estate, its land within the same limits; and it has been the universal decision that the mode of purchasing land, the mode of conveying land, and the right to purchase were all within the jurisdiction of the State in which the subject of the purchase was located. Now, if I understand this bill, it is not confined to persons of African descent. The language of the first part of the first section is:

That there shall be no discrimination in civil rights or immunities among the inhabitants of any State or Territory of the United States on account of race, color, or previous condition of slavery.

That is to say, that no State shall discriminate at all between any inhabitants within her limits on account of any race to which they may belong, whether white or black, on account of color, if they are not white, or on account of their having been previously in a state of slavery, so that the white as well as the black is included in this first section; and if this passes, and we have the authority to pass it, then it would be impossible, as I think, for any State in the Union to draw any distinction as between her citizens who have been there from birth or who have been residents there for any length of time, and he who comes into the State now for the first time as a foreigner; he becomes an "inhabitant." If he comes from England or from any of the countries of the world and settles in the State of Illinois, that moment he becomes an inhabitant, and being an inhabitant, if this bill is to pass in the shape in which it stands, he can buy, he can sell, he can hold, and he can be inherited from.

MR. TRUMBULL. If the Senator will allow me, that is the law of Illinois to-day.

MR. JOHNSON. That may be; but it is not necessarily the law of Illinois. That is the law of Illinois, and Illinois has a right to make it her law; but I am speaking now of the question of power. Illinois has a right now to repeal that law. What Illinois has done has not been done by a great many of the States, or perhaps by a majority of the States. They will not permit aliens to purchase or to hold, or if they do, they do not permit others to inherit through them. It is subject now in all the States as far as I am aware—in the absence of legislation I am sure it must be so—to escheat at the instance of the Government.

But that is not all. That observation applies to everybody, without distinction of color or without reference to their antecedent condition; but in terms we are not left to infer that it was not intended to apply it to the blacks, because that is its chief provision, and no doubt is the provision for which the bill was supposed to be necessary. I take it for granted that neither the honorable member from Illinois nor any other member of the Senate would perhaps have thought it necessary to introduce such a bill as this but for the condition in which the blacks are; so that the object of the bill is, mainly to provide for the case of blacks. Now, what does it do? There exists in the States of the Union, and there must exist in every Government clothed with the power of governing well and of preserving the peace and harmony of society, a police power; there exists a power to legislate in relation to the prejudices of the people, a power not to legislate against their prejudices. Everybody knows that if a Legislature blindly legislates upon a subject which is obnoxious to the whole community that is subject to its power for a time, it is an act of no practical importance. How has it been in the eastern States with regard to the fugitive slave law of 1850? I mention it not with a view to find fault with the feeling on the subject that has existed in what have been called the free States.

The original fugitive slave law of 1793, which was passed at the instance of General Washington, was of itself very obnoxious at the time to a great many; but the author of the law of 1850—I do not like to name him, because I am willing, for his sake, that his name in that connection should be forgotten—admitted, as we have it from the authority of Mr. Clay, that he had made that law as obnoxious as he could in order to prevent its being observed in the States where slavery did not exist, and he accomplished his purpose. The law in one or two instances was enforced in one sense, but how enforced? Enforced by power, by military or civil power, threatening upon each occasion when resort was had to it to involve the particular community where the attempt was made in civil strife and bloodshed. The result was that no man who lost a slave, unless he wanted to make it the subject of political agitation in the South, dreamed of going to the North to recover him; it could not be done. Even the honorable member from Massachusetts [Mr. Sumner] here upon the floor of the Senate, as he has over and over admitted, said that he was not a dog, and not being a dog, he would not comply with the provisions of that law; and he spoke, no doubt, the sentiment of a large proportion of the people of Massachusetts, and perhaps what is the universal opinion of the people of that State at this moment and of all the loyal States. The law, therefore, became a dead letter, not because Congress had not the authority to pass it, for, as was stated just now in debate, the Supreme Court by a unanimous decision ruled that that law was constitutional, and Mr. Webster, whose feelings were all the other way no doubt, and who said his feelings were all the other way, admitted in his celebrated speech of the 7th of March that it was a constitutional law, however much he regretted its provisions.

I mention that for the purpose of applying it to one of the provisions of this bill. What is to be its application? There is not a State in which these negroes are to be found where slavery existed until recently, and I am not sure that there is not the same legislation in some of the States where slavery has long since been abolished, which does not make it criminal for a black man to marry a white woman, or for a white man to marry a black woman; and they do it not for the purpose of denying any right to the black man or to the white man, but for the purpose of preserving the harmony and peace of society. The demonstrations going on now in your free States show that a relation of that description cannot be entered into without producing some disorder. Do you not repeal all that legislation by this bill? I do not know that you intend to repeal it; but is it not clear that all such legislation will be repealed, and that consequently there may be a contract of marriage entered into as between persons of these different races, a white man with a black woman, or a black man with a white woman? If you are prepared to repeal it, do you think that the repeal will answer any practical purpose? Are you not, on the contrary, rather inclined to believe that, like the fugitive slave law of 1850, if enforced at all, and if these parties are to be protected at all, it must be enforced and the protection must be given by the bayonet? Is not that the effect of the law? Still confining myself to the first section, it says that these parties, without distinction of color, "shall have the same right to make and enforce contracts," to make contracts of any and every description.

WILLIAM FESSENDEN [R., ME.]. Where is the discrimination against color in the law to which the Senator refers?

REVERDY JOHNSON [DEM., MD.]. There is none; that is what I say; that is the very thing I am finding fault with.

MR. TRUMBULL. This bill would not repeal the law to which the Senator refers, if there is no discrimination made by it.

MR. JOHNSON. Would it not? We shall see directly. Standing upon this section, it will be admitted that the black man has the same right to enter into a contract of marriage with a white woman as a white man has, that is clear, because marriage is a contract. I was speaking of this without reference to any State legislation.

MR. FESSENDEN. He has the same right to make a contract of marriage with a white woman that a white man has with a black woman.

MR. JOHNSON. Just wait a moment. My friend from Maine is so quick that he cannot wait for the operation of slower minds. If there were no laws in Maryland on the subject, then the black man could marry a white woman, but there are laws. What is the effect of those laws? The first section of this bill says that there is to be no discrimination. The second section says that "any person who, under color of any law, statute, ordinance, regulation, or custom, shall subject or cause to be subjected any inhabitant of any State or Territory to the deprivation of any right secured or protected by this act, or to different punishment," shall be proceeded against under this bill. Now, there is a State law which says to the black man, "You shall not marry a white woman," and says to the white man, "You may." There is therefore in Maryland one law in relation to this question for the white man, and another law for the black man. The black man marries a white woman and we try to enforce our laws against him. We say to him, "You have done an illegal act, you have offended against the legislation of Maryland by marrying a white woman." He says, "I have done no such thing; I would have done it but for the legislation of Congress; I would have been liable to trial and conviction but for the legislation of Congress; but I set up the legislation of Congress; you may tell me you are prosecuting me under a law of the State of Maryland which makes it a crime in me, but Congress says that that State legislation shall be of no avail; the law of Maryland in reference to the question is at an end." It means that if it means anything. If the honorable member does not mean that he can change the language. I do not understand my friend from Maine or the honorable member from Illinois himself as denying that, looking to the provisions in the first section, supposing there was no law in Maryland on the subject—and I single out Maryland merely for the purpose of illustration—the contract of marriage would be embraced. White and black are considered together, put in a mass, and the one is entitled to enter into every contract that the other is entitled to enter into. Of course, therefore, the black man is entitled to enter into the contract of marriage with a white woman; but the law of Maryland prevents it; the law of Maryland punishes him for attempting it; and when the man is tried for having violated the law of Maryland, the court will say, "How is the prosecution to be supported under any law of Maryland—that law which is inconsistent with the provisions of the first section of this law of Congress, and the second section of which provides, virtually, that he who prevents a black man from marrying a white woman under any law of Maryland is to be subject to the penalties imposed by it?" That is the way I understand it. I do not think I can be wrong.

But whether I am wrong or not, upon a careful and correct interpretation of the provisions of these two sections, I suppose all the Senate will admit that the error is not so gross a one that the courts may not fall into it. Then what is the result? The whole of this legislation to be found in almost every State in the Union where slavery has existed, and to be found, I believe, in several of the other States, is done away with. You do not mean to do that. I am sure the Senate is not prepared to go to that extent; and I submit to the honorable chairman, without proclaiming myself to be right beyond all possible question of doubt, which would be in bad taste, and certainly very far from what I am disposed to do when I find that a different opinion is entertained by two gentlemen whose opinions I hold in so much respect—I submit to the honorable chairman of the Judiciary Committee whether he had not better make it so plain that the difficulty which I suggest in the execution of the law will be obviated.

But to come back to the amendment that is now before the Senate; I do not know what will be the effect of the amendment upon the Indians. The honorable member from Kansas [Mr. Lane] supposes he avoids the difficulty which he thinks would have existed under the original amendment by inserting the words, "or tribal authority." First, what would be the meaning of the amendment without those words? I understood the honorable chairman of the committee to say that these Indians are not citizens of the United States, and never have been. That is a mistake, as I think. The Indian tribes upon that portion of the American continent that belonged to Great Britain were always subject to the dominion of England. England could have done what she thought proper to do with them, but all she did in the execution of that, her sovereign right, was to prohibit them from entering into any contracts in relation to their lands with any other nation than England or the dependencies of England. When we obtained our independence, the whole authority that England had over the tribes became vested in the United States; and since then the uniform view that has been taken of the relation in which these Indians stand to the United States is, that they are but the wards of the United States. They have no sovereign power whatever; they are not a nation in the general acceptation of that term; they cannot sell their lands without the authority of the United States; they are not at liberty to sell their lands to anybody but to citizens of the United States, and under such regulations as the United States may impose.

If the honorable member will refresh his memory by consulting the case of Worcester *vs.* The State of Georgia, reported in 6 Peters, I think, he will find that Mr. Chief Justice Marshall, who gave the opinion of the court, deciding that the legislation of Georgia or the acts of Georgia were unconstitutional, admits that the Government of the United States could do with the Indians, as far as the question of power was concerned, just what it thought proper; that the absolute dominion was in the United States; the possessory title, with a *quasi* dominion, was with the Indians, but that *quasi* dominion was only that they could sell their lands and were not subject to be taxed by the United States, but only because the United States themselves had agreed that they should have those rights; but it was not pretended in that case that they were not citizens of the United States. The result, therefore, would be that an Indian child, born within the territorial limits of these tribes, would be a citizen of the United States, because the territory is part of the United States. Nobody ever doubted that the whole of the Indians who are subject to our control are now located upon territory belonging to the United States, and the result would necessarily follow, so far as citizenship depends upon birth, that, if you make it depend upon birth, the child who is born within the territorial limits of the United States, whether that portion be or be not within the temporary or partial control of the Indians, would be a citizen of the United States. Would the suggestion made by my friend from Kansas obviate it? The language of the amendment as proposed is, "all persons born in the United States." That would certainly include the Indians if I am right in saying the Indian country is part of the United States.

MR. TRUMBULL. "And not subject to any foreign Power."

MR. JOHNSON. I have not come to that. You and the Senator from Maine are always too fast for me. "Born in the United States"—I suppose that it will be admitted that that will include them—"and not subject to any foreign Power." The amendment suggested by the Senator from Kansas is to add the words, "or tribal authority."

JAMES LANE [R., KAN.]. Does not that restrict it?

MR. JOHNSON. It does to a certain extent, but does it go as far as you want it to go?

CHARLES SUMNER [R., MASS.]. Allow me to ask the Senator whether we do not always deal with the Indians through the treaty-making power?

MR. JOHNSON. We have done so, but not necessarily.

MR. SUMNER. Is it not the habit?

MR. JOHNSON. Certainly it is; but I am dealing with it now as a question of power. We have dealt with them as a treaty-making power, but it is not because there ever was a doubt that Congress could deal with them by legislation; and, in point of fact, although we have dealt with them as a treaty-making power, we have done so by making them make the treaty. It is no treaty-making power in the ordinary acceptation of the term; that is to say, the parties are not equal.

MR. SUMNER. With the Senator's permission, I will remind him that we act upon our treaties with the Indians in this Chamber with precisely the same forms that we do upon our treaties with the European Powers, and they must be ratified by a vote of two thirds of this body.

MR. JOHNSON. I understand that; but what I mean to say is, and I do not think the honorable member will contradict me, that there is nothing in the Constitution of the United States defining the treaty-making power, or in any other branch of it, which says that Congress cannot legislate in regard to them. That is what I mean to say. Now to what period does the phrase, "not subject to any foreign Power or tribal authority" relate? Does it mean at the time of the birth, or the time the controversy arises? My friend from Illinois seems to think, and perhaps he is right, that it means the time of the birth; but it admits of a different interpretation. "All persons born in the United States and not subject to any foreign Power or tribal authority shall be citizens of the United States"—when?

MR. TRUMBULL. When born.

MR. JOHNSON. I know that that is your interpretation.

MR. LANE. That is not the way I want it.

MR. JOHNSON. I know it is not; that is the reason that I suggest it. My friend from Kansas has a very clear perception upon all matters, particularly those relating to the Indians. [Laughter.]

MR. LANE. In answer to the suggestion of the Senator from Maryland, I will state the reason why I do not want it so to apply. A large portion of our Indians have recently taken allotments of land, and our supreme court have decided, as I understand—I have not seen the decision—that the act of accepting the allotments makes them citizens so far as to subject the allotments to taxation. Now, what I desire of the Senate is that the Indians who have taken the allotments and thereby separated themselves from the tribal authority may become citizens of the United States. My colleague and myself have consulted on the subject, and we think it wise legislation that they may have the privilege of holding these allotments and selling them. That is the object.

MR. JOHNSON. The honorable member does not suppose that I am opposed to that. I admit with him that those Indians who have separated themselves from their tribes, and have acquired lands in the State of Kansas, or anywhere else, ought to be citizens. The only question is whether you have done it by this provision. I throw it out as a suggestion that may or may not have weight, just as the Senate may think it entitled to weight or not. If my friend, the chairman of the committee, is right in his construction of the clause, that it means the time of the birth, then the honorable member from Kansas will not have effected his purpose. I think I can satisfy the Senator that he is quite short of his designed mark, provided the honorable chairman is right—and perhaps he is, I rather think he is—in his interpretation of his amendment, that it means to refer to the date of the birth as the time when the foreign allegiance exists.

The honorable member from Kansas makes the allegiance or tribal authority take the same date. Then the Indians whom you want to make citizens and who have recently come to Kansas, and, who have purchased land, but who were born under tribal authority, will not become citizens unless it be by treaty; and that cannot be true so far as citizenship of the United States is concerned, where they become citizens by buying lands in Kansas. If they are aliens before they buy the land, and nothing is done by them to obtain the character of citizens except buying the land, then they do not become citizens; that is very clear. They can only become citizens by a bill like this, which will provide in words for such cases as exist in Kansas; and I think they ought to be provided for.

EDGAR COWAN [R., PA.]. Will it not have to be a uniform law under the Constitution?

MR. JOHNSON. It would be uniform of course with reference to those buying lands in any State and separating themselves from their tribes.

MR. COWAN. But not as to all people—Irishmen, Germans, Indians, and everybody.

MR. JOHNSON. That is uniformity with a vengeance; but that is not the uniformity which the Constitution renders necessary, if I understand it. One or two of my friends on this side of the Chamber who have spoken seem to suppose that this citizenship cannot be obtained through the legislation of Congress. I entertain a different opinion. The clause in the Constitution to which reference has been made—one of the provisions of the eighth section of the first article—gives to Congress the right to establish uniform laws of naturalization; and the view taken of the effect of that clause, considered in connection with the whole Constitution, is that they cannot become citizens in any other way. That is not true. How did the residents of Louisiana at the time of the cession in 1803, and the residents of Florida at the time of the cession of 1819, became citizens of the United States? It was by treaty. The treaties in those cases provided that all the inhabitants of the ceded territory should be entitled in the United States to the same privileges, immunities, and rights that belonged to the citizens of the United States. No naturalization was ever supposed to be necessary in those cases, and none of those inhabitants have since applied for naturalization; and they have been in the courts time after time and recognized as citizens.

MR. COWAN. I should like to ask the honorable Senator whether that was not done by treaty; whether it can be done in any other way except according to some uniform rule which is to operate equally upon all people?

MR. JOHNSON. That rule in relation to Louisiana could not be considered uniform, because it did not provide in relation to all Territories afterward to be acquired; it only covered that case. That, however, is a question which I am not now discussing. I understood the argument to be that the only way in which a person born abroad could become a citizen of the United States was through the naturalization power, so to speak; that Congress must exercise by legislation the power conferred upon that body of establishing a uniform rule of naturalization. Now, in the case which I have stated, as I suppose my friend will admit, it was done not by that means, but by the treaty-making power.

MR. TRUMBULL. Does the Senator mean to say that we acquired Texas by treaty? Did we acquire Texas by treaty, and make its citizens citizens of the United States by treaty?

MR. JOHNSON. I did not say so. I said Louisiana and Florida, not Texas.

MR. TRUMBULL. I thought the Senator included Texas.

MR. JOHNSON. No sir, I did not refer to Texas. It was proposed at one time to acquire Texas by treaty, but it was subsequently annexed by joint resolution of the two Houses. That establishes the precedent which I was about to suppose might be established under the Constitution. The citizens of Texas, who of course were aliens, it has never been doubted became citizens of the United States by the annexation of Texas; and that was not done by treaty, it was done by legislation. If the power was in Congress by legislation to make citizens of all the inhabitants of the State of Texas, why is it not in the power of Congress to make citizens by legislation of all who are inhabitants of the United States and who are not citizens? That is what this bill does, or what it proposes to do. There are within the United States millions of people who are not citizens, according to the view of the Supreme Court of the United States. Ought they to be citizens? I think they ought. I think it is an anomaly that says there shall not be the rights of citizenship to any of the inhabitants of any State of the United States.

While they were slaves it was a very different question; but now, when slavery is terminated, and by terminating it you have got rid of the only obstacle in the way of citizenship, two questions arise: First, whether that fact itself does not make them citizens? Before they were not citizens, because of slavery, and only because of slavery. Slavery abolished, why are they not just as much citizens as they would have been if slavery had never existed? My opinion is that they become citizens, and I hold that opinion so strongly that I should consider it unnecessary to legislate on the subject at all as far as that class is concerned, but for the ruling of the Supreme Court to which I have adverted. They held that the Constitution of the United States in no part of it in which the word citizen was used was intended to embrace the African; or to state it still more strongly, but not more strongly than the court stated it, they held that, looking to the contemporaneous history and to the contemporaneous legislation of the several States at the time the Constitution was adopted, the use of the word "citizen" as employed in that Constitution was to exclude the African.

MR. COWAN. And every other race but the white.

MR. JOHNSON. Every race but the white—to exclude the African. That decision stands unreversed. Nobody can say that it will be reversed. It is the decision of the highest court to which we are bound to submit with all proper deference, not binding upon us perhaps as legislating in very many particulars; but still, after such a decision has been pronounced, it is our duty, as I think, to avoid its results if we think that decision in the present state of the country would produce mischievous results, by providing that these people, notwithstanding their African descent, shall be citizens of the United States now that they are free.

As to the propriety of passing the bill itself, that is another question. I do not propose now, nor perhaps at any time, to trouble the Senate with any remarks upon the question of the propriety of the passage of the bill. According to my views, which I may or may not explain, if there shall be time at some future period in the session, I think we have not the power to pass this bill; but conceding that the power exists, what I desire, as I hope I shall ever desire, is that the Senators who think they have the power to pass the bill should make it as acceptable and as free from doubt as their wisdom will allow them to do. . . .

MR. SAULSBURY. I want to test that very fact. I may be mistaken, but for twenty years I have had to use the law as an instrument, as the workman uses his instruments, to make a living, and I do hold that under the words "civil rights" the power to vote is given, because it is a civil right. The honorable chairman of the Judiciary Committee who has this bill under charge says he does not mean to confer that right. His meaning cannot control the operation or the effect of this law, if the bill shall become a law. I believe that if this bill is enacted into a law your judges in most of the States will determine that under these words the power of voting is given. The honorable Senator cited an authority the other day, from Maryland I think it was, in which it was decided that that right was conferred after domicile had been acquired according to the laws of the State. Sir, I wish to exclude that very idea; and if you do not mean to confer that power I want you to say so. However highly I esteem the learning of the honorable chairman of the Judiciary Committee, I am not willing to trust to his declaration that that power is not to be conferred, and I want this Congress to say that in conferring these civil rights they do not mean to confer the right to vote.

Talk to me, sir, about the words "civil rights" not including the right to vote! What is a civil right? It is a right that pertains to me as a citizen. And how do I get the right to vote? I get it by virtue of citizenship, and I get it by virtue of nothing else. When this act is passed into a law, and I find a Republican judge in any of the States of this country deciding that under it a negro has the right to vote, I am not going to quarrel with the opinion of that judge, because I believe he is deciding the law correctly. Sir, if you do not intend to confer that right, say so. If you do not mean to invade the States of this Union, and take from them the right to prescribe the qualifications of voters, say so. That is all I ask. Do not leave it in doubt.

As I said the other day, I know but two foundations of right that any man has: one is a right founded in nature; the other is a right founded in law. Under the law of nature I have got no right to vote. Under the law regulating society and government I have a right to vote. I get it simply on the ground of my citizenship; and your bill confers that right.

It will not do for the honorable chairman of the Judiciary Committee to say that by specifying in other lines of the first section the right to sue and be sued, and to give evidence, to lease and to hold property, he limits these rights. He does no such thing. He may think that that is the intention; but when you come to look at the powers conferred by this section, and when you consider the closing words of the section, giving to everybody, without distinction of race or color, the same rights to protection of property and person and liberty, when these rights are given to the negro as freely as to the white man, I say, as a lawyer, that you confer the right of suffrage, because, under our republican form and system of government, and according to the genius of our republican institutions, one of the strongest guarantees of personal rights, of the rights of person and property, is the right of the ballot.

Now, gentlemen, let us deal fairly, squarely, and honestly with each other. If you do not mean to confer this power, say so. I only ask you to say, by my amendment, that you do not mean by this bill to confer that power. If you vote down my proposition, what will be the interpretation put upon your law? If it shall go before any judicial tribunal of this country, and they find that you voted down this amendment, what is the interpretation they will put upon it? That you meant to confer the power, simply because you refused to say that you did not.

But, sir, I will not argue the question. It is a foregone conclusion that this bill is to pass, and I shall not detain the Senate. . . .

House of Representatives-39th Congress, 1st Session
March 1-13, 1866

JAMES WILSON [R., IOWA]. This bill has been considered by the Committee on the Judiciary, and I have been instructed by that committee to offer several amendments to it. The first amendment is in the seventh line of the first section, to strike out the words "inhabitants of" and insert the words "citizens of the United States in;" so that that portion will read:

There shall be no discrimination in civil rights or immunities among the citizens of the United States in any State or Territory, &c.

This amendment is intended to confine the operation of this bill to citizens of the United States, instead of extending it to the inhabitants of the several States, as there seems to be some doubt concerning the power of Congress to extend this protection to such inhabitants as are not citizens. . . .

Mr. Speaker, the importance of this bill, the magnitude of the questions involved in it, the objects sought to be reached and secured by it, will insure for it the most deliberate consideration of this House. Few measures of graver import have ever commanded the attention of Congress. It is a very positive bill, and I expect it to meet with most positive opposition, but I believe it will survive this and triumph.

Some of the questions presented by this bill are not entirely free from difficulties. Precedents, both judicial and legislative, are found in sharp conflict concerning them. The line which divides these precedents is generally found to be the same which separates the early from the later days of the Republic. The further the Government drifted from the old moorings of equality and human rights, the more numerous became judicial and legislative utterances in conflict with some of the leading features of this bill.

The Committee on the Judiciary bestowed on this subject a degree of careful examination which we believe will enable us to maintain successfully our conclusions both as to the propriety and constitutionality of this measure.

The first section of the bill contains the following declaration concerning citizenship:

That all persons born in the United States and not subject to any foreign Power, excluding Indians not taxed, are hereby declared to be citizens of the United States without distinction of color.

This provision, I maintain, is merely declaratory of what the law now is. This, I presume, would not be disputed if the language were qualified by the presence of the word "white." In the absence of this word, I am sure that my proposition will be disputed by every member of this House who believes that this Government is exclusively a "white man's Government." . . .

It is in vain we look into the Constitution of the United States for a definition of the term "citizen." It speaks of citizens, but in no express terms defines what it means by it. We must depend on the general law relating to subjects and citizens recognized by all nations for a definition, and that must lead us to the conclusion that every person born in the United States is a natural-born citizen of such States, except it may be that children born on our soil to temporary sojourners or representatives of foreign Governments, are native-born citizens of the United States. Thus it is expressed by a writer on the Constitution of the United States:

Every person born within the United States, its Territories, or districts, whether the parents are citizens or aliens, is a natural-born citizen in the sense of the Constitution, and entitled to all the rights and privileges appertaining to that capacity. [*Rawle on the Constitution* 80]

And this writer continues, as if he intended a refutation of the position assumed by some persons at this time, that a negro is neither a citizen nor an alien, but a mere person with no definable national character, and adds:

It is an error to suppose, as some have done, that a child is born a citizen of no country, and subject of no Government, and that he so continues till the age of discretion, when he is at liberty to put himself under what Government he pleases. [*Ibid* 80, 81]

No nation, I believe, ever did recognize this absurd doctrine; and the only force it ever had in this country, was that given it by the Democratic party which used the negro as a football for partisan games. The growing importance of the colored race in the United States, now that the entire race is free, will soon cause even the Democratic party to abandon the indefensible position it occupies on this question. That we have six million persons in this Government subject to its laws, and liable to perform all the duties and support all the obligations of citizens, and yet who are neither citizens nor aliens, is an absurdity which cannot surive long in the light of these days of progressive civilization. . . .

But, sir, suppose I should admit for the sake of an argument that negroes are not citizens, would that be an objection to the power of Congress to enact the provision of this bill to which I have called the attention of the House? If they are not citizens may we not naturalize them? If this can be done, then in either view of the case the provision of the bill which I am now discussing is proper, and is not obnoxious to the objection that we do not possess the power to pass it.

The Constitution, in article one, section eight, provides that Congress shall have power "to establish a uniform rule of naturalization." This does not mean that the power of Congress exhausts itself by being once used, nor that there can be but one rule, nor that the rule established must provide that the naturalization shall be by action upon single or individual cases, nor yet that only foreigners can be thus made citizens. The practice of the Government is against all these positions. . . .

Mr. Speaker, these authorities are sufficient upon this point, and I will leave the question of citizenship as presented in the first part of this section, and call the attention of the House to the next proposition of the section as proposed to be amended by the committee. It is in these words:

There shall be no discrimination in civil rights or immunities among citizens of the United States in any State or Territory of the United States on account of race, color, or previous condition of slavery; and such citizens of every race and color, without regard to any previous condition of slavery or involuntary servitude, except as a punishment for crime whereof the party shall have been duly convicted, shall have the same right to make and enforce contracts, to sue, be parties and give evidence, to inherit, purchase, lease, sell, hold, and convey real and personal property, and to full and equal benefit of all laws and proceedings for the security of person and property as is enjoyed by white citizens, and shall be subject to like punishment, pains, and penalties, and to none other, any law, statute, ordinance, regulation, or custom, to the contrary notwithstanding.

This part of the bill will probably excite more opposition and elicit more discussion than any other; and yet to my mind it seems perfectly defensible. It provides for the equality of citizens of the United States in the enjoyment of "civil rights and immunities." What do these terms mean? Do they mean that in all things civil, social, political, all citizens, without distinction of race or color, shall be equal? By no means can they be so construed. Do they mean that all citizens shall vote in the several States? No; for suffrage is a political right which has been left under the control of the several States, subject to the action of Congress only when it becomes necessary to enforce the guarantee of a republican form of government. Nor do they mean that all citizens shall sit on the juries, or that their children shall attend the same schools. These are not civil rights or immunities. Well, what is the meaning? What are civil rights? I understand civil rights to be simply the absolute rights of individuals, such as—

The right of personal security, the right of personal liberty, and the right to acquire and enjoy property." "Right itself, in civil society, is that which any man is entitled to have, or to do, or to require from others, within the limits of prescribed law." [1 Kent's Commentaries 199]

To use the language of Attorney General Bates, in the opinion already cited, "The word rights is generic, common, embracing whatever may be lawfully claimed." The definition given to the term "civil rights" in Bouvier's Law Dictionary is very concise, and is supported by the best authority. It is this:

> Civil rights are those which have no relation to the establishment, support, or management of government.

From this it is easy to gather an understanding that civil rights are the natural rights of man; and these are the rights which this bill proposes to protect every citizen in the enjoyment of throughout the entire dominion of the Republic.

But what of the term "immunities?" What is an immunity? Simply "freedom or exemption from obligation;" an immunity is "a right of exemption only," as "an exemption from serving in an office, or performing duties which the law generally requires other citizens to perform." This is all that is intended by the word "immunities" as used in this bill. It merely secures to citizens of the United States equality in the exemptions of the law. A colored citizen shall not, because he is colored, be subjected to obligations, duties, pains, and penalties from which other citizens are exempted. Whatever exemptions there may be shall apply to all citizens alike. One race shall not be more favored in this respect than another. One class shall not be required to support alone the burdens which should rest on all classes alike. This is the spirit and scope of the bill, and it goes not one step beyond.

Mr. Speaker, I think I may safely affirm that this bill, so far as it declares the equality of all citizens in the enjoyment of civil rights and immunities, merely affirms existing law. We are following the Constitution. We are reducing to statute form the spirit of the Constitution. We are establishing no new right, declaring no new principle. It is not the object of this bill to establish new rights, but to protect and enforce those which already belong to every citizen. I am aware, sir, that this doctrine is denied in many of the States; but this only proves the necessity for the enactment of the remedial and protective features of this bill. If the States would all observe the rights of our citizens, there would be no need of this bill. . . .

MARTIN THAYER [R., PA.]. It would have afforded me, Mr. Speaker, much more satisfaction if my public duties had allowed me time to present what I have to say to the House in reference to this bill in a somewhat more orderly and methodical manner than I shall be able to do. I cannot, however, consistently with what I conceive to be the duty which I owe to the loyal constituency which I have the honor to represent upon this floor, allow the opportunity which now presents itself to pass without expressing in such manner as I may be able the reasons which govern me in giving, as I do, my cordial assent to the principles and the details of this great measure.

Sir, this bill is the just sequel to, and the proper completion of, that great measure of national redress which opened the dungeon doors of four million human beings. Without this, in my judgment, that great act of justice will be paralyzed and made useless. With this it will have practical effect, life, vigor, and enforcement. It has been the fashion of gentlemen holding a certain set of opinions in this House to characterize that great measure to which I have referred as a revolutionary measure.

Sir, it was a revolutionary measure. It was one of the greatest, one of the most humane, one of the most beneficial revolutions which ever characterized the history of a free State; but it was a revolution which, though initiated by the conflict of arms and rendered necessary as a measure of war against the public enemy, was accomplished within and under the provisions of the Constitution of the United States. It was a revolution for the relief of human nature, a revolution which gave life, liberty, and hope to millions whose condition until then appeared to be one of hopeless despair. It was a revolution of which no freeman need be ashamed, of which every man who assisted in it will, I am sure, in the future be proud, and which will illumine with a great glory the history of this country.

The bill which now engages the attention of the House has for its object to carry out and guaranty the reality of that great measure. It is to give to it practical effect and force. It is to prevent that great measure from remaining a dead letter upon the constitutional page of this country. It is to carry to its legitimate and just result the great humane revolution to which I have referred. The events of the last four years, the convulsions through which this country has passed, the fortunes of war, the progress of ideas, the triumph of republican liberty, have changed this large class of people who dwell within the confines of the United States from a condition of slavery to that of freedom. The practical question now to be decided is whether they shall be in fact freemen. It is whether they shall have the benefit of this great charter of liberty given to them by the American people.

Sir, if it is competent for the new-formed Legislatures of the rebel States to enact laws which oppress this large class of people who are dependent for protection upon the United States Government, to retain them still in a state of real servitude; if it is practicable for these Legislatures to pass laws and enforce laws which reduce this class of people to the condition of bondmen; laws which prevent the enjoyment of the fundamental rights of citizenship; laws which declare, for example, that they shall not have the privilege of purchasing a home for themselves and their families; laws which impair their ability to make contracts for labor in such manner as virtually to deprive them of the power of making such contracts, and which then declare them vagrants because they have no homes and because they have no employment; I say, if it is competent for these Legislatures to pass and enforce such laws, then I demand to know, of what practical value is the amendment abolishing slavery in the United States? Tell me when you boast of the glorious character of that addition to your Constitution what benefit you have conferred upon the men who are liberated from slavery by it, if these things are to be done under the flag of the United States and in the face of the authority of the Federal Constitution.

For one, sir, I thought when I voted for the amendment to abolish slavery that I was aiding to give real freedom to the men who had so long been groaning in bondage. I did not suppose that I was offering them a mere paper guarantee. And when I voted for the second section of the amendment, I felt in my own mind certain that I had placed in the Constitution and given to Congress ability to protect and guaranty the rights which the first section gave them.

The simple principle of the bill under consideration and its whole essence is contained in its first section. The rest is all matter of detail. The whole life and substance of the bill is in its first section. That section enacts that—

All persons born in the United States and not subject to any foreign Power, excluding Indians not taxed, are hereby declared to be citizens of the United States, without distinction of color, and there shall be no discrimination in civil rights or immunities among the inhabitants of any State or Territory of the United States on account of race, color, or previous condition of slavery.

Now, sir, what is there in that? Let me appeal to the common sense and judgement of every member of this House when I put the question. What is there in that to challenge the denunciation which the House listened to yesterday from the gentleman from New Jersey, [Mr. Rogers?] Is any man to be injured by it? Are any man's rights to be invaded or taken away by it? Who will pretend that such is the case? It is an enactment simply declaring that all men born upon the soil of the United States shall enjoy the funda-mental rights of citizenship. What rights are these? Why, sir, in order to avoid any misapprehension they are stated in the bill. The same section goes on to define with greater particularity the civil rights and immunities which are to be protected by the bill. They are—

The right to make and enforce contracts, to sue, be parties and give evidence, to inherit, purchase, lease, sell, hold, and convey real and personal property, and to full and equal benefit of all laws and proceedings for the security of person and property, and to be subject to like punishment, pains, and penalties, and to none other.

Now, sir, I will pay so high a compliment to the intelligence of the gentleman who addressed us yesterday, as to say that I do not think he can believe that this bill extends or alters, or can be construed to extend or alter, the laws regulating suffrage in any of the States. Sir, no lawyer who is acquainted with the use of terms and the rules which regulate the construc-tion of laws will, I think, seriously contend that the language of this bill can by any possibility, or by any forced construction, produce any such result.

In the first place, the words themselves are "civil rights and immunities," not political privileges; and nobody can successfully contend that a bill guarantying simply civil rights and immunities is a bill under which you could extend the right of suffrage, which is a political privilege and not a civil right.

Then, again, the matter is put beyond all doubt by the subsequent particu-lar definition of the general language which has been just used; and when those civil rights which are first referred to in general terms in the bill are subsequently enumerated, that enumeration precludes any possibility that the general words which have been used can be extended beyond the particulars which have been enumerated.

It is well for gentlemen at the outset to disabuse themselves of any such idea as that which has been suggested in regard to the point which I am now considering. I tell gentlemen that no man upon this floor can successfully defend himself before the country for voting against this bill upon the ground that it impairs the rights of States in determining the qualifications of electors. It has no such effect, and I tell those gentlemen that when they vote against this bill they will have to answer to their constituents for voting, not to protect the rights of States in the regulation of suffrage, but for voting against the protection of the fundamental rights of citizenship and nothing else. If they can stand at home upon any such platform as that, they may safely vote against this bill, but there is nothing else in the bill but this.

Now, sir, why should not this be done? Why should not these fundamental rights and immunities which are common to the humblest citizen of every free State, to be extended to these citizens? Why should they be deprived of the right to make and enforce contracts, of the right to sue, of the right to be parties and give evidence in courts of justice, of the right to inherit, purchase, lease, hold, and convey real and personal property? And why should they not have full and equal benefit of all laws and proceedings for the security of person and property? . . .

MICHAEL KERR [DEM., IND.]. . . . The gentleman from Pennsylvania [Mr. Thayer] has fairly won the distinction, in this debate, of having discovered a new fountain of congressional power. He informs us in effect that the first eleven amendments to the Constitution are grants of power to Congress; that they contain guarantees which it is the right and duty of Congress to secure and enforce in the States. Hitherto those amendments have been supposed, by lawyers, statesmen, and courts, to contain only *limitations* on the power of Congress. The history of the country teaches us that the people of the States feared that, by such vicious constructions as we now daily hear, Congress might usurp powers not granted to it, and thus peril the rights of the States and of their citizens; and *therefore* the States demanded these amendments as safeguards against encroachments on the part of the General Government. In almost every convention by which the Constitution was adopted, amendments to guard against the abuse of power by the General Government were recommended. They were not intended to be, and they are not, limitations on the powers of the States. They are bulwarks of freedom, erected by the people between the States and the Federal Government, and this bill is an attempt to prostrate them. What right has Congress to invade a State, and dictate to it *how* it shall protect its citizens in their right not to be deprived of life, liberty, or property without due process of law? Or what right has it to assume that a State will not do its duty to its citizens in these particulars, and then, upon such assumption, to usurp the functions of the

State government? This bill attempts to do this thing. It applies to every State in this Union. Are the States supposed to have lost all interest in the welfare and protection of their own citizens? . . .

This bill is liable to the very great objection that its provisions are uncertain as to their meaning. Its intentions are expressed in terms which are alike undefined and indefinable. For example, what does the word *citizen* mean in the first section? Etymologically, it is said to mean a person who enjoys the freedom and privileges of a city. In American law, one writer says it means a person, native or naturalized, who has the privilege of voting for public officers and of being elected to office. Another says it means any person, native-born or naturalized, of either sex, who is entitled to full protection in the exercise and enjoyment of the so-called private rights, but does not define what those rights are. This bill says:

> There shall be no discrimination in civil rights or immunities among citizens of the *United States* in any State or Territory, on account of race, color, or previous condition of slavery.

But it does not define the term "civil rights and immunities." What are such rights? One writer says civil rights are those which have no relation to the establishment, support, or management of the Government. Another says they are the rights of a citizen; rights due from one citizen to another, the privation of which is a *civil injury* for which redress may be sought by a *civil action.* Other authors define all these terms in different ways, and assign to them larger or narrower definitions according to their views. Who shall settle these questions? Who shall define these terms? Their definition here by gentlemen on this floor is one thing; their definition after this bill shall have become a law will be quite another thing. The anti-slavery amendment of the Constitution had one very simple object to accomplish when gentlemen on the other side of this House desired to secure its adoption; but now it is confidently appealed to as authority for this bill and almost every other radical and revolutionary measure advocated by the majority in this Congress. Those gentlemen often have strange visions of constitutional law, and it is not safe to judge from their opinions to-day what they will be to-morrow.

This bill forbids any discrimination in civil rights and immunities on account of *race* or *color.* Under the laws of Indiana no person except white male inhabitants can be allowed to engage in the business of retailing spirituous liquors. But a negro procures the requisite petition and applies to a county board for a license to retail liquors. It is refused. Now, this discrimination is based both upon color and race. And the county board, by refusing the license, violates the second section of this act, and thereby commit a misdemeanor, for which they may be fined each not exceeding $1,000, or imprisoned not exceeding one year, or both, in the discretion of the court.

But this punishment shall not be administered in the courts of Indiana, but must be in the Federal courts at the capital of the State, as prescribed in the third section of this bill. Or, the city of New Albany, in which I live, whose ordinances follow the State law, might refuse a license to a negro under the same circumstances, and the common council would thus become wrongdoers, subject to the same punishments. Now, it cannot be said that selling liquor according to law in Indiana is not a civil right. It certainly is; but if it is not, yet a license is a contract, and this bill says the negro shall have "the same right to make and enforce contracts" as the white man. It is as much a contract or civil right as would be a license to sell meat in their market-house or to run a dray in their streets or to carry on any other business.

Again, the constitution of Indiana has dedicated a munificent fund to the support of common schools for the education of the children of the State. But negro and mulatto children are by law excluded from those schools. Negroes and mulattoes are exempt by law from school tax. They are denied a civil right, on account of race and color, and are granted an immunity, (from school taxation,) but are taxed for all other purposes. Now, a negro or mulatto takes his child to the common schoolhouse and demands of the teacher that it be admitted to the school and taught as the white children are, which is refused. The teacher then becomes a wrong-doer and is liable to the same punishments, to be administered in the same way; because all the persons referred to would be acting under *color* of some law, statute, ordinance, regulation, or custom.

The constitution of Indiana, adopted in 1851, forbids any negro or mulatto to come into or settle in that State after the adoption of that constitution, and declares all contracts made with any negro or mulatto coming into the State contrary to the provisions of that constitution shall be void. This bill proposes to annul those constitutional provisions and all State laws passed to secure their execution. A negro comes into the State in defiance of them, and makes contracts, and the courts of Indiana, acting under *color* of those provisions and laws, refuse to enforce those contracts. There will thus arise, not only a conflict of authority, which may lead to most unhappy results, but the officers refusing to enforce such contracts would, under the provisions of this bill, at once become criminals, subject to the penalties already mentioned. Or if a State court or officer refused in any such proceeding to receive the testimony of any negro, where he was forbidden by the State law to receive it, he too would incur the penalties of this bill. It cannot be claimed that the persons to whom I have referred could not be punished under the provisions of this bill because they were acting as officers and their conduct was the result of errors of judgment only. That would be no valid defense—no defense at all—against the positive terms of this law. I hold that the only persons intended to be punished by this bill are persons acting under State authority in some sort of official capacity. By its very terms, it only applies to persons who shall do these prohibited acts "under *color* of any law, statute, ordinance, regulation, or *custom.*" Who can act under such *color* but officers of some kind?

I might go on and in this manner illustrate the practical working of this extraordinary measure. But I have said enough to indicate the inherent viciousness of the bill. It takes a long and fearful step toward the complete obliteration of State authority and the reserved and original rights of the States. It puts the local policy and officers, executive, ministerial, and judicial, of the States, at the mercy of the petty Federal officers, who, under this bill, may be made to swarm over the whole country, exercising both ministerial and judicial functions, by arresting, examining, and imprisoning persons charged or suspected of having done any of the forbidden things under *color* of local laws or policy. Then the things attempted to be prohibited are in themselves so extraordinary and anomalous, so unlike anything ever attempted before by the Federal Government, that the authors of this bill feared, very properly too, that the system of laws heretofore administered in the Federal courts might fail to supply any precedent to guide the courts in the enforcement of the strange provisions of this bill, and not to be thwarted by this difficulty, they confer upon the courts the power of judicial legislation, the power to make such other laws as they may think necessary. . . .

Our Federal courts are thus to be made *itinerant,* and speedy justice administered at each offender's own door, and if he is found guilty he may perhaps enjoy the singular felicity of being executed at home. But courts do not consist of judges alone. It will be the duty of the judges, district attorneys, marshals, clerks, grand and petit juries, and the bailiffs of the courts, with the records, to accompany each other in these remarkable visitations and perambulations. It seems to me the framer of this section of the bill has left at least one defect in it. He should have provided for an executioner, who should be of the favored race and color, and should march in the forefront of the procession with a guillotine. . . .

JOHN BINGHAM [R., OHIO]. . . . Having said this much, Mr. Speaker, I proceed to present to the consideration of the House my objections to the bill. And, first, I beg gentlemen to consider that I do not oppose any legislation which is authorized by the Constitution of my country to enforce in its letter and its spirit the bill of rights as embodied in that Constitution. I know that the enforcement of the bill of rights is the want of the Republic. I know if it had been enforced in good faith in every State of the Union the calamities and conflicts and crimes and sacrifices of the past five years would have been impossible.

But I feel that I am justified in saying, in view of the text of the Constitution of my country, in view of all its past interpretations, in view of the manifest and declared intent of the men who framed it, the enforcement of the bill of rights, touching the life, liberty, and property of every citizen of the Republic within every organized State of the Union, is of the reserved powers of the States, to be enforced by State tribunals and by State officials acting under the solemn obligations of an oath imposed upon them by the Constitution of the United States. Who can doubt this conclusion who considers the words of the Constitution: "the powers not delegated to the United States by the Constitution, nor prohibited by it to the States, are reserved to the States respectively, or to the people?" The Constitution does not delegate to the United States the power to punish offenses against the life, liberty, or property of the citizen in the States, nor does it prohibit that power to the States, but leaves it as the reserved power of the States, to be by them exercised. The prohibitions of power by the Constitution to the States are express prohibitions, as that no State shall enter into any treaty, &c., or emit bills of credit, or pass any bill of attainder, &c. The Constitution does not prohibit States from the enactment of laws for the general government of the people within their respective limits.

Mr. Speaker, I would further remark in this connection, I honor the mover of this bill for the purpose he seeks to attain, which is to compel the exercise in good faith by the States of this reserved power. I cast no reflection upon the honorable committee of this House, in seeking to remedy, if possible, the great wrongs that have hitherto been inflicted upon citizens of the United States, I may say in almost every State of the Union, by State authority, and inflicted, too, in the past, without redress. I am with him in an earnest desire to have the bill of rights in your Constitution enforced everywhere. But I ask that it be enforced in accordance with the Constitution of my country.

Has the Congress of the United States the power to pass and enforce the bill as it comes to us from the committee? Has the Congress of the United States the power to declare, as this bill does declare, in the words which I propose to strike out, that there shall be no discrimination of civil rights among citizens of the United States in any State of the United States, on account of race, color, or previous condition of slavery?

I find no fault with the introductory clause, which is simply declaratory of what is written in the Constitution, that every human being born within the jurisdiction of the United States of parents not owing allegiance to any foreign sovereignty is, in the language of your Constitution itself, a natural-born citizen; but, sir, I may be allowed to say further, that I deny that the Congress of the United States ever had the power or color of power to say that any man born within the jurisdiction of the United States, not owing a foreign allegiance, is not and shall not be a citizen of the United States. Citizenship is his birthright, and neither the Congress nor the States can justly or lawfully take it from him. But while this is admitted, can you declare by congressional enactment as to citizens of the United States within the States that there shall be no discrimination among them of civil rights?

What are civil rights? I know the learning and ability of the honorable chairman of the Judiciary Committee, [Mr. Wilson.] It was my good fortune to be associated with him two years on that important and responsible committee, and I take pleasure in bearing witness to-day to the integrity, fidelity, and ability with which he discharged all his duties. I respectfully submit to that gentleman, that by all authority the term "civil rights" as used in this bill does include and embrace every right that pertains to the citizen as such.

Why, sir, the very origin of the term "civil" ought to satisfy gentlemen on this point, that it has relation to the rights and all the rights of the citizen. I submit that the term civil rights includes every right that pertains to the citizen under the Constitution, laws, and Government of this country. The term "citizen" has had a definite meaning among publicists ever since the days of Aristotle. He interpreted and rendered that term to signify a person who was a partner in the government of the country. Under the Constitution of the United States every natural-born citizen of the Republic is, in some sense, a partner in the Government, although he may take no active part in it. A distinction is taken, I know very well, in modern times, between civil and political rights. I submit with all respect that the term "political rights" is only a limitation of the term "civil rights," and by general acceptation signifies that class of civil rights which are more directly exercised by the citizen in connection with the government of his country. If this be so, are not political rights all embraced in the term "civil rights," and must it not of necessity be so interpreted? Blackstone, whose Commentaries on the common law are so exact in definition, uses in that classic of the law the terms "civil liberty" and "political liberty" everywhere as synonymous. It never occurred to him that there was a colorable distinction between them.

If civil rights has this extent, what, then, is proposed by the provision of the first section? Simply to strike down by congressional enactment every State constitution which makes a discrimination on account of race or color in any of the civil rights of the citizen. I might say here, without the least fear of contradiction, that there is scarcely a State in this Union which does not, by its constitution or by its statute laws, make some discrimination on account of race or color between citizens of the United States in respect of civil rights.

I know there are some exceptions. I cannot stop to mention them within the thirty minutes of time allowed me or to make clearer what I have said. I say with some few exceptions every State in the Union does make some discrimination between citizens of the United States, either by its constitution or its statute laws, in respect of civil rights on account of race or color. I desire to call the attention of the House to the fact that the honorable gentleman who reported this bill in the Senate, and for whom I have the highest respect, had the candor to admit to me the other day that the franchise of office, according to all the authorities, is a civil right, and in my opinion by every fair interpretation of the Constitution it can rightfully be conferred upon no man in any State save upon a citizen of the United States.

By the constitution of my own State neither the right of the elective franchise nor the franchise of office can be conferred upon any citizen of the United States save upon a white citizen of the United States. What do you propose to do by this bill? You propose to make it a misdemeanor, punishable upon conviction by fine and imprisonment in the penitentiary, for the Governor of Ohio to obey the requirements of the constitution of the State, which requires that none shall be elected, and therefore none commissioned, to office in that State save white citizens of the United States.

I understand very well, from private conversation that I have had with my learned friend, the chairman of the Judiciary Committee, that he does not look on this clause in the first section as an obligatory requirement. I have no time to undertake to discuss that question, but I submit that it is as much obligatory as any other clause of the section. The clause is imperative. It is in the language of law. It provides that—

There shall be no discrimination in civil rights or immunities among citizens of the United States in any State or Territory of the United States on account of race, color, or previous condition of slavery.

That is as obligatory as any other portion of the section. If it is not obligatory, what objection has the gentleman to striking it out? If it is obligatory, it must be stricken out or the constitutions of the States are to be abolished by your act, or, what is the same thing, their enforcement by the State officers charged with that duty made a crime for which they are to be imprisoned. I deny the power of Congress to make an error of judgment in a State officer a crime to be punished by imprisonment. However honest, however just, however humane the purposes of the gentleman may be in presenting this penal provision of the bill, I deny the power of Congress to enact obedience to a State law which has been passed and is enforced in good faith into a crime. This is the further provision of the first section:

And such citizens of every race and color, without regard to any previous condition of slavery or involuntary servitude, except as a punishment for crime whereof the party shall have been duly convicted, shall have the same right to make and enforce contracts, to sue, be parties and give evidence, to inherit, purchase, lease, sell, hold, and convey real and personal property, and to full and equal benefit of all laws and proceedings for the security of person and property as is enjoyed by white citizens, and shall be subject to like punishment, pains, and penalties, and to none other, any law, statute, ordinance, regulation, or custom, to the contrary notwithstanding.

I say, with all my heart, that that should be the law of every State, by the voluntary act of every State. The law in every State should be just; it should be no respecter of persons. It is otherwise now, and it has been otherwise for many years in many of the States of the Union. I should remedy that not by an arbitrary assumption of power, but by amending the Constitution of the United States, expressly prohibiting the States from any such abuse of power in the future. Instead of sending out such amendment to the people we are asked to remedy this State wrong by enacting in the second section of this bill as follows:

> That any person who, under color of any law, statute, ordinance, regulation, or custom shall subject or cause to be subjected any inhabitant [citizen] of any State or Territory to the deprivation of any right secured or protected by this act, or to different punishment, pains, or penalties on account of such person having at any time been held in a condition of slavery or involuntary servitude, except as a punishment for crime whereof the party shall have been duly convicted, or by reason of his color or race, than is prescribed for the punishment of white persons, shall be deemed guilty of a misdemeanor, and on conviction shall be punished by a fine not exceeding $1,000, or imprisonment not exceeding one year, or both.

Mr. Speaker, the word "inhabitant" is printed in the second section in mistake for "citizen." I say this upon the suggestion of the chairman of the committee. If this is to be the language of the bill, by enacting it are we not committing the terrible enormity of distinguishing here in the laws in respect to life, liberty, and property between the citizen and stranger within your gates? Do we not thereby declare the States may discriminate in the administration of justice for the protection of life against the stranger irrespective of race or color?

Sir, that is forbidden by the Constitution of your country. The great men who made that instrument, when they undertook to make provision, by limitations upon the power of this Government, for the security of the universal rights of man, abolished the narrow and limited phrase of the old Magna Charta of five hundred years ago, which gave the protection of the laws only to "free men" and inserted in its stead the more comprehensive words, "no person;" thereby obeying that higher law given by a voice out of heaven: "Ye shall have the same law for the stranger as for one of your own country." Thus, in respect to life and liberty and property, the people by their Constitution declared the equality of all men, and by express limitation forbade the Government of the United States from making any discrimination.

This bill sir, with all respect I submit, departs from that great law. The alien is not a citizen. You propose to enact this law, you say, in the interests of the freedmen. But do you propose to allow these discriminations to be made in States against the alien and stranger? Can such legislation be sustained by reason or conscience? With all respect to every gentleman who may be a supporter of it, I ask, can it be sanctioned? Is it not as unjust as the unjust State legislation you seek to remedy? Your Constitution says "no person," not "no citizen," "shall be deprived of life, liberty, or property," without due process of law.

If the bill of rights, as has been solemnly ruled by the Supreme Court of the United States, does not limit the powers of States and prohibit such gross injustice by States, it does limit the power of Congress and prohibit any such legislation by Congress.

But, sir, on yesterday, the honorable gentleman from Pennsylvania [Mr. Broomall]—than whom there is no more candid or just gentleman in the House—treated this measure as though it was a bill simply for the protection of freedmen in their rights for the time being in the late insurrectionary States. That is a great mistake. It applies to every State in the Union, to States which have never been in insurrection, and is to be enforced in every State of the Union, not only for the present but for all future time, or until it shall be repealed by some subsequent act of Congress. It does not expire by virtue of its own limitation; it is intended to be permanent.

And let me here suggest to the House that this bill stands in strange contrast with the solemn action of the Senate and of the House in that just and righteous bill known as the Freedmen's Bureau bill. I shall not now take up the time of the House to read the seventh and eighth sections of that bill. But I beg leave to remark to the House, and I ask consideration to the fact, that the seventh and eighth sections of the Freedmen's Bureau bill enumerate the same rights and all the rights and privileges that are enumerated in the first section of this bill, and for a violation of those rights and privileges within any of the insurrectionary States they impose the same penalty, and no other, than that which is imposed by the second section of this bill. But it contains this remarkable provision, that the jurisdiction conferred by the seventh and eighth sections upon the Freedmen's Bureau to inflict these penalties and enforce the rights enumerated shall cease and determine upon the restoration of those insurrectionary States to their constitutional relations with the United States, and the establishment therein of the courts.

The two sections referred to of the Freedmen's Bureau bill, so recently passed and vetoed, are as follows:

SEC. 7. *And be it further enacted,* That whenever in any State or district in which the ordinary course of judicial proceedings has been interrupted by the rebellion, and wherein, in consequence of any State or local law, ordinance, police or other regulation, custom, or prejudice, any of the civil rights or immunities belonging to white persons, including the right to make and enforce contracts, to sue, be parties, and give evidence, to inherit, purchase, lease, sell, hold, and convey real and personal property, and to have full and equal benefit of all laws and proceedings for the security of person and estate, including the constitutional right of bearing arms, are refused or denied to negroes, mulattoes, freedmen, refugees, or any other persons, on account of race, color, or any previous condition of slavery or involuntary servitude, or wherein they or any of them are subjected to any other or different punishment, pains, or penalties for the commission of any act or offense, than are prescribed for white persons committing like acts or offenses, it shall be the duty of the President of the United States, through the Commissioner, to extend military protection and jurisdiction over all cases affecting such persons so discriminated against.

SEC. 8. *And be it further enacted,* That any person who, under color of any State or local law, ordinance, police or other regulation, or custom, shall, in any State or district in which the ordinary course of judicial proceedings has been interrupted by the rebellion, subject, or cause to be subjected, any negro, mulatto, freedman, refugee, or other person, on account of race or color, or any previous condition of slavery or involuntary servitude, or for any other cause, to the deprivation of any civil right secured to white persons, or to any other or different punishment than white persons are subject to for the commission of like acts or offenses, shall be deemed guilty of a misdemeanor, and be punished by fine not exceeding $1,000, or imprisonment not exceeding one year, or both; and it shall be the duty of the officers and agents of this bureau to take jurisdiction of, and hear and determine all offenses committed against the provisions of this section, and also of all cases affecting negroes, mulattoes, freedmen, refugees, or other persons who are discriminated against in any of the particulars mentioned in the preceding section of this act, under such rules and regulations as the President of the United States, through the War Department, shall prescribe. The jurisdiction conferred by this and the preceding section on the officers and agents of this bureau shall cease and determine whenever the discrimination on account of which it is conferred ceases, and in no event to be exercised in any State in which the ordinary course of judicial proceedings has not been interrupted by the rebellion, nor in any such State after said State shall have been fully restored in all its constitutional relations to the United States, and the courts of the State and of the United States within the same are not disturbed or stopped in the peaceable course of justice.

This jurisdiction shall cease, and in no event be exercised *in any State*, after said State shall have been fully restored in all its constitutional relations to the United States. What was that but a solemn declaration by the Senate and House of Representatives to the whole world that during the insurrectionary condition of the States we have the power, and the duty rests upon us, to enforce these rights of person and citizen, in behalf not only of those freedmen but of refugees and of all men within the limits of the insurrectionary district, by the establishment of this extraordinary bureau of justice known as the Freedmen's Bureau? What was it but the solemn conviction and declaration of Congress that with the restoration of those States to their constitutional relations, and the establishment of courts of justice therein, our powers in the premises cease, and under the Constitution of the country freedmen and refugees alike are dependent for justice and their rights upon the civil administrators of the law within those respective States? Why did not the Congress declare in that bill that upon the restoration of the civil authority within those States and when the courts of the United States therein shall no longer "be stopped in the peaceable course of justice," the jurisdiction thus conferred should be exercised by the courts of the United States? Why, on the contrary, did the Congress solemnly enact by that bill that upon such restoration this jurisdiction for the protection of refugees and freedmen should cease and determine? It was a confession by solemn and formal enactment that in that event your judicial power in the premises is ended.

It was that, sir, and nothing but that. I would be ashamed, sir, to go to your tribune, and take upon my soul the oath prescribed by the Constitution, if I thought this Government had not the power to establish tribunals of justice within the insurrectionary districts during the time of insurrection and until the duly organized State governments were restored for the protection of life, liberty, and property, to all men alike. Hence, sir, I stand by the Freedmen's Bureau bill; and standing by that bill I hold it up this day before the House as a point blank condemnation of the attempt to assert this great power over States duly organized, and sustaining their full constitutional relation to the Government of the United States, and in which the courts are not "disturbed or stopped in the peaceable course of justice."

This brings me, sir, to the closing remark which I propose to make on this subject, and that is this: that in the language of the "old man eloquent," which I have had occasion more than once to quote upon this floor in the hearing of some of those who now honor me with their attention, in time of war, whether it be civil or foreign war, the public safety becomes the highest law; and tribunals of States and institutions of States, to use his own terse words, "go by the board for the time being." But when peace is restored; when the courts of justice are opened; when her white-robed ministers take the golden scales into their hands, justice is to be administered under the Constitution, according to the Constitution, and within the limitation of the Constitution.

What is that limitation, sir? Simply this, that the care of the property, the liberty, and the life of the citizen, under the solemn sanction of an oath imposed by your Federal Constitution, is in the States, and not in the Federal Government. I have sought to effect no change in that respect in the Constitution of the country. I have advocated here an amendment which would arm Congress with the power to compel obedience to the oath, and punish all violations by State officers of the bill of rights, but leaving those officers to discharge the duties enjoined upon them as citizens of the United States by that oath and by that Constitution. Standing upon this position, I may borrow the words of the most distinguished man who was ever sent hither from the Old World to make a personal observation of the workings of our institutions, as truly descriptive of the American system: "centralized government, decentralized administration." That, sir, coupled with your declared purpose of equal justice, is the secret of our strength and power.

I hold, sir, that our Constitution never conferred upon the Congress of the United States the power—sacred as life is, first as it is before all other rights which pertain to man on this side of the grave—to protect it in time of peace by the terrors of the penal code within organized States; and Congress has never attempted to do it. There never was a law upon the United States statute-book to punish the murderer for taking away in time of peace the life of the noblest, and the most unoffending as well, of your citizens, within the limits of any State of the Union. The protection of the citizen in that respect was left to the respective States, and there the power is to-day. What you cannot do by direction you cannot do by indirection.

To show that I am not mistaken on this subject, I desire to read the language of one of those grand intellects who during life illustrated the jurisprudence of our country, and has left in his works a perpetual monument of his genius, his learning, and his wisdom. I read from the text of Chancellor Kent:

The judicial power of the United States is necessarily limited to national objects. The vast field of the law of property, the very extensive head of equity jurisdiction, the principal rights and duties which flow from our civil and domestic relations fall within the control, and we might almost say the exclusive cognizance of the State governments. We look essentially to the State courts for protection to all these momentous interests. They touch, in their operation, every chord of human sympathy, and control our best destinies. It is their province to reward and to punish. Their blessings and their terrors will accompany us to the fireside, and be in constant activity before the public eye. [1 Kent, Lecture 19, sec. 446]

Sir, I have always so learned our dual system of Government by which our own American nationality and liberty have been established and maintained. I have always believed that the protection in time of peace within the States of all the rights of person and citizen was of the powers reserved to the States. And so I still believe.

Now, what does this bill propose? To reform the whole civil and criminal code of every State government by declaring that there shall be no discrimination between citizens on account of race or color in civil rights or in the penalties prescribed by their laws. I humbly bow before the majesty of justice, as I bow before the majesty of that God whose attribute it is, and therefore declare there should be no such inequality or discrimination even in the penalties for crime; but what power have you to correct it? That is the question. You further say that in the courts of justice of the several States there shall, as to the qualifications of witnesses, be no discrimination on account of race or color. I agree that, as to persons who appreciate the obligation of an oath—and no others should be permitted to testify—there should be no such discrimination.

But whence do you derive power to cure it by a congressional enactment? There should be no discrimination among citizens of the United States in the several States, of like sex, age, and condition, in regard to the franchises of office. But such a discrimination does exist in nearly every State. How do you propose to cure all this? By a congressional enactment? How? Not by saying, in so many words, which would be the bold and direct way of meeting this issue, that every discrimination of this kind, whether existing in State constitution or State law, is hereby abolished. You propose to make it a penal offense for the judges of the States to obey the constitution and laws of their States, and for their obedience thereto to punish them by fine and imprisonment as felons. I deny your power to do this. You cannot make an official act, done under color of law, and without criminal intent and from a sense of public duty, a crime. . . .

MR. WILSON. . . This bill, sir, has met with opposition in both Houses on the same ground that in times gone by, before this land was drenched in blood by the slaveholders' rebellion, was urged by those who controlled the destinies of the southern portion of the country, and those who adhered to their fortunes in the North, for the purpose of riveting the chain of slavery and converting this Republic into a great slave nation. The arguments which have been urged against this bill in both Houses are but counterparts of the arguments used in opposition to the authority the Government sought to exercise in controlling and preventing the spread of slavery. But I have not time in the few minutes allotted to me to go over the general ground, and I shall confine myself to the points which have been made by the gentleman from Ohio, [Mr. Bingham,] who addressed the House this morning.

Now, sir, I do not intend to be driven or lured from the position I took at the opening of this discussion in justification of this bill by any of the "glittering generalities" which have been drawn into the discussion. I affirmed on that occasion, and I reaffirm here to-day, that citizens of the United States, as such, are entitled to certain rights; and I stand here to-day to affirm that being entitled to those rights it is the duty of the Government to protect citizens in the perfect enjoyment of them. The citizen is entitled to life, liberty, and the right to property. The gentleman from Ohio tells us in the protection of these rights the citizen must depend upon the "honest purpose of the several States," and that the General Government cannot interpose its strong right arm to defend the citizen in the enjoyment of life, liberty, and in possession of property. In other words, if the States of this Union, in their "honest purpose," like the honesty of purpose manifested by the southern States in times past, should deprive the citizen, without due process of law, of life, liberty, and property, the General Government, which can draw the citizen by the strong bond of allegiance to the battle-field, has no power to intervene and set aside a State law, and give the citizen protection under the laws of Congress in the courts of the United States; that at the mercy of the States lie all the rights of the citizen of the United States; that while it was deemed necessary to constitute a great Government to render secure the rights of the people, the framers of the Government turned over to the States the power to deprive the citizen of those things for the security of which the Government was framed. In other words, the little State of Delaware has a hand stronger than the United States; that revolted South Carolina may put under lock and key the great fundamental rights belonging to the citizen, and we must be dumb; that our legislative power cannot be exercised; that our courts must be closed to the appeal of our citizens. That is the doctrine this House of Representatives, representing a great free people, just emerged from a terrible war for the maintenance of American liberty, is asked to adopt.

The gentleman from Ohio tells the House that civil rights involve all the rights that citizens have under the Government; that in the term are embraced those rights which belong to the citizen of the United States as such, and those which belong to a citizen of a State as such; and that this bill is not intended merely to enforce equality of rights, so far as they relate to citizens of the United States, but invades the States to enforce equality of rights in respect to those things which properly and rightfully depend on State regulations and laws. My friend is too sound a lawyer, is too well versed in the Constitution of his country, to indorse that proposition on calm and deliberate consideration. He knows, as every man knows, that this bill refers to those rights which belong to men as citizens of the United States and none other; and when he talks of setting aside the school laws and jury laws and franchise laws of the States by the bill now under consideration, he steps beyond what he must know to be the rule of construction which must apply here, and as the result of which this bill can only relate to matters within the control of Congress.

He says that we cannot interpose in this way for the protection of rights. Can we not? What are the great civil rights to which the first section of the bill refers? I find in the bill of rights which the gentleman desires to have enforced by an amendment to the Constitution that "no person shall be deprived of life, liberty, or property without due process of law." I understand that these constitute the civil rights belonging to the citizens in connection with those which are necessary for the protection and maintenance and perfect enjoyment of the rights thus specifically named, and these are the rights to which this bill relates, having nothing to do with subjects submitted to the control of the several States. . . .

Now, sir, in relation to the great fundamental rights embraced in the bill of rights, the citizen being possessed of them is entitled to a remedy. That is the doctrine of the law as laid down by the courts. There can be no dispute about this. The possession of the rights by the citizen raises by implication the power in Congress to provide appropriate means for their protection; in other words, to supply the needed remedy.

The citizen is entitled to the rights of life, liberty, and property. Now, if a State intervenes and deprives him, without due process of law, of these rights, as has been the case in a multitude of instances in the past, have we no power to make him secure in his priceless possessions? When such a case is presented can we not provide a remedy? Who will doubt it? Must we wait for the perpetration of the wrong before acting? Who will affirm this? The power is with us to provide the necessary protective remedies. If not, from whom shall they come? From the source interfering with the right? Not at all. They must be provided by the Government of the United States, whose duty it is to protect the citizen in return for the allegiance he owes to the Government. Justice, reason, everything, asserts this as the true theory for the guidance of our action. This is in accord with the dignity of government. Without it the Republic becomes an oppressor, exacting a discharge of duty by the citizen, in the absence of the power to return a protective compensation.

I will now notice particularly the provisions of the amendment proposed by the gentleman from Ohio [Mr. Bingham] to the motion to recommit. I want no more complete assertion of the power to pass this bill as reported from the committee than the gentleman's own amendment. What does he propose? To instruct the committee to report back this bill, striking out of the first clause the words "and there shall be no discrimination of civil rights or immunities among citizens of the United States, in any State or Territory of the United States, on account of race, color, or previous condition of slavery;" and to insert in the eighth line of the first section, after the word "right," the words "in every State and Territory of the United States;" leaving the section in every other respect precisely as reported by the committee.

Now, sir, what rights does the gentleman propose to protect? Let his own instructions answer for him:

And such citizens of every race and color, without regard to any previous condition of slavery or involuntary servitude, except as a punishment for crime whereof the party shall have been duly convicted, shall have the same right in every State and Territory of the United States to make and enforce contracts, to sue, be parties and give evidence, to inherit, purchase, lease, sell, hold, and convey real and personal property, and to have equal benefit of all laws and proceedings for the security of person and property as is enjoyed by white citizens, and shall be subject to like punishment, pains, and penalties, and to none other, any law, statute, ordinance, regulation, or custom to the contrary notwithstanding.

Now, I want to know whether these rights are any greater than the rights which are included in the general term "life, liberty, and property." And yet the gentleman admits by his instructions, and asks this House to indorse his admission, that the General Government may secure to citizens of the United States in every State the possession of these enumerated rights. I take the gentleman's own instructions, and his argument in favor of them, and I apply them as arguments in support of the report of the Judiciary Committee. They go as far as we have gone, and assert the identical powers and principles which we have asserted.

But he says the second section is objectionable. Well, I want no more direct authority than his own in vindication of the principle involved in the second section. What does he propose in regard to it? He moves—

Also to strike out all parts of said bill which are penal, and which authorize criminal proceedings, and in lieu thereof to give to all citizens injured by denial or violation of any of the other rights secured or protected by said act an action in the United States courts, with double costs in all cases of recovery, without regard to the amount of damages; and also to secure to such persons the privilege of the writ of *habeas corpus.*

What difference in principle is there between saying that the citizen shall be protected by the legislative power of the United States in his rights by civil remedy and declaring that he shall be protected by penal enactments against those who interefere with his rights? There is no difference in the principle involved. If we may adopt the gentleman's mode we may also select the mode provided in this bill. There is a difference in regard to the expense of protection. There is also a difference as to the effectiveness of the two modes. Beyond this, nothing. This bill proposes that the humblest citizen shall have full and ample protection at the cost of the Government, whose duty it is to protect him. The amendment of the gentleman recognizes the principle involved, but it says that the citizen despoiled of his rights, instead of being properly protected by the Government, must press his own way through the courts and pay the bills attendant thereon. This may do for the rich, but to the poor, who need protection, it is mockery. The highest obligation which the Government owes to the citizen in return for the allegiance exacted of him is to secure him in the protection of his rights. Under the amendment of the gentleman the citizen can only receive that protection in the form of a few dollars in the way of damages, if he shall be so fortunate as to recover a verdict against a solvent wrong-doer. This is called protection. This is what we are asked to do in the way of enforcing the bill of rights. Dollars are weighed against the right of life, liberty, and property. The verdict of a jury is to cover all wrongs and discharge the obligations of the Government to its citizens.

Sir, I cannot see the justice of that doctrine. I assert that it is the duty of the Government of the United States to provide proper protection, and to pay the costs attendant on it. We have gone out with the strong arm of the Government and drawn from their homes all over this land, in obedience to the bond of allegiance which the Government holds on the citizen, hundreds of thousands of men to the battlefield; and yet while we may exercise this extraordinary power, the gentleman claims that we cannot extend the protecting hand of the Government to these men who have been battling for the life of the nation, but can only send them at their own cost to juries for verdicts of a few dollars in compensation for the most flagrant wrong to their most sacred rights. Let those support that doctrine who will, I cannot.

Sir, in the votes upon the several propositions now before us I expect to have the indorsement of most, if not all, of the members of this House of the great principle involved in the bill. Of course our Democratic friends will vote for the motion of the gentleman from Ohio [Mr. Bingham] to recommit the bill with instructions, and thereby direct the committee to report a bill which shall declare all persons, negroes included, citizens of the United States, and we shall have the gentleman from Ohio who addressed the House yesterday voting in favor of instructing the committee to report the bill back so amended as to still embrace all the specified rights to which he objected. And we shall have the gentleman from New York, [Mr. Raymond,] who addressed the House yesterday, voting in favor of instructions which will compel the Committee on the Judiciary to report back a bill which shall involve the identical principle of the second section of this bill, upon which he based his opposition. Every vote in favor of these instructions will be a vote in favor of the principles of this bill. And, sir, although it may result in the defeat of what I regard to be most important legislation, I shall at least have the consolation of knowing that this intelligent House accepts the conclusion that the Committee on the Judiciary arrived at—that all these rights belong to the citizen and should be protected, the only difference between us being that the committee insists that the protection should be extended at the cost of the Government, while those in favor of the instructions believe that we should compel the citizen to seek his remedy at his own cost.

Now, sir, in relation to the remainder of the bill which the gentleman from Ohio proposes to strike out, we have had an indorsement of that by our Democratic friends for very many years. Those provisions are made up of the several sections of the old fugitive slave law, modified in such a manner as to exclude therefrom the features to which many of us formerly objected. I am not prepared to cast a vote which shall declare that all the powers exercised by this Government in former times in behalf of slavery shall not be exercised in behalf of the freedom of the citizen and his ample protection in all his fundamental rights. . . .

MR. WILSON reported back from the Committee on the Judiciary, with amendments, the bill (S. No. 61) entitled "An act to protect all persons in the United States in their civil rights and furnish the means of their vindication."

The first amendment reported by the committee on the Judiciary was read, as follows:

Strike out, in lines six, seven, eight, and nine of section one, the following words:

Without distinction of color, and there shall be no discrimination in civil rights or immunities among citizens of the United States in any State or Territory of the United States on account of race, color, or previous condition of slavery.

So that the section will read as follows:

That all persons born in the United States and not subject to any foreign Power, excluding Indians not taxed, are hereby declared to be citizens of the United States; and such citizens of every race and color, without regard to any previous condition of slavery or involuntary servitude, except as a punishment for crime whereof the party shall have been duly convicted, shall have the same right to make and enforce contracts, to sue, be parties, and give evidence, to inherit, purchase, lease, sell, hold, and convey real and personal property, and to full and equal benefit of all laws and proceedings for the security of person and property as is enjoyed by white citizens, and shall be subject to like punishment, pains, and penalties, and to none other, any law, statute, ordinance, regulation, or custom to the contrary notwithstanding. . . .

Mr. Speaker, the amendment which has just been read proposes to strike out the general terms relating to civil rights. I do not think it materially changes the bill; but some gentlemen were apprehensive that the words we propose to strike out might give warrant for a latitudinarian construction not intended. . . .

RALPH HILL [R., IND.]. What has become of the amendment the gentleman promised me to move, that nothing in this bill contained should be construed to affect or interfere with the right of suffrage in the several States?

MR. WILSON. When the bill was up before I did offer such an amendment, that nothing in the bill contained should be construed to affect the rights of suffrage in the several States. I will explain. Some members of the House thought, in the general words of the first section in relation to civil rights, it might be held by the courts that the right of suffrage was included in those rights. To obviate that difficulty and the difficulty growing out of any other construction beyond the specific rights named in the section, our amendment strikes out all of those general terms and leaves the bill with the rights specified in the section. Therefore the amendment referred to by the gentleman is unnecessary. . . .

THE VETO MESSAGE
March 27, 1866

I regret that the bill, which has passed both Houses of Congress, entitled "An act to protect all persons in the United States in their civil rights and furnish the means of their vindication," contains provisions which I can not approve consistently with my sense of duty to the whole people and my obligations to the Constitution of the United States. I am therefore constrained to return it to the Senate, the House in which it originated, with my objections to its becoming a law.

By the first section of the bill all persons born in the United States and not subject to any foreign power, excluding Indians not taxed, are declared to be citizens of the United States. This provision comprehends the Chinese of the Pacific States, Indians subject to taxation, the people called gypsies, as well as the entire race designated as blacks, people of color, negroes, mulattoes, and persons of African blood. Every individual of these races born in the United States is by the bill made a citizen of the United States. It does not purport to declare or confer any other right of citizenship than Federal citizenship. It does not purport to give these classes of persons any status as citizens of States, except that which may result from their status as citizens of the United States. The power to confer the right of State citizenship is just as exclusively with the several States as the power to confer the right of Federal citizenship is with Congress.

The right of Federal citizenship thus to be conferred on the several excepted races before mentioned is now for the first time proposed to be given by law. If, as is claimed by many, all persons who are native born already are, by virtue of the Constitution, citizens of the United States, the passage of the pending bill can not be necessary to make them such. If, on the other hand, such persons are not citizens, as may be assumed from the proposed legislation to make them such, the grave question presents itself whether, when eleven of the thirty-six States are unrepresented in Congress at the present time, it is sound policy to make our entire colored population and all other excepted classes citizens of the United States. Four millions of them have just emerged from slavery into freedom. Can it be reasonably supposed that they possess the requisite qualifications to entitle them to all the privileges and immunities of citizens of the United States? Have the people of the several States expressed such a conviction? It may also be asked whether it is necessary that they should be declared citizens in order that they may be secured in the enjoyment of the civil rights proposed to be conferred by the bill. Those rights are, by Federal as well as State laws, secured to all domiciled aliens and foreigners, even before the completion of the process of naturalization; and it may safely be assumed that the same enactments are sufficient to give like protection and benefits to those for whom this bill provides special legislation. Besides, the policy of the Government from its origin to the present time seems to have been that persons who are strangers to and unfamiliar with our institutions and our laws should pass through a certain probation, at the end of which, before attaining the coveted prize, they must give evidence of their fitness to receive and to exercise the rights of citizens as contemplated by the Constitution of the United States. The bill in effect proposes a discrimination against large numbers of intelligent, worthy, and patriotic foreigners, and in favor of the negro, to whom, after long years of bondage, the avenues to freedom and intelligence have just now been suddenly opened. He must of necessity, from his previous unfortunate condition of servitude, be less informed as to the nature and character of our institutions than he who, coming from abroad, has, to some extent at least, familiarized himself with the principles of a Government to which he voluntarily intrusts "life, liberty, and the pursuit of happiness." Yet it is now proposed, by a single legislative enactment, to confer the rights of citizens upon all persons of African descent born within the extended limits of the United States, while persons of foreign birth who make our land their home must undergo a probation of five years, and can only then become citizens upon proof that they are "of good moral character, attached to the principles of the Constitution of the United States, and well disposed to the good order and happiness of the same."

The first section of the bill also contains an enumeration of the rights to be enjoyed by these classes so made citizens "in every State and Territory in the United States." These rights are "to make and enforce contracts; to sue, be parties, and give evidence; to inherit, purchase, lease, sell, hold, and convey real and personal property," and to have "full and equal benefit of all laws and proceedings for the security of person and property as is enjoyed by white citizens." So, too, they are made subject to the same punishment, pains, and penalties in common with white citizens, and to none other. Thus a perfect equality of the white and colored races is attempted to be fixed by Federal law in every State of the Union over the vast field of Etatetion covered by these enumerated rights. In no one of these can any State ever exercise any power of discrimination between the different races. In the exercise of State it has frequently been thought expedient to discriminate between the two races. By the statutes of some of the States, Northern as well as Southern, it is enacted, for instance, that no white person shall intermarry with a negro or mulatto. Chancellor Kent says, speaking of the blacks, that—

> Marriages between them and the whites are forbidden in some of the States where slavery does not exist, and they are prohibited in all the slaveholding States; and when not absolutely contrary to law, they are revolting, and regarded as an offense against public decorum.

I do not say that this bill repeals State laws on the subject of marriage between the two races, for as the whites are forbidden to intermarry with the blacks, the blacks can only make such contracts as the whites themselves are allowed to make, and therefore can not under this bill enter into the marriage contract with the whites. I cite this discrimination, however, as an instance of the State policy as to discrimination, and to inquire whether if Congress can abrogate all State laws of discrimination between the two races in the matter of real estate, of suits, and of contracts generally, Congress may not also repeal the State laws as to the contract of marriage between the two races. Hitherto every subject embraced in the enumeration of rights contained in this bill has been considered as exclusively belonging to the States. They all relate to the internal police and economy of the respective States. They are matters which in each State concern the domestic condition of its people, varying in each according to its own peculiar circumstances and the safety and well-being of its own citizens. I do not mean to say that upon all these subjects there are not Federal restraints—as, for instance, in the State power of legislation over contracts there is a Federal limitation that no State shall pass a law impairing the obligations of contracts; and, as to crimes, that no State shall pass an *ex post facto* law; and, as to money, that no State shall make anything but gold and silver a legal tender; but where can we find a Federal prohibition against the power of any State to discriminate, as do most of them, between aliens and citizens, between artificial persons, called corporations, and natural persons, in the right to hold real estate? If it be granted that Congress can repeal all State laws discriminating between whites and blacks in the subjects covered by this bill, why, it may be asked, may not Congress repeal in the same way all State laws discriminating between the two races on the subjects of suffrage and office? If Congress can declare by law who shall hold lands, who shall testify, who shall have capacity to make a contract in a State, then Congress can by law also declare who, without regard to color or race, shall have the right to sit as a juror or as a judge, to hold any office, and, finally, to vote "in every State and Territory of the United States." As respects the Territories, they come within the power of Congress, for as to them the lawmaking power is the Federal power; but as to the States no similar provision exists vesting in Congress the power "to make rules and regulations" for them.

The object of the second section of the bill is to afford discriminating protection to colored persons in the full enjoyment of all the rights secured to them by the preceding section. It declares—

That any person who, under color of any law, statute, ordinance, regulation, or custom, shall subject, or cause to be subjected, any inhabitant of any State or Territory to the deprivation of any right secured or protected by this act, or to different punishment, pains, or penalties on account of such person having at any time been held in a condition of slavery or involuntary servitude, except as a punishment for crime whereof the party shall have been duly convicted, or by reason of his color or race, than is prescribed for the punishment of white persons, shall be deemed guilty of a misdemeanor, and on conviction shall be punished by fine not exceeding $1,000, or imprisonment not exceeding one year, or both, in the discretion of the court.

This section seems to be designed to apply to some existing or future law of a State or Territory which may conflict with the provisions of the bill now under consideration. It provides for counteracting such forbidden legislation by imposing fine and imprisonment upon the legislators who may pass such conflicting laws, or upon the officers or agents who shall put or attempt to put them into execution. It means an official offense, not a common crime committed against law upon the persons or property of the black race. Such an act may deprive the black man of his property, but not of the *right* to hold property. It means a deprivation of the right itself, either by the State judiciary or the State legislature. It is therefore assumed that under this section members of State legislatures who should vote for laws conflicting with the provisions of the bill, that judges of the State courts who should render judgments in antagonism with its terms, and that marshals and sheriffs who should, as ministerial officers, execute processes sanctioned by State laws and issued by State judges in execution of their judgments could be brought before other tribunals and there subjected to fine and imprisonment for the performance of the duties which such State laws might impose. The legislation thus proposed invades the judicial power of the State. It says to every State court or judge, If you decide that this act is unconstitutional; if you refuse, under the prohibition of a State law, to allow a negro to testify; if you hold that over such a subject-matter the State law is paramount, and "under color" of a State law refuse the exercise of the right to the negro, your error of judgment, however conscientious, shall subject you to fine and imprisonment. I do not apprehend that the conflicting legislation which the bill seems to contemplate is so likely to occur as to render it necessary at this time to adopt a measure of such doubtful constitutionality.

In the next place, this provision of the bill seems to be unnecessary, as adequate judicial remedies could be adopted to secure the desired end without invading the immunities of legislators, always important to be preserved in the interest of public liberty; without assailing the independence of the judiciary, always essential to the preservation of individual rights; and without impairing the efficiency of ministerial officers, always necessary for the maintenance of public peace and order. The remedy proposed by this section seems to be in this respect not only anomalous, but unconstitutional; for the Constitution guarantees nothing with certainty if it does not insure to the several States the right of making and executing laws in regard to all matters arising within their jurisdiction, subject only to the restriction that in cases of conflict with the Constitution and constitutional laws of the United States the latter should be held to be the supreme law of the land. . . .

I do not propose to consider the policy of this bill. To me the details of the bill seem fraught with evil. The white race and the black race of the South have hitherto lived together under the relation of master and slave—capital owning labor. Now, suddenly, that relation is changed, and as to ownership capital and labor are divorced. They stand now each master of itself. In this new relation, one being necessary to the other, there will be a new adjustment, which both are deeply interested in making harmonious. Each has equal power in settling the terms, and if left to the laws that regulate capital and labor it is confidently believed that they will satisfactorily work out the problem. Capital, it is true, has more intelligence, but labor is never so ignorant as not to understand its own interests, not to know its own value, and not to see that capital must pay that value.

This bill frustrates this adjustment. It intervenes between capital and labor and attempts to settle questions of political economy through the agency of numerous officials whose interest it will be to forment discord between the two races, for as the breach widens their employment will continue, and when it is closed their occupation will terminate.

In all our history, in all our experience as a people living under Federal and State law, no such system as that contemplated by the details of this bill has ever before been proposed or adopted. They establish for the security of the colored race safeguards which go infinitely beyond any that the General Government has ever provided for the white race. In fact, the distinction of race and color is by the bill made to operate in favor of the colored and against the white race. They interfere with the municipal legislation of the States, with the relations existing exclusively between a State and its citizens, or between inhabitants of the same State—an absorption and assumption of power by the General Government which, if acquiesced in, must sap and destroy our federative system of limited powers and break down the barriers which preserve the rights of the States. It is another step, or rather stride, toward centralization and the concentration of all legislative powers in the National Government. The tendency of the bill must be to resuscitate the spirit of rebellion and to arrest the progress of those influences which are more closely drawing around the States the bonds of union and peace.

My lamented predecessor, in his proclamation of the 1st of January, 1863, ordered and declared that all persons held as slaves within certain States and parts of States therein designated were and thenceforward should be free; and further, that the executive government of the United States, including the military and naval authorities thereof, would recognize and maintain the freedom of such persons. This guaranty has been rendered especially obligatory and sacred by the amendment of the Constitution abolishing slavery throughout the United States. I therefore fully recognize the obligation to protect and defend that class of our people whenever and wherever it shall become necessary, and to the full extent compatible with the Constitution of the United States.

Entertaining these sentiments, it only remains for me to say that I will cheerfully cooperate with Congress in any measure that may be necessary for the protection of the civil rights of the freedmen, as well as those of all other classes of persons throughout the United States, by judicial process, under equal and impartial laws, in conformity with the provisions of the Federal Constitution.

I now return the bill to the Senate, and regret that in considering the bills and joint resolutions—forty-two in number—which have been thus far submitted for my approval I am compelled to withhold my assent from a second measure that has received the sanction of both Houses of Congress.

Andrew Johnson

THE ANTI-PEONAGE ACT

Commentary

The Thirteenth Amendment itself categorically prohibits the existence of either slavery or involuntary servitude within the United States. Like the other post-Civil War amendments, it contains a section expressly empowering the Congress to enforce its provisions by appropriate legislation. The congressional authority thus granted was promptly exercised by the Anti-Peonage Act of 1867, making it a crime to hold or return "any person to a condition of peonage" or to arrest "any person with the intent of placing him in or returning him to a condition of peonage."

The Anti-Peonage Act was aimed primarily at the system of peonage that still existed in the Territory of New Mexico in 1867—a system largely inherited from the days of Spanish rule. Like the Thirteenth Amendment itself, however, the 1867 statute uses language that goes beyond the immediate evil involved and prohibits the holding of anyone to peonage or involuntary servitude throughout the United States. As such, it is the congressional complement of the Thirteenth Amendment's prohibition. The legislative history of the statute indicates that it was largely noncontroversial in nature, considered by virtually all as a necessary measure to curb an evil left untouched by the Thirteenth Amendment's general prohibition.

The constitutional power of the Congress to enact the 1867 statute cannot be doubted, for the Thirteenth Amendment grants the explicit authority to enact laws enforcing the amendment's prohibition. Nor can it be argued that the statute sweeps too far, since it reaches the acts proscribed, regardless of whether they are committed by purely private persons or by those acting under color of governmental authority. In this respect, the Thirteenth, unlike the Fourteenth and Fifteenth Amendments, is not addressed solely to state action. Consequently, legislation to enforce the Thirteenth Amendment may operate directly upon the acts of individuals, whether sanctioned by state legislation or not.

In line with what has just been said, the highest Court has had no difficulty in upholding the federal statute punishing the holding of a person in peonage. Said the Court in *Clyatt* v. *United States,* 197 U.S. 207 (1905), "We entertain no doubt of the validity of this legislation, or its applicability to the case of any person holding another in a state of peonage. . . . It operates directly on every citizen of the Republic, wherever his residency may be."

The Thirteenth Amendment and the 1867 enforcing statute are broader than a proscription of Negro slavery as it had existed in the antebellum South. Their purpose was not only to end slavery but to maintain a system of completely free and voluntary labor. As such, their effect was to do away with all forms of forced labor—"to abolish all practices whereby subjection having some of the incidents of slavery was legally enforced." [*United States* v. *Shackney,* 333 F.2d 475 (2d Cir. 1964).]

The Thirteenth Amendment and the 1867 statute enforcing the amendment by making peonage and involuntary servitude a crime, taken together, raise both a sword and a shield against all forms of forced labor in this country. An illustrative case in which they were used "as a sword" is *United States* v. *Reynolds,* 235 U.S. 133 (1914). The Supreme Court there upheld an indictment charging that an employer had a laborer convicted under an Alabama statute making it à crime for a convict "working out" a fine paid by the surety to refuse to labor further. The Alabama statute was ruled unconstitutional and employers acting under it subject to federal prosecution.

In the case that follows (infra p. 172) —*Bailey* v. *Alabama*, 219 U.S. 219 (1911) —on the other hand, the Thirteenth Amendment and the anti-peonage law were raised "as a shild" to invalidate the conviction of a laborer under a state law. The state law at issue made the refusal to perform the labor called for in a written contract of employment, under which the employee had obtained money advanced thereunder which was not refunded, *prima facie* evidence of an intent to defraud and therefore punishable as a criminal offense. The effect of the statute was to make it a crime for servants owing debts or other types of debtors to leave their employment. Yet, if the Thirteenth Amendment and 1867 statute mean anything, they must, at the least, invalidate all such laws which require compulsory service in payment of a debt.

THE ANTI-PEONAGE ACT
March 2, 1867

Be it enacted by the Senate and House of Representatives of the United States of America in Congress assembled, That the holding of any person to service or labor under the system known as peonage is hereby declared to be unlawful, and the same is hereby abolished and forever prohibited in the Territory of New Mexico, or in any other Territory or State of the United States; and all acts, laws, resolutions, orders, regulations, or usages of the Territory of New Mexico, or of any other Territory or State of the United States, which have heretofore established, maintained, or enforced, or by virtue of which any attempt shall hereafter be made to establish, maintain, or enforce, directly or indirectly, the voluntary or involuntary service or labor of any persons as peons, in liquidation of any dent or obligation, or otherwise, be, and the same are hereby, declared null and void; and any person or persons who shall hold, arrest, or return; or cause to be held, arrested, or returned, or in any manner aid in the arrest or return of any person or persons to a condition of peonage, shall, upon conviction, be punished by fine not less than one thousand nor more than five thousand dollars, or by imprisonment not less than one or more than five years, or both, at the discretion of the court.

SEC. 2. *And be it further enacted,* That it shall be the duty of all persons in the military or civil service in the Territory of New Mexico to aid in the enforcement of the foregoing section of this act; and any person or persons who shall obstruct or attempt to obstruct, or in any way interfere with, or prevent the enforcement of this act, shall be liable to the pains and penalties hereby provided; and any officer or other person in the military service of the United States who shall so offend, directly or indirectly, shall, on conviction before a court-martial, be dishonorably dismissed the service of the United States, and shall thereafter be ineligible to reappointment of any office of trust, honor, or profit under the government.

Approved, March 2, 1867.

THE DEBATE

CHARLES SUMNER [R., MASS.]. Mr. President, I offer the following resolution:

Resolved, That the Committee on the Judiciary be directed to consider if any further legislation is needed to prevent the enslavement of Indians in New Mexico or any system of peonage there, and especially to prohibit the employment of the Army of the United States in the surrender of persons claimed as peons.

I ask for the present consideration of the resolution.

The Senate, by unanimous consent, proceeded to its consideration.

MR. SUMNER. Mr. President, I desire to call the attention of the Senate to important facts under that resolution. I think you will be astonished when you know that the evidence is complete that at this moment in a Territory of the United States there is a system of slavery which a proclamation of the President has down to this day been unable to root out. During the life of Mr. Lincoln I more than once appealed to him to exercise his power as the head of the executive, to root this evil out of the Territory of New Mexico. The result was a proclamation and also definite orders from the Department of War; but in the face of that proclamation and of those definite orders this abuse has continued, and according to the official evidence it seems to have increased. I have in my hand the report of the Commissioner of Indian Affairs, from which I will read a short passage. I read from page 33:

On the subject of peonage, the qualified slavery still prevalent in New Mexico, authorized by its laws and encouraged and practiced by its people, officials of Government, and natives of the United States as well as those who have been 'to the manor born.' Mr. Graves's statements, with the evidence presented therewith, are such as to leave no doubt of the duty of Congress to take the matter in hand and deal with it effectually. This office has done all that lay in its power by promulgating the order of the President forbidding the practice, and all the other Departments of the Government issued like directions to the officers responsible to them; but in spite of all this it is clear that the practice still continues to a greater or less extent.

JOHN CONNESS [R., CAL.]. Will the Senator state the date of the report he reads from?

MR. SUMNER. It is the report of this year just made—the report of the Commissioner of Indian Affairs submitted to Congress at the opening of this session.

Then there is the report of the special agent, J. K. Graves, which is made to the Commissioner of Indian Affairs, in which he expresses himself as follows:

Upon the subject of peonage I have given considerable thought; and inasmuch as this pernicious system of slavery still exists to an alarming extent in all parts of the Territory of New Mexico Government should at once adopt vigorous measures tending to its immediate abolition.

The citizens here, although strictly enjoined to give recompense for all service, will nevertheless cling tenaciously to their old customs, and unless the Government, in adopting a definite policy relative to this remaining blot upon the otherwise fair scroll of freedom, sends a special power to the Territory to direct and superintend the practical details of the work of improvement the system will continue for years to come, and be marked with all its present degrading tendencies.

A practice, sanctioned by territorial law, has obtained by which the whites are encouraged to make volunteer expeditions or campaigns against the Indians. Theoretically those participating in these raids are rewarded with the plunder obtained, but should report at the territorial offices all the captives; while practically, in most cases, the captives are either sold at an average of seventy-five to four hundred dollars, or held in possession in practical slavery. This state of things of course keeps up a state of hostility among the Indians. The intervention of Congress is asked to put a stop to this practice.

Again, in another place he says:

This system, either in the ordinary Mexican form, that of a state of continual imprisonment or service for debt, or in that of practical enslavement of captive Indians, "is the universally recognized mode of securing labor and assistance." No less than four hundred Indians are thus held in Santa Fé alone. Their treatment varies with the whims and feelings of their holders. Sometimes they are doubtless better off than when free. The arguments to sustain the system are the same as those formerly used in behalf of slavery. In spite of the stringent orders of the Government the system continues, and nearly every Federal officer held peons in service. The superintendent of Indian affairs had half a dozen. The practice of Federal officers sustained it.

It is to that that I desire to call particular attention. In the resolution which is now on your table, sir, I specially ask the action of the committee with reference to the employment of the Army of the United States in the surrender of fugitive peons. A correspondence is given in the report of the Commissioner of Indian Affairs which illustrates this. Here, for instance, is a letter from N. H. Davis, assistant inspector general United States Army:

Las Cruces, August 22, 1865.

The commanding officer of Fort Selden will allow, and assist if necessary, the bearer, Don Pedro Garcia, and retain and take in his charge his peon, Antonio Rodriguez, if at said post.

By command of General Carleton:

N. H. Davis,
Assistant Inspector General United States Army.

To that we have the following reply:

Headquarters Fort Selden,
New Mexico, August 22, 1865.

Colonel: Yours of to-day requiring me to assist in my official capacity in taking or delivering to a citizen a peon is received. I desire to be informed explicitly whether I am to take this as a precedent and to deliver to any person claiming the person of another.

This is directly contrary to civil law. The laws of the Territory, according to my recollection, have made it a penal offense to return a man to another claiming him as his own. The President of the United States has abolished involuntary servitude; it is certainly contrary to the established rules and regulations of the Government under which we live.

I should like some instructions on this point, if you require me to return those who have escaped from involuntary servitude. It is directly contrary to my opinion of law and justice, and I will only do it on positive and unmistakable orders.

I am, colonel, very respectfully, your obedient servant,

J. H. Whitlock,
Captain First Veteran Infantry, California Volunteers, Commanding.

Colonel N. H. Davis,
Assistant Inspector General, Las Cruces, New Mexico.

Then to that we have the reply of this assistant inspector general of the United States, in which he undertakes to lay down the law and the Constitution; and I am sorry to understand that he is a Massachusetts man:

Inspector General's Department,
Department of New Mexico,
Concordia, Texas, September 1, 1865.

Your letter of the 22d ultimo has been received, in which your premises taken are wrong and your reasoning fallacious. Peonage is voluntary and not involuntary servitude. The Constitution of the United States or the proclamation of the President does not prohibit it. The statute law of the land expressly recognizes this servitude. It is an apprenticeship, or an agreement between the master and servant, and not only can the master arrest and take his servant peon, but the civil authorities are commanded to arrest and deliver the peon to his master when deserting him. (See Laws of New Mexico, chapter twelve: contracts between master and servant, passed by the Legislative Assembly, 1858 and 1859.)

MR. CONNESS. Those statutes have been repealed, have they not?

MR. SUMNER. The Senator from California reminds me that they have been repealed.

MR. CONNESS. I think so.

MR. SUMNER. But this learned officer who lays down the law treats them as still existing.

MR. CONNESS. I will state to the Senator that, if repealed—and it is my impression they have been—it has been only very recently.

MR. SUMNER. This learned officer then proceeds:

You now hold a civil prisoner arrested by military authority. The question is not whether peonage is a good or bad kind of servitude; it is whether it is recognized by law, and whether when a peon had swindled his master out of a large sum of money and deserted him, taking shelter at a military post, the commander thereof would, by extending the courtesy of aiding or acting for the civil authorities in surrendering the culprit, violate any obligation of law or duty. It seems that in the case in question he would not.

You ask for explicit instructions, and make use of disrespectful and threatening language. The first will be granted, and the latter this time overlooked.

You are hereby directed so far to aid in the rendition of peons when claimed by their masters, or there is a reasonable cause to believe they have deserted them, as not to allow them to remain on the military reservation. These instructions will be faithfully executed, in spirit as well as letter, without evasion.

By command of General Carleton, commanding Department of New Mexico.

I am, very respectfully, your obedient servant,

N. H. Davis,
Assistant Inspector General United States Army.

Captain J. H. Whitlock,
Commanding Fort Selden, New Mexico.

The special Indian agent who reports this correspondence very aptly adds: "The aid of Congress is invoked to stop the practice."

I hope the Department of War will communicate directly with General Carleton, under whose sanction this order has been made, and I hope that our Committee on the Judiciary will consider carefully if any further legislation is needed in order to meet this case. A presidential proclamation has failed; orders of the War Department thus far have failed; the abuse still continues, and we have a very learned officer in the Army of the United States undertaking to vindicate it.

MR. CONNESS. I wish to say a single word (as the morning hour is nearly closed and we cannot go to other business) in connection with the pending resolution offered by the Senator from Massachusetts. The officer spoken of and mentioned, Captain Whitlock, is personally known to me, and his communication, which has been read, is but additional evidence to me of his great personal and official rectitude as a public servant. It is also known to me, as it has been for perhaps four years past, that the administration of military affairs in the Territory of New Mexico has been a standing disgrace to this Government. I have made efforts in the direction of a change—all the efforts that I was capable of making; but in all the applications and in all the presentations I have made, both to the President and to the War Department, I have found that at every point the case was, to use a common term, blocked. There was no such thing as even inquiring into the administration of General Carleton in New Mexico. While the war went on I had supposed there was some excuse for this, but now when it is over there is no longer excuse, and this record presented here this morning is but one single additional fact in the whole line of maladministration in that Territory. I think it is a fact. I think I have evidence in my possession that this officer, high in command in the United States Army and in the administration of its military affairs, is personally interested at this time, and has been, in leasing and letting to the Government of the United States the houses they use and the posts they occupy upon their own land.

But, sir, I did not intend to more than call attention to the matter. I have failed utterly in all the attempts I have been able to make in getting such attention to the subject as would lead to a correction. I hope that this inquiry will go in that direction and finally be effective. . . .

HENRY WILSON [R., MASS.]. I now call up the bill (S. No. 543) to abolish and forever prohibit the system of peonage in the Territory of New Mexico and other parts of the United States.

The motion was agreed to; and the Senate, as in Committee of the Whole, proceeded to consider the bill.

MR. WILSON. I have an amendment to offer to the bill in two sections, as a substitute for the entire bill. I do not think it necessary, therefore, to read the original bill, but merely the amendment, which is more carefully drawn.

THE PRESIDENT PRO TEMPORE [La Fayette Foster, R., Conn.]. The reading of the original bill will be dispensed with if there be no objection.

MR. WILSON. I move to strike out all of the bill after the enacting clause, and to insert the following in lieu thereof:

That the holding of any person to service or labor under the system known as peonage is hereby declared to be unlawful, and the same is hereby abolished and forever prohibited in the Territory of New Mexico, or in any other Territory or State of the United States; and all laws, resolutions, orders, regulations, or usages of the Territory of New Mexico, or of any other Territory or State of the United States, which have heretofore established, maintained, or enforced, or by virtue of which any attempt shall hereafter be made to establish, maintain, or enforce, directly or indirectly, the voluntary or involuntary service or labor of any persons as peons, in liquidation of any debt or obligation, or otherwise, be, and the same are hereby, declared null and void; and any person or persons who shall hold, arrest, or return, or cause to be held, arrested, or returned, or in any manner aid in the arrest or return of any person or persons to a condition of peonage, shall, upon conviction, be punished by fine not less than $1,000 nor more than $5,000, and by imprisonment not less than one or more than five years, or both, at the discretion of the court.

SEC. 2. And be it further enacted, That it shall be the duty of all persons in the military or civil service in the Territory of New Mexico to aid in the enforcement of the foregoing section of this act; and any person or persons who shall obstruct or attempt to obstruct, or in any way interfere with or prevent the enforcement of this act, shall be liable to the pains and penalties hereby provided; and any officer or other person in the military service of the United States who shall so offend, directly or indirectly, shall, on conviction before a court-martial, be dishonorably dismissed the service of the United States, and shall thereafter be ineligible to reappointment to any office of trust, honor, or profit under the Government.

GARRET DAVIS [R., KY.]. I will thank the mover of this bill to inform the Senate what this thing called peonage is; to give us a clear, succinct, and comprehensible definition of the term.

MR. WILSON. It is a condition of modified servitude, which we have inherited from Mexico. It exists in New Mexico at this time, the only part of the country where I know it does exist. In some cases it is voluntary, but in most cases forcible. In the larger towns it is disappearing, but in a portion of the country it still exists; and what is more, officers of the United States, military and civil, have been carrying it out. The object of this bill is to arrest it, to make it the duty of the civil and military officers of the United States in the Territory to put an end to the system and not support it. A report was made by one of the officers of the Government, one of the Indian agents, to the Indian Bureau, showing how persons were held in service; that officers of the United States held these persons in service; and that Colonel Davis, under the direction of General Carleton, had undertaken to enforce this law or custom in New Mexico. We intend by this bill to put an end to the system. It is a system of modified servitude which is carried on to a great extent in New Mexico, and especially to a lamentable extent with the Indians. A great many Indians are captured and forcibly held in servitude.

MR. DAVIS. The Senator says that it is a system of modified servitude, sometimes voluntary and sometimes involuntary. I suppose that to the extent that it is voluntary there is no necessity and no power on the part of Congress to interfere with it. But how far and to what extent is it voluntary? The system of apprenticeship is a servitude, and an involuntary servitude. I have seen a great deal of general statement about peonage in Mexico, but I have never yet met with any precise definition of it giving me a fair idea of what it was. I admit that my want of information on the subject has not been supplied much by the explanation of the Senator. In what form is it involuntary to what extent; what are the rights of the peon, and what are the rights of the man who claims his services? How can it be terminated? I suppose all these are matters that are governed by the system itself. I think we are about to legislate on a subject that we know very little about; at least that is my case.

HENRY LANE [R., IND.]. By the laws of Mexico which were existing in New Mexico at the time of the conquest peonage was established. The system was simply this, as I understand it: that where a Mexican owed a debt his creditor had a right to his labor and services until that debt was paid. The debtor became a domestic servant, and he and his family were supported by the creditor, and the peonage never ended until the debt was discharged. It was a kind of servitude for debt, which the committee thought was inconsistent with our institutions. We simply say by this bill that peonage shall be abolished, and the creditor shall be left to all his legal means of collecting his debt, but he shall not hold the peon in slavery. I understand also that by this system the creditor not only had a right by an involuntary process to the labor of the peon, but the debtor if he chose might become the servant of the creditor and serve until the debt was paid. A very small debt with the interest, where the peon has a family to support and the creditor supports him, amounts to a servitude for life. We now simply say that the creditor in New Mexico shall have all the means of collecting their debts known to the law, but that peonage or servitude for debt shall cease. That is the whole of it.

MR. DAVIS. Well, Mr. President, I have been for a good many years of my life in about the same state of slavery that my friend from Indiana represents the peons of Mexico to have been; I have owed considerable debts and I have worked mighty hard to pay them. All the proceeds of my labor went to the payment of my debts, and I had not the advantage which the peon has; the creditor was not supporting me during the time I was laboring to discharge my debts; I had to support myself.

I rather think this matter might as well be postponed till the 4th of March. I believe every difficult question is proposed to be referred over to that time. I once heard of an Irishman who stole an old woman's turkey, and he put it under his arm and was traveling off pretty rapidly to make his escape with his booty. She followed him some distance, but he outran her. When she discovered that she could not overtake him, she said, "Oh, you thief, never mind; you will pay for this on the day of judgment." "Well, madam," said he, "if you will trust me that long I will take another." [Laughter.] I think we may as well trust this system of peonage till the 4th of March, when I suppose the honorable Senator from Massachusetts will have time to investigate the whole subject, and to present it just as it exists clearly to the Senate, and inform us what there is in it that deserves correction or reformation, and what there is in it that ought to remain. I think this feature of a man's working to pay the debts that he owes to his creditors, in a modified form at least, ought to exist.

MR. WILSON. I do not suppose the Senator from Kentucky needs information in regard to what peonage is in New Mexico or Mexico or anywhere else. I do not desire to take up time in defining what it is. It is simply a system of slavery, as I said, a modified slavery. The creditor cannot sell the peon, but he holds his services. The system has been of the most wretched and degrading character, degrading all that class of population. In the larger towns in New Mexico they are getting emancipated from it, and the peons are being elevated by that emancipation.

MR. LANE. If the Senator will pardon me one moment, I will say that the creditor cannot sell the peon, but he can transfer him just as he would a mule or a horse and give his services to anybody else. It is a system of serfdom worse than the Russian system ever was.

EDGAR COWAN [R., VA.]. If he assigns him is it not on a consideration?

MR. LANE. Certainly.

MR. WILSON. The other day my colleague read from a report of one of the officers of the Indian Bureau an account of the state of things in New Mexico. That officer pressed upon the Government the importance of prompt action in this matter; that a great number of persons were held in that condition; that the system exists in a large portion of New Mexico, and is in force to-day. It has disappeared in the large towns, and peons who once worked for two or three dollars a month are now able to command respectable wages, to support their families, elevate themselves, and improve their condition. It is certainly a most wretched system. It applies not to negroes, but to white men; and while I have great faith in the negro, I believe a white man is as good as a negro; and while I have been against negro slavery, I am also against slavery of this kind for white men. I hope we shall put the bill on its passage, and I have no doubt good results will grow out of it.

JAMES DOOLITTLE [R., WIS.]. I will state for the information of the Senate that while examining into the Indian affairs of New Mexico, as a member of the committee on that subject, of which the present Presiding Officer was also a member, we reported some testimony bearing on this state of affairs in the Territory of New Mexico. It appeared, I think, from my best recollection without now reading from the report, that it was believed there were about two thousand of the Navajo and Ute Indians who were held in New Mexico as domestic servants in a state of bondage or slavery. The Navajoes, a large and powerful tribe of Indians, numbering nearly ten thousand, had been almost constantly at war with the Mexicans; and it will be remembered that a majority of the Mexicans are of Indian blood, with some Spanish blood intermixed. These wars had continued for hundreds of years probably. They were raiding upon each other, stealing each other's flocks and herds, and stealing each other's women and children. The Mexicans, it is said, rather got the advantage of the Navajoes in the number of women and children, but the Navajoes got the advantage of the Mexicans in stealing sheep and cattle, and running them off into their fastnesses. The sum and substance of the testimony was that probably there were about two thousand Indians held in New Mexico under this system. But, sir, you will recollect the testimony of Judge Benedict, the chief justice of the Territory. He stated that the question having arisen before the United States court in New Mexico upon a *habeas corpus,* it was decided that these persons were free, and the court had discharged them upon *habeas corpus.* The court had decided that there was no power in the law of New Mexico which would hold a person against his will in servitude; but he stated that as a practical fact these persons remained in the families and in the service of their former masters or employers. Not knowing their rights, not being in a position to go into court to assert their rights, or not having a desire to do so, they were generally remaining in the families of their masters, and probably there were about two thousand of them in the Territory; that is, so far as Indian slavery is concerned. Some of these Indians were captured by the Mexicans, and some were captured by other tribes of Indians and sold to the Mexicans.

Then, as to the system of peonage, it is true that by the law of Mexico before we acquired the Territory of New Mexico the system of peonage existed there; a system by which a person indebted to another is compelled specifically to perform labor until the debt is discharged. The debtor has the privilege, under their law, of hiring himself out to another man; to get another man or master, if you please, to purchase the debt; and then he goes along with his debt to another master; but as long as the debt remains he is compelled to serve. According to the custom of that country with that class of people, in the development of civilization which they have attained, the practical fact was that almost always when one desired to hire out, the first thing the laborer desired to do was to get in debt to his master, and get in debt as much as he could, and go and live with him. Generally they are in the employ of wealthy persons owning the lands, and the peons live upon the lands and cultivate them as serfs. It is a system of serfdom. I understood, however, from the chief justice of the Territory, that in the decision which was given by the court they had decided against the power to hold these persons against their will; they were not compelled to remain any longer than they desired to remain; but as a practical fact they do reside with the landholders throughout New Mexico to a considerable extent.

I state this simply as the information which came to us upon our examination. The testimony of Chief Justice Benedict and Governor Connolly and various others in relation to the system will be found in the appendix to the report which we have made. I think I have stated substantially just how it stands.

CHARLES BUCKALEW [DEM., MASS.]. There is no doubt of our jurisdiction in the Territory of New Mexico to enact such a law as the one proposed. I have some knowledge of this system and I think the necessity for this law is evident. Eventually the courts will weed out this system in that Territory, and do it effectually; but it will remain lingering there for a considerable time unless Congress shall interpose by a law of this kind. Upon the publication of such a statute in that Territory the whole system will fall to the ground at once. I think anywhere within the limits of the United States, with our ideas and our civilization, it is a disgrace that it should be permitted to continue where the power of this Government can extend. In practice, this is not a system of service for the payment of a debt, in view of which the servitude commences. As already explained, the almost invariable fact is that the peon continues accumulating debt, and as that debt is formed while he is subject to a master the terms of it are always exceedingly unfavorable to him, and for a very nominal consideration he is continued in this system of service during his whole lifetime. It is a system which degrades both the owner of the labor and the laborer himself, and in my opinion the sooner we terminate it the better.

MR. WILSON. I hope the bill will now be put on its passage.

THE PRESIDENT PRO TEMPORE. The question is on the amendment offered as a substitute for the bill.

The amendment was agreed to.

The bill was reported to the Senate as amended, and the amendment was concurred in.

The bill was ordered to be engrossed for a third reading; was read the third time, and passed.

House of Representatives-39th Congress, 2nd Session
March 2, 1867

The next business upon the Speaker's table was Senate bill No. 543, to abolish and forever prohibit the system of peonage in the Territory of New Mexico and other parts of the United States; which was read a first and second time.

JOHN BINGHAM [R., OHIO]. I move that that bill be put on its passage.

The bill provides that the holding of any person to service or labor under the system known as peonage is hereby declared to be unlawful, and the same is hereby abolished and forever prohibited in the Territory of New Mexico, or in any other Territory or State of the United States; and all laws, resolutions, regulations, or usages of the Territory of New Mexico, or of any other Territory or State of the United States, which have heretofore established, maintained, or enforced, or by virtue of which any attempt shall hereafter be made to establish, maintain, or enforce, directly or indirectly, the involuntary or involuntary service of labor of any persons as peons, in liquidation of any debt or obligation, or otherwise, be, and the same are hereby, declared null and void; and any person or persons who shall hold, arrest, or return, or cause to be held, arrested, or returned, or in any manner aid in the arrest or return of any person or persons to a condition of peonage, shall, upon conviction, be punished by fine not less than $1,000 nor more than $5,000, and by imprisonment not less than one nor more than five years, or both, at the discretion of the court.

It further provides that it shall be the duty of all persons in the civil and military service of the United States in the Territory of New Mexico to aid in the enforcement of the foregoing section of this act; and that any person or persons who shall obstruct or attempt to obstruct, or in any way interfere with or to prevent the enforcement of this act, shall be liable to the pains and penalties hereby provided, and any officer or other person in the military service of the United States who shall obstruct or interfere with the duties of the said assistant commissioner, directly or indirectly, shall, on conviction before a court-martial, be dishonorably dismissed the service of the United States, and shall thereafter be ineligible to reappointment to any office of trust, honor, or profit under the Government.

The bill was ordered to be read a third time; and it was accordingly read the third time, and passed.

THE DECISION

BAILEY V. ALABAMA
219 U.S. 219 (1911)

Mr. Justice Hughes delivered the opinion of the Court.

This is a writ of error to review a judgment of the Supreme Court of the State of Alabama, affirming a judgment of conviction in the Montgomery City Court. The statute, upon which the conviction was based, is assailed as in violation of the Fourteenth Amendment of the Constitution of the United States upon the ground that it deprived the plaintiff in error of his liberty without due process of law and denied him the equal protection of the laws, and also of the Thirteenth Amendment and of the act of Congress providing for the enforcement of that Amendment, in that the effect of the statute is to enforce involuntary servitude by compelling personal service in liquidation of a debt.

The statute in question is § 4730 of the Code of Alabama of 1896, as amended in 1903 and 1907. The section of the Code as it stood before the amendments provided that any person who with intent to injure or defraud his employer entered into a written contract for service and thereby obtained from his employer money or other personal property, and with like intent and without just cause, and without refunding the money or paying for the property refused to perform the service, should be punished as if he had stolen it. In 1903 [Gen. Acts, Ala., p. 345] the section was amended so as to make the refusal or failure to perform the service, or to refund the money or pay for the property, without just cause, *prima facie* evidence of the intent to injure or defraud. This amendment was enlarged by that of 1907. [Gen. Acts, Ala., p. 636] The section, thus amended, reads as follows:

"Any person, who with intent to injure or defraud his employer, enters into a contract in writing for the performance of any act of service, and thereby obtains money or other personal property from such employer, and with like intent, and without just cause, and without refunding such money, or paying for such property, refuses or fails to perform such act or service, must on conviction be punished by a fine in double the damage suffered by the injured party, but not more than $300, one-half of said fine to go to the county and one-half to the party injured; and any person, who with intent to injure or defraud his landlord, enters into any contract in writing for the rent of land, and thereby obtains any money or other personal property from such landlord, and with like intent, without just cause, and without refunding such money, or paying for such property, refuses or fails to cultivate such land, or to comply with his contract relative thereto, must on conviction be punished by fine in double the damage suffered by the injured party, but not

172

more than $300, one-half of said fine to go to the county and one-half to the party injured. And the refusal or failure of any person, who enters into such contract, to perform such act or service or to cultivate such land, or refund such money, or pay for such property without just cause shall be *prima facie* evidence of the intent to injure his employer or landlord or defraud him. That all laws and parts of laws in conflict with the provisions hereof be and the same are hereby repealed."

There is also a rule of evidence enforced by the courts of Alabama which must be regarded as having the same effect as if read into the statute itself, that the accused, for the purpose of rebutting the statutory presumption, shall not be allowed to testify "as to his uncommunicated motives, purpose or intention." [*Bailey* v. *The State,* 161 Alabama, 77, 78]

Bailey, the plaintiff in error, was committed for detention on the charge of obtaining fifteen dollars under a contract in writing with intent to injure or defraud his employer. He sued out a writ of *habeas corpus* challenging the validity of the statute. His discharge was refused and the Supreme Court of the State affirmed the order, holding the statute to be constitutional. 158 Alabama, 18. On writ of error from this court it was held that the case was brought here prematurely, and the questions now presented were expressly reserved. [*Bailey* v. *Alabama,* 211 U. S. 452]

Having failed to obtain his release on *habeas corpus*, Bailey was indicted on the following charge:

"The Grand Jury of said County charge, that before the finding of this indictment Alonzo Bailey with intent to injure or defraud his employer The Riverside Company, a corporation, entered into a written contract to perform labor or services for The Riverside Company, a corporation and obtained thereby the sum of Fifteen Dollars from the said The Riverside Company, and afterwards with like intent, and without just cause, failed or refused to perform such labor or services or to refund such money against the peace and dignity of the State of Alabama."

Motion to quash and a demurrer to the indictment were overruled. Upon the trial the following facts appeared: On December 26, 1907, Bailey entered into a written contract with the Riverside Company, which provided:

"That I Lonzo Bailey for and in consideration of the sum of Fifteen Dollars in money, this day in hand paid to me by said The Riverside Co., the receipt whereof, I do hereby acknowledge, I, the said Lonzo Bailey do hereby consent, contract and agree to work and labor for the said Riverside Co. as a farm hand on their Scotts Bend Place in Montgomery County, Alabama, from the 30 day of Dec. 1907, to the 30 day of Dec. 1908, at and for the sum of 12.00 per month.

"And the said Lonzo Bailey agrees to render respectful and faithful service to the said The Riverside Co. and to perform diligently and actively all work pertaining to such employment, in accordance with the instructions of the said The Riverside Co., or ag't.

"And the said The Riverside Co. in consideration of the agreement above mentioned of the said Lonzo Bailey hereby employs the said Lonzo Bailey as such farm hand for the time above set out, and agrees to pay the said Lonzo Bailey the sum of $10.75 per month."

The manager of the employing company testified that at the time of entering into this contract there were present only the witness and Bailey and that the latter then obtained from the company the sum of fifteen dollars; that Bailey worked under the contract throughout the month of January and for three or four days in February, 1908, and then, "without just cause and without refunding the money, ceased to work for said Riverside Company, and has not since that time performed any service for said Company in accordance with or under said contract, and has refused and failed to perform any further service thereunder, and has, without just cause, refused and failed to refund said fifteen dollars." He also testified, in response to a question from the attorney for the defendant and against the objection of the State, that Bailey was a negro. No other evidence was introduced.

The court, after defining the crime in the language of the statute, charged the jury, in accordance with its terms, as follows:

"And the refusal of any person who enters into such contract to perform such act or service, or refund such money, or pay for such property, without just cause, shall be *prima facie* evidence of the intent to injure his employer, or to defraud him."

Bailey excepted to these instructions, and requested the court to instruct the jury that the statute, and the provision creating the presumption, were invalid, and further that "the refusal or failure of the defendant to perform the service alleged in the indictment, or to refund the money obtained from the Riverside Co. under the contract between it and the defendant, without cause, does not of itself make out a prima facie case of the defendant's intent to injure or defraud said Riverside Company."

The court refused these instructions and Bailey took exception.

The jury found the accused guilty, fixed the damages sustained by the injured party at fifteen dollars, and assessed a fine of thirty dollars. Thereupon Bailey was sentenced by the court to pay the fine of thirty dollars and the costs, and in default thereof to hard labor "for twenty days in lieu of said fine and one hundred and sixteen days on account of said costs."

On appeal to the Supreme Court of the State the constitutionality of the statute was again upheld and the judgment affirmed. [161 Alabama, 75.]

We at once dismiss from consideration the fact that the plaintiff in error is a black man. While the action of a State through its officers charged with the administration of a law, fair in appearance, may be of such a character as to constitute a denial of the equal protection of the laws, [*Yick Wo* v. *Hopkins,* 118 U. S. 356, 373] such a conclusion is here neither required nor justified. The statute, on its face, makes no racial discrimination, and the record fails to show its existence in fact. No question of a sectional character is presented, and we may view the legislation in the same manner as if it had been enacted in New York or in Idaho. Opportunities for coercion and oppression, in varying circumstances, exist in all parts of the Union, and the citizens of all the States are interested in the maintenance of the constitutional guarantees, the consideration of which is here involved. . . .

In the present case it is urged that the statute as amended, through the operation of the presumption for which it provides, violates the Thirteenth Amendment of the Constitution of the United States and the act of Congress passed for its enforcement. . . .

The language of the Thirteenth Amendment was not new. It reproduced the historic words of the ordinance of 1787 for the government of the Northwest Territory and gave them unrestricted application within the United States and all places subject to their jurisdiction. While the immediate concern was with African slavery, the Amendment was not limited to that. It was a charter of universal civil freedom for all persons, of whatever race, color or estate, under the flag.

The words involuntary servitude have a "larger meaning than slavery." "It was very well understood that in the form of apprenticeship for long terms, as it had been practiced in the West India Islands, on the abolition of slavery by the English government, or by reducing the slaves to the condition of serfs attached to the plantation, the purpose of the article might have been evaded, if only the word slavery had been used." [*Slaughter House Cases,* 16 Wall. 69.] The plain intention was to abolish slavery of whatever name and form and all its badges and incidents; to render impossible any state of bondage; to make labor free, by prohibiting that control by which the personal service of one man is disposed of or coerced for another's benefit which is the essence of involuntary servitude.

While the Amendment was self-executing, so far as its terms were applicable to any existing condition, Congress was authorized to secure its complete enforcement by appropriate legislation. As was said in the *Civil Rights cases*: "By its own unaided force and effect it abolished slavery, and established universal freedom. Still, legislation may be necessary and proper to meet all the various cases and circumstances to be affected by it, and to prescribe proper modes of redress for its violation in letter or spirit. And such legislation may be primary and direct in its character; for the Amendment is not a mere prohibition of state laws establishing or upholding slavery, but an absolute declaration that slavery or involuntary servitude shall not exist in any part of the United States." [109 U. S. 20.]

The act of March 2, 1867 (Rev. Stat., §§ 1990, 5526, *supra*), was a valid exercise of this express authority. [*Clyatt v. United States,* 197 U. S. 207] It declared that all laws of any State, by virtue of which any attempt should be made "to establish, maintain, or enforce, directly or indirectly, the voluntary or involuntary service or labor of any persons as peons, in liquidation of any debt or obligation, or otherwise," should be null and void.

Peonage is a term descriptive of a condition which has existed in Spanish America, and especially in Mexico. The essence of the thing is compulsory service in payment of a debt. A peon is one who is compelled to work for his creditor until his debt is paid. And in this explicit and comprehensive enactment, Congress was not concerned with mere names or manner of description, or with a particular place or section of the country. It was concerned with a fact, wherever it might exist; with a condition, however named and wherever it might be established, maintained or enforced.

The fact that the debtor contracted to perform the labor which is sought to be compelled does not withdraw the attempted enforcement from the condemnation of the statute. The full intent of the constitutional provision could be defeated with obvious facility if, through the guise of contracts under which advances had been made, debtors could be held to compulsory service. It is the compulsion of the service that the statute inhibits, for when that occurs the condition of servitude is created, which would be not less involuntary because of the original agreement to work out the indebtedness. The contract exposes the debtor to liability for the loss due to the breach, but not to enforced labor. This has been so clearly stated by this court in the case of *Clyatt, supra,* that discussion is unnecessary. The court there said:

"The constitutionality and scope of sections 1990 and 5526 present the first questions for our consideration. They prohibit peonage. What is peonage? It may be defined as a status or condition of compulsory service, based upon the indebtedness of the peon to the master. The basal fact is indebtedness. As said by Judge Benedict, delivering the opinion in *Jaremillo* v. *Romero,* 1 N. Mex. 190, 194: 'One fact existed universally; all were indebted to their masters. This was the cord by which they seemed bound to their masters' service.' Upon this is based a condition of compulsory service. Peonage is sometimes classified as voluntary or involuntary, but this implies simply a difference in the mode of origin, but none in the character of the servitude. The one exists where the debtor voluntarily contracts to enter the service of his creditor. The other is forced upon the debtor by some provision of law. But peonage, however created, is compulsory service, involuntary servitude. The peon can release himself therefrom, it is true, by the payment of the debt, but otherwise the service is enforced. A clear distinction exists between peonage and the voluntary performance of labor or rendering of services in payment of a debt. In the latter case the debtor, though contracting to pay his indebtedness by labor or service, and subject like any other contractor to an action for damages for breach of that contract, can elect at any time to break it, and no law or force compels performance or a continuance of the service. We need not stop to consider any possible limits or exceptional cases, such as the service of a sailor, *Robertson* v. *Baldwin,* 165 U. S. 275, or the obligations of a child to its parents, or of an apprentice to his master, or the power of the legislature to make unlawful and punish criminally an abandonment of an employé of his post of labor in any extreme cases. That which is contemplated by the statute is compulsory service to secure the payment of a debt." [197 U. S. 215, 216]

The act of Congress, nullifying all state laws by which it should be attempted to enforce the "service or labor of any persons as peons, in liquidation of any debt or obligation, or otherwise," necessarily embraces all legislation which seeks to comple the service or labor by making it a crime to refuse or fail to perform it. Such laws would furnish the readiest means of compulsion. The Thirteenth Amendment prohibits involuntary servitude except as punishment for crime. But the exception, allowing full latitude for the enforcement of penal laws, does not destroy the prohibtion. It does not permit slavery or involuntary servitude to be established or maintained through the operation of the criminal law by making it a crime to refuse to submit to the one or to render the service which would constitute the other. The State may impose involuntary servitude as a punishment for crime, but it may not compel one man to labor for another in payment of a debt, by punishing him as a criminal if he does not perform the service or pay the debt.

If the statute in this case had authorized the employing company to seize the debtor and hold him to the service until he paid the fifteen dollars, or had furnished the equivalent in labor, its invalidity would not be questioned. It would be equally clear that the State could not authorize its constabulary to prevent the servant from escaping and to force him to work out his debt. But the State could not avail itself of the sanction of the criminal law to supply the compulsion any more than it could use or authorize the use of physical force. "In contemplation of the law the compulsion to such service by the fear of punishment under a criminal statute is more powerful than any guard which the employer could station." [Ex parte Hollman (S. Car.), 60 S. E. Rep. 24]

What the State may not do directly it may not do indirectly. If it cannot punish the servant as a criminal for the mere failure or refusal to serve without paying his debt, it is not permitted to accomplish the same result by creating a statutory presumption which upon proof of no other fact exposes him to conviction and punishment. Without imputing any actual motive to oppress, we must consider the natural operation of the statute here in question [Henderson v. Mayor, 92 U. S. 268], and it is apparent that it furnishes a convenient instrument for the coercion which the Constitution and the act of Congress forbid; an instrument of compulsion peculiarly effective as against the poor and the ignorant, its most likely victims. There is no more important concern than to safeguard the freedom of labor upon which alone can enduring prosperity be based. The provisions designed to secure it would soon become a barren form if it were possible to establish a statutory presumption of this sort and to hold over the heads of laborers the threat of punishment for crime, under the name of fraud but merely upon evidence of failure to work out their debts. The act of Congress deprives of effect all legislative measures of any State through which directly or indirectly the prohibited thing, to wit, compulsory service to secure the payment of a debt may be established or maintained; and we conclude that § 4730, as amended, of the Code of Alabama, in so far as it makes the refusal or failure to perform the act or service, without refunding the money or paying for the property received *prima facie* evidence of the commission of the crime which the section defines, is in conflict with the Thirteenth Amendment and the legislation authorized by that Amendment, and is therefore invalid.

In this view it is unnecessary to consider the contentions which have been made under the Fourteenth Amendment. As the case was given to the jury under instructions which authorized a verdict in accordance with the statutory presumption, and the opposing instructions requested by the accused were refused, the judgment must be reversed.

Reversed and cause remanded for further proceedings not inconsistent with this opinion.

THE FOURTEENTH AMENDMENT

Commentary

The landmark enactment in the field of civil rights is the Fourteenth Amendment—the most important of the additions made to the Constitution in the period following the Civil War. The postbellum amendments themselves constituted the first changes in the organic text in over sixty years. The Thirteenth Amendment (*supra* p. 21) abolished slavery; the Fifteenth Amendment (*infra* p. 371) gave the emancipated race the right of suffrage. But these were scarcely enough to vest the Negro with anything like the civil status of others in the community or to deal with the gross discriminations against the freedmen that were so graphically described in the Report of the Joint Committee on Reconstruction, which drafted the Fourteenth Amendment (*infra* p. 285). What was needed, according to the committee, was an addition to the organic law to protect the civil rights of all persons, including the emancipated race, against state infringements.

The result was the adoption of the Fourteenth Amendment, which deals specifically with civil rights in its key first section. That section, on its face, was intended to have two principal effects. The first was to sweep away the decision in *Dred Scott* v. *Sandford,* 19 How. 393 (1857) barring citizenship for the Negro. Hence Section one's first sentence providing citizenship for all persons born or naturalized in this country. In addition, the intent was to make it illegal for the states to deny equal civil rights to those thus made citizens by the provision that no state was to "deprive any person of life, liberty, or property without due process of law" or to "deny to any person within its jurisdiction the equal protection of the laws." These two clauses of the Fourteenth Amendment were completely to transform the American constitutional system. Much of the stuff of our constitutional law in the century that has followed has, in truth, been in the nature of mere gloss upon those two pregnant provisions.

To understand the true impact of the Fourteenth Amendment, one should understand the situation with regard to constitutional protection of civil rights before the Civil War. The only part of the antebellum Constitution that was relevant to such protection was the Bill of Rights and, before the Civil War, it was of little practical effect as a restraint upon governmental power. It should not be forgotten, in the first place, that the first amendments to the organic instrument were applicable only as restrictions upon the federal government. So the Supreme Court had held in one of Chief Justice John Marshall's last important opinions—that delivered in *Barron* v. *Baltimore,* 7 Pet. 243 (1833)—and its decision to that effect was never questioned. This meant that the federal Constitution was, prior to the Civil War, of small moment as a curb upon state infringements upon civil rights.

In the actual operation of the constitutional system, during the first years of the Republic, there was little occasion for application of the guaranties

181

contained in the Bill of Rights against the federal government. That was the case because there were then relatively few interferences from Washington with the personal and property rights of the individual. It is true that the danger of abridgement of such rights has always existed at the state and local levels. Until the Civil War, nevertheless, it was felt that such danger could be dealt with adequately through enforcement by the states of their own organic guaranties.

It was after the Civil War that demand arose for national protection against alleged abuses of state power. The Civil War itself clearly marked a crucial turning point in American development, the true import of which we are only now beginning to comprehend. As such, it was bound to have important constitutional, as well as other, effects. By far the most important of these was the inclusion in the Constitution of the guaranties contained in the post-Civil War amendments, particularly the Fourteenth Amendment. It was that amendment which made the protection of life, liberty, and property a national responsibility—federalizing, as it were, the vindication of individual rights throughout the land.

From a constitutional point of view, the adoption of the Fourteenth Amendment was of cardinal consequence. Like the victory of the North during the war itself, it constituted the culmination of the nationalistic theory which had first taken root eighty years earlier in Philadelphia.

From the founding of the Republic to the end of the Civil War, it was the states which were the primary guardians of the rights and liberties of their citizens, and they alone could determine the character and extent of such rights. That was true because the federal Bill of Rights, as we emphasized, was binding upon the federal government alone—not the states. As far as the federal Constitution was concerned, the states were free to encroach upon civil rights as they chose. With the adoption of the Fourteenth Amendment, all this was changed. That amendment called upon the national government to protect the citizens of a state against the state itself. Thenceforth, the safeguarding of civil rights was to become primarily a federal function.

Before Fort Sumter, the great theme in American constitutional history was the nation-state problem. Nation and states all too often appeared to confront each other as equals, and all was overshadowed by the danger that centrifugal forces would tear the nation apart. The surrender at Appomattox put an end to such danger. Thenceforth, the Union was, as the highest bench itself put it, in 1869, "indestructible" and the supremacy of federal power was insured. The law could now turn from the federal-state problem which had been resolved by the Union victory. The focus of constitutional concern could be transferred from the protection of federal power to the safeguarding of individual rights against governmental power.

Yet, even when the Fourteenth Amendment began to be given effect as a restraint upon state power, its impact was almost entirely confined to the economic sphere. When the Supreme Court came over to the view that the Fourteenth Amendment was intended to work an essential change in the organic framework, its decisions on the matter all but limited the change effected to the area of property rights. Such limitations may have been understandable in an era of explosive industrial expansion, which so drastically altered the whole social and economic fabric. In such an era, it was not unnatural for the dominant emphasis to be placed upon the proper relationship between government and business. To the law, as to the society which it mirrored, the danger that state sovereignty would impair the power of the nation was replaced by the danger that government would unduly impede industry in its destined economic conquest of a continent.

The result was that the Fourteenth Amendment was converted into a Magna Carta for business, in place of the Great Charter for individual rights which its framers had intended. For the next half century, property rather than personal rights were the primary concern of the courts. In 1922, a federal judge could state, "It should be remembered that of the three fundamental principles which underlie government, and for which government exists, the protection of life, liberty, and property, the chief of these is property." [*Childrens Hospital* v. *Adkins*, 284 Fed. 613, 622 D. C. Cir. (1922)]

If such judicial comment was not at variance with reality in 1922, the same is no longer true. The constitutional emphasis in our own day has shifted to one of ever growing concern for "life and liberty," as the really basic rights which the Constitution was meant to safeguard. The earlier stress upon the protection of *property* rights against what were conceived as governmental violations of due process has given way to one which has increasingly focused on *personal* rights. It is not, indeed, too much to say that the Fourteenth Amendment has now become (as its framers intended), in its most important aspect, the shield of individual liberties throughout the nation. Civil rights have become the very stuff of which our constitutional law is now made.

The shift in emphasis from property to personal rights makes the material which follows on the legislative history of the Fourteenth Amendment of particular pertinence. A knowledge of such history is essential to an understanding of what the men who framed and voted for the amendment intended it to accomplish. Such understanding is necessary, too, for a judgment on whether the Supreme Court has construed the amendment in accordance with the intent expressed by its framers. The legislative history is of special interest to one concerned with the high Court's recent change in construction. The earlier restrictive interpretation in the field of civil rights (which made equal protection a mere slogan for the Negro) has been replaced by a more hospitable approach which makes of the equal protection clause a Great Charter for civil rights, and also gives to Congress the broadest powers to enforce the civil rights provisions of section one.

AMENDMENT XIV

Proposed: June 16, 1866
Ratified: July 28, 1868

SEC. 1. All persons born or naturalized in the United States, and subject to the jurisdiction thereof, are citizens of the United States and of the State wherein they reside. No State shall make or enforce any law which shall abridge the privileges or immunities of citizens of the United States; nor shall any State deprive any person of life, liberty, or property, without due process of law, nor deny to any person within its jurisdiction the equal protection of the laws.

SEC. 2. Representatives shall be apportioned among the several States according to their respective numbers, counting the whole number of persons in each State, excluding Indians not taxed. But when the right to vote at any election for the choice of electors for President and Vice-President of the United States, representatives in Congress, the executive and judicial officers of a State, or the members of the legislature thereof, is denied to any of the male inhabitants of such State, being twenty-one years of age, and citizens of the United States, or in any way abridged, except for participation in rebellion or other crime, the basis of representation therein shall be reduced in the proportion which the number of such male citizens shall bear to the whole number of male citizens twenty-one years of age in such State.

SEC. 3. No person shall be a senator or representative in Congress, or elector of President and Vice-President, or hold any office, civil or military, under the United States, or under any State, who, having previously taken an oath, as a member of Congress, or as an officer of the United States, or as a member of any State legislature, or as an executive or judicial officer of any State, to support the Constitution of the United States, shall have engaged in insurrection or rebellion against the same, or given aid or comfort to the enemies thereof. But Congress may, by a vote of two-thirds of each house, remove such disability.

SEC. 4. The validity of the public debt of the United States, authorized by law, including debts incurred for payment of pensions and bounties for services in suppressing insurrection or rebellion, shall not be questioned. But neither the United States nor any State shall assume or pay any debt or obligation incurred in aid of insurrection or rebellion against the United States, or any claim for the loss or emancipation of any slave; but all such debts, obligations and claims shall be held illegal and void.

SEC. 5. The Congress shall have power to enforce, by appropriate legislation, the provisions of this article.

Commentary

The Fourteenth Amendment has its origin in the resolution offered by Congressman Thaddeus Stevens [R., Pa.] on December 4, 1865—the day on which the Thirty-ninth Congress convened for its first session—to create a Joint Committee of nine representatives and six senators to "inquire into the condition of the States which formed the so-called Confederate States of America, and report whether they, or any of them, are entitled to be represented in either house of Congress." This measure was adopted on December 13, and brought into being the Joint Committee on Reconstruction (popularly known as the "Committee of Fifteen"), vested with authority "to report at any time, by bill or otherwise." It was in this Committee that the Fourteenth Amendment originated.

The Joint Committee interpreted its broad mandate to include the drafting of constitutional amendments. Among these were proposed amendments submitted at the Committee's third meeting, on January 12, 1866, by Representatives John Bingham [R., Ohio] and Thaddeus Stevens. Their proposals sought to ensure to the newly emancipated Negro equality with the white in the operation of the laws. The Bingham draft is of particular interest both because of the key role played by its author in the writing of section 1 of the Fourteenth Amendment and the fact that it contained the first use of the phrase "equal protection" in a proposed constitutional provision.

The proposals were referred to a subcommittee, which, on January 20, reported a new draft of the Bingham version. This was rejected by the Committee and a new version was reported by Bingham on January 27. This poorly drafted proposal was also not approved by the Committee. Then, on February 3, Bingham moved a new draft as a substitute amendment. This measure was accepted by the Committee and was introduced in each House on February 13.

The following extracts from the Journal of the Joint Committee on Reconstruction trace the draft constitutional amendments referred to from their first submission on January 12, 1866, to the Committee approval of the Bingham draft on February 3. They should be read for what they tell us about the developing language of the Fourteenth Amendment. In particular, we should note the improvements made in the proposed drafts. Yet it is fair to say that even the February 3 version reported to Congress is much inferior to the amendment finally voted, even though it had (as the parentheses inserted by Bingham indicate) come to use language adapted from the original Constitution—thus pointing the way to the seminal inclusion of a due process clause such as that contained in the Fifth Amendment.

THE ORIGINS

The Joint Committee on Reconstruction
House of Representatives-39th Congress, 1st Session
1865-1867

December 4, 1865.

On motion of Mr. Stevens:

Be it resolved, by the Senate and House of Representatives in Congress assembled, That a joint committee of fifteen members shall be appointed, nine of whom shall be members of the House, and six members of the Senate, who shall inquire into the condition of the States which formed the so-called Confederate States of America, and report whether they, or any of them, are entitled to be represented in either House of Congress, with leave to report at any time, by bill or otherwise; and until such report shall have been made, and finally acted on by Congress, no member shall be received into either House from any of the so-called Confederate States; and all papers relating to the representation of said States shall be referred to the said Committee without debate.

Attest,

Edw'd McPherson, Clerk.

December 12, 1865.

Amended in the Senate, on motion of Mr. Anthony, so as to read,

Resolved by the House of Representatives, (the Senate concurring) That a joint committee of fifteen members shall be appointed, nine of whom shall be members of the House, and six members of the Senate, who shall inquire into the condition of the States which formed the so-called Confederate States of America, and report whether they, or any of them, are entitled to be represented in either House of Congress, with leave to report at any time, by bill or otherwise.

Attest,

J. W. Forney, Secretary.

Dec. 13, 1865.

In the House of Representatives, on motion of Mr. Stevens, the amendments of the Senate were concurred in.

Attest,

Edw'd McPherson, Clerk.

Members on the part of the Senate.
Mr. William P. Fessenden, of Maine.
Mr. James W. Grimes, of Iowa.

Mr. Ira Harris, of New York.
Mr. Jacob M. Howard, of Michigan.
Mr. Reverdy Johnson, of Maryland.
and Mr. George H. Williams, of Oregon.
Members on the part of the House of Rep's.
Mr. Thaddeus Stevens, of Penn'a.
Mr. Elihu B. Washburne, of Illinois.
Mr. Justin S. Morrill, of Vermont.
Mr. Henry Grider, of Kentucky.
Mr. John A. Bingham, of Ohio.
Mr. Roscoe Conkling, of New York.
Mr. George S. Boutwell, of Massachusetts.
Mr. Henry T. Blow, of Missouri.
and Mr. Andrew J. Rogers, of New Jersey.

Friday, January 12, 1866.

The committee met pursuant to adjournment; absent Mr. Rogers. . . .

Mr. Morrill submitted the following:

Ordered, That a sub-committee, to consist of five members, including the Chairman of the Committee on the part of the Senate, and the Chairman of the Committee on the part of the House, (Messrs. Fessenden and Stevens) be appointed, to which shall be referred the various propositions submitted by members of this Committee in relation to apportionment of representatives in Congress, with instructions to prepare and report to this Committee a proposition upon that subject.

The motion was agreed to.

Mr. Bingham submitted the following proposed amendment of the Constitution of the United States, and moved that the same be referred to the sub-committee just authorized:

The Congress shall have power to make all laws necessary and proper to secure to all persons in every state within this Union equal protection in their rights of life, liberty and property.

The motion was agreed to.

Mr. Stevens submitted the following proposed amendment of the Constitution, and moved that the same be referred to the sub-committee just authorized:

All laws, state or national, shall operate impartially and equally on all persons without regard to race or color.

The motion was agreed to.

On motion of Mr. Stevens:

Ordered, That the remaining members of the sub-committee, authorized at this meeting, be appointed by the Chairman of the Joint Committee.

The motion was agreed to.

The Chairman announced the following as members of the sub-committee:

Messrs. Fessenden and Stevens (named in the order of the Joint Committee) and Messrs. Howard, Conkling and Bingham.

On motion of Mr. Stevens:

Ordered, That the Chairman be instructed to introduce into the Senate a concurrent resolution authorizing the Joint Committee to send for persons and papers. . . .

Saturday, January 20, 1866.

The committee met pursuant to call of its Chairman; absent, Mr. Johnson. . . .

The Chairman, from the sub-committee on the basis of representation, reported that the sub-committee had directed him to report the following for the action of the Joint Committee; the first two as alternative propositions, one of which, with the third proposition, to be recommended to Congress for adoption:

"*Resolved,* by the Senate and House of Representatives of the United States of America in Congress assembled, two-thirds of both Houses concurring, that the following Articles be proposed to the Legislatures of the several States, as amendments to the Constitution of the United States, which, when they, or either of them, shall be ratified by three-fourths of the said Legislatures, shall be valid as part of said Constitution; viz:

ARTICLE A. Representatives and direct taxes shall be apportioned among the several States within this Union, according to the respective numbers of citizens of the United States in each State; and all provisions in the Constitution or laws of any State, whereby any distinction is made in political or civil rights or privileges, on account of race, creed or color, shall be inoperative and void.

Or the following:

ARTICLE B. Representatives and direct taxes shall be apportioned among the several States which may be included within this Union, according to their respective numbers, counting the whole number of citizens of the United States in each State; provided that, whenever the elective franchise shall be denied or abridged in any State on account of race, creed or color, all persons of such race, creed or color, shall be excluded from the basis of representation.

ARTICLE C. Congress shall have power to make all laws necessary and proper to secure to all citizens of the United States, in every State, the same political rights and privileges; and to all persons in every State equal protection in the enjoyment of life, liberty and property."

The Joint Committee proceeded to consider the report of the sub-committee.

Mr. Stevens moved that the last article be separated from whichever of the other two should be adopted by the Committee, and be considered by itself.

The question was taken by yeas and nays, and decided in the affirmative, yeas 10, nays 4. . . .

Wednesday, January 24, 1866.

The Committee met pursuant to call of its Chairman; absent Messrs. Harris and Johnson. . . .

The Committee proceeded to the consideration of the following amendment to the Constitution proposed by the sub-committee on the basis of representation:

"Congress shall have power to make all laws necessary and proper to secure to all citizens of the United States in each State the same political rights and privileges; and to all persons in every State equal protection in the enjoyment of life, liberty and property."

Mr. Howard moved to amend by inserting the words "and elective" after the word "political."

The question was taken by yeas and nays, and decided in the negative, yeas 2, nays 10, absent and not voting 3, as follows:

Yeas—Messrs, Howard and Rogers—2.

Nays—The Chairman, Messrs. Williams, Stevens, Washburne, Morrill, Grider, Bingham, Conkling, Boutwell and Blow—10.

Absent and not voting—Messrs. Grimes, Harris and Johnson.

So the amendment was not agreed to. . . .

Saturday, January 27, 1866.

The Committee met pursuant to the call of its Chairman; absent Messrs. Blow and Rogers.

Mr. Bingham from the sub-committee on the powers of Congress, reported back the proposed amendment of the Constitution, referred to them, in the following form:

"Congress shall have power to make all laws which shall be necessary and proper to secure all persons in every state full protection in the enjoyment of life, liberty and property; and to all citizens of the United States in any State the same immunities and also equal political rights and privileges."

The Chairman moved to strike out the word "also" in the last clause.

The motion was agreed to.

Mr. Johnson moved to amend the last clause by striking out the word "any" and inserting the word "every" before the word "state."

The motion was agreed to.

Mr. Johnson moved to strike out the word "all" before the word "laws."

The motion was agreed to.

Mr. Johnson moved to strike out the last clause of the proposed amendment.

The question was taken by yeas and nays, and it was decided in the negative, yeas 4, nays 6, absent and not voting 5, as follows:

Yeas—Messrs. Harris, Johnson, Grider and Conkling—4.

Nays—The Chairman, Messrs. Williams, Stevens, Morrill, Bingham and Boutwell—6.

Absent and not voting—Messrs. Grimes, Howard, Washburne, Blow and Rogers—5.

So the amendment was not agreed to. . . .

Saturday, February 3, 1866.

The Committee met pursuant to call of its Chairman; absent Messrs. Johnson and Blow.

The Committee resumed the consideration of the prosed amendment of the Constitution of the United States, reported from the sub-committee on powers of Congress; the same having been amended, when last under consideration by the Committee (January 27, 1866) to read as follows:

"Congress shall have power to make laws which shall be necessary and proper to secure to all persons in every State full protection in the enjoyment of life, liberty and property; and to citizens of the United States in every State the same immunities, and equal political rights and privileges."

Mr. Bingham moved the following as a substitute by way of amendment:

"The Congress shall have power to make all laws which shall be necessary and proper to secure to the citizens of each state all privileges and immunities of citizens in the several states (Art. 4, Sec. 2); and to all persons in the several States equal protection in the rights of life, liberty and property (5th Amendment)."

After discussion,

The question was taken by yeas and nays, and it was determined in the affirmative, yeas 7, nays 6, absent and not voting 2, as follows:

Yeas—Messrs. Howard, Williams, Washburne, Morrill, Bingham, Boutwell and Rogers—7.

Nays—The Chairman, Messrs. Grimes, Harris, Stevens, Grider and Conkling—6.

Absent and not voting—Messrs. Johnson and Blow—2.

So the amendment was agreed to. . . .

Saturday, February 10, 1866.

The Committee met pursuant to the call of its Chairman; absent Mr. Washburne.

The Committee resumed the consideration of the joint resolution proposing an amendment to the Constitution of the United States, as amended on motion of Mr. Bingham at the last meeting.

Mr. Stevens moved that the same be reported to the two Houses of Congress.

The question was taken by yeas and nays, and it was decided in the affirmative, yeas 9, nays 5. . . .

Commentary

On February 26, 1866, the proposed amendment drafted by Congressman Bingham, approved by the Joint Committee on Reconstruction on February 3, and introduced in each House on February 13, came up for debate in the House. After three days of debate, it was evident that the Bingham resolution could not secure the necessary two-thirds majority, and its further consideration was deferred. In effect, this particular proposal was never considered again, though it did appear a few weeks later, phrased differently, as Section 1 of the Fourteenth Amendment.

The February 26-8 debate on the Bingham proposal remains of interest because of the important speeches made by Bingham in support of his amendment. Bingham himself was a central figure in the drafting of the Fourteenth Amendment; Justice Hugo Black has, indeed, said that "Bingham may, without extravagance, be called the Madison of the first section of the Fourteenth Amendment." As such, Bingham's point of view is of particular significance to one concerned with the legislative history of the Fourteenth Amendment.

In assessing the following extracts from Bingham's addresses defending his amendment, it should be borne in mind that his proposal, unlike the Fourteenth Amendment itself, was framed only in terms of a grant of power to Congress to secure the privileges and immunities of state citizens and equal protection for all persons. His speeches indicate that he intended to give Congress the authority to protect the rights of life, liberty, and property. Had this Bingham proposal been adopted, the subsequent controversy over the reach of the Fourteenth Amendment would have been avoided. That is true because the Bingham draft would not, of its own force, have been a restriction on state action, thus barring the need for judicial interpretation of the scope of the amendment in the absence of congressional action. In addition, the power given to Congress would not have been limited to "state action" but could have reached individual discriminatory action. Under the broad grant to Congress in the Bingham resolution, there could have been no decision such as that in the 1883 *Civil Rights Cases* (*infra* p. 780). Nor could there have been any doubt about the congressional power to enforce the Bill of Rights in the states.

Bingham's speeches themselves indicate some confusion in his mind on the crucial question of the force of the Bill of Rights upon the states. He seems to assert that its provisions have always been binding, but Congress had not been given power to force the states to observe them. Such assertion is plainly inaccurate, in view of the established law that the Bill of Rights was a limitation only upon the federal government. It is also not clear whether Bingham, in referring to "this immortal bill of rights embodied in the Constitution" was talking, in the precise legal sense, of the first eight amendments and their specific provisions. It should, at the same time, be noted how the draft amendment had progressed from a provision intended to protect the emancipated Negro to one whose broad language would cover all persons in the United States.

THE DEBATE

JOHN BINGHAM [R., OHIO]. From the select joint committee on reconstruction, reported back a joint resolution (H. R. No. 63) proposing an amendment to the Constitution of the United States.

The joint resolution was read, as follows:

Resolved by the Senate and House of Representatives of the United States of America in Congress assembled, (two thirds of both Houses concurring,) That the following article be proposed to the Legislatures of the several States as an amendment to the Constitution of the United States, which, when ratified by three fourths of the said Legislatures, shall be valid as part of said Constitution, namely:

ARTICLE

The Congress shall have power to make all laws which shall be necessary and proper to secure to the citizens of each State all privileges and immunities of citizens in the several States, and to all persons in the several States equal protection in the rights of life, liberty, and property.

Mr. Speaker, this resolution, as the House is aware, has received its first and second readings. It comes back from the committee in the precise form in which it was originally reported. I do not propose at present to detain the House with any very extended remarks in support of it. I ask, however, the attention of the House to the fact that the amendment proposed stands in the very words of the Constitution of the United States as it came to us from the hands of its illustrious framers. Every word of the proposed amendment is to-day in the Constitution of our country, save the words conferring the express grant of power upon the Congress of the United States. The residue of the resolution, as the House will see by a reference to the Constitution, is the language of the second section of the fourth article, and of a portion of the fifth amendment adopted by the First Congress in 1789, and made part of the Constitution of the country. The language of the second section of the fourth article is—

The citizens of each State shall be entitled to all privileges and immunities of citizens in the several States.

The fifth article of the amendment provides that—

No person shall be deprived of life, liberty, or property, without due process of law.

Sir, it has been the want of the Republic that there was not an express grant of power in the Constitution to enable the whole people of every State, by congressional enactment, to enforce obedience to these requirements of the Constitution. Nothing can be plainer to thoughtful men than that if the

193

grant of power had been originally conferred upon the Congress of the nation, and legislation had been upon your statute-books to enforce these requirements of the Constitution in every State, that rebellion, which has scarred and blasted the land, would have been an impossibility.

I ask the attention of the House to the further consideration that the proposed amendment does not impose upon any State of the Union, or any citizen of any State of the Union, any obligation which is not now enjoined upon them by the very letter of the Constitution. I need not remind gentlemen here that the Constitution, as originally framed, and as adopted by the whole people of this country, provides that—

This Constitution, and the laws of the United States which shall be made in pursuance thereof, and all treaties made, or which shall be made, under the authority of the United States, shall be the supreme law of the land; and the judges in every State shall be bound thereby, anything in the constitution or laws of any State to the contrary notwithstanding.

Could words be stronger, could words be more forceful, to enjoin upon every officer of every State the obligation to obey these great provisions of the Constitution, in their letter and their spirit? I submit to the judgment of the House, that it is impossible for mortal man to frame a formula of words more obligatory than those already in that instrument, enjoining this great duty upon the several States and the several officers of every State in the Union.

And, sir, it is equally clear by every construction of the Constitution, its contemporaneous construction, its continued construction, legislative, executive, and judicial, that these great provisions of the Constitution, this immortal bill of rights embodied in the Constitution, rested for its execution and enforcement hitherto upon the fidelity of the States. The House knows, sir, the country knows, the civilized world knows, that the legislative, executive, and judicial officers of eleven States within this Union within the last five years, in utter disregard of these injunctions of your Constitution, in utter disregard of that official oath which the Constitution required they should severally take and faithfully keep when they entered upon the discharge of their respective duties, have violated in every sense of the word these provisions of the Constitution of the United States, the enforcement of which are absolutely essential to American nationality.

By order, then, of the committee, sir, and for the purpose of giving to the whole people the care in future of the unity of the Government which constitutes us one people, and without which American nationality would cease to be, I propose the adoption of this amendment to the House, and through the House I press it upon the consideration of the loyal people of the whole country. . . .

WILLIAM HIGBY [R., CAL.]. Mr. Speaker, I differ from a great many members of this House, and I presume that I shall differ from a great many in authority as to the question of amending the Constitution of the United States. I do not believe in making any amendments that are going by very slow degrees to a proper conclusion. Neither do I believe in making such amendments as will occasion a division in the public mind as to whether any improvement has been made or not. But an amendment that will give strength to the Government of the United States, an increased strength over what it may have now under the present Constitution, will meet with my hearty concurrence.

I understand this joint resolution, should it become part of the Constitution of the United States, will only have the effect to give vitality and life to portions of the Constitution that probably were intended from the beginning to have life and vitality, but which have received such a construction that they have been entirely ignored and have become as dead matter in that instrument. When we read this proposed amendment we will think it already embraced in the Constitution, but so scattered through different portions of it that it has no life or energy. But by condensing it, as we find it in this joint resolution, should it become a portion of the Constitution, it will then become operative and beneficial.

Mr. Speaker, the article proposed, the adoption of which by two thirds of this House and of the other branch of Congress would be only a preliminary step to its becoming a part of the Constitution, is in these words:

The Congress shall have power to make all laws which shall be necessary and proper to secure to the citizens of each State all privileges and immunities of citizens in the several States, and to all persons in the several States equal protection in the rights of life, liberty, and property.

Well, sir, I find in the beginning of the eighth section of the first article the words, "Congress shall have power;" and in the latter portion of the same section are the words, "to make all laws which shall be necessary and proper." "To secure to" are new words embraced in this amendment. "The citizens of each State," and "all privileges and immunities of citizens in the several States," are words which are found in the Constitution in another place.

The fifth article of the amendments of our present Constitution provides that, "No person shall be deprived of life, liberty, or property without due process of law."

The language of this proposed amendment is very little different. It provides that Congress shall secure—"To all persons in the several States equal protection in the rights of life, liberty, and property."

Thus, sir, we find by an examination of the Constitution that it was intended to provide in these separate portions precisely what will be provided by this article, should it become a portion of the Constitution.

Why, sir, what force or value is there in article four, section one, of the Constitution, in these words:

The citizens of each State shall be entitled to all privileges and immunities of citizens of the several States.

If that provision had been enforced heretofore, how different would have been the condition of the various States of this Union. Had that provision been enforced, a citizen of New York would have been treated as a citizen in the State of South Carolina; a citizen of Massachusetts would have been regarded as a citizen in the State of Mississippi or Louisiana. The man who was a citizen in one State would have been considered and respected as a citizen in every other State of the Union.

But, sir, that provision of the Constitution has been trampled under foot; it has been considered in certain States of this Union as nugatory and of no force whatever. The intent of this amendment is to give force and effect and vitality to that provision of the Constitution which has been regarded heretofore as nugatory and powerless. . . .

Now, sir, the Government of the United States cannot do away with the force of the exceptional portion of that article [i.e., the Thirteenth Amendment] which allows a State to frame its laws so that a man may be sold into slavery "as a punishment for crime." The legislation of a State may prescribe as the penalty for a particular offense, that the offender shall pay a fine, or be imprisoned in the State prison, or be sold into slavery. Is there any power in the Government of the United States by which it can declare that a State shall punish crime in only one certain way? Is there in this Union a single State whose criminal code does not provide alternative penalties? The law of my own State provides that for an assault with a deadly weapon with an intent to commit bodily injury, the offender on conviction may be sent to the State prison for two years, or be fined in the sum of $5,000. If the judge who pronounces the sentence sees fit to impose a fine, the offender, if he be able to pay it, suffers no other penalty. By paying the fine, he saves himself from imprisonment.

Now, let me suppose a case which not only may happen, but has happened, in the southern States. Grant that the laws must be made equal; that they must be administered equally upon all classes, without regard to color or race. Suppose that a State enacts a provision that a party guilty of a particular offense shall, on conviction, be imprisoned in the State prison for two years or be sold into slavery. Such a provision operates equally upon all classes, but the judge could discriminate, and could say to the white offender, "Go to the State prison," while he could say to the black man, "Go into slavery." You cannot prevent such things as that by any legislation in these Halls. Such things are being done now in the southern States, as organized under executive authority. Let Congress admit that those are States of this Union, with the right of representation, and we shall have given that system an irrevocable sanction beyond the future control of the Government of the United States, because those States are acting under the amendment of the

Constitution, and can pass such laws in spite of anything which we may do in this Hall, and you leave slavery sealed upon the Government. That is one of the results, if the Executive is right in his position. We are tied and bound, and we cannot get by it; but if it requires legislation, then we hold the power. But we cannot, except we can get through an amendment of the character of the one now pending before this body, if they are States now, and have the right to come upon this floor, and we can only judge of the elections, returns, and qualifications of our own members. . . .

WILLIAM NIBLACK [R., IND.]. I beg to inquire of the gentleman whether the amendment to the Constitution he is advocating is intended or calculated to have any effect on the condition of the Chinamen in California. If it is to have any effect upon the Chinese population there, let us know what effect it is to have?

MR. HIGBY. If the Government will annul the treaty with China, the people of California will get rid of the Chinese. I know something of the Chinese, and do not believe the gentleman from Indiana does.

MR. NIBLACK. I want information.

MR. HIGBY. The Chinese are nothing but a pagan race. They are an enigma to me, although I have lived among them for fifteen years. You cannot make good citizens of them; they do not learn the language of the country; and you can communicate with them only with the greatest difficulty, as their language is the most difficult of all those spoken; they even dig up their dead while decaying in their graves, strip the putrid flesh from the bones, and transport the bones back to China. They bring their clay and wooden gods with them to this country, and as we are a free and tolerant people, we permit them to bow down and worship them.

Sir, they do not propagate in our country. A generation is not growing up in the State, except an insignificant few in comparison with the great number among us. Judging from the daily exhibition in our streets, and the well established repute among their females, virtue is an exception to the general rule. They buy and sell their women like cattle, and the trade is mostly for the purpose of prostitution. That is their character. You cannot make citizens of them. . . .

MR. NIBLACK. I understand that gentlemen on the other side have taken the position that intelligence is not at all necessary to the exercise of the right of voting; that a man, from the fact of belonging to the human race, is entitled to vote and to be called a man and brother. I understand them to urge it is a question of manhood and not a question of morals, not a question of religion. If a Chinaman is one of the human race, why should he be degraded below the negro? Why should he not receive the same right as the negro? I should like to understand it. The negro is of pagan race, and is a pagan before he comes here.

MR. HIGBY. But he is not a pagan now. The negro is as much a native of this country as the gentleman or myself. I will say, from what I have seen of the gentleman, when he knows that people as well as I do, I would abide by his judgment in reference to the position they should take in any civilized community.

MR. NIBLACK. One word. The gentleman is very kind. I have no difficulty myself in arriving at a conclusion upon this question; and I was aware that the gentleman knew more about the Chinese people in this country and in the country from which they come than I do. I asked for information. I want to understand why we should exclude one race and include another, why we should deny to these people the right of naturalization, for instance, and allow it to others.

MR. HIGBY. I will tell him. They are foreigners and the negro is a native.

MR. NIBLACK. Why do you not naturalize them?

MR. HIGBY. I have given a very good reason. . . .

ROBERT HALE [R., N.Y.]. . . . it does seem to me, with the little knowledge that I possess of constitutional law, and with the very brief and hasty examination that I have been enabled to give to this matter, that no weight or authority of members of this House to-day ought to bring us to pass this amendment without at least a most careful and scrutinizing examination. It does seem to me that the tenor and effect of the amendment proposed here by this committee is to bring about a more radical change in the system of this Government, to institute a wider departure from the theory upon which our fathers formed it than ever before was proposed in any legislative or constitutional assembly. Listening to the remarks of the distinguished member of the committee [Mr. Bingham] who reported this joint resolution to the House, one would be led to think that this amendment was a subject of the most trivial consequence. He tells us, and tells us with an air of gravity that I could not but admire, that the words of the resolution are all in the Constitution as it stands, with the single exception of the power given to Congress to legislate. A very important exception, it strikes me, but one to which the gentleman seems to attach very little weight.

My friend from California, [Mr. Higby], who addressed the House this morning in support of this resolution of the committee, (and I speak of that gentleman with the most entire respect and friendship,) went a little further, and succeeded in showing that the exception of the honorable gentleman from Ohio [Mr. Bingham] was unnecessary; for, said the gentleman from California, the words of this joint resolution are all in the Constitution as it now stands. He turns to the eighth section of the first article, and in the first clause of it he finds the words "the Congress shall have power." He turns to the last clause of the same section, and there he finds the words "to make all laws which shall be necessary and proper." He turns to the second section of the fourth article, and there finds the words: "The citizens of each State shall be entitled to all privileges and immunities of citizens in the several States."

He turns to the fifth article of the amendments to the Constitution, and there finds the words: "No person shall be deprived of life, liberty, or property without due process of law."

Thus, he says, you have included in the Constitution as it stands all the words of the amendment proposed by the committee. The ingenuity of the argument was admirable. I never heard it paralleled except in the case of the gentleman who undertook to justify suicide from the Scripture by quoting two texts: "Judas went and hanged himself;" "Go thou and do likewise."

Now, Mr. Speaker, what is the theory of our Constitution? I will not undertake to elaborate this matter too far; but briefly, imperfectly, and within very scanty limits, let me attempt an answer to this question. In general terms, is it not that all powers relating to the existence and sovereinty of the nation, powers relating to our foreign relations, powers relating to peace and war, to the enforcement of the law of nations and international law, are the powers given to Congress and to the Federal Government by the Constitution, while all powers having reference to the relation of the individual to the municipal government, the powers of local jurisdiction and legislation, are in general reserved to the States?

What is the effect of the amendment which the committee on reconstruction propose for the sanction of this House and the States of the Union? I submit that it is in effect a provision under which all State legislation, in its codes of civil and criminal jurisprudence and procedure, affecting the individual citizen, may be overridden, may be repealed or abolished, and the law of Congress established instead. I maintain that in this respect it is an utter departure from every principle ever dreamed of by the men who framed our Constitution.

THADDEUS STEVENS [R., PA.]. Does the gentleman mean to say that, under this provision, Congress could interfere in any case where the legislation of a State was equal, impartial to all? Or is it not simply to provide that, where any State makes a distinction in the same law between different classes of individuals, Congress shall have power to correct such discrimination and inequality? Does this proposition mean anything more than that?

MR. HALE. I will answer the gentleman. In my judgment it does go much further than the remarks of the gentleman would imply; but even if it goes no further than that—and I will discuss this point more fully before I conclude—it is still open to the same objection, that it proposes an entire departure from the theory of the Federal Government in meddling with these matters of State jurisdiction at all.

I now come directly, as I was coming in due order when the gentleman's very pertinent inquiry arrested my attention, to the consideration whether this is as has been maintained by the gentleman who reported the resolution, and by others, simply a provision for the equality of individual citizens before the laws of the several States. I submit, Mr. Speaker, that it means much more than that. Let me read the language of the resolution, striking out, for the purpose of making it more clear, that part which is simply irrelevant to the matter which I here discuss:

> The Congress shall have power to make all laws which shall be necessary and proper to secure to all persons in the several States equal protection in the rights of life, liberty, and property.

Now, I say to the gentleman from Pennsylvania [Mr. Stevens] that reading the language in its grammatical and legal construction it is a grant of the fullest and most ample power to Congress to make all laws "necessary and proper to secure to all persons in the several States protection in the rights of life, liberty, and property," with the simple proviso that such protection shall be equal. It is not a mere provision that when the States undertake to give protection which is unequal Congress may equalize it; it is a grant of power in general terms—a grant of the right to legislate for the protection of life, liberty, and property, simply qualified with the condition that it shall be equal legislation. That is my construction of the proposition as it stands here. It may differ from that of other gentlemen. . . .

Mr. Speaker, let me go a little further here. If it be true that the construction of this amendment, which I understand to be claimed by the gentleman from Ohio, [Mr. Bingham,] who introduced it, and which I infer from his question is claimed by the gentleman from Pennsylvania, [Mr. Stevens;] if it be true that that is the true construction of this article, is it not even then introducing a power never before intended to be conferred upon Congress? For we all know it is true that probably every State in this Union fails to give equal protection to all persons within its borders in the rights of life, liberty, and property. It may be a fault in the States that they do not do it. A reformation may be desirable, but by the doctrines of the school of politics in which I have been brought up, and which I have been taught to regard was the best school of political rights and duties in this Union, reforms of this character should come from the States, and not be forced upon them by the centralized power of the Federal Government.

Take a single case by way of illustration, and I take it simply to illustrate the point, without expressing any opinion whatever on the desirability or undesirability of a change in regard to it. Take the case of the rights of married women; did any one ever assume that Congress was to to be invested with the power to legislate on that subject, and to say that married women, in regard to their rights of property, should stand on the same footing with men and unmarried women? There is not a State in the Union where disability of married women in relation to the rights of property does not to a greater or less extent still exist. Many of the States have taken steps for the partial abolition of that distinction in years past, some to a greater extent and others to a less. But I apprehend there is not to-day a State in the Union where there is not a distinction between the rights of married women, as to property, and the rights of *femmes sole* and men.

MR. STEVENS. If I do not interrupt the gentleman I will say a word. When a distinction is made between two married people or two *femmes sole*, then it is unequal legislation; but where all of the same class are dealt with in the same way then there is no pretense of inequality.

MR. HALE. The gentleman will pardon me; his argument seems to me to be more specious than sound. The language of the section under consideration gives to *all persons* equal protection. Now, if that means you shall extend to one married woman the same protection you extend to another, and not the same you extend to unmarried women or men, then by parity of reasoning it will be sufficient if you extend to one negro the same rights you do to another, but not those you extend to a white man. I think, if the gentleman from Pennsylvania claims that the resolution only intends that all of a certain class shall have equal protection, such class legislation may certainly as easily satisfy the requirements of this resolution in the case of the negro as in the case of the married woman. The line of distinction is, I take it, quite as broadly marked between negroes and white men as between married and unmarried women.

It was not within the purview of the original Constitution to grant the power of legislation to Congress on subjects of this character. Mr. Speaker, the powers conferred on Congress are all contained in the eighth section of the first article of the Constitution. I ask the House to look at these provisions, their nature, their general scope, the accuracy, precision, and care with which they are defined, and compare them with what I cannot but characterize, with all my respect and deference for the committee on reconstruction, as the extremely vague, loose, and indefinite provisions of the proposed amendment.

By the eighth section of the first article the subjects upon which Congress is to have power to legislate are enumerated. Congress is to have power to lay and collect taxes, duties, imposts, and excises; to pay the debts and provide for the common defense and general welfare of the United States; to borrow money; to regulate commerce with foreign nations, among the several States, and with the Indian tribes, (which are regarded in many respects as foreign nations;) to establish a system of naturalization and bankruptcy; to coin money; fix the standard of weights and measures; provide for the punishment of counterfeiting the coin and securities of the United States; establish post offices and post roads; provide for copyrights and patents; constitute certain judicial tribunals; punish piracy on the high seas outside of the jurisdiction of the States, &c.

Go through that section carefully and you will find no general power granted to Congress to legislate upon matters of a municipal nature, or matters relating to the social or civil rights of citizens of the States, but everywhere it points most strictly and carefully to the legitimate objects for which the national Government was created. And the last clause that is often quoted, and which I have heard quoted to-day in this House, but which is almost as often misquoted as quoted, gives to Congress only the power to make all laws which shall be necessary and proper for the carrying into execution the foregoing powers, and all other powers vested by the Constitution in the Government of the United States, or in any department or officer thereof. In that sweeping, comprehensive clause, as it is ordinarily deemed, covering all the powers essential to carry out the other powers granted by the instrument and the other powers conferred upon any department of the Government of the United States, we find that it is limited directly to these powers; it is not a general power to enact all laws for carrying out the provisions of the Constitution.

Again, the gentleman from Ohio [Mr. Bingham] refers us to the fifth article of the amendments to the Constitution as the basis of the present resolution, and as the source from which he has taken substantially the language of that clause of the proposed amendment I am considering. Now, what are these amendments to the Constitution, numbered from one to ten, one of which is the fifth article in question? What is the nature and object of these articles? They do not contain, from beginning to end, a grant of power anywhere. On the contrary, they are all restrictions of power. They constitute the bill of rights, a bill of rights for the protection of the citizen, and defining and limiting the power of Federal and State legislation. They are not matters upon which legislation can be based. They begin with the proposition that "Congress shall make *no law,*" &c.; and if I were to follow the example of my friend from California, [Mr. Higby], I might perhaps claim that here was a sufficient prohibition against the legislation sought to be provided for by this amendment. Throughout they are prohibitions against legislation. Throughout they provide safeguards to be enforced by the courts, and not to be exercised by the Legislature. And they provide in this noble fifth article, among others—provisions which at this time especially deserve the attention of the American people—that no person shall be deprived of life, liberty, or property, without due process of law.

MR. BINGHAM. Will the gentleman refer to the second section of the fourth article?

MR. HALE. The gentleman from Ohio refers me to the second section of the fourth article. I omit the consideration of that section for the reason that my argument is directed exclusively to the consideration of the final clause of the amendment proposed, which is founded on the fifth article of the amendments, without referring at all to the other clause, founded on the section to which the gentleman from Ohio refers me. The last-named section is therefore outside the range of my remarks on this occasion.

Now, I suggest to gentlemen: is it wise at this time, after the experience we have had of the working of this Constitution, with all the reverence in which we have been accustomed to hold it, after having it tested as it has been by this mighty rebellion—through peace, through foreign war, through civil war, having found its strength, its elasticity, its sufficiency for all circumstances and all trials—is it wise for us to alter it thus rashly, to alter it in its most vital and essential principle, to amend it by substituting a new principle for the very soul that animates the system created by it?

MR. BINGHAM. The gentleman will allow me to ask him to point to a single decision. The gentleman says that the sufficiency of the Constitution has been tested and found in the past. I ask him now if he knows of a single decision in which the sufficiency of the Constitution to secure to a party aggrieved in his person within a State the right to protection by the prosecution of a suit, which by the organic law of the State was denied to him, has ever been affirmed, either by Federal statute or Federal decision, or whether the nation has not been dumb in the presence of the organic act of a State which declares that eight hundred thousand natural-born citizens of the United States shall be denied the right to prosecute a suit in their courts, either for the vindication of a right or the redress of a wrong? Where is the decision? I want an answer.

MR. HALE. The gentleman will always get an answer when he asks me a question. It is never necessary for him to accompany his questions with a warning.

I have not been able to prepare a brief for this argument, and therefore I cannot refer the gentleman to any case. As I never claim to be a very learned constitutional lawyer I have no hesitation in making the admission that I do not know of a case where it has ever been decided that the United States Constitution is sufficient for the protection of the liberties of the citizen. But still I have, somehow or other, gone along with the impression that there is that sort of protection thrown over us in some way, whether with or without the sanction of a judicial decision that we are so protected. Of course, I may be entirely mistaken in all this, but I have certainly some how had that impression.

CHARLES ELDREDGE [DEM., WIS.]. I wish to know if the gentleman from Ohio [Mr. Bingham] has found or heard of a case in which the Constitution of the United States has been pronounced to be insufficient?

MR. HALE. I would rather leave these gentlemen to answer one another at some other time, if it will answer their purposes as well.

MR. BINGHAM. I beg leave to say that I am ready to answer the gentleman now, and to produce such a decision, whether the gentleman from New York is or is not.

MR. HALE. This is no doubt a very interesting side issue; but the gentlemen will pardon me if I prefer to go on with my own speech now, and leave them to make theirs in proper order.

I insist that the American people have not yet found that their State governments are insufficient to protect the rights and liberties of the citizen. If the gentleman from Ohio has found it so, I recommend him to emigrate to New York, where he will find it very different.

MR. BINGHAM. The gentleman will excuse me. I do not cast any imputation upon the State of New York. The gentleman knows full well, from conversations I have had with him, that so far as I understand this power, under no possible interpretation can it ever be made to operate in the State of New York while she occupies her present proud position.

MR. HALE. The gentleman has the reply, and I hope he will pardon me for saying that I think he ought not to interrupt me now.

MR. BINGHAM. I ought not to do so, and I do not wish to do it.

MR. HALE. It is claimed that this constitutional amendment is aimed simply and purely toward the protection of "American citizens of African descent" in the States lately in rebellion. I understand that to be the whole intended practical effect of the amendment.

MR. BINGHAM. It is due to the committee that I should say that it is proposed as well to protect the thousands and tens of thousands and hundreds of thousands of loyal white citizens of the United States whose property, by State legislation, has been wrested from them under confiscation, and protect them also against banishment.

MR. HALE. I trust that when the gentleman comes to reply, he will give me as much of his time as he takes of mine. As he has the reply, I do not think he ought to interject his remarks into my speech. I will modify my statement and say that this amendment is intended to apply solely to the eleven States lately in rebellion, so far as any practical benefit to be derived from it is concerned. The gentleman from Ohio can correct me if I am again in error.

MR. BINGHAM. It is to apply to other States also that have in their constitutions and laws to-day provisions in direct violation of every principle of our Constitution.

ANDREW ROGERS [DEM., N.J.]. I suppose the gentleman refers to the State of Indiana?

MR. BINGHAM. I do not know; it may be so. It applies unquestionably to the State of Oregon.

MR. HALE. Then I will again modify my correction and say that it is intended to apply to every State which, in the judgment of the honorable member who introduced this measure, has failed to provide equal protection to life, liberty, and property. And here we come to the very thing for which I denounce this proposition, that it takes away from these States the right to determine for themselves what their institutions shall be. Oregon has not been contumacious toward this Union; Oregon has not been in rebellion; the gentleman has no charge to bring against her, except that she has incorporated into her constitution and laws provisions that to him are distasteful, and which he thinks unjust. I submit that that should never be a question for us to pass upon here in Congress. It is a question under the Constitution of the United States, and under the whole theory of our Government, for the people of Oregon to pass upon and to remedy, if remedy is required, and not for the gentleman from Ohio in his capacity as a member of this House, or for Congress. . . .

Now, I put it to the gentleman [Mr. Bingham] if at a single stride we take such a step as this, if we confer upon the Federal Congress powers, in such vague and general language as this amendment contains, to legislate upon all matters pertaining to the life, liberty, and property of all the inhabitants of the several States, I put it to the gentleman, whom I know sometimes at least to be disposed to criticise this habit of liberal construction, to state where he apprehends that Congress and the courts will stop in the powers they may arrogate to themselves under this proposed amendment.

It has been settled judicially, as well as legislatively, that the words "necessary and proper," which are found in this amendment, as well as in the original Constitution, by no means imply indispensable necessity; that the legislation "necessary" for carrying into execution powers is not the legislation without which the thing cannot be done. But it has been expressly settled that it means simply "needful," "requisite," "conducive to," and under that settled interpretation of his language I ask the gentleman where he will draw the line as to the powers which Congress may exercise as the "necessary and proper" legislation to attain these very general results?

It seems to me, sir, that this is, of all kinds of legislation, the most dangerous. I believe that the tendency in this country has been from the first too much toward the accumulation and strengthening of central Federal power. During the last five years of war and rebellion, that tendency has necessarily and inevitably increased. It must always happen that when the life of the nation is menaced the strength and extent of central power will be augmented. In such emergencies the nation arrogates to itself powers which it never thought of possessing or exercising in time of peace. We have become habituated to yielding to such things as matters of inexorable necessity. I submit to gentlemen whether it is not now time that we should check that current. I believe that this is, of all times the last when we should undertake a radical amendment of the Constitution, so immensely extending the power of the Federal Government, and derogating from the power of the States. . . .

MR. BINGHAM. Mr. Speaker, I approach the discussion of this subject, aware that it will be utterly impossible for me, within the time allotted me by the rules of the House, to do justice to the proposition reported by the joint committee.

I think, sir, that the honorable gentleman from Vermont [Mr. Woodbridge] has uttered words that ought to be considered and accepted by gentlemen of the House, when he says that the action of this Congress in its effect upon the future prosperity of the country will be felt by generations of men after we shall all have paid the debt of nature. I believe, Mr. Speaker, as I have had occasion to say more than once, that the people of the United States have intrusted to the present Congress in some sense the care of the Republic, not only for the present, but for all the hereafter. Your committee, sir, would not have sent to this House for its consideration this proposition but for the conviction that its adoption by Congress and its ratification by the people of the United States is essential to the safety of all the people of every State. I repel the suggestion made here in the heat of debate, that the commmittee or any of its members who favor this proposition seek in any form to mar the Constitution of the country, or take away from any State any right that belongs to it, or from any citizen of any State any right that belongs to him under that Constitution. The proposition pending before the House is simply a proposition to arm the Congress of the United States, by the consent of the people of the United States, with the power to enforce the bill of rights as it stands in the Constitution today. It "hath that extent—no more." It is in these words:

Joint resolution proposing an amendment to the Constitution of the United States.
Resolved by the Senate and House of Representatives of the United States of America in Congress assembled, (two thirds of both Houses concurring.) That the following article be proposed to the Legislatures of the several States as an amendment to the Constitution of the United States, which, when ratified by three fourths of the said Legislatures, shall be valid as part of said Constitution, namely:

ARTICLE
The Congress shall have power to make all laws which shall be necessary and proper to secure to the citizens in the several States, and to all persons in the several States equal protection in the rights of life, liberty, and property.

Gentlemen who seem to be very desirous (although it has very recently come to them) to stand well with the President of the United States, if they will look narrowly into the message which he addressed to this Congress at the opening of the session will find that the proposition pending is approved in that message. The President in the message tells this House and the country that "the American system rests on the assertion of the equal right of every man to life, liberty, and the pursuit of happiness.

But, sir, that statement rests upon higher authority than that of the President of the United States. It rests upon the authority of the whole people of the United States, speaking through their Constitution as it has come to us from the hands of the men who framed it. The words of that great instrument are:

The citizens of each State shall be entitled to all privileges and immunities of citizens in the several States.
No person shall be deprived of life, liberty, or property, without due process of law.

What do gentlemen say to these provisions? "Oh, we favor that; we agree with the President that the basis of the American system is the right of every man to life, liberty, and the pursuit of happiness; we agree that the Constitution declares the right of every citizen of the United States to the enjoyment of all privileges and immunities of citizens in the several States, and of all persons to be protected in life, liberty, and property."

Gentlemen admit the force of the provisions in the bill of rights, that the citizens of the United States shall be entitled to all the privileges and immunities of citizens of the United States in the several States, and that no person shall be deprived of life, liberty, or property without due process of law; but they say, "We are opposed to its enforcement by act of Congress under an amended Constitution, as proposed." That is the sum and substance of all the argument that we have heard on ths subject. Why are gentlemen opposed to the enforcement of the bill of rights, as proposed? Because they aver it would interfere with the reserved rights of the States! Who ever before heard that any State had reserved to itself the right, under the Constitution of the United States, to withhold from any citizen of the United States within its limits, under any pretext whatever, any of the privileges of a citizen of the United States, or to impose upon him, no matter from what State he may have come, any burden contrary to that provision of the Constitution which declares that the citizen shall be entitled in the several States to all the immunities of a citizen of the United States?

What does the word immunity in your Constitution mean? Exemption from unequal burdens. Ah! say gentlemen who oppose this amendment, we are not opposed to equal rights: we are not opposed to the bill of rights that all shall be protected alike in life, liberty, and property; we are only opposed to enforcing it by national authority, even by the consent of the loyal people of all the States.

MR. ROGERS. Will the gentleman yield to me?

MR. BINGHAM. The gentleman must excuse me.

MR. ROGERS. Only for a question. I only wish to know what you mean by "due process of law."

MR. BINGHAM. I reply to the gentleman, the courts have settled that long ago, and the gentleman can go and read their decisions.

MR. HALE. Allow me to put a question.

MR. BINGHAM. Excuse me. Mr. Speaker, we have had some most extraordinary arguments against the adoption of the proposed amendment. Amongst others we have the argument of the gentleman from New Jersey, [Mr. Rogers,] that he is opposed to it because he says it comes from a joint committee more tyrannical than any tyranny which disgraced the times of Louis XIV. I do not see if the amendment be good, that that is any objection to its adoption. The gentleman seemed to think it was an objection. He must have spoken sportively; he must have spoken ironically of the committee of which the gentleman himself is a member. The gentleman unwittingly echoed the speech made at the other end of the avenue, and I regret to say by the President, in which he denounced to a party of the gentleman's choosing this joint committee of reconstruction, raised by the action of both Houses of Congress, as a central dictator unconstitutional and unauthorized by law. Why, sir, if the gentleman was not speaking sportively, if he was not speaking ironically, one would suppose he would make haste to withdraw himself from all connection with such a committee as that of which he thus speaks. Surely the gentleman does not mean by this denunciation of the committee to boast, like certain men of eighteen centuries ago, that he is better than other men, who lifted up their hands and thanked God that they were not like other men. If that be the gentleman's opinion of himself, it is time he should exclaim, "My soul, be not thou united with their assembly or sit in the council of the ungodly!"

We have the extraordinary argument of the gentleman from Pennsylvania, [Mr. Randall,] that however just the amendment may be we ought not to pass it in the absence of the Representatives of the eleven States lately in insurrection against the country. Mr. Speaker, when the gentleman comes to reflect upon that remark of his he will see by using it he casts an imputation upon the very men who framed the matchless Constitution of the country under which we are assembled here to-day. It was written in the Articles of Confederation that they "should be articles of perpetual Union" between the original thirteen States who were parties to it. It was written in the Constitution that, if adopted by nine States, it should become the Constitution for those nine States, the covenant of the Articles of Confederation to the contrary notwithstanding. It thence resulted that the Constitution did become the supreme law of some ten States, in the absence of assent thereto on the part of three, and in direct violation of the express covenant of the Confederation itself. And when the question was asked of one of the fathers of the Constitution, how can you break up the Confederation without the consent of all the States, and against the protest of some of them; how can you break the covenant "of perpetual Union" under the Articles of Confederation? he gave for answer, that the right of the people to self-preservation justifies it; it rests upon the transcendent right of nature, and nature's God. That right is still in the people and has justified their action through all this trial. It is the inherent right of the people. It cannot be taken from them. It has survived the storms and tempests of this great conflict of arms. Hence, if the gentleman's logic be true, that you cannot amend the Constitution without the assent of Representatives in Congress of the rebel States, you could not have passed any bill during all these four years of war, if it affected in any sense the interests of the eleven rebel States.

In that objection the gentleman, like the gentleman who preceded him, is simply following the argument of the President, who has said something of that kind in his veto message of the Freedmen's Bureau bill.

We have, then, sir, the calmer and more deliberate utterance of the honorable gentleman from New York, [Mr. Hale.] He says that the Constitution does contemplate equality in the protection of the rights of life, liberty, and property in every State. He admits it does contemplate that the citizen of each State shall be entitled to all the privileges and immunities of citizens in the several States. It will be noticed, the gentleman takes care not to utter one single word in opposition to that part of the amendment which seeks the enforcement of the second section of the fourth article of the Constitution of the United States, but by his silence he gives his assent to it. But the gentleman reiterates the old cry of State rights, and says, "You are impairing State rights." I would like to know, and when the gentleman comes to make another argument on this subject, I respectfully ask him to inform us whence he derives the authority for supposing, if he does so suppose, that any State has the right to deny to a citizen of any other State any of the privileges or immunities of a citizen of the United States. And if a State has not the right to do that, how can the right of a State be impaired by giving to the people of the United States by constitutional amendment the power by congressional enactment to enforce this provision of their Constitution?

The gentleman did not utter a word against the equal right of all citizens of the United States in every State to all privileges and immunities of citizens, and I know any such denial by any State would be condemned by every sense of his nature. If a State has not the right to deny equal protection to any human being under the Constitution of this country in the rights of life liberty, and property, how can State rights be impaired by penal prohibitions of such denial as proposed?

But, says the gentleman, if you adopt this amendment you give to Congress the power to enforce all the rights of married women in the several States. I beg the gentleman's pardon. He need not be alarmed at the condition of married women. Those rights which are universal and independent of all local State legislation belong, by the gift of God, to every woman, whether married or single. The rights of life and liberty are theirs whatever States may enact. But the gentleman's concern is as to the right of property in married women.

Although this word property has been in your bill of rights from the year 1789 until this hour, who ever heard it intimated that anybody could have property protected in any State until he owned or acquired property there according to its local law or according to the law of some other State which he may have carried thither? I undertake to say no one.

As to real estate, every one knows that its acquisition and transmission under every interpretation ever given to the word property, as used in the Constitution of the country, are dependent exclusively upon the local law of the States, save under a direct grant of the United States. But suppose any person has acquired property not contrary to the laws of the State, but in accordance with its law, are they not to be equally protected in the enjoyment of it, or are they to be denied all protection? That is the question, and the whole question, so far as that part of the case is concerned.

The gentleman seemed to think that all persons could have remedies for all violations of their rights of "life, liberty, and property" in the Federal courts.

I ventured to ask him yesterday when any action of that sort was ever maintained in any of the Federal courts of the United States to redress the great wrong which has been practiced, and which is being practiced now in more States than one of the Union under the authority of State laws, denying to citizens therein equal protection or any protection in the rights of life, liberty, and property.

MR. HALE. Will the gentleman allow me to ask him a question?

MR. BINGHAM. No, sir; the gentleman will please excuse me.

MR. HALE. If he is relating what took place in the debate—

MR. BINGHAM. I am relating what I asked the gentleman yesterday.

MR. HALE. In the debate?

MR. BINGHAM. Yes, sir, in the debate. A gentleman on the other side interrupted me and wanted to know if I could cite a decision showing that the power of the Federal Government to enforce in the United States courts the bill of rights under the articles of amendment to the Constitution had been denied. I answered that I was prepared to introduce such decisions; and that is exactly what makes plain the necessity of adopting this amendment.

Mr. Speaker, on this subject I refer the House and the country to a decision of the Supreme Court, to be found in 7 Peters 247, in the case of *Barron* v. The *Mayor and City Council of Baltimore,* involving the question whether the provisions of the fifth article of the amendments to the Constitution are binding upon the State of Maryland and to be enforced in the Federal courts. The Chief Justice says:

The people of the United States framed such a Government for the United States as they supposed best adapted to their situation and best calculated to promote their interests. The powers they conferred on this Government were to be exercised by itself; and the limitations of power, if expressed in general terms, are naturally, and we think necessarily, applicable to the Government created by the instrument. They are limitations of power granted in the instrument itself, not of distinct governments, framed by different persons and for different purposes.

If these propositions be correct, the fifth amendment must be understood as restraining the power of the General Government, not as applicable to the States.

I read one further decision on this subject—the case of the *Lessee of Livingston* v. *Moore and others,* 7 Peters 551. The court, in delivering its opinion, says:

As to the amendments of the Constitution of the United States, they must be put out of the case, since it is now settled that those amendments do not extend to the States; and this observation disposes of the next exception, which relies on the seventh article of those amendments.

What have gentlemen to say to that? Sir, I stand relieved to-day from entering into any extended argument in answer to these decisions of your courts, that although as ruled the existing amendments are not applicable to and do not bind the States, they are nevertheless to be enforced and observed in States by the grand utterance of that immortal man, who, while he lived, stood alone in intellectual power among the living men of his country, and now that he is dead, sleeps alone in his honored tomb by the sounding sea. I refer to that grand argument never yet answered, and never to be answered while human language shall be spoken by living man, wherein Mr. Webster says:

> There is no language in the Constitution applicable to a confederation of States. If the States be parties, as States, what are their rights, and what their respective covenants and stipulations? And where are their rights, covenants, and stipulations expressed? The States engage for nothing, they promise nothing. In the Articles of Confederation, they did make promises, and did enter into engagements, and did plight the faith of each State for their fulfillment, but in the Constitution there is nothing of that kind. The reason is, that in the Constitution it is the people who speak, and not the States. . . . They address themselves to the States and to the Legislatures of States in the language of injunction and prohibition. The Constitution utters its behests in the name and by authority of the people, and it does not exact from States any plighted public faith to maintain it. On the contrary, it makes its own preservation depend on individual duty and individual obligation. . . . It lays its hand on individual duty and individual conscience. It incapacitates any man to sit in the Legislature of a State who shall not first have taken his solemn oath to support the Constitution of the United States. From the obligation of this no State power can discharge him. [3 Webster's *Works* 471]

Why, I ask, should not the "injunctions and prohibitions," addressed by the people in the Constitution to the States and the Legislatures of States, be enforced by the people through the proposed amendment? By the decisions read the people are without remedy. It is admitted in the argument of Mr. Webster, just cited, that the State Legislatures may by direct violations of their duty and oaths avoid the requirements of the Constitution, and thereby do an act which would break up any government.

Those oaths have been disregarded; those requirements of our Constitution have been broken; they are disregarded to-day in Oregon; they are disregarded to-day, and have been disregarded for the last five, ten, or twenty years in every one of the eleven States recently in insurrection.

The question is, simply, whether you will give by this amendment to the people of the United States the power, by legislative enactment, to punish officials of States for violation of the oaths enjoined upon them by their Constitution? That is the question, and the whole question. The adoption of the proposed amendment will take from the States no rights that belong to the States. They elect their Legislatures; they enact their laws for the punishment of crimes against life, liberty, or property; but in the event of the adoption of this amendment, if they conspire together to enact laws refusing equal protection to life, liberty, or property, the Congress is thereby vested with power to hold them to answer before the bar of the national courts for the violation of their oaths and of the rights of their fellow-men. Why should it not be so? That is the question. Why should it not be so? Is the bill of rights to stand in our Constitution hereafter, as in the past five years within eleven States, a mere dead letter? It is absolutely essential to the safety of the people that it should be enforced.

Mr. Speaker, it appears to me that this very provision of the bill of rights brought in question this day, upon this trial before the House, more than any other provision of the Constitution, makes that unity of government which constitutes us one people, by which and through which American nationality came to be, and only by the enforcement of which can American nationality continue to be.

The imperishable words of Washington ought to be in the minds of all of us touching this great question whether the unity of the Government shall be enforced hereafter by just penal enactments when the Legislatures of States refuse to do their duty or keep inviolate their oath. Washington, speaking to you and to me and to the millions who are to come after us, says:

> The unity of the Government which constitutes you one people is a main pillar in the edifice of your real independence, the support of your tranquillity at home, your peace abroad, of your safety, of your prosperity, of that very liberty which you so highly prize.

Is it not essential to the unity of the people that the citizens of each State shall be entitled to all the privileges and immunities of citizens in the several States? Is it not essential to the unity of the Government and the unity of the people that all persons, whether citizens or strangers, within this land, shall have equal protection in every State in this Union in the rights of life and liberty and property?

Why, sir, what an anomaly is presented today to the world! We have the power to vindicate the personal liberty and all the personal rights of the citizen on the remotest sea, under the frowning batteries of the remotest tyranny on this earth, while we have not the power in time of peace to enforce the citizens' rights to life, liberty, and property within the limits of South Carolina after her State government shall be recognized and her constitutional relations restored.

I commend especially to the honorable gentleman from New York [Mr. Hale] the paper issued by his distinguished fellow-citizen, when he was acting as Secretary of State for the United States, the lamented Marcy, touching the protection of the rights of Martin Koszta, a citizen of the United States, whose rights were invaded abroad, within the jurisdiction of the empire of Austria. Commodore Ingraham gave notice that he would fire upon their town and their shipping unless they respected the rights of a declared citizen of the American Republic. You had the power to enforce your demand. But you are powerless in time of peace, in the presence of the laws of South Carolina, Alabama, and Mississippi, as States admitted and restored to the Union, to enforce the rights of citizens of the United States within their limits.

Do gentlemen entertain for a moment the thought that the enforcement of these provisions of the Constitution was not to be considered essential? Consider the triple safeguards interposed in the Constitution itself against their denial. It is provided in the Constitution, in the first place, that "this Constitution," the whole of it, not a part of it, "shall be the supreme law of the land." Supreme from the Penobscot in the farthest east, to the remotest west where rolls the Oregon; supreme over every hamlet, every State, and every Territory of the Union.

As the whole Constitution was to be the supreme law in every State, it therefore results that the citizens of each State, being citizens of the United States, should be entitled to all the privileges and immunities of citizens of the United States in every State, and all persons, now that slavery has forever perished, should be entitled to equal protection in the rights of life, liberty, and property.

As a further security for the enforcement of the Constitution, and especially of this sacred bill of rights, to all the citizens and all the people of the United States, it is further provided that the members of the several State Legislatures and all executive and judicial officers, both of the United States and of the several States, shall be bound by oath or affirmation to support this Constitution. The oath, the most solemn compact which man can make with his Maker, was to bind the State Legislatures, executive officers, and judges to sacredly respect the Constitution and all the rights secured by it. And yet there is still another provision lest a State Legislature, with the approval of a State Executive, should, in disregard of their oath, invade the rights of any citizen or person by unjust legislation, violative alike of the Constitution and the rights secured by it, which is very significant and not to be overlooked, which is,

And the judges of every State shall be bound to the Constitution of the United States, anything in the constitution and laws of any State to the contrary notwithstanding.

With these provisions in the Constitution for the enforcement in every State of its requirements, is it surprising that the framers of the Constitution omitted to insert an express grant of power in Congress to enforce by penal enactment these great canons of the supreme law, securing to all the citizens in every State all the privileges and immunities of citizens, and to all the people all the sacred rights of person—those rights dear to freemen and formidable only to tyrants—and of which the fathers of the Republic spoke, after God had given them the victory, in that memorable address in which they declared, "Let it be remembered that the rights for which America has contended were the rights of human nature?" Is it surprising that essential as they held the full security to all citizens of all the privileges and immunities of citizens, and to all the people the sacred rights of person, that having proclaimed them they left their lawful enforcement to each of the States, under the solemn obligation resting upon every State officer to regard, respect, and obey the constitutional injunction?

What more could have been added to that instrument to secure the enforcement of these provisions of the bill of rights in every State, other than the additional grant of power which we ask this day? Nothing at all. And I am perfectly confident that that grant of power would have been there but for the fact that its insertion in the Constitution would have been utterly incompatible with the existence of slavery in any State; for although slaves might not have been admitted to be citizens they must have been admitted to be persons. That is the only reason why it was not there. There was a fetter upon the conscience of the nation; the people could not put it there and permit slavery in any State thereafter. Thank God, that fetter has been broken; it has turned to dust before the breath of the people, speaking as the voice of God and solemnly ordaining that slavery is forever prohibited everywhere within the Republic except as punishment for crime on due conviction. Even now for crimes men may be enslaved in States, notwithstanding the new amendment.

As slaves were not protected by the Constitution, there might be some color of excuse for the slave States in their disregard for the requirement of the bill of rights as to slaves and refusing them protection in life or property; though, in my judgment, there could be no possible apology for reducing men made like themselves, in the image of God, to a level with the brutes of the field, and condemning them to toil without reward, to live without knowledge, and die without hope.

But, sir, there never was even colorable excuse, much less apology, for any man North or South claiming that any State Legislature or State court, or State Executive, has any right to deny protection to any free citizen of the United States within their limits in the rights of life, liberty, and property. Gentlemen who oppose this amendment oppose the grant of power to enforce the bill of rights. Gentlemen who oppose this amendment simply declare to these rebel States, go on with your confiscation statutes, your statutes of banishment, your statutes of unjust imprisonment, your statutes of murder and death against men because of their loyalty to the Constitution and Government of the United States.

That is the issue that is before the American people; and God helping me, without respect for persons in high places who show a disposition to betray this great cause, I will not betray it, so long as it is given me to know the right. . . .

THE ORIGINS

Commentary

The legislative scene now shifted back to the Joint Committee on Reconstruction. It had done nothing on the subject of civil rights since it had voted on February 3, 1866, to approve Congressman Bingham's ill-fated proposal. On April 21, Congressman Stevens reopened the subject with a draft amendment, "one not of his own framing." The draft had actually been submitted to him by Robert Dale Owen, the English reformer who had come to this country before the Civil War. The Owen draft covered most of the matters dealt with by the Fourteenth Amendment. Its key first section was, however, framed only in terms of discrimination against the Negro—a backward step from the Bingham drafts previously put forward. Bingham then moved to include a new section 5, which contained, for the first time, the language of section 1 of the Fourteenth Amendment (except for its clause providing citizenship for all persons born or naturalized in the United States, which was added later in the Senate). After the Committee had first accepted and then declined to recommend Bingham's new proposal, it was accepted by the Committee on April 28 as section 1 of the recommended Fourteenth Amendment.

At last, the Committee was able to report the essential text of what was to become the Fourteenth Amendment. As far as its crucial first section was concerned, it cannot be doubted that the draft Bingham induced the Committee to accept on April 28 marked a real advance upon earlier proposals. This was no longer a mere grant of power to Congress, but a self-executing positive provision barring the states from restricting civil rights. There was now a privileges and immunities clause—with all the uncertainties inherent in that vague phrase. The equal protection requirement was retained—in form omitting the trilogy of life, liberty, and property. And their protection was to be secured by a due process clause—the single clause copied from the Bill of Rights into the new draft.

THE FOURTEENTH AMENDMENT

The Joint Committee on Reconstruction
House of Representatives-39th Congress, 1st Session
1865-1867

Washington, April 21, 1866.

The Committee met pursuant to adjournment; absent: Messrs. Ira Harris [R., N.Y.] and Roscoe Conkling [R., N.Y.]. . . .

Mr. Stevens said he had a plan of reconstruction, one not of his own framing, but which he should support, and which he submitted to the Committee for consideration.

It was read as follows:

A joint resolution proposing an amendment to the Constitution, and to provide for the restoration to the states lately in insurrection of their full political rights.

Whereas, It is expedient that the States lately in insurrection should, at the earliest day consistent with the future peace and safety of the Union, be restored to full participation in all political rights; therefore,

Be it resolved, by the Senate and House of Representatives of the United States of America in Congress assembled (two-thirds of both Houses concurring), that the following Article be proposed to the Legislatures of the several states as an amendment to the Constitution of the United States, which, when ratified, by three-fourths of said legislatures, shall be valid as part of the Constitution, namely:

Article—

SEC. 1. No discrimination shall be made by any state, nor by the United States, as to the civil rights of persons because of race, color, or previous condition of servitude.

SEC. 2. From and after the fourth day of July, in the year one thousand eight hundred and seventy-six, no discrimination shall be made by any state, nor by the United States, as to the enjoyment by classes of persons of the right of suffrage, because of race, color, or previous condition of servitude.

SEC. 3. Until the fourth day of July, one thousand eight hundred and seventy-six, no class of persons, as to the right of any of whom to suffrage discrimination shall be made by any state, because of race, color, or previous condition of servitude, shall be included in the basis of representation.

SEC. 4. Debts incurred in aid of insurrection or of war against the Union, and claims of compensation for loss of involuntary service or labor, shall not be paid by any state nor by the United States.

SEC. 5. Congress shall have power to enforce by appropriate legislation, the provisions of this article.

And be it further resolved, That whenever the above recited amendment shall have become part of the Constitution, and any state lately in insurrection shall have ratified the same, and shall have modified its constitution and laws in conformity with the first section thereof, the Senators and Represen- tatives from such state, if found duly elected and qualified, shall, after having taken the usual oath of office, be admitted as such:

Provided, That no person who, having been an officer in the army or navy of the United States, or having been a member of the Thirty-sixth Congress, or of the Cabinet in the year one thousand eight hundred and sixty, took part in the late insurrection, shall be eligible to either branch of the national legislature until after the fourth day of July, one thousand eight hundred and seventy-six. . . .

Mr. Bingham moved to insert as section five the following:

"SEC. 5. No state shall make or enforce any law which shall abridge the privileges or immunities of citizens of the United States; nor shall any state deprive any person of life, liberty or property without due process of law, nor deny to any person within its jurisdiction the equal protection of the laws."

After discussion thereon,

The question was taken, and it was decided in the affirmative, yeas 10, nays 2. . . .

Washington, April 25, 1866.

The Committee met pursuant to adjournment (Mr. Reverdy Johnson [Dem., Md.] in the chair); absent Messrs. William Fessenden [R., Me.] and Elihe Washburne [R., Ill.]. . . .

Mr. George Williams [R., Ore.] moved to amend the joint resolution by striking out the fifth section of the proposed amendment to the Constitution, as follows:

"SEC. 5. No state shall make or enforce any law which shall abridge the privileges or immunities of citizens of the United States; nor shall any state deprive any person of life, liberty, or property without due process of law; nor deny to any person within its jurisdiction the equal protection of the laws."

After discussion,

The question was taken, and it was decided in the affirmative, yeas 7, nays 5. . . .

Washington, April 28, 1866.

The Committee met pursuant to adjournment; all the members present. . . .

Mr. Bingham moved to strike out the first section of the proposed amend- ment to the Constitution, which was as follows:

"SEC. 1. No discrimination shall be made by any State, or by the United States, as to the civil rights of persons, because of race, color or previous condition of servitude."

and to insert in lieu thereof the following:

"SEC. 1. No State shall make or enforce any law which shall abridge the privileges or immunities of citizens of the United States; nor shall any State deprive any person of life, liberty, or property, without due process of law, nor deny to any person within its jurisdiction the equal protection of the laws."

After discussion,

The question was taken, and it was decided in the affirmative, yeas 10, nays 3. . . .

The joint resolution and bills adopted are as follows:

A joint resolution proposing an amendment to the Constitution of the United States.

Be it resolved, by the Senate and House of Representatives of the United States of America in Congress assembled (two-thirds of both Houses concurring), That the following article be proposed to the Legislatures of the several States as an amendment to the Constitution of the United States, which, when ratified by three-fourths of said Legislatures, shall be valid as part of the Constitution, namely:

Article—

SEC. 1. No state shall make or enforce any law which shall abridge the privileges or immunities of citizens of the United States; nor shall any State deprive any person of life, liberty, or property without due process of law; nor deny to any person within its jurisdiction the equal protection of the laws.

SEC. 2. Representatives shall be apportioned among the several States which may be included within this Union according to their respective numbers, counting the whole number of persons in each State, excluding Indians not taxed. But whenever in any State the elective franchise shall be denied to any portion of its male citizens not less than twenty-one years of age, or in any way abridged, except for participation in rebellion or other crime, the basis of representation in such State shall be reduced in the proportion which the number of male citizens shall bear to the whole number of such male citizens not less than twenty-one years of age.

SEC. 3. Until the 4th day of July, in the year 1870, all persons who voluntarily adhered to the late insurrection, giving it aid and comfort, shall be excluded from the right to vote for Representatives in Congress and for electors for President and Vice-President of the United States.

SEC. 4. Neither the United States nor any State shall assume or pay any debt or obligation already incurred, or which may hereafter be incurred, in aid of insurrection or of war against the United States, or any claim for compensation for loss of involuntary service or labor.

SEC. 5. The Congress shall have power to enforce by appropriate legislation the provisions of this article. . . .

Commentary

On May 8, 1866, the proposed Fourteenth Amendment, with the crucial Section 1 in its final form (except for the definition of citizenship to be included by the Senate later that month), was debated in the House. The extracts from the debates which follow begin with Mr. Stevens' speech as head of the House delegation on the Joint Committee on Reconstruction, introducing the proposed amendment. There follow pertinent portions of the other House speeches during the three days of debate, concluding with Congressman Bingham's closing address on May 10, after which the amendment was passed by the House—yeas 128, nays 37, not voting 19.

Certain things should be borne in mind in considering the House debate extracts which follow. It should, in the first place, be pointed out that, in the debates themselves, the time was divided more evenly between supporters and opponents of the amendment than the extracts chosen indicate. To one interested in the amendment's history, it is primarily the views expressed in support of adoption that are of present-day interest. Hence, the extracts that follow (as well as those given later from the Senate debates) are primarily devoted to the speeches made in favor of the amendment.

In addition, it should be noted that much of the contemporary interest expressed in the legislative debates was focused upon provisions of the proposed amendment that are of much less concern a century later. A good part of the debate was centered around Sections 2, 3, and 4 of the amendment, especially their punitive intent vis-a-vis the southern states. These provisions are of only academic interest to the present-day observer concerned with the Fourteenth Amendment's impact upon civil rights. In the debate extracts that follow, we have omitted almost all of the discussion relating to these sections. In operation, the key provision of the Fourteenth Amendment has been Section 1. Its draftsmanship has been traced in the prior pages and now there are presented those parts of the debates which are devoted to it. They are of crucial importance to an understanding of what impact the men who passed the Fourteenth Amendment intended its first section to have upon civil rights.

Of the House speeches which follow, the most important are those of Congressmen Stevens, Garfield, and Bingham. To Stevens, the great object of Section 1 was *discrimination*—its goal to ensure that "the law which operates upon one man shall operate *equally* upon all." To him, as to many of the Radical Republicans, Section 1 was not nearly as important as Section 2 (on representation), which explains why he and other speakers devoted tantalizingly little time to the provision which most concerns the student of civil rights today. Garfield was already one of the leaders of the House and his views were listened to with great respect. To him, Section 1 was intended to give permanence to the Civil Rights Act of 1866 by incorporating its provisions "in the eternal firmament of the Constitution."

Garfield's speech actually summarizes the main theme of almost all the speakers supporting the amendment with regard to Section 1—that Section 1 is essentially the elevation to the constitutional plane of the provisions of the 1866 civil rights statute. It will be recalled that, in the debate on the statute, the main objection of many opponents had to do, not with desirability, but with constitutionality. Now the constitutional question is to be settled by inclusion of the rights established by the 1866 Act within the protection of the new amendment and the grant of organic authority to Congress to enact legislation enforcing such rights. Certainly, it is fair to say that the participants in the House debate did not even consider whether the proposed Section 1 would make the first eight amendments binding upon the states.

The one possible exception was Representative John Bingham, whose speech on May 10 closed the debate. In his view, Section 1 of the new amendment would supply "That great want of the citizen and stranger, protection by national law from unconstitutional State enactment." As an example of such unconstitutional state enactment, he refers to the fact that, "Contrary to the express letter of your Constitution, 'cruel and unusual punishments' have been inflicted under State laws within this Union upon citizens." This implies that the Eighth Amendment was already binding upon the states and the new amendment would give Congress power to repress such state action inconsistent with the Constitution. Such view had already been expressed by Bingham in his February 26 speech (*supra* p. 193). It is wholly contrary to the rule established in Supreme Court decisions that the first eight amendments restrict only the federal government, not the states. If Bingham erroneously believed that the states had always been bound by a Bill of Rights provision like the Eighth Amendment, his whole approach to the effect of the new section was based upon a legal misconception.

THE DEBATE

House of Representatives-39th Congress, 1st Session
May 8-10, 1866

THADDEUS STEVENS [R., PA.]. The short time allowed by our resolution will suffice to introduce this debate. If unexpectedly there should be any objection to the proposed amendment to the Constitution I may ask the indulgence of the House to reply.

The committee are not ignorant of the fact that there has been some impatience at the delay in making this report; that it existed to some extent in the country as well as among a few members of the House. It originated in the suggestions of faction, no doubt, but naturally spread until it infected some good men. This is not to be wondered at or complained of. Very few could be informed of the necessity for such delay. Beside, we are not all endowed with patience; some men are naturally restive, especially if they have active minds and deep convictions.

But I beg gentlemen to consider the magnitude of the task which was imposed upon the committee. They were expected to suggest a plan for rebuilding a shattered nation—a nation which though not dissevered was yet shaken and riven by the gigantic and persistent efforts of six million able and ardent men; of bitter rebels striving through four years of bloody war. It cannot be denied that this terrible struggle sprang from the vicious principles incorporated into the institutions of our country. Our fathers had been compelled to postpone the principles of their great Declaration, and wait for their full establishment till a more propitious time. That time ought to be present now. But the public mind has been educated in error for a century. How difficult in a day to unlearn it. In rebuilding, it is necessary to clear away the rotten and defective portions of the old foundations, and to sink deep and found the repaired edifice upon the firm foundation of eternal justice. If, perchance, the accumulated quicksands render it impossible to reach in every part so firm a basis, then it becomes our duty to drive deep and solid the substituted piles on which to build. It would not be wise to prevent the raising of the structure because some corner of it might be founded upon materials subject to the inevitable laws of mortal decay. It were better to shelter the household and trust to the advancing progress of a higher morality and a purer and more intelligent principle to underpin the defective corner.

I would not for a moment inculcate the idea of surrendering a principle vital to justice. But if full justice could not be obtained at once I would not refuse to do what is possible. The commander of an army who should find his enemy intrenched on impregnable heights would act unwisely if he insisted on marching his troops full in the face of a destructive fire merely to show his courage. Would it not be better to flank the works and march round

221

and round and besiege, and thus secure the surrender of the enemy, though it might cost time? The former course would show valor and folly; the latter moral and physical courage, as well as prudence and wisdom.

This proposition is not all that the committee desired. It falls far short of my wishes, but it fulfills my hopes. I believe it is all that can be obtained in the present state of public opinion. Not only Congress but the several states are to be consulted. Upon a careful survey of the whole ground, we did not believe that nineteen of the loyal States could be induced to ratify any proposition more stringent than this. I say nineteen, for I utterly repudiate and scorn the idea that any State not acting in the Union is to be counted on the question of ratification. It is absurd to suppose that any more than three-fourths of the States that propose the amendment are required to make it valid; that States not here are to be counted as present. Believing, then, that this is the best proposition that can be made effectual, I accept it. I shall not be driven by clamor or denunciation to throw away a great good because it is not perfect. I will take all I can get in the cause of humanity and leave it to be perfected by better men in better times. It may be that that time will not come while I am here to enjoy the glorious triumph; but that it will come is as certain as that there is a just God.

The House should remember the great labor which the committee had to perform. They were charged to inquire into the condition of eleven States of great extent of territory. They sought, often in vain, to procure their organic laws and statutes. They took the evidence of every class and condition of witness, from the rebel vice president and the commander-in-chief of their armies down to the humblest freedman. The sub-committees who were charged with that duty—of whom I was not one, and can therefore speak freely—exhibited a degree of patience and diligence which was never excelled. Considering their other duties, the mass of evidence taken may well be considered extraordinary. . . .

Let us now refer to the provisions of the proposed amendment.

The first section prohibits the States from abridging the privileges and immunities of citizens of the United States, or unlawfully depriving them of life, liberty, or property, or of denying to any person within their jurisdiction the "equal" protection of the laws.

I can hardly believe that any person can be found who will not admit that every one of these provisions is just. They are all asserted, in some form or other, in our Declaration or organic law. But the Constitution limits only the action of Congress, and is not a limitation on the States. This amendment supplies that defect, and allows Congress to correct the unjust legislation of the States, so far that the law which operates upon one man shall operate *equally* upon all. Whatever law punishes a white man for a crime shall punish the black man precisely in the same way and to the same degree. Whatever law protects the white man shall afford "equal" protection to the black man. Whatever means of redress is afforded to one shall be afforded to all. Whatever law allows the white man to testify in court shall allow the man of color to do the same. These are great advantages over their present codes. Now different degrees of punishment are inflicted, not on account of the magnitude of the crime, but according to the color of the skin. Now color disqualifies a man from testifying in courts, or being tried in the same way as white men. I need not enumerate these partial and oppressive laws. Unless the Constitution should restrain them those States will all, I fear, keep up this discrimination, and crush to death the hated freedmen. Some answer, "Your civil rights bill secures the same things." That is partly true, but a law is repealable by a majority. And I need hardly say that the first time that the South with their copperhead allies obtain the command of Congress it will be repealed. The veto of the President and their votes on the bill are conclusive evidence of that. And yet I am amazed and alarmed at the impatience of certain well-meaning Republicans at the exclusion of the rebel States until the Constitution shall be so amended as to restrain their despotic desires. This amendment once adopted cannot be annulled without two thirds of Congress. That they will hardly get. And yet certain of our distinguished friends propose to admit State after State before this becomes a part of the Constitution. What madness! Is their judgment misled by their kindness; or are they unconsciously drifting into the haven of power at the other end of the avenue? I do not suspect it, but others will.

The second section I consider the most important in the article. It fixes the basis of representation in Congress. If any State shall exclude any of her adult male citizens from the elective franchise, or abridge that right, she shall forfeit her right to representation in the same proportion. The effect of this provision will be either to compel the States to grant universal suffrage or so to shear them of their power as to keep them forever in a hopeless minority in the national Government, both legislative and executive. If they do not enfranchise the freedmen, it would give to the rebel States but thirty-seven Representatives. Thus shorn of their power, they would soon become restive. Southern pride would not long brook a hopeless minority. True it will take two, three, possibly five years before they conquer their prejudices sufficiently to allow their late slaves to become their equals at the polls. That short delay would not be injurious. In the mean time the freedmen would become more enlightened, and more fit to discharge the high duties of their new condition. In that time, too, the loyal Congress could mature their laws and so amend the Constitution as to secure the rights of every human being, and render disunion impossible. Heaven forbid that the southern States, or *any one of them,* should be represented on this floor until such muniments of freedom are built high and firm. Against our will they have been absent for four bloody years; against our will they must not come back until we are ready to receive them. Do not tell me that there are loyal representatives waiting for admission—until their States are loyal they can have no standing here. They would merely *mis*represent their constituents.

I admit that this article is not as good as the one we sent to death in the Senate. In my judgment, we shall not approach the measure of justice until we have given every adult freedman a homestead on the land where he was born and toiled and suffered. Forty acres of land and a hut would be more valuable to him than the immediate right to vote. Unless we give them this we shall receive the censure of mankind and the curse of Heaven. That article referred to provided that if *one* of the injured race was excluded the State should forfeit the right to have any of them represented. That would have hastened their full enfranchisement. This section allows the States to discriminate among the same class, and receive proportionate credit in representation. This I dislike. But it is a short step forward. The large stride which we in vain proposed is dead; the murderers must answer to the suffering race. I would not have been the perpetrator. A load of misery must sit heavy on their souls.

The third section may encounter more difference of opinion here. Among the people I believe it will be the most popular of all the provisions; it prohibits rebels from voting for members of Congress and electors of President until 1870. My only objection to it is that it is too lenient. I know that there is a morbid sensibility, sometimes called mercy, which affects a few of all classes, from the priest to the clown, which has more sympathy for the murderer on the gallows than for his victim. I hope I have a heart as capable of feeling for human woe as others. I have long since wished that capital punishment were abolished. But I never dreamed that all punishment could be dispensed with in human society. Anarchy, *treason,* and violence would reign triumphant. Here is the mildest of all punishments ever inflicted on traitors. I might not consent to the extreme severity denounced upon them by a provisional governor of Tennessee—I mean the late lamented Andrew Johnson of blessed memory—but I would have increased the severity of this section. I would be glad to see it extended to 1876, and to include all State and municipal as well as national elections. In my judgment we do not sufficiently protect the loyal men of the rebel States from the vindictive persecutions of their victorious rebel neighbors. Still I will move no amendment, nor vote for any, lest the whole fabric should tumble to pieces.

I need say nothing of the fourth section, for none dare object to it who is not himself a rebel. To the friend of justice, the friend of the Union, of the perpetuity of liberty, and the final triumph of the rights of man and their extension to every human being, let me say, sacrifice as we have done your peculiar views, and instead of vainly insisting upon the instantaneous operation of all that is right accept what is possible, and "all these things shall be added unto you."

WILLIAM FINCK [DEM., OHIO]. Mr. Speaker, I promise to trespass upon the attention of the House but a very few minutes in what I have to say on this question.

An amendment to the Constitution is at all times a matter of grave importance, and should command calm and patient deliberation.

It is of the last importance to the prosperity and happiness of a people that stability in the great organic laws of the nation should be maintained. Amendments sometimes, I agree, become necessary to the constitution of every nation; but they should not be hurriedly made, and never without considering the interests and opinions of the whole people.

To me, Mr. Speaker, this of all others seems the most inauspicious time to propose or make changes in our Constitution.

We are just at the close of the most stupendous war which has ever scourged any nation, and the passions and alienations which have been engendered by this strife have not yet completely passed away.

The amendments proposed are to affect the people of this whole country, but more especially are they intended to affect the people of the States lately in insurrection; and it would seem not only to be an act of even-handed justice, but of the highest wisdom, if we would consult the teachings of the wise and pure men who established our Government, that these people should have an opportunity of considering and discussing these amendments here, and to record their votes through their representatives either for or against them before they are finally submitted to the States for their action. Now, what is the condition in which we to-day find ourselves?

The war terminated over a year ago. The people of the late insurgent States have fully and completely yielded obedience to the Constitution and laws of the United States. Their State governments are completely restored. Their courts are in the full exercise of their jurisdiction, and profound peace reigns throughout our borders. To show that these people are in earnest, and acting in good faith, I need only refer to the fact that they have ratified the amendment abolishing slavery, abandoned the pretended claim to the right of secession, and elected members of Congress.

But, sir, the men who control this Congress have failed, in my judgment, to meet these people in that true spirit of kindness and forgiveness dictated by a wise and enlarged statesmanship, and which now alone are necessary to restore cordial relations between the two sections.

At the commencement of this session a most extraordinary resolution was adopted, creating a joint committee of fifteen on reconstruction, and to which it was ordered that everything relating to the admission of members from the late insurgent States should be referred, and none of their representatives were to be admitted until this committee should report on the subject. Thus this House, in the face of that provision of the Constitution, which declares that each House shall be the judge of the elections, returns, and qualifications of its own members, surrendered the exercise of that right to a joint committee, the distinguished chairman of which [Mr. Stevens] had already pronounced these States conquered territories and their citizen aliens.

We have been advised from time to time, with an air of supreme defiance at the restoration policy of the President, that Congress must first ascertain and declare that these were States really in the Union, with governments republican in form; and that until these things were satisfactorily declared by Congress, no Senator or Representative could be admitted from any of these States.

Well, sir, we have waited, and the country has waited, with feverish anxiety for the period when this committee should report on these questions and the congressional plan should be finally presented. Witnesses have been brought from all parts of the country and examined by the committee, to ascertain and report on the loyalty of the southern people and the condition of their State governments. At last, after five months' labor, this committee has brought in its report, and what information do they bring us? And what do they propose that Congress shall do? Do they tell us whether these States are in or out of the Union; or whether they have governments republican in form? Not a bit of it. But they report an amendment to the Constitution, containing four or five sections, with two bills accompanying it, and these are to constitute the congressional plan, as opposed to the policy of the President.

The time to which I am limited by the resolution of the House regulating this discussion will prevent me from entering into an elaborate examination of this plan of the committee; and I shall have, therefore, to content myself with a very brief examination of it.

The first section provides that—

No State shall make or enforce any law which shall abridge the privileges or immunities of citizens of the United States: nor shall any State deprive any person of life, liberty, or property without due process of law, nor deny to any person within its jurisdiction the equal protection of the laws.

Well, all I have to say about this section is, that if it is necessary to adopt it, in order to confer upon Congress power over the matters contained in it, then the civil rights bill, which the President vetoed, was passed without authority, and is clearly unconstitutional. . . .

I ask gentlemen to pause and reflect before they commit themselves to so monstrous and revolutionary a scheme as this.

I may be deluded and mistaken when I assume that we are still legislating under a Constitution which we have all sworn to support. Or can it be possible that while the forms and provisions. of that sacred instrument are still contained in our books, that its whole spirit and binding authority have been destroyed, and that the rich heritage of our fathers, of a free Government regulated by law, has become already a mere machine by which the majority in Congress are left free and untrammeled to do just what they please?

Mr. Speaker, I trust that we are still in possession, not only of the Constitution of our fathers, but that we will be animated and controlled, at least in some degree, by their wisdom and patriotism.

Sir, I deny wholly that there exists under our Constitution any right whatever for any number of States to combine together to exclude the rest from their constitutional representation in Congress, and to say to these States so excluded that they shall only exercise the right of representation on the terms and conditions of adopting certain proposed amendments to the Constitution, because by the recognition of such a principle you at once sanction the right of three fourths of the States, not to make amendment merely, but to adopt a provision which they may call an amendment, and then drive the remaining one fourth of the States out of the Union, unless they shall also adopt the same proposition.

For that is virtually what is assumed may be done by the proposition of this committee. Nay, more than this is assumed. It is the assertion of the right of three fourths of the States to say to the other fourth, you shall be held in this Union for the purposes of taxation; you shall be subjected to all the burdens and duties of States in the Union, but you shall never be represented in Congress unless you agree to the conditions which we shall see proper to impose on you, although the Constitution expressly declares that "no State without its consent shall be deprived of its equal suffrage in the Senate," and that each State shall have at least one Representative in the House.

Sir, the whole scheme is revolutionary and a most shallow pretext for an excuse to exclude the vote of eleven States in the next presidential election. You cannot exact conditions in this way from any State in the Union; no more from Georgia, than from Massachusetts. They are each equal States in the Union, held together by the same Constitution, neither being the superior of the other in their relation to the Federal Government as States.

I cannot pretend to say, Mr. Speaker, what will be the action of these States, on these proposed changes, but I trust they will have spirit enough left to reject, with firm and manly independence, a scheme which disfranchises a large majority of their citizens and brands with the humiliating marks of inferiority States which are constitutionally the equals of any other States in this Union. . . .

Mr. Speaker, the North and the South are destined to live together as one people, in the same Union, and under a common Constitution. Let us, I beseech you, endeavor to live together as true friends and brothers.

Let us rise equal to the great occasion and imitate the noble example of our brave armies in the field, who, when the conflict had ended, no longer regarded the southern people as enemies, but as friends. "Enemies in war, in peace friends." Let us welcome into these Halls representatives from all the States who may be true to the Constitution and the Union; and when all these States shall once more gather around this common council chamber of the nation, then, and not till then, let the great questions of amendment be fairly discussed and voted upon. . . .

JAMES GARFIELD [R., OHIO]. Mr. Speaker, I do not rise to speak at length upon the pending measure, but for the purpose of entering a motion and submitting a few practical suggestions on the bill, and particularly in reference to the third section.

With almost every proposition in the report of the joint committee on reconstruction I am pleased; yes, more than pleased, I am delighted that we have at least reached the firm earth, and planted our feet upon the solid granite, on enduring and indubitable principle. I believe we have at last a series of propositions which, in the main, will meet the approval of the American people as no others have ever done since the beginning of this struggle.

I will not go into a general discussion of the reconstruction policy, but will confine myself in the few words I shall say to the joint resolution and the amendment to the Constitution proposed by it now before the House, and more particularly to one section of it. First let me say I regret more than I shall be able to tell this House that we have not found the situation of affairs in this country such, and the public virtue such that we might come out on the plain, unanswerable proposition that every adult intelligent citizen of the United States, unconvicted of crime, shall enjoy the right of suffrage.

Sir, I believe that the right to vote, if it be not indeed one of the natural rights of all men, is so necessary to the protection of their natural rights as to be indispensable, and therefore equal to natural rights. I believe that the golden sentence of John Stuart Mill, in one of his greatest works, ought to be written on the constitution of every State, and on the Constitution of the United States, as the greatest and most precious of truths, "That the ballot is put into the hands of men, not so much to enable them to govern others as that he may not be misgoverned by others." I believe that suffrage is the shield, the sword, the spear, and all the panoply that best befits a man for his own defense in the great social organism to which he belongs. And I profoundly regret that we have not been enabled to write it and engrave it upon our institutions, and imbed it in the imperishable bulwarks of the Constitution as a part of the fundamental law of the land.

But I am willing, as I said once before in this presence, when I cannot get all I wish to take what I can get. And therefore I am willing to accept the propositions that the committee have laid before us, though I desire one amendment which I will mention presently.

I am glad to see this first section here which proposes to hold over every American citizen, without regard to color, the protecting shield of law. The gentleman who has just taken his seat [Mr. Finck] undertakes to show that because we propose to vote for this section we therefore acknowledge that the civil rights bill was unconstitutional. He was anticipated in that objection by the gentleman from Pennsylvania, [Mr. Stevens.] The civil rights bill is now a part of the law of the land. But every gentleman knows it will cease to be a part of the law whenever the sad moment arrives when that gentleman's party comes into power. It is precisely for that reason that we propose to lift that great and good law above the reach of political strife, beyond the reach of the plots and machinations of any party, and fix it in the serene sky, in the eternal firmament of the Constitution, where no storm of passion can shake it and no cloud can obscure it. For this reason, and not because I believe the civil rights bill unconstitutional, I am glad to see that first section here.

As the nearest approach to justice which we are likely to be able to make, I approve of the second section that bases representation upon voters. I believe the section is now free from the objections that killed it in the Senate, and I have no doubt it will now pass that body.

I am glad to see the fourth section here, which forever forbids the payment of the rebel debt. I am quite sure that on the proposition no man in this House will vote in the negative. Some may think the section unnecessary, but for abundant caution, and "to make assurance doubly sure," let it become a part of the Constitution.

It is to the third section that I wish to call the attention of the House for a moment. The gentleman from Maine [Mr. Blaine] has made a point against it, which has at least this value; that whatever may be the intention of the committee or of the House, the section is least susceptible of double construction. Some may say that it revokes and nullifies in part the pardons that have already been granted in accordance with law and the proclamations of the President. Others may say that it does not affect them, and will not apply to rebels who have been thus pardoned. . . . if the section does not apply to those who have been pardoned, then it will apply to so small a number of people as to make it of no practical value; for the excepted classes in the general system of pardons from a very small fraction of the rebels. If the section does apply to those who have received the pardon, the objection of the gentleman from Maine [Mr. Blaine] may be worthy of consideration.

But, without entering into the question of construction at all, and if there were no doubt or difference on that score, there are still other points to which I wish to call the attention of the House. If the proposition had been that those who had been in rebellion should be ineligible to any office under the Government of the United States, and should be ineligible to appointment as electors of the President and Vice President of the United States, or if all who had voluntarily borne arms against the United States had been declared forever incapable of voting for a United States officer, it would, in my judgment, be far more defensible. But what is the proposition? It is that—

Until the 4th day of July, in the year 1870, all persons who voluntarily adhered to the late insurrection, giving it aid and comfort, shall be excluded from the right to vote for Representatives in Congress and for electors for President and Vice President of the United States.

Now, Mr. Speaker, this, in my judgment, is the only proposition in this resolution that is not bottomed clearly and plainly upon principle—principle that will stand the test of centuries, and be as true a thousand years hence as it is to-day. If the persons referred to are not worthy to be allowed to vote in January of 1870, will they be worthy in July of that year? If the franchise were withheld until they should perform some specific act of loyalty, if it were conditioned upon any act of theirs, it would commend itself as a principle, but the fixing of an ordinary date, without any regard to the character or conduct of the parties themselves, is indefensible, and will not commend itself to the judgment of reflecting men. What is worse, it will be said everywhere that this is purely a piece of political management in reference to a pesidential election.

Now, I desire that what goes into our Constitution shall be the pure gold, unalloyed, untainted, having mingled with it nothing that will not stand the test of the ages. I fear that the proposition to which I have just referred might not stand that crucial test.

But, sir, I invite the attention of the House to another consideration. Suppose this section should become a part of the Constitution, and suppose that it were entirely defensible as a matter of principle, I ask gentlemen how it is to be carried out in practice. If, under its operation in eleven States of the Union, nine tenths, and, in some instances, ninety-nine hundredths of the adult population are to be disfranchised for four years, how do you propose to carry its provisions into practical execution? Will nine tenths of the population consent to stay at home and let one tenth do the voting? Will not every ballot-box be the scene of strife and bloodshed? It may well be doubted whether this section can be carried out except by having a military force at every ballot-box in eleven States of the Union. Are you ready to make the South a vast camp for four years more? I am ready to do that or anything else in the way of expense, if it is necessary as means of securing liberty and union; but I believe that great result can be achieved in a less expensive way. But it is evident to me that if this section becomes a part of the Constitution, it must either remain a dead letter or we must maintain a large army to enforce it. I do not, therefore, think it wise or prudent, both for practical reasons and for reasons of construction, as suggested by the gentleman from Maine, that the third section shall stand as a part of the Constitution in its present form.

I am sure no member of this House will think that I make this motion with the least desire to favor or excuse in any way the men who have been in arms against the Government. I trust I do not need to make such a disclaimer to any person here, or among Union men anywhere. But I desire that any proposition which may be submitted by us for ratification by the States shall be so grounded in practical wisdom, that when it is presented to the American people, any man who votes against it will need to hide his face in shame. And there are thousands of men who only need some little excuse to justify themselves in voting against this great and good measure. I had nearly completed a substitute for this section providing that no person who had voluntarily adhered to the late insurrection should ever be eligible to any office under the United States, but as I have not perfected it I will not present it now. I hope, however, we may begin by striking out the section as it now stands.

Is it now in order, Mr. Speaker, to move an amendment? . . .

They have undertaken to reject and resist our scheme of restoring the Union for five years, and they propose now, and the gentleman by his own confession invites them to continue to unite and reject the scheme of the great Union party and of the people to build up liberty in this country and put down traitors and treason everywhere. I call upon the great Union party to stand together, and with all their manhood resist the revolutionary schemes not only of these rebels at the South, but of their coadjutors and abettors on this floor and everywhere who would unite with them and trample not only upon the prostrate body of the Union party, but, as I believe, of liberty herself. I have done.

MARTIN THAYER [R., PA.] obtained the floor.

MR. FINCK. Will the gentleman allow me just one moment?

MR. THAYER. I will yield to the gentleman for a moment.

MR. FINCK. I desire to say to my colleague, for whom I have the highest respect, that in my judgment there is but one party in this country that is a disunion party, and he belongs to it. [Laughter on the Republican side of the House.]

MR. GARFIELD. I am willing to stand by my record as a Union man.

MR. THAYER. Mr. Speaker, the proceedings of the House to-day will, I trust, silence, at once and forever, the clamorous calumnies which have been industriously propagated by designing persons ever since this Congress convened, in which it was asserted that this Congress had no intention of taking any steps the object of which was the restoration of peace and concord to this whole country.

There have been persons, sir, very wise in their own conceit, great builders of States in their own judgment, and great law-makers, if their own opinions are to be received as truth, who have supposed that the great work upon which this Congress has entered was a work which might be accomplished with as much facility as a justice of the peace would dispose of an insignificant case in his court; and who saw, in the subject which engages the attention of this House, a matter of no grander dimensions than those which characterize the ordinary legislation of Congress. In the opinion of these persons the accumulated ruin of four years of civil war was to be remedied in an hour; States which were disorganized and rent from the parent Government by organized secession; by the deliberate and solemn act of conventions of the people; by the passage of laws during a period of four years; by the formation of new local governments; and by the exercise of every *de facto* sovereign power, were, in the opinion of these wiseacres, to be regenerated and restored to their normal relations to the Government, whose laws they had overthrown and trampled under foot, with as much facility as you would pass the most unimportant bill, and with as little delay as it would require to call the yeas and nays in this House.

Let the American people, Mr. Speaker, understand, as I doubt not they do generally understand, the magnitude of the ruin which has been caused by the rebellion, and they will comprehend the labors and the difficulties which attend the reconstruction of those old relations of loyalty and fidelity to the Constitution which once characterized these States.

Sir, for one, I have never lost my faith in the wisdom and discretion of the able committee to whom, at the outset of this Congress, this most important subject was committed. For one, I have not doubted that as soon as it could be accomplished, within as short a compass of time as the nature of the subject and the extent of the labors devolved upon them would permit, they would present to this House some scheme upon which the loyal people of the country might unite to effect a perfect restoration of peace and harmony throughout the United States. To the scheme which they have presented for that purpose, with the exception of one feature contained in it, and upon which I will presently remark, I am prepared, after due deliberation, to give my cordial assent and approval. The exception to which I refer is the provision of the third section of the proposed amendment to the Constitution.

With regard to the first section of the proposed amendment to the Constitution, I cannot conceive that any loyal man can hold any other view upon that subject than that which is indicated in the proposed amendment. The Constitution of the United States apportioned Representatives and direct taxes among the several States according to their respective numbers, and ordained that those numbers should be determined by adding to the whole number of free persons, including those held to service for a term of years and Indians not taxed, three fifths of all other persons. So stood the Constitution at the commencement of the rebellion. By that instrument three fifths of the class of persons known as slaves were counted in the enumeration which fixed the basis of representation in this House.

How stands the Constitution now? Why, sir, the literal application of the Constitution to the present state of affairs makes this late slave population of the rebel States count in the representation in this body, not as three fifths, but as five fifths. Will any man say that that was contemplated by the framers of the Constitution? Will any man say that it was within the intention of the framers of that instrument that the late slaves in this country should, by an unforeseen state of public affairs, under a provision which enacted that they should count in the basis of representation as three fifths, come to count as five fifths, while at home they are counted politically as nothing? Yet this is what is proposed by those who oppose this amendment. It seems to me no man can maintain that proposition upon any principle of justice or sound political reasoning. What number of Representatives will this bring into this Chamber from the rebel States by way of increase over the former number that came here under the terms of the Constitution? About thirteen members. Is it not preposterous that after all the trials, the sacrifices, the sufferings, and the hardships caused by this great war for the Union the result of the success of the Government should be the increase of representation in this House on the part of those who made the rebellion, by adding thirteen members which they had not before the war? Is there a man here who dare go before the northern people and tell them that they are to be rewarded for the losses and sufferings which they have sustained by having thirteen additional members admitted into this body from the rebel States. I want to see the northern constituency that will send a Representative here who declares in plain terms that that is just and that he is in favor of it.

Now, I ask gentlemen on the other side of the House why that should be done. If you say that this large class of persons have been transformed from their late condition of chattels to a condition in which they constitute a part of the element of the political fabric, then I can conceive that having added that much in population to the thinking, voting men of the southern States, it would be just and proper that that addition should be represented in this body. But we all know that such is not the case. In those States themselves the late slaves do not enter into the basis of local representation. In South Carolina they do not enter into the basis of representation in the Legislature of that State. And anybody who will read the new constitution of South Carolina will see that such is the case.

Would it not be a most unprecedented thing that when this population are not permitted where they reside to enter into the basis of representation in their own State, we should receive it as an element of representation here; that when they will not count them in apportioning their own legislative districts, we are to count them as five fifths (no longer as three fifths, for that is out of the question) as soon as you make a new apportionment? I am not going to dwell upon that proposition. I believe it to be a proposition which the people of this country will understand without much discussion. You have only to enunciate that proposition in plain terms in order to secure for it the unqualified rebuke of every man who sustained the Government during the war for the Union.

With regard to the second section of the proposed amendment to the Constitution, it simply brings into the Constitution what is found in the bill of rights of every State of the Union. As I understand it, it is but incorporating in the Constitution of the United States the principle of the civil rights bill which has lately become a law, and that, not as the gentleman from Ohio [Mr. Finck] suggested, because in the estimation of this House that law cannot be sustained as constitutional, but in order, as was justly said by the gentleman from Ohio who last addressed the House, [Mr. Garfield,] that that provision so necessary for the equal administration of the law, so just in its operation, so necessary for the protection of the fundamental rights of citizenship, shall be forever incorporated in the Constitution of the United States. But, sir, that subject has already been fully discussed, I have upon another occasion expressed my views upon it and I do not propose to detain the House with any further remarks of my own upon it. . . .

WILLIAM KELLEY [R., PA.]. Mr. Speaker, I know not that I am called specially to give utterance to my thoughts on this measure. The report of the committee does not meet my expectation, and one of its propositions is in conflict with some of my well-considered convictions. If, however, those with whom I am sent to cooperate in this House deem this measure wise and expedient, I will vote for it. I am prompted to speak because it will enable me to gratify gentlemen on the other side of the House, by allowing them to hear voices from one of the disfranchised States. They will, I know, be gratified to learn that they are not entirely voiceless or powerless on this floor.

One thing attracted my attention and doubtless that of others while listening to the speech of the gentleman from Ohio [Mr. Finck] and that of my eloquent colleague, [Mr. Boyer,] and that was that neither of them embodied in the text of his speech the text of the amendment they were discussing. I do not think this omission was accidental. I apprehend they would rather their constituents should read their denunciatory remarks than the language of the propositions under consideration. They have not discussed any provision of the proposed amendment. I will not say they dare not discuss them clause by clause and denounce them as they have, but it would evince a high degree of political courage.

Let us look at these provisions so fearfully denounced by the gentlemen. Does my colleague think he could go safely through his district in Pennsylvania denouncing the proposition to embody in the Constitution of the United States a provision that—

No State shall make or enforce any law which shall abridge the privileges or immunities of citizens of the United States; nor shall any State deprive any person of life, liberty, or property without due process of law; nor deny to any person within its jurisdiction the equal protection of the laws?

There is not a man in Montgomery or Lehigh county that will not say those provisions ought to be in the Constitution if they are not already there.

Again, sir, dare he read to his constituents the language of the second section and reiterate his denunciations of it? It is as follows:

SEC. 2. Representatives shall be apportioned among the several States which may be included within this Union according to their respective numbers, counting the whole number of persons in each State, excluding Indians not taxed. But whenever in any State the elective franchise shall be denied to any portion of its male citizens not less than twenty-one years of age, or in any way abridged, except for participation in rebellion or other crime, the basis of representation in such State shall be reduced in the proportion which the number of such male citizens shall bear to the whole number of male citizens not less than twenty-one years of age.

Shall the pardoned rebels of the South include in the basis of representation four million people to whom they deny political rights, and to no one of whom is allowed a vote in the selection of a Representative? Can he tell the men of the boroughs of Norristown and Allentown that one red-handed rebel in South Carolina is of right and ought to be the equal of three of the best and most patriotic of them on the floor of Congress or in the college for the election of President and Vice President? He dare not do it. They would spurn him and the insulting proposition. The men who fought the rebels and crushed their confederacy would say, give us at least equal consideration and power with the traitors against whom we fought, and who caused the death of three hundred thousand of our patriotic brethren.

I come, sir, to the third section. To strike that out would, in my judgment, be to emasculate the amendment. It is as follows:

SEC. 3. Until the 4th day of July, 1870, all persons who voluntarily adhered to the late insurrection, giving it aid and comfort, shall be excluded from the right to vote *for Representatives in Congress and for electors for President and Vice President of the United States.*

Who ought to govern this country? The men who for more than four years sustained bloody war for its overthrow, or they whom my colleague designates as "that proscriptive body of men known as the great Union party" who maintained the Government against the most gigantic rebellion since that which Satan led? I quote my colleague's language, and I ask him whether he dare go before our fellow citizens and argue that magnanimity requires us to hand the Government over immediately to the vanquished but unconverted rebels of the South. . . .

JOHN BROOMALL [R., PA.]. Mr. Speaker, it was to be expected that the measure now before the House would meet the opposition and denunciation of the unrepentant thirty-three of this body. The gentlemen who have voted on all occasions upon the rebel side of all questions that have been before the country for six years could hardly be expected to change their position at this time.

LEWIS ROSS [DEM., ILL.]. Will the gentleman allow me to ask him a question?

MR. BROOMALL. Allow me at once to say that I have but thirty minutes, and will not yield any of my time to anybody.

I say, Mr. Speaker, that it was not to be expected that those gentlemen would change their front upon short notice at this late day. But it is useless to waste arguments upon them in favor of this measure.

It was also to be expected that the six Johnsonian new converts to Democracy would also oppose and vote against this measure; commencing with the gentleman from New York, [Mr. Raymond,] who, I believe, has the disease in the most virulent form, thence down to the gentleman from Kentucky, [Mr. Smith,] who preceded me on this question, and who has the mildest and most amiable type of the infection. Upon them, too, arguments are useless.

There must then be thirty-nine votes against the measure, and I want there to be no more. I want every member of this House outside of those thirty-nine to vote for it heartily and earnestly. I want every man to come to the conclusion to which I have come, to vote, if not for that which he wants, for the best that he can get; to vote for the report of the committee if he can get it, just as he would have voted for someting better; and if he cannot get the measure reported, then to vote for the next best.

It is not what I wanted. How far short of it! But the necessity is urgent, and we must take what will obtain the votes of two thirds of both Houses of Congress, and the ratification of three fourths of the actual States of this Union, those entitled to a voice upon the question.

Now, what is this that is submitted for our action? I will consider the several propositions briefly; I am only sorry that I am limited to so short a space of time. We propose, first, to give power to the Government of the United States to protect its own citizens within the States, within its own jurisdiction. Who will deny the necessity of this? No one. The fact that all who will vote for the pending measure, or whose votes are asked for it, voted for this proposition in another shape, in the civil rights bill, shows that it will meet the favor of the House. It may be asked, why should we put a provision in the Constitution which is already contained in an act of Congress? The gentleman from Ohio [Mr. Bingham] may answer this question. He says the act is unconstitutional. Now, I have the highest respect for his opinions as a lawyer, and for his integrity as a man, and while I differ from him upon the law, yet it is not with that certainty of being right that would justify me in refusing to place the power to enact the law unmistakably in the Constitution. On so vital a point I wish to make assurance doubly sure.

I know that the unrepentant Democracy of this body voted against the civil rights bill upon the allegation that it was unconstitutional. And I rather expect to see them exhibit their usual consistency by voting against making it constitutional upon the ground that it is so already.

That measure, however, will meet with no opposition from those on whom the country depends for its safety, because if it is not necessary it is at least harmless. If we are already safe with the civil rights bill, it will do no harm to become the more effectually so, and to prevent a mere majority from repealing the law and thus thwarting the will of the loyal people.

The second proposition is, in short, to limit the representation of the several States as those States themselves shall limit suffrage. That measure has already received the sanction of all who can possibly be expected to vote for the proposition now before the House; because the joint resolution which passed this body by more than two thirds, and was defeated in the Senate, proposed to submit a similar change in the Constitution to the States for ratification. There is, therefore, little necessity for argument upon this point. . . .

GEORGE SHANKLIN [DEM., KY.]. Mr. Speaker, the subject now before the House for its consideration is a matter, perhaps, of as much importance, and involves as many important interests to the American people, as any subject upon which the Congress of the United States can have to pass. Upon its solution may depend the weal or woe of the American people and their descendants. Those institutions, republican and free in their character, reared by the wisdom, the patriotism, and the sufferings of our revolutionary sires, and consecrated by their blood, may depend upon the action of this Congress upon this subject.

It becomes us, then, as the Representatives of a generous and confiding people, who hold these important interests and trusts in our hands, to divest ourselves as far as is possible of every angry passion, to banish every sectional prejudice or partiality, to discard personal interest and considerations, to break the lines of party, and to rise above considerations of that kind to a higher and purer sphere, that we may act for the general good of the whole country now and forever. If we could but do this our labors would be easy, our task would be more than half performed in its very commencement. But if, from the frailty of our natures and our passions, we are unable to assume a position of this sort let us at least approach our task with clean hands, pure hearts, and patriotic intentions. . . .

Mr. Speaker, there are two prominent and distinct ideas contained in this proposition. The first idea is to strike down the reserved rights of the States, those rights which were declared by the framers of the Constitution to belong to the States exclusively and necessary for the protection of the property and liberty of the people. The first section of this proposed amendment to the Constitution is to strike down those State rights and invest all power in the General Government. It is then proposed to disfranchise the people of the southern States who have gone into this rebellion, until the party in power could fasten and rivet the chains of oppression for all time to come, and hedge themselves in power, that they may rule and control those people at will. Those are the two ideas contained in this proposition.

Now, how do you propose to carry out that second idea? Is it by degrading, by humbling, by humiliating these people, and rendering them unworthy of the blessings of liberty or of being recognized as citizens? Do you expect to effect the object in that way? Do you expect, by the terms you propose to impose on those people, to render them willing serfs and slaves to your power? If they will submit to the burdens which you propose, then they ought not to come back into this Union; for they will be unworthy to hold the position of American citizens.

But how are you going to humble and degrade these people? By disfranchising them, by oppressing them with taxes, by denying them representation, by dragging them down to the loyal political and social equality with the servile African race. You may impoverish them, you may exterminate them, but you can never reduce them to the condition when they will kiss the hand that strikes them. . . .

HENRY RAYMOND [R., N.Y.]. Mr. Speaker, I took occasion at an early stage of the session, while making some remarks on the general subject of restoration, to say that, in my judgment, the joint committee to which it had been referred, ought to lay the whole of their plan upon our tables before asking us to act upon any of its specific parts. I congratulate myself, sir, that, although when first made the demand was received with anything but favor, the committee now concede its justice by complying with it. It seemed to me then, as it seems to the committee now, that when a proposition embracing several branches more or less interdependent and all essential to the object sought to be attained, justice and fair dealing required that Congress should have possession of the whole case before being required to act upon any of its parts. We may see the result of a different course in the recent experience of the British House of Commons. That House was called on to consider a scheme of parliamentary reform, consisting of two branches, one an extension of the suffrage, and the other a reapportionment of representation, or, as they style it, a redistribution of seats. The ministry submitted its programme for the first but withheld the second. Thereupon a portion of the ministerial party demanded to see the whole plan before acting upon part of it. The ministry refused to comply, and the result of their refusal was that, although they commenced the session with a majority of sixty, they carried the bill on its second reading by the meager majority of five, in a House of over six hundred members.

I am glad to see that the reconstruction committee does not imitate the obstinacy of the British ministry. After long delay and several attempts to carry single parts of its proposition, it now submits the whole of the plan by which it proposes to restore the Union. I must say that I see nothing in the report which required any such delay, nothing which depends for its validity or force upon the evidence which, with such protracted pain, the committee has spent five months in collecting. And it is fortunate for us that this is so, for Congress is not yet in possession of any considerable portion of the testimony. It has not yet been printed and laid upon our tables to guide our action.

But, sir, without dwelling further upon these preliminary matters, I will proceed to state the nature of the report which has thus been made. The programme of reconstruction reported by the committee consists of three parts: first, a series of five constitutional amendments, upon as many different subjects, each distinct from the other; and then two bills, one providing for the admission into Congress of Representatives from the States lately in rebellion upon certain conditions, and the other excluding from Federal offices for all time to come certain classes of persons who have been engaged in that rebellion. The House has ordered that these three propositions shall be taken up in succession, and the proposed amendments to the Constitution are the only topics which are properly before us for our action now. I concur fully in the suggestion of the President of the United States, that it would be wise, when acting upon amendments to the Constitution, that all the States to be affected by them should be represented in the debate. I do not understand him to hold, I certainly do not hold myself, that the presence of them all is essential to the validity of the action we may take; and inasmuch as they are to be submitted, if adopted by us, to all the States of the Union for their ratification, and as the assent of three fourths of all those States will be required to make them valid as parts of the Constitution, I am quite willing to take action upon them here even in the absence of those States which are as yet without representation.

And now, sir, with regard to these amendments, five in form, but only four in substance, I have this to say: that, with one exception, they are such as commend themselves to my approval. The principle of the first, which secures an equality of rights among all the citizens of the United States, has had a somewhat curious history. It was first embodied in a proposition introduced by the distinguished gentleman from Ohio, [Mr. Bingham,] in the form of an amendment to the Constitution, giving to Congress power to secure an absolute equality of civil rights in every State of the Union. It was discussed somewhat in that form, but, encountering considerable opposition from both sides of the House, it was finally postponed, and is still pending. Next it came before us in the form of a bill, by which Congress proposed to exercise precisely the powers which that amendment was intended to confer, and to provide for enforcing against State tribunals the prohibitions against unequal legislation. I regarded it as very doubtful, to say the least, whether Congress, under the existing Constitution, had any power to enact such a law; and I thought, and still think, that very many members who voted for the bill also doubted the power of Congress to pass it, because they voted for the amendment by which that power was to be conferred. At all events, acting for myself and upon my own conviction on this subject, I did not vote for the bill when it was first passed, and when it came back to us from the President with his objections I voted against it. And now, although that bill became a law and is now upon our statute-book, it is again proposed so to amend the Constitution as to confer upon Congress the power to pass it.

Now, sir, I have at all times declared myself heartily in favor of the main object which that bill was intended to secure. I was in favor of securing an equality of rights to all citizens of the United States, and of all persons within their jurisdiction; all I asked was that it should be done by the exercise of powers conferred upon Congress by the Constitution. And so believing, I shall vote very cheerfully for this proposed amendment to the Constitution, which I trust may be ratified by States enough to make it part of the fundamental law.

The second amendment which is proposed to the Constitution relates to the basis of representation. That has also been already before this House for its action, and I have always declared myself in favor of the object it seeks to accomplish. As I remarked on a previous occasion, I do not think the South ought to gain a large increase of political power in the councils of the nation from the fact of their having rebelled, as they will do if the basis of representation remains unchanged. But when it was presented before it came in a form which recognized by implication the right, of every State to disfranchise a portion of its citizens on account of race, color, or previous condition of servitude, and provided that whenever any portion of any race should be thus disfranchised by any State, the whole of that race within that State should be excluded from enumeration in fixing the basis of representation. As the gentleman from Pennsylvania [Mr. Stevens] said yesterday, it provided that "if a single one of the injured race was excluded from the right of suffrage, the State should forfeit the right to have any of them represented;" and he added that he preferred it on that account. Well, sir, I did not. When it was presented before, the distinguished gentleman from Ohio [Mr. Schenck] made a very powerful argument against it. He showed that it tended directly to discourage every southern State from preparing its colored population for enfranchisement; that it deprived them of all inducement for their gradual admission to the right of suffrage, inasmuch as it exacted universal suffrage as the only condition upon which they should be counted in the basis of representation at all. I thought that argument entitled to great weight. I have never yet heard it answered. The gentleman from Ohio converted me to that view of the subject, and although he relinquished or waived it himself, I could not. I voted against a proposition which seemed to me so unjust and so injurious, not only to the whites of the southern States, but to the colored race itself. Well, sir, that amendment was rejected in the Senate, and the proposition, as embodied in the committee's report, comes before us in a very different form. It is now proposed to base representation upon suffrage, upon the number of voters, instead of upon the aggregate population in every State of the Union. And as I believe that to be essentially just, and likely to remedy the unequal representation of which complaint is so justly made, I shall give it my vote. . . .

RUFUS SPAULDING [DEM., OHIO.]. Mr. Speaker, the report of the committee has elicited in this House a most searching criticism. It is approved and disapproved, either wholly or in part, according to the views entertained by the particular individuals who have obtained the floor.

It does not, in all respects, come up to the standard which my imperfect judgment had erected, but I have lived long enough to know that very few things of a public character can be accomplished without some abnegation of one's own notions of propriety, and a respectful deference to the opinions of others.

The joint committee on reconstruction was made up of able and patriotic men. They have labored assiduously for nearly six months, and have now given to us the result of their deliberations in certain proposed amendments of the Constitution, and sundry propositions for legislative enactment.

Regarding it as more important that some definite *project* be presented by Congress to the people of the United States than that the plan itself approach very nearly to perfection, and fearing the effect of amendments upon the successful passage of the measures proposed through Congress, I have brought my mind to the conclusion that I shall best subserve the cause of patriotism and the country's good by voting severally and collectively for the measures reported by the committee. . . .

Now, sir, we propose to amend the Constitution of the United States in several respects. As to the first measure proposed, a person may read it five hundred years hence without gathering from it any idea that this rebellion ever existed. The same may be said of the second proposition, for it only proposes that, the bondsmen being made free, the apportionment of Representatives in Congress shall be based upon the whole number of persons who exercise the elective franchise, instead of the population. . . .

But, sir, there is another reason why we should ingraft this provision upon the Constitution. All our congressional legislation may be considered as ephemeral. I know that my friends on the other side of the House always take courage when we advance the idea that at some remote period they may gain possession of the controlling power in these Halls and carry measures according to the dictates of their own wisdom and sense of patriotism. Sir, let the effect fall where it may, and give consolation to whom it will, I still declare that all these matters are within the bounds, not only of possibility, but of probability, that at some not very remote period, if we admit Representatives from the rebel States into this Hall without qualification, the prospect is that, in conjunction with their friends who have so strongly sympathized with them during the four years of this recent strife, they will repeal many, if not all, of the measures which we have adopted for the welfare and the salvation of the country. Hence I insist that something of this sort should go into the Constitution, where it shall require not only the action of the Senate and the House of Representatives, but the action of the State Legislatures to erase it. . . .

GEORGE MILLER [R., PA.]. Mr. Speaker, I am glad that the committee on reconstruction, through their honorable chairman, [Mr. Stevens,] have reported to this House a proposition for certain amendments to the Constitution of the United States, which, if approved by two thirds of both Houses and then ratified by the Legislatures of three fourths of the several States, will become a part thereof. . . .

As to the first, it is so just that no State shall deprive any person of life, liberty, or property without due process of law, nor deny equal protection of the laws, and so clearly within the spirit of the Declaration of Independence of the 4th of July, 1776, that no member of this House can seriously object

The next, as to representation, I deem the most important amendment, and is in fact the corner-stone of the stability of our Government. In the Constitution of the United States of 17th of September, 1787, in section two, under article one, it is provided that—

Representatives and direct taxes shall be apportioned among the several States which may be included within this Union according to their respective numbers, which shall be determined by adding to the whole number of free persons, including those bound to service for a term of years, and excluding Indians not taxed, three fifths of all other persons.

The word "slave" was not very palatable to the venerable gentlemen who framed that Constitution, and therefore they used the words "all others," which, of course, meant slaves. Before the rebellion the slave States had a representation in Congress of nineteen for slaves and about five for free blacks, and slavery being now abolished, the other two fifths would add say thirteen more, making about thirty-seven Representatives from the black man's population. Now, conceding to each State the right to regulate the right of suffrage, they ought not to have a representation for male citizens not less than twenty-one years of age, whether white or black, who are deprived of the exercise of suffrage. This amendment will settle the complication in regard to suffrage and representation, leaving each State to regulate that for itself, so that it will be for it to decide whether or not it shall have a representation for all its male citizens not less than twenty-one years of age.

The amendment, Mr. Speaker, if adopted, will give the country a sufficient guarantee against any contingency that might arise in the admission of representatives from the States lately in rebellion—I mean such men as did not voluntarily engage in the rebellion, and can take the oath prescribed by existing laws. I do not regard the amendment of the constitutions of those States of much practical importance, for the same power that makes the amendments may unmake; but to annul an amendment to the Constitution of the United States requires the consent of two thirds of both Houses of Congress and a ratification by the Legislatures of three fourths of the several States or by a convention in three fourths thereof, as the one or the other mode of ratification may be proposed by Congress; and if this amendment is adopted it is not likely it will ever be altered so as to endanger the loyal States—I mean by the loyal States those States that aided us in putting down the rebellion. . . .

THOMAS ELIOT [R., MASS.]. And now, Mr. Speaker, I shall very briefly give my reasons for sustaining the report of the committee and voting for the amendment which they offer to the House.

I support the first section because the doctrine it declares is right, and if, under the Constitution as it now stands, Congress has not the power to prohibit State legislation discriminating against classes of citizens or depriving any persons of life, liberty, or property without due process of law, or denying to any persons within the State the equal protection of the laws, then, in my judgment, such power should be distinctly conferred. I voted for the civil rights bill, and I did so under a conviction that we have ample power to enact into law the provisions of that bill. But I shall gladly do what I may to incorporate into the Constitution provisions which will settle the doubt which some gentlemen entertain upon that question.

The second section, Mr. Speaker, is, in my judgment, as nearly correct as it can be without being fully, in full measure, right. But one thing is right, and that is secured by the amendment. Manifestly no State should have its basis of national representation enlarged by reason of a portion of citizens within its borders to which the elective franchise is denied. If political power shall be lost because of such denial, not imposed because of participation in rebellion or other crime, it is to be hoped that political interests may work in the line of justice, and that the end will be the impartial enfranchisement of all citizens not disqualified by crime. Whether that end shall be attained or not, this will be secured: that the measure of political power of any State shall be determined by that portion of its citizens which can speak and act at the polls, and shall not be enlarged because of the residence within the State of portions of its citizens denied the right of franchise. So much for the second section of the amendment. It is not all that I wish and would demand; but odious inequalities are removed by it and representation will be equalized. . . .

SAMUEL RANDALL [R., PA.]. Mr. Speaker, in discussing this question briefly, as I am compelled to do by reason of the limited time allowed me, I shall advert to the proposition now before the House as a whole, not undertaking a lengthy discussion of the various amendments which have been proposed, and I trust the chairman of the committee [Mr. Stevens] will, when the proper time arrives, call the previous question, and in that manner induce a vote upon the main proposition as embraced in the whole five sections of the proposed amendment to the Constitution.

And for that purpose I desire to analyze the various sections of the proposed amendment. The first section proposes to make an equality in every respect between the two races, notwithstanding the policy of discrimination which has heretofore been exclusively exercised by the States, which in my judgment should remain and continue. They relate to matters appertaining to State citizenship, and there is no occasion whatever for the Federal power to be exercised between the two races at variance with the wishes of the people of the States. For myself, I would wish that the colored race should be placed in the same political condition as it occupies in Pennsylvania; but I would leave all this to the States themselves, just in the same manner as the elective franchise is permitted. If you have the right to interfere in behalf of one character of rights—I may say of every character or rights, save the suffrage—how soon will you be ready to tear down every barrier? It is only because you fear the people that you do not now do it. I consider the Federal restraints upon the States in reference to rights of citizens as now in the Constitution safe and sufficient. I feel it, in consequence, my imperative duty to oppose this section. Grant this power, insert it in the Constitution, and how soon will the privilege of determining who must vote within the States be assumed by the Federal power? Gentlemen here admit that they desire this, but that the weak kneed of their party are not equal to the issue. Your purpose is the same, and but for that timidity you would now ingraft negro suffrage upon our Constitution and force it on the entire people of this Union. . . .

Such is the plan of the committee of fifteen, or what may perhaps be described as the congressional view of this vexed question. It is a plan of disunion, and it is a deception to call it otherwise; and the friends of the Union, by whatever name, must cooperate to defeat this measure, or the Union will sooner or later be destroyed by those who have arrogated to themselves to be its special defenders.

This proposition is worthy of having emanated from the tower of Babel. It carries with it a confusion of tongues and a confusion of purposes. One design, however, is clearly apparent, and that is to secure the success of the Republican party, even in the event of the overthrow of the Union. . . .

ANDREW ROGERS [DEM., N.J.] [member of Joint Reconstruction Committee]. . . .

Now, sir, I have examined these propositions with some minuteness, and I have come to the conclusion different to what some others have come, that the first section of this programme of disunion is the most dangerous to liberty. It saps the foundation of the Government; it destroys the elementary principles of the States; it consolidates everything into one imperial despotism; it annihilates all the rights which lie at the foundation of the Union of the States, and which have characterized this Government and made it prosperous and great during the long period of its existence.

This section of the joint resolution is no more nor less than an attempt to embody in the Constitution of the United States that outrageous and miserable civil rights bill which passed both Houses of Congress and was vetoed by the President of the United States upon the ground that it was a direct attempt to consolidate the power of the States and to take away from them the elementary principles which lie at their foundation. It is only an attempt to ingraft upon the Constitution of the United States one of the most dangerous, most wicked, most intolerant, and most odious propositions ever introduced into this House or attempted to be ingrafted upon the fundamental law of the Federal Union.

It provides that no State shall make or enforce any law which shall abridge the privileges or immunities of citizens of the United States; nor shall any State deprive any person of life, liberty, or property without due process of law, nor deny to any person within its jurisdiction the equal protection of the laws. What are privileges and immunities? Why, sir, all the rights we have under the laws of the country are embraced under the definition of privileges and immunities. The right to vote is a privilege. The right to marry is a privilege. The right to contract is a privilege. The right to be a juror is a privilege. The right to be a judge or President of the United States is a privilege. I hold if that ever becomes a part of the fundamental law of the land it will prevent any State from refusing to allow anything to anybody embraced under this term of privileges and immunities. If a negro is refused the right to be a juror, that will take away from him his privileges and immunities as a citizen of the United States, and the Federal Government will step in and interfere, and the result will be a contest between the powers of the Federal Government and the powers of the State. It will result in a revolution worse than that through which we have just passed. It will rock the earth like the throes of an earthquake until its tragedy will summon the inhabitants of the world to witness its dreadful shock.

I believe it will be, if that contest comes between Federal and State powers, a time when nature will bleed with agony in every part. That, sir, will be an introduction to the time when despotism and tyranny will march forth undisturbed and unbroken, in silence and in darkness, in this land which was once the land of freedom, where the sound of freedom once awakened the souls of the sons and daughters of America, when from the mountain-tops to the shore of the ocean they drank in the love of liberty.

I assert that the second section of this proposed amendment is unparalleled in ferocity. It saps the foundation of the rights of the States, by taking away the representation to which they would be entitled under the present Constitution. When the gentleman from Ohio [Mr. Bingham] brought forward a proposition from the committee on reconstruction to amend the Constitution of the United States, interfering with the elementary principles of taxation and representation, the principles for which our fathers fought when they rebelled against the tyranny of King George and the English Parliament who undertook to tax the people of the colonies without representation, the proposition was defeated in this House upon the ground that it would destroy a fundamental principle, that there should be taxation only according to representation.

This, sir, is precisely such a proposition as that. It declares that if the southern people refuse to allow the negroes to vote, then all that portion of the male colored population of twenty-one years of age and upward shall be excluded in the basis of representation—shall not be counted in ascertaining how many Representatives the States are entitled to.

The honorable gentleman from Pennsylvania [Mr. Stevens] has the frankness to state to the House what the object and purpose of the second clause are. He says:

The effect of this provision will be either to compel the States to grant universal suffrage or so to shear them of their power as to keep them forever in a hopeless minority in the national Government, both legislative and executive.

Yes, gentlemen, it is but the negro again appearing in the background. The only object of the constitutional amendment is to drive the people of the South, ay, and even the people of the North, wherever there is much of a negro population, to allow that population not qualified but universal suffrage, without regard to intelligence or character, to allow them to come to the ballot-box and cast their votes equally with the white men.

Why do you not meet this question boldly and openly? Why do you undertake to deceive the people by offering to them an amendment which you say is based upon a principle of justice, that only the voting population shall be represented, when you admit by your leader in this House, the honorable gentleman [Mr. Stevens] who introduced into the committee this whole scheme of disunion and despotism, that the object of this amendment is to force the southern States to grant to the negro unrestricted suffrage?

Sir, I want it distinctly understood that the American people believe that this Government was made for white men and white women. They do not believe, nor can you make them believe—the edict of God Almighty is stamped against it—that there is a social equality between the black race and the white.

I have no fault to find with the colored race. I have not the slightest antipathy to them. I wish them well, and if I were in a State where they exist in large numbers I would vote to give them every right enjoyed by the white people except the right of a negro man to marry a white woman and the right to vote. But, sir, this proposition goes further than any that has ever been attempted to be carried into effect. Why, sir, even in Rhode Island to-day there is a property qualification in regard to the white man's voting as well as the negro. And yet Representatives of the eastern, middle, western, and some of the border States come here and attempt in this indirect way to inflict upon the people of the South negro suffrage. God deliver this people from such a wicked, odious, pestilent despotism! God save the people of the South from the degradation by which they would be obliged to go to the polls and vote side by side with the negro! . . .

JOHN FARNSWORTH [R., ILL.]. Mr. Speaker, in my half hour I shall confine myself to the amendments of the Constitution now under consideration. When the bill reported by the committee of fifteen comes up for action by this House I may desire to say something in regard to it.

I intend to vote for this amendment in the form reported, with the exception of the third section. It is not all I could wish; it is not all I hope may yet be adopted and ratified; for I am not without hope that Congress and the people of the several States may yet rise above a mean prejudice and do equal and exact justice to all men, by putting in practice that "self-evident truth" of the Declaration of Independence, that Governments "derive their just powers from the consent of the governed," and giving to every citizen, white or black, who has not forfeited the right by his crimes, the ballot. But I do not think it is becoming in a legislator to oppose some good because the measure is not all he wants.

The first section of the amendment proposed is as follows:

SEC. 1. No State shall make or enforce any law which shall abridge the privileges or immunities of citizens of the United States; nor shall any State deprive any person of life, liberty, or property, without due process of law; nor deny to any person within its jurisdiction the equal protection of its laws.

So far as this section is concerned, there is but one clause in it which is not already in the Constitution, and it might as well in my opinion read, "No State shall deny to any person within its jurisdiction the equal protection of the laws." But a reaffirmation of a good principle will do no harm, and I shall not therefore oppose it on account of what I may regard as surplusage.

"Equal protection of the laws;" can there be any well-founded objection to this? Is not this the very foundation of a republican government? Is it not the undeniable right of every subject of the Government to receive "equal protection of the laws" with every other subject? How can he have and enjoy equal rights of "life, liberty, and the pursuit of happiness" without "equal protection of the laws?" This is so self-evident and just that no man whose soul is not too cramped and dwarfed to hold the smallest germ of justice can fail to see and appreciate it. . . .

JOHN BINGHAM [R., OHIO]. The want of the Republic to-day is not a Democratic party, is not a Republican party, is not any party save a party for the Union, for the Constitution, for the supremacy of the laws, for the restoration of all the States to their political rights and powers under such irrevocable guarantees as will forevermore secure the safety of the Republic, the equality of the States, and the equal rights of all the people under the sanctions of inviolable law.

I trust, Mr. Speaker, that after the roll shall have been called this day, and the departing sun shall have gilded with its last rays the dome of the Capitol, it will not be recorded by the pen of the historian that the sad hour had come to this great Republic which, in the day of its approaching dissolution, came to the republic of ancient Rome, when it was said Caesar had his party, Antony had his party, Brutus had his party, but the Commonwealth had none!

I speak to-day, Mr. Speaker, to the party that is for the Republic; to the party that is for the Constitution; to the party that is for the speedy restoration to their constitutional relations of the late insurrectionary States, under such perpetual guarantees as will guard the future of the Republic by the united voice of a united people against the sad calamities which have in these late years befallen it.

Mr. Speaker, the final settlement of this grave question which touches the nation's life is at last with the people of the loyal States—the loyal people of the Union. To the end, therefore, knowing, as the committee did know, that parties must dissolve, that men must perish from the earth, but that the Commonwealth is for all time, if its laws be just and its people be faithful, they propose to the several States a perpetual covenant in the form of a constitutional amendment, never to be broken so long as the people adhere to their cherished forms of government, which, when ratified, will secure the safety of all and the rights of each, not only during the present generation, but throughout all generations, until this grand example of free government shall itself be forgotten. The amendment reported by the committee is as follows:

ARTICLE

SEC. 1. No State shall make or enforce any law which shall abridge the privileges or immunities of citizens of the United States; nor shall any State deprive any person of life, liberty, or property without due process of law; nor deny to any person within its jurisdiction the equal protection of the laws.

SEC. 2. Representatives shall be apportioned among the several States which may be included within this Union according to their respective numbers, counting the whole number of persons in each State, excluding Indians not taxed. But whenever, in any State, the elective franchise shall be denied to any portion of its male citizens not less than twenty-one years of age, or in any way abridged, except for participation in rebellion or other crime, the basis of representation in such State shall be reduced in the proportion which the number of such male citizens shall bear to the whole number of male citizens not less than twenty-one years of age.

SEC. 3. Until the 4th day of July, in the year 1870, all persons who voluntarily adhered to the late insurrection, giving it aid and comfort, shall be excluded from the right to vote for Representatives in Congress and for electors for President and Vice President of the United States.

SEC. 4. Neither the United States nor any State shall assume or pay any debt or obligation already incurred, or which may hereafter be incurred, in aid of insurrection or of war against the United States, or any claim for compensation for loss of involuntary service or labor.

SEC. 5. The Congress shall have power to enforce by appropriate legislation the provisions of this article.

The necessity for the first section of this amendment to the Constitution, Mr. Speaker, is one of the lessons that have been taught to your committee and taught to all the people of this country by the history of the past four years of terrific conflict—that history in which God is, and in which He teaches the profoundest lessons to men and nations. There was a want hitherto, and there remains a want now, in the Constitution of our country, which the proposed amendment will supply. What is that? It is the power in the people, the whole people of the United States, by express authority of the Constitution to do that by congressional enactment which hitherto they have not had the power to do, and have never even attempted to do; that is, to protect by national law the privileges and immunities of all the citizens of the Republic and the inborn rights of every person within its jurisdiction whenever the same shall be abridged or denied by the unconstitutional acts of any State.

Allow me, Mr. Speaker, in passing, to say that this amendment takes from no State any right that ever pertained to it. No State ever had the right, under the forms of law or otherwise, to deny to any freeman the equal protection of the laws or to abridge the privileges or immunities of any citizen of the Republic, although many of them have assumed and exercised the power, and that without remedy. The amendment does not give, as the second section shows, the power to Congress of regulating suffrage in the several States.

The second section excludes the conclusion that by the first section suffrage is subjected to congressional law; save, indeed, with this exception, that

as the right in the people of each State to a republican government and to
choose their Representatives in Congress is of the guarantees of the Constitution, by this amendment a remedy might be given directly for a case
supposed by Madison, where treason might change a State government from
a republican to a despotic government, and thereby deny suffrage to the
people. Why should any American citizen object to that? But, sir, it has been
suggested, not here, but elsewhere, if this section does not confer suffrage the
need of it is not perceived. To all such I beg leave again to say, that many
instances of State injustice and oppression have already occurred in the State
legislation of this Union, of flagrant violations of the guarantied privileges of
citizens of the United States, for which the national Government furnished
and could furnish by law no remedy whatever. Contrary to the express letter
of your Constitution, "cruel and unusual punishments" have been inflicted
under State laws within this Union upon citizens, not only for crimes committed, but for sacred duty done, for which and against which the Government of the United States had provided no remedy and could provide none.

Sir, the words of the Constitution that "the citizens of each State shall be
entitled to all privileges and immunities of citizens in the several States"
include, among other privileges, the right to bear true allegiance to the
Constitution and laws of the United States, and to be protected in life,
liberty, and property. Next, sir, to the allegiance which we all owe to God
our Creator, is the allegiance which we owe to our common country.

The time was in our history, thirty-three years ago, when, in the State of
South Carolina, by solemn ordinance adopted in a convention held under the
authority of State law, it was ordained, as a part of the fundamental law of
that State, that the citizens of South Carolina, being citizens of the United
States as well, should abjure their allegiance to every other government or
authority than that of the State of South Carolina.

That ordinance contained these words:

> The allegiance of the citizens of this State is due to the State; and no allegiance is due
> from them to any other Power or authority; and the General Assembly of said State is
> hereby empowered from time to time, when they may deem it proper, to provide for the
> administration to the citizens and officers of the State, or such of the said officers as they
> may think fit, of suitable oaths or affirmations, binding them to the observance of such
> allegiance, and abjuring all other allegiance; and also to define what shall amount to a
> violation of their allegiance, and to provide the proper punishment for such violation.

There was also, as gentlemen know, an attempt made at the same time by
that State to nullify the revenue laws of the United States. What was the
legislation of Congress in that day to meet this usurpation of authority by
that State, violative alike of the rights of the national Government and of the
rights of the citizen?

In that hour of danger and trial to the country there was as able a body of
men in this Capitol as was ever convened in Washington, and of these were
Webster, Clay, Benton, Silas Wright, John Quincy Adams, and Edward

Livingston. They provided a remedy by law for the invasion of the rights of the Federal Government and for the protection of its officials and those assisting them in executing the revenue laws. (See 4 Statutes-at-Large, 632-33.) No remedy was provided to protect the citizen. Why was the act to provide for the collection of the revenue passed, and to protect all acting under it, and no protection given to secure the citizen against punishment for fidelity to his country? But one answer can be given. There was in the Constitution of the United States an express grant of power to the Federal Congress to lay and collect duties and imposts and to pass all laws necessary to carry that grant of power into execution. But, sir, that body of great and patriotic men looked in vain for any grant of power in the Constitution by which to give protection to the citizens of the United States resident in South Carolina against the infamous provision of the ordinance which required them to abjure the allegiance which they owed their country. It was an opprobrium to the Republic that for fidelity to the United States they could not by national law be protected against the degrading punishment inflicted on slaves and felons by State law. That great want of the citizen and stranger, protection by national law from unconstitutional State enactments, is supplied by the first section of this amendment. That is the extent that it hath, no more; and let gentlemen answer to God and their country who oppose its incorporation into the organic law of the land.

The second section of the amendment simply provides for the equalization of representation among all the States of the Union, North, South, East, and West. It makes no discrimination. New York has a colored population of fifty thousand. By this section, if that great State discriminates against her colored population as to the elective franchise, (except in cases of crime,) she loses to that extent her representative power in Congress. So also will it be with every other State.

Upon the third section of the amendment gentlemen are divided upon this side of the House as well as upon the other. It is a provision that until the year 1870 all persons who voluntarily adhered to the late insurrection, giving it aid and comfort, shall be excluded from the right to vote for Representatives in Congress or for electors for President or Vice President of the United States. This section imposes no other or further disability.

It seems to me, Mr. Speaker, that this section can bring no strength to the amendment, although I fully agree with the honorable gentleman from Massachusetts [Mr. Banks] in the words which he so fitly uttered, it is within the authority of the people of the United States to disfranchise these parties. But, sir, I submit to the honorable gentleman, and I submit to the House, that if we have the power by a mere act of Congress, (as is conceded by the committee,) to take from rebels the franchise of office under the Government of the United States for life, as is provided in the bill reported by the committee, we can as well take from them until 1870, by an act of

Congress, the right to vote for Representatives in Congress or for presidential electors, as is provided in the third section of this amendment.

MR. STEVENS. And have it vetoed.

MR. BINGHAM. My friend from Pennsylvania says, "and have it vetoed." I am not fearful of any veto at the other end of the avenue. I believe no veto can defeat the final passage of either of the measures reported to the House, nor can a veto defeat the final triumph of this constitutional amendment before the people. The success of the amendment here depends upon no veto. It does not go to the President for his sanction. Touching, however, the other question, the veto of the bill, even with the provision of the third section added to it, I do not believe for a moment, that the President will veto it, and for the reasons suggested, which I have not time to enumerate now, by the gentleman from Massachusetts in the citations he made from the President's proclamation of the 29th of May last and the just deductions he drew therefrom. I can vote for the amendment with the third section in as readily as without it. It raises no question of power; it imposes no unjust disability. It involves a question of policy, not of power. The sovereignty of the nation can unquestionably disfranchise the persons referred to, not only until 1870, but until seventy times seventy shall have passed over them, if it pleases God to allow them so long to live upon the earth.

The question upon the third section, and the only question, is, what do we gain by putting it in the constitutional amendment? If thereby we endanger the adoption of the amendment in the Senate, or its final ratification by the requisite number of States, we should omit it. It has been said that the third section is incapable of execution if adopted. I beg leave to say to the House that in my opinion an amendment that is not to be executed to the full, and which is incapable of full execution, ought not to be put into the Constitution. My honorable colleague from the Columbus district, [Mr. Shellabarger,] in my judgment, suggested, in the few remarks which he made yesterday, the only method by which the Government of the United States can enforce the first clause of that section, and that is by making a registry law for congressional districts, and the election of Representatives to Congress all over the country, and appointing election officers to conduct the same. The first clause only of the third section can in that way be executed; but is there anybody here who proposes to send Federal election officers into Massachusetts or New York to control the elections of Representatives to Congress? The amendment, sir, is of universal application, and if adopted, it is to be enforced in every State in the Union. There are voters within the operation of this section in every State. I have no objection to their disfranchisement, but are you going to enforce the provision if adopted? If not, why retain it? Is it to be retained simply to furnish demagogues a pretext for raising the howl that we exclude rebels for four years only that we may control the next presidential election? Honest, intelligent, and reflecting men will scout such a suggestion, but the calculating and the careless or thoughtless may accept and act upon it to the hurt, the lasting hurt, of the sacred cause this day in your hands. How, I ask, can the last clause of this third section be enforced?

That clause of the section excludes until 1870 all rebels from voting for electors for President and Vice President of the United States.

I venture to say that by the very letter and intendment of the Constitution of our country, the great seal of a State, duly organized and exercising its functions within this Union touching the appointment of electors for President and Vice President of the United States, is final and conclusive upon Congress, except when the certificate shows that the electors were appointed on a day other than that prescribed by the Constitution or the laws. The Constitution has provided that these electors shall be appointed by each State in such manner as the Legislature thereof may direct; that the Congress may determine the time of choosing the electors and the day on which they shall give their votes, which day shall be the same throughout the United States, and that the electors shall certify their action.

If the State and the electors' certificates show that all these provisions have been complied with, Congress cannot go behind them and inquire who voted for the electors. If, on the contrary, the certificate from any State discloses that the electors did not meet on the day prescribed by law, as was the fact in the Wisconsin case, to which the gentleman from Massachusetts [Mr. Banks] referred, of course the Congress could reject the vote from that State, but where the certificates are regular, where they show a due appointment of electors, that the electors were chosen on the day prescribed by law, and met and voted for President and Vice President on the day prescribed by law, Congress cannot go behind the certificates; neither can the two Houses of Congress, in joint convention or separately, investigate the question. The appointment of electors for President and Vice President of the United States is the act of a State and not of individuals. "Each State shall appoint," says the Constitution; therefore the act can be evidenced only by the certificate of the State officials, under its great seal, which imports absolute verity. How could Congress say the appointment was not the act of the State against the certificate and seal of the State?

The remarks of some gentlemen to the effect that under the Constitution we could enforce the first clause of the section by inquiring into the election of members of the House or of the Senate, do not apply to the last clause, because the express language of the Constitution is that "each House shall be the judge of the elections and returns" as well as the "qualifications of its own members." There is no like grant in the Constitution that each House or both Houses in joint convention may inquire into the appointment of electors; therefore the second clause of the third section of the amendment is useless.

I venture to say that clause is useless unless, indeed, by implication Congress is to declare the express text of the Constitution as I have cited it repealed by the proposed amendment when adopted, and that by virtue of it Congress will prescribe by law the mode and manner of appointing electors for President and Vice President of the United States, in the face of the existing provision of the Constitution that "each State shall appoint the electors in such manner as the Legislature thereof may direct." Who will say, if this amendment is adopted, that the State Legislatures may not direct the manner and each State appoint electors? To what, then, are we reduced? This amendment does not disqualify any rebel or aider of the rebellion from voting at all the State elections for all State officers, nor does it disqualify them from being appointed presidential electors. It amounts, therefore, to this: though it be adopted, and made part of the Constitution, yet all persons "who voluntarily adhered to the late insurrection, giving it aid and comfort," may vote at all the State elections for State officers, and, being largely in the majority in every insurrectionary State, may elect the State Legislature, which may appoint electors for President and Vice President of the United States, and from aught in the amendment may appoint rebels as such electors.

It seems to me, sir, that it must by this time be apparent to members of the House that this clause of the amendment is never to be executed until that will require another amendment to the Constitution to enforce this clause if adopted.

I trust, therefore, that when the vote comes to be taken on the pending motion to strike out which is offered by way of instruction to the motion to recommit, it will be adopted, and that afterward the House will, if it deems it important, put such a provision as to the election of Representatives to Congress as it has the lawful right to do in the bill of disfranchisement.

Mr. Speaker, there is another section which simply prohibits the United States or any State of this Union from ever assuming or paying any part of the rebel debt or making compensation for emancipated slaves. I do not believe that there is a man on this floor who can answer to his constituency for withholding his vote from that proposition. It involves the future fidelity of the nation. It is a declaration in solemn form, if accepted by the people, that the resources of this great country shall be used in the future, not to liquidate debts contracted in aid of rebellion, not to pay for emancipated slaves, but to maintain inviolate the plighted faith of the nation to all the world and especially to its dead and its living defenders.

Mr. Speaker, I trust that this amendment, with or without the third section, will pass this House. I trust that the disfranchisement bill, with or without additions, will pass this House. I trust that the enabling act for the restoration of the States that have been in rebellion will, with amendment, pass this House; so that the day may soon come when Tennessee—loyal Tennessee, loyal in the very heart of the rebellion, her mountains and plains blasted by the ravages of war and stained with the blood of her faithful children fallen in the great struggle for the maintenance of the Union—having already conformed her constitution and laws to every provision of this amendment, will at once upon its submission by Congress irrevocably ratify it, and be without further delay represented in Congress by her loyal Representatives and Senators, duly elected and duly qualified and ready to take the oath of office prescribed by existing law.

Let that great example be set by Tennessee and it will be worth a hundred thousand votes to the loyal people in the free North. Let this be done and it will be hailed as the harbinger of that day for which all good men pray, when the fallen pillars of the Republic shall be restored without violence or the noise of words or the sound of the hammer, each to its original place in the sacred temple of our national liberties, thereby giving assurance to all the world that for the defense of the Republic it was not in vain that a million and a half of men, the very elect of the earth, rushed to arms; that the Republic still lives, and will live forevermore, the sanctuary of an inviolable justice, the refuge of liberty, and the imperishable monument of the nation's dead, from the humblest soldier who perished on the march, or went down amid the thunder and tempest of the dread conflict, up through all the shining roll of heroes, and patriots, and martyrs, to the incorruptible and immortal Commander-in-Chief, who fell by an assassin's hand in the capital, and thus died that his country might live. . . .

On May 23, 1866, the Senate began its consideration of the proposed Fourteenth Amendment. Much of what was said about the extracts from the House debate of May 8-10 is also relevant here. The Senate debate began with the speech of Senator Jacob Howard [R., Mich.] introducing the amendment. The debate itself was shorter and less informative than that in the House, though it extended over a longer period of time. It was not till June 8 that the vote was taken, with the amendment passing by 33 to 11, with 5 not voting.

The Senate made one important change in Section 1 of the proposed amendment, as it had been reported by the Joint Committee—the addition of the first sentence defining citizenship. Critics had asserted that an amendment designed to clarify the rights of citizenship should itself make clear who were citizens. The addition was made without debate on May 29, as one of the changes which had been agreed on in a Republican caucus (which gave rise to Senator Hendricks' caustic animadversions on June 4). The addition to Section 1 was really only an improved version of the citizenship definition in the 1866 Civil Rights Act. Its primary purpose was to lend constitutional sanction to the citizenship status of the Negro, and thus hammer the last nail in the coffin of the by-then thoroughly discredited *Dred Scott* decision.

In the Senate debate itself, the most important speech was the introductory address of Senator Howard. Called upon to substitute for the ailing Joint Committee chairman, Howard delivered what is, in many ways, the most significant legislative statement on the purpose of Section 1 of the Fourteenth Amendment. In his speach, we have the only specific assertion that the aim of the new provision was to make the Bill of Rights binding upon the states. Referring to the "privileges and immunities" guaranteed by the amendment, he tells us that they include the privileges and immunities spoken of in Article IV, Section 2, as well as "the personal rights guaranteed and secured by the first eight amendments." He then goes on to declare: "The great object of the first section of this amendment is, therefore, to restrain the power of the States and compel them at all times to respect these great fundamental guarantees."

Certain important points are relevant in considering Howard's assertion on the purpose of the new amendment. His claim is based upon the privileges and immunities clause of Section 1; he states that it is that clause that is intended to incorporate the Bill of Rights. It should, however, be observed that the more recent controversy over whether the Fourteenth Amendment makes the Bill of Rights binding upon the states (as exemplified by the opinions in *Adamson* v. *California, infra* p. 342) has turned on the scope of the amendment's due process clause. As other speakers in the Senate debate (notably Reverdy Johnson, perhaps the ablest lawyer in the chamber) pointed out, the term "privileges and immunities" itself was far from clear and it was difficult, if not impossible, to say what the effect of the new privileges and immunities clause would be. Certainly no participant in the congressional debates so much as even hinted that the due process clause of the proposed amendment would have the drastic impact that has since been claimed for it.

Even though he was only a substitute for the Joint Committee chairman, Senator Howard did occupy the position of sponsor of the amendment and, as such, his views on its effect are entitled to particular weight. At the same time, it is most pertinent to note that his assertion that the amendment was intended to make the Bill of Rights binding upon the states was concurred in by no other senator. On the contrary, the position taken by many of the participants in the Senate debate was inconsistent with Howard's view. This was true particularly of some of the senators whose legal backgrounds were especially impressive, such as Senators Luke Poland [R., Vt.] (for many years Chief Justice of Vermont), Reverdy Johnson [Dem., Md.], and John Henderson [Dem., Mo.]. They asserted either that the new privileges and immunities clause secured nothing beyond what was intended by Article IV, section 2, or that its effect was uncertain.

After the Senate debate, the proposed amendment was returned to the House for its concurrence in the changes made in the upper chamber, notably the addition of the citizenship clause to section 1. The House considered the Senate changes during a single day and voted its concurrence 132 to 120, 32 absent. Thus, the Fourteenth Amendment was approved by the required majority, by Congress. The next step was ratification by the states, which was completed in 1868, and the amendment was certified as part of the Constitution on July 21, 1868.

THE DEBATE

Senate-39th Congress, 1st Session
May 23-June 8, 1866

JACOB HOWARD [R., MICH.]. Mr. President, I regret that the state of the health of the honorable Senator from Maine [Mr. Fessenden] who is chairman, on the part of the Senate, of the Joint Committee of Fifteen, is such as to disable him from opening the discussion of this grave and important measure. I was anxious that he should take the lead, and the prominent lead, in the conduct of this discussion, and still entertain the hope that before it closes the Senate will have the benefit of a full and ample statement of his views. For myself, I can only promise to present to the Senate, in a very succinct way, the views and the motives which influenced that committee, so far as I understand those views and motives, in presenting the report which is now before us for consideration, and the ends it aims to accomplish.

The joint resolution creating that committee intrusted them with a very important inquiry, an inquiry involving a vast deal of attention and labor. They were instructed to inquire into the condition of the insurgent States, and authorized to report by bill or otherwise at their discretion. I believe that I do not overstate the truth when I say that no committee of Congress has ever proceeded with more fidelity and attention to the matter intrusted to them. They have been assiduous in discharging their duty. They have instituted an inquiry, so far as it was practicable for them to do so, into the political and social condition of the insurgent States. It is very true, they have not visited any localities outside of the city of Washington in order to obtain information; but they have taken the testimony of a great number of witnesses who have been summoned by them to Washington, or who happened to be in Washington, and who had some acquaintance with the condition of affairs in the insurgent States. I think it will be the judgment of the country in the end that that committee, so far as the procuring of testimony upon this subject is concerned, has been not only industrious and assiduous, but impartial and entirely fair. I know that such has been their aim. I know that it has not been their purpose to present to Congress and the country in their report anything unfair or one-sided, or anything of a party tendency. Our anxiety has been to ascertain the whole truth in its entire length and breadth, so far as the facilities given us would warrant.

One result of their investigations has been the joint resolution for the amendment of the Constitution of the United States now under consideration. After most mature deliberation and discussion, reaching through weeks and even months, they came to the conclusion that it was necessary, in order to restore peace and quiet to the country and again to impart vigor and efficiency to the laws, and especially to obtain something in the shape of a security for the future against the recurrence of the enormous evils under

257

which the country has labored for the last four years, that the Constitution of the United States ought to be amended; and the project which they have now submitted is the result of their deliberations upon that subject.

The first section of the amendment they have submitted for the consideration of the two Houses relates to the privileges and immunities of citizens of the several States, and to the rights and privileges of all persons, whether citizens or others, under the laws of the United States. It declares that—

No State shall make or enforce any law which shall abridge the privileges or immunities of citizens of the United States; nor shall any State deprive any person of life, liberty, or property without due process of law; nor deny to any person within its jurisdiction the equal protection of the laws.

It will be observed that this is a general prohibition upon all the States, as such, from abridging the privileges and immunities of the citizens of the United States. That is its first clause, and I regard it as very important. It also prohibits each one of the States from depriving any person of life, liberty, or property without due process of law, or denying to any person within the jurisdiction of the State the equal protection of its laws.

The first clause of this section relates to the privileges and immunities of citizens of the United States as such, and as distinguished from all other persons not citizens of the United States. It is not, perhaps, very easy to define with accuracy what is meant by the expression, "citizen of the United States," although that expression occurs twice in the Constitution, once in reference to the President of the United States, in which instance it is declared that none but a citizen of the United States shall be President, and again in reference to Senators, who are likewise to be citizens of the United States. Undoubtedly the expression is used in both those instances in the same sense in which it is employed in the amendment now before us. A citizen of the United States is held by the courts to be a person who was born within the limits of the United States and subject to their laws. Before the adoption of the Constitution of the United States, the citizens of each State were, in a qualified sense at least, aliens to one another, for the reason that the several States before that event were regarded by each other as independent Governments, each one possessing a sufficiency of sovereign power to enable it to claim the right of naturalization; and, undoubtedly, each one of them possessed for itself the right of naturalizing foreigners, and each one, also, if it had seen fit so to exercise its sovereign power, might have declared the citizens of every other State to be aliens in reference to itself. With a view to prevent such confusion and disorder, and to put the citizens of the several States on an equality with each other as to all fundamental rights, a clause was introduced in the Constitution declaring that "the citizens of each State shall be entitled to all privileges and immunities of citizens in the several States."

The effect of this clause was to constitute ipso facto the citizens of each one of the original States citizens of the United States. And how did they antecedently become citizens of the several States? By birth or by naturalization. They became such in virtue of national law, or rather of natural law which recognizes persons born within the jurisdiction of every country as being subjects or citizens of that country. Such persons were, therefore, citizens of the United States as were born in the country or were made such by naturalization; and the Constitution declares that they are entitled, as citizens, to all the privileges and immunities of citizens in the several States. They are, by constitutional right; entitled to these privileges and immunities, and may assert this right and these privileges and immunities, and ask for their enforcement whenever they go within the limits of the several States of the Union.

It would be a curious question to solve what are the privileges and immunities of citizens of each of the States in the several States. I do not propose to go at any length into that question at this time. It would be a somewhat barren discussion. But it is certain the clause was inserted in the Constitution for some good purpose. It has in view some results beneficial to the citizens of the several States, or it would not be found there; yet I am not aware that the Supreme Court have ever undertaken to define either the nature or extent of the privileges and immunities thus guarantied. Indeed, if my recollection serves me, that court, on a certain occasion not many years since, when this question seemed to present itself to them, very modestly declined to go into a definition of them, leaving questions arising under the clause to be discussed and adjudicated when they should happen practically to arise. But we may gather some intimation of what probably will be the opinion of the judiciary by referring to a case adjudged many years ago in one of the circuit courts of the United States by Judge Washington; and I will trouble the Senate but for a moment by reading what that very learned and excellent judge says about these privileges and immunities of the citizens of each State in the several States. It is the case of *Corfield* v. *Coryell,* found in 4 Washington's Circuit Court Reports 380. Judge Washington says:

The next question is whether this act infringes that section of the Constitution which declares that "the citizens of each State shall be entitled to all privileges and immunities of citizens in the several States?"

The inquiry is, what are the privileges and immunities of citizens in the several States? We feel no hesitation in confining these expressions to those privileges and immunities which are in their nature fundamental, which belong of right to the citizens of all free Governments, and which have at all times been enjoyed by the citizens of the several States which compose this Union from the time of their becoming free, independent, and sovereign. What these fundamental principles are it would, perhaps, be more tedious than difficult to enumerate. They may, however, be all comprehended under the following general heads: protection by the Government, the enjoyment of life and liberty, with the right to acquire and possess property of every kind, and to pursue and obtain happiness and safety, subject nevertheless to such restraints as the Government may justly prescribe for the general good of the whole. The right of a citizen of one State to pass through or to reside in any other State, for purposes of trade, agriculture, professional pursuits, or otherwise; to claim the benefit of the writ of *habeas corpus;* to institute and maintain action of any kind in the courts of the State; to take, hold, and dispose of property, either real or personal, and an exemption from higher taxes or impositions than are paid by the other citizens of the State, may be mentioned as some of the particular privileges and immunities of citizens which are clearly embraced by the general description of privileges deemed to be fundamental, to which may be added the elective franchise, as regulated and established by the laws or constitution of the State in which it is to be exercised. These, and many others which might be mentioned, are, strictly speaking, privileges and immunities, and the enjoyment of them by the citizens of each State in every other State was manifestly calculated (to use the expressions of the preamble of the corresponding provision in the old Articles of Confederation) the better to secure and perpetuate mutual friendship and intercourse among the people of the different States of the Union.

Such is the character of the privileges and immunities spoken of in the second section of the fourth article of the Constitution. To these privileges and immunities, whatever they may be—for they are not and cannot be fully defined in their entire extent and precise nature—to these should be added the personal rights guarantied and secured by the first eight amendments of the Constitution; such as the freedom of speech and of the press; the right of the people peaceably to assemble and petition the Government for a redress of grievances, a right appertaining to each and all the people; the right to keep and to bear arms; the right to be exempted from the quartering of soldiers in a house without the consent of the owner; the right to be exempt from unreasonable searches and seizures, and from any search or seizure except by virtue of a warrant issued upon a formal oath or affidavit; the right of an accused person to be informed of the nature of the accusation against him, and his right to be tried by an impartial jury of the vicinage; and also the right to be secure against excessive bail and against cruel and unusual punishments.

Now, sir, here is a mass of privileges, immunities, and rights, some of them secured by the second section of the fourth article of the Constitution, which I have recited, some by the first eight amendments of the Constitution; and it is a fact well worthy of attention that the course of decision of our courts and the present settled doctrine is, that all these immunities, privileges, rights, thus guarantied by the Constitution or recognized by it, are secured to the citizen solely as a citizen of the United States and as a party in their courts. They do not operate in the slightest degree as a restraint or prohibition upon State legislation. States are not affected by them, and it has been repeatedly held that the restriction contained in the Constitution against the taking of private property for public use without just compensation is not a restriction upon State legislation, but applies only to the legislation of Congress.

Now, sir, there is no power given in the Constitution to enforce and to carry out any of these guarantees. They are not powers granted by the Constitution to Congress, and of course do not come within the sweeping clause of the Constitution authorizing Congress to pass all laws necessary and proper for carrying out the foregoing or granted powers, but they stand simply as a bill of rights in the Constitution, without power on the part of Congress to give them full effect; while at the same time the States are not restrained from violating the principles embraced in them except by their own local constitutions, which may be altered from year to year. The great object of the first section of this amendment is, therefore, to restrain the power of the States and compel them at all times to respect these great fundamental guarantees. How will it be done under the present amendment? As I have remarked, they are not powers granted to Congress, and therefore it is necessary, if they are to be effectuated and enforced, as they assuredly ought to be, that additional power should be given to Congress to that end. This is done by the fifth section of this amendment, which declares that "the Congress shall have power to enforce by appropriate legislation the provisions of this article." Here is a direct affirmative delegation of power to Congress to carry out all the principles of all these guarantees, a power not found in the Constitution.

The last two clauses of the first section of the amendment disable a State from depriving not merely a citizen of the United States, but any person, whoever he may be, of life, liberty, or property without due process of law, or from denying to him the equal protection of the laws of the State. This abolishes all class legislation in the States and does away with the injustice of subjecting one caste of persons to a code not applicable to another. It prohibits the hanging of a black man for a crime for which the white man is not to be hanged. It protects the black man in his fundamental rights as a citizen with the same shield which it throws over the white man. Is it not time, Mr. President, that we extend to the black man, I had almost called it the poor privilege of the equal protection of the law? Ought not the time to be now passed when one measure of justice is to be meted out to a member of one caste while another and a different measure is meted out to the member of another caste, both castes being alike citizens of the United States, both bound to obey the same laws, to sustain the burdens of the same Government, and both equally responsible to justice and to God for the deeds done in the body?

But, sir, the first section of the proposed amendment does not give to either of these classes the right of voting. The right of suffrage is not, in law, one of the privileges or immunities thus secured by the Constitution. It is merely the creature of law. It has always been regarded in this country as the result of positive local law, not regarded as one of those fundamental rights lying at the basis of all society and without which a people cannot exist except as slaves, subject to a despotism.

As I have already remarked, section one is a restriction upon the States, and does not, of itself, confer any power upon Congress. The power which Congress has, under this amendment, is derived, not from that section, but from the fifth section, which gives it authority to pass laws which are appropriate to the attainment of the great object of the amendment. I look upon the first section, taken in connection with the fifth, as very important. It will, if adopted by the States, forever disable every one of them from passing laws trenching upon those fundamental rights and privileges which pertain to citizens of the United States, and to all persons who may happen to be within their jurisdiction. It establishes equality before the law, and it gives to the humblest, the poorest, the most despised of the race the same rights and the same protection before the law as it gives to the most powerful, the most wealthy, or the most haughty. That, sir, is republican government, as I understand it, and the only one which can claim the praise of a just Government. Without this principle of equal justice to all men and equal protection under the shield of the law, there is no republican government and none that is really worth maintaining.

The second section of the proposed amendment reads as follows:

SEC. 2. Representatives shall be apportioned among the several States which may be included within the Union, according to their respective numbers, counting the whole number of persons in each State, excluding Indians not taxed. But whenever, in any State, the elective franchise shall be denied to any portion of its male citizens not less than twenty-one years of age, or in any way abridged, except for participation in rebellion or other crime, the basis of representation in such State shall be reduced in the proportion which the number of such male citizens—

That is, citizens as to whom the right of voting is denied or abridged—
"shall bear to the whole number of male citizens not less than twenty-one years of age."

It is very true, and I am sorry to be obliged to acknowledge it, that this section of the amendment does not recognize the authority of the United States over the question of suffrage in the several States at all; nor does it recognize, much less secure, the right of suffrage to the colored race. I wish to meet this question fairly and frankly; I have nothing to conceal upon it; and I am perfectly free to say that if I could have my own way, if my preferences could be carried out, I certainly should secure suffrage to the colored race to some extent at least; for I am opposed to the exclusion and proscription of an entire race. If I could not obtain universal suffrage in the popular sense of that expression, I should be in favor of restricted, qualified suffrage for the colored race. But, sir, it is not the question here what will we do; it is not the question what you, or I, or half a dozen other members of the Senate may prefer in respect to colored suffrage; it is not entirely the question what measure we can pass through the two Houses; but the question really is, what will the Legislatures of the various States to whom these amendments are to be submitted do in the premises; what is it likely will meet the general approbation of the people who are to elect the Legislatures, three fourths of whom must ratify our propositions before they have the force of constitutional provisions?

Let me not be misunderstood. I do not intend to say, nor do I say, that the proposed amendment, section two, proscribes the colored race. It has nothing to do with that question, as I shall show before I take my seat. I could wish that the elective franchise should be extended equally to the white man and to the black man; and if it were necessary, after full consideration, to restrict what is known as universal suffrage for the purpose of securing this equality, I would go for a restriction; but I deem that impracticable at the present time, and so did the committee.

The colored race are destined to remain among us. They have been in our midst for more than two hundred years; and the idea of the people of the United States ever being able by any measure or measures to which they may resort to expel or expatriate that race from their limits and to settle them in a foreign country, is to me the wildest of all chimeras. The thing can never be done; it is impracticable. For weal or for woe, the destiny of the colored race in this country is wrapped up with our own; they are to remain in our midst, and here spend their years and here bury their fathers and finally repose themselves. We may regret it. It may not be entirely compatible with our taste that they should live in our midst. We cannot help it. Our forefathers introduced them, and their destiny is to continue among us; and the practical question which now presents itself to us is as to the best mode of getting along with them.

The committee were of opinion that the States are not yet prepared to sanction so fundamental a change as would be the concession of the right of suffrage to the colored race. We may as well state it plainly and fairly, so that there shall be no misunderstanding on the subject. It was our opinion that three fourths of the States of this Union could not be induced to vote to grant the right of suffrage, even in any degree or under any restriction, to the colored race. We may be right in this apprehension or we may be in error. Time will develop the truth; and for one I shall wait with patience the movements of public opinion upon this great and absorbing question. The time may come, I trust it will come, indeed I feel a profound conviction that it is not far distant, when even the people of the States themselves where the colored population is most dense will consent to admit them to the right of suffrage. Sir, the safety and prosperity of those States depend upon it; it is especially for their interest that they should not retain in their midst a race of pariahs, so circumstanced as to be obliged to bear the burdens of Government and to obey its laws without any participation in the enactment of the laws.

The second section leaves the right to regulate the elective franchise still with the States, and does not meddle with that right. Its basis of representation is numbers, whether the numbers be white or black; that is, the whole population except untaxed Indians and persons excluded by the State laws for rebellion or other crime. Formerly under the Constitution, while the free States were represented only according to their respective numbers of men, women, and children, all of course endowed with civil rights, the slave States had the advantage of being represented according to their number of the same free classes, increased by three fifths of the slaves whom they treated not as men but property. They had this advantage over the free States, that the bulk of their property in the proportion of three fifths had the right of representation in Congress, while in the free States not a dollar of property entered into the basis of representation. John Jacob Astor, with his fifty millions of property, was entitled to cast but one vote, and he at the ballot-box would meet his equal in the raggedest beggar that strolled the streets. Property has been rejected as the basis of just representation; but still the advantage that was given to the slave States under the Constitution enabled them to send at least twenty-one members to Congress in 1860, based entirely upon what they treated as property—a number sufficient to determine almost every contested measure that might come before the House of Representatives.

The three-fifths principle has ceased in the destruction of slavery and in the enfranchisement of the colored race. Under the present Constitution this change will increase the number of Representatives from the once slaveholding States by nine or ten. That is to say, if the present basis of representation, as established in the Constitution, shall remain operative for the future, making our calculations upon the census of 1860, the enfranchisement of their slaves would increase the number of their Representatives in the other House nine or ten, I think at least ten; and under the next census it is easy to see that this number would be still increased; and the important question now is, shall this be permitted while the colored population are excluded from the privilege of voting? Shall the recently slaveholding States, while they exclude from the ballot the whole of their black population, be entitled to include the whole of that population in the basis of their representation, and thus to obtain an advantage which they did not possess before the rebellion and emancipation? In short, shall we permit it to take place that one of the results of emancipation and of the war is to increase the Representatives of the late slaveholding States? I object to this, I think they cannot very consistently call upon us to grant them an additional number of Representatives simply because in consequence of their own misconduct they have lost the property which they once possessed, and which served as a basis in great part of their representation.

The committee thought this should no longer be permitted, and they thought it wiser to adopt a general principle applicable to all the States alike, namely, that where a State excludes any part of its male citizens from the elective franchise, it shall lose Representatives in proportion to the number so excluded; and the clause applies not to color or to race at all, but simply to the fact of the individual exclusion. Nor did the committee adopt the principle of making the ratio of representation depend upon the number of voters, for it so happens that there is an unequal distribution of voters in the several States, the old States having proportionally fewer than the new States. It was desirable to avoid this inequality in fixing the basis. The committee adopted numbers as the most just and satisfactory basis, and this is the principle upon which the Constitution itself was originally framed, that the basis of representation should depend upon numbers; and such, I think, after all, is the safest and most secure principle upon which the Government can rest. Numbers, not voters; numbers, not property; this is the theory of the Constitution.

By the census of 1860, the whole number of colored persons in the several States was four million four hundred and twenty-seven thousand and sixty-seven. In five of the New England States, where colored persons are allowed to vote, the number of such colored persons is only twelve thousand one hundred and thirty-two. This leaves of the colored population of the United States in the other States unrepresented, four million four hundred and fourteen thousand nine hundred and thirty-five, or at least one seventh part of the whole population of the United States. Of this last number, three million six hundred and fifty thousand were in the eleven seceding States, and only five hundred and forty-seven thousand in the four remaining slave States which did not secede, namely, Delaware, Maryland, Kentucky, and Missouri. In the eleven seceding States the blacks are to the whites, basing the calculation upon the census of 1860, nearly as three to five. A further calculation shows that if this section shall be adopted as a part of the Constitution, and if the late slave States shall continue hereafter to exclude the colored population from voting, they will do it at the loss at least of twenty-four Representatives in the other House of Congress, according to the rule established by the act of 1850. I repeat, that if they shall persist in refusing suffrage to the colored race, if they shall persist in excluding that whole race from the right of suffrage, they will lose twenty-four members of the other House of Congress. Some have estimated their loss more and some less; but according to the best calculation I have been able to make, I think that will be the extent. It is not to be disguised—the committee have no disposition to conceal the fact—that this amendment is so drawn as to make it the political interest of the once slaveholding States to admit their colored population to the right of suffrage. The penalty of refusing will be severe. They will undoubtedly lose, and lose so long as they shall refuse to admit the black population to the right of suffrage, that balance of power in Congress which has been so long their pride and their boast. . . .

MR. HOWARD. I now offer a series of amendments to the joint resolution under consideration, which I will send to the Chair.

WILLIAM FESSENDEN [R., ME.]. Take them one section at a time.

MR. HOWARD. I will state very briefly what they are. I propose to amend section one of the article by adding after the words "section one" the following words, which will of course constitute a part of section one:

All persons born in the United States and subject to the jurisdiction thereof are citizens of the United States and of the States wherein they reside.

The second amendment—

MR. FESSENDEN. Let us take a vote on the first one.

LYMAN TRUMBULL [R., ILL.]. The Senator had better state all the amendments.

REVERDY JOHNSON [R., MD.]. I hope we shall hear them all.

MR. HOWARD. The second amendment is to amend the second section by striking out the word "citizens," in the twentieth line, where it occurs, and inserting after the word "male" the words "inhabitants, being citizens of the United States;" and by inserting at the end of that section the words "any such State."

The third section has already been stricken out. Instead of that section, or rather in its place, I offer the following:

SEC. 3. No person shall be a Senator or Representative in Congress, or an elector of President and Vice President, or hold any office, civil or military, under the United States, or under any State, who, having previously taken an oath as a member of Congress, or as an officer of the United States, or as a member of any State Legislature, or as an executive or judicial officer of any State, to support the Constitution of the United States, shall have engaged in insurrection or rebellion against the same, or given aid or comfort to the enemies hereof; but Congress may by a vote of two thirds of each House, remove such disability.

The following is to come in as section four:

The obligations of the United States incurred in suppressing insurrection, or in defense of the Union, or for payment of bounties or pensions incident thereto, shall remain inviolate.

Section four, as it now stands, will be changed to section five, and I propose to amend that section as follows: strike out the word "already," in line thirty-four, and also the words "or which may hereafter be incurred," in line thirty-five, and also the words "or of war" in lines thirty-five and thirty-six, and insert the word "rebellion" in lieu thereof; and also strike out the words "loss of involuntary service or labor" in line thirty-seven, and insert "the loss or emancipation of any slave; but all such debts, obligations, and claims shall be forever held illegal and void."

After consultation with some of the friends of this measure it has been thought that these amendments will be acceptable to both Houses of Congress and to the country, and I now submit them to the consideration of the Senate.

THE PRESIDENT PRO TEMPORE [LA FAYETTE FOSTER, R., CONN.]. . . . The question now is on the amendments proposed by the Senator from Michigan.

WILLARD SAULSBURY [DEM., DEL.]. It is very well known that the majority of the members of this body who favor a proposition of this character have been in very serious deliberation for several days in reference to these amendments, and have held some four or five caucuses on the subject. Perhaps they have come to the conclusion among themselves that the amendments offered are proper to be made, but this is the first intimation that the minority of the body has had of the character of the proposed change in the constitutional amendment. Now, sir, it is nothing but fair, just, and proper that the minority of the Senate should have an opportunity to consider these amendments; and I rise for the purpose of moving that these amendments, together with the original proposition, be printed, so that we may see them before we are called upon to vote on them. Certainly there can be no graver question, no more serious business that can engage the attention of this Senate than a proposed change in the fundamental law.

MR. FESSENDEN. I will say to the Senator that if any gentleman on that side of the Chamber desires that these amendments be laid upon the table and printed, there is no objection to that.

MR. SAULSBURY. Then I will defer any further remarks, and make that motion.

THE PRESIDENT PRO TEMPORE. It is moved that the amendments be printed and that the further consideration of the joint resolution be postponed until to-morrow.

The motion was agreed to. . . .

THOMAS HENDRICKS [DEM., IND.]. Mr. President, nothing but a sense of imperative duty induces me to address the Senate upon this occasion. The Constitution is to be changed; the foundations of the Government are to be disturbed; some of the old oak timbers are to be removed, and timber of recent growth is to be substituted. Upon the foundations fixed by the fathers our institutions have rested firmly and securely for three quarters of a century. They have stood unmoved by the contests of ambitious leaders, the angry strife of parties, and the rolling waves of war. In peace and in war; in the turbulence of times of financial embarrassment, and the corruptions attendant upon the accumulation of great wealth; in every possible state and condition of our society, the Constitution has borne the test; and the fact now stands conceded that it established a system of government entirely adapted to our wants and condition as a people. This is proven beyond cavil and question by the prosperity and individual happiness that attended our growth, and the greatness and power to which we attained. The prosperity of the citizen, his security and happiness, and the might and grandeur of the nation attest the excellence of our form of government. The blessings of the past are our guarantee for the future if we but maintain our institutions as they are.

And now, sir, in this the most unsafe period of our history; when the passions excited by the war are yet fierce; when sectional controversies run high, and party strife is raging; when eleven States are absent from this Chamber, and other sections, seizing the opportunity, see to aggrandize their power, and to fasten upon the country a partial and unequal policy; when the lust for power and gain carries men beyond the restraints of justice and right; at such a time I cannot remain wholly silent when I see the hand of the partisan and the self-constituted reformer laid upon the sacred work of the fathers. In such a case to speak is a man's duty, though none may heed. But, Mr. President, it is hard work to speak when one knows in advance that no argument, however just and forcible, and no appeal, however patriotic, can influence a single vote; that the authority and law of a political party is over every Senator of the majority; and that it remains now only to register the decree of the secret caucus.

At the meeting of Congress, but before the President had delivered his message, and before his views had been officially communicated, the Republican members, in caucus, determined to raise a committee of fifteen to "inquire into the condition of the States which formed the so-called confederate States of America, and report whether they or any of them are entitled to be represented in either House of Congress." In most indecent haste the resolution passed both branches, and the committee became fastened upon Congress and the country. Because of its party origin, the work it had to do, and the secret character of its proceedings, that committee came to be known in the country as the "revolutionary tribunal," the "directory," and the "star chamber." Its first report was made some months since, in which it was proposed to reduce the representation of the southern States, but by the aid of the distinguished Senator from Massachusetts, [Mr. Sumner,] who submits to party restraints upon his judgment with impatience, that measure was defeated. Its second report is now upon our desks. It passed the House, but when it came under discussion in the Senate, and had to bear the test of the independent judgment of Senators, it was found wanting, and its defeat became almost certain. A second defeat of a party programme could not be borne; its effect upon the fall elections would be disastrous. A caucus was called, and we witnessed the astounding spectacle of the withdrawal, for the time, of a great legislative measure, touching the Constitution itself, from the Senate, that it might be decided in the secret councils of a party. For three days the Senate Chamber was silent, but the discussions were transferred to another room of the Capitol, with closed doors and darkened windows, where party leaders might safely contend for a political and party policy.

When Senators returned to their seats I was curious to observe who had won and who lost in the party lottery. The dark brow of the Senator from New Hampshire [Mr. Clark] was lighted with a gleam of pleasure. His proposed substitute for the third section was the marked feature of the measure. But upon the lofty brow of the Senator from Nevada [Mr. Stewart] there rested a cloud of disappointment and grief. His bantling, which he had named universal amnesty and universal suffrage, which he had so often dressed and undressed in the presence of the Senate, the darling offspring of his brain, was dead; it had died in the caucus; and it was left to the sad Senator only to hope that it might not be his last. Upon the serene countenance of the Senator from Maine, the chairman of the fifteen, there rested the composure of the highest satisfaction; a plausible political platform had been devised, and there was yet hope for his party.

Mr. President, I recognize the propriety and necessity of conventions and caucuses to regulate all questions of organization and political policy; but I have never felt myself authorized to subordinate my judgment as a representative of the people to the decision of any body of men other than those I represent. To me it seems clear that each Senator owes it to the country to vote upon every important measure and every proposed modification thereof according to the dictates of his own judgment and conscience. The Constitution requires that two thirds of the Senators, each answering for himself, shall agree to a proposed amendment before it can be submitted to the States. In this weighty business now before us what are the facts? The House sent us four propositions to change the Constitution in one bill. Upon discussion it was found that probably no one of the propositions, nor any proposed modification thereof, could receive the required vote. Two thirds of the Senators, belonging to one political party, retired from the Senate to consider and agree upon a bill. Each Senator, by going into the secret caucus, agreed and became bound to vote for whatever the majority of the caucus should adopt. A section or an entire bill may be adopted by a bare majority of the caucus, much less than one half the Senate, but the entire two thirds must vote for it in the Senate, not because it is right, but because the majority of the caucus has said so; and thus an amendment of the Constitution may be adopted by the Senate when a majority of the body would vote against it if no party obligation rested upon them. What Senator would dare propose to shut these doors against the people, that we in secret might take steps to change their great charter of liberty? The people would not endure it, but in congregating thousands would burst them open and demand to know all that was said and done upon a matter of such interest to them. The present proposed amendment has been decided upon in a conclave more secret than has ever been known in this country.

So carefully has the obligation of secrecy been observed that no outside Senators, not even the sharp-eyed men of the press, have been able to learn one word that was spoken, or one vote given. An Egyptian darkness covers the proceeding. The secret could not be more profound had the conclave assembled down in the deep and dark caverns of the earth. If you change the Constitution have the people not the right to know how and why it is done, what was proposed and said, and how each Senator voted? Is it not their business? Or indeed have they masters, party chieftains, who may say to them "We govern, you obey?" Is it not a fact that shall arrest attention that since this measure was reported from the caucus scarce an explanation has been conceded, and not one amendment offered or voted for by a single Senator who was in the caucus, so exacting and imperative is the obligation, and so literally is party authority obeyed. Sir, if the people can only come to know how this thing has been done, I believe they will refuse their indorsement.

I now propose a brief examination of the measure as it came from the caucus. It proposes an additional article of five sections, making that number of amendments or additions to the Constitution.

For the first section the virtue is claimed that it defines citizenship of the United States and of the States. I will read that part of the section:

All persons born in the United States, and subject to the jurisdiction thereof, are citizens of the United States and of the State wherein they reside.

What citizenship is, what are its rights and duties, its obligations and liabilities, are not defined or attempted to be defined; but these vexed questions are left as unsettled as during all the course of our history, when they have occupied the attention and taxed the learning of the departments of Government. But this is certain, that the section will add many millions to the class of persons who are citizens. We have been justly proud of the rank and title of our citizenship, for we understood it to belong to the inhabitants of the United States who were descended from the great races of people who inhabit the countries of Europe, and such emigrants from those countries as have been admitted under our laws. The rank and title conferred honor at home and secured kindness, respect, and safety everywhere abroad; but if this amendment be adopted we will then carry the title and enjoy its advantages in common with the negroes, the coolies, and the Indians. When the Senator from Wisconsin proposed an amendment excluding the savage Indians of the forest I believe every Senator who had been in the caucus voted against it. No one was authorized to change a word that the caucus had used, but I am not quite sure that the people of Minnesota will regard the obligation to a caucus as a sufficient reason why the Senator from that State [Mr. Ramsey] should seek to confer the rank, privileges, and immunities of citizenship upon the cruel savages who destroyed their peaceful settlements and massacred the people with circumstances of atrocity too horrible to relate. How our citizenship will be esteemed at home and abroad should this amendment be adopted we may judge by consulting the sentiments with which we regard Mexican citizenship. We feel that it defines a mixed population, made up of races that ought not to mingle—whites, negroes, and Indians—of whom twenty thousand could not cope with four thousand soldiers of the United States of pure white blood on the field of Buena Vista. It was the work of many generations to place the name and fame of our citizenship so high that it ranked with the proudest titles on earth; but the mad fanaticism and partisan fury of a single year may so degrade it as there shall be: "None so poor to do it reverence."

The second section now demands our attention. The intent and effect of that section is to take away representation in Congress in all the States in which the right of voting is not given to the negroes. The purpose is to constrain every State to confer the right of voting upon the negroes; and in case of refusal, the penalty is loss of representation. The section does not rest upon the proposition that those whom the States treat as unfit to vote shall not be represented, for it is so framed as to continue to the northern and eastern States their twenty Representatives that are based upon a non-voting population. It is so framed, also, as to continue to the States of Maryland, Tennessee, West Virginia, and Missouri their full representation, although during the war the military power was so used in those States as to place the political power in the hands of a few, who so exercised it as to exclude the residue of the people from the ballot-box. You say that if the States treat the negroes as unfit to vote, then they shall not be voted for; that no representation shall be allowed for them; then, I ask, if in some of the northern States the foreigner is denied a vote for five years, why shall he be voted for? If in Maryland, West Virginia, Tennessee, and Missouri the majority are treated as unfit to vote, why shall the minority vote for them and be represented for them? Come, now, let candor and truth have full sway, and answer me, is it not because you believe that the few in these States now allowed to vote will send radicals to Congress, and therefore you allow them to send full delegations that it may add to your political party power? And I now submit to your patriotism, to your love of our country, if we have not come upon most dangerous times, when our Constitution is to be torn up and remodeled that a political party may make its power more secure, that it may hold on to the offices, and shape and control sectional policies.

Mr. President, I now venture the prediction that this thing cannot succeed; that in this land of intelligence and love of liberty and right permanent power cannot be built upon inequality, injustice, and wrong. If the principle be right that none but voters ought to be represented, why do you not say so? If you think the negro ought to have the right of voting; if you are in favor of it, and intend it shall be given, why do you not in plain words confer it upon them? It is much fairer than to seek it by indirection, and the people will distinctly understand you when you propose such a change of the Constitution. I am not for it directly, nor will I coerce the States to its allowance. If conferred by the free action of the States, I am content. Within the limits of constitutional right and power I will support all measures necessary and proper for the protection and elevation of the colored race; measures safe and just to both races; but I do not believe that it is for the good of either race that they should be brought into close social and political relations. God has marked the peculiarities of each. He has put them asunder, and it is not the right, much less the duty, of man to join them together. Our institutions rest for their support upon the intelligence and virtue of the people, and who may say that the untaught negroes, so lately manumitted, are qualified to exercise the privileges and discharge the duties of an American citizen? Why then coerce the States to their enfranchisement? . . .

LUKE POLAND [R., VT.]. Mr. President, the few observations which I propose to make are addressed to the general merits of the proposition which is before the Senate, but some of them are addressed to the very point of this pending amendment. I read in a morning paper that it was expected that I would present some important and new views upon the subject. The views that I shall present, Mr. President, may be important in the sense that almost any view that any man may present who has a vote to give on such a subject is important; but that I shall be able to say, after six months' discussion of this subject, anything new is more than I expect.

Mr. President, all the questions involved in the proposed amendments to the Constitution have been so elaborately and ably discussed on former occasions during the present session that I do not feel at liberty to attempt to argue them at length and in detail. I do not propose to do more than to state, in the shortest and plainest manner I am able, some of the reasons for my action upon the propositions submitted to us by the committee.

The clause of the first proposed amendment, that "no State shall make or enforce any law which shall abridge the privileges or immunities of citizens of the United States," secures nothing beyond what was intended by the original provision in the Constitution, that "the citizens of each State shall be entitled to all privileges and immunities of citizens in the several States."

But the radical difference in the social systems of the several States, and the great extent to which the doctrine of State rights or State sovereignty was carried, induced mainly, as I believe, by and for the protection of the peculiar system of the South, led to a practical repudiation of the existing provision on this subject, and it was disregarded in many of the States. State legislation was allowed to override it, and as no express power was by the Constitution granted to Congress to enforce it, it became really a dead letter. The great social and political change in the southern States wrought by the amendment of the Constitution abolishing slavery and by the overthrow of the late rebellion render it eminently proper and necessary that Congress should be invested with the power to enforce this provision throughout the country and compel its observance.

Now that slavery is abolished, and the whole people of the nation stand upon the basis of freedom, it seems to me that there can be no valid or reasonable objection to the residue of the first proposed amendment:

Nor shall any State deprive any person of life, liberty, or property without due process of law, nor deny to any person within its jurisdiction the equal protection of the law.

It is the very spirit and inspiration of our system of government, the absolute foundation upon which it was established. It is essentially declared in the Declaration of Independence and in all the provisions of the Constitution. Notwithstanding this we know that State laws exist, and some of them of very recent enactment, in direct violation of these principles. Congress has already shown its desire and intention to uproot and destroy all such partial State legislation in the passage of what is called the civil rights bill. The power of Congress to do this has been doubted and denied by persons entitled to high consideration. It certainly seems desirable that no doubt should be left existing as to the power of Congress to enforce principles lying at the very foundation of all republican government if they be denied or violated by the States, and I cannot doubt but that every Senator will rejoice in aiding to remove all doubt upon this power of Congress. . . .

JOHN HENDERSON [DEM., MO.]. I propose to discuss the first section only so far as citizenship is involved in it. I desire to show that this section will leave citizenship where it now is. It makes plain only what has been rendered doubtful by the past action of the Government. If I be right in that, it will be a loss of time to discuss the remaining provisions of the section, for they merely secure the rights that attach to citizenship in all free Governments.

Justice McLean, in the *Dred Scott* case, said:

Being born under our Constitution and laws, no naturalization is required, as one of foreign birth, to make him a citizen. The most general and appropriate definition of the term citizen is a "freeman."

So the learned judge held that Dred Scott, having his domicile in a State different from that of the defendant, and being a freeman, is a citizen within the act of Congress, and the courts of the Union are open to him.

From his argument it follows that any person, black or white, born upon the soil of a State, is a citizen of that State, unless he be born in slavery, and if he be born a slave, he becomes a citizen so soon as by the laws of the State he becomes a freeman. His opinion leads to the conclusion that citizens of States are necessarily citizens of the United States. All born on the soil free are citizens of the respective States of their birth, and therefore citizens of the United States. Those born on foreign soil, he holds, cannot be invested with rights of citizenship without naturalization.

He says further:

While I admit the Government was not made especially for the colored race, yet many of them were citizens of the New England States, and exercised the rights of suffrage when the Constitution was adopted.

Judge McLean might have gone further and enumerated other than New England States that acknowledged the citizenship of African freemen at that date. . . .

Judge Curtis, in his dissenting opinion in the *Dred Scott* case, says: "To determine whether any free persons descended from Africans held in slavery were citizens of the United States under the Confederation, and consequently at the time of the adoption of the Constitution of the United States, it is only necessary to know whether any such persons were citizens of either of the States under the Confederation. Of this," he said, "there can be no doubt."

At the time of the ratification of the Articles of Confederation free native-born inhabitants of the States of New Hampshire, Massachusetts, New York, New Jersey, and North Carolina, though descended from African slaves, were not only called citizens of those States, but such of them as had the other necessary qualifications possessed the franchise of electors on equal terms with other citizens.

In conclusive proof of his reasoning on this subject Judge Curtis cites the action of Congress when framing the Articles of Confederation. The fourth article, it will be remembered, provides "that the free inhabitants of each of these States, paupers, vagabonds, and fugitives from justice excepted, shall be entitled to all privileges and immunities of free citizens in the several States." While this provision was under consideration, June 25, 1778, the South Carolina delegates moved to insert the word "white" after "free" and before "inhabitants," thereby securing the privileges only to white persons. The motion was voted down by eight States to two, one State being divided. This proves beyond doubt that the privileges and immunities of citizenship were at that time willingly accorded to all men who were free, who were not slaves, whether white or black.

Judge Curtis, after stating that in five States at least free negroes enjoyed the elective franchise when the Constitution was adopted, concludes very justly that they became "citizens of the new Government," and "so in every sense part of the people of the United States," and "among those for whom and whose posterity the Constitution was ordained and established."

> There can scarcely be a doubt that all persons residing in the several States at the time of the adoption of the Federal Constitution became citizens of the United States, and no State thereafter can deprive them or their prosterity of this right. The power to naturalize is exclusive in Congress, and the foreigner naturalized becomes a citizen of the United States, and necessarily is a citizen of the State in which he is domiciled. The posterity of such foreigner so dominciled becomes a citizen of the State and of the United States by virtue of his birth alone.

If the opinion of Judge Curtis be open to criticism at all it consists in the conclusion to which he arrives—

> That it is left to each State to determine what free persons born within its limits shall be citizens of such State, and thereby be citizens of the United States.

He leaves the inference that Federal citizenship may be given or taken away by State action. He admits that being a State citizen confers the Federal right. If once the character of citizen of the United States attaches, no State, I apprehend, can take it away. . . .

The Federal Constitution failed to define United States citizenship, and equally failed to declare what classes of persons should be entitled to its privileges. If those persons who enjoyed "all the privileges and immunities" of State citizenship at the adoption of the Constitution were not by the Constitution made citizens of the United States, it would be difficult to ascertain who were to be considered such. To deny it in such cases would lead to a total denial of such a thing as United States citizenship at all. But that cannot be the case, for, in defining the qualifications of a Representative in Congress, the Constitution requires that he shall "have been seven years a citizen of the United States." The same instrument, prescribing the qualifications of a Senator in Congress, declares that he "shall have been nine years a citizen of the United States." It is also fixed in the instrument that no person shall be President except a "natural-born citizen or a citizen of the United States at the time of the adoption of the Constitution." These clauses show that such a thing as United States citizenship existed at and prior to the time when the Constitution was adopted. Another curious fact may be seen in this, that while the Senator and Representative must be a citizen of the United States at the time of their election, it is only necessary that they be "inhabitants" of their respective States. One may be a Senator or Representative in Congress before he has acquired the rights of citizenship in his State. But he must have once been a State citizen. For instance, if an individual, seven years before the adoption of the Constitution, had been recognized a citizen of one of the States, acquiring the right either by birth or by naturalization therein, and had continued to remove from one State to another, failing to remain in any one of them long enough to acquire "all the privileges and immunities" of a citizen therein, he would yet have been a citizen of the United States and eligible to a seat in Congress from the State in which he was domiciled at the time. And so would one have been eligible to the Senate who nine years before had enjoyed State citizenship in one of the States under the Articles of Confederation.

In the clause fixing the qualifications of the President, the language is changed from "citizenship" to "residence." It says no person shall be elected President who shall not have been "fourteen years a resident of the United States." Fourteen years went back to the period of the battle of Lexington. It must be that a higher evidence of attachment to the country was intended to be secured in the President than in a member of Congress, but unless "residence" in the States be regarded as furnishing that evidence equally with citizenship itself, then the qualification of the President is not of so high a character as that of a member of Congress.

It cannot be otherwise than that all free natural-born residents of the States and all who had been naturalized by the States became, at the adoption of the Constitution, citizens of the United States. Their descendants of course followed their condition. All born of such parents became citizens at their birth. The States, after the adoption, could no longer naturalize. This power, by the Constitution, was given to Congress. But now upon the moment of naturalization the foreigner becomes a citizen of the United States, and may become a citizen of any one of the States by the same residence and under the same circumstances as native-born citizens of other States.

Now, if there be any force in the reasoning to which I have referred, or any weight in the authorities cited, United States citizenship is just what it is defined to be in the first section of this amendment. I mean that those persons who are to be made citizens by this amendment are the persons, and none others, who have ever been citizens of the United States under a fair and rational interpretation of the Constitution since its adoption in 1789.

I now proceed to consider briefly the second section of this amendment. It materially changes the Constitution as respects representation in the lower House of Congress. The same change, of course, will be produced in the Electoral Colleges. The Constitution, as it now stands, apportions Representatives and direct taxes among the States according to the number of their inhabitants; but this number is to be ascertained by taking the whole number of free persons, male and female, including apprentices, and adding thereto three fifths of the slaves and excluding all Indians not taxed. It is upon this enumeration, ascertained by the census every ten years, that Representatives have been apportioned to the States since the formation of the Government. At the time the Constitution was framed the large slaveholding States desired that the whole number of their slaves should enter into the basis of representation. This was resisted by States having few or no slaves. The question was one of great difficulty. It was finally compromised, however, by estimating each slave as three fifths of a person for purposes of representation. But it was insisted that if he were three fifths of a person for representation he should also be three fifths of a person for purposes of taxation. The controversy was therefore settled by imposing direct taxation upon the States in the same proportion in which they might be represented upon their slave population. The clause was so adjusted that whenever a slave became free he necessarily became a full person for purposes of representation and taxation. He then was included in the list of "free persons," and not in that of "other persons." Therefore, whenever a State emancipated its slaves, as many did before the late war, it increased its representative power in Congress and fell subject to increased taxation to the extent of two fifths of all persons so emancipated.

The recent war of rebellion has terminated in the abolition of slavery in all the southern States. This emancipation, of course, was against the will of those States; but it none the less increases their representative power because it was forced on them.

This provision of the Constitution, like many others, looked to the ultimate extinction of slavery in all the States. It was so worded, of course, as to be adapted to either state of affairs. It compromised a present difficulty growing out of a state of slavery, but anticipated a period when it would cease to exist. When the former slave became a freeman he was to become one of the people. He ceased to be property, and became a person. I confess I can see no good reason why the negro thus emancipated should be excluded from the basis of representation. I believe that no one in the Federal Convention asked the exclusion of any person, white or black, citizen or alien, provided he were a freeman. Indeed, in the fifty-fourth number of the Federalist, Mr. Madison, commending the Constitution to the people, says:

It is not contended that the number of people in each State ought not to be the standard for regulating the proportion of those who are to represent the people of each State.

And in the same connection he remarks:

That if the laws were to restore the rights which have been taken away the negroes could no longer be refused an equal share of representation with the other inhabitants.

For myself, I cannot refrain from expressing regret that it becomes necessary for me to give apparent indorsement to a principle contained in this second section. It departs from the views of the framers of the Constitution in several particulars. The first prominent objection is that it separates representation from taxation. If it were proposed to base taxation upon wealth instead of numbers it would be much better. Mr. Madison said that the rule of representation referred to the "personal rights of the people," and therefore should be based upon numbers, irrespective of their political condition. But he remarked that the rule basing taxation upon numbers is "in no case a precise measure, and in ordinary cases a very unfit one." The amendment, as proposed, does not base taxation upon wealth, but leaves the Constitution in this respect as it now stands. If direct taxation be hereafter levied it will be apportioned among the States, according to their numbers, including free negroes as well as all other persons. If I believed it probable that direct taxation would be resorted to in the future legislation of the country, nothing could induce me to support this proposition. A second objection to it consists in the argument furnished, that we admit the necessity, or at least the propriety, of excluding arbitrarily a freeman from the elective franchise; and it will be contended that we render a present doubtful power of the States to do so certain. A third objection which is urged consists in the fact that while it inflicts punishment for the exclusion of the negro from the ballot, it permits the white citizen and the alien inhabitant to be excluded by the States without loss of representative power. A fourth objection will be urged that it presents too great an incentive to the States to extend suffrage to persons who are ignorant and uneducated for the mere purpose of acquiring power, inasmuch as those who may be excluded under this provision on account of the want of intelligence will be equally excluded from the basis of representation.

The amendment fixes representation upon numbers, precisely as the Constitution now does, but when a State denies or abridges the elective franchise to any of its male inhabitants who are citizens of the United States and not less than twenty-one years of age, except for participation in rebellion or other crime, then such State will lose its representation in Congress in the proportion which the male citizen so excluded bears to the whole number of male citizens not less than twenty-one years of age in the State. . . .

MR. HENDRICKS. It is not my purpose to delay the vote but a moment. I have desired to accommodate the Senator who wishes to leave, and shall not be in the way of that result, but it is my duty to call the attention of the Senator from Michigan to the language of the first section. He says that the word "abridged" as found in the second section in its connection with the right of suffrage, is of such uncertain meaning that it ought not to be used in the Constitution; that it would carry cases into the courts; and therefore the word ought not to be used. Now, I find the same word used in the first section of this article, and in a very important connection, if possible in a more important connection than that in which it is found in the second section:

No State shall make or enforce any law which shall abridge the privileges or immunities of citizens of the United States.

If the chairman—I was going to say the chairman of the caucus, but I will not say that—if the distinguished Senator who has this measure now in charge says to the Senate that the word "abridged," in its connection with the right of suffrage, is of such uncertain meaning that it should not be used in the Constitution in that connection, is it proper that that word shall be used in the first section in relation to the rights and privileges and immunities of citizens?

MR. HOWARD. I think so, undoubtedly; because it is easy to apply the term "abridged" to the privileges and immunities of citizens, which necessarily include within themselves a great number of particulars. They are not a unit, an indivisible unit, like the right to vote. . . .

MR. HENDRICKS. The language of the first section would be identical with the second if it were "denied or abridged." Now the Senator says he cannot understand what it means when we speak of "abridging" the right of suffrage. Then I ask what it means when we speak of "abridging" the rights and immunities of citizenship. It is a little difficult to say, and I have not heard any Senator accurately define, what are the rights and immunities of citizenship; and I do not know that any statesman has very accurately defined them; but even in reference to that, which of itself is not very certain but to some extent vague, a word is now used, as the Senator says, of uncertain legal meaning. He is willing that we shall say "abridge" the rights and immunities of citizens, but not willing that we shall use the word "abridge" the right of suffrage. Of course, the abridgment of the right of suffrage does not apply to the particular individual when he comes to cast his vote, that he shall cast a part of a vote. It does not mean that. It must relate to the class that shall enjoy it. An abridgment of the right of suffrage must relate to the class to which it applies or extends.

Mr. President, my purpose in calling attention to this is to say that this proceeding by the amendment of the Constitution is not so safe as it ought to be. What have we witnessed within the last two days? The measure first came from the committee of fifteen, where it was considered for long sessions of the committee, and brought before us, as it was claimed, in a very perfect state. A little discussion showed that it would not stand the test. Senators were opposed to this and that of the different propositions. Then it went to a peculiar assembly, and was considered there. It comes back, and even the Senator who brings in the report is now dissatisfied. . . .

Now, sir, this measure, which I believe can accomplish no good for the country, is condemned in part by the Senator from Ohio, in part by the Senator from Illinois, in part by the Senator who now proposes an amendment; but all three of these Senators say they will vote for it, not that it is right, but that it is the best they can get under the circumstances. I do not expect the judgment of each man to be perfectly satisfied with every proposition; but, sir, the Constitution ought not to be amended for the purpose of making a platform for a political campaign. The Constitution of the country ought to be amended that it shall be the permanent fundamental law of the country. The embarrassment here is, not that it is difficult to define such general propositions as ought to find their way into the Constitution, but the difficulty in the phraseology here is to include this, and to exclude that, to leave general propositions, to leave a principle, and to fix up a thing for a particular purpose. When the Senator from Michigan says that the southern negroes ought not to be counted if they are regarded as unfit to be voters, I understand that proposition; but when he turns around and says that the people of Missouri, who are decreed by the rest of the people of that State as unfit to be voters, shall be represented, I do not understand such a proposition; and where you undertake to express opposite thoughts in the same sentence you find difficulty of phraseology. If you will say in plain words that nobody shall be represented in Congress who is not recognized by the State as a voter, I understand it; but when you say that a man in the State of Georgia shall not be represented because the people of Georgia count him unfit to be a voter, and in the State of Missouri, a man, who is counted as unfit to be a voter, shall be represented there, I do not understand the principle. When you have to fix up a Constitution to include some things and exclude others, for partisan purposes, you do find difficulties of phraseology. It cannot be made easy. The difficulty is in the thought, not in the use of the English language; and that is the very difficulty that we have in this case. How do you want to "abridge" the right of suffrage? What is meant by it? What is meant by "abridging" the rights and immunities of citizens? We do not know, the Senator from Michigan says. Why shall we allow representation to a non-voter in one State, and disallow it in another, upon principle? You say that the negro in Georgia, because he is not allowed to be a voter by the people of Georgia, shall not be represented, and you say that the criminals, because they are criminals, in Missouri, excluded from the right of voting, shall be represented. Where is the principle and the right of it?

Sir, this thing will be discussed before the people. Although it is clothed in doubtful sentences, it will come to be understood. I believe the people of this country are just; and I do not think the people of this country will say that the voter in Missouri ought to represent two men, when the voter in another State is denied that. But, sir, my purpose was simply to suggest to the distinguished Senator from Michigan that the same doubtful word was used in the first section that he objects to in the second. . . .

MR. JOHNSON. I am decidedly in favor of the first part of the section which defines what citizenship shall be, and in favor of that part of the section which denies to a State the right to deprive any person of life, liberty, or property without due process of law, but I think it is quite objectionable to provide that "no State shall make or enforce any law which shall abridge the privileges or immunities of citizens of the United States," simply because I do not understand what will be the effect of that.

MR. FESSENDEN. We have agreed to that.

MR. JOHNSON. I understand not.

DANIEL CLARK [R., N.H.]. We have concurred in the amendments made as in Committee of the Whole to the first section.

MR. JOHNSON. That is all. You have not agreed to the words to which I now object. I move, therefore, to amend the section as it now stands by striking out the words "make or enforce any law which shall abridge the privileges or immunities of citizens of the United States; nor shall any State;" so as to make it read:

No State shall deprive any person of life, liberty, or property without due process of law, nor deny to any person within its jurisdiction the equal protection of the laws.

JOHN CONNESS [R., CAL.]. Have all the amendments made as in Committee of the Whole been voted upon?

THE PRESIDING OFFICER. They have not been.

MR. CONNESS. Are they not first in order?

MR. CLARK. Oh, we may as well vote on this amendment now as it is moved; it saves time.

The amendment was rejected. . . .

THE PRESIDING OFFICER. This joint resolution having been read three times, the question is on its passage.

MR. JOHNSON. I ask for the yeas and nays.

Several Senators. The yeas and nays must be taken, of course.

The yeas and nays were ordered; and being taken, resulted—yeas 33, nays 11; as follows:

YEAS—Messrs. Anthony, Chandler, Clark, Conness, Cragin, Creswell, Edmunds, Fessenden, Foster, Grimes, Harris, Henderson, Howard, Howe, Kirkwood, Lane of Indiana, Lane of Kansas, Morgan, Morrill, Nye, Poland, Pomeroy, Ramsey, Sherman, Sprague, Stewart, Sumner, Trumbull, Wade, Willey, Williams, Wilson, and Yates—33.

NAYS—Messrs. Cowan, Davis, Doolittle, Guthrie, Hendricks, Johnson, McDougall, Norton, Riddle, Saulsbury, and Van Winkle—11.

ABSENT—Messrs. Brown, Buckalew, Dixon, Nesmith, and Wright—5.

THE PRESIDING OFFICER. The joint resolution is passed, having received the votes of two thirds of the Senate.

House of Representatives-39th Congress, 1st Session
June 13,1866

AARON HARDING [DEM., KY.]. . . . In regard to this constitutional amendment a great many things might be said. It is provided in the first section that all persons born or naturalized in the United States, and subject to the jurisdiction thereof, are citizens of the United States and of the State wherein they reside. No State shall make or enforce any law which shall abridge the privileges or immunities of citizens of the United States; nor shall any State deprive any person of life, liberty, or property without due process of law, nor deny to any person within its jurisdiction the equal protection of the laws.

And the last section provides that Congress shall have power to enforce by appropriate legislation the provisions of this article. This at once transfers all powers from the State governments over the citizens of a State to Congress. You will see that it is only a preparation for an interminable conflict between the Federal and State jurisdictions. We know what the result of this will be, for we have already seen it tested. Will not Congress then virtually hold all power of legislation over your own citizens and in defiance of you?

But how does this agree with the memorable language of the Chicago platform, which declares in so many words that "the right of each State to order and control its own domestic affairs according to its own judgment exclusively is essential to that balance of power on which the perfection and endurance of our political fabric depend?" This amendment is in direct contravention of that platform, because it transfers to Congress from the States all power of control over their own citizens. Let me tell you, you are preparing for revolutions after revolutions. They may be peaceful, and I hope they will. I warn you there will be no peace in this country until each State be allowed to control its own citizens. If you take that from them what care I for the splendid machinery of a national Government? My constituents are able to judge of their own wants, but you propose to take this power from them and to transfer it to Congress, and to let Congress judge of their wants and what legislation should be enacted for their government.

I think I should be sustained by high authority if I were to announce that this amendment is a mere political platform, and that it is not approved by many who will vote for it, because they do not believe it ought to pass. It is a mere platform upon which the party is to go before the country to fight the political battles of next fall. I should have high authority if I were to say that those who vote for these constitutional amendments were opposed to them, and that they are about to go before the country with them masked and veiled in hypocrisy and deceit.

THADDEUS STEVENS [R., PA.]. Mr. Speaker, I do not intend to detain the House long. A few words will suffice.

We may, perhaps, congratulate the House and the country on the near approach to completion of a proposition to be submitted to the people for the admission of an outlawed community into the privileges and advantages of a civilized and free Government.

When I say that we should rejoice at such completion, I do not thereby intend so much to express joy at the superior excellence of the scheme, as that there is to be a scheme—a scheme containing much positive good, as well, I am bound to admit, as the omission of many better things.

In my youth, in my manhood, in my old age, I had fondly dreamed that when any fortunate chance should have broken up for awhile the foundation of our institutions, and released us from obligations the most tyrannical that ever man imposed in the name of freedom, that the intelligent, pure and just men of this Republic, true to their professions and their consciences, would have so remodeled all our institutions as to have freed them from every vestige of human oppression, of inequality of rights, of the recognized degradation of the poor, and the superior caste of the rich. In short, that no distinction would be tolerated in this purified Republic but what arose from merit and conduct. This bright dream has vanished "like the baseless fabric of a vision." I find that we shall be obliged to be content with patching up the worst portions of the ancient edifice, and leaving it, in many of its parts, to be swept through by the tempests, the frosts, and the storms of despotism.

Do you inquire why, holding these views and possessing some will of my own, I accept so imperfect a proposition? I answer, because I live among men and not among angels; among men as intelligent, as determined, and as independent as myself, who, not agreeing with me, do not choose to yield their opinions to mine. Mutual concession, therefore, is our only resort, or mutual hostilities.

We might well have been justified in making renewed and more strenuous efforts for a better plan could we have had the cooperation of the Executive. With his cordial assistance the rebel States might have been made model republics, and this nation an empire of universal freedom. But he preferred "restoration" to "reconstruction." He chooses that the slave States should remain as nearly as possible in their ancient condition, with such small modifications as he and his prime minister should suggest, without any impertinent interference from Congress. He anticipated the legitimate action of the national Legislature, and by rank usurpation erected governments in the conquered provinces; imposed upon them institutions in the most arbitrary and unconstitutional manner; and now maintains them as legitimate governments, and insolently demands that they shall be represented in Congress on equal terms with loyal and regular States.

To repress this tyranny and at the same time to do some justice to conquered rebels requires caution. The great danger is that the seceders may soon overwhelm the loyal men in Congress. The haste urged upon us by some loyal but impetuous men; their anxiety to embrace the representatives of rebels; their ambition to display their dexterity in the use of the broad mantle of charity; and especially the danger arising from the unscrupulous use of patronage and from the oily orations of false prophets, famous for sixty-day obligations and for protested political promises, admonish us to make no further delay.

A few words will suffice to explain the changes made by the Senate in the proposition which we sent them.

The first section is altered by defining who are citizens of the United States and of the States. This is an excellent amendment, long needed to settle conflicting decisions between the several States and the United States. It declares this great privilege to belong to every person born or naturalized in the United States.

The second section has received but slight alteration. I wish it had received more. It contains much less power than I could wish; it has not half the vigor of the amendment which was lost in the Senate. It or the proposition offered by Senator Wade would have worked the enfranchisement of the colored man in half the time.

The third section has been wholly changed by substituting the ineligibility of certain high offenders for the disfranchisement of all rebels until 1870.

This I cannot look upon as an improvement. It opens the elective franchise to such as the States choose to admit. In my judgment it endangers the Government of the country, both State and national; and may give the next Congress and President to the reconstructed rebels. With their enlarged basis of representation, and exclusion of the loyal men of color from the ballot-box, I see no hope of safety unless in the prescription of proper enabling acts, which shall do justice to the freedmen and enjoin enfranchisement as a condition-precedent.

The fourth section, which renders inviolable the public debt and repudiates the rebel debt, will secure the approbation of all but traitors.

The fifth section is unaltered.

You perceive that while I see much good in the proposition I do not pretend to be satisfied with it. And yet I am anxious for its speedy adoption, for I dread delay. The danger is that before any constitutional guards shall have been adopted Congress will be flooded by rebels and rebel sympathizers. Whoever has mingled much in deliberative bodies must have observed the mental as well as physical nervousness of many members, impelling them too often to injudicious action. Whoever has watched the feelings of this House during the tedious months of this session, listened to the impatient whispering of some and the open declarations of others; especially when able and sincere men propose to gratify personal predilections by breaking the ranks of the Union forces and presenting to the enemy a ragged front of stragglers, must be anxious to hasten the result and prevent the demoralization of our friends. Hence, I say, let us no longer delay; take what we can get now, and hope for better things in further legislation; in enabling acts or other provisions.

I now, sir, ask for the question.

THE SPEAKER [SCHUYLER COLFAX, R., IND.]. The question before the House is on concurring in the amendments of the Senate; and as it requires by the Constitution a two-thirds vote, the vote will be taken by yeas and nays. . . .

The question was put on concurring with the amendments of the Senate; and there were—yeas 120, nays 32, not voting 32; as follows:

YEAS—Messrs. Alley, Allison, Ames, Delos R. Ashley, James M. Ashley, Baker, Baldwin, Banks, Barker, Baxter, Beaman, Bidwell, Bingham, Blaine, Boutwell, Bromwell, Buckland, Bundy, Reader W. Clarke, Sidney Clarke, Cobb, Conkling, Cook, Cullom, Darling, Davis, Dawes, Defrees, Delano, Dodge, Donnelly, Driggs, Dumont, Eckley, Eggleston, Eliot, Farnsworth, Farquhar, Ferry, Garfield, Grinnell, Griswold, Hale, Abner C. Harding, Hart, Hayes, Henderson, Higby, Holmes, Hooper, Hotchkiss, Asahel W. Hubbard, Chester D. Hubbard, John H. Hubbard, James R. Hubbell, Jenckes, Julian, Kelley, Kelso, Ketcham, Kuykendall, Laflin, Latham, George V. Lawrence, Loan, Longyear, Lynch, Marvin, McClurg, McKee, McRuer, Mercur, Miller, Moorhead, Morrill, Morris, Moulton, Myers, Newell, O'Neill, Orth, Paine, Perham, Phelps, Pike, Plants, Pomeroy, Price, William H. Randall, Raymond, Alexander H. Rice, John H. Rice, Sawyer, Schenck, Scofield, Shellabarger, Sloan, Smith, Spalding, Stevens, Stilwell, Thayer, Francis Thomas, John L. Thomas, Trowbridge, Upson, Van Aernam, Robert T. Van Horn, Ward, Warner, Henry D. Washburn, William B. Washburn, Weckler, Wentworth, Whaley, Williams, James F. Wilson, Stephen F. Wilson, Windom, and the Speaker—120.

NAYS—Messrs. Ancona, Bergen, Boyer, Chandler, Coffroth, Dawson, Denison, Eldredge, Finck, Glossbrenner, Grider, Aaron Harding, Hogan, Edwin N. Hubbell, James M. Humphrey, Kerr, Le Blond, Marshall, Niblack, Nicholson, Samuel J. Randall, Ritter, Rogers, Ross, Sitgreaves, Strouse, Taber, Taylor, Thornton, Trimble, Winfield, and Wright—32.

NOT VOTING—Messrs. Anderson, Benjamin, Blow, Brandegee, Broomall, Culver, Deming, Dixon, Goodyear, Harris, Hill, Demas Hubbard, Hulburd, James Humphrey, Ingersoll, Johnson, Jones, Kasson, William Lawrence, Marston, McCullough, McIndoe, Noell, Patterson, Radford, Rollins, Rousseau, Shanklin, Starr, Burt Van Horn, Elihu B. Washburne, and Woodbridge—32.

THE SPEAKER. Two thirds of both Houses having concurred in the joint resolution (H.R. No. 127) proposing an amendment to the Constitution of the United States, the joint resolution has passed.

Commentary

Just before the final vote in both houses on June 8 and 13, 1866, the Report of the Joint Committee on Reconstruction was submitted to Congress. This report came too late to influence the congressional debates; but it was widely distributed and undoubtedly helped muster support in the states for the new amendment. The lengthy testimony appended to the report, with its graphic description of gross discriminations against Negroes in the South, undoubtedly helped persuade the public of the need to prevent such discriminations by the proposed constitutional amendment. Yet, though the Committee report is an able document as far as it goes, it furnishes little aid to the present-day student of civil rights concerned with the Fourteenth Amendment's impact upon that field. All it really tells us is that conditions in the former Confederate states are such that they should not be allowed congressional representation without "adequate security for future peace and safety," and that such security can be found only "in such changes in the organic law as shall determine the civil rights and privileges of all citizens." The Fourteenth Amendment is put forward as the provision to meet the need referred to: it will protect the civil rights of all, including the freedmen, against state infringements.

REPORT OF THE
JOINT COMMITTEE ON RECONSTRUCTION

That they have attended to the duty assigned them as assiduously as other duties would permit, and now submit to Congress, as the result of their deliberations, a resolution proposing amendments to the Constitution, and two bills, of which they recommend the adoption.

Before proceeding to set forth in detail their reasons for the conclusion to which, after great deliberation, your committee have arrived, they beg leave to advert, briefly, to the course of proceedings they found it necessary to adopt, and to explain the reasons therefor.

The resolution under which your committee was appointed directed them to inquire into the condition of the Confederate States, and report whether they were entitled to representation in Congress. It is obvious that such an investigation, covering so large an extent of territory and involving so many important considerations, must necessarily require no trifling labor, and consume a very considerable amount of time. It must embrace the condition in which those States were left at the close of the war; the measures which have been taken towards the reorganization of civil government, and the disposition of the people towards the United States; in a word, their fitness to take an active part in the administration of national affairs.

As to their condition at the close of the rebellion, the evidence is open to all and admits of no dispute. They were in a state of utter exhaustion. Having protracted their struggle against federal authority until all hope of

285

successful resistance had ceased, and laid down their arms only because there was no longer any power to use them, the people of those States were left bankrupt in their public finances, and shorn of the private wealth which had before given them power and influence. They were also necessarily in a state of complete anarchy, without governments and without the power to frame governments except by the permission of those who had been successful in the war. The President of the United States, in the proclamations under which he appointed provisional governors, and in his various communications to them, has, in exact terms, recognized the fact that the people of those States were, when the rebellion was crushed, "deprived of all civil government," and must proceed to organize anew. In his conversation with Mr. Stearns, of Massachusetts, certified by himself, President Johnson said, "the State institutions are prostrated, laid out on the ground, and they must be taken up and adapted to the progress of events." Finding the southern States in this condition, and Congress having failed to provide for the contingency, his duty was obvious. As President of the United States, he had no power, except to execute the laws of the land as Chief Magistrate. These laws gave him no authority over the subject of reorganization, but by the Constitution he was commander-in-chief of the army and navy of the United States. The Confederate States embraced a portion of the people of the Union who had been in a state of revolt, but had been reduced to obedience by force of arms. They were in an abnormal condition, without civil government, without commercial connexions, without national or international relations, and subject only to martial law. By withdrawing their representatives in Congress, by renouncing the privilege of representation, by organizing a separate government, and by levying war against the United States, they destroyed their State constitutions in respect to the vital principle which connected their respective States with the Union and secured their federal relations; and nothing of those constitutions was left of which the United States were bound to take notice. For four years they had a *de facto* government, but it was usurped and illegal. They chose the tribunal of arms wherein to decide whether or not it should be legalized, and they were defeated. At the close of the rebellion, therefore, the people of the rebellious States were found, as the President expresses it, "deprived of all civil government." . . .

Your committee came to the consideration of the subject referred to them with the most anxious desire to ascertain what was the condition of the people of the States recently in insurrection, and what, if anything, was necessary to be done before restoring them to the full enjoyment of all their original privileges. It was undeniable that the war into which they had plunged the country had materially changed their relations to the people of the loyal States. Slavery had been abolished by constitutional amendment. A large proportion of the population had become, instead of mere chattels, free men and citizens. Through all the past struggle these had remained true and loyal, and had, in large numbers, fought on the side of the Union. It was impossible to abandon them, without securing them their rights as free men and citizens. The whole civilized world would have cried out against such base ingratitude, and the bare idea is offensive to all right-thinking men. Hence it became important to inquire what could be done to secure their rights, civil and political. It was evident to your committee that adequate security could only be found in appropriate constitutional provisions. By an original provision of the Constitution, representation is based on the whole number of free persons in each State, and three-fifths of all other persons. When all become free, representation for all necessarily follows. As a consequence the inevitable effect of the rebellion would be to increase the political power of the insurrectionary States, whenever they should be allowed to resume their positions as States of the Union. As representation is by the Constitution based upon population, your committee did not think it advisable to recommend a change of that basis. The increase of representation necessarily resulting from the abolition of slavery was considered the most important element in the questions arising out of the changed condition of affairs, and the necessity for some fundamental action in this regard seemed imperative. It appeared to your committee that the rights of these persons by whom the basis of representation had been thus increased should be recognized by the general government. While slaves they were not considered as having any rights, civil or political. It did not seem just or proper that all the political advantages derived from their becoming free should be confined to their former masters, who had fought against the Union, and withheld from themselves, who had always been loyal. Slavery, by building up a ruling and dominant class, had produced a spirit of oligarchy adverse to republican institutions, which finally inaugurated civil war. The tendency of continuing the domination of such a class, by leaving it in the exclusive possession of political power, would be to encourage the same spirit, and lead to a similar result. Doubts were entertained whether Congress had power, even under the amended Constitution, to prescribe the qualifications of voters in a State, or could act directly on the subject. It was doubtful, in the opinion of your committee, whether the States would consent to surrender a power they had always exercised, and to which they were attached. As the best if not the only method of surmounting the difficulty, and as eminently just and proper in itself, your committee came to the conclusion that political power should be possessed in all the States exactly in proportion as the right of suffrage should be granted, without distinction of color or race. This it was thought would leave the whole question with the people of each State, holding out to all the advantage of increased political power as an inducement to allow all to participate in its exercise. Such a provision would be in its nature gentle and persuasive, and would lead, it was hoped, at no distant day, to an equal participation of all, without distinction, in all the rights and privileges of citizenship, thus affording a full and adequate protection to all classes of citizens, since all would have, through the ballot-box, the power of self-protection.

Holding these views, your committee prepared an amendment to the Constitution to carry out this idea, and submitted the same to Congress. Unfortunately, as we think, it did not receive the necessary constitutional support in the Senate, and therefore could not be proposed for adoption by the States. The principle involved in that amendment is, however, believed to be sound, and your committee have again proposed it in another form, hoping that it may receive the approbation of Congress. . . . It seems to your committee not unreasonable to require satisfactory evidence that the ordinances and constitutional provisions which the President deemed essential in the first instance will be permanently adhered to by the people of the States seeking restoration, after being admitted to full participation in the government, and will not be repudiated when that object shall have been accomplished. And here the burden of proof rests upon the late insurgents who are seeking restoration to the rights and privileges which they willingly abandoned, and not upon the people of the United States who have never undertaken, directly or indirectly, to deprive them thereof. It should appear affirmatively that they are prepared and disposed in good faith to accept the results of the war, to abandon their hostility to the government, and to live in peace and amity with the people of the loyal States, extending to all classes of citizens equal rights and privileges, and conforming to the republican idea of liberty and equality. They should exhibit in their acts something more than an unwilling submission to an unavoidable necessity—a feeling, if not cheerful, certainly not offensive and defiant. And they should evince an entire repudiation of all hostility to the general government, by an acceptance of such just and reasonable conditions as that government should think the public safety demands. Has this been done? Let us look at the facts shown by the evidence taken by the committee. . . .

Looking still further at the evidence taken by your committee, it is found to be clearly shown by witnesses of the highest character and having the best means of observation, that the Freedmen's Bureau, instituted for the relief and protection of freedmen and refugees, is almost universally opposed by the mass of the population, and exists in an efficient condition only under military protection, while the Union men of the south are earnest in its defence, declaring with one voice that without its protection the colored people would not be permitted to labor at fair prices, and could hardly live in safety. They also testify that without the protection of United States troops, Union men, whether of northern or southern origin, would be obliged to abandon their homes. The feeling in many portions of the country towards emancipated slaves, especially among the uneducated and ignorant, is one of vindictive and malicious hatred. This deep-seated prejudice against color is assiduously cultivated by the public journals, and leads to acts of cruelty, oppression, and murder, which the local authorities are at no pains to prevent or punish. There is no general disposition to place the colored race, constituting at least two-fifths of the population, upon terms even of civil equality. While many instances may be found where large planters and men of the better class accept the situation, and honestly strive to bring about a better order of things, by employing the freedmen at fair wages and treating them kindly, the general feeling and disposition among all classes are yet totally averse to the toleration of any class of people friendly to the Union, be they white or black; and this aversion is not unfrequently manifested in an insulting and offensive manner. . . .

With such evidence before them, it is the opinion of your committee—

1. That the States lately in rebellion were, at the close of the war, disorganized communities, without civil government, and without constitutions or other forms, by virtue of which political relations could legally exist between them and the federal government.

2. That Congress cannot be expected to recognize as valid the election of representatives from disorganized communities, which, from the very nature of the case, were unable to present their claim to representation under those established and recognized rules, the observance of which has been hitherto required.

3. That Congress would not be justified in admitting such communities to a participation in the government of the country without first providing such constitutional or other guarantees as will tend to secure the civil rights of all citizens of the republic; a just equality of representation; protection against claims founded in rebellion and crime; a temporary restoration of the right of suffrage to those who have not actively participated in the efforts to destroy the Union and overthrow the government, and the exclusion from positions of public trust of, at least, a portion of those whose crimes have proved them to be enemies to the Union, and unworthy of public confidence. . . .

We now propose to re-state, as briefly as possible, the general facts and principles applicable to all the States recently in rebellion:

1. The seats of the senators and representatives from the so-called Confederate States became vacant in the year 1861, during the second session of the thirty-sixth Congress, by the voluntary withdrawal of their incumbents, with the sanction and by direction of the legislatures or conventions of their respective States. This was done as a hostile act against the Constitution and government of the United States, with a declared intent to overthrow the same by forming a southern confederation. This act of declared hostility was speedily followed by an organization of the same States into a confederacy, which levied and waged war, by sea and land, against the United States. This war continued more than four years, within which period the rebel armies besieged the national capital, invaded the loyal States, burned their towns and cities, robbed their citizens, destroyed more than 250,000 loyal soldiers, and imposed an increased national burden of not less than $3,500,000,000, of which seven or eight hundred millions have

already been met and paid. From the time these confederated States thus withdrew their representation in Congress and levied war against the United States, the great mass of their people became and were insurgents, rebels, traitors, and all of them assumed and occupied the political, legal, and practical relation of enemies of the United States. This position is established by acts of Congress and judicial decisions, and is recognized repeatedly by the President in public proclamations, documents, and speeches.

2. The States thus confederated prosecuted their war against the United States to final arbitrament, and did not cease until all their armies were captured, their military power destroyed, their civil officers, State and confederate, taken prisoners or put to flight, every vestige of State and confederate government obliterated, their territory overrun and occupied by the federal armies, and their people reduced to the condition of enemies conquered in war, entitled only by public law to such rights, privileges, and conditions as might be vouchsafed by the conqueror. This position is also established by judicial decisions, and is recognized by the President in public proclamations, documents, and speeches.

3. Having voluntarily deprived themselves of representation in Congress for the criminal purpose of destroying the federal Union, and having reduced themselves, by the act of levying war, to the condition of public enemies, they have no right to complain of temporary exclusion from Congress; but, on the contrary, having voluntarily renounced the right to representation, and disqualified themselves by crime from participating in the government, the burden now rests upon them, before claiming to be reinstated in their former condition, to show that they are qualified to resume federal relations. In order to do this, they must prove that they have established, with the consent of the people, republican forms of government in harmony with the Constitution and laws of the United States, that all hostile purposes have ceased, and should give adequate guarantees against future treason and rebellion—guarantees which shall prove satisfactory to the government against which they rebelled, and by whose arms they were subdued.

4. Having, by this treasonable withdrawal from Congress, and by flagrant rebellion and war, forfeited all civil and political rights and privileges under the federal Constitution, they can only be restored thereto by the permission and authority of that constitutional power against which they rebelled and by which they were subdued.

5. These rebellious enemies were conquered by the people of the United States, acting through all the co-ordinate branches of the government, and not by the executive department alone. The powers of conqueror are not so vested in the President that he can fix and regulate the terms of settlement and confer congressional representation on conquered rebels and traitors. Nor can he, in any way, qualify enemies of the government to exercise its law-making power. The authority to restore rebels to political power in the federal government can be exercised only with the concurrence of all the

departments in which political power is vested; and hence the several procla-mations of the President to the people of the Confederate States cannot be considered as extending beyond the purposes declared, and can only be regarded as provisional permission by the commander-in-chief of the army to do certain acts, the effect and validity whereof is to be determined by the constitutional government, and not solely by the executive power.

6. The question before Congress is, then, whether conquered enemies have the right, and shall be permitted at their own pleasure and on their own terms, to participate in making laws for their conquerors; whether conquered rebels may change their theatre of operations from the battle-field, where they were defeated and overthrown, to the halls of Congress, and, through their representatives, seize upon the government which they fought to de-stroy; whether the national treasury, the army of the nation, its navy, its forts and arsenals, its whole civil administration, its credit, its pensioners, the widows and orphans of those who perished in the war, the public honor, peace and safety, shall all be turned over to the keeping of its recent enemies without delay, and without imposing such conditions as, in the opinion of Congress, the security of the country and its institutions may demand.

7. The history of mankind exhibits no example of such madness and folly. The instinct of self-preservation protests against it. The surrender by Grant to Lee, and by Sherman to Johnston, would have been disasters of less magnitude, for new armies could have been raised, new battles fought, and the government saved. The anti-coercive policy, which, under pretext of avoiding bloodshed, allowed the rebellion to take form and gather force, would be surpassed in infamy by the matchless wickedness that would now surrender the halls of Congress to those so recently in rebellion until proper precautions shall have been taken to secure the national faith and the national safety.

8. As has been shown in this report, and in the evidence submitted, no proof has been afforded to Congress of a constituency in any one of the so-called Confederate States, unless we except the State of Tennessee, qualified to elect senators and representatives in Congress. No State constitu-tion, or amendment to a State constitution, has had the sanction of the people. All the so-called legislation of State conventions and legislatures has been had under military dictation. If the President may, at his will, and under his own authority, whether as military commander or chief executive, qualify persons to appoint Senators and elect Representatives, and empower others to appoint and elect them, he thereby practically controls the organi-zation of the legislative department. The constitutional form of government is thereby practically destroyed, and its powers absorbed in the Executive. And while your committee do not for a moment impute to the President any such design, but cheerfully concede to him the most patriotic motives, they cannot but look with alarm upon a precedent so fraught with danger to the republic.

9. The necessity of providing adequate safeguards for the future, before

restoring the insurrectionary States to a participation in the direction of public affairs, is apparent from the bitter hostility to the government and people of the United States yet existing throughout the conquered territory, as proved incontestably by the testimony of many witnesses and by undisputed facts.

10. The conclusion of your committee therefore is, that the so-called Confederate States are not, at present, entitled to representation in the Congress of the United States; that, before allowing such representation, adequate security for future peace and safety should be required; that this can only be found in such changes of the organic law as shall determine the civil rights and privileges of all citizens in all parts of the republic, shall place representation on an equitable basis, shall fix a stigma upon treason, and protect the loyal people against future claims for the expenses incurred in support of rebellion and for manumitted slaves, together with an express grant of power in Congress to enforce those provisions. To this end they offer a joint resolution for amending the Constitution of the United States, and the two several bills designed to carry the same into effect, before referred to.

Before closing this report, your committee beg leave to state that the specific recommendations submitted by them are the result of mutual concession, after a long and careful comparison of conflicting opinions. Upon a question of such magnitude, infinitely important as it is to the future of the republic, it was not to be expected that all should think alike. Sensible of the imperfections of the scheme, your committee submit it to Congress as the best they could agree upon, in the hope that its imperfections may be cured, and its deficiencies supplied, by legislative wisdom; and that, when finally adopted, it may tend to restore peace and harmony to the whole country, and to place our republican institutions on a more stable foundation.

Commentary

In many ways, the most provocative legislative statements on the purpose of the framers of the Fourteenth Amendment in the field of civil rights were made five years after the congressional debates already given. Such statements were made in an 1871 debate in the House on a bill to enforce the provisions of the Fourteenth Amendment. The bill in question became the Act of April 20, 1871, more popularly known as the Ku Klux Act (*infra* p. 593). The remarks referred to are so pertinent to the legislative history of the Fourteenth Amendment that the relevant extracts from the 1871 debate are included here. For our purposes, we must agree with then Representative James Garfield [R., Ohio] when he said that the 1871 debate "will become historical," since, in it, some of the key men in the drafting and passage of the Fourteenth Amendment sought to explain the purpose of its crucial Section 1.

Of particular interest is the lengthy address of Congressman John Bingham [R., Ohio], who stated his understanding of the purpose of Section 1 as he had originally drafted it. The most important part of his speech is his explanation of why he changed the form of his draft amendment from the affirmative version first introduced by him (giving Congress the power to secure equal protection) to the negative version ultimately substituted and adopted (prohibiting the states from abridging privileges and immunities or denying due process or equal protection). He tells how, after his first version had failed to receive House approval, he had re-examined "the great decision of Marshall" in *Barron* v. *Baltimore,* 7 Peters 243,—the 1833 decision which had held the first eight amendments binding only upon the federal government, not upon the states. He says that he then understood, as never before, certain words in John Marshall's opinion—notably where the great Chief Justice declared that had the framers of the Bill of Rights intended them to limit the states, they "would have imitated the framers of the original Constitution." Acting upon such suggestion, Bingham said that he did imitate the original framers in their drafting of Article I, Section 10, containing express limitations upon state power. Imitating their example "to the letter," he recast his proposal so that it began, "No State shall . . . ."

The change thus explained by Bingham has been of the greatest consequence. It converted the Fourteenth Amendment from a grant authorizing Congress to protect civil rights to a self-operative prohibition which could be enforced by the courts though there had been no congressional action in the matter. The amendment could thus develop into the great charter of civil rights that it has since become, something that would have been impossible if it had remained only a delegation of legislative power. In addition, the change made by Bingham was what made possible the development of the doctrine of judicial supremacy that was to occur toward the end of the century. In practice, enforcement of the Fourteenth Amendment's provisions was, until our own day, to be almost entirely a judicial function.

293

As indicated, the 1871 speech explains why Bingham changed Section 1 of the Fourteenth Amendment from an affirmative to its present negative form. What was it, according to him, that the states were now prohibited from doing? Bingham's answer was given in terms of the Bill of Rights. According to him, "the privileges and immunities of citizens of the United States, as contradistinguished from citizens of a State, are chiefly defined in the first eight amendments." And it is these eight articles that were never limitations upon the states, but were now made so by the Fourteenth Amendment. Here we have from the man who drafted Section 1 of the amendment (except for its citizenship clause) an explicit statement that it was intended to bind the states by the Bill of Rights.

It should, however, be pointed out that Bingham's 1871 statement, while surely entitled to weight, is far from conclusive on the issue. After all, what was adopted by Congress and submitted for ratification was Bingham's proposal, not his speech—a speech made more than five years after the event. The 1871 remarks were made in the midst of a heated debate, in which the constitutionality of the measure Bingham was then supporting was challenged. He not unnaturally stated his recollection of what had transpired five years earlier in terms which would support the measure he was advocating in 1871. Perhaps Garfield (who had also participated in the Fourteenth Amendment debates) was unfair when he declared, "My colleague can make but he cannot unmake history." But his retort goes to the heart of the matter. One may doubt whether the Bingham recollection alone justifies the ex post facto rewriting of the crucial section of the Fourteenth Amendment. Never in the 1866 debates did Bingham refer specifically to the now-claimed incorporation of the Bill of Rights in the new amendment, though, as already indicated, there were confused intimations to such effect in some of his 1866 speeches. Again, it should be emphasized that apart from Senator Jacob Howard [R., Mich.] (*supra* p. 257), no other speaker in the Fourteenth Amendment debates even remotely supported the view expressed in Bingham's 1871 address, and members of both houses made statements inconsistent with it. Perhaps the best answer to Bingham in the 1871 debate was that given by Congressman John Storm [Dem., Pa.] when he declared (in a speech not reprinted here), "If the monstrous doctrine now set up as resulting from the provisions of that Fourteenth Amendment had ever been hinted at, that Amendment would have received an emphatic rejection at the hands of the people."

THE DEBATE

The House having under consideration the bill (H. R. No. 320) to enforce the provisions of the fourteenth amendment to the Constitution of the United States, and for other purposes—

JOHN BINGHAM [R., OHIO] said: Mr. Speaker: No man is equal to the task of discussing, as it ought to be discussed, the issue before this House within the limits of a single hour. I scarcely hope that I shall have done more than touch the hem of the garment of the argument when my hour shall have expired. But, sir, whatever I may fail to do, the great people behind me will not fail to supply. They, sir, constitute the tribunal before whom this issue is on trial.

It is the old issue with which the people have become familiar within the last ten years. It presents itself, sir, this day only in another form. In substance it is precisely the issue which was presented ten years ago upon this floor, and was discussed ably and exhaustively upon this side of the House and upon that. The question then, sir, and the question now, is, whether it is competent for the Congress of the United States, under the Constitution of the United States, in pursuance of its provisions, and in the exercise of the powers vested by it "in the Government of the United States or in any department or officer thereof," to provide by law for the enforcement of the Constitution, on behalf of the whole people, the nation, and for the enforcement as well of the Constitution on behalf of every individual citizen of the Republic in every State and Territory of the Union to the extent of the rights guarantied to him by the Constitution.

Until this issue was raised, in 1860–61, the constitutional power of Congress to provide for the common defense and the enforcement of the Constitution and laws of the United States had not been seriously questioned in this House. Now, as then, this power, essential to the nation's life and the safety of the people, is here challenged. It amazes me that, after all that has transpired in this country for the final settlement of this very question, gentlemen on either side of the House would dare to open it again. It has been settled by your courts of justice; it has been settled by the repeated action of your Congress within the last ten years; it has been settled by the people themselves, by the ballot and by battle, by laws and by arms; and from their decision thus made there cannot rightfully lie an appeal. And yet gentlemen substantially again open this question to-day.

The question as presented here and now may be stated thus: is it competent for Congress to provide by law for the better enforcement of the Constitution and laws of the United States and the better security of the life, liberty, and property of the citizens of the United States in the several States of the Union? The Constitution is not self-executing, therefore laws must be enacted by Congress for the due execution of all the powers vested by the Constitution in the Government of the United States, or in any department or any officer thereof. No man can successfully deny the power of Congress so to legislate, for it is expressly provided in the Constitution that "Congress shall have power to make all laws which shall be necessary and proper for carrying into execution" the powers therein expressly granted to Congress, "and all other powers vested by this Constitution in the Government of the United States, or in any department or officer thereof."

My honorable friend from Indiana [Mr. Kerr] discussed this question, upon the Constitution as it was and not upon the Constitution as it is. In the progress of his remarks the gentleman [Mr. Kerr] did disclose to this House and to the country the fact that under the Constitution as it was, it always was competent for the Congress of the United States, by law, to enforce every affirmative grant of power and every express negative limitation imposed by the Constitution upon the States. The great case from which the gentleman read in 6 Wheaton, pages 375-447, (*Cohens* v. *Virginia.*) is a judicial ruling that clearly, distinctly, and beyond all question, to the extent of all the affirmative grants of power in the Constitution, and of all the express negative limitations of power imposed by the Constitution upon the States, it is competent for Congress to legislate. From the opinion in this case, delivered by Marshall, C. J., I read the following:

America has chosen to be, in many respects and to many purposes, a nation; and for all these purposes, her Government is complete; to all these objects it is competent. The people have declared that in the exercise of all powers given for these objects it is supreme. It can then, in effecting these objects, legitimately control all individuals or governments within the American territory. The constitution and laws of a State, so far as they are repugnant to the Constitution and laws of the United States, are absolutely void. These States are constituent parts of the United States. They are members of one great empire. [6 Wheat. 414]

Mr. Speaker, I have not the time to read from that opinion further. I will state, however, to the House that in this opinion, scarcely second in importance to any of the opinions that emanated from that matchless Chief Justice whose full-orbed intellect for thirty years illumined the jurisprudence of his country, you will find incorporated the words of Hamilton, who was second to no man in gifts of mind and second to no man in the service which he rendered to the people of his own day and to the millions who have come after him in framing the Constitution of the United States. Marshall incorporates the words of Hamilton with approval, words in which Hamilton, while the Constitution was on trial for adoption or rejection before all the people of the States, referring to the dual system of government, national government, and State governments, and the judicial powers of each for the administration of the laws of the Union, declared "that the national and State systems are to be regarded as one whole," and that "the courts of the latter [the

States] will, of course, be national auxiliaries to the execution of all the laws of the Union."

The States exercise their judicial power under the Constitution, and in subordination to the Constitution, and subject to the express limitations of the Constitution, but for the purpose of aiding its enforcement, not of breaking it. The Constitution declares—

This Constitution, and the laws of the United States which shall be made in pursuance thereof, and all treaties made or which shall be made in pursuance thereof, and all treaties made, or which shall be made, under the authority of the United States, shall be the supreme law of the land; and the judges in every State shall be bound thereby, anything in the constitution or laws of any State to the contrary notwithstanding.

By the legislation of the First Congress, passed by the votes of many of the eminent men who framed the Constitution, then members of Congress, and approved by Washington, the power was given to the humblest citizen aggrieved by the final decision of State courts against his guaranteed rights under the Constitution and laws of the United States, to bring the same for review and reversal before the Supreme Court of the United States, and thereby set aside the usurpations of a State. The judiciary act of 1789 asserts this power of the Government of the United States fully and expressly.

The act of 1789, the validity and constitutionality of which has never been challenged by a respectable court in America, ought to have satisfied gentlemen that it is too late to raise the question they are raising here to-day, the power of Congress to provide by law for the enforcement of the powers vested by the Constitution in the Government of the United States, both against individuals and States, as Marshall expressed it. I desire to read, merely for the purpose of recalling the recollection of the members of the House to its provisions, from the twenty-fifth section of that act, under which the case of *Cohens* v. *Virginia,* to which the honorable gentlemen from Indiana [Mr. Kerr] referred, came into the Supreme Court of the United States for review. That section is as follows:

A final judgment or decree in any suit, in the highest court of law or equity of a State in which a decision in the suit could be had, where is drawn in question the validity of a treaty or statute of, or an authority exercised under the United States, and the decision is against their validity; or where is drawn in question the validity of a statute of, or an authority exercised under any State, on the ground of their being repugnant to the Constitution, treaties, or laws of the United States, and the decision is in favor of such, their validity; or where is drawn in question the construction of any clause of the Constitution, or of a treaty, or statute of, or commission held under the United States, and the decision is against the title, right, privilege, or exemption specially set up or claimed by either party, under such clause of the said Constitution, treaty, statute, or commission, may be reëxamined and reversed or affirmed in the Supreme Court of the United States upon a writ of error, the citation being signed by the Chief Justice, or judge or chancellor of the court rendering or passing the judgment or decree complained of, or by a justice of the Supreme Court of the United States, in the same manner and under the same regulations; and the writ shall have the same effect as if the judgment or decree complained of had been rendered or passed in a circuit court; and the proceeding upon the reversal shall also be the same, except that the Supreme Court, instead of remanding the cause for a final decision, as before provided, may, at their discretion, if the case shall have been once remanded before, proceed to a final decision of the same, and award execution. But no other error shall be assigned or regarded as a ground of refusal in any such case, as aforesaid, than such as appears on the face of the record. &c. [1 *Brightly* 259, 260]

Notwithstanding the express grant of power in the Constitution, and the rulings of Marshall, and this legislation of the First Congress, gentlemen still aver that Congress cannot constitutionally make laws to enforce the rights of the nation against either States or unlawful combinations of men. I answer that the power to suppress combinations to obstruct the execution of the laws of the United States, was asserted under the administration of Washington by the Congress of the United States, and with his approval. I refer now to the act of 1795, which brings in question the discretion in the Executive of which the gentleman from New York [Mr. Wood] so loudly complained. The act of 1795 provided—

That whenever the United States shall be invaded, or be in imminent danger of invasion. &c., it shall be lawful for the President of the United States to call forth such number of the militia of the State or States as he may judge necessary to repel such invasion, and to issue his orders for that purpose to such officer or officers of the militia as he may think proper.

In the second section of this act it is further provided:

Whenever the laws of the United States shall be opposed, or the execution thereof obstructed in any State by combinations too powerful to be suppressed by the ordinary course of judicial proceedings, or by the powers vested in the marshals by this act, it shall be lawful for the President of the United States to call forth the militia of such State, or of any other State or States, as may be necessary to suppress such combinations and to cause the laws to be duly executed, and the use of the militia so to be called forth may be continued, if necessary, until the expiration of thirty days after the commencement of the then next session of Congress.

In the third section it is provided that:

Whenever it may be necessary, in the judgment of the President, to use the military force hereby directed to be called forth, the President shall forthwith, by proclamation, command such insurgents to disperse, and retire peaceably to their respective abodes, within a limited time.

Then, again, in a further provision of that act, which I shall not stop to read, it is provided that the militia being called out, under the discretion of the President, "and employed in the service of the United States, shall for the time being be subject to the same Rules and Articles of War as the troops of the United States," and liable, therefore, to trial and punishment and execution, even to death, by military commission or court-martial. "Whenever in the judgment of the President it is necessary," says this act, approved by Washington and never challenged until these controversies arose in these latter days, to which I have referred, by any patriot anywhere in the nation, all the arms bearing population of the United States, at the discretion of the President, might be called and coerced into the service of the nation, and neither *habeas corpus* nor any other civil process known either to the State tribunals of justice or to the national civil tribunals of justice could interfere in the premises.

In support of what I have just said I refer in passing to the ruling made in 12 Wheaton, page 19, by the Supreme Court of the United States, in the case of *Martin* v. *Mott,* in which it was decided that the President is the exclusive and final judge whether the exigency contemplated by the law has arisen; a decision the legal soundness of which has never to this day been authoritatively questioned.

What becomes, sir, in the light of this early legislation, this contemporaneous exposition of the Constitution, of that outcry of the gentleman from New York [Mr. Wood] about discretion confided to the President being usurpation? I can well understand the significance of an unlimited discretion in a monarchy, where, by the constitution of the State, the king can do no wrong, and no man may challenge his decree, which awes a prostrate and defenseless people into submission. But I do not understand what significance is to be attached to this clamor of the gentleman from New York about discretion being vested in a President of the United States by the people's laws, when the President is but the servant of the people, created by the breath of their power.

FERNANDO WOOD [DEM., N.Y.]. You would make him their master.

MR. BINGHAM. Oh, the gentleman thinks that the people are not capable of being their own masters, that the servant may be greater than his lord! The significance of the gentleman's last remark, if there is any possible significance in it, (and I say this with all respect,) is that the system of civil polity known as the Constitution of the United States is a failure, that the people are incapable of self government. The gentleman, I perceive, inclines to absolute power in a single hand! Discretionary power in a President is dangerous to the people who intrust it to him as their mere servant! The people cannot all assemble at the Capitol. The people cannot in person exercise the powers by them expressly delegated to their agents. If their agents abuse the trust the people are not without remedy. They can bring to trial and judgment either a recusant President or a recusant Congress. "Discretion dangerous to the people!"

Why, sir, the gentleman strikes at the essential features of your Constitution. The largest discretion under the Constitution of the United States is vested in a Congress, consisting of a Senate and House of Representatives, in which body the honorable gentleman himself holds a distinguished place. Consider the discretion which is vested in Congress. If anything is to be proved by the gentleman's outcry, if indeed discretionary power is dangerous to the public liberty, the people, enlightened by the gentleman, should reform their Constitution and strip Congress of all discretionary power. That

Congress is left to exercise all its great powers at discretion is undoubted. The Congress of the United States, under the Constitution, is invested with power to determine, in their discretion, the issues of life and death to the people of the Republic.

By the Constitution of the country you have the discretion, when, in your judgment it is needful and proper, to declare war. In pursuance of the exercise of that power you have the other great power to pass your conscription act, when, in your judgment, you deem it needful; to drag from his home every man capable of bearing arms in the Republic, to subject him to the perils of the march or the greater perils of the battle, and also to the despotism, as the gentleman calls it, of martial or military law. After you have declared war, after you have summoned the whole able-bodied population of the country to the field, you have granted to you expressly the further power to provide by law, to turn out of their homes the wives and children whom your citizens may have left behind and quarter your soldiers upon the hearthstone. Who trembles at the magnitude of this power?

The people are equal to the task of redressing all wrongs which may be inflicted upon them either by President or by Congress. If the President violates the discretionary powers vested in him the people by their Representatives summon him to the bar of the Senate to answer for high crimes and misdemeanors, and on conviction not only depose him from his great office, but make him as one dead among living men, by pronouncing their irrevocable decree, from which there is no pardon on this side of the grave, that never again shall he hold office of trust, honor, or profit, in the United States.

As for the members of this House, if they be false to their trust they must answer every second year at the bar of public opinion, and an offended, betrayed, and outraged people, having the power, know how to make such betrayers of their rights and their interests powerless for all the future. The gentleman cannot trust discretionary power to the President! The people grant discretionary power to the President, they trust and confide in him, and have reason to believe that he will faithfully do his duty.

Additional to this legislation of 1795, Mr. Speaker, is the act of 1861, which declares in express words that whenever, in the judgment of the President, there are unlawful obstructions, combinations, or assemblages of persons against the authority of the United States too powerful to be restrained or controlled by ordinary judicial process, it shall be lawful for the President to employ the Army, the Navy, and the militia of all the States to enforce the faithful execution of the laws of the United States. [2 Brightley 191] The President's power under these acts does not wait on the call of States, or Legislatures, or Governors. The President acts upon his own judgment and discretion under the law. I agree with the suggestion of my honorable and learned friend from Wisconsin, [Mr. Eldredge,] that the provision of the Constitution as to the protection of the States against invasion and insurrection, upon the call of their Legislature or their Governor, is in full force; but it in no wise touches this power of providing by law for the protection of all the guarantied rights of the people, under the Constitution of the United States, without asking any favor of the Legislature or the Governor of any State.

Mr. Speaker, having said this much on this subject, I refer to the bill under consideration to say, that I do not propose now to discuss the provisions of the bill in detail. The bill incorporates in general the provisions, adapting them, however, to the existing condition of things, which have been law from the foundation of the Government, and to which I have referred. There may be provisions in the bill pending which are not necessary or proper. If there be, I shall ask the privilege, and I have no doubt it will be accorded to me, to attempt to amend by the favor of the House.

Of the general power of Congress to legislate for the better enforcement of all the powers vested by the Constitution in the Government of the United States, and for the better protection of the people in the rights thereby guarantied to them against States and combinations of individuals, I have no doubt, for the reason that it is a closed question, absolutely closed—

CHARLES ELDREDGE [DEM., WIS.]. Will I interrupt my friend—

MR. BINGHAM. The gentleman will excuse me.

MR. ELDREDGE. I wish to ask him to apply that second section to his statement and see if it does conform to the provision of the Constitution—

MR. BINGHAM. I have already stated, Mr. Speaker, that I have spoken of the provisions of the bill in general, and not in detail. I do not propose to be diverted from my line of argument. I have been endeavoring to demonstrate that the legislation of the country in all the past was an exercise of the general power to legislate as proposed by this bill. If it was competent heretofore to give the President power to enforce by arms the faithful execution of the laws against unlawful combinations of men, surely it is equally competent, to make the fact of such combinations a crime punishable in your courts. The powers of the States have been limited and the powers of Congress extended by the last three amendments of the Constitution. These last amendments—thirteen, fourteen, and fifteen—do, in my judgment, vest in Congress a power to protect the rights of citizens against States, and individuals in States, never before granted. It is my purpose, as far as I may be able in the limited time allowed me, to make this statement good.

Mr. Speaker, the honorable gentleman from Illinois [Mr. Farnsworth] did me unwittingly, great service, when he ventured to ask me why I changed the form of the first section of the fourteenth article of amendment from the form in which I reported it to the House in February, 1866, from the Committee on Reconstruction. I will answer the gentleman, sir, and answer him truthfully. I had the honor to frame the amendment as reported in February, 1866, and the first section, as it now stands, letter for letter and syllable for syllable, in the fourteenth article of the amendments to the

Constitution of the United States, save the introductory clause defining citizens. The clause defining citizens never came from the joint Committee on Reconstruction, but the residue of the first section of the fourteenth amendment did come from the committee precisely as I wrote it and offered it in the Committee on Reconstruction, and precisely as it now stands in the Constitution, to wit:

No State shall make or enforce any law which shall abridge the privileges or immunities of citizens of the United States; not shall any State deprive any person of life, liberty, or property, without due process of law, nor deny to any person within its jurisdiction the equal protection of the laws.

The Fourteenth Amendment concludes as follows:

The Congress shall have power, by appropriate legislation, to enforce the provisions of this article.

That is the grant of power. It is full and complete. The gentleman says that amendment differs from the amendment reported by me in February; differs from the provision introduced and written by me, now in the fourteenth article of amendments. It differs in this: that it is, as it now stands in the Constitution, more comprehensive than as it was first proposed and reported in February, 1866. It embraces all and more than did the February proposition.

JOHN FARNSWORTH [R., ILL.]. I wish simply to call your attention—

MR. BINGHAM. Well, what is it?

MR. FARNSWORTH. The Fourteenth Amendment embraced other provisions which require legislation. The last clause gives Congress power—

MR. BINGHAM. I thank the gentleman for that word. The Fourteenth Amendment closes with the words, "the Congress shall have power to enforce, by appropriate legislation, the provisions of this article"—the whole of it, sir; all the provisions of the article; every section of it.

MR. FARNSWORTH rose.

MR. BINGHAM. The gentleman from Illinois must not further interrupt me. He is not now enlightening me on this subject, though doubtless he is capable of doing so when he has the time.

The gentleman ventured upon saying that this amendment does not embrace all of the amendment prepared and reported by me with the consent of the committee in February, 1866. The amendment reported in February, and to which the gentleman refers, is as follows:

The Congress shall have power to make all laws which shall be necessary and proper to secure to the citizens of each State all the privileges and immunities of citizens in the several States, and to all persons in the several States equal protection in the rights of life, liberty, and property.

That is the amendment, and the whole of it, as reported in February, 1866. That amendment never was rejected by the House or Senate. A motion was made to lay it on the table, which was a test vote on the merits of it, and the motion failed—only forty-one votes for the motion, and one hundred and ten against it. I consented to and voted for the motion to postpone it till the second Tuesday of April. Afterward, in the Joint Committee on Reconstruction, I introduced this amendment, in the precise form, as I have stated, in which it was reported, and as it now stands in the Constitution of my country. It contains the words, among others—"Nor deny to any person within its jurisdiction the equal protection of the laws."

The gentleman inquires, what does this mean? It ought to have occurred to the gentleman that it means that no State shall deny to any person within its jurisdiction the equal protection of the Constitution of the United States, as that Constitution is the supreme law of the land, and, of course, that no State should deny to any such person any of the rights which it guaranties to all men, nor should any State deny to any such person any right secured to him either by the laws and treaties of the United States or of such State. The gentleman, if he had consulted Magna Charta, which England's brilliant and profound constitutional historian, Hallam, has well said "is the keystone of English liberty," would have found, in the forty-sixth clause, these words: "We will sell to no man, we will not deny or delay to any man right or justice."

After all the past, is it needful to say what it means to deny right or justice to any man? The words in the first section of the fourteenth amendment are quite as comprehensive as these words of Magna Charta, to wit:

No State shall make or enforce any law which shall abridge the privileges or immunities of citizens of the United States; nor shall any State deprive any person of life, liberty, or property, without due process of law, nor deny to any person within its jurisdiction the equal protection of the laws.

These are the words of Magna Charta, "we will not deny to any man right or justice," the great words of England's constitution, out of which has come all that grand system of English law and growth and development which has made the elder branch of our house, only second to America, her child, in the family nations. I affirm that by the equal justice of her laws, by the strength, maturity, and splendor of her intellect, by the purity of her life, by her inventive genius, by her power on land and sea, by her triumphs in production, greater in proportion to population than that of any other people now or at any time upon this globe, England is foremost of the nations of the Old World. It was her Magna Charta, sir, which, when faithfully enforced, made it impossible for a slave to breathe in England, and by force of it, it came to be that the moment a slave set foot upon her soil his fetters turned to dust and he was free. A people to be great must be just.

The gentleman asked what mean the words in the fourteenth article "nor shall any State deny to any person the equal protection of the laws." Sir, the gentleman seems to have taken a step backward, either in knowledge of the right or fidelity to it. No man regrets this more than I do. When this fourteenth amendment was under discussion before the House, the gentleman endeavored to impress upon the House that the adoption of this very amendment, and especially the first section of it, which he says now we have no power to enforce, was essential to the protection of the poor emancipated slaves in the several States. I shall do no injustice to the gentleman. I shall quote his words exactly from the Globe as they there stand recorded.

At that day, speaking of this amendment, the gentleman from Illinois [Mr. Farnsworth] said:

> Equal protection by the laws! Can there be a well-founded objection to this? Is not this the very foundation of a republican government? Is it not the undeniable right of every subject of the Government to receive equal protection of the laws with every other subject? This is so self-evident and just that no man whose soul is not too cramped and dwarfed to hold the smallest germ of justice can fail to see and appreciate it." [58 *Globe* 2539]
>
> The preservation of the Government requires it. The rights and liberties of the loyal poor cannot be preserved without it. [*Ibid.* 2510]

Surely the gentleman then supposed the words "the equal protection of the laws" were more than a glittering generality; that they were to be enforced to the extent of securing to all the guarantees of life, liberty, and property as provided in the supreme law of the land, the Constitution of the United States. Well might the gentleman inquire, as he does to-day, "What means that language if we adopted the amendment without power to enforce it?" There is not a line or a letter in the fourteenth amendment that looks to the protection of the rights of these poor unfortunates, "the loyal poor," as the gentleman called them, who were subjected to the torture of human bondage, but the provisions of the first and fifth sections of the fourteenth article of amendment. The power to enforce this provision by law is as full as any other grant of power to Congress. It is, "the Congress shall have power, by appropriate legislation," to enforce this and every other provision of this article.

Mr. Speaker, allow me to say, further, that by the text of the Constitution as you remember it, and as all thoughtful Representatives remember it, there are negative limitations upon the power of the States; as, for example, that no State shall make an *ex post facto* law; that no State shall pass any law impairing the obligation of contracts; that no State shall grant any title of nobility; that no State shall make anything a legal tender but gold and silver coin; that no State shall enter into any treaty, alliance, or confederation, nor any compact or agreement with another State, or with a foreign Power, etc.

These are of the negative limitations on the power of the States in the original text of the Constitution. Does the gentleman undertake to tell me that they have not always been enforced against State constitutions and State statutes, and the judgment of the highest courts of the States, in the Supreme Court of the United States, under the twenty-fifth section of the act of 1789? Why, sir, if I were to read the decisions that have been made in the exercise of this very power, under that law, enforcing these negative prohibitions upon States, the sun would go down before I had read even a syllabus of the cases. Is not the gentleman answered now? But, says the gentleman to me, why did you change the amendment of February, 1866? Sir, I sat at the feet of one who, though departed this life, still lives among us in his immortal spirit, and still speaks to us from the reports of the highest judicial tribunal on earth, which he so long adorned as the Chief Justice of the Supreme Court of the United States. I took counsel, sir, of that great man, John Marshall, foremost of all the judges, in the hope that by his guidance, the amendment might be so framed that in all the hereafter, it might be accepted by the historian of the American Constitution and her Magna Charta "as the keystone of American liberty."

I answer the gentleman, how I came to change the form of February to the words now in the first section of the fourteenth article of amendment, as they stand, and I trust will forever stand, in the Constitution of my country. I had read—and that is what induced me to attempt to impose by constitutional amendments new limitations upon the power of the States—the great decision of Marshall in Barron *vs.* the Mayor and City Council of Baltimore, wherein the Chief Justice said, in obedience to his official oath and the Constitution as it then was:

The amendments [to the Constitution] contain no expression indicating an intention to apply them to the State governments. This court cannot so apply them [7 Peters 250]

In this case the city had taken private property for public use, without compensation as alleged, and there was no redress for the wrong in the Supreme Court of the United States; and only for this reason, the first eight amendments were not limitations on the power of the States.

And so afterward, in the case of the *Lessee of Livingston* v. *Moore and others,* (7 Peters 552,) the court ruled, "it is now settled that the amendments [to the Constitution] do not extend to the States." They were but limitations upon Congress. Jefferson well said of the first eight articles of amendments to the Constitution of the United States, they constitute the American Bill of Rights. Those amendments secured the citizens against any deprivation of any essential rights of person by any act of Congress, and among other things thereby they were secured in their persons, houses, papers, and effects against unreasonable searches and seizures, in the inviolability of their homes in times of peace, by declaring that no soldier shall in time of peace be quartered in any house without the consent of the owner. They secured trial by jury; they secured the right to be informed of the nature and cause of accusations which might in any case be made against them; they secured compulsory process for witnesses, and to be heard in defense by counsel. They secured, in short, all the rights dear to the American citizen. And yet it was decided, and rightfully, that these amendments, defining and protecting the rights of men and citizens, were only limitations on the power of Congress, not on the power of the States.

In reëxamining that case of Barron, Mr. Speaker, after my struggle in the House in February, 1866, to which the gentleman has alluded, I noted and apprehended as I never did before, certain words in that opinion of Marshall. Referring to the first eight articles of amendments to the Constitution of the United States, the Chief Justice said: "Had the framers of these amendments intended them to be limitations on the powers of the State governments they would have imitated the framers of the original Constitution, and have expressed that intention." [*Barron* v. *The Mayor,* etc., 7 Peters 250]

Acting upon this suggestion I did imitate the framers of the original Constitution. As they had said "no State shall emit bills of credit, pass any bill of attainder, *ex post facto* law, or law impairing the obligations of contracts;" imitating their example and imitating it to the letter, I prepared the provision of the first section of the Fourteenth Amendment as it stands in the Constitution, as follows:

No State shall make or enforce any law which shall abridge the privileges or immunities of the citizens of the United States, nor shall any State deprive any person of life, liberty, or property without due process of law, nor deny to any person within its jurisdiction the equal protection of the laws.

I hope the gentleman now knows why I changed the form of the amendment of February, 1866.

Mr. Speaker, that the scope and meaning of the limitations imposed by the first section, fourteenth amendment of the Constitution may be more fully understood, permit me to say that the privileges and immunities of citizens of the United States, as contradistinguished from citizens of a State, are chiefly defined in the first eight amendments to the Constitution of the United States. Those eight amendments are as follows:

ARTICLE I
Congress shall make no law respecting an establishment of religion, or prohibiting the free exercise thereof, or abridging the freedom of speech, or of the press, or the right of the people peaceably to assemble, and to petition the Government for a redress of grievances.

ARTICLE II
A well-regulated militia being necessary to the security of a free State, the right of the people to keep and bear arms shall not be infringed.

ARTICLE III
No soldier shall, in time of peace, be quartered in any house, without the consent of the owner, nor in time of war, but in the manner to be prescribed by law.

ARTICLE IV
The right of the people to be secure in their persons, houses, papers, and effects, against unreasonable searches and seizures, shall not be violated, and no warrant shall issue but upon probable cause, supported by oath or affirmation, and particularly describing the place to be searched and the persons or things to be seized.

ARTICLE V
No person shall be held to answer for a capital or otherwise infamous crime, unless on a presentment or indictment of a grand jury, except in cases arising in the land or naval

forces, or in the militia, when in actual service in time of war or public danger; nor shall any person be subject for the same offense to be twice put in jeopardy of life or limb, nor shall be compelled on any criminal case to be a witness against himself, nor be deprived of life, liberty, or property, without due process of law; nor shall private property be taken for public use without just compensation.

ARTICLE VI

In all criminal prosecutions, the accused shall enjoy the right to a speedy and public trial, by an impartial jury of the State and district wherein the crime shall have been committed, which district shall have been previously ascertained by law, and to be informed of the nature and cause of the accusation; to be confronted with the witnesses against him; to have compulsory process for obtaining witnesses in his favor; and to have the assistance of counsel for his defense.

ARTICLE VII

In suits at common law, where the value in controversy shall exceed twenty dollars, the right of trial by jury shall be preserved, and no fact tried by jury shall be otherwise reëxamined in any court of the United States, than according to the rules of the common law.

ARTICLE VIII

Excessive bail shall not be required, nor excessive fines imposed, nor cruel and unusual punishments inflicted.

These eight articles I have shown never were limitations upon the power of the States, until made so by the fourteenth amendment. The words of that amendment, "no State shall make or enforce any law which shall abridge the privileges or immunities of citizens of the United States," are an express prohibition upon every State of the Union, which may be enforced under existing laws of Congress, and such other laws for their better enforcement as Congress may make.

Mr. Speaker, that decision in the fourth of Washington's Circuit Court Reports, to which my learned colleague [Mr. Shellabarger] has referred is only a construction of the second section, fourth article of the original Constitution, to wit, "The citizens of each State shall be entitled to all privileges and immunities of citizens in the several States." In that case the court only held that in civil rights the State could not refuse to extend to citizens of other States the same general rights secured to its own.

In the case of The *United States* v. *Primrose,* Mr. Webster said that—

For purposes of trade, it is evidently not in the power of any State to impose any hinderance or embarrassment, &c., upon citizens of other States, or to place them, on coming there, upon a different footing from her own citizens. [6 Webster's *Works* 112].

The learned Justice Story declared that—

The intention of the clause ("the citizens of each State shall be entitled to all privileges and immunities of citizens in the several States.") was to confer on the citizens of each State a general citizenship, and communicated all the privileges and immunities which a citizen of the same State would be entitled to under the same circumstances. [2 *Story on the Constitution* 605].

Is it not clear that other and different privileges and immunities than those to which a citizen of a State was entitled are secured by the provision of the fourteenth article, that no State shall abridge the privileges and immunities of citizens of the United States, which are defined in the eight articles of amendment, and which were not limitations on the power of the States before the fourteenth amendment made them limitations?

Sir, before the ratification of the Fourteenth Amendment, the State could deny to any citizen the right of trial by jury, and it was done. Before that the State could abridge the freedom of the press, and it was so done in half of the States of the Union. Before that a State, as in the case of the State of Illinois, could make it a crime punishable by fine and imprisonment for any citizen within her limits, in obedience to the injunction of our divine Master, to help a slave who was ready to perish; to give him shelter, or break with him his crust of bread. The validity of that State restriction upon the rights of conscience and the duty of life was affirmed, to the shame and disgrace of America, in the Supreme Court of the United States; but nevertheless affirmed in obedience to the requirements of the Constitution. [*Moore v. The People,* 14 How. 19-20]

Under the Constitution as it is, not as it was, and by force of the Fourteenth Amendment, no State hereafter can imitate the bad example of Illinois, to which I have referred, nor can any State ever repeat the example of Georgia and send men to the penitentiary, as did that State, for teaching the Indian to read the lessons of the New Testament, to know that new evangel, "The pure in heart shall see God."

Mr. Speaker, this House may safely follow the example of the makers of the Constitution and the builders of the Republic, by passing laws for enforcing all the privileges and immunities of citizens of the United States, as guarantied by the amended Constitution and expressly enumerated in the Constitution. Do gentlemen say that by so legislating we would strike down the rights of the State? God forbid. I believe our dual system of government essential to our national existence. That Constitution which Washington so aptly said made us one people, is essential to our nationality and essential to the protection of the rights of all the people at home and abroad. The State governments are also essential to the local administration of the law, which makes it omnipresent, visible to every man within the vast extent of the Republic, in every place, whether by the wayside or by the fireside, restraining him by its terrors from the wrong, and protecting him by its power, in the right.

Who is there here to say that any State ever had the right to defeat the very object for which all government is made?

The nation cannot be without that Constitution, which made us "one people;" the nation cannot be without the State governments to localize and enforce the rights of the people under the Constitution. No right reserved by the Constitution to the States should be impaired, no right vested by it in the

Government of the United States, or in any Department or officer thereof, should be challenged or violated. "Centralized power, decentralized administration," expresses the whole philosophy of the American system. You say it is centralized power to restrain by law unlawful combinations in States against the Constitution and citizens of the United States, to enforce the Constitution and the rights of United States citizen by national law, and to disperse by force, if need be, combinations too powerful to be overcome by judicial process, engaged in trampling under foot the life and liberty, or destroying the property of the citizen.

The people of the United States are entitled to have their rights guarantied to them by the Constitution of the United States, protected by national law. I enter upon no new construction. I follow this day, in its letter and its spirit, the utterance of that mightiest man of our time, to whom God gave such gifts of intellect as are but seldom given to man. The intellectual giant of the North, in the most elaborate argument of his public life, vindicated the Constitution of his country to the extent of all the grants and limitations of power which it then contained, and asserted the rightful authority of Congress to enforce them by law. The Supreme Court of the United States, and the legislative and executive departments, as I have shown, fully supported all that he said.

To the right understanding of Mr. Webster's words, the House will bear in mind that the Constitution of the United States required, that every State officer, legislative, executive, and judicial, should be bound by oath or affirmation to support it; that it declared that:

This Constitution and the laws of the United States which shall be made in pursuance thereof, and all treaties made or which shall be made under the authority of the United States, shall be the supreme law of the land, and the judges in every State shall be bound thereby, anything in the constitution or laws of any State to the contrary notwithstanding.

I now quote Mr. Webster's words:

The maintenance of this Constitution does not depend on the plighted faith of the States as States to support it. It relies on individual duty and obligation.

The Constitution of the United States creates direct relations between this Government and individuals. This Government may punish individuals for treason, and all other crimes in the code, when committed against the United States.

On the other hand, the Government owes high and solemn duties to every citizen of the country. It is bound to protect him in his most important rights and interests. It makes war for his protection, and no other government in the country can make war. It makes peace for his protection, and no other government can make peace. He goes abroad beneath its flag, and carries with him a national character imparted to him by this Government, which no other government can impart. [3 Webster's Works 469, 470]

Has the Congress any clearer grant of power to make war for the protection of the citizen than it has to make laws to enforce his guarantied "privileges" under the Constitution, as defined therein and assured by the fourteenth amendment?

The significant remark in that profound speech of Mr. Webster is, that, in which he says that the maintenance of this Constitution does not depend on the plighted faith of the States as States to support it. It relies on individual duty and obligation. That was his judgment; and logically it was followed by his other words, "The Government owes high and solemn duties to every citizen of the country. It is bound to protect him in his most important rights." Has he rights any more important than the rights of life, liberty, and property?

Sir, what would this Government be worth if it must rely upon States to execute its grants of power, its limitations of power upon States, and its express guarantees of rights to the people. Admitting that the States have concurrent power to enforce the Constitution of the United States within their respective limits, must we wait for their action? Are not laws preventive, as well as remedial and punitive? Is it not better to prevent a great transgression in advance, than to engage in the terrible work of imprisonment, and confiscation, and execution after the crime has been done? Our fathers in the beginning set us the example of legislating in advance. Yet gentlemen say, now that the Constitution is amended and new powers have been vested in Congress, we must wait until these combinations are made. Why, sir, if we pass this bill and these offenses are not attempted or actually committed anywhere, no man is hurt, no State is restrained in the exercise of any of the powers which rightfully belong to it. Why not in advance provide against the denial of rights by States, whether the denial be acts of omission or commission, as well as against the unlawful acts of combinations and conspiracies against the rights of the people?

The States never had the right, though they had the power, to inflict wrongs upon free citizens by a denial of the full protection of the laws; because all State officials are by the Constitution required to be bound by oath or affirmation to support the Constitution. As I have already said, the States did deny to citizens the equal protection of the laws, they did deny the rights of citizens under the Constitution, and except to the extent of the express limitations upon the States, as I have shown, the citizen had no remedy. They denied trial by jury, and he had no remedy. They took property without compensation, and he had no remedy. They restricted the freedom of the press, and he had no remedy. They restricted the freedom of speech, and he had no remedy. They restricted the rights of conscience, and he had no remedy. They bought and sold men who had no remedy. Who dare say, now that the Constitution has been amended, that the nation cannot by law provide against all such abuses and denials of right as these in States and by States, or combinations of persons?

I respectfully ask my friend from Illinois [Mr. Farnsworth] to review all that he has said on this subject. If I am not right in asserting that the negative limitations imposed by the Constitution on States can be enforced by law against individuals and States, then the Government was wrong from the administration of Washington down, and the Supreme Court of the United States was wrong every time this question has come before it.

Let gentlemen consider the last three amendments and the new limitations thereby imposed upon the power of the States, and the new powers thereby vested in Congress. The first of these (the thirteenth) provides that involuntary servitude, or slavery, shall not exist in the United States. That is negative. Then we have the further provision that Congress shall have power to enforce, by appropriate legislation, this amendment. That is affirmative. Do gentlemen undertake to say to-day that this does not impose a new limitation upon the power of the States, and grant a new power to Congress?

Does the gentleman from Indiana [Mr. Kerr] wish to be understood as affirming that there is no new grant of power here to Congress and no new limitation on the States? I rather think not. Let any State try the experiment of again enslaving men, and we will see, whether it is not competent for the Congress of the United States to make it a felony punishable by death to reduce any man, white or black, under color of State law, to a system of enforced human servitude or slavery; that system which converts a man, endowed with immortal life, into a thing of trade, an article of merchandise, with no acknowledged rights in the present and no hope of a heritage in the great hereafter. In such case the nation would inflict the penalty for this crime upon individuals, not upon States.

Will gentlemen undertake to tell the country that we cannot enforce by positive enactment that negative provision, the thirteenth article of amendment?

We have fully considered the fourteenth amendment. We have seen that it expressly grants the power to Congress to enforce its provisions, all its provisions, by appropriate legislation. Consider the fifteenth amendment, which declares, "No State shall deny to any citizen of the United States the right to vote on account of race, color, or previous condition of servitude." Here is a negative provision, a mere limitation, like the thirteenth and fourteenth amendments, on the power of the States, but coupled with a grant of power to Congress to enforce it. Did not a large majority of this House vote for the enforcement act of last May, which set aside the constitutions as well as the statutes of half the States of the Union because they denied rights guarantied to citizens by this negative provision, and which also declared combinations in States to deprive citizens of their rights, felony, punishable in the courts of the United States? I undertake to say, as to those sections of that law which enforce this provision and define and provide for the punishment of conspirators against the guarantied rights of the people, that there has never been found in America, anywhere, a court weak enough or wicked enough to question their validity, not one.

I am not speaking of all the details of that act. I am speaking of the provisions of it which declare that the right shall not be denied, nor challenged, nor violated by individuals or States. What difference is there between enforcing the negative provision of the fifteenth amendment and enforcing a negative provision of the thirteenth and fourteenth amendments? There is no difference, sir. No man can find any difference. There the three new amendments stand, imposing limitations, as I have said, upon the powers of the States which never were imposed on them before, and granting to the Congress of the United States express powers which never were in Congress before.

Mr. Speaker, I respectfully submit to the House and country that, by virtue of these amendments, it is competent for Congress to-day to provide by law that no man shall be held to answer in the tribunals of any State in this Union for any act made criminal by the laws of that State without a fair and impartial trial by jury. Congress never before has had the power to do it. It is also competent for Congress to provide that no citizen in any State shall be deprived of his property by State law or the judgment of a State court without just compensation therefor. Congress never before had the power so to declare. It is competent for the Congress of the United States to-day to declare that no State shall make or enforce any law which shall abridge the freedom of speech, the freedom of the press, or the right of the people peaceably to assemble together and petition for redress of grievances, for these are of the rights of citizens of the United States defined in the Constitution and guarantied by the fourteenth amendment, and to enforce which Congress is thereby expressly empowered. . . .

MR. FARNSWORTH. . . . Now, Mr. Speaker, I wish to call the attention of the House to the history of this fourteenth amendment of the Constitution of the United States. Let us see what was understood to be its meaning at the time of its adoption by Congress, for it is the first section of that amendment which is relied on by the advocates of this bill as its authority.

I will premise by calling the attention of the House to an amendment which was reported by the gentleman from Ohio [Mr. Bingham] who is to follow me, and who was then a member of the Committee on Reconstruction, February 26, 1866, which preceded the reporting of the fourteenth amendment. That amendment is in this language:

ARTICLE—. The Congress shall have power to make all laws which shall be necessary and proper to secure to the citizens of each State all privileges and immunities of citizens in the several States, and to all persons in the several States equal protection in the rights of life, liberty, and property.

Mark you, Mr. Speaker, that amendment was first reported by the Committee on Reconstruction, February, 1866. What was the fate of that amendment? The gentleman from Ohio [Mr. Bingham] says that it was incorporated in the fourteenth amendment. By no means. This, it will be observed, confers power directly upon Congress to legislate on this subject.

SAMUEL SHELLABARGER [R., OHIO]. So does the fifth section of the fourteenth amendment.

MR. FARNSWORTH. Let us see; we will come to that. This is what Mr. Bingham said about that amendment at the time—

MR. BINGHAM. What page?

MR. FARNSWORTH. Page 1034. This is what he said:

Every word of the proposed amendment is to-day in the Constitution of our country, save the words conferring the express grant of power upon the Congress of the United States.

The gentleman from Ohio is an able constitutional lawyer. He goes on:

The residue of the resolution, as the House will see by a reference to the Constitution, is the language of the second section of the fourth article, and of a portion of the fifth amendment adopted by the First Congress in 1789, and made part of the Constitution of the country. The language of the second section of the fourth article is:
The citizens of each State shall be entitled to all privileges and immunities of citizens in the several States.
The fifth article of the amendment provides that—
No person shall be deprived of life, liberty, or property without due process of law.
Sir, it has been the want of the Republic that there was not an express grant of power in the Constitution to enable the whole people of every State, by congressional enactment, to enforce obedience to these requirements of the Constitution.

What was the fate of that amendment? It was postponed a day or two and ordered to be printed. Then it came up for debate. But few speeches were made on it, and nearly all of them against it. The gentleman from Pennsylvania [Mr. Kelley] who addressed the House the other day favored it, taking the bull by the horns then, as now, in favor of the largest possible constitutional powers. He said:

In conclusion, Mr. Speaker, I repeat that I hold that all the power this amendment will give is already in the Constitution. I admit that it has lain dormant—

Whatever a "dormant" power is. Judge Hale, a very able lawyer from New York, said:

What is the effect of the amendment which the Committee on Reconstruction propose for the sanction of this House and the States of the Union? I submit that it is in effect a provision under which all State legislation, in its codes of civil and criminal jurisprudence and procedure, affecting the individual citizen, may be overriden, may be repealed or abolished, and the law of Congress established instead. I maintain that in this respect it is an utter departure from every principle ever dreamed of by the men who framed our Constitution.

MR. SHELLABARGER. He was a mild Republican.

MR. FARNSWORTH. Mr. Stewart, of Nevada, in the Senate, in reference to that amendment, incidentally—it was not acted on in the Senate at all—used this language:

There is another proposition of the committee of fifteen, which, if passed, will obviate the necessity of passing this, and obviate the necessity of any further constitutional amendment, and I think obviate the necessity of any more State Legislatures or conventions.

Judge Davis, a Republican member of this House from New York, said:

> Now, sir, the distinguishing feature in our Government is this: the Federal Government has its peculiar and restrictive duties. It is a Government of limited power and authority, extending over the whole country, providing for general and national interests; and in everything relating to the affairs which pertain to the Union that Government is supreme; but within that jurisdiction are erected many different States bound to allegiance to the Federal Government in all matters pertaining to the Union, yet in respect of social arrangement, in respect of the rights of property and control of persons, are entirely independent. And it is this feature which has given greater security and greater liberty to this country than was ever conferred before by any system of government which human wisdom has devised.

Senator Conkling, then a member of this House and a member of the Committee on Reconstruction, used this language:

> Mr. Speaker, I have not sought the floor for the purpose of discussing the merits of this amendment. It was introduced several weeks ago and considered in the committee of fifteen. At that time and always I felt constrained to withhold from it my support as one of the committee; and when the consent of the committee was given to its being reported I did not concur in the report. So much I deem it fair and right to say.

Mr. Hotchkiss, of New York, another member, and who was a member of the last Congress, says:

> I understand the amendment, as now proposed, by its terms to authorize Congress to establish uniform laws throughout the United States upon the subject named—the protection of life, liberty, and property. I am unwilling that Congress shall have any such power. Congress already has the power to establish a uniform rule of naturalization and uniform laws upon the subject of bankruptcy. That is as far as I am willing that Congress shall go. The object of a Constitution is not only to confer power upon the majority, but to restrict the power of the majority and to protect the rights of the minority. It is not indulging in imagination to any great stretch to suppose that we may have a Congress here who would establish such rules in my State as I should be unwilling to be governed by. Should the power of this Government, as the gentleman from Ohio fears, pass into the hands of the rebels, I do not want rebel laws to govern and be uniform throughout this Union.

The gentleman from Ohio [Mr. Bingham] who reported that bill made a speech in advocacy of it. In that speech he quoted this from James Madison:

> The powers reserved to the Federal States will extend to all the objects which, in the ordinary course of affairs, concern the lives, liberties, and properties of the people, and the internal order, improvement, and prosperity of the State.

He quoted this for the purpose of showing that there is no power in the Federal Constitution to legislate except where the express power is conferred upon Congress. He quoted from Madison to show that Congress had no power to legislate in the matter, and for that reason the committee reported that article of amendment. A motion was made by the gentleman from Wisconsin [Mr. Eldredge] to lay the resolution on the table, which was voted down—every Republican, I believe, voting against laying it on the table by a general understanding; Mr. Conkling, Mr. Hale, Mr. Davis, and Mr.

Hotchkiss with the rest. But then, by the concerted action of the Republicans, it was given its quietus by a postponement for two months, where it slept the sleep that knows no waking. It was postponed until the second Tuesday of April. The gentleman from Ohio [Mr. Bingham] knows what that meant.

MR. BINGHAM. I made the motion myself to postpone and make it an order for that day, but I did not choose to call it up.

MR. FARNSWORTH. No; the gentleman never called it up. And thus ended that attempt to give to Congress the power which is claimed for it by this bill.

MR. BINGHAM. Because I put it in another form; and I am prepared to demonstrate to the House and to the country that it is in a better form now than it was then.

MR. FARNSWORTH. Why was it put in another form? Did the gentleman put it in another form to deceive somebody?

MR. BINGHAM. No, sir; I shall show why it was put in another form.

MR. FARNSWORTH. It was abandoned and a different amendment substituted, different in form and substance, and so understood by Congress, as I will show. On the 30th of April, 1866, Mr. Stevens, of Pennsylvania, chairman of the Committee on Reconstruction, reported the fourteenth amendment, but not in the shape in which it passed finally.

JAMES GARFIELD [R., OHIO]. Everything was there except the "citizens" clause of the first section.

MR. FARNSWORTH. The amendment was adopted by the House as reported; the additional declaration of citizenship in the first section, and other changes, were made in the Senate. I shall show what Mr. Stevens said in reporting it. But, before coming to that, I may state that the amendment as he reported it contained five sections, the third of which provided that the rebels should be disfranchised until 1870. That was changed afterward in the Senate to its present shape. It was ordered to be printed, and was then postponed until May 8, when Mr. Stevens called it up. And this is what he said:

The first section prohibits the States from abridging the privileges and immunities of citizens of the United States, or unlawfully depriving them of life, liberty, or property, or of denying to any person within their jurisdiction the 'equal' protection of the laws.

I can hardly believe that any person can be found who will not admit that every one of these provisions is just. They are all asserted, in some form or other, in our declaration or organic law. But the Constitution limits only the action of Congress, and is not a limitation on the States. This amendment supplies that defect, and allows Congress to correct—

Mark the words—

allows Congress to correct the unjust legislation of a State, so far as the law which operates upon one man shall operate equally upon all.

To correct unjust, discriminating, partial legislation so that the law shall be equal. Was he a mild Republican, the gentleman from Pennsylvania, Mr. Stevens? I never supposed that he had it in a very mild form. "Whatever law punishes a white man for crime shall punish a black man precisely in the same way and to the same degree;" that is, the law shall do so. Whatever law protects the one shall protect the other, and the same redress shall be afforded by law to one as to the other.

MR. SHELLABARGER. There the gentleman gets at fault.

MR. FARNSWORTH. "Whatever law allows the white man to testify in court shall allow the man of color to do the same."

MR. SHELLABARGER. Read that just as Mr. Stevens said it.

MR. FARNSWORTH. I am reading it.

MR. SHELLABARGER. You put in two words.

MR. FARNSWORTH. I did, yes. The gentleman is very captious; he certainly stands upon slippery ground if he needs to be so technical.

MR. SHELLABARGER. Read just what Mr. Stevens said.

MR. FARNSWORTH. Does not every man in the House know that Mr. Stevens is talking about the law of the State, not the administration of the law? This is what he says: "That the law which allows a white man to testify shall allow a black man also."

MR. SHELLABARGER. Mr. Stevens said that every man should have equal means of protection, and if my friend says the administration of the law is not the means of protection—

MR. FARNSWORTH. This is what he says: "Whatever law protects the white man shall afford 'equal' protection to the black man. Whatever means of redress." What does he mean by "means of redress?"

MR. SHELLABARGER. Execution of the laws.

MR. FARNSWORTH. My friend is a very able lawyer; why is he so technical? Mr. Stevens in speaking of the means of redress afforded by the law, not by the justice of the peace, or the constable, or the jury. Not that all officers and juries shall have equal intelligence or all be of one color.

MR. SHELLABARGER. By the administration of the law also.

MR. FARNSWORTH. I quote further:

These are great advantages over their present codes. Now, different degrees of punishment are inflicted, not on account of the magnitude of the crime, but according to the color of the skin. Now color disqualified a man from testifying in courts, or being tried in the same way as white men. I need not enumerate these partial and oppressive laws.

Why, sir, we all know, and especially those of us who were members of Congress at that time, that the reason for the adoption of this amendment was because of the partial, discriminating, and unjust legislation of those States under governments set up by Andrew Johnson, by which they were punishing and oppressing one class of men under different laws from another class.

That is pretty much all Mr. Stevens said upon that section. He passes on and lays great stress upon the disfranchising clause of the amendment. He reported it so as to disfranchise everybody engaged in the rebellion until 1870; and then to allow everybody to vote and to hold office.

But other gentlemen discussed it; among others, Mr. Eliot, of Massachusetts. I will not stop to read what he says, but I will only refer to his remarks. It was to the same general tenor the unjust and discriminating legislation of those States; never claiming that this provision thus reported to the House gave any power to Congress to legislate except to correct this unjust legislation of the States.

I took a little part myself in that discussion; saying very little about that section, but complaining of the third section, which disfranchised everybody until 1870, as being unjust, impolitic, and difficult to execute. The gentleman from Massachusetts near me, [Mr. Dawes,] took the same ground substantially, only that he presented it more ably. I took ground that we did not go so far at that time as we ought to have gone; that we ought to adopt an amendment which should confer the franchise upon the black people of the United States, but which Congress had not then come quite up to the mark of doing. But I said I was willing to do what I could; that I would vote for what I could get, though it was not all that I wanted.

The House failed to vote down the previous question by a close vote; and the previous question being seconded and the main question ordered, the Republicans on this floor all voted for the amendment as it was reported, and it went to the Senate. However, before I refer to that I will quote again from the gentleman from Ohio, [Mr. Bingham,] upon this amendment as it was finally reported. He says, after quoting the amendment as reported:

The necessity for the first section of this amendment to the Constitution, Mr. Speaker, is one of the lessons that have been taught to your committee and taught to all the people of this country by the history of the past four years of terrific conflict, that history in which God is, and in which He teaches the profoundest lessons to men and nations. There was a want hitherto, and there remains a want now, in the Constitution of our country, which the proposed amendment will supply.

What is that? It is the power in the people, the whole people of the United States, by express authority, to do that by congressional enactment which hitherto they have not ad the power to do and have never even attempted to do; that is, to protect by national law the privileges and immunities of all citizens of the Republic and the inborn rights of every person within its jurisdiction whenever the same shall be abridged or denied by the unconstitutional acts of any State.

MR. SHELLABARGER. That is what the third section says.

MR. FARNSWORTH. The third section makes no reference to the unconstitutional acts of a State. It refers to the unlawful acts of a combination of two or more persons.

MR. SHELLABARGER. No; it assumes that the State has denied protection to some of its citizens.

MR. FARNSWORTH. No; it assumes that an unlawful act of some of its citizens is the act of the State. It will be seen that the language of the gentleman from Ohio, [Mr. Bingham,] in speaking upon this amendment as finally adopted, is very different from what it was upon the amendment which he first reported, and which was sent to the "tomb of the Capulets." He claims that the amendment supplies a want which has been felt—the correction of unjust and unconstitutional legislation of the States.

Mr. Speaker, I have somewhat carefully looked through the debate on this question by the Democratic members at that time, and I do not find that any of them claimed, or made it an argument against the amendment, that it conferred any such power upon Congress as is now claimed by the authors of this bill.

MR. GARFIELD. If the gentleman will allow me to interrupt him for a moment, I wish to say that I have read over these debates carefully, and it will be found that there were two Democrats, Mr. Shankland, of Kentucky, and Mr. Rogers, of New Jersey, who said, in a broad and sweeping way, that this amendment also broke down the barriers of State law and State authority. I believe, however, they are the only two who took any such ground; and they did not make their charge specific; they only made the statement in a broad, general, and rather "stump speech" way.

MR. FARNSWORTH. Now, let us see what was done in the Senate. The first section was amended by prefacing it with the declaration of citizenship; but little was said in the debate concerning that section. The gentleman from Vermont, [Mr. Poland,] who was then in the Senate, made some remarks upon it, which I will quote. He said:

> The clause of the first proposed amendment, that no State shall make or enforce any law that shall abridge the privileges or immunities of citizens of the United States, secures nothing beyond what was intended by the original provision in the Constitution, that the citizens of each State shall be entitled to all the privileges and immunities of citizens in the several States.

The gentleman from Vermont did not dream that the provision went any further than that. Mr. Reverdy Johnson, of Maryland, a Democrat, in discussing this amendment, said:

> I am decidedly in favor of the first part of the section, which defines what citizenship shall be, and in favor of that part of the section which denies to a State the right to deprive any person of life, liberty, or property without due process of law.

Mr. Reverdy Johnson, whatever else may be said of him, is undoubtedly one of the ablest constitutional lawyers in this country; and can any one suppose that he understood this amendment as conferring upon Congress the power to legislate? By no means. He moved to amend by striking out the other clause; and on that point he said:

But I think it is quite objectionable to provide that no State shall make or enforce any law which shall abridge the privileges and immunities of citizens of the United States, simply because I do not understand what would be the effect of that.

But as to the remainder of the section he declared himself in favor of it. The amendment was discussed by Senators Hendricks, Doolittle, Davis of Kentucky, and other able Democratic lawyers in the Senate, none of whom claimed that it conferred upon Congress any power to legislate in the manner now proposed.

Mr. Speaker, I cannot pursue this branch of the discussion further, for my time does not permit. But in the light of this discussion, in view of the history of this amendment, which I have thus rapidly sketched, can there be any doubt as to what was understood to be the interpretation of this amendment at the time it was adopted? The gentleman from Ohio has referred to the civil rights bill and said that I have supported it. I have no doubt of it.

MR. SHELLABARGER. The section is in the revenue laws, an independent section punishing all conspiracies for violation of the laws of the United States.

MR. FARNSWORTH. I do not doubt the power of Congress to provide for the enforcement of its own constitutional laws; but that I had given votes and done things during my twelve years' service in the House of Representatives which I cannot defend, I have no doubt; otherwise I would be more than human. I know we have done things during the war and during the process of reconstruction to save the Republic which could not be defended if done in peace. We were obliged to do some things because of the bad influence of Andrew Johnson's administration which will scarcely bear the test of the calm light of peace and constitutional law. We passed laws, Mr. Speaker, and the country knows it, which we did not like to let go to the Supreme Court for adjudication. And I am telling no tales out of school. Since the adoption of this amendment, because of scruples in regard to the constitutionality of the civil rights bill we have reenacted it.

Sir, we have done some things under the necessity of the case, and under the war powers, and I am ready to do them again to save the nation's life, which may be a little beyond the verge of the constitutional power possessed by Congress in time of peace. But, sir, this is not the time to overstep those bounds. . . . It is said that this bill applies only to the protection of the rights of the citizens of the United States as such. But the Constitution makes every man a citizen who was either born or naturalized in the United States; and they are all likewise citizens of the States where they reside. There is no distinction. Every citizen is a citizen of the United States and of some State; and every citizen of a State is "subject to the jurisdiction of the United States." It is claimed that the concluding clause of the fourteenth amendment, which says that "Congress shall have power to enforce the provisions of the amendment by appropriate legislation," gives authority for this bill. I deny it, sir.

The first section of the amendment requires no legislation; "it is a law unto itself;" and the courts can execute it. If it requires "enforcing" legislation, what kind does it require? Certainly not a law which goes a long way beyond the scope of the provision. The Constitution cannot be extended by the law. It is very clear to my mind that the only "legislation" we can do is to "enforce" the provisions of the Constitution upon the laws of the State. There are other provisions in that amendment which require legislation by Congress. Apportioning Representatives and relieving from disabilities by Congress are required by the amendment.

Thus then the question presents itself, as has been said before, the question whether we shall obliterate State lines and abolish State constitutions and State Legislatures, and centralize all the power of these States of ours in one grand despotic, central Government at Washington, or, will we preserve the State governments, wherein resides, as I think, the chief protection of the rights of the citizen as well as the source of the powers of the General Government.

MR. GARFIELD. . . . I presume it will not be denied, that before the adoption of the last three amendments it was the settled interpretation of the Constitution that the protection of the life and property of private citizens within the States belonged to the State governments exclusively. . . .

Now, three amendments, the thirteenth, fourteenth, and fifteenth, have been added to the Constitution, and it will not be denied that each of these amendments has so modified the Constitution as to change the relation of Congress to the citizens of the States. They have to some extent enlarged the functions of Congress, and, within prescribed limits, have extended its jurisdiction within the States.

I now inquire how far this jurisdiction has been extended. The thirteenth amendment provides that slavery shall never exist within the United States, or any place subject to their jurisdiction, and Congress is empowered to enforce this provision on every inch of soil covered by our flag. Congress may by its legislation prevent any person from being made a slave by any law, usage, or custom, or by any act direct or indirect. This, I presume, will not be denied; and Congress has effectually carried out this provision.

In the fifteenth amendment, the last of the three, the rights of citizens of the United States to vote shall not be denied or abridged, either by the United States or by any State, in consequence of race, color, or previous condition of servitude. And that, taken in connection with the clause in the main text of the Constitution, which authorizes Congress to regulate the time, place, and manner of holding elections, arms Congress with the full power to protect the ballot-box at all elections, at least of officers of the United States, and to protect the right of all men within the limit of that clause to the suffrage. On this point, I presume, there will be no difference of opinion, at least on this side of the House. In pursuance of this power we passed the act of May 31, 1870, and the amendatory act of February 28, 1871.

I now come to consider last in order, for it is the basis of the pending bill, the fourteenth amendment. I ask the attention of the House to the first section of that amendment, as to its scope and meaning. I hope gentlemen will bear in mind that this debate, in which so many have taken part, will become historical, as the earliest legislative construction given to this clause of the amendment. Not only the words which we put into the law, but what shall be said here in the way of defining and interpreting the meaning of the clause, may go far to settle its interpretation and its value to the country hereafter.

No thorough discussion of this clause is possible which does not include a history of some of the leading facts connected with its origin and its adoption by Congress. I will therefore state briefly the proceedings of this House on the first form of amendment proposed on the subject embraced in the first section of the fourteenth amendment, as it now stands in the Constitution.

On the 13th February, 1866, Mr. Bingham reported, from the joint Committee on Reconstruction, a joint resolution proposing the following amendment to the Constitution of the United States:

ARTICLE: The Congress shall have power to make all laws which shall be necessary and proper to secure to the citizens of each State all the privileges and immunities of citizens in the several States; and to all persons in the several States .equal protection in the rights of life, liberty, and property.

The debate proceeded at great length, and the necessity for increased protection to those who had lately been slaves, against the hostile legislation of the States, was strongly urged. I will quote a few paragraphs from the debate, to show some of the leading reasons that were urged for and against the proposition.

Mr. Higby, of California, insisted that this amendment was necessary in order to protect the lives and property of the citizens in the South. He showed how, under the thirteenth amendment, the laws of the States might be so administered as to put black men into slavery under pretense of sentencing them for crime, and that without additional power given to Congress the General Government could not prevent such a result. [*Globe,* February 27, 1056]

Others urged the amendment on the same and similar grounds.

Mr. Hale, of New York, opposed the amendment. He said that under it—

All State legislation, in its codes of civil and criminal jurisprudence and procedure, affecting the individual citizen, may be overriden, may be repealed, and abolished, and the law of Congress established instead. I maintain that in this respect it is an utter departure from every principle ever dreamed of by the men who framed our Constitution.—*Globe,* page 1963.

On the 28th of February my colleague [Mr. Bingham] made a very able and elaborate speech in defense of the amendment. He based its necessity on the fact that Congress had then no power to legislate for life, liberty, and property within the States. He affirmed, also, that the guarantees of the rights of property and person named in the fifth article of amendments to the Constitution were not limitations on the State governments, but only on Congress. To support this position he quoted the case of *Barron* v. *The Mayor and City Council of Baltimore*, (7 Peters, page 247;) also, *Lessee of Livingston* v. *Moore*, (7 Peters, page 251;) also, 3 Webster, page 471; and then said:

The question is simply whether you will give by this amendment, to the people of the United States, the power, by legislative enactment, to punish officials of States for violation of the oaths enjoined upon them by their Constitution. [*Globe* 1090]

In the course of Mr. Bingham's speech, Judge Hale, of New York, asked him—

Whether, in his opinion, this proposed amendment to the Constitution does not confer upon Congress a general power of legislation for the purpose of securing to all persons in the several States protection of life, liberty, and property, subject only to the qualification that that protection shall be equal.

Mr. BINGHAM. I believe it does in regard to life, liberty, and property, as I have heretofore stated it, the right to real estate being dependent on the State law, except when granted by the United States.

Mr. HALE. I desire to know if he means to imply that it extends to personal estate.

Mr. BINGHAM. Undoubtedly it is true.

Mr. Conkling, now a Senator from the State of New York, during the same debate said of this amendment:

It was introduced several weeks ago, and considered in a committee of fifteen. At that time and always I felt constrained to withhold from it my support as one of the committee, and when the consent of the committee was given to its being reported I did not concur in the report. [*Globe* 1094]

Mr. Hotchkiss, of New York, said:

I understand the amendment, as now proposed by its terms, to authorize Congress to establish uniform laws throughout the United States upon the subject named, the protection of life, liberty, and property. I am unwilling that Congress shall have any such power.

I have been thus particular in reviewing the history of this debate, in order to show the sentiment that then prevailed in this House in regard to one of the theories which we are asked to adopt in this debate.

Now, let it be remembered that the proposed amendment was a plain, unambiguous proposition to empower Congress to legislate directly upon the citizens of all the States in regard to their rights of life, liberty, and property. Mark the action of the House. After a debate of two weeks, the record of which covers more than one hundred and fifty columns of the Globe, and in which the proposed amendment was subjected to a most searching examination, it became evident that many leading Republicans of this House would not consent to so radical a change in the Constitution, and the bill was recommitted to the joint select committee.

MR. BINGHAM. The gentleman is mistaken. A motion was made to lay that amendment on the table. There were 41 votes in favor of the motion and 110 against it. I voted myself in favor of a postponement; but the measure was not recommitted, for I was a member of the committee and knew what it could do.

MR. GARFIELD. My colleague is technically right in saying that the measure was postponed. Of course the majority did not allow it to be laid on the table on motion of a member of the opposite party, and the motion was voted down, as my colleague has said. But the consideration of the measure was postponed on motion of Mr. Conkling, who had opposed it from the start, and it did in fact go back to the committee, and was never again discussed in this House. What is more, it was never debated at all in the Senate, though it was introduced into that body by Mr. Fessenden the same day that Mr. Bingham introduced it into the House. The whole history of the case shows that it became perfectly evident, both to the members of the Senate and of the House, after the House debate, that the measure could not command a two thirds vote of Congress, and for that reason the proposition was virtually withdrawn. Its consideration was postponed February 28 by a vote of 110 to 37.

More than a month passed after this postponement, or recommittal, without further action in either House. On the 30th April, 1866, the fourteenth amendment was introduced into the House, and the first section was precisely as it now stands in the Constitution, except that the first sentence of the present text was not in the draft. The new form of amendment was also debated at great length. The gentleman who reported it from the committee, the late Mr. Stevens, of Pennsylvania, said that it came far short of what he wished, but after full consideration, he believed it the most that could be obtained.

MR. BINGHAM. My colleague will allow me to correct him again. The remark of Mr. Stevens had no relation whatever to that provision, none at all. That is all I have to say on that point now.

MR. GARFIELD. My colleague can make but he cannot unmake history. I not only heard the whole debate at the time, but I have lately read over, with scrupulous care, every word of it as recorded in the Globe. I will show my colleague that Mr. Stevens did speak specially of this very section.

The debate on this new proposition, which afterward became the fourteenth amendment, was opened by Mr. Stevens, May 8th, in a characteristic and powerful speech. He spoke of the difficulties which the joint committee on reconstruction had encountered, and of the long struggle they had had to reach any proposition on which the friends of the amendment could unite. He said:

> The proposition is not all that the committee desired. It falls far short of my wishes, but it fulfills my hopes. I believe it is all that can be obtained in the present state of public opinion.
>
> The first section prohibits the States from abridging the privileges and immunities of

citizens of the United States, or unlawfully depriving them of lefe, liberty, and property, or of denying to any person within their jurisdiction the "equal" protection of the laws.

I can hardly believe that any person can be found who will not admit that every one of these provisions is just. They are all asserted, in some form or other, in our Declaration or organic law. But the Constitution limits only the action of Congress, and is not a limitation on the States. This amendment supplies that defect and allows Congress to correct the unjust legislation of the States, so far that the law which operates upon one man shall operate equally upon all. Whatever law punishes a white man for a crime shall punish the black man precisely in the same way and to the same degree. Whatever law protects the white man shall afford "equal" protection to the black man. Whatever means of redress is afforded to one shall be afforded to all. Whatever law allows the white man to testify in court shall allow the man of color to do the same. These are great advantages over their present codes. Now different degrees of punishment are inflicted, not on account of the magnitude of the crime, but according to the color of the skin. Now color disqualifies a man from testifying in the courts or being tried in the same way as white men. I need not enumerate these partial and oppressive laws. Unless the Constitution should restrain them, those States will all, I fear, keep up this discrimination and crush to death the hated freedmen. [*Globe* 2459]

In the long debate which followed this section of the amendment was considered as equivalent to the first section of the civil rights bill, except that a new power was added in the clause which prohibited any State from depriving any person within its jurisdiction of the equal protection of the laws. The interpretation of this first section, as given by Mr. Stevens, was the one followed by almost every Republican who spoke on the measure. It was throughout the debate, with scarcely an exception, spoken of as a limitation of the power of the States to legislate unequally for the protection of life and property. On the 9th of May Mr. Eliot, of Massachusetts, said:

I support the first section because the doctrine it declares is right, and if under the Constitution as it now stands Congress has not the power to prohibit State legislation discriminating against any classes of citizens or depriving any persons of life, liberty, and property without due process of law, or denying to any persons within the State the equal protection of the laws, then, in my judgment, such power should be distinctly conferred. [*Globe* 2511]

Mr. Farnsworth approved the amendment but said that the first section might as well be reduced to these words: "No State shall deny to any person within its jurisdiction the equal protection of the laws," for that was the only provision in it which was not already in the Constitution. [*Globe* 2539].

It is noticeable also that no member of the Republican party made any objection to this section on the grounds on which so many had opposed the former resolution of amendment; but many expressed their regret that the article was not sufficiently strong.

Mr. Shankling, of Kentucky, a Democrat, said:

The first section of this proposed amendment to the Constitution is to strike down the reserved rights of the States and invest all the power in the Federal Government. [*Globe* 2500]

Mr. Rogers, of New Jersey, a Democrat, took similar ground. [*Globe* 2538]

These are the only declarations I find in the House debates, either by Democrats or Republicans, indicating that this clause was regarded as placing the protection of the fundamental rights of life and property directly in the control of Congress; and these declarations of Shankling and Rogers were general and sweeping charges, not sustained even by specific statement.

I close this citation of speeches on the amendment by quoting the view taken of the scope and meaning of this first section by my colleague, [Mr. Bingham.] He said:

> This section gives power to protect by national law the privileges and immunities of all the citizens of the Republic and the inborn rights of every person within its jurisdiction whenever the same shall be abridged or denied by unconstitutional acts of any State.
>
> Allow me, Mr. Speaker, in passing, to say that this amendment takes from no State any right that ever pertained to it. No State ever had the right, under the forms of law or otherwise, to deny to any freeman the equal protection of the laws, or to abridge the privilges or immunities of any citizen of the Republic, although many of them have assumed and exercised the power, and that without remedy. [*Globe* 2542]

After a debate on this new proposition which lasted several days and evenings, the amendment passed the House May 10, 1866, by a vote of 128 ayes to 37 noes, not one Republican voting against it. It will not be denied, as a matter of history, that this form of amendment received many Republican votes that the first form to which I have referred could not have received. In the Senate there was but little debate on the first section and no change was made in it, except that, on the motion of Mr. Howard, of Michigan, these words were added at the beginning of the section:

> All persons born or naturalized in the United States and subject to the jurisdiction thereof are citizens of the United States and of the States wherein they reside.

Other changes were made by the Senate in other sections of the amendment, and the whole, as amended, passed June 8, by a vote of 33 to 11.

On the 13th of June the House passed the article, with the Senate amendments, by a vote of 120 to 32, every Republican present voting for it.

With this review of the history of the clause rejected and that adopted in our minds, I ask gentlemen to consider the difference between the two. Putting the fifth clause of the amendment first, and, to make the comparison closer, omitting the definition of citizenship, the section as adopted reads thus:

> The Congress shall have power to enforce, by appropriate legislation, the following provisions—

To wit:

> No State shall make or enforce any law which shall abridge the privileges or immunities

of citizens of the United States; nor shall any State deprive any person of life, liberty, or property without due process of law, nor deny to any person within its jurisdiction the equal protection of the laws.

And this is the rejected clause:

The Congress shall have power to make all laws which shall be necessary and proper to secure to the citizens of each State all the privileges and immunities of citizens in the several States, and to all persons in the several States equal protection in the rights of life, liberty, and property.

The one exerts its force directly upon the States, laying restrictions and limitations upon their power and enabling Congress to enforce these limitations. The other, the rejected proposition, would have brought the power of Congress to bear directly upon the citizens, and contained a clear grant of power to Congress to legislate directly for the protection of life, liberty, and property within the States. The first limited but did not oust the jurisdiction of the State over these subjects. The second gave Congress plenary power to cover the whole subject with its jurisdiction, and, as it seems to me, to the exclusion of the State authorities.

Mr. Speaker, unless we ignore both the history and the language of these clauses we cannot, by any reasonable interpretation, give to the section, as it stands in the Constitution, the force and effect of the rejected clause.

Mr. Speaker, I now inquire to what extent this section does enlarge the powers of Congress. On the proper answer to this inquiry will chiefly rest our power of legislation on the subject before us. The first sentence of the section defines citizenship.

It declares that—

All persons born and naturalized in the United States and subject to the jurisdiction thereof are citizens of the United States and of the State wherein they reside.

On this threshold of the section, we find a conflict of opinion. In his very able speech, my colleague [Mr. Shellabarger] has given us his interpretation of this first sentence. He says:

The United States added to its Constitution what was not in it before; because never before was it found in the Constitution in express words that all people in this country were citizens of the United States as well as of the States. This was added, and added for a purpose.

He also says:

The making of them United States and authorizing Congress by appropriate law to protect that citizenship gave Congress power to legislate directly for enforcement of such rights as are fundamental elements of citizenship.

This, sir, is the foundation idea on which this section and the whole bill rest for their constitutional warrant. If right, it solves every possible doubt and difficulty in every part of this great inquiry.

Now, Mr. Speaker, I desire to call the attention to this statement, that in putting into the Constitution a definition of citizenship there was given to Congress a great power which did not before exist in the Constitution. Can my colleague by any possibility forget that provision of the Constitution which declares that "no person shall be a Representative who shall not have been seven years"—what? "A citizen of the United States." Can he forget that other clause which declares that "no person shall be a Senator of the United States who shall not have been nine years a citizen of the United States?" Can he forget that in article two, section one, it is declared that "no person except a natural-born citizen, or a citizen of the United States at the adoption of the Constitution, shall be eligible to the office of President?" Were there no citizens of the United States until the fourteenth amendment passed? Was my colleague any less a citizen of the United States when he sat in the Thirty-Ninth Congress than he is to-day? Sir, the citizens of the United States made this Constitution. It was not the Constitution that made us citizens. The people who ordained and established the Constitution were citizens when they made that instrument.

I know my colleague limits his statement by saying that the Constitution did not before say, "in express words, that all the people in this country were citizens of the United States;" but I ask him and all who hear me to say whether this was not as true before the adoption of the Fourteenth Amendment as it is to-day. The only doubt I ever heard expressed on this point was whether slaves became citizens of the United States by the act of emancipation. If they did, the proposition was wholly true, before as well as after the adoption of the amendment.

I hold in my hand Paschal's annotated edition of the Constitution, four pages and a half of which are filled with references to decisions of the courts, from the beginning of the century until now, declaring in the plainest terms that all free persons, born or naturalized in the United States, are citizens thereof. A weak attempt was made in the Dred Scott case to exclude free colored persons from the rights of citizenship, but that feature of the opinion was in opposition to the main body of previous precedents and to all subsequent decisions. I will quote but one or two of the many declarations of our constitutional teachers. Chancellor Kent says:

> Citizens, under our Constitution and laws, mean free inhabitants born within the United States or naturalized under the laws of Congress.
>
> If a slave born in the United States be manumitted or otherwise lawfully discharged from bondage, or if a black man born in the United States becomes free he becomes thenceforward a citizen, but under such disabilities as the laws of the several States may deem it expedient to prescribe to persons of color. [*Ibid* 1; Kent's *Commentaries* 292 note]

In the admirable opinion of Attorney General Bates, delivered to President Lincoln, November 29, 1862, this whole subject is thoroughly discussed. He says:

The Constitution does not make the citizen; it is, in fact, made by them. Every person born in the country is, at the moment of birth, *prime facie,* a citizen.

We have recognized this principle of citizenship in all our naturalization laws. We transform the subjects of foreign Governments into citizens of the United States whenever they comply with the terms of our naturalization laws. The civil rights bill broadly and fully affirms the doctrine I am here contending for.

I remember the able speech of my colleague [Mr. Shellabarger] in favor of the civil rights bill, in the spring of 1866, before this fourteenth amendment had been adopted. The first sentence of that law is in these words:

*Be it enacted,*etc., That all persons born in the United States, and not subject to any foreign Power, excluding Indians not taxed, are hereby declared to be citizens.

My colleague and I then believed, as I now believe, that we were fully empowered to make this declaration of citizenship, and so the Republicans in this House and in the Senate believed.

I do not by any means underrate the value and importance of the first sentence of the amendment. It set at rest forever a vexed and troublesome question. It brushed away all the legal subtleties and absurdities that were based on the supposed difference between citizenship of the United States and citizenship of the States; and by declaring that every person born on the soil and subject to the jurisdiction of the United States is a citizen both of the nation and of the State wherein he resides. It lifted into undoubted citizenship those who had been slaves, and thus resolved all doubts as to their civil condition. It is clear to my mind that this had already been done by the provisions of the civil rights bill.

It was held by Mr. Justice Swayne, in his learned opinion on the case of Rhodes *vs.* The United States, that the civil rights bill naturalized all negroes born in this country who had been slaves, made them citizens, and gave them all the rights, privileges, and immunities to which white men were entitled under the laws. The rights of the white citizens were made the standard to which all others were lifted. But neither the civil rights bill nor the first sentence of the fourteenth amendment added to the rights already guarantied to the white citizen by the Constitution.

If the view I have taken of citizenship be correct, it follows that my colleague is in error when he attempts to find in the first sentence of this first section, the power to protect by congressional enactment, all the fundamental rights of persons and property within the States—a power which had theretofore, without question, belonged exclusively to the State governments. If my colleague's reasoning on this point be valid, I do not see how he can stop short of ousting completely the jurisdiction of the States over these subjects. He makes the clause go to the full extent of the one which was rejected.

I shall not be able in the hour assigned me to discuss with thoroughness all the paragraphs of this section, but I will notice them briefly.

The next clause is this:

No State shall make or enforce any law which shall abridge the privileges and immunities of the citizens of the United States.

The substance of this provision is in the main text of the Constitution, and has again and again been interpreted by the courts.

MR. BINGHAM. The gentleman will please excuse me if I interrupt him.

MR. GARFIELD. My time is more than half expired, and I hope my colleague will not unnecessarily consume it.

MR. BINGHAM. The first, in the first section of the fourteenth article of amendment, to wit, "no State shall make or enforce any law which shall abridge the privileges or immunities of citizens of the United States," never were in the original text of the Constitution. The original text of the Constitution reads that the citizens of each State shall be entitled to the privileges and immunities of citizens of the several States; which were always interpreted, even by Judge Story, from whom the gentleman cited in the outset, to mean only privileges and immunities of citizens of the States, not of the United States.

MR. GARFIELD. I have made no statement which requires this criticism of my colleague. It is true that the main text of the Constitution which he quotes speaks of State citizenship; but as all persons free born or naturalized were citizens of the United States, it brings us to the same result as though national citizenship had been expressed in the section quoted. Indeed, the Supreme Court declared, forty years ago, that "a citizen of the United States residing in any State of the Union is a citizen of that State." [*Gassies* v. *Ballon,* 6 Peters 761]

My colleague, [Mr. Shellabarger,] and also the gentleman from Massachusetts, [Mr. Hoar,] have given a breadth of interpretation to the force of these words "privileges" and "immunities" which, in my judgment, are not warranted, and which go far beyond the intent and meaning of those who framed and those who amended the Constitution. The gentleman from Massachusetts said in his speech:

Congress is empowered by the Fourteenth Amendment to pass all appropriate legislation to secure the privileges and immunities of the citizen. Now, what is comprehended in this term privileges and immunities? Most clearly it comprehends all the privileges and immunities declared to belong to the citizen by the Constitution itself. Most clearly, also, it seems to me, it comprehends those privileges and immunities which all republican writers of authority agree in declaring fundamental and essential to citizenship.

He then quotes from Judge Washington's opinion in the case of *Corfield* v. *Coryell* a statement that the fundamental rights of citizenship "are protection by the Government, the enjoyment of life and liberty, with the right to acquire and possess property of every kind, and to pursue and obtain happiness and safety."

Now, sir, if this is to be the construction of the clause, the conclusion is irresistible that Congress may assert and maintain original jurisdiction over all questions affecting the rights of the person and property of all private citizens within a State, and the State government may legislate upon this subject only by sufferance of Congress. It must be remembered that Judge Washington was interpreting the second section of the fourth article of the Constitution, and that neither he in 1820, nor any other judge before or since, has authorized so broad a construction of the power of Congress as that proposed by the gentlemen to whom I refer.

The next clause of the section under debate declares:

Nor shall any State deprive any person of life, liberty, or peroperty, without due process of law.

This is copied from the fifth article of amendments, with this difference: as it stood in the fifth article it operated only as a restraint upon Congress, while here it is a direct restraint upon the governments of the States. The addition is very valuable. It realizes the full force and effect of the clause in Magna Charta, from which it was borrowed; and there is now no power in either the State or the national Government to deprive any person of those great fundamental rights on which all true freedom rests, the rights of life, liberty, and property, except by due process of law; that is, by an impartial trial according to the laws of the land. This very provision is in the constitution of every State in the Union; but it was most wise and prudent to place it in the serene firmament of the national Constitution, high above all the storms and tempests that may rage in any State.

Mr. Speaker, I come now to consider the last clause of this first section, which is, as I believe, the chief and most valuable addition made to the Constitution in the section. That clause declares that no State shall "deny to any person within its jurisdiction the equal protection of the laws." This thought was never before in the Constitution, either in form or in substance. It was neither expressed in any words in the instrument, nor could it be implied from any provision. It is a broad and comprehensive limitation on the power of the State governments, and, without doubt, Congress is empowered to enforce this limitation by any appropriate legislation. Taken in connection with the other clauses of this section, it restrains the States from making or enforcing laws which are not on their face and in their provisions of equal application to all the citizens of the State. It is not required that the laws of a State shall be perfect. They may be unwise, injudicious, even unjust; but they must be equal in their provisions, like the air of heaven, covering all and resting upon all with equal weight. The laws must not only be equal on their face, but they must be so administered that equal protection under them shall not be denied to any class of citizens, either by the courts or the executive officers of the State.

It may be pushing the meaning of the words beyond their natural limits, but I think the provision that the States shall not "deny the equal protection of the laws" implies that they shall afford equal protection.

Now, Mr. Speaker, to review briefly the ground traveled over: the changes wrought in the Constitution by the last three amendments in regard to the individual rights of citizens are these: that no person within the United States shall be made a slave; that no citizen shall be denied the right of suffrage because of his color or because he was once a slave; that no State, by its legislation or the enforcement thereof, shall abridge the privileges or immunities of citizens of the United States; that no State shall, without due process of law, disturb the life, liberty, or property of any person within its jurisdiction; and finally, that no State shall deny to any person within its jurisdiction the equal protection of the laws.

Thanks to the wisdom and patriotism of the American people, these great and beneficent provisions are now imperishable elements of the Constitution, and will, I trust, remain forever among the irreversible guarantees of liberty.

How can these new guarantees be enforced? In the first place, it is within the power of Congress to provide, by law, that cases arising under the provisions of these amendments may be carried up on appeal from the State tribunals to the courts of the United States, where every law, ordinance usage, or decree of any State in conflict with these provisions may be declared unconstitutional and void. This great remedy covers nearly all the ground that needs to be covered in time of peace; and this ground has already been covered, to a great extent, by the legislation of Congress.

The civil rights act of 1866, as reenacted by the law of May 21, 1870, opens the courts of the United States to all who were lately slaves, and to all classes of persons who by any State law or custom are denied the equal rights and privileges of white men. By the stringent and sweeping act of May 21, 1870, known as the enforcement act, and by the supplementary act of February 28, 1871, Congress has provided the amplest protection of the ballot-box and of the right of voters to enjoy the suffrage as guarantied to them in the main text of the Constitution and in the fifteenth amendment.

In the second place, it is undoubtedly within the power of Congress to provide by law for the punishment of all persons, official or private, who shall invade these rights, and who by violence, threats, or intimidation shall deprive any citizen of their fullest enjoyment. This is a part of that general power vested in Congress to punish the violators of its laws.

Under this head I had supposed that the enforcement act of May 21, 1870, made ample provision. I quote the sixth section:

SEC. 6. *And be it further enacted,* That if two or more persons shall band or conspire together, or go in disguise upon the public highway, or upon the premises of another, with intent to violate any provision of this act, or to injure, oppress, threaten, or intimidate any citizen with intent to prevent or hinder his free exercise and enjoyment of any right or privilege granted or secured to him by the Constitution or laws of the United States, or because of his having exercised the same, such persons shall be held guilty of felony, and, on conviction thereof, shall be fined or imprisoned, or both, at the discretion of the court—the fine not to exceed $5,000, and the imprisonment not to exceed ten years—and shall, moreover, be thereafter ineligible to and disabled from holding any office or place of honor, profit, or trust created by the Constitution or laws of the United States.

The sixteenth and seventeenth sections add still further safeguards for the protection of the people.

For the protection of all officers of the United States in the discharge of their duties, and for the enforcement of all the laws of the United States, our statutes make ample provisions. The President is empowered to use all the land and naval forces if necessary to execute these laws against all offenders.

But, sir, the President has informed us in his recent message, that in some portions of the Republic wrongs and outrages are now being perpetrated, under circumstances which lead him to doubt his power to suppress them by means of existing laws. That new situation confronts us. I deeply regret that we were not able to explore the length, breadth, and depth of this new danger before we undertook to provide a legislative remedy. The subject is so obscured by passion that it is hardly possible for Congress, with the materials now in our possession, to know the truth of the case, to understand fully the causes of this new trouble, and to provide wisely and intelligently the safest and most certain remedy.

But enough is known to demand some action on our part. To state the case in the most moderate terms, it appears that in some of the southern States there exists a wide-spread secret organization, whose members are bound together by solemn oaths to prevent certain classes of citizens of the United States from enjoying these new rights conferred upon them by the Constitution and laws; that they are putting into execution their design of preventing such citizens from enjoying the free right of the ballot-box and other privileges and immunities of citizens, and from enjoying the equal protection of the laws. Mr. Speaker, I have no doubt of the power of Congress to provide for meeting this new danger, and to do so without trenching upon those great and beneficent powers of local self-government lodged in the States and with the people. To reach this result is the demand of the hour upon the statesmanship of this country. This brings me to the consideration of the pending bill.

The first section provides, in substance, that any person who, under color of any State law, ordinance, or custom, shall deprive any person of any rights, privileges, or immunities secured by the Constitution, the offender shall be liable to an action at law, or other proper proceeding, for redress in the several district or circuit courts of the United States. This is a wise and salutary provision, and plainly within the power of Congress.

But the chief complaint is not that the laws of the State are unequal, but that even where the laws are just and equal on their face, yet, by a systematic maladministration of them, or a neglect or refusal to enforce their provisions, a portion of the people are denied equal protection under them. Whenever such a state of facts is clearly made out, I believe the last clause of the first section empowers Congress to step in and provide for doing justice to those persons who are thus denied equal protection.

Now if the second section of the pending bill can be so amended that it shall clearly define this offense, as I have described it, and shall employ no terms which assert the power of Congress to take jurisdiction of the subject until such denial be clearly made, and shall not in any way assume the original jurisdiction of the rights of private persons and of property within the States—with these conditions clearly expressed in the section, I shall give it my hearty support. These limitations will not impair the efficiency of the section, but will remove the serious objections that are entertained by many gentlemen to the section as it now stands.

I have made these criticisms, not merely for the purpose of securing such an amendment to the section, but because I am unwilling that the interpretation which some gentlemen have given of the constitutional powers of Congress shall stand as the uncontradicted history of this legislation. Amendments have been prepared which will remove the difficulties to which I have alluded; and I trust that my colleague [Mr. Shellabarger] and his committee will themselves accept and offer these amendments. I am sure my colleague will understand that I share all his anxiety for the passage of a proper bill. It is against a dangerous and unwarranted interpretation of the recent amendments to the Constitution that I feel bound to enter my protest.

As indicated in our discussion of the legislative debates above, the framers of the Fourteenth Amendment (especially Representative John Bingham [R., Ohio], who drafted most of Section 1 and Senator Jacob Howard [R., Mich.], who opened the Senate debate) placed particular stress upon Section 1's privileges and immunities clause prohibiting the states from abridging "the privileges and immunities of citizens of the United States." It is possible, indeed, that the "privileges and immunities" sought to be protected comprehended all the rights included in the first eight amendments, with the privileges and immunities clause intended to make the Bill of Rights binding upon the states. Yet, if such was the intent of the draftsmen of the Fourteenth Amendment, it was soon to be frustrated. As Professor Edward Corwin once put it, "Unique among constitutional provisions, the privileges and immunities clause of the Fourteenth Amendment enjoys the distinction of having been rendered a 'practical nullity' by a single decision of the Supreme Court rendered within five years after its ratification."

The decision referred to was that rendered in the 1873 *Slaughter-House Cases,* 16 Wall. 36 (1873). The Court there found crucial decisional significance in the difference in language between the amendment's citizenship clause (inserted, it will be recalled, during the Senate debate) and its privileges and immunities clause (part of the original draft of Bingham's final version of Section 1). Justice Samuel Miller's opinion which follows stresses the fact that, while the first sentence of the amendment makes all persons born or naturalized in this country both "citizens of the United States and of the State wherein they reside," the next sentence protects only "the privileges or immunities of citizens of the United States" from state abridgment. The distinction, said the Court, was intended to leave the fundamental rights of life and property untouched by the amendment, and they remained, as always, in the hands of the states.

Under *Slaughter-House,* the privileges and immunities clause did not transform the rights of citizens of each state into rights of national citizenship enforceable as such in the federal courts. Instead, it only protected against state encroachment those rights "which owe their existence to the federal government, its national character, its Constitution, or its laws." The rights protected are solely those which would not have existed but for the presence of the federal government. Rights which antedate and thus do not owe their existence to such government are privileges and immunities only of state citizenship. The right to earn a livelihood was such a right. Hence, the Louisiana law at issue in *Slaughter-House,* which restricted the right of New Orleans butchers to earn a living, was ruled not violative of the Fourteenth Amendment's privileges and immunities clause.

The *Slaughter-House* decision, in effect, read the privileges and immunities clause out of the Fourteenth Amendment—at least so far as its practical impact was concerned. Under *Slaughter-House,* the amendment created no new privileges and immunities of United States citizenship. The relevant clause was reduced to a mere reiteration of a prohibition already operative against the states. In particular, a state violation of the rights guaranteed in the Bill of Rights does not contravene the privileges and immunities clause. The cases have consistently ruled that the inclusion in the first eight amendments of a specific right does not make such right a federal privilege or immunity secured by the Fourteenth Amendment against state action.

SLAUGHTER-HOUSE CASES
16 WALL. 36 (1873)

MR. JUSTICE MILLER, now, April 14th, 1873, delivered the opinion of the Court.

These cases are brought here by writs of error to the Supreme Court of the State of Louisiana. They arise out of the efforts of the butchers of New Orleans to resist the Crescent City Live-Stock Landing and Slaughter-House Company in the exercise of certain powers conferred by the charter which created it, and which was granted by the legislature of that State. . . .

The statute thus assailed as unconstitutional was passed March 8th, 1869, and is entitled "An act to protect the health of the city of New Orleans, to locate the stock-landings and slaughter-houses, and to incorporate the Crescent City Live-Stock Landing and Slaughter-House Company."

The first section forbids the landing or slaughtering of animals whose flesh is intended for food, within the city of New Orleans and other parishes and boundaries named and defined, or the keeping or establishing any slaughter-houses or *abattoirs* within those limits except by the corporation thereby created, which is also limited to certain places afterwards mentioned. Suitable penalties are enacted for violations of this prohibition.

The second section designates the corporators, gives the name to the corporation, and confers on it the usual corporate powers.

The third and fourth sections authorize the company to establish and erect within certain territorial limits, therein defined, one or more stock-yards, stock-landings, and slaughter-houses, and imposes upon it the duty of erecting, on or before the first day of June, 1869, one grand slaughter-house of sufficient capacity for slaughtering five hundred animals per day.

It declares that the company, after it shall have prepared all the necessary buildings, yards, and other conveniences for that purpose, shall have the sole and exclusive privilege of conducting and carrying on the live-stock landing and slaughter-house business within the limits and privilege granted by the act, and that all such animals shall be landed at the stock-landings and slaughtered at the slaughter-houses of the company, and nowhere else.

Penalties are enacted for infractions of this provision, and prices fixed for the maximum charges of the company for each steamboat and for each animal landed.

Section five orders the closing up of all other stock-landings and slaughter-houses after the first day of June, in the parishes of Orleans, Jefferson, and St. Bernard, and makes it the duty of the company to permit any person to slaughter animals in their slaughter-houses under a heavy penalty for each refusal. Another section fixes a limit to the charges to be made by the company for each animal so slaughtered in their building, and another provides for an inspection of all animals intended to be so slaughtered, by an officer appointed by the governor of the State for that purpose.

These are the principal features of the statute, and are all that have any bearing upon the questions to be decided by us.

This statute is denounced not only as creating a monopoly and conferring odious and exclusive privileges upon a small number of persons at the expense of the great body of the community of New Orleans, but it is asserted that it deprives a large and meritorious class of citizens—the whole of the butchers of the city—of the right to exercise their trade, the business to which they have been trained and on which they depend for the support of themselves and their families; and that the unrestricted exercise of the business of butchering is necessary to the daily subsistence of the population of the city. . . .

The first section of the fourteenth article, to which our attention is more specially invited, opens with a definition of citizenship—not only citizenship of the United States, but citizenship of the States. No such definition was previously found in the Constitution, nor had any attempt been made to define it by act of Congress. It had been the occasion of much discussion in the courts, by the executive departments, and in the public journals. It had been said by eminent judges that no man was a citizen of the United States, except as he was a citizen of one of the States composing the Union. Those, therefore, who had been born and resided always in the District of Columbia or in the Territories, though within the United States, were not citizens. Whether this proposition was sound or not had never been judicially decided. But it had been held by this court, in the celebrated Dred Scott case, only a few years before the outbreak of the civil war, that a man of African descent, whether a slave or not, was not and could not be a citizen of a State or of the United States. This decision, while it met the condemnation of some of the ablest statesmen and constitutional lawyers of the country, had never been overruled; and if it was to be accepted as a constitutional limitation of the right of citizenship, then all the negro race who had recently been made freemen, were still, not only not citizens, but were incapable of becoming so by anything short of an amendment to the Constitution.

To remove this difficulty primarily, and to establish a clear and comprehensive definition of citizenship which should declare what should constitute citizenship of the United States, and also citizenship of a State, the first clause of the first section was framed.

All persons born or naturalized in the United States, and subject to the jurisdiction thereof, are citizens of the United States and of the State wherein they reside.

The first observation we have to make on this clause is, that it puts at rest both the questions which we stated to have been the subject of differences of opinion. It declares that persons may be citizens of the United States without regard to their citizenship of a particular State, and it overturns the Dred Scott decision by making *all persons* born within the United States and subject to its jurisdiction citizens of the United States. That its main purpose was to establish the citizenship of the negro can admit of no doubt. The phrase, "subject to its jurisdiction" was intended to exclude from its operation children of ministers, consuls, and citizens or subjects of foreign States born within the United States.

The next observation is more important in view of the arguments of counsel in the present case. It is, that the distinction between citizenship of the United States and citizenship of a State is clearly recognized and established. Not only may a man be a citizen of the United States without being a citizen of a State, but an important element is necessary· to convert the former into the latter. He must reside within the State to make him a citizen of it, but it is only necessary that he should be born or naturalized in the United States to be a citizen of the Union.

It is quite clear, then, that there is a citizenship of the United States, and a citizenship of a State, which are distinct from each other, and which depend upon different characteristics or circumstances in the individual.

We think this distinction and its explicit recognition in this amendment of great weight in this argument, because the next paragraph of this same section, which is the one mainly relied on by the plaintiffs in error, speaks only of privileges and immunities of citizens of the United States, and does not speak of those of citizens of the several States. The argument, however, in favor of the plaintiffs rests wholly on the assumption that the citizenship is the same, and the privileges and immunities guaranteed by the clause are the same.

The language is, "No State shall make or enforce any law which shall abridge the privileges or immunities of citizens of *the United States.*" It is a little remarkable, if this clause was intended as a protection to the citizen of a State against the legislative power of his own State, that the word citizen of the State should be left out when it is so carefully used, and used in contradistinction to citizens of the United States, in the very sentence which precedes it. It is too clear for argument that the change in phraseology was adopted understandingly and with a purpose.

Of the privileges and immunities of the citizen of the United States, and of the privileges and immunities of the citizen of the State, and what they respectively are, we will presently consider; but we wish to state here that it is only the former which are placed by this clause under the protection of the Federal Constitution, and that the latter, whatever they may be, are not intended to have any additional protection by this paragraph of the amendment. . . .

It would be the vainest show of learning to attempt to prove by citations of authority, that up to the adoption of the recent amendments, no claim or pretence was set up that those rights depended on the Federal government for their existence or protection, beyond the very few express limitations which the Federal Constitution imposed upon the States—such, for instance, as the prohibition against ex post facto laws, bills of attainder, and laws impairing the obligation of contracts. But with the exception of these and a few other restrictions, the entire domain of the privileges and immunities of citizens of the States, as above defined, lay within the constitutional and legislative power of the States, and without that of the Federal government. Was it the purpose of the fourteenth amendment, by the simple declaration that no State should make or enforce any law which shall abridge the privileges and immunities of *citizens of the United States*, to transfer the security and protection of all the civil rights which we have mentioned, from the States to the Federal government? And where it is declared that Congress shall have the power to enforce that article, was it intended to bring within the power of Congress the entire domain of civil rights heretofore belonging exclusively to the States?

All this and more must follow, if the proposition of the plaintiffs in error be sound. For not only are these rights subject to the control of Congress whenever in its discretion any of them are supposed to be abridged by State legislation, but that body may also pass laws in advance, limiting and restricting the exercise of legislative power by the States, in their most ordinary and usual functions, as in its judgment it may think proper on all such subjects. And still further, such a construction followed by the reversal of the judgments of the Supreme Court of Louisiana in these cases, would constitute this court a perpetual censor upon all legislation of the States, on the civil rights of their own citizens, with authority to nullify such as it did not approve as consistent with those rights, as they existed at the time of the adoption of this amendment. The argument we admit is not always the most conclusive which is drawn from the consequences urged against the adoption of a particular construction of an instrument. But when, as in the case before us, these consequences are so serious, so far-reaching and pervading, so great a departure from the structure and spirit of our institutions; when the effect is to fetter and degrade the State governments by subjecting them to the control of Congress, in the exercise of powers heretofore universally conceded to them of the most ordinary and fundamental character; when in fact it radically changes the whole theory of the relations of the State and Federal governments to each other and of both these governments to the people; the argument has a force that is irresistible, in the absence of language which expresses such a purpose too clearly to admit of doubt.

We are convinced that no such results were intended by the Congress which proposed these amendments, nor by the legislatures of the States which ratified them.

Having shown that the privileges and immunities relied on in the argument are those which belong to citizens of the States as such, and that they are left to the State governments for security and protection, and not by this article placed under the special care of the Federal government, we may hold ourselves excused from defining the privileges and immunities of citizens of the United States which no State can abridge, until some case involving those privileges may make it necessary to do so.

But lest it should be said that no such privileges and immunities are to be found if those we have been considering are excluded, we venture to suggest some which owe their existence to the Federal government, its National character, its Constitution, or its laws.

One of these is well described in the case of *Crandall v. Nevada,* 6 Wall. 35 (1868). It is said to be the right of the citizen of this great country, protected by implied guarantees of its Constitution, "to come to the seat of government to assert any claim he may have upon that government, to transact any business he may have with it, to seek its protection, to share its offices, to engage in administering its functions. He has the right of free access to its seaports, through which all operations of foreign commerce are conducted, to the sub-treasuries, land offices, and courts of justice in the several States." And quoting from the language of Chief Justice Taney in another case, it is said "that *for all the great purposes for which the Federal government* was established, we are one people, with one common country, *we are all citizens of the United States;*" and it is, as such citizens, that their rights are supported in this court in *Crandall* v. *Nevada.*

Another privilege of a citizen of the United States is to demand the care and protection of the Federal government over his life, liberty, and property when on the high seas or within the jurisdiction of a foreign government. Of this there can be no doubt, nor that the right depends upon his character as a citizen of the United States. The right to peaceably assemble and petition for redress of grievances, the privilege of the writ of *habeas corpus*, are rights of the citizen guaranteed by the Federal Constitution. The right to use the navigable waters of the United States, however they may penetrate the territory of the several States, all rights secured to our citizens by treaties with foreign nations, are dependent upon citizenship of the United States, and not citizenship of a State. One of these privileges is conferred by the very article under consideration. It is that a citizen of the United States can, of his own volition, become a citizen of any State of the Union by a *bona fide* residence therein, with the same rights as other citizens of that State. To these may be added the rights secured by the thirteenth and fifteenth articles of amendment, and by the other clause of the fourteenth, next to be considered.

But it is useless to pursue this branch of the inquiry, since we are of opinion that the rights claimed by these plaintiffs in error, if they have any existence, are not privileges and immunities of citizens of the United States within the meaning of the clause of the fourteenth amendment under consideration. . . .

The *Slaughter-House Cases*, just given, effectively frustrated the intent expressed by Congressman Bingham and Senator Howard (if such was, indeed, their true intent at the time the Fourteenth Amendment was written and debated) to include the rights secured by the Bill of Rights in the privileges and immunities which might not be abridged by the states. The *Slaughter-House* decision did not, however, prevent the Fourteenth Amendment from reviving the constitutional question that had been laid to rest in *Barron* v. *Baltimore*, 7 Pet. 243 (1833), where the Supreme Court had ruled that the Bill of Rights placed restraints only on the Federal Government, not the states. After *Slaughter-House*, the claim that the Fourteenth Amendment made the Bill of Rights binding upon the states was based primarily upon the amendment's due process clause. The claim was first made and rejected in the Supreme Court in *Hurtado* v. *California*, 110 U.S. 516 (1884). Since that case, the high bench has consistently refused to accept the view that the Bill of Rights is, as such, incorporated into the Fourteenth Amendment.

Adamson v. *California*, 332 U.S. 46 (1947), contains the most important consideration by the Supreme Court of the question of whether the Fourteenth Amendment does make the provisions of the first eight amendments binding upon the states as well as the federal government. Of particular interest to us is Justice Hugo Black's dissent, which urges that the Supreme Court has not adequately considered the historical background of the Fourteenth Amendment. Such background, he asserts, indicates clearly that those who sponsored and favored the amendment intended its first section to make the Bill of Rights applicable to the states. The appendix which Justice Black appended to his opinion (not reprinted here) contains a summary of the legislative history of the Fourteenth Amendment (i.e., an abbreviated version of the extracts printed above).

One who has read the pages just referred to has the basis for making a judgment on who was correct in the *Adamson* case—the Court majority (whose view was best expressed in Justice Felix Frankfurter's concurring opinion) or Justice Black. At a minimum, however, it should be noted that the historical record drawn from the Congressional debates is not nearly as clear as the Black dissent asserts. It may well be that Senator Howard and Congressman Bingham had the intent asserted by Black (yet even their views on the matter, we saw, were confused), but it is certainly not accurate to say that the Black view is borne out by the statements of other participants in the 1866 debates.

Yet, whatever one may think of the correctness of Justice Black's historical interpretation, it is clear that his view on the wholesale incorporation of the Bill of Rights into the Fourteenth Amendment has yet to command a majority of the Supreme Court. Instead the Court has followed a rule of selective incorporation, under which only those rights secured by the Bill of

341

Rights which may be considered *fundamental* are included within the due process clause of the Fourteenth Amendment, and as such, are binding upon the states. It should, at the same time, be noted that the tendency in recent years has been to consider as fundamental evermore the rights protected by the first eight amendments. Such tendency may ultimately render all but academic the controversy between the majority and dissent in *Adamson* itself.

(Parenthetically, it should be pointed out that the narrow holding of *Adamson*—that the comment by Court and prosecutor on defendant's failure to testify in a state criminal case does not violate the Fourteenth Amendment— has been overruled by *Griffin* v. *California,* 380 U.S. 609 (1965), though that decision does not change *Adamson's* answer to the broader question of the extent to which the Fourteenth Amendment imposes the requirements of the Bill of Rights upon the states.)

ADAMSON v. *CALIFORNIA*
332, U. S. 46 (1947)

MR. JUSTICE REED delivered the opinion of the Court.

The appellant, Adamson, a citizen of the United States, was convicted, without recommendation for mercy, by a jury in a Superior Court of the State of California of murder in the first degree. After considering the same objections to the conviction that are pressed here, the sentence of death was affirmed by the Supreme Court of the state. 27 Cal. 2d 478, 165 P. 2d 3. Review of that judgment by this Court was sought and allowed under Judicial Code § 237; 28 U.S.C. § 344. The provisions of California law which were challenged in the state proceedings as invalid under the Four- teenth Amendment to the Federal Constitution are those of the state consti- tution and penal code in the margin. They permit the failure of a defendant to explain or to deny evidence against him to be commented upon by court and by counsel and to be considered by court and jury. The defendant did not testify. As the trial court gave its instructions and the District Attorney argued the case in accordance with the constitutional and statutory provisions just referred to, we have for decision the question of their constitutionality in these circumstances under the limitations of § 1 of the Fourteenth Amend- ment. . . .

In the first place, appellant urges that the provision of the Fifth Amend- ment that no person "shall be compelled in any criminal case to be a witness against himself" is a fundamental national privilege or immunity protected against state abridgment by the Fourteenth Amendment or a privilege or immunity secured, through the Fourteenth Amendment, against deprivation by state action because it is a personal right, enumerated in the federal Bill of Rights.

Secondly, appellant relies upon the due process of law clause of the Fourteenth Amendment to invalidate the provisions of the California law, set out in note 3 *supra*, and as applied (a) because comment on failure to testify is permitted, (b) because appellant was forced to forego testimony in person because of danger of disclosure of his past convictions through cross-examination, and (c) because the presumption of innocence was infringed by the shifting of the burden of proof to appellant in permitting comment on his failure to testify.

We shall assume, but without any intention thereby of ruling upon the issue, that permission by law to the court, counsel and jury to comment upon and consider the failure of defendant "to explain or to deny by his testimony any evidence or facts in the case against him" would infringe defendant's privilege against self-incrimination under the Fifth Amendment if this were a trial in a court of the United States under a similar law. Such an assumption does not determine appellant's rights under the Fourteenth Amendment. It is settled law that the clause of the Fifth Amendment, protecting a person against being compelled to be a witness against himself, is not made effective by the Fourteenth Amendment as a protection against state action on the ground that freedom from testimonial compulsion is a right of national citizenship, or because it is a personal privilege or immunity secured by the Federal Constitution as one of the rights of man that are listed in the Bill of Rights.

The reasoning that leads to those conclusions starts with the unquestioned premise that the Bill of Rights, when adopted, was for the protection of the individual against the federal government and its provisions were inapplicable to similar actions done by the states. *Barron* v. *Baltimore*, 7 Pet. 243; *Feldman* v. *United States*, 322 U. S. 487, 490. With the adoption of the Fourteenth Amendment, it was suggested that the dual citizenship recognized by its first sentence secured for citizens federal protection for their elemental privileges and immunities of state citizenship. The *Slaughter-House Cases* decided, contrary to the suggestion, that these rights, as privileges and immunities of state citizenship, remained under the sole protection of the state governments. This Court, without the expression of a contrary view upon that phase of the issues before the Court, has approved this determination. *Maxwell* v. *Bugbee*, 250 U. S. 525, 537; *Hamilton* v. *Regents*, 293 U. S. 245, 261. The power to free defendants in state trials from self-incrimination was specifically determined to be beyond the scope of the privileges and immunities clause of the Fourteenth Amendment in *Twining* v. *New Jersey*, 211 U. S. 78, 91—98. "The privilege against self-incrimination may be withdrawn and the accused put upon the stand as a witness for the state." The *Twining* case likewise disposed of the contention that freedom from testimonial compulsion, being specifically granted by the Bill of Rights, is a federal privilege or immunity that is protected by the Fourteenth Amendment against state invasion. This Court held that the inclusion in the Bill of Rights of this protection against the power of the national government did not make the privilege a federal privilege or immunity secured to citizens by the Constitution against state action. *Twining* v. *New Jersey, supra,* at 98—99; *Palko* v. *Connecticut, supra,* at 328. After declaring that state and national citizenship co-exist in the same person, the Fourteenth Amendment forbids a state from abridging the privileges and immunities of citizens of the United States. As a matter of words, this leaves a state free to abridge, within the limits of the due process clause, the privileges and immunities flowing from state citizenship. This reading of the Federal Constitution has heretofore found favor with the majority of this Court as a natural and logical interpretation. It accords with the constitutional doctrine of federalism by leaving to the states the responsibility of dealing with the privileges and immunities of their citizens except those inherent in national citizenship. It is the construction placed upon the amendment by justices whose own experience had given them contemporaneous knowledge of the purposes that led to the adoption of the Fourteenth Amendment. This construction has become embedded in our federal system as a functioning element in preserving the balance between national and state power. We reaffirm the conclusion of the *Twining* and *Palko* cases that protection against self incrimination is not a privilege or immunity of national citizenship.

Appellant secondly contends that if the privilege against self incrimination is not a right protected by the privileges and immunities clause of the Fourteenth Amendment against state action, this privilege, to its full scope under the Fifth Amendment, inheres in the right to a fair trial. A right to a fair trial is a right admittedly protected by the due process clause of the Fourteenth Amendment. Therefore, appellant argues, the due process clause of the Fourteenth Amendment protects his privilege against self-incrimination. The due process clause of the Fourteenth Amendment, however, does not draw all the rights of the federal Bill of Rights under its protection. That contention was made and rejected in *Palko* v. *Connecticut,* 302 U. S. 319, 323. It was rejected with citation of the cases excluding several of the rights, protected by the Bill of Rights, against infringement by the National Government. Nothing has been called to our attention that either the framers of the Fourteenth Amendment or the states that adopted intended its due process clause to draw within its scope the earlier amendments to the Constitution. *Palko* held that such provisions of the Bill of Rights as were "implicit in the concept of ordered liberty," p. 325, became secure from state interference by the clause. But it held nothing more. . . .

We find no other error that gives ground for our intervention in California's administration of criminal justice.

Affirmed.

MR. JUSTICE FRANKFURTER, concurring.

Less than ten years ago, Mr. Justice Cardozo announced as settled constitutional law that while the Fifth Amendment, "which is not directed to the states, but solely to the federal government," provides that no person shall be compelled in any criminal case to be a witness against himself, the process of law assured by the Fourteenth Amendment does not require such immunity from self crimination: "in prosecutions by a state, the exemption will fail if the state elects to end it." *Palko* v. *Connecticut,* 302 U. S. 319, 322, 324. Mr. Justice Cardozo spoke for the Court, consisting of Mr. Chief Justice Hughes, and McReynolds, Brandeis, Sutherland, Stone, Roberts, Black, JJ. (Mr. Justice Butler dissented.) The matter no longer called for discussion; a reference to *Twining* v. *New Jersey,* 211 U. S. 78, decided thirty years before the *Palko* case, sufficed.

Decisions of this Court do not have equal intrinsic authority. The *Twining* case shows the judicial process at its best—comprehensive briefs and powerful arguments on both sides, followed by long deliberation, resulting in an opinion by Mr. Justice Moody which at once gained and has ever since retained recognition as one of the outstanding opinions in the history of the Court. After enjoying unquestioned prestige for forty years, the *Twining* case should not now be diluted, even unwittingly, either in its judicial philosophy or in its particulars. As the surest way of keeping the *Twining* case intact, I would affirm this case on its authority.

The circumstances of this case present a minor variant from what was before the Court in *Twining* v. *New Jersey, supra.* The attempt to inflate the difference into constitutional significance was adequately dealt with by Mr. Justice Traynor in the court below. *People* v. *Adamson,* 27 Cal. 2d 478, 165 P. 2d 3. The matter lies within a very narrow compass. The point is made that a defendant who has a vulnerable record would, by taking the stand, subject himself to having his credibility impeached thereby. See *Raffel* v. *United States,* 271 U. S. 494, 496—97. Accordingly, under California law, he is confronted with the dilemma, whether to testify and perchance have his bad record prejudice him in the minds of the jury, or to subject himself to the unfavorable inference which the jury might draw from his silence. And so, it is argued, if he chooses the latter alternative, the jury ought not to be allowed to attribute his silence to a consciousness of guilt when it might be due merely to a desire to escape damaging cross-examination.

This does not create an issue different from that settled in the *Twining* case. Only a technical rule of law would exclude from consideration that which is relevant, as a matter of fair reasoning, to the solution of a problem. Sensible and just-minded men, in important affairs of life, deem it significant that a man remains silent when confronted with serious and responsible evidence against himself which it is within his power to contradict. The notion that to allow jurors to do that which sensible and right-minded men do every day violates the "immutable principles of justice" as conceived by a civilized society is to trivialize the importance of "due process." Nor does it make any difference in drawing significance from silence under such circumstances that an accused may deem it more advantageous to remain silent than to speak, on the nice calculation that by taking the witness stand he may expose himself to having his credibility impugned by reason of his criminal record. Silence under such circumstances is still significant. A person in that situation may express to the jury, through appropriate requests to charge, why he prefers to keep silent. A man who has done one wrong may prove his innocence on a totally different charge. To deny that the jury can be trusted to make such discrimination is to show little confidence in the jury system. The prosecution is frequently compelled to rely on the testimony of shady characters whose credibility is bound to be the chief target of the defense. It is a common practice in criminal trials to draw out of a vulnerable witness's mouth his vulnerability, and then convince the jury that nevertheless he is telling the truth in this particular case. This is also a common experience for defendants.

For historical reasons a limited immunity from the common duty to testify was written into the Federal Bill of Rights, and I am prepared to agree that, as part of that immunity, comment on the failure of an accused to take the witness stand is forbidden in federal prosecutions. It is so, of course, by explicit act of Congress. 20 Stat. 30; see *Bruno* v. *United States*, 308 U. S. 287. But to suggest that such a limitation can be drawn out of "due process" in its protection of ultimate decency in a civilized society is to suggest that the Due Process Clause fastened fetters of unreason upon the States. (This opinion is concerned solely with a discussion of the Due Process Clause of the Fourteenth Amendment. I put to one side the Privileges or Immunities Clause of that Amendment. For the mischievous uses to which that clause would lend itself if its scope were not confined to that given it by all but one of the decisions beginning with the *Slaughter-House Cases,* 16 Wall. 36, see the deviation in *Colgate* v. *Harvey*, 296 U. S. 404, overruled by *Madden* v. *Kentucky*, 309 U. S. 83)

Between the incorporation of the Fourteenth Amendment into the Constitution and the beginning of the present membership of the Court—a period of seventy years—the scope of that Amendment was passed upon by forty-three judges. Of all these judges, only one, who may respectfully be called an eccentric exception, ever indicated the belief that the Fourteenth Amendment was a shorthand summary of the first eight Amendments theretofore limiting only the Federal Government, and that due process incorporated those eight Amendments as restrictions upon the powers of the States. Among these judges were not only those who would have to be included among the greatest in the history of the Court, but—it is especially relevant to note—they included those whose services in the cause of human rights and the spirit of freedom are the most conspicuous in our history. It is not invidious to single out Miller, Davis, Bradley, Waite, Matthews, Gray, Fuller, Holmes, Brandeis, Stone and Cardozo (to speak only of the dead) as judges who were alert in safeguarding and promoting the interests of liberty and human dignity through law. But they were also judges mindful of the relation of our federal system to a progressively democratic society and therefore duly regardful of the scope of authority that was left to the States even after the Civil War. And so they did not find that the Fourteenth Amendment, concerned as it was with matters fundamental to the pursuit of justice, fastened upon the States procedural arrangements which, in the language of Mr. Justice Cardozo, only those who are "narrow or provincial" would deem essential to "a fair and enlightened system of justice." *Palko* v. *Connecticut*, 302 U. S. 319, 325. To suggest that it is inconsistent with a truly free society to begin prosecutions without an indictment, to try petty civil cases without the paraphernalia of a common law jury, to take into consideration that one who has full opportunity to make a defense remains silent is, in De Tocqueville's phrase, to confound the familiar with the necessary.

The short answer to the suggestion that the provision of the Fourteenth Amendment, which ordains "nor shall any State deprive any person of life, liberty, or property, without due process of law," was a way of saying that every State must thereafter initiate prosecutions through indictment by a grand jury, must have a trial by a jury of twelve in criminal cases, and must have trial by such a jury in common law suits where the amount in controversy exceeds twenty dollars, is that it is a strange way of saying it. It would be extraordinarily strange for a Constitution to convey such specific commands in such a roundabout and inexplicit way. After all, an amendment to the Constitution should be read in a "sense most obvious to the common understanding at the time of its adoption. . . . For it was for public adoption that it was proposed." See Mr. Justice Holmes in *Eisner* v. *Macomber*, 252 U. S. 189, 220. Those reading the English language with the meaning which it ordinarily conveys, those conversant with the political and legal history of the concept of due process, those sensitive to the relations of the States to the central government as well as the relation of some of the provisions of the Bill of Rights to the process of justice, would hardly recognize the Fourteenth Amendment as a cover for the various explicit provisions of the first eight Amendments. Some of these are enduring reflections of experience with human nature, while some express the restricted views of Eighteenth Century England regarding the best methods for the ascertainment of facts. The notion that the Fourteenth Amendment was a covert way of imposing upon the States all the rules which it seemed important to Eighteenth Century statesmen to write into the Federal Amendments, was rejected by judges who were themselves witnesses of the process by which the Fourteenth Amendment became part of the Constitution. Arguments that may now be adduced to prove that the first eight Amendments were concealed within the historic phrasing of the Fourteenth Amendment were not unknown at the time of its adoption. A surer estimate of their bearing was possible for judges at the time than distorting distance is likely to vouchsafe. Any evidence of design or purpose not contemporaneously known could hardly have influenced those who ratified the Amendment. Remarks of a particular proponent of the Amendment, no matter how influential, are not to be deemed part of the Amendment. What was submitted for ratification was his proposal, not his speech. Thus, at the time of the ratification of the Fourteenth Amendment the constitutions of nearly half of the ratifying States did not have the rigorous requirements of the Fifth Amendment for instituting criminal proceedings through a grand jury. It could hardly have occurred to these States that by ratifying the Amendment they uprooted their established methods for prosecuting crime and fastened upon themselves a new prosecutorial system.

Indeed, the suggestion that the Fourteenth Amendment incorporates the first eight Amendments as such is not unambiguously urged. Even the boldest innovator would shrink from suggesting to more than half the States that how they are lost. As judges charged with the delicate task of subjecting the government of a continent to the Rule of Law we must be particularly mindful that it is "a *constitution* we are expounding," so that it should not be imprisoned in what are merely legal forms even though they have the sanction of the Eighteenth Century.

It may not be amiss to restate the pervasive function of the Fourteenth Amendment in exacting from the States observance of basic liberties. See *Malinski* v. *New York*, 324 U. S. 401, 412 *et seq.*; *Louisiana* v. *Resweber*, 329 U. S. 459, 466 *et seq.* The Amendment neither comprehends the specific provisions by which the founders deemed it appropriate to restrict the federal government nor is it confined to them. The Due Process Clause of the Fourteenth Amendment has an independent potency, precisely as does the Due Process Clause of the Fifth Amendment in relation to the Federal Government. It ought not to require argument to reject the notion that due process of law meant one thing in the Fifth Amendment and another in the Fourteenth. The Fifth Amendment specifically prohibits prosecution of an "infamous crime" except upon indictment; it forbids double jeopardy; it bars compelling a person to be a witness against himself in any criminal case; it precludes deprivation of "life, liberty, or property, without due process of law. . . ." Are Madison and his contemporaries in the framing of the Bill of Rights to be charged with writing into it a meaningless clause? To consider "due process of law" as merely a shorthand statement of other specific clauses in the same amendment is to attribute to the authors and proponents of this Amendment ignorance of, or indifference to, a historic conception which was one of the great instruments in the arsenal of constitutional freedom which the Bill of Rights was to protect and strengthen.

A construction which gives to due process no independent function but turns it into a summary of the specific provisions of the Bill of Rights would, as has been noted, tear up by the roots much of the fabric of law in the several States, and would deprive the States of opportunity for reforms in legal process designed for extending the area of freedom. It would assume that no other abuses would reveal themselves in the course of time than those which had become manifest in 1791. Such a view not only disregards the historic meaning of "due process." It leads inevitably to a warped construction of specific provisions of the Bill of Rights to bring within their scope conduct clearly condemned by due process but not easily fitting into the pigeon-holes of the specific provisions. It seems pretty late in the day to suggest that a phrase so laden with historic meaning should be given an improvised content consisting of some but not all of the provisions of the first eight Amendments, selected on an undefined basis, with improvisation of content for the provisions so selected.

And so, when, as in a case like the present, a conviction in a State court is here for review under a claim that a right protected by the Due Process Clause of the Fourteenth Amendment has been denied, the issue is not whether an infraction of one of the specific provisions of the first eight Amendments is disclosed by the record. The relevant question is whether the criminal proceedings which resulted in conviction deprived the accused of the due process of law to which the United States Constitution entitled him. Judicial review of that guaranty of the Fourteenth Amendment inescapably imposes upon this Court an exercise of judgment upon the whole course of the proceedings in order to ascertain whether they offend those canons of decency and fairness which express the notions of justice of English-speaking peoples even toward those charged with the most heinous offenses. These standards of justice are not authoritatively formulated anywhere as though they were prescriptions in a pharmacopoeia. But neither does the application of the Due Process Clause imply that judges are wholly at large. The judicial judgment in applying the Due Process Clause must move within the limits of accepted notions of justice and is not to be based upon the idiosyncrasies of a merely personal judgment. The fact that judges among themselves may differ whether in a particular case a trial offends accepted notions of justice is not disproof that general rather than idiosyncratic standards are applied. An important safeguard against such merely individual judgment is an alert deference to the judgment of the State court under review.

MR. JUSTICE BLACK, dissenting.

The appellant was tried for murder in a California state court. He did not take the stand as a witness in his own behalf. The prosecuting attorney, under purported authority of a California statute, Cal. Penal Code, § 1323 (Hillyer-Lake, 1945), argued to the jury that an inference of guilt could be drawn because of appellant's failure to deny evidence offered against him. The appellant's contention in the state court and here has been that the statute denies him a right guaranteed by the Federal Constitution. The argument is that (1) permitting comment upon his failure to testify has the effect of compelling him to testify so as to violate that provision of the Bill of Rights contained in the Fifth Amendment that "No person . . . shall be compelled in any criminal case to be a witness against himself"; and (2) although this provision of the Fifth Amendment originally applied only as a restraint upon federal courts, *Barron* v. *Baltimore,* 7 Pet. 243, the Fourteenth Amendment was intended to, and did, make the prohibition against compelled testimony applicable to trials in state courts.

The Court refuses to meet and decide the appellant's first contention. But while the Court's opinion, as I read it, strongly implies that the Fifth Amendment does not, of itself, bar comment upon failure to testify in federal courts, the Court nevertheless assumes that it does in order to reach the second constitutional question involved in appellant's case. I must consider the case on the same assumption that the Court does. For the discussion of the second contention turns out to be a decision which reaches far beyond the relatively narrow issues on which this case might have turned.

This decision reasserts a constitutional theory spelled out in *Twining* v. *New Jersey,* 211 U. S. 78, that this Court is endowed by the Constitution with boundless power under "natural law" periodically to expand and contract constitutional standards to conform to the Court's conception of what at a particular time constitutes "civilized decency" and "fundamental liberty and justice." Invoking this *Twining* rule, the Court concludes that although comment upon testimony in a federal court would violate the Fifth Amendment, identical comment in a state court does not violate today's fashion in civilized decency and fundamentals and is therefore not prohibited by the Federal Constitution as amended.

The *Twining* case was the first, as it is the only, decision of this Court which has squarely held that states were free, notwithstanding the Fifth and Fourteenth Amendments, to extort evidence from one accused of crime. I agree that if *Twining* be reaffirmed, the result reached might appropriately follow. But I would not reaffirm the *Twining* decision. I think that decision and the "natural law" theory of the Constitution upon which it relies degrade the constitutional safeguards of the Bill of Rights and simultaneously appropriate for this Court a broad power which we are not authorized by the Constitution to exercise. Furthermore, the *Twining* decision rested on previous cases and broad hypotheses which have been undercut by intervening decisions of this Court. See Corwin, *The Supreme Court's Construction of the Self-Incrimination Clause,* 29 Mich. L. Rev. 1, 191, 202. My reasons for believing that the *Twining* decision should not be revitalized can best be understood by reference to the constitutional, judicial, and general history that preceded and followed the case. That reference must be abbreviated far more than is justified but for the necessary limitations of opinion-writing.

The first ten amendments were proposed and adopted largely because of fear that Government might unduly interfere with prized individual liberties. The people wanted and demanded a Bill of Rights written into their Constitution. The amendments embodying the Bill of Rights were intended to curb all branches of the Federal Government in the fields touched by the amendments—Legislative, Executive, and Judicial. The Fifth, Sixth, and Eighth

Amendments were pointedly aimed at confining exercise of power by courts and judges within precise boundaries, particularly in the procedure used for the trial of criminal cases. Past history provided strong reasons for the apprehensions which brought these procedural amendments into being and attest the wisdom of their adoption. For the fears of arbitrary court action sprang largely from the past use of courts in the imposition of criminal punishments to suppress speech, press, and religion. Hence the constitutional limitations of courts' powers were, in the view of the Founders, essential supplements to the First Amendment, which was itself designed to protect the widest scope for all people to believe and to express the most divergent political, religious, and other views.

But these limitations were not expressly imposed upon state court action. In 1833, *Barron v. Baltimore, supra,* was decided by this Court. It specifically held inapplicable to the states that provision of the Fifth Amendment which declares: "nor shall private property be taken for public use, without just compensation." In deciding the particular point raised, the Court there said that it could not hold that the first eight Amendments applied to the states. This was the controlling constitutional rule when the Fourteenth Amendment was proposed in 1866.

My study of the historical events that culminated in the Fourteenth Amendment, and the expressions of those who sponsored and favored, as well as those who opposed its submission and passage, persuades me that one of the chief objects that the provisions of the Amendment's first section, separately, and as a whole, were intended to accomplish was to make the Bill of Rights, applicable to the states. With full knowledge of the import of the *Barron* decision, the framers and backers of the Fourteenth Amendment proclaimed its purpose to be to overturn the constitutional rule that case had announced. This historical purpose has never received full consideration or exposition in any opinion of this Court interpreting the Amendment.

In construing other constitutional provisions, this Court has almost uniformly followed the precept of *Ex parte Bain*, 121 U. S. 1, 12, that "It is never to be forgotten that, in the construction of the language of the Constitution . . . , as indeed in all other instances where construction becomes necessary, we are to place ourselves as nearly as possible in the condition of the men who framed that instrument." See also *Everson v. Board of Education*, 330 U. S. 1, 8, 28, 33; *Thornhill v. Alabama*, 310 U. S. 88, 95, 102; *Knowlton v. Moore*, 178 U. S. 41, 89, 106; *Reynolds v. United States*, 98 U. S. 145, 162; *Barron v. Baltimore, supra* at 250—251; *Cohens v. Virginia*, 6 Wheat. 264, 416—420.

Investigation of the cases relied upon in *Twining v. New Jersey* to support the conclusion there reached that neither the Fifth Amendment's prohibition of compelled testimony, nor any of the Bill of Rights, applies to the States, reveals an unexplained departure from this salutary practice. Neither the briefs nor opinions in any of these cases, except *Maxwell v. Dow*, 176 U. S.

581, make reference to the legislative and contemporary history for the purpose of demonstrating that those who conceived, shaped, and brought about the adoption of the Fourteenth Amendment intended it to nullify this Court's decision in *Barron* v. *Baltimore, supra,* and thereby to make the Bill of Rights applicable to the States. In *Maxwell* v. *Dow, supra,* the issue turned on whether the Bill of Rights guarantee of a jury trial was, by the Fourteenth Amendment, extended to trials in state courts. In that case counsel for appellant did cite from the speech of Senator Howard, Appendix, *infra,* p. 104, which so emphatically stated the understanding of the framers of the Amendment—the Committee on Reconstruction for which he spoke— that the Bill of Rights was to be made applicable to the states by the Amendment's first section. The Court's opinion in *Maxwell* v. *Dow, supra,* 601, acknowledged that counsel had "cited from the speech of one of the Senators," but indicated that it was not advised what other speeches were made in the Senate or in the House. The Court considered, moreover, that "What individual Senators or Representatives may have urged in debate, in regard to the meaning to be given to a proposed constitutional amendment, or bill or resolution, does not furnish a firm ground for its proper construction, nor is it important as explanatory of the grounds upon which the members voted in adopting it." *Id.* at 601-602.

In the *Twining* case itself, the Court was cited to a then recent book, Guthrie, *Fourteenth Amendment to the Constitution* (1898). A few pages of that work recited some of the legislative background of the Amendment, emphasizing the speech of Senator Howard. But Guthrie did not emphasize the speeches of Congressman Bingham, nor the part he played in the framing and adoption of the first section of the Fourteenth Amendment. Yet Congressman Bingham may, without extravagance, be called the Madison of the first section of the Fourteenth Amendment. In the *Twining* opinion, the Court explicitly declined to give weight to the historical demonstration that the first section of the Amendment was intended to apply to the states the several protections of the Bill of Rights. It held that that question was "no longer open" because of previous decisions of this Court which, however, had not appraised the historical evidence on that subject. *Id.* at 98. The Court admitted that its action had resulted in giving "much less effect to the Fourteenth Amendment than some of the public men active in framing it" had intended it to have. *Id.* at 96. With particular reference to the guarantee against compelled testimony, the Court stated that "Much might be said in favor of the view that the privilege was guaranteed against state impairment as a privilege and immunity of National citizenship, but, as has been shown, the decisions of this court have foreclosed that view." *Id.* at 113. Thus the Court declined, and again today declines, to appraise the relevant historical evidence of the intended scope of the first section of the Amendment. Instead it relied upon previous cases, none of which had analyzed the evidence showing that one purpose of those who framed, advocated, and adopted the Amendment had been to make the Bill of Rights applicable to the States. None of the cases relied upon by the Court today made such an analysis.

For this reason, I am attaching to this dissent an appendix which contains a résumé, by no means complete, of the Amendment's history. In my judgment that history conclusively demonstrates that the language of the first section of the Fourteenth Amendment, taken as a whole, was thought by those responsible for its submission to the people, and by those who opposed its submission, sufficiently explicit to guarantee that thereafter no state could deprive its citizens of the privileges and protections of the Bill of Rights. Whether this Court ever will, or whether it now should, in the light of past decisions, give full effect to what the Amendment was intended to accomplish is not necessarily essential to a decision here. However that may be, our prior decisions, including *Twining,* do not prevent our carrying out that purpose, at least to the extent of making applicable to the states, not a mere part, as the Court has, but the full protection of the Fifth Amendment's provision against compelling evidence from an accused to convict him of crime. And I further contend that the "natural law" formula which the Court uses to reach its conclusion in this case should be abandoned as an incongruous excrescence on our Constitution. I believe that formula to be itself a violation of our Constitution, in that it subtly conveys to courts, at the expense of legislatures, ultimate power over public policies in fields where no specific provision of the Constitution limits legislative power. And my belief seems to be in accord with the views expressed by this Court, at least for the first two decades after the Fourteenth Amendment was adopted.

In 1872, four years after the Amendment was adopted, the *Slaughter-House* cases came to this Court. 16 Wall. 36. The Court was not presented in that case with the evidence which showed that the special sponsors of the Amendment in the House and Senate had expressly explained one of its principal purposes to be to change the Constitution as construed in *Barron* v. *Baltimore, supra,* and make the Bill of Rights applicable to the states. Nor was there reason to do so. For the state law under consideration in the *Slaughter-House* cases was only challenged as one which authorized a monopoly, and the brief for the challenger properly conceded that there was "no direct constitutional provision against a monopoly." The argument did not invoke any specific provision of the Bill of Rights, but urged that the state monopoly statute violated "the natural right of a person" to do business and engage in his trade or vocation. On this basis, it was contended that "bulwarks that have been erected around the investments of capital are impregnable against State legislation." These natural law arguments, so suggestive of the premises on which the present due process formula rests, were flatly rejected by a majority of the Court in the *Slaughter-House* cases. What the Court did hold was that the privileges and immunities clause of the Fourteenth Amendment only protected from state invasion such rights as a person has because he is a citizen of the United States. The Court enumerated some, but refused to enumerate all of these national rights. The majority of the Court emphatically declined the invitation of counsel to hold that the Fourteenth Amendment subjected all state regulatory legislation to continuous censorship by this Court in order for it to determine whether it collided with this Court's opinion of "natural" right and justice. In effect, the *Slaughter-House* cases rejected the very natural justice formula the Court today embraces. The Court did not meet the question of whether the safeguards of the Bill of Rights were protected against state invasion by the Fourteenth Amendment. And it specifically did not say as the Court now does, that particular provisions of the Bill of Rights could be breached by states in part, but not breached in other respects, according to this Court's notions of "civilized standards," "canons of decency," and "fundamental justice."

Later, but prior to the *Twining* case, this Court decided that the following were not "privileges or immunities" of national citizenship, so as to make them immune against state invasion: the Eighth Amendment's prohibition against cruel and unusual punishment, *In re Kemmler*, 136 U. S. 436; the Seventh Amendment's guarantee of a jury trial in civil cases, *Walker* v. *Sauvinet*, 92 U. S. 90; the Second Amendment's "right of the people to keep and bear Arms . . . ," *Presser* v. *Illinois*, 116 U. S. 252; the Fifth and Sixth Amendments' requirements for indictment in capital or other infamous crimes and for trial by jury in criminal prosecutions, *Maxwell* v. *Dow*, 176 U.S. 581. While it can be argued that these cases implied that no one of the provisions of the Bill of Rights was made applicable to the states as attributes of national citizenship, no one of them expressly so decided. In fact, the Court in *Maxwell* v. *Dow, supra* at 597-598, concluded no more than that "the privileges and immunities of citizens of the United States do not necessarily include all the rights protected by the first eight amendments to the Federal Constitution against the powers of the Federal Government." *Cf. Palko* v. *Connecticut*, 302 U. S. 319, 329.

After the *Slaughter-House* decision, the Court also said that states could, despite the "due process" clause of the Fourteenth Amendment, take private property without just compensation, *Davidson* v. *New Orleans*, 96 U. S. 97, 105; *Pumpelly* v. *Green Bay Co.*, 13 Wall., 166, 176-177; abridge the freedom of assembly guaranteed by the First Amendment, *United States* v. *Cruikshank*, 92 U. S. 542; see also *Prudential Ins. Co.* v. *Cheek*, 259 U. S. 530, 543; *Patterson* v. *Colorado*, 205 U. S. 454; *cf. Gitlow* v. *New York*, 268 U. S. 652, 666 (freedom of speech); prosecute for crime by information rather than indictment, *Hurtado* v. *People of California*, 110 U. S. 516; regulate the price for storage of grain in warehouses and elevators, *Munn* v. *Illinois*, 94 U. S. 113. But this Court also held in a number of cases that colored people must, because of the Fourteenth Amendment, be accorded equal protection of the laws. See, *e. g., Strauder* v. *West Virginia*, 100 U. S. 303; *cf. Virginia* v. *Rives*, 100 U. S. 313; see also *Yick Wo* v. *Hopkins*, 118 U. S. 356.

Thus, up to and for some years after 1873, when *Munn* v. *Illinois, supra,* was decided, this Court steadfastly declined to invalidate states' legislative regulation of property rights or business practices under the Fourteenth Amendment unless there were racial discrimination involved in the state law challenged. The first significant breach in this policy came in 1889, in *Chicago, M. & St. P. R. Co.* v. *Minnesota,* 134 U. S. 418. A state's railroad rate regulatory statute was there stricken as violative of the due process clause of the Fourteenth Amendment. This was accomplished by reference to a due process formula which did not necessarily operate so as to protect the Bill of Rights' personal liberty safeguards, but which gave a new and hitherto undiscovered scope for the Court's use of the due process clause to protect property rights under natural law concepts. And in 1896, in *Chicago, B. & Q. R. Co.* v. *Chicago,* 166 U. S. 226, this Court, in effect, overruled *Davidson* v. *New Orleans, supra,* by holding, under the new due process-natural law formula, that the Fourteenth Amendment forbade a state from taking private property for public use without payment of just compensation.

Following the pattern of the new doctrine formalized in the foregoing decisions, the Court in 1896 applied the due process clause to strike down a state statute which had forbidden certain types of contracts. *Allgeyer* v. *Louisiana,* 165 U. S. 578. *Cf. Hoopeston Canning Co.* v. *Cullen,* 318 U. S. 313, 316, 318—319. In doing so, it substantially adopted the rejected argument of counsel in the *Slaughter-House* cases, that the Fourteenth Amendment guarantees the liberty of all persons under "natural law" to engage in their chosen business or vocation. In the *Allgeyer* opinion, *id.* at 589, the Court quoted with approval the concurring opinion of Mr. Justice Bradley in a second *Slaughter-House* case, *Butchers' Union Co.* v. *Crescent City Co.,* 111 U. S. 746, 762, 764, 765, which closely followed one phase of the argument of his dissent in the original *Slaughter-House* cases—not that phase which argued that the Bill of Rights was applicable to the States. And in 1905, three years before the *Twining* case, *Lochner* v. *New York,* 198 U. S. 45, followed the argument used in *Allgeyer* to hold that the due process clause was violated by a state statute which limited the employment of bakery workers to sixty hours per week and ten hours per day.

The foregoing constitutional doctrine, judicially created and adopted by expanding the previously accepted meaning of "due process," marked a complete departure from the *Slaughter-House* philosophy of judicial tolerance of state regulation of business activities. Conversely, the new formula contracted the effectiveness of the Fourteenth Amendment as a protection from state infringement of individual liberties enumerated in the Bill of Rights. Thus the Court's second-thought interpretation of the Amendment was an about-face from the *Slaughter-House* interpretation and represented a failure to carry out the avowed purpose of the Amendment's sponsors. This reversal is dramatized by the fact that the *Hurtado* case, which had rejected the due process clause as an instrument for preserving Bill of Rights liberties and privileges, was cited as authority for expanding the scope of that clause so as to permit this Court to invalidate all state regulatory legislation it believed to be contrary to "fundamental" principles.

The *Twining* decision, rejecting the compelled testimony clause of the Fifth Amendment, and indeed rejecting all the Bill of Rights, is the end product of one phase of this philosophy. At the same time, that decision consolidated the power of the Court assumed in past cases by laying broader foundations for the Court to invalidate state and even federal regulatory legislation. For the *Twining* decision, giving separate consideration to "due process" and "privileges or immunities," went all the way to say that the "privileges or immunities" clause of the Fourteenth Amendment "did not forbid the States to abridge the personal rights enumerated in the first eight Amendments . . . ." *Twining* v. *New Jersey, supra,* 99. And in order to be certain, so far as possible, to leave this Court wholly free to reject all the Bill of Rights as specific restraints upon state action, the decision declared that even if this Court should decide that the due process clause forbids the states to infringe personal liberties guaranteed by the Bill of Rights, it would do so, not "because those rights are enumerated in the first eight Amendments, but because they are of such a nature that they are included in the conception of due process of law." *Ibid.*

At the same time that the *Twining* decision held that the states need not conform to the specific provisions of the Bill of Rights, it consolidated the power that the Court had assumed under the due process clause by laying even broader foundations for the Court to invalidate state and even federal regulatory legislation. For under the *Twining* formula, which includes non-regard for the first eight Amendments, what are "fundamental rights" and in accord with "canons of decency," as the Court said in *Twining,* and today reaffirms, is to be independently "ascertained from time to time by judicial action . . . ." *Id.* at 101; "what is due process of law depends on circumstances." *Moyer* v. *Peabody*, 212 U. S. 78, 84. Thus the power of legislatures became what this Court would declare it to be at a particular time independently of the specific guarantees of the Bill of Rights such as the right to freedom of speech, religion and assembly, the right to just compensation for property taken for a public purpose, the right to jury trial or the right to be secure against unreasonable searches and seizures. Neither the contraction of the Bill of Rights safeguards nor the invalidation of regulatory laws by this Court's appraisal of "circumstances" would readily be classified as the most satisfactory contribution of this Court to the nation. In 1912, four years after the *Twining* case was decided, a book written by Mr. Charles Wallace Collins gave the history of this Court's interpretation and application of the Fourteenth Amendment up to that time. It is not necessary for one fully to agree with all he said in order to appreciate the sentiment of the following comment concerning the disappointments caused by this Court's interpretation of the Amendment.

. . . It was aimed at restraining and checking the powers of wealth and privilege. It was to be a charter of liberty for human rights against property rights. The transformation has been rapid and complete. It operates today to protect the rights of property to the detriment of the rights of man. It has become the Magna Carta of accumulated and organized capital. Collins, the Fourteenth Amendment and the States, (1912) 137-8.

That this feeling was shared, at least in part, by members of this Court is revealed by the vigorous dissents that have been written in almost every case where the *Twining* and *Hurtado* doctrines have been applied to invalidate state regulatory laws.

Later decisions of this Court have completely undermined that phase of the *Twining* doctrine which broadly precluded reliance on the Bill of Rights to determine what is and what is not a "fundamental" right. Later cases have also made the *Hurtado* case an inadequate support for this phase of the *Twining* formula. For despite *Hurtado* and *Twining*, this Court has now held that the Fourteenth Amendment protects from state invasion the following "fundamental" rights safeguarded by the Bill of Rights: right to counsel in criminal cases, *Powell* v. *Alabama*, 287 U. S. 45, 67, limiting the *Hurtado* case; see also *Betts* v. *Brady*, 316 U. S. 455, and *De Meerleer* v. *Michigan*, 329 U. S. 663; freedom of assembly, *De Jonge* v. *Oregon*, 299 U. S. 353, 364; at the very least, certain types of cruel and unusual punishment and former jeopardy, *State of Louisiana ex rel. Francis* v. *Resweber*, 329 U. S. 459; the right of an accused in a criminal case to be informed of the charge against him, see *Snyder* v. *Massachusetts*, 291 U. S. 97, 105; the right to receive just compensation on account of taking private property for public use, *Chicago, B. & Q. R. Co.* v. *Chicago*, 166 U. S. 226. And the Court has now through the Fourteenth Amendment literally and emphatically applied the First Amendment to the States in its very terms. *Everson* v. *Board of Education*, 330 U. S. 1; *Board of Education* v. *Barnette*, 319 U. S. 624, 639; *Bridges* v. *California*, 314 U. S. 252, 268.

In *Palko* v. *Connecticut, supra*, a case which involved former jeopardy only, this Court re-examined the path it had traveled in interpreting the Fourteenth Amendment since the *Twining* opinion was written. In *Twining* the Court had declared that none of the rights enumerated in the first eight amendments were protected against state invasion because they were incorporated in the Bill of Rights. But the Court in *Palko, supra*, at 323, answered a contention that all eight applied with the more guarded statement, similar to that the Court had used in *Maxwell* v. *Dow, supra* at 597, that "there is no such general rule." Implicit in this statement, and in the cases decided in the interim between *Twining* and *Palko* and since, is the understanding that some of the eight Amendments do apply by their very terms. Thus the Court said in the *Palko* case that the Fourteenth Amendment may make it unlawful for a state to abridge by its statutes the "freedom of speech which the

First Amendment safeguards against encroachment by the Congress . . . or the like freedom of the press . . . or the free exercise of religion . . . , or the right of peaceable assembly . . . or the right of one accused of crime to the benefit of counsel . . . . In these and other situations immunities that are valid as against the federal government by force of the specific pledges of particular amendments have been found to be implicit in the concept of ordered liberty, and thus, through the Fourteenth Amendment, become valid as against the states." *Id.* at 324-325. The Court went on to describe the Amendments made applicable to the States as "the privileges and immunities that have been taken over from the earlier articles of the federal bill of rights and brought within the Fourteenth Amendment by a process of absorption." *Id.* at 326. In the *Twining* case fundamental liberties were things apart from the Bill of Rights. Now it appears that at least some of the provisions of the Bill of Rights in their very terms satisfy the Court as sound and meaningful expressions of fundamental liberty. If the Fifth Amendment's protection against self-incrimination be such an expression of fundamental liberty, I ask, and have not found a satisfactory answer, why the Court today should consider that it should be "absorbed" in part but not in full? *Cf.* Warren, The New "Liberty" under the Fourteenth Amendment, 39 Harv. L. Rev. 431, 458—461 (1926). Nothing in the *Palko* opinion requires that when the Court decides that a Bill of Rights' provision is to be applied to the States, it is to be applied piecemeal. Nothing in the *Palko* opinion recommends that the Court apply part of an Amendment's established meaning and discard that part which does not suit the current style of fundamentals. . . .

I cannot consider the Bill of Rights to be an outworn 18th Century "strait jacket" as the *Twining* opinion did. Its provisions may be thought outdated abstractions by some. And it is true that they were designed to meet ancient evils. But they are the same kind of human evils that have emerged from century to century wherever excessive power is sought by the few at the expense of the many. In my judgment the people of no nation can lose their liberty so long as a Bill of Rights like ours survives and its basic purposes are conscientiously interpreted, enforced and respected so as to afford continuous protection against old, as well as new, devices and practices which might thwart those purposes. I fear to see the consequences of the Court's practice of substituting its own concepts of decency and fundamental justice for the language of the Bill of Rights as its point of departure in interpreting and enforcing that Bill of Rights. If the choice must be between the selective process of the *Palko* decision applying some of the Bill of Rights to the States, or the *Twining* rule applying none of them, I would choose the *Palko* selective process. But rather than accept either of these choices, I would follow what I believe was the original purpose of the Fourteenth Amendment—to extend to all the people of the nation the complete protection of the Bill of Rights. To hold that this Court can determine what, if any, provisions of the Bill of Rights will be enforced, and if so to what degree, is to frustrate the great design of a written Constitution.

Conceding the possibility that this Court is now wise enough to improve on the Bill of Rights by substituting natural law concepts for the Bill of Rights, I think the possibility is entirely too speculative to agree to take that course. I would therefore hold in this case that the full protection of the Fifth Amendment's proscription against compelled testimony must be afforded by California. This I would do because of reliance upon the original purpose of the Fourteenth Amendment.

It is an illusory apprehension that literal application of some or all of the provisions of the Bill of Rights to the States would unwisely increase the sum total of the powers of this Court to invalidate state legislation. The Federal Government has not been harmfully burdened by the requirement that enforcement of federal laws affecting civil liberty conform literally to the Bill of Rights. Who would advocate its repeal? It must be conceded, of course, that the natural law due process formula, which the Court today reaffirms, has been interpreted to limit substantially this Court's power to prevent state violations of the individual civil liberties guaranteed by the Bill of Rights. But this formula also has been used in the past, and can be used in the future, to license this Court, in considering regulatory legislation, to roam at large in the broad expanses of policy and morals and to trespass, all too freely, on the legislative domain of the States as well as the Federal Government.

Since *Marbury* v. *Madison*, 1 Cranch 137, was decided, the practice has been firmly established, for better or worse, that courts can strike down legislative enactments which violate the Constitution. This process, of course, involves interpretation, and since words can have many meanings, interpretation obviously may result in contraction or extension of the original purpose of a constitutional provision, thereby affecting policy. But to pass upon the constitutionality of statutes by looking to the particular standards enumerated in the Bill of Rights and other parts of the Constitution is one thing; to invalidate statutes because of application of "natural law" deemed to be above and undefined by the Constitution is another. "In the one instance, courts proceeding within clearly marked constitutional boundaries seek to execute policies written into the Constitution; in the other, they roam at will in the limitless area of their own beliefs as to reasonableness and actually select policies, a responsibility which the Constitution entrusts to the legislative representatives of the people." *Federal Power Commission* v. *Pipeline Co.*, 315 U. S. 575, 599, 601, n. 4.

Commentary

If one thing is clear from the legislative history of the Fourteenth Amendment, it is that its provisions were intended, as a minimum, to protect the civil rights of the newly-emancipated Negro. So much was, indeed, conceded by the Supreme Court itself in the *Slaughter-House Cases* (*supra* p. 335). It cannot, however, be disputed that, until our own day, the Fourteenth Amendment fell far short of its primary purpose of ensuring equal rights for the Negro. The anomaly here results from the fact that, during the same period, while the amendment was of little value to the Negro, for whose benefit it had immediately been intended, it was being developed by the Supreme Court as the legal safeguard of property rights, particularly those of corporations.

The Fourteenth Amendment provision designed directly to prevent discrimination against the emancipated race was the equal protection clause. In *Plessy* v. *Ferguson*, 163 U.S. 537 (1896), however, the Supreme Court construed that clause in a manner which enabled discrimination against the Negro to be condoned by law. At issue in *Plessy* was the claim that a Louisiana statute requiring separate railroad accommodations for Negro and white passengers violated the Fourteenth Amendment's requirement of equal protection of the laws. The Court rejected the contention and held, on the contrary, that mere segregation in transportation did not violate the equal protection clause. The Court refused to accept "the assumption that the enforced separation of the two races stamps the colored race with a badge of inferiority." Under the Court's doctrine, so long as laws requiring segregation did not establish unequal facilities for the Negro, he was not denied the equal protection of the laws. As the Court explained it in *Brown* v. *Board of Education* (*infra* p. 361), "Under that doctrine, equality of treatment is accorded when the races are provided substantially equal facilities, even though these facilities be separate."

Plessy v. *Ferguson* gave the lie to the American ideal, so eloquently stated by Justice John Harlan in dissent there: "Our Constitution is color-blind, and neither knows nor tolerates classes among citizens." Upon *Plessy* was built the whole structure of segregation that has been at the heart of the Southern system of racial discrimination.

It was not until the 1954 case of *Brown* v. *Board of Education* that the "separate but equal" doctrine of *Plessy* v. *Ferguson* was overruled by the Supreme Court. Paradoxically, perhaps, the road to the *Brown* decision was pointed to by the proviso of equality laid down in *Plessy* v. *Ferguson* itself, whose doctrine had been the legal cornerstone of Southern segregation. Starting in 1937, the Supreme Court began to emphasize the requirement of equality in the separate facilities provided for the Negro in the field of education. The cases from 1937 to 1954 placed ever increasing stress upon the judicial implementation of the requirement of equality in facilities. The

360

Court's decisions tended toward the doctrine that, where higher education is concerned, separate facilities for the Negro are inherently unequal. From there, it was a short (though vital) step to the *Brown* decision itself, for what is true of segregation in higher education is also true of segregation as such. There can never be real equality in separated facilities, for the mere fact of segregation makes for discrimination. The arbitrary separation of the Negro, solely on the basis of race, is, in the phrase of the *Plessy* dissent, a "badge of servitude" and must generate in him a feeling of inferior social status, regardless of the formal equality of the facilities provided for him. And if that be the case, then, as the *Brown* decision ruled, segregation as such is discriminatory and hence a denial of the equal protection of the laws demanded by the Fourteenth Amendment.

What is true of segregation in education is equally true of other types of racial segregation. Under *Brown*, all segregation must be ruled violative of the Fourteenth Amendment's equal protection clause, thus removing the legal prop for the whole pattern of southern discrimination against the Negro. The *Brown* decision outlawing segregation in schools was thus as momentous as any ever rendered by a judicial tribunal. For make no mistake about it, it will ultimately have an impact upon a whole community's way of life comparable to that caused by the most drastic political revolution or military conflict. That is, of course, exactly what was intended by the framers of the Fourteenth Amendment, and, under *Brown*, their intent in the field of civil rights has, for the first time, been given full effect by the law.

BROWN v. *BOARD OF EDUCATION,*
347 U. S. 483 (1954)

MR. CHIEF JUSTICE WARREN delivered the opinion of the Court.

These cases come to us from the States of Kansas, South Carolina, Virginia, and Delaware. They are premised on different facts and different local conditions, but a common legal question justifies their consideration together in this consolidated opinion.

In each of the cases, minors of the Negro race, through their legal representatives, seek the aid of the courts in obtaining admission to the public schools of their community on a nonsegregated basis. In each instance, they had been denied admission to schools attended by white children under laws requiring or permitting segregation according to race. This segregation was alleged to deprive the plaintiffs of the equal protection of the laws under the Fourteenth Amendment. In each of the cases other than the Delaware case, a three-judge federal district court denied relief to the plaintiffs on the so-called "separate but equal" doctrine announced by this Court in *Plessy* v. *Ferguson,* 163 U.S. 537. Under that doctrine, equality of treatment is accorded when the races are provided substantially equal facilities, even though these facilities be separate. In the Delaware case, the Supreme Court of Delaware adhered to that doctrine, but ordered that the plaintiffs be admitted to the white schools because of their superiority to the Negro schools.

The plaintiffs contend that segregated public schools are not "equal" and cannot be made "equal," and that hence they are deprived of the equal protection of the laws. Because of the obvious importance of the question presented, the Court took jurisdiction. Argument was heard in the 1952 Term, and reargument was heard this Term on certain questions propounded by the Court.

Reargument was largely devoted to the circumstances surrounding the adoption of the Fourteenth Amendment in 1868. It covered exhaustively consideration of the Amendment in Congress, ratification by the states, then existing practices in racial segregation, and the views of proponents and opponents of the Amendment. This discussion and our own investigation convince us that, although these sources cast some light, it is not enough to resolve the problem with which we are faced. At best, they are inconclusive. The most avid proponents of the post-War Amendments undoubtedly intended them to remove all legal distinctions among "all persons born or naturalized in the United States." Their opponents, just as certainly, were antagonistic to both the letter and the spirit of the Amendments and wished them to have the most limited effect. What others in Congress and the state legislatures had in mind cannot be determined with any degree of certainty.

An additional reason for the inconclusive nature of the Amendment's history, with respect to segregated schools, is the status of public education at that time. In the South, the movement toward free common schools, supported by general taxation, had not yet taken hold. Education of white children was largely in the hands of private groups. Education of Negroes was almost nonexistent, and practically all of the race were illiterate. In fact, any education of Negroes was forbidden by law in some states. Today, in contrast, many Negroes have achieved outstanding success in the arts and sciences as well as in the business and professional world. It is true that public school education at the time of the Amendment had advanced further in the North, but the effect of the Amendment on Northern States was generally ignored in the congressional debates. Even in the North, the conditions of public education did not approximate those existing today. The curriculum was usually rudimentary; ungraded schools were common in rural areas; the school term was but three months a year in many states; and compulsory school attendance was virtually unknown. As a consequence, it is not surprising that there should be so little in the history of the Fourteenth Amendment relating to its intended effect on public education.

In the first cases in this Court construing the Fourteenth Amendment, decided shortly after its adoption, the Court interpreted it as proscribing all state-imposed discriminations against the Negro race. The doctrine of "separate but equal" did not make its appearance in this Court until 1896 in the case of *Plessy* v. *Ferguson, supra,* involving not education but transportation. American courts have since labored with the doctrine for over half a century. In this Court, there have been six cases involving the "separate but equal" doctrine in the field of public education. In *Cumming* v. *County Board of Education,* 175 U. S. 528, and *Gong Lum* v. *Rice,* 275 U. S. 78, the validity of the doctrine itself was not challenged. In more recent cases, all on the graduate school level, inequality was found in that specific benefits enjoyed by white students were denied to Negro students of the same educational qualifications. *Missouri ex rel. Gaines* v. *Canada,* 305 U. S. 337; *Sipuel* v. *Oklahoma,* 332 U. S. 631; *Sweatt* v. *Painter,* 339 U. S. 629; *McLaurin* v. *Oklahoma State Regents,* 339 U. S. 637. In none of these cases was it necessary to re-examine the doctrine to grant relief to the Negro plaintiff. And in *Sweatt* v. *Painter, supra,* the Court expressly reserved decision on the question whether *Plessy* v. *Ferguson* should be held inapplicable to public education.

In the instant cases, that question is directly presented. Here, unlike *Sweatt* v. *Painter,* there are findings below that the Negro and white schools involved have been equalized, or are being equalized, with respect to buildings, curricula, qualifications and salaries of teachers, and other "tangible" factors. Our decision, therefore, cannot turn on merely a comparison of these tangible factors in the Negro and white schools involved in each of the cases. We must look instead to the effect of segregation itself on public education.

In approaching this problem, we cannot turn the clock back to 1868 when the Amendment was adopted, or even to 1896 when *Plessy* v. *Ferguson* was written. We must consider public education in the light of its full development and its present place in American life throughout the Nation. Only in this way can it be determined if segregation in public schools deprives these plaintiffs of the equal protection of the laws.

Today, education is perhaps the most important function of state and local governments. Compulsory school attendance laws and the great expenditures for education both demonstrate our recognition of the importance of education to our democratic society. It is required in the performance of our most basic public responsibilities, even service in the armed forces. It is the very foundation of good citizenship. Today it is a principal instrument in awakening the child to cultural values, in preparing him for later professional training, and in helping him to adjust normally to his environment. In these days, it is doubtful that any child may reasonably be expected to succeed in life if he is denied the opportunity of an education. Such an opportunity, where the state has undertaken to provide it, is a right which must be made available to all on equal terms.

We come then to the question presented: Does segregation of children in public schools solely on the basis of race, even though the physical facilities and other "tangible" factors may be equal, deprive the children of the minority group of equal educational opportunities? We believe that it does.

In *Sweatt* v. *Painter, supra*, in finding that a segregated law school for Negroes could not provide them equal educational opportunities, this Court relied in large part on "those qualities which are incapable of objective measurement but which make for greatness in a law school." In *McLaurin* v. *Oklahoma State Regents, supra*, the Court, in requiring that a Negro admitted to a white graduate school be treated like all other students, again resorted to intangible considerations: ". . . his ability to study, to engage in discussions and exchange views with other students, and, in general, to learn his profession." Such considerations apply with added force to children in grade and high schools. To separate them from others of similar age and qualifications solely because of their race generates a feeling of inferiority as to their status in the community that may affect their hearts and minds in a way unlikely ever to be undone. The effect of this separation on their educational opportunities was well stated by a finding in the Kansas case by a court which nevertheless felt compelled to rule against the Negro plaintiffs:

Segregation of white and colored children in public schools has a detrimental effect upon the colored children. The impact is greater when it has the sanction of the law; for the policy of separating the races is usually interpreted as denoting the inferiority of the negro group. A sense of inferiority affects the motivation of a child to learn. Segregation with the sanction of law, therefore, has a tendency to [retard] the educational and mental development of negro children and to deprive them of some of the benefits they would receive in a racial [ly] integrated school system.

Whatever may have been the extent of psychological knowledge at the time of *Plessy* v. *Ferguson,* this finding is amply supported by modern authority. Any language in *Plessy* v. *Ferguson* contrary to this finding is rejected.

We conclude that in the field of public education the doctrine of "separate but equal" has no place. Separate educational facilities are inherently unequal. Therefore, we hold that the plaintiffs and others similarly situated for whom the actions have been brought are, by reason of the segregation complained of, deprived of the equal protection of the laws guaranteed by the Fourteenth Amendment. This disposition makes unnecessary any discussion whether such segregation also violates the Due Process Clause of the Fourteenth Amendment. . . .

THE FIFTEENTH AMENDMENT

Commentary

According to perhaps the most famous passage in Aristotle, man is by nature a political animal. That being the case, it is scarcely surprising that among the most precious rights of citizenship are those denoted as political. Without such rights, indeed, it may be doubted that an individual can be said truly to attain the dignity of citizenship. The essential aspect of citizenship is the ability to share in government. Such ability is patently lacking in one who does not possess basic political rights.

The Fourteenth Amendment (*supra* p. 184) vested the emancipated Negro with the dignity of citizenship. But it did not expressly extend the franchise to the freedmen. In the congressional debates, opponents of the Fourteenth Amendment had asserted, and its supporters strongly denied, that the amendment's first section would have the effect of conferring the right to vote upon Negroes. The lack of express provision in it on the right of suffrage has prevented the Fourteenth Amendment by itself from affecting state power to restrict the franchise on racial grounds. For such power to be eliminated, further constitutional provision was necessary. The need was met by the Fifteenth Amendment, which specifically prohibits both the Federal Government and the states from denying or abridging the right of citizens to vote "on account of race, color, or previous condition of servitude."

There can be no doubt of the primary purpose of the Fifteenth Amendment. As one of the three post-Civil War amendments, it was a vital part of the program to emancipate the Negro and guarantee to him a full and equal legal status in the society, by, as Justice John Harlan once put it, protecting "all the civil rights that pertain to freedom and citizenship." The Fifteenth Amendment was written into the Constitution to open to the recently liberated race full participation in the process of government. Such participation was to be ensured by securing to the Negro the same political franchise as others in the community.

The significance of the Fifteenth Amendment is to be found in the crucial position of the right to vote as the most important attribute of citizenship in a system of representative government. For a racial minority like the Negro, indeed, the right of suffrage is more than a symbol of its role in a democracy. In a system such as ours, political action is a principal instrument for the protection of individual and group rights. As a disenfranchised minority, the Negro would have little hope to exert political pressure to bring about an end to discriminatory practices.

The Fifteenth Amendment itself has its origins in some of the proposals considered by the Joint Committee on Reconstruction, which (as seen *supra* p. 186) drafted the Fourteenth Amendment. An early version of that amendment provided for the striking down of state laws "whereby any distinction is made in *political* or civil rights or privileges, on account of race, creed, or color" (*supra* p. 188, emphasis added). Such proposal was voted down in the committee. Another approach—that of prospective guaranty of suffrage—was taken in the proposed Fourteenth Amendment introduced by Congressman Thaddeus Stevens [R., Pa.] on April 21, 1866. Under it, after 1876, no discrimination was to be made by the Federal Government or any state "as to the enjoyment by classes or persons of the right of suffrage, because of race, color, or previous condition of servitude."

The Stevens proposal was adopted by the Joint Committee; but strong opposition soon developed among the more moderate congressional Republicans, who felt that Negro suffrage tied to the party program would be a handicap in the coming elections. The committee receded from its position and (as already seen) the Fourteenth Amendment ultimately reported by it and voted by the Congress contained no express reference to the right of suffrage, except in its second section, which provides for indirect enforcement of the right to vote through congressional power to reduce the representation of states in which the right to vote is abridged. The congressional power thus granted has, however, never been exercised and the Fourteenth Amendment has had little practical impact upon the right of suffrage.

The next stage in the federal effort to extend the suffrage to the Negro was through the Reconstruction Act of 1867. Under it, the southern states could escape from military occupation only by adopting constitutions which guaranteed the elective franchise to all males over twenty-one years, "of whatever race, color, or previous condition." By statutes of 1868, the southern states were admitted to representation only upon condition that their constitutions would never be so altered as to deprive the enfranchised Negro of the right to vote.

After the ratification of the Fourteenth Amendment, July 28, 1868, and the Presidential election of 1868, a new effort was made to protect Negro suffrage by constitutional guaranty. Such effort culminated in the Fifteenth Amendment, which passed Congress in 1869 and was ratified in 1870.

The Congressional history of the Fifteenth Amendment starts with the introduction in the two houses of proposed amendments reported by the House and Senate Judiciary Committees. The House version was introduced on January 11 (infra p. 372), and the Senate version on January 15, 1869 (infra p. 372). Both provided for prohibitions against denial or abridgment of the right to vote on racial grounds. The Senate version was drafted in almost exactly the language that ultimately became the Fifteenth Amendment, with the important difference that, as introduced in the upper House, the proposed amendment would have protected both "The right . . . to vote and hold office," while the version finally passed guarantees only "The right . . . to vote."

The proposed Fifteenth Amendment was opposed by two principal groups in the Congress. First, there were those who were completely hostile to any constitutional protection of the right of suffrage. The more moderate of these opponents focused their attack upon the alleged invasion of states' rights that would be involved in federalizing the right of suffrage. The more extreme opponents denied the authority to amend the Constitution in this respect—an argument that today, at least, seems without any constitutional basis, in view of the unrestrained reach of the amending power under Article V (except for the two specific restrictions mentioned there, which have nothing to do with the subject of suffrage). Relatively few in the congressional debates attacked the amendment on the ground of alleged Negro inferiority—which is itself surprising, considering that the Negro was still a slave less than a decade earlier.

More influential in the Fortieth Congress than those who opposed any constitutional protection of the right to vote were those who went to the opposite extreme and attacked the proposed Fifteenth Amendment as not going far enough. They sought a broader provision guaranteeing universal male suffrage, rather than one limiting its protection to those denied the right to vote on racial grounds. Led by Representative John Bingham [R., Ohio] (who had, as seen *supra* p. 185, played so important a part in the drafting of the Fourteenth Amendment), they sought to substitute an amendment prohibiting any state from denying to United States citizens the right to vote, except on the grounds of sex, age, residence, or crime. Substitute amendments to such effect were introduced in both Houses, but were overwhelmingly defeated. The proponents of universal male suffrage then tried another substitute (reminiscent of the early version of the Fourteenth Amendment drafted by Bingham, *supra* p. 189), which gave Congress the power to abolish any state restrictions upon the right to vote. This, too, was defeated and the attempt to impose a uniform rule of universal male suffrage was given up.

The universal suffragists urged, as Senator Willard Warner [R., Ala.] put it, that "The question before us is not one of Negro suffrage. It is the question of suffrage in itself." To others who sought to change the draft amendment, however, the only issue was that of Negro suffrage, and they urged that the provision should be worded only to make the Negro a voter. Such was the purpose of the substitute introduced by Senator Jacob Howard [R., Mich.], under which citizens of African descent were given the same right to vote as other citizens. This proposal was supported by senators from the Pacific Coast, since it eliminated the problem of Chinese suffrage. But it was opposed by the bulk of those in favor of extending the right of suffrage on the ground that, if the principle involved was correct, it should not be restricted to one named race—as Senator William Stewart [R., Nev.] put it, "Why a distinction against the descendants of other countries?"

The only important question remaining in the Congressional debate was whether the version of the proposed amendment reported by the House or Senate Judiciary Committee was to be adopted. The House passed the version reported by its committee. The Senate ultimately passed the version reported by its committee as a substitute for the House bill. A conference committee was appointed and it recommended that the Senate version be adopted with the deletion of the words "or hold office." Thus was drafted the final form of the Fifteenth Amendment, as a protection of the right to vote against discrimination on grounds of race, color, or previous condition of servitude. The conference report was concurred in by the House almost without debate on February 23, 1869, by 144 to 44 (35 not voting). It was bitterly attacked by some senators, but was finally agreed to on February 26, by 39 to 13 (14 absent). The Fifteenth Amendment thus passed by Congress became part of the Constitution on March 30, 1870.

One point remains to be noted with regard to the legislative history of the Fifteenth Amendment—and it is one that is of particular interest in view of recent civil rights legislation. One of the substitute amendments offered during the congressional debates would have prohibited discrimination in voting "on account of race, color, nativity, property, *education,* or religious belief" (*infra* p. 408, emphasis added). Such prohibition, if adopted, would plainly have outlawed all educational qualifications upon the right to vote, including literacy tests. It was actually passed by the Senate, which feared that the South might still be able to disenfranchise the Negro by the imposition of educational tests. Though such fear was to prove well founded, at the time it was taken the Senate action aroused a storm of protest. Despite the strong support of Congressman Bingham, the House rejected the substitute amendment, and the Senate itself then voted in its place the version originally recommended by its Judiciary Committee.

It can be argued that the congressional rejection of the substitute amendment barring educational qualifications upon suffrage indicates a clear legislative intent not to have the Fifteenth Amendment affect state power to impose such qualifications, including literacy tests. If that is true, it can be said that the original intent in this respect has been frustrated by the Voting Rights Act of 1965 provisions which do override state literacy requirements (*infra* vol. II) and the Supreme Court decisions upholding Congressional power to enact such provisions (*infra* vol. II). It may be doubted, however, whether those who wrote and voted the Fifteenth Amendment realized the extent to which their command of racial equality in the electoral process would be thwarted by state literacy tests. From such point of view, the Supreme Court today is correct in holding that the congressional authority to enforce the Fifteenth Amendment includes the power to proscribe literacy tests where they are used as vehicles of racial discrimination.

AMENDMENT XV

March 30, 1870

SEC. 1. The right of citizens of the United States to vote shall not be denied or abridged by the United States or by any State on account of race, color, or previous condition of servitude.

SEC. 2. The Congress shall have power to enforce this article by appropriate legislation.

THE DEBATE

GEORGE BOUTWELL [DEM., MASS.]. I now report from the Committee on the Judiciary joint resolution (H. R. No. 363) proposing an amendment to the Constitution of the United States. . . .

The joint resolution (H. R. No. 402) proposing an amendment to the Constitution of the United States was read a first and second time.

RUFUS SPALDING [DEM., OHIO]. I ask that the joint resolution be read in full.

The joint resolution was read, as follows:

Be it resolved by the Senate and House of Representatives of the United States of America in Congress assembled, (two thirds of both Houses concurring,) That the following article be proposed to the Legislatures of the several States as an amendment to the Constitution of the United States, which, when ratified by three fourths of said Legislatures, shall be held as part of said Constitution, namely:

ARTICLE

SEC. 1. The right of any citizen of the United States to vote shall not be denied or abridged by the United States or any State by reason of the race, color, or previous condition of slavery of any citizen or class of citizens of the United States.

SEC. 2. The Congress shall have power to enforce by proper legislation the provisions of this article.

MR. BOUTWELL. I move that the joint resolution be printed and recommitted to the Committee on the Judiciary.

The motion was agreed to. . . .

CHARLES SUMNER [R., MASS.]. What disposition does the Senator propose of those papers [ie., petitions for protection of the right to vote]?

WILLIAM STEWART [R., NEV.]. I ask that the committee be discharged from the further consideration of these petitions. We have reported a constitutional amendment on the subject.

MARTIN THAYER [R., PA.]. Providing for universal suffrage?

MR. STEWART. Yes, sir. The amendment reported is very short; I ask that it be read.

The Secretary read the amendment reported by the Committee on the Judiciary to Senate joint resolution No. 8. The committee propose the following article of amendment to the Constitution:

ART. 15. The right of citizens of the United States to vote and hold office shall not be denied or abridged by the United States, or any State, on account of race, color, or previous condition or servitude. And Congress shall have power to enforce the provisions of this article by appropriate legislation. . . .

House of Representatives-40th Congress, 3rd Session
January 27, 1869

JOHN BINGHAM [R., OHIO]. Before the question is put on that motion I desire to ask that an amendment which I design to offer as a substitute for the proposed constitutional amendment be ordered to be printed.

There being no objection, the amendment was ordered to be printed. It is as follows:

Insert in lieu of section one of the article proposed to be added to the Constitution the following:

No State shall make or enforce any law which shall abridge or deny to any male citizen of the United States, of sound mind, and over twenty-one years of age, the equal exercise of the elective franchise at all elections in the State wherein he shall have actually resided for a period of one year next preceding such election, except such of said citizens as shall hereafter engage in rebellion or insurrection, or who may have been or shall be duly convicted of treason or other crime of the grade of felony at common law.

HAMILTON WARD [R., N.Y.]. I ask that an amendment which I propose to offer be also printed.

There being no objection, the amendment was ordered to be printed. It is as follows:

In lieu of section one of the article proposed to be added to the Constitution insert the following:

No State shall make or enforce any law which shall deny to any male citizen of the United States over twenty-one years of age, who has been such citizen for three months, the free exercise of the elective franchise in the State of his residence, except to punishment for treason or other crime of the grade of felony at common law, whereof the person shall have been duly convicted. But this article shall not affect persons now disfranchised for participation in rebellion, nor prevent the execution of such proper registration and naturalization laws as may be needed to protect the people in a just exercise of the elective franchise, nor to affect such qualifications of electors as to time of residence as may be imposed by law for a period of one year or less. . . .

SHELBY CULLOM [R., KY.]. . . . And, sir, in the work of reconstruction, and in our efforts to establish the Government upon just principles, a constitutional amendment regulating the question of suffrage throughout the land should be passed and sent to the States for their consideration without delay. Nothing but a Constitution guarantying impartial laws and impartial liberty will satisfy the demands of justice or the people and place the Government on a sure foundation. An amendment declaring the immunities of citizens, and guarantying a republican form of government by securing the elective franchise to citizens deprived of it by reason of race or color or previous condition, if sent to the States without unreasonable delay, may be acted upon by the State Legislatures of the Union, which are now or will very soon be, in session, and it will be but a short time before the Government will be substantially just in giving civil and political rights to all its citizens. If in less than a century from the adoption of the Declaration of Independence this nation guaranties by constitutional provision perfect civil and political rights to all its citizens we may justly be proud, and believe that our trials and sufferings may not have been all in vain.

I am for the constitutional amendment reported by the gentleman from Massachusetts from the Reconstruction Committee and now before the House for consideration. I am not sure but it may be improved. The language should be such as to cover the case and not require amending again when in a short time some other injustice grows up among the people not based upon the question of race, color, or previous condition of slavery. I am getting tired of that expression. May there not be need of making the amendment broader? There are to-day many people in the country who have amassed fortunes, who are living in luxury, who look down with scorn upon the poor. They believe the poor man has no right to impose taxes upon them for schools, railroads, or anything else. They do not believe the poor man ought to vote. Some of the States now have property qualifications, and a colored man cannot vote unless he happens to own a certain amount of property. Again, there is a large portion of the educated people of the country who believe that they are the people who are peculiarly fitted to do all the voting, and that the unlettered man ought not to have the right to vote; they are willing to let the man who cannot read do the fighting, but desire his exclusion from the ballot. This is all wrong; and in my judgment this proposed amendment ought to be broader and more comprehensive, so that we may not be called upon soon again to support another.

Men may say there is no danger from these causes. There may not be at present, though I do not admit it; but if there is not we should look to possibilities in the future as we seek to amend the great Magna Charta of the country. As the country gets older and riches accumulate in families from generation to generation it will become less and less interested in the condition of the people, and aristocracy, backed up by wealth, will seek to make the poor subservient to its demands, and then the oppressed will cry out for protection, and ask that it shall be guarantied by the Constitution. Already, sir, the monopolies of the country are becoming the chief rulers of the land. Capital thrown together and fostered and aided by legislation, State and national, in the shape of railroad charters, organizing companies, and allowing consolidations, and aided by enormous land grants and money subsidies, are ruling the country from one end of it to the other, and the galleries and lobbies of every Legislature, State and national, are thronged with men seeking to procure an advantage over the mass of the people by legislation, adding to their already overgrown fortunes. The people have these things to fear. These monopolies are to be used in the future as mighty engines to oppress the people who, remain at home pursuing an honest avocation scarcely imagining what oppressions may be in store for them in the future. I hope the committee who reported this amendment will take it back, by consent of the House, and make it broad enough to protect the people in the future against oppressive legislation either on account of race, color, or previous condition, or by capital, or any other element that may seek to oppress any portion of the people of the land. . . .

Senate-40th Congress, 3rd Session
January 28-9, 1869

THE PRESIDENT PRO TEMPORE [BENJAMIN WADE, R., OHIO]. The order of the day, the joint resolution (S. R. No. 8) proposing an amendment to the Constitution of the United States, is now before the Senate as in Committee of the Whole, and the pending question is on the amendment reported by the Committee on the Judiciary.

WILLIAM STEWART [R., NEV.]. I do not propose to occupy the time of the Senate in discussing this great question at any length. It is the culmination of a contest which has lasted for thirty years. It is the logical result of the rebellion, of the abolition of slavery, and of the conflicts in this country during and before the war. Every person in the country has discussed it; it has been discussed in every local paper, by every local speaker; it has been discussed at the firesides; and now we are to place the grand result, I hope, in the Constitution of the United States. And let me remind my fellow-Senators that it is well that this work be now done, for we have realized the force of the very pointed sentence which was read here from the Swiss address, that "undetermined questions have no pity for the repose of mankind." This question can never rest until it is finally disposed of. This amendment is a declaration to make all men, without regard to race or color, equal before the law. The arguments in favor of it are so numerous, so convincing, that they carry conviction to every mind. The proposition itself has been recognized by the good men of this nation; and it is important, as the new administration enters upon the charge of the affairs of this country, that it should start on this high and noble principle that all men are free and equal, that they are really equal before the law. We cannot stop short of this.

It must be done. It is the only measure that will really abolish slavery. It is the only guarantee against peon laws and against oppression. It is that guarantee which was put in the Constitution of the United States originally, the guarantee that each man shall have a right to protect his own liberty. It repudiates that arrogant, self-righteous assumption, that one man can be charged with the liberties and destinies of another. You may put this in the form of legislative enactment; you may empower Congress to legislate; you may empower the States to legislate, and they will agitate the question. Let it be made the immutable law of the land; let it be fixed; and then we shall have peace. Until then there is no peace. I cannot add to the many eloquent speeches that have been made on this great question in this House. I will not attempt it. I want a vote. I will not occupy time. The proposition itself is more eloquent than man can be. It is a declaration too high, too grand, too noble, too just, to be ornamented by oratory. I hope we shall soon have a vote upon the question. . . .

THE PRESIDING OFFICER [THOMAS FERRY, R., MICH.]. The question is on the amendment reported by the Committee on the Judiciary, to strike out:

No State shall deny or abridge the right of its citizens to vote and hold office on account of race color, or previous condition.

And in lieu thereof to insert:

The right of citizens of the United States to vote, and hold office shall not be denied or abridged by the United States or any State on account of race, color, or previous condition of servitude.

The amendment was agreed to. . . .

JOSEPH FOWLER [R., TENN.]. . . . . In regard to the proposition to amend the Constitution, I will say that it is known that I am altogether in favor of manhood suffrage, and have been for years. I do not know, however, that I prefer to see the Constitution changed to perfect that purpose. It is a matter that to some extent ought to be left to the reflection of the people, and the change ought to be made by the people of the various States themselves. I would rather see an indication on the part of the people of the United States expressive of their entire confidence in the freedom of the individual than to see us put into the Constitution an arbitrary and fixed rule that cannot be changed and cannot be reformed without revolution.

Besides that, there is another objection in my mind to this provision going into the Constitution, and that is this: if it is intended to be an expression of the fact that the American people have risen to the point of acknowledging the freedom of the individual—that the individual is free—if this is to be an expression of individual freedom, it does not go far enough. While I am in favor of all citizens of the United States having the right to vote and hold office, without respect to race or color, I would rather go a little further than that. I would not by any means be willing to debar the women of the country from giving their suffrage or their expression in regard to the authority of laws to control or govern them, as I do not believe that any responsible person can be controlled by the authority of any other one. There is no reason why you, sir, should be governed by any other person; and if there is any argument why you should vote, that argument will apply equally well to any intelligent woman in the country. I cannot see the force of the argument which would give to natives of China, of Africa, and of India a right to control the destinies of the women of this country—and recollect I am an advocate of that right—and exclude from a voice my mother or my sister or my wife, an American woman, from the exercise of this inestimable privilege. I intend, when the proper stage is reached, to move an amendment to this proposition for the benefit of the women of the country. . . .

THE PRESIDENT PRO TEMPORE. The order of the day is the joint resolution (S. R. No. 8) proposing an amendment to the Constitution of the United States, which is now before the Senate as in Committee of the Whole, upon which question the Senator from Connecticut [Mr. Dixon] is entitled to the floor.

JAMES DIXON [R., CONN.]. Mr. President, the importance and the gravity of the subject now under consideration by the Senate ought to lift its discussion out of the region of mere party politics, and elevate the Senate in its consideration into an atmosphere purer and higher than that of mere party controversy; for, sir, it is not, perhaps, too much to say that this is the most important question in many of its bearings which has ever been presented to Congress in the shape of a proposed constitutional amendment.

What is the question? It is not merely a question of suffrage. That of itself is a subject of vast importance, and is now agitating the public mind of this country to a very great extent. The question whether the female sex should be permitted to participate in the privilege of suffrage, whether other restrictions should be removed, the question of age, the question of property, a multitude of questions are or may be raised which are vastly important and interesting in connection with the right of suffrage. But, sir, we are not now dealing merely with the qualification of voters. The question is not what shall be the qualifications of the voter, but who shall create, establish, and prescribe those qualifications; not who shall be the voter, but who shall make the voter.

In considering that question we ought to remember that it is utterly impossible that any State should be an independent republic which does not entirely control its own laws with regard to the right of suffrage. Nor does it make the slightest difference with regard to this that any abdication or abnegation of its power is voluntary. It may be said that it is proposed that the States shall voluntarily relinquish their power to control the subject of suffrage within their respective limits. Sir, suppose a State should voluntarily assume upon itself a foreign yoke, or declare by a majority of its own people, or even by a unanimous vote, that it would prefer a monarchy, would the fact of its being voluntary at all affect the question whether it was still an independent republic?

Now, sir, it may be that the people of this country in their present condition of mind are ready to relinquish the power in the States of regulating their own laws with regard to suffrage; and if it should so prove, and the result should show that your own State (Ohio) and my State, (Connecticut), having once or twice voted against extending the right of suffrage to the negro race, should now consent that a central power should regulate that question, and should do this voluntarily and freely, nevertheless they would by that action lose their character as republican governments. And, sir, that is the reason why it was that in the formation of the Constitution of the United States there was an entire neglect to interfere in the slightest degree with the question of suffrage in the several States. Look through the Constitution as it was formed, and you find no allusion whatever to the question of suffrage, except by reference to existing laws and qualifications in the then existing States. . . . when it is proposed to amend the Constitution of the United States in this respect it is very questionable whether it is not an amendment which subverts the whole foundation and principle of the Government. Suppose an amendment were offered here to-day proposing that this Government, instead of being a Republic, should be a monarchy; suppose it were proposed to strike out the clause of the Constitution guarantying a republican form of government to each State, and instead of that to insert a guarantee of a monarchy to each State. I do not know that this amendment would not be within the power of Congress to propose. The Constitution provides that Congress may propose such amendments as in its own judgment it shall think best and proper. If a proposition of that kind were made it is very true it might be objected "this goes to the foundation of your Government; this is not amendment; it is revolution, it is subversion." Can that not be said in this instance? Is the proposed amendment any more a fair carrying out of the intendment of the Constitution when it provides for its own amendment than it would be if it proposed directly to subvert the form of government, if it be true that the right of exercising and controlling the power of suffrage must necessarily exist in a State or it ceases to be a Republic?

Sir, when we view the question in this light it must be acknowledged that it rises far above the question of any mere detail as to suffrage; far higher in importance than the question even of abolishing slavery in the States; far higher than any proposition which has ever been made with regard to the amendment of the Constitution, because it is in its truest sense radical and revolutionary. It strikes at the very root and foundation of the Government; it removes its corner stone, and changes the entire character of the State governments. Nor does it relieve this difficulty at all to say that the interference is not by this amendment perfect and complete; that some shadow of liberty is left to the States to control their own suffrage laws. The proposition submitted by the Committee on the Judiciary provides that no restriction on the right of suffrage shall be made by a State on account of race, color, or previous condition of servitude. It may be said that in all other respects the State is left free to prescribe its own restrictions. The first answer to that is that when you once begin to interfere with the right of a State to regulate for itself independently the question of what shall be the qualifications of the voter, you abandon the whole principle. It is not necessary to utterly subvert the power of the State in this respect and make it wholly dependent upon a foreign—and when I use the word "foreign," I mean merely external power outside of itself. But, sir, in this case it so happens that the very question upon which the public mind has mainly been agitated is the question of the extension of the right of suffrage in respect to race and color—I should say, perhaps mainly with respect to race. I do not acknowledge that in the State of Connecticut any man is disfranchised merely on account of his color, although the word "white" is used in the Constitution. It is precisely as if it had been said, "none shall vote but those of the white race." That this is so is shown by the fact that it excludes negroes and Indians. Certainly the Indian patriarch who once lived in the neighborhood of Norwich had as good a natural right to vote as any imported African, but in the State of Connecticut the right has always been claimed and exercised entirely to control the Indian race; to keep them in a state of tutelage; to refuse them even the power of making a contract, much more the power of governing the State. It was a question of race; it was not merely a question of color.

Although it may be said that in this case the intention is not entirely to deprive the various States of the right to control their own suffrage laws, it so happens that in some of those States most interested, as, for example, the State of Ohio and the State of Connecticut, this is the very question. It is therefore a subterfuge and an evasion to say, "We do not interfere in any other respect," when there is no other respect in which it is possible to interfere, or in regard to which anybody ever proposed to interfere. . . .

Mr. President, I have already said that the question before the Senate is not merely a question of suffrage, but that it goes to the very foundation of republican government and strikes at the power of the States to determine and establish, each for itself, the qualification of its own voters. It is important to bear in mind this distinction. There are in the State of Connecticut, and doubtless in all the States, many who are in favor of universal suffrage without distinction of race or color, who yet cling to the right of each State to decide as to the qualifications of its own voters. The pending constitutional amendment proposes to transfer this power from the States to the General Government by the consent of three-fourths of the States; but the character of the Government is no less changed by this mode of effecting the alteration than if it were done by act of Congress. All the States will not consent to the change, and those States which do not thus consent will be deprived by external power of the essential characteristic of self-government as completely as if the change were made by a mere law of Congress.

Furthermore, those States which consent to the amendment are merely the artificers of their own ruin as communities entitled to local self-government. They destroy freely and voluntarily, but yet they not the less destroy their character as independent States of this Union. Even the consent of a State, however freely rendered, would not prevent the necessary consequence, namely, the loss of the vital and essential element of self-government, consisting in the power of deciding freely, independently, and without appeal upon the qualifications of voters. Therefore it will be found that many

advocates of negro suffrage will condemn and oppose this attempt to overthrow the State governments and reduce them to utter insignificance by the
establishment of the principle involved in this amendment. They are unwilling to see the ancient Commonwealths which won our national independence and formed our national Government, together with their younger
sisters who fill up the number of our United States, reduced from the proud
position of independent, self-governing republics to the humble and helpless
condition of subject provinces whose people exercise the right of suffrage
under conditions and regulations imposed by a central power. . . .

SAMUEL POMEROY [R., KAN.]. . . . But I have had read the amendment
which I propose to offer to the present consitutional amendment for the
purpose of discussing this question still further. My amendment provides that
no State nor the United States shall make any inequalities that are not
equally applicable to all citizens. If you want a condition of intelligence, of
education, of any quality that applies equally to all, it can be adopted by the
States under the amendment that I have proposed. I shall now take it upon
me in a few brief words to demonstrate the proposition that inequality of
rights secured in either constitution or law is a source of weakness.

Mr. President, by this amendment I mean something more than an hour's
delay in the passage of this joint resolution. To delay it is no pleasure to me;
I am but too anxious for it to become part of the fundamental law. And I
would not support this amendment to the amendment but from the conviction I entertain that the Constitution will be incomplete without it. Indeed, I
hold it will be radically defective without this amendment. The great error of
the past, when the Constitution was formed, grew out of inequalities among
men, as it respects their rights. It has been the contest of the century, and it
finally culminated in a legal dogma, pronounced some years ago by one of
the justices of the Supreme Court, that one class had no rights which the
other was bound to respect. To deprive a citizen of any one right will tend to
produce the extinction of all. And the right to take the least prepares, if not
justifies, the way to take the whole. I know Senators are in haste to pass this
resolution, but the opportunity does not often occur to amend the organic law
of a nation. It may not come to us again in a lifetime, and what is worth
doing at all is worth doing well and right.

We have hauled up the old ark of the Constitution for repairs, and I want
above all other things to secure it against the possibility of the admission that
there can be inequalities of rights among citizens. It matters not in what
those inequalities consist; if they relate to and impair the rights of the citizen,
even the poorest and the weakest, they are fatal and destructive to the safety
and peace of the Government and to its character as a model of republicanism to the world, and also to the well-being of those whose rights are
destroyed or abridged. Amend the Constitution to-day and leave in the
possibility of the rights of any of our citizens being insecure or destroyed or
neglected, and you have perfected nothing. A contest will go on until we or

some more faithful men who come after us shall complete the work neglected at this moment by us. . . .

The irresistible tendency of modern civilization is in the direction of the extension of the right of suffrage, and not at all toward proscription. The day when a few men did the voting and governing for the many has gone by. Seven hundred thousand colored men were enfranchised in a day, and they have not disappointed the reasonable expectations which were entertained by them. They were unlearned and, for the most part, ignorant men. But instinct is wiser than logic. The negro has blended and is lost sight of in the man. Manhood suffrage is now held to be the native and the inherent right of every male citizen of a prescribed age; and some there are who claim the enfranchisement of negro and rebel together. But is there no injustice in completing the work of reconstruction upon such a basis? Are not the men and the women citizens of the Republic alike? And how can there be in a just Government an equality of citizens with a proscription of rights? I mean, of any of their rights. . . .

Now, if this question of suffrage is to be settled, and settled by the law of the Constitution, it is of the highest importance that it be settled upon the right basis and upon one entirely in harmony with the genius and spirit of our Government and institutions. I only claim the logical sequence of our political organization. All other Governments save ours have their privileged men or classes and their unprivileged; some are citizens, others are mere subjects; one class control public affairs, the other bear its burdens with voices silenced. But in this Government, ordained by the people, the citizens, their right to administer it should not be questioned. And how can this Government be administered but by the ballot? Laws are made and executed by the representatives of the ballot. An elective officer is but a consolidated ballot; one person exercising the voice and will of many. . . .

I now come to this point to say that to deprive any citizen of the right of suffrage is a violation of the principles of our Government as it was ordained, and is a blow direct at the Government itself. I have studied this form of government to no purpose if its logic does not lead me to universal and impartial suffrage. The Constitution places all the powers of the Government in the people who ordained it, (and it resided in them in any event); but while they delegated the exercise of certain powers to departments, State and national, still they held the reins of modification of all that was delegated, and provided for the exercise of that right. Hence it is that I can say that this is not only no "white man's Government," but it is no male Government; and it is a historical fact that in the early days of our history both colored men and white women were admitted to the ballot upon precisely the same terms as white men. This was done in some instances, but their number being few does not affect the principle. If you admit but one woman to vote or one negro it is a confession that there is no legal bar to all. . . .

GARRETT DAVIS [DEM., KY.]. Does the Constitution say that its provisions are silent in the midst of arms? No, sir. That was a powerful expression, not of sentiment but of fear, by Cicero when Pompey's soldiers were present in the Forum. There is no such maxim, no such principle, no such monstrosity in our system. Here we have a Government of law founded upon a Constitution and law subordinate to that Constitution. Among the principles of the Constitution is this: that one State of the Union has as much power, as much right to proceed in all of its processes in the important business of altering the fundamental law as any other State. Where States are in insurrection, where they are making *flagrante bello* against the Government of the United States, you cannot in that condition of things proceed to alter the Constitution at all. You must first reduce the insurgent States to obedience to the Constitution and the authority of the United States, and then you may proceed to amend your Constitution. You cannot do it under any other state of case.

But the present condition of things is incomparably stronger than that. Here there is no war; there is no rebellion; there is no insurgent in arms against the authority of the Government of the United States. All have submitted. The law reigns supreme, except so far as it is violated by the machinery of the party in power. At any rate, the insurgents have all submitted. They are no longer in resistance to the laws of the United States or its authority. They have been vanquished in battle, and they have submitted in the best and noblest faith that ever was professed by a discontented people who had been warring on the Government of their country and all of its authority. Now, when peace and order reign, except so far as they are disturbed by the revolutionary movements of the party in power; when, if they were disposed to perform their functions under and according to the Constitution there would not be a ripple upon the surface of our great political sea, but it would be as placid and as transparent as a mirror, as peaceful as though there was not a breeze stirring—when this is the condition of things you have a right to claim the representation and the presence of the representation, both in the House of Representatives and the Senate, from every State in the Union. They are anxious to be represented; craving, beseeching, praying, adjuring you to allow them to be represented; and yet you still, by lawless force, keep them out of your councils, and in their absence, under the operation of this force, you proceed to alter the fundamental law, the Constitution of our common Government, when that Constitution gives to all the States the free and perfect right to take part in this important business.

Sir, your amendments to the Constitution are all void; they are of no effect. They were proposed by a mutilated Congress; they were proposed by a mutilated House of Representatives and Senate. That mutilation at one time was voluntary, but now, since it has been healed by the submission and obedience of the insurgents to the Constitution and laws of the United States, you have proceeded to continue it, to enlarge it, to protect it indefinitely; and with all this violence done by you to the Constitution, and to the rights of the people and the sovereign States of the United States to take part in this important business of amending the Constitution, you still continue the mockery of your amendments. How ridiculous! How absurd!

Sir, these amendments of the Constitution, your Freedmen's Bureau bill, your civil rights bill, and all your monstrous and unconstitutional laws will be decided in the course of a few years by the sovereign people of the United States of America in their paramount power and sovereignty, to be null and void, mere *debris* that you have thrown over the Constitution. They will be swept away from it. You are now indulging a dream of power as did Belshazzar before the inscription appeared upon the wall of his palace. That inscription will come to you. You will be weighed in the balance and you will be found wanting, and another Cyrus will sweep you from power. Mr. President, I do not expect to live many years, but I expect to live to see the day of that deliverance of our country and of our glorious Constitution. When I have seen that day I shall then be prepared to exclaim, Simeon-like, "Lord, now lettest thou thy servant depart in peace." . . .

House of Representatives-40th Congress, 3rd Session
January 30, 1869

SAMUEL SHELLABARGER [R., OHIO]. I withdraw the modifications of amendment which I offered yesterday, so as to leave the amendment as it was originally printed, and I ask that it may be read.

The Clerk read the amendment, as follows:

No State shall make or enforce any law which shall deny or abridge to any male citizen of the United States of the age of twenty-one years or over, and who is of sound mind, an equal vote at all elections in the State in which he shall have such actual residence as shall be prescribed by law, except to such as have engaged or may hereafter engage in insurrection or rebellion against the United States, and to such as shall be duly convicted of treason, felony, or other infamous crime. . . .

ROBERT SCHENCK [R., OHIO]. Knowing how many of us are represented by my colleague [Mr. Shellabarger] in the substitute he has offered, I need not say I approve the form, that it shall be in the shape of an inhibition to the States. Yesterday, when the proposition was pending, many gentlemen, among them the gentleman from Massachusetts [Mr. Boutwell] and his colleague, [Mr. Butler,] objected that unless there was something saving to the States the power to regulate the exercise of the elective franchise this noted proposition would virtually repeal or be repugnant to the passage of any registry law. Now, I conceive there is nothing in that objection. At first it seemed to be plausible, and yielding to that plausibility my colleague, [Mr. Shellabarger,] with the consent of others, agreed to modify the proposition. He now withdraws the modification. I think it necessary to have the modification withdrawn, because if there be anything in the argument presented by the gentleman from Massachusetts, [Mr. Boutwell,] that it interferes with the possibility of having registry laws, then upon the same argument we could have no registration laws now.

Look, for instance, at the constitution of Massachusetts. What does it provide? It provides in absolute terms that every male citizen who has attained the age of twenty-one years, who has resided in the Commonwealth one year, and within the district six months, and who has paid certain taxes, shall be permitted to vote; and to this is added by the twentieth article of the amendments an educational requirement. Now, a man in Massachusetts goes to the polls and offers to vote. He shows that he is twenty-one years of age; that he has always resided within the State; that he is a citizen; that he can read the Constitution in the English language and write his name, yet objection is made to the reception of his vote. Why? Because he has not registered. He points to the Constitution and says, "By the Constitution it is provided that every man having these qualifications, which I possess, shall have the right to vote." The reply is, "That Constitution implies the necessity of prescribing by law regulations under which the votes shall be cast." If this were not so, the registry law now in force in Massachusetts would be unconstitutional. But does any gentleman here pretend to say that it is so? A man possessing all the qualifications which by the express terms of the Constitution are requisite to make him an elector, presents himself at the polls, and is told, "Stand back, because you are not registered." This goes to show that these provisions as to the qualifications of electors do not, in the slightest degree, interfere with the power of the Legislature of the State to adopt proper regulations under which the votes shall be cast. Hence, any exception of the kind proposed here for the purpose of saving that right to the States is unnecessary. Besides, sir, the language of this amendment is still stronger, because it contains the word "equal;" it provides for securing to citizens an "equal" right to vote. . . .

GEORGE BOUTWELL [DEM., MASS.]. I think I had better bring the debate to a close; and I may as well make an example in the case of my colleague by refusing to yield to him.

Mr. Speaker, I only wish to say that the distinctions and differences of opinion which have been evolved by the debate in regard to the effect of the amendment proposed by the gentleman from Ohio [Mr. Bingham] afford to my mind conclusive evidence that if we submit the amendment in that form to the country we shall introduce in every State confusion, discord, and contention as to what the effect of the provision will be. But the amendment reported by the Judiciary Committee is directed against those distinctions which have been brought prominently before the country, and on which substantially public opinion, as entertained by the Republican party, has been expressed. We are safe if we stand upon the resolution reported by the committee; and, in my judgment, we are unsafe if we accept what we ourselves confessedly are unable to understand in such a way as to come to an agreement upon it. . . .

The main question was ordered; which was first upon Mr. Shellabarger's amendment to the amendment of Mr. Bingham.

The amendment was read, as follows:

Strike out in the amendment of Mr. BINGHAM the provision proposed to be inserted in lieu of section one of the proposed new article of the Constitution, and insert in lieu thereof the following:

No State shall make or enforce any law which shall deny or abridge to any male citizen of the United States of the age of twenty-one years or over, and who is of sound mind, an equal vote at all elections in the State in which he shall have such actual residence as shall be prescribed by law, except to such as have engaged or may hereafter engage in insurrection or rebellion against the United States, and to such as shall be duly convicted of treason, felony, or other infamous crime. . . .

The yeas and nays were ordered.

The question was taken; and it was decided in the negative—yeas 61, nays 126, not voting 35. . . .

The question then recurred on Mr. Bingham's amendment, as follows:

Strike out all of article one and insert as follows:

SEC. 1. No State shall make or enforce any law which shall deny or abridge to any male citizen of the United States of sound mind and twenty-one years of age or upward the equal exercise of the elective franchise at all elections in the State wherein he shall have actually resided for a period of one year next preceding such election, subject to such registration laws and laws prescribing local residence as the State may enact, except such of said citizens as shall engage in rebellion or insurrection, or who may have been, or shall be, duly convicted of treason or other infamous crime.

HAMILTON WARD [R., N.Y.] demanded the yeas and nays.

The yeas and nays were ordered.

The question was taken; and it was decided in the negative—yeas 24, nays 160, not voting 38. . . .

JAMES BROOKS [DEM., N.Y.]. Will the gentleman from Massachusetts yield to me to have a vote on my amendment for the enfranchisement of women and children over twelve years of age?

MR. BOUTWELL. The gentleman is not serious in that inquiry. . . .

The result having been announced as above, the joint resolution, being engrossed, was read the third time.

I move the previous question on the passage, and demand the yeas and nays. . . .

The question was taken; and it was decided in the affirmative—yeas 150, nays 42, not voting 31. . . .

So (two thirds having voted in favor thereof) the joint resolution was passed.

Senate-40th Congress, 3rd Session
February 3-9, 1869

WILLIAM STEWART [R., NEV.]. I am instructed by the Committee on the Judiciary to move to amend the resolution by striking out the whole of section one of the proposed article and inserting in lieu thereof:

The right of citizens of the United States to vote and hold office shall not be denied or abridged by the United States, or by any State, on account of race, color, or previous condition of servitude.

GEORGE WILLIAMS [R., ORE.]. I move to amend the amendment by inserting the words "natural born" before "citizens."

MR. STEWART. I hope that will not prevail.

THOMAS FERRY [R., MICH.]. I suppose, in accordance with the ordinary practice of the Senate, upon this subject again coming to its consideration I would be entitled, by courtesy, at least, to the floor. If there are other amendments which gentlemen desire to submit I will give way. I rose to move an adjournment; but I will postpone that motion for other amendments if gentlemen desire to offer them.

CHARLES BUCKALEW [DEM., PA.]. I desire to give notice of an amendment that I intend to propose, to come in at the end of the resolution. It is to add the words:

That the foregoing amendment shall be submitted to the Legislatures of the several States, the most numerous branches of which shall be chosen next after the passage of this resolution.

JACOB HOWARD [R., MICH.]. I desire to offer a substitute for the resolution of the Judiciary Committee, and I ask to have it printed. My proposition is to strike out the first section of the proposed article and insert:

Citizens of the United States of African descent shall have the same right to vote and hold office as other citizens.

JAMES DOOLITTLE [R., WIS.]. I suggest to the Senator from Oregon, [Mr. Williams,] whose amendment I understand is pending, that instead of the words "natural born" he shall say "native born citizens."

MR. WILLIAMS. No; I have followed the language of the Constitution.

HENRY CORBETT [R., ORE.]. I desire to give notice of an amendment that I shall propose to come in at the end of the first section of the proposed article:

But Chinamen not born in the United States, and Indians not taxed, shall not be deemed or made citizens.

JOSEPH FOWLER [R., TENN.]. I desire to submit an amendment which at the proper time I shall propose. It is to substitute for the first section of the proposed article of amendment—

All citizens of the United States residents of the several States now or hereafter comprehended in the Union, of the age of twenty-one years and upward, shall be entitled to an equal vote in all elections in the State wherein they shall reside, (the period of such residence as a qualification for voting to be decided by each State,) except such citizens as shall engage in rebellion or insurrection, or shall be duly convicted of treason or other infamous crime.

FREDERICK SAWYER [R., S.C.]. I wish to give notice of an amendment which I shall propose in lieu of the first section of the proposed article:

The right to vote and hold office shall belong to all male citizens of the United States who are twenty-one years old and of sound mind, and who have not been or shall not have been duly convicted of treason or other infamous crime: *Provided,* That nothing herein contained shall deprive the several States of the right to prescribe terms of residence which shall precede the exercise of the right to vote, to fix the age at which said citizens shall become eligible to hold office, and to make such registration laws as may be necessary to guard the purity of elections; which conditions of residence and age and registration laws shall be uniformly applicable to all male citizens of the United States.

THE PRESIDENT PRO TEMPORE [BENJAMIN WADE, R., OHIO]. The question now is on the amendment offered by the Senator from Oregon [Mr. Williams] to the amendment of the Senator from Nevada, [Mr. Stewart.]

JAMES DIXON [R., CONN.]. I desire at the proper time to move the same amendment to this resolution which I proposed to the Senate resolution, and that is to strike out the word "Legislatures" and insert "conventions" at the respective places where the word "Legislatures" occurs.

SAMUEL POMEROY [R., KAN.]. I moved an amendment to the former proposition, and as that proposition seems to have been superseded by this, I desire to give notice that at a suitable time I shall offer the same amendment to this resolution. I desire to have it read for information.

THE CHIEF CLERK. The proposed amendment is to strike out all of the first article of the contemplated constitutional amendment, and to insert in lieu of it:

The right of citizens of the United States to vote and hold office shall not be denied or abridged by the United States or any State for any reason not equally applicable to all citizens.

MR. DIXON. I move that all these proposed amendments be printed.

The motion was agreed to. . . .

The Senate, as in Committee of the Whole, resumed the consideration of the joint resolution (H. R. No. 402) proposing an amendment to the Constitution of the United States.

MR. FERRY. Mr. President, I ask the Clerk to read the resolution of the House of Representatives as it will stand if amended as proposed by the Senator from Nevada, [Mr. Stewart.]

THE CHIEF CLERK. The resolution if amended as proposed will read as follows:

ARTICLE XV

SEC. 1. The right of citizens of the United States to vote and hold office shall not be denied or abridged by the United States or by any State on account of race, color, or previous condition of servitude.

MR. FERRY. Mr. President, it was my intention, when I sought the floor upon this resolution as reported by the Committee on the Judiciary, to address myself to a considerable degree to the merits of the proposed amendment to the Constitution; but the course which the debate has taken seems to have rendered such a discussion in a degree superfluous. Every Senator who has spoken against the resolution has placed his opposition not upon its merits or demerits, but upon the particular mode of submission to the people provided for, or upon other technicalities surrounding the subject, instead of upon the subject itself.

The Senator from Kentucky, [Mr. Davis,] lifting no voice now against the extension of the suffrage, simply denies the capacity of Congress to propose amendments to the Constitution at all, because here yet remain a few of the States unrepresented in the national Legislature. The Senator from Indiana, [Mr. Hendricks,] silent now with regard to the capacity of the disfranchised class for self-government, bases his opposition to the resolution of the committee on the technical doctrine of estoppel, drawn from his familiarity with the law. And my colleague, [Mr. Dixon,] twice during the last fifteen years committed by his votes to the extension of the suffrage to the extent proposed in the resolution, cannot oppose himself to its principle, but seeks by indirection to accomplish its defeat.

A great change has come over the minds of the Opposition since the voice of the people of this land was heard last autumn upon the questions involved in this amendment. A year ago opprobrious nicknames applied to the class of citizens whom it is now proposed to enfranchise, denials of the capacity and almost of the humanity of the negro, appeals to popular prejudice, were the staple of the argument which we heard against the beneficent measure now brought to the consideration of this body.

But since that period a change has come over the vision of the opponents of this measure; and now no voice is raised in denial of its expediency or its justice considered in itself, but only against the method in which it is proposed that the measure shall be accomplished. And, sir, there is good reason for this change. Within a year the people of the United States, in their ratification at the polls of the action of Congress upon the question of reconstruction, have decided that four fifths of the colored men of this country shall henceforth enjoy all the civil and political rights of American citizens. To-day five hundred thousand ballots in the hands of colored citizens have a voice more potent than had a year ago the unsupported claims of right upon the consciences and the action of those who then as now opposed the extension of the suffrage.

But although the hostility which is developed to the resolution is changed in the mode of its manifestation, it is not changed in itself in any particular. As I have intimated, what formerly it sought to attain by a denial of the common rights of manhood it now seeks to accomplish by indirection and by technicalities.

The first of the technicalities is the one which was urged by the Senator from Indiana [Mr. Hendricks.] We are estopped, is the purport of his argument, from proposing to the people of the nation a great and beneficent change in the fundamental law, because a convention of a political party almost a year ago pledged that party, according to the construction of the Senator, against any such change. This doctrine of estoppel, which lawyers who have no other defense in their causes find so easy to set up, and whose principle is that though the defendant has no just ground to resist the claim that is made upon him yet the plaintiff has said or done something which shall preclude him from enforcing it—this technical doctrine of estoppel is gravely urged upon the consideration of the Senate as if any action of a political convention were competent to bind the action of the Congress of the United States. No matter what parties in convention may declare to be their view of what ought to be the course of legislation in this nation, I as a legislator have the right to propose what changes in our law, ordinary or organic, I may choose; and I and all of us have the right, and it is our bounden duty; if those changes are required by grave considerations of public interest, to advocate and to vote for those changes.

But, sir, it is not true that the Chicago platform does contain anything in contravention of the amendment to the Constitution which is now proposed by the Committee on the Judiciary. The Senator read from the second resolution of the Chicago platform as follows:

> The guarantee by Congress of equal suffrage to all loyal men at the South was demanded by every consideration of public safety, of gratitude, and of justice, and must be maintained, while the question of suffrage in all the loyal States properly belongs to the people of those States.

And he avers that the concluding portion of this resolution binds the Republican members of Congress neither to adopt nor propose any amendment to the Constitution of the United States looking to the extension of the suffrage. Why, sir, the resolution is of directly the contrary purport. What is it in sum and substance? It makes a distinction between the loyal and the lately rebel States in regard to the extension of the suffrage in them respectively. Adhering—for at that time the fourteenth article of amendment to the Constitution of the United States had not been fully ratified—to the construction of the Constitution familiar to every one since the foundation of the Government on that question, it declared that in those States whose people had renounced their rights under the Federal Constitution, by rebellion against the sovereignty of the United States, must submit to the legislation of

Congress in regard to their social reorganization; while at the same time it declared that the people of the loyal States, in which all the guarantees of the Constitution retained their vigor, should themselves have control of any change of their organic laws in this respect, whether effected by amendment of the Constitution of the United States or of any individual State.

The substantial thing declared was, that in the loyal States any change of the suffrage should be wrought out by constitutional amendment to be submitted to the people; in the rebel States, whose people had abjured their privileges under the Constitution by rebellion, they must submit to the legislation of Congress in their social reorganization; and that is all there is of it. The sole distinction is this distinction between the people of these two classes of States; and as to which mode of submitting the question to the people of the loyal States should be adopted, through an amendment to the Constitution of the United States or through an amendment to the constitutions of their respective States, is a simple question of expediency. In the language of the Chicago resolution, the proposal to the people of the United States of an amendment extending suffrage is a giving to the people of the States the decision of that question. The fathers meant to give it to them when they framed the Constitution. By fourteen successive articles of amendment we have submitted alteration after alteration in this mode to the people, and now upon this question of the extension of the suffrage we have only to ask, is it better and wiser and more expedient to submit an amendment of the Constitution of the United States, to be ratified by the people at once, or amendments of the State constitutions, to be ratified at various periods by the people of the States respectively? In deciding this question of expediency the answer seems to me to be apparent. What do we want to change the constitution of a State or of the United States at all for in this respect? If we need the change at all it is because there is an evil existing in the land which calls for a remedy. Those of us who sustain this amendment believe that such an evil exists; and that evil is, that in eighteen out of the thirty-seven States a class of citizens of the United States is deprived of its natural rights by local laws; and we believe that this oppression—a remnant of slavery—should be removed from an innocent, a law-abiding, and a useful class of our fellow-citizens.

If it be such an evil it should be removed in the manner speediest and surest. It may be removed by constitutional means, either by an amendment to the Constitution of the United States or by the process of successive amendments of the constitutions of the several States. But it exists in eighteen States. The action of no one State can affect the action of any other. Nothing can reach them all so quickly or in a manner so accordant with a wise expediency as an amendment to the fundamental law of the Republic itself which shall place all its citizens upon the same footing of equal political rights.

It is in this respect similar to the amendment, for which my colleague voted, abolishing slavery in the States. That was a matter within State jurisdiction and which might have been left for the several States themselves to remove by amendment of their respective constitutions; but it existed in fifteen States; the experience of the nation from its very beginning had shown that the evil was real, and the intervention of Congress by the proposal to the whole people of an amendment to the Constitution of the United States was the mode adopted here and approved by the people. The same reason which then called for the intervention of this power to amend the Constitution of the United States so that slavery should be abolished now calls for the intervention of the same power so that disfranchisement shall also be abolished. . . .

But leaving the ground taken by the Senator from Indiana I come to the position occupied by my colleague. Whether anything which has been done by the Chicago convention operates as an estoppel upon us or not, whether the objections to details presented by the Senator from Indiana ought to prevail or not, my colleague has an additional objection to it that the mode of submitting the proposed amendment is somehow unjust, unfair, and improper; and to obviate this he proposes to amend the resolution by striking out the word "Legislatures" and inserting the word "conventions," so that the amendment shall be referred to conventions of the people of the States for ratification instead of being referred to the Legislatures. I confess that I felt some degree of surprise at the language employed by my colleague, and echoed by the Senator from Indiana, as to the effect of the resolution in the manner of its submission of the amendment to the Legislatures; for the whole tenor of their argument was to denounce such a mode of submission as contrary to what my colleague termed the fundamental principles of republican government and calculated to subvert republican institutions everywhere. Sir, these gentlemen, since I have been in this body, have been stout sticklers for the Constitution of the United States. My colleague has walked *non passibus equis* in the footsteps of the occupant of the White House in his devotion to that instrument, and yet it would be hard to believe, after listening to his denunciation of the proposed mode of submission in this resolution, that that mode is in strict conformity with the Constitution; that it is the mode in which fourteen amendments, one after the other, have been submitted to the people, and that never before has any man dreamed that when the Legislatures had ratified an amendment to the Constitution it had not received the popular sanction. But my colleague would submit this amendment to conventions of delegates of the people of the States.

Why has that mode never been adopted hitherto? The answer to this question will show why it ought not to be adopted now. Where an evil exists of such grave magnitude as to demand the interposition of the people themselves by way of change of their organic law it is an evil which ought to be corrected speedily. The Constitution has provided for its speediest correction by the submission of an amendment to the Legislatures. It has given the power indeed of submission to conventions; but Congress and the people never have used that power, because the machinery of conventions was dilatory, expensive, and unwise. . . .

But my colleague, as a final stroke in his assault upon this beneficent measure, lifts up again that old battle-cry which I thought had gone down forever with the overthrow of the rebellion. Adopt your amendment to the Constitution, he says, and Connecticut ceases to be an independent republic. When was she one? If my State has ever been an independent republic, in his life time or in mine, I have not known it. I heard in the other House before the war began men who were plotting to wrench this Republic asunder talk about the independent republics of South Carolina and Georgia and Mississippi and Alabama—those utterances came from the lips of such men as Keitt and Crawford and Barksdale and Davis—but, sir, I did not expect now, after that fierce struggle is over, that my colleague would strike hands with those who in the spring of 1861, claiming to represent the Democracy of Connecticut, and under the lead of Burr and Seymour and Eaton proclaimed that this Government was without the power to put down a rebellion, because every State was an independent republic, and had a right to secede at its pleasure. No, sir; the people of Connecticut, when South Carolina proclaimed that doctrine, did not believe it. I resisted it in Congress before the war; I resisted it before my people in the spring of 1861; and when the assertion of the sovereignty of the independent republics of the South flamed out into rebellion and threatened to devour the national sovereignty a million of the young men of this nation went out to meet it, and to trample it down in bloody mire forever; and now when we simply propose to extend to an innocent, a law-abiding, an industrious, a peaceful portion of the citizens of the United States rights which God gave them, and of which man for generations has deprived them, my colleague raises the old cry of State sovereignty and independent republics to cast odium upon it. . . .

No, sir; this pretense that the independence of Connecticut is to be demolished by doing right to a portion of her citizens seems to me like the politician's afterthought, as I said before; for, committed as he is to the rectitude of the principle involved in this amendment, some mode must be devised of awakening prejudice other than by the old cry against the negro, in order to escape from the position in which he is placed by his new party affiliations. . . .

WILLARD WARNER [R., ALA.]. Mr. President, I have proposed an amendment to the joint resolution now before the Senate, in the following words:

ARTICLE XV

SEC. 1. The right of citizens of the United States to hold office shall not be denied or abridged by the United States or any State on account of property, race, color, or previous condition of servitude; and every male citizen of the United States of the age of twenty-one years or over, and who is of sound mind, shall have an equal vote at all elections in the State in which he shall have actually resided for a period of one year next preceding such election, except such as may hereafter engage in insurrection or rebellion against the United States, and such as shall be duly convicted of treason, felony, or other infamous crime.

SEC. 2. Congress shall have power to enforce this article by appropriate legislation.

The Senator from Connecticut [Mr. Dixon] rightly states the question. The question before us is not one of negro suffrage. It is the question of suffrage in itself. It is the broad question who shall be the voters of this country, in whose hands shall rest the political power. I take issue squarely with the Senator from Connecticut when he claims that Connecticut is a sovereign State, and that to her rightfully belongs the privilege of determining who of the citizens of this Republic shall have the right to vote and hold office. If it be a question of humiliation, it is, on the one hand, whether Connecticut shall be humiliated, or, on the other, whether Connecticut shall have the right to humiliate every citizen of the Republic who shall choose to dwell within her borders.

Mr. President, in all governments sovereign power resides somewhere, limited only by God's justice, which is over all. Men and governments violating justice sooner or later come to ruin. In our Government the sovereignty is in the people; hence the question, "Who are the people?" is of practical and vital importance. When you settle that you settle the basis of government. The Constitution of our country is but the expressed will of the people, fixing certain great fundamental principles and defining a certain general organization under and by which Government shall be, by the people, administered.

The organic law, to avoid confusion and conflict, provides the manner of its own amendment or change. In the manner provided in the Constitution we are about to proceed to the most responsible and solemn of all our duties to change it. Laws of Congress passed to-day may, if faulty, be amended, or, if radically wrong, repealed to-morrow. But provisions put into the Constitution must stand, in the nature of things, as the rule of action for many years. Not only are we proposing to amend the organic law, but to amend it in its most vital part. We are about to put into it words which shall define and declare for years, perhaps for centuries, to come in whose hands the power of this great Republic shall rest—who shall vote, who shall elect its officers, make its laws, shape its policy, and control its destinies. In our action is bound up the welfare of the present and the coming millions of our country, and corelated with it are the interests of all the sons of men. Let us, then, approach our task solemnly and gravely, having in view not only the interests of our present population, but also the well-being of the multitudes who press on our track with remorseless tread.

The theory of our Government is that power, the sovereign power, belongs to the people, not to a portion of the people, not to the learned, not to the ignorant, not to the rich, not to the poor, not to the great, not to the weak, but to all the people. We eschew in our system of government all aristocracies, whether of birth, of wealth, or of learning. Based as are our institutions on the idea that the right of self-government is inherent in manhood, we profess to give to each individual an equal share of political power.

Years ago, in this Capitol and in this body, was fought, with the weapons of reason, the great battle of State and national sovereignty. Hayne stood up in these Halls as the champion of the former, while the great Webster, following the lead of Hamilton, and standing on the principle that "we, the people of the United States," "do ordain and establish this Constitution," with triumphant and irresistible logic maintained the "solidarity" of the Republic. From this court appeal was taken to the arbitrament of arms, and on more than a hundred battle-fields the conclusions of Webster were reaffirmed, and from that decision there is to be, I conclude, no appeal.

I think that it is a proposition too clear for argument that to the people, the whole people, the nation, belongs the decision of the question who shall exercise political power—in other and plainer words, who shall vote and hold office. And I think that it is equally clear that, to be true to our system and to the ideas upon which it is based, we must conclude that all men of sound mind are entitled to these rights.

To allow States to determine who of the citizens of the nation shall have political power is to give away the most essential and vital attribute of sovereignty—to concede a power which may be used to build up an aristocracy or to change and destroy our system of government. To give to States the power to disfranchise and disqualify for crime is a very limited and possibly not dangerous concession; but that a citizen living in Massachusetts should lose his right to vote for President by moving to Connecticut, or that different qualifications for voting for President, for instance, should be required in different parts of the country, is so manifestly wrong and so clearly at variance with that provision of the Constitution which declares that "the citizens of each State shall be entitled to all privileges and immunities of citizens in the several States," that it needs but to be stated to be condemned.

Now, what are the words proposed by the committee to be put into the Constitution to settle this vital question? They are as follows:

No State shall deny or abridge the right of its citizens to vote and hold office on account of race, color, or previous condition.

To propose to put into the Constitution any words which shall control the action of the States in this matter is to concede the great principle for which I argue, that to the nation belongs the determination of the question who shall have political power. Then the only question remaining is, do these words settle it aright? Let us examine the force and scope of this provision.

First, it does not determine who shall vote and hold office. Secondly, it does not protect any class of citizens against disfranchisement or disqualification. It simply and only provides that certain classes indicated shall not be disfranchised or disqualified for certain reasons, namely, race, color, or condition. For any other reason any State may deprive any portion of its citizens of all share in the Government. The *animus* of this amendment is a desire to protect and enfranchise the colored citizens of the country; yet, under it and without any violation of its letter or spirit, nine tenths of them might be prevented from voting and holding office by the requirement on the part of the States or of the United States of an intelligence or property qualification.

Is this the Dead Sea fruit which we are to gather from the plantings of a hundred years? Is this to be the sum of the triumph of the grand struggle of a century past in this country for equal rights, a struggle whose pathway is marked by the graves of unnumbered martyrs, and whose culmination rocked the Republic to its base and reddened a thousand fields with the blood of its best sons?

Lame and impotent conclusion. You fail to protect the only classes of your citizens who need protection. Knowledge is power. Wealth is power. The learned and the rich scarcely need the ballot for their protection. The great farmer who has his three to five score laborers has a power and influence which no law can take away. It is his landless and dependent tenants, in their cabins and in their ignorance, who need the ballot for their safety. The millionaire in his money, and the man of education in his knowledge and his brain, have each a power in government greater than a hundred ballots, a power which the Constitution neither gives nor can take away. It is the poor, unlearned man, who has nothing but the ballot, to whom it is a priceless heritage, a protection and a shield.

Mr. President, now that the grand opportunity occurs of settling this question of equal rights, I would improve it to put into the organic law provisions which shall determine the qualifications of electors, and give to every citizen the right to vote, thus making suffrage uniform, equal, and universal, and putting it out of the power of the small portion of the people living within the bounds of each single State to make a different rule. Surely none less than the whole people of the nation should have the right to say who shall be their partners in the Government; and, as one of the people, I am in favor of giving equally to all citizens of the Republic of sound mind and unstained by great crimes the right to vote and hold office.

Mr. President, I would admit woman, the most beautiful, the purest and best of God's creations, to an equal voice with us in the Government. As she is now the sharer of all our pleasures, the partner of all our joys, I would have her share with us the powers, the duties, and the responsibilities of government. Suppose, Mr. President, that one of the many sorrow-stricken women made widows by the late war should walk into this Chamber and say, "Senators, my husband and two sons lie in yonder national cemetery—their graves marked, cared for, cherished gratefully and tenderly by the nation—as the last resting-place of the heroic defenders of its life. I have no husband, no son, no brother, no father, no man left to represent me. I pay taxes; every law you pass affects me and mine, and I demand a voice in this Government." What answer shall you give her?

But I know that woman's suffrage is not now attainable, and I would not, as a practical legislator, jeopardize the good which is attainable by linking with it that which is impossible. Besides, whenever the women of this country ask with anything like unanimity for the ballot they will get it.

JOSEPH ABBOTT [R., N.C.]. . . . Mr. President, I do not intend to discuss this question at any length, much less with reference to its legal aspect, but rather to give a general expression of opinion in regard to it as it appears in my own mind. When we incorporate the principles of this proposed amendment into the Constitution we are only applying and carrying out the very earliest assumptions of the men who laid the foundations of our political system. Recent events within the nation for which few, if any, in this Chamber were responsible, and which threw forward to the front questions which had been remote, have rendered it necessary for the nation to take this additional step toward the establishment of the rights of men. I refer, of course, in thus speaking, to the events of the late war. While the principles on which this amendment is based were well understood and definitely announced in the inception of the Government, in declarations which could not be misinterpreted, the opportunity, or rather the necessity, for planting them in the fundamental law had not until lately arisen. . . .

The question for us to consider now is, whether we shall move still further in the same direction and confer equal political privileges upon all our citizens wherever found. In considering this matter the following questions necessarily present themselves to our minds:

First. Have we a constitutional authority to do it?

Second. Is it equitable to do it under the terms of the Constitution?

Third. Is it expedient to do it?

As to the first question, there is not enough of doubt to admit of discussion. We are bound by no obligation of fundamental law not to insert this provision in the Constitution. On the other hand, it is expressly provided in that law how it may be changed or amended; and we are pursuing the mode prescribed to accomplish the result toward which we are aiming. Our Constitution having been made by the people, may be modified by the same authority. Nothing is more false than that the organic law of a nation may not grow with the growth of a people. It has a right to take coloring from the development of civilization, and especially, as in this case, when all the prescribed formulas are complied with. I therefore dismiss that point without further notice.

The second question, whether it is equitable under our governmental compact to insert this amendment, is broader and involves the whole question of political rights under our Government or as modified by our political compact. Whether each man has a natural right to participate in controlling society, which is government, is not a question which it is necessary to examine here. Various opinions are held on this subject; one class believing that the right to vote is a natural and inherent right correlative with the inherent right of liberty, of which a man cannot be rightfully deprived by any compact or bargain among men; and the other believing that it is a mere conventional right, which may be withheld or conferred according as it may be deemed a benefit or an injury to the State. Whichever of these opinions may be correct, it is certain that this Government was founded on the idea that all political power was vested in the people—not a third or a half or any fraction, but all the people. Hence it was said in the Declaration of Independence that all men were "created equal; that they were endowed by their Creator with certain inalienable rights;" and that "to secure these rights governments were instituted among men, deriving their just powers from the consent of the governed." And hence the preamble of the Constitution declared that "we, the people of the United States"—not a part, but all—for certain purposes proceed to establish our fundamental law. And these original declarations, uttered in the stress of impending trials, are now fortified by the utterances of a century, wherein all our legislation and the sayings of our wisest and best statesmen and philosophers have given them assent. It is true that in practice we have made distinctions depriving certain classes in different States of the privileges of participating in public affairs, and until recently depriving a whole race of those privileges, all of which has been in conflict with the declarations of the founders of the Government. The founders of this nation undoubtedly meant what they said, that this was a Government of the people, deriving its just powers from the consent of the governed, not one, but all. So much for the equity of the matter as considered in connection with our system of government.

I now proceed to consider the expediency of passing this resolution; and I shall take latitude enough possibly to examine further whether the right exists outside the compacts of Government, as well as the expediency of it. I say, then, at the threshold, that in my opinion we are bound to conduct this Government on the basis of permitting the ballot to every male citizen. It is my opinion that the motive power which moves this vast machine, the primary force in the body politic, the original fountain from which springs all law-making authority, is hereafter to be found in the great mass of the people, without distinction of color or race or personal qualities. While aiding in rebuilding the shattered ruins of States in the southern part of this Union, the attention of some of us has been called to this subject in all its aspects; and I confess that, for one, I have come to the conclusion, first, that we could not resist the overwhelming current of public opinion in favor of universal suffrage if we would; and, second, that it is absolutely right and expedient that suffrage be bestowed upon all men within this nation; so that we have necessity as well as right impelling us to this action. . . .

When it was proposed to confer the right to vote upon the colored people of the South, we all remember what evils were predicted. It was said that these people were ignorant; that they were incapable of exercising this function of citizens; that the local State governments were to pass into the hands of the mob, and that confusion and disorder, if not anarchy, would ensue. What is the result? Why, sir, in several of those States in which the former slaves had by their votes a controlling voice there have been adopted constitutions which embody the highest principles that relate to Government, which are more liberal and beneficent than the old ones which they superseded, while the governments move on equably, justice being well administered, public order being well preserved, and liberty permanently established. I think that our late experience in the southern States has demonstrated that the Republic is safe in the hands of all her people. We have now conferred citizenship upon nearly all of this nation. Let us go on and complete the work, until we shall really have a Government by the people, of the people, and for the people.

I am therefore in favor of this amendment, first, because we have constitutional authority to present it; second, because it is equitable, under the early assumptions of the Government, to insert it; and third, because it is expedient to do so. . . .

I have purposely passed over the subterfuges by which it has been attempted to defeat this amendment, such as that of the Senator from Kentucky, [Mr. Davis,] who sets up the objection that all the States are not represented here, and that therefore this action would be null; and such as that of the Senator from Indiana, [Mr. Hendricks,] who contends that the amendment ought to be submitted to a convention; and also such as that of the Senator from Connecticut, [Mr. Dixon,] who contends that the States are independent, and that therefore suffrage cannot be controlled by the United States within their limits. All these ought to be classed among the trivial expedients of politicians rather than among the weighty reasons which should influence the minds of those who constitute the highest branch of the law-making power of the nation. I suppose it were better to brush all these special pleadings away, put them into concealment, and look straight forward to the consummation of this amendment. . . .

Sir, I now desire to say a few words in regard to the apprehensions expressed during this debate that the Federal Government is making too great encroachments upon the reserved rights of the States, and that this proposed amendment is a special evidence of that tendency in the Government. It is said that we are in danger from the centralization of power; that a great consolidated tyranny may arise which will overawe the separate States and finally trample upon the rights of the people. I confess that I do not participate in these apprehensions. Our dangers heretofore as a nation and the dangers which have arisen to safe and just government have not arisen from centralization, but from decentralization. Human liberty and the very existence of the nation have been menaced for many years under the guise of States rights. Why should there be danger to the liberties of the people from the General Government? The lower House of Congress is elected directly from the people, and is as purely a representative body as can be found in the world; while the Senate is elected by the governments of States, and is representative also. The chief executive officer of the nation is elected directly by the vote of the people. The Congress and the Government are but an expression of the whole people's will. There is no basis in its structure on which to found a tyranny. When the people of these States shall be oppressed, and when the nation itself shall break into fragments, I believe it will be, not from the tyranny of the central power, but from the colliding interests and local animosities of sections, even as the universe is not jarred by the sun which hangs forever firmly in space, but by some planet which may burst from its orbit.

I believe that the time has arrived when the power of the General Government should be felt within every foot of its territory. I believe that the time has come when it is the duty of the Government to assert its supremacy and protect life and property everywhere in the United States; and if it has not authority enough for the purpose now, I desire to see it conferred. The Republic must be in America the permanent paramount authority. . . .

ADONIJAH WELCH [R., FLA.]. Mr. President, I desire to offer a mere fragment of thought, not by any means wearisome in length, but bearing upon a point not, as it seems to me, sufficiently noticed by those who favor the measure before the Senate. I should hesitate to prolong this discussion even by the few minutes I shall venture to occupy if the reasons which may be urged for the adoption of the proposed amendment had been completely stated, leaving the general argument of right of Congress to pass this amendment to others. I propose to address myself to the answering of a specific objection to negro suffrage, which has been reiterated in various phraseology during the last three days. This objection, stripped of its verbiage and stated syllogistically, reads as follows: intelligence and virtue are indispensable to the safe exercise of the right of suffrage; the African race in this country is inferior in respect to intelligence and virtue; and consequently it should be denied the right of suffrage.

Now, the fallacy of this reasoning ought to be apparent upon its simple statement. The premise with which it starts nobody denies. It is, indeed, an axiom lying at the basis of our republican Government and national prosperity. But intelligence and virtue are not the distinctive characteristics of races; they are not peculiar to any race; they are not monopolized by nor wholly excluded from any people on the round earth. Intelligence and virtue are individual possessions, inconstant qualities varying *ad infinitum* among the individuals of every people, attaining their highest manifestations in the great and the good and being partially or wholly wanting in the degraded and the vicious. Those constant qualities which mark the different races are mainly physical, consisting of peculiarities of color, feature, figure, and the like; but as these peculiarities are not the qualifications for the voter, nor indicate the presence or absence of such qualifications, they cannot without absurdity be assumed as the ground for withholding or bestowing the right of suffrage. I do not share the prejudice of Senators against race; my prejudices are for or against individuals according to their merits or demerits. . . .

MR. HOWARD. Mr. President, I do not intend at this late hour of the night to enter largely into the discussion of this question, but rise rather for the purpose of presenting, as briefly as possible, some views which I entertain upon it.

It will not escape the attention of any man that there is an anomaly in the Constitution of the United States. While to all other Governments that I know of in the world, properly called governments, pertains the faculty of regulating and pescribing the qualifications of voters, it is a very singular fact that no such faculty belongs to the Government of the United States. The first clause of the Constitution, although it does not impart any power to the States in reference to the qualification of electors, recognizes the undoubted fact that the States then possessed the right to prescribe qualifications for the electors within their own limits, and authorizes those same electors to be the electors of the Representatives in Congress, and of the electors of President and Vice President, so that it has always been out of the power of Congress under the Constitution to prescribe who shall and who shall not vote for Representatives in Congress or for electors of President and Vice President.

In this respect the Government of the United States is subject entirely to the action of the State governments; and herein consists this strange anomaly. Certainly, ordinarily speaking, the power of regulating suffrage ought to pertain to the Government which is to be affected by it. Our fathers, however, did not see fit to grant to the Federal Government any such authority; and I believe the present is the only attempt which has been made since the foundation of the Government to interfere with this right of the States to prescribe the qualifications of voters not only within their own limits, but as to the Federal Government.

Now, sir, on looking over the amendment which has been proposed to us by the Committee on the Judiciary, although I am in favor of conferring the right of suffrage on the colored man as such, I do not find the provision expressed so clearly in that amendment as I wish it were. Indeed, sir, the frame of the amendment, its form, its legal intendment, interpretation, and effect are to me all very objectionable. It declares that "the right of citizens of the United States to vote and hold office shall not be denied or abridged by the United States, or by any State on account of race, color, or previous condition of servitude." Observe, sir, and I call the attention of Senators to the clause, "shall not be denied or abridged by the United States." Sir, the United States have never granted to any citizen of the United States in the States, nor abridged to him, the right to vote. The Government of the United States has not intermeddled, nor has it the right to intermeddle, with the right of voting; and it is hardly proper language, therefore, to say that this right, with which the Government of the United States cannot intermeddle, shall not be denied or abridged by the United States. It is hardly intelligible language to me as a lawyer.

Again there arises from that peculiar form of expression, "shall not be denied or abridged by the United States," what, to my mind, is a very plain implication that in respect to other matters except race, color, or previous condition of servitude, the United States may, through its proper organs, if the Government shall see fit, abridge or deny to citizens of the United States in a State the right to vote or to hold office. For instance, the implication arises that for any other cause, whether it be religious belief, or a want of moral training, or defect of education, or whatever other test Congress may see fit to prescribe, the right to vote may be taken away from the citizen of the United States by act of Congress. Certainly I do not apprehend that the Committee on the Judiciary intended any such thing; but so plain to me is this implication that under such a clause Congress would have the right to deny or abridge the right of voting for some other causes than those mentioned in the article, that I certainly can never give that amendment my vote, for I will never agree, here or elsewhere, that the Congress of the United States or any State government shall have it in its power to say to a citizen of the United States "You shall not vote or hold office because your religious creed is not so and so, or because you do not belong to and commune with this, that, or the other religious denomination." I prefer to adhere to the present provisions of the Constitution of the United States in all these respects—the Constitution which prohibits utterly and forever the setting up of any religious test.

I am willing, as I have already remarked, to extend to the colored man, who is a citizen of the United States, the right to vote and to hold office, like any other citizen; but I prefer to do it in direct and plain terms, so that he who runs may read, without circumlocution, without indirection, but plainly, in terms that are intelligible to the lowest capacity. I shall, therefore, at the proper time, propose an amendment to the amendment now before us, which will be in the following words:

> Citizens of the United States, of African descent, shall have the same right to vote and hold office in States and Territories, as other citizens, electors of the most numerous branch of their respective Legislatures.

Thus adopting the constitutional language of electors having the qualifications of electors of the most numerous branch of the State Legislatures. It seems to me that this expression meets exactly the case which is before us. Why not come out plainly, manfully, and frankly to the world and say what we mean, and not endeavor to darken counsel with words without knowledge, by circumlocution, by concealing or endeavoring to conceal, the real thing which we aim at? Give us, then, the colored man, for that and that only is the object that is now before us. The sole object of this whole proceeding is to impart by a constitutional amendment to the colored man who has become free in the United States the ordinary right of citizens of the United States, and that is the whole of it. I do not wish by any form of words to conceal the fact or to blur the fact that I am in favor of extending to this class of men the right to vote and to hold office in the United States. Sir, they exist among us at this time, not by their own consent, but by the fault of our fathers and of our mother country, whose merchants, moved by the love of gain, brought them to this country and consigned them to slavery. They have ever been a disturbing element in our politics. The fact of the American people holding in bondage so large a number of human beings has been a blot upon our national reputation, has been a source of discredit to the American people abroad. That long and great controversy finally culminated in the recent rebellion. That rebellion necessarily led to the emancipation of the slaves. They are now free. More than four million of that race have become emancipated, and are now enjoying, under an act of Congress and under an amendment of the Constitution of the United States the rights of citizens of the United States. We have made them such. Whether it be for their benefit or our benefit, for their disadvantage or our disadvantage, the fact has become fixed; they are free and are citizens of the United States, endowed with all the civil rights which belong to white men who are citizens of the United States, and the only question now before us and before the country in reference to them is, shall they not only be allowed their civil rights, but shall they for all future time find in the Constitution of their country a guarantee of their political rights as citizens and as political equals with you and me?

Sir, it is impossible in the very nature of things that so large a portion of citizens of the United States as the black portion now are can for any considerable length of time remain in our midst without enjoying the right of suffrage. That would be a great anomaly in our condition. It would be a state of things entirely inconsistent with the genius and mild, beneficent, democratic spirit of our Government. Sir, if they are to remain citizens of the United States, to have the right of eating the bread which they earn, of having a title to the clothes which they earn; if they are to be permitted to purchase houses and lands, to become fathers and mothers, with all the domestic rights which pertain to that condition belonging to them, we must sooner or later see to it that they are citizens possessed of the right to vote and to be represented in the legislative bodies who have control of their persons and their property. Upon the principle of republican government they are entitled thus to be represented; and it will be impossible for the American people, however strong may be the spirit of caste, however odious the black man may be in the eyes of some of our fellow-citizens—it will be utterly impossible to continue this black race in a state of pupilage, of inferiority in respect to political rights for any considerable length of time; and I think, therefore, for their security, for our own security, as an act of justice to them and of security and strength to the Union itself, and the glory of the American people, this thing ought to be done, and I am prepared to vote for it. . . .

I shall vote to impart to the colored man, wherever he may be found within the limits of the United States, if he be a citizen of the United States, the same rights both in regard to his property and liberty and to his political rights and privileges, as pertain to the white man; and I shall do it because we have made him a citizen of the United States; and on this question I have no fear of going before my constituents or any constituency in the United States and before the tribunal of history.

I have thus, Mr. President, as briefly as possible, expressed my objections to the form which this amendment has received at the hands of the Committee on the Judiciary. I think it contains within itself a grant of power to the Congress of the United States to set up other tests for voting and holding office; any other tests, if you please, but those specifically mentioned in the clause. I am quite sure that neither the Senate nor the House of Representatives, if they look upon this matter in that light, will ever agree to any such proposition; and I am entirely certain that the Legislatures of the several States to whom this amendment may be transmitted will entirely dissent from it; while I have no doubt that if the proposition is plainly submitted of giving to the citizens of African descent the right to vote and hold office like other citizens of the United States the amendment will be carried by a handsome majority.

THOMAS HENDRICKS [DEM., IND.]. . . . I have not been satisfied, as many gentlemen of the Republican party recently were not satisfied, that it is wise to extend the suffrage to the colored people. If any State chooses to do it under the existing Constitution it is her own right to do so. I make no war upon that. That is right, because it is in the sense of the Constitution right, the State having the power to do so. But I am not satisfied, I never have been satisfied, that it is wise to make suffrage universal so as to include that race; and I think upon this subject there are some Senators in this Hall who are going to vote for this amendment who will agree with me. I will come to that directly.

I do not believe that the negro race and the white race can mingle in the exercise of political power and bring good results to society. We are of different races. Men may argue about it as much as they please; we know that in many respects there is a great difference between the races. There is a difference not only in their physical appearance and conformation, but there is a difference morally and intellectually; and I do not believe that the two races can mingle successfully in the management of government. I believe that it will bring strife and trouble to the country. That is my conviction upon the subject. I do not believe that they will add to the common intelligence of the country when we make them voters.

Some Senator this evening said that intelligence and virtue were essential to the safe exercise of the suffrage. I think that race does not now bring to the mass of the intelligence of this country an addition. I do not think it ever will. That race in its whole history has furnished no evidence of its capacity to lift itself up. It has never laid the foundation for its own civilization. Any elevation that we find in that race is when we find it coming in contact with the white race. The influence of the white race upon the colored man has carried him up somewhat in the scale of civilization, but when dependent upon himself he has never gone upward. I am willing that that shall be tested by the history and experience of two thousand years back. While the tendency of the white race is upward, the tendency of the colored race is downward; and I have always supposed it is because in that race the physical predominates over the moral and intellectual qualities. I may be mistaken in that; I will not undertake to say that that is certainly so. But I believe that the tendency of that race is downward when not supported by the intelligence of the white race.

MR. WELCH. May I ask the Senator, are the qualities of the voter—which are qualifications—in the individual or in the race? Is the white villain, if there is such a character, qualified to vote, while the intelligent negro—for there are intelligent negroes—is unqualified to vote? The question is on the individuals, not on the race.

MR. HENDRICKS. I listened to the Senator discuss the question of individual intelligence and individual virtue this evening. I am not speaking of it in that relation just now, because the amendment that is pending before the Senate is not considering the race in regard to the individuals that make it. This is a proposition to extend the suffrage to an entire race. I am speaking of that race, whether it is a wise thing to bring into the political Government of this country this race, which has shown in its history an incapacity to elevate itself or to establish a civilization for itself. . . .

OLIVER MORTON [R., IND.]. Mr. President, we have just heard from my distinguished colleague, we heard it this evening from the Senator from Kentucky, [Mr. Davis,] and this afternoon from the Senator from Delaware, [Mr. Saulsbury], the argument against this constitutional amendment that the African is an inferior race, incapable of development, and a race that never invented anything. Suppose we admit this statement to be true; suppose we confess this argument in its length and breadth; I ask if it is an argument against this amendment or in its favor?

It is admitted by all these Senators at the same time that the negro is a kindly race; it is not a savage race; and it is a Christian race in this country, as much so as the white people; but they say that they are of inferior intellectual power, not capable of the same development and progress as the whites. Suppose we grant all this; I ask if it is not a reason why these men should have the ballot put into their hands by which they may protect and take care of themselves? The strong can protect themselves; the weak require to be furnished with the means of protection. In this country there is no protection for political and civil rights outside of the ballot. If men have a natural right to life, liberty, and the pursuit of happiness, they have a natural right to the use of the means by which life, liberty, and the pursuit of happiness can be enjoyed. Sir, the argument is against these Senators. If we admit the inferiority of this race, which I am not now prepared to do, surely it is a reason why we should give to that race the ballot, by which it can protect itself from the powerful and from the majority.

We are told, as an evidence of the inferiority of the race, that they have never invented anything. My colleague would seem to wish to establish a new test or qualification of suffrage, that no man shall be allowed to vote who has not invented something. I wonder how many inventors there are here in this body to-night.

Sir, all these illustrations that have been given of the inferiority of this race are foreign to the question; they are, in fact, begging the question; for admitting them all to be true, the argument comes with ever-increasing force that we ought to give to this weaker, this inferior race, the means of self-protection. . . .

CHARLES SUMNER [R., MASS.]. If we are to have a constitutional amendment now, I want to have it as complete as possible, so that it shall provide against any possible necessity of any amendment hereafter. It will be observed that this amendment of my friend from Michigan, [Mr. Howard,] like the amendment of the committee, is confined simply to the right to vote and hold office. It seems to me that we ought to make a complete work, and to provide for full equality of rights in all respects. If there be any other particular under the head of right, we ought to secure it to all persons, without distinction of color. I propose, therefore, to add to the amendment of my friend from Michigan these words:

"And there shall be no discrimination in rights on account of race or color."

Of course the object of this is to broaden the proposition, not merely to make it a guarantee of the right to vote and to hold office, but a guarantee of equal rights universally.

CHARLES DRAKE [R., MO.]. I would ask the honorable Senator. . . what is the necessity for that, in view of the language of the first section of the fourteenth article of the amendment to the Constitution, which says:

Nor shall any State deprive any person of life, liberty, or property without due process of law, nor deny to any person within its jurisdiction the equal protection of the laws.

MR. SUMNER. I should answer the Senator's question by putting him another. What is the use of the constitutional amendment on which you are now to vote?

MR. DRAKE. Just the very use that it expresses on its face, to secure the right of suffrage to these men whose personal and legal rights we had guaranteed in the previous amendment, but had not guaranteed to them the right of suffrage.

MR. SUMNER. I differ radically and entirely from my friend, and I think there is just the same necessity for the supplementary provision that I propose as there is for the provision which has his support. If the clause to which he calls attention is inadequate to protect persons in their rights of citizenship, including the right to vote, it is inadequate to protect them in anything; the clause is so much waste paper. Now are we in earnest? Are we disposed to close this question up so that no petitions hereafter shall come to us asking equal rights protected either by Congress or by constitutional amendment? I say I want to make complete work and finish it so that hereafter there shall be no question. It is on that account that I would make the addition to the proposition of my friend from Michigan. . . .

MR. EDMUNDS. I hope the Senate will not agree to that amendment. It does not, as it seems to me, stand on any principle. It limits constitutional privileges to persons of African descent, selecting one particular and peculiar nationality. It does appear to me that there is nothing republican in that. It may do as an expedient for to-day. It may be said that it covers all that to-day embarrasses people in the United States, and we ought to put into the Constitution, if we are to put anything in, something which will be broader than one race and be longer in its duration and application than any limited period of time. I do not wish to occupy time, of course, but these are objections which to me are perfectly insuperable to the amendment of the Senator from Michigan. . . .

MR. WARNER. I hope this amendment will not be adopted. I hope the Congress of this country will not single out one race for protection; but that we shall go at once to the broad, grand, affirmative proposition which shall secure the object the Senator from Vermont so well states— that of securing to all the citizens of this country their rights. I think this proposition to single out one race is the weakest one that can be put before the country. If we want to strengthen it and give it a chance of adoption, we ought to amend it and insert the Irish and Germans. I think to single out one race is unworthy of the country and unworthy of the great opportunity now presented to us. We ought to go to the root of the matter by putting in the fundamental law a provision which will make the Constitution beyond doubt mean what the Senators from Vermont and Massachusetts now understand it to mean.

JAMES PATTERSON [R., N.H.]. I hope that this proposition will be adopted; for of all the amendments which have been offered I think it is the best. Our object is to meet a wrong done to a class of black native citizens; to give them the same privileges that other citizens of the United States possess. The Constitution gives to the United States the right to establish a uniform system of naturalization; so that Europeans and Asiatics coming to our coast may be naturalized upon the same conditions in California and in New York. So by the passage of this proposition we shall relieve these black citizens, native to the soil, from the wrong which is done them, without doing any wrong to the Asiatics who may flow in upon our western shores. I prefer, for one, to leave that question open, so that if a war springs up in Asia and these increasing tides of immigration from Asia pour upon our Pacific coast in such numbers as to endanger the welfare of those States, they may have it in their power to guard themselves against the threatened evils, and then, if any evil should result, it will be in our power to remedy it. "Sufficient unto the day is the evil thereof." Let us meet this evil, and not in attempting to meet it provide others that we know not of. . . .

MR. WARNER. I wish to move a substitute for the whole proposition.

THE CHIEF CLERK. The proposed amendment is to strike out all after "section one" and to insert the following:

The right of citizens of the United States to hold office shall not be denied or abridged by the United States or any State on account of property, race, color, or previous condition of servitude; and every male citizen of the United States of the age of twenty-one years, or over, and who is of sound mind, shall have an equal vote at all elections in the State in which he shall have actually resided for a period of one year next preceding such election, except such as may hereafter engage in insurrection or rebellion against the United States, and such as shall be duly convicted of treason, felony, or other infamous crimes. . . .

GEORGE WILLIAMS [R., ORE.]. I would inquire of the author of this amendment if he has carefully considered its effect in the States? I suppose that if this is made a part of the Constitution every citizen will have an equal right to vote with every other citizen in every school district and in every municipality and in every sort of an organization that may exist in the States. Then there is another election, the election of United States Senators, which may, perhaps, be reached by the general term "elections" here employed. It seems to me that it is dangerous to say by a provision of the Constitution of the United States that in all possible or conceivable elections which may be held in the States for any local purpose every citizen shall have an equal right to vote. There may be elections held where it would operate greatly to the injury of all concerned to let every person have an equal right to vote. Sometimes it becomes necessary to regulate elections in school districts; persons who own property in the district pay taxes, and it is thought advisable sometimes that they should have the control of the elections. I do not undertake to justify such legislation as that, but I say there is danger that we may put a rule in the Constitution of the United States that will produce great embarrassment in the States. I am a little afraid to vote for it.

JOHN SHERMAN [R., OHIO]. Mr. President, I thought nothing would tempt me to say one word in this debate on the constitutional amendment, but Senators have already perceived the difficulty we are approaching, and we might as well at once face the issue. There are five different causes of exclusion from the right to vote in this and other countries. The first is race. This cause of exclusion has existed in this country in nearly all the States until recently. The second is property, and that has existed in England since the foundation of their Government. The third is religion, which exists in almost all countries except our own. The fourth is nativity, and that exists in nearly all countries. The fifth is education, and that is an experiment of ours, I believe, in Massachusetts.

Now, Mr. President, if we are endeavoring to settle this question once for all, I think it would be wiser and better to declare that every male citizen of the United States, native or naturalized, above the age of twenty-one years, shall have the right to vote, unless he is excluded for crime; and that no State shall exclude any one from the right to vote because of his race, because of his property or want of property, because of his religion, because of his birthplace, or because of the misfortune of want of education. As this amendment makes the nearest approach to that, I have made up my mind to vote for it, or I shall vote for the amendment of the Senator from Massachusetts, [Mr. Wilson.] I do not like to apply a rule so narrow and limited as to guaranty rights to the African race which we refuse to the Asiatic race or to other races. I do not wish to include the ignorant masses of our southern population and exclude the partially intelligent classes of the State of Massachusetts. I do not want to include the negroes and exclude or allow a State to exclude foreigners who are declared to be citizens of the United States under the laws of the United States.

Therefore, it does seem to me that if we intend to now prescribe a rule for suffrage in this country, we ought to make it operate universally and withdraw from the States all power to exclude any portion of the male citizens of the United States, leaving them, if they choose, to regulate the length of residence, whether females shall participate in the elective franchise, at what age males shall vote, etc.; but to exclude from them all power to deprive any portion of our male citizens above the age of twenty-one years of the right to vote, unless where the right has been forfeited by crime. If the amendment of the Senator from Massachusetts is voted down and this amendment is voted down, then the next best proposition, I think, is that report of the Committee on the Judiciary, which I shall then vote for. . . .

MR. WILSON. I desire to offer an amendment to the amendment. It is a modification of the proposition that was acted on a short time ago. It is to strike out all of section one of the article reported by the committee, and to insert:

No discrimination shall be made in any State among the citizens of the United States in the exercise of the elective franchise or in the right to hold office in any State on account of race, color, nativity, property, education, or religious creed.

I will simply say that this amendment is more comprehensive, fuller, and juster than any amendment that has been offered, I think, and therefore I think it is strong enough, and I hope the Senate will adopt it.

MR. SHERMAN. We have debated the phraseology of this amendment so long, and so much debate has been exhausted upon it, that it is not worth while to spend any more time. I am satisfied that the report of the Judiciary Committee, which only extends to the African race and secures to them the elective franchise, is not broad enough when we are about to change the Constitution. I much prefer the language read by the Senator from Maine a while ago as the report of the Committee on Reconstruction two years ago; but now I believe it is wise to wipe out a multitude of discriminations in the constitutions of the several States that make discriminations on account of religious faith, color, property, etc. In the State of New Hampshire no man is allowed to hold office by her constitution unless he believes in the Protestant faith, although I believe that provision is now practically a dead letter. In Rhode Island naturalized citizens are not allowed to hold office or to vote in certain cases. In Massachusetts they exclude people who cannot read by a test that is not practical in character and is useless.

It seems to me, as the Republican party are about to lay the foundation for a political creed, that the broadest and safest and best foundation for it is universal suffrage, protecting all men above the proper age and with the proper residence in the right to share in the elective franchise and in the right to hold office. The amendment of the Senator from Massachusetts [Mr. Wilson] is carefully worded so as not to exclude or change the Constitution of the United States in prescribing the qualifications of the President of the United States or of a Senator. The Constitution requires that the President must be a native-born citizen of the United States. No one wishes to change that. It provides also that a Senator shall have resided in his State so many years, and shall, if he be a naturalized citizen, be more than nine years a citizen. This amendment does not change that provision. It only requires that in a State for local offices no discrimination shall be made against any citizen of the United States, because when a person is naturalized the theory of our law is that he should be placed on an equal footing in all respects with the native-born citizen, except where he has been expressly excluded by the provisions of the Constitution of the United States. It seems to me, if we are to have a party platform, that this proposition will give us the best one. Senators have made this a party question undoubtedly. The debate last night shows that it is intended to make this a party question, and to oppose it as a party creed. I am willing myself to accept as a party creed the broad general principle that every man of a given age and prescribed residence shall have an equal voice in making the laws and enforcing the laws of the United States. . . .

MR. MORTON. Mr. President, we are now about to amend the fundamental law in regard to suffrage. The amendment, as it is proposed by the House of Representatives and as it is reported by the Committee on the Judiciary of the Senate, confines the limitation upon State power to the single subject of race or color, just as if that was the only subject upon which there could be an abuse; just as if that was the only important consideration. Now, sir, that we are at work on this subject, can we stand justified before the people of this nation if we do not make this limitation apply to other possible abuses? This amendment, as offered by the Senator from Massachusetts, proposes to say that there shall be no discrimination on account of race, color, nativity, property, education, or creed. I think there is no more principle, there is no more justice in requiring a man to have a certain amount of property before he shall be allowed to exercise this right that is indispensable to the protection of his life, liberty, and happiness, than there is in requiring him to have a white skin. If the right of suffrage is a natural right, if it belongs to all men because they have a right to have a voice in the Government that controls their action, if it is necessary to all men as a means of protecting other acknowledged natural rights, how can you make it depend upon property?

Now, sir, this question is before us, and we cannot refuse to adopt the pending amendment without saying substantially to the States, "While you shall not disfranchise a man on account of color, you may disfranchise him because he has not got property." Are we willing to place ourselves as a Senate, and are my Republican friends willing to place themselves as a party, before the country on that ground? I will not do it for one.

The same may be said in regard to educational tests. I believe all educational tests in this country are humbugs. They do no good. When you come to consider the question of voting as a natural right, what right have you to take it from a man because he cannot read and write? He may be, nevertheless, a very intelligent man, and he has his rights to defend and preserve just like other men, and the right of suffrage is just as important to him as it is to anybody else. What right have you to say that he shall not have it because he cannot read and write?

The same is true in regard to the qualification of religious faith. The State of New Hampshire now excludes any man from her house of representatives unless he belongs to the Protestant faith. That exclusion is contrary to the whole spirit of our institutions; and now that we are at work on this subject, and the question is brought before us, are we at liberty to reject this amendment, and thus say to New Hampshire, in substance and by implication, that she may continue to exclude men from office on account of their faith?

In regard to nativity, if we reject this amendment we say to the States, "You cannot exclude men because of their color, but you are still left at liberty to exclude them because of their nativity." Are we prepared to say that? I am aware that the question of colored suffrage has brought the subject before Congress; but, now that it is here, we are bound, as wise legislators, if we are entitled to that character, to consider and to guard against all the abuses that may arise upon that subject.

MR. HOWARD. Mr. President, it seems to me that this amendment of the Senator from Massachusetts is entirely too sweeping. It contemplates a complete revolution in the State constitutions. It takes away from the States the right to require any particular residence of a citizen of the United States before he is permitted to hold office. Let me give you a single instance. Take the clause in the constitution of my own State which declares that —

> No person shall be eligible to the office of Governor or Lieutenant Governor who shall not have been five years a citizen of the United States and a resident of this State two years next preceding the election.

He must have been a citizen of the United States at least five years from the date of his naturalization before he can be elected Governor of that State; and I presume an analogous provision is contained in most of the constitutions of the States. If it is not it certainly ought to be, in my judgment. But this amendment abolishes all discrimination of this kind as to holding office. It gives the right to hold office to one citizen as much as to another, if I understand it rightly.

There is another view to be taken of this. In my own State, as is the case in Indiana, I think, and probably many of the new States in the West, persons who have simply declared their intention to become naturalized citizens are allowed, after a certain residence in the State, to vote and to hold office. What is to be the condition of that class of persons under such an amendment as this? No discrimination can be made against citizens, and that clause would leave to the Legislatures the right to discriminate in favor of unnaturalized foreigners, and prefer them, if they saw fit to do so unwise a thing, even to citizens of the United States, whether native-born or naturalized. Sir, this amendment is entirely too sweeping; it runs a plowshare through all the State constitutions and overturns the most important State regulations that can be found. For my part I am not prepared to go so far as that. I am willing to cure the evil of which complaint has been made, and to give to the black man the right to vote, if situated within the United States, in all cases in which I would give a white citizen of the United States the right to vote. But I will not go so far as to overthrow and uproot the very foundations of the State constitutions. . . .

MR. PATTERSON. Mr. President, allusion has been made several times in the debate to the religious test in the constitution of New Hampshire. The restriction is that none but those of the Protestant religion shall be members of the house of representatives. It is true that there is such a restriction in our constitution, but as a matter of fact it is a dead letter as I have said once before. Catholics are allowed to hold seats in our Legislature and to hold office in the State, and I presume the people of the State would not object to having that restriction in our constitution set aside.

But, sir, I am opposed to the amendment of the Senator from Massachusetts for another reason. I do not oppose it because it overrides that part of our constitution particularly, nor am I against it because it sets aside conditions of suffrage generally. I want no distinction of caste, or color, or property, but I have always been in favor of the law of Massachusetts. I have hitherto been in favor of an educational test as a restriction upon the right of suffrage; nor am I prepared to say now, as one gentleman has said, that this is an idle restriction; that it is doing violence to the civilization and the Christianity of the age to retain an educational test in our constitution or in our law.

Suffrage is the most sacred of all our rights; and why should we throw open this portal of political power and let into the strongholds of our Government the emissaries of arbitrary power, the minions of despotism? Why should we let barbarism come in like a flood? If you do that the period may not be far distant when you will have so degraded the intelligence of your people that they will be unequal to self-government, and then, like the early republics, you will roll down the bloody grade of revolution into the most abject and absolute despotism.

I know that as we stand to-day an educational test may not be necessary; but it will do no harm. If the people have the intelligence prerequisite to self-government an educational test will not limit very much the extent of suffrage. There will be about as many votes cast with it as without it. It is simply a safeguard against a possible evil. I would have the intelligence prerequisite to the exercise of suffrage very low, so that it may be easily reached by our foreign population or by any of our native population who may lack the means of education. I desire it, among other things, as an encouragement to popular intelligence. I say simply this, that the way to suffrage should be open to all. To deny it on account of race or color or want of property is doing violence to the civilization of our age, and insults Christianity; but to protect and guard it against the incoming floods of ignorance and barbarism is simply to preserve the jewel of liberty. This is my view of this subject, both as an abstract and practical question. For this and for no other reason am I opposed to the amendment of the gentleman from Massachusetts. . . .

MR. WILSON. I hope Senators will allow me a single instant to allude to one point. I wish to say to the Senator from New Hampshire, who has referred to the State of Massachusetts, that the educational test in that State is practically of no value whatever. I do not believe it keeps five hundred men from the elections in that State. I was opposed to it when it was adopted. I did not believe a word in it, and I believe less in it now. Last autumn, I remember, we had several hundred foreigners where I live who became voters. Our friends supposed we might have a pretty sharp contest, and they came to me and said "Probably fifteen or twenty of these men cannot read and write; do you not think we had better put the educational test to them?'' I said to my friends what I have always said, "Never do it." I would be ashamed to look a man in the face when I put such a test to him. I believe in manhood, and I believe the ballot is an educator, and I do not believe in any such petty tests. I think it is anything but creditable to any part of the country.

MR.PATTERSON. Will the gentleman allow me to ask him a question?

MR. WILSON. Certainly.

MR. PATTERSON. I wish to ask the gentleman if he thinks self-government is possible among the Hottentots or the Micronesians?

MR. WILSON. No; I do not think it is. I am sorry that my friend should put such a question as that. We are not talking about Hottentots; we are talking about the people who come here from western Europe, who are of our race, who are naturalized in the United States. I wish to say one single word to the Senator upon this point. We have heard to-day, since we have been here, a great deal said about barbarians in Africa. The answer is that we are not dealing with barbarians in Africa; we are dealing with four million men whose ancestors have been for two hundred years in this country, and we are not dealing with Hottentots. . . .

ROSCOE CONKLING [R., N.Y.]. Mr. President, I have been silent during the long debate which still proceeds, and I promise to occupy but few moments now. The original proposition pending came from the Committee on the Judiciary. I was not present in committee, although I am regular in my attendance there, when the action, whatever it may have been upon this subject was taken, and therefore I had no part in the phraseology, the form, or the substance which has occupied the Senate. It follows that I have no preference by way of pride, of paternity, or relationship for any of the multiplied versions before us.

The honorable Senator from Ohio [Mr. Sherman] tells us that he sees among all these forms a preference due to the amendment proposed by the Senator from Massachusetts, [Mr. Wilson,] and now immediately pending. But for this announcement by the Senator from Ohio I should have deemed this amendment open to much question and uncertainty. Let us see in part, at least, what it is. It consists of two members. I read the first member separated from the second:

No discrimination shall be made in any State among the citizens of the United States in the exercise of the elective franchise on account of race, color, nativity, property, education, or creed.

I omit for the moment the words relative to eligibility to office. Had the Senator considered how far this may revolutionize and undo the constitutions, the enactments, and the customs of the States? Take the test of property. No discrimination in the exercise of the elective franchise in case of any election shall be made on the score of property. What becomes of all the elections held under provisions of municipal charters, which are participated in by freeholders or tax-payers alone? What becomes, in the cities of the State of New York, of wholesome restrictive provisions in municipal charters, restraining the expenditure of moneys beyond a certain sum, unless a majority or two-thirds of the tax-payers of the city, that is to say the stockholders in the corporation, at an election to be held for that purpose, shall authorize additional expenditure? Is there anything in the history of the last few years which demands of this body a proposition to molest safeguards such as these?

But again, no discrimination whatever in the exercise of the elective franchise—I emphasize the expression "in the exercise of the elective franchise"—shall be made on account of nativity. Will some Senator tell me what the effect of this would be upon the reforms now suggested in reference to naturalization? For example, the honorable Senator from Massachusetts does not intend to deprive the State of New York of the power to make regulations concerning registry and other incidents in the exercise of the elective franchise. Suppose the State of New York requires that naturalized citizens shall produce their certificates of naturalization when their names go down upon the registry, and when their ballots go down into the box. Would not that, I submit to Senators, be a discrimination touching the exercise of the elective franchise on account of nativity? If it would not, why not? All naturalized persons being required to produce proof of their naturalization—required, if you please, to produce proof not demanded of other citizens of the place where they live, of the length of time for which they have lived in a precinct or at the number of a street in a city,—would not that be a discrimination touching the exercise of their rights, and touching the exercise of the elective franchise, and does it not rest upon reasons of nativity?

Again, suppose the laws of naturalization shall provide that nine months or six months, so as to remove the act from proximity to an election, shall intervene between the act of naturalization and the deposit of a vote by the recipient of the certificate, would not that be a discrimination peculiar to that class of citizens, and would it not be made on the ground and solely on the ground of foreign nativity? I know it may be said that the provision touching naturalization might be that the certificate itself should not take effect, that no vigor should be imparted to it when it was granted, nor until a certain period had elapsed. It is possible—probable, if you please—that by some careful arrangement of legislative provisions by way of circumlocution or circumvention you could navigate around a constitutional amendment of this sort; but is it well, is it wise to imbed in the bulwarks of the Constitution requirements or impediments which are to become the occasions of skill in the department of evasion?

I will not multiply words, however, but will come to the second member of the proposition: "No discrimination shall be made as to the right to hold office in any State on account of"—I do not read all the exclusions— "property, education, or creed." Can a State provide that a judge shall be a lawyer? I doubt it if the language I have read be imported into the Constitution. Can you provide that law and the classics together must be pursued as a study for three years or seven years to entitle an applicant to admission to practice in the courts? The honorable Senator may say that the profession of the law, or the right to exercise it, is not an office or the holding of an office. The Supreme Court has gone very near overruling him upon that point, should he rely upon it. But let us suppose that attorneys and counselors would not be embraced, can you provide that a man to hold an office requiring medical skill shall be educated and licensed as a surgeon? Can you provide that a chaplain in a State prison shall be a clergyman of some Christian denomination? Can you provide that no man shall be eligible to election as surrogate or as recorder unless he has the skill, even the readiness of penmanship and grammatical composition, or the legal attainments fitting him for the place?

In the jurisprudence and in the arrangements, statutory and municipal, general and endemic, to which I am most accustomed, nothing is more common, nothing is more inwrought in the system than the idea that the requisite skill and attainments shall be a part of the merit of the person to be selected or appointed to office. But all this is to disappear in the face of this amendment.

Education in any degree whatever, either as a qualification of suffrage or officeholding, a standard of intelligence above the most groveling and besotted ignorance is to be beyond and above the power, above the prerogative of the States. Sir, licentiousness is not liberty and excess is not wisdom; and if it be true that an amendment such as this is the best which has been hammered out on the anvil of this debate, perhaps that fact may prove, as I have silently suspected for several days, that a small number of Senators, such as this body can furnish in large numbers, might take the various propositions suggested and from them all or beyond them all deduce something better, some simple thing, preserving all that need not be disturbed, and rejecting all that is ambiguous and hurtful. As I was not present in the Judiciary Committee when assent was given to one form of amendment I hesitate to suggest any course in derogation of the wish or the view of the committee. I refrain, therefore, from making a motion or making more than a general suggestion; but it seems to me that with so many propositions before us, and with a proposition so open to criticism as this, receiving the preferential approval of several Senators, we might profitably consider whether it would not be well to resort to some more exact and speedy mode of perfecting a proposition than has been found in the long-continued debate conducted so ably by those who have shared it. . . .

MR. SHERMAN. Mr. President, I regret very much to prolong this discussion. I feel very much as the Senator from New York does, that we have already exhausted our time and our patience; but there are a few observations made by him to which I will reply very briefly.

The House of Representatives sent to us an amendment to the Constitution proposing to abrogate and change the constitutions of at least thirty States in the Union. It proposes to declare that all distinctions made in those constitutions on account of race, color, or previous condition of slavery shall be swept away. It deals, therefore, with the most difficult problem of political economy, the right of suffrage. The Committee on the Judiciary, of which the honorable Senator from New York is a member, report to us an amendment changing the House resolution somewhat by extending this provision to those holding office, so that no discrimination shall be made against a person of African descent holding any office of honor, trust, or profit in the United States. This changes the constitutions of at least thirty States of the Union. Among others it changes the constitution of the State of Ohio. This is a very sensitive question with our people. The great body of the party to which I belong have long been in favor of dispensing with and repealing all discriminations on account of color, but we made an appeal to the people two years ago on this subject and were defeated; and I may say that no change can be made in the Constitution likely to excite so much popular feeling as this proposed change to extend to the negro race in the State of Ohio the elective franchise. I say this freely, because I am in favor of giving to them every right which is conferred by the Constitution and laws on white people.

When we proposed to deal with this question of suffrage we were met with this difficulty: here is an amendment to the Constitution that must be acted on by two thirds of both Houses of Congress and must get the assent of three fourths of the States of the Union; and yet we put this proposition on so narrow a ground that we are constantly apologizing for its weakness. Why should we protect the African in the enjoyment of suffrage, when in certain States of the Union even naturalized citizens cannot vote? Why should we protect the descendant of the African, when in certain States of the Union a man who has the misfortune not to be able to read and write cannot vote? Why should we apply this supreme remedy of the Constitution only in favor of this particular class of citizens? Senators must see at once that to rest this constitutional amendment upon so narrow a ground is not defensible, and therefore it has been sought to extend the operation of this constitutional amendment so as to reach other abuses. We know that in certain States of the Union there are educational tests, and there are tests growing out of birth, tests growing out of color, tests growing out of religious belief. None of these exist in the State of Ohio, except as to color. None of these exist in the more modern constitutions. Most of them are the relic of the same sentiment that incorporated property qualifications in all the constitutions of the old States. They have been swept away by time. Now, when we are dealing with the question of suffrage, why not sweep them all away, and say that a man of proper age and proper residence, whatever may be his color or religious opinions, shall vote? . . .

We ought to deny to States the right to discriminate between citizens on account of anything except age, residence, and sex. In all other respects citizens should have an equal right to vote. We ought to regard it as a fundamental principle of our Government that all persons arriving at a certain age are entitled to equal rights. We can fairly base our action upon that fundamental principle and submit that action to the people with a certainty that it will be adopted. But, sir, if I go before the people of Ohio with a constitutional amendment such as that which is sent to us by the House of Representatives, or that which is proposed by the Judiciary Committee, how shall I be met? Take the prejudice and feeling of that people known to me and known to all Senators, and when I go before them how shall I be met? I shall be told "Here are white citizens excluded from voting in Massachusetts because they cannot read and write; here are people excluded from office in New Hampshire because they are not Protestants. Why do you not correct these evils at your own door, evils brought upon the country by your own friends, and why should you protect only and seek to extend only the right of suffrage to the colored race, who are just emancipated from bondage, who are ignorant, who are without the capacity, probably, for self-government unless they become enlightened?" How can you answer it? It is impossible to answer, especially when you meet a prejudiced people who have got to vote on this question. The people of Ohio come from all the old States, many of them from Virginia and Maryland and other of the old slave States. They are full of prejudices. Unless you show that you are willing to adopt a universal rule which tramples down their prejudices, and the prejudices of the people of other portions of the old States where they have not adopted, probably, the more advanced rules on this subject—unless you can show that you have dealt with this question in an enlightened spirit of statesmanship, you will be borne down by popular clamor. It will be said this is a mere party expedient to accomplish party ends, and not a great fundamental proposition upon which you should base your superstructure. . . .

THE PRESIDENT PRO TEMPORE [BENJAMIN WADE, R., OHIO]. The question is on the amendment of the Senator from Massachusetts [Mr. Wilson] to the amendment proposed by the Senator from Nevada, [Mr. Stewart.]

JOHN CONNESS [R., CAL.]. On that amendment I call for the yeas and nays.

The yeas and nays were ordered; and being taken, resulted—yeas 31, nays 27. . . .

So the amendment to the amendment was agreed to. . . .

House of Representatives-40th Congress, 3rd Session
February 15, 1869

. . . (two thirds voting in favor thereof) the rules were suspended, and the amendments of the Senate were taken up and read, as follows:

Line two add the letter "s" to the word "article."
Line three strike out the word "an" and add "s" to "amendment."
Line four, after "State," insert "either of."
After line six insert "first amendment."
Strike out the first section and insert in lieu thereof:

No discrimination shall be made in any State among the citizens of the United States in the exercise of the elective franchise or in the right to hold office in any State on account of race, color, nativity, property, education, or creed. . . .

GEORGE BOUTWELL [DEM., MASS.]. Mr. Speaker, I think there are two fatal objections to the proposition coming from the Senate. I could enumerate many others of great magnitude; but in regard to the proposition concerning suffrage, if there is any one purpose we have had in view in regard to this amendment of the Constitution it has been to secure to the slave class the right to vote. Now, then, this amendment, as it comes from the Senate, says there shall be no discrimination in the right to vote or hold office on account of race, color, nativity, education, property, or creed. But the point I make against this proposition is that it leaves it open to the States to declare by law that persons who have been held in slavery, or whose mothers were slaves, shall neither vote nor hold office; and this amendment to the Constitution, if adopted, would furnish no means by which that evil could be remedied, because the slave class, as is well known, are of no specific color and are of no particular race, and can only be described by the use, in substance, of that phrase, which gentlemen here seem to avoid, but which has grown out of the historical fact of the age, and which we must meet by the use of language explicit and clear. We must say that there shall be no discrimination on account of the previous condition of slavery. There is no security in the proposition, as it comes from the Senate, for this great class of American citizens. And this is but one objection to the first amendment of the Senate. . . .

JOHN BINGHAM [R., OHIO]. If I understand the remarks of the gentleman from Massachusetts [Mr. Boutwell], he objects because this proposed amendment of the Constitution does not also contain the words "or on account of previous condition of servitude." Do I understand the gentleman correctly? . . .

Mr. Speaker, if I thought those who were once slaves, and, in the words of Kent, natural-born citizens of the United States under disability, but who are now freemen and therefore citizens of the United States under no disability, were not upon an equal footing with other natural-born citizens, I would agree with the gentleman and never vote for this amendment at all even if it received the assent of the House; but I differ from the gentleman *toto coelo* in his premises. I say that since the adoption of the thirteenth and fourteenth articles of amendment to the Constitution those who were once slaves—citizens, in the language of Kent, under disability—are as much free citizens without disability as any other citizens in the Republic and under the equal protection of the law. I only quote the words of the great commentator himself when I say further, in addition to what I have already said, that the moment the condition of slavery ceases they become citizens without disability. The words "natural born" occur in the Constitution. It also provides that all persons born in the Republic, and also all persons of foreign birth who may become naturalized, shall be citizens of the United States. . . .

If the amendment should be concurred in, and it should afterwards be ratified, I will undertake to say, as a Representative of the American people, that it would be henceforth out of the power of any State of the Union to discriminate against any class of natural-born citizens of the Republic on account of slavery or servitude. For one, having reflected much on this subject, I am now ready to pass a law which shall be effective, and enforcing it in our own courts, against any such despotism being attempted by any State in the Union, in the event of the adoption and ratification of this amendment.

I will add further, Mr. Speaker, that when you come to consider an amendment to the fundamental law the question is, what is the grievance to be remedied, what is the injury, what is the wrong you wish to redress? I ask the gentleman from Massachusetts to consider that there is not a State constitution in America which disqualifies from office any human being on account of previous condition of servitude. The disqualification is on account of color, on account of the accident of birth, on account of want of educational qualifications, on accout of creed, and on account of want of property; and all these grievances are remedied and covered by this amendment, every one of them. One reason why I ask the House to concur is that this Congress is in the last days of its existence, and every man knows that unfinished business does not survive, but perishes with it. By refusing to concur with the Senate you may never have another opportunity of presenting this question to the consideration of the American people. It is equal and just and right, for it puts the political privileges of the natural born and naturalized citizens alike under the protection of the laws, irrespective of color. It is just and right in this, that it disposes of discriminations made on account of faith in the laws of New Hampshire; it disposes of the discrimination on account of nativity in the constitution of Rhode Island, and of New York on account of property. It disposes of the discrimination in twenty or more States in the Union on account of color; it puts the citizens of the United States upon an equal footing, and I repeat, it puts it beyond the power of any State to disfranchise any natural born or naturalized citizen on account of nativity, color, education, property, or creed.

As to servitude, that is embraced in the words color, race, and nativity. It will be in vain to look into any of the State constitutions for any such disability, for they never undertook to discriminate against any man on account of previous condition of servitude. Every man knows that it would be a violation of the letter and spirit of the proposed amendment, and the thirteenth and fourteenth articles already ratified. . . .

HENRY BROMWELL [R., ILL.]. I wish to call the gentleman's attention to one thing. I should like to know whether there is any provision incorporated anticipating the objection on account of previous condition of servitude, and putting it out of the power of any State to prevent any citizen of the United States from voting on account of former condition of servitude? The gentleman from Ohio states, because the Constitution makes them all citizens it is all right; but cannot a State prevent a citizen from actually voting on account of this very circumstance?

MR. BINGHAM. Not at all. That is what I anticipated; that if this amendment be passed a State can do no such thing, and the suggestion of the gentleman ought to be a reason why we should not send the amendment back to the Senate for its action. I will make this suggestion in connection with it; although I admit that if the additional words "previous condition of servitude" were put in I still would vote for it, for the reason that I do not think it changes the legal effect of it at all.

MR. BROMWELL. But striking it out might change the legal effect of it.

MR. BINGHAM. Not all all; it is not there now to be stricken out. I will make this suggestion: that if you put these words in the Constitution, "shall not discriminate on account of previous condition of servitude," then by every known rule of construction it would imply that discrimination might be made on account of some future condition of servitude. . . .

CHARLES ELDREDGE [DEM., WIS.]. I call for the yeas and nays.

The yeas and nays were ordered.

The first amendment of the Senate was to make the article in relation to suffrage read as follows:

SEC. 1. No discrimination shall be made in any State among the citizens of the United States in the exercise of the elective franchise or in the right to hold office in any State on account of race, color, nativity, property, education or creed.

SEC. 2. The Congress shall have power to enforce by appropriate legislation the provisions of this article.

The question was taken; and there were—yeas 37, nays 133, not voting 52. . . .

So (two thirds not voting in favor thereof) the amendment was not concurred in. . . .

Senate-40th Congress, 3rd Session
February 17-23, 1869

The action of the House of Representatives was read, as follows:

In the House of Representatives, February 15, 1869:

Resolved, That the House non-concur in the amendments of the Senate to the joint resolution (H. R. No. 402) proposing an amendment to the Constitution of the United States, and ask a conference with the Senate on the disagreeing votes of the two Houses thereon.

Ordered, That Mr. Boutwell, Mr. Shellabarger, and Mr. Eldredge be the committee on the part of the House.

WILLIAM STEWART [R., NEV.]. I move that the Senate insist on its amendments, and agree to the conference asked by the House of Representatives. . . .

CHARLES BUCKALEW [DEM., PA.]. . . . I have noticed, sir, for several years that upon political issues which appear here in Congress, whether in the form of propositions to amend the Constitution of the United States, or in the forms of ordinary legislation, whether by bill or joint resolution, the House of Representatives always insists that its particular views shall prevail, and in nine cases out of ten the House has its way; its will and its opinions prevail; and it is very possible now that upon this question of amending the Constitution, or rather of forming a proposition of amendment, the House of Representatives, according to the accepted practice of Congress for many years upon political questions, will again prevail. . . .

If, therefore, sir, on the present occasion the Senate shall conclude to take back all that it has done upon this subject, to withdraw its proposition entirely from the field of debate and from the field of action, and assent to what was originally proposed by the House, if gentlemen conclude to bend their wills to the will of the House, their opinions to the opinion of the House, it will be in exact accord and in perfect consistency with the political history of Congress for the last half dozen years, and it will be another proof added to many former ones that in this country the ideas which obtain in Parliament as to the relative importance of the two Houses are year after year to obtain more and more completely. There, sir, in Parliament, although the theory of the Constitution of Great Britain is that the House of Lords shall participate in legislation, and it has always been conceded even by the Commons that it has power to amend bills, yet whenever the House of Commons has made up its mind to insist upon a measure the upper House must give way. They cannot resist the demand of the Commons when that demand is persisted in, and why? Because the House of Commons represents the people of Great Britain; the House of Lords represents only a caste or a class of population; the voice of the British nation is heard through the lower House, and is heard through it alone. The upper House is a sort of consulting body, and it has certain judicial functions imposed upon it by the British system; but it is not, in point of fact, an efficient member of the legislative body.

The Senate of the United States by its course and conduct upon all questions bearing a political complexion now for many years past, and by the action proposed to it upon this measure before us, is to subside into the position of a House of Lords in this country; is not to be taken as representing the majesty of our great political Commonwealths called States, or as representing in any sense the voice of that mighty people whose tides of population are swelling from ocean to ocean by many millions in each decade of our progress. No, sir; it is to subside into a body of consultation with whom the popular branch of Congress may confer occasionally by committees of conference and by messages through its Clerk, but it is to have no efficient, actual, thorough, realized power in this Government to control and direct the action of its political department. . . .

HENRY WILSON [R., MASS.]. I desire to say a word, and I shall be very brief, for I am acting in this matter in no factious spirit certainly, but with an earnest desire to get what I believe to be right. In my judgment, nine tenths of our friends in and out of Congress who are in favor of submitting this question to the country at all are in favor of so submitting it as to settle both the right to vote and the right to be voted for. I do hope that we shall adopt that plan here, and that the fear of failing in this measure will not drive us, in a panic, to send out to the country an immature proposition—a proposition that is not complete within itself.

Now, in several of the States of this Union the colored men have the right by their constitutions to hold office. There is a controversy in Georgia about it, and why has that controversy arisen? Because it is not expressed in their constitution; it was left to be inferred; and what is the result? Disorganization, injustice, and wrong; and we have held Georgia up here during this whole session. Now, sir, suppose we submit this imperfect proposition which says to seven hundred and fifty thousand colored men in this country, "You shall have the right to vote, but you shall not have the right to sit upon a jury or the right to hold office," how will they feel in regard to it?

THE PRESIDENT PRO TEMPORE [THOMAS FERRY, R., MICH.]. If the Senator will permit me, I will tell him that it says no such thing.

MR. WILSON. It is true it does not say that expressly, but it leaves that inference. It does not say that a State shall not deny to colored men the right to hold office; and will it not be an inspiration to some to keep or take that right from them? Will not that be the tendency? I do not know that it will; all that I say is that I fear it will. Now, sir, I want to accomplish the work of making these citizens equal to other citizens in rights and in privileges.

I do not wish to trespass upon the Senate further, but it does seem to me that this measure should have been referred to a committee of conference, and I think there we could have amended satisfactorily the House proposition or the proposition of the Judiciary Committee, which I like a great deal better and am perfectly willing to like. The Senator from Vermont [Mr. Edmunds] suggests that we lay this upon the table and pass immediately the resolution of the Committee on the Judiciary. I would be happy to do that, for it does seem to me that what we are now doing is wrong, and suppose two thirds should not vote for this, where is the amendment then?

MR. STEWART. I wish to say just one word. I think the Senator from Massachusetts is as much responsible as any other person for the condition in which we are placed. In the first place, the proposition of the Judiciary Committee was conceded by a large number of our friends to be the best. It contained the simple proposition that the right to vote and hold office should not be denied on account of race, color, or previous condition of servitude. It did not attempt to extend any further than to the right to vote and hold office. The Senator from Massachusetts moved to put upon that several other propositions which loaded it down. He voted to put upon it the proposition with regard to electing the President; he voted to put upon it a proposition with regard to religious tests; he voted to put upon it a proposition with regard to education; he voted to put upon it all of those propositions which went to the House of Representatives and were rejected by them. It came here. A majority of our friends here this morning, on consultation and by a large vote, said we had better take this than to have nothing, and the votes have been very emphatic on that point. Every vote has been a test on the proposition that we will take this rather than have nothing. To throw it open to further discussion is to get nothing. The true way to get the right to hold office included in this proposition was by standing by the Judiciary Committee of the Senate in their amendment. I stood by it; I refrained from speaking, and protested against loading that down as it was loaded down by the vote of the Senator from Massachusetts and others. It is now in such a shape that to send it to a committee of conference at this late day will cause the loss of everything. I am for doing something for the colored man in earnest, and I am not so anxious to have a proposition of mine go into the Constitution as I am to accomplish some good. This is not my proposition, but it is the best I can get, and therefore I am for taking it now rather than getting nothing. . . .

CHARLES SUMNER [R., MASS.]. When interrupted I was about to observe that we are pressed now for a vote on a proposition from the other House which in the opinion of many Senators is immature in its form, which does not touch one of the important questions that ought to be settled by the proposed amendment. My colleague has already stated his view on that point, and I must say I subscribe entirely to it. I feel that it would be wrong for us now while undertaking to settle this great question to leave it in any of its forms open to doubt. Do you not leave it so open if you adopt the proposition from the House, especially in view of recent transactions in the South generally, and particularly in the State of Georgia? It is our duty, I submit now, to foreclose all those questions; and now it is proposed that we shall be pressed to a vote leaving one of those questions open.

Sir, I do not think that wise. I think that in putting this great article into the Constitution we ought to be careful that it is complete in form and that it does meet all the exigencies of the occasion. Does this meet those exigencies? Is it complete in power? Is there a single Senator who is in favor of a constitutional amendment who will say that it is complete in form, or that it meets all the exigencies of the occasion? I believe there is not one Senator that I have now the honor of addressing who will affirm that it does. Now, sir, shall we, under the circumstances of the case, in this peculiar exigency, be driven to adopt this imperfect proposition? I hope not. I think therefore that it would be better for the Senate to retrace its steps, to go back, if it could, to a committee of conference; but if it is not disposed to do that, let it commit the whole question to that committee of this body from which it originally proceeded—the Judiciary Committee—expecting from them an early report on the form which this proposition should finally assume when it is voted upon.

Sir, this seems to me to be the practical way of getting out of our present embarrassments. I know no other way; either go to a committee of conference or go to a committee of this body that shall review the whole matter this evening and make an early report to-morrow morning. It is on that account that I have moved that this whole subject be recommitted to the Committee on the Judiciary.

THE PRESIDENT PRO TEMPORE. The question is on concurring in the resolution of the House of Representatives.

GEORGE EDMUNDS [R., VT.]. Mr. President, the Committee on the Judiciary have reported to this body a Senate resolution on this very subject, in which, I believe by the unanimous vote of the Republican members of that committee, they recommended that there should be no distinction among citizens of the United States touching the right to hold office any more than touching the right to vote for officeholders. The House of Representatives has sent over this proposition which limits—

JOSEPH ABBOTT [R., N.C.]. Will the Senator from Vermont allow me to interrupt him for a moment?

MR. EDMUNDS. Certainly.

MR. ABBOTT. The proposition of the Senate as it passed included the right to hold office, as I understood.

MR. EDMUNDS. I have not stated that it did not. I said that the Senate resolution as reported to this body by the Committee on the Judiciary relieved all classes of the citizens of the United States from discriminations as it respects political rights to be voted for as well as to vote. Then the House of Representatives sent over a proposition which was short of that, and which said that no State should discriminate against any citizen of the United States touching the right to vote, and which implied, as this proposition fairly does—and you can put no other construction upon it—that while you give every citizen of a State a right to vote you leave it to the majority of that State to determine whether he shall have any right to be voted for. I know no distinction in philosophy, in politics, for in justice between the right to select in a republican government the agent who is to execute your will and the right to be selected by our fellow-citizens as that agent.

But now the question is what we are to do. The Senator from Massachusetts [Mr. Sumner] suggests that this ought to be recommitted to some committee. A committee has exercised and exhausted its functions upon it in the way that the honorable Senator desires, but when its proposition was amended by the Senate contrary to the wishes of the committee, and there were imported into it two entirely different propositions, one of which to be sure covered this question and a great deal more, and another entirely new to us, those of us who stood up here to resist it found that those who should have been our friends and who should have gotten us out of the difficulty by voting it down, had gone away and we were left in the minority and the thing passed. Now it comes back. What are we to do? As one of the representatives of the people of a State that does not believe in any political distinction among citizens, I feel it to be my duty to vote against this proposition, and if it fails, as I hope it will, all we have to do is to take up from your table, matured and ready, the very proposition that covers the whole ground that my friend from Massachusetts stands for as well as myself. Why should any friend of that proposition therefore hesitate for a moment to vote against this one and then go on and send over to the House a proposition that a majority of us really believe in?

MR. STEWART. I will tell the Senator the very reason why. As soon as he gets that proposition up again does he not expect that the same men who loaded it before will load it again?

MR. EDMUNDS. No, sir.

MR. STEWART. Does he not expect that the Senator from Massachusetts and the Senators from the other States will load it down so as to destroy it? Does he not expect that the rest of the session will be spent at cross purposes?

MR. EDMUNDS. No.

MR. STEWART. Is he not willing to take the proposition which the House of Representatives sends to us, which accomplishes a great deal, rather than to take the risk of having our proposition again loaded down? I tell you that voting against this proposition is voting against any constitutional amendment for this session, for there are men in the Senate—I am not among them, I prefer the Senate proposition—but there are plenty of men here who do not prefer it, and you will have them turning around and playing the same game of delay that you are playing now. There are two sides to this question, and those who are responsible for loading the Senate proposition are going by the same votes to bury that, and we lose the only hope we have. The only hope for getting anything is to vote for this proposition, and I appeal to those who are willing to take something in favor of the colored man to vote for it. I appeal to the Senators who are willing to take something to vote for this, and then I will go with them and stand by them as faithfully as I can for another proposition that will give the right to hold office. I will work with them for that, and let us save what we have got. . . .

THE PRESIDENT PRO TEMPORE. The question now is on concurring in the resolution of the House of Representatives, on which question the yeas and nays have been ordered.

The question being taken by yeas and nays resulted—yeas 31, nays 27. . . .

THE PRESIDENT PRO TEMPORE. Two thirds of the Senate not having voted in the affirmative, the resolution is rejected. . . .

WILLARD SAULSBURY [DEM., DEL.],. . . . Mr. President, I have such a regard for the Constitution of my country framed by the great men of the past that I confess I do not like any attempt whatever to touch, even after the greatest consideration, the work of their hands. The Constitution as framed by them with the twelve original amendments as they are called, is a charter of liberty and of human freedom sufficiently expansive for any people.

But I suggest, Mr. President, that this whole difficulty in which we are now placed does not arise from any imperfect work of the fathers, nor even so much from any imperfect work of yours, as it does from a great original imperfection before any of us or our fathers had an existence upon earth. The origin of the difficulty goes even beyond the institution of human society. Now, if we correct that by an amendment to the Constitution I guess you may have one a little more perfect than you have before you. The difficulty to which I allude results from what was done away back in the bosom of time when a Being whom we have been taught to regard as the great Ruler and Governor of the universe, the Creator of all, never having made anything before, so far as there is any recorded history, came to the conclusion and in council it was determined upon that man should be made. First, the earth for him to live upon was made; then the sun and moon and stars; and then man was made. "Let us make man" was the council of Heaven. And when He proceeded to make man He had not seen that you had actually lived upon the earth and in your wisdom had discovered what He did not see as having actually occurred, whether He foresaw it or not, and that was the equality of all men, and that there should be no distinction between men; and He created man, and we find when we come on the stage of action that this creation of His has different hues of skin, different mental and moral organizations; we find them inhabiting the earth in different societies, with different orders of intellect; and I would say different orders of beings. Now, sir, if he had only been as wise as you are and had the experience you have, He might have made them all just alike, and that would have got rid of all this difficulty. [Laughter].

Mr. President, is there any way to get rid of the difficulty? If you get rid of that difficulty you will have no need for any of these proposed amendments to the Constitution of the United States. I suggest, therefore, Mr. President, as a mode of solving the difficulty, that you do not incorporate any of these proposed amendments in the Constitution, but that you have instead of a fifteenth or sixteenth amendment one that will perfect the whole system, and let it read: "ARTICLE XV.— "That there is not now and never shall be hereafter any distinction of color." [Laughter].

If you will just incorporate that into the Constitution it will be a panacea for all our political evils; it will obviate the necessity of any legislation growing out of the distinction of color. But if you think that would not do it, you may put in "that there is not now and never has been any distinction of race." If that will not do, you may put in "that there never has been any such thing as servitude in the world, and never shall be," and you will have it all cured! . . .

THE PRESIDENT PRO TEMPORE. The question now is on disagreeing to the amendment of the House of Representatives, and asking a committee of conference; on which question the yeas and nays have been ordered.

The question being taken by yeas and nays, resulted—yeas 32, nays 17. . . .

So the motion was agreed to.

THE PRESIDENT PRO TEMPORE. How shall the committee be appointed?

MR. STEWART. By the Chair.

THE PRESIDENT PRO TEMPORE. If no objection be made that course will be pursued.

Mr. Stewart, Mr. Conkling, and Mr. Edmunds were subsequently appointed the committee of conference on the disagreeing votes of the two Houses on the amendments to the joint resolution (S. R. No. 8) proposing an amendment to the Constitution of the United States. . . .

House of Representatives-40th Congress, 3rd Session
February 23, 1869

GEORGE BOUTWELL [DEM., MASS.]. I rise to make the following privileged report:

The committee of conference on the disagreeing votes of the two Houses on the joint resolution (S. No. 8) proposing an amendment to the Constitution of the United States having met, after full and free conference, have agreed to recommend and do recommend to their respective Houses as follows:

That the House recede from their amendments and agree to the resolution of the Senate, with an amendment, as follows:

In section one, line two, strike out the words "or hold office;" and that the Senate agree to do the same.

> *George S. Boutwell,*
> *John A. Bingham,*
> *John A. Logan,*
> Managers on the part of the House,
> *William M. Stewart,*
> *Roscoe Conkling,*
> Managers on the part of the Senate.

I propose to let the House understand what this report of the committee of conference is. It is the original proposition of the Senate with the words "and hold office" stricken out; so that if the report be agreed to the proposed amendment will read:

The right of citizens of the United States to vote shall not be denied or abridged by the United States or by any State on account of race, color, or previous condition of servitude.

I am happy to be able to say, as the report shows, that it is unanimous so far as the managers on the part of the House are concerned, and I presume that the House is ready to vote upon the report of the committee. I demand the previous question unless some gentleman desires to debate the report, which I hope will not be the case at this late hour of the session. . . .

Mr. Boutwell and Mr. Niblack called for the yeas and nays on agreeing to the report of the committee of conference.

The yeas and nays were ordered.

The question was taken; and there were—yeas 144, nays 44, not voting 85. . . .

Senate-40th Congress, 3rd Session
February 26, 1869

THE PRESIDENT PRO TEMPORE [BENJAMIN WADE, R., OHIO]. A special order is before the Senate, being the report of the committee of conference on joint resolution (S. R. No. 8) proposing an amendment to the Constitution of the United States. . . .

The report of the committee of conference was read, as follows:

WILLIAM STEWART [R., NEV.]. I call for the reading of the joint resolution as it will read if amended.

The Chief Clerk read as follows:

Resolved by the Senate and House of Representatives of the United States of America in Congress assembled, (two thirds of both Houses concurring,) That the following article be proposed to the Legislature of the several States as an amendment to the Constitution of the United States, which when ratified by three fourths of said Legislatures shall be valid as part of the Constitution, namely:

ARTICLE XV.

SEC. 1. The right of citizens of the United States to vote shall not be denied or abridged by the United States or by any State on account of race, color, or previous condition of servitude.

SEC. 2. The Congress by appropriate legislation may enforce the provisions of this article . . .

JACOB HOWARD [R., MICH.]. The question is upon concurring in the report of the committee of conference. I shall vote to concur in the report not because this amendment of the Constitution as presented is entirely satisfactory to me, but because I think that it is at present the best that can be obtained. I must content myself, therefore, with the best I can get and run the risk of the future.

I desire to call the attention of Senators to the peculiar wording of this amendment and to its application in the future. I had hoped that the amendment which we should adopt at this session of Congress would have the effect to put an end to all further discussions throughout the country as to the political status of the colored man. I think that has really been the great object at which we have all aimed. I wish this amendment accomplished that object. It possibly may do so; possibly it may not. It will be observed from the language of the report now before us that it does not confer upon the colored man the right to vote. I wish it did; because if it had that effect it would for the future put an end to all controversy respecting his political right as a voter in the United States. As to his right to hold office that, in my judgment, would follow almost as a matter of course. At any rate it would be a subject about which I should have no concern for the future; for a person possessing the right of voting at the polls is inevitably in the end vested with the right to hold office under the Government of which he is a voter. This, however, confers no right to vote. It declares that "the right of citizens of the United States to vote shall not be denied or abridged," etc., without imparting the right itself.

Suppose that after the reorganization of the Government in the State of South Carolina, for example, the voters in the State shall see fit to divest the colored man there of his right to vote. They certainly have a right to do so, under the reserved rights of the States as one of the States of the Union; and the only mode in which the right to vote could be restored to the colored man in that State would be under the subsequent clause in this amendment giving to Congress power to carry out and effectuate this clause by appropriate legislation, so that Congress would then, if it saw fit, step in and remedy the defect of the State law and restore to the colored man his right to vote. This might be the case in more than one of the States of this Union. It might, indeed, be the case in all States of the Union; and Congress would be called upon to exercise an authority under the second clause of this amendment, and to impart by direct congressional legislation to the colored man his right to vote. No one can dispute this.

Suppose that after having passed such an act of Congress thus conferring the right upon the colored man a subsequent Congress should see fit to overhaul our action on the subject and take away from the colored man the right to vote. That might be done, because the action of one Congress does not necessarily bind a subsequent Congress in regard to its action. So that this question of negro suffrage, as it is called, will still be a subject for political discussion and wrangling for perhaps all time to come; and this amendment, as to which its authors fondly hope will put an end to all this discussion for the future, in my judgment does no such thing, but rather holds out to the future the same subject as a theme for political wrangling and discussion; and there is no possibility of foreseeing the time at which the great negro question will be put to rest.

These are some of the difficulties, and the main difficulties, which I see growing out of this particular form of the amendment. I hope it will work well; I trust it will; but I cannot refrain from pointing out to the Senate the difficulties which I foresee may take place in the future growing out of this same amendment of the Constitution.

GEORGE EDMUNDS [R., VT.]. Mr. President, I understood the Senator from
Kansas to raise the question of order whether under parliamentary law we
were entitled to pass upon this question which is now submitted to us in this
report. Certainly, if there be anything in the question, as I think there is, it
can be no other than a question of parliamentary order.

The history of the proposition is this: the Senate passed a joint resolution—
which is the original proposition now before us—and sent it to the House,
declaring that the right of citizens of the United States to vote and hold office
should not be denied or abridged by the United States or by any State by
reason of race, color, or previous condition of servitude. I believe I quote the
exact language, or substantially, sufficiently for my purpose. The House of
Representatives agreed to that with two proposals of amendment. The first
was to strike out the words "the United States," so as to leave the prohibition
applying to the States in their individual political capacity alone; and second,
to add to the enumerated grounds of prohibition three others than those
proposed by the Senate—nativity, creed, property. The Senate disagreed to
those proposals of amendment, and a conference was the result.

Now, what were the powers of that conference committee? If there is
anything that is settled in parliamentary law, if there is anything that is
settled in the proprieties of legislative proceedings, it is that there was
confided to those gentlemen only the question of discussing the points of
disagreement arising between the two Houses. Now, was the question of
office-holding one of those points of disagreement? No man will say that,
because both bodies had voted for it. The points of disagreement were first
on striking out the words "the United States," which may be set aside as not
material to this inquiry; and second, as to modifying or restraining what we
had proposed on the subject of the causes of exclusion—race, color, or
previous condition of servitude—and adding further and other causes in
respect to which we would deny to the States the power of legislation or
political action. These were the only things that were sent to this committee
of conference; they were the only subjects which the Senate and House of
Representatives were willing or could have been willing to confide to their
discretion, because they were the only points and causes of disagreement.
Now we find that the committee report that they have agreed to recommend
that the House of Representatives recede from both its proposals of amendment and agree to the resolution of the Senate to which it had already
agreed, with an alteration of the substance, I may say because I feel it, the
life of the text of the resolution.

My friend from Kansas has shown from the Journals of this body that
there never has been an instance so far as he has gone in which a committee
of conference has attempted to go outside of the subjects of disagreement
and to change that which had already been agreed to except where both
Houses, dispensing by unanimous consent with all rules of order, have
agreed unanimously to make some phraseological change.

Now, what does this propose to do? It proposes to strike out from this constitutional amendment one half of all it contains. It proposes to say, "While we will leave to the States of this Union the power to deny one class or many classes of their citizens the right to be voted for, the right to represent and to protect in a legislative way their own citizens, we will deny to a State the power of saying that they shall not choose." If this were a mere question of technicality, if it did not involve a great principle, I certainly should not raise any point of order upon it; but feeling, as I did in committee, that it was merely asserting the shadow while it wiped out the substance, that it was flying in the face, so far as peace and progress are concerned, of all history and all experience, I felt obliged to decline to sign this report on the ground, among others, that it had gone entirely beyond any authority that the committee had to treat upon the subjects of disagreement between the two Houses. . . .

No Senator has raised his voice to defend the right of any State to say while you give a man the right to vote you shall not permit him to be voted for. I do not know but that we shall hear it yet, though nobody has heard it so far. What is the reason, then? Some vague fear, I suppose, fills the mind of some trembling convert to liberty that his people will not be satisfied to give the negro the right to run against themselves for some office, but they are willing to confer upon him the boon of voting for them. I do not believe in that, sir. As I have said, I believe it to be ruinous to the Government if it is carried out. I believe it to be an outrage upon the good sense and the patriotism of the country; and so believing—though I do not wish to occupy time in stopping its progress if my political friends think it best to pass it—I have felt bound to say so.

MR. STEWART. I have refrained during this discussion from occupying time. I will not now occupy time, and I ask the friends of the proposition not to occupy time; but I must submit a few considerations to the Senate; I must make a few remarks just now upon the condition of the case as it has arisen.

It is said that if you cannot have it right do not have it at all. The question of what is right I suppose must be determined by the majority of the two Houses. There are no two Senators who agree as to exactly the thing which should be done. The Senator from Kansas has been pressing his motion for female suffrage; the Senator from Vermont wants to have office holding included; the Senator from Massachusetts wants to have nativity and creed inserted. Neither of these concurs with the other; one wants a t crossed this way, and another wants an i dotted that way; and thus it is that we lose time discussing little things that do not enter into the main question. . . .

Mr. President, I have labored hard for this constitutional amendment. I have been earnest in my efforts to obtain it. I have not been a stickler for words. I have been willing to take any proposition that seemed likely to succeed, whether it was a House proposition or a Senate proposition. I was not anxious to be the author of the words. I accepted every proposition that was brought forward so long as there was any prospect of its success. But it is now so late in the session that if this proposition cannot be adopted none can be in my judgment. There is not time for another conference and another action of the House and Senate upon it. The appropriation bills are not disposed of. The chairman of the Committee on Appropriations notifies me that he is about to antagonize his bill against this measure, and it must inevitably go. Every Senator must see that there is not time for further action.

FREDERICK FRELINGHUYSEN [R., N.J.]. And no chance at the next session.

MR. STEWART. And no chance at the next session? Your Legislatures are waiting now, ready to act. Send it to another conference and the whole thing is lost.

MR. FRELINGHUYSEN. There will be no chance at the next session, because there will not be a two-thirds vote there for it.

MR. STEWART. And there must be two thirds in the other House. The proposition on your table received in the other House 143 votes to 43 votes, and it will receive in this body the entire Republican vote, as I understand, when they believe that nothing else can be obtained. I have labored here to obtain something else. I have labored to have the right to hold office inserted in the amendment, because I was willing to do the whole right; but that is impossible, and now I want to secure to all men the right to protect themselves with the ballot. The ballot has shown that it has potent effects in bringing loyal Senators to this Hall from the South. It has shown that it had potent effect in the South in reorganizing that country. It was the only expedient that could be substituted for the military power there; and it has worked better than we had any reason to anticipate. Now, I say, give to all men, regardless of race or color, the ballot, and they will secure to themselves all other rights. I appeal to the friends of the measure to vote for concurrence in the report of the committee. It is the only hope I have. I am willing to work night and day for any other proposition that shall be more acceptable to gentlemen until the end of the session; but I have no hope that we can go through the various stages of another proposition with any chance of success. . . .

THE PRESIDENT PRO TEMPORE [SCHUYLER COLFAX, R., IND.]. The question is on concurring in the report of the committee; and on this question the yeas and nays must be called.

On this question the yeas are 39, and the nays are 13. Two thirds of the Senators present having voted in the affirmative, the report is agreed to.

THE DECISION

Commentary

Before the Fifteenth Amendment, no one disputed the state power to exclude individuals from voting on the ground of race. Nor can it be gainsaid that the adoption of the amendment completely terminated such state power. The very language of the amendment, the Supreme Court has said, "bans racial discrimination in voting by both state and nation. It thus establishes a national policy, obviously applicable to the right of Negroes not to be discriminated against as voters in elections to determine public governmental policies or to select public officials, national, state, or local." [*Terry* v. *Adams,* 345 U.S. 461 (1953).]

The Fifteenth Amendment has thus invested citizens with a new constitutional right—that of freedom from discrimination in the exercise of the elective franchise on account of race, color, or previous condition of servitude. If citizens of one race having certain qualifications are permitted by a state to vote, those of another having the same qualifications must be. The Fifteenth Amendment secures the right to vote to all citizens, irrespective of race or color.

Without any doubt, the Fifteenth Amendment automatically put an end to all state constitutional and statutory provisions expressly limiting the franchise at general elections to persons of the white race. "Beyond question," declared the Supreme Court in 1881, "the adoption of the Fifteenth Amendment had the effect, in law, to remove from the State Constitution, or render inoperative, that provision which restricts the right of suffrage to the white race." [*Neal* v. *Delaware,* 103 U.S. 370 (1881).] And such would be the automatic effect on any future provision which should give the right of voting exclusively to members of one race, or burden such right when exercised by members of another.

Although the Fifteenth Amendment legally prohibits racial discrimination, this prohibition in voting in general elections has not, however, of itself, been enough to insure the effective participation of the Negro in the elective process. After the Fifteenth Amendment, efforts aimed at disenfranchising the Negro in the South made use of the so-called "white primary," by which participation in the primary election of the Democratic party was limited to white citizens. Since the Democratic primary has been the only election of real significance in most of the southern states, the device of the white primary was intended to result in effective exclusion of the Negro from the political process in those states.

Does disenfranchisement of the Negro at the primary stage come within the prohibition of the Fifteenth Amendment? The answer to this question depends upon whether state action is involved in such disenfranchisement, for it is only such state action which is affected by the Fifteenth Amendment.

In *Nixon* v. *Herndon,* 273 U.S. 536 (1927), the highest bench dealt with a Texas statute which provided that "in no event shall a Negro be eligible to participate in a Democratic party primary election held in the State." The discrimination against the Negro in this case was clearly caused by the action of the state legislature, and the statute was consequently held to violate the constitutional prohibition.

Nothing daunted, the Texas legislature enacted a new statute which gave the state executive committee of a political party the power to prescribe the qualification of its members for voting or other participation. The state executive committee of the Democratic party then adopted a resolution that white Democrats and no others might participate in the primaries of that party. The Supreme Court held that this, too, transgressed the constitutional command, for whatever power of exclusion had been exercised by the members of the Democratic executive committee had come to them, "not as the delegates of the party, but as the delegates of the State." [*Nixon* v. *Condon,* 286 U.S. 73 (1932).]

The decision in this case was based upon the theory that the Texas statute vested in the executive committee an authority independent of the will of the party as a whole, and that, therefore, its discriminatory acts amounted to state action within the constitutional prohibition. Three weeks after the decision of the Court, a state convention of the Democratic party in Texas adopted a resolution to the effect that in the future only white citizens might vote in the party primaries. A Negro who had been refused a ballot in the Democratic primary brought an action for damages, and the case having been carried to the Supreme Court, that tribunal held in *Grovey* v. *Townsend,* 295 U.S. 45 (1935), that the convention resolution was not state action within the meaning of the Fifteenth Amendment, but was only the action of the political party in exercising its inherent right to determine its own policies and membership. Here the matter seemed to rest, and the southern states appeared to have found a legally condoned method of precluding the Negro from effectively exercising his right to vote.

Such a result might well be satisfying to those who believe that the law must be imprisoned in formal fictions. But it cannot be denied that it is pure fiction to assimilate the Democratic party in a southern state to any purely private club and to assert that the qualifications for membership established by it are as far aloof from the impact of constitutional restraints as are those for membership in a golf club or a Masonic lodge. Regardless of the technical form, the result of such approach was to bar the Negro from participation in the only stage of the election procedure which was of practical significance in the South. It was, therefore, not surprising that the Supreme Court itself in 1944 refused to countenance what was really a transparent violation of the Fifteenth Amendment. At that time, the highest bench overruled *Grovey* v. *Townsend* in *Smith* v. *Allwright,* 321 U.S. 649 (1944), which follows this note. The *Smith* case holds that, while the privilege of membership in a political party may be no concern of the state in certain circumstances, when that privilege is made a necessary qualification for voting in a primary to select candidates for a general election, the state makes the action of the party the action of the state. *Smith* v. *Allwright* makes it the governing rule that any primary election is a vital part of the machinery of government and, as such, fully within the reach of the Fifteenth Amendment.

Under *Smith* v. *Allwright,* and more recent cases applying its holding, the concept of racial equality in the voting booth contained in the Fifteenth Amendment extends to all phases of state elections. And that is true whether the particular phase be one operated by a state, a political party, or even a formally private association or club. The courts have consistently held that, regardless of the form used, no election machinery could be sustained under the Fifteenth Amendment if its purpose or effect was to deny Negroes on account of their race an effective voice in the governmental affairs of their country, state, or community.

SMITH v. ALLWRIGHT
321 U. S. 649 (1944)

MR. JUSTICE REED delivered the opinion of the Court.

This writ of certiorari brings here for review a claim for damages in the sum of $5,000 on the part of petitioner, a Negro citizen of the 48th precinct of Harris County, Texas, for the refusal of respondents, election and associate election judges respectively of that precinct, to give petitioner a ballot or to permit him to cast a ballot in the primary election of July 27, 1940, for the nomination of Democratic candidates for the United States Senate and House of Representatives, and Governor and other state officers. The refusal is alleged to have been solely because of the race and color of the proposed voter.

The actions of respondents are said to violate §§ 31 and 43 of Title 8 of the United States Code in that petitioner was deprived of rights secured by §§ 2 and 4 of Article I and the Fourteenth, Fifteen and Seventeenth Amendments to the United States Constitution. The suit was filed in the District Court of the United States for the Southern District of Texas, which had jurisdiction under Judicial Code § 24, subsection 14.

The District Court denied the relief sought and the Circuit Court of Appeals quite properly affirmed its action on the authority of *Grovey* v. *Townsend,* 295 U. S. 45. We granted the petition for certiorari to resolve a claimed inconsistency between the decision in the *Grovey* case and that of *United States* v. *Classic,* 313 U. S. 299. 319 U. S. 738.

The State of Texas by its Constitution and statutes provides that every person, if certain other requirements are met which are not here in issue, qualified by residence in the district or county "shall be deemed a qualified elector." Constitution of Texas, Article VI, § 2; Vernon's Civil Statutes (1939 ed.), Article 2955. Primary elections for United States Senators, Congressmen and state officers are provided for by Chapters Twelve and Thirteen of the statutes. Under these chapters, the Democratic party was required to hold the primary which was the occasion of the alleged wrong to petitioner. A summary of the state statutes regulating primaries appears in the footnote. These nominations are to be made by the qualified voters of the party. Art. 3101. . . .

The Democratic party on May 24, 1932, in a state convention adopted the following resolution, which has not since been "amended, abrogated, annulled or avoided":

"*Be it resolved* that all white citizens of the State of Texas who are qualified to vote under the Constitution and laws of the State shall be eligible to membership in the Democratic party and, as such, entitled to participate in its deliberations."

It was by virtue of this resolution that the respondents refused to permit the petitioner to vote.

Texas is free to conduct her elections and limit her electorate as she may deem wise, save only as her action may be affected by the prohibitions of the United States Constitution or in conflict with powers delegated to and exercised by the National Government. The Fourteenth Amendment forbids a State from making or enforcing any law which abridges the privileges or immunities of citizens of the United States and the Fifteenth Amendment specifically interdicts any denial or abridgement by a State of the right of citizens to vote on account of color. Respondents appeared in the District Court and the Circuit Court of Appeals and defended on the ground that the Democratic party of Texas is a voluntary organization with members banded together for the purpose of selecting individuals of the group representing the common political beliefs as candidates in the general election. As such a voluntary organization, it was claimed, the Democratic party is free to select its own membership and limit to whites participation in the party primary. Such action, the answer asserted, does not violate the Fourteenth, Fifteenth or Seventeenth Amendment as officers of government cannot be chosen at primaries and the Amendments are applicable only to general elections where governmental officers are actually elected. Primaries, it is said, are political party affairs, handled by party, not governmental, officers. No appearance for respondents is made in this Court. Arguments presented here by the Attorney General of Texas and the Chairman of the State Democratic Executive Committee of Texas, as amici curiae, urged substantially the same grounds as those advanced by the respondents. . . .

The statutes of Texas relating to primaries and the resolution of the Democratic party of Texas extending the privileges of membership to white citizens only are the same in substance and effect today as they were when *Grovey* v. *Townsend* was decided by a unanimous Court. The question as to whether the exclusionary action of the party was the action of the State persists as the determinative factor. In again entering upon consideration of the inference to be drawn as to state action from a substantially similar factual situation, it should be noted that *Grovey* v. *Townsend* upheld exclusion of Negroes from primaries through the denial of party membership by a party convention. A few years before, this Court refused approval of exclusion by the State Executive Committee of the party. A different result was reached on the theory that the Committee action was state authorized and the Convention action was unfettered by statutory control. Such a variation in the result from so slight a change in form influences us to consider anew the legal validity of the distinction which has resulted in barring Negroes from participating in the nominations of candidates of the Democratic party in Texas. Other precedents of this Court forbid the abridgement of the right to vote. *United States* v. *Reese,* 92 U. S. 214, 217; *Neal* v. *Delaware,* 103 U. S. 370, 388; *Guinn* v. *United States,* 238 U. S. 347, 361; *Myers* v. *Anderson,* 238 U. S. 368, 379; *Lane* v. *Wilson,* 307 U. S. 268.

It may now be taken as a postulate that the right to vote in such a primary for the nomination of candidates without discrimination by the State, like the right to vote in a general election, is a right secured by the Constitution. *United States* v. *Classic,* 313 U. S. at 314; *Myers* v. *Anderson,* 238 U. S. 368; *Ex parte Yarbrough,* 110 U. S. 651, 663 *et seq.* By the terms of the Fifteenth Amendment that right may not be abridged by any State on account of race. Under our Constitution the great privilege of the ballot may not be denied a man by the State because of his color.

We are thus brought to an examination of the qualifications for Democratic primary electors in Texas, to determine whether state action or private action has excluded Negroes from participation. Despite Texas' decision that the exclusion is produced by private or party action, *Bell* v. *Hill, supra,* federal courts must for themselves appraise the facts leading to that conclusion. It is only by the performance of this obligation that a final and uniform interpretation can be given to the Constitution, the "supreme Law of the Land." *Nixon* v. *Condon,* 286 U. S. 73, 88; *Standard Oil Co.* v. *Johnson,* 316 U. S. 418, 483; *Bridges* v. *California,* 314 U. S. 252; *Lisenba* v. *California,* 314 U. S. 219, 238; *Union Pacific R. Co.* v. *United States,* 313 U. S. 450, 467; *Drivers Union* v. *Meadowmoor Co.,* 312 U. S. 287, 294; *Chambers* v. *Florida,* 309· U. S. 227, 228. Texas requires electors in a primary to pay a poll tax. Every person who does so pay and who has the qualifications of age and residence is an acceptable vote for the primary. Art. 2955. As appears above in the summary of the statutory provisions set out in note 6, Texas requires by the law the election of the county officers of a party. These compose the county executive committee. The county chairmen so selected are members of the district executive committee and choose the chairman for the district. Precinct primary election officers are named by the county executive committee. Statutes provide for the election by the voters of precinct delegates to the county convention of a party and the selection of delegates to the district and state conventions by the county convention. The state convention selects the state executive committee. No convention may place in platform or resolution any demand for specific legislation without endorsement of such legislation by the voters in a primary. Texas thus directs the selection of all party officers.

Primary elections are conducted by the party under state statutory authority. The county executive committee selects precinct election officials and the county, district or state executive committees, respectively, canvass the returns. These party committees or the state convention certify the party's candidates to the appropriate officers for inclusion on the official ballot for the general election. No name which has not been so certified may appear upon the ballot for the general election as a candidate of a political party. No other name may be printed on the ballot which has not been placed in nomination by qualified voters who must take oath that they did not participate in a primary for the selection of a candidate for the office for which the nomination is made.

The state courts are given exclusive original jurisdiction of contested elections and of mandamus proceedings to compel party officers to perform their statutory duties.

We think that this statutory system for the selection of party nominees for inclusion on the general election ballot makes the party which is required to follow these legislative directions an agency of the State in so far as it determines the participants in a primary election. The party takes its character as a stage agency from the duties imposed upon it by state statutes; the duties do not become matters of private law because they are performed by a political party. The plan of the Texas primary follows substantially that of Louisiana, with the exception that in Louisiana the State pays the cost of the primary while Texas assesses the cost against candidates. In numerous instances, the Texas statutes fix or limit the fees to be charged. Whether paid directly by the State or through state requirements, it is state action which compels. When primaries become a part of the machinery for choosing officials, state and national, as they have here, the same tests to determine the character of discrimination or abridgement should be applied to the primary as are applied to the general election. If the State requires a certain electoral procedure, prescribes a general election ballot made up of party nominees so chosen and limits the choice of the electorate in general elections for state offices, practically speaking, to those whose names appear on such a ballot, it endorses, adopts and enforces the discrimination against Negroes, practiced by a party entrusted by Texas law with the determination of the qualifications of participants in the primary. This is state action within the meaning of the Fifteenth Amendment. *Guinn* v. *United States,* 238 U. S. 347, 362.

The United States is a constitutional democracy. Its organic law grants to all citizens a right to participate in the choice of elected officials without restriction by any State because of race. This grant to the people of the opportunity for choice is not to be nullified by a State through casting its electoral process in a form which permits a private organization to practice racial discrimination in the election. Constitutional rights would be of little value if they could be thus indirectly denied. *Lane* v. *Wilson,* 307 U. S. 268, 275.

The privilege of membership in a party may be, as this Court said in *Grovey* v. *Townsend,* 295 U. S. 45, 55, no concern of a State. But when, as here, that privilege is also the essential qualification for voting in a primary to select nominees for a general election, the State makes the action of the party the action of the State. In reaching this conclusion we are not unmindful of the desirability of continuity of decision in constitutional questions. However, when convinced of former error, this Court has never felt constrained to follow precedent. In constitutional questions, where correction depends upon amendment and not upon legislative action this Court throughout its history has freely exercised its power to reexamine the basis of its constitutional decisions. This has long been accepted practice, and this practice has continued to this day. This is particularly true when the decision believed erroneous is the application of a constitutional principle rather than an interpretation of the Constitution to extract the principle itself. Here we are applying, contrary to the recent decision in *Grovey* v. *Townsend,* the well-established principle of the Fifteenth Amendment, forbidding the abridgement by a State of a citizen's right to vote. *Grovey* v. *Townsend* is overruled.

Judgment reversed.

THE ENFORCEMENT ACT OF 1870

Commentary

The Enforcement Act of 1870 was enacted on May 31, 1870—only two months after ratification of the Fifteenth Amendment. Its background has recently been described by the Supreme Court as follows:

> The purpose and scope of the . . . 1870 enactment must be viewed against the events and passions of the time. The Civil War had ended in April 1865. Relations between Negroes and whites were increasingly turbulent. Congress had taken control of the entire governmental process in former Confederate States. It had declared the governments in 10 "unreconstructed" States to be illegal and had set up federal military administrations in their place. Congress refused to seat representatives from these States until they had adopted constitutions guaranteeing Negro suffrage, and had ratified the Fourteenth Amendment. Constitutional conventions were called in 1868. Six of the 10 States fulfilled Congress' requirements in 1868, the other four by 1870.
>
> For a few years "radical" Republicans dominated the governments of the Southern States and Negroes played a substantial political role. But countermeasures were swift and violent. The Ku Klux Klan was organized by southern whites in 1866 and a similar organization appeared with the romantic title of the Knights of the White Camellia. In 1868 a wave of murders and assaults was launched including assassinations designed to keep Negroes from the polls. The States themselves were helpless, despite the resort by some of them to extreme measures such as making it legal to hunt down and shoot any disguised man.
>
> Within the Congress pressures mounted in the period between the end of the war and 1870 for drastic measures. *United States* v. *Price*, 383 U.S. 787, 803-4 (1966).

The congressional pressures referred to led directly to the Enforcement Act of 1870. The congressional debates on that statute contain two principal themes: (1) protection of the right to vote, so recently guaranteed in the Fifteenth Amendment; (2) the problem of violence aimed at keeping Negroes from the polls.

As originally introduced, the proposed statute sought to deal primarily with the first of the themes mentioned. As explained by Congressman John Bingham [R., Ohio] in introducing the measure, its object was "to enforce the legal right of the citizens of the United States to vote in the several States of this Union"—a right which had been "defiantly denied" in violation of the Constitution. To attain such object, the bill barred state officers from restricting suffrage on racial grounds and provided criminal sanctions for enforcement of its prohibitions. The House version of such bill passed the lower chamber on May 16, 1870, on Mr. Bingham's motion to suspend the rules and pass the bill by a two-thirds vote without debate.

In the Senate, there was a full debate, extending over several days. Senator William Stewart [R., Nev.], who introduced the debate, urged that the House bill was defective and that something more was needed "if we intend to enforce the fifteenth amendment." The House bill dealt only with official action; there was nothing in it to reach the case of mob violence or other action by private individuals designed to prevent Negroes from voting.

443

To remedy the deficiencies of the House bill in this respect, Stewart urged the substitution of the stronger measure recommended by the Senate Judiciary Committee. Unlike the House bill, the Senate version was not limited to official action; its key section was aimed at "any person" who sought to prevent or obstruct any citizen from exercising his right to vote.

Of particular significance in the Senate debate was the speech of Senator John Pool [R., N.C.], in sponsoring, as an amendment, what became Sections 5, 6, and 7 of the 1870 Act. His remarks constitute the sole legislative explanation of the only parts of the Enforcement Act that are still part of the statute book (his Sections 5 and 6, have survived later revisions and repeals, are now contained, with some changes, in the Federal Criminal Code, 18 U.S.C. §241, and have increasingly been used to protect civil rights in recent years). The sections introduced by Pool went further than either the House bill or the Senate version in dealing with the problem of nonofficial action (individual or mob) aimed at preventing Negro exercise of constitutional rights. The Pool sections, in the form in which they were finally adopted, made it an offense for "any person" to prevent or hinder anyone in the exercise of the right of suffrage guaranteed by the Fifteenth Amendment, or for two or more persons from conspiring together, or going in disguise, to injure, oppress, or intimidate any citizen in the free exercise or enjoyment of any right or privilege guaranteed him by the Constitution or federal laws.

The theory offered by Senator Pool in support of his sections was as interesting as it was far-reaching. According to him, the rights secured by the Fifteenth Amendment could be abridged either by positive legislation or by acts of omission. The former was reached directly by the constitutional provision; the latter was not. If a state should omit to act to prevent private individuals from contravening the rights of citizens under the amendment, it was the congressional duty "to supply that omission, and by its own laws and by its own courts to go into the states for the purpose of giving the amendment vitality there." In the view so enunciated, state omission or failure to act may be treated as "state action" for purposes of congressional power to enforce the Fifteenth Amendment. Congress might thus act directly against private individuals who were able to violate constitutional rights because of the omission of state officials to protect those rights. What gives the Pool view in this respect such significance is the recent tendency of the Supreme Court drastically to expand the "state action" notion—a trend that may culminate one day in the acceptance of the extreme Pool view in the matter.

In addition to its further extension of the Enforcement Act beyond the traditional limits of "state action," the Pool amendment had the effect of greatly broadening the reach of the 1870 statute itself. As Congressman James Beck [Dem., Ky.] plaintively put it, when the bill came back to the House, "The bill which left us was simply a bill to enforce the fifteenth amendment;" now it was a bill to enforce the Fourteenth Amendment as well. The broadening of the bill was ultimately to prove of great consequence. When (as will be seen *infra* p. 805) the Democratic-controlled Congress in 1894 repealed the voting right provisions of the 1870 act, it left alone the broader sections introduced by Senator Pool, which now survive as general prohibitions against deprivation of constitutional rights.

As already stressed, the Senate version, plus the Pool amendment, converted the 1870 statute from a law aimed at official action restricting Negro voting rights (as provided in the House bill) to one which reached private action as well and action interfering with rights under both the Fourteenth and Fifteenth Amendments. This led naturally to strong attacks by opponents of the bill, who urged that the constitutional amendments were aimed only at state action, and that laws enforcing them could not consequently be directed at the acts of purely private individuals. The best presentation of the argument to such effect was by Senator Eugene Casserly [Dem., Cal.], who urged that the power to punish private individuals was in violation of the relevant rights.

At the end of the Senate debate (including an all night session because of an attempted filibuster), that chamber voted overwhelmingly (43-8) to pass its bill (now containing the Pool amendment) as a substitute for the House bill. The House refused to accept the Senate version and a conference committee was agreed to. The conference report recommended acceptance of the Senate bill, with some minor amendments (as fully explained by Senator William Stewart). The report was passed in both Houses—by 43 to 11 in the Senate, and 133 to 58 in the House. It became law on May 31, 1870.

THE ENFORCEMENT ACT
May 31, 1870

Be it enacted by the Senate and House of Representatives of the United States of America in Congress assembled, That all citizens of the United States who are or shall be otherwise qualified by law to vote at any election by the people in any State, Territory, district, county, city, parish, township, school district, municipality, or other territorial subdivision, shall be entitled and allowed to vote at all such elections, without distinction of race, color, or previous condition of servitude; any constitution, law, custom, usage, or regulation of any State or Territory, or by or under its authority, to the contrary notwithstanding.

SEC. 2. *And be it further enacted,* That if by or under the authority of the constitution or laws of any State, or the laws of any Territory, any act is or shall be required to be done as a prerequisite or qualification for voting, and by such constitution or laws persons or officers are or shall be charged with the performance of duties in furnishing to citizens an opportunity to perform such prerequisite, or to become qualified to vote, it shall be the duty of every such person and officer to give to all citizens of the United States the same and equal opportunity to perform such prerequisite, and to become qualified to vote without distinction of race, color, or previous condition of servitude; and if any such person of officer shall refuse or knowingly omit to give full effect to this section, he shall, for every such offence, forfeit and pay the sum of five hundred dollars to the person aggrieved thereby, to be recovered by an action on the case, with full costs, and such allowance for counsel fees as the court shall deem just, and shall also, for every such offence, be deemed guilty of a misdemeanor, and shall, on conviction thereof, be fined not less than five hundred dollars, or be imprisoned not less than one month and not more than one year, or both, at the discretion of the court.

SEC. 3. *And be it further enacted,* That whenever, by or under the authority of the constitution or laws of any State, or the laws of any Territory, any act is or shall be required to [be] done by any citizen as a prerequisite to qualify or entitle him to vote, the offer of any such citizen to perform the act required to be done as aforesaid shall, if it fail to be carried into execution by reason of the wrongful act or omission aforesaid of the person or officer charged with the duty of receiving or permitting such performance of offer to perform, or acting thereon, be deemed and held as a performance in law of such act; and the person so offering and failing as aforesaid, and being otherwise qualified, shall be entitled to vote in the same manner and to the same extent as if he had in fact performed such act; and any judge, inspector, or other officer of election whose duty it is or shall be to receive, count, certify, register, report, or give effect to the vote of any such citizen who shall wrongfully refuse or omit to receive, count, certify, register, report, or give effect to the vote of such citizen upon the presentation by him of his affidavit stating such offer and the time and place thereof, and the name of the officer or person whose duty it was to act thereon, and that he was wrongfully prevented by such person or officer from performing such act, shall for every such offence forfeit and pay the sum of five hundred dollars to the person aggrieved thereby, to be recovered by an action on the case, with full costs, and such allowance for counsel fees as the court shall deem just, and shall also for every such offence be guilty of a misdemeanor, and shall, on conviction thereof, be fined not less than five hundred dollars, or be imprisoned not less than one month and not more than one year, or both, at the discretion of the court.

SEC. 4. *And be it further enacted,* That if any person, by force, bribery, threats, intimidation, or other unlawful means, shall hinder, delay, prevent, or obstruct, or shall combine and confederate with others to hinder, delay, prevent, or obstruct, any citizen from doing any act required to be done to qualify him to vote or from voting at any election as aforesaid, such person shall for every such offence forfeit and pay the sum of five hundred dollars to the person aggrieved thereby, to be recovered by an action on the case, with full costs, and such allowance for counsel fees as the court shall deem just, and shall also for every such offence be guilty of a misdemeanor, and shall, on conviction thereof, be fined not less than five hundred dollars, or be imprisoned not less than one month and not more than one year, or both, at the discretion of the court.

SEC. 5. *And be it further enacted,* That if any person shall prevent, hinder, control, or intimidate, or shall attempt to prevent, hinder, control, or intimidate, any person from exercising or in exercising the right of suffrage, to whom the right of suffrage is secured or guaranteed by the fifteenth amendment to the Constitution of the United States, by means of bribery, threats, or threats of depriving such person of employment or occupation, or of ejecting such person from rented house, lands, or other property, or by threats of refusing to renew leases or contracts for labor, or by threats of violence to himself or family, such person so offending shall be deemed guilty of a misdemeanor, and shall, on conviction thereof, be fined not less than five hundred dollars, or be imprisoned not less than one month and not more than one year, or both, at the discretion of the court.

SEC. 6. *And be it further enacted,* That if two or more persons shall band or conspire together, or go in disguise upon the public highway, or upon the premises of another, with intent to violate any provision of this act, or to injure, oppress, threaten, or intimidate any citizen with intent to prevent or hinder his free exercise and enjoyment of any right or privilege granted or secured to him by the Constitution or laws of the United States, or because of his having exercised the same, such persons shall be held guilty of felony, and, on conviction thereof, shall be fined or imprisoned, or both, at the discretion of the court,—the fine not to exceed five thousand dollars, and the imprisonment not to exceed ten years,—and shall, moreover, be thereafter ineligible to, and disabled from holding, any office or place of honor, profit, or trust created by the Constitution or laws of the United States.

SEC. 7. *And be it further enacted,* That if in the act of violating any provision in either of the two preceding sections, any other felony, crime, or misdemeanor shall be committed, the offender, on conviction of such violation of said sections, shall be punished for the same with such punishments as are attached to the said felonies, crimes, and misdemeanors by the laws of the State in which the offence may be committed.

SEC. 8. *And be it further enacted,* That the district courts of the United States, within their respective districts, shall have, exclusively of the courts of the several States, cognizance of all crimes and offences committed against the provisions of this act, and also, concurrently with the circuit courts of the United States, of all causes, civil and criminal, arising under this act, except as herein otherwise provided, and the jurisdiction hereby conferred shall be exercised in conformity with the laws and practice governing United States courts; and all crimes and offences committed against the provisions of this act may be prosecuted by the indictment of a grand jury, or, in cases of crimes and offences not infamous, the prosecution may be either by indictment or information filed by the district attorney in a court having jurisdiction.

SEC. 9. *And be it further enacted,* That the district attorneys, marshals, and deputy marshals of the United States, the commissioners appointed by the circuit and territorial courts of the United States, with powers of arresting, imprisoning, or bailing offenders against the laws of the United States, and every other officer who may be specially empowered by the President of the United States, shall be, and they are hereby, specially authorized and required, at the expense of the United States, to institute proceedings against all and every person who shall violate the provisions of this act, and cause him or them to be arrested and imprisoned, or bailed, as the case may be, for trial before such court of the United States or territorial court as has cognizance of the offense. And with a view to afford reasonable protection to all persons in their constitutional right to vote without distinction of race, color, or previous condition of servitude, and to the prompt discharge of the duties of this act, it shall be the duty of the circuit courts of the United States, and the superior courts of the Territories of the United States, from time to time, to increase the number of commissioners, so as to afford a speedy and convenient means for the arrest and examination of persons charged with a violation of this act; and such commissioners are hereby authorized and required to exercise and discharge all the powers and duties conferred on them by this act, and the same duties with regard to offences created by this act as they are authorized by law to exercise with regard to other offences against the laws of the United States.

SEC. 10. *And be it further enacted,* That it shall be the duty of all marshals and deputy marshals to obey and execute all warrants and precepts issued under the provisions of this act, when to them directed; and should any marshal or deputy marshal refuse to receive such warrant or other process when tendered, or to use all proper means diligently to execute the same, he shall, on conviction thereof, be fined in the sum of one thousand dollars, to the use of the person deprived of the rights conferred by this act. And the better to enable the said commissioners to execute their duties faithfully and efficiently, in conformity with the Constitution of the United States and the requirements of this act, they are hereby authorized and empowered, within their districts respectively, to appoint, in writing, under their hands, any one or more suitable persons, from time to time, to execute all such warrants and other process as may be issued by them in the lawful performance of their respective duties, and the persons so appointed to execute any warrant or process as aforesaid shall have authority to summon and call to their aid the bystanders or *posse comitatus* of the proper county, or such portion of the land or naval forces of the United States, or of the militia, as may be necessary to the performance of the duty with which they are charged, and to insure a faithful observance of the fifteenth amendment to the Constitution of the United States; and such warrants shall run and be executed by said officers anywhere in the State or Territory within which they are issued.

SEC. 11. *And be it further enacted*, That any person who shall knowingly and wilfully obstruct, hinder, or prevent any officer or other person charged with the execution of any warrant or process issued under the provisions of this act, or any person or persons lawfully assisting him or them from arresting any person for whose apprehension such warrant or process may have been issued, or shall rescue or attempt to rescue such person from the custody of the officer or other person or persons, or those lawfully assisting as aforesaid, when so arrested pursuant to the authority herein given and declared, or shall aid, abet, or assist any person so arrested as aforesaid, directly or indirectly, to escape from the custody of the officer or other person legally authorized as aforesaid, or shall harbor or conceal any person for whose arrest a warrant or process shall have been issued as aforesaid, so as to prevent his discovery and arrest after notice or knowledge of the fact that a warrant has been issued for the apprehension of such person, shall, for either of said offences, be subject to a fine not exceeding one thousand dollars, or imprisonment not exceeding six months, or both, at the discretion of the court, on conviction before the district or circuit court of the United States for the district or circuit in which said offence may have been committed, or before the proper court of criminal jurisdiction, if committed within any one of the organized Territories of the United States.

SEC. 12. *And be it further enacted*, That the commissioners, district attorneys, the marshals, their deputies, and the clerks of the said district, circuit, and territorial courts shall be paid for their services the like fees as may be allowed to them for similar services in other cases. The person or persons authorized to execute the process to be issued by such commissioners for the arrest of offenders against the provisions of this act shall be entitled to the usual fees allowed to the marshal for an arrest for each person he or they may arrest and take before any such commissioner as aforesaid, with such other fees as may be deemed reasonable by such commissioner for such other additional services as may be necessarily performed by him or them, such as attending at the examination, keeping the prisoner in custody, and providing him with food and lodging during his detention and until the final determination of such commissioner, and in general for performing such other duties as may be required in the premises; such fees to be made up in conformity with the fees usually charged by the officers of the courts of justice within the proper district or county as near as may be practicable, and paid out of the treasury of the United States on the certificate of the judge of the district within which the arrest is made, and to be recoverable from the defendant as part of the judgment in case of conviction.

SEC. 13. *And be it further enacted*, That it shall be lawful for the President of the United States to employ such part of the land or naval forces of the United States, or of the militia, as shall be necessary to aid in the execution of judicial process issued under this act.

SEC. 14. *And be it further enacted*, That whenever any person shall hold office, except as a member of Congress or of some State legislature, contrary to the provisions of the third section of the fourteenth article of amendment of the Constitution of the United States, it shall be the duty of the district attorney of the United States for the district in which such person shall hold office, as aforesaid, to proceed against such person, by writ of *quo warranto* returnable to the circuit or district court of the United States in such district, and to prosecute the same to the removal of such person from office; and any writ of *quo warranto* so brought, as aforesaid, shall take precedence of all other cases on the docket of the court to which it is made returnable, and shall not be continued unless for cause proved to the satisfaction of the court.

SEC. 15. *And be it further enacted*, That any person who shall hereafter knowingly accept or hold any office under the United States, or any State to which he is ineligible under the third section of the fourteenth article of amendment of the Constitution of the United States, or who shall attempt to hold or exercise the duties of any such office, shall be deemed guilty of a misdemeanor against the United States, and, upon conviction thereof before the circuit or district court of the United States, shall be imprisoned not more than one year, or fined not exceeding one thousand dollars, or both, at the discretion of the court.

SEC. 16. *And be it further enacted*, That all persons within the jurisdiction of the United States shall have the same right in every State and Territory in the United States to make and enforce contracts, to sue, be parties, give evidence, and to the full and equal benefit of all laws and proceedings for the security of person and property as is enjoyed by white citizens, and shall be subject to like punishment, pains, penalties, taxes, licenses, and exactions of every kind, and none other, any law, statute, ordinance, regulation, or custom to the contrary notwithstanding. No tax or charge shall be imposed or enforced by any State upon any person immigrating thereto from a foreign country which is not equally imposed and enforced upon every person immigrating to such State from any other foreign country; and any law of any State in conflict with this provision is hereby declared null and void.

SEC. 17. *And be it further enacted*, That any person who, under color of any law, statute, ordinance, regulation, or custom, shall subject, or cause to be subjected, any inhabitant of any State or Territory to the deprivation of any right secured or protected by the last preceding section of this act, or to different punishment, pains, or penalties on account of such person being an alien, or by reason of his color or race, than is prescribed for the punishment of citizens, shall be deemed guilty of a misdemeanor, and, on conviction, shall be punished by fine not exceeding one thousand dollars, or imprisonment not exceeding one year, or both, in the discretion of the court.

SEC. 18. *And be it further enacted,* That the act to protect all persons in the United States in their civil rights, and furnish the means of their vindication, passed April nine, eighteen hundred and sixty-six, is hereby re-enacted; and sections sixteen and seventeen hereof shall be enforced according to the provisions of said act.

SEC. 19. *And be it further enacted,* That if at any election for representative or delegate in the Congress of the United States any person shall knowingly personate and vote, or attempt to vote, in the name of any other person, whether living, dead, or fictitious; or vote more than once at the same election for any candidate for the same office; or vote at a place where he may not be lawfully entitled to vote; or vote without having a lawful right to vote; or do any unlawful act to secure a right or an opportunity to vote for himself or any other person; or by force, threat, menace, intimidation, bribery, reward, or offer, or promise thereof, or otherwise unlawfully prevent any qualified voter of any State of the United States of America, or of any Territory thereof, from freely exercising the right of suffrage, or by any such means induce any voter to refuse to exercise such right; or compel or induce by any such means, or otherwise, any officer of an election in any such State or Territory to receive a vote from a person not legally qualified or entitled to vote; or interfere in any manner with any officer of said elections in the discharge of his duties; or by any of such means, or other unlawful means, induce any officer of an election, or officer whose duty is is to ascertain, announce, or declare the result of any such election, or give or make any certificate, document, or evidence in relation thereto, to violate or refuse to comply with his duty, or any law regulating the same; or knowingly and wilfully receive the vote of any person not entitled to vote, or refuse to receive the vote of any person entitled to vote; or aid, counsel, procure, or advise any such voter, person, or officer to do any act hereby made a crime, or to omit to do any duty the omission of which is hereby made a crime, or attempt to do so, every such person shall be deemed guilty of a crime, and shall for such crime be liable to prosecution in any court of the United States of competent jurisdiction, and, on conviction thereof, shall be punished by a fine not exceeding five hundred dollars, or by imprisonment for a term not exceeding three years, or both, in the discretion of the court, an I shall pay the costs of prosecution.

SEC. 20. *And be it further enacted,* That if, at any registration of voters for an election for representative or delegate in the Congress of the United States, any person shall knowingly personate and register, or attempt to register, in the name of any other person, whether living, dead, or fictitious, or fraudulently register, or fraudulently attempt to register, not having a lawful right so to do; or do any unlawful act to secure registration for himself or any other person; or by force, threat, menace, intimidation, bribery, reward, or offer, or promise thereof, or other unlawful means, prevent or hinder any person having a lawful right to register from duly exercising such right; or compel or induce, by any of such means, or other unlawful means, any officer of registration to admit to registration any person not legally entitled thereto, or interfere in any manner with any officer of registration in the discharge of his duties, or by any such means, or other unlawful means, induce any officer of registration to violate or refuse to comply with his duty, or any law regulating the same; or knowingly and wilfully receive the vote of any person not entitled to vote, or refuse to receive the vote of any person entitled to vote, or aid, counsel, procure, or advise any such voter, person, or officer to do any act hereby made a crime, or to omit any act, the omission of which is hereby made a crime, every such person shall be deemed guilty of a crime, and shall be liable to prosecution and punishment therefor, as provided in section nineteen of this act for persons guilty of any of the crimes therein specified: *Provided,* That every registration made under the laws of any State or Territory, for any State or other election at which such representative or delegate in Congress shall be chosen, shall be deemed to be a registration within the meaning of this act, notwithstanding the same shall also be made for the purposes of any State, territorial, or municipal election.

SEC. 21. *And be it further enacted,* That whenever, by the laws of any State or Territory, the name of any candidate or person to be voted for as representative or delegate in Congress shall be required to be printed, written, or contained in any ticket or ballot with other candidates or persons to be voted for at the same election for State, territorial, municipal, or local officers, it shall be sufficient prima facie evidence, either for the purpose of indicting or convicting any person charged with voting, or attempting or offering to vote, unlawfully under the provisions of the preceding sections, or for committing either of the offenses thereby created, to prove that the person so charged or indicted, voted, or attempted or offered to vote, such ballot or ticket, or committed either of the offenses named in the preceding sections of this act with reference to such ballot. And the proof and establishment of such facts shall be taken, held, and deemed to be presumptive evidence that such person voted, or attempted or offered to vote, for such representative or delegate, as the case may be, or that such offense was committed with reference to the election of such representative or delegate, and shall be sufficient to warrant his conviction, unless it shall be shown that any such ballot, when cast, or attempted or offered to be cast, by him, did not contain the name of any candidate for the office of representative or delegate in the Congress of the United States, or that such offense was not committed with reference to the election of such representative or delegate.

SEC. 22. *And be it further enacted,* That any officer of any election at which any representative or delegate in the Congress of the United States shall be voted for, whether such officer of election be appointed or created by or under any law or authority of the United States, or by or under any State, territorial, district, or municipal law or authority, who shall neglect or refuse to perform any duty in regard to such election required of him by any law of the United States, or of any State or Territory thereof; or violate any duty so imposed, or knowingly do any act thereby unauthorized, with intent to affect any such election, or the result thereof; or fraudulently make any false certificate of the result of such election in regard to such representative or delegate; or withhold, conceal, or destroy any certificate of record so required by law respecting, concerning, or pertaining to the election of any such representative or delegate; or neglect or refuse to make and return the same as so required by law; or aid, counsel, procure, or advise any voter, person, or officer to do any act by this or any of the preceding sections made a crime; or to omit to do any duty the omission of which is by this or any of said sections made a crime, or attempt to do so, shall be deemed guilty of a crime and shall be liable to prosecution and punishment therefor, as provided in the nineteenth section of this act for persons guilty of any of the crimes therein specified.

SEC. 23. *And be it further enacted*, That whenever any person shall be defeated or deprived of his election to any office, except elector of President or Vice-President, representative or delegate in Congress, or member of a State legislature, by reason of the denial to any citizen or citizens who shall offer to vote, of the right to vote, on account of race, color, or previous condition of servitude, his right to hold and enjoy such office, and the emoluments thereof, shall not be impaired by such denial; and such person may bring any appropriate suit or proceeding to recover possession of such office, and in cases where it shall appear that the sole question touching the title to such office arises out of the denial of the right to vote to citizens who so offered to vote, on account of race, color, or previous condition of servitude, such suit or proceeding may be instituted in the circuit or district court of the United States of the circuit or district in which such person resides. And said circuit or district court shall have, concurrently with the State courts, jurisdiction thereof so far as to determine the rights of the parties to such office by reason of the denial of the right guaranteed by the fifteenth article of amendment to the Constitution of the United States, and secured by this act.

Approved, May 31, 1870.

THE DEBATE

JOHN BINGHAM [R., OHIO]. I ask the House, under instructions from the Committee on the Judiciary, to allow me to report and put on its passage, with an amendment in the nature of a substitute, which has been fully considered by the House, bill No. 1293, to enforce the rights of citizens of the United States to vote in the several States of this Union who have heretofore been denied that right on account of race, color, or previous condition of servitude. This bill has been printed and upon the tables of members for nearly three months. The object of the bill is to enforce the legal right of the citizens of the United States to vote in the several States of this Union—a right which is defiantly denied in my own State and in others, in direct contravention of the express letter of the Constitution of the United States. . . .

I move that the rules be suspended to allow me to report the bill with an amendment and put the same on its passage. . . .

AARON SARGENT [R., CAL.]. I rise to make a parliamentary inquiry. If the motion of the gentleman from Ohio [Mr. Bingham] prevails, does it cut off the opportunity to offer amendments?

THE SPEAKER [JAMES BLAINE, R., ME.]. It does, and passes the bill by a single vote of two thirds of the House.

CHARLES ELDREDGE [DEM., WIS.]. Is it proposed to put through such an important bill without allowing any opportunity for amendment or discussion?

SAMUEL RANDALL [DEM., PA.]. That is the proposition. . . .

The question recurred on Mr. Bingham's motion, that the rules be suspended and the bill passed.

MR. ELDREDGE called for the yeas and nays.

The yeas and nays were ordered.

The question was taken; and there were—yeas 131, nays 44, not voting 53.

So (two thirds voting in favor thereof) the rules were suspended, and the bill was passed.

The Senate, as in Committee of the Whole, proceeded to consider the bill (H.R. No. 1293) to enforce the rights of citizens of the United States to vote in the several States of this Union, who have hitherto been denied that right on account of race, color, or previous condition of servitude.

WILLIAM STEWART [R., NEV.]. I wish to call the attention of the Senate to the provisions of this bill, to show that it will not answer the purpose; that we need something more if we intend to enforce the fifteenth amendment. I wish any bill on this subject to contain all the requisites. It will be necessary to glance at each section of the bill to see what the proposition contained in it is, which will take me but a few moments.

The first section provides:

That any officer of the United States, or of any State, Territory, or district, and every officer of any city, county, town, township, borough, ward, parish, or hundred, in any State, Territory, or district, who shall by any official act whatever, or by the omission, neglect, or refusal to perform any official act or duty whatever, whether under color or pretext of any provision of any State constitution, or any law of any State, Territory, or district whatsoever, or of any local, municipal, or other law, rule, or ordinance, deny or abridge the right of any citizen of the United States to vote, on account of race, color, or previous condition of servitude, at any Federal, State, county, municipal, or other election, etc.

That is made a misdemeanor. That is very well so far as it goes. It should be a misdemeanor if the officer fails to perform that act, or does anything by which the right to vote is denied to a citizen.

Then the second section provides—

That all colored citizens of the United States resident in the several States of the United States shall be entitled to vote at all elections in the State, county, parish, town, township, ward, or hundred of their residence, subject only to the same conditions which now are or may hereafter be required to qualify white citizens to vote therein. And any person who shall by force, fraud, intimidation, or other unlawful means whatsoever, prevent any colored citizen from voting at any such election, who possesses the qualifications, except in respect of color, requisite to enable a white citizen to vote thereat, shall, upon conviction thereof, be adjudged guilty of a misdemeanor, etc.

Those two sections relate simply to voting. If an officer fails or refuses to perform an official act necessary to give a voter the right to vote he is guilty of a misdemeanor. It provides for the case of any person who shall by fraud, intimidation, or other unlawful means prevent a citizen from voting. That has nothing to do with registration and the preliminary matters which are necessary prior to voting; so that something else must be provided to reach that.

The third section provides "that in case the constitution or law of any State shall require the assessment or payment of a tax as a qualification of an elector," and the assessor or other officer shall refuse or willfully neglect to assess the person or property of any colored citizen, he shall be punished for that offense.

The fourth section also relates to the same system of the assessment of a tax, put in another form.

The fifth section provides "that if any clerk or other officer required by the law of any State to register, record, or transcribe any list of persons upon whom taxes have been assessed," &c., shall refuse to register a colored voter, if he is properly assessed for taxes, then such officer shall forfeit $500 and be deemed guilty of a misdemeanor.

The sixth section provides a penalty for any collector of taxes who does not do this duty with regard to the taxes.

The seventh section provides for the punishment of any officer who, at any election for President and Vice President of the United States or members of the House of Representatives, shall fail to receive the vote of a voter on account of race or color.

The eighth section goes on to prescribe the penalty for refusing to register the voter again.

The ninth section provides the penalty in case "any person shall by threats, violence, or intimidation prevent or attempt to prevent any citizen of the United States from the free exercise of his right to vote in any election at which members of Congress, or electors for President or Vice President of the United States may be voted for." It provides that such person shall be liable to indictment and punishment. That is fixing it for a particular election.

These are the provisions of the House bill. It provides for the two cases mentioned; and now let me state some cases that it does not provide for. There is nothing in the world in this bill to punish outsiders for preventing the registration of voters altogether. That is the great difficulty. A mob may prevent registration, as they have done over in Virginia, and there is no penalty provided. There is nothing to reach that case at all. And in case a mob should prevent registration altogether, and not allow a colored man to register, then under this bill there is nothing to entitle him to vote when he comes to the poll. There is nothing to interfere with the power of a mob to drive him away from the registrar's office; and that being conclusive evidence upon the right to vote, and there being no penalty provided for that, the whole bill is good for nothing; the whole bottom is out of the bill. I tell you, Senators, it will not answer the purpose at all.

Now, in order that the bill reported by the Committee on the Judiciary may be understood, I desire to call the attention of the Senate to it. Perhaps it may be improved. The Senator from North Carolina [Mr. Pool] has made some suggestions, and has prepared one or two sections which strike me very favorably. One of those sections provides against unlawful combinations to intimidate voters, which would come in properly in connection with this bill. It prevents intimidation outside of the immediate relation to registration and to voting, going upon the plantations, Kuklux Klans, &c. He has prepared some sections which may be necessary to make the Senate bill a complete bill. Let me analyze for a moment the bill prepared by the Committee on the Judiciary and see what cases it provides for.

The first section is the simple declaration of the principle that all men shall be entitled to vote without distinction of race or color.

The second section provides:

> That if by or under the authority of the constitution or laws of any State, or the laws of any Territory, any act is or shall be required to be done as a prerequisite or—

I want to call attention to this thing, and Senators will see the difficulty in framing anything. If anything is required to be done as a prerequisite or—

> qualification for voting, and by such constitution or laws persons or officers are or shall be charged with the performance of duties in furnishing to citizens an opportunity to perform such prerequisite, or to become qualified to vote, it shall be the duty of every such person and officer to give to all citizens of the United States the same and equal opportunity to perform such prerequisite, and to become qualified to vote, without distinction of race, color, or previous condition of servitude.

We have undertaken to enumerate some prerequisites. There may be a thousand other things invented outside of them not referred to by the first section.

JOHN SHERMAN [R., OHIO]. The House bill makes it an offense for any officer "by any official act whatever, or by omission, neglect, or refusal to perform any official act or duty whatever, whether under color or pretext of any provision of any State constitution, or any law of any State, Territory, or district whatsoever, or of any local, municipal, or other law, rule, or ordinance," &c., to "deny or abridge" the right to vote.

MR. STEWART. The third—

JACOB HOWARD [R., MICH.]. Let me call the attention of the Senator from Nevada to the second clause of section two of the House bill. Does not that cover every case of a mob or other illegal violence by which a colored citizen is prevented from voting?

MR. STEWART. The second clause of section two is, "and any person who shall by force, fraud, intimidation, or other unlawful means whatsoever, prevent any colored citizen from voting"—

MR. HOWARD. "From voting."

MR. STEWART. But not from registering. That is·the point. I say they have provided a penalty against those who prevent colored citizens from voting, but not for forming a mob to prevent them from performing the prerequisites required to entitle them to vote.

MR. HOWARD. Suppose a colored citizen has been prevented from registering by mob violence.

MR. STEWART. Under the House bill there is no remedy.

MR. HOWARD. In that case he is not entitled to vote, and he is thereby prevented from voting. Does not that bring the offense within the language of that clause?

MR. STEWART. No.

MR. HOWARD. I am inclined to think it would.

MR. STEWART. It will never be so construed. Criminal laws are strictly construed. If a colored man was prevented from registering, an indictment would not lie against the party so preventing him, for having prevented him from voting.

MR. HOWARD. I am inclined to think it would.

MR. STEWART. Most certainly not. No criminal law would be construed in that way.

MR. HOWARD. Why not, if registering is a prerequisite for voting, as I suppose it to be?

MR. SHERMAN. I wish to call the attention of the Senator from Michigan to the first section of the House bill.

MR. STEWART. I hope I shall be allowed to go on. I undertake to say that there is nothing whatever in the House bill to prevent intimidation and fraud by outsiders to prevent a party from performing the prerequisites necessary to qualify him to vote. Such a provision cannot be found in the bill. But in the third section of the bill that is reported by the Judiciary Committee we have this provision:

> That whenever, by or under the authority of the constitution or laws of any State, or the laws of any Territory, any act is or shall be required to be done by any citizen as a prerequisite to qualify or entitle him to vote, the offer of any such citizen to perform the act required to be done, as aforesaid, shall, if it failed to be carried into execution by reason of the wrongful act or omission aforesaid of the person or officer charged with the duty of receiving or permitting such performance or offer to perform or acting thereon, be deemed and held as a performance in law of such act, and the person so offering and failing as aforesaid and being otherwise qualified, shall be entitled to vote in the same manner and to the same extent as if he had in fact performed such act.

That is not provided for in the House bill. We say in this section that if the man offers to perform the prerequisites required by State law, and is prevented, that offer shall be equivalent to a performance, and when he presents his affidavit his vote shall be received. It has been criticised and suggested that great injustice may be done by this section. It has been severely criticised by the Senator from Ohio, [Mr. Thurman.] All this section provides is that if a man is otherwise qualified, and has offered to become registered or to perform any other act necessary as a prerequisite under the local laws, his vote shall be received. What is the objection to receiving his vote under those circumstances? If he is a legal voter, in every other way qualified, his vote ought to be received, whether he is actually registered or not. No injustice can be done if his vote is received, because he is otherwise qualified, a legal voter. The Senator from Ohio [Mr. Thurman] says this is a bounty to swear falsely. The man presents an affidavit showing the fact that he has offered to perform the prerequisite; but then he can be objected to for any other reason. He can be objected to because he is not otherwise qualified; but if he is otherwise qualified, and he presents an affidavit that he offered to register or to do any other act required, and was not allowed to do it, what is the harm in receiving his vote? It ought to be received. I say that those who drive colored men from the polls should not reap the advantage of their own wrong, and this section, which does not appear in the House bill at all, is a very important one.

I did not intend to occupy a moment's time, but I do not want the Senate to lay aside one bill and take up another without knowing what they are doing. The fourth section of the bill presented by the Judiciary Committee provides:

> That if any person by force, bribery, threats, intimidation, or otherwise, shall hinder, delay, prevent, or obstruct, or attempt to hinder, delay, prevent or obstruct any citizen from doing any act authorized by this act to be done—

I will say "required to be done"—I propose to amend that phraseology at the proper time—

> to qualify him to vote or from voting at any election as aforesaid, such person shall for every such offense forfeit and pay the sum of $500 to the person aggrieved thereby.

Here, if any person by any means—by fraud, force, or violence—prevents a man either from registering or paying taxes, or doing any act necessary to qualify him to vote, or if by fraud or violence he prevents him from voting, he is guilty of a misdemeanor; and I undertake to say that that fourth section alone is worth three times the whole House bill. It will meet three times as many cases as the House bill. The fourth section standing alone is worth more than the whole House bill put together. It makes it an offense to interfere with the registration by outsiders and for outsiders or anybody to interfere with voters.

Then the fifth section contains this provision:

> That any person who shall be deprived of any office except that of member of Congress or member of a State Legislature, by reason of the violation of the provisions of this act, shall be entitled to recover possession of such office by writ of *mandamus* or other appropriate proceeding; and the circuit and district courts of the United States shall have concurrent jurisdiction of all cases arising under this section. . . .

Now, for the rest of our bill, it is simply providing the machinery to put the bill in motion; and I want to call the attention of the Senate to that. We have the machinery, substantially, of the civil rights act to put the bill in motion. The House bill merely makes it an offense to do certain things, covering about one half the ground; and it makes it an offense punishable in the United States district courts. Who is going to do it? What is that going to amount to? Who is going to be prosecutor? The Senate bill goes on and not only gives the United States courts jurisdiction, but requires the circuit judges to appoint commissioners wherever it may be necessary—if necessary, in every precinct—to arrest and punish parties. It empowers the marshal to aid those commissioners, and to summon the *posse comitatus* whenever it may be necessary. It further empowers the commissioners to appoint special officers to enforce their writs, and it empowers the President of the United States to aid the courts in the enforcement of the law. You have got the agents here in this bill—a system which was matured when the civil rights act was passed, giving agencies the power to enforce the bill. Merely declaring it an offense, and leaving anybody to prosecute it that pleases, and making no further provision, will be a dead letter. It also provides for paying these officers.

Now, suppose you have a district in the South where they refuse to allow the negro to vote, where men are combined together against it. Suppose that the United States judge is applied to, and he appoints a local commissioner for that district. That commissioner can appoint his officers. When these offenses are committed, when there is an attempt to prevent registration, the guilty parties can be arrested. You have got the whole power of the Government in aid of your law.

All this machinery is left out of the House bill. The House bill would be just as good if it simply said that all men should vote, being otherwise qualified, without distinction of race or color, and that if any officer should interfere with them in any way he should be guilty of a misdemeanor. That is all there is of it. It will fall a dead letter.

I apprehend if you pass a bill that has the elements of success in it, that has machinery whereby it can be enforced, it will enforce itself. If it is known that where there is resistance in a locality the United States circuit judge can appoint commissioners, and that those commissioners are judges for that purpose, have all the power of local magistrates, that they can appoint police officers, and that those police officers can be paid and the commissioners can be paid by the United States, and that guilty parties can be arrested there on the spot, and the power of the Government he brought to bear to sustain them, a bill with that machinery, I apprehend, will be respected. You may create as many offenses as you please, but if you provide no machinery for punishing them, as there is not in the House bill, it will amount to nothing.

I do not want to occupy the time of the Senate in the particular discussion of this bill; but before any Senator undertakes to amend a bill here in the Senate it will be well for him to spend some time in examining each expression carefully, and to see to it that his amendment covers the case, that it meets the case he intends to meet. I can tell the effect of the Senate bill in a moment. In the first place, it makes it the duty of all officers charged with doing any act which is a prerequisite to voting to furnish to all men, without distinction of color, an equal opportunity of performing it. In the next place, if a person is otherwise qualified to vote, and attempts to qualify himself by registering, or paying taxes, performing the acts required, and he fails by reason of being unlawfully prevented, then he shall go to the polls with his vote. The next section provides that if any person—this goes outside of the officers—intimidate him while he is attempting to qualify himself by performing the prerequisites, or by any other unlawful means attempt to prevent him from performing that prerequisite, or if any person shall prevent him unlawfully from voting by threats or by any other mode of obstruction, then that person shall be guilty of an offense. The next section provides that the candidate who is entitled to his office by reason of the refusal of boards of canvassers, or otherwise, to count the colored vote, may have his action to obtain possession of his office. The rest of it is the machinery of the civil rights bill modified to suit the emergencies of the case, whereby you have agents to enforce the law, and the power of the Government to protect the voters in a fair opportunity to record their votes.

Now, Mr. President, I propose to offer as a substitute for the House bill the Senate bill, together with the amendments which I offered to that bill. . . .

MR. HOWARD. Mr. President, on reading the second section of the House bill more carefully than I was able to do before I have come to the conclusion that it does not restrain and punish violent opposition to the registration of voters. I can hardly conceive how that was omitted by the party who drafted this bill. The language is:

And any person who shall, by force, fraud, intimidation, or other unlawful means whatsoever, prevent any colored citizen from voting at any such election who possesses the qualifications, except in respect of color, requisite to enable a white citizen to vote thereat, shall, upon conviction thereof, etc.

I rather think that that section would not apply to violent opposition made to a party offering to register himself simply, because I think the word "qualifications" here must refer, if it refers to anything, to the registration of the voter. I think that is a very serious omission; and if it be in order, I beg to offer an amendment to it so as to bring that sort of violence within the operation of the clause. I will offer the following amendment, after the word "from," in line nine of the second section, to insert:

Registering his name preparatory to voting, or from doing any other act required by law as a prerequisite to voting, or from.

So as to read:

And any person who shall by force, fraud, intimidation, or other unlawful means whatsoever, prevent any colored citizen from registering his name preparatory to voting, or from doing any other act required by law as a prerequisite to voting, or from voting at any such election, etc. . .

MATTHEW CARPENTER [R., WIS.]. I do not desire to detain the Senate at any length on this subject, but it seems to me that this Senate bill is the better bill of the two. If there are any particular provisions in it which need amendment let them be amended; but the general scope and purpose of the Senate bill seem to me far preferable to the one which has been sent to us by the House. This House bill is confined almost exclusively, and I think exclusively, to punishing officers and persons who shall intimidate or hinder or delay voting in the methods pointed out by the bill, or permitting the performance of some duty which is enjoined on them as officers under the law. In that particular it is in no way remedial; it punishes the crime after it is complete and done, but it gives no remedy to the person who has been injured by the wrongful act.

Now, the fifth section of the Senate bill is in my judgment worth the whole House bill together. It provides that

Any person who shall be deprived of any office, except that of member of Congress or member of a State Legislature . . .

Of course that exception is because the Congress and the Legislature are the exclusive judges of the qualifications and elections of their members—

by reason of the violation of the provisions of this act, shall be entitled to recover possession of such office by writ of *mandamus* or other appropriate proceeding, and the circuit and district courts of the United States shall have concurrent jurisdiction of all cases arising under this section.

Here is the great distinction in doctrine and philosophy between the two bills, and the question now is which course of action the Senate choose to take. If we are simply to follow on after the violation of law and punish the man who has violated it, in each particular case, by fine and imprisonment, then the House bill is the best conceived bill. If we design to do something more than that; if we design to go beyond merely punishing specific violations of the law, and to carry out and enforce the principle of this amendment to the Constitution, and give effect to the votes of colored persons offered at the polls, then we should have some such provision as is contained in the Senate bill. . . .

We design to do one of two things: we design to carry out and enforce and secure, not merely the observance of the letter, but to accomplish the spirit and object of this amendment, in which case we must have some remedy like that provided in the fifth section of the Senate bill; or we mean to say to men all over the country, "If you choose to violate the law we will punish you simply by fine and imprisonment, and that shall square the account."

MR. HOWARD. If you can find a jury that will convict.

MR. CARPENTER. If you can find a jury to convict, the Senator from Michigan suggests. That is not enough. This amendment to the Constitution is ample and full, and clothes Congress with all power to secure the end which it declares shall be accomplished; and in this case, by this section, we have a remedy which secures to the man who has been injured redress for the wrong he has suffered.

There are several things about this Senate bill, some things in its phraseology, perhaps some in its substantial and important provisions, that may be improved by amendment; but it seems to me to be a far better bill if we desire to do anything. If we merely wish to pretend to do something and not accomplish anything substantial and important, the House bill is an excellent recipe for doing that; but if we mean to carry out, execute, and secure the performance and observance of this amendment to the Constitution, it is certain to my mind that the Senate bill is far preferable to the bill that comes from the House; and for that reason I hope the Senate will not adopt it as a substitute. Let us take this Senate bill and go through with it, perfect it by additions or subtractions, but act upon it as the basis of the legislation called for at the present time.

MR. HOWARD. I think upon the whole I will withdraw my amendment for the present, and I hope the Senate will come to a vote on the question of substituting the Senate for the House bill. . . .

JOHN POOL [R., N.C.]. I desire to say a word in regard to the particular amendment now pending. This bill is for the purpose of enforcing the fifteenth amendment, which applies to colored voters, most of whom reside in the section of the country from which the Senator from Alabama and myself come. The great and most effectual means used to interfere with their exercise of the right secured to them by the fifteenth amendment is by intimidation, by violence. I think that the penalty which is named in this second section, to be enforced by the party aggrieved, would never be put into operation at all. The purpose of the bill is to protect those citizens against intimidation from voting.

I confess that there is something in the suggestion of the Senator from Vermont, that there is no intimidation in this particular section aimed at. But, sir, it is perfectly sure that the very same means of intimidation which prevents a colored citizen from voting will be resorted to to prevent him from bringing this penal action, and unless the section is amended as suggested by the Senator from Alabama I do not believe that an action will ever be brought in those States, because it is much more difficult for one of those citizens to bring and maintain a criminal action than it is for him to perform the single act of voting.

MR. EDMUNDS. Will my friend permit me to make a suggestion right there?

MR. POOL. Certainly.

MR. EDMUNDS. If you take out this penalty, as it is called, really liquidated damages, from the person who is aggrieved, whose right is denied, and who has suffered injury, and give it to anybody who will sue for it, it becomes a pure penalty. Then the question is, whether you can have a bill which contains double penalties; whether you are to punish, in the strict sense of punishment, a man twice for the same offense; because my friend will see that the section, in addition to giving these damages to the party aggrieved as damages, makes it a criminal misdemeanor, punishable on indictment and conviction by a fine of not less than $500 and imprisonment not less than a month nor more than a year. I suggest to my friend, who is a cultivated and educated lawyer, whether he would not in court find himself in great difficulty with a bill of double penalties, which were purely such. . . .

ALLEN THURMAN [DEM., OHIO]. Mr. President, I confess I was not prepared
to hear my friend from Wisconsin [Mr. Carpenter] place his chief advocacy
of the Senate bill upon the fifth section of the bill. Let us see what the fifth
section is:

> That any person who shall be deprived of any office, except that of member of Congress or
> member of a State Legislature, by reason of the*violation of the provisions of this act, shall be
> entitled to recover possession of such office by writ of *mandamus* or other appropriate proceeding,
> and the circuit and district courts of the United States shall have concurrent jurisdiction of all cases
> arising under this section.

And by the next section it is provided:

> That the district courts of the United States, within their respective districts, shall have,
> exclusively of the courts of the several States, cognizance of all crimes and offenses committed
> against the provisions of this act.

The idea, then, of the bill is that the enforcement of this act, and of the
rights of persons under this act, is to be exclusively in the courts of the
United States, and that all persons who shall be deprived of office by any
violation of this act may recover their offices by some appropriate remedy in
the courts of the United States. Now, the first point to which I wish to call
the attention of my friend is quite a practical consideration. How many
officers will this cover who may thus be deprived of their offices by a
violation of this act; that is, by somebody not being registered who would
have voted for them, or somebody being prevented from voting at the
elections who would have voted for them, or any other of the grounds that
may be stated under this bill? How many such officers are there? I will speak
for my own State. This bill embraces every officer except members of the
Legislature in the State of Ohio. It takes, therefore, all the State officers to
begin with. It then takes all the judiciary of the State; then all the county
officers; then all the city officers and town officers; and then all the township
officers. Now, let me say to my friend from Wisconsin that that will make
about two hundred persons in the county in which I live who are to be
entitled to go into the circuit or district court of the United States to test the
election of the persons who are declared elected.

MR. CARPENTER. Let me ask my friend from Ohio whether he expects that
whole number will be defrauded out of their election very often in his
county?

MR. THURMAN. I do not expect any such thing, but I know there have
been a great many contested-election cases in Ohio, and I know if they had
all been tried in the district court of the United States for the district of Ohio
that court would have had very little time to attend to anything else. But
now, when you have increased the jurisdiction of that court, and increased
the causes for which you may proceed, and allow two hundred persons in a

single county, or more than twenty thousand persons in the single State of Ohio, or, taking the whole United States through, about half a million persons, to go into the district courts to contest elections and try the title to office there, I want to know what is to become of your district courts?

MR. STEWART. Does the Senator understand that the jurisdiction is confined to the district courts of the United States in this fifth section?

MR. THURMAN. Well, sir, whether it is confined to them or not, parties may go into those courts, and they would be likely enough to go there. I do not know exactly what construction is to be put upon the bill, taking that section in connection with the sixth section. Perhaps the sixth section only relates to criminal procedure, and therefore it is only in relation to that that it is exclusive. But if it is not exclusive, then I want to put to my friend from Nevada this question: what are you to do if a contest is begun under the State law? Then may not a contest be begun in the district court of the United States? Which has the superior jurisdiction? Under our State law it is not necessary that the party who has lost the office shall contest, but any elector may contest the election. Now, suppose a contest is commenced under the State law, and another proceeding is commenced in the United States district court "by writ of *mandamus* or other appropriate proceeding;" which jurisdiction is the superior? Which decision is to be obeyed? Here you put it in the power of at least half a million people who may be defeated for office in the United States to load down the docket of your district courts, if you pass this fifth section; and as I said yesterday, it applies in terms even to the election of President of the United States; and you may have the spectacle of seeing a contest for the Presidency in a district court of the United States. It applies to the election of every Governor of a State. . . .

As I have said, the first remarkable feature that strikes me about this House bill is that the first section covers all the other sections down to the ninth. I ask Senators to look at the first section. It provides:

That any officer of the United States, or of any State, Territory, or district, and every officer of any city, county, town, township, borough, ward, parish, or hundred, in any State, Territory, or district, who shall by any official act whatever, or by the omission, neglect, or refusal to perform any official act or duty whatever, whether under color or pretext of any provision of any State constitution, or any law of any State, Territory, or district whatsoever, or of any local, municipal, or other law, rule, or ordinance, deny or abridge the right of any citizen of the United States to vote, on account of race, color, or previous condition of servitude, at any Federal, State, county, municipal, or other election, shall, upon conviction thereof, be adjudged guilty of a misdemeanor, and shall be punished by imprisonment of not less than one year and not exceeding three years, or by a fine not less than $500 nor exceeding $5,000, or both such fine and imprisonment, at the discretion of the court.

That covers every conceivable case of official misconduct or official negligence that can be found in this bill, or that can exist at all. There is not one single supposable case of official negligence, whether it is in a registrar, whether it is in a tax assessor, whether it is in a tax collector, whether it is in a judge of election, whether it is in a board of canvassers, or whether it is in any other official functionary whomsoever, that is not covered by this first section. That being the case, there is no necessity at all for the other sections which follow in the bill, until you come to the ninth.

The second thing that strikes one as curious about the House bill is that, after leaving the first section, every other section in the bill down to the ninth is confined to a refusal to permit a colored citizen to register or to vote. That is the whole of it. It is only for the protection of colored citizens. If this bill passes the man who by intimidation prevents a white citizen from voting or from registering goes without any punishment whatsoever.

MR. EDMUNDS. That is in the House bill, not the Senate bill.

MR. THURMAN. I am speaking of the House bill. In such a case he goes without any punishment, unless he is punished under the State law. The man who interferes with the rights of a white citizen, and deprives him of his right to register or to vote, is subject to no punishment except that which the State law affords.

THOMAS FERRY [R., MICH.]. But the ninth section provides for all citizens.

MR. THURMAN. The ninth section it is true provides for all citizens. That section reads:

That if any person shall by threats, violence, or intimidation prevent or attempt to prevent any citizen of the United States from the free exercise of his right to vote in any election at which members of Congress or electors for President or Vice President of the United States may be voted for, etc.

My friend from Connecticut will observe that this section applies only to the election of members of Congress, or electors of President and Vice President; but the preceding part of the bill punishes anybody who interferes with the right of the colored citizen who offers his vote at any State election whatsoever, or any election held under any State constitution or law, down to the lowest municipal election that can be held. The ninth section only refers to Federal elections. So the Senator will see that I am right in saying that the sections from one to nine, both exclusive, do not protect the right of any white man whatsoever, but are simply limited to the protection of the colored race. If the Senate is prepared to say that a white man is less entitled to protection in his right of suffrage than is a colored man, then this House bill is all right; but if the Senate is not prepared to say that, then the word "colored" should be stricken out wherever it occurs, in every one of these sections, so as to make them apply to all citizens alike. That is an amendment that can very easily be made, and then the bill would not be obnoxious to the criticism I am now making upon it.

But in point of truth there is no necessity, after the first section, for any one of these sections in the House bill until you come to section nine. What, then, is section nine?

That if any person shall, by threats, violence, or intimidation, prevent or attempt to prevent any citizen of the United States from the free exercise of his right to vote in any election at which members of Congress or electors for President or Vice President of the United States may be voted for, such person so offending shall be liable to indictment, and on conviction thereof, shall be subject to a fine not exceeding $1,000, or to imprisonment not less than one year nor more than three years, or both, at the discretion of the court.

Then the tenth section provides:

That the circuit courts of the United States shall have jurisdiction of the suits for forfeitures imposed and causes of action created by this act, and the circuit and district courts of the United States shall have jurisdiction of the misdemeanors created by this act.

In my opinion, if you would strike out of this House bill all the sections but the first and ninth and tenth sections it would be more unique, and then would be a bill that some one with some reason might support. Whether or not it would be perfectly right then I do not say. I should like to reflect upon that before I could vote for it; but it certainly would then be a bill not obnoxious to the objections to which both the Senate bill and the House bill as it now stands are. I hope we shall go on, however, and perfect the House bill. The more I reflect upon the Senate bill the more surprised I am that anybody can give it his support.

Now, I wish to say one word in respect to the Senate bill, and I do not know that I shall trouble the Senate again with remarks upon this subject. I wish to say a word upon the twelfth section, to which I briefly alluded the day before yesterday in the remarks that I then submitted. That section is in these words:

That it shall be lawful for the President of the United States, or such person as he may empower for that purpose, to employ such part of the land or naval forces of the United States, or of the militia, as shall be deemed necessary to prevent the violation and enforce the due execution of this act.

I expected that the gentleman who has this bill in charge would explain that section and let us know how these troops were to act, how they were to enforce the provisions of this bill, how they were to prevent its violation. Let me ask the attention of that gentleman. There are in the State of Ohio about fifteen hundred election precincts. I suppose, taking the whole United States together, there are not less than twenty-five or thirty thousand election precincts in the whole United States and the Territories thereof, all of which are covered by this bill. Now, what are you going to do with your troops? It will be said that it will not be necessary to send them to every one of these election precincts. Manifestly not. You would have to increase the Army twentyfold, fifty-fold, to do that. It is supposed, then, that there are some places only to which it will be necessary to send troops; and you put it entirely in the discretion of the Chief Magistrate of this country, whoever may be that Chief Magistrate, in a law which you intend to be permanent— it ought to be permanent or not be a law at all—to interfere with the military at any poll where he may see fit so to interfere.

In any section of the country, in any State, in any district, in any closely-contested State or closely-contested district, you put it in the power of one man, the President of the United States, who may be directly interested in the result, who may be a candidate at that very election, to surround the polls with the troops of the United States, to do what? To see that this act be not violated; to see that this act be enforced. Nay, more, you put it in his power to delegate to some person, not an officer at all either of the State or of the United States, and in a district where there is no domestic violence, no insurrection, no rebellion, but perfect peace; you put it in the power of the President to give to some single individual the delegated power of employing the whole Army of the United States to see that this act be not violated; to see that there is no cheating at elections. Why, sir, what a power is that!

I asked the gentleman who has this bill in charge, the day before yesterday, what the troops were to do when they surrounded the poll. I will take a case. Here is an election poll, and here are a hundred troops of the United States under the command of a captain or lieutenant of infantry. He is sent there to do what? In the language of this bill, "to prevent the violation and enforce the due execution of this act." What then is to be prevented? The violation of the act. What is to be the violation of the act? The improper rejection of the vote of some colored man, or other citizen of the United States. That is the violation that is to be prevented. What is the enforcement of the act? To compel the reception of that man's vote. To prevent the violation of the act is to prevent the rejection of the vote. To enforce the act is to enforce the reception of his vote. When the judges of election, the sworn officers of election, decide that a man is not entitled to vote, then, and not until then, can this military officer be called into requisition. And what then? Is his judgment to override that of the judges of election?

Is he to adjudge that they have wrongly decided? Is he to decide that they have violated the act? Is this military man to decide this question of law under the constitution of Ohio, or the constitution of New York, or the constitution and statutes of Kentucky, and to hold that the judges of election— men versed in the election law—have decided the question wrongly, and therefore it is necessary for him to interfere, and do what? Interfere and compel them at the point of the bayonet to receive the vote that they, under their oaths as sworn officers have rejected. If it is not that, it is nothing. If it is not that, it is simply intimidation. If it is not that, it is simply holding the bayonet to the throat of the civil officer, and holding it there by command of the President of the United States. Show me something that these troops are to do; show me how they are to prevent the violation of this act; show me how they are to enforce this act, unless you give the military man the right to override the judgment of the civil officer; to override the solemn judgment of the sworn judge of election deciding as to the law of his own State and the constitution of his own State and the right of voters thereunder. . . .

Sir, I say once more, if this can be done in a free country, let us hear no more talk about the one-man power; let us hear no more talk about the power of the President of the United States; make a monarch of him at once. Louis Napoleon has been charged with controlling the elections in France. Louis Napoleon never surrounded every polling place in France with the troops of the empire, or the troops of the republic before it was an empire. Never did he dare to do that. Not a soldier appeared at the voting places in Paris even, where there was the strongest opposition that existed to the emperor at the late election there; but the votes of the soldiers were taken in their own barracks, their own camps. Throughout all France the people were allowed to vote without any bayonets in sight, without any soldiers to make them afraid, without anything to intimidate the voters in the shape of military coercion. And yet here in a Republic you propose to confer upon one man, who may be a candidate for election himself, the power to surround any poll he pleases in the whole United States with his troops to see that the election law is not violated! I say again, if that can be done, it is idle to talk about free institutions any more.

MR. EDMUNDS. My friend from Ohio, speaking for that great mass of our countrymen whom he so well represents, and being, as they are, so much in favor of enforcing the fifteenth amendment, reminds me of one of Shakespeare's characters, Falstaff by name, who insisted upon it that he would not give a reason for anything, I believe it was, upon compulsion. My friend from Ohio is very much interested in favor of carrying out this constitutional amendment; but he does not want to have any law that will compel him to do so. He wants to do it of his own free will and accord.

If my friend had made the speech that he has now favored us with, (and it is a very ingenious one, and in many respects a sound one,) twenty years ago when his own party was pressing almost exactly such a section as the eighth section of this bill, in order to aid in the rendition of fugitive slaves back to slavery, he would have performed a greater service to his country than he performs now. I ask the Secretary, in order that the Senate may see the comparison between these two sections, to read the fifth section of the act of 1850, passed by the party of which my friend from Ohio is the exponent; and I ask Senators to take the eighth section of this bill and compare it as the Secretary reads to see if we have not pretty good authority for that kind of legislation.

The Secretary read as follows from the act of September 18, 1850:

MR. EDMUNDS. Now, Mr. President, the only possible difference in substance and almost in phraseology between the fifth section of the act of 1850 and this eighth section is that the eighth section contains a statement that "such portion of the land or naval forces of the United States, or of the militia, as may be necessary," may also be called upon. Upon that point we have the settled determination of a Democratic administration and a Democratic Attorney General, and a correct interpretation, too, under the act of 1850, on this very point. The statute of 1850 provided that all the bystanders or *posse comitatus* of the proper county may be called upon . . .

Therefore we have a very excellent model of legislation to carry into force one of the provisions of the Constitution of the United States; and when one of those provisions was in favor of slavery, in favor of carrying back an escaping fugitive to servitude and to the lash, it was very convenient for a party that then controlled the country to pass acts of Congress to carry out such an odious provision of the Constitution, and to authorize commissioners to call upon the whole body of the country, soldiers and sailors, marines, Army, and everything, to help carry the poor hunted fugitive back. Now, times have changed after twenty years; and with the fugitive liberated and made a free and independent man of, when we apply the same machinery to protect him in the rights that the Constitution gives him, my friend from Ohio changes with the tune of his party, and sings that this is outrage and oppression!

MR. THURMAN. Mr. President, times have changed when the Senator from Vermont goes to the fugitive slave law of 1850 to find a model for legislation, and times have changed wonderfully. Now, Mr. President, if I had the slightest doubt in the world that I was right I could entertain that doubt no longer. When so astute and able a man as the Senator from Vermont can give no better reason for the defense of this section than that which he has given, I know my objections to it must be well taken. What possible connection, or parallel, or similitude has the use of the troops of the United States to enforce the execution of the writ of a court against resistance to the case provided for in this bill, of surrounding the ballot-boxes with the troops of the United States to compel the judges of election to receive the votes or to compel them to reject them? . . .

OLIVER MORTON [R., IND.]. Mr. President, I think it my duty to call the attention of the Senate to one question that seems to me to affect this Senate bill in nearly every section, and which does not affect the House bill. My attention was called to it by the remarks of the Senator from New Jersey. Our theory is that the question of suffrage is under the control of the States, and was left to the several States by the Constitution of the United States; and that being the case, Congress had no power to pass a law conferring suffrage on colored men, and it was necessary to amend the Constitution of the United States for that purpose. We therefore provided in the fifteenth amendment that "the right of citizens of the United States to vote shall not be denied or abridged by the United States, or by any State, on account of race, color, or previous condition of servitude." The proposition to which I call attention is this: that the question of suffrage is now, as it was before, completely under the control of the several States to punish violations of the right of suffrage, just as they had the power before, except that we take away their power to deny suffrage on account of race, color, or previous condition of servitude, and have given to Congress the power to enforce this amendment.

The question now to which I call the attention of the Senate is whether it is in the power of Congress to make provision for punishing violations of the right of suffrage except those violations which go to the question of color, race, or previous condition of servitude.

MR. EDMUNDS. But it does not make any difference which the color is, black or white.

MR. MORTON. Not a bit. It does not make any difference which; but if a man is denied the right of suffrage because he is a white man, if any State shall assume to deny a man the right of suffrage because he is a white man, then we have a right to interfere; or if because he is a colored man, then we have a right to interfere. But suppose the denial of the right of suffrage by a board of registration or a board of inspectors has nothing whatever to do with color; suppose it is for an offense that existed by State law before the enactment of this fifteenth amendment, what power have we got to interfere with that any more than we had before?

MR. EDMUNDS. Nobody, I think, would claim that we have. I should not say so. . . .

CARL SCHURZ [R., MO.]. Mr. President, as the Senate will remember, the honorable Senator from New Jersey [Mr. Stockton] addressed yesterday, in the course of his speech, a personal appeal to me, with so much eloquent earnestness that I am not permitted to doubt its sincerity; and I think courtesy requires that I should respond to it in the same spirit. He expressed his belief that I and thousands of the children of my native land had come to these shores for the purpose of enjoying the blessings of liberty and self-government; and in arguing against this bill, he intimated that we would certainly consider it our duty to do all in our power to preserve and perpetuate these inestimable blessings. In all these suppositions he was right; but I apprehend there may be a serious difference of opinion between the Senator from New Jersey and myself as to what those blessings of liberty and self-government consist in, and as to the manner in which they can and ought to be preserved and perpetuated; and inasmuch as he has appealed to me from his point of view I think it is proper that I should appeal to him and to his associates from mine.

I have listened to the arguments of Democratic Senators against this bill with mingled pleasure and pain; pleasure, when I noticed how my honorable friend from Ohio, [Mr. Thurman,] whose shrewdness on this floor nobody is disposed to doubt, thought it proper to confine himself to an attack on the details of this bill, instead of launching into that general denunciation of the constitutional amendments and the legislation based thereon with which Democratic Senators had made us so familiar on former occasions. I might have considered that a good omen had not some of his associates, less discreet and more impulsive than he, hoisted the true colors of their party and boldly declared that they did not believe in the validity of the fifteenth amendment, and openly proclaimed their desire to see it overthrown. Then I could not but remember that even the Senator from Ohio, in the opening remarks of his speech, spoke of the fifteenth amendment as a thing of only supposed legality, though he, as a practical man, was willing to base his argument upon that supposition, for the reason that the ruling majority of the Senate were united upon that point. Well, sir, this, it seems to me, opens to us a view rather wider than the discussion of the technical points which we have been listening to in the course of this debate.

It brings back to our memories again the fierce declamation hurled aginst all the constitutional amendments by our Democratic associates in this body; the bitter opposition raised against all legislation designed to enforce them; the vehement appeals in the name of liberty, of self-government, of State rights, and of all that is great and good, to leave the rights of the newly-enfranchised class to the legislative action of the States exclusively; the acrimonious charge that we were a revolutionary party; that we had already revolutionized the Constitution of the United States, and that we were about to subvert the whole system of self-government and all the political institutions to which this country owes so many of its blessings.

Now, sir, in responding to the appeal of the Senator from New Jersey, and desiring to say to him what I conceive to be the blessings of liberty and self-government, and the manner in which they ought to be sustained, preserved, and perpetuated, I beg him to review with me the field covered by the bill before us. We are charged with having revolutionized the Constitution of the country by the amendments recently ratified; and that charge is reiterated so often that we have reason to suppose our opponents must consider it a crushing argument. Well, sir, I do not deem it necessary to enter a plea of "not guilty." On the contrary, I acknowledge the fact, and I suppose the Republican party is by no means ashamed of it. Yes, sir, this Republic has passed through a revolutionary process of tremendous significance. Yes, the Constitution of the United States has been changed in some most essential points; that change does amount to a great revolution, and this bill is one of its legitimate children. Let us look those facts in the face, and I think we may derive from them some conclusions which may be of service in the discussion of the provisions of this bill. What was that constitutional revolution which the Democrats denounce as so fearful an outrage? In order to understand it fully, we must cast a look back and see what the constitutional polity of the United States was before the civil war, according to the Democratic interpretation of the Constitution then prevailing.

Constitutions and constitutional constructions do not spring from a mere process of philosophical speculation and reasoning. They grow out of conditions, circumstances, events, sympathies, prevailing interests. We all remember that the most powerful political interest in this country for a long period previous to the war was that of slavery. We remember also that the slave power, finding itself at war with the conscience of mankind, condemned by the enlightened spirit of this age, menaced by adverse interests growing stronger and stronger every day, sought safety behind the bulwark of what they euphoniously called local self-government, and intrenched itself in the doctrine of State sovereignty. To be sure, it made, from that defensive position, offensive sallies, encroaching on the rights of the nonslaveholding States, as for instance in the case of the notorious fugitive slave law and the attempt to take possession of the whole territorial domain of this Republic; but the doctrine of State sovereignty was its main citadel, its base of operations. . . .

Finally that structure of fallacies, still so overshadowing but ten short years ago, tumbled down. It fell after having heaped outrage after outrage upon the dignity of human nature; after having for generations befogged the minds, corrupted the logic, and debauched the moral sense of the American people; after having well-nigh poisoned our whole political life; after having involved this country in the most irrepressible of conflicts. It fell after having arrayed man against man in bloody struggle; after having devoured five hundred thousand of the children of this Republic and untold millions of our treasure. It was finally overthrown by the shock of the great revolution. And what did that revolution put in its place? It gave us three great amendments to the national Constitution. The first ordains that no State shall henceforth have the power to introduce or maintain slavery or involuntary servitude. The second ordains that all persons born or naturalized in the United States are citizens of the United States and of the States in which they reside, and that no State shall henceforth have the power to make or enforce any law abridging the privileges and immunities of citizens of the Republic. The third ordains that no State shall abridge the right of suffrage of any citizen on account of race, color, or previous condition of servitude. And all three empower Congress to pass appropriate legislation for their enforcement.

That is the result of the great constitutional revolution. What does this result signify? The war grew out of the systematic violation of individual rights by State authority. The war ended with the vindication of individual rights by the national power. The revolution found the rights of the individual at the mercy of the States; it rescued them from their arbitrary discretion, and placed them under the shield of national protection. It made the liberty and rights of every citizen in every State a matter of national concern. Out of a republic of arbitrary local organizations it made a republic of equal citizens—citizens exercising the right of self-government under and through the States, but as to their rights as citizens not subject to the arbitrary will of the States. It grafted upon the Constitution of the United States the guarantee of national citizenship; and it empowered Congress, as the organ of the national will, to enforce that guarantee by national legislation. That is the meaning of that great revolution; and if Democratic Senators denounce the bill at present before us as its offspring they are welcome. I accept the name.

Now, sir, what is the scope and purpose of this bill? It provides that no State shall enforce a law with regard to elections, or the processes preliminary to elections, in which in any way, either directly or indirectly, discrimination is made against any citizen on account of race, color, or previous condition; and when any citizen is hindered in the exercise of the right of suffrage by means of fraud, intimidation, or violence, or misuse of official power, the offender shall be brought to trial and punishment by a court of the United States. And for this the bill provides the necessary machinery. In other words, neither a State nor an individual shall deprive any citizen of the United States, on account of race or color, of the free exercise of his right to participate in the functions of self-government; and the national Government assumes the duty to prevent the commission of the crime, and to correct its consequences when committed. That is all.

If we were to judge the character and tendency of this bill from the expressions used by our Democratic associates in denouncing it we should think that we were about to perpetrate the most horrible crime against the rights of man and human liberty ever conceived by the human imagination. It is as if the democratic institutions of this country were about to receive their death-blow, while we contemplate nothing but to secure every citizen of the United States in the free and full enjoyment of those democratic institutions.

What are the objections? It is, I believe, not pretended that the bill in its general scope and purpose runs against the Constitution as improved by the fifteenth amendment; but it is objected that the bill is uncalled for, on the ground that nothing has been done in the different States to show the necessity of any such legislation. Sir, is this true? Can this assertion be maintained even a single moment? For generations the practices of slavery have controlled the minds and moral views of the people of the southern States. Popular prejudice, so long nourished by those practices, was naturally arrayed against the enfranchisement of the former slave, and the beneficient agency of time has by no means been sufficient yet to allay it, whatever improvement we may observe. Joined to the prejudice of race, the jealousy of political power conspires against a fair execution of the fifteenth amendment, and in view of these opposing forces, who will deny that this legislation to enforce it is necessary?

Nay, more than that. The very Senators on this floor who pretend that the passage of this bill is not called for by circumstances go so far as to throw doubt upon the validity of the fifteenth amendment, thus exciting the worst passions of the disturbing element in the South to do all within their power to defeat the purposes of this constitutional provision. Is it not so? And while on the one hand themselves fanning the flame, they on the other hand deny the necessity of quenching it. Will it be unfair to assume under such circumstances that while denouncing this legislation as uncalled for they merely desire to defeat the purposes of the fifteenth amendment?

The Senator from Maryland urged another argument, which at first sight seems to have some plausibility. He says that the constitutional amendment is one of the great prohibitory clauses, as we find them in several places and on several subjects in the Constitution of the United States, and that with regard to them enforcing legislation had never been thought necessary. Suppose this to be so; can he tell me why it was deemed indispensable to affix to the thirteenth, fourteenth, and fifteenth amendments the express provision that Congress should have the power to enforce them by appropriate legislation? The Senator from Maryland says that Congress had that power anyhow. I suppose so; but why was the power never so emphatically and expressly asserted as in these three cases? Simply because it was known that the recent three amendments had to be enforced in the States lately in armed insurrection, against the opposition of prejudice, habit, and political passion. Is not the distinction obvious? Is not the intent of those who drafted the amendments and provided for the express grant of power clear as sunlight? Is not the necessity of using that grant of power equally evident?

Now, sir, I will not go into the discussion of the argument offered by Democratic Senators against the details of this bill. I know there are several provisions which are objectionable. I admit it frankly. I do think that the section which confers by implication upon the President power to surround the polls with the military forces of the United States ought not to be raised to the dignity of a permanent law. I know that such a law would be repugnant to the genius of free institutions, and that it is considered so all over the world. So it is with the other clause providing that the President shall have the power to command a judge to go here and to go there; and further, it is in my opinion of doubtful propriety to stimulate the desire of a citizen to secure his rights by the mercenary consideration of money. It does appear to me if a man has not spirit enough to do it for the sake of his rights, he ought not to be permitted to do it for the sake of so many dollars. And I here express my hope that the Senate will strike out these obnoxious provisions.

But as to the whole machinery of the bill, I think the Senator from Ohio was not quite justified in waving off so lightly the argument which was employed against him by my friend from Vermont that the Democrats had found that legal machinery not only constitutional, but positively admirable when it was used to enforce the fugitive-slave law, while they denounce it as detestable and infamous now. The Senator from Ohio knows very well that a legal machinery used for a laudable purpose may be very praiseworthy, while it is most reprehensible when used for evil; and so the Senator from Vermont was certainly right when he blamed the Democrats for calling this machinery all possible bad names when it is to be used in the service of the constitutional rights of freemen, while they had upheld it as most rightful and necessary, and denounced everybody as a traitor who would not help in executing it when it was to serve in the unholy work of returning fugitive slaves, who sought their freedom, to bondage and misery.

But here is another question of interest. Does this bill really take away from the States the power to legislate on the subject? Look at it closely. Does it? Not at all, sir. It leaves the States just as free as they ever were to legislate for the prompt and vigorous enforcement of protection of the right of every voter to the free exercise of the suffrage. Does it not? In that respect it does not impose the least restriction on the power of the States. In that direction the States may go just as far as they please. But the bill does provide that a State shall no longer have the power to swindle any of its citizens out of their rights.

A State shall have full power to do that which is right in its own way; but it is prohibited from doing that which is wrong in any way. It is this, I suppose, what Democrats will insist upon calling an arbitrary limitation of State rights. Or is it true, what is asserted also, that this legislation does not find anything analogous in the Constitution of the United States? In the Constitution, sir, we find one clause which ordains that no State shall have the power to grant titles of nobility. What does that mean? It means that no State shall elevate by the grant of privileges, one class of its citizens above the rest. And what is contemplated by the fifteenth amendment and by the law designed to enforce it? That no State shall have the power to degrade, by the withholding of rights, any portion of its citizens below the rest. Is not the correspondence here evident? But here suddenly the indignation of our Democratic friends is aroused, and in the prohibition to degrade men they find an intolerable encroachment on State rights and local self-government. And just there, I apprehend, is the rub. It is not so much the technicalities of the bill; it is the spirit, the purpose of the bill they oppose. It is, as the Senator from Maryland has just openly and boldly proclaimed, that if the bill were ever so perfect, he would vote against it on general principles. He nods his assent; and I am sure I cannot mistake him; and the same thing we have been given to understand by every Democratic Senator who has addressed the Senate on this question.

Let us see what their complaints are, then. Strip them of all the verbiage of technical points, sift them to the bottom, and you will find there a residue of the old pro-slavery logic still. As they once asserted that true liberty implied the right of one man to hold another man as his slave, they will tell you now that they are no longer true freemen in their States because under the authority of the States they can no longer deprive other men of their rights. As they once asserted that true self-government consisted in the power of a State to exclude a large portion of its citizens from self-government, so they will say now that we strike a blow at self-government because we insist upon legislation securing every citizen of the States in the enjoyment of self-government. Is it not so?

Destruction of self-government! What a prodigious discovery our Democratic associates have made! Sir, it is not because this bill lays its hands upon self-government to destroy it, but because by the fifteenth amendment, and the legislation made in pursuance thereof, the general sway of self-government is to be for the first time established all over this country, that I am in favor of the principles of this act. What is true self-government? What does it consist in? True self-government consists in a political organization of society which secures to the generality of its members, that is to say, to the whole people, and not to a part of them only, the right and the means to cooperate in the management of their common affairs, either directly, or, where direct action is impossible, by a voluntary delegation of power. It ceases to be true self-government as soon as the powers of government are conferred as an exclusive privilege on one portion of the people and is withheld from the rest. And how is self-government exercised? By the right of suffrage. The representative system knows no other instrumentality. Suffrage is the means by which it lives and breathes. . . .

The time is past, sir, when the cry of State rights will serve as a guise for such pretensions. I, too, am a friend and earnest advocate of State rights, as far as State rights are the embodiment of true local self-government. True, I do not cling to those traditional notions which an historical period now passed by and absolved has brought down to us. I do not cherish that sentimental—I might almost say that supersititious—reverence for individual States, which attributes to them as historical persons a sort of transcendental sanctity; but I do believe that their value can hardly be over-estimated as compact political sub-organizations, through which and in which the self-government of the people is exercised, and within which it finds its most appropriate and efficient organs. I am therefore in favor of leaving to the States as large a scope of independent action as may be consistent with the safety of the Republic and the rights of the citizens. . . .

But the constitutional revolution has enlarged the powers of Congress for the purpose of establishing and securing true and general self-government in all of these States, not for the purpose of circumscribing its scope and functions within narrower limits. It has indeed overthrown what I call State wrongs; but it was not designed to abolish what I would call the legitimate sphere of State rights. And I venture to say—and I cannot repeat this warning too often—the party which would attempt to carry that revolution much farther in the direction of an undue centralization of power would run against a popular instinct far stronger than party allegiance has ever proved to be.

But, sir, on the other hand, the party that would refuse to recognize and acquiesce in the great results of this beneficent revolution, the party that would attempt to subvert the institution of general self-government under national protection, as now established in the Constitution; the party that would strive to overthrow this new order of things, such a party certainly cannot fail to encounter the condemnation of the people and to meet disgrace and destruction, for such a party openly by its own confession constitutes itself the enemy of the peace and glory of this Republic. And I would say to my friend from New Jersey that I did not come to this country, where I hope to enjoy the blessings of liberty and self-government, to aid any party in designs like these. . . .

You tell us also, gentlemen, that legislation like this is odious to you. Look around you and see how much you can do to make it superfluous. We, too, should be glad never to be under the necessity of resorting to it. If you want to avoid it the means is simple. Prevail upon your friends never to threaten or trouble any class of voters in the free exercise of their rights, have those rights secured and protected by appropriate State legislation, and that State legislation respected by your friends, and such measures as this will never be practically applied. Nay, more than that, if you are really in earnest, then I would advise you to accept this measure as a gage of good faith instead of opposing it. It would be far better than your attempts to throw doubt upon the legality of the constitutional amendments, your studious efforts to hold out to your partisans the prospect of their overthrow, and of the subversion of all that has been accomplished for the final settlement of our controversies and the peace of the country. . . .

JOHN POOL [R., N.C.]. Mr. President, the question involved in the proposition now before the Senate is one in which my section of the Union is particularly interested; although since the ratification of the fifteenth amendment, which we are now about to enforce by appropriate legislation, other sections of the country have become more or less interested in the same question. It is entering upon a new phase of reconstruction; that is, to enforce by appropriate legislation those great principles upon which the reconstruction policy of Congress was based. . . .

The equality which by the thirteenth, fourteenth, and fifteenth amendments has been attempted to be secured for the colored men, has not only subjected them to the operation of the prejudices which had theretofore existed, but it has raised against them still stronger prejudices and stronger feelings in order to fight down the equality by which it is claimed they are to control the legislation of that section of the country. They were turned loose among those people, weak, ignorant, and poor. Those among the white citizens there who have sought to maintain the rights which you have thrown upon that class of people, have to endure every species of proscription, of opposition, and of vituperation in order to carry out the policy of Congress, in order to lift up and to uphold the rights which you have conferred upon that class. It is for that reason not only necessary for the freedmen, but it is necessary for the white people of that section that there should be stringent and effective legislation on the part of Congress in regard to these measures of reconstruction.

We have heard on former occasions on the floor of the Senate that there were organizations which committed outrages, which went through communi-

ties for the purposes, of intimidating and coercing classes of citizens in the
exercise of their rights. We have been told here that perhaps it might be well
that retaliation should be resorted to on the part of those who are oppressed.
Sir, the time will come when retaliation will be resorted to unless the
Government of the United States interposes to command and to maintain the
peace; when there will be retaliation and civil war; when there will be
bloodshed and tumult in various communities and sections. It is not only
necessary for the freedmen, but it is important to the white people of the
southern section, that by plain and stringent laws the United States should
interpose and preserve the peace and quiet of the community.

The fifteenth amendment to the Constitution of the United States provides
that the right of citizens of the United States to vote shall not be denied or
abridged by the United States, or by any State on account of race, color, or
previous condition of servitude. It speaks of "the right of citizens to vote." It
has been said that voting is a privilege; but this amendment recognizes it as a
right in the citizen; and this right is not to "be denied or abridged by the
United States, or by any State." What are we to understand by that? Can
individuals abridge it with impunity? Is there no power in this Government
to prevent individuals or associations of individuals from abridging or contravening that provision of the Constitution? If that be so, legislation is
unnecessary. If our legislation is to apply only to the States, it is perfectly
clear that it is totally unnecessary, inasmuch as we cannot pass a criminal
law as applicable to a State; nor can we indict a State officer as an officer. It
must apply to individuals. A State might attempt to contravene that provision
of the Constitution by passing some positive enactment by which it would be
contravened, but the Supreme Court would hold such enactment to be
unconstitutional, and in that way the State would be restrained. But the word
"deny" is used. There are various ways in which a State may prevent the full
operation of this constitutional amendment. It cannot—because the courts
would prevent it—by positive legislation, but by acts of omission it may
practically deny the right. The legislation of Congress must be to supply acts
of omission on the part of the States. If a State shall not enforce its laws by
which private individuals shall be prevented by force from contravening the
rights of the citizen under the amendment, it is in my judgment the duty of
the United States Government to supply that omission, and by its own laws
and by its own courts to go into the States for the purpose of giving the
amendment vitality there.

The word "deny" is used not only in this fifteenth amendment, but I
perceive in the fourteenth amendment it is also used. When the fourteenth
amendment was passed there was in existence what is known as the civil
rights bill, a part of which has been copied in the Senate bill now pending.
The civil rights bill recognized all persons born or naturalized in the United
States as citizens, and provided that they should have certain rights which
were enumerated. They are, "to make and enforce contracts, to sue, be made

parties, give evidence, to inherit, purchase, lease, sell, hold and convey real and personal property," and to "the full and equal benefit of all laws and proceedings for the security of person and property."

The civil rights bill was to be enforced by making it criminal for any officer, under color of any State law, "to subject, or cause to be subjected, any citizen to the deprivation of any of the rights secured and protected" by the act. If an officer of any State were indicted for subjecting a citizen to the deprivation of any of those rights he was not to be indicted as an officer; it was as an individual. And so, under the fourteenth amendment to the Constitution, "no State shall make or enforce any law which shall abridge the privileges or immunities of citizens of the United States; nor shall any State deprive any person of life, liberty, or property without due process of law, nor deny to any person within its jurisdiction the equal protection of the laws." There the word "deny" is used again; it is used in contradistinction to the first clause, which says, "No State shall make or enforce any law" which shall do so and so. That would be a positive act which would contravene the right of a citizen; but to say that it shall not deny to any person the equal protection of the law it seems to me opens up a different branch of the subject. It shall not deny by acts of omission, by a failure to prevent its own citizens from depriving by force any of their fellow-citizens of these rights. It is only when a State omits to carry into effect the provisions of the civil rights act, and to secure the citizens in their rights, that the provisions of the fifth section of the fourteenth amendment would be called into operation, which is, "that Congress shall enforce by appropriate legislation the provisions of this article."

There is no legislation that could reach a State to prevent its passing a law. It can only reach the individual citizens of the State in the enforcement of law. You have, therefore, in any appropriate legislation, to act on the citizen, not on the State. If you pass an act by which you make it an indictable offense for an officer to execute any law of a State by which he trespasses upon any of these rights of the citizen it operates upon him as a citizen, and not as an officer. Why can you not just as well extend it to any other citizen of the country?

It is, in my judgment, incumbent upon Congress to pass the most stringent legislation on this subject. I believe that we have a perfect right under the Constitution of the United States, not only under these three amendments, but under the general scope and features and spirit of the Constitution itself, to go into any of these States for the purpose of protecting and securing liberty. I admit that when you go there for the purpose of restraining liberty, you can go only under delegated powers in express terms; but to go into the States for the purpose of securing and protecting the liberty of the citizen and the rights and immunities of American citizenship is in accordance with the spirit and whole object of the formation of the Union and the national Government.

There are, Mr. President, various ways in which the right secured by the fifteenth amendment may be abridged by citizens in a State. If a State should undertake by positive enactment, as I have said, to abridge the right of suffrage, the courts of the country would prevent it; and I find that in section two of the bill which has been proposed as a substitute by the Judiciary Committee of the Senate provision is made for cases where officers charged with registration or officers charged with the assessment of taxes and with making the proper entries in connection therewith, shall refuse the right to register or to pay taxes to a citizen. I believe the language of the Senate bill is sufficiently large and comprehensive to embrace any other class of officers that might be charged with any act that was necessary to enable a citizen to perform any prerequisite to voting. But, sir, individuals may prevent the exercise of the right of suffrage; individuals may prevent the enjoyment of other rights which are conferred upon the citizen by the fourteenth amendment, as well as trespass upon the right conferred by the fifteenth. Not only citizens, but organizations of citizens, conspiracies, may be and are, as we are told, in some of the States formed for that purpose. I see in the fourth section of the Senate bill a provision for cases where citizens by threats, intimidation, bribery, or otherwise prevent, delay, or hinder the exercise of this right; but there is nothing here that strikes at organizations of individuals, at conspiracies for that purpose. I believe that any bill will be defective which does not make it a highly penal offense for men to conspire together, to organize themselves into bodies, for the express purpose of contravening the right conferred by the fifteenth amendment. . . .

But, sir, there is a great, important omission in this bill as well as in that of the House. It seems not to have struck those who drew either of the two bills that the prevention of the exercise of the right of suffrage was not the only or the main trouble that we have upon our hands. Suppose there shall be an organization of individuals, or, if you please, a single individual, who shall take it upon himself to compel his fellow-citizens to vote in a particular way. Suppose he threatens to discharge them from employment, to bring upon them the outrages which are being perpetrated by the Kuklux organizations, so as not to prevent their voting, but to compel them to vote in accordance with the dictates of the party who brings this coercion upon them. It seems to me it is necessary that we should legislate against that. That is a more threatening view of the subject than the mere preventing of registration or of entering men's names upon the assessment books for taxation or of depositing the ballot in the box. I think the bill cannot be perfected to meet the emergencies of the occasion unless there be a section which meets that view of the case.

The Senator from Indiana [Mr. Morton] asks whether I have drawn an amendment to that effect. I have, but I cannot offer it at this time, for the simple reason that there is an amendment to an amendment pending.

MR. MORTON. Let it be read for information.

MR. POOL. It has been printed, and I send it to the desk to be read for information.

The Chief Clerk read the amendment intended to be proposed by Mr. Pool, as follows:

Insert after section four of the Senate bill the following sections:

SEC. 5. *And be it further enacted,* That it shall be unlawful for any person, with intent to hinder or influence the exercise of the right of suffrage as aforesaid, to coerce or intimidate, or attempt to coerce or intimidate any of the legally qualified voters in any State or Territory. Any person violating the provisions of this section shall be held guilty of a misdemeanor, and on conviction thereof shall be fined or imprisoned, or both, in the discretion of the court: the fine not to exceed $1,000, and the imprisonment not to exceed one year.

SEC. 6. *And be it further enacted,* That if two or more persons shall band or conspire together, or go in disguise upon the public highway, or upon the premises of another, with intent to violate any provision of this act, or to injure, oppress, threaten, or intimidate any citizen with intent to prevent or hinder his free exercise and enjoyment of any right or privilege granted or secured to him by the Constitution or laws of the United States, such person shall be held guilty of felony, and on conviction thereof shall be fined and imprisoned; the fine not to exceed $5,000 and the imprisonment not to exceed ten years; and shall, moreover, be thereafter ineligible to and disabled from holding any office or place of honor, profit, or trust created by the Constitution or laws of the United States.

SEC. 7. *And be it further enacted,* That if in the act of violating any provision in either of the two preceding sections, any other felony, crime, or misdemeanor shall be committed, the offender may be indicted or prosecuted for the same in the courts of the United States, as hereinafter provided, for violations of this act, and on conviction thereof shall be punished for the same with such punishments as are attached to like felonies, crimes, and misdemeanors by the laws of the State in which the offense may be committed.

Strike out section twelve and substitute therefor the following:

And be it further enacted, That the President of the United States, or such person as he may empower for that purpose, may employ in any State such part of the land and naval forces of the United States, or of the militia, as he may deem necessary to enforce the complete execution of this act: and with such forces may pursue, arrest, and hold for trial all persons charged with the violation of any of the provisions of this act, and enforce the attendance of witnesses upon the examination or trial of such persons.

WILLARD SAULSBURY [DEM., DEL.]. Mr. President

THE VICE PRESIDENT [SCHUYLER COLFAX, R., IND.]. Does the Senator from North Carolina yield to the Senator from Delaware?

MR. POOL. Yes, sir.

MR. SAULSBURY. It has been my intention to address the Senate on this bill—

MR. POOL. I meant to yield only temporarily. I thought the gentleman desired to ask a question.

MR. SAULSBURY. Then I will suggest to the Senator's legal mind a proposition, and I should like to hear him discuss it. The fifteenth amendment provides that Congress shall by appropriate legislation enforce it. I should like to hear the Senator from North Carolina upon that question. That legislation is not appropriate which is prohibited. The Constitution of the United States provides that upon application of the Governor, when the

Legislature is not in session, or of the Legislature when in session, the President may use the military force of the country in a State. This bill provides that the President, of his own motion, without application either from the Governor or the Legislature of a State, may use the military force of the country. I wish the Senator from North Carolina, who is a clear-headed man in his advocacy of this measure, to demonstrate to the Senate the constitutional right of the Congress of the United States to make such an enactment as this. . . .

MR. POOL. The Senator from Indiana asked if I had an amendment prepared which met the view of the case I was presenting in regard to the compelling of citizens to vote in a particular way. The first section of the amendment which I have offered uses this language:

That it shall be unlawful for any person with intent to hinder or influence the exercise of the right of suffrage as aforesaid, to coerce or intimidate or attempt to coerce or intimidate any of the legally qualified voters in any State or Territory.

But, Mr. President, there is another view which seems to have been lost sight of entirely by those who have drawn both the House bill and the bill now pending before the Senate, and from which we apprehend very much danger. It is this: the oppression of citizens because of having voted in a particular way, or having voted at all. It may often happen, as it has happened up to this time already, that upon the close of an election colored persons will be discharged from employment by their employers. They may be subjected to outrages of various kinds because they have participated in an election, and cast their votes in a particular way. That is not done for the purpose of punishment so much as for the purpose of deterring them from voting in any succeeding election, or from voting in a way that those who perpetrate these outrages do not desire them to do. I find that branch of the subject is entirely left out of view in the bill.

There is another feature of my amendment which I deem of some importance. It is this:

That if in the act of violating any provision in either of the two preceding sections any other felony, crime, or misdemeanor shall be committed, the offender may be indicted or prosecuted for the same in the courts of the United States.

I think the most effective mode of preventing this intimidation and these attempts at coercion, as well as the outrages which grow out of these attempts, would be found in making any offense committed in the effort to violate them indictable before the courts of the United States. As was said before, in the discussion of the Georgia question in the Senate, the juries in the communities where these outrages are committed are often composed of men who are engaged in them, or of their friends, or of those who connive at them, or of persons who are intimidated by them, and in many instances they dare not bring in a true bill when there is an attempt to indict, or if a true bill be found, they dare not go for conviction on the final trial. It is for that reason that I believe it will be better, it will be the only effective remedy, to take such offenders before the courts of the United States, and there have them tried by a jury which is not imbued with the prejudices and interests of those who perpetrate the crimes.

These are the principal features of the amendment which I have drawn in the effort to perfect this bill; and there is another one to which I will call the attention of the Senate. It is that in regard to calling out the military forces of the United States. I find that in the civil rights bill, as in the bill which has been introduced by the Senate Judiciary Committee, the President is authorized, either by himself or by such person as he may empower for that purpose, to use the military forces of the United States to enforce the act. There in both instances it stops. It has been objected to here that the expression, "or such other person as he may empower for that purpose," should not be in the bill; that it may be subject to abuse. I think it would have no good effect to keep that language in. The President may send his officers and he may empower whomsoever he pleases to take charge of his forces without any such provision.

But there is a use for these forces which seems not to have been adverted to in either the civil rights bill or in the bill that is now pending before the Senate. It is the holding of these offenders for examination and trial after they are arrested. Their confederates, if they are put in the common prisons of the State, will in nine cases out of ten release them. But more important still is it to use these forces to compel the attendance of witnesses; for a subterfuge resorted to is to keep witnesses away from the trial. In many instances witnesses are more or less implicated in the commission of the offense. In other cases the witnesses are intimidated and cannot be obtained upon the trial. So in the amendment which I have prepared I have proposed that these forces may be used to enforce the attendance of witnesses both upon the examination and the trial. My purpose in introducing this was to perfect the Senate bill. I think, as I said yesterday, that that bill is liable to less objection than the House bill. I think it is more efficacious in its provisions. I think it is better that the Senate should direct its attention to perfecting that bill, in order that it may be made, when perfected, a substitute for the bill that came from the House.

That much being said upon the purpose of perfecting the bill and making it efficacious, I have very little more to say. I did not intend when I rose to say much upon the general power, which has been questioned here, to pass any law at all. I think it is better to do nothing than to do that which will not have the proper effect. To do that which will not accomplish the purpose would be worse than doing nothing at all. That the United States Government has the right to go into the States and enforce the fourteenth and the fifteenth amendments is, in my judgment, perfectly clear, by appropriate legislation that shall bear upon individuals. I cannot see that it would be possible for appropriate legislation to be resorted to except as applicable to individuals who violate or attempt to violate these provisions. Certainly we cannot legislate here against States. As I said a few moments ago, it is upon individuals that we must press our legislation. It matters not whether those individuals be officers or whether they are acting upon their own responsibility; whether they are acting singly or in organizations. If there is to be appropriate legislation at all, it must be that which applies to individuals.

I believe that the United States has the right, and that it is an incumbent duty upon it, to go into the States to enforce the rights of the citizens against all who attempt to infringe upon those rights when they are recognized and secured by the Constitution of the country. If we do not possess that right the danger to the liberty of the citizen is great indeed in many parts of this Union. I think this question will come time and again as years pass by, perhaps before another year, in different forms before the Senate. It is well that we should deal with it now and deal with it squarely, and I hope that the Senate will not hesitate in doing so.

Mr. President, the liberty of a citizen of the United States, the prerogatives, the rights, and the immunities of American citizenship, should not be and cannot be safely left to the mere caprice of States either in the passage of laws or in the withholding of that protection which any emergency may require. If a State by omission neglects to give to every citizen within its borders a free, fair, and full exercise and enjoyment of his rights it is the duty of the United States Government to go into the State, and by its strong arm to see that he does have the full and free enjoyment of those rights.

Upon that ground the Republican party must stand in carrying into effect the reconstruction policy, or the whole fabric of reconstruction, with all the principles connected with it, amounts to nothing at all; and in the end it will topple and fall unless it can be enforced by the appropriate legislation, the power to enact which has been provided in each one of the great charters of liberty which that party has put forth in its amendments to the Constitution. Unless the right to enforce it by appropriate legislation is enforced stringently and to the point, it is clear to my mind that there will be no efficacy whatever in what has been done up to this time to carry out and to establish that policy.

I did not rise, sir, for the purpose of arguing the question very much in detail. I did not rise for the purpose of making any appeals to the Senate; but more for the purpose of asserting here and arguing for a moment the general doctrine of the right of the United States to intervene against individuals in the States who attempt to contravene the amendment to the Constitution which we are now endeavoring to enforce, and for the purpose of calling attention to the defects in the bill and offering a remedy for them. . . .

GEORGE WILLIAMS [R., ORE.]. Mr. President, I desire to say a few words upon the motion made by the Senator from Nevada before the vote is taken; but there is very little satisfaction in trying to explain the provisions of these two bills, or compare one with the other, when there are so few Senators to listen. Perhaps I could not enlighten anybody on the subject if I should try. But I must say that I prefer the House bill to the bill reported by the Judiciary Committee of the Senate, because it is a plain, straightforward, intelligible piece of legislation. By it remedies are provided for all existing evils; and that is as far as in my judgment it is safe or prudent to go at this time; for this legislation undertakes to occupy a new field, one that has not heretofore been occupied by the legislation of Congress. Laws of thirty-seven States, differing from each other, are to be modified, or perhaps repealed by this legislation. Laws, with the provisions of which we are not at all familiar, are to be more or less affected by this legislation. It therefore appears to me that prudence requires that we should proceed in a careful manner in this legislation, and only do that now which the necessities of the case seem to require.

The House bill provides that the officer whose duty it is to assess persons, who refuses to assess a man on account of his color, if the assessment be a prerequisite for voting, shall be punished. It also provides that if an officer whose duty it is to collect or receive a tax shall refuse to do so on account of color he shall be punished. And it also provides that if a person whose duty it is to register an elector, or a candidate for elector, shall refuse to act in conformity to law, he shall be punished. And so ample provision, it appears to me, is made in the House bill to enable all citizens of the United States, without distinction of race or color, to prepare themselves for voting and to vote; and I know of no legal obstacles that can be thrown in the way except those that are provided for by the bill that has been sent to the Senate from the House of Representatives.

Now, is it advisable for us to go into the regions of imagination or conjecture with this legislation? Is it advisable for us to suppose some possible but not probable case that may arise, and attempt to provide for it in the provisions of this bill?

MR. STEWART. I inquire of the Senator from Oregon if it is improbable that men will try to prevent the registration of colored voters? Is it not a fact that they are trying to do that now in Virginia and other places? Is it not probable that they will prevent some from voting? These things are not provided for in the House bill.

MR. WILLIAMS. I say that provision is made in the House bill, explicitly made, to punish any officer who shall refuse to register a person on account of race, color, or previous condition of servitude.

MR. STEWART. It does not touch outsiders who interfere—mobs.

MR. WILLIAMS. Sir, does the Senator expect that he can by any legislation which can be devised here prevent the existence of mobs; prevent the existence of violence such as sometimes arises at the polls, and will occasionally arise at the polls at all elections?

MR. STEWART. I expect to do just this thing: if they interfere with the colored man, and will not allow him to go to the place of registration and register, I want to make that an offense, and punish it, if we can enforce the law. That is what we mean to do.

MR. WILLIAMS. Mr. President, the bill that has been sent to the Senate from the House of Representatives makes ample provision for such a case, I say, because it provides that if any person, by threats, fraud, or intimidation, shall attempt to prevent a person from voting on account of his race, color, or previous condition of servitude, he shall be subjected to a punishment.

MR. STEWART. "From voting;" but not from doing these other things. . . .

MR. WILLIAMS. I think I understand these two bills; I have read them both carefully, and I am endeavoring to show that the House bill provides for all probable cases where persons may seek to interfere with the right of suffrage on account of race, color, or previous condition of servitude; and if any Senator will take the bill that has been sent here from the House and read its different provisions he will find that in that respect it is quite as effective as the bill that has been reported by the Judiciary Committee.

This bill is intended as a criminal code upon the subject of elections by Congress, and the House bill distinctly defines and describes the crimes, and distinctly defines and describes the punishments that shall be inflicted; and in that respect it commends itself to my judgment. I cannot approve of legislation that is so vague, indefinite, and uncertain as not to be understood, and not to be understood by the committee who have reported it to the Senate, for the different members of this committee differ here as to the meaning of their bill, and different Senators outside of the committee entertain different opinions as to its meaning; and if such a piece of legislation is put before the country it will lead to infinite controversy and litigation.

The Senator from Nevada proposes a bill to enforce the fifteenth amendment, and upon that he piles another bill which is intended to enforce the fourteenth amendment, and upon that he piles another which is intended to protect citizens in the enjoyment of their civil rights; and this conglomerated mass of incongruities and uncertainties is to be put through here in the name of a bill to enforce the fifteenth amendment!

I object to the Senate bill, because it is indefinite and vague in all or nearly all of its provisions. It seems to be a sort of scoop-net that has been thrown out for the purpose of catching some conceivable cases that may arise; and it is not a bill applicable to existing mischiefs, which can be distinctly understood and can be easily and directly remedied. Take the second section as an illustration of the bill. . . .

This section provides that officers who are charged with certain duties in reference to elections shall give all persons an equal opportunity to qualify themselves for voting. Now, as to whether certain persons have or have not an equal opportunity to do a thing is a matter of opinion about which men may very honestly differ; and where there is a poll or place of registration, where there are a thousand, or it may be five thousand persons desiring to be registered, to say that it shall be a crime if the officer does not give to each one of those five thousand persons an equal opportunity to register is to describe an offense, it seems to me, without any precedent in criminal jurisprudence. And then it provides that the officer shall "give full effect to this section." The crime consists in not giving full effect to a certain section of a law. Who can tell whether a man gives full effect or not to a provision of law like that? Many persons who are interested may suppose that the officer does not give full effect to it and he may suppose that he does. Room is left here for unbounded controversy and contention over the meaning of this section. If this law defined exactly what the crime should be, if a refusal to assess a person upon application was defined as a crime, then there would be no difficulty in inflicting the punishment; and so in reference to registration; and so in reference to the different acts required. If each preparatory act was described, and if it was declared that any officer who should prevent the performance of that preparatory act should be punished, then the officer would understand his duty, and the person seeking the benefit of the law would understand his rights.

I think section three is subject to the same objection. Much controversy has arisen here between different Senators as to what this section means. Sir, the members of this committee differ as to whether it applies to all persons, or whether it applies exclusively to persons of color. I understand the honorable Senator who has charge of the bill to say that it applies exclusively to persons of color, while other members of the committee contend that it applies to all persons. So under this section, according to the construction put upon it by some members of the committee, one of the famous New York "repeaters" may, upon his affidavit anywhere in that city, compel the judges to receive his vote. We all know that those persons are capable of doing any act or committing any crime for the purpose of swelling the majority of the party to which they belong; and if one of those persons in the city of New York goes to the voting place and files his affidavit, then the judge is bound to receive his vote if it applies to all persons. If it applies only to colored persons, then of course that objection would not apply to the section.

But, sir, in any event, as has been suggested by the Senator from Michigan, it seems to me that it opens the door to abuse and to fraud. It in effect repeals to a great extent the registration acts of many of the States, for those acts provide, where persons are prevented by anything that may occur from registering their names, ways and means by which they can secure the right to vote. I object to the section particularly because it is so indefinite, and so vague and so uncertain that nobody can understand it; and because there is such a difference of opinion as to its meaning as to make it almost impossible to apply or enforce it.

But without going into details as to the different provisions of the Senate bill, I will say that it seems to me it is subject to two objections which will be urged against it by the popular voice of the country. One is that it opens the door to a perfect torrent of litigation. There is no end to the lawsuits that will spring up under this bill, and nearly all of these lawsuits will be conducted at the expense of the United States. . . .

Everybody familiar with elections knows that whenever they are fairly conducted there are more or less persons who feel aggrieved by the result. Is it not usual for persons to complain that they have not been allowed to vote, or that they have not been allowed to register themselves? Is it not usual for defeated parties to complain in that way, and find fault with the judges and with other persons connected with the election? And does not this bill invite all such persons in every precinct in these United States to commence suits, and promises and declares that if any individual will bring such suit, with the necessary evidence to sustain it, he shall receive $500 compensation for his services in the litigation? Sir, it seems to me that this bill opens up a field of speculation for persons who are disposed to occupy it without any precedent in the history of this country.

This bill, too, is open to another objection which has been suggested by several Senators; and that is, that it appears, whatever its precise object may be, to subordinate the elections in the country to the military power of the Government. I do not, of course, participate in those fears and apprehensions which have been expressed; but, at the same time, if there is one feeling among the people of the United States stronger than another it is that the elections of this country should be free, as free as possible, and that they should not be controlled by military influence and power. True, we have been compelled by the exigencies of the war to depart from this time-honored rule of the country; but it is our duty, as it appears to me, as soon as practicable to go back to the old system of allowing as far as practicable all elections in this country to be entirely free from external influence, and particularly free from military influence.

Sir, let it be remembered that this bill is not made exclusively for the southern States, but it is to apply equally in every State of this Union. There is not a precinct in New York or Maine or Oregon where the military may not be summoned by some subordinate of some commissioner to go to the polls for the purpose in some way of influencing or controlling an election.

This bill provides that attorneys, marshals, and deputy marshals shall be employed and shall act; that the courts shall have unlimited power to appoint commissioners. The courts may appoint one commissioner, or they may appoint a thousand commissioners in every state in the Union; and those commissioners are allowed to appoint subordinates in such numbers as they may see proper and these persons are authorized by this bill to summon the military power of the country to their aid at elections. . . .

These commissioners may appoint any number of suitable persons without limit, and these suitable persons, who may be perfectly irresponsible, may exercise the power of the President of the United States, and summon the military to enforce the provisions of the fifteenth amendment of the Constitution. I do not know that any danger will grow out of this provision; but it has a very bad look, and it should be remembered in reference to this bill that its doctrines and provisions are to be defended everywhere in the United States; and I am afraid that in our effort to do something for Louisiana or Mississippi, or some one of those States, we may lose sight of the other parts of the United States, where the people have not been accustomed to have elections in any way influenced by military power; and, sir, I doubt very much whether the people of the country will acquiesce in any such legislation.

Mr. President, these are two popular objections that will be made to the provisions of this bill. Such provisions, it seems to me, are unnecessary at this time. Let us take the House bill. If we do that it may perhaps need some amendment. I do not pretend to say it is a perfect bill; but it is a plain, concise, clear, systematic piece of legislation, which looks to me like law. But this Senate bill, as it has been proposed, looks to me like a sort of moral essay that has been thrown into something like the shape of legislation. Let us take the House bill. Let us adopt it. Information has been received here from various parts of the country that expedition in this legislation is necessary; and if we take the House bill, with such amendments as may be proposed to it if it be imperfect, then there is a probability that at some time before we adjourn we can obtain some legislation for the enforcement of the fifteenth amendment. Senators have already seen what a vast field of discussion the bill reported by the Judiciary Committee opens. Senators upon this floor, grave and learned Senators, whose Republicanism is beyond question, have expressed doubts as to the constitutionality of many of its provisions. Sir, in the House bill there can be no question, it seems to me, about the constitutionality of every one of its provisions. Let us adopt that bill. It meets existing mischiefs, and if experience shall demonstrate that it is in any respect defective, if any State Legislature shall devise any scheme to avoid the provisions of that bill, then it can be amended so as to meet that device; and so we can learn from experience what may be necessary for this sort of legislation. . . .

MR. STEWART. I have no pride of opinion in connection with this bill, and I wish that others were as free from it as I am; but it does seem to me that there is a great deal of pride of opinion in connection with this House bill, a bill which is utterly defective. The question is simply this: does the Senate mean, after having passed the fifteenth amendment, that the colored man shall have the right to vote? I undertake to say that under the House bill I can invent a hundred modes whereby he can be deprived of his vote and nobody be punished. I undertake to say that the House bill is no better than the amendment I have offered, as it now stands; and if any gentleman will sit down with me for half an hour I can demonstrate to him that there is no use whatever in passing the House bill; that it does not meet any of the requirements; that there is no proper machinery in it for enforcing the fifteenth amendment.

The Senator from Oregon [Mr. Williams] objects that we have made it the duty of the marshals, the commissioners, and the courts to go on and execute this law, and that it will be expensive to the Government. The House bill, I admit, would be cheaper, because it would never be executed. It simply defines a few offenses, and can be gotten over very easily. Let us look at it a moment and see what is left out. The first section of the House bill provides that any officer of the United States or of any State, Territory, or district, etc., who shall fail or refuse to do his duty in regard to the right of citizens to vote, shall be punished for it as an offense. That is very well. The next section is:

That all colored citizens of the United States resident in the several States of the United States shall be entitled to vote at all elections, etc.

That is very well. Then it makes it an offense to interfere with their votes. Then the third, fourth, fifth, and sixth sections relate to the question of taxation; that if there is a tax to be levied a colored citizen shall be taxed the same as anybody else, so as to entitle him to be registered. The sixth section is to meet the case in Delaware on the taxing question.

Then the seventh section relates to elections of members of Congress and electors for President and Vice President of the United States, and makes any interference with those elections an offense.

The eighth section makes it an offense for any officer to refuse to register any citizen.

There is the whole House bill. Let me show you the cases that may arise that do not fall under it. In the first place there may be combinations to prevent the colored voters from going to the registration. Anobody else can prevent the registration, and then they will not become voters. That is one thing that can be done that is not provided for at all. If they are thus prevented from registering there is no remedy, and they lose their votes. That is not provided against at all. The outside world are not forbidden to interfere with the registration; and if they do interfere with it then their votes are lost and the citizens' rights are taken away.

Then again the House bill speaks of registration and the payment of taxes as the only prerequisites that can be invented. There may be a hundred prerequisites invented by the States. Those two the House happened to think of, and provided for; but there may be others. It is very easy for a State to provide that each man shall have a certificate. That is not an enrollment or anything of the kind. The House have undertaken to enumerate the prerequisites to voting, and have only enumerated two or three, when a hundred can be invented. Talk about a definite law! Why, sir, this bill is a regularly-invented machine how not to do it.

Then it provides that the offenders shall be guilty of a misdemeanor and shall be punished by the United States courts; and you have got but one United States court and one marshal in a State. It does not provide for the appointment of any more commissioners than there are now; it does not provide for increasing the number of officers if it should be necessary to enforce it. There is no machinery whatever for its enforcement.

The Senator from Oregon has objected several times to the additions that are made to this Senate bill, as if they were hard to understand. One of them is simply a requirement that all citizens shall obey the fourteenth amendment and shall not violate the provisions of that amendment while it is in force. Everybody wants that amendment enforced while it is in force, both those who are in favor of amnesty and those who are opposed to amnesty. I think while it is a part of the Constitution we ought to observe it and see that it is observed. That section does not involve any other question. . . .

I do not know that I ought to complain about the way in which the recommendations of the Committee on the Judiciary are received in this body; but somehow or other it seems that they are always either too radical or too conservative. This measure is too radical. By and by we shall come in with something else, and that will be too conservative. Is it impossible to suit the taste of the Senate upon a question of this kind?

In this Senate bill we speak of "any act" which "is or shall be required to be done as a prerequisite or qualification for voting." Why do we say that? Because it is impossible to enumerate over-specifically all the requirements that might be made as prerequisites for voting, and so we use general language, which covers any act necessary to qualify the voter to vote. The States can invent just as many requirements as you have fingers and toes. They could make one every day. Here the House bill is confined to two prerequisites, registration and taxation. If there is any other prerequisite to be performed, which the States can require, then they can avoid the House bill. There is no machinery for enforcing it. It will amount to nothing. It is true it is perfectly harmless. We had better let the fifteenth amendment stand just as it does, and let it enforce itself, than attempt legislation which we know cannot succeed, which we know will not meet the contingencies that will arise.

The Senator from North Carolina [Mr. Pool] explained very clearly yesterday that the House bill does not reach any of the cases that are likely to arise; that it does not reach any of the cases that are arising to-day. The Senate bill may not be altogether perfect. I am inclined to think that we ought to accept one or two of the sections offered by that Senator to meet the case where the Kuklux Klan go upon plantations and intimidate people. I think that ought to be made an offense specifically. I think it is under this bill. I think it is "hindering" or "preventing;" but perhaps it would be well enough to specify it particularly; but certainly we do not want less than we have got in this Senate bill. . . .

EUGENE CASSERLY [DEM., CAL.], addressed the Senate in opposition to the bill. [His remarks will be published in the Appendix (See *infra* p.   )].

MR. STEWART. I wish to occupy a few moments in correcting some statements made by the Senator from California, and then I shall move a recess. He says there is no necessity for this legislation because there is no opposition to carrying the fifteenth amendment into execution. The Governor of his State says that if the fifteenth amendment goes through all the forms necessary to its adoption, and receives the vote of every State but California, it is still—

MR. CASSERLY. The Senator ought to state that that was before the adoption of the amendment was announced.

MR. STEWART. Here is his language:

"It seems clear, then, upon principle and authority, that if the proposed amendment went through the forms of adoption, it would be mere *brutum fulmen*, destitute of any validity whatever."

And since its adoption the attorney general of California has delivered an opinion advising Democratic registrars and Democratic officers who conduct the elections not to register colored voters, and not to receive their votes.

This idea of sleeping on the matter for a little while is a mere trap. The Democratic party do not intend that the elections next fall shall be fairly conducted; and I say from their conduct in the past we have a right so to judge. What did the Democratic party in Louisiana do at the last election? Colored men were there entitled to vote by law. They did not let them vote at all. Talk about there being no necessity for applying a remedy! Why, sir, all the colored voters were excluded in Louisiana. What did they do in Georgia? In almost every county they did precisely the same thing. The same thing is true of portions of Mississippi. What did they do in Tennessee? Notwithstanding that by their own constitution, a constitution which they themselves had adopted, the negro was entitled to the ballot, they drove him from it last fall *en masse*. . . .

Sir, the object is to lull us to sleep, to allow this session to pass by, saying there is no necessity for legislation, so that the Democrats may obtain possession of the other House by driving voters from the polls this fall. When the fifteenth amendment was pending I warned you that if it was not got through at that session it never would be passed. You passed it, and we have got it. Now, I say that if you do not pass a law at this session to enforce the fifteenth amendment the negro will not get the ballot for many, many years. Pass this law, appoint your agents under it, make it effective, and there will be no trouble at all. It will be submitted to then, and it will cost nothing. There will be no lawsuits when you have the machinery and the power to enforce it. But if you allow this session of Congress to pass by without action, and the elections come on next fall for members of the other House, you will find that House filled without the vote of the black man. That is the opinion of every southern man with whom I have conversed on this subject. They all agree that this is the *animus*.

Now, I wish to reply to one or two criticisms that have been made upon the bill. It is stated that the affidavit which the voter is to make under the second section authorizes an arrest. That is not so. The voter makes his affidavit, and that entitles him to vote, if he is otherwise qualified; but in order to arrest the party who offends against the law it must be set forth that the voter has made this affidavit, and he must show that he was otherwise qualified. It simply serves the place of registration if he has been driven from the registration office; it is to provide then that he shall not be required to register. That is all there is about it. That is fair. If he is otherwise qualified and a legal voter, and is driven away from the registration office, he should not be required to register. A man should not be required to do an impossible thing, and other parties should not be allowed by fraud to take from him the opportunity to register, and thus deprive him of his vote.

The Senator from California says, or uses words to that effect, that the parties who are to enforce this law will be a horde of bad men. Who are they, and who are to appoint them? The commissioners are to be appointed by your circuit judges. I think I have heard that Senator, as I have heard most Senators here, commend the new circuit judges who have been appointed by the President. Can they not be trusted to appoint commissioners to execute this law? Are they all to be bad men? I believe that a better set of appointments has rarely ever been made than the circuit judges who have recently been appointed. The country is satisfied with them and willing to trust them. The bill is guarded in that particular. Shall we not use those instruments?

But Senators tell us it is no use to pass this legislation. Make a declaration that the negro ought to vote, but do not have any machinery whereby that declaration can be put into force. Sir, I care for no bill unless it secures the vote to the negro. That is what I am after, and that is what I propose to do. . . .

MR. THURMAN. Mr. President, if no one feels disposed to speak on this bill, I wish before the vote is taken to say a very few words in addition to those so well said by the Senator from California [Mr. Casserly] this afternoon [See *supra* p. 292], on the question whether Congress has power to pass a measure of this character, which involves a consideration of the terms of the fifteenth amendment. It will be recollected that when I addressed the Senate before I said nothing on that question, in order that I might proceed at once to consider the details of the bill.

After listening to the remarks of the Senator from California, I am wholly at a loss to see how any one can come to a different conclusion than that which he has announced. What is the language of this amendment? "The right of citizens of the United States to vote shall not be denied or abridged by," whom? Not by an individual acting in breach of the law; that is not the language. Not by a combination of individuals constituting a mob; that is not the language. It is not against them that this provision of the Constitution is directed; but it is explicit, "shall not be denied or abridged by the United States, or by any State, on account of race, color, or previous condition of servitude."

It is a prohibition upon the United States and upon the States, and no stretch of ingenuity can extend it one hair's breadth further. Why the prohibition to the United States? Because the Congress of the United States fixes the qualifications of voters in the District of Columbia and also in the Territories of the United States; and therefore the prohibition upon the United States is proper. Why the prohibition upon the States? Because the States, each for itself, fixes the qualification of voters in the States. Before the passage of this amendment to the Constitution the power of a State to fix the qualifications of its voters was without any limit or restriction whatsoever. It was so completely without limit or restriction that in several of the States persons not citizens of the United States were allowed to vote; as, for instance, foreigners who had declared their intention to become citizens, but had not completed their naturalization by a residence of five years and taking the final oath. That was the case, if I mistake not, formerly in the State of Illinois, and perhaps in some other States where foreign-born persons who had declared their intention to become citizens were allowed to vote before they had fully become citizens of the United States. I may be mistaken in respect to that particular State, but I know that that was the case in some of the States.

GARRETT DAVIS [DEM., KY.]. On a residence of six months.

MR. THURMAN. Then comes this provision, the sole provision in the Constitution of the United States which limits that heretofore complete and plenary and unconditional power of a State to fix the qualification of the voters in that State; and what is it? How can any man say that it is anything more than a limitation upon the power of the State? Is it not just as much a limitation on the power of the State as is the provision in the Constitution that no State shall coin money; that no State shall keep or maintain an army or a navy without the consent of Congress? Just as these are limitations on the powers of the States, so is this fifteenth amendment a limitation on the power of the State, and nothing else, so far as the State is concerned.

What is the effect? Simply this, that if there is in a State constitution a discrimination on account of race, color, or previous condition of servitude, that provision in the State constitution becomes null and void, because it becomes repugnant to this provision of the Constitution of the United States. So if there are laws of the States that discriminate against any person otherwise qualified to vote, because of his race, color, or previous condition of servitude, those laws *ipso facto* become void, because they are repugnant to this provision of the Constitution of the United States.

If a State should hereafter attempt to pass such laws it would be attempting to do an unconstitutional thing, and its action would be absolutely null and void, and for a remedy against any such violation whatsoever the courts afford precisely the same redress that they do against the violation of any other portion of the Constitution of the Union. If there is a necessity for passing a stringent bill to enforce this amendment of the Constitution, the very same reason would require bills of pains and penalties and persecutions to enforce every other prohibition of the Constitution, for there is not one of them that may not be violated. This, then, being simply a limitation on the power of the State, simply withholding from it one of the powers which it heretofore possessed, the power of fixing the qualifications of electors, or restricting that power in a single particular, it is as plain, it seems to me, as the sun at noon-day in a cloudless sky; that this amendment can only be held to speak of a State as a State; as a State in her political character, as a distinct autonomy, and does not deal with individuals at all.

Now, sir, there is a case in which Congress might, perhaps, deal with individuals, the case supposed by my friend from California. Suppose, for instance, the State of Ohio should pass a law that no colored man should vote; or, to change it, suppose it should pass a law that no white man should vote, and the officers charged with the execution of that law should attempt to carry it into effect, they would be liable to civil actions without any act passed by Congress at all; but possibly in a case like that Congress might by law reach those individuals thus executing a State law, and therefore, acting in pursuance of an act of the State, which the Constitution of the United States forbids.

That is one thing; but a wholly different thing from that is the unauthorized act of an individual, which tends to interfere with the right of another man to vote, and which unauthorized act is even in violation of the law of the State itself. . . .

It is amazing to me that any lawyer can think for a moment that this bill in this respect where it acts on individuals—not officers of a State at all, mere private individuals, mere trespassers, mere breakers of the peace, mere violators of the State law—that this bill which seizes them and punishes them under this act of Congress and in the Federal courts is warranted by the fifteenth amendment of the Constitution. . . .

But now what is proposed to be done? Now you propose to seize hold of a mere idler; now you propose to seize hold of a mere ruffian; now you propose to seize hold of some man who is simply a cheater at the election; all of whom are punishable under the State law; and under the pretense of restricting the power of the State, which declares the very acts complained of to be unlawful, and punishes those acts, you take the individual from under the State law, send him before the Federal court, and punish him in virtue of an act of Congress.

Why, sir, if you can do this, if this is to be the interpretation of the fifteenth amendment and the right to pass appropriate legislation in support of it, then you may go the whole length. It is only a question, then, of discretion with you. You are foolish to talk about such a bill as this if this interpretation is right. Why not go the whole length at once? Why not take all the elections in your own hands? Why not provide by Federal law for the whole registration? Why not provide Federal judges of election, Federal boards of canvassers, and Federal machinery for the whole of the process of election from the time the voter goes to register until the time that the successful candidate is inaugurated into his office? You can do that just as constitutionally as you can pass this bill. . . .

MR. POOL. I desire to ask the Senator, for whose opinion I have very great respect, this question: suppose a State should pass a law that no registrar or poll-keeper should be punished for declining to register a colored man or to receive his vote, by what legislation should we reach that case?

MR. THURMAN. Well, sir, let us suppose that the State passes no law to punish any man for failing to register any one—

MR. POOL. That was not the case I put. I said suppose a State passes a law that no registrar or poll-keeper shall be punished for refusing to register a colored man or refusing to receive his vote?

MR. THURMAN. I once more say suppose the State provides that no man shall be punished for failing to register anybody. Let us go further, and suppose that the State will not pass a registry law at all—suppose the State will not pass any law for elections at all. Does that give you any authority to provide by act of Congress for the election of State officers in the State? Suppose a State does not pass any law to elect any State officers whatever, does that give Congress any right over the subject because of that omission of duty on the part of the State?

But let me say to my friend, who is a lawyer, that he makes nothing in the world by supposing cases so improbable that they come under that well-known axiom of the law, that nothing is proved by extreme cases. You are not at liberty to suppose that any State will pass a law in direct violation of the Constitution of the United States. If you can do that in respect to this provision you can do it in respect to any other provision. You may say that you will assume that a State will pass a law that no man shall be punished for counterfeiting, or no man shall be punished for coining money, or the like. You may go on with the whole series of cases in which there are prohibitions on the States, or any other matter that would be unconstitutional, and suppose that a State is going to do it. It is a thing not to be supposed.

MR. POOL. But if the Senator will allow me, I think that very thing is supposed in the fifteenth amendment. It declares that this right shall not be denied or abridged by any State, and that it shall be enforced by appropriate legislation by Congress. What is the need of appropriate legislation unless it was supposed that a State might either by positive act, as I have named, or by omission, fail to carry out and perfect this right? . . .

What will you do in a case where a State omits either to compel these officers to receive that vote, or to punish them when they refuse to receive it, by which the whole efficacy and value of the fifteenth amendment is broken down? If the United States cannot come in then and enforce it, of what value is the clause which says that by appropriate legislation this right may be enforced?

MR. THURMAN. Why, Mr. President, of great value. It has already been proved, in my judgment, that that provision about appropriate legislation is nothing more than the old provision in the Constitution which gives Congress power to pass all necessary and proper laws for carrying the provisions of the Constitution into effect, and is to be interpreted in the same light. For instance, suppose a State should pass a law, and it is no more extreme case than the one my friend has supposed, that would make it punishable for a black man or a white man either to vote or to offer to vote; you may pass laws by which that question can be tried before the Federal tribunals, and the State law can be declared null and void. That would be appropriate legislation. If a State should pass laws that would make it a penal crime for citizens to be placed upon precisely the same footing, you can pass laws by which you can bring them before the Federal judiciary and have it determined whether those laws are correct or not. That is appropriate legislation.

But because you can do such a thing as that, because you can pass such laws as that to provide the machinery by which State laws in conflict with this provision are to be declared to be null and void, because you can clothe your judicial tribunals with the necessary power to hold all such laws to be null and void, it does not follow at all that you can invade the rights of the States to regulate their own elections, their own mode and manner of elections, much less that under the provisions of this bill you can seize hold of individuals who have no color of office under the State, no color of authority under the State, but are simply private breakers of the law, punishable under the law of the State. . . .

MR. MORTON. Mr. President, I desire to say but a few words. I simply wish to inquire now, in general terms, what is the position of the Democratic Senators on this floor with regard to this amendment? . . .

I understood it to be this: that the fifteenth amendment contains no grant of power, but is simply in the nature of a prohibition; that its effect is simply and solely to deny to the United States the power to abridge suffrage on account of race, color, or previous condition of servitude, and to deny to any State the power to do it for those reasons; but that the Congress of the United States has no power to legislate to enforce that right. That I understand to be the general position; and if I am not correct I should be glad to be corrected. . . .

The first observation I have to make upon this general position occupied by our Democratic friends is that it is in accordance with the position they have taken in nearly all constitutional powers. They assert a want of power in the General Government. Now, sir, what is the spirit and the true intent of the fifteenth amendment, as we all remember it when it passed in this Chamber, as will be shown by the Congressional Globe, by all the discussions, as it is understood by the country? What is the true intent and spirit of that amendment? It is that the colored man, so far as voting is concerned, shall be placed upon the same level and footing with the white man, and that Congress shall have the power to secure to him that right. Is not that the spirit and the intent of that amendment as we all remember it when it passed this Chamber, that the colored man shall be placed on the same footing in regard to voting with the white man, and that Congress shall have the power to secure him in the enjoyment of that right?

Now, the ground these Democratic Senators take is, that any law passed by Congress abridging the right of the colored man to vote is simply unconstitutional and void; that any law or constitution adopted by a State to abridge the right of the colored man to vote is simply unconstitutional and void; and there it stops. If it stops there, what is the use of the second section of the article, which declares that Congress shall have the power by appropriate legislation to enforce it? That second section is intended to give to Congress the power of conferring upon the colored man the full enjoyment of his right. We so understood it when we passed it. The debates will show that that was the understanding.

If the construction adopted by the Senator from Tennessee and others is correct the second section is a nullity; the whole effect of the fifteenth amendment is that any State law prohibiting colored suffrage is void; and there it stops. That is their argument. If it stops there, the second section is nugatory and unnecessary. We know that the second section was put there for the purpose of enabling Congress itself to carry out the provision. It was not to be left to State legislation. If there is any doubt about the understanding with which that was passed we can refer to the debates in the Globe, for it is but little over a year ago since it was done. We know that it was put there for the purpose of enabling Congress to take every step that might be necessary to secure the colored man in the enjoyment of these rights.

Now, sir, we take both of these sections together, we construe them in harmony with each other, and they give to us all the power that is claimed by this bill. But we are met by the same narrow rule of construction, that there is no power to do anything; it must all be left to the States. . . .

MR. CASSERLY. It would seem from the drift of the Senator's remarks that he includes me as one of those who take the ground which he is now assailing. I do not wish to occupy the time of the Senate at this late hour; but I ought to say, in response to the challenge of the Senator from Indiana, that that is not precisely my position as I endeavored to state it. My position was this: that the fifteenth amendment operates upon the United States and upon the States; that the fifteenth amendment operates to make invalid and void any legislation of the United States or of any State that is in conflict with its provisions. That is the primary effect and operation of the amendment. I said, if it does operate upon persons it can only operate upon such persons as are officially related to the United States or to the States, and who, under color of some statute or ordinance of the United States, or of a State, undertake to infringe the fifteenth amendment. That was my position.

MR. MORTON. Mr. President, I understood the Senator substantially that way, and I suggest that his explanation does not vary materially my statement. I understood the Senator to take the position that this amendment operates upon the constitutional power of Congress and upon the power of the State, denying the power to pass any law abridging the right of suffrage, but that it does not operate upon individuals as such. He makes this explanation, that if it does operate upon individuals, which I do not understand him to admit even now, it would be because they were operating under color of some United States law or a law of some State. That brings him back to the same position. I state the position as being in conflict with that which we intended by that amendment, to place the colored man upon the same footing, with regard to suffrage, that the white man occupies, and to give to Congress the power necessary to enable him to enjoy it fully; and that involves the exercise of the power upon individuals. I repeat again, and it must be fresh in the recollection of most members of the Senate, that the debates upon the adoption of that constitutional amendment will show that it was adopted with that understanding and spirit. I never heard the construction that has been given to it in the argument on this bill, that it operated only upon States as municipal corporations and upon the United States. I never heard that position taken, I believe, throughout the long and interesting debate which took place on the passage of the amendment. I never heard it until to-day. . . . I should like to ask the Senator a question. He admits that Congress may prescribe the manner of holding the election; that is to say, to prescribe that it may be by ballot.

MR. THURMAN. Yes.

MR. MORTON. If Congress has the power to say that the election shall be by ballot, I ask if it has not the power to protect the ballot, to protect men in the exercise of that right? If it has not got that power, then the right to say that the election shall be by ballot amounts to nothing. Congress may say that the election may be by ballot; but according to the argument of the Senator from Ohio it has no power to punish offenses against the ballot. Perhaps the State will refuse to enact any laws on that subject. Then the power given to Congress goes for nothing. Now, the power to say that the election may be held by ballot implies the power to protect the ballot, and the power to protect the ballot carries with it the right to provide the particular way in which the ballot shall be cast, and to determine what persons shall cast the ballot. If Congress has the right to determine what persons shall cast the ballot, in determining that the election shall be by ballot, then it has a right to provide registration as a test or as a means of fixing that right; and if it has a right to provide registration, then it has a right to punish offenses against the registration. In other words, the right to do a thing implies the right to protect the thing to be done, and that is the whole of it; and when the Senator admits that, he admits every right that is necessary to the enjoyment or protection of it.

MR. THURMAN. Mr. President, that is a favorite argument of my friend from Indiana. I think I have heard it now for about the sixth time. I did not know before, though, that it was so extensive. I think I have heard him say again and again that the right to reconstruct included the right to protect reconstruction; and having got the right to reconstruct upon an inference from the Constitution, he then draws another inference from that and gets the right to protect reconstruction; and so he goes on until there is not one single right left to the States or to the people of this country that is not at the mercy of Congress.

MR. MORTON. That is no answer.

MR. THURMAN. The Senator says Congress may prescribe that the election for members of Congress shall be by ballot. I say so, too. . . .

But now what does the Senator from Indiana say? That the right to prescribe the manner of holding the election involves the right to say who shall vote. That is what the Senator said, and he says that in the face—

MR. MORTON. I did not say that.

MR. THURMAN. The Senator said that. If he takes it back, well and good.

MR. MORTON. I did not mean to speak in general terms of determining the qualifications of the voter. That matter is to be determined by the State law, except so far as it may be changed by the fifteenth amendment. My whole argument goes to this point, that the right to prescribe a regulation carries with it the right to protect the regulation; otherwise it is nonsense. If Congress has the right to prescribe the ballot, it must have the power to protect the ballot, or else prescribing it goes for nothing. . . .

If Congress has the right to prescribe the manner of holding elections, it has a right to prescribe the test by which it will determine who has the right to vote according to the State law. That is what I mean: that Congress has the right to say that the men who have a right to vote under the State law shall vote by ballot. Then how are you to determine the question who has the right to vote under the State law? I would say—but that is not perhaps involved in this question—that Congress has a right to prescribe registration as a mode of determining the question who has a right to vote under the laws of the State; in other words, as furnishing the evidence as to who shall cast the ballot. . . .

MR. THURMAN. I give the Senator the benefit of his explanation; but I do not at all agree with him upon his theory. His theory is that if Congress has the right to prescribe the manner of holding elections, and that includes the right to prescribe that the election shall be by ballot, that gives to Congress a complete and plenary power to pass a criminal code in regard to elections. I say it does no such thing. It is an utter confounding of the jurisdiction of the States and of the Federal Government. It is a perfect ignoring of all the history of this country. If there was one thing about which our forefathers were more jealous than another it was that the States each for itself should determine the qualifications of electors, and should prescribe the laws which were to preserve the purity of elections. . . .

MR. THURMAN. Mr. President, I think I hazard nothing in saying that there is not one Senator in this Chamber who knows what this bill now is. I see Senators here who have gone to their homes and had a comfortable rest, while others of us have sat up through the weary hours of the night. I see other Senators here who have quietly slept on sofas while amendment after amendment has been made to this bill, and only aroused from their slumbers when there was a division of the Senate or when their presence was necessary in order to make a quorum. I do not believe there is a Senator here who will stand up and on his honor declare that he knows what this bill is. And yet we are asked here now to vote on this question; we are asked to pass this bill—such a bill as never was passed or thought of being passed since this Government has had an existence. If anybody will say that it was not thought of being passed, because the fifteenth amendment was only lately adopted, let me say to him that one half of this bill has no relevancy whatever to the fifteenth amendment; it does not depend upon the fifteenth amendment, but is placed upon a provision in the Constitution that is as old as the Constitution itself. I refer to the amendment offered first by my colleague, and afterward, in a modified form, by the Senator from Maine.

But while I like the rest of you do not know what this bill is in its present shape, there are some things that I do know about it. I do know that for precisely the same offense this bill, as it now stands, provides in one part of it that the punishment shall be $500 to the informer, $500 to the United States, and not less than one month's imprisonment and not more than one year; and that in another provision of the bill for that identical offense the punishment is three years in the penitentiary. That I know; and I know that no ingenuity can get rid of it. I know that this bill is, as the Senator from Oregon, even before this amendment, truly characterized it, a conglomeration of incongruities and contradictions. That I know, with all respect to its supporters, this bill is.

Sir, I have fought this bill to the best of my poor ability; not for the purpose of delay. What interest had I in making myself sick by sitting here the whole night for the mere purpose of delay? What good will it bring to me or to any Senator on this floor to delay action on this bill against the will of the majority? No, sir; I have stayed here during the long and weary vigils of this night with the honest purpose of trying to make this bill less objectionable than it was as reported from the committee. I have sought to divest it of features that in my mind shock every principle of wisdom and provision after provision in the Constitution of the United States. I have endeavored to do my duty in this respect. I have not sought to filibuster here simply for delay; nothing of that kind. Now, the result is that after the sun has risen this bill is before this Senate, without one Senator knowing what it is; and it is here, as the Senator from Oregon properly characterized it, a conglomeration of incongruities and contradictions. That is what is is. . . .

The Chief Clerk read the report of the committee of conference, as follows:

The committee of conference on the disagreeing votes of the two Houses on the amendment of the Senate to the bill (H. R. No. 1293) to enforce the right of citizens of the United States to vote in the several States of this Union, who have hitherto been denied that right on account of race, color, or previous condition of servitude, having met, after full and free conference have agreed to recommend, and to recommend to their respective Houses, as follows:

That the House recede from its disagreement to the amendment of the Senate, and agree to the same with the following amendments:

Section three, line nineteen after the word "shall" insert the word "wrongfully;" in line nineteen strike out the word "knowingly."

Section eleven, line twenty-two, strike out the words "by indictment and," and in lieu thereof insert the word "on."

Section thirteen, strike out all of the section after the word "be" in line four, and in lieu thereof insert "necessary to aid in the execution of judicial process issued under this act."

Section sixteen, line fourteen, strike out "emigrating," and in lieu thereof insert "immigrating;" line sixteen, strike out "emigrating," and in lieu thereof insert "immigrating."

Section nineteen, line thirty-nine, strike out "indictment," and in lieu thereof insert "prosecution."

Section twenty, line thirty, strike out "indictment," and in lieu thereof insert "prosecution."

Section twenty, at the end of the section add the following proviso:

Provided, That every registration made under the laws of any State or Territory, for any State or other election at which such Representative or Delegate in Congress shall be chosen, shall be deemed to be a registration within the meaning of this act, notwithstanding the same shall also be made for the purposes of any State, territorial, or municipal election.

Insert the following, to come in as section twenty-one:

SEC. 21. *And be it further enacted,* That whenever by the laws of any State or Territory the name of any candidate or person to be voted for as Representative or Delegate in Congress shall be required to be printed, written, or contained in any ticket or ballot with other candidates or persons to be voted for at the same election for State, territorial, municipal, or local officers, it shall be sufficient *prima facie* evidence, either for the purpose of indicting or convicting any person charged with voting or attempting or offering to vote unlawfully under the provisions of the preceding sections, or for committing either of the offenses thereby created, to prove that the person charged or indicted voted, or attempted or offered to vote, such ballot or ticket, or committed either of the offenses named in the preceding sections of this act with reference to such ballot. And the proof and establishment of such fact shall be taken, held, and deemed to be presumptive evidence that such person voted, or attempted or offered to vote, for such Representative or Delegate, as the case may be, or that such offense was committed with reference to the election of such Representative or Delegate, and shall be sufficient to warrant his conviction, unless it shall be shown that any such ballot when cast, or attempted or offered to be cast, by him did not contain the name of any candidate for the office of Representative or Delegate in the Congress of the United States, or that such offense was not committed with reference to the election of such Representative or Delegate.

Insert the following, to come in as section twenty-two:

SEC. 22. *And be it further enacted,* That any officer of any election at which any Representative or Delegate in the Congress of the United States shall be voted for, whether such officer on election be appointed or created by or under any law or authority of the United States, or by or under any State, territorial, district, or municipal law or authority, who shall neglect or refuse to perform any duty in regard to such election required of him by any law of the United States. or of any State or Territory thereof, or violate any duty so imposed, or knowingly do any act thereby unauthorized. with intent to affect any such election or the result thereof: or fraudulently make any false certificate of the result of such election in regard to such Representative or Delegate; or withhold, conceal, or destroy any certificate or record so required by law respecting, concerning, or pertaining to the election of any such Representative or Delegate; or neglect or refuse to make and return the same as so required by law; or aid, counsel, procure, or advise any voter, person, or officer to do any act by this or any of the preceding sections made a crime: or to omit to do any duty the omission of which is by this or any of said sections made a crime. or attempt to do so, shall be deemed guilty of a crime, and shall be liable to prosecution and punishment therefor. as provided in the nineteenth section of this act for persons guilty of any of the crimes therein specified.

Strike out all of the twenty-first section, and in lieu thereof insert the following. to come in as section twenty-three:

And be it further enacted, That whenever any person shall be defeated or deprived of his election to any office, except elector of President or Vice President. Representative or Delegate in Congress, or member of a State Legislature, by reason of the denial to any citizen or citizens who shall offer to vote of the right to vote on account of race, color, or previous condition of servitude. his right to hold and enjoy such office and the emoluments thereof shall not be impaired by such denial: and such person may bring any appropriate suit or proceeding to recover possession of such office: and in cases where it shall appear that the sole question touching the title to such office arises out of the denial of the right to vote to citizens who so offered to vote. on account of race, color, or previous condition of servitude, such suit or proceeding may be instituted in the circuit or district court of the United States of the circuit or district in which such person resides; and said circuit or district court shall have, concurrently with the State courts, jurisdiction thereof so far as to determine the rights of the parties to such office by reason of the denial of the right guarantied by the fifteenth article of amendments to the Constitution of the United States and secured by this act.

And that the Senate agree to the same.

That the House agree to the Senate amendment to the title of the bill.

William M. Stewart,
George F. Edmunds,
Managers on the part of the Senate.
John A. Bingham,
Noah Davis,
Managers on the part of the House.

MR. STEWART. I will proceed to explain the points of this report. The House substantially adopt our bill with some slight modifications.

In section three of the Senate bill the word "wrongfully" is introduced after the word "shall." As it now reads, in line seventeen, it is "who shall refuse or wrongfully omit to receive and count votes," etc. As amended, it reads "who shall wrongfully refuse or omit."

In section eleven the word "indictment" is stricken out and the word "on" inserted. I will explain the object of this. In the eighth section there is a general provision that where the offense is infamous it must be prosecuted by indictment, and where it is not infamous it may be either by indictment or information. In some of the sections we have stricken out "indictment" and put in "prosecution" simply to harmonize the bill. It will be governed by the provisions of the eighth section, which declares that where the crime is infamous it must be prosecuted by indictment, according to the Constitution, and when not infamous it may be by information or indictment, as the prosecution may elect to pursue. These changes are only to make the bill harmonious in that regard, not intending to change its effect.

In section thirteen there is an amendment of some little importance, although it makes it just what the Judiciary Committee intended it originally should be. Section thirteen reads as follows:

That it shall be lawful for the President of the United States to employ such part of the land or naval forces of the United States, or of the militia, as shall be deemed necessary to prevent the violation and enforce the due execution of this act.

The conference committee recommend the striking out of all this section after the word "be" in the fourth line and inserting "necessary to aid in the execution of judicial process issued under this act;" so that the section will read, when amended:

That it shall be lawful for the President of the United States to employ such part of the land or naval forces of the United States, or of the militia, as shall be necessary to aid in the execution of judicial process issued under this act. . . .

Then in section sixteen the word "emigrating," where it occurs twice in that section, is stricken out, and "immigrating" inserted, which is a mere verbal correction.

Then in section nineteen we strike out "indictment" and insert "prosecution." That is for the purpose of accomplishing the same purpose I have already explained, to make the bill uniform.

In section twenty the same change again occurs. At the end of section twenty we insert a proviso. That section relates to registration. . . .

It was suggested that the registration mentioned in the last sections of the Senate bill and the provisions included in those sections against fraudulent voting, repeating, etc., only related to the election of members of Congress; whereas at the same election State officers were in some States elected. They are voted for on one ticket, and men are registered for the purpose of voting not only for members of Congress, but for State officers. This proviso is intended to simplify the evidence. If a person registers in order to vote at a general election where a member of Congress is to be chosen, the provision is that it shall be regarded as a violation of the act, if he fraudulently registers, although other persons are to be elected besides members of Congress. The proviso is:

Provided, That every registration made under the laws of any State or Territory for any State or other election, at which such Representative or Delegate in Congress shall be chosen, shall be deemed a registration within the meaning of this act, notwithstanding the same shall also be made for the purpose of any State, territorial, or municipal election.

Sections twenty and twenty-one also apply to that matter of evidence. For instance, if a person goes to the polls and fraudulently votes or offers to vote a whole ticket the burden of proof shall not be on the Government to prove that in that ticket the name of a member of Congress was contained; but if he votes or offers to vote fraudulently at an election where tickets with the names of members of Congress are being received, it shall be presumed that he voted for member of Congress; and it is incumbent on him then to prove that his ticket did not have the name of a member of Congress oń it. It is a mere regulation of the matter of evidence. That is all there is of these sections. It is a very important matter, because it might be impossible to prove what was on the ticket; but if a man casts a fraudulent vote, or offers to vote fraudulently at a poll where votes for members of Congress are being received, it shall be presumed that he voted for members of Congress, and he must show he did not.

Then the final section of the amendment passed by the Senate was intended by the Senate undoubtedly to give a remedy in a specific case; that is, when persons offering to vote were denied the right to vote by reason of color the candidate defeated by reason of that denial might go into the United States courts on that particular question, so that effect should be given to the voice of the voters. For instance, if a sheriff was to be elected in one of the southern States, and he received one thousand white votes, and there were fifteen hundred colored voters all ready to vote for him, but who were excluded, he might go to the United States court and recover the office; but in order that that section should not cover any other case than that specific one, to give effect to votes denied for this reason, the committee of conference have redrawn the section very carefully, narrowing it down to the particular issue where the right to vote is denied for that specific reason; not drawing anything else before the United States courts, and for the purpose of giving effect to this fifteenth amendment. I will read the section as reported by the conference committee; it will explain itself probably better than I can explain it:

And be it further enacted, That whenever any person shall be defeated or deprived of his election to any office, except elector of President or Vice President, Representative or Delegate in Congress, or member of a State Legislature, by reason of the denial to any citizen or citizens who shall offer to vote of the right to vote on account of race, color, or previous condition of servitude, the right to hold and enjoy such office and the emoluments thereof shall not be impaired by such denial; and such person may bring any appropriate suit or proceeding to recover possession of such office; and in cases where it shall appear that the sole question touching the title to such office arises out of the denial of the right to vote to citizens who so offered to vote, on account of race, color, or previous condition of servitude, such suit or proceeding may be instituted in the circuit or district court of the United States of the circuit or district in which such person resides; and said circuit or district court shall have concurrently with the State courts jurisdiction thereof so far as to determine the right of the parties to such office by reason of the denial of the right guaranteed by the fifteenth article of amendments to the Constitution of the United States, and secured by this act.

That is, it carries out the design of the section, as it was adopted by the Senate, precisely, but in a little more guarded language, narrowing it down to the particular issue to give effect to the fifteenth amendment, allowing the voter not only the right to vote, but the right to have his vote counted and to be made effective.

These are all the amendments. They do not change any of the essential features of the bill as it passed the Senate, but make it a little more harmonious, and carry out the design of the Senate precisely in the bill passed by them. . . .

JOHN STOCKTON [DEM., N.J.]. . . . I could not sign the report because I disapproved of the bill itself and in very serious particulars of many of the amendments, yet my impression is, as I was going to say, that the bill is better than it left the Senate; but it would, perhaps, be a little more proper for me to say that it is not quite so bad. But certainly in regard to a bill of this importance, involving great constitutional questions, as it certainly does, and in some respects new constitutional questions, we should be allowed to see it in print and know what the changes are before we vote upon it.

Mr. President, recollect that this bill was hurried through the Senate at a prolonged night session; that it was asserted on the floor in the middle of that night that Senators voting for that bill did not know what it was; that a bill which came from the Committee on the Judiciary, a bill to enforce the fifteenth amendment, became a bill to enforce the fourteenth and fifteenth amendments and with something about Chinese immigration, and also a bill for the military possession of the election polls. The circumstance which has been stated by the Senator from Nevada, that the section giving the President the right to take military possession of the polls has been so altered by the committee of conference as only to permit him to do so in pursuance of legal process, shows the importance of consideration and deliberation. . . .

I stated . . . that I thought this bill had been improved by the conference committee; but it does not seem to me that the fact that in my judgment it has been improved should be a reason why the Senate should not have it printed, when I also asserted, as I did, that large portions of new matter are inserted, attempting to reach new difficulties in the way of the proper enforcement of the fifteenth amendment.

For example, the reports reads: "In line nineteen, after the word "shall," insert the word "wrongfully."

The Senate will recollect that in many places in this bill and in the various bills that were before the Senate I tried to induce the Senate to insert the words "with intent to violate the fifteenth amendment," or "with intent to violate this act." The insertion of that word "wrongfully" covers, to my mind, a great danger that was contained in the original bill. The insertion of that word will prevent persons who do not intend to violate the law from being drawn into a net. Therefore I say in that respect the bill is decidedly improved, and it is in some other respects.

The amendment made to the last section of the original Senate bill is quite an improvement. That section authorized the President to call out the Army and the naval forces to enforce this bill. The committee of conference have attached to it a clause that he may only do so in pursuance of judicial process. That is a great safeguard. He has little more power by that than he has now. But then here are some new sections altogether, which no gentleman in the Senate has ever considered; and I do not believe any gentleman who was not on the conference committee, unless perhaps he has been informed by the Senator from Nevada, knows what the committee intended by putting them in. If there is any gentleman who does not know it, I should like to have this bill printed, in order that I might explain to him what those clauses were put in for.

Then the report goes on: "Insert the following, to come in as section twenty-one."

And there [exhibiting the report] is a large portion of a bill that was printed and introduced into the other House, inserted here, pasted on, and we are to adopt that as part of this bill, without knowing why it was put there, a new feature entirely, intended to reach a new difficulty, which I never heard suggested by anybody until we got into · the committee of conference:

SEC. 21. *And be it further enacted,* That whenever, by the laws of any State or Territory, the name of any candidate or person to be voted for as Representative or Delegate in Congress, shall be required to be printed, written, or contained in any ticket or ballot with other candidates or persons to be voted for at the same election for State, territorial, municipal, or local officers, it shall be sufficient *prima facie* evidence, either for the purpose of indicting or convicting any person charged with voting or attempting or offering to vote unlawfully under the provisions of the preceding sections. or for committing either of the offenses thereby created. to prove that the person so charged or indicted voted. or attempted or offered to vote. such ballot or ticket. or committed either of the offenses named in the preceding sections of this act with reference to such ballot.

It appears that in many States of this Union it is provided by law, or if not by law by custom, that the elections for members of Congress shall be held at the same time that the local elections are held. The tickets are in many cases printed as State tickets. It was suggested that there might be difficulty in convicting a man of voting illegally for a member of Congress. The plain and natural way to meet that difficulty was to provide by law that the elections should be held separately. As you only have the right to reach one of them by your enactment, you should provide by law that it should be held separately, and then, if a man votes, the natural presumption of law, of course, is that he votes for the member of Congress whose name is upon the ticket. But in this case the man may scratch his ticket, and every one knows that at some elections the natural presumption is altogether that he did not vote for a member of Congress. But you come in and provide a new rule of presumptions, an unnatural rule, and give no reason for it. It is in violation of the ordinary principles of evidence, and you give no reason whatever for it.

There is no reason, I should say, for it but the difficulty of attaining this end. The end is a proper end, I admit; the end we all want to attain by proper means and through the proper jurisdiction. The end is to punish the man who attempts to vote illegally. But it is not necessary, it is awkward, it is clumsy to go about forcing a presumption on the courts and forcing the person accused to rebut it. How is he to rebut it if he never showed his ticket to anybody? It will require him to do that. The very object of the ballot is that it shall be secret and private; that no man shall pry into the voter's affairs or how he shall vote. If you do not so pry into his affairs, if he has a right to keep his ballot secret, then when he comes and puts it in the ballot-box there is no human being who by any possibility can prove the contrary. When you presume it, when you make it a *prima facie* case, you really make it conclusive; and really if you charge a man with this offense the evidence is conclusive against him. That is really the meaning of it. You absolutely, according to my construction, take away all power of defense from the man who is charged in that way. I am sure Senators will see that the proper course to attain the object desired is that which I suggest, to make them vote at separate times, make them vote on separate ballots.

This matter has never been examined; it has never been before the Senate; it has never been before the Judiciary Committee; it has never been considered by any committee of the Senate, and I doubt whether it has been considered by any committee of the House, but it is simply put in here after a few moments' conversation which ought to have been on other subjects. When this is dragged in as new matter in the committee of conference, why should the Senate vote upon it and adopt a clause of that kind which violates all the principles of evidence as we have them in the common law? . . .

JAMES BAYARD [DEM., DEL.]. . . . The result of the report of this committee of conference is to change this bill in most important particulars. Senators are aware that in the bill passed by the Senate last week, laid within five minutes upon our desks fresh from the hands of the printer, there are twenty-one sections. In the bill brought before us by this report in manuscript by the committee of conference there are twenty-three sections; and not only that, but whole previous sections have been taken out and others have been substituted, entirely changing their character. I do say that it is impossible for a man, unless he was a member of the committee of conference, to understand what their action has been; and we should have an opportunity, the ordinary, reasonable, legal opportunity, of seeing in print a measure of this importance. I trust, therefore, that the Senate will suffer this bill to be printed. The majority have, as has been said by the honorable Senator from Ohio, the numerical power in this Chamber to do just as they please in regard to calling up and passing measures. I trust they will at least regard the rights of the minority sufficiently to let us see what we are to vote for, and to speak our minds, however feebly, against it. . . .

MR. BAYARD. Mr. President, on yesterday there seemed to be a disposition in the Senate at one time to force this bill, reported from the committee of conference of the two Houses, to its passage. Among the gentlemen in this

Chamber who objected to any delay was the Senator from Michigan, not now in his seat, [Mr. Howard,] who considered that no more light could be thrown on the subject, and therefore further discussion of it would be entirely useless, simply fatiguing those who were already weary, and in his view entirely unnecessary. I do not suppose, I never did suppose, myself able to give light to that Senator's mind; nor do I think now, in the temper of this body and its method of discussing questions, that much is to be expected to be gained by the weight of mere argument where party spirit or a party measure intervenes. . . .

Light, whether from any poor remarks I shall submit, or to be found by having the measure upon which we are to vote placed in a printed form before the Senate, would seem alike to be unnecessary to the mind of that Senator and his colleagues who wished to force a vote yesterday afternoon. The bill upon which we are called this morning to vote was not then in print. It consisted of a piece of mosaic work of the various bills of the two Houses, with complicated amendments, and a great portion of them created in this committee of conference, existing only in manuscript, and that in an exceedingly hasty and carelessly arranged form, with interlineations and omissions. Therefore it would seem that the majority of the Senate represented by that Senator were perfectly willing to vote upon this measure, although it was a human impossibility that they could know precisely what they were voting upon.

At about eleven o'clock this morning this bill for the first time may be said to have seen daylight. It was placed on our tables about an hour before the Senate convened. In that time I have read it; and I propose to discuss it as well as the short time given to me will permit.

On the 30th of March, 1870, the Secretary of State of the United States proclaimed the ratification by three fourths of the States of the Union of a fifteenth amendment to the Constitution of the United States. I do not propose now to enumerate the well-known matters of public fact, matters of history, the record of which cannot be gainsaid, which make that proclamation, in my honest opinion, a huge untruth; a mere mockery upon the letter, spirit, and intent of our constitution of government; that from first to last it has lacked, and lacks to-day, those essentials which make it binding upon the States and the people of this country. I do not now propose to discuss those reasons. They are there. They cannot be evaded; and in their own time they will come up for consideration.

In the course of the debate that occurred here last week, and while I was compelled by the pressure of other duties to be absent, I saw the sketch of a speech made, I think, by the honorable Senator from Missouri, [Mr. Schurz], in which he talked of "dark threats" on the part of members of the party with whom I am associated and act on this floor in respect to the fate of this amendment. Sir, if it be a "dark threat" to declare that amendment a fraud, then make the most of a declaration. I deem it a fraud; I deem it an act of revolution; and although I am perfectly well aware that there are acts which, having an illegitimate origin, by time and the acquiescence of the people will harden into accepted law, yet I say by such means, and such means alone, will that amendment ever become entitled to the respect and confidence of the States or the United States.

I leave it to its fate, being convinced that if it be, as I believe, false it will in time share the fate of all falsehood; that, being in its nature contrary to the genius of our institutions, abnormal, and inconsistent, it will have but a short and stormy existence, a brief period of control, and then be overwhelmed by the returning tread of a free and intelligent people seeking to renew their allegiance to the governmental compact of their fathers. In that compact were embodied principles of civil and religious liberty which the fell spirit of party and of warfare in our own day has dethroned from their just and lawful supremacy.

Sir, what was this amendment? It provides:

That the right of citizens of the United States to vote shall not be denied or abridged by the United States or by any State on account of race, color, or previous condition of servitude.

And secondly:

Congress shall have power to enforce this article by appropriate legislation.

Now, what is the power given to Congress and the duty enjoined upon it by this amendment? The sole, natural, reasonable intent of the words therein contained was that discrimination at the polls on account of race, color, or previous condition should not exist. But this bill as reported grasps the whole control of elections, and is intended, not to prevent discrimination between the various races of men, but to discriminate directly against the white race and in favor of the black. Turn to section five of this bill, and there you will see:

That if any person shall prevent, hinder, control, or intimidate, or shall attempt to prevent, hinder, control, or intimidate, any person from exercising or in exercising the right of suffrage—

Does it stop there? No, sir—

to whom the right of suffrage is secured or guarantied by the fifteenth amendment to the Constitution of the United States.

To what class of people does the fifteenth amendment guaranty or secure the right of suffrage? Simply to those who by reason of race or color had been previously discriminated against. Therefore, this bill allows, intends to allow, hinderance, control, intimidation of any white citizen; but it makes that a crime as against the black which is not a crime against the white. Then, in section twenty-three there is a provision of like character:

That whenever any person shall be defeated or deprived of his election to any office, except elector of President or Vice President, Representative or Delegate in Congress, or member of a State Legislature, by reason of the denial to any citizen or citizens who shall offer to vote of the right to vote on account of race, color, or previous condition of servitude.

What does that mean? It is a clear discrimination that if a candidate for any of the offices named shall lose his office by reason of the denial of the right of suffrage to white men there shall be no remedy for him; but if he loses it because of the denial to black men then this law is to come in and do that which the very language of your amendment was intended to prevent; that is to say, you do discriminate, and yet your fifteenth amendment declares that you shall not.

I consider this bill not an act of "appropriate legislation" fairly to enforce that amendment; but it is only another attempt to bolster up by violence and intimidation, in the shape of penal enactments, the inferior capacities of the negro race in the struggle for social and political equality. Each step made by the Radical party shows the false nature of their proposition. If this race had been fit to take part in the political councils of the country they would have vindicated that fact by their own action long ago. But they are not fit; and the longer the foolish attempt is made to govern a nation by such means the more patent will be its impossibility. The spectacle of the southern States to-day is a melancholy proof of the truth of the facts I here state. Sir, your premises are false, and your conclusions therefore will have the usual melancholy disappointment of error.

Why, sir, what becomes of registration laws? You here permit an *ex parte* oath to take the place of every guard which heretofore existed; and characteristically by this bill the *ex parte* affidavit of any man who wants to vote, and who has not complied with the prerequisites for casting his vote, if made falsely, has no punishment provided for it. A bill that in almost every section contains a severe and excessive penalty for the violations of the act, yet contains no punishment for the most flagitious of all offenses, the taking of a false oath for the purpose either of injuring a fellow-being, or of gaining some right to which the party is not entitled.

Now, sir, for whom has all this been done? For whose protection? It has been only for the ignorant, semi-barbarous race unfit for voting, manufactured into voters and allies of the Republican party to sustain themselves a little longer in power. Why cannot a word be said in this bill for the white naturalized citizen of the United States, say those in Rhode Island, for instance, where negroes now, as for a long time past, have been permitted to vote and exempted from qualifications that the constitution and laws of that State impose on all white naturalized citizens?

With what measure is it that you propose to replace the well-tested, adjudicated laws of the States, by them ordained in past years for the protection of this franchise? I ask the Senate, I ask the country still more, to contemplate the outrageous severity of the punishments and fines contained in this bill. It was said that the code of Draco was so severe that it was written rather in human blood than in ink. It might almost be said in regard to this law. Compare the provisions of this law with the acts of the State Legislatures relating to offenses of a similar character. I know the penalties prescribed by the State in which I live, one of the original thirteen, a State where law has been respected as much as in any other in the Union; where property, life, and person all have been equally protected with any other; where a man's right to hold office has been subjected to as little interference that was wrong, so far as the people of the State were concerned, as in any other State in this Union; and yet compare the heavy penalties exacted by the law now under consideration of an officer of election, who, acting in a judicial capacity, one requiring the exercise of discretion, and acting under oath, is to be punished, and punished, as I will presently show, for crimes so illy defined, that I hope for that reason, if for none other, your law will turn out to be utterly impracticable in its operation.

The fines and penalties are to be found in twelve sections out of the twenty-three sections of this law. Twelve sections of this law contain the most extravagant punishments for failures to perform certain duties or the commission of forbidden acts, not less than $500 fine and imprisonment not less than a month. There is no limitation to the fine, none whatever; it may be $50,000; imprisonment may tend to a year; and for similar offenses in the State of Delaware men are fined from fifty to one hundred dollars, and no man was ever imprisoned for such a transgression, and no law there ever required it.

Not only that, sir, but these penalties are cumulative; you not only fine the man in an amount to be given to the informer, but you then make him guilty of a public offense and fine him again for the misdemeanor; and after all that the party aggrieved has his action on the case at common law to recover for such damages as might be due him—a right that has always existed; that exists now, whether with this law or without it.

There is another commentary upon this law. It is that the offenses, whether of omission or commission, are indefinite, and that tends to injustice. *Dolus latet in generalibus,* every lawyer recognizes as true; and it is more dangerous in criminal than other legislation. In criminal pleading there must be certainty to a particular intent—that certainty which is the life of criminal justice, which courts insist upon always, that the party shall have his offense defined in order that he may know precisely wherein to meet the allegation.

What do you find here? Look at section two and see the character of the offense for which an officer of election shall not only "forfeit and pay the sum of $500 to the person aggrieved thereby, to be recovered by an action on the case, with full costs and such allowance for counsel fees as the court shall deem just," but "shall also, for every such offense, be deemed guilty of a misdemeanor, and shall, on conviction thereof, be fined not less than $500, or be imprisoned not less than one month and not more than one year, or both, at the discretion of the court."

What is that offense? In line thirteen it is, "if he shall refuse or knowingly omit to give full effect to this section." Is it not an absurdity to draw an indictment upon such a law as that? No judge would sustain such a conviction; he would arrest instantly any such attempt to convict a man upon so vague a phrase as that, "omit to give full effect to this section." The section contains some twenty-one lines, and upon that a man is to be fined in an amount without limit, or imprisoned for a time, which may be one year, or both fined and imprisoned.

Again, section six provides:

That if two or more persons shall band or conspire together, or go in disguise upon the public highway, or upon the premises of another, with intent to violate any provision of this act, or to injure, oppress, threaten, or intimidate any citizen with intent to prevent or hinder his free exercise and enjoyment of any right or privilege granted or secured to him by the Constitution or laws of the United States, or because of his having exercised the same—

What a proposition! What are the "rights or privileges secured to citizens by the Constitution and laws of the United States?" If you mean to make it an offense to invade these rights, it is your duty as legislators to point out the precise offense intended. That could be made the basis, with a partial court, with an excited and partial jury, to convict a man for an act apparently the most innocent, by raking up some possible right, throwing a dragnet over all the laws of the United States, over the Constitution of the United States, and from all those extracting some possible exercise of a right or privilege which this party intimidated another from enjoying, and upon conviction of such an offense as that, the party is to be made infamous as a felon—

Shall be fined or imprisoned, or both, at the discretion of the court, the fine not to exceed $5,000, and the imprisonment not to exceed ten years, and shall, moreover, be thereafter ineligible to, and disabled from, holding any office or place of honor, profit, or trust created by the Constitution or laws of the United States.

Here, with this utterly indefinite charge against a man, something that no man could discover if he talked for a week, and undertook to point out all the possibilities that partisan ingenuity could define, the partiality of prejudiced jurors or judges may create that a felony of which no man dreams at this time, and which no man can define with that certainty which criminal justice requires you to exercise in creating statutory offenses of a high grade.

Furthermore, sir, this law proposes to enforce the laws of the States—to act upon State officers. I thought it long ago was settled by the Supreme Court of the United States, in the leading case of Prigg vs. The Commonwealth of Pennsylvania, that Congress cannot impose any duty on a State officer, or enforce the performance by a State officer of any duty; and yet, in the face of that explicit decision, here is the attempt to do this by the seventh section!

That if in the act of violating any provision in either of the two preceding sections, any other felony, crime, or misdemeanor shall be committed, the offender, on conviction of such violation of said sections, shall be punished for the same with such punishments as are attached to the said felonies, crimes, and misdemeanors, by the laws of the State in which the offense may be committed.

Crimes are evil in themselves, and they are prohibited. These are the two generic classes. The States may make acts offenses which are not wrong in their own nature; and under this clause the Congress of the United States undertakes to punish a man with penalties created only by the laws of the States, and those laws not even recited in the act under which you pretend to make them efficient. In section twenty two the same thing occurs. Here is again the attempt in lines seven, eight, and nine of the twenty-second section, that declares:

That any officer of any election at which any Representative or Delegate in the Congress of the United States shall be voted for, whether such officer of election be appointed or created by or under any law or authority of the United States, or by or under any State, territorial, district, or municipal law or authority.

That is to say, whether he is created by the laws of any State or Territory, or by municipal law—

who shall neglect or refuse to perform any duty in regard to such election required of him by any law of the United States, or of any State or Territory thereof.

That is again an attempt to enforce upon a State officer duties that you did not institute and that you cannot compel him to perform, because he is not your officer nor your creature; and yet in defiance of the fixed decisions of the court of last resort in this country, in defiance of what I may term the explicit sense of the country on this subject, here is the attempt to use State officers for Federal purposes in defiance of the decisions of the judicial branch of your own Government.

Sir, this bill deserves the name of a pestiferous law. It is a law calculated to promote litigation. It is a law designed to promote persecutions and prosecutions. It gives premiums and fees to pettifogging attorneys and unscrupulous litigants, and that in cases where they are to be themselves benefited by their own testimony.

Why, sir, look at section three. It provides that where a man has not been assessed, or has not been registered, or has not performed any other prerequisite required by the constitution or laws of a State before he shall vote, he may come forward, and on making his *ex parte* affidavit that he has proposed to do these things and has been prevented, and that his vote has been refused by a person whose sense of duty compels him to refuse it, then the party is to recover $500, "with full costs and such allowance of counsel fees as the court shall deem just." That provision for paying these parties-claimant counsel feels is certainly something new, so far as my knowledge extends in the legislation of the United States. I know there has been an evil practice of paying that wretched class of persons called public informers. I know that this country has been disgraced by the creation of a class of social spies and informers upon their fellow-citizens who have made a base living by undertaking to inform upon their fellow-men, destroying all confidence in social intercourse between man and man. But even under those laws never yet was it proposed that you should bring the pettifogging attorney in and give him fees in addition to the fine which the informer is to pocket upon procuring a conviction.

These features run all through the act. Twelve sections out of twenty-three establish fines and penalties, and every section contains an additional reward for the man who shall stimulate litigation. There is a maxim well known, and no more wholesome one is known to the law, than that "it is for the benefit of the Republic that there should be an end to lawsuits." What a commentary is that maxim upon this proposed law! . . .

Another thing this bill does. It creates a new army of officials, a swarm of officials who are to cover the country and eat out the substance of the people by their costs and legal expenses. These classes are provided for without limit, and the discretion to create such officers is reposed in one of the humblest classes of Government officials. I mean by that those who are subject to removal by an immediate superior, who are low in grade of office. Section nine provides:

That the district attorneys, marshals, and deputy marshals of the United States, the commissioners appointed by the circuit and territorial courts of the United States, with powers of arresting, imprisoning, or bailing offenders against the laws of the United States, and every other officer who may be specially empowered by the President of the United States, shall be, and they are hereby, specially authorized.

Here, then, is the power of appointment by the President without limitation as to number. One might have supposed that the dignity of the presidential office, the confiding of the power to a single man, might possibly limit the number of such appointments; but we find in line nineteen of the same section that—

With a view to afford reasonable protection to all persons in their constitutional right to vote without distinction of race, color, or previous condition of servitude, and to the prompt discharge of the duties of this act, it shall be the duty of the circuit courts of the United States, and the superior courts of the Territories of the United States, from time to time, to increase the number of commissioners, so as to afford a speedy and convenient means for the arrest and examination of persons charged with a violation of this act.

Here, then, is the second source from which a new swarm of these officers is to be created. But the bill does not stop there. Having shown you that the

President can appoint as many as he pleases, that the courts can appoint as many as they please, we find in section ten, the better to enable these appointees of the President and of the courts, the commissioners—

To execute their duties faithfully and efficiently, in conformity with the Constitution of the United States and the requirements of this act, they are hereby authorized and empowered, within their districts respectively, to appoint, in writing under their hands, any one or more suitable persons, from time to time, to execute all such warrants.

Here is another unlimited power of appointment: "one or more suitable persons," at the convenience and the discretion of these commissioners. This is an act which is leveled chiefly against the southern States, but it is one that will be paid for out of the public Treasury of the United States; for all these fees, and all these rewards, and all these expenses must be paid in the first instance out of the public Treasury, although the law provides for their subsequently being included in the judgment in case of conviction. How many men would be able to pay them? We all know the class of men who would be capable of committing the offense of preventing another from exercising his due franchises; and what would your judgment against them be worth? These parties would have received their money, and the attempt to collect the money from men who are commonly insolvent would be worthless.

I do believe and have my hopes that the very severities of this law will stand in the way of its execution. I believe that its severities, its illegalities, and enormities will be rectified in great part by just judges. I believe its cruelties will in a great degree be curbed by that sentiment of humanity which will pervade the juries of our country; and that in this way, when it has been exposed in all its enormity, there will be a returning sense of reason and proper feeling among our people that will not long suffer it to disgrace the statute-book. . . .

MR. STEWART. Mr. President, I congratulate the Senate and the country that we are about to assert some of the powers of Congress for the protection of voters; for the protection of the down-trodden; for the protection of persons in their political and civil rights; that we are about to get a bill which asserts something of the dignity and power of this nation.

It has been stated by some in the course of the debate that no legislation is necessary, and by others that this fifteenth amendment is a fraud and shall be of short duration. I tell the Opposition that it is no fraud, and that its duration will be perpetual. Rights guarantied and granted to the people cannot be taken from them. No party can stand on the basis of taking away such rights. When the high-sounding phrase came from certain pretended or real leaders of the Democratic party that they intended to acquiesce in the fifteenth amendment, I did not then believe in the good faith of the declarations so made. The statements which have come from the other side since this debate has begun convince me that I was right; that they did not intend to do it in good faith, but intended to pass by this Congress and then break it down. I congratulate the Senate and the country that we have this legislation in time to head off these designs, in time to give force and effect to this great amendment, in time to secure to all citizens of the United States an equal right to vote without regard to race or color. I believe we have a bill that will effect that object; and it is certainly a bill that will injure no man who does not desire to prevent the fulfillment of that object. It is certainly a bill that will injure no man who does not desire to do something wrong. He who is willing that the true spirit of the Constitution and laws of his country shall be administered, that the rights of man shall be respected, need not fear this law. . . .

We have more in this bill. We have an attempt to enforce the fourteenth amendment while it remains a part of your Constitution. Passing constitutional amendments and not enforcing them is trifling. Let them be enforced while they are part of the Constitution. It is trifling to allow a rebel to hold office in violation of the fourteenth amendment. Let it be enforced while it is a part of the Constitution.

We have more in this bill. We have commenced legislation in the right direction by attempting to guard the ballot-box in New York against the trampling of it down by the Democratic party. Why should gentlemen talk about our want of faith in the people? Sir, our faith in the people is unlimited; but we have no faith in a Democratic oligarchy in New York city or New Orleans or Georgia which by its power shall drive loyal men from the polls.

We believe that it is the duty of this Government to see that republican institutions prevail in this country. Talk not to us about not desiring to protect the ballot-box, when in New York frauds by the thousand and tens of thousands are committed at every election and are regarded as a good joke! In the presidential election of 1868 at least four States of this Union were carried by fraud for the Democratic candidate—New York, New Jersey, Georgia, and Louisiana. Shall we tolerate that? Who has faith in the people? Is it a Democratic oligarchy, who want their favorites or their tools to vote eight or ten or a hundred times a day, who would strike at the ballot-box itself? Our law is only for the protection of the ballot-box. We proclaim now and here that we will exert all the power we can exert under the Constitution to protect the ballot-box in every State of the Union. We probably have not got enough legislation in this bill on that subject, but if the occasion arises we will invent more. We will make the effort to see if it is in the power of this Government to prevent its being turned into anarchy and confusion by a conspiracy in New York or Georgia or Louisiana.

That is one feature of this bill. It is a good bill. I say, "let us have peace;" but peace upon what terms? The terms upon which we want peace and upon which we intend to have it, and the only terms upon which peace can be had, are that every citizen of the United States, without regard to color, shall have an equal opportunity to vote; that no State shall deny to any person, whether he is an alien or a native-born citizen, the equal protection of the laws; that while we have the power to regulate the time and the manner of elections for members of Congress we will not allow repeaters, if we can help it, but will have a fair vote of the people. We will have peace on the terms of protecting the citizens of the United States and by respecting the Constitution; and these are the only terms on which we can have peace.

The other side say, "Give us Kuklux, give us repeaters, give us Chinese, robbers, and murderers; let them have their way and you shall have peace." I say no; upon those terms there is no peace. There is no peace except in submitting to the laws, and in the equal protection of all persons by the law. There is no need of the Democratic party here resorting to special pleading, and talking about the time and manner of passing bills. Let me say to those gentlemen, advise your constituents to obey the law; advise your constituents to stop robbing and murdering Chinese; advise your constituents to let the negroes vote as other men vote; advise your constituents that it will not do in the great city of New York to poll seventy-five or one hundred thousand fraudulent votes at an election; advise them that that cannot be done; stop protesting against this legislation which seeks to prevent such things, and then we shall have peace. I tell my Democratic friends that if you ever expect to succeed you must turn your attention more to the justice of the case, and stop your technical pleas. The same technical pleas have been made ever since the war began. You have been all the time trying to find in the Constitution "how not to do it."

Ever since the war closed you have been trying to point out how we could not reconstruct. You have been quibbling and complaining at every attempt we have made. You have been occupying whole nights here in uttering condemnations of the just and liberal measures of a patriotic Congress. You have failed, and you will fail again. Let me advise you now to turn your attention to enforcing the laws, to turn our attention to the only means by which peace can be had, and we will meet you in brotherly love. We have no enmity against the Democratic party as such; but while it goes wrong, while its motto is anarchy, injustice, inequality, fraud, we will conquer it every time. Change your motto, protect the oppressed, and be a Democratic party in fact; be for justice, for humanity, for progress, and then you will have some chance. Your now fighting the fifteenth amendment is only another of your usual blunders. Some of the party thought it was not best to do it, but finally at the close of this debate you treat it as a fraud. Such things will kill you all the time. Come out on the side of humanity, justice, peace, law, the Constitution; take the Constitution as it is, uphold it and defend it, and you will have peace. . . .

THE VICE PRESIDENT. The hour of three o'clock has now arrived. The question is on agreeing to the conference report, upon which the yeas and nays have been ordered. The Secretary will call the roll.

The question being taken by yeas and nays, resulted—yeas 48, nays 11. . . .

So the report was concurred in.

House of Representatives-41st Congress, 2nd Session
May 27, 1870

THE SPEAKER [JAMES BLAINE, R., ME.]. The House now resumes the consideration of the report of the committee of conference on the disagreeing votes of the two Houses on the amendment of the Senate to the bill (H. R. No. 1293) to enforce the right of citizens of the United States to vote in the several States of this Union who have hitherto been denied that right on account of race, color, or previous condition of servitude. By unanimous consent it was agreed that there should be two and a half hours of debate on this report, of which the Opposition should have one hour and a half. The gentleman from Ohio [Mr. Bingham] is first entitled to the floor.

JOHN BINGHAM [R., OHIO]. I propose to occupy a very brief time in stating the substance of the report submitted by the committee of conference. The House is doubtless aware that the Senate amendment, which was the subject of the conference, included substantially all that had been embraced in the bill reported to this House by the Judiciary Committee, and which had received the approval of the House. In addition to that, the Senate amendment contained various provisions for the enforcement of certain sections of the fourteenth article of the amendments to the Constitution. It contained also a provision authorizing the President of the United States to employ the Army, the Navy, and the militia, at his discretion, in elections. It also contained a provision regulating the imposition of taxes upon immigrants by the legislation of the respective States. And it contained, further, a provision giving jurisdiction to the district and circuit courts of the United States, concurrently with the State courts, in all contested elections, save elections of members of Congress and elections of members of the State Legislatures. The report of the conference committee, in so far as it changes the Senate bill, is confined to the matters which I have just enumerated, and in the addition of two or three more sections designed to prevent fraudulent registration at all elections in the United States at which Federal officers shall be voted for, and also to prevent fraudulent voting at such elections.

This statement, Mr. Speaker, places the House, I believe, in possession of the changes and new provisions proposed and agreed upon by a majority of the conference committee. Touching the power which was proposed to be conferred upon the President by the Senate amendment, to employ, at his discretion, the Army, the Navy, and the militia at elections in the several States of this Union, I beg leave to inform the House that the conference committee have substantially struck out that section and inserted in its stead a simple provision that the President of the United States may employ the military force, so far as may be necessary, to execute the judicial process authorized by the proposed act.

Touching the provision of the Senate amendment limiting the power of the States to impose taxes upon immigrants, I wish to say that the only change made by the conference committee is the change of the word "emigrants" to "immigrants;" and that the only effect of the section is to assert the power of the United States, under the express provision of the national Constitution, over the several States of this Union to this extent and no further, that hereafter the taxes imposed by the several States upon immigrants thereto shall be equal; that the States shall not hereafter discriminate against the immigrant from China and in favor of the immigrant from Prussia, nor against the immigrant from France and in favor of the immigrant from Ireland; that immigrants being persons within the express words of the fourteenth article of the constitutional amendments, shall, whenever they may be found within the jurisdiction of any of the States of the Union, be entitled to the equal protection of the laws, not simply of the State itself, but of the Constitution of the United States as well.

The additional sections to the Senate bill, incorporated by the action of the conference committee, are, as I have already remarked, provisions to prevent fraudulent registration and fraudulent voting at all elections in the several States of this Union and in the several Territories at which a member or Delegate to Congress shall be voted for. I do not deem it important to explain at any length the provisions of these sections; but I deem it due to the committee to say that as to the constitutionality of the provisions that have been thus added, and the necessity for such legislation, I do not allow myself to entertain for one moment the belief that any thoughtful man of this House, fully advised of the nature of the provisions, can doubt for one moment their necessity and constitutionality.

While the general power of the States to "regulate," in the language of the Constitution, the election of Representatives to Congress is conceded by all who have ever read that instrument, it must at the same time be admitted that by the very same clause the power is conferred upon Congress to make regulations for the election of members of Congress, or to alter the regulations which have been or may hereafter be made in that behalf by the States. The amendments proposed to prevent fraudulent registration or fraudulent voting, in so far as I am advised, do not alter any of the existing regulations of the States touching registration; they are but a simple exercise of the power expressly conferred on the Congress of the United States to regulate elections of members and Delegates to Congress. They are expressly limited to elections of these officers. I do not deem it important to say anything further on that point.

I may as well say, however, in passing, so that no one may have occasion to complain that I have omitted to call attention to anything new in the proposed legislation arising out of the action of the conference committee, that there is in section twenty-one a provision which makes the fact that a Federal officer was voted for at an election *prima facie* evidence, with certain limitations, against the party accused of having violated the provisions of the act who actually voted at the same election.

I have only to say, Mr. Speaker, of this section that this provision corresponds with like provisions now found on the statute-books of the United States, the validity of which, I believe, has never yet been successfully challenged in any court of the United States. The express condition, making a certain condition of facts *prima facie* evidence, already finds a place on your statute-book, and the constitutionality thereof remains to this day, so far as I am advised, unquestioned.

I have only one further remark to make in opening this case to the House, and that is in relation to the twenty-first and last section of the Senate amendment. The House doubtless will remember, the Senate amendment having been printed in full in the Globe, what that provision was. It was in substance that all contested-election cases, except the election of members of Congress and members of the State Legislatures, might be tried and determined in the district and circuit courts of the United States concurrently with the courts of the several States. The House will take notice that in the amendments substituted for this section by the conference committee all of this section has been excluded and a section inserted in its stead which excepts from the operation of the act electors for President and Vice President of the United States, Representative or Delegate in Congress, and members of a State Legislature. It was thought important by the conference committee that the courts of the United States under no possible condition of things should be authorized to intervene to settle any case of contest whatever about the election of members of Congress, about the election of electors for President or Vice President of the United States, or about the election of the members of a State Legislature, leaving the last under the constitutions of the several States to be settled exclusively by the bodies to which they were elected.

The gentleman says, How about the word constables? I will come to that directly. It was also deemed essential that the contest of the election of members of Congress should not be allowed by the courts, leaving the decision of such question precisely where the express words of the Constitution leave it, to the Houses of Congress severally to which the members are respectively chosen. So also as to the election of electors of President and Vice President of the United States. Mr. Speaker, the report of the conference committee excludes the courts of the United States, or, in other words, does not confer on the courts of the United States any power whatever to intervene in the matter of any election whatever, either of ward constables or of anybody else, save in the words of the report of the conference, to wit:

In cases where it shall appear that the sole question touching the title to such office arises out of the denial of the right to vote to citizens who so offered to vote on account of race, color, or previous condition of servitude, such suit or proceeding may be instituted in the circuit or district court of the United States of the circuit or district in which such person resides. And said circuit or district court shall have, concurrently with the State courts, jurisdiction thereof so far as to determine the rights of the parties to such office by reason of the denial of the right guarantied by the fifteenth article of amendment to the Constitution of the United States, and secured by this act; and that the Senate agree to the same.

I should have preferred, because I do not deem it essential to the success of this measure, that the Senate had not raised this question with the House of contesting any election in the courts; but having raised it, I am content to enact the provision, with the limitation now put upon it (into a law) and leave it thus forevermore, assured as I am it can work no possible harm: because in any event and in every event it leaves in the courts of the United States no power save to determine the single question where the person offering his vote shall have it rejected simply on the ground that his right, guarantied under the fifteenth article of amendment to the Constitution of the United States, is denied. I do not deem it necessary to enter on any argument in support of this section of the report. With the limitation expressed I am satisfied, never intending myself to extend, as at present advised, the power of the courts of the United States over any question whatever of election beyond the express letter of this section itself. I look upon the word "necessary" as incorporated in the Constitution of the United States in the grant of powers, as a grant and limitation as well of power. I do not believe under any possible condition of things it would be necessary, as the Constitution now stands, to vest in any of the courts of the United States any jurisdiction over the question of contested elections beyond the express jurisdiction with the express limitation contained in the twenty-third section of the report.

Here, Mr. Speaker, for the present I leave the question for further discussion to my honorable colleagues. . . .

MICHAEL KERR [DEM., IND.]. Mr. Speaker, as a member on the part of the House of the conference committee, to which this bill was referred to by the Senate and House, I was unable to concur with the majority of the committee in the report which was made by them, and I did not sign it. I desire now to say that the reason why I could not concur in that report, very briefly expressed, is this: that in my judgment every single section of this bill— twenty-three in number—save only the first, involves a palpable violation of the spirit and letter of the Constitution; that every section except the first is grossly wrong in principle, is demanded by no existing condition in the country, is condemned by every consideration of just expediency, and ought not to be enacted into the form of a law.

The bill, as it stands, is loose and uncertain in its structure and composition, full of ambiguous propositions, of repetitions, and of mere partisan legislation. Its pretended purpose is to execute the fifteenth amendment, but its provisions have very little relation to that amendment. They serve very well to illustrate the revolutionary and partisan spirit in which the amendment was conceived and ratified. When the amendment was originally under discussion here I predicted that it would soon lead to this vicious brood of partisan enactments. Any one unfamiliar with the history and progress of Radical legislation might well be amazed that upon so narrow a basis as that amendment so fearful a superstructure could be erected. But the truth is, that amendment only supplies the pretext, not the constitutional authority, for this bill.

I desire to state briefly why I think some of its sections are unconstitutional. I inquire first, then, and I desire the attention of the gentlemen who were my colleagues on the committee, what the fifteenth amendment, in pretended execution of which this bill was framed, authorizes Congress to do? It provides that—"The right of citizens of the United States to vote"— Mark that "to vote"—

shall not be denied or abridged by the United States or by any State on account of race, color, or previous condition of servitude.

What is it that neither Congress nor any State may deny or abridge? It is not the right to be registered under any system of State registration, or to be enrolled in any particular way, or to be taxed preparatory to voting under State laws. It does not confer the right to vote. It only forbids the denial by the States or by Congress of the right to vote on account of race, color, or previous condition of servitude. But the right itself must be derived from and enjoyed in accordance with the laws of the States. Suffrage is the gift of the States. Its regulation pertains to them alone. This amendment does not say they may not deny or abridge suffrage at their pleasure, but only that they shall not do so "on account of race, color, or previous condition of servitude." For all other causes, applicable alike to citizens of all colors, races, and conditions, the powers of the States are as plenary as they were before the pretended ratification of the amendment.

Now, look at the second, third, and fourth sections of this bill, and you will find that they relate to the right of registration and other formalities under State laws. They create numerous new offenses and prescribe many punishments extraordinary, extreme, and in my judgment clearly excessive. They forbid the doing of things not mentioned in the amendment nor embraced within its spirit or intent. The right of citizens to vote is what shall not be denied or abridged "on account of race, color, or previous condition of servitude." Not the right to register or do any other thing as a mere prerequisite to the right to vote. Those matters are left, where they have always belonged, to the sole regulation of the States. This attempt to bring them within congressional power and to make a new catalogue of crimes to be punished in Federal courts is most dangerous and unwarranted.

It was never contemplated by the people that Congress would attempt to usurp control of the elections in the States, to dictate in what manner they should be conducted, to put them under the supervision of Federal officers, and give all judicial power over them to Federal courts. . . .

I hold, Mr. Speaker, in reference not alone to this fifteenth amendment, but to the fourteenth amendment, and to all like provisions in the Constitution of the United States, and I hold this upon the authority of a long line of adjudicated cases, that all the power of the Federal Government that can be rightfully exercised in such cases may be exercised and exhausted against the persons who offend, and against the persons alone; not against the State, nor against the State law, nor by the overthrow of the ordinary machinery or regulations of civil government in any State. It was no part of the purpose of the people in ratifying either amendment to invade or destroy the original right of local self-government in the States; and to assume any such thing is, in my judgment, to strike down the most vital security that remains to the people of this country. . . .

But, Mr. Speaker, there are other provisions in the bill which, in my judgment, are fraught with tenfold greater danger and mischief than those to which I have referred. If this bill becomes a law, in some sections of the country it will become a fruitful source of trouble, confusion, disturbance, strife, litigation, and injustice. There is no telling what may be the extent of the evil and agitation which may grow out of this bill if it becomes a law in some sections of this country. I will read one section of the bill, the fourth section:

SEC. 4. *And be it further enacted,* That if any person, by force, bribery, threats, intimidation, or other unlawful means, shall hinder, delay, prevent, or obstruct, or shall combine and confederate with others to hinder, delay, prevent, or obstruct, any citizen from doing any act required to be done to qualify him to vote or from voting at any election as aforesaid, such person shall for every such offense forfeit and pay the sum of $500 to the person aggrieved thereby, to be recovered by an action on the case, with full costs, and such allowance for counsel fees as the court shall deem just, and shall also for every such offense be guilty of a misdemeanor, and shall, on conviction thereof, be fined not less than $500, or be imprisoned not less than one month and not more than one year, or both, at the discretion of the court.

Gentlemen will observe from the reading of this section to what a remarkable extent there has been incorporated in this bill the miserable cant pretense which now prevails in some sections of this country, and which is daily resorted to in order to defeat the will of the people and to overthrow and override the laws of the States and the right of representation, not alone in the States, but in this House. By this section there is presented to the minds of a certain class of people in this country, and especially in the South, a direct pecuniary inducement, a direct bribe to stir up and cultivate strife, to use base means to entrap good citizens, and then prefer criminal charges and drag the people into the courts of justice of the United States for the purpose of prosecuting and persecuting and plundering white people who may be their neighbors, who may be in the exercise only of their rights and acting in precise accordance with the laws of the country. Yet the burden of their offense may consist in the fact that they have only desired by legitimate and honorable means to save themselves and their society from domination of ignorance and vice, controlled by political adventurers, agitators, and camp-followers, who are unfit to control any community or any class of people anywhere.

Yet to these fellows, by this action of Congress, is presented an inducement to harass, oppress, and persecute all persons who in the exercise of their ordinary and just political rights, privileges, and immunities shall attempt by legitimate means to control the suffrage of the colored men in the South; because, sir, it need not be disguised that this bill, with its prosecutions and punishments, fines, penalties, and imprisonments, is aimed at the people of the South. It is conceived in a spirit of malignity against the people of the South. It is designed to perpetuate in that section the power of the Radical party, and to perpetuate the power and domination of the colored element in these States. Let this law be enacted, and let a knowledge of its existence be brought to the minds of the negroes of the South, who are under the guidance of these political adventurers, and with the aid of the pestiferous pack of shysters and pettifoggers who hang on the outskirts of the Republican party in the South, and infest the courts of justice in that section, under the guidance and with the aid of such men, of such animals, what will become of the peace and order of that section?

It is worse than would be a direct proposition to incorporate into this law the odious and horrible principle of employing informers to go about the country and institute prosecutions and divide the spoils with a grasping Government. This bill gives to each complainant $500, "with full costs, and such allowance for counsel fees as the court shall deem just." Thus, further to encourage these prosecutions and the disturbance of society, the parties suing are promised exemption from all costs in the employment of counsel, and the court is permitted to pay lawyers for them at the expense of the people of the entire country. Let any gentleman read section four again— and in these respects it is a copy of sections two and three—and ask himself if a more mischievous and damnable policy could be devised for the destruction of the public peace? The evil results of this law will not be confined to the South. They will be experienced in a less degree all over the country where negroes and mean Radical white men abound.

But they are not content with these remarkable provisions. They further provide in the seventh section of this bill, with the most extraordinary disregard of long-established and never-questioned principles of constitutional law—

That if in the act of violating any provision in either of the two preceding sections any other felony, crime, or misdemeanor shall be committed, the offender, on conviction of such violation of said sections, shall be punished for the same with such punishments as are attached to the said felonies, crimes, and misdemeanors by the laws of the State in which the offense may be committed.

After enacting these multitudinous crimes and offenses in this law, it is then attempted by a direct violation of the Constitution to transplant into a Federal law the preexisting laws of a State of this Union, as well as laws which may hereafter be enacted by States, and to provide that in addition to these congressional crimes, penalties, and punishments, if the State law shall impose any other punishments, then those other punishments shall also be considered a part of this law, for the purpose of their execution as being a part of this law, and shall be so considered by the officers and courts of the United States, and any violations of those State laws shall be made a basis of indictment or information in Federal courts against citizens of the several States, enforced in Federal courts, and the penalties, fines, and punishments in execution of State laws to be enforced by the Federal Government against the citizens of the States.

I ask gentlemen of intelligence on this floor if such a proposition as that was ever before tolerated in an American Congress? I say without hesitation that for it there is no example in our legislative or judicial history. This is the first instance of the kind in our history; it is as extraordinary as it is novel, and it is as vicious and lawless and revolutionary as it is extraordinary. It ought to be rejected by this House, not only with the judicial emphasis of condemnation which it deserves, but with indignation and contempt.

The gentleman from Ohio [Mr. Bingham] says that this bill is intended for the purpose of executing the fourteenth and fifteenth articles of amendment to the Constitution of the United States. Yet one section only has any logical relation to the fourteenth article of amendment, that is the fourteenth section; and one section alone has direct and logical reference to the enforcement of the fifteenth article of amendment; and that is all. Yet there are twenty-three sections in this bill, twenty-one of which relate to powers and to purposes outside both the fourteenth and fifteenth articles of amendment. They might be better and more truly denominated twenty-one sections designed to perpetuate the power of the Republican party in this country.

In my judgment that is the purpose of all those sections. It is impossible to turn to any one of them without finding violations of established principles of law. I will invite attention briefly to one of those sections. The fifteenth section of this bill undertakes to create a new offense, a new misdemeanor, and a new punishment. Not only by deposition from office in the case of any person who shall hold office in violation of the provisions of the third section of the fourteenth article of amendment to the Constitution, but also by declaring such person guilty of a misdemeanor and subjecting him to indictment and prosecution in a Federal court, and to trial, conviction, and fine not exceeding $1,000, and imprisonment not exceeding one year, or both, in the judgment of the court.

In what does the crime consist for which these punishments are to be inflicted? I wish some gentleman would point out to me in what element or part of such an act he can find moral turpitude or wrong or dishonesty, or anything worthy of such punishments. He is chosen or appointed to the office by reason of his recognized intelligence, fitness, and qualification, his conceded integrity and purity of personal character; and in order to promote the best interests of society, in order to carry on and maintain civil government, in order to protect the rights of person and property, he accepts the office to which he is chosen or appointed. He enters into it, and proceeds to perform its duties in precise accordance with the laws of his State and of the United States, except only the inhibition against his holding office, which is contained in the third section of the fourteenth article of the constitutional amendments. On what principle of human justice would you denounce against a citizen thus acting these severe and repeated and most excessive penalties and prosecutions? I am utterly unable to understand on what principle of right it can be justified. Such legislation seems to me to mock the spirit of the age, to be inhuman and barbarous, and a direct and most cruel thrust at the very existence of well-regulated government. . . .

JAMES BECK [DEM., KY.]. I do not profess to be able to discuss this measure in ten minutes, but as the people I represent are perhaps as much interested in its defeat and will be as much oppressed by its passage as the people of any other section, I desire to enter my protest against it, as being fraught with evil, and evil only. I desire to protest against the action of the conference committee, and especially of the majority of the conferees on the part of the House, for having abandoned the bill passed by the House, and not only adopted the more odious and oppressive measure passed by the Senate, but because they have framed and adopted new legislation, which neither the House nor the Senate ever thought of, in order to make it more iniquitous still.

I have before objected, and shall hereafter still more strenuously object, to these committees of conference, whereby the absolute right to legislate without restriction or control is vested in two Radical members of each House, who are generally known beforehand to be willing to go any lengths to carry out whatever scheme it may be desired to put through. This report is a specimen. The bill which left us was simply a bill to enforce the fifteenth amendment, and we had a right to suppose the gentleman from Ohio [Mr. Bingham] would insist on maintaining it in that form; instead of that it is abandoned, and he urges us to pass this bill of abominations hatched and concocted in the conference committee room, in part, at least, which pretends to reenact the infamous civil rights bill, and enforce the fourteenth as well as the fifteenth amendment. We are required to swallow it all at one dose. I have no doubt we will be compelled to do it.

MR. BINGHAM. Mr. Speaker, if I had entertained doubts before this discussion upon the constitutionality of this bill, or upon the question whether the rights of the people or the rights of the States were invaded by it, those doubts would have been removed after I had listened to the torrent of declamation against the bill from gentlemen learned in the law and not wanting in knowledge of the rights of the people and of the rights of the States. No man, sir, who gave attention to this discussion could gather from the utterances of a single gentleman who lifted his voice in denunciation of this bill wherein it invades any right of any citizen or any reserved right of any State. . . .

What more, sir, have you heard from these gentlemen, so urgent here in demanding the attention of the House to their fierce invective against this bill or any kindred enactment? Why, sir, that the negro is to be crushed between the upper and the nether millstone by the proposed legislation, and in the next breath you are told that by the proposed legislation you glorify the negro at the expense of the poor white man. There is logic for you! Gentlemen seem to intimate that this bill protects the elective franchise only in citizens of color, as they are called; they intimate that the equal right of the citizen of the United States to vote, having like qualifications under the laws of the several States, is not protected by it from disfranchisement on account of race! Sir, men will look in vain for a single utterance from any gentleman who puts forth this unconsidered denunciation of the bill for a single reference to any line in it that justifies their denunciation.

Mr. Speaker, every section of this bill applies alike to all citizens of the United States, irrespective of color, race, or previous condition of servitude, who are or shall be otherwise qualified to vote; and yet the gentleman from Kentucky, [Mr. Beck,] in the fury of his excitement, ventured to say in the presence of this House that the penalties of the bill do not apply and could not be denied his right to vote under color, if you please, or State constitutions or State laws, on account of race! Is there any man who will calmly and deliberately so stultify himself as to say that upon the enactment into law of this bill by the Congress of the United States any State of this Union can thereafter lawfully deny on account of race the right to vote to any white citizen of the United States resident therein and otherwise having the qualifications required by such State of voters? Does this bill propose, in the interests of white citizens, not to impose the same restraint on the majority of the people of South Carolina, who are colored, as upon the majority of the people of New York, who are white? So much for the fairness of the presentation of that objection, that white citizens are not protected. . . .

Why, sir, I remember a time, not very long ago, when I heard gentlemen on this floor in the excitement of debate declare that it was unconstitutional to defend the Constitution, and now to-day we are taught the new lesson that it is unconstitutional to enforce the Constitution.

On that point we have had the learned and profound utterances of the gentleman from New York, [Mr. Cox,] supported, as the gentleman alleges, by the great name of Jeremy Bentham. Does not the gentleman know that Jeremy Bentham was wise enough and learned enough to understand that a law is utterly worthless—worth, at most, no more than the parchment on which it is written—without a sanction? Yet the gentleman complains here because the Representatives of the people of the United States provide in this bill penal sanctions to enforce its prohibitions, and thereby make answerable at the bar of the courts of the United States any person who by threat, intimidation, or violence shall attempt to interfere with the lawful exercise of the ballot by any citizen of the United States in any State of the Union.

The gentleman grew eloquent when he talked of liberty. He is not unread in the history of the human race; he is not unread in the history of those struggles in which men have glorified human nature and attested their claim to immortality by vindicating their right to civil and religious liberty. I pray that gentleman to inform this House, when he again speaks on that subject, when or where liberty found a refuge upon this planet save under the shelter of law—law enforced by sanctions.

CHARLES ELDREDGE [DEM., WIS.]. Not under an empire.

MR. BINGHAM. "An empire!" The word "empire," sir, has no terrors for me when applied to that empire whose scepter is knowledge and whose power is the ballot in the hands of freemen—the empire of reason, the empire of justice, asserted by freemen through written law for the equal protection of themselves and the protection as well of the "stranger within their gates."

MR. ELDREDGE. This bill establishes the empire of despotism; and that is what the gentleman is advocating.

MR. BINGHAM. I decline to be further interrupted by the gentleman. I have said enough to show that the sum total of the outcry against this bill is that by it the equal rights of the people of this country are to be enforced, for the first time in the history of the Republic, by a national statute and by the whole power of the Union and of the people of all the States. It is to be made a crime hereafter for men, by violence or intimidation, to interfere with that right "formidable to tyrants only"—the right of an unrestrained ballot in the hands of freemen.

MR. ELDREDGE. Under the sword!

MR. BINGHAM. "Under the sword!" There is no such word in the bill. The gentleman had better undertake to gibbet in infamy the memory of the founders of the Republic, who gave us the example of this legislation by enacting under the administration of Washington the very same provision that is incorporated in this bill—the only provision in it which authorizes the employment of military force. Talk about "the sword!" Sir, the sword is well enough when needful as the avenger of the wrongs inflicted upon a free people.

I do not forget in this discussion that grand utterance which, when the

American people first struck for independence and self-government, they borrowed from England's martyred hero, Sydney, graved it on their guns, and read it in the lurid light of battle, "Resistance to tyrants in obedience to God." I repeat it, "Resistance to tyrants is obedience to God," even though that resistance be made with the sword, with shot and shell and bayonet.

Let the people speak by the ballot unawed. Let them exercise their equal right to the ballot, that power under which your Constitution was ordained, by which your Constitution has been maintained, by which your Congresses are chosen, by which your armies are organized and supported, and by which your tribunals of justice are established. We propose to enforce that right; and by the help of the American people we will do it.

[Here the hammer fell].

THE SPEAKER. . . . The agreement was that after two hours and a half spent in debate the vote should be taken upon the question, "Will the House agree to the report of the committee of conference?" On that question the gentleman from New York [Mr. Cox] has called for the yeas and nays.

The yeas and nays were ordered. . . .

The question was taken; and it was decided in the affirmative—yeas 133, nays 58, not voting 39. . . .

So the report of the committee of conference was agreed to.

Senate-41st Congress, 2nd Session
May 20, 1870

EUGENE CASSERLY [DEM., CAL.]. . . . My purpose was to bring to the notice of Senators a view of the subject which, if accepted by them, must control their action. That view is, that there is nothing in the fifteenth amendment which under the most liberal construction authorizes any of the legislation proposed by the bill of the Senate, or any of the provisions of the House bill after the first section. I ask the attention of Senators to this view because I deem it to be vital. . . .

In considering the effect of this amendment the first inquiry is, what was its object, what was the policy of its adoption? We cannot differ as to the answer. It was the last of three amendments promulgated since the war. The first of these, the thirteenth amendment, abolished slavery. The fourteenth amendment declared all persons born or naturalized in the United States to be citizens of the United States. The fifteenth amendment forbids the United States, or any State, to deny to citizens of the United States the right to vote "on account of race, color, or previous condition of servitude." The thirteenth amendment made all persons free. The fourteenth amendment conferred citizenship on all native or naturalized persons, and on all persons equal protection before the law. The fifteenth amendment is more limited in its language. It merely forbids "the United States or any State to deny or abridge the right of citizens to vote"—not generally, but for a limited class of causes—"on account of race, color, or previous condition of servitude." Not all "citizens" are protected in "the right to vote," but only those whose right might be "abridged or denied" on account of one special class of grounds, "race, color, or previous condition of servitude." This class of grounds is not only special in itself, but it limits the effect of the amendment to a special class of "citizens;" those, namely, of the negro race, whether previously slave or free.

"The right to vote" of that class of persons had been "denied or abridged" in many, perhaps most of the States, and might be again in all. Hence there was an evil, real or supposed, to be remedied and prevented. There was in the country another large class of persons, of the white race, natives of Europe, who though declared to be "citizens" of the United States by the fourteenth amendment, had been or were still denied, or at least abridged of "the right to vote" in one or more States, and might be in all, on account of nativity or the want of a property qualification, or both. By the peculiar wording of the fifteenth amendment all this class was and is excluded from its benefits. All this makes it quite clear that the intent of the fifteenth amendment was single; to protect one race of people in the country, and only one, that known as "the colored race." To that class of citizens, therefore, its effects are confined.

Its operation upon the United States and the States, and the powers of Congress under it, are of course limited in like manner.

Another vital consequence follows also. The control of the subject of the suffrage remains in the States full and uncontrolled, as it was before the fifteenth amendment, except only that they shall not "abridge or deny the right to vote" to persons of the African race on account of their "race, color, or previous condition of servitude." This will be apparent from a few considerations. Before the fifteenth amendment the control of the whole subject of suffrage had been conceded to and exercised by the States, under the Constitution, from the foundation of the Government. It was a right peculiarly cherished by the people of the States. The Republican party fully and solemnly recognized and affirmed all this, not once, but often; but most clearly and with the greatest binding force at its last presidential convention, though it limited the declaration to those States which did not go into secession. The language was that "the question of suffrage in all the loyal States properly belongs to the people of those States."

We have seen how guarded the amendment is in its language, how closely restricted to a particular class of "citizens" and of causes of abridgment or denial. Except as to that class of citizens and causes, the amendment leaves the whole subject of suffrage, including qualifications of voters, in the control of the States as fully as it had been for nearly eighty years before the amendment was thought of. . . .

The prohibition is laid upon "the United States" or "any State." It is with these, as States, that in terms the amendment deals. Clearly its primary general operation is to make void any law of the United States or any constitution or law of any State which contravenes its provisions. This has always been held with regard to the many prohibitions in the Constitution of the United States upon the power of the States; as, for example, those in article one, section ten:

No State shall, etc., coin money; emit bills of credit; make anything but gold and silver coin a tender in payment of debts; pass any, etc., *ex post facto* law, or law impairing the obligation of contracts, etc.

This language is identical in legal effect with that of the fifteenth amendment:

The right, etc., to vote shall not be denied or abridged by the United States, or by any State, etc.

In each case the State is prohibited from exercising certain specified powers.

In the case of State laws "impairing the obligation of contracts," the question has very frequently arisen as to the mode of operation of the constitutional prohibition. It has always been understood that the prohibition operated directly upon the State law and made it void. The remedy has always been asserted through the courts, State or Federal, to the entire satisfaction of all parties interested. Let me remind Senators that it has always been left there, even in cases where the controversy gave rise to great popular excitement. No such tremendous apparatus of coercion as is now brought forward was ever thought of.

The same remarks apply to laws of the United States in violation of express constitutional prohibitions. They have been disposed of by the parties affected through the ordinary remedial processes of the courts.

Besides making void all provisions, constitutional or statutory, that violate it, does the fifteenth amendment go further? Does it operate upon individuals, and authorize Congress to pass laws affecting them? The strongest argument that it does is found by Senators who so affirm in section two of the amendment:

Congress shall have power to enforce this article by appropriate legislation.

But this is no argument. It is an effort to argue backward. The congressional power to enforce is one thing, and is a power to legislate merely. The constitutional provisions to be enforced are something entirely different. They are the principal thing, and must be found, if at all, in the first section of the amendment. They furnish the subject and the limit of the power to legislate. That power is merely incident and executory. It would exist in Congress without an express grant, just as much as the power to legislate in execution of the numerous powers given to Congress in section eight of article one would exist without the express authority at the foot of the section

To make all laws which shall be necessary and proper for carrying into execution the foregoing powers, etc.

In short, a power in Congress to legislate in execution of constitutional provisions never can be held to enlarge those provisions. Otherwise, as such a power always exists in Congress, it can always be used to enlarge the Constitution.

The argument is that unless the amendment affects individuals as well as States the power to legislate given to Congress has nothing to operate on. It is not well founded. The amendment is in terms a prohibition, and is negative merely. Congress may well give to its brief words the sanction of positive law, declaring fully what provisions of constitutional or statutory law are void for conflict. It may also provide means in the Federal courts for the more easy and prompt vindication, by the civil remedies known to the law, of the rights protected by the fifteenth amendment. All this would be "appropriate legislation" under section two.

But, sir, the subject is new, grave, and difficult. Let me concede for the argument that the amendment authorizes Congress to legislate against individuals. What individuals, let me ask? Clearly, only those individuals who, as officers under State laws, judges of election and of registration, canvassers, and returning officers, for instance, have official relations to the State. What more, sir? You may say that the State can act only through her agents, that is, her officers; and that under the amendment you can deal with those agents. But you can do this only so far as they can claim to be the agents of the State. That is, only so far as, being officers of the State, they act under or by color of State laws, which "deny or abridge the right to vote" under the fifteenth amendment, but no further. If there is no such State law; if, as in Massachusetts, the law has been for a long time in accord with the amendment; or if it has been changed to conform to it, as in New York, then it is not a case of a State acting either by a law or by her officers under her law. It is a case of a naked trespass by a private wrong-doer, of his own mere motion.

His case is within the jurisdiction of his own State, whose laws he has violated. To them his correction belongs. To them the remedy of the injured person must be left. Congress has no authority in such a case. It has nothing to do with it. It had not before the fifteenth amendment and it has not since. The amendment acts upon the State, or, if you will, upon the agents and officers of the State acting under State authority. It does not act at all nor in any way on the case of a private person committing a wrong out of his own head, not only without any authority from the State but in violation of its laws. To say of such a man's offense that it falls within the scope of an amendment which provides that "the right of a citizen to vote shall not be abridged or denied by the United States or by any State," is an absurdity in terms. If it is not, and if Congress can legislate for every such wrong, then it follows that any ruffian inflamed with drink who drives away a colored voter from the polls in the city of New York presents a case of the State of New York, despite all her laws in accord with the fifteenth amendment, "denying the right of a citizen to vote on account of his race or color," within the amendment.

Can the force of nonsense further go? Yet if this is nonsense, as it clearly is, a great part of the Senate bill is neither sense nor law; for it deals with precisely such cases. An unlawful interference by any idle person with a voter of African race, may or may not be on account of his race. The State law does not aid you to ascertain, for it is in the voter's favor. Like any other trespass upon a personal right, it is a matter for the State jurisdiction, civil or criminal, or both, according to the facts. The police of the polls and of the elections generally, against private individuals violating the right of colored men to vote, belongs to the States. The fifteenth amendment has not given it to Congress. It leaves it where it found it—in the States.

No, sir; except perhaps in the single case of a State officer acting under a State constitution or law, Congress has acquired no right, under the fifteenth amendment, to deal with individuals who interfere with the right of voters of African race. You must leave to the States the correction of all such cases. . . .

MATTHEW CARPENTER [R., WIS.]. I should like to ask my friend from California a question. I wish to call his attention to the language of the fourteenth amendment, and ask him if, in his opinion, that does not authorize the passage of this Senate bill? If he will read the first three or four lines of that amendment he will come to the clause to which I am calling his attention.

MR. CASSERLY. I supposed that the bill of the Committee on the Judiciary and the House bill were both of them bills to enforce the fifteenth amendment. Now, one of the most distinguished members of the Senate Judiciary Committee asks me whether there is not enough in the fourteenth amendment to justify the Senate bill? Why, sir, have we been discussing the Senate bill under a total mistake as to its object, or is this a change of front to meet the exigencies of the contest? Certainly the Senate bill is not a bill to enforce the fourteenth amendment; it is a bill to enforce the fifteenth amendment. Even if it were to enforce the fourteenth amendment, the suggestion of the Senator from Wisconsin does not help the matter. . . .

Both amendments are the same in their mode of operation. Both refer expressly to States. Both in terms operate on States as such. Both deal with the act of a State; with the constitution or law of a State; and if you will, for the sake of argument, with an officer of the State acting under color of a State law or constitution against the prohibitions of either amendment. Under neither amendment has Congress even a color of authority to go any further and deal with private individuals violating either amendment out of their own heads. Under the fourteenth amendment it is extremely plain that the criminal or illegal acts of a private person in a State, in depriving another of his life by murder, or of his liberty by false imprisonment, or of his property by stealing it, all "without due process of law," could never give to Congress the right to interfere. Otherwise Congress might take to itself, under pretense of enforcing the fourteenth amendment, the entire criminal and civil jurisdiction in the States of offenses and trespasses against life, liberty, and property by private persons acting without any color of State authority.

All this is perfectly clear under the fourteenth amendment; and as the language of the two amendments as to the point in discussion is identical in legal effect, it is equally clear as to the fifteenth amendment.

The same construction, therefore, binds you as to that amendment. Under pretense of enforcing it you cannot, besides dealing with States and the agents and officers of States, legislate for the unlawful proceedings of individuals having no official character. You cannot thus draw to yourselves, as in a great degree you do in this bill, the entire jurisdiction, civil and criminal, of offenses against the right to vote of citizens of the African race, still less of citizens of the white race.

I thank the Senator from Wisconsin for calling my attention to the fourteenth amendment and to the flood of light which it throws upon our subject.

The comparison of the two amendments makes my ground as to the fifteenth amendment impregnable. It shows beyond any plausible or even rational doubt that the fifteenth amendment operates in the manner and to the extent I have stated, and not otherwise or further. Primarily it operates on the United States and on the States, and makes void any law or constitution contrary to its provisions, which are for the protection of citizens of the African race in their right to vote. If it operates on persons it is only on those who are officers, and hence the agents of the State. In all other respects the subject of the suffrage and the right to it is untouched by the amendment, and remains as fully as before within the exclusive jurisdiction of the States. . . .

THE DECISION

Commentary

It is frequently said that the post-Civil War civil rights legislation was all but nullified by the strict interpretation given to the Thirteenth, Fourteenth, and Fifteenth Amendments by the Supreme Court, starting with the *Slaughter-house Cases* (*supra p.* 335) and culminating in the *Civil Rights Cases* (*infra p.* 780). It can scarcely be denied that the highest Court did, in the period from 1873-1883, restrict the reach of the postbellum amendments, particulary in limiting the operation of the Fourteenth Amendment guaranty of equality to "state action," in accord with its literal language. At the same time, a close reader of these pages can see that the high-bench doctrines articulated in the cases referred to were anything but manufactured by the Justices out of whole cloth. The theme of limited power conferred by the relevant amendments is one that runs through all the debates on the civil rights legislation covered in these pages, from the Enforcement Act of 1870 to the Civil Rights Act of 1875. If, in the congressional debates, that theme was stated principally by Democratic legislators, it was soon to be taken up by a Supreme Court whose members had, with one exception, been appointed by Republican Presidents.

In addition, critics of the high Court's post-Civil War performance in the civil rights field too frequently forget that important provisions of the postbellum statutes under consideration were upheld by the Court. This is more important than is generally realized, for the decisions sustaining key provisions of the 1870 Enforcement Act and 1871 Force Act relating to protection of the suffrage have been precedents upon which recent congressional efforts to protect the right to vote have been based.

Among the decisions sustaining provisions of the post-bellum civil rights laws, *Ex parte Yarbrough,* 110 U.S. 651 (1884) which follows, is of particular interest. In it, the Supreme Court upheld an indictment charging defendants with conspiring to intimidate a Negro citizen in the exercise of his right to vote at a congressional election and, in execution of such conspiracy, using force and violence against him. The Government, according to the opinion, plainly has the power to enact appropriate laws to secure a congressional election from the influence of violence. Under the Court's reasoning, indeed, such power exists, even independently of the Fifteenth Amendment in the congressional power to punish crimes where that is "necessary and proper" to effectuate the objects of the federal government. And, if that be the case, the reach of the statute at issue in *Yarbrough* need not be limited by the "state action" requirement of the Fourteenth and Fifteenth Amendments.

EX PARTE YARBROUGH
110 U. S. 651 (1884)

MR. JUSTICE MILLER delivered the opinion of the Court.

This case originates in this court by an application for a writ of *habeas corpus* on the part of Jasper Yarbrough and seven other persons, who allege that they are confined by the jailer of Fulton County, in the custody of the United States marshal for the Northern District of Georgia, and that the trial, conviction, and sentence in the Circuit Court of the United States for that district, under which they are held, were illegal, null and void. . . .

This, however, leaves for consideration the more important question—the one mainly relied on by counsel for petitioners—whether the law of Congress, as found in the Revised Statutes of the United States, under which the prisoners are held, is warranted by the Constitution, or being without such warrant, is null and void.

If the law which defines the offence and prescribes its punishment is void, the court was without jurisdiction and the prisoners must be discharged.

Though several different sections of the Revised Statutes are brought into the discussion as the foundation of the indictments found in the record, we think only two of them demand our attention here, namely, sections 5508 and 5520. They are in the following language:

SEC. 5508. If two or more persons conspire to injure, oppress, threaten, or intimidate any citizen in the free exercise or enjoyment of any right or privilege secured to him by the Constitution or laws of the United States, or because of his having so exercised the same, or if two or more persons go in disguise on the highway, or on the premises of another, with intent to prevent or hinder his free exercise or enjoyment of any right or privilege so secured, they shall be fined not more than five thousand dollars and imprisoned not more than ten years; and shall, moreover, be thereafter ineligible to any office or place of honor, profit, or trust created by the Constitution or laws of the United States.

SEC. 5520. If two or more persons in any State or Territory conspire to prevent by force, intimidation, or threat, any citizen who is lawfully entitled to vote, from giving his support or advocacy, in a legal manner, toward or in favor of the election of any lawfully qualified person as an elector for President or Vice President, or as a member of the Congress of the United States; or to injure any citizen in person or property on account of such support or advocacy; each of such persons shall be punished by a fine of not less than five hundred nor more than five thousand dollars, or by imprisonment, with or without hard labor, not less than six months nor more than six years, or by both such fine and imprisonment. . . .

Stripped of its technical verbiage, the offence charged in this indictment is that the defendants conspired to intimidate Berry Saunders, a citizen of African descent, in the exercise of his right to vote for a member of the Congress of the United States, and in the execution of that conspiracy they beat, bruised, wounded and otherwise maltreated him; and in the second

538

count that they did this on account of his race, color, and previous condition of servitude, by going in disguise and assaulting him on the public highway and on his own premises.

If the question were not concluded in this court, as we have already seen that it is by the decision of the Circuit Court, we entertain no doubt that the conspiracy here described is one which is embraced within the provisions of the Revised Statutes which we have cited.

That a government whose essential character is republican, whose executive head and legislative body are both elective, whose most numerous and powerful branch of the legislature is elected by the people directly, has no power by appropriate laws to secure this election from the influence of violence, of corruption, and of fraud, is a proposition so startling as to arrest attention and demand the gravest consideration.

If this government is anything more than a mere aggregation of delegated agents of other States and governments, each of which is superior to the general government, it must have the power to protect the elections on which its existence depends from violence and corruption.

If it has not this power it is left helpless before the two great natural and historical enemies of all republics, open violence and insidious corruption.

The proposition that it has no such power is supported by the old argument often heard, often repeated, and in this court never assented to, that when a question of the power of Congress arises the advocate of the power must be able to place his finger on words which expressly grant it. The brief of counsel before us, though directed to the authority of that body to pass criminal laws, uses the same language. Because there is no *express* power to provide for preventing violence exercised on the voter as a means of controlling his vote, no such law can be enacted. It destroys at one blow, in construing the Constitution of the United States, the doctrine universally applied to all instruments of writing, that what is implied is as much a part of the instrument as what is expressed. This principle, in its application to the Constitution of the United States, more than to almost any other writing, is a necessity, by reason of the inherent inability to put into words all derivative powers— a difficulty which the instrument itself recognizes by conferring on Congress the authority to pass all laws necessary and proper to carry into execution the powers expressly granted and all other powers vested in the government or any branch of it by the Constitution. . . .

The frequent failures of the legislatures of the States to elect senators at the proper time, by one branch of the legislature voting for one person and the other branch for another person, and refusing in any manner to reconcile their differences, led Congress to pass an act which compelled the two bodies to meet in joint convention, and fixing the day when this should be done, and requiring them so to meet on every day thereafter and vote for a senator until one was elected.

In like manner Congress has fixed a day, which is to be the same in all the States, when the electors for President and Vice-President shall be appointed.

Now the day fixed for electing members of Congress has been established by Congress without regard to the time set for election of State officers in each State, and but for the fact that the State legislatures have, for their own accommodation, required State elections to be held at the same time, these elections would be held for congressmen alone at the time fixed by the act of Congress.

Will it be denied that it is in the power of that body to provide laws for the proper conduct of those elections? To provide, if necessary, the officers who shall conduct them and make return of the result? And especially to provide, in an election held under its own authority, for security of life and limb to the voter while in the exercise of this function? Can it be doubted that Congress can by law protect the act of voting, the place where it is done, and the man who votes, from personal violence or intimidation and the election itself from corruption and fraud?

If this be so, and it is not doubted, are such powers annulled because an election for State officers is held at the same time and place? Is it any less important that the election of members of Congress should be the free choice of all the electors because State officers are to be elected at the same time? *Ex parte Siebold,* 100 U. S. 371.

These questions answer themselves; and it is only because the Congress of the United States, through long habit and long years of forbearance, has, in deference and respect to the States, refrained from the exercise of these powers, that they are now doubted.

But when, in the pursuance of a new demand for action, that body, as it did in the cases just enumerated, finds it necessary to make additional laws for the free, the pure, and the safe exercise of this right of voting, they stand upon the same ground and are to be upheld for the same reasons.

It is said that the parties assaulted in these cases are not officers of the United States, and their protection in exercising the right to vote by Congress does not stand on the same ground.

But the distinction is not well taken. The power in either case arises out of the circumstance that the function in which the party is engaged or the right which he is about to exercise is dependent on the laws of the United States.

In both cases it is the duty of that government to see that he may exercise this right freely, and to protect him from violence while so doing, or on account of so doing. This duty does not arise solely from the interest of the party concerned, but from the necessity of the government itself, that its service shall be free from the adverse influence of force and fraud practised on its agents, and that the votes by which its members of Congress and its President are elected shall be the *free* votes of the electors, and the officers thus chosen the free and uncorrupted choice of those who have the right to take part in that choice.

This proposition answers also another objection to the constitutionality of the laws under consideration, namely, that the right to vote for a member of Congress is not dependent upon the Constitution or laws of the United States, but is governed by the law of each State respectively.

If this were conceded, the importance to the general government of having the actual election—the voting for those members—free from force and fraud is not diminished by the circumstance that the qualification of the voter is determined by the law of the State where he votes. It equally affects the government, it is as indispensable to the proper discharge of the great function of legislating for that government, that those who are to control this legislation shall not owe their election to bribery or violence, whether the class of persons who shall vote is determined by the law of the State, or by law of the United States, or by their united result.

But it is not correct to say that the right to vote for a member of Congress does not depend on the Constitution of the United States.

The office, if it be properly called an office, is created by that Constitution and by that alone. It also declares how it shall be filled, namely, by election. Its language is:

The House of Representatives shall be composed of members chosen every second year by the people of the several States, and the electors in each State shall have the qualifications requisite for electors of the most numerous branch of the State legislature. [Article I., Section 2.]

The States in prescribing the qualifications of voters for the most numerous branch of their own legislatures, do not do this with reference to the election for members of Congress. Nor can they prescribe the qualification for voters for those *eo nomine*. They define who are to vote for the popular branch of their own legislature, and the Constitution of the United States says the same persons shall vote for members of Congress in that State. It adopts the qualification thus furnished as the qualification of its own electors for members of Congress.

It is not true, therefore, that electors for members of Congress owe their right to vote to the State law in any sense which makes the exercise of the right to depend exclusively on the law of the State. . . .

The Fifteenth Amendment of the Constitution, by its limitation on the power of the States in the exercise of their right to prescribe the qualifications of voters in their own elections, and by its limitation of the power of the United States over that subject, clearly shows that the right of suffrage was considered to be of supreme importance to the national government, and was not intended to be left within the exclusive control of the States. It is in the following language:

SEC. 1. The right of citizens of the United States to vote shall not be denied or abridged by the United States, or by any State, on account of race, color, or previous condition of servitude.

SEC. 2. The Congress shall have power to enforce this article by appropriate legislation.

While it is quite true, as was said by this court in *United States* v. *Reese,* 92 U.S. 214, that this article gives no affirmative right to the colored man to vote, and is designed primarily to prevent discrimination against him whenever the right to vote may be granted to others, it is easy to see that under some circumstances it may operate as the immediate source of a right to vote. In all cases where the former slave-holding States had not removed from their Constitutions the words "white man" as a qualification for voting, this provision did, in effect, confer on him the right to vote, because, being paramount to the State law, and a part of the State law, it annulled the discriminating word *white,* and thus left him in the enjoyment of the same right as white persons. And such would be the effect of any future constitutional provision of a State which should give the right of voting exclusively to white people, whether they be men or women. *Neal* v. *Delaware,* 103 U. S. 370.

In such cases this fifteenth article of amendment does, *proprio vigore,* substantially confer on the negro the right to vote, and Congress has the power to protect and enforce that right.

In the case of *United States* v. *Reese,* so much relied on by counsel, this court said in regard to the Fifteenth Amendment, that "it has invested the citizens of the United States with a new constitutional right which is within the protecting power of Congress. That right is an exemption from discrimination in the exercise of the elective franchise on account of race, color, or previous condition of servitude." This new constitutional right was mainly designed for citizens of African descent. The principle, however, that the protection of the exercise of this right is within the power of Congress, is as necessary to the right of other citizens to vote as to the colored citizen, and to the right to vote in general as to the right to be protected against discrimination:

The exercise of the right in both instances is guaranteed by the Constitution, and should be kept free and pure by congressional enactments whenever that is necessary.

The reference to cases in this court in which the power of Congress under the first section of the Fourteenth Amendment has been held to relate alone to acts done under State authority, can afford petitioners no aid in the present case. For, while it may be true that acts which are mere invasions of private rights, which acts have no sanction in the statutes of a State, or which are not committed by any one exercising its authority, are not within the scope of that amendment, it is quite a different matter when Congress undertakes to protect the citizen in the exercise of rights conferred by the

Constitution of the United States essential to the healthy organization of the government itself.

It is as essential to the successful working of this government that the great organisms of its executive and legislative branches should be the free choice of the people as that the original form of it should be so. In absolute governments, where the monarch is the source of all power, it is still held to be important that the exercise of that power shall be free from the influence of extraneous violence and internal corruption.

In a republican government, like ours, where political power is reposed in representatives of the entire body of the people, chosen at short intervals by popular elections, the temptations to control these elections by violence and by corruption is a constant source of danger.

Such has been the history of all republics, and, though ours has been comparatively free from both these evils in the past, no lover of his country can shut his eyes to the fear of future danger from both sources.

If the recurrence of such acts as these prisoners stand convicted of are too common in one quarter of the country, and give omen of danger from lawless violence, the free use of money in elections, arising from the vast growth, of recent wealth in other quarters, presents equal cause for anxiety.

If the government of the United States has within its constitutional domain no authority to provide against these evils, if the very sources of power may be poisoned by corruption or controlled by violence and outrage, without legal restraint, then, indeed, is the country in danger, and its best powers, its highest purposes, the hopes which it inspires, and the love which enshrines it, are at the mercy of the combinations of those who respect no right but brute force, on the one hand, and unprincipled corruptionists on the other.

The rule is discharged, and the writ of habaes corpus is denied.

THE FORCE ACT OF 1871

Commentary

The Enforcement Act of 1870 sought to give effect to the right of suffrage established by the Fifteenth Amendment through the machinery of the criminal law. It provided for criminal sanctions against those who interfered with the constitutionally guaranteed right to vote; enforcement of such sanctions was to be left to the traditional processes of the criminal law. The purpose of the so-called Force Act of 1871 was to supplement the 1870 statute by supplying independent enforcement machinery which would affirmatively insure vindication of the right to vote in all congressional elections. The machinery contemplated was to be provided by the appointment of federal officials to supervise the election process in each election district (in cities or towns of over 20,000 inhabitants). In effect, the Force Act provided for the supersession of the normal state electoral process by the federal officers to be appointed under the statute. Such extreme measure was justified by its supporters as necessary to protect Negro suffrage and to prevent election frauds in the actual climate that prevailed in the Reconstruction South. It should, however, be noted that the 1871 statute was not limited in its application to the southern states. On the contrary, as the remarks of John Churchill [R., N.Y.] in the debate extracts which follow show, the law was intended to apply in New York as fully as in the South. In actual fact, among the most striking uses of the election machinery set up by the Force Act were to be those in elections in New York City.

The Force Act of 1871 was introduced in the House by Congressman Churchill. The debate on it was all but perfunctory. The Republican leadership had plainly decided upon its speedy passage, and only one day, February 15, 1871, was devoted to its consideration. Only one amendment, modifying Section 12 to eliminate a provision for military forces to be employed to aid federal election officials, was agreed to, or even considered. In the Senate, too, the debate took only one day. Most of it was devoted to Democratic amendments designed to soften the bill's drastic impact upon state electoral processes (some of which are given for illustrative purposes, in the extracts that follow). The haste with which the Congress acted is shown by the refusal of the majority to accept even amendments correcting obvious misprints in the bill (notably that offered by Senator James Bayard [Dem., Del.]). The votes in both Houses, on party lines, were overwhelmingly in favor of the bill.

In the debates themselves, almost all the time was taken by opponents of the bill; as Senator John Sherman [R., Ohio] put it, "the minority have had the field before them with no one to reply to them." As had been true of the Enforcement Act of 1870, the opposition articulated was based both upon the claim of unconstitutionality and lack of need for so drastic a measure.

Emphasis was placed upon the overriding of the states in a manner never before deemed necessary. As in the case of the other civil rights laws passed in the Reconstruction period, however, the majority had resolved to enact the bill regardless of any objections. In the words of Senator Allen Thurman [Dem., Ohio], "the fiat of caucus has gone forth that this bill is to be passed."

Until recently, we might have considered the Force Act of 1871 as an extreme measure justified, if at all, only by the conditions that prevailed in the Reconstruction South. However, in our own day, too, the Congress has seen fit to provide for a comparable supersession of state by federal authority in the electoral process in the Voting Rights Act passed in 1965. In some ways, indeed, as we shall see, the 1965 statute is even more far-reaching than its 1871 predecessor. Yet the abuses which called forth the 1965 law were not nearly as great as those which existed in the post-Civil War period. Perhaps we can now look with more toleration at the work of the Radical Republicans in the Reconstruction period than would have been possible not too long ago.

THE FORCE ACT
February 28, 1871

Be it enacted by the Senate and House of Representatives of the United States of America in Congress assembled, That section twenty of the "Act to enforce the rights of citizens of the United States to vote in the several States of this Union, and for other purposes," approved May thirty-one, eighteen hundred and seventy, shall be, and hereby is, amended so as to read as follows:

"SEC. 20. *And be it further enacted,* That if, [at] any registration of voters for an election for representative or delegate in the Congress of the United States, any person shall knowingly personate and register, or attempt to register, in the name of any other person, whether living, dead, or fictitious, or fraudulently register, or fraudulently attempt to register, not having a lawful right so to do; or do any unlawful act to secure registration for himself or any other person; or by force, threat, menace, intimidation, bribery, reward, or offer, or promise thereof, or other unlawful means, prevent or hinder any person having a lawful right to register from duly exercising such right; or compel or induce, by any of such means, or other unlawful means, any officer of registration to admit to registration any person not legally entitled thereto, or interfere in any manner with any officer of registration in the discharge of his duties, or by any such means, or other unlawful means, induce any officer of registration to violate or refuse to comply with his duty or any law regulating the same; or if any such officer shall knowingly and wilfully register as a voter any person not entitled to be registered, or refuse to so register any person entitled to be registered: or if any such officer or other person whose duty it is to perform any duty in relation to such registration or election, or to ascertain, announce, or declare the result thereof, or give or make any certificate, document, or evidence in relation thereto, shall knowingly neglect or refuse to perform any duty required by law, or violate any duty imposed by law, or do any act unauthorized by law relating to or affecting such registration or election, or the result thereof, or any certificate, document, or evidence in relation thereto, or if any person shall aid, counsel, procure, or advise any such voter, person, or officer to do any act hereby made a crime, or to omit any act the omission of which is hereby made a crime, every such person shall be deemed guilty of a crime, and shall be liable to prosecution and punishment therefor as provided in section nineteen of said act of May thirty-one, eighteen hundred and seventy, for persons guilty of any of the crimes therein specified: *Provided,* That every registration made under the laws of any State or Territory for any State or other election at which such representative or delegate in Congress shall be chosen, shall be deemed to be a registration within the meaning of this act, notwithstanding the same shall also be made for the purposes of any State, territorial, or municipal election."

SEC. 2. *And be it further enacted.* That whenever in any city or town having upward of twenty thousand inhabitants, there shall be two citizens thereof who, prior to any registration of voters for an election for representative or delegate in the Congress of the United States, or prior to any election at which a representative or delegate in Congress is to be voted for, shall make known, in writing, to the judge of the circuit court of the United States for the circuit wherein such city or town shall be, their desire to have said registration, or said election, or both, guarded and scrutinized, it shall be the duty of the said judge of the circuit court, within not less than ten days prior to said registration, if one there be, or, if no registration be required, within not less than ten days prior to said election, to open the said circuit court at the most convenient point in said circuit. And the said court, when so opened by said judge, shall proceed to appoint and commission, from day to day and from time to time, and under the hand of the said circuit judge, and under the seal of said court, for each election district or voting precinct in each and every such city or town as shall, in the manner herein prescribed, have applied therefor, and to revoke, change, or renew said appointment from time to time, two citizens, residents of said city or town, who shall be of different political parties, and able to read and write the English language, and who shall be known and designated as supervisors of election. And the said circuit court, when opened by the said circuit judge as required herein, shall therefrom and thereafter, and up to and including the day following the day of election, be always open for the transaction of business under this act, and the powers and jurisdiction hereby granted and conferred shall be exercised as well in vacation as in term time; and a judge sitting at chambers shall have the same powers and jurisdiction, including the power of keeping order and of punishing any contempt of his authority, as when sitting in court.

SEC. 3. *And be it further enacted,* That whenever, from sickness, injury, or otherwise, the judge of the circuit court of the United States in any judicial circuit shall be unable to perform and discharge the duties by this act imposed, it shall be his duty, and he is hereby required, to select and to direct and assign to the performance thereof, in his place and stead, such one of the judges of the district courts of the United States within his circuit as he shall deem best; and upon such selection and assignment being made, it shall be lawful for, and shall be the duty of, the district judge so designated to perform and discharge, in the place and stead of the said circuit judge, all the duties, powers, and obligations imposed and conferred upon the said circuit judge by the provisions of this act.

SEC. 4. *And be it further enacted,* That it shall be the duty of the supervisors of election, appointed under this act, and they and each of them are hereby authorized and required, to attend at all times and places fixed for the registration of voters, who, being registered, would be entitled to vote for a representative or delegate in Congress, and to challenge any person offering to register; to attend at all times and places when the names of registered voters may be marked for challenge, and to cause such names registered as they shall deem proper to be so marked; to make, when required, the lists, or either of them, provided for in section thirteen of this act, and verify the same; and upon any occasion, and at any time when in attendance under the provisions of this act, to personally inspect and scrutinize such registry, and for purposes of identification to affix their or his signature to each and every page of the original list, and of each and every copy of any such list of registered voters, at such times, upon each day when any name may or shall be received, entered, or registered, and in such manner as will, in their or his judgment, detect and expose the improper or wrongful removal therefrom, or addition thereto, in any way, of any name or names.

SEC. 5. *And be it further enacted,* That it shall also be the duty of the said supervisors of election, and they, and each of them, are hereby authorized and required, to attend at all times and places for holding elections of representatives or delegates in Congress, and for counting the votes cast at said elections; to challenge any vote offered by any person whose legal qualifications the supervisors, or either of them, shall doubt; to be and remain where the ballot-boxes are kept at all times after the polls are open until each and every vote cast at said time and place shall be counted, the canvass of all votes polled be wholly completed, and the proper and requisite certificates or returns made, whether said certificates or returns be required under any law of the United States, or any State, territorial, or municipal law, and to personally inspect and scrutinize, from time to time, and at all times, on the day of election, the manner in which the voting is done, and the way and method in which the poll-books, registry-lists, and tallies or check-books, whether the same are required by any law of the United States, or any State, territorial, or municipal law, are kept; and to the end that each candidate for the office of representative or delegate in Congress shall obtain the benefit of every vote for him cast, the said supervisors of election are, and each of them is, hereby required, in their or his respective election districts or voting precincts, to personally scrutinize, court, and canvass each and every ballot in their or his election district or voting precinct cast, whatever may be the indorsement on said ballot, or in whatever box it may have been placed or be found; to make and forward to the officer who, in accordance with the provisions of section thirteen of this act, shall have been designated as the chief supervisor of the judicial district in which the city or town wherein they or he shall serve shall be, such certificates and returns of all such ballots as said officer may direct and require, and to attach to the registry list, and any and all copies thereof, and to any certificate, statement, or return, whether the same, or any part or portion thereof, be required by any law of the United States, or of any State, territorial, or municipal law, any statement touching the truth or accuracy of the registry, or the truth or fairness of the election and canvass, which the said supervisors of election, or either of them, may desire to make or attach, or which should properly and honestly be made or attached, in order that the facts may become known, any law of any State or Territory to the contrary notwithstanding.

SEC. 6. *And be it further enacted,* That the better to enable the said supervisors of election to discharge their duties, they are, and each of them is, hereby authorized and directed, in their or his respective election districts or voting precincts, on the day or days of registration, on the day or days when registered voters may be marked to be challenged, and on the day or days of election, to take, occupy, and remain in such position or positions, from time to time, whether before or behind the ballot-boxes, as will, in their judgment, best enable them or him to see each person offering himself for registration or offering to vote, and as will best conduce to their or his scrutinizing the manner in which the registration or voting is being conducted; and at the closing of the polls for the reception of votes, they are, and each of them is, hereby required to place themselves or himself in such position in relation to the ballot-boxes for the purpose of engaging in the work of canvassing the ballots in said boxes contained as will enable them or him to fully perform the duties in respect to such canvass provided in this act, and shall there remain until every duty in respect to such canvass, certificates, returns, and statements shall have been wholly completed, any law of any State or Territory to the contrary notwithstanding.

SEC. 7. *And be it further enacted,* That if any election district or voting precinct in any city, town, or village, for which there shall have been appointed supervisors of election for any election at which a representative or delegate in Congress shall be voted for, the said supervisors of election, or either of them, shall not be allowed to exercise and discharge, fully and freely, and without bribery, solicitation, interference, hinderance, molestation, violence, or threats thereof, on the part of or from any person or persons, each and every of the duties, obligations, and powers conferred upon them by this act and the act hereby amended, it shall be the duty of the supervisors of election, and each of them, to make prompt report, under oath, within ten days after the day of election, to the officer who, in accordance with the provisions of section thirteen of this act, shall have been designated as the chief supervisor of the judicial district in which the city or town wherein they or he served shall be, of the manner and means by which they were, or he was, not so allowed to fully and freely exercise and discharge the duties and obligations required and imposed by this act. And upon receiving any such report, it shall be the duty of the said chief supervisor, acting both in such capacity and officially as a commissioner of the circuit court, to forthwith examine into all the facts thereof; to subpoena and compel the attendance before him of any witnesses; administer oaths and take testimony in respect to the charges made; and prior to the assembling of the Congress for which any such representative or delegate was voted for, to have filed with the clerk of the House of Representatives of the Congress of the United States all the evidence by him taken, all information by him obtained, and all reports to him made.

SEC. 8. *And be it further enacted,* That whenever an election at which representatives or delegates in Congress are to be chosen shall be held in any city or town of twenty thousand inhabitants or upward, the marshal of the United States for the district in which said city or town is situated shall have power, and it shall be his duty, on the application, in writing, of at least two citizens residing in any such city or town, to appoint special deputy marshals, whose duty it shall be, when required as provided in this act, to aid and assist the supervisors of election in the verification of any list of persons made under the provisions of this act, who may have registered, or voted, or either; to attend in each election district or voting precinct at the times and places fixed for the registration of voters, and at all times and places when and where said registration may by law be scrutinized, and the names of registered voters be marked for challenge; and also to attend, at all times for holding such elections, the polls of the election in such district or precinct. And the marshal and his general deputies, and such special deputies, shall have power, and it shall be the duty of such special deputies, to keep the peace, and support and protect the supervisors of elections in the discharge of their duties, preserve order at such places of registration and at such polls, prevent fraudulent registration and fraudulent voting thereat, or fraudulent conduct on the part of any officer of election, and immediately, either at said place of registration or polling-place, or elsewhere, and either before or after registering or voting, to arrest and take into custody, with or without process, any person who shall commit, or attempt or offer to commit, any of the acts or offences prohibited by this act, or the act hereby amended, or who shall commit any offence against the laws of the United States: *Provided,* That no person shall be arrested without process for any offence not committed in the presence of the marshal or his general or special deputies, or either of them, or of the supervisors of election, or either of them, and, for the purposes of arrest or the preservation of the peace, the supervisors of election, and each of them, shall, in the absence of the marshal's deputies, or if required to assist said deputies, have the same duties and powers as deputy marshals: *And provided further,* That no person shall, on the day or days of any such election, be arrested without process for any offence committed on the day or days of registration.

SEC. 9. *And be it further enacted,* That whenever any arrest is made under any provision of this act, the person so arrested shall forthwith be brought before a commissioner, judge, or court of the United States for examination of the offences alleged against him; and such commissioner, judge, or court shall proceed in respect thereto as authorized by law in case of crimes against the United States.

SEC. 10. *And be it further enacted,* That whoever, with or without any authority, power, or process, or pretended authority, power, or process, of any State, territorial, or municipal authority, shall obstruct, hinder, assault, or by bribery, solicitation, or otherwise, interfere with or prevent the supervisors of election, or either of them, or the marshal or his general or special deputies, or either of them, in the performance of any duty required of them, or either of them, or which he or they, or either of them, may be authorized to perform by any law of the United States, whether in the execution of process or otherwise, or shall by any of the means before mentioned hinder or prevent the free attendance and presence at such places of registration or at such polls of election, or full and free access and egress to and from any such place of registration or poll of election, or in going to and from any such place of registration or poll of election, or to and from any room where any such registration or election or canvass of votes, or of making any returns or certificates thereof, may be had, or shall molest, interfere with, remove, or eject from any such place of registration or poll of election, or of canvassing votes cast thereat, or of making returns or certificates thereof, any supervisor of election, the marshal, or his general or special deputies, or either of them, or shall threaten, or attempt, or offer so to do, or shall refuse or neglect to aid and assist any supervisor of election, or the marshal or his general or special deputies, or either of them, in the performance of his or their duties when required by him or them, or either of them, to give such aid and assistance, he shall be guilty of a misdemeanor, and liable to instant arrest without process, and on conviction thereof shall be punished by imprisonment not more than two years, or by fine not more than three thousand dollars, or by both such fine and imprisonment, and shall pay the costs of the prosecution. Whoever shall, during the progress of any verification of any list of the persons who may have registered or voted, and which shall be had or made under any of the provisions of this act, refuse to answer, or refrain from answering, or answering shall knowingly give false information in respect to any inquiry lawfully made, such person shall be liable to arrest and imprisonment as for a misdemeanor, and on conviction thereof shall be punished by imprisonment not to exceed thirty days, or by fine not to exceed one hundred dollars, or by both such fine and imprisonment, and shall pay the costs of the prosecution.

SEC. 11. *And be it further enacted,* That whoever shall be appointed a supervisor of election or a special deputy marshal under the provisions of this act, and shall take the oath of office as such supervisor of election or such special deputy marshal, who shall thereafter neglect or refuse, without good and lawful excuse, to perform and discharge fully the duties, obligations, and requirements of such office until the expiration of the term for which he was appointed, shall not only be subject to removal from office with loss of all pay or emoluments, but shall be guilty of a misdemeanor, and on conviction shall be punished by imprisonment for not less than six months nor more than one year, or by fine not less than two hundred dollars and not exceeding five hundred dollars, or by both fine and imprisonment, and shall pay the costs of prosecution.

SEC. 12. *And be it further enacted,* That the marshal, or his general deputies, or such special deputies as shall be thereto specially empowered by him, in writing, and under his hand and seal, whenever he or his said general deputies or his special deputies, or either or any of them, shall be forcibly resisted in executing their duties under this act, or the act hereby amended, or shall, by violence, threats, or menaces, be prevented from executing such duties, or from arresting any person or persons who shall commit any offence for which said marshal or his general or his special deputies are authorized to make such arrest, are, and each of them is hereby, empowered to summon and call to his or their aid the bystanders or posse comitatus of his district.

SEC. 13. *And be it further enacted,* That it shall be the duty of each of the circuit courts of the United States in and for each judicial circuit, upon the recommendation in writing of the judge thereof, to name and appoint, on or before the first day of May, in the year eighteen hundred and seventy-one, and thereafter as vacancies may from any cause arise, from among the circuit court commissioners in and for each judicial district in each of said judicial circuits, one of such officers, who shall be known for the duties required of him under this act as the chief supervisor of elections of the judicial district in and for which he shall be a commissioner, and shall, so long as faithful and capable, discharge the duties in this act imposed, and whose duty it shall be to prepare and furnish all necessary books, forms, blanks, and instructions for the use and direction of the supervisors of election in the several cities and towns in their respective districts; to receive the applications of all parties for appointment to such positions; and upon the opening, as contemplated in this act, of the circuit court for the judicial circuit in which the commissioner so designated shall act, to present such applications to the judge thereof, and furnish information to said judge in respect to the appointment by the said court of such supervisors of election; to require of the supervisors of election, where necessary, lists of the persons who may register and vote, or either, in their respective election districts or voting precincts, and to cause the names of those upon any such list whose right to register or vote shall be honestly doubted to be verified by proper inquiry and examination at the respective places by them assigned as their residences; and to receive, preserve, and file all oaths of office of said supervisors of election, and of all special deputy marshals appointed under the provisions of this act, and all certificates, returns, reports, and records of every kind and nature contemplated or made requisite under and by the provisions of this act, save where otherwise herein specially directed. And it is hereby made the duty of all United States marshals and commissioners who shall in any judicial district perform any duties under the provisions of this act, or the act hereby amended, relating to, concerning, or affecting the election of representatives or delegates in the Congress of the United States, to, from time to time, and with all due diligence, forward to the chief supervisor in and for their judicial district all complaints, examinations, and records pertaining thereto, and all oaths of office by them administered to any supervisor of election or special deputy marshal, in order that the same may be properly preserved and filed.

SEC. 14. *And be it further enacted,* That there shall be allowed and paid to each chief supervisor, for his services as such officer, the following compensation, apart from and in excess of all fees allowed by law for the performance of any duty as circuit court commissioner: For filing and caring for every return, report, record, document, or other paper required to be filed by him under any of the provisions of this act, ten cents; for affixing a seal to any paper, record, report, or instrument, twenty cents; for entering and indexing the records of his office, fifteen cents per folio; and for arranging and transmitting to Congress, as provided for in section seven of this act, any report, statement, record, return, or examination, for each folio, fifteen cents; and for any copy thereof, or of any paper on file, a like sum. And there shall be allowed and paid to each and every supervisor of election, and each and every special deputy marshal who shall be appointed and shall perform his duty under the provisions of this act, compensation at the rate of five dollars per day for each and every day he shall have actually been on duty, not exceeding ten days. And the fees of the said chief supervisors shall be paid at the treasury of the United States, such accounts to be made out, verified, examined, and certified as in the case of accounts of commissioners, save that the examination or certificate required may be made by either the circuit or district judge.

SEC. 15. *And be it further enacted,* That the jurisdiction of the circuit court of the United States shall extend to all cases in law or equity arising under the provisions of this act or the act hereby amended; and if any person shall receive any injury to his person or property for or on account of any act by him done under any of the provisions of this act or the act hereby amended, he shall be entitled to maintain suit for damages therefor in the circuit court of the United States in the district wherein the party doing the injury may reside or shall be found.

SEC. 16. *And be it further enacted,* That in any case where suit or prosecution, civil or criminal, shall be commenced in a court of any State against any officer of the United States, or other person, for or on account of any act done under the provisions of this act, or under color thereof, or for or on account of any right, authority, or title set up or claimed by such officer or other person under any of said provisions, it shall be lawful for the defendant in such suit or prosecution, at any time before trial, upon a petition to the circuit court of the United States in and for the district in which the defendant shall have been served with process, setting forth the nature of said suit or prosecution, and verifying the said petition by affidavit, together with a certificate signed by an attorney or counsellor at law of some court of record of the State in which such suit shall have been commenced, or of the United States, setting forth that as counsel for the petition [er] he has examined the proceedings against him, and has carefully inquired into all the matters set forth in the petition, and that he believes the same to be true, which petition, affidavit, and certificate shall be presented to the said circuit court, if in session, and, if not, to the clerk thereof at his office, and shall be filed in said office, and the cause shall thereupon be entered on the docket of said court, and shall be thereafter proceeded in as a cause originally commenced in that court; and it shall be the duty of the clerk of said court, if the suit was commenced in the court below by summons, to issue a writ of certiorari to the State court, requiring said court to send to the said circuit court the record and proceedings in said cause; or if it was commenced by capias, he shall issue a writ of habeas corpus cum causa, a duplicate of which said writ shall be delivered to the clerk of the State court, or left at his office by the marshal of the district, or his deputy, or some person duly authorized thereto; and thereupon it shall be the duty of the said State court to stay all further proceedings in such cause, and the said suit or prosecution, upon delivery of such process, or leaving the same as aforesaid, shall be deemed and taken to be moved to the said circuit court, and any further proceedings, trial, or judgment therein in the State court shall be wholly null and void; and any person, whether an attorney or officer of any State court, or otherwise, who shall thereafter take any steps, or in any manner proceed in the State court in any action so removed, shall be guilty of a misdemeanor, and liable to trial and punishment in the court to which the action shall have been removed, and upon conviction thereof shall be punished by imprisonment for not less than six months nor more than one year, or by fine not less than five hundred nor more than one thousand dollars, or by both such fine and imprisonment, and shall in addition thereto be amenable to the said court to which said action shall have been removed as for a contempt; and if the defendant in any such suit be in actual custody on mesne process therein, it shall be the duty of the marshal, by virtue of the writ of habeas corpus cum causa, to take the body of the defendant into his custody, to be dealt with in the said cause according to the rules of law and the order of the circuit court, or of any judge thereof in vacation. And all attachments made and all bail or other security given upon such suit or prosecution shall be and continue in like force and effect as if the same suit or prosecution had proceeded to final judgment and execution in the State court. And if upon the removal of any such suit or prosecution it shall be made to appear to the said circuit court that no copy of the record and proceedings therein in the State court can be obtained, it shall be lawful for said circuit court to allow and require the plaintiff to proceed de novo, and to file a declaration of his cause of action, and the parties may thereupon proceed as in actions originally brought in said circuit court; and on failure of so proceeding judgment of non prosequitur may be rendered against the plaintiff, with costs for the defendant.

SEC. 17. *And be it further enacted,* That in any case in which any party is or may be by law entitled to copies of the record and proceedings in any suit or prosecution in any State court, to be used in any court of the United States, if the clerk of said State court shall, upon demand and the payment or tender of the legal fees, refuse or neglect to deliver to such party certified copies of such record and proceedings, the court of the United States in which such record and proceedings may be needed, on proof by affidavit that the clerk of such State court has refused or neglected to deliver copies thereof on demand as aforesaid, may direct and allow such record to be supplied by affidavit or otherwise, as the circumstances of the case may require and allow; and thereupon such proceeding, trial, and judgment may be had in the said court of the United States, and all such processes awarded, as if certified copies of such records and proceedings had been regularly before the said court; and hereafter in all civil actions in the courts of the United States either party thereto may notice the same for trial.

SEC. 18. *And be it further enacted,* That sections five and six of the act of the Congress of the United States approved July fourteen, eighteen hundred and seventy, and entitled "An act to amend the naturalization laws, and to punish crimes against the same," be, and the same are hereby, repealed; but this repeal shall not affect any proceeding or prosecution now pending for any offence under the said sections, or either of them, or any question which may arise therein respecting the appointment of the persons in said sections, or either of them, provided for, or the powers, duties, or obligations of such persons.

SEC. 19. *And be it further enacted,* That all votes for representatives in Congress shall hereafter be by written or printed ballot, any law of any State to the contrary notwithstanding; and all votes received or recorded contrary to the provisions of this section shall be of none effect.

Approved, February 28, 1871.

THE DEBATE

House of Representatives-41st Congress, 3rd Session
February 15, 1871

The House proceeded to the consideration of the bill (H. R. No. 2634) to amend an act approved May 31, 1870, entitled "An act to enforce the rights of citizens of the United States to vote in the several States of this Union, and for other purposes," reported with amendments by the Committee on the Judiciary. . . .

CHARLES ELDREDGE [DEM., WIS.]. Of all the legislation proposed by this or any other Congress, there is none, in my judgment, more unwarrantable and unjustifiable than that proposed by this bill. It is absolutely atrocious. It has no warrant in the Constitution, and no precedent unless it be in the act to which this is amendatory, in any previous practice of the Government. Aside from that it stands alone, original as it is hideous and revolting. It has not the merit of one redeeming provision or quality. It will bind the several States hand and foot, and deliver them over to the Federal Government subjugated and helpless, the mere tools and slaves of Congress. This bill a law, and the law acquiesced in by the people, the States and all State institutions and laws, so far as rights and powers are concerned, are absolutely overthrown and blotted out. The existence of the States and all their institutions can only be in the name; they cannot act or move except by the permission and will of the Federal power.

Sir, this bill is the crowning act of centralization and consolidation. Stealthily and by somewhat measured step heretofore has been the march of Federal power upon the rights and jurisdiction of States; but this reaches the point and accomplishes State destruction by a single bound, by one grand act. It brushes away at once and finally all State machinery and local authority and substitutes in their place the Federal bayonets. It not only subjugates and subjects all local and State offices and officers to the Federal will, making them the instruments of its execution, loading them with pains, penalties, and forfeitures for its neglect, but makes them criminals for obedience to the laws of the State whose officers they are and to which they are bound by their solemn oaths. It creates a host of new offices before unknown, and fills the land with spies and informers with large pay and emoluments for their filthy work. It establishes and ordains a multitude of crimes heretofore not known to our law. It seeks to overawe free American citizens and control their votes by the menace of the sword and the presence at the voting precinct of the soldier of the Army. It places for ten days at and before the time of elections paid agents, two or more at each voting place; in the interest of the majority of Congress, to "scrutinize," manage, and control the votes of the people, to secure by fair means or foul the continuation in power of a corrupt and radical Congress.

Mr. Speaker, no fair-minded man, no disinterested, unprejudiced man, can read the provisions of this bill without being convinced that it has its origin in the interest of an unscrupulous and desperate party. It bears on its face and in all its provisions the clearest evidence of its origin and purpose, not to secure, but to prevent pure and fair elections, not to aid the voter to express his own unbiased judgment, but to awe him into submission and control him against his conviction. Its very title is a false pretense, if not a lie, adopted for the purpose of defrauding the people and cheating them into the support of a most infamous measure:

An act to enforce the rights of citizens of the United States to vote in the several States of this Union.

The falsity of this title will be perceived by reference to only a few of the provisions of the bill imposing conditions upon and throwing impediments in the way of free suffrage.

In the first place, by the first section of the bill, the Federal Government takes full and absolute possession of the registry of voters provided for by any of the States of the Union. It takes possession and control of all the State officers provided by State laws for the administration of the registry laws of the States. It adopts the registrations made by the States in the following proviso:

That every registration made under the laws of any State or Territory, for any State or other election at which such Representative or Delegate in Congress shall be chosen, shall be deemed to be a registration within the meaning of this act, notwithstanding the same shall also be made for the purposes of any State, territorial, or municipal election.

Notwithstanding this it imposes penalties, and denounces as crimes acts of such officers in conformity with and in obedience to the registry laws of the States.

It provides for the appointment of supervisors to guard and "scrutinize" the registrations and elections, whose duties among others, as provided by the fourth section, are thus defined:

They and each of them are hereby authorized and required to attend at all times and places fixed for the registration of voters, who being registered would be entitled to vote for Representative or Delegate in Congress, and to challenge any person offering to register.

Let it be observed: "required to attend and to challenge any person offering to register." How far this is calculated to enforce the right of citizens of the United States to vote, how far it goes to sustain the truthfulness of the title, I leave for the present to the candid mind to judge.

The bill further requires these tools of party and of the Federal power to attend at all times and places where the names of registered voters may be marked for challenge, and upon any occasion and at any time when so in attendance to personally inspect and scrutinize such registry; and this without regard to and to the exclusion of the officers of the State in charge. By the fifth section of the bill these supervisors are "required" to attend at all times and places for holding elections for Representatives in Congress, and for counting the votes cast, "to challenge any vote offered," to remain with the ballot-box till the last vote is counted, and to themselves count and canvass each and every ballot what ever may be the indorsement on said ballot or in "whatever box it may be found." And these supervisors are authorized and required to make and attach to the returns any statement touching the truth or accuracy of the registry or the truth or fairness of the election, any law of any State notwithstanding.

The sixth section provides that these supervisors shall, on the day or days of registration, on the day or days when registered voters may be marked for challenge, and on the day or days of election, take, occupy, and remain in such position or positions before or behind the ballot-boxes as their judgment may dictate. And when the polls shall be closed they are required to place themselves in such position with reference to the ballot-boxes as they may choose for the purpose of canvassing the votes. All these things may be done without regard for and to the exclusion of the State officers appointed to do the work.

Mr. Speaker, I might stop here. I have shown by the mere statement of these provisions of this bill that the title is an untruth. In view of these provisions alone no sane man can believe this is a bill "to enforce the right of citizens of the United States to vote." It must be seen that it is a bill to prevent, hinder, and delay citizens in voting. It provides a system to drive citizens from the polls, and to disgust all honest men with our elections.

But the worst of it is yet to be considered. And first let me remark that this new and cumbersome machinery is not confined, as some have supposed, to cities having upward of twenty thousand inhabitants. The bill is drawn, I apprehend, to suggest this view, and to divert attention from its true intent and meaning. The language of the bill is: "that whenever, in any city or town having upward of twenty thousand inhabitants," etc. The word "town" must be taken in its popular sense, and will be construed in this bill as synonymous with township.

It will extend to any rural town or township, and every town having a population of twenty thousand will be covered by this provision. These officers then can be appointed in the great majority of the election precincts of the United States. They will swarm over and throughout the length and breadth of the land, and their name will be legion. They will be an electioneering force such as was never before organized in any country on earth; such as no free country can or ever ought to tolerate. But two of these partisan agents in each election district in cities and towns having upward of twenty thousand inhabitants are only a small number of these creatures of the Federal power authorized by this bill, as we shall see when we have looked it through, when we shall consider the other appointments by the United States marshals which will be made and to which there is no limitation.

I said the worst is yet to come. By the eighth section the marshal of the United States is empowered, and it is made his duty, on application of two citizens of any such city or town, to appoint "special deputies" whose duty it shall be to attend at all the times and places specified for the attendance of the supervisors. The pretense of their appointment is to preserve order, keep the peace, and support and protect the supervisors in the discharge of their duties. They are to prevent fraudulent registration and fraudulent voting, or fraudulent conduct on the part of any officer of election, and immediately, either at said registration or polling place or elsewhere, and either before or after registering or voting to arrest and take into custody, with or without process, any person who shall commit, or attempt, or offer to commit any of the acts prohibited by this act or the act hereby amended, or who shall commit any offense against the laws of the United States.

The power to arrest is also conferred upon the supervisors. In addition to all this, the tenth section provides "that whoever, with or without any authority, power, or process of any State, territorial, or municipal authority," shall in any wise "interfere with or prevent the supervisors of elections, or either of them, or the marshal or his general or special deputies, or either of them," in any duty required of them, "or shall molest, interfere with, remove or eject from any such place of registration or poll of election" "any supervisor of election, the marshal, or his general or special deputies," or attempt to offer so to do, or shall refuse or neglect to aid and assist any supervisor of election or the marshal or any of his deputies when required, shall be guilty of a misdemeanor and liable to instant arrest, with or without process, and on conviction thereof shall be punished by imprisonment not less than one year nor more than two years, or by fine not less than $1,000 or more than $3,000, or by both such fine and imprisonment, and shall pay the cost of prosecution.

But to cap the climax of the enormity, to outrage every sense of honor, propriety, and decency, to insult and trample upon all law, and make the liberty of the citizen a delusion and suffrage a pretense and a snare, it is provided by the twelfth section that all these great and little satraps, the supervisors, the marshal and his deputies, may, when they shall see fit, summon to their aid the bystanders, a *posse comitatus*, and require the commanding officer of the nearest United States military or naval forces to enable them to accomplish the purposes of their appointment. Yes, sir; the bill requires it; the biggest fool the marshal shall be able to appoint his deputy will be in command of the Army and Navy of the United States. "And it shall be" (I use the words of the bill) "the duty of such commanding officer upon such requisition being made to obey it without delay." There is no alternative, no discretion, no delay. The highest and lowest military or naval commander must instantly obey the deputy marshals created under this act. The President of the United States, the Commander-in-Chief, must be subject to such order. The voice of Congress is the voice of omnipotence.

It has made the rule, it has established the regulation. President, generals, lieutenant generals, major generals, brigadier generals, and all are subject to the command of the most insignificant deputy marshal of the United States. Was there ever so supremely ridiculous and absurd a proposition? This bill not only places the States, State officers, and all local State authorities, but the United States, all United States officers, civil and military, and all the powers of the Federal Government, under the control and at the disposal of these election officers.

Mr. Speaker, it may perhaps be deemed undignified and small to look into the lesser details of this grand scheme, this grand electioneering scheme, as I look upon it; this scheme for propping up the waning fortunes of the Republican party; but it ought to be understood. It will do no harm to look into and count the cost of this new departure in politics, and see as well as we can about how much of an "elephant" we shall have on our hands.

There is to be in each judicial district one chief supervisor of elections, who is to furnish all necessary books, blanks, forms, etc., and do and perform a great many other duties, with most extravagant fees for his services, the aggregate of which will depend upon the work he will find to do, and which no man can estimate in advance.

As we have already seen, there will be two supervisors of elections in each election precinct in every city and town of upward of twenty thousand inhabitants. The marshal will, in each of these election precincts, appoint at least two special deputies and as many more as he shall see fit. Being a partisan, and anxious to carry the elections in favor of his party, he will of course appoint just as many as the exigencies of the case may seem to require. He is not limited by the act. I estimate, without pretending to entire accuracy, that there will be of supervisors and marshals from forty to fifty thousand throughout the United States. It may be more. These are exclusive of all those who may be pressed into service from among the bystanders at elections. The bill provides that "there shall be allowed and paid to each and every supervisor of elections, and each and every special deputy marshal" compensation "at the rate of five dollars per day" for each and every day he shall "actually have been on duty not exceeding ten days." Here, then, it will be seen is a grand army of electioneers, of tens of thousands of party politicians, and a fund of millions of dollars to be paid from the public Treasury for the work to be performed.

Every one of these supervisors and deputy marshals will receive at least fifty dollars. It is of little account that one of these supervisors is of "different politics" from the other. Scarcely any two men can be found who are not of somewhat different politics; so there will be no difficulty in having them all of one party. And if this be not so, no such thing is required in the selection of the deputy marshals. They will certainly all be on one side, and all ready and willing to do the work of their masters, and may outnumber the supervisors by thousands. There will be but two supervisors in each precinct, whereas there will be of deputy marshals ten, twenty, or any other indefinite number the marshal may be induced to appoint. But enough of the details of this infernal bill. They are sickening in the extreme. The cloven foot of blinded, bigoted party appears in every line. It tells of the consciousness of the party itself that it is doomed, that its hour of dissolution is at hand. It is one of many desperate efforts to avert a fate it long has merited, and which this very measure betokens and will hasten.

Mr. Speaker, I have said this bill is obnoxious to the Consitution. Who will argue that it is not? Who will contend that the Constitution of this great Republic warrants such a measure? Who will admit that the States, the grand, glorious States of this Union, the very pillars upon which the Union is built and by which it is upheld and sustained, are sunk so low; have become so insignificant, as to be trifled with and humiliated and contemned as by this bill? Is there any one in this House or elsewhere to stand up and assert the right of the Federal Government to intermeddle as proposed in the registration of the citizens of the States? Is there a statesman in all the land who will attempt, under our Constitution, to defend the wanton and arbitrary arrests, arrests without complaint and without warrant, provided for by this bill? Is it pretended that our bill of rights is repealed by the "fifteenth amendment?" Has the adoption into our Constitution (even if it were legally and validly done, which I deny) of the declaration that "the right of citizens of the United States to vote shall not be denied or abridged by the United States, or by any State, on account of race, color, or previous condition of servitude," given authority to the United States to arrest any and all citizens without warrant and imprison them without a trial or hearing? In giving the right to vote to the negro have we subjected every citizen of the United States to the indignities and outrages provided for by this bill, in attending the polls for the mere purpose of trying to vote?

By conferring suffrage upon the colored race have we lost the rights our fathers secured to us by the Constitution? In giving freedom to the slaves have we become slaves ourselves? It must be apparent to all that the language of this pretended fifteenth amendment confers no power upon Congress to pass such a measure as this bill. It is at most only a prohibition upon the United States and the States as such—upon them in their legislative capacity, the only capacity in which they can act—prohibiting them from discriminating against any citizen on account of "race, color, or previous condition of servitude." It makes void any act of the United States and the States that should make this discrimination. The power to punish individuals and impose penalties for the violation of law or obedience to State laws must be found if at all in some other provision. . . .

Sir, the proposition and all such propositions are too absurd and preposterous for a candid answer. There is no constitutional warrant for this measure. It is rank usurpation and revolution; it is an insult to every citizen of the Republic; it is hostile in every feature to liberty, and violates every fundamental idea of republican government; it will bring war and bloodshed; it is intended to awe the free men of the States and drive them from the polls. They will not submit without a struggle. There will be many a man, accustomed to cast his vote without hinderance or molestation; many a good and true citizen, faithful, law-abiding, and patriotic, who will feel more like firing a bullet than casting a ballot through the spy and informer paid from the people's Treasury, which this bill places before and behind the ballot-box, to obstruct not facilitate voting. The hypocritical cry of "Let us have peace" will not avail in the face of such measures as this. The people cannot be humiliated much further; they will soon have borne all they can; they will ere long assert their sovereign right and power to be free; and they will teach Congress, too, that its members are the servants not the masters of the people, and that the people have, under our system, the right to govern themselves. . . .

JOHN CHURCHILL [R., N.Y.]. Mr. Speaker, the Government of the United States was founded upon a principle which, although not new in theory to the speculators upon political rights, was certainly new in practice, the principle that government depends upon the will of the governed; in other words, that the will of the majority of the people of any State, when that will can be ascertained, is the proper law of the country. The whole value, the whole moral force of this principle depends, however, upon the question whether or not, after the election shall be held, the people believe that the result of the election, as declared by the authorities who preside over it, expresses truly the wishes of the majority of the people. We have for eighty years submitted quietly to the result of elections on the assumption that this principle has been faithfully observed. Elections have been held for the highest and the lowest officers in the State, and whoever has been declared elected has been obeyed as the rightful officer.

But, Mr. Speaker, for some years past grave doubts have prevailed in different portions of this country as to whether the declared results of elections have truly expressed the will of the people. With regard to officers of States and officers of minor communities this doubt, so far as it exists, is left to be determined, as it can only be determined, by the laws existing in those States or communities. But so far as regards members of the Congress of the United States, although the first legislation in regard to the matter is intrusted by the Constitution of the United States to the States themselves, the power is properly reserved to Congress itself to determine by what rules these elections shall be conducted; and if, in regard to elections held under State laws for national officers, this doubt exists, if in this way the principle of representative government is threatened, then the power is by the Constitution reserved to Congress to determine the manner in which elections shall be held, and thereby to insure that the result, when declared, shall be the real will of the majority of the people.

Mr. Speaker, the bill before the House is intended to do nothing more than to remove the doubts which have arisen as to whether the declared results of elections held in different parts of the country represent truly the will of the majority of the people.

FERNANDO WOOD [DEM., N.Y.]. Just here I would like to ask my colleague one question. Has any doubt been expressed by either of the political parties as to the entire integrity and honesty of the late election in our State? Is it not admitted by the leaders of the Republican party in that State that the election was entirely fair? This being so, how can there be any justification for the passage of this bill at the present time?

MR. CHURCHILL. Mr. Speaker, in answer to the question of my colleague, I will say that under the provisions of the laws which this act is intended to amend and extend we had in the State of New York and in its doubtful districts last fall a fairer election than we have had for years.

Now, Mr. Speaker, in order to show the occasion for this measure, I will send to the Clerk's desk to be read the report of a committee of elections in our own State of New York, upon an election in the city of New York, where two Democrats were contesting the right to a seat in the Assembly, and where there was an opportunity to learn the fraudulent means for carrying elections which could not be had under other circumstances; and as at the election at which this case arose members of Congress were elected as well as members of the Assembly, it will be seen that the frauds which deprived a member of the Assembly of his seat also affected the right to seats upon this floor. . . .

CLARKSON POTTER [DEM., N.Y.]. My colleague yields to me for a question. He has just stated that under the act passed at the last session, the operation of which this bill is intended to enlarge and extend, we had a more honest election in the State of New York than we ever had before. Now I desire to ask my colleague, if that be so, what is the purpose of enlarging and extending the operation of the act of the last session, and whether it be not, under the pretense of securing an honest election, to put obstacles in the way of a fair and full vote?

MR. CHURCHILL. I will answer the question of my colleague. The object of this bill is simply to perfect the bill of last summer and to make it more likely to accomplish the real object which was desired and intended to be accomplished by it; and that is, that while it shall exclude no honest man from the polls and hinder no honest man in his effort to vote, it shall prevent the repetition of such acts and many other acts of offense against the elective franchise as have been detailed. . . .

I desire now to call attention to the features of this bill to show that there is nothing in it, so far as the principle is concerned, which has not already been fully considered both in the House and Senate, and, after such consideration, adopted as the sense of the two Houses of Congress. The first section of this bill, Mr. Speaker, is intended as a substitute for the twentieth section of the act of May 31, 1870, entitled "An act to enforce the rights of citizens of the United States to vote in the several States of this Union, and for other purposes," and simply adds to the misdemeanors which were created by that section. It makes it a misdemeanor knowingly to register a person not entitled to registration and knowingly to exclude from registration a person entitled to registration.

Mr. Speaker, I do not believe that there is a gentleman upon either side of this House who will hesitate for one moment to declare that for an officer of registration to exclude from registration a person he knows is entitled to be registered, or to permit to be registered a person he knows is not entitled to be registered, is a crime, a crime against the Government of the United States, a crime against that principle which lies at the very foundation of our representative institutions. That is the first section, Mr. Speaker.

The sections which follow, from two to seven, are intended to make more precise the duties and the rights of supervisors of elections, officers who are authorized to be appointed by the fifth section of the act passed on the 14th July, 1870, entitled "An act to amend the naturalization laws and to punish crimes against the same." And they do nothing further than simply to define the powers, the rights, and the duties of these officers, in order that they may not only understand themselves what their rights are, but also in order that whoever may desire to interfere with them in the performance of their duties may also know what the rights of these officers are under the laws of the United States.

The sections which follow, eight and nine, are in lieu of section six of the same act to which I last referred, authorizing the appointment of deputy marshals to attend elections in places where it was believed and certified that their attendance might be necessary; to attend those elections for the purpose of protecting the supervisors of elections in the performance of their duties. And they are required to be members of different political parties, so that they may act each as a check upon the other, and that they may secure, as far as possible, by their joint action, this result: that when the election shall be closed and its result declared that declaration shall state truly what the will of the majority of the people voting at that election was. . . .

The tenth section of this bill makes it a misdemeanor that there shall be any improper interference with these supervisors of elections and marshals in the performance of their duties. If it be true that the office which is to be conferred upon these parties is an important one, and one essential to the safety of the Government and its continuance, then certainly it is a crime to interfere with them, and this declaration, that such interference shall be a misdemeanor, is proper.

The twelfth section provides that in case of forcible resistance to the attendance of these parties upon their duties, then the military and naval authority of the United States may be employed for the purpose of preserving the peace.

The thirteenth section creates, it is true, a new officer; to wit, chief supervisors of election, who are to be appointed in each judicial district where it is believed that the necessity for officers of this kind may exist, and whose duty it is to recommend to the circuit judge proper persons to act as supervisors of election, to assist the supervisors, to acquaint them with their duties, to furnish them the blanks which may be necessary in the performance of their duties, and to assist generally in carrying this law into effect.

Now, I do not care to take up any more of the time of the House in the discussion of this bill. As I have stated, the whole principle of the bill has been fully discussed in both branches of Congress and has been accepted by the House, and accepted, I believe, by the sentiment of a great majority of the American people. . . .

JOHN BINGHAM [R., OHIO]. . . . The debate to-day has taken so wide a range that it would be utterly impossible for any man, within the time alloted me, to even refer intelligibly to all that has been said by way of objection to this bill. I shall have accomplished my purpose if I shall succeed in putting the House in possession of the views which I entertain in regard to the constitutionality of this bill and the necessity for its enactment.

Gentlemen have asked here where is your authority to make this legislation? That question was answered in the beginning by the commanding minds of the Republic who had more to do with framing that admirable system of civil polity known as the Constitution of the United States than any other. I refer to those great minds of the Constitutional Convention, Alexander Hamilton and James Madison.

In reference to the meaning of this provision in the original text of the Constitution, "the Congress shall have power to make or to alter such regulations" fixing the time, place, and manner of holding elections for Representatives in Congress, each of them notified the country that without it the system would be defective; that without it the national Government would be at the mercy of the States; that without it it would be in the power of the States, acting separately and without violence, to demolish the national Government. I cannot make their words stronger by any words of mine. . . . Mr. Speaker, those last words constitute a key to this whole controversy. Your Constitution would have been only a glittering bauble if it had not conferred, as it did confer, upon the national Legislature the power of self-preservation. Why, sir, who does not know that the power of the nation is the national power to legislate? Who does not know that those who are to exercise the legislative power can only be chosen by the people in organized States? Who does not know that if the State Legislature should choose to incumber the exercise of this power with inconvenient or impossible conditions, and if the national Congress had not the power to overrule or alter such conditions, the nation would perish? How could the Republic live one hour without the legislative department, through which and by which the people may exercise the power to make law for their protection?

Mr. Speaker, I esteem as highly as any gentleman on this floor the rights of the people to their local State governments. While I intend here and now, at all times and everywhere, according to the measure of my strength, to vindicate those rights in their just extent, I beg leave to say that I esteem as well the national power to correct the abuses of State legislation and to secure and enforce by the silent operation of law the equal rights of all the people of the United States.

Mr. Speaker, the people of this country learned wisdom in that terrible ordeal through which they passed during the four years of our strange, unmatched, and unnatural rebellion. There was not a thoughtful man in the country who did not learn from that terrible trial the weakness of the Constitution. Thus instructed, men did gird themselves to the work of providing against that weakness by the Constitution in the future by incorporating into the text of the instrument the power of the national Congress to correct and restrain by law the abuses of State authority. It is written there so plainly that no man can mistake the effect and strength of the amendment. The words are "No State shall make or enforce any law which shall abridge the immunities and privileges of citizens of the United States," "and the Congress shall have power by appropriative legislation to enforce" the amendment.

The very first article of your Constitution, sir, provides that the people of the several States shall every two years choose Representatives to Congress. According to the whole number of representative population in each this representation is to be apportioned. The additional amendment to the Constitution is, that citizens of the United States hereafter, having like qualifications of age, residence, sex, property, etc., shall, without regard to race, color, or previous condition of servitude, have the equal right to vote as citizens of the United States in the several States of this Union. Surely that secures the equal right to vote to all citizens resident in each State, without distinction of race, color, or previous condition of servitude, who have the other qualifications required by the State for Representatives in Congress. This amendment having become part of the Constitution, the act to which the bill now pending is amendatory, approved on the 31st day of last May, by its first section, for the first time in our history, declares this equal right to the ballot among citizens of the United States having equal qualifications, without regard to race, color, or previous condition of servitude, in the several States of this Union. Chiefly, sir, to make good this provision of the Constitution, chiefly to secure the equal right on the part of citizens in other respects qualified, the act of the 31st of May was passed.

Here we are to-day, Mr. Speaker, engaged in the unseemly spectacle of wild and angry debate, in which the spirit of party seems stronger than the spirit of patriotism. It is true, sir, the question in controversy is, shall we, by good and just legislation, enforce this inestimable right of the equal enjoyment on the part of citizens of the United States to vote as guaranteed by our amended Constitution? That is the whole of this quarrel, sir. . . .

Mr. Speaker, the other objection is raised here that officers charged with the performance of a very important duty, to wit, to secure to the feeble, the aged, and infirm an equal right with the strong and influential at the ballot-box, when they go to choose Representatives in Congress, shall, in case they are forcibly resisted in the discharge of this duty, be permitted to call upon the *posse comitatus* to aid them. In order to do what? In order to secure by the presence of the people a decent respect to their own laws and silence the cry of violence and force.

Mr. Speaker, this public opinion, which manifests itself by the silent uprising of the people in obedience to the express letter of their own law is mightier than arms. It is because from the beginning it has been the custom and right of the people to incorporate just such language in their legislation that it finds place in this twelfth section of this bill. The provision is: if the officer charged with the duty prescribed shall be forcibly resisted in the execution thereof he shall summon to his aid the people themselves. When the people come in their might for the vindication of their own rightful authority, the voice of the mob is hushed into silence; the law speaks and is obeyed. That is, we are told, oppressive and wrong! As obedience to law is the duty of all, its enforcement, if need be, is surely a right of the people. . . .

The residue of this bill in its main features has received the sanction and the very strong vote of both branches of Congress. This is only a change in detail of what is already on the statute-book, save and except the last section of the bill, which declares that hereafter in all elections for Representatives of Congress the vote shall be by ballot, written or printed, anything in the law of any State to the contrary notwithstanding, and that the votes given or recorded contrary to the provisions of this section shall be of none effect.

The power thus to regulate is given to Congress by the provision of the Constitution to which I referred before, which declares that Congress shall have power to alter the State regulations as to the manner of holding elections for Congress. It is so interpreted by the argument of Madison, from which I read. He declared in that argument expressly that it was deemed important to vest this power in the Congress of the United States, whether the vote should be *viva voce* or by ballot. . . .

SAMUEL COX [DEM., N.Y.]. I would like to ask my friend, when he seeks to make uniformity as to suffrage in this country, what sort of provision he would make for Rhode Island, for instance, where there is a real estate qualification of $134 over and above all incumbrances; or with reference to Massachusetts, where the ability to read and write is a qualification? I would ask him, Mr. Speaker—

MR. BINGHAM. That is all the gentleman needs to say on that subject. I am speaking, Mr. Speaker, upon another and different subject. The qualification of electors and the manner of holding or conducting elections are as distinct from each other as light and darkness. . . . Mr. Speaker, it did not occur to the gentleman from New York [Mr. Cox] when he asked his question that the qualifications of the elector and the manner of holding or conducting an

election are very different things. The State prescribes the qualifications of
the electors, subject to the limitation of the Constitution which I cited at the
outset, and subject, if you choose, to the other general limitation that
Congress shall guaranty a republican form of government. But the manner of
exercising this power by the elector in the choice of Representatives to
Congress is the very power conferred by the Constitution upon Congress, and
which the framers of the Constitution deemed essential to the security and
the stability of the national Government. That, sir, is the power we are
asserting here to-day.

We do not make registration laws by this bill. We provide, however, in
order that there may be no abuse, no corruption, no fraud on the part of the
State officials in the execution of the registration law, that there shall be at
the registration of electors for Representatives to Congress Federal officers,
chosen from the opposing parties, and who shall also participate in conducting the election, simply to the end that there may be fair play and the
enjoyment of equal rights under the laws of the State. That is prescribing the
manner simply in which the election shall be conducted.

The object of the bill is very manifest, and in my judgment just as it is
manifest. It is to prevent, under the law and by virtue of the law, any
violation of the rights of the citizen by fraud or corruption on the part of any
one to whom is intrusted the conduct of the election or the registration of
voters. . . .

I am speaking of the means provided by this bill to secure an equal right
to be registered and vote, where that right is acknowledged both by the
national Constitution and the State law. I am speaking also of the other
provision of this bill which secures an honest acknowledgment of the clearly
expressed will of the qualified electors at the election of Representatives in
Congress. I am speaking of the wholesome provisions of this law, in short,
which by wise and just enactments put an end, I hope for ever in the future,
to fraud and bribery and intimidation and corruption on the part of officials
or hired interveners, when the people assemble to elect their Representatives
in Congress.

As gentlemen choose to talk about an appeal on this question from our
action to the people, I choose to strike hands with them and go to the people
on the question, shall we have guarded and sheltered by national law
hereafter the rights of the people at elections, their equal rights as secured by
the national and the State Constitutions in the choice of national Representatives, and shall we have the will of the people carried out after it is so
declared at the ballot-box by a fair count and fair return? I have no doubt,
Mr. Speaker, how that issue will terminate. Gentlemen have taken upon
themselves the role of prophets, and have undertaken to tell us what sort of a
fate awaits us if we dare to adopt the proposed legislation to protect the
ballot-box against bribery and fraud and perjury, and to protect each citizen
in his equal right with every other citizen to vote, free of undue restraint or

nenace or intimidation, for national Representatives. I believe, sir, that the people are equal to the task of first requiring the enactment of just such laws here, and of sustaining them elsewhere, at the ballot-box, by their suffrages.

I am willing that the issue shall be made up, and let the people speak upon this question. The bill interferes with no reserved rights of the States. If the States do not choose to hold their elections on the same day for mere State officials, be it so; but with regard to the vote for Representatives in Congress, I take it that the great majority of the people of every State in the Union will admit that the nation has a right to be represented at every election for Congress by its own law and by its own officials as well as the State. I have given the words, the thoughtful words of the makers of the Constitution in support of that right. No law of any State by this bill is in any manner wrongfully impaired. . . .

Senate-41st Congress, 3rd Session
February 24, 1871

GEORGE VICKERS [DEM., MD.]. Mr. President, this bill seems to be the offspring of a bill passed at the last session of Congress with the specious title of an act to enforce the right of citizens of the United States to vote in the several States of the Union, and for other purposes. The effect if not the object of the bill of the last session was to intimidate and overawe the free citizens of the United States who were entitled to the right of suffrage; but the people were so prudent, forbearing, and discreet, that no disturbance was created, and therefore no pretext furnished for an attempted interference with the freedom of elections or to set aside the elections which were held in the States.

Thus the bill failed of its effect; the results of the elections were not such as the farmers of the bill contemplated when they introduced and passed it in Congress. It became necessary therefore to bring forward the present bill to strengthen the weaknesses of the bill of last session and to supply additional and stringent measures in reference to future elections to be held in the States. Both bills are obnoxious to constitutional objections; they are bills inexpedient, unjust, and unfit to be executed in the States. . . .

It will be seen that the qualification of electors or voters is to be ascertained and fixed by the States, independent of any action or control of the Federal Government. The power to prescribe these qualifications is inherent in the States, and is to be exercised in perfect independence of Congress.

The fifteenth amendment comes in as a proviso or addendum to the power originally reserved to the States, and says that in fixing the qualifications for voters the States must not discriminate among the people on account of race, color, or previous condition of servitude. The States have the constitutional power to-day to prescribe any condition to the right to vote, except as to race or color and former condition of the person. They may prescribe as qualifications for voters for the house of delegates, or representatives to the popular branch of the State Legislature, education, and define the branches and extent of it; also a property qualification; also that a voter shall have been a citizen of the State for five, ten, or any number of years, looking back beyond your fifteenth amendment. Age and residence are completely in their province to declare. When these qualifications are fixed by the States according to their taste and pleasure, limited only by race or color, as alluded to, the voters for members of Congress are made by the Constitution to conform to those fixed and regulated by the States. It will be seen that the primary and essential power is in the States. The General Government in this respect is secondary, and made to accept and adopt the action and legislation of the States in reference to this important matter of the qualification of voters. . . .

Congress now proposes, not to legislate for the election of members of Congress separately and distinctly from the State elections, which, if they have any power to legislate at all on the subject, is the only mode in which that power can be exercised, but to permit the State laws to be in force which regulate the time, places, and manner of holding elections, Congress does not now propose to change the time, or the place, or the manner, but it proposes to interfere with elections to be conducted under State authority.

But what semblance of right has Congress to pass this bill? It is claimed under the fifteenth amendment. . . .

It declares that the right to vote shall not be denied or abridged by any State. Has any State attempted by her legislation to deny, abridge, or impair, in any sense, the right of any one to vote? No State has done so, or essayed to do so; on the contrary, every State has furnished facilities to voters to enable them to exercise their suffrage. Elections have been held in all the States, and the free exercise of the elective franchise has been freely enjoyed by all. The States have modified their registration and election laws in conformity to the fifteenth amendment by striking out the word "white." But the only restriction upon a State is that by her legislation she shall not deny this privilege of franchise on account of race, color, or previous condition of servitude. She may virtually deny it, by prescribing educational or property qualification, or residence or citizenship for a period of time, or any other, except that of race or color.

This restriction or denial is to be done by State authority; by the legislative power of the State in the form of law. It is only after State action denying or abridging the right to vote that the second clause of the fifteenth amendment can be exercised by Congress, namely: Congress shall have the power to enforce this provision by appropriate legislation.

This last power only springs into action from the exercise of power by a State. It is latent, and must forever remain so, in a constitutional sense, until it is warmed into activity and energy by State authority.

It exists only conditionally, contingently. It is not an isolated, independent power, to be exercised at will; but it is a subsidary, secondary, inferior power, to be used in reference to the condition or contingency which is annexed to the principal power.

This secondary or contingent power, when called into action, must be used only to the extent of securing the elective franchise to such persons as may have been deprived of it by a State on account of race, color, or previous condition of servitude.

This power cannot mount higher than its principal; the accessory cannot do more than that principal; the stream cannot rise higher than the fountain. . . .

But what is proposed by this bill? You propose to send United States marshals to superintend State registrations and elections held and regulated by State laws. You propose to make them spies and informers upon State officers and authorities. You propose to prescribe the manner in which these State officers shall perform their duties, and to punish any one by fine and imprisonment who violates a law of a State. You assume the right to write upon and identify the books and papers of judges and registration officers; to challenge persons offering to register; to mark upon the book such challenges; to challenge voters at elections; to inspect and scrutinize at all times during the election the manner in which the voting is done and poll-books kept; to scrutinize, count, and canvass each and every ballot; to remain before and behind the ballot-boxes; to have appointed marshals, deputy marshals, and special deputies without number, and in their discretion, before or after registration or voting, to arrest and take into custody, with or without process, any person who shall in their judgment commit any offense under this act. It punishes any one who, by authority of any sovereign State, shall obstruct these high functionaries of the Federal Government in performing their duties as they may choose to understand them; and any who shall not in humble submission get out of the way in their "full and free access and egress to and from any such place of registration or poll of election;" and also punishes any one "who shall refuse to aid and assist any supervisor of election, or the marshal, or his general or special deputies, or either of them, in the performance of his or their duties, when required by him or them;" and shall be subject to immediate arrest without process, and on conviction to be punished by imprisonment not less than one nor more than two years, or by fine not less than $1,000 nor more than $3,000, or by both fine and imprisonment, and to pay the costs of prosecution! Every special deputy is to be paid five dollars per day; and in case any citizen shall sue any of these high dignitaries in any of the State courts for assault and battery, or false imprisonment, or if any grand jury shall indict any such Federal officer or deputy for an offense against the peace and order of the State, the defendant at his mere will and pleasure, without an affidavit, can put all the State courts at defiance, and remove his case to a United States court, distant from the scene of outrage and oppression, and in which the jury is to be selected by a partisan officer in full sympathy and accord with these supervisors, deputies, and special deputies, and overseers of State elections. Did any bill ever before presented to an American Congress contain such a catalogue of oppressions and enormities as that under consideration? The alien and sedition laws of the elder Adams were mild and benignant compared with the provisions of this bill. They were intended as aids to prop a failing Administration; these, to perpetuate party ascendency under the guise of a disposition to prevent or punish frauds. The first proved to be a lever to overthrow those whom they were intended to subserve; the latter will contribute much to the discomfiture and destruction of a party which, for partisan ends, will inflict so many and such dangerous wounds upon the Constitution of the country and the liberties of the people. . . .

But what right has Congress to interfere with the registration of voters? What clause of the Constitution gives them the right? The States have the exclusive power to judge of and fix the qualifications of voters; not denying or abridging the right by reason of race, color, or previous condition of servitude. The States are to fix the age and residence. The "manner" of conducting an election refers to a different subject. . . .

ALLEN THURMAN [DEM., OHIO]. I move to amend the bill by striking out all of the first section after the enacting clause.

Mr. President, this section is a bill of pains and penalties. It is a section that imposes punishment for what are defined in it as offenses. It is a section that punishes officers of registration for a failure to perform their duty, for malfeasance in the performance of their duty, and other persons not officers, for depriving any one of the right to register, or for procuring any one fraudulently to register, and also any one who shall fraudulently register as a voter.

Now, Mr. President, there is scarcely an offense in this section that is not punishable under the laws of the States. Mark it: this bill provides for no registration; no law of Congress provides for any registration. The only registration in this country is under State laws. There is no other registration known to the laws of this land; and the laws of the State that provide for registration provide for punishing exactly this class of offenses which is provided for in this section.

What, then, is the consequence of passing this section? It is simply to punish a man twice for the same offense. It is to punish him first under State authority, and next to punish him under the authority of the United States. It is to make him pay the penalty of his offense twice, once under indictment in the State courts and then again under an indictment in the Federal courts. . . .

Here is a provision for registration. Does registration belong to Congress? There is no congressional registration act. Registration is left to the States entirely. Registration is for the purpose of determining who are electors, not simply of Representatives or Delegates to Congress, but also of State, county, city, and township officers. It is a State statute that provides for registration; and the same State statute provides the punishment for those who shall be guilty of fraudulent registration or obstructing registration. That subject, all admit, is within the jurisdiction of the States. This very bill admits that it is within the jurisdiction of the States. It is a State law that is made upon the subject, over a subject within the jurisdiction of the State, over a subject that is not given to Congress at all; for there is no man who will dare to say that there is one word in the Constitution of the United States which authorizes Congress to pass a law for registration. This subject of registration is wholly within State jurisdiction. Congress has no more power to pass a bill for the registration of voters in the States than it has to pass such a bill for the registration of voters in France. It is a subject wholly within the jurisdiction of the States; and in respect to this subject the States have passed their laws and inflicted their penalties upon those who offend against them; and now this Congress asserts that it has power to inflict double punishment upon the man who violates those State laws over which Congress has no jurisdiction whatever.

Mr. President, it is mournful to think what all this is. I know it is only another step in that march toward the centralization of all power in the Federal Government. I know it is only another step toward the annihilation of the States. I know that the Senator from the greatest State in the Union, one of the largest in territory and greatest in population and the greatest in wealth, is the first one to lay down his State at the feet of Federal power and annihilate it from our system. Ah, sir, that was not the spirit of New York in the olden time. That was not the spirit of New York when the Federal Constitution was framed. Not then was she so debased, not then was she so humble that she could crawl in the dust and be trodden under foot and see her own citizens punished twice for a violation of her own State law. No, no; the State of the Livingstons, of the Schuylers, of the Morrises; of the Hamiltons, did not then lay down her proud escutcheon in the dust to be walked and trampled down whenever a mere partisan majority in the Congress of the United States should see fit to trample upon her.

Here is the subject of registration over which Congress has no more power than it has over elections in France. You have power to regulate the time and manner of electing members of Congress. That the Constitution has given you. That does not affect the question of registration at all. Over that subject the States are supreme. That subject belongs to them alone. . . .

JOHN SHERMAN [R., OHIO]. In reply to that suggestion, let me now, with great kindness and a desire to promote a speedy adjournment tonight, make a single remark. It is manifest to the Senator that the majority of this body are not inclined to make the agreement. They are satisfied of their power to pass the bill, their right to pass it, and that it is their duty to pass it to secure fair elections in cities containing twenty thousand inhabitants. No speech will be made on this side. That is manifest already.

The minority have rights. They have the right undoubtedly to make their objections to this bill, to make them in the most complete manner, to present them as fully as they think proper. But it seems to me, after they have done that, considering the enormous labor that we have to pass through until the end of this session, they ought to be satisfied, especially as they have had the field before them with no one to reply to them. We are all actuated by a sense of duty in the course that we pursue. . . .

ROSCOE CONKLING [R., N.Y.]. *De minimis non cura lex.* . . .

MR. THURMAN. I wish to make one remark. The Senator from Delaware called the attention of the Senate to the fact that there is an omission of a word necessary to the sense in one part of this bill; I do not know what section it is. I have heard it suggested that that is a mere clerical error which may be corrected by the Committee on Enrollment. I wish to enter my protest against any such doctrine. The most that any Committee on Enrollment can do is to correct bad spelling. That they may do; but I deny the power of any Committee on Enrollment to supply any word whatsoever.

THE VICE PRESIDENT. The Chair coincides with the Senator from Ohio; but the Chair will remind him, familiar with the Statutes-at Large as he is, that by usage, not by law, the Secretary of State supplies words necessary to make the text complete.

MR. THURMAN. I know how the Secretary of State does that, in brackets, to signify that they are not in the bill as it passed. I understand the custom perfectly.

THE VICE PRESIDENT. The enrolling clerk has no authority to do it.

MR. THURMAN. The enrolling clerk has no authority to supply anything, and the enrolling committee has no authority to supply anything. The Secretary of State has nothing but the original roll, and in giving a copy to the printer he may put in brackets the omitted words. That is a mere suggestion. He puts them in brackets, which shows that they are not in the original bill. . . .

THE DECISION

Commentary

As already pointed out, the Force Act of 1871 provided for the supersession of the normal state electoral process by federal officers to be appointed under the statute. Though doubtless extreme, such measure was ruled within the congressional power to enforce the Fourteenth Amendment in *Ex parte Siebold,* 100 U.S. 371 (1880). Petitioners there were state election officials who had been convicted of preventing federal supervisors of election, appointed under the 1871 statute, from performing their duties. They applied for habeas corpus, contending that the 1871 law was invalid. Such contention was rejected in a strong opinion by Justice Joseph P. Bradley. The congressional power to pass laws to regulate congressional elections and for securing the purity thereof and the rights of citizens to vote therein peaceably and without molestation was categorically affirmed. The Court's language was so far reaching as to put to rest doubts about the congressional authority to protect the voting process—if need be, by setting up its own electoral machinery to supplement or displace that of the states. The full implications of such authority are to be seen in the 1965 Voting Rights Act and the Supreme Court decision *South Carolina* v. *Katzenback,* 383 U. S. 301 (1966).

EX PARTE SIEBOLD,
100 U.S. 371 (1880)

MR. JUSTICE BRADLEY delivered the opinion of the Court.

The petitioners in this case, Albert Siebold, Walter Tucker, Martin C. Burns, Lewis Coleman, and Henry Bowers, were judges of election at different voting precincts in the city of Baltimore, at the election held in that city, and in the State of Maryland, on the fifth day of November, 1878, at which representatives to the Forty-sixth Congress were voted for.

At the November Term of the Circuit Court of the United States for the District of Maryland, an indictment against each of the petitioners was found in said court, for offences alleged to have been committed by them respectively at their respective precincts whilst being such judges of election; upon which indictments they were severally tried, convicted, and sentenced by said court to fine and imprisonment. They now apply to this court for a writ of *habeas corpus* to be relieved from imprisonment. . . .

The indictments commence with an introductory statement that, on the 5th of November, 1878, at the Fourth [or other] Congressional District of the State of Maryland, a lawful election was held, whereat a representative for that congressional district in the Forty-sixth Congress of the United States was voted for; that a certain person [naming him] was then and there a supervisor of election of the United States, duly appointed by the Circuit Court aforesaid, pursuant to sect. 2012 of the Revised Statutes, for the third [or other] voting precinct of the fifteenth [or other] ward of the city of Baltimore, in the said congressional district, for and in respect of the election aforesaid, thereat; that a certain person [naming him] was then and there a special deputy marshal of the United States, duly appointed by the United States marshal for the Maryland district, pursuant to sect. 2021 of the Revised Statutes, and assigned for such duty as is provided by that and the following section, to the said precinct of said ward of said city, at the congressional election aforesaid, thereat. Then come the various counts.

The petitioner, Bowers, was convicted on the second count of the indictment against him, which was as follows:

"That the said Henry Bowers, afterwards, to wit, on the day and year aforesaid, at the said voting precinct within the district aforesaid, unlawfully did obstruct, hinder, and, by the use of his power and authority as such judge as aforesaid (which judge he then and there was), interfere with and prevent the *said supervisor of election* in the performance of a certain duty in respect to said election required of him, and which he was then and there authorized to perform by the law of the United States, in such case made and provided, to wit, that of personally inspecting and scrutinizing, at the beginning of said day of election, and of the said election, the manner in which the voting was done at the said poll of election, by examining and seeing whether the ballot first voted at said poll of election was put and placed in a ballot-box containing no ballots whatever, contrary to sect. 5522 of said statutes, and against the peace, government, and dignity of the United States."

Tucker, who was indicted jointly with one Gude, was convicted upon the second and fifth counts of the indictment against them, which were as follows:

"2. That the said Justus J. Gude and the said Walter Tucker afterwards, to wit, on the day and year aforesaid, at the said voting precinct of said ward of said city, unlawfully and by exercise of their power and authority as such judges as aforesaid, did prevent and hinder the free attendance and presence of the said James N. Schofield (who was *then and there such deputy marshal* as aforesaid, in the due execution of his said office), at the poll of said election of and for the said voting precinct, and the full and free access of the same deputy marshal to the same poll of election, contrary to the said last-mentioned section of said statutes (sect. 5522), and against the peace, government, and dignity of the United States.

"5. That the said Justus J. Gude and said Walter Tucker, on the day and year aforesaid, at the precinct aforesaid, within the district aforesaid (they being then and there such officers of said election as aforesaid), knowingly and unlawfully at the said election did a certain act, not then and there authorized by any law of the State of Maryland, and not authorized then and there by any law of the United States, by then and there fraudulently and clandestinely putting and placing in the ballot-box of the said precinct twenty (and more) ballots (within the intent and meaning of sect. 5514 of said statutes), which had not been voted at said election in said precinct before the ballots, then and there lawfully deposited in the same ballot-box, had been counted, with intent thereby to affect said election and the result thereof, contrary to sect. 5515 of said statutes, and against the peace, government, and dignity of the United States."

This charge, it will be observed, is for the offence commonly known as "stuffing the ballot-box." . . .

The sections of the law on which these indictments are founded, and the validity of which is sought to be impeached for unconstitutionality, are summed up by the counsel of the petitioners in their brief as follows (omitting the comments thereon):

The counsel say:

"These cases involve the question of the constitutionality of certain sections of title xxvi. of the Revised Statutes, entitled 'The Elective Franchise.'

"SEC. 2011. The judge of the Circuit Court of the United States, wherein any city or town having upwards of twenty thousand inhabitants is situated, upon being informed by two citizens thereof, prior to any registration of voters for, or any election at which a representative or delegate in Congress is to be voted for, that it is their desire to have *such registration or election guarded and scrutinized*, shall open the Circuit Court at the most convenient point in the circuit.

"SEC. 2012. The judge shall appoint two supervisors of election for every election district in such city or town.

"SEC. 2016. The supervisors are authorized and required to attend all times and places fixed for registration of voters to challenge such as they deem proper; to cause such names to be registered as they may think proper to be so marked; to inspect and scrutinize such register of voters; and for purposes of identification to affix their signatures to each page of the original list.

"SEC. 2017. The supervisors are required to attend the times and places for holding elections of representatives or delegates in Congress, and of counting the votes cast; to challenge any vote the legality of which they may doubt; to be present continually where the ballot-boxes are kept, until every vote cast has been counted, and the proper returns made, required under any law of the United States, or any State, territorial, or municipal law; and to personally inspect and scrutinize at any and all times, on the day of election, the manner in which the poll-books, registry lists, and tallies are kept; whether the same are required by any law of the United States, or any State, territorial, or municipal laws.

"SEC. 2021. requires the marshal, whenever any election at which representatives or delegates in Congress are to be chosen, upon application by two citizens in cities or towns of more than twenty thousand inhabitants, to appoint special deputy marshals, whose duty it shall be to aid and assist the supervisors in the discharge of their duties, and attend with them at all registrations of voters or election at which representatives to Congress may be voted for.

"SEC. 2022. requires the marshal, and his general and special deputies, to keep the peace and protect the supervisors in the discharge of their duties; preserve order at such place of registration and at such polls; prevent fraudulent registration and voting, or fraudulent conduct on the part of any officer of election, and immediately to arrest any person who commits, or attempts to commit, any of the offences prohibited herein, or any offence against the laws of the United States."

The counsel then refer to and summarize sects. 5514, 5515, and 5522 of the Revised Statutes. Sect. 5514 merely relates to a question of evidence, and need not be copied. Sects. 5515 and 5522, being those upon which the indictments are directly framed, are proper to be set out in full. They are as follows:

"SEC. 5515. Every officer of an election at which any representative or delegate in Congress is voted for, whether such officer of election be appointed or created by or under any law or authority of the United States, or by or under any State, territorial, district, or municipal law or authority, who neglects or refuses to perform any duty in regard to such election required of him by any law of the United States, or of any State or Territory thereof, or who violates any duty so imposed; or who knowingly does any acts thereby unauthorized, with intent to affect any such election, or the result thereof; or who fraudulently makes any false certificate of the result of such election in regard to such representative or delegate; or who withholds, conceals, or destroys any certificate of record so required by law respecting the election of any such representative or delegate; or who neglects or refuses to make and return such certificate as required by law; or who aids, counsels, procures, or advises any voter, person, or officer to do any act by this or any of the preceding sections made a crime, or to omit to do any duty the omission of which is by this or any of such sections made a crime, or attempts to do so, shall be punished as prescribed in sect. 5511."

"SEC. 5522. Every person, whether with or without any authority, power, or process, or pretended authority, power, or process, of any State, Territory, or municipality, who obstructs, hinders, assaults, or by bribes, solicitation, or otherwise, interferes with or prevents the supervisors of election, or either of them, or the marshal or his general or special deputies, or either of them, in the performance of any duty required of them, or either of them, or which he or they, or either of them, may be authorized to perform by any law of the United States, in the execution of process or otherwise, or who, by any of the means before mentioned, hinders or prevents the free attendance and presence at such places of registration, or at such polls of election, or full and free access and egress to and from any such place of registration or poll of election, or in going to and from any such place of registration or poll of election, or to and from any room where any such registration or election or canvass of votes, or of making any returns or certificates thereof, may be had, or who molests, interferes with, removes, or ejects from any such place of registration or poll of election, or of canvassing votes cast thereat, or of making returns or certificates thereof, any supervisor of election, the marshal, or his general or special deputies, or either of them; or who threatens, or attempts, or offers so to do, or refuses or neglects to aid and assist any supervisor of election, or the marshal or his general or special deputies, or either of them, in the performance of his or their duties, when required by him or them, or either of them, to give such aid and assistance, shall be liable to instant arrest without process, and shall be punished by imprisonment not more than two years, or by a fine of not more than $3,000, or by both such fine and imprisonment, and shall pay the cost of the prosecution."

These portions of the Revised Statutes are taken from the act commonly known as the Enforcement Act, approved May 31, 1870, and entitled "An Act to enforce the right of citizens of the United States to vote in the several States of this Union, and for other purposes;" and from the supplement of that act, approved Feb. 28, 1871. They relate to elections of members of the House of Representatives, and were an assertion, on the part of Congress, of a power to pass laws for regulating and superintending said elections, and for securing the purity thereof, and the rights of citizens to vote thereat peaceably and without molestation. It must be conceded to be a most important power, and of a fundamental character. In the light of recent history, and of the violence, fraud, corruption, and irregularity which have frequently prevailed at such elections, it may easily be conceived that the exertion of the power, if it exists, may be necessary to the stability of our frame of government. . . .

The clause of the Constitution under which the power of Congress, as well as that of the State legislatures, to regulate the election of senators and representatives arises, is as follows: "The times, places, and manner of holding elections for senators and representatives shall be prescribed in each State by the legislature thereof; but the Congress may at any time, by law, make or alter such regulations, except as to the place of choosing Senators."

It seems to us that the natural sense of these words is the contrary of that assumed by the counsel of the petitioners. After first authorizing the States to prescribe the regulations, it is added, "The Congress may *at any time*, by law, *make or alter* such regulations." "*Make or alter*." What is the plain meaning of these words? If not under the prepossession of some abstract theory of the relations between the State and national governments, we should not have any difficulty in understanding them. There is no declaration that the regulations shall be made either wholly by the State legislatures or wholly by Congress. If Congress does not interfere, of course they may be made wholly by the State; but if it chooses to interfere, there is nothing in the words to prevent its doing so, either wholly or partially. On the contrary, their necessary implication is that it may do either. It may either make the regulations, or it may alter them. If it only alters, leaving, as manifest convenience requires, the general organization of the polls to the State, there results a necessary co-operation of the two governments in regulating the subject. But no repugnance in the system of regulations can arise thence; for the power of Congress over the subject is paramount. It may be exercised as and when Congress sees fit to exercise it. When exercised, the action of Congress, so far as it extends and conflicts with the regulations of the State, necessarily supersedes them. This is implied in the power to "make or *alter*. . . ."

As to the supposed conflict that may arise between the officers appointed by the State and national governments for superintending the election, no more insuperable difficulty need arise than in the application of the regulations adopted by each respectively. The regulations of Congress being constitutionally paramount, the duties imposed thereby upon the officers of the United States, so far as they have respect to the same matters, must necessarily be paramount to those to be performed by the officers of the State. If both cannot be performed, the latter are *pro tanto* superseded and cease to be duties. If the power of Congress over the subject is supervisory and paramount, as we have seen it to be, and if officers or agents are created for carrying out its regulations, it follows as a necessary consequence that such officers and agents must have the requisite authority to act without obstruction or interference from the officers of the State. No greater subordination, in kind or degree, exists in this case than in any other. It exists to the same extent between the different officers appointed by the State, when the State alone regulates the election. One officer cannot interfere with the duties of another, or obstruct or hinder him in the performance of them. Where there is a disposition to act harmoniously, there is no danger of disturbance between those who have different duties to perform. When the rightful authority of the general government is once conceded and acquiesced in, the apprehended difficulties will disappear. Let a spirit of national as well as local patriotism once prevail, let unfounded jealousies cease, and we shall hear no more about the impossibility of harmonious action between the national and State governments in a matter in which they have a mutual interest.

As to the supposed incompatibility of independent sanctions and punishments imposed by the two governments, for the enforcement of the duties required of the officers of election, and for their protection in the performance of those duties, the same considerations apply. While the State will retain the power of enforcing such of its own regulations as are not superseded by those adopted by Congress, it cannot be disputed that if Congress has power to make regulations it must have the power to enforce them, not only by punishing the delinquency of officers appointed by the United States, but by restraining and punishing those who attempt to interfere with them in the performance of their duties; and if, as we have shown, Congress may revise existing regulations, and add to or alter the same as far as it deems expedient, there can be as little question that it may impose additional penalties for the prevention of frauds committed by the State officers in the elections, or for their violation of any duty relating thereto, whether arising from the common law or from any other law, State or national. Why not? Penalties for fraud and delinquency are part of the regulations belonging to the subject. If Congress, by its power to make or alter the regulations, has a general supervisory power over the whole subject, what is there to preclude it from imposing additional sanctions and penalties to prevent such fraud and delinquency? . . .

The objection that the laws and regulations, the violation of which is made punishable by the acts of Congress, are State laws and have not been adopted by Congress, is no sufficient answer to the power of Congress to impose punishment. It is true that Congress has not deemed it necessary to interfere with the duties of the ordinary officers of election, but has been content to leave them as prescribed by State laws. It has only created additional sanctions for their performance, and provided means of supervision in order more effectually to secure such performance. The imposition of punishment implies a prohibition of the act punished. The State laws which Congress sees no occasion to alter, but which it allows to stand, are in effect adopted by Congress. It simply demands their fulfilment. Content to leave the laws as they are, it is not content with the means provided for their enforcement. It provides additional means for that purpose; and we think it is entirely within its constitutional power to do so. It is simply the exercise of the power to make additional regulations.

That the duties devolved on the officers of election are duties which they owe to the United States as well as to the State, is further evinced by the fact that they have always been so regarded by the House of Representatives itself. In most cases of contested elections, the conduct of these officers is examined and scrutinized by that body as a matter of right; and their failure to perform their duties is often made the ground of decision. Their conduct is justly regarded as subject to the fullest exposure; and the right to examine them personally, and to inspect all their proceedings and papers, has always been maintained. This could not be done, if the officers were amenable only to the supervision of the State government which appointed them. . . .

It must also be remembered that we are dealing with the question of power, not of the expediency of any regulations which Congress has made. That is not within the pale of our jurisdiction. In exercising the power, however, we are bound to presume that Congress has done so in a judicious manner; that it has endeavored to guard as far as possible against any unnecessary interference with State laws and regulations, with the duties of

State officers, or with local prejudices. It could not act at all so as to accomplish any beneficial object in preventing frauds and violence, and securing the faithful performance of duty at the elections, without providing for the presence of officers and agents to carry its regulations into effect. It is also difficult to see how it could attain these objects without imposing proper sanctions and penalties against offenders. . . .

Several other questions bearing upon the present controversy have been raised by the counsel of the petitioners. Somewhat akin to the argument which has been considered is the objection that the deputy marshals authorized by the act of Congress to be created and to attend the elections are authorized to keep the peace; and that this is a duty which belongs to the State authorities alone. It is argued that the preservation of peace and good order in society is not within the powers confided to the government of the United States, but belongs exclusively to the States. Here again we are met with the theory that the government of the United States does not rest upon the soil and territory of the country. We think that this theory is founded on an entire misconception of the nature and powers of that government. We hold it to be an incontrovertible principle, that the government of the United States may, by means of physical force, exercised through its official agents, execute on every foot of American soil the powers and functions that belong to it. This necessarily involves the power to command obedience to its laws, and hence the power to keep the peace to that extent.

This power to enforce its laws and to execute its functions in all places does not derogate from the power of the State to execute its laws at the same time and in the same places. The one does not exclude the other, except where both cannot be executed at the same time. In that case, the words of the Constitution itself show which is to yield. "This Constitution, and all laws which shall be made in pursuance thereof, . . . shall be the supreme law of the land."

This concurrent jurisdiction which the national government necessarily possesses to exercise its powers of sovereignty in all parts of the United States is distinct from that exclusive power which, by the first article of the Constitution, it is authorized to exercise over the District of Columbia, and over those places within a State which are purchased by consent of the legislature thereof, for the erection of forts, magazines, arsenals, dock-yards, and other needful buildings. There its jurisdiction is absolutely exclusive of that of the State, unless, as is sometimes stipulated, power is given to the latter to serve the ordinary process of its courts in the precinct acquired.

Without the concurrent sovereignty referred to, the national government would be nothing but an advisory government. Its executive power would be absolutely nullified.

Why do we have marshals at all, if they cannot physically lay their hands on persons and things in the performance of their proper duties? What functions can they perform, if they cannot use force? In executing the processes of the courts, must they call on the nearest constable for protection? Must they rely on him to use the requisite compulsion, and to keep the peace whilst they are soliciting and entreating the parties and bystanders to allow the law to take its course? This is the necessary consequence of the positions that are assumed. If we indulge in such impracticable views as these, and keep on refining and re-refining, we shall drive the national government out of the United States, and relegate it to the District of Columbia, or perhaps to some foreign soil. We shall bring it back to a condition of greater helplessness than that of the old confederation.

The argument is based on a strained and impracticable view of the nature and powers of the national government. It must execute its powers, or it is no government. It must execute them on the land as well as on the sea, on things as well as on persons. And, to do this, it must necessarily have power to command obedience, preserve order, and keep the peace; and no person or power in this land has the right to resist or question its authority, so long as it keeps within the bounds of its jurisdiction. Without specifying other instances in which this power to preserve order and keep the peace unquestionably exists, take the very case in hand. The counsel for the petitioners concede that Congress may, if it sees fit, assume the entire control and regulation of the election of representatives. This would necessarily involve the appointment of the places for holding the polls, the times of voting, and the officers for holding the election; it would require the regulation of the duties to be performed, the custody of the ballots, the mode of ascertaining the result, and every other matter relating to the subject. Is it possible that Congress could not, in that case, provide for keeping the peace at such elections, and for arresting and punishing those guilty of breaking it? If it could not, its power would be but a shadow and a name. But, if Congress can do this, where is the difference in principle in its making provision for securing the preservation of the peace, so as to give to every citizen his free right to vote without molestation or injury, when it assumes only to supervise the regulations made by the State, and not to supersede them entirely? In our judgment, there is no difference; and, if the power exists in the one case, it exists in the other. . . .

The doctrine laid down at the close of counsel's brief, that the State and national governments are co-ordinate and altogether equal, on which their whole argument, indeed, is based, is only partially true.

The true doctrine, as we conceive, is this, that whilst the States are really sovereign as to all matters which have not been granted to the jurisdiction and control of the United States, the Constitution and constitutional laws of the latter are, as we have already said, the supreme law of the land; and, when they conflict with the laws of the States, they are of paramount authority and obligation. This is the fundamental principle on which the authority of the Constitution is based; and unless it be conceded in practice, as well as theory, the fabric of our institutions, as it was contemplated by its founders, cannot stand. The questions involved have respect not more to the autonomy and existence of the States, than to the continued existence of the United States as a government to which every American citizen may look for security and protection in every part of the land.

We think that the cause of commitment in these cases was lawful, and that the application for the writ of *habeas corpus* must be denied.

Application denied.

THE KU KLUX ACT

Commentary

On March 28, 1871, President Ulysses S. Grant sent Congress a special message urging the enactment of legislation to deal with "A condition of affairs. . . in some of the States of the Union rendering life and property insecure." The President was, of course, referring to the rising tide of terrorism in the southern states, led by the Ku Klux Klan (established 1866). The extent of such terrorism was fully documented in extensive Senate hearings. The type of testimony given in such hearings may be seen from the extracts contained in the speech of Representative William Stoughton [R., Mich.] early in the debate extracts that follow. Similar extracts were contained in the addresses of many Republicans, though, for our purposes, the Stoughton speech is enough to give the reader an illustrative idea of their flavor.

When the President's message was received, the House moved to take speedy action. Instead of the more elaborate measures that had previously been urged (notably a bill proposed by Congressman Benjamin Butler [R., Mass.] which had just failed to pass the House a year earlier), the House Judiciary Committee reported out a short bill, which contained the essential provisions of the law finally enacted as the so-called Ku Klux Act of 1871. The five sections of the original House bill were succinctly explained by Representative Samuel Shellabarger [R., Ohio] in introducing the measure in the lower chamber.

The Ku Klux Act, as introduced and ultimately passed, had two broad purposes: (1) to provide civil and criminal sanctions to deter infringements upon civil rights; and (2) to provide authority to the government to meet with force unlawful combinations and violence which interfered with civil rights or the execution of justice or federal law.

The first purpose was behind Section 1, providing for a lawsuit in a federal court by any person deprived of the rights given him by the Constitution or federal law or authority against any person who subjected him to such deprivation (such provision still exists as 42 U.S.C. §1983, and was derived from a comparable section of the 1866 Civil Rights Act); as well as Section 2 (which, in revised form, is now 42 U.S.C. §1985), which provided for a criminal penalty against any person who committed a listed series of acts, ranging from conspiring to overthrow the government to deprivation or violation of constitutional rights, particularly those secured by the Fourteenth and Fifteenth Amendments.

The aim of providing the federal government with the authority needed to cope with mob violence was met by these two sections. The President had the power to use the armed forces to suppress any violence which deprived any class of people of their constitutional rights if the state authorities refused or were unable to protect such rights. He could also suspend habeas corpus. These provisions, in effect, gave the President the power to declare martial law in places where he deemed federal troops necessary to protect Negro rights, particularly the right to vote. The power thus granted was used

591

by President Grant when, in October, 1871, he sent in troops to deal with the situation in nine South Carolina counties.

As was true of all of the post-Civil War civil rights legislation, the legislative proceedings leading to passage of the Ku Klux Act were essentially ratifications of what had already been decided upon by the Radical Republican leadership. This is not to say, however, that the debate itself did not go fully into the legal and other issues raised by the 1871 statute. As the Supreme Court has pointed out in *Collins* v. *Hardyman*, 341 U.S. 651 (1951), "The Act, popularly known as the Ku Klux Act, was passed by a partisan vote in a highly inflamed atmosphere. It was preceded by spirited debate which pointed out its grave character and susceptibility to abuse."

While Section 1 of the Ku Klux Act, by its terms, was limited in operation to persons who violated constitutional rights under color of state law, Section 2 imposed its criminal sanctions upon "any person" who so acted, regardless of whether his action was connected with action of the state in which he acted. This, of course, opened the door to opponents of the measure to contend that the law went beyond the constitutional language which, in the Fourteenth and Fifteenth Amendments, was limited to "state action" alone. The argument the other way proceeded upon the theory that state failure to act to protect constitutional rights furnished a sufficient basis for congressional action. In such view (best expressed in the remarks of Representative John Coburn [R., Ind.]) "state inaction" was elevated to the "state action" called for by the Fourteenth Amendment. (Such argument, it should be noted, has recently been revived by those who urge a much wider reach for the Fourteenth Amendment than is possible under prevailing legal principles.)

Congressional attacks were also made on the Ku Klux Act's provisions authorizing the President to use armed force and suspend habeas corpus. It was claimed that the Fourteenth Amendment provided no constitutional basis for conferring so far-reaching a power. Supporters of the bill relied here upon the notion that Congress could step in (even by so drastic a measure) when state failure to act resulted in a deprivation (even by otherwise private action) of constitutional rights.

To one interested in constitutional law, the remarks of Senator Lyman Trumbull [R., Ill.] on the privileges and immunities clause of the Fourteenth Amendment are of particular interest. According to him, that clause "did not extend the rights and privileges of citizenship one iota." The view thus articulated by the then-Chairman of the Senate Judiciary Committee anticipated, in substance, the basic holding in the matter two years later in the *Slaughter-house* cases, *supra* p. 335. In view of the criticism to which the Supreme Court decision has been subjected, it is most pertinent to note that the same answer to the question of the effect of the privileges and immunities clause was given in 1871 by the man who headed the Senate Judiciary Committee when the Fourteenth Amendment was passed.

The Ku Klux Act itself was passed by the House on April 6, 1871, by 118 to 91. It was passed by the Senate with amendments, on April 14, 45 to 19. The House refused to concur in the Senate amendments and a conference committee was appointed. The House refused to concur in the conference report, largely because it opposed a Senate amendment making cities and counties where violence occured liable in damages to those injured. The second conference committee watered down such provision to provide liability only for persons who knew of a conspiracy to violate civil rights and who could have prevented it. The second conference report was concurred in by both Houses on April 19, and the Ku Klux Act became law the next day.

THE KU KLUX ACT
April 20, 1871

Be it enacted by the Senate and House of Representatives of the United States of America in Congress assembled, That any person who, under color of any law, statute, ordinance, regulation, custom, or usage of any State, shall subject, or cause to be subjected, any person within the jurisdiction of the United States to the deprivation of any rights, privileges, or immunities secured by the Constitution of the United States, shall, any such law, statute, ordinance, regulation, custom, or usage of the State to the contrary notwithstanding, be liable to the party injured in any action at law, suit in equity, or other proper proceeding for redress; such proceeding to be prosecuted in the several district or circuit courts of the United States, with and subject to the same rights of appeal, review upon error, and other remedies provided in like cases in such courts, under the provisions of the act of the ninth of April, eighteen hundred and sixty-six, entitled "An act to protect all persons in the United States in their civil rights, and to furnish the means of their vindication"; and the other remedial laws of the United States which are in their nature applicable in such cases.

SEC. 2. That if two or more persons within any State or Territory of the United States shall conspire together to overthrow, or to put down, or to destroy by force the government of the United States, or to levy war against the United States, or to oppose by force the authority of the government of the United States, or by force, intimidation, or threat to prevent, hinder, or delay the execution of any law of the United States, or by force to seize, take, or possess any property of the United States contrary to the authority thereof, or by force, intimidation, or threat to prevent any person from accepting or holding any office or trust or place of confidence under the United States, or from discharging the duties thereof, or by force, intimidation, or threat to induce any officer of the United States to leave any State, district, or place where his duties as such officer might lawfully be performed, or to injure him in his person or property on account of his lawful discharge of the duties of his office, or to injure his person while engaged in the lawful discharge of the duties of his office, or to injure his property so as to molest, interrupt, hinder, or impede him in the discharge of his official duty, or by force, intimidation, or threat to deter any party or witness in any court of the United States from attending such court, or from testifying in any matter pending in such court fully, freely, and truthfully, or to injure any such party or witness in his person or property on account of his having so attended or testified, or by force, intimidation, or threat to influence the verdict, presentment, or indictment, of any juror or grand juror in any court of the United States, or to injure such juror in his person or property on account of any verdict, presentment, or indictment lawfully assented to by him, or on account of his being or having been such juror, or shall conspire together, or go in disguise upon the public highway or upon the premises of another for the purpose, either directly or indirectly, of depriving any person or any class of persons of the equal protection of the laws, or of equal privileges or immunities under the laws, or for the purpose of preventing or hindering the constituted authorities of any State from giving or securing to all persons within such State the equal protection of the laws, or shall conspire together for the purpose of in any manner impeding, hindering, obstructing, or defeating the due course of justice in any State or Territory, with intent to deny to any citizen of the United States the due and equal protection of the laws, or to injure any person in his person or his property for lawfully enforcing the right of any person or class of persons to the equal protection of the laws, or by force, intimidation, or threat to prevent any citizen of the United States lawfully entitled to vote from giving his support or advocacy in a lawful manner towards or in favor of the election of any lawfully qualified person as an elector of President or Vice-President of the United States, or as a member of the Congress of the United States, or to injure any such citizen in his person or property on account of such support or advocacy, each and every person so offending shall be deemed guilty of a high crime, and, upon conviction thereof in any district or circuit court of the United States or district or supreme court of any Territory of the United States having jurisdiction of similar offences, shall be punished by a fine not less than five hundred nor more than five thousand dollars, or by imprisonment, with or without hard labor, as the court may determine, for a period of not less than six months nor more than six years, as the court may determine, or by both such fine and imprisonment as the court shall determine. And if any one or more persons engaged in any such conspiracy shall do, or cause to be done, any act in furtherance of the object of such conspiracy, whereby any person shall be injured in his person or property, or deprived of having and exercising any right or privilege of a citizen of the United States, the person so injured or deprived of such rights and privileges may have and maintain an action for the recovery of damages occasioned by such injury or deprivation of rights and privileges against any one or more of the persons engaged in such conspiracy, such action to be prosecuted in the proper district or circuit court of the United States, with and subject to the same rights of appeal, review upon error, and other remedies provided in like cases in such courts under the provisions of the act of April ninth, eighteen hundred and sixty-six, entitled "An act to protect all persons in the United States in their civil rights, and to furnish the means of their vindication."

SEC. 3. That in all cases where insurrection, domestic violence, unlawful combinations, or conspiracies in any State shall so obstruct or hinder the execution of the laws thereof, and of the United States, as to deprive any portion or class of the people of such State of any of the rights, privileges, or immunities, or protection, named in the Constitution and secured by this act, and the constituted authorities of such State shall either be unable to protect, or shall, from any cause, fail in or refuse protection of the people in such rights, such facts shall be deemed a denial by such State of the equal protection of the laws to which they are entitled under the Constitution of the United States; and in all such cases, or whenever any such insurrection, violence, unlawful combination, or conspiracy shall oppose or obstruct the laws of the United States or the due execution thereof, or impede or obstruct the due course of justice under the same, it shall be lawful for the President, and it shall be his duty to take such measures, by the employment of the militia or the land and naval forces of the United States, or of either, or by other means, as he may deem necessary for the suppression of such insurrection, domestic violence, or combinations; and any person who shall be arrested under the provisions of this and the preceding section shall be delivered to the marshal of the proper district, to be dealt with according to law.

SEC. 4. That whenever in any State or part of a State the unlawful combinations named in the preceding section of this act shall be organized and armed, and so numerous and powerful as to be able, by violence, to either overthrow or set at defiance the constituted authorities of such State, and of the United States within such State, or when the constituted authorities are in complicity with, or shall connive at the unlawful purposes of, such powerful and armed combinations; and whenever, by reason of either or all of the causes aforesaid, the conviction of such offenders and the preservation of the public safety shall become in such district impracticable, in every such case such combinations shall be deemed a rebellion against the government of the United States, and during the continuance of such rebellion, and within the limits of the district which shall be so under the sway thereof, such limits to be prescribed by proclamation, it shall be lawful for the President of the United States, when in his judgment the public safety shall require it, to suspend the privileges of the writ of habeas corpus, to the end that such rebellion may be overthrown: *Provided*, That all the provisions of the second section of an act entitled "An act relating to habeas corpus, and regulating judicial proceedings in certain cases," approved March third, eighteen hundred and sixty-three, which relate to the discharge of prisoners other than prisoners of war, and to the penalty for refusing to obey the order of the court, shall be in full force so far as the same are applicable to the provisions of this section: *Provided further*, That the President shall first have made proclamation, as now provided by law, commanding such insurgents to disperse: *And provided also*, That the provisions of this section shall not be in force after the end of the next regular session of Congress.

SEC. 5. That no person shall be a grand or petit juror in any court of the United States upon any inquiry, hearing, or trial of any suit, proceeding, or prosecution based upon or arising under the provisions of this act who shall, in the judgment of the court, be in complicity with any such combination or conspiracy; and every such juror shall, before entering upon any such inquiry, hearing, or trial, take and subscribe an oath in open court that he has never, directly or indirectly, counselled, advised, or voluntarily aided any such combination or conspiracy; and each and every person who shall take this oath, and shall therein swear falsely, shall be guilty of perjury, and shall be subject to the pains and penalties declared against that crime, and the first section of the act entitled "An act defining additional causes of challenge and prescribing an additional oath for grand and petit jurors in the United States courts," approved June seventeenth, eighteen hundred and sixty-two, be, and the same is hereby, repealed.

SEC. 6. That any person or persons, having knowledge that any of the wrongs conspired to be done and mentioned in the second section of this act are about to be committed, and having power to prevent or aid in preventing the same, shall neglect or refuse so to do, and such wrongful act shall be committed, such person or persons shall be liable to the person injured, or his legal representatives, for all damages caused by any such wrongful act which such first-named person or persons by reasonable diligence could have prevented; and such damages may be recovered in an action on the case in the proper circuit court of the United States, and any number of persons guilty of such wrongful neglect or refusal may be joined as defendants in such action: *Provided* That such action shall be commenced within one year after such cause of action shall have accrued; and if the death of any person shall be caused by any such wrongful act and neglect, the legal representatives of such deceased person shall have such action therefor, and may recover not exceeding five thousand dollars damages therein, for the benefit of the widow of such deceased person, if any there be, or if there be no widow, for the benefit of the next of kin of such deceased person.

SEC. 7. That nothing herein contained shall be construed to supersede or repeal any former act or law except so far as the same may be repugnant thereto; and any offences heretofore committed against the tenor of any former act shall be prosecuted, and any proceeding already commenced for the prosecution thereof shall be continued and completed, the same as if this act had not been passed, except so far as the provisions of this act may go to sustain and validate such proceedings.

Approved, April 20, 1871.

THE DEBATE

House of Representatives-42d Congress, 1st Session
March 28-April 6, 1871

SAMUEL SHELLABARGER [R., OHIO]. Mr. Speaker, I am directed by the select committee to which was referred the late message of the President of the United States to report a bill (H. R. No. 320) to enforce the provisions of the fourteenth amendment to the Constitution of the United States, and for other purposes.

The bill was read a first and second time and ordered to be printed.

The bill, which was read, provides in the first section that any person who, under color of any law, statute, ordinance, regulation, custom, or usage of any State, shall subject, or cause to be subjected, any person within the jurisdiction of the United States to the deprivation of any rights, privileges, or immunities secured by the Constitution of the United States, shall, any such law, statute, ordinance, regulation, custom, or usage of the State to the contrary notwithstanding, be liable to the party injured in any action at law, suit in equity, or other proper proceeding for redress, such proceeding to be prosecuted in the several district or circuit courts of the United States, with and subject to the same rights of appeal, review upon error, and other remedies provided in like cases in such courts, under the provisions of the act of the 9th of April, 1866, entitled "An act to protect all persons in the United States in their civil rights, and to furnish the means of their vindication," and the other remedial laws of the United States which are in their nature applicable in such cases. The second section provides that if two or more persons shall, within the limits of any State, band, conspire, or combine together to do any act in violation of the rights, privileges, or immunities of any person, to which he is entitled under the Constitution and laws of the United States, which, committed within a place under the sole and exclusive jurisdiction of the United States, would, under any law of the United States then in force, constitute the crime of either murder, manslaughter, mayhem, robbery, assault and battery, perjury, subornation of perjury, criminal obstruction of legal, process or resistance of officers in discharge of official duty, arson, or larceny, and if one or more of the parties to said conspiracy or combination shall do any act to effect the object thereof, all the parties to or engaged in said conspiracy or combination, whether principals or accessories, shall be deemed guilty of a felony, and upon conviction thereof shall be liable to a penalty of not exceeding $10,000, or to imprisonment not exceeding ten years, or both, at the discretion of the court; provided, that if any party or parties to such conspiracy or combination shall, in furtherance of such common design, commit the crime of murder, such party or parties so guilty shall, upon conviction thereof, suffer death; and provided also, that

597

any offense punishable under this act, begun in one judicial district of the
United States and completed in another, may be dealt with, inquired of,
tried, determined, and punished in either district. The third section provides
that in all cases where insurrection, domestic violence, unlawful combinations, or conspiracies in any State shall so far obstruct or hinder the execution of the laws thereof as to deprive any portion or class of the people of
such State of any of the rights, privileges, or immunities named in and
secured by this act, and the constituted authorities of such State shall either
be unable to or shall from any cause fail in or refuse protection of the people
in such rights, and shall fail or neglect, through the proper authorities, to
apply to the President of the United States for aid in that behalf, such facts
shall be deemed a denial by such State of the equal protection of the laws to
which they are entitled under the fourteenth article of amendments to the
Constitution of the United States; and in all such cases it shall be lawful for
the President, and it shall be his duty, to take such measures, by the
employment of the militia or the land and naval forces of the United States,
or of either, or by other means, as he may deem necessary for the suppression of such insurrection, domestic violence, or combinations; and any person
who shall be arrested under the provisions of this and the preceding section
shall be delivered to the marshal of the proper district, to be dealt with
according to law. The fourth section provides that whenever in any State or
part of a State the unlawful combinations named in the preceding section of
this act shall be organized and armed, and so numerous and powerful as to
be able, by violence, to either overthrow or set at defiance the constituted
authorities of such State, or when the constituted authorities are in complicity
with or shall connive at the unlawful purposes of such powerful and armed
combinations; and whenever, by reason of either or all of the causes aforesaid, the conviction of such offenders and the preservation of the public
safety shall become in such district impracticable, in every such case such
combinations shall be deemed a rebellion against the Government of the
United States, and during the continuance of such rebellion, and within the
limits of the district which shall be so under the sway thereof, such limits to
be prescribed by proclamation, it shall be lawful for the President of the
United States, when in his judgment the public safety shall require it, to
suspend the privileges of the writ of *habeas corpus*, and to declare and
enforce, subject to the Rules and Articles of War, and other laws of the
United States now in force applicable in case of rebellion, martial law, to the
end that such rebellion may be overthrown, provided that the President shall
first have made proclamation, as now provided by law, commanding such
insurgents to disperse; and provided also, that the provisions of this section
shall not be in force after the 1st day of June, 1872. The fifth and concluding
section provides that nothing herein contained shall be construed to supersede or repeal any former act or law except so far as the same may be

repugnant thereto; and any offenses heretofore committed against the tenor of any former act shall be prosecuted, and any proceeding already commenced for the prosecution thereof shall be continued and completed, the same as if this act had not been passed, except so far as the provisions of this act may go to sustain and validate such proceedings. . . .

WILLIAM STOUGHTON [R., MICH.]. Mr. Speaker, the moderation and forbearance of the American people upon the final subjugation of the rebellion are without a parallel in the history of the world. The lives of the insurgents were spared and their property was restored. If this magnanimity of a generous conqueror was an error, as subsequent events seem to indicate, we ought at least to take care that there shall be no future exemption from punishment for crimes against the peace and safety of the nation. It has been the earnest hope of the Republican party and of all good men everywhere that the spirit of violence and outrage had passed away in the South and that a better order of things would be established. With this view the State governments have been reorganized and put in operation and all local power freely placed in the hands of the people. The right of suffrage has been generously extended to all classes of men, subject only to the provision that the disloyal white man should never disfranchise the loyal black man. The broadest political privileges have been granted, with the single restriction, provided in the fourteenth amendment to the Constitution, that those who added perjury to the crime of treason should be prohibited from again holding office under the Government; and even this disability has been removed by Congress whenever it has been asked for in good faith. Under these circumstances we have a right to expect and demand at least a quiet submission to just and wholesome laws from our late enemies. Unfortunately, however, our reasonable expectations have not been realized. There exists at this time in the southern States a treasonable conspiracy against the lives, persons, and property of Union citizens, less formidable it may be, but not less dangerous, to American liberty than that which inaugurated the horrors of the rebellion. The existence of this organization and its treasonable character are proved by the sworn testimony of an array of witnesses from all parts of the South, which must carry conviction to the minds of the most skeptical.

The evidence taken before the Senate committee in relation to the outrages, lawlessness, and violence in North Carolina establishes the following propositions:

1. That the Ku Klux organization exists throughout the State, has a political purpose, and is composed of the members of the Democratic or Conservative party.

2. That this organization has sought to carry out its purposes by murders, whippings, intimidation, and violence against its opponents.

3. That it not only binds its members to execute decrees of crime, but

protects them against conviction and punishment, first by disguises and secrecy, and second, by perjury, if necessary, upon the witness-stand and in the jury-box.

4. That of all the offenders in this order, which has established a reign of terrorism and bloodshed throughout the State not one has yet been convicted.

James E. Boyd, a witness before this committee, against whom nothing can be alleged except that he was a confederate soldier, a supporter of Seymour and Blair in 1868, and initiated into the Ku Klux Klan as an auxiliary of the Democratic party, testifies, in answer to a question as to the designs and regulations of that order, as follows:

The meetings were to be held in secret places—in the woods, or some other place distant from any habitation, in order to avoid detection. The disguise prescribed was a long white gown and a mask for the face. A county was divided into a certain number of districts, and each district composed a camp, which was under the command of a captain. The whole county constituted a klan, under the command of a chief. No person could be initiated as the member of any camp until his name had been submitted to the camp and his application unanimously agreed to by the members of the camp. The manner of making raids was prescribed by the regulations. No raid was to be made, no person punished, no execution done, unless it had first been unanimously agreed upon at a regular meeting of a camp of the klan and duly approved by the officers and the chief of the klan. The sign of recognition of the White Brotherhood was by sliding the right hand down along the opposite lappel of the coat. If the party to whom the sign was made was a member of the organization he returned it by sliding the left hand in the same manner down along the opposite lappel of the coat. The word of distress was "Shiloh." There was a sign of distress to be made when a brother was in distress and wanted assistance. I do not remember the sign, it was some sign made by the hand. But if the person was so situated that the sign made by the hand could not be seen, then the word "Shiloh" was used to denote distress.

Question. Upon the oath administered, the mode of procedure prescribed, and the government of the organization, so far as you have observed, are the members bound to carry out the decrees of the order, if they involve murder and assassination?

Answer. I think so, sir. If it was decided to take the life of a man a camp is ordered to execute the sentence, and is bound to do it.

Question. What would be the penalty if any member refused?

Answer. I do not know that any penalty was prescribed for that. A member could excuse himself from attendance at meetings or from going upon raids if he had a proper excuse. The penalty prescribed in the regulations for the punishment of any member who should disclose the secrets of the order was death. Each member was informed upon his initiation that if he disclosed the secrets of the organization he should be the first victim.

Question. If any arrests should be made by the civil authorities for murders or other crimes committed in pursuance of the decrees of a camp, to what extent did the obligations of members bind them to assist and protect each other?

Answer. To whatever extent was in their power.

Question. Did it go to the extent of giving testimony in behalf of each other or of acquitting if upon a jury?

Answer. I think that was one of the objects and intentions of the organization, that a person on the witness-stand or in the jury-box should disregard his oath in order to protect a member of the organization.

Question. Do you know of any instances of wrong or outrage perpetrated upon persons in pursuance of the decrees or orders of this organization?

Answer. I do not know of any decrees or decisions they made. I know of punishments that were inflicted by the organization.

Question. State any of them that you now remember.

Answer. The most serious instance in my county, I believe, was the hanging of a negro man by the name of Outlaw, who was taken from his house, in the town where I live, about one o'clock at night, by a band of from eighty to a hundred men, and hung upon an elm tree, not very far from the courthouse door.

Question. When was that?

Answer. On the night of the 26th of last February.

Question. What was the offense charged against him?

Answer. I never heard of any. The newspapers have said that he was guilty of having shot at a band of Ku Klux that passed through the town some time previous, but that was not true. . . .

Question. What is your knowledge of the object and extent of this organization throughout the State?

Answer. I can only state from heresay—what I have heard from members of the organization. The number of the members of the organization is supposed to be forty thousand. Their object was the overthrow of the reconstruction policy of Congress and the disfranchisement of the negro. There are two other organizations besides that of the White Brotherhood, as I said before. I was a full member of one of them and partly a member in the other. I cannot say that I considered myself really a member of the other. One organization was called the Invisible Empire. There is another organization which rather superseded the White Brotherhood in my county, after it had gone on for some time, and was called the Constitutional Union Guards, whose oaths and manner of operation were about the same. There was very little difference; some change in the signs. The sign of recognition was by crossing the hand on the breast. . . .

Question. In speaking about the punishing of men, on these raids, in the first part of your testimony, what do you mean?

Answer. Whatever punishment was passed upon in the camp.

Question. For what were they punished?

Answer. I do not know; just whatever they saw proper. If they thought the man ought to be killed for being too prominent in politics, they would have a meeting and pass sentence upon him. I have no doubt in my own mind (though I have no information from others that such was the case) but what Outlaw was killed in order to break up the organization of the colored voters in my own county, or frighten them away from voting.

Question. Were other punishments inflicted in your county besides this?

Answer. Yes, sir. In consequence of Outlaw's murder, a negro by the name of William Puryear, a half simple fellow, who, it was said, saw some of his neighbors returning in disguise from Graham the night that Outlaw was hung, was drowned in the millpond.

Question. Were there any whippings in the county?

Answer. Yes, sir. I believe there were one hundred or one hundred and fifty in the last two years in the county, white and black. Some have been whipped two or three times.

I have quoted largely from the testimony of this witness for the purpose of showing the dangerous character of this organization. I also make an extract from the testimony of Hon. Thomas Settle, one of the judges of the supreme court, showing the same state of things and strongly corroborating the material statements of Mr. Boyd:

By the Chairman:

Question. Give us your belief as to the true position of the political organizations with reference to this organization.

Answer. Well, sir, I must think that the present Democratic party there, judging from the circumstances, are encouraging it. I do not think it is accidental. In the course of our investigation last summer it leaked out in the testimony that Hamilton C. Jones, present member of the Legislature, gave the signs of the Invisible Empire to James E. Boyd, who was then a Democratic candidate for the house of commons for Alamance county. Dr. Moore, also, who had been a member of the previous house, gave the signs of the Invisible Empire. Mr. Boyd had belonged to the White Brotherhood, and this was a new organization to make it more compact, it was said. After Dr. Moore had given the signs to Mr. Boyd they walked down to the Yarboro hotel and went into the room of Colonel Jones, who also gave Mr. Boyd the signs. It was not proved that they were members, but Mr. Boyd said in his testimony that Mr. Jarvis was in the room when Hamilton C. Jones gave him the signs. It was further stated by Mr. Boyd that he learned from Dr. Moore that Frederick N. Strudwick, a grandson of a former chief justice, Frederick Nash, was on his way to assassinate Senator Shoffner, who had introduced the stringent militia bill. Well, at the next session of the Legislature, Mr. Jarvis was made speaker. He is speaker of the present house. No person swore positively that Mr. Jarvis was a member of the organization, but Mr. Boyd swore that Dr. Moore informed him that Jarvis was a member, and that Jarvis was in the room when Jones gave the signs. Mr. Jones is a prominent member of the senate, and Judge Warren, who is presiding officer, being in feeble health, Mr. Jones frequently presides in that body. It is notorious that the resolution of impeachment of Governor Holden was passed in caucus. Mr. Strudwick was charged with introducing, and did introduce, the resolution. He was also prominent in bringing forward a bill, which passed and became a law forthwith, to repeal the act which had been passed, introduced by Mr. Shoffner. I draw from these facts the inference that the Legislature must be controlled by those men who were honored by the party, and who were elected last summer as members of the party, and I think that is the general opinion.

Question. Do I understand you, then, to say that the weight of what is known as the Conservative or Democratic party at present gives encouragement to this organization, and that those of that party who denounce it are exceptions?

Answer. Yes, sir; that is the general opinion there.

Question. What has been the effect on the public mind with reference to the security of person and property, of these outrages, and the difficulty in the way of punishment?

Answer. Well, sir, I suppose any candid man in North Carolina would tell you it is impossible for the civil authorities, however vigilant they may be, to punish those who perpetrate these outrages. The defect lies not so much with the courts as with the juries. You cannot get a conviction; you cannot get a bill found by the grand jury, or, if you do, the petit jury acquits the parties. In my official capacity I sit with Judge Pearson and Judge Dick. Judge Pearson issued a bench warrant last summer for some parties, and had them brought before him at Raleigh. He requested Judge Dick and myself to meet him. We did so, and the trial extended over three weeks, and there it came to our knowledge that it was the duty and obligation of members of this secret organization to put themselves in the way to be summoned as jurors, to acquit the accused, or to have themselves summoned as witnesses to prove an *alibi*. This they swore to; and such is the general impression. Of course it must be so, for there has not been a single instance of conviction in the State.

Question. Upon investigations made before you in your official capacity, have you any doubt that a state of things exists requiring men to shield themselves in the way you have mentioned?

Answer. None whatever. I am satisfied, from their own declarations and from the effect visible in all the courts, that it is so.

Question. Where they are charged with offenses, is there any probability of securing justice against them in counties where the organization exists at all?

Answer. Well, sir, my belief is that the organization extends to every county in the State. I am satisfied that the organization is a very extensive one. I have no doubt it is much more numerous in some counties than others, and I believe the middle or Piedmont region of the State is the chief nucleus, and that there the outrages have been the most numerous.

Judge Logan, of the ninth district, and Judge Henry, of the eleventh district, express substantially the same views. Their opinions are mainly founded upon the effects visible in the courts over which they preside and about which they can neither be mistaken nor deceived. Certain it is that these criminals are able to baffle and set at defiance all the ordinary appliances of the law. The testimony of Thomas W. Willeford, formerly a member of the Ku Klux Klan, throws additional light upon the secret workings of this order and discloses the means by which these results are brought about in the State and local courts. This witness testifies as follows:

Question. Did they tell you what the object was?
Answer. Yes, sir; in the first meeting. I was initiated in Kennedy's barn.
Question. Did you take the oath?
Answer. Yes, sir; and then the next Saturday went to the meeting.
Question. What did they tell you then was the object of the organization?
Answer. They told me it was to damage the Republican party as much as they could—burning, stealing, whipping niggers, and such things as that.
Question. Murder?
Answer. The leading men it was to murder.

Question. Have you ever heard of a Ku Klux being convicted of any offense there?
Answer. No, sir.
Question. Was there anything in the obligation you took or the rules of the order as to your being obliged to defend men by your oaths, or otherwise?
Answer. Yes, sir; if he could get you in as a witness you had to swear him out, let you be swearing a lie or not. If you swore against him, why you might just as well be a-traveling at onct.
Question. You mean by that you would be in danger of your life from the order?
Answer. Yes, sir.
Question. Anything about getting on the jury?
Answer. Yes, sir; if we could get on the jury we could save him, do what you please.
Question. No matter what the proof?
Answer. Yes, sir; you could not bring proof enough to convict.

The following testimony of Caswell Holt, a poor and ignorant, but honest and conscientious negro, who was twice visited by the Ku Klux, will show the manner in which these outrages are executed:

By the Chairman:
Question. Were these men disguised?
Answer. Yes, sir.
Question. How?
Answer. They all had long white robes on, all of them, loose gowns, and caps on their heads with three horns. I went to my house; my wife said, "What did they do to you?" I said, "Don't talk to me; they pretty nigh killed me." She kept on at me, and asked me what they said and did to me. At last she said, "Must I go down to the house for Mr. Holt?" I told her, "Yes, you may go down there and tell him to come up; I want to see him." I could neither sit, lie down, nor stand; I was up and down all night, trying to get some ease some way.
Question. To what extent was your back injured?
Answer. It was cut all to pieces; and my wife pulled a splinter out of me here [putting his hand on his right hip] as long as my finger, from one of the sticks they hit me with.
Question. Now go on and tell us about the time when you were visited again.
Answer. It went on in that way until the crop was gathered again; it was about two weeks before Christmas. I had done gathered the crop and sowed a little wheat on the place. I was going to move the next week. I would have left the week before they shot me, but there was a little road they wanted to cut out from Gun Creek to Company Shops, and I went there on Saturday and worked on that. I had been chopping very hard, and came home that night and laid down on the bed. The boys were all up there that night. The dog broke out after I laid down. There was a hole in the walls of the house; it was a log house; and the boys peeped out and said, "Here, pap, the Ku Klux are all around the house." I said, "They are?" They said, "Yes." By this time they were at the door, and said, "Open the door."

They struck against the door with a stick, or something—bang against the door. I said, "No, sir; I don't open my door for no man, unless he tells me who he is and what he wants." He said, "God damn you, open the door." I thought when he come that way he wouldn't get me to open it, sure. I said, "No, sir." He said, "Strike a light before you open it." I said, "I've nothing to make a light of, and if I had I wouldn't do it, and I won't open the door." I then went to the door; it was a little thin poplar door, about three quarter inch plank. I stood at the door. My biggest boy was standing a little piece off from me. There was an ax sitting there, and I picked it up and went to reach it to him, so that if they should break in we would hurt some of them before they did too much mischief. I had a bowie-knife in my hand, standing there at the door. I was standing there as close as I am now to this table. They said, "Open the door." I said I shouldn't do it. Then one said, "Blow his brains out." Just as he said that they all fired through the door, just red-hot, just flaming red when they came through. I didn't think it was but one crack; but they said they shot a half a dozen times or more. I clapped my hand on here [placing his hand on his breast] and said, "There, they've shot me." My boy knew where there were some loose planks in the floor. He jerked up two of them, and they all run through under the house—all the biggest of them; all but the three little girls I had.

Question. What occurred afterward?

Answer. The next morning I sent for the doctor to come and take out the balls, Dr. Montgomery. He came and took out the balls, and told them they had better move me to Graham, if I was to be moved, or else they wouldn't move me at all. That evening they carried me to Graham, and got me there just at night.

Question. How many balls did they fire into you?

Answer. [The witness indicated where he had been shot—in both arms and in his chest.] There were five balls and two shot.

Question. What has been the effect of such proceedings upon the colored people of that county; do they feel safe?

Answer. They don't feel safe there at all, I can tell you that; and a great many of them have taken the notion to leave; they could hardly stay about there. They wanted to run them all off because the principal part of them voted the Radical ticket.

By Mr. Nye:

Question. Wanted to run all off who voted the Radical ticket.

Answer. Yes, sir.

Question. Did you hear that said?

Answer. Yes, sir; I heard it talked, and I saw them try it. They tried to turn me from voting the Republican ticket: but I didn't turn, and that is what they shot me for I reckon. That is the case every election that has been there. They have been trying to get us to vote the Conservative ticket; some they would get to vote it, and some they wouldn't.

Question. Were those that would not vote the Conservative ticket the ones that had these outrages committed on them?

Answer. Yes, sir. You never saw one bothered at all that voted the Conservative ticket.

Can any one, Mr. Speaker, contemplate these disclosures without surprise and well-founded alarm? Yet, sir, the Democratic party have from the first denied, and then palliated and excused these outrages. In Tennessee and other southern States the laws which had been passed by Republican Legislatures to suppress and punish the Ku Klux were repealed as soon as the Democratic party came into power. The relation of the Democracy to this order is precisely that of the receiver of stolen property to the thief. The murder of leading Republicans, terrifying the colored population, and putting whole neighborhoods in fear so that the Ku Klux can control an election, is heralded as a Democratic victory. . . .

We may as well concede, Mr. Speaker, that if this system of violence is to continue in the South the Democratic party will secure the ascendency. If political opponents can be marked for slaughter by secret bands of cowardly assassins who ride forth with impunity to execute the decrees upon the unarmed and defenseless, it will be fatal alike to the Republican party and civil liberty. But, sir, we may well ask where this will end. How long will it be before the Tammany Hall Democracy, who are now furnishing arms to the Ku Klux of the South to murder southern Republicans, will introduce this new element of Democratic success into northern politics?

The report, Mr. Speaker, to which I have referred shows over one hundred and fifty authenticated cases where persons have either been murdered, brutally beaten, or driven away at the peril of their lives. And the same deplorable state of things exists in South Carolina, Georgia, Mississippi, Louisiana, Kentucky, Tennessee, and Texas. Jails have been broken open, the officers of the law killed while attempting to discharge their sworn duty, and the criminals turned loose upon the community. Revenue officers and mail agents of the United States have in some instances been murdered, and in others driven away from their posts. But a few days ago, over a hundred Alabama Ku Klux made a raid upon Meridian, Mississippi, and carried off their victims for execution. A meeting of the citizens was called to protest against these outrages. The Ku Klux became alarmed. At their instigation warrents were issued for the arrest of peaceable and well-disposed negroes upon the charge of "using seditious language." When the court convened they again assembled in force, and commenced the work of death. Judge Bramlette, the presiding magistrate, was shot and the scene closed by driving the Republican mayor out of the city. . . .

The whole South, Mr. Speaker, is rapidly drifting into a state of anarchy and bloodshed, which renders the worst Government on the face of the earth respectable by way of comparison. There is no security for life, person, or property. The State authorities and local courts are unable or unwilling to check the evil or punish the criminals. It is not a question of power or numbers. If the cowardly miscreants who conceal their crimes by hideous disguises, the dark pall of night and the darker pall of perjury, would give the loyal people of the South an open field and a fair fight they would protect themselves. But, sir, the Ku Klux system is ingeniously devised for the express purpose of enabling a few bad men to intimidate the masses of the people, to avoid any conflict with the military power, and to control the State courts and local authorities by perjury and fraud.

It is an extraordinary combination to commit crime, and requires extraordinary legislation for its suppression. What that legislation shall be imposes a grave responsibility upon Congress. It is a fundamental principle of law that while the citizen owes allegiance to the Government he has a right to expect and demand protection for life, person, and property. But we are not compelled to rest upon this inherent and undeniable right to protect our own citizens. The Constitution of the United States contains an express grant of power coupled with an imperative injunction for its exercise. The first section of the fourteenth article of the amendments to the Constitution provides that no State shall "deny to any person within its jurisdiction the equal protection of the laws."

When thousands of murders and outrages have been committed in the southern States and not a single offender brought to justice, when the State courts are notoriously powerless to protect life, person, and property, and when violence and lawlessness are universally prevalent, the denial of the equal protection of the laws is too clear to admit of question or controversy. Full force and effect is therefore given to section five, which declares that "Congress shall have power to enforce by appropriate legislation the provisions of this article." The authority thus conferred is subject to no restrictions or limitations. It is for Congress in its discretion to determine what legislation is appropriate, and its decision is binding upon every other department of the Government. The inquiry, if any arises, is not what Congress may do, but what it may not do.

It is certain that under this provision of the Constitution Congress has power to declare martial law in the insurrectionary districts, to fully investigate these outrages, and to provide for their trial and punishment in the United States courts where perjury in the jury box and on the witness-stand can be guarded against, and where the military power can be called upon to aid in the enforcement of the laws.

I believe, Mr. Speaker, that the wisdom of enlightened statesmanship can prescribe a remedy for any crime which the ingenuity of bad men can invent, and that a failure on our part to provide "appropriate legislation" for the fearful disorders which prevail throughout the South would be an admission, false in fact and disgraceful in character, that our criminal law is a mockery and our Government a failure. . . .

GEORGE MORGAN [DEM., OHIO]. Mr. Speaker, in a government of delegated powers, clearly defined by a written constitution, it matters little what may be the name of the party in power, provided it administers the government in conformity with the fundamental law. But a party which assumes powers not granted, no matter what may be its name, is a party of usurpation. The party to-day in power calls itself "Republican;" and yet its President, its leader in the Senate, and its master, if not its leader in this House, were but a few years ago proud of the appellation of Democrats. Hence names are of little import; for it is principles which constitute a party, not a name. Names are as often chosen to conceal principles as to represent them.

That crimes are committed is true. The existence of jails and penitentiaries, the frequent announcement of murders and executions, the number of persons mysteriously assassinated, the assassin escaping without detection, as in the Nathan murder in New York, and in similar outrages in the South, all prove that crime exists in the land. But, sir, when did not crime exist?

But the number and character of offenses are willfully exaggerated. For my own part I am no apologist for crime, whether committed in the South or in the North. When committed in the South or in the North I trust that the criminals may be brought to speedy justice by trial and condemnation before tribunals of competent jurisdiction. For, if they be not tried by such tribunals, then the act of condemnation is itself a crime, and the greater, because committed under the pretended guise of law. . . .

But we were told that not only are common murders and common crimes committed in the South, but that there are political offenses committed there. If such be the truth, and in some cases it probably is so, who is responsible, who is to blame? There is no justification for them. But I maintain, sir, that if such offenses are committed they have been caused in good part by the mistaken legislation of Congress; for the Federal Legislature, forgetting that ours is a republican Government, a Confederacy of republican States, under a written Constitution, based, as all republics are, upon public virtue, upon the principle of reason and consent—the Federal Legislature, I say, in 1866, commenced what is known as reconstruction, a system based on the vital principle of despotism—fear, fear inspired by force. . . .

I have not time to go through this bill section by section, and only propose to glance at the third and fourth sections and of the articles of the Constitution under which it is claimed to be framed.

The third section of this bill proposes to invest the President of the United States with discretionary power, without any check of any kind, either State or Federal, to determine under what circumstances he shall employ the Army, the Navy, the militia, or use any other means to suspend the laws of a State, to abolish its courts and to establish military commissions in their stead. What, sir, is a military commission? It is a tribunal which may try, convict, and execute a man within the same hour; it has absolute control over life, liberty, and property. And you propose by this bill to confer upon one man the power to abolish your courts, not only in the South, but in every State of the North and the West, at his own discretion, by his own unrestrained will, without any official information from any State as to what may be its internal condition!

Now, sir, I deny that there is in the fourteenth article of amendment to the Constitution of the United States any power conferred which authorizes the President to use the Army, the Navy, and the militia against the people of a State without having been first called upon by the Legislature, or the Governor of that State, there being no time to convene the Legislature. The fourteenth article of amendment, under which it is claimed by the advocates of this bill that this power is given, is as follows:

No State shall make or enforce any law which shall abridge the privileges or immunities of citizens of the United States; nor shall any State deprive any person of life, liberty, or property without due process of law.

Is there any power conferred there, unless it be to go into the courts for redress against a violation of these rights? And if there be domestic violence which the State cannot suppress, how is the President to know whether within the limits of any State life, liberty, and property have been taken from the citizen without due process of law? The Constitution itself provides how it shall be done. We find in the fourth section of the fourth article of the Constitution that it is provided that:

The United States shall guaranty to every State in this Union a republican form of government, and shall protect each of them against invasion; and on application of the Legislature, or the Executive (when the Legislature cannot be convened) against domestic violence.

Here it will be observed that so jealous is the Constitution of the rights and liberties of the people, that it does not allow the President to interfere, even on the application of the Governor of a State, except when the Legislature cannot be convened. The power proposed by this bill to be conferred on the President is despotic. It is to place him on a footing with the Czar, the Sultan, and the Mogul. And do you intend to break down all the barriers which protect your constituents, to place the President above the Constitution, and announce to the world that this is a Government of force, and not of law?

So, in the fourth section of the bill, the President is authorized, at his own discretion, of his own will and option, to suspend the writ of *habeas corpus* in time of peace, and establish martial law in any district, in any State or States of the Union, either North or South, at his sole discretion. . . .

Now, sir, if you want to preserve peace to the South, if you want to preserve peace and tranquillity to the whole country, if you are not determined to strike a blow which may end in the total subversion of our free institutions, change your policy to the South; instead of disabilities give amnesty; instead of vengeance offer reconciliation; instead of hostility tender the olive branch, and peace, prosperity, and happiness will bless our whole country.

Sir, I, with you, with every good citizen, denounce the violation of the law wherever the law is violated. But, to punish an individual crime or to punish a few crimes, do not strike down the institutions of our country. Stop sending to the South your tax-gatherers from Ohio and from Massachusetts and from other States of the North. When you know that the people of the North themselves are restive under the burdens of taxation, is it strange that the people of the South should be equally so when you require them to pay taxes to support the Government which has kept them under political disabilities during a period of six years after the close of the war, and sends strangers among them as conquerors and tax-gatherers? . . .

WILLIAM ARTHUR [DEM., KY.]. . . .

From the commencement of the present session of this Congress the gentleman from Massachusetts [Mr. Butler] vainly endeavored to introduce and bring forward his bill upon the subject of alleged disorders in the South. That bill was most atrocious in its character. It shocked every conservative Republican in this House, and many of the bolder sort hesitated to give it countenance. But, unabashed by all these unfriendly manifestations, the author adhered first to his bill and finally to the spirit and substance of it (when he found he could not get its form and details) with the audacity, subtlety, and tenacity for which he is distinguished as a Republican leader. It seemed to us, on this side of the House, that the better genius of the Republican party would prevail, and that malevolence, factiousness, and imposture would be discountenanced.

Subsequently followed the recent message of the Executive upon alleged southern disorders; the select committee of the House was formed, to whom it was referred, who, upon consideration, have, by the gentleman from Ohio, [Mr. Shellabarger,] reported the pending bill to the House. If the gentleman from Massachusetts, [Mr. Butler,] in the loss of his own bill experienced the pangs of unrequited paternity, he did not lose his vitality; and now, in the sequel, his temporary loss has been more than compensated in his signal triumph over the better men of his party in this House and on that committee, as proven by the pending bill, which, in spirit and in substance, is identical in atrocity. . . .

Proposed legislation by Congress is properly subjected to two cardinal tests, namely: first, is it constitutional; second, is it expedient? I shall not now go into the constitutionality of this section. It is cumulative, as far as it goes, with certain provisions in the civil rights bill. The opinion of the country is formed upon that bill. I believe it to be a flagrant violation of the spirit and letter of that revered instrument. We are aware that it has undergone to some extent judicial construction in State and Federal judicatures; that its constitutionality has been affirmed on the one hand and denied on the other; and that the Supreme Court has not as yet, so far as I am advised, passed upon it. It is therefore an open question, and is at least of doubtful constitutionality, and therefore to be condemned.

But having the section subjected to the second cardinal test, to wit, is it expedient? It must upon the slightest reflection fall under the sternest condemnation of the jurist, the statesman, the philanthropist, of every lover of the divine and political axiom of peace and good will to men. It overrides the reserved powers of the States. It reaches out and draws within the despotic circle of central power all the domestic, internal, and local institutions and offices of the States, and then asserts over them an arbitrary and paramount control as of the rights, privileges, and immunities secured and protected, in a peculiar sense, by the United States in the citizens thereof. Having done this, having swallowed up the States and their institutions, tribunals, and functions, it leaves them the shadow of what they once were. They are nominally what they should be as of sovereign right. And so long as they remain servile, suppliant, and subservient, the mailed hand of central power is stayed. But if the Legislature enacts a law, if the Governor enforces it, if the judge upon the bench renders a judgment, if the sheriff levy an execution, execute a writ, serve a summons, or make an arrest, all acting under a solemn, official oath, though as pure in duty as a saint and as immaculate as a seraph, for a mere error of judgment, they are liable, and most certain, at the suit of any knave, plain or colored, under the pretext of the deprivation of his rights, privileges, and immunities as a citizen, *par excellence*, of the United States, to be summarily stripped of official authority, dragged to the bar of a distant and unfriendly court, and there placed in the pillory of vexations, expensive, and protracted litigation, and heavy damages and amercements, destructive of health and exhaustive of means, for the benefit of unscrupulous adventurers or venal minions of power.

Hitherto, in all the history of this country and of England, no judge or court has been held liable, civilly or criminally, for judicial acts, and the ministerial agents of the law have been covered by the same aegis of exemption. Willfulness and corruption in error alone created a liability; and the judiciary has always remained in justice and equity, in intellect and learning, in freedom and in courage, far, far uplifted above the turmoils, the passions, and the vicissitudes of parties and partisan creeds, the central orb of the highest civilization, and the sheet-anchor of law and order. But no tribunal is sacred in the eye of existing usurpation, and every character, however excellent, must go down under the baleful progress of despotic power. Under the provisions of this section every judge in the State court and every other officer thereof, great or small, will enter upon and pursue the call of official duty with the sword of Damocles suspended over him by a silken thread, and bent upon him the scowl of unbridled power, the forerunner of the impending wrath, which is gathering itself to burst upon its victim.

But I can dwell on this section no longer, and I hasten on to section two. . . .

This section, like the first, absorbs the entire jurisdiction of the States over their local and domestic affairs: the first section as to civil rights and remedies, and the second as to wrongs and punishments; and it broadly asserts the same exclusive and plenary authority and jurisdiction in Congress and the United States courts over these subjects in and over all the States which the Federal Government possesses over places acquired by the consent of the States "for the erection of forts, magazines, arsenals, dock-yards, and other needful buildings."

It enumerates certain offenses now, under existing laws, punished as such in the United States courts, when committed in places under exclusive Federal jurisdiction, such as enumerated above. It then proceeds to create and define the particular offense, to wit:

First, banding, conspiring, or combining together to commit any one of the following offenses in the States, namely: murder, manslaughter, mayhem, robbery, perjury, subornation of perjury.

All heretofore of the sole jurisdiction of the States, within their limits, and punished as felonies.

Secondly, criminal obstruction of legal process or resistance of officers in discharge of official duty.

All this, I suppose, whether the officers or process be State or Federal, legal or illegal, for such is the vagueness and generality of the terms of the bill. Those offenses are such in the States, and uniformly punished there by the State laws and courts as felonies or misdemeanors, according to the circumstances of the particular case.

Thirdly and last, upon which I will dwell but for a moment, by way of illustration of the temper of the bill, assault and battery, for the most part the lowest grade of offense, being often no graver than a mere breach of the peace; and if any one of such persons, so combining to commit an assault and battery, shall do any act, shall so much as raise his hand, though it descend not, or advance his foot, though it step not, and no harm ensues to person or thing, all and each are declared to be guilty of a felony, and, upon conviction, fined $10,000 and imprisoned ten years, either or both, at the discretion of the court.

Shades of Draco and of Jeffreys! where is the parallel to this wickedness?.

The House and country will observe that by section three the Executive is to be the sole judge when to take military occupation of a State. The fourth section provides that such occupation shall be conclusive proof of rebellion. The President may intervene on a pretext, on a breach of the peace, assault and battery, or, peradventure, a fomented riot; and instantly, by the operation of this law that intervention by the President is held to be of itself conclusive proof of rebellion, and rebellion so held to exist with all the dire consequences in the train of this bill. . . .

GEORGE MCKEE [R., MISS.]. Mr. Speaker, I did not intend to take part in this debate, but statements have been made upon this floor that demand refutation, expecially from southern Republicans. The Republicans of the South have been held up as knaves and thieves; every crime has been charged upon them. This wholesale denunciation of the millions of Republicans in the southern States is but carrying out on the floor of this House on a grander scale the Ku Klux policy. They first murder their victim, and then with lying charges blacken his name and fame, in order to escape some of the odium attaching among civilized men to their wicked deeds. The country has become familiar with this mode of defense in individual cases, and now it is proposed to familiarize us with this policy on a national scale, as the circle of the infamous Klan widens in influence and begins to exert a controlling power among that northern Democracy of which it has been the efficient servant and ally and which it now aspires to rule. . . .

And now a short word as to Mississippi affairs. Both branches of our State

Legislature have passed a joint resolution calling for United States troops to enforce law and maintain order. For myself, I prefer regular troops to put down lawlessness. It does not breed the ill-feeling which must result from using militia. It does not engender the same strife between neighbors and neighborhoods and counties. Governor Alcorn has sent for troops without waiting for legislative action. Whatever other disagreements may exist between the executive and legislative departments of Mississippi, they agree in this. I shall not go into a detailed statement of the state of affairs in Mississippi; I have neither time nor inclination to do so. . . .

The Meridian massacre was in my own district; it has often been alluded to in this debate, and I cannot pass it in silence. The Alabama Ku Klux have made frequent incursions into our State. They participated in this bloody massacre at Meridian, invited there, as it is understood, by our home Ku Klux. They had been in that county before that time. Prior to the late butchery two colored officials had been murdered. Other outrages had been committed. But still it was deemed that enough had not been done, and the bloody work of death culminated in that infamous scene of riot and blood at Meridian which can neither be denied, excused, nor palliated.

I do not care to go into details. One single statement tells the whole story. One, and perhaps two white men killed, eight or ten colored men killed, according to Democratic authority, while Republicans claim that twenty-five or thirty have been killed in the streets and shot or hung in the swamps; and yet among all this red list of slaughter you do not find the name of a single Democrat. The dead and the wounded, the maimed and the scourged, are all, all Republicans. Not even the hair of the head of a single Democrat was harmed. No logic and no partisan passion can avail against this single fact. In this, as in all similar cases, lying dispatches come up here, claiming that colored men begin a riot. But when later news comes it is always found that colored men and Republicans alone have been killed. The colored men of Meridian were shot in the streets and hunted and hung in the swamp. They fled to the forest, and their path was lit up by the light of the blazing roof trees of their lowly cabins, and by the burning church around which their little homes were clustered. And now the widow and the orphan and the refugee are scattered far and wide. The homes so dear to them are desolate and they dare not return. The church which, with prayer and toil, they had reared, to the erection of which I have often seen them giving their illy-spared mite out of their scanty earnings, and beneath the heaven-pointing spire of which they have so often gathered to worship God in their simple way—that too is destroyed. Their husbands and fathers are slain; and houseless and homeless, weary and tired, poor and hungry, they know not what to do! And yet gentlemen on the other side say these outrages are "got up by Republicans for the occasion." May God forgive them for the lying slander upon a stricken people! . . .

Gentlemen are opposing this bill on constitutional grounds who claimed they had a legal constitutional right to secede and set up the confederate government, and yet they hold that this law to protect citizens of the United States by United States authority is against that Constitution, which in the interests of rebellion has been so widely interpreted; and others of the Opposition ransack the archives of the past, and with labored effort make long speeches to prove that this Government cannot protect its citizens; but the people are not to be deceived by all the musty lore of the past, nor by all the cobwebbed precedents they may rake out of the dust of ages, and which are not precedents at all in a case like this. The people know that the people must be protected; that the Constitution is created for the people, not the people for the Constitution; and I would rather trust the clear, honest, simple judgment of the people than that of any legal quibbler who ever split a constitutional hair on either side of this House. I would rather have the judgment of the people than that of all the Democratic jurists, from Chief Justice Taney down.

Gentlemen may talk of "the theory of our Government" and quote sage but obsolete precedents of constitutional law, (often obsolete because of the fourteenth and fifteenth amendments,) they may bring up against this bill their obscure maxims, but there is an old maxim of law, yes, and of statesmanship, too, which no one will gainsay, which is better, broader, and higher than all others, and which should be written in lines of living light all over every free republic of the people: *Salus populi suprema est lex*—the safety of the people should be the supreme law; and I hope that this House will declare under our Constitution that the safety of the people shall be the supreme law. This Government is of the people, by the people, and for the people, and every right of the lowliest citizen must be protected, or our much-vaunted Government and Constitution is a miserable failure. . . .

BENJAMIN BUTLER [R., MASS.]. . . .

There seem to me two controlling propositions on this question.

First. If the Federal Government cannot pass laws to protect the rights, liberty, and lives of citizens of the United States in the States, why were guarantees of those fundamental rights put in the Constitution at all, and especially by acts of amendment?

All agree that the mere constitutional assertion of affirmative guarantees not made operative by law, are ineffectual to aid the citizen. How, then, can the citizen avail himself of those constitutional guarantees and affirmative declarations of his rights, if Congress cannot pass laws to make them operative? How can it be an interference with the rights of the States for the laws of the United States to afford that protection to its citizens which the State fails or neglects to do for itself?

Is it one of the rights of a State not to protect its citizens in the enjoyment of life, liberty, and property, and thereby deny him the equal protection of the laws, so that, when the General Government attempts to do for the protection of the citizen what the State has failed to do, is it to be held an interference with the rights of the State? Pardon me; it seems to me that such action is only a necessary and proper interference with the wrongs of a State. A State has no constitutional or other right reserved to itself to deny or neglect to its citizen the equal protection of the laws.

Secondly. If the General Government has not the constitutional power to protect the lives, liberty, and property of its citizens upon its own soil when such protection is needed, then it ought to have such power; it should reside somewhere in the Government. For without the power to protect the lives of its citizens, a republican government is a failure, and if such be constitutional law, to be a citizen of the United States is to be the most unprotected of all mankind.

Wherever a citizen of the United States may be, upon a foreign soil or upon a foreign sea, however remote, the Constitution and laws of the United States are around and about him, guarding him from outrage and injury as fully as the cherubim and the flaming sword kept the way of the tree of life. There is no nation so weak or savage, none so cultivated, rich, or powerful, that it can unjustly lay its hand upon an American citizen in arrest or anger without calling down upon it the whole power of the Republic to protect him and redress his wrongs. "I am an American citizen" is the passport of safety of all his rights throughout the world, save only in his own country. Can this be so? . . .

Can it be, then, that an American citizen is protected in his rights of person and property by the Constitution and laws of the United States, with the whole power of the Government, everywhere, except on our own soil, under his own roof-tree, and covered by our own flag? Does that proposition need more argument than the statement of it? If the converse be true, then again I repeat, the Government of the United States is a failure; and better monarchy, better despotism, better anything than systematized anarchy, organized murder, outrage, and wrong, done at the will of remorseless bands upon defenseless citizens. . . .

Early in February last a bill was referred to the Committee on Reconstruction to meet the status of the South as it then appeared.

It will be observed that many of these most violent outrages have been brought to the attention of Congress since that date. It then seemed to the Committee on Reconstruction that provision might be made for relief against crime through the ordinary channels of judicial administration, provided with a sufficient number of judicial officers charged in due form of law with the detection of such crimes and staying and arresting the offenders. But it also appeared to that committee that, in order to give the judicial tribunals of the United States jurisdiction of such acts of wrong and violence, they must be made specific crimes against the laws, sovereignty, peace, and dignity of the United States. Therefore, a bill was considered in that committee, which provided, first, that there should be a commissioner of a United States court in every county of the South where the state of lawlessness rendered his presence necessary, whose duty it should be to ferret out crime, stay the offenders, and bring them to justice.

The bill further provided that the wrongs committed against the citizens of the United States, for the purpose of depriving such citizens of enjoyment of life, liberty, and property, guarantied to him by the Constitution, be made crimes against the laws of the United States and cognizable by its courts. The bill further provided that every citizen should have remedy in the Federal courts against the party depriving him of such rights, immunities, and privileges; and that where the community connived at such crimes and allowed its citizens to be plundered of such rights without any sufficient attempt to stay the marauders, so that by their stealth or their poverty the citizen was left without remedy, then he should have a remedy against the locality whose duty it was to protect him and which had failed on its part, for the wrongs suffered by him, with proper penalties and provisions to put the judicial machinery in motion to carry out the provisions of law.

Such are all the punitive or remedial provisions of the bill which the Committee on Reconstruction of the last Congress, by a vote of every true Republican present, ordered to be reported to the House, and which received a vote of but two less than two thirds that it should be considered in preference to all other business.

That bill I am proud to have called after my name. There is no provision of it that I would alter or change, except to make them more stringent, had I the power to make them the supreme law of the land. There is no provision in it but what was agreed to be within the constitutional power of Congress by some of the best lawyers of both Senate and House, to whom it was submitted; and the only criticism upon it by such lawyers was, it seemed to me, the puerile one that it might shock the prejudices of the people, and so injure the Republican party. . . .

Failing to be considered by the House at the last session, for reasons which have been heretofore sufficiently discussed, that same bill substantially was submitted to a joint committee of the two Houses of Congress, consisting of ten members, again fully considered, and again agreed to by a two-thirds majority of that committee, all concluding that the provisions of the bill were within the constitutional power of Congress, and the chairman of the committee was directed to report it to a caucus of the Republican party of each House, to be called for that purpose.

At a caucus, wherein eighty-four Republican members were present, there being but little over a hundred such members in town, that bill was reported and considered, section by section, and explained and debated for nearly three hours. Whereupon the caucus ordered the bill to be reported to the House and pressed for passage, and that order is certified in words following, that is to say:

That the report be accepted and adopted as the sense of this convention and that the committee be instructed to introduce it in the House of Representatives and press it to its passage.

Eighty-four members present.

A true copy:

Austin Blair
Chairman

After this statement in regard to the bill prepared in the manner above stated who shall dare say that it has not been approved by a majority of the Republicans of this House?

Certainly it was open to no objection in regard to its constitutionality or stringency that does not with equal force apply to the bill under discussion. As a matter of constitutional law there is no escaping the proposition, that if Congress has a right to declare a conspiracy to deprive a citizen of the United States of the rights guarantied to him by the Constitution and laws within the limits of a State, for doing of an act which is an offense, a crime against the United States, it is equally constitutional to declare an act done by one man with like intent and purpose a crime where the State denies equal protection of the laws to the citizen.

But, for one, I am quite content to take the bill before the House, because the recent developments of lawlessness and crime show an extent of organization, a fixedness of purpose, and a ruthlessness in execution of that purpose which demonstrate that the ordinary machinery of judicial tribunals is entirely inadequate to meet the great emergency which has arisen and erected itself into incipient war, even under the stringent provisions of the bill which I have been discussing—and which for shortness of designation I beg leave hereafter to refer to as my bill, although it is the bill of two Republican committees. Nothing but the strong arm of military power will put down military organizations such as the evidence discloses now exist in the South. True, in my bill I had enforced the judicial power by provisions drawn from the fugitive slave law, which caused some well-meaning Republicans to declare they could not vote for that provision of the bill. Let me tell them, however, that the Republicans voted for every substantial provision I have drawn from the fugitive slave law in the enforcement bill of the fifteenth amendment, reported by the Judiciary Committee of the last House, passed May 31, 1870. The difference is, only they apparently did not know it when they voted for it, while when my bill was before the House I was frank enough to tell them the origin of its provisions which seem so distasteful to them.

For myself, I cannot see why stringent provisions, declared to be constitutional by the courts, framed by the Democracy, to take away the liberty of the slave negro, should not be used to save the lives of free citizens, any more than John Wesley, when he set some of his stirring hymns to dancing-tunes, could see why the devil should have all the good tunes. . . .

In their eager denunciations of our bill to repose in the hands of the

President the power to suspend the writ of *habeas corpus* when the exigency arises, and to declare martial law and establish military commissions, our Democratic opponents seem to forget that that power is reposed now in every one of the Governors of the thirty-seven States, whenever either one of the thirty-seven Legislatures chooses to exercise it; and in some States the Governor is authorized to exercise it, when in his judgment the exigency arises, by standing laws. . . .

I see before me on the Democratic side of the House—and I ardently wish there were more—gentlemen who fought for the Union in 1861, including the gentleman from Ohio, [Mr. Morgan,] and who are now denying the constitutionality of the legislation we propose. Will they answer me one or two questions? Was the war of 1861 in which they fought a constitutional war? Did not Lincoln call out his troops under the act of 1795? Did not the Supreme Court of the United States declare that that was the "legal and proper beginning of war?" For what purpose were the troops called out? To suppress combinations against the laws of the United States too powerful to be resisted by the ordinary process of judicial tribunals, as we are now providing by law. Did the Governors or Legislatures of any of the southern States call upon President Lincoln to send such troops down there? If, as they claim, Congress cannot constitutionally empower the President to send troops to suppress insurrection in the southern States, pray, why did they march at the call of President Lincoln and take a commission in that war to unconstitutionally oppress their brethren of the South? Will the gentleman from Ohio suspend for a moment his vituperation of the Republican party and President Grant to reflect upon these questions? . . .

The gentleman from Ohio, [Mr. Morgan,] in his speech the other day, was kind enough to say that, "If the gentleman from Massachusetts [Mr. Butler] is not leader here, it was evident that he is master somewhere else."

He does me honor overmuch. I claim no influence nor power save that of a Representative of the people, striving to do his duty without fear or favor, in urging the passage of such laws as in his best judgment are for the good of his country. It is the highest position to which I can aspire, and one of which I am justly proud. Would to God the taunt of the gentleman from Ohio were true! That President Grant could, under the laws, and would make me "master somewhere else." Oh, for an hour of such power to rule the right and suppress the wrong; to save and defend the oppressed and down-trodden; to stay and punish the evil-doer. Then indeed should midnight raider and the murderous Ku Klux smiter of defenseless women and children and the disguised assassin and burner of quiet men's houses hang on the trees like ripe fruit ready to be plucked, until every man's rights, however humble, should be respected, and every roof tree, however lowly, should be the safe castle of refuge for its occupant from Mason and Dixon's line to Mexico.

We hear many fears expressed lest our bill to punish conspiracies for murder, arson, robbery, and other felonies, when it becomes law, shall be used as an instrument for the oppression of the people. No good and just man need fear its provisions. But let the wicked conspirators tremble. Every man can escape the stringency of its action by remaining a quiet and peaceful citizen, and not infringing the rights of person, property, or liberty of another, and voting the Democratic ticket only once at one election, and suffering his neighbor to exercise freely the same privilege if he is so benighted as to wish so to do. Let that be done, and every Democrat, rebel, and Ku Klux will be safe from its terrors. It is "the wicked who flee when no man pursueth." No hard-working and industrious white man or negro at the South, who is laboring to support himself, his wife, and family, to lay up his share of the three and a half millions of accumulations already deposited by the blacks in their savings-banks since the war—a greater amount derived from earnings of their labor since their late masters ceased, in part, from robbing them of its products than the entire banking capital, outside of their principal cities, invested by the whole southern white population since the war—but what will applaud and bless our action. . . .

JOHN COBURN [R., IND.]. . . .

Such occurrences show that there is a preconcerted and effective plan by which thousands of men are deprived of the equal protection of the laws. The arresting power is fettered, the witnesses are silenced, the courts are impotent, the laws are annulled, the criminal goes free, the persecuted citizen looks in vain for redress. This condition of affairs extends to counties and States; it is, in many places, the rule, and not the exception.

What, then, can be done? The States cannot or do not act. Some other power must be invoked. Where does it reside? How can it be exercised? Can it be made effectual? These are questions of the gravest import and which are forced upon us by the present circumstances.

That power resides in the General Government. The Constitution was framed in order to establish justice and insure domestic tranquillity, among other things. What is "to establish?" It is to fix firmly, safely, and permanently; not to intrust the matter to others, but attend to that duty promptly and fully; to secure justice to all, to use whatever power is necessary, to use it at the right time and in the right way. To insure domestic tranquillity. What is that; what is "to insure?" It is to leave no room for doubt or failure; it is to provide for it; it is to erect barriers against wrongdoers; it is to cause peace to prevail. What nobler or broader exercise of sovereign power can there be than this? Whenever the guarantys of the Constitution are broken, whenever there is a failure of a republican form of government, wherever there is domestic violence and aid is asked by the State authorities, where ever the equal protection of the laws is denied, in all such cases the General Government must exert its power to establish justice and insure tranquillity. There is no other power known under heaven. Without such a superintending and overruling authority our Government is chaos, is anarchy, is an unfinished ruin, fails where it is most needed.

In the matter before us the republican form of government is preserved, but much of its essence is denied. It may be safely said that a republican government, to exist, must be able to use the means to suppress lawlessness. If it does not, it is no government at all, much less a republican one. It is a vain thing to assert the right of suffrage, of representation, and of equality of protection as to person and property if none is given to them. Just as well have anti-republican institutions; they might be safer and better. The guaranty of republican institutions is made for the good that is in them, and not as a mere empty declaration.

But, to proceed a step further. Where there is domestic violence and aid is asked by the State, the nation must exercise its authority. Can it do so without invitation? Before the fourteenth amendment it could not unless that violence amounted to an overthrow of republican institutions; then it could; then the invitation is needless, the guaranty must be fulfilled. But now, where the equal protection of the law, as in case of an overthrow of republican institutions, is denied by domestic violence or any other cause, the nation may interpose to afford it, by legislation, directing the use of military power and the interposition of the courts of the United States; and this effort may be aimed at the particular case or State where the difficulty exists, or at all cases of that character whenever and wherever arising. The failure to afford protection equally to all is a denial of it.

Affirmative action or legislation is not the only method of a denial of protection by a State, State action not being always legislative action. A State may by positive enactment cut off from some the right to vote, to testify or to ask for redress of wrongs in court, to own or inherit or acquire property, to do business, to go freely from place to place, to bear arms, and many other such things. This positive denial of protection is no more flagrant or odious or dangerous than to allow certain persons to be outraged as to their property, safety, liberty, or life; than to overlook offenders in such cases; than to utterly disregard the sufferer and his persecutor, and treat the one as a nonentity and the other as a good citizen. How much worse is it for a State to enact that certain citizens shall not vote, than allow outlaws by violence, unpunished, to prevent them from voting? How much more effectual is the denial of justice in a State where the black man cannot testify, than in a State where his testimony is utterly disregarded when given on behalf of his race? How much more oppressive is the passage of a law that they shall not bear arms than the practical seizure of all arms from the hands of the colored men? A systematic failure to make arrests, to put on trial, to convict, or to punish offenders against the rights of a great class of citizens is a denial of equal protection in the eye of reason and the law, and justifies, yes, loudly demands, the active interference of the only power that can give it. If, in addition to all this, the State should fail to ask the aid of the General Government in putting down the existing outlawry, would not a more complete and perfect case of denial of protection be made out? Indeed, it would be difficult to conceive of a more glaring instance of the denial of protection.

It may be safely said, then, that there is a denial of the equal protection of the law by many of these States. It is therefore the plain duty of Congress to enforce by appropriate legislation the rights secured by this clause of the fourteenth amendment of the Constitution. So far it has not been found necessary to do this; but the emergency has at last arisen, and there is but one course to take. How can this thing be done? Shall we deal with individuals, or with the State as a State? If we can deal with individuals, that is a less radical course, and works less interference with local governments. To punish a particular individual is less troublesome than to set aside a whole State government, declare martial law, suspend the writ of *habeas corpus*, and substitute, generally, national for State authority. Can this be done? Or must the nation in every case of this kind deal with the State alone? Must we allow outrages to proceed till State authority is prostrated? It would seem more accordant with reason that the easier, more direct, and more certain method of dealing with individual criminals was preferable, and that the more thorough method of superseding State authority should only be resorted to when the deprivation of rights and the condition of outlawry was so general as to prevail in all quarters in defiance of or by permission of the local government.

In my judgment Congress has both remedies, and can use both or either as the emergency may require. . . .

Senate-42d Congress, 1st Session
April 11-14, 1871

GEORGE EDMUNDS [R., VT.]. I now move to take up the bill (H. R. No. 320) to enforce the provisions of the fourteenth amendment to the Constitution of the United States, and for other purposes.

The motion was agreed to; and the Senate, as in Committee of the Whole, proceeded to consider the bill. . . .

THE VICE PRESIDENT. The Secretary will now report the amendments of the Committee on the Judiciary.

MR. EDMUNDS. Before the amendments are reported I should like to ascertain the pleasure of the Senate, if I can, as to the method of considering them. If there is no special objection to any of the amendments, I should like to go forward and have them agreed to or disposed of; but if there is objection, perhaps it might be as well not to undertake to act upon the amendments until discussion shall have been had upon the nature and scope of the bill. However, the Secretary may read the first amendment, and I shall then, perhaps, be able to ascertain what the view of the Senate is on the subject.

THE CHIEF CLERK. The first amendment is in line nine of the second section to strike out the words "against the will and."

MR. EDMUNDS. Perhaps I should say a few words in explanation of the amendments. The committee did not undertake to exercise any matter of taste in making these amendments, and did not intend to go beyond the scope of the House bill. All that it undertook to do was to do those things that it thought essential to make the bill, within its present constitutional scope and within the scope of its expediency also, so perfect that it would stand the test of a criminal inquiry in the courts of justice, and to embrace within its reach some of the objects which seem to have been accidentally omitted in the preparation of it in the House of Representatives.

Our effort, therefore, has been, as to all these amendments, to do only so much as seemed to us to be indispensable to make the bill a perfect working bill upon the basis on which it was framed. For instance, look at the amendment on the second page, in the second section, where the House bill had provided merely for a conspiracy to injure a person on account of the lawful discharge of his duties as an officer of the United States, that being the cause and made no provision for a conspiracy to injure him while engaged in the course of their discharge. The old statutes of the United States make it a crime now to assault any officer of the United States or beat him while in the discharge of the duties of his office. This bill, acting upon the same subject, seemed by implication to repeal that provision and to provide only for punishing a conspiracy to attack or injure him on account of the performance of the duties of his office, leaving it to the uncertain circumstantial testimony which must always exist in cases of conspiracy, and leaving it to a jury to guess, if they can, whether this interference with him was occasioned by reason of the performance of his duties, instead of leaving to the jury the plain fact that he was interfered with when in the performance of his duty as the law now stands in respect to actual interference; I do not know that there is any provision for conspiracy. That illustrates one amendment.

So when you go to the bottom of the same page you find that we have inserted in the protective and punitory clauses of this bill the word "party" as well as "witness." The House had made no provision for punishing a conspiracy to hinder any person who was obliged to resort to the courts for redress, but they had undertaken to make provision for securing the witnesses and the jurors. It appeared to us that it would be a somewhat singular course of legislation to afford no protection to parties who had been hindered and oppressed and who were undertaking to resort to the judiciary for their protection, while we undertook to protect the agencies through which that protection was to be obtained, leaving the conspirators to conspire against the life of the party; and if they should succeed in that conspiracy there would be no occasion for them to conspire against his liberties, for he would be dead and gone.

The amendments on the top of the third page are in the same spirit, which I need not enlarge upon. Then toward the foot of the third page comes an amendment, somewhat longer, which provides for punishing a conspiracy for the purpose of impeding and obstructing and defeating the due course of justice in any State or Territory with intent to deny any citizen of the United States the due and equal protection of the laws. This we understood to have been intended to be reached by the preceding provision of the House bill providing for punishing a conspiracy for the purpose of preventing or hindering the constituted authorities of any State from giving and securing to all persons within that State the equal protection of the laws; but we were very much afraid that the vagueness and generality of those phrases, they not being such as have been used in criminal statutes before, would lead to extreme difficulty in the prosecution and punishment of offenders, even if it might not break down altogether on account of its vagueness. We therefore thought it desirable, carrying out the same view and intending to reach the same end, to introduce as an amendment the words to which I have referred, being well-known and well settled words used in the statutes and used at the common law as covering conspiracies for any purpose the design of which through any means should be to defeat the regular and due administration of justice. We regard that amendment as of considerable importance to the security of the very ends which this section has attempted to reach.

Then the next amendment of real substance is on the fifth page, where we propose to strike out the words from section three "so far obstruct or hinder the execution of the laws thereof and of the United States as to." As the section now stands, coming from the House of Representatives, these insurrections and unlawful combinations or conspiracies, in order to be interfered with by the President of the United States by military power, must not only reach the point of depriving as a matter of fact portions and classes of the people of a State of their constitutional rights of life, liberty, and property, and the protection of the laws, but they must go to the point of obstructing and hindering in the technical sense (when anybody is interfered with under it) the execution of the laws of that State and also the laws of the United States, putting it in the conjunctive. Therefore as the section stood it appeared to us that the President would have no right to interfere at all under this section unless these combinations and conspiracies should not only have spread desolation and terror and death through any given section of a State, but also should have gone to the point in connection with that of, in the technical sense, hindering and obstructing the execution of the law, which should be brought to bear upon the subject, not only of the State itself, but of the United States.

In a case of that kind it would involve a great deal of difficulty and require a great deal of proof to reach the point where the President could interfere at all. We thought it desirable to leave his right to interfere under this third section upon a plain and simple state of facts, as follows: first, that there should be a conspiracy, an unlawful combination which should be so far carried into effect as to deprive as a matter of fact some portion or class of the people of a State of the rights and privileges which the Constitution of the United States secures to them, so that the President would have a plain and simple case to act upon, which nobody could misunderstand, which the people of the State would understand, which the conspirators would understand, which the Executive would understand; that is to say, first, a conspiracy, and second, a conspiracy carried into effect depriving classes of the community of their constitutional rights.

OLIVER MORTON [R., IND.]. I ask the Senator whether, in the seventh and eighth lines of that section where the words "or obstruct the equal and impartial course of justice" are used, that clause is intended to embrace the State courts.

MR. EDMUNDS. Certainly, referring to "the equal and impartial course of justice" mentioned in the second section on the third page. This obstruction of the equal and impartial course of justice, however, must, under the provisions of all this bill, go so far as to deny and withhold from citizens of the United States that equality of protection in seeking justice which the Constitution of the United States gives to them. We do not undertake in this bill to interfere with what might be called a private conspiracy growing out of a neighborhood feud of one man or set of men against another to prevent one getting an indictment in the State courts against men for burning down his barn; but, if in a case like this, it should appear that this conspiracy was formed against this man because he was a Democrat, if you please, or because he was a Catholic, or because he was a Methodist, or because he was a Vermonter, (which is a pretty painful instance that I have in my mind in the State of Florida within a few days where a man lost his life for that reason,) then this section could reach it.

Then we think it of considerable importance in the eleventh, twelfth, and thirteenth lines of the third section on the fifth page to strike out the cumulative words—

And shall fail or neglect, through the proper authorities, to apply to the President of the United States for aid in that behalf.

The scope of that portion of the section is that after this conspiracy shall have been formed, after it shall have been carried into execution by violence so as to deprive classes or portions of the people of a State of their constitutional right to protection and equality, the President shall not interpose unless the constituted authorities of the State shall be unable or unwilling—that is the substance of it—to give them protection, and shall also have failed to apply to the President of the United States for that protection. With that clause in, if any State, through its Legislature or through its Governor, shall apply to the President of the United States for protection, in such a case the President, under this section, has no right to interfere and give the very protection that they call for, for the reason that his only right to interfere is based upon the condition that there shall have been no application made to him; and therefore, in such a case, if application were sincerely made by some Governor or Legislature who were desirous of assistance, or insincerely made by some Governor or Legislature who wished to trammel the powers of the Executive under this section, his only power then would be to interfere under preexisting laws purely and solely in aid of the State authorities and turn the prisoner whom he should have caught over to the State authorities to be tried by a State jury in the very county where he and his brethren had formed the conspiracy.

It appeared to us that it was right to provide that when this extreme condition of things should have arisen, of a conspiracy carried into effect to destroy the rights of citizens of the United States to the equal protection of the laws, and should have gone so far that, as a matter of fact, the State authorities were unable to give the protection which they ought to do as well as we, then it would be quite time for the President to interfere, and that he ought not to be trammeled and impeded in that interference to protect the national rights of a citizen by any call of a State Executive, either sincere or insincere, upon him, which would oust the very jurisdiction which the section gives.

MR. MORTON. Will the Senator allow me to ask him a question on a point of detail?

MR. EDMUNDS. With pleasure.

MR. MORTON. I call his attention to the third section beginning with the fifteenth line:

And in all such cases it shall be lawful for the President, and it shall be his duty, to take such measures, by the employment of the militia or the land and naval forces of the United States, or of either, or by other means, as he may deem necessary for the suppression of such insurrection, domestic violence, or combinations; and any person who shall be arrested under the provisions of this and the preceding section shall be delivered to the marshal of the proper district to be dealt with according to law.

Now, in the absence of the suspension of the writ of *habeas corpus*, I should like to inquire what can be done under that section. . . .

MR. EDMUNDS. My answer to that is that, under this section, without the suspension of the writ of *habeas corpus* the President and his forces really act as a *posse comitatus*, although they are entitled to act under this bill just as police officers are entitled to act, as a *posse comitatus*, so to speak, without a warrant; that is, the President may go in with his forces and seize the conspirators and turbulent and wicked men who are engaged in these acts of violence, without waiting for anybody to swear out a warrant against these people before a commissioner or a judge. He may capture them, as we always do in such cases. He occupies in fact, seeing the thing go on and being called upon to repress it by force, precisely the position that a body of police would occupy in seeing a riot in the streets of a city, who would seize the rioters and take them before a judge without going to the judge first for a warrant. That is the effect of it. Then the party being brought into court would be tried under the preceding sections of this act for being engaged in a conspiracy of the nature named, and would be tried in that case under the second and third sections in the circut court of the United States for that State or the district court, as the case might be, and wherever that court should be held, instead of being tried in the very county, as always by State laws it is provided, where the offense was committed.

The only amendment which we have recommended to the fourth section, providing for the power to suspend the *habeas corpus* in certain cases, is, in the last lines of it, that that section shall continue in force until the end of the next regular session of Congress, instead of expiring on the 1st day of June, 1872, by its own limitation. We think it right and desirable that that subject shall not pass from the control of Congress by its own limitation until the end of its next session, unless Congress itself shall, as it may do at any time, see fit to do it. Although we are unwilling to suppose that anybody would resort to such an expedient, yet we are unwilling to leave it to the power of anybody in either House of Congress by a course of unfair practice, if the state of the country at that time should require that this power should be exercised, to allow this section to lapse, by sheer force of argument and debate, when a majority of both Houses should think it fit to continue it. In other words, to use language which I do not very much admire, we should prefer not to have this section expire by its own limitation at the next session on account of any filibustering to prevent an act to continue it, if it should be necessary. We therefore hold it as in force until the expiration of the next regular session of Congress, unless it should please a majority of the two Houses to change it before. . . .

Having said this about these amendments, and having stated, I believe, that the committee regard almost all of them as essential to the perfectness and proper and easy operation of the statute, I will now, while I am up, say a word in respect to the scope of the bill as it stands and as it will be, as to its general scope if amended.

The first section is one that I believe nobody objects to, as defining the rights secured by the Constitution of the United States when they are assailed by any State law or under color of any State law, and it is merely carrying out the principles of the civil rights bill, which have since become a part of the Constitution.

The second section, it will be observed, only provides for the punishment
of a conspiracy. It does not provide for the punishment of any act done in
pursuance of the conspiracy, but only a conspiracy to deprive citizens of the
United States, in the various ways named, of the rights which the Constitution and the laws of the United States made pursuant to it give to them; that
is to say, conspiracies to overthrow the Government, conspiracies to impede
the course of justice, conspiracies to deprive people of the equal protection of
the laws, whatever those laws may be. It does not provide, as I say, for any
punishment for any act which these conspirators shall do in furtherance of
the conspiracy. It punishes the conspiracy alone, leaving the States, if they
see fit, to punish the acts and crimes which may be committed in pursuance
of the conspiracy. I confess that I thought myself it was desirable, to make
the bill complete, to make it completely logical and completely effective, that
a section should have been added providing not only for punishing the
conspiracy, but providing also in the same way for punishing any act done in
pursuance of the conspiracy. This section gives a civil action to anybody who
shall be injured by the conspiracy, but does not punish an act done as a
crime.

Then the third section is, as we think, one in entire conformity to
precedents and in entire conformity to the principles of the Constitution and
of the laws, authorizing the President when the lawful rights of citizens of the
United States shall be interfered with and overthrown by unlawful conspiracies, combinations, and insurrections, and when the State shall fail to
protect the people in those rights and put down these insurrections, to bring
to bear the power of the nation for the purpose of repressing such tumults
and disorders, and handing the violators of the law over to justice.

The fourth section provides that when these unlawful conspiracies and
combinations shall have proceeded to that extreme extent as really to become general in a State, covering more than one combination and being so
powerful as to be able to overthrow the State authorities and to set them at
defiance, then it shall be treated as in the character of a local rebellion, and
the President, in that case, shall be authorized, as the Constitution gives us
the power to authorize him, to bring the military to bear upon it, and for the
time being within the district where the power of the courts and the power of
the States are both set at defiance, to suspend the writ of *habeas corpus*. But
even then the bill does not go so far in that direction as upon a mere reading
it would be supposed it did, because there is attached to this suspension of
the *habeas corpus* the provision that the act of 1863 relating to *habeas
corpus* shall apply even to a case of this kind; and that provides that in all
cases in States where the *habeas corpus* is suspended, and the Federal
judiciary is still able to hold sway at the places where it holds courts, any
person arrested and seized under the suspension of the *habeas corpus* shall
be reported to the Federal judiciary within a limited time, or as soon as
practicable, and if the Federal judiciary shall not deal with the offenders thus

reported by finding indictments or other prosecution, then, upon the order of a judge, the persons thus seized under the suspension of *habeas corpus* shall be set at liberty.

In substance and fact it leaves a Federal *habeas corpus* in effect, although not in precise form, still operating for a limited time. So that really the sharpest criticism, with this proviso, could scarcely say that in a substantial sense we authorize the President to suspend the writ of *habeas corpus* at all. About all that we do is to authorize him to proclaim that he has suspended it, and then, as soon as he has caught anybody, to report him and hand him over to the Federal judge. It is much less than I should have wished for myself; but as the House had chosen to so limit it, we thought it not wise to undertake to change it.

The fifth section of course explains itself, as to not repealing any former law.

The sixth section provides for an inquiry into the character and conduct of persons who may be summoned to sit on juries in cases arising under the provisions of this act. There is an amendment which seems to be a mere verbal one, but which carries a great deal of effect in it, in the sixth section, which I did not call attention to in that connection.

As the House passed the bill, this inquiry into the conduct of juries was only in suits or prosecutions based upon this act. All civil suits, as every lawyer understands, which this act authorizes, are not based upon it; they are based upon the right of the citizen. The act only gives a remedy. The suit, therefore, in the technical sense, instead of being based upon the statute, as it would be if it were debt for a penalty, is a suit arising under the statute, and the consequence would be when you come to get before a judge and undertake to challenge a jury, without inserting the words "arising under" the provisions of this act, as well as based upon it, any private party would find himself debarred of having this inquiry made for his protection at all, and it would be only in criminal prosecutions based upon the provisions of the statute that this challenging of jurors could occur. We thought it important, therefore, to use words which would enable a judge in all the cases of civil redress to see that the party aggrieved should have a pure and uncontaminated jury.

The last clause of this last section is also of considerable importance, and I ought to explain it to the Senate. It provides that "the act entitled 'An act defining additional causes of challenge, and prescribing an additional oath for grand and petit jurors in the United States courts,' approved June 17, 1862, be, and the same is hereby, repealed." That act provides that it shall be a good cause of challenge, upon suitable and proper inquiry made in the way pointed out by the statute, to any grand or petit juror, that he has been engaged in the rebellion. This section repeals that act, so that it will be no disqualification in cases arising under this act, or arising under any other act in the courts of the United States, either criminal or civil, hereafter, that the person summoned as a juror and who is proposed to be put in the panel has been engaged in the rebellion; so that in no possible case can participation in the late rebellion be made the ground for setting aside a juror. I am bound to say that that does not meet with my individual approval, but I am instructed by the committee, and shall do so with pleasure, to report the bill in that respect as it stands.

This, Mr. President, explains, I believe, the general scope, and, perhaps I might, say the detailed operation of this bill. I feel some confidence in saying that, upon discussion, I think it will turn out that this bill is clearly within the provisions of the Constitution of the United States, and in respect to the matters upon which it operates, and over which it undertakes to exercise sway, it is much more moderate and limited in its application and in its remedies and punishments than the state of the case—if it be one half as bad as the newspapers in the southern States of all parties, collating and putting together their facts, represent the case to be—it is much more moderate and limited than the case would justify. . . .

JOHN STOCKTON [DEM., N.J.]. Mr. President, this act provides that any person who, under color of any law of any State, shall subject or cause to be subjected any person within the jurisdiction of the United States to the deprivation of any rights, privileges, or immunities secured by the Constitution of the United States, shall be liable to the party injured for redress, the proceedings to obtain which shall be in the Federal courts. In the second section, that if two or more persons, within any State or Territory of the United States, shall conspire to put down or destroy the Government of the United States by force, or levy war against the United States, or to oppose by force the authority of the United States, or by force, intimidation, or threat to prevent, hinder, or delay the execution of any law of the United States, or take any property of the United States against the will of the United States, or prevent any person from accepting or holding any office or trust or place of confidence under the United States, or injure any witness in his person or property, etc., or go in disguise upon the public highway or upon the premises of another for the purpose, either directly or indirectly, of depriving any person of the equal protection of the laws, or hindering the constituted authorities of any State from giving or securing to all persons within such State the equal protection of the laws, etc., such person shall be deemed guilty of a high crime, and shall be punished in the Federal courts by a fine not less than $500 nor more than $5,000, or by imprisonment with or without hard labor, as the court may determine, for a period not less than six months nor more than six years. A civil remedy is also given to the party injured. By section three it is provided that in all cases where insurrection, domestic violence, unlawful combinations, or conspiracies in any State shall so far obstruct or hinder the execution of the laws thereof, and of the United States, as to deprive any portion or class of the people of such State of any of the rights, privileges, immunities, or protection named in the Constitution and secured by this act, or obstruct the equal and impartial course of justice, and the constituted authorities of such State shall either be unable to protect or shall from any cause fail to protect or neglect to apply to the President, such facts shall be deemed a denial by such State of the equal protection of the laws to which they are entitled under the Constitution of the United States; and in all such cases it shall be lawful for the President, and it shall be his duty, to take such measures, by the employment of the militia or the land and navy forces of the United States, etc. It is further provided by section four that whenever in any State or part of a State unlawful combinations shall set at defiance the constituted authorities, or when the constituted authorities are in complicity with or connive at the unlawful purpose, and conviction shall become impracticable, it shall be deemed a rebellion against the Government of the United States, and it shall be lawful for the President to suspend the privileges of the writ of *habeas corpus*. It further provides that no person shall be a grand or petit juror who shall, in the judgment of the court, be in complicity with such combination, and each jury must take an oath that he never aided, etc.

Mr. President, the Constitution provides that the privilege of the writ of *habeas corpus* shall not be suspended unless when, in cases of rebellion or invasion, the public safety may require it. This act avoids the whole prohibition by defining what shall be construed to be a rebellion, and leaving the question of public safety requiring it entirely to the President.

The fourteenth amendment provides that no State shall deprive any person of life, liberty, or property without due process of law, nor deny to any person within its jurisdiction the equal protection of the laws. But the act authorizes the President to do what is forbidden by this clause to the States, and, notwithstanding the constitutional restraints on the executive power, takes the whole question away from the courts by construing what shall be deemed a denial by a State of the equal protection of the law.

The Constitution provides that in all criminal prosecutions the accused shall enjoy the right to a speedy and public trial by an impartial jury of the State and district wherein the crime shall have been committed. The bill deprives him altogether of trial by jury, for the qualifications of the juror are left to the judgment of the court. It does not exclude those only who shall not be able to take a certain oath; it does not exclude only those in complicity or who may have aided, but who in the judgment of the court be in complicity. The court selects the jury.

Thus, at the outset, we find the judgment of the President as to its necessity; his will alone is substituted for a constitutional protection as to the suspension of the privilege of the writ of *habeas corpus*. Congress defines, instead of the courts, the meaning of rebellion and what shall be deemed a denial by a State of equal protection, thus amending the Constitution at pleasure.

That although the President is not permitted by section four, article four, to interfere in a State against domestic violence except on application of the Legislature, or the Executive when it cannot be convened, he is by this bill authorized to use the militia, the Army, and Navy whenever he thinks the congressional definition justifies him, which is really whenever he sees fit.

"If any one obstructs the equal and impartial course of justice" is added by the Senate committee in place of the words "and shall fail or neglect, through the proper authorities, to apply to the President of the United States for aid in that behalf."

What is the meaning of obstructing the equal and impartial course of justice? I apprehend that it has no legal, definite meaning; that it may mean anything required. I doubt whether there are many people in the United States who do not obstruct the equal and impartial course of justice. It is not its administration by judicial or executive officers, but the impartial course of justice. Any man who is unjust himself in word or deed violates this law, commits this offense; the man that lies and does not pay his debts violates it; the man who does not obey the golden rule violates it. What does it mean? Yet whether you know its meaning or not, it is that crime the commission of which by one man creates the constructive crime called "a denial by a State of equal protection of the laws," and upon the occurrence of which it is declared not only to be lawful for the President, but it is made his duty, "to take such measures by the employment of the militia, or the land and naval forces of the United States, or of either, or by other means, as he may deem necessary, for the suppression of such insurrection, domestic violence, or combinations."

But, Mr. President, this act is entitled "An act to enforce the provisions of the fourteenth amendment to the Constitution of the United States, and for other purposes." And, first, Mr. President, let me observe that the act is, in my judgment, much more for other purposes than to enforce the fourteenth amendment. What those purposes are has been spread before the country, not only by speeches, but has been plainly pointed out by the history of this whole movement, from its initiation to the present time. It is an act for other purposes, undoubtedly. Whether it is properly in any sense an act to enforce the fourteenth amendment is quite questionable.

It is for other, and, as it seems to me, for very bad purposes, but it is not an act to enforce the fourteenth amendment in the view that I take of it. The fourteenth amendment says that no State shall make or enforce any law which shall abridge the privileges or immunities or citizens of the United States; having previously declared that all persons born or naturalized in the United States and subject to the jurisdiction thereof are citizens of the United States and of the State wherein they reside. Mr. President, has it been asserted anywhere, by anybody, that any State had made or enforced any law to abridge the privileges or immunities of citizens? No, sir. If it has, I have not heard it.

How, then, is the power to pass this bill obtained? Not certainly by section five of the amendment, for this is not in any sense appropriate legislation to enforce the provisions of the article.

Mr. President, the construction of the fourteenth amendment necessary to make this bill constitutional is simply this: that as the amendment provided that no State should deprive any person of life, liberty, or property without due process of law, nor deny to any person within its jurisdiction the equal protection of the laws, therefore Congress can, whenever it pleases, interfere with all these rights, restrict and deny them in despite of all the express reservations and prohibitions contained in the amendments, articles one, four, five, nine, and ten; or, in other words, because no State can, Congress may; or, in other words, the denial of power to a State confers it on Congress. Nay, more; you claim the power to subordinate the whole Bill of Rights to the absolute and uncontrolled will of one man, who is the commander of the Army and Navy, and whose executive powers are limited and defined by article two, and who, if he steps beyond these powers without authority of an amendment to the Constitution, is simply a usurper. . . .

It is insisted that when the fourteenth amendment declares that "all persons born or naturalized in the United States shall be citizens of the United States" the privileges of that citizenship attach to every individual, and the United States Government is bound to protect them. These privileges are alleged to be such as are asserted in the Declaration of Independence, namely, "the enjoyment of life and liberty, with the right to acquire and possess property." That this makes it the duty of the General Government to protect all its citizens in all their rights, therefore, if some of them are alleged in small localities to be interfered with, Congress may destroy the whole framework of the States, the whole machinery of self-government, and violate, as to the whole body of the people, every provision of the Bill of Rights, make itself omnipotent, and place the life and liberty of every human being at the absolute mercy of the President, thus destroying the Constitution absolutely, everything of value in it, in order that they may do the work of local self-government, thereby changing the whole theory of our Government.

Under this construction it is claimed you may give any power you please to the President, and make his will the law of the land, overriding the constitutional restraints imposed on the executive power, notwithstanding Congress is absolutely in terms prohibited from doing it. He may assume by your direction the judicial power and hold the assizes in the State of North Carolina under the absolute claims made under this construction of the fourteenth amendment, and which construction is needed to support this bill.

It is said that, whatever might have been the case before, under the fourteenth amendment Congress is bound to protect United States citizens in all their privileges, the enjoyment of life, liberty, etc., under which I believe the Radical party include the right to vote, the exercise of the right of suffrage. This was declared to be a God-given, natural right; it was dignified by the name of "manhood suffrage;" the simple fact being that who shall vote and who shall not vote is nothing but a question of expediency, dependent, not upon race or color, but upon fitness, which determines properly who shall exercise the right of choosing their representative, indirectly assisting in making the law, and governing the country. But to prevent any State from passing laws or using their constitutions to abridge the rights of citizens of the United States, (who are therein declared to be all persons born or naturalized therein,) whether suffrage be one or not, is the object of this amendment; to abrogate any clause in the State constitutions which would operate to do it; to prevent State laws from being passed whose object might be to do it, and to enforce the amendment; that is, to attain this end by such constitutional legislation as Congress may deem necessary, through constitutional means, through the United States courts and marshals and judges, authorized to call for aid whenever necessary, and protected already with the whole power of our Government, but not to claim, as is done by the advocates of this bill, that the power to prevent the State from doing these constitutional acts gives authority to the United States to destroy the autonomy of the States and make war on the people thereof, when it is not and never has been even alleged that any State ever had contemplated any of the acts forbidden, but simply that crimes against the laws of the United States of various grades and kinds, as well as the States, had occurred in all the States, as they always have and will do. . . .

Mr. President, there is no proof that all the crimes alleged to have been committed cannot be punished by a proper organization of the United States courts. Every one of these offenses are punishable by the State courts; they are in full operation, with all their processes served without hindrance from any one. So far from that supreme necessity existing which, in times of sudden and violent political shocks, justifies the resort to the maxim, on the ground that law no longer exists, (for it is a revolutionary maxim in such cases,) it is not suggested that any necessity exists except a want of ability or zeal by the Government in executing the laws, which laws, without alteration, are ample for the purpose, and can be enforced at any moment without this bill, in accordance with the Constitution, by the whole military power of the Government.

Under these circumstances, I cannot but consider the precedent about to be set most dangerous. I cannot but believe that there must be, as the title says, other objects in view besides the enforcement of the fourteenth amendment. . . .

THE PRESIDING OFFICER. [JAMES HARLAN, R., IOWA]. Is the Senate ready for the question on the first amendment to this bill reported by the Committee on the Judiciary?

WILLIAM HAMILTON [DEM., MD.]. What is the amendment?

THE PRESIDING OFFICER. The amendment will be reported.

THE CHIEF CLERK. In section two, line nine, it is proposed to strike out the words "against the will and," and in line ten to strike out the words "of the United States" and insert "thereof;" so as to read, "or delay the execution of any law of the United States, or by force to seize, take, or possess any property of the United States contrary to the authority thereof, or by force, intimidation," etc.

LYMAN TRUMBULL [R., ILL.]. To that particular amendment there would, perhaps, be no objection. Probably it is a proper amendment to make, as it corrects the phraseology and does not alter the meaning of the bill; but as I thought it was better not to attempt to amend the bill as it came from the House of Representatives, I had intended to object to all these amendments upon that ground. It is not my purpose to go into any general argument upon this bill, and I am not in a condition to do so this afternoon, if I designed to do so at any time. I shall content myself with stating merely what I suppose to be the principle involved in the bill, and what the effect of these amendments is. I shall do this without any considerable argument or attempt at illustration.

I am sorry that while a bill of so much importance is under consideration the Senate is so thin, and should give so little attention to the principles which are involved in it; principles which go to the foundation of the Government; principles which, if carried out, may change the character of the Government. Whether it may be best to change the character of the Government is a very serious question for the consideration of the American people. It should not be lightly done. Whether we have done so in the amendments which have been made to the Constitution of the United States since the war, is a question that deserves and should receive serious consideration, before, by legislation, we adopt a policy that virtually does make such a change. . . .

Subsequently to the enactment of the civil rights act [of 1866] the fourteenth constitutional amendment was adopted. That amendment in its first clause is but a copy of the civil rights act, declaring that all persons born in the United States and not subject to any foreign jurisdiction are citizens of the United States. This had been previously declared by act of Congress, and it was so without any act of Congress. Every person born within the jurisdiction of a nation must be a citizen of that country. Such persons are called subjects of the Crown in Great Britain, in this country citizens of the United States. It is an entire mistake to suppose that there was no such thing as an American citizen until the adoption of the fourteenth amendment to the Constitution of the United States. American citizenship existed from the moment that the Government of the United States was formed. . . .

It was because of the idea which obtained before the adoption of the thirteenth amendment to the Constitution of the United States, that slaves were property and not persons, that it was thought proper to embody in the civil rights bill the declaration that all persons born in the United States were citizens. I did not think at that time that it was necessary. I recollect that I had a discussion on that very point with the then Senator from Maryland, Mr. Reverdy Johnson, as to the propriety of inserting in the civil rights act those words declaring that all persons born in the United States were citizens. We both agreed that after the abolition of slavery everybody born in and subject to the jurisdiction of the United States was a citizen of the United States; but we both thought that in consequence of the declaration which had been enunciated in the Dred Scott case, and also in order that there might be no cavil about it, it was better to declare it by law.

MR. EDMUNDS. That decision was flatly the other way, that they were not citizens, although free persons.

MR. TRUMBULL. Yes, sir, there is a decision, I think, that even free colored persons were not citizens. After the abolition of slavery and of the distinction in regard to colored persons I do not think such a decision could have been maintained. It was advisable, at any rate, to put such an express declaration in the law. After that bill was passed it will be remembered that the President of the United States vetoed it, and one of the reasons that he gave for the veto was that Congress could not by law declare that these persons were citizens of the United States. I remember very well the answer which I gave to that suggestion of the President, which was twofold: first, that it was competent to make persons citizens by statute; second, that the statute was but declaratory of what the law already was. I agreed that they were citizens. The President said in his veto message that if that was true the law was of no use, and if it was not true the law could not make them citizens; the answer to which was that the statute was declaratory of what the law was before, and numerous statutes were referred to to show that it had been the practice, almost from the origin of the Government, to make persons citizens of the United States by act of Congress. It had been done in reference to Indian tribes; it had been done in regard to Mexicans; and different classes of persons had been made citizens by act of Congress before, and the act was a proper one to settle the question.

Then, when we came to the adoption of the fourteenth amendment it was suggested by some persons that there might still be a cavil upon this question as to whether all persons born in the United States were citizens, and it was thought advisable, for the purpose of putting that question once and forever at rest, to insert the words which are in the fourteenth amendment, declaring that all persons born within the United States and subject to its jurisdiction were citizens of the United States. In my opinion, that has not changed at all the fact that after the abolition of slavery, and after the authority of the States to deprive persons of liberty ceased, every person born in the United States was a citizen of the United States. I do not think there could have been any question that they were all citizens without the declaration in the civil rights act or without the declaration in the fourteenth amendment. . . .

I come now, Mr. President, to those clauses of the fourteenth amendment which, it is supposed, have changed the Constitution as it was originally formed. The next is:

No State shall make or enforce any law which shall abridge the privileges or immunities of citizens of the United States.

That is substantially what the Constitution was before, and I do not know that it enlarged at all the provision of the Constitution as it before existed, which declared that:

The citizens of each State shall be entitled to all privileges and immunities of citizens in the several States.

In my judgment, that amounts to the same thing. It is a repetition of a provision in the Constitution as it before existed. It states it in a little different language by saying that "no State shall make or enforce any law which shall abridge the privileges or immunities of citizens of the United States." The section, as it originally stood in the Constitution, read:

The citizens of each State shall be entitled to all privileges and immunities of citizens in the several States.

MR. EDMUNDS. If my friend will pardon me, I do not wish to interrupt the course of his remarks, but on that point I should like to suggest to him that the language changes entirely in the description of the class of persons who are entitled to protection. The old clause provided that the citizens of each State, as citizens of a State, should be entitled to the rights of citizenship in any other State to which they might go. The new amendment provides that the citizens of the United States, whether they are the citizens of any particular State or not, shall have universal citizenship in the United States.

MR. TRUMBULL. That is true; but it is limited in another respect to an infringement by law.

MATTHEW CARPENTER [R., WIS.]. Let me ask my friend if it does not very much enlarge it in this respect: the old Constitution merely provided, for instance, that a citizen of Wisconsin removing to Illinois should have all the rights and privileges of a citizen of Illinois, leaving it still to that State to determine what should be the rights of a citizen. For instance, a colored man going from Wisconsin to Illinois was a voter or not according to the laws of Illinois. Now the Constitution does not leave the man going into another State at the mercy of that State as to his rights; but it says that from and after the passage of this amendment—that is the legal effect of it—no State shall make, or, if it has one in its statute-book, enforce any law which shall abridge the privileges or immunities of a citizen of the United States. Now the question is upon that amendment of the Constitution. Are not the privileges and immunities of every citizen of the United States put on a par in every State of the Union?

MR. TRUMBULL. The words "privileges and immunities," as the Senator well knows, if he will think for a moment, have nothing to do with voting. They refer to civil rights. His illustration about the right to vote has no application. Women do not vote.

MR. CARPENTER. I am aware they do not, and I simply resorted to that illustration to show what was meant by the old provision. I did not mean that "privileges and immunities" covered voting.

MR. TRUMBULL. The "privileges and immunities" referred to in the Constitution are of a civil character, applying to civil rights, and not political rights, and were never so understood. The Senator from Wisconsin asks if they are not protected in all the privileges and immunities of citizens of the United States. Undoubtedly; but we have not advanced one step by that admission. The fourteenth amendment does not define the privileges and immunities of a citizen of the United States any more than the Constitution originally did.

MR. CARPENTER. If my friend will allow me, I heard him say a moment ago that there were some things so plain in this country that they need not be in the Constitution, and I claim this to be exactly illustrative of that remark. There are certain privileges and immunities of American citizens that are recognized in every State of the Union and by every American as being peculiarly and especially the privileges of an American citizen, and that Constitution means to protect those, or else it is mere idle talk and protects nothing.

MR. TRUMBULL. The protection which the Government affords to American citizens under the Constitution as it was originally formed is precisely the protection it affords to American citizens under the Constitution as it now exists. The fourteenth amendment has not extended the rights and privileges of citizenship one iota. They are right where they always were. The citizen of the United States was to be defended as against foreign aggression, as against foreign nations, in all his rights of a national character, under the old Constitution. The fourteenth amendment has not defined what the privileges and immunities of citizenship are. Was not Martin Van Buren, or Zachary Taylor, or James K. Polk just as much a citizen, and a native-born citizen, of the United States before the fourteenth amendment as the Senator from Wisconsin is to-day since the adoption of the fourteenth amendment? They were citizens, and they were clothed with all the rights of American citizenship, and the Federal Government was bound to protect them in whatever immunity and privilege belonged to them as citizens of the nation; but that did not have reference to the protection of those persons in individual rights in their respective States, except so far as being citizens of one State entitled them to the privileges and immunities of citizens in every other. . . .

This Constitution says no such thing as that a State shall not abridge the privileges of any citizen. It speaks of citizens of the United States, and you have not advanced one step in the argument unless you can define what the privileges and immunities of citizens of the United States are. If the Senator from Wisconsin had honored me with his attention when I commenced, he would have observed that I stated at the commencement that this national Government was not formed for the purpose of protecting the individual in his rights of person and of property.

MR. CARPENTER. That is what I understand to be the very change wrought by the fourteenth amendment. It is now put in that aspect and does protect them.

MR. TRUMBULL. Then it would be an annihilation entirely of the States. Such is not the fourteenth amendment. The States were, and are now, the depositaries of the rights of the individual against encroachment.

MR. CARPENTER. And that Constitution forbids them to deny them, and authorizes Congress to legislate so as to carry that prohibition into execution.

MR. TRUMBULL. If the Constitution had said that the privileges and immunities of citizens of the United States embraced all the rights of person and property belonging to an individual, then the Senator would be right; but it says no such thing. In my judgment, the fourteenth amendment has not changed an iota of the Constitution, as it was originally framed, in that respect. . . .

The difference between the Senator from Wisconsin and myself is, as to what are the privileges and immunities of citizens of the United States. I insist that the privileges and immunities belonging to the citizen of the United States as such are of a national character, and such as the nation is bound to protect, whether the citizen be in foreign lands, or in any of the States of the Union. The Government of the United States protects the citizen of the United States to the same extent in Carolina or Massachusetts as it protects him in Portugal or in England. National citizenship is one thing, and State citizenship another; and before this constitutional amendment was adopted the same obligation, in my judgment, rested upon the Government of the United States to protect citizens of the United States as now.

The next clause of the fourteenth amendment is this:

Nor shall any State deprive any person of life, liberty, or property, without due process of law.

That was the Constitution applicable to the Government of the United States before the adoption of the late amendments. The Federal Government had no authority under the Constitution as it was amended, in 1791 I think, to deprive any person of life, liberty, or property without due process of law. That inhibition did not extend to the States, but all the States had adopted a similar clause in their State constitutions. Every one of them, as far as I have examined, had done so; but there was no clause in the Constitution of the United States binding them to carry out this provision. There is no change in that respect so far as the States are concerned, and the Federal Government cannot interfere with the States so long as they do not deprive some person of life, liberty, or property without due process of law. If they should, then the power is given to the Federal Government to correct that violation of the Constitution of the United States. It may now prevent any State from depriving any person of life, liberty, or property without due process of law. I am not now speaking of the machinery for doing it; but the power is now in the Federal Government under the fourteenth amendment to prevent a State doing what no State would undertake to do without a violation of its own constitution.

Then follows the other clause:

Nor deny to any person within its jurisdiction the equal protection of the laws.

That is a new provision, and the Federal Government is now vested with power to see to it that no State deprives any person of life, liberty, or property without due process of law, or denies to any person within its jurisdiction the equal protection of the laws; just as, under the old Constitution, no State could pass a law impairing the obligation of contracts. The Federal Government was vested with power to see that no State did pass a law impairing the obligation of contracts. But suppose a State did do it? Suppose a State passed an *ex post facto* law or a law impairing the obligation of contracts? That act was void, and it was the duty of the State courts to pronounce it void, which, in some instances, they did. But suppose the State courts upheld this void act of the State Legislature, which impaired the obligation of contracts; what then? The Federal Government interfered and declared the law invalid and afforded to the party the means to enforce his contract as it had been made.

Now, suppose in the cases arising under the fourteenth amendment that a State attempts to deprive a person of life, liberty, or property without due process of law, or suppose that a State denies to a person within its jurisdiction the equal protection of the laws, then the Federal Government has a right to set aside this action of the State authorities and see to it that the person is protected in his life and his liberty and his property, unless they are taken from him by due process of law, and that he receives the equal protection of the laws, just as it furnished the means to give him the enforcement of his contract under the old Constitution.

MR. CARPENTER. Will my friend allow me a question at that point?

MR. TRUMBULL. Certainly.

MR. CARPENTER. The prohibition in the old Constitution that no State should pass a law impairing the obligation of contracts was a negative prohibition laid upon the State. Congress was not authorized to interfere in case the State violated that provision. It is true that when private rights were affected by such a State law, and that was brought before the judiciary, either of the State or nation, it was the duty of the court to pronounce the act void; but there the matter ended. Under the present Constitution, however, in regard to those rights which are secured by the fourteenth amendment, they are not left as the right of the citizen in regard to laws impairing the obligation of contracts was left, to be disposed of by the courts as the cases should arise between man and man, but Congress is clothed with the affirmative power and jurisdiction to correct the evil.

I think there is one of the fundamental, one of the great, the tremendous revolutions effected in our Government by that article of the Constitution. It gives Congress affirmative power to protect the rights of the citizen, whereas before no such right was given to save the citizen from the violation of any of his rights by State Legislatures, and the only remedy was a judicial one when the case arose.

MR. TRUMBULL. Mr. President, I am not specially upon the question of remedies at this moment, as to how the United States should afford the remedy; but let me say to the Senator from Wisconsin that the authority of the United States was just as positive under the Constitution, as originally framed, as it is under the fourteenth amendment. What says the Constitution of the United States? It says—this is the original Constitution:

No State shall pass any *ex post facto* law, or law impairing the obligation of contracts.

That is what the Constitution said. What else did it say?

The Congress shall have power to make all laws which shall be necessary and proper for carrying into execution the foregoing powers, and all other powers vested by this Constitution in the Government of the United States, or in any department or officer thereof.

What was vested in the Government of the United States? The power to carry out the clause declaring that no State should pass a law impairing the obligation of contracts. This was a power conceded by the people to the Government of the United States when they made it, and with that concession went along the power to make all laws necessary and proper to carry it into effect. . . .

I come now, Mr. President, to the bill under consideration about which I shall make a few suggestions, and but few. I wish to premise at the outset that I am going into no statement about the outrages in the South. Whether they have been exaggerated, as some contend, or whether they are as bad as others insist, is not a question that I propose at all to discuss. The President of the United States has thought it questionable at any rate whether he had sufficient power to put down organizations which exist in some of the States of the Union, which are encroaching on the rights of person and property, which are committing outrages and sacrificing life. Now, sir, I want it understood that I am ready to go as far as he who goes farthest to maintain the authority of the Government of the United States.

Show me that it is necessary to exercise any power belonging to the Government of the United States in order to maintain its authority and I am ready to put it forth. But, sir, I am not willing to undertake to enter the

States for the purpose of punishing individual offenses against their authority committed by one citizen against another. We, in my judgment, have no constitutional authority to do that. When this Government was formed, the general rights of person and property were left to be protected by the States, and there they are left to-day. Whenever the rights that are conferred by the Constitution of the United States on the Federal Government are infringed upon by the States, we should afford a remedy. That was done in 1789 by the twenty-fifth section of the judiciary act, which afforded a remedy against a State statute in violation of the Constitution of the United States, as in the case of a State law impairing the obligation of contracts. I have no objection now to a law which shall protect a person in the same way against inequality of legislation in any of the States of the Union against any laws that deprive him of life, liberty, or property except by the judgment of his peers or the law of the land. I am ready to pass appropriate legislation on that subject; and I understand that this bill as it passed the House of Representatives was framed on this principle. As originally introduced, it went to the extent of punishing offenses against the States; and there was objection to it on the part of some of the most thoughtful minds in the House of Representatives. Those provisions were changed, and as the bill passed the House of Representatives, it was understood by the members of that body to go no further than to protect persons in the rights which were guarantied to them by the Constitution and laws of the United States, and it did not undertake to furnish redress for wrongs done by one person upon another in any of the States of the Union in violation of their laws, unless he also violated some law of the United States, nor to punish one person for an ordinary assault and battery committed on another in a State.

To that extent I felt that I could give my support to the bill. I regretted that the Committee on the Judiciary thought it necessary to amend the bill; but a majority came to that conclusion, and I think (although I believe in that the Senator from Vermont who reports the bill with the amendments does not agree with me) that these amendments make the bill obnoxious to the very objection which was made to it in the House of Representatives in its original shape, that it does go to the extent of undertaking to punish persons for violating State laws, without reference to any violation of the Constitution or laws of the United States.

I do not believe the Senator from Vermont entertains the opinion that the Congress of the United States has a right to pass a general criminal code for the States of the Union, and I am sure if he does maintain that they have the right to do it, he would think it impolitic to exercise that power. I do not suppose there is a single person on this floor who would be in favor of Congress passing a law punishing larceny, assault and battery, and all sorts of crime in the different States of the Union, and taking control of all the contracts made between individuals, because that would be destructive at once of the State governments. The only use of governments, the only purpose for which they are instituted, is to protect persons in their rights of person and property. That is all any one of us wants; and if the Federal Government takes to itself the entire protection of the individual in his rights of person and property, what is the need of the State governments? It would be a change in our form of government, and an unwise one, in my judgment, because I believe that the rights of the people, the liberties of the people, the rights of the individual are safest among the people themselves, and not in a central Government extending over a vast region of country. I think the nearer you can bring the administration of justice between man and man to the people themselves, the safer the people will be in their rights of person and property.

I should like now to get the attention of Senators a moment, and especially of the lawyers of the body, to a single amendment in the seventeenth line of the second section. The Judiciary Committee propose to insert the words "or while engaged in the." I think that changes the whole character of that section. Let me show how.

As the bill originally stood as it came from the House, it provided for the punishment of a conspiracy to injure a person holding a United States office in his person or property on account of his lawful discharge of the duties of his office. That is legitimate. I can vote for a law that punishes a conspiracy to injure a United States officer on account of his lawful discharge of the duties of his office. But what is the amendment? Its effect is to punish a conspiracy to injure his property "while he is engaged in the lawful discharge of his duties." Is not that very different? To illustrate: the Senator who sits before me [Mr. Hamilton of Maryland] has a very valuable farm over in Maryland, I assume; I suppose he has; if he has not he ought to have half a dozen. Suppose while he is here in the discharge of the duties of his office somebody trespasses upon his farm; suppose two or three persons get together and make a combination for the purpose of breaking into his barn and stealing his grain, if you please; that is made a United States offense, and they are to be punished in the United States courts with imprisonment for not less than six months nor more than six years. . . .

I wish now to call attention to another amendment in the same section, section two, on lines thirty-six, thirty-seven, thirty-eight, thirty-nine, and forty, which is obnoxious to the same objection that I have made to the other amendment. That amendment proposes to punish two or more persons who "conspire together for the purpose of in any manner impeding, hindering, obstructing, or defeating the due course of justice in any State or Territory, with intent to deny to any citizen of the United States the due and equal protection of the laws."

I do not deny the authority to punish a conspiracy for the purpose of denying to any citizen of the United States the due and equal protection of the laws. We have a right to punish such a conspiracy; but that is not this amendment. This amendment punishes a conspiracy to impede or obstruct the due course of justice in a State. That is the conspiracy that it punishes; not the conspiracy to deny the citizen the equal protection of the laws, but the conspiracy to defeat the due course of justice, with intent, it is true, to deny to any citizen the equal protection of the laws. That must be the intent; but the intent is not the thing that is punished. It is not the substantive part of the offense. If it is, then it is provided for in the four preceding lines. If this clause simply means to punish a conspiracy to deny the equal protection of the laws, that is provided for in the previous lines, commencing with line thirty-four.

MR. EDMUNDS. Is not that the due course of justice of the State courts?

MR. TRUMBULL. The language of the amendment is:

For the purpose of in any manner impeding, hindering, obstructing, or defeating the due course of justice in any State or Territory, with intent to deny to any citizen of the United States the due and equal protection of the laws.

A conspiracy to deny to citizens of the United States the due and equal protection of the laws, I submit to the Senator from Vermont, comes within lines thirty-four, thirty-five, and thirty-six, which provide for punishing a conspiracy "for the purpose of preventing or hindering the constituted authorities of any State from giving or securing to all persons within such State the equal protection of the laws." So that if that is all that the Senator means, it is already provided for. If he means more than that, and to punish a conspiracy against the State, then I am opposed to it.

MR. EDMUNDS. Now will the Senator allow me to say a word if it does not interrupt him?

MR. TRUMBULL. Certainly.

MR. EDMUNDS. We are both of us in favor of the general principle of this bill, I have no doubt thoroughly, and we are both of us equally sincere in the desire to make it, as far as it goes, effectual, so that the violent people we design to repress will be taught to behave themselves. Now, I submit to my friend whether those three lines, thirty-four, thirty-five, and thirty-six, beginning in the disjunctive at the end of line thirty-three, do not, in express terms, provide for punishing a conspiracy formed "for the purpose of preventing or hindering the constituted authorities of any State from giving or securing to all persons within such State the equal protection of the laws." What laws? The laws of that State. Therefore the bill as it came from the House, of which I understand my friend to be in favor, expressly provides for punishing a conspiracy to obstruct the State authorities by a general name, (the Executive, the military, the judiciary, every department of the State,) in giving to everybody the equal protection of their own laws.

Now, if my friend will pardon me a little further, I wish to ask him this question: I ask if he does not know that the object of this amendment was, in the same spirit and with the same scope, instead of using those vague generalities, which it might be thought would be difficult in a court of justice to define and enforce, to take up, as another mode of expressing the same general idea, words that are known to previous statutes, that are known to the courts, technically defining an offense that is well known of obstructing the State authorities in the course of executing justice. That was all that we meant, and with the intent we have named, which really, it seems to me, narrows what is the point of the scope of the previous clause.

MR. TRUMBULL. If this last clause is embraced within the other, as I have said, there is no occasion for it. If it is not embraced within the other then it means something more than the other, and is the punishment of a conspiracy against the execution of a State law, and that I do not think we can punish. If that provision were in the original bill, if it were susceptible of that construction, I think it would be objectionable.

MR. EDMUNDS. What do you understand that to mean?

MR. TRUMBULL. I should have to read the whole section back, and I do not care to go into that at this moment.

Section three, I think, is made objectionable by striking out the words in the third line "so far obstruct or hinder the execution of the laws thereof and of the United States as to." In order to make myself understood I will read that section as I now understand it with the amendment that has been made striking out the words I have just read and including the words in lines seven and eight, which are inserted in the bill, or a portion of those words. Of course I cannot be understood in the remarks I am making except by Senators who have the bill before them. The Senator from Vermont will see the point I make. I will read the section leaving out the surplusage:

That in all cases where domestic violence in any State shall obstruct the impartial course of justice, and the constituted authorities of such State shall from any cause fail in protection of the people in such rights, it shall be lawful for the President to employ the land and naval forces, etc.

Can we do that? That is this section of the bill when you leave out the verbiage. It declares that in all cases where domestic violence in any State obstructs the impartial course of justice—that means in the State—and the constituted authorities of such State shall from any cause fail in protection of the people in such rights, it shall be lawful for the President to employ the land and naval forces of the United States for the purpose of putting down such domestic violence.

Why, Mr. President, can that be possible? Is it not our duty to endeavor first to enforce the law through the civil tribunals of the country? Are you going to call upon the Army and Navy of the United States to put down domestic violence, because the impartial administration of justice is interfered with, or obstructed, in a particular locality when the United States courts are open? Why, sir, formerly, when in 1795 the law was passed authorizing the Army and Navy to be used, it was only when the judicial tribunals of the United States were overborne. Here is a proposition, without any call from the States for assistance, to put down domestic violence, that the President of the United States may, whenever the course of justice is not impartially administered in any State of this Union, march the Army and Navy there and use them to put down domestic violence. That was not the bill as it passed the House of Representatives. The bill as it passed that body provided that where this insurrection or domestic violence in any State should so far obstruct or hinder the execution of the laws thereof and of the United States as to deprive any portion or class of the people of any of the rights, privileges, or immunities secured by the Constitution, the President might interpose. That we have a right to do.

When there is a conspiracy that obstructs the laws of the United States so that persons cannot have the rights to which they are entitled under the Constitution of the United States, we have a right then, when the courts cannot afford the requisite protection, to call for the military assistance; but as the bill is altered, it provides for giving this assistance to put down domestic violence in any locality in a State whenever the impartial administration of justice is interfered with. . . .

MR. TRUMBULL. I should like to ask the Senator from Vermont if the United States were not bound, before the fourteenth amendment, to protect all the privileges and immunities of citizens of the United States, whatever they were? Under the general clause giving Congress authority to carry out and protect whatever powers are vested in the United States, if there was such a thing as a citizen of the United States, which the Senator will of course admit, whatever his privileges and immunities were, was not the Government of the United States bound to protect them everywhere?

MR. EDMUNDS. That is what I have been trying to show for half an hour, in the best way I could.

MR. TRUMBULL. Then, if the Senator assents to that, I desire to ask him whether the privileges and immunities of a citizen of the United States were not precisely the same before the adoption of the fourteenth amendment, and if not, wherein do they differ?

MR. EDMUNDS. My friend sees where he is coming out, and so I will wait a moment before I answer the question in form. I say, and have endeavored to maintain, that the United States was bound, is bound, and always must be bound, like every other sovereign Government, to protect every right that it gives to its citizens. There can be no doubt of it. That is precisely the position upon which I stand. But what I said was that a citizen only became a citizen of the United States, under the language of this Constitution that I have read, through the fact that he was a citizen of a State, to begin with, except in the case of naturalization, and then he became, by the act of the nation, a citizen of the State; that the national citizenship was the consequence of the State citizenship, and therefore that the privileges of a national citizen must always be measured by and controlled by, the rules that applied to State citizenship; and hence if the State of South Carolina wished to enslave a portion of its citizens, if any citizen of another State chose to go there and be enslaved, if he came within the description of the enslaved persons, he must take his chance and the Constitution could not help him. That is the position. As I go along I will answer the other part of the question of my friend, and he will presently see what the answer is.

Now, sir, to put this question at rest as to what was the nature of national citizenship, whether it was fundamental because the person was an inhabitant of the nation itself, or born in it, or naturalized to it, or whether it was the mere consequence of the fact that he was a citizen of a State, the thirteenth and fourteenth amendments came in. The fourteenth amendment declared that:

All persons born or naturalized in the United States, and subject to the jurisdiction thereof, are citizens of the United States and of the State wherein they reside.

The order of the language of the old Constitution is reversed absolutely. Instead of declaring, as it did before, that a citizen of a State was entitled to the privileges of a citizen in another State, it declared that every person born within the territory of the United States was a citizen of the nation, and, by consequence, a citizen of any State in which he might from time to time reside.

MR. TRUMBULL. If the Senator will allow me again, did that do anything more than give citizenship to a class of persons who before that time did not have it, and did it give anybody any privileges and immunities beyond those possessed by a confessed citizen of the United States before its enactment?

MR. EDMUNDS. I declare most emphatically that it did; that it gave the man who had been a citizen of Vermont or of Massachusetts before, and who under the old Constitution, becoming a citizen of South Carolina, only had such rights as the constitution of South Carolina chose to give to their citizens, either to be a slave or a free man, or whatever condition they might impose upon him, a national citizenship as an original and fundamental right that no State could regulate or destroy or impede, because it says so; and as a consequence of that, it said wherever he went he became a citizen of the State to which he emigrated. . . .

Now, sir, let us see what rights these new amendments have given to citizens; and I am sorry to have troubled the Senate so long in discussing this general principle; but inasmuch as the whole constitutionality of our legislation has been made to turn, as I have said, upon the denial of our right to exercise direct powers over the citizens as such, I have felt justified in demonstrating, as I think I have, from history, from the Constitution, from the statutes, and from the decisions, that this pretense is a sheer delusion.

Now, what do these amendments provide?

The thirteenth amendment provided that there should be neither slavery nor involuntary servitude except for crime. That was a prohibition. It did not name a State at all. Under the old decisions, to which I have referred, protecting life, liberty, and property against invasion without due process of law, Democratic Senators and my friend from Illinois might have contended that this was only a prohibition against slavery under the authority of the United States, and that any State could now deprive a citizen of his liberty for the reason that the thirteenth amendment only operated as against the Government of the United States as it was held under the old one which I have read.

But that has not been contended, and everybody knows that it would be scouted, for there is added—if there could have been any doubt about it before—the provision that "Congress shall have power to enforce this article by appropriate legislation." Therefore, when the prohibition against slavery was enacted and the power was expressly put into the hands of Congress to carry out that enactment, to see that it was made effectual, was it not the right and the duty of Congress, too, to the last point of its power, to protect the liberty of all people wherever it might be assailed by that form of crime? Nobody questions it. Even my honorable friend from Ohio who sits farthest from me [Mr. Thurman] I think will admit, I believe he did the other day—I do not know that the conversation was public, although it was a business conversation—that under the thirteenth amendment there is no question but that Congress may take all necessary means to prevent the reestablishment of slavery.

ALLEN THURMAN [DEM., OHIO]. In my judgment, that provision that Congress shall have power by appropriate legislation to give effect to this article which is found in each of the thirteenth, fourteenth, and fifteenth articles of amendment confers no power upon Congress that would not exist in Congress if those words were stricken out of the Constitution. They are not a particle broader than the clause in the original Constitution that Congress shall have power to pass all laws necessary and proper, etc; and this very word "appropriate" is derived from the opinion of Judge Marshall in *McCulloch* v. *Maryland*, in which he says that Congress, under that authority to pass all proper and necessary laws, could use any appropriate means;

MR. EDMUNDS. Very good; then my purpose is answered; and let me tell my friend that there is a wide distinction, if he will study the Constitution a little more closely, between this phraseology of the second section of the thirteenth article and the old phraseology. This says that "Congress shall have power to enforce this article by appropriate legislation." That said that Congress should have power by all necessary legislation to carry into effect the powers therein granted. The prohibitions upon the States were not granted powers; they were denied powers; not denied powers of the national Government, but denied powers of the States; and therefore the strict language of the old grant of power to legislate did not cover those cases at all.

MR. THURMAN. The Senator will pardon me for saying that I think I could convince him that there is no difference; but it would require an argument, and I do not want to interrupt his speech.

MR. EDMUNDS. My friend knows that when he goes to an argument or threatens one I am always convinced at once. [Laughter.] But the chief point now is, as my friend agrees, that here is, whether necessary or unnecessary, an express grant of power to us, the national Legislature, to defend the rights of citizens of the United States and all inhabitants of the country, whether citizens or not, against slavery. Now, how are you going to do it? Are you going to do it by passing a proclamation to the State of Georgia when she may choose to reenslave her negroes? Or, are you going to do it by making war upon her? Or, are you going to do it, as we by this bill do it under the fourteenth amendment, by declaring that any man who infracts that article shall be punished?

I take it, there is only one answer to that question. If any State should undertake to set up slavery, or any man in a State should undertake to set it up, (because the old theory was that the States did not set it up at all, that it was a kind of hereditary personal right that came down from the patriarchs in some undefined way,) my friend from Ohio would be among the most earnest opponents of any legislation which should address itself to the State of Georgia. He would say, "The State of Georgia is not in fault; she cannot as a State be in fault at all, because her officers, her Legislature, her Governor, her judiciary, all together as such, have no power or authority to do anything of the kind, and their acts, therefore, are utterly void, and the people in their collective capacity are not responsible for them at all; and you have no right to make war upon the people because their officers, their mere agents whom they have selected, have exceeded their jurisdiction and authority. Go," he would say, "to the guilty ones. Address yourselves to the criminal who has violated this article of the Constitution and the statutes of the United States by doing that which the Constitution forbids."

Thus you will have enforced the thirteenth article of amendments and secured liberty and punished slavery. It would be an extreme case which could justify any other answer; and inasmuch as slavery is so odious to mankind now, gentlemen of all political shades would acquiesce, and there would not be a debate or a party division upon the passage of a bill which should provide for the punishment of the act of reducing any man to slavery, under the thirteenth amendment. Nobody, I venture to say, would have been heard to open his lips to condemn such legislation, however much some portion of the people might desire to see slavery restored, or to question the propriety or the constitutionality of enacting it.

But when you take the next step and come to the next article of the Constitution, which secures the rights of white men as much as of colored men, you touch a tender spot in the party of our friends on the other side. If you wish to employ the powers of the Constitution to preserve the lives and liberties of white people against attacks by white people, against raping and murder and assassination and conspiracy, contrived in order to drive them from the States in which they have been born or have chosen to settle, contrived in order to deprive them of the liberty of having a political opinion,

contrived for the purpose of driving them from a city or town where they have
endeavored to carry on a peaceable and lawful business or to cultivate the
soil, then the whole strength of the Democratic party and all its allies is
arrayed against the constitutionality and propriety of such an act.

Sir, what did the fourteenth amendment say, taking it a little in detail? The
first section of it is all that I need to read. It has four distinct and separate
clauses. The first is the one upon which I have commented, and I will now
only state it:

> All persons born or naturalized in the United States, and subject to the jurisdiction thereof, are
> citizens of the United States, and of the State wherein they reside.

I have said prematurely, in answer to my friend from Illinois, and out of
the order of the proper discussion of this subject, all that I will take the time
to say about it. The next is the provision that:

> No State shall make or enforce any law which shall abridge the privilege or immunities of
> citizens of the United States.

There is a direct prohibition to the State; it is a direct prohibition against
the making of a law; it is a direct prohibition against the enforcing of a law;
and that perhaps brings me to the question here as well as anywhere else,
what is a State?

My honorable friend from Ohio [Mr. Thurman] said yesterday, my friend
from New Jersey [Mr. Stockton] said the other day, and everybody says on
that side, that a State is the legislative department, and that all the prohibitions and commands of this section are addressed to the law-making power of
a State, and that any omission of the Governor to give rights under his
department, any omission of the judiciary to grant rights under their department, any violation by either of these departments of a State government of
any right secured by this section, is not a violation by the State, for that must
be by the law-making power. Now, apply it to this:

> No State shall make or enforce any law which shall abridge the privileges or immunities of
> citizens of the United States.

Not "abridge the privileges and immunities of citizens of one State going to
another," as the old language was, but "which shall abridge the privileges and
immunities of citizens of the United States," whether they are citizens of one
State or another—absolute and complete. But what is the State? Is it the
Legislature? It is as to making law, with the aid of a Governor. As to
enforcing a law, is the Legislature the State? How do Legislatures enforce
laws? I had been taught in my little reading and experience in the profession
of the law that the enforcement of the law belonged to the judiciary and the
executive combined. I had never heard before that it was a part of the
legislative functions of a government to enforce laws; and yet, if my friend is
right, although the very word "enforce" is used in this prohibition, it is after

all only a command to the members of the Legislature that they shall not enforce any such law; and therefore the executive and the judicial departments of the State are not prohibited from enforcing any law they please which violates the privileges and immunities of citizens of the United States.

Why, Mr. President, this is absurd; it flies in the face of the very language, it flies in the face of everything we know of the nature and constitution of a government, be it State or national. . . .

The next provision is the one that "no State shall deprive any person of life, liberty, or property without due process of law." Under the old Constitution a similar provision existed, not using the word "State," and, as I have already stated, the courts decided that that prohibition did not apply to the States at all, and that therefore it only applied to the United States. Hence this clause in the amendment, which also Congress is to enforce by appropriate legislation, "no State shall deprive any person of life, liberty, or property, without due process of law." So that, taking the two clauses together, the old one and the new one, you have in the Constitution of the United States a sweeping declaration that neither the United States nor any one under them, nor any State nor any one under it, shall deprive any person of life, liberty, or property, without due process of law. Is not that, then, as complete as any language can make it? Does it not cover all the power of the nation in every department of the Government, both national and State? Nobody can dispute it; it says so in terms. Taking the two together, the States are prohibited, the nation is prohibited, everybody is prohibited from denying the rights of citizens to life, liberty, and property, without the regular and due process of law—constitutional law.

Now we come to the next clause, "Nor deny to any person within its jurisdiction the equal protection of the laws." And here, again, after this clause, follows the potent, although my friend from Ohio and my friend from Illinois think the unnecessary, declaration that "Congress may enforce this provision by appropriate legislation." Now, what is a State to do? It is not to deny to any person within its jurisdiction the equal protection of its laws; not the equal making of its laws, which had been provided for before, not the right to life, liberty, and property, which had been provided for before; but it is not to deny the protection of its laws.

What is protection of law? Do I need to weary the patience of the Senate with undertaking to define what is the protection of the law? I take it any, the humblest, citizen in the land knows what the protection of the law is. The meanest criminal in the land knows what it is to violate the protection of the law. I shall assume, therefore, that if there has been any, or if there may be any of the offenses named in this act committed in any State, those offenses will deprive citizens of the United States and every one else upon whom they are committed of the protection of the law, unless the criminal who shall commit those offenses is punished and the person who suffers receives that redress which the principles and spirit of the laws entitle him to have.

"No State is to deny," say the gentlemen. That means, they say, the State in its collective capacity. What part of the State? My friend from Ohio says the Legislature. Then the Legislature, reading it in that way, shall not deny to any person within its jurisdiction the equal protection of the laws. It had said that before. The very second provision in this section declares that no State shall make or enforce any law which shall interfere with the privilege and immunity of a citizen of the United States; and everybody agrees that that privilege and that immunity is the very same thing that is mentioned in other language in the next clause—the privilege of life, the privilege of liberty, the privilege of the acquirement of property. So that, on the theory of my friend from Ohio, a great constitutional amendment, carefully prepared, discussed in both branches of Congress, passed by two thirds of each House, ratified by three fourths of the States, committed the awkward blunder of stating over again, in obscure language, what it had stated in its second provision only four lines above in clear language: that it had said that no State (which can only act through its Legislature) shall make any law which shall do this thing, and when it had, then, coming to the last clause, had restated the same thing in vaguer language, that they should not deny to any person the equal protection of the law. That cannot be maintained. A Legislature acting directly does not afford to any person the protection of the law; it makes the law under which and through which, being executed by the functionaries appointed by the State for that purpose, citizens receive the protection of the law. . . .

House of Representatives-42d Congress, 1st Session
April 19, 1871

The committee of conference of the two Houses on their disagreeing votes upon the bill of the House entitled (H. R. No. 320) "An act to enforce the provisions of the fourteenth amendment to the Constitution of the United States, and for other purposes," respectfully report that, having met, after full and free conference thereon they do recommend that the two Houses agree to a substitute for the twenty-first amendment of the Senate, as follows:

That if any house, tenement, cabin, shop, building, barn, or granary shall be unlawfully or feloniously demolished, pulled down, burned, or destroyed, wholly or in part, by any persons riotously and tumultuously assembled together; or if any person shall unlawfully and with force and violence be whipped, scourged, wounded, or killed by any persons riotously and tumultuously assembled together, with intent to deprive any person of any right conferred upon him by the Constitution and laws of the United States, or to deter him or punish him for exercising such right, or by reason of his race, color, or previous condition of servitude, in every such case the county, city, or parish in which any of the said offences shall be committed shall be liable to pay full compensation to the person or persons damnified by such offense, if living, or to his widow or legal representative if dead; and such compensation may be recovered in an action on the case by such person or his representative in any court of the United States of competent jurisdiction in the district in which the offense was committed, such action to be in the name of the person injured, or his legal representative, and against said county, city, or parish; and in which action any of the parties committing such acts may be joined as defendants. And any payment of any judgment, or part thereof unsatisfied, recovered by the plaintiff in such action, may, if not satisfied by the individual defendant therein within two months next after the recovery of such judgment upon execution duly issued against such individual defendant in such judgment, and returned unsatisfied, in whole or in part, be enforced against such country, city, or parish, by execution, attachment, mandamus, garnishment, or any other proceeding in aid of execution or applicable to the enforcement of judgments against municipal corporations: and such judgment shall be a lien as well upon all moneys in the treasury of such county, city, or parish, as upon the other property thereof. And the court in any such action may on motion cause additional parties to be made therein prior to issue joined, to the end that justice may be done. And the said county, city, or parish, may recover the full amount of such judgment, by it paid, with costs and interest, from any person or persons engaged as principal or accessory in such riot, in an action in any court of competent jurisdiction. And such country, city, or parish, so paying, shall also be subrogated to all the plaintiff's rights under such judgment.

And that the same stand as section six of the said bill, and that section six stand as section five, and that section five be transferred to the end of the bill as section seven.

George F. Edmunds,
John Sherman,
Managers on the part of the Senate.
S. Shellabarger,
G. W. Scofield,
Managers on the part of the House.

JOHN FARNSWORTH [R., ILL.]. . . .

What have we now presented to us for our action? We have a section which authorizes suits to be brought against counties and cities in every case of destruction of property or injury of the person by two or more persons in a riotous or tumultuous manner, when it is done in derogation of the exercise of some constitutional right of the person, or done on account of color, or race, or previous condition of servitude; such, for instance, Mr. Speaker, as this: if a Chinaman should be mobbed by three or four miners in California or Nevada on account of being a Chinaman, he may sue the county in the United States courts and recover damages. Or, to take another case of a man mobbed in Illinois on account of race or color, suppose a colored and a white person get married, and some of the young men of the village get up a *charivari*, not for the purpose of preventing any right to vote, but because of color, then the person claiming that he is injured may sue the county and recover damages.

The Supreme Court of the United States has decided repeatedly that Congress can impose no duty on a State officer. We can impose no duty on a sheriff or any other officer of a county or city. We cannot require the sheriff to read the riot act or call out the *posse comitatus* or perform any other act or duty. Nor can Congress confer any power or impose any duty upon the county or city. Can we then impose on a county or other State municipality liability where we cannot require a duty? I think not. Suppose a judgment obtained under this section, and no property can be found to levy upon except the court-house, can we levy on the court-house and sell it? So this section provides, and that too in an action of tort, in an action *ex delicto*, where the county has never entered into any contract, where the State has never authorized the county to assume any liability of the sort or imposed any liability upon it. It is in my opinion simply absurd. . . .

BENJAMIN BUTLER [R., MASS.]. . . .

The bill now presents itself with three features which, in my judgment, are worth preserving. First, the right to punish through the courts of the United States crimes against citizens of the United States to prevent the exercise of their rights; second, the power of the President to use the strong arm of military power to suppress all outrages and wrong upon citizens; and, third, a definition of what are the powers of the General Government, because this amendment, as reported by the committee, has in it, in my judgment, some virtue in this: it goes further in the direction of interfering with the individual rights of citizens by law of Congress than ever I attempted to do or desired to do, and makes a precedent for us in the future. I attempted heretofore to report a bill which would allow men who did the act of depriving a citizen of his right to be punished in courts of the United States. I thought the constitutional power was with us to do that.

Now, my friends, who have constitutional scruples about doing that, have reported an amendment to give a remedy by taking the property of a citizen of the United States because he knows somebody who has committed an offense, or is about to commit an offense, or happens to know about an offense about to be committed, and has not prevented it. For gentlemen who have constitutional scruples, this is going further than anything I have done or know. I have known men in my time who mistook dyspepsia for conscience. [Laughter.] I have known men who mistook their doubts and qualms for constitutional law, who are quite willing to go very far, if they do not happen to go under the lead they do not like, and if you give them their own head will go further than the farthest. So far as this particular provision is concerned, now substituted for what is known as the Sherman amendment, I look upon it as utterly useless, a mere illusion and delusion. . . .

Here is not the slightest pretense of remedy. There is not a man who believes there will ever be a verdict under it. It is put in here that we may throw dust into the eyes of the people, and for no other purpose. But, for all that, I will vote for the bill as a whole, precisely as I voted for the deficiency bill, although opposed to many things in it because I must take the bill *commodum cum onere*—the bitter with the sweet. . . .

Senate-42d Congress, 1st Session
April 19, 1871

GEORGE EDMUNDS [R., VT.]. . . .

As to the last section, in the way it stood originally, being the amendment offered by the Senator from Ohio, [Mr. Sherman,] the conferees of the Senate found it impossible to bring the Representatives of the House to agree to that section in the form in which it stood, on account of difficulties which had occurred to a majority of the House of Representatives respecting our power to deal with the particular organization in a State called a county or a town and for such other reasons as it is not necessary now to state. Thereupon, in order to aid in the repression of these outrages by tumults and conspiracies, the conferees on the part of the House of Representatives and ourselves agreed to substitute for that the provision which the Secretary has read, the substance and effect of which is to make the whole body of the inhabitants of the vicinity who have knowledge that a conspiracy is formed to destroy the property or to injure the person of any peaceable inhabitant, and who refuse or neglect to exert all lawful means to repress it, having the power to assist in preventing it, responsible. It is, in other words, dealing with the citizen under the Constitution.

Every citizen in the vicinity where any such outrages as are mentioned in the second section of this bill, which I need not now describe, are likely to be perpetrated, he having knowledge of any such intention or organization, is made a peace officer, and it is made his bounden duty as a citizen of the United States to render positive and affirmative assistance in protecting the life and property of his fellow citizens in that neighborhood against unlawful aggression; and if, having this knowledge and having power to assist by any reasonable means in preventing it or putting it down or resisting it, he fails to do so, he makes himself an accessory, or rather a principal in the outrage itself, and his fellow-citizen, who is thus wronged on account of his refusal to help him to protect himself, is made responsible for it. I think, Mr. President, that in substance and effect this reaches the same result; and I am not at all sure but that it is quite as effectual as the redress against the county, without liability against the inhabitants of it, would have been. Therefore I hope the Senate will agree to the report which we have made. . . .

THE CIVIL RIGHTS ACT OF 1875

Commentary

The Civil Rights Act of 1875 was the most important of the post-Civil War statutes designed to ensure equal rights for the Negro. As such, it constituted the culmination of the program of the Radical Republicans, which had begun with the Thirteenth Amendment and the Civil Rights Act of 1866—what one scholar has termed the "capstone of the congressional civil rights program." The 1875 statute climaxed a decade of efforts by the Radical Republicans to elevate the ideal of racial equality to the legal plane. One may go further and see in the 1875 law the last victory for the egalitarian ideal of the Reconstruction period. From 1875 to 1954, there were to be no further statutory gains for racial equality. On the contrary, the civil rights legislation enacted during the post-Civil War decade was soon to be virtually emasculated by both Congress and the Supreme Court.

To the twentieth-century observer, the Civil Rights Act of 1875 is of particular interest, for it constitutes what James M. McPherson has aptly termed an historical bridge between the Fourteenth Amendment and the Civil Rights Act of 1964. The goal of equality in public accommodations, which Congress (as we shall see in volume II) sought to attain by enactment of the 1964 statute, was the very same that had been intended by the 1875 law. A reading of the legislative history of the 1875 law that follows will demonstrate that the legislators of the post-Civil War period were intimately concerned with many of the key problems that are still with us today in the field of civil rights: integration versus segregation, particularly in education; legal versus social equality; and the crucial question of whether an ideal such as racial equality can really be achieved by legislative action, especially in a society bitterly opposed to practical implementation of such an ideal.

The key figure in the enactment of the Civil Rights Act of 1875 was Senator Charles Sumner [R., Mass.]. That is true even though Sumner himself died in March, 1874—a year before the 1875 statute became law. As the sponsor of the measure in the House pointed out (*infra* p. 727), the bill was originated by Sumner and he regarded it as the main legacy left by him to his country. On his deathbed, he is siad to have told Judge Ebenezer R. Hoar, then a Republican Congressman from Massachusetts, "You must take care of the civil rights bill,—my bill, the civil rights bill,—don't let it fail!"

Sumner's efforts to secure legislative implementation of racial equality go back to the Civil War period itself. During the postwar decade, he was a leader in the congressional struggle to secure legal equality for the freedmen. He felt, however, that the measures enacted prior to the 1875 statute (which have been covered in the preceding portions of this work) were scarcely adequate to attain the goal of full racial equality. As he put it in an 1870 speech, "It remains that equal rights shall be secured in all the public conveyances, and on the railroads. . . . All schools must be opened to all, without distinction of color." Enactment of federal legislation to secure these rights remained the dominant theme of Sumner's life in the four years that followed.

In 1870, Sumner introduced the first version of what was to become the 1875 Civil Rights Act—a bill to prohibit discrimination by railroads, steamboats, public conveyances, hotels, restaurants, licensed theaters, public schools, juries, and church organizations or cemetery associations "incorporated by national or State authority." Though the bill did not get out of committee, Sumner reintroduced his bill in subsequent sessions and succeeded in securing its passage by the Senate (though in weakened form) in 1872. The House refused to pass the bill, and Sumner's illness during the next session left the measure without the leadership needed for action.

Sumner returned for what was to be his final effort in the first session of the Forty-third Congress. This time the growing demand for a civil rights law was supported by President Ulysses S. Grant's recommendation in his 1873 annual message to Congress of a statute "to better secure the civil rights which freedom should secure, but has not effectually secured, to the enfranchised slave." In addition, the Republicans, by now committed to enactment of civil rights legislation, had an overwhelming majority in both Houses.

At the same time, however, the movement for civil rights legislation was seriously jolted by the Supreme Court decision in the *Slaughter-House Cases* (*supra* p. 335). The Court there ruled that the privileges and immunities clause of the Fourteenth Amendment protected only the privileges and immunities of national citizenship and that protection of the rights of state citizenship was left to the states alone. The *Slaughter-House* decision added a new dimension to the congressional debate on Sumner's civil rights bill. Opponents of the bill speedily seized upon the high bench decision to demonstrate that the measure was unconstitutional, urging that the rights protected by it were only those of state, not national, citizenship. In fact, as will be noted, the debates on the constitutional issues were to be among the most interesting in the legislative history of the Civil Rights Act of 1875.

It was the bill introduced by Sumner in December, 1873, in the first session of the Forty-third Congress, that was finally to reach the statute book. Paradoxically perhaps, the crucial catalyst that led to Senate enactment was the death of Sumner himself in March, 1874. Only two months later, the Senate passed Sumner's bill, virtually as it had originally been introduced—with the exception only of the clause covering discrimination in churches. It has been said that the speedy Senate passage was intended as a memorial to the dead senator. In the House, however, no action was taken before adjournment. Instead, the measure was recommitted to the House Judiciary Committee, with instructions that it not be reported at that session.

It remained for the second session of the Forty-third Congress to complete passage of the civil rights bill. For advocates of the measure, indeed, that session appeared to be the last chance to enact the bill. That was true because more than half of the Republican members of the House had been defeated in the 1874 election. As it turned out, then, the civil rights bill was passed by a lame-duck House on February 3, 1875; ninety of the one hundred and sixty Republicans who voted for it had actually been retired by the voters at the last election. In the House debates, the opponents of the bill constantly stressed the election results to demonstrate what they considered the overwhelming popular support for their position.

With two exceptions, the House bill was substantially similar to the Sumner bill passed by the Senate, and the latter body was able to vote for the House bill on February 27, 1875, with comparatively little debate, since it had fully debated the comparable Sumner measure the year earlier. The exceptions referred to were the cemetery and school provisions, which were removed by the House. The debate over the school provision was (as will be pointed out) of particular importance; it is, in fact, most relevant to our present-day problems with segregation.

To the student of civil rights in the mid-twentieth century, two features of the 1874-75 debates are particularly pertinent. The first is the discussion of the constitutional issues. That is true for two reasons. The first stems from the striking down by the Supreme Court of the key public accommodations provisions of the 1875 Act in the *Civil Rights Cases* (*infra* p. 780). Critics of the Court, especially in recent years, have contended that the high bench decision amounted to virtual judicial usurpation, with the justices emasculating the post-Civil War amendments to nullify the broad remedial intent of their framers. The congressional debates on the 1875 civil rights law demonstrate that such a view is unfounded. There is ample indication in the debates that a substantial number of legislators considered the bill before them unconstitutional—many of them (notably Senators James Kelly [DEM., ORE.], Allen Thurman [DEM., OHIO], and Matthew Carpenter [R., WIS.]) for the very reason stated by the Supreme Court—i.e., that it sought to reach individual, rather than state action.

The second reason why the constitutional discussions during the 1874-75 congressional debates are of such interest today is their relevance to recent developments in the field of civil rights. In the Senate debate in February, 1875, Senator Carpenter stated that Congress might try to accomplish the public-accommodation purposes of the 1875 act under its commerce power. "Such provision in regard to theaters," he asserted, "would be somewhat fantastic as a regulation of commerce." In 1964, the Congress enacted a Civil Rights Act (*infra* Vol. II) based upon the commerce power, of the very type which Senator Carpenter had termed "fantastic" in 1875. And, as Carpenter prophesied, such statute was actually to be upheld by the Supreme Court.

Even more interesting to the present-day observer are those portions of the 1874-75 debates dealing with discrimination in education. Discussed in them are the very problems that have become so important since the 1954 Supreme Court decision in *Brown* v. *Board of Education* (*supra* p. 361) — integration versus segregation, the threat of the South to close down the public school system rather than have "mixed" schools, and the claim that all that is really needed is to have "separate but equal" facilities for the two races.

Without a doubt, the sharpest congressional controversy over the 1875 statute arose over the provision of the original Sumner bill prohibiting racial discrimination, not only in public accommodations, but also in all "common schools and public institutions of learning or benevolence supported in whole or part by general taxation." Though a strong effort was made to strike out such prohibition in the Senate, it was defeated, and the bill as passed by the upper chamber in 1874 contained the school provision as it had been drafted by Sumner.

The situation was different when the House considered the bill a year later. Public opposition, as shown by the 1874 election results already discussed, led the House to vote to strike out the clause prohibiting racial discrimination in educational institutions and cemeteries. The actual vote on the amendment introduced by William Kellogg [R., Pa.] to strike out the school provision was overwhelmingly in favor (128 to 48). Interestingly enough, the consensus against the school prohibition was now so great that no effort was made in the Senate to reinsert such prohibition in the bill. Instead (as already noted), the Senate speedily passed the House-voted bill and it thus became the 1875 Civil Rights Act. (Mention should also be made of the fact that both houses considered and decisively defeated amendments to permit "separate but equal" facilities for whites and Negroes.)

The 1874-75 debates on the proposed prohibition of racial discrimination in schools are directly relevant to the question of the intent of those who wrote the Fourteenth Amendment with regard to segregation in education. One who reads what is said in the debates that follow cannot help but conclude that the Congress that sat less than a decade after ratification of the Fourteenth Amendment did not think that the amendment had the effect of prohibiting school segregation which the Supreme Court was to attribute to it in the *Brown* v. *Board of Education* case of 1954. Certainly, if such effect had been considered to flow from the amendment, the whole debate on the proposed school provision in 1874-75 would have been irrelevant, for integrated schools would have been constitutionally required, regardless of any congressional provision in the matter. Yet, it is fair to say that no participant in the congressional debates took such a view. Once again, however, this does not mean that the decision in *Brown* was wrong. On the contrary, in *Brown* the Court was interpreting the Constitution to meet society's needs in 1954—which were not necessarily the same as those which existed in 1875. Only those who seek the unattainable of making the Constitution as inflexible as the laws of the Medes and Persians can object to constitutional construction that is not cast in a rigid mold. Stability and change are the twin sisters of the law. To yield slavishly only to the demands of the former would scarcely enable the Constitution to serve to meet the nation's needs through the ages.

THE CIVIL RIGHTS ACT
MARCH 1, 1875

Whereas, it is essential to just government we recognize the equality of all men before the law, and hold that it is the duty of government in its dealings with the people to mete out equal and exact justice to all, of whatever nativity, race, color, or persuasion, religious or political; and it being the appropriate object of legislation to enact great fundamental principles into law: Therefore,

Be it enacted by the Senate and House of Representatives of the United States of America in Congress assembled, That all persons within the jurisdiction of the United States shall be entitled to the full and equal enjoyment of the accommodations, advantages, facilities, and privileges of inns, public conveyances on land or water, theaters, and other places of public amusement; subject only to the conditions and limitations established by law, and applicable alike to citizens of every race and color, regardless of any previous condition of servitude.

SEC. 2. That any person who shall violate the foregoing section by denying to any citizen, except for reasons by law applicable to citizens of every race and color, and regardless of any previous condition of servitude, the full enjoyment of any of the accommodations, advantages, facilities, or privileges in said section enumerated, or by aiding or inciting such denial, shall, for every such offense, forfeit and pay the sum of five hundred dollars to the person aggrieved thereby, to be recovered in an action of debt, with full costs; and shall also, for every such offense, be deemed guilty of a misdemeanor, and, upon conviction thereof, shall be fined not less than five hundred nor more than one thousand dollars, or shall be imprisoned not less than thirty days nor more than one year: *Provided,* That all persons may elect to sue for the penalty aforesaid or to proceed under their rights at common law and by State statutes; and having so elected to proceed in the one mode or the other, their right to proceed in the other jurisdiction shall be barred. But this proviso shall not apply to criminal proceedings, either under this act or the criminal law of any State: *And provided further,* That a judgment for the penalty in favor of the party aggrieved, or a judgment upon an indictment, shall be a bar to either prosecution respectively.

SEC. 3. That the district and circuit courts of the United States shall have, exclusively of the courts of the several States, cognizance of all crimes and offenses against, and violations of, the provisions of this act; and actions for the penalty given by the preceding section may be prosecuted in the territorial, district, or circuit courts of the United States wherever the defendant may be found, without regard to the other party; and the district attorneys, marshals, and deputy marshals of the United States, and commissioners appointed by the circuit and territorial courts of the United States, with powers of arresting and imprisoning or bailing offenders against the laws of the United States, are hereby specially authorized and required to institute proceedings against every person who shall violate the provisions of this act, and cause him to be arrested and imprisoned or bailed, as the case may be, for trial before such court of the United States, or territorial court, as by law has cognizance of the offense, except in respect of the right of action accruing to the person aggrieved; and such district attorneys shall cause such proceedings to be prosecuted to their termination as in other cases: *Provided*, That nothing contained in this section shall be construed to deny or defeat any right of civil action accruing to any person, whether by reason of this act or otherwise; and any district attorney who shall willfully fail to institute and prosecute the proceedings herein required, shall, for every such offense, forfeit and pay the sum of five hundred dollars to the person aggrieved thereby, to be recovered by an action of debt, with full costs, and shall, on conviction thereof, be deemed guilty of a misdemeanor, and be fined not less than one thousand nor more than five thousand dollars: *And provided further*, That a judgment for the penalty in favor of the party aggrieved against any such district attorney, or a judgment upon an indictment against any such district attorney, shall be a bar to either prosecution respectively.

SEC. 4. That no citizen possessing all other qualifications which are or may be prescribed by law shall be disqualified for service as grand or petit juror in any court of the United States, or of any State, on account of race, color, or previous condition of servitude; and any officer or other person charged with any duty in the selection of summoning of jurors who shall exclude or fail to summon any citizen for the cause aforesaid shall, on conviction thereof, be deemed guilty of a misdemeanor, and be fined not more than five thousand dollars.

SEC. 5. That all cases arising under the provisions of this act in the courts of the United States shall be reviewable by the Supreme Court of the United States, without regard to the sum in controversy, under the same provisions and regulations as are now provided by law for the review of other causes in said court.

Approved, March 1, 1875.

THE DEBATE

Senate-43d Congress, 1st Session
April 29-May 22, 1874

The Senate, as in Committee of the Whole, proceeded to consider the bill (S. No. 1) supplementary to an act entitled "An act to protect all citizens of the United States in their civil rights, and to furnish the means for their vindication," passed April 9, 1866.

The Committee on the Judiciary reported the bill with an amendment. . . .

FREDERICK FRELINGHUYSEN [R., N.J.]. . . .

Mr. President, the Committee on the Judiciary have devolved on me, on whom it should not have been imposed, the duty of presenting and explaining this bill, which I shall do in the most concise manner, even pruning from my remarks such comment as a measure having for its object the civil rights of all might naturally inspire in the councils of a free people.

I invoke for the bill a calm, impartial, and unpartisan consideration, and ask its adoption only as it commends itself as consistent with the permanent interests of the nation, with the Constitution, and with justice to all classes of citizens. Would that the author of the measure was here to present and defend it! To our views it would have been becoming that he who was in the forum the foremost leader of the grandest victory of the nineteenth century in the western himisphere, the victory of freedom over slavery, should have completed the work he so efficiently aided. But it was otherwise decreed.

I call the attention of the Senate to but two sections of this measure—the first section and the fourth section of the amendment; the other parts of the bill being mere machinery to carry those into effect. The first section provides:

> That all persons within the jurisdiction of the United States shall be entitled to the full and equal enjoyment of the accommodations, advantages, facilities, and privileges of inns, public conveyances on land or water, theaters, and other places of public amusement; and also of common schools and public institutions of learning or benevolence, supported in whole or in part by general taxation, and of cemeteries so supported; subject only to the conditions and limitations established by law, and applicable alike to citizens of every race and color, regardless of any previous condition of servitude.

The fourth section provides:

> That no citizen possessing all other qualifications which are or may be prescribed by law shall be disqualified for service as grand or petit juror in any court of the United States or of any State on account of race, color, or previous condition of servitude; and any officer or other person charged with any duty in the selection or summoning of jurors who shall exclude or fail to summon any citizen for the cause aforesaid shall, on conviction thereof, be deemed guilty of a misdemeanor, and be fined not more than $5,000.

663

Thirteen years ago in this Republic, the foundation principles of which are freedom and political equality, there were four million slaves. There came a bloody war between those who theretofore had striven together for the glory of the Republic—a war rendered the more terrific and destructive by the universal bravery and heroism of the American character. This war was followed by amendments to the Constitution which were discussed and contested in the national councils and on the public platforms with an energy and ability not inferior to those which had characterized the then recent contest of arms. That whole struggle in field and forum was one between freedom and slavery, between national sovereignty and State sovereignty, a struggle between United States citizenship and State citizenship, and the superiority of the allegiance due to each. We all know how the contest was decided.

It is the one purpose of this bill to assert, or rather to reassert, "freedom from all discrimination before the law on account of race, as one of the fundamental rights of United States citizenship." If, sir, we have not the constitutional right thus to legislate, then the people of this country have perpetrated a blunder amounting to a grim burlesque over which the world might laugh were it not that it is a blunder over which humanity would have occasion to mourn. Sir, we have the right, in the language of the Constitution, to give "to all persons within the jurisdiction of the United States the equal protection of the laws."

This bill when enacted, it is believed, will be a finality, removing from legislation, from politics, and from society, an injurious agitation, and securing to every citizen that proud equality which our nation declares to be his right, and which is a boon in defense of which most men would die.

It is the friction created by discrimination among citizens in the administration of law that disturbs the harmony of government. Let us take away the foreign substance. We know we have proven that equality is the true principle on which to run society; give it full play with no obstruction, and the machine will run noiselessly and without a jar. On the contrary, keep four millions impressed with the conviction that they are denied the full and perfect enjoyment of that equality which all others have guaranteed to them, and that by a nation they are taxed to support, and to defend which they fought, and they will be dissatisfied, asserting, and obtrusive; and their obtrusions will engender prejudice and augment the evil.

The colored citizens ask this legislation, not because they seek to force themselves into associations with the whites, but because they have their prides and emulations among themselves, and wish there in those associations to feel that there is no ban upon them, but that they are as fully enfranchised as any who breathe the air of heaven.

I ask you, should the colored citizens be content to demand less than full and equal enfranchisement; should they say "We are content that we and our children shall wear forever the badge of political inferiority," would they not thereby prove themselves to you to be unfit for the high dignity to which the nation has called them? Let us not doubt the foundation principle of our Government; it has always proved true. Give equality to all. Our confidence will not be abused.

This bill applies alike to the white citizen and to the colored citizen.

I am aware that the majority of the Supreme Court in the Slaughter-house case, (16 Wallace,) giving construction to the thirteenth, fourteenth, and fifteenth amendments in the light of the history which called them into being, make them apply especially, though not exclusively I think to the enfranchisement of the colored race. There can be no doubt they apply equally to all races. . . .

This bill therefore properly secures equal rights to the white as well as to the colored race.

Again let me say that this measure does not touch the subject of social equality. That is not an element of citizenship. The law which regulates that is found only in the tastes and affinities of the mind; its law is the arbitrary, uncontrolled human will. You cannot enact it.

This bill does not disturb any laws, whether statute or common, relating to the administration of inns, places of public amusement, schools, institutions of learning or benevolence, or cemeteries, supported in whole or in part by general taxation, (and it is only to these that it applies,) excepting to abrogate such laws as make discrimination on account of race, color, or previous servitude.

Inns, places of amusement, and public conveyances are established and maintained by private enterprise and capital, but bear that intimate relation to the public, appealing to and depending upon its patronage for support, that the law has for many centuries measurably regulated them, leaving at the same time a wide discretion as to their administration in their proprietors. This body of law and this discretion are not disturbed by this bill, except when the one or the other discriminates on account of race, color, or previous servitude.

As the capital invested in inns, places of amusements, and public conveyances is that of the proprietors, and as they alone can know what minute arrangements their business requires, the discretion as to the particular accommodation to be given to the guest, the traveler, and the visitor is quite wide. But as the employment these proprietors have selected touches the public, the law demands that the accommodation shall be good and suitable, and this bill adds to that requirement the condition that no person shall, in the regulation of these employments, be discriminated against merely because he is an American or an Irishman, a German or a colored man.

I have called attention to inns, places of amusements, and public conveyances, separately from schools, institutions of learning and benevolence, and cemeteries, supported in whole or in part by general taxation, because the condition of the existence of the former, differs from that of the latter, I assume that no one can question that schools, institutions of learning and benevolence, and cemeteries, which are supported by the taxation of all, should be subject to the equal use of all. Subjecting to taxation is a guarantee of the right to use. Even as to these institutions, which are the fruit of taxation, the bill does not disturb the established law, statute or common, or the discretion of their managers, except so far as the one or the other, in violation of the fundamental principles of our Government, discriminates against some one under our jurisdiction because of his blood, because of his complexion, or because of the cruel wrong of slavery which he may have suffered.

Uniform discrimination may be made in schools and institutions of learning and benevolence on account of age, sex, morals, preparatory qualifications, health, and the like. But the son of the poorest Irishman in the land, who has sought our shores to better the condition of his offspring, shall have as good a place in our schools as the scion of the chief man of the parish. The old blind Italian, who comes otherwise within the regulations of an asylum for the blind supported by taxation, shall have as good a right to its relief as if he were an American born.

There is but one idea in the bill and that is: The equality of races before the law.

The inquiry may arise whether this bill admits of the classification of races in the common-school system; that is, having one school for white and another for colored children. . . .

The language of this bill secures full and equal privileges in the schools, subject to laws which do not discriminate as to color.

The bill provides that full and equal privileges shall be enjoyed by all persons in public schools supported by taxation, subject only to the limitation established by law, applicable alike to citizens of every race and color and regardless of previous servitude.

The bill does not permit the exclusion of one from a public school on account of his nationality alone.

The object of the bill is to destroy, not recognize, the distinctions of race.

When in a school district there are two schools, and the white children choose to go to one and the colored to the other, there is nothing in this bill that prevents their doing so.

And this bill being a law, such a voluntary division would not in any way invalidate an assessment for taxes to support such schools.

And let me say that from statements made to me by colored Representatives in the other House, I believe that this voluntary division into separate schools would often be the solution of difficulty in communities where there still lingers a prejudice against a colored boy, not because he is ignorant, or untidy, or immoral, but because of his blood.

The colored race have in the last ten years manifested such noble and amiable qualities, judiciously adapting themselves to the demands of their peculiar position, that we should not hesitate to believe that they will in the future conciliate and remove rather than provoke unworthy prejudices; and there is nothing in this law which would affect the legality of schools which were voluntarily thus arranged, one for the white and the other for the colored children.

We were told that to give the colored people freedom was to subject the whites of the South to murder, rapine, and violence. But instead of this— while not forgetting those from whom they had received the boon of freedom—they as a general rule had a tender regard for the comfort and well-being of those to whom they were formerly enslaved, which fact, in passing, let me say, is strong evidence that those who held them in bondage were not, as a general rule, hard task-masters.

We were told that if you placed them in the Army they would not fight; but in the front ranks they gave proof of their claims to high manhood.

We were told that they would abuse the elective franchise; but unless a large majority of the Senate are in error, they have most wisely employed their privilege.

So now, invest them by this bill with full and unqualified privileges, and they will so enjoy them as not to provoke, but so as to remove prejudice.

If it be asked what is the objection to classification by race, separate schools for colored children, I reply, that question can best be answered by the person who proposes it asking himself what would be the objection in his mind to his children being excluded from the public schools that he was taxed to support on account of their supposed inferiority of race.

The objection to such a law in its effect on the subjects of it is that it is an enactment of personal degradation.

The objection to such a law on our part is that it would be legislation in violation of the fundamental principles of the nation.

The objection to the law in its effect on society is that "a community is seldom more just than its laws;" and it would be perpetuating that lingering prejudice growing out of a race having been slaves which it is as much our duty to remove as it was to abolish slavery.

Then, too, we know that if we establish separate schools for colored people, those schools will be inferior to those for the whites. The whites are and will be the dominant race and rule society. The value of the principle of equality in government is that thereby the strength of the strong inures to the benefit of the weak, the wealth of the rich to the relief of the poor, and the influence of the great to the protection of the lowly. It makes the fabric of society a unit, so that the humbler portions cannot suffer without the more splendid parts being injured and defaced. This is protection to those who need it. And it is just that it should be so; for of what value is the wealth and talent and influence of the individual if you isolate him from society? Great as he may be, he is the debtor to society. Let him pay.

Sir, if we did not intend to make the colored race full citizens, if we purpose to place them under the ban of any legalized disability of inferiority, and there to hold them, we should have left them slaves.

I saw this forcible and truthful sentiment a few days since:

When men are completely sunk in degradation. they are apt to be content with their lot; but raise them a few degrees, and they immediately grow dissatisfied with their state. and are wretched indeed if they are not daily rising higher.

In the name of Justice let us now take our depressing hand from long wronged people. Look at their history. It was the rapacity of our fathers that brought them here. They have been docile and submissive to our laws. They have never been pensioners on our charity; they have cleared the forest, reclaimed the morass, developed our wealth, brought in yearly one hundred millions of dollars in cotton—one year one hundred and forty-four millions—and cotton is the equivalent of the much-coveted gold; and without return have supported in affluence many of our people and educated their children, and they have helped fight our battles.

Now let them rise. Let them realize the assurance that Providence seems to be giving them—that higher, still higher, they shall go.

I believe that there is before that race a great future, a future which will render plain the mysterious past. They will not only here develop the vast hidden resources of our illimitable territory and here become and remain respectable citizens; but under the tropics, where the darts of the Pale Rider visit with death the temerity of the white man who braves that vertical sun, there are more than a hundred million of their race. Elevated here, it may be that it is designed that some of them shall of their own volition there sow the seed of a free government and a pure religion.

It may be that in the morbid imagination of the proud some one may fear that the result of this measure will be to place alongside of him in inn or theater some one in every respect his peer except that he differs in complexion. And he may feel that such an event would be an indignity and humiliation. Be it so, sir. The dissatisfaction of a vain pride does not have the weight of the dust in the balance in the eye of reason or in the sight of Him who made of one blood all nations of men when contrasted with the political and consequently the intellectual and moral elevation of a race. Think for yourselves what is the import of that word "race," with its one hundred and twenty millions, its ever-succeeding generation moving on a state that is probationary to immortality. I trust that in legislating on this subject the horizon of our reflections may not be limited by a few short years, or this brief generation, but that it may compass the long life of the nation, and the welfare of mankind.

Now let me call attention to the law. It is claimed that the enactment of the bill would be in violation of the Constitution, because the regulation of inns, public conveyances, and places of amusement, common schools, institutions of learning and benevolence, and cemeteries, supported by taxation, are under the regulation of the States and not of the General Government. The bill proposes to leave them under State control, and expressly says that all persons are to have the full and equal enjoyment of inns, etc., subject to the conditions and limitations established by law—State statutes and common law—with the exception that such laws must be applicable alike to citizens of every race and color and regardless of previous servitude.

Is it constitutional for the General Government to legislate to prevent discrimination on account of race, etc.? We maintain that the General Government has this right under three different grants of power.

1. Under the thirteenth, fourteenth, and fifteenth amendments, considered together and in connection with the contemporaneous history;

2. Under the provision of the fourteenth amendment which prohibits a State from enforcing any law which abridges the privileges and immunities of citizens of the United States; and also,

3. Under the provision of article fourteen which requires a State to give to every person within its jurisdiction the equal protection of the laws; and under the general power given Congress to enforce these provisions by appropriate legislation. . . .

I insist that the principles upon which the thirteenth, fourteenth, and fifteenth amendments are stated by the court to have been based and founded make this bill constitutional. They were passed, the court says, to give "additional guarantees of human rights; additional powers to the Federal Government; additional restraints upon those of the States." They say that after slavery was abolished it was developed that "the condition of the slave race would, without further protection of the Federal Government, be almost as bad as it was before;" that State laws were passed imposing on the colored race "onerous disabilities and burdens, curtailing their rights in the pursuits of life, liberty, and property to such an extent that their freedom was of little value;" that they were prohibited from living in towns, denied the right to purchase lands, to give testimony in courts, or to follow occupations of gain; that it was to relieve from these evils the fourteenth amendment was passed. The three amendments were passed as we insist, and as the reasoning of the court admits, to destroy all discrimination in the law among citizens of the United States.

This bill is authorized, too, by the provision of the fourteenth amendment which prohibits a State from enforcing any law which abridges the privileges and immunities of citizens of the United States. . . .

The fourteenth amendment goes much further than the old Constitution. It makes United States citizenship primary, and State citizenship derivative, dependent on United States citizenship and residence. A citizen of the United States comes under the protection of the Federal Government as to his fundamental rights. It also makes all persons born or naturalized in the United States and subject to its jurisdiction citizens of the United States, and it prevents the privileges and immunities of a citizen of the United States from being abridged. The provision that "the citizens of each State shall be entitled to all privileges and immunities of citizens in the several States" is to prevent in the qualified manner stated discrimination as to the particular class to which he belongs. Though a colored man was a citizen of Massachusetts, he would not formerly be such in South Carolina, because it was against their law for a colored man to be one of their citizens. A State formerly could reduce the rights of its own citizens, and all others fell with them. Now, the fundamental privileges and immunities of citizens of the United States are beyond the caprice of State legislation. This idea is well expressed by Justice Bradley in The Live Stock Association *vs.* The Crescent City Live Stock Company, in 1 Abbott, page 38:

The "privileges and immunities" secured by the original Constitution were only such as each State gave to its own citizens. Each was prohibited from discriminating in favor of its own citizens and against the citizens of other States. But the fourteenth amendment prohibits any State from abridging the privileges or immunities of the citizens of the United States, whether its own citizens or any others. It not merely requires equality of privileges, but it demands that the privileges and immunities of all citizens shall be absolutely unabridged, unimpaired.

And now, Mr. President, what is the remedy? How is the United States, how are we, to protect the privileges of citizens of the United States in the States? We cannot deal with the States or with their officials to compel proper legislation and its enforcement; we can only deal with the offenders who violate the privileges and immunities of citizens of the United States.

By so doing, so far as this bill goes, we do not interfere with the States passing and enforcing just such laws as they see proper as to inns, public conveyances, schools, institutions of learning and benevolence, places of amusement, and cemeteries—they may modify or abolish them at pleasure; but as no State under the old Constitution could discriminate in law against a citizen of another State as to fundamental rights to any greater degree than it did against a citizen of its own State, of the same class, so now no State must discriminate against a citizen of the United States merely on account of his race.

As to the civil remedies for a violation of these privileges, we know that when the courts of a State violate the provisions of the Constitution or the law of the United States there is now relief afforded by a review in the Federal courts. And since the fourteenth amendment forbids any State from making or enforcing any law abridging these privileges and immunities, as you cannot reach the Legislatures, the injured party should have an original action in our Federal courts, so that by injunction or by the recovery of damages he could have relief against the party who under color of such law is guilty of infringing his rights. As to the civil remedy no one, I think, can object. And there is the same propriety in punishing by indictment those who violate the established equality of citizens of the United States by depriving them of the privileges of inns, schools, and burial, merely because of their race, as there is for punishing criminally those who violate postal or currency laws of the United States.

A word now as to the fourth section, which relates to jurors. The provision that a citizen shall not be discriminated against as a juror on account of his race should commend itself to the good judgment of the Senate.

The large majority of issues of fact in this country are tried by the jury. It is an institution that has come to us from England as the companion of civil liberty. The advantages of this mode of trial over that by officers appointed for the purpose are, that the jury are acquainted with the mode of life, habits, and customs of the locality; that they know the witnesses, have sympathy with the parties; and going immediately from the jury-box to the community, they feel their responsibility and the importance of doing justice.

The jury is an institution for the trial of issues of fact by the people, in contradistinction of trial by officers. The juror is in no sense an officer. The performance of this duty, or the enjoyment of this privilege, appertained in England to citizens generally. The jurors were not required to take the test oaths as all officers were. They must be of the people, of the vicinage or body of the county to which the cause of action belonged; so the sixth article of amendment to the Constitution requires that the jury shall be of the district wherein the crime was committed. So that it is very clear that a juror is not an officer, but is of the people.

I do not know that a citizen has a right to be a juror; but has he not a right not to be discriminated against, a right not to be disqualified on account of his blood?

A law which should exclude all naturalized citizens of the United States from the jury-box would deny to naturalized citizens the equal protection of the law. Is it equal protection, that from the tribunal that is to pass on one's life, liberty, and property those who would naturally have an interest in him shall be excluded?

A State may make such qualifications of jurors as it pleases. It may require that they be freeholders; that they read and write; that they submit to an examination in the rudiments of law. But when a State says one class of citizens of the United States shall be tried by a jury which is or may be composed in part or in whole by those of their own blood, and that another class of citizens of the United States shall never be tried by a jury that has one of their race upon it, I submit the discrimination violates a fundamental right of a citizen of the United States, and denies them the equal "protection of the laws."

I have thus discharged, most imperfectly, the duty assigned me, and commend the bill to the favorable consideration of the Senate. . . .

ALLEN THURMAN [DEM., OHIO]. . . .

Soon after the Constitution was ratified the people saw fit to adopt ten amendments to it about the same time. Every one of those amendments is a limitation, not upon the powers of the States, but upon the powers of the Federal Government. The people were so jealous then of encroachments by the Federal Government, so fearful that it would usurp authority detrimental to the best interests, if not to the existence of the States, and also detrimental to the liberties and the prosperity of the people, that they required it to be put in solemn form in these amendments that the Federal Government should be restricted as therein declared and that "the powers not delegated to the United States by the Constitution, nor prohibited by it to the States, are reserved to the States respectively, or to the people."

In the course of time the people proceeded to further amend the Constitution by articles 13, 14, and 15, and now I ask the particular attention of the Senate to what the prohibitions in these articles are in order to show that they are precisely of the same nature as the prohibitions in the original Constitution and in the first eight amendments thereof; prohibitions some of them upon the Federal Government as a Government, and the others prohibitions upon the States as sovereign States, and nothing else, nowhere prohibitions upon individuals as individuals, nowhere treating individuals as mere members of the community, but everywhere, in every line and sentence of the amendments, treating the States as corporations, as sovereign States, and acting upon them as States, and treating the Federal Government in its sphere as a sovereign Government, and acting upon it in its sovereign capacity. What is the thirteenth article of amendment?

Neither slavery nor involuntary servitude, except as a punishment for crime whereof the party shall have been duly convicted, shall exist within the United States, or any place subject to their jurisdiction.

There is a prohibition upon both the Federal and the State governments. It is not directed against an individual, for how could any individual constitute slavery? Slavery can only exist by operation of law, and law could only be enacted by either the Federal or the State governments. The prohibition then is upon these governments as governments, and in no other sense whatsoever.

Now, let us come to article 14, section 1:

All persons born or naturalized in the United States, and subject to the jurisdiction thereof, are citizens of the United States and of the State wherein they reside.

That is mere definition. Then comes the prohibition: "No State"—
Not "no individual," but "no State"—

shall make or enforce any law which shall abridge the privileges or immunities of citizens of the United States.

An individual cannot make law; it is the State alone that can make law, and it is the State alone that can enforce law; and therefore the prohibition is directly upon that sovereign being, the State, that it shall neither make or enforce any law that "shall abridge the privileges or immunities of citizens of the United States;" and proceeding, it says:

Nor shall any State deprive any person of life, liberty, or property, without due process of law; nor deny to any person within its jurisdiction the equal protection of the laws.

Mr. President, is not that plainly a prohibition directed to the States in their capacity as States? Is that provision a mere statute of murder, etc.? Is that merely a provision that no man in the United States shall commit murder, that no man in the United States shall kidnap, that no man in the United States shall unlawfully arrest and detain? Is that it? In other words, is this great provision of the Constitution degraded to the mere office of an ordinary criminal code? No, sir; but it is a limitation on the power of the States and its prohibition is addressed to the States.

What next? I need not speak of sections 2, 3, and 4 of that article, because they are not necessary to illustrate what I am endeavoring to prove. I therefore proceed to article 15; and what is that?

The right of citizens of the United States to vote shall not be denied or abridged by the United States or by any State on account of race, color, or previous condition of servitude.

OLIVER MORTON [R., IND.]. Will the Senator allow me to ask him a question before he passes from the fourteenth amendment?

MR. THURMAN. If it is not a speech. I wish to be very brief this evening. If the Senator has only a question to ask I will yield.

MR. MORTON. Only a question. The Senator states that the prohibitions in the first section of the fourteenth amendment are addressed to the States as corporations and not to individuals. Calling his attention to the fact that the last section provides that Congress may enforce the amendment by appropriate legislation, I ask him how Congress may enforce the prohibitions against a State?

MR. THURMAN. Just precisely as it enforces the prohibition against a State that it shall not pass any law impairing the obligation of contracts, contained in the original Constitution. It enforces it by providing for the making of a case for the judicial tribunals of the United States, in which that law impairing the obligation of contracts may be declared to be null and void. So, too, any law which any State may pass or enforce in violation of the thirteenth, fourteenth, or fifteenth amendments may be declared void in precisely the same way; and the only proper and constitutional mode in my judgment for Congress to adopt is to provide for bringing any such cases that it sees proper to provide for decision before the judicial tribunals of the Federal Government. That was the mode under the Constitution before these amendments were adopted; and it is the proper mode yet.

The Constitution is not so imperfect an instrument as some seem to suppose. It provides not simply for an executive and legislative department, but also for a judicial department, and provides that the judicial power shall extend to all cases arising under this Constitution or the laws and treaties made in pursuance thereof. That gives the judicial power ample cognizance of every case that can possibly arise that brings into discussion the validity of any State law which is said to be in contravention of the Constitution of the United States, or the laws of Congress passed in pursuance thereof.

And now, in regard to this clause that "Congress shall have power by appropriate legislation to enforce this article," Congress would have exactly the same power if that clause were not in the Constitution at all. That does not add one iota to the power of Congress.

The section is:

The Congress shall have power to enforce this article by appropriate legislation.

That does not add, as I say, one iota to the power of Congress; and if it were stricken out of each of the thirteenth and fourteenth and fifteenth amendments, the power of Congress would be precisely what it now is. For what is "appropriate legislation?" It is the very same thing that is provided for by the eighth section of article 1, as construed by the Supreme Court in McCulloch *vs.* Maryland, the wellknown and familiar provision as to the power of Congress to made necessary laws, and which reads:

The Congress shall have power to make all laws which shall be necessary and proper for carrying into execution the foregoing powers. and all other powers vested by this Constitution in the Government of the United States. or in any department or officer thereof.

That provision covers the amendments adopted afterward, just as much as it covers the powers conferred by the original Constitution. . . .

The provision at the close of section 8 of article 1, "that Congress shall have power to make all laws," etc., applies to all provisions of the Constitution that may be in it in all time to come. It is a standing, speaking power that continues for all time as long as the Constitution shall endure, and reaches every particle of it, however it may be added to by amendment. We all know perfectly well that that provision "to make all laws which shall be necessary and proper for carrying into execution the foregoing powers," and so on, is wholly and absolutely unnecessary. It was so declared—and no man ever contradicted it—in the Federalist, and proved to be wholly unnecessary, and it was put in only out of abundant caution. In no debate whatever, either in the Federal Convention or in the conventions of the States, have I ever seen, nor do I believe it has ever been found, the position that that was a substantive, independent power of Congress. It was nothing but putting in words, in the form of an express grant, that power which would have resulted by necessary implication even if those words were stricken out of the Constitution; and so it is expressly stated in the Federalist. There is no question about that. . . .

I have said that these are prohibitions upon the powers of the States. But what does this bill undertake to do? Does this bill undertake to treat with laws made or enfored by States that deprive any citizen of the United States of any privilege or immunities of a citizen of the United States, or that deny him the equal protection of the laws? Does it do any such thing as that? Let us see. Mark it, this bill must rest, if it have any constitutional warrant at all, upon these words: "No State shall make or enforce any law which shall abridge the privileges or immunities of citizens of the United States." And again: "Nor shall any State deprive any person of life, liberty, or property, without due process of law: nor deny to any person within its jurisdiction the equal protection of the laws."

"No State shall make or enforce any law which shall abridge the privileges or immunities of citizens of the United States." Does this bill deal with any such law of a State? No, sir; it does not profess to do so. It is not aimed at any law of a State. It is aimed against the acts of individuals; it is aimed against keepers of theaters, keepers of circuses, keepers of hotels, managers of railroads, stagecoaches, and the like. There is not one single sentence in the whole bill which is leveled against any law made or enforced by a State. The Constitution says that no State shall make or enforce any such law. This bill says to a State, "Although you do not make any such law, although you do not enforce any such law, although your law is directly the opposite, although you punish every man who does any one of the acts mentioned in this bill, and punish him never so severely, yet the Congress of the United States will step in and under that clause of the Constitution which says that you, the State, shall not make or enforce any such law, we, the Federal power, will seize the man whom you have punished for this very act, and will punish him again; we will treat the keeper of a theater as the State; we will treat the hotel keeper as the State; we will treat the railroad conductor as the State, we will treat the stage-driver as the State; and although you may have punished each and every one of these men for the very acts enumerated in this bill, we, under the pretense that the States do make or enforce a law which deprives a citizen of his equal privileges and immunities, will seize that citizen again and subject him to a double punishment for the offense for which he has already suffered." That is what this bill is; and no sophistry can make it anything else.

Take the case of Louisiana. If I am rightly informed—and if I am not the Senator from Louisiana can correct me—there is not one single act or omission in this bill which is not already punishable in Louisiana under her State statute. And now, sir, you are to go with the Federal power into the State of Louisiana and under pretense that that State has made and enforced laws which violate the fourteenth amendment, when every law that she has made and every law that she does enforce is in strict consonance and accordance with that amendment, you are to go there and seize her citizens who have already been punished by the State authority and punish them a second time by the Federal arm!

Why, sir, if it is constitutional reasoning that supports this bill, then I confess that all my studies of the Constitution have been wholly in vain. If this is justice, then I confess that forty years and more of study of the law have all been thrown away upon me. If this is not monstrous, if this is not inhuman, if it is not a violation of the first principles of right, if it is not a violation of the spirit of that provision in the Constitution that no man shall be put in jeopardy twice for the same offense, if it is not legislation utterly disgraceful to a civilized people, then I confess, Mr. President, that I am not able to see correctly what is the scope or purpose of this legislation, or what are the principles of right and justice that should prevail under a civilized government.

PRESIDENT PRO TEMPORE [MATTHEW CARPENTER, R., WIS.]. Will the Senator pardon me for asking him a question?

THE PRESIDING OFFICER [MATT RANSOM, DEM., N.C.]. Does the Senator from Ohio yeild to the Senator from Wisconsin?

MR. THURMAN. Yes, sir.

MR. CARPENTER. The concluding clause in the legislative article is that Congress shall have power—

To make all laws which shall be necessary and proper for carrying into execution the foregoing powers, and all other powers vested by this Constitution in the Government of the United States, or in any department or officer thereof.

Turn now to the other provision of the Constitution which says that no State shall make any law "impairing the obligation of contracts." Does this clause in the legislative article cover that case, or authorize Congress to pass any law in regard to it? The provision is that Congress shall have power to make laws "necessary and proper for carrying into execution the foregoing powers"—that is, the power just preceding in this legislative article conferred by the Constitution upon Congress—

And all other powers vested by this Constitution in the Government of the United States, or in any department or officer thereof.

Now, does the provision in the other section, that "no State shall coin money," vest any power in the United States or in any department or officer thereof? Clearly not. It is an inhibition laid upon the State; but no power with reference to it is conferred upon the General Government. My honorable friend is entirely sound undoubtedly in saying that this clause adds nothing to the legislative article; that all which is covered by it would be raised by necessary implication. But do not these words go in the other direction and do they not restrict? When this clause was put in, that Congress shall have power to make all laws necessary and proper for a certain purpose, that is to execute the powers conferred by the Constitution upon Congress and the powers vested by the Constitution in the United States Government, or in any department or officer thereof, does not that fairly exclude any power to legislate in regard to a State's impairing the obligation of contracts or coining money?

Come now to the fifteenth amendment:

The right of citizens of the United States to vote shall not be denied or abridged by the United States or by any State on account of race. color. or previous condition of servitude.

There is nothing in the world but a clear and clean prohibition upon the States. But then it adds:

The Congress shall have power to enforce this article by appropriate legislation.

If this means simply that Congress shall have power to declare by law that no State shall deny this right, that is nonsense, because the Constitution declares it already, and no legislation is required for that. Therefore the Senator, in order to maintain his argument, must convict those who framed and those who adopted this constitutional amendment of nonsense when he says that this provision gives no power to legislate affirmatively upon the subject, because a mere prohibition repeated in a statute would be wholly worthless, it being already in the Constitution. Therefore, being bound to presume that this provision in the Constitution was intended to grant some power, and some substantial beneficial power, must we not say that it meant to empower Congress to see to it that the State did not in any way do the thing which the Constitution says no State shall do? In other words, may not Congress under this provision enter into that field and see to it that every citizen has a right to vote in every State and that he is not deprived of that right either by law, or by a fraud at the polls systematically carried on over the State, or by any other means, by which the citizen might lose his right. In other words, was this clause put in here merely to tie down a State by act of Congress or statute which was already tied down by the Constitution itself; or was it put there to carry out the substantial end, to act affirmatively, and to see not only that the State did not do it negatively, but that we might see that the fact itself, the right to vote, should be enjoyed?

MR. THURMAN. I do not object to this question, although it has taken immense proportions, and the Senator has set up a man of straw to knock it down by putting in my mouth an argument that I never made. I certainly did not say or mean to say that the power of Congress is merely to re-enact the terms of the Constitution. I do not think the Constitution ever contemplated any such thing as that. If the Senator will listen to me a little while, I think I shall make my idea clear to him, which I evidently did not do before; and if I did not make it clear to him, I should doubt having made it clear to anybody else.

My proposition is that this provision, that "the Congress shall have power to enforce this article by appropriate legislation," means nothing more in respect to the amendments to which it is attached, the thirteenth, fourteenth, and fifteenth, than does the last clause in the eighth section of the first article in reference to the provisions to which that referred. If the Senator will follow me through, he will see how that works. . . .

Mr. President, I do not wish to speak further about that. I have no hope whatever that any reasoning that I can urge will be of the least avail; and why not? First, for the reason I have already stated, and next for the reason that the Supreme Court of the United States has rendered a solemn decision that is as plainly in the face of this bill as I am in the presence of this Senate; and if Senators will pay no regard to that decision I cannot hope that they will be influenced by any arguments of mine. I allude to the decision in what are known as the Slaughter-house cases. There is no refinement or hair-splitting that can get rid of the opposition of that decision to this bill. I must content myself with referring to only a few passages from the opinion of the majority, remarking, however, that the opinion of the dissenting judges, as explained afterward in the Bartmeyer case shows, as it seems to me, that they did not intend to support any such bill as this by the weight of their authority; but, be that as it may, what demands our attention is the opinion of the majority of the court.

HENRY PEASE [R., MISS.]. I desire to ask the gentleman a question.

THE PRESIDENT PRO TEMPORE. Does the Senator from Ohio yield to the Senator from Mississippi?

MR. THURMAN. If it is only a question.

MR. PEASE. If I understand the position taken by the honorable Senator, it is that under the Constitution Congress is only authorized to provide such legislation as shall enable the citizen to bring any abridgement of his rights into the courts or under the judicial action of the United States. I desire to ask the Senator if the bill under consideration does not provide for just such a state of things, does it not provide that a man who is abridged in any of his rights as a citizen can get redress in the Federal courts of the United States?

MR. THURMAN. The Senator certainly could not have heard what I said before or he would not have asked me that question. The bill undoubtedly provides for making cases enough, God knows. It provides for making a great many too many cases for Federal jurisdiction; but it does not provide for making that case which the Constitution is aimed at, the case where a State makes or enforces a law that deprives a citizen of the United States of his privileges or immunities. It does not touch any such case at all. It is not aimed at any such case; but, as I have said before and repeated once, and I do not like to repeat it again, it applies to a State in which the laws punish the very acts that are provided for in this bill just as much as it does to any State that should make or enforce a law contrary to either one of these amendments to the Constitution.

To return to the decision of which I was speaking. The judge delivering the opinion of the majority of the court in the Slaughter-house cases goes on to show, and in this exposes the error of the argument of the Senator from Indiana, [Mr. Pratt,] delivered to-day, that the privileges and immunities of citizens of the United States are distinct from the privileges and immunities of citizens of the States; that the privileges and immunities of citizens of the United States must of necessity be derived from the Constitution of the United States, but the privileges and immunities of citizens of a State are derived under her constitution, and therefore they are different things. It may be that a citizen may have the same immunities as a citizen of the United States that he has in Ohio as a citizen of Ohio, because the provisions constituting a bill of rights in the Federal and State constitutions are in many particulars the same; and so the same remark might be made of many other States, perhaps the most of them, but still the distinction remains between privileges and immunities of citizens of the United States as citizens of the United States, and privileges and immunities that belong to a citizen of a State in virtue of his character of State citizenship. This is made extremely clear in the opinion of the judge who delivered the opinion in that case. I desire to call the particular attention of the Senate to some of his reasoning upon the fourteenth amendment. The first sentence of that amendment is:

All persons born or naturalized in the United States, and subject to the jurisdiction thereof, are citizens of the United States and of the State wherein they reside.

That secures two citizenships to a person born or naturalized in the United States. It secures to him, in the first place, a citizenship of the United States. For instance, if he were born in the District of Columbia it secures him citizenship of the United States. The old argument, which never seemed to me to be sound, was that a man could not be a citizen of the United States unless he were a citizen of a State—that was the extreme view taken by the State-rights men—and consequently that a man born in a Territory could not become a citizen of the United States until he became a citizen of some State, and in the same way that all persons born and residing in the District of Columbia were not citizens of the United States. That was the old argument. It necessarily resulted in that. This provision puts an end to that, and says that wherever you are born, whether in the District of Columbia, in a Territory, or in a fortress, you are a citizen of the United States; or wherever you are naturalized, whether in the District of Columbia or in a Territory, you are a citizen of the United States. Then it goes further, and provides that the same person shall be a citizen of the State wherein he resides, and thus secures to him State citizenship.

But the next sentence contains the prohibition upon which this bill is founded, and mark what it is:

No State shall make or enforce any law which shall abridge the privileges or immunities of citizens of the United States.

Limiting it to United States citizenship alone. It is not provided that "no State shall make or enforce any law which shall abridge the privileges or immunities of citizens of the United States or of the State." There are no such words there as "or of the State." It is only a limitation on the power of the State to make a law which shall abridge the privileges and immunities of citizens of the United States, and leaves the State to deal with its citizens as it has the power to do in regard to their privileges and immunities as citizens of the *State*. This distinction is very clearly pointed out by the judge who delivered the opinion of the majority in that case, and he then goes on and says:

> It is quite clear, then, that there is a citizenship of the United States, and a citizenship of a State, which are distinct from each other, and which depend upon different characteristics or circumstances in the individual.
>
> We think this distinction and its explicit recognition in this amendment of great weight in this argument, because the next paragraph of this same section, which is the one mainly relied on by the plaintiffs in error, speaks only of privileges and immunities of citizens of the United States—

That is the clause which is now under consideration—

> and does not speak of those of citizens of the several States. The argument, however, in favor of the plaintiffs rests wholly on the assumption that the citizenship is the same, and the privileges and immunities guaranteed by the clause are the same.

That is, the argument of the plaintiffs in error in the Slaughter-house cases went upon the theory that the privileges and immunities of citizens of the State and of citizens of the United States were identical, were the same. The court show that this is not the case, and then they go on to say:

> The language is, "No State shall make or enforce any law which shall abridge the privileges or immunities of citizens of *the United States.*" It is a little remarkable, if this clause was intended as a protection to the citizens of a State against the legislative power of his own State, that the word, "citizen of the State" should be left out when it is so carefully used, and used in contradistinction to citizens of the United States, in the very sentence which precedes it. It is too clear for argument that the change in phraseology was adopted understandingly and with a purpose.
>
> Of the privileges and immunities of the citizen of the United States, and of the privileges and immunities of the citizens of the State, and what they respectively are, we will presently consider.

Now I ask the attention of the Senate to this:

> But we wish to state here that it is only the former—

That is, the immunities and privileges of citizens of the United States as such—

> which are placed by this clause under the protection of the Federal Constitution, and that the latter, whatever they may be, are not intended to have any additional protection by this paragraph of the amendment.
>
> If, then, there is a difference between the privileges and immunities belonging to a citizen of the United States as such, and those belonging to the citizen of the State as such, the latter—

That is the privileges and immunities belonging to him as the citizen of a State—

must rest for their security and protection where they have heretofore rested; for they are not embraced by this paragraph of the amendment.

The court next proceeds to show what is meant by the privileges and immunities of the citizen of a State; and to that I beg leave to call the careful attention of the Senate. To do this Mr. Justice Miller refers to the decisions upon this article in the original Constitution:

The citizens of each State shall be entitled to all privileges and immunities of citizens in the several States.

That is section 2 of the fourth article of the original Constitution. Now mark it, that deals with State citizenship alone; it has nothing to do with citizenship of the United States. It deals with State citizenship alone, and the very words are "privileges and immunities," just as they are in the fourteenth amendment, and the question arose first in Corfield vs. Coryell, reported in Washington's Circuit Court Reports, and afterward in Ward vs. The State of Maryland, (12 Wallace,) and in Paul vs. Virginia, (8 Wallace.) What are the privileges and immunities of citizens of the States which under this article of the original Constitution are to be respected by the other States?

TIMOTHY HOWE [R., WIS.]. Privileges of citizens of the United States.

MR. THURMAN. No; privileges of citizens of the State. The question arose, what were the privileges of citizens of the State—not of the United States, but of the State. Let me read the section again:

The citizens of each State shall be entitled to all privileges and immunities of citizens in the several States.

That is to say, they shall be entitled to the privileges and immunities of State citizenship. That is the provision of the original Constitution. Now the question comes, what are those privileges and immunities that appertain to men as citizens of the State? If they appertain to them as citizens of the State, they are not those peculiar privileges that appertain to them as citizens of the United States, but they are privileges and immunities that belong to them in virtue of their State citizenship. The first definition was by Justice Washington in the case of Corfield vs. Coryell, decided in 3 Washington's Circuit Court Reports, 371.

MR. MORTON. I wish to call the attention of the Senator to the fact that the privileges and immunities of citizens of the State, spoken of in the article of the Constitution he has just read, are treated as being identical with the privileges of citizens of the United States under the fourteenth article, and the judge reads from the case of Coryell to show that those rights were identical in their character.

MR. THURMAN. There is nothing in the world to show that under the fourteenth amendment they are treated as identical at all, but on the contrary this very case decides that they are not identical. This very decision which I have read decides that they are not identical.

MR. MORTON. The Senator does not understand me. The court draws a distinction between the privileges of citizens of the United States and of citizens of a State, but the privileges meant by the original article referred to are those which are now treated as the privileges of a citizen of the United States.

MR. THURMAN. Yes, in this Hall, but in no court.

MR. MORTON. In that decision.

MR. THURMAN. No, sir; not a bit of it.

MR. MORTON. I will show it.

MR. THURMAN. On the contrary, the Senator cannot find one word in the opinion of the majority of the court that sustains any such proposition, but directly the reverse.

MR. FRELINGHUYSEN. Will the Senator allow me a word?

MR. THURMAN. Yes, sir.

MR. FRELINGHUYSEN. As I understand the Slaughter-house cases, the majority of the court hold that it is one of the privileges of a citizen of the United States to have the benefit of the provision of the fourteenth amendment which declares that no State shall "deny to any person within its jurisdiction the equal protection of the laws," and I will call the attention of the Senator to the eightieth page of the decision. The majority of the court, commencing on the seventy-ninth page, run over a list of what they consider the privileges of United States citizenship; and then at the end of the first clause on the eightieth page the court say:

To these may be added the rights secured by the thirteenth

That is, freedom—

and fifteenth articles of amendment, and by the other clause of the fourteenth, next to be considered.

That clause is:

Nor shall any State deprive any person of life, liberty, or property, without due process of law; nor deny to any person within its jurisdiction the equal protection of the laws.

The court go on and say:

The existence of laws in the States where the newly emancipated negroes resided, which discriminated with gross injustice and hardship against them as a class, was the evil to be remedied by this clause, and by it such laws are forbidden.

MR. THURMAN. I am astonished, I must confess, after the court made an elaborate argument to show that these rights of citizens of the State must depend upon the State, and that they are wholly distinct from the rights, privileges, and immunities which belong to a man in his character of citizen of the United States, and basing the very decision upon that ground, that the

Senator from New Jersey should take hold of a single sentence, separated from its context, to draw directly an opposite conclusion to that at which the majority of the court arrived.

MR. FRELINGHUYSEN. I only read one sentence, but it extends over two or three pages.

MR. THURMAN. Not only that; the judge proceeded to show that the very ground taken now by the Senator from New Jersey could be reduced to absurdity, and he went into an elaborate *reductio ad absurdum* of the very identical proposition that is now started by the Senator from New Jersey. . . .

I know there are certain gentlemen who have been in the Congress of the United States, who thought it their duty to shear the Supreme Court of its powers under the Constitution and the laws, and by the repeal of statutes to prevent questions affecting the liberty, nay, the lives of citizens from being determined by that high judicial tribunal; but with the oath that I have taken to support the Constitution of the United States, and with the provision of the Constitution that the judicial power of the Government shall extend to all cases arising under the Constitution and all laws and treaties made in pursuance thereof, I consider it to be a part of my sworn duty not to deprive that court of the power to decide questions of that character, and that it is my duty to provide by law that such questions shall take the form of a case in order that they may be thus decided.

But, sir, enough of this. I beg the attention of the lawyers of the Senate to the opinion of the judges, including those of the dissenting judges, as explained in the Bartmeyer case, to show that as they there interpret the powers of Congress, those powers do not cover this bill.

A few words more and I will have done. I have spoken three times as long as I should have done but for the interruptions to which I have been subjected, of which, however, I make not the slightest complaint. I have no desire but to arrive at the truth. I have no feeling on this subject. I believe that I have far less prejudice against this colored race than perhaps half the people that reside in States where a colored man's face never was seen or where it was so seldom seen that the man who bore it was rather a novelty and a show. I have lived all my life surrounded by the colored race, and there is not one of them living on the face of this earth that can say that I ever treated him unkindly or with disrespect. I entertain for them none but the kindest feelings. They are human beings, as I am, and I am willing to see them enjoy every civil right that I enjoy. In my State they have enjoyed these rights for many a long year by the universal consent of all the people, and they will so continue to enjoy them; and now, speaking in their interest, I say that this bill is injurious and prejudicial to them. I say nothing about any hostile feeling that the bill itself may create that may lead to acts of oppression or violence. I speak not of that now. I shall confine myself mainly if not altogether to the question of the common schools. In regard to that, if I understood the Senator from Indiana, [Mr. Pratt,] he said that this bill did not require mixed schools. I may have misunderstood him; but if I apprehended his remarks clearly he said this bill does not require mixed schools. I do not think that any one of the majority of the Judiciary Committee who reported the bill will sustain that assertion. I know that the first section of the bill may to a careless reader seem ambiguous, but I do not think there is one member of the majority of the Judiciary Committee who will not say, if the question is put directly to him, that the meaning of the section is that there shall be mixed schools. Let us see:

That all persons within the jurisdiction of the United States shall be entitled to the full and equal enjoyment of the accommodations, advantages, facilities, and privileges of inns, public conveyances on land or water, theaters, and other places of public amusement

Let us stop there for a moment. That means mixed audiences, does it not? That means mixed guests at a hotel, does it not? That means mixed travelers on a railway or in a stage-coach, does it not? If not, it does not mean anything. It certainly was not intended by the committee that Mr. Saville should build another theater for the entertainment of the colored people of Washington City, or that the Baltimore and Ohio Railway or the Baltimore and Potomac Railway is to run separate cars to carry colored persons. These are the very things that are complained of. Therefore, mixture is meant in inns, in public conveyances on land or water, in theaters, in other places of public amusement, and then it goes right on, "and"—there is the copulative conjunction, and as if to make that more emphatic the word "also" is added—

and also of common schools and public institutions of learning or benevolence supported, in whole or in part, by general taxation.

If it means a mixed audience in a theater, if it means mixed guests at an inn, if it means mixed travelers on a railway, it means mixed colors in public schools and public institutions of learning and benevolence supported in whole or in part by general taxation. There is no getting rid of it. But that is not all

And of cemeteries so supported—

And then comes—

subject only to the conditions and limitations established by law.

If it stopped there it would possibly, but by no means certainly, leave it to the law-making power of the State to make a discrimination on the basis of color; but it does not stop there. For the very purpose of preventing any such discrimination on the basis of color, this sentence is added:

and applicable alike to citizens of every race and color, regardless of any previous condition of servitude.

That is to say, you may make conditions and limitations by law, but they must be conditions and limitations "applicable alike to citizens of every race and color regardless of any previous condition of servitude." You may provide by law that a negro man for certain sufficient causes may be excluded from an inn, a railway car, or a theater; but you must for the same causes exclude white men also. In other words, the prohibition is against any discrimination on the basis of race or color. There is no question about that. There cannot be. Therefore my friend from Indiana, if he has understood this first section as allowing the State of Indiana to provide by law that the children of colored people and of white people shall be educated in different schools, is entirely mistaken. This is intended to prohibit that very thing. Take my own State. Ohio was the first of the Western States that established a common-school system, and she established it long before it was established in a majority of the States lying east of the Alleghanies. She has nurtured it with all the care that ever a mother nurtured her offspring until there are $12,000,000 raised annually in the State of Ohio for the support of common schools. Twelve million dollars by taxation her people pay every year for the erection of school-houses and the support of common schools. If any other State can show a better record, let it be produced. She has provided always that the colored children should have equal advantages with the whites; and although $999 out of every $1,000 of those $12,000,000 come from the pockets of the white people, yet she gives to the negro child *per capita* precisely the same amount for his education that she gives to the child of the white parent.

GEORGE EDMUNDS [R., VT.]. May I ask the Senator a question? Is that given as a matter of grace and genorosity, or is it given as a matter of right that the colored citizen has to have the State protect him and educate him?

MR. THURMAN. I do not care whether it is a matter of right or whether it is a matter of generosity, it is a matter of fact; and it does not become the Senator from Vermont to be questioning the motive when the fact exists.

MR. MORTON. I should like to inquire of the Senator whether the laws of Ohio provide for the establishment of separate schools now?

MR. THURMAN. Yes, sir; they do; that is the statute to this day, and I hold in my hand a decision pronounced by the supreme court of that State, composed of five eminent republicans, every one of them a republican; and it is the unanimous decision of that court, pronounced in December, 1871— only two years ago—in which the very question was whether that law of Ohio was in violation of the fourteenth amendment of the Constitution; and the court, after stating the case, say:

It is quite apparent from this state of the case that the proceeding is brought, not because the children of the plaintiff are excluded from the public schools, but to test the right of those having charge of them to make a classification of scholars on the basis of color.

It was not a question of their being excluded, because they were not excluded from the school which was established for colored children.

This is the principal question in the case, and we propose to consider it without reference to the question made as to the proper parties to the proceeding, for in the view we take of the case this becomes unnecessary.

Then the court go on to show that if this provision of the law making separate schools on the basis of the distinction of color were in violation of the fourteenth amendment, it must be in violation of certain similar provisions in the constitution of Ohio of 1851, and of the first constitution of that State adopted in 1802, and then they cite uniform decisions directly upon the point by the supreme court of that State that that classification on the basis of color was not a violation of the constitution of 1851, or of the constitution of 1802, nor was it a violation of the provisions of the grants by the United States to the State of Ohio of land for purposes of education. . . .

That decision was followed by the decision of the Slaughter-house cases, which is on all-fours with that unanimous decision of the supreme court of Ohio. Now, I need not say to any Senator that if the exlusion of colored children from white schools is not a violation of the fourteenth amendment, then you have no right to punish such exclusion. You cannot get the right to punish it unless it is a violation of the Constitution, and the Supreme Court of the United States has said in effect that it is no violation of the Constitution of the United States. The supreme court of Ohio, by a unanimous decision of judges strongly sympathizing with the colored people and belonging to that party which sets itself up as their great champion, has said the same thing. And yet you seek to overthrow the law of my State and force upon her people what her Legislature, her courts, her constitutional conventions, and her people have always opposed and ever will oppose.

Mr. President, I said some time ago, so long ago that I had almost forgotten it, that this bill is prejudicial to the interests of the colored race. Every man in this Senate I have no doubt desires to see that race educated. It is for the best interests of the whole people, not simply of that race but of the white race also, that they should be educated. How are they to be educated in the Southern States which lately were slave-holding States? Unless the Federal Government is to assume the right to set up schools there and carry on education on the doctrine to which I have alluded, that there is no express prohibition against their doing it in the Constitution, if the Federal Government is not to set up and pay for schools there, those schools must be set up and maintained by the State Legislatures and paid for out of the property of the white people of those States. The property belongs to the white people, almost the whole of it; the taxes come out of their pockets; and it is their Legislatures that must pass the laws to levy those taxes, with the exception of perhaps two States, or at the most three, in which the negroes predominate. Now, I ask you, Senators, if you, treating as utterly unworthy of regard this thing which you call a prejudice, and which you felt yourselves not a great while ago and which was as strong in your States, Senators from New England, as it was in the Southern States in the days of your fathers—if treating that as a mere prejudice you require that there shall be mixed schools in those States, I ask you what will be the result? The result will be that schools will not be established; the taxes will not be laid; the laws for the common-school system will be repealed or rendered nugatory; and the consequence will be that both the negro children and the poor white children too will go without education. There never was so fatal a blow aimed at the common-school system, never so fatal a blow aimed at the education of the poor, never so fatal a blow aimed at the education and elevation of the children of this colored race, conceived by the mind of man as this civil-rights bill. . . .

JOHN STOCKTON [DEM., N.J.]. I propose now, Mr. President, to examine this bill in some little detail to see what its propositions are and what its effect will be, and then to conclude the remarks I have to make to the Senate by an examination of its constitutionality, in which connection I shall consider the decision in the Slaughter-house case and a case decided since.

What is this bill? The fourteenth constitutional amendment declares that no State shall pass any law that interferes with the equal rights of any citizen, and it gives power to enforce by appropriate legislation this deprivation of authority to the States. The bill sets out by declaring that all men shall have equal rights in inns, public conveyances, cemeteries, and schools. The bill purports, in the first place, to pass a statute which, if it means nothing but what it appears to mean in reference to common carriers and innkeepers, is the law now. If it mean nothing else but what it is insisted upon by the advocates of this bill, or some of them, that it means, it is the law now. Every man knows that a common carrier by his contract with the public when he becomes a common carrier, when he gets his right to take toll and freight, is bound to carry all; that every railroad company and steamboat company is so bound by the law of common carriers as it prevailed in England and has been adopted or amended in this country. He knows that the best accommodation to be had for the same money is the right and title of every citizen of this country. He knows that when the constitutional amendment was adopted making persons of African descent citizens, it gave them every right that a white man had as a citizen of the United States. He has a right to precisely as good accommodations and equal accommodations. But the construction given by this bill, the construction given by the late Senator from Massachusetts, [Mr. Sumner,] the construction given when you come to apply it to schools, makes that word "equal" mean "the same;" and there is where the difficulty lies.

If by the clause empowering "appropriate legislation" you can carry out that construction, you gain more power than the Constitution had itself and get more power from the words "appropriate legislation" given to Congress than the clause itself contains. By the same process of reasoning it is very easy then to make "equal" mean "the same," and that has already been avowed in this Chamber. On an occasion when this bill was brought up here before, the late Senator from Massachusetts insisted that the colored children were entitled to go to the same schools. That is insisted on by the convention whose resolutions have been read; and that was insisted on yesterday by the Senator from Massachusetts now on this floor, [Mr. Boutwell,] who said that the very object was to educate the people together, that this miserable prejudice that existed should be rooted out of the hearts of the young as they grow up; that was the very object of it. They were to have the same schools, not equal schools. When it was asserted on this floor that the schools in this District, for example, were equally good, the answer was, what a dreadful thing it is to the feelings of a colored parent who knows that his child cannot go into that building because white children go there! There must be the same schools for both, we are told; and so there must be the same grave-yard because it is my grave-yard and contains graves of my loved ones. It is the same school because it is my school and the school of my children. Let the colored man love his school as he loves his children; and the more he worships and mourns at the graves of his loved ones, the more I respect him; but he, unstirred up by bad men who do it for the very purpose of agitation, does not seek or desire the violation of a natural feeling deeply implanted in the bosom of every man, be his skin white or black.

I have said that if the interpretation of the bill were not in the very words of gentlemen who advocate it that which I have suggested, the simple fact of establishing equal rights would amount to nothing; for they have them now by law, and they have redress in the State courts for any violation of them. But, Mr. President, let us go further. This bill which gives equal rights guards and protects us somewhat. It is equal rights where the school or the cemetery is established or kept up in whole or in part by general taxation. The provision in regard to the inn or tavern or conveyance does not contain that clause. There you can go into a man's own domestic affairs. The innkeeper, by the common law of England and by the common law of most of the States of this land, altered by the statutes of the States though altered but very slightly, goes to the county court; he proves that he has so many beds, accommodations for so many wayfarers, and he gets his license from the county court, with a recommendation from his neighbors and friends, to keep a way-side inn, wherein the weary traveler may rest. He is called upon every year to renew that license; for no man is authorized to keep a bar-room exclusively so on the highway; but he may keep a house of entertainment for those who are weary, for those who need it. Unless he agrees to do that, he cannot have a license. Now, Mr. President, you propose to do what? Not to say that no State shall pass any law, as the amendment provides, but to pass a law yourself making the man who does not keep that hotel according to the orders of Congress, according to such arbitrary rules as you may lay down in

Congress, a criminal, liable to fine and imprisonment. You make those who authorize him to keep the inn, those who give him the license, inciters of that crime; and you make the very courts of the State, the judges of the common pleas sitting on the bench in the counties of my State and licensing these inns and taverns under the laws of the State, under the common law of their fathers as they brought it to this country, criminals.

The colored people are already, as I have said, equal before the law. They vote for the school superintendent, and if they have the majority they elect a colored man. They vote in every respect as the white man does. They elect indirectly the judges of the common pleas who grant these licenses. They have their full right in the Government, their full right in the country, their full representation by the right of suffrage. They are equal before the law. What do you propose to do with them? To make them superior to the law, superior to the majority that make the rules and say a man may keep such and such a house of entertainment by congressional action.

Under the laws of the States as they now exist an innkeeper would have no right to drive out of his house when he had the accommodations, and he is obliged to have the accommodations provided by law, any man of any color. If Congress does not interfere with the manner in which the hotel is kept he might regulate its discipline. He might say that the servant in that house, be he white or black, should eat in the kitchen, that the guests of the house should eat in another room, that the ladies should have separate apartments; he might make such rules and distinctions as common decency and propriety make proper in a well-regulated hotel; and if he did not make those rules his license would be taken from him, for his house would become a disorderly one. In making those rules and regulations he would have a right to say that a man who had a contagious disease could not come into his house, for that is for the security of the public health. He might say that a man who contaminated the morals of the community, who desired to come into his house to gamble, could not come in, for that would hurt the public morals. So you admit that under the power granted by the State he stands there the regulator of his own hotel and only accountable to the law of the State and the municipal corporation which granted his license. And yet if a negro fancies that he is not treated properly, or if he goes into a hotel and is not put in such a place as would interfere with the regular discipline which all admit is necessary for that house, that innkeeper and all who incite him, which means anybody, are liable to be punished with fines and penalties, in which the Senator from Indiana glories.

One step further, Mr. President. These parties must be indicted; for it is made the duty of the marshal, it is made the duty of the district attorney, it is made the duty of the commissioner appointed by this act with power to arrest and imprison the body of any citizen, to hear these complaints and act immediately upon them on the testimony of any man who may pretend that his feeling have been wounded on account of race or color; and thus the citizen may be imprisoned in the State where he has committed no offense against its laws, in the body of the county of Essex, in the city of Newark, in the State of New Jersey, by an order from a United States commissioner, with power of arrest and imprisonment.

But a step further. When the creatures created by this act have done their work, that man at least has one bulwark left—a bulwark the establishment and protection of which have raised many and many a revolution among our ancestors who were freer than we are to-day—I mean the right to be tried by his peers, to be tried by a fair and impartial jury; the last bulwark left him from the attack of Federal authority under the pretense of equal rights; and even there, in violation of the most solemn guarantees of the Constitution, you tamper with that jury and put in the box a jury that you know to be prejudiced, and you do it intentionally. You use the machinery of the United States courts; you bring men, as you did in the State of North Carolina, under a reign of terror that they cannot resist; you bring them to be tried by a jury on a question of race and color which you make, and before a jury that you oblige to be composed of a part of this minority race, and whose battle you admit and tell them you are fighting. I ask any man learned in the law, any man who has ever practiced in our courts, particularly our Federal *nisi prius* courts at the present day, whether he thinks that any man under a charge under this act of violating equal rights would have a fair trial before a jury called under the act, half of which might be colored people, who went there for the very purpose of protecting under the impulse of the feelings, natural perhaps but not proper for an impartial juror, which they evince in the resolutions passed at Nashville? . . .

Mr. President, one of the saddest things about the whole of this business, one of the saddest things that I trust and hope at last the people will begin to see, is the utter recklessness of this proposition. The gentlemen who advocate the bill do not seem to see its results or its effect. They seem perfectly willing to throw life, liberty, and everything else that we have or care for on a sea of uncertainty. The offense is no offense, it has no definition; it requires the construction of your courts which is against the ordinary liberal rules of the common law; and it requires the definition given here to frame any sort of imaginary crime, and when an indictment is framed it may cover nearly every harmless act of life.

Mr. President, I do not know that I ever interfered with the equal rights of any colored man. I certainly never have done so intentionally, and I certainly never intended to do so. I think they are a very kind and a very gentle race. I have quite as much personal regard for colored people, and quite as much desire that their condition shall be improved and that they shall go on improving and progressing, as any other gentleman on the other side of the Chamber. I think I am a little wiser in my course than they are, and I trust that I am guided by no prejudice.

This bill, if passed, will, among other things, break up the whole common-school system in this country; it will leave uneducated the colored people, a million of whose children, it is said, are now being educated under the benign laws of the State governments and under the protection of those laws by the money of the white people who are bound to make their subscriptions. It will leave them no free schools; it will leave them without education and without the hope of it for years to come. For what? If you make this system go on compulsorily, then what do you do? You establish the system which has made revolution after revolution in England; you establish the system against which Ireland protested until finally the spirit of the age made England give it up—taxing one class of men to educate the other people's children, and taxing for an established church those who believe in another faith. That is to be done here. The poor German and Irishman, who you have invited to these shores, is to be deprived of his liberties and privileges and of the blessings of those laws to which he was invited, and he is to see his children turned out of the school-houses because he does not wish them to associate with the colored people, whether from prejudice or otherwise, and then you continue to tax him to make him support the school-houses of colored persons. That may be done by State legislation where the colored are in the majority, but it follows that an attempt to do it arbitrarily against the will of the whites when they are in the majority would make it the duty of the Government to interfere in behalf of the white minority in South Carolina and Louisiana; and as I said before it is unwise and inexpedient, with no end on earth to be accomplished by it except to delude the poor colored man.

But, Mr. President, let me state the legal propositions on which I rely. The fourteenth amendment makes all persons born or naturalized in the United States citizens of the United States, and of the State wherein they reside, and declares that *no State* shall make or enforce any law which shall abridge the privileges or immunities of citizens of the United States.

No State shall make or enforce any law which shall abridge the privileges or immunities of citizens of the United States; nor shall any State deprive any person of life, liberty, or property, without due process of law; nor deny to any person within its jurisdiction the equal protection of the laws.

Now the bill before us professes to declare that all persons are *entitled* to the full and equal enjoyment of accommodations in inns, schools, cemeteries, etc.

It proposes under the pretense of *appropriate* legislation to enforce the fourteenth article to destroy its whole character and meaning. The fourteenth amendment operates on the States—forbids them from *abridging*, etc.; forbids them from denying *equal protection of the law* to citizens of the United States, which citizenship it created.

The fifteenth amendment took the control of suffrage from the States. But both the amendments from the very fact that they were amendments, and were necessary, admit the entire and exclusive control the States had over the subject—both subjects, except where the amendments restrict and forbid it.

And yet, under the pretense of enforcing these amendments by appropriate legislation, this bill proposes for the first time to interfere with the municipal and police powers of not only the States, but the counties, cities, towns, and school districts, and make all violations of the act misdemeanors and punishable in the courts of the United States by fine and imprisonment, acting directly on the *individual*.

It is a destruction of the rule that the *majority governs*. An arbitrary order from a central consolidated despotism creating an unknown crime which is not *defined*, which is a *negative act*, the definition of which depends upon the mere caprice of the petty tyrant set up by the act and clothed with powers of arresting the body and depriving citizens of their liberty.

Why is not the State Legislature asked to make such a law? Because South Carolina needs no such law to accomplish the object desired; because the majority are of the colored race.

Why are not New York and New Jersey asked? Because it is well known that the majority of the people, irrespective of race or color, would not change the whole form of government, and tyrannically deprive the individual, the school district, the town meeting, the city government, the county court, of managing their own affairs and administering their municipal laws as they have been wont to do.

Knowing that the State will not do it, knowing it is not the will of the people, on the ground that because the State is forbidden to pass any law depriving or denying, etc., equal rights, the United States undertakes to make it a crime against the General Government for individuals to control their own affairs, for corporations to be controlled by the majority of its members, for the State courts to see that all *are equal before the law*, which means properly the government of the majority. Because the States are forbidden to pass laws depriving a citizen of the United States of his rights, it follows, it is insisted, that Congress can make police regulations for every locality, and that an act of omission, which is no interference whatever with the fourteenth amendment; and no crime, but a duty by the law of the State, which permits the people to assemble in town meetings and vote by a majority the sum to be collected for public education, and elect the school superintendent, who has duties assigned him by law, makes it a crime for that superintendent to regulate the necessary discipline of the school, to determine what ages, sexes, and colors may best be taught in the same class. . . .

The construction of the fourteenth amendment which makes this act constitutional, which makes it *appropriate legislation*, is said by the Supreme Court [in the *Slaughter-House Cases*] to be a construction not only unwarranted by the words, but a departure from the structure and spirit of our institutions, and its effect to *fetter and degrade* the State governments, by subjecting them to the control of Congress. . . .

My colleague also fails to observe that the whole operation of the amendment, in words and by every rule of construction, is to prohibit *State legislation* from a certain kind of legislation, precisely as by the Constitution it is forbidden a State to pass an *"ex post facto* law." While this bill acts directly on the citizen and the individual by municipal and police regulations—a power never before claimed—and creates a crime against the United States by any act which comes within the definition.

Neither my colleague nor any one else has or can show any authority for this despotic assumption of power. The Supreme Court says it degrades the States and changes the whole structure of government. . . .

MR. PEASE. Mr. President, I had intended while this question was before the Senate to submit some remarks, but owing to the lateness of the hour, and the further fact that every Senator has made up his mind as to the manner in which he shall vote upon this question, I shall not attempt to detain the Senate by any extended remarks.

I desire briefly to give some of the reasons why I shall support this bill. I shall vote for the bill, first, because I believe that the Congress of the United States has the power under the Constitution to enact a law of this kind. I shall vote for this measure because I believe that it is the bounden duty of the American Congress to enforce the provisions of the fourteenth amendment to the Constitution. So far as the relation of the citizen to the General Government and to the several States that make up the Government is concerned, I am satisfied that the policy of this Government has been changed and that the thirteenth, fourteenth, and fifteenth amendments to the Constitution have provided a new policy in this Government, a policy that defines, recognizes, and protects the rights, the privileges, and the immunities of American citizenship, and has given to Congress the power and the right to legislate for their protection in those several rights and privileges. I believe that the fourteenth amendment to the Constitution clearly indicates that it was the policy of this Government to protect by all needful legislation every citizen, high or low, rich or poor, white or black, native or foreign, who should comply with the terms of citizenship; that all classes should have the equal protection of American law and be protected in their inalienable rights, those rights which grow out of the very nature of society, and the organic law of this country.

Arguments have been presented here intended to show that this measure is unconstitutional. I have listened patiently and attentively to the ingenious and able efforts that have been made by the opposition, and I am perfectly satisfied that the position taken and the arguments advanced by the friends of this bill are unanswered and are unanswerable. I shall not at this late hour attempt to recapitulate them; it is unnecessary.

But, sir, I have heard what it might have been expected we should hear from the opposition, a party which has opposed every measure looking to the protection and elevation of a certain class of American citizens. Why, sir, in every step and stage of the history of this country from the breaking out of the war up to the present day, in every measure looking to the preservation of the Government and protection of the citizen, we have been met with the cry of unconstitutionality. When the thirteenth amendment was proposed to the several States, the democratic party of this country met it with the cry, "It is unconstitutional." When the fourteenth amendment was submitted to the several States, we were met with the same objection. So we the fifteenth amendment, and so with all legislation looking to the enforcement of these amendments to the Constitution, we have been met by that party with the cry of unconstitutionality.

Believing that we have the constitutional right to enact this bill, there is but one other phase of the question to be considered, and that is the question of expediency. I believe that it is expedient for the Congress of the United States now to fix a remedy for existing evils and settle forever the question of the rights, privileges, and immunities of American citizens. There is no more opportune time than the present hour. I believe that this measure has the indorsement of the popular sense to-day. I believe that the American people are prepared for it and are desirous that the question of the status of the negro in this country shall be fixed. I believe that if this measure were to-day submitted to the American people for their suffrages it would meet with an overwhelming approval. The American people are disposed to establish justice and the equality of the citizen before the law.

The main objection that has been brought forward by the opponents of this bill is the objection growing out of mixed schools. Every one who has spoken in opposition to this measure has expressed very serious solicitude as to its effect upon the colored people of the South. Now, I have been somewhat familiar with their condition; I have been familiar with their educational interest for the last ten or twelve years, and I undertake to say that none of the difficulties that have been portrayed will obtain in the South. I believe that the southern people recognize the importance of educating the masses of the people. There has been a great revolution in public sentiment in the South during the last three or four years, and I believe that to-day a majority of the southern people are in favor of supporting, maintaining, and fostering a system of common education, a system of common schools, that shall extend the benefits of the rudiments of an English education to all her people; and I believe that the people of the South so fully recognize this, that if this measure shall become a law, there is not a State south of Mason and Dixon's line that will abolish its school system. Men are governed by their interests. There is not a southern planter but knows that it is for his interest to encourage the education and protection of the lately emancipated people. It is for his interest to have a school-house near his plantation, for his interest to encourage the building of churches, because it will secure labor, it will secure contentment and permanency among the laboring class. In those States the history of the last two or three years proves, and the people of the South are not blind to that fact, that in the State of Georgia, where unjust discriminations have been practiced against the colored people, and where they have been denied school advantages and other privileges of citizenship, there has been a tide of emigration from the State. The colored people, who constitute the mass of the laboring classes, are leaving that State and going to those sections of the country where their rights are protected and educational facilities are provided. If by no higher motive, the southern people will be governed by their own self-interest, and will continue to foster a system of public schools. They recognize the fact that under the new order of government their property and their personal interests are in the hands of an ignorant populace. They recognize the fact that the great interests of society under a form of government like ours depend upon the virtue and intelligence of the people; and in proportion as the people are educated the State will prosper and the general welfare of the people be secured.

Now, sir, in the State of Mississippi we have a system of schools, and under the law regulating the system the child of the colored man can enter the school where white children are taught, and the laws of the State will protect him. We have in that State probably one of the finest colleges in the South, an institution which has been the pride of the Southwest—I refer to Oxford University—and to-day the son of the black man can enter the halls of that institution under the laws of our State. But, sir, with this law, with these provisions, and with a civil-rights law passed two years ago, more stringent in its provisions than the one that is before us to-day, not one instance has come to my knowledge where a colored man has attempted to enforce the law in this respect. The colored people asked for the establishment of a similar university, and the State granted it. The colored man of the South understands and appreciates the situation. All he asks and wants is that there shall be no discrimination against him, that there shall be no legislation based upon color tending to debase and degrade him on account of his color or previous condition. He asks simply that he shall be placed upon the same footing with the white man, and his own good sense teaches him to adapt himself to the circumstances. The humblest and the most ignorant colored man in the South, if he has not an idea above the hoe-handle he wields, knows enough, and appreciates fully the situation, not to force himself into a position where he is to become the victim of prejudice. But he wants as a citizen of the United States that he shall be equally protected under the law; that all legislation, whether it be by the State or by the national Government, shall not discriminate against him on account of his color.

Gentlemen say that if equal advantages in separate schools are provided the law is met so far as privileges and immunities are concerned. I say that whenever a State shall legislate that the races shall be separated, and that legislation is based upon color or race, there is a distinction made; it is a distinction the intent of which is to foster a concomitant of slavery and to degrade him. The colored man understands and appreciates his former condition; and when laws are passed that say that "because you are a black man you shall have a separate school," he looks upon that, and justly, as tending to degrade him. There is no equality in that.

I do not propose to extend my remarks longer. I believe that the country to-day and the American Senate are satisfied that we have the right under the Constitution to pass this enforcement law; and believing this, I shall support the measure, . . . because when this question is settled I want every college and every institution of learning in this broad land to be open to every citizen, that there shall be no discrimination. I want Harvard to throw open her doors; I want Dartmouth to do the same thing. I desire to see such legislation as shall require every institution of learning which is supported in whole or in part by taxation or by public endowment to give to every citizen equal privileges and equal rights in those institutions. I am therefore opposed to that amendment.

In conclusion, I appeal to the Senate in behalf of four millions of citizens of the United States whose rights and immunities are abridged in many of the States. The people of the State I have the honor to represent in this Senate desire that when they pass beyond the limits of their own State they shall not be subjected to indignities upon railroads, steamboats, or the highways on account of color; they ask such legislation shall be had as shall afford the protection guaranteed to them in the Constitution. I should prove recreant to the trust imposed on me if I failed to urge the adoption and vote for this measure. . . .

WILLARD SAULSBURY [DEM., DEL.]. Mr. President, I am fully aware of the unfavorable circumstances under which I rise to discuss this question. We have already been in session fully nine hours, and human nature cannot endure the fatigues of a continuous session for so long a period without feeling some degree of weariness, which in a measure disqualifies for a proper discussion of the subject under consideration. I am also aware that at this hour of the night, when every member of the Senate is exhausted, when there is no disposition to listen to debate, it is calculated to discourage and embarrass very considerably any one that may attempt to address the Senate.

Again, I have been an observer of what has been transpiring while this discussion has been proceeding, the discussion upon a question involving some of the dearest rights of the people of this country, and very frequently, as at present, only a few members of the dominant party are present. I will not say that they are absent, for the reason that they belong to that class of men who love "darkness rather than light, because their deeds are evil." It may be that they do not wish to listen to the exposure of this measure, which a party caucus has decreed shall become a law, or perhaps they are taking their repose. So far as I am concerned, I say to them sleep on; take your rest now; there is coming a day when the American people will hold you and your party to a strict responsibility for present indifference to their wishes, and for the great wrong you propose by this bill to inflict upon them.

Mr. President, on a former occasion, when a measure very similar in its provisions to the bill now before the Senate was under consideration, I took occasion to state some of the objections which I had to its provisions; and perhaps that fact, together with the very embarrassing circumstances to which I have alluded under which I rise to address myself to this question, would justify me in giving upon this bill a silent vote; and yet, regarding this matter as one affecting the interests of the people whom I have the honor in part to represent, I can do nothing less than trespass on the patience of the Senate, for a few moments at least, while I state some of the objections that I think properly arise to the measure before the Senate.

Let me say that if the American people had not ceased to be astonished at anything that takes place in this Chamber or in the other House of Congress, they certainly would be very much surprised at the introduction of a proposition of this kind from one of the committees of this body. Whatever folly any individual member of the Senate may commit in the introduction and pressure of measures upon his own responsibility, it was not to be presumed that any committee of the Senate, especially the Judiciary Committee, heretofore regarded as the highest committee of the Senate, could have committed so grave a mistake as to bring forward a proposition so revolting to the sense and so injurious to the interests of the American people. What is this measure? Disguise it as you may, it is nothing more nor less than an attempt on the part of the American Congress to enforce association and companionship between the races in this country. The object of this bill is not to confer upon the colored race any political rights. The thirteenth, the fourteenth, and the fifteenth amendments have conferred political rights upon the colored people. The thirteenth amendment secured them against the bondage of slavery; the fourteenth amendment constituted them citizens of the United States, and the fifteenth amendment secured to them the right to the elective franchise. But this measure goes further. It proposes not, I say again, to confer any political rights upon the people of African descent, but it proposes to enforce familiarity, association, companionship between the white and the colored people of this country. Is not that true?

That is the object of the bill. It proposes, so far as hotels are concerned, that the white and the colored people shall have the same advantages, equal advantages; that they shall enter with equal right into every part of the inn; that the keeper of the inn shall make no discrimination on account of their race or color; that colored men shall sit at the same table beside the white guest, that he shall enter the same parlor and take his seat beside the wife and daughters of the white man, whether the white man is willing or not, because you prohibit any discrimination against him. He is entitled, under the privileges of this bill, to go into every part of that hotel; he may not be excluded from any part thereof, even though a better separate place should be assigned him by the landlord. If the object was not to enforce companionship, why do you not permit in this bill the landlord to set apart a portion of his hotel, so that he might have one parlor for colored people and another parlor for white people, so that he might have one table for the colored man and another table for the white man, giving to one as good accomodations as to the other? Why is it that there is not a provision which allows that? Simply because, I say, the object and purpose of this bill is to force association and companionship between the races.

Is not that true of the theater? Do you not require that every facility, every advantage which the white man may have may be invaded by the colored man, that he may enter and have the same privileges—not privileges and accommodations assigned to him in a separate part of the theater, but the same privileges—that he may go wherever the white man goes; he may go wherever the white lady goes; no one shall discriminate and set apart one portion for colored people and another portion for white people? Why is it that you in this bill declare that there shall be no such discrimination? I repeat again, it is found only in the fact that you desire to enforce familiarity, association, and companionship between the races.

So, again, with your common schools and institutions of learning. Why is it under the provisions of this bill that you may not have separate schools? I am aware that some of the gentlemen who advocate this bill have said that it might be so, but I am equally aware that the distinguished Senator from Massachusetts [Mr. Boutwell] declared that it might not be so, and my own interpretation of the provisions of this bill is that there is no authority under it to make any assignment for colored schools and for white schools, but that every colored child under the provisions of this bill has the right to enter into the white school though there may be a better school provided for the colored people.

I ask what is the reason of this provision? I maintain that no reason can be found other than the fact that the friends and supporters of this bill desire to enforce the intermixture, the association, and companionship between the races. . . .

Mr. President, I have no unkind feeling to the colored people. On the contrary, without boasting of any particular friendship for them, I have never yet seen a human being, white or black, in distress whose sufferings I would not relieve if I could. I have been as kind to the colored people with whom I have been brought in contact as other gentlemen. I have defended them at the bar against the gravest charges when they needed counsel; and, sir, under any circumstances of life I would be as kind to the colored people as any one. Therefore in what I have to say against the mixed schools, I wish no one to understand that I cherish the least unkind feeling toward any colored man or any living being on earth. I would promote his interests in every proper way. By advice and by other means I would assist him in the progress and advance of life; but I have some respect also for my own race, and when you ask me to aid in the passage of a bill which I know is not only to injure, if it does not destroy, the common schools of the white people, but which I am satisfied will injure the colored schools scattered throughout the States, I am compelled to decline your invitation and to express my objection to the bill, and shall do so with a sincere desire to promote the best interests of both races, acknowledging, however, a higher regard for my own race than any other.

But, Mr. President, the provisions of this bill do not stop with the common schools. It is to apply to all benevolent institutions. Now, sir, there are benevolent institutions in this land into which white persons and colored persons can go, and in all those institutions separate arrangements are made so that the one shall not be brought in contact with the other. In many of your hospitals and in your almshouses these arrangements exist. This bill proposes not only that you shall have association and companionship in taverns, in theaters, in the common schools, in the institutions of learning, but even the home which is prepared for the old and infirm, the common almshouse and the home for the indigent and poor. When the old matron, unable to support herself, is compelled to accept the charities of the public and seeks a home in the common almshouse, the provisions of this bill consign her to the same apartments that are assigned to colored people. Through life she may have maintained a separate and distinct existence from them; she may not have been their associate at all; but when she comes in her advanced age and in her misfortune to be supported by the hand of charity, you propose to follow her into the very almshouse of the country; you propose to make the old man and the old woman of the Caucasian race the companions of negroes, with whom they have never associated in life, if compelled to spend the evening of their days in the almshouse. Not only unfortunate old age but helpless and afflicted infancy is not exempt. The orphan asylum where charitable ladies gather the unprotected and helpless children that they may administer to their comfort, if supported in whole or in part by taxation, is brought within the terms of this bill. Even there you admit of no discrimination, separate apartments, but compel the association of the white children with the colored that are taken there by their friends.

Do not say that you can make any separate arrangement under the provisions of this bill. The object and purport of the measure is to have association in all these places, in the hospital and in the almshouse, everywhere. Companionship and association are the great object sought to be accomplished. You admit of no discrimination, but prohibit it by pains and penalties.

But, Mr. President, without dwelling longer upon this point, let me ask where does the Congress of the United States get the power, the authority, to enact any such law? The constitutional amendments have been appealed to. Prior to the adoption of those amendments a Senator on this floor would have contended that there was anything in the Constitution that would warrant such legislation. By universal consent prior to the adoption of the recent amendments the States and the right to make any laws recognizing distinctions between the races. It is therefore only under the amendments to the Constitution that this power is claimed.

What are those amendments? No one will contend that the thirteenth amendment, which simply prohibited slavery or involuntary servitude in this country, confers any power upon Congress to enact this bill. No one will contend that the fifteenth amendment, which simply confers the elective franchise upon the colored people, confers upon Congress the authority to enact this bill. It is therefore the fourteenth amendment, and that alone, under which the power to enact this proposed law is derived, if it can be derived at all. What was the purport and intent of that amendment of the Constitution? The Supreme Court have said in the very Slaughter-house case which has been brought here in support of this bill that the primary object and purport and intent of that amendment was to confer citizenship upon the colored race, to make them citizens of the United States. That it accomplished that purpose no one questions; but that it does not warrant this legislation is a proposition which I think it is not hard to demonstrate both from argument and from authority. But I will not trespass upon the time of the Senate by reasoning upon this subject abstractly, because the matter is *res adjudicata*. The Supreme Court have passed upon the true intent and purport of the fourteenth amendment. In the Slaughter-house case for the first time that amendment came in review before that court. What said the court? After stating the object of that amendment to be to confer the right of citizenship upon the colored people, distinguishing between the citizenship of the United States and State citizenship, they went on to define what were the rights of citizenship created by the amendment, and then declared that the rights of citizenship of the State as contradistinguished from citizenship of the United States might be regulated—that is the substance of it—by the State; and that such regulation was no infringement of the fourteenth article of the Constitution. . . .

With these views expressed so clearly not only by the majority of the court in the Slaughter-house case, but by the dissenting judges in that case, I am at a loss to know how any legal mind in this body can claim to find within the fourteenth amendment or within any clause of the Constitution the authority for this proposed enactment. . . .

Mr. President, what is the true character of this measure? I say, first, it is a matter of injustice. Northern Senators residing in communities where there are but few colored people, and who, therefore, are not to be affected by this measure, come into the Senate and by their legislation force upon the people in States where there are large colored populations a measure which will most grievously affect them. Sir, if the provisions of this bill were to reach to the same extent the communities which they represent, they would not be here the advocates of the measure. They are here to press upon others that which they would not accept for themselves provided there were as many colored people in their States and communities as there are in the States in this Union which will be affected by this bill. It is therefore a measure of injustice, gross, flagrant injustice.

Sir, what are the facts? Are these Northern Senators and the constituencies they represent any more careful of the rights of other people than those in the former slaveholding States? How is it in Massachusetts to-day? Is everybody entitled to the elective franchise in Massachusetts? It was conferred on the colored race without any conditions, and yet I ask was it not the law in Massachusetts and is it not the case still that a man in order to vote in the city of Boston must be able to read the Bible? I have a letter now from a gentleman from Boston stating to me that that is the fact, and that he must be able to read it to the satisfaction of the clerk of the court, and that a thousand men in that city for that reason cannot vote.

How is it in Rhode Island? Why, sir, that State discriminates against foreign-born citizens and requires a property qualification of them which is not required of others. How is it in Connecticut? Under the law of that State every man must be registered before he can vote, and before he can be registered and qualified to vote he must prove that he can read. Here is the law. The voter "shall tell whether he is an alien or native born, and when he became twenty-one years of age, and before his admission to be registered he shall read at least one line of the Constitution or statutes in such manner as to show that he is not prompted and not reciting from memory." So that if a man has been unfortunate and unable to acquire any education you discriminate against him in the State of Connecticut and in the State of Massachusetts and do not permit his registration and qualification as an elector; and yet those who represent those sections of the country, under the plea of justice to the negro, come here to enforce upon the States having a large colored population measures which they would not accept for themselves if similarly situated, and which they know will be unjust to white people of those States.

It is not only a measure of injustice, it is a measure of inhumanity. What will it do? It will break up the schools in the States. Even the Senator from Wisconsin [Mr. Howe] said this morning he was afraid it might have that effect. Why, sir, the public judgment of the people of the States will compel their Legislatures to abolish the school system, and then alike the free schools for white and for colored will be abolished, and, in that view of it, this measure is a measure of inhumanity—of inhumanity not only to the poor white people who are dependent upon public schools, but it is a measure of inhumanity to the colored people, who are not able to maintain schools sufficient to educate all their children.

The people in the Southern States are doing liberal things for the education of the colored people. The recent Legislature of Maryland appropriated $100,000 exclusively to colored schools in that State. That is about equal to $5,000 to each county in the State to maintain colored schools. Does any man suppose that with this law upon the statute-book, when the white and colored pupils are compelled to mix in schools, the people of Maryland will make such liberal provision for the education of the colored people? No, sir. The white people of Maryland, the most of them, can educate their children at select schools, and they will do it. I know that that will be the case in the State which I have the honor in part to represent; and I say here that, sooner than see mixed schools in the State of Delaware, I would be glad to see the Legislature destroy the common-school system in the State.

The Senator from Indiana farthest from me, [Mr. Pratt,] as well as the Senator from New Jersey, [Mr. Frelinghuysen,] said that this measure is demanded by the colored people. If this legislation is in obedience to their behests, if they are not willing that the white people shall make provision for them in their own way, but demand to be forced into the white schools, then I say upon them must fall the consequences. I deplore the consequences to result from this measure, but I would not willingly see the white children of the State in which I live compelled to go to mixed schools. It would be the poor men alone who would be compelled to send their children to such schools. Men who are able in my State now maintain a large number of select schools notwithstanding we have a good common-school system. Those who now patronize the common schools will forego their advantages sooner than see their children compelled to associate with colored boys and girls. . .

JAMES KELLY [DEM., ORE.]. Before this vote is taken I desire to say a few words. I do not wish to prolong the discussion, because I know that it is determined that the vote must be taken to-night, and I have no particular complaint to make of this, as my brother from North Carolina has done. If I were in the majority, perhaps I would act in the same way; especially if I had a pet measure that I wished to put through; and therefore I will not complain of anything they do in this matter. Indeed, there is another reason why I am reconciled to it. It appears that the length of the session is determined; that is, a month hence we are to adjourn; and there is a great deal of legislation to be done, and therefore it is perhaps well enough that we should do what we can, even though we stay late at night; and yet upon so grave a constitutional question as this is I would much rather that we should have another day to discuss it. It is not every day that a question of this importance arises in the Senate, one that is so far-reaching in its consequences as this certainly will be. In matters of ordinary legislation I would not ask the Senate, if it desired to terminate the discussion of any topic, to prolong it; but I must confess in this case I do. I would rather the bill should go over until to-morrow or Monday, if we do not sit to-morrow; not that I wish any factious opposition to be made to the passage of the bill. I shall content myself, as I suppose all my brethren on this side will, with giving our votes against it and raising what protest we can against its passage. But there is no use in fighting fate. It is decreed, decreed I suppose by caucus, that the bill shall go through, that it shall become the law of the land. I must confess that I do not like that mode of determining grave questions of constitutional law, that a man's voice and vote shall be bound by the dictum of a caucus. I have an admiration for a man who upon questions of this kind can forget party, can rise above the action of those with whom he is associated, and I have a corresponding contempt for the decrees of a caucus to settle questions of this kind and say to every man, "You must vote so and so whatever your opinions may be."

So much for that. I do not propose to discuss this question at any length to-night. Indeed, it would be an unpardonable waste of time, now that it is decided the vote must take place, to go into a discussion and repeat matters that have already been presented to the Senate. I do not propose to discuss what may be the probable effects of the passage of this bill. Indeed, so far as any partisan advantage or disadvantage may come from it, I think it will result entirely to the advantage of the party to which I belong. I have no fears of the result. I think many Senators who now are swift in their advocacy of this measure, who think that they will reap rich rewards from it will only find in the end that they have been digging their political graves. I may be mistaken. They think otherwise; I think differently from them. I think the coming elections in the fall will perhaps depend somewhat upon this very question of the centralizing tendencies of the General Government. I do not look upon it in the light that some do, that it is simply a question whether the negro shall go to the public schools or shall not go, whether he shall go to a public inn or shall not. I do not look at it in that light at all. That is a minor view; but the main point here that will attract the attention of the country is the centralizing disposition of the Federal Government to usurp and take away from the States rights which they have enjoyed since the formation of the Government; and that is the issue presented to the people at large.

As I said a while ago, I do not wish to repeat anything that has already been said. I wish to call the attention of the Senate simply to some matters of constitutional law. I care nothing about what the consequences of this act may be. They have been spoken of by other Senators. Whether it will have an evil tendency if the bill be passed, as I have no doubt it will be, whether it will destroy the public schools in the Southern or other States, I do not know; but gentlemen have referred to it who know more about it than I do. I leave that altogether and call attention to the constitutional question.

It is admitted, I believe by all Senators, both on this side and on the other, that prior to the fourteenth amendment of the Constitution there was no power whatever in Congress to legislate upon this subject, and that all the power of legislation is derived from two sections of the fourteenth article, section 1 and section 5 of the fourteenth article of amendment. The first is that:

All persons born or naturalized in the United States, and subject to the jurisdiction thereof, are citizens of the United States and of the State wherein they reside. No State shall make or enforce any law which shall abridge the privileges or immunities of citizens of the United States; nor shall any State deprive any person of life, liberty, or property, without due process of law; nor deny to any person within its jurisdiction the equal protection of the laws.

That is coupled with a section which gives to Congress power to enforce by appropriate legislation the provisions of the article. These I understand from the arguments which have been made are the powers which it is claimed authorize Congress to legislate on this subject. It seems to me very apparent, indeed I have no doubt so far as I am concerned myself that this clause is simply an inhibition upon the right of the States to legislate upon this subject, that it was intended that no State should make or enforce by its act, by its legislation, any law which should abridge the privileges or immunities of citizens of the United States. It is an inhibition on the States; and the fifth section, that "Congress shall have power to enforce by appropriate legislation the provisions of this article," was simply giving the authority to Congress to make a case and present it so that it might be taken to the highest court of the United States by appeal from the State courts if there should be any attempt to enforce any obnoxious law of a State. It was intended simply to give the right of appeal, to make a case and transfer it from the courts of a State to the Federal courts to decide upon it; and that when the decision was made that would be a finality in the matter. It was supposed, I dare say, that the State courts have some virtue, some intelligence, and that if the United States courts decide the State law to be unconstitutional the State courts would bow to that decree. They have heretofore done it; and I do not see that their integrity should be questioned now.

It seems, however, that our republican friends place an entirely different construction upon this section. They claim that it is not simply an inhibition against State legislation, but that it gives Congress the affirmative power to legislate upon individuals and to enforce the rights that are supposed to be protected by punishing an individual for their infringement; in other words, that Congress can legislate upon the citizens throughout the United States in the same way that they may legislate for citizens who are within dock-yards, forts, arsenals, or wherever the United States may have exclusive jurisdiction, that the power of legislation in the one case is the same as in the other. I do not look at it so.

It is claimed that the right of every citizen of the United States to go to an inn, or to a public school, or to a theater, is a privilege and immunity, that it is embraced within those two words "privileges and immunities" of citizens of the United States; and therefore Congress has a right to protect these privileges and immunities. That has been a disputed point; but conceding it for the sake of the argument, let me go a little further. There is no question that a man's right to his property is a privilege; and he has a right and immunity from its destruction. So is his liberty, and so is his life; and indeed they are mentioned in this section, for it says: "No State shall deprive any person of life, liberty, or property, without due process of law." Now, I will put a question to our friends across the way, and especially I call the attention of the Senator in charge of the bill, the honorable Senator from New Jersey, to it. If these are privileges and immunities, as unquestionably they are, then Congress has power to protect the life of a citizen, and to punish individuals who may take away the life of a man maliciously; Congress has the power to protect individuals in their property, and to punish for its theft; Congress has the right in case any person is deprived of his liberty and put in prison unlawfully to pass laws to protect that man in his liberty, and to punish any individual who may falsely imprison him or do so without just cause. There can be no escape from this; because if Congress has the power to punish for these minor infractions of law, unquestionably it can protect the privileges and immunities of citizens so far as their lives, their property, and their liberties are concerned. Any one can see that if that be so this Senate and the House of Representatives have the power now to pass a law to punish a man for committing murder, to punish a man for committing burglary, robbery, arson. Such acts are certainly an invasion of the right of an individual; and will it be contended—and I ask the Senator from New Jersey to explain whether this is so or whether it is not so—that Congress can pass a law to punish murder, to punish manslaughter, to punish arson, simply because any individual may be so far lost to his sense of duty as to commit a breach of the law in that respect? If we have a right to pass this bill, unquestionably the whole subject of criminal legislation has been taken away from the States and conferred upon the Federal Government.

Now let us look at this bill. It proposes that a man shall be punished by a fine not less than $500 nor more than $1,000, and by an imprisonment not less than thirty days nor more than a year for simply depriving a person of the privilege of attending a public theater or of going to a common school; or in case a hotel-keeper refuses to allow another to set down at his table whenever he may choose, he is liable to the penalty this law imposes. It is not confined to the African race, but if any citizen deprives him of the right to sit down at a public table or to claim to occupy a particular seat at the opera, he is liable to the penalties imposed by this bill.

ROSCOE CONKLING [R., N.Y.]. If he does it by reason of race.

MR. KELLY. No. I beg pardon, it is not on account of race; and if the Senator will read it carefully I think he will come to the conclusion that if one citizen deprives another of the privileges and immunities specified in the first section, he is to be punished so and so; it is not, as the Senator suggests in case he shall do so on account of race. I maintain that under the provisions of this bill if one citizen deprives another white citizen of his right to sit down at a public inn he is liable to the penalties imposed. I maintain that a careful reading of the bill will show that that is so. Nay, more; it will reach so far as this: that if some thoughtless boy should annoy his fellow in school, or in an insulting way treat him as he ought not to do, he can be punished because he is a citizen of the United States and he can be visited with all the penalties imposed by this bill. It says that any person aiding, inciting, or abetting these acts shall be liable to the penalties of the bill. As I said, a school-boy who ought to be punished by his master's whip is liable to be seized by the marshal and taken out of school and tried in the district court of the United States and the penalty imposed. This bill will warrant that punishment.

Mr. President, if for these minor offenses such penalties can be imposed, what shall we say when a man steals another's property? Certainly this Congress is not going to allow the State governments that are so derelict in their duty, that have failed to perform those functions of government which have been assigned to them, to try the right to property, to punish a man for taking the property of another. This Congress that assumes jurisdiction over cases of this kind will surely protect a man in his right of property and life by imposing penalties on the wrong-doer. It would be an unpardonable wrong, it seems to me, if this great assembly, the Congress of the United States, should undertake to protect individuals in these minor rights, as to the manners of the table or a seat in an opera, and yet be forgetful of the right of the citizens to protection in their lives, their liberty, and their property, and intrust all that field to the State governments. Can it be possible that we are going to legislate on these matters, and yet be forgetful of the rights of the citizens in other respects? I think not.

I simply refer to this view of the power of Congress to protect citizens in their rights of property and life to show the absurdity of this rule of construction, because if the Federal Government has a right to punish in the one case it has in the other, and therefore a man may be tried and punished for taking another's life by depriving him of his privilege and immunity to life, and the penalty no doubt, if it is corresponding to this penalty, would be by execution at the hangman's hand. Failing to convict there, I ask could a State court try him a second time? Can a man be tried twice for the same offense? Certainly not. There is a constitutional provision that protects a man from a second trial for any and every offense.

Mr. President, this Government of ours is a divided sovereignty. The States when they formed the Federal Government ceded to it certain of their sovereign rights, retaining others. Wherever the States have a right to punish an offense, the Federal Government has not. Wherever the Federal Government has a right, it has been taken away from the States. Now, one thing is very certain; there can be no mistake about it: if the States have a right to punish for infractions of a law like this, the Federal Government has not. If on the other hand that right has been ceded, has been granted to the Federal Government, then the States have no right whatever to prosecute for the same offense. There can be no debatable ground, no divided sovereignty, no joint occupation of this legal domain. It either belongs to one sovereignty or the other, not to both. There is no such thing as concurrent jurisdiction in criminal cases. That is well settled now. Whatever concurrent jurisdiction there may be between the Federal and State governments in civil matters, so far as criminal jurisdiction is concerned, it either belongs to the States or to the Federal Government.

What, then, will be the result? Whenever such a bill as this is brought to the proper decision of the highest tribunal of the country, I have no fears of the result. But this is certain: if the Federal Government has a right to pass these laws and impose these penalties for refusing to permit any citizen of the United States to ride on any particular railway car, or to go to a theater, or to go to a common school, then all the laws that have been passed by the State governments to protect individuals in these respects amount to a nullity. The Senator from Mississippi said to-day that they had a more stringent law in that State than this is. I say it amounts to nothing; they cannot enforce that law there, and then have the Federal Government enforce it a second time. No man can be punished twice for the same offense, as I stated, and it is simply a question for the colored people whether they are willing to renounce the protection that their own States give them, where they can be tried in perhaps fifty or one hundred counties, where all these matters can be litigated at their own doors, or whether a single Federal court in a State shall have complete jurisdiction over them. . .

But the sole objection that I have to this bill is that it is an aggression on the part of the Federal Government upon the reserved rights of the States, and that if we can legislate upon this subject now, we can next year legislate so as to prevent one man from assailing another, one citizen from doing an injury to another by taking away his property. It will be simply a question of time. If we allow this first encroachment upon the reserved rights of the States, no one can tell where it will end. It will not depend upon the written Constitution of the country, but upon the simple will of Congress how far they will say that they have a right to go in protecting the privileges and immunities of citizens of the United States by direct legislation under the clause which gives power to enforce by appropriate legislation the provisions of the fourteenth article. I say there will be no limit to the jurisdiction of the United States Government. If Congress usurp jurisdiction in this case, if they punish offenses of this kind, it will be but the commencement of that usurpation which will draw all the criminal jurisdiction of the country into this great maelstrom, and you will legislate for thirty-seven States and nine Territories, and make the laws to punish for any infraction of rights in this chamber and in the Hall at the other end of the Capitol; and then, instead of having legislation at home, where every person can have not only the laws made at his door or near his home, but justice administered in the county where he lives, we shall have it administered in but one court in a State and that the Federal court, and every person must go to that court for the redress of his wrongs or to defend himself against unjust prosecution.

There was an intimation made here that legislation of this kind would have a tendency and that the result necessarily would be that the common schools in many of the States would be discontinued. It was said that the people would not submit to this dictatorial legislation of Congress, and that consequently the result would be that the public schools would cease to exist. The Senator from Wisconsin [Mr. Howe] who addressed the Senate this afternoon, as I understood him, seemed to intimate—I do not know whether it was intended as a threat—that if the States should deprive these citizens of the rights and privileges of the common schools, Congress would find some way to enforce these rights. I do not know whether I misunderstood him or not; but I suppose he meant that if the States should abolish the common schools, the Federal Government would undertake to coerce the people of the States, to levy taxes to support common schools, or perhaps acting upon this principle that they have a right to coerce individuals, Congress would pass a law compelling the States to levy a tax to support common schools within their limits. I do not know that any Senator has advocated that, but that will be I have no doubt the result in the end.

If the Southern States or any State in this Union, on account of the legislation which takes place here, on account of the passage of this law, shall destroy or take away the common schools from their citizens, I have no doubt that other Congresses more obsequious than this, courting the popular vote, will say that Congress has the right by appropriate legislation to guarantee the privilege and immunity of citizens to go to school, and that therefore it is incumbent upon Congress to pass some law authorizing the assessment and collection of taxes in the States for that purpose. It would certainly not be stranger than this kind of legislation. Indeed I do not see how any one with a legal mind or reasoning faculties can make the distinction that we have a right to say who shall attend public schools, and yet that we cannot say that they shall be supported in a certain way and enforce taxation for that purpose.

I can see what all this legislation tends to. It is to centralization. It is to that which the framers of the Constitution dreaded when it was first submitted for the approval of the States. We know that in the early days many of those thoughtful statesmen, when it was proposed to adopt the Federal Constitution, said, and said very truly, and they seem to have had the gift of prophecy, that the Federal Government would in the end usurp the reserved rights of the States, and destroy their liberty. How prophetic it has been! Step by step it goes on: year by year one right and another right is taken from States and vested in the Federal courts and in the first Federal Legislature. It is for this reason, and this only, that I have risen to protest, so far as my voice and so far as my vote will go, against this legislation. The other minor matters I care nothing about, because as I said, in my own judgment, on a careful reading of this bill it applies to the infringement of a white man's rights by another white man just as much as to depriving a negro of his rights by a white man. It applies to one citizen taking another's rights away; and as I said, so far as this matter is concerned, it is a mere nothing; it is a bagatelle. The great object that we ought all to have is to preserve that strict line of jurisdiction between the State and Federal Government which it was the object of the framers of the Constitution to continue. . . .

AARON SARGENT [R., CAL.]. I now move the amendment of which I gave notice this afternoon. It is to add to the first section the following proviso:

Provided, That nothing herein contained shall be construed to prohibit any State or school district from providing separate schools for persons of different sex or color, where such separate schools are equal in all respects to others of the same grade established by such authority, and supported by an equal pro rata expenditure of school funds.

MR. EDMUNDS. On that question I ask for the yeas and nays.

The yeas and nays were ordered, and the Secretary proceeded to call the roll. . . .

The roll-call being concluded, the result was announced—yeas 21, nays 26. . . .

So the amendment to the amendment was rejected. . . .

THE CHIEF CLERK. The amendment is to strike out in section 1, commencing in line 9, the following words:

And also of common schools and public institutions of learning or benevolence, supported, in whole or in part, by general taxation.

JOHN JOHNSTON [CONS., VA.]. I call for the yeas and nays on that.

The yeas and nays were ordered, and the Secretary proceeded to call the roll. . . .

The roll-call having been concluded, the result was announced—yeas 14, nays 30. . . .

MR. SARGENT. My amendment would make the section read "and also of the common-school system." I am willing to give the colored people the full benefit of the system. I think they should have the full benefit of the system.

MR. EDMUNDS. So do I; and I think they should also have the benefit of the system of railways; and if you have the word "system" in one part you ought to have it in the other. The whole effect of this proposition is to authorize States on account of color to deny the right to ride in a particular railroad car, or to go to a particular common school. If there is anything in the bill, it is exactly contrary to that. If there is anything in the fourteenth amendment it is exactly opposite to that. The fourteenth amendment does not authorize us to make any trades with States either way on the subject, or regulate the action of States. What the Constitution authorizes us to do is to enforce equality; and it is not half-equality, for there is no such thing as half-equality. It is entire equality or nothing at all. Now, the Senator proposes to say that everybody shall have an equal right in a system of common schools. That is the law of all the States now. Everybody has an equal right, and always had in old slave times in the system of railways; that is, one car was provided for the colored men and another for the white man, and so on. To put in these words here or in any part of the bill is merely to say in substance and effect that this bill shall have no force in asserting the equality that the fourteenth amendment to the Constitution asserts, if that asserts any equality at all; and of course the bill goes on the theory that it does. This amendment, therefore, ought not to be adopted, in my opinion.

MR. SARGENT. I do not know that the fourteenth amendment enjoins upon us that we shall have mixed schools. I do not know that the fourteenth amendment performs any of the offices the Senator speaks of. If it requires that there shall be an equal education commonly extended to all people of the United States of any color, the section certainly, with this amendment of mine, enforces that right. I doubt if the office of the fourteenth amendment is to provide that I should receive any man into my house; that my liberties shall be encroached upon for the benefit of any man, be he white or black. I doubt if the fourteenth amendment provides that females shall be intruded into male schools or males into females schools; and yet this would be the office of the fourteenth amendment under the logic of the Senator from Vermont.

There is one thing more important to the people of the United States, to its future, to the future of its institutions, than any other, and that is the education of the coming generation, the education of the present and the future. Senators very well know that there are inveterate and determined assaults upon the common-school system in every part of the country by powerful religious organizations. I do not criticise their right to entertain the suspicion which they have of the public-school system, or their right to declare against it, or their right to assault it. I suppose they have the same right to think that the system should be overthrown, and to teach that doctrine in pastoral letters and enjoin it upon their followers and those who believe in their faith, as I have to say that I think the common-school system is the very safety of our institutions. But, sir, this is a powerful and most potent influence, working day by day to strike down your common-school system, not merely in the city of New York and Boston and Philadelphia, but in the State of California, of Missouri, in every State in this Union. Senators know that it is one of the serious questions of the times whether the common-school system can be maintained against this most powerful, far-reaching influence; an influence that is inflamed or inspired by strong religious sentiment, even fanaticism; which has at its back vast wealth, which has as its weapon a strong sway over the minds of its devotees. This influence levels its blows continuously. It is an influence that never dies, but goes on week after week and month after month and year after year. It is as immortal as any human force or institution can be. I am not criticising it; I am merely stating a fact, and your common schools in this country are standing up with difficulty under this continuous assault.

Now, sir, you propose to re-enforce that adverse influence against your common-school system. You propose to bring what may be perhaps an unreasonable prejudice, but a prejudice nevertheless—a prejudice powerful, permeating every part of the country, and existing more or less in every man's mind; I dare say existing in the mind of the Senator from Massachusetts who made his enthusiastic speech a few moments ago for the abolition of the idea in the minds of our children that there is any distinction of race or color or sex. I say that that powerful prejudice exists in every part of the country. If you now bring this re-enforcement to the forces which assault your common-school system and strive to strike it down, the result is not hard to predict.

Senators know that there are States in the Union, not merely in the South but in the North, where this influence set at work will break up and utterly destroy, certainly for some time to come and perhaps for a long time to come, the efficiency of the common-school system. I have no doubt this is true of the State of New Jersey, and that the Senator from New Jersey on my left [Mr. Stockton] when speaking on this matter was prophetic. I have no doubt it is the case in the State of Maryland. It was stated on this floor and was not contradicted, and I believe it cannot be contradicted, that there are in Maryland liberal endowments for the colored normal school, and so down to the very infant school for the education of the colored persons, as liberal, as fair, as munificently provided as those for the whites; and that both classes, the whites and the blacks, are gaining a valuable education under this system. But by the effect of this legislation, which is insisted on here for political purposes, in order to gain the eye of the colored people and encourage them to adhere to the republican party—for that is what it amounts to, for political purposes—we are sacrificing the higher interests of the country, and we are giving occasion to the enemies of our common-school system to bring an argument against it that cannot be withstood. I consider that these are more important considerations than the question whether the republican party shall have more or less of the colored vote of this country. I think it is more important both to the colored race and to the white race that the means of education which are now being extended throughout this country, and in most of the country are so perfect in their operation, are so well supported by public opinion, shall not be endangered, shall not be overthrown. It is more important to the colored race and to the white that these shall be maintained in their present vigor and increased, rather than that we shall bring against them for doubtful advantages the irresistible passions of mankind; the prejudices which, however we may deny it, still operate with great force, to result in destroying the system or curtailing its usefulness.

The Senator from Massachusetts says that we ought to overlook any temporary inconvenience; that we ought to overlook, for the sake of the principle which he asserts exists here, any consequences in the present. I say that these consequences are too great, both now and for the future, for us to overlook them. We ought to legislate here as statesmen, having in view not merely abstract ideas or theoretical principles or sublimated ideas, but to observe the condition of the times and know whether by any law which we may pass here we inflict an injury upon the country; whether we retard its prosperity; whether we overthrow its educational systems; whether we entail ignorance upon the coming generations; whether we destroy institutions which have proved their value, and which no man in his good senses, unbiased by bigotry, can deny are of inestimable value, ay, indispensable to the country. We can talk in an enthusiastic manner if we see fit, and pretend to be regardless of consequences. We may insist that we are led in a certain direction by our principles and should disregard all prudence in order to follow them; but that is not wise statesmanship. We ought to look to the condition of the country, to see where this legislation leaves its great interests; and for that reason I offer this amendment, giving to all persons of any race, of any color, of any sex, equal rights in our common-school system. Who asks more than that asks too much. That certainly is sufficient, and I do not think there is good judgment in making it a penal offense to prevent the intrusion either of a boy into a girl's school or of a colored person into a white school or of a white person into a colored school. If you say that the fourteenth amendment absolutely levels all distinctions and justifies you in putting heavy penalties to prevent a system of separate schools, then I say you cannot separate your sexes; you must put them all into the same school, and the boy who demands to enter a female school has just as much right to do it under the fourteenth amendment. Following your principle, lauded here, you are required to enforce this by a law and penalties just as much as you are that a person of a particular color shall be allowed to enter into schools of another color. I would give all the full benefit of the school system, and I would do no more.

MR. EDMUNDS. I shall not detain the Senate at this early or late hour of the morning, whichever it is, with any very formal reply to the Senator from California; but he unfortunately I think adopts the democratic idea of the fourteenth amendment, and that is that it does not level absolutely and destroy distinctions of race, color, and previous condition of servitude. He holds with the gentlemen of the other party that all the fourteenth amendment means is just what the Constitution meant before, and that is that every man, woman, and child in a State shall have whatever rights the laws of that State choose to give every man, woman, and child in that State.

MR. SARGENT. The Senator misrepresents me entirely. . . .

MR. EDMUNDS. . . .

I repeat what I said before, that in my judgment the Senator from California, from the tenor of his remarks, occupies the position that the gentlemen on the other side of the Chamber generally do; and I will say for his benefit that I did not thereby intend to impute to him any personal wrong or other thing. He has just as good a right to his opinions as the democrats have to theirs and as I have to mine. I do not quarrel with that. That is one of the rights which the fourteenth amendment secures to him as it does to me. But the Senator's argument results in exactly this: that the fourteenth amendment does not, as it respects common schools, level a distinction which a State may have a right to make on account of race and color. If it does not level that distinction, then it does not level a distinction that a State has a right to make on the same account in respect to a railway, or a highway, or a steamboat, or any other thing; for the fourteenth amendment is general and sweeping. It either means that there shall be equality of right—not a trade or a business of expediency which is left to Congress, but a declaration of the right of a citizen which no distinction of race or origin can affect—or else it does not touch on the subject at all. There cannot be any dodging that. I suppose that both sides agree to that: either that the democratic view of the amendment is right, that it does not touch these subjects at all, and therefore we cannot interfere with the right of the State to regulate its common schools, discriminating against color, discriminating against race, discriminating against religion, or anything that the State chooses to discriminate against; or else it does confer upon citizens of the United States a right, and that right is inherent, one that cannot be divided or paltered with or traded away. It is either an absolute right that the Constitution gives to the citizen, or it is nothing at all and does not touch the case.

This bill proceeds upon the idea that the Constitution does secure to the citizen certain inherent rights, because they are rights, and then it merely undertakes to enforce those rights, not to enter into a parley with the States about them and say "you may or may not enforce them as you may think is desirable," or say "you may enforce them in this way or that way." It only undertakes to declare that whatever right the citizen has under the fourteenth amendment that right shall be protected, and the bill asserts, implies, assumes that that right is one which enables the Congress to say, and makes it its duty to say, that no citizen shall be discriminated against on account of his origin or on account of his color.

If that is so, then the Senator's argument is the democratic argument, inasmuch as he says the State has the right to regulate this business of common schools and to exclude people on account of their color one way or the other. If the State has that right, we cannot interfere with it. If the State has not that right, we cannot confer it by an act of Congress, because such an act of Congress would be in violation of the fourteenth amendment itself.

The Senator's amendment proposes to recognize the right in a State to discriminate on account of color, and if it does recognize that right, it recognizes it as a right inherent in the State and which the fourteenth amendment does not touch. If it does not touch it, then there is not a right in your bill that is constitutional. On the other hand, if the fourteenth amendment does touch it, and this right to discriminate on account of color is not in the State, then I repeat, the Congress of the United States has no power to confer such a right upon a State to make discriminations between its citizens on account of color. It does not undertake to confer any rights at all on the States. That is a misapprehension. . . .

Now, Mr. President, let me refer for a single moment to a practical question which has not yet been stated here, and I shall have done. It is said that this bill is likely to do injury by breaking up schools in the places where, for the sake of the colored people, they are most needed. What sort of comfort do the colored people get in the schools of the Southern States now? Ostensibly there is a system, as the Senator from California very properly characterized it, of common schools, which on the statute-book is for all, the white on the one side, and the colored on the other; but when the officers of the law come to apply that system, when the power of the State comes to execute the law, you find everywhere—I do not say everwhere, speaking by the book, because I have not looked into the records of every State—but you find in three of the chief States whose Senators, some of them, have participated in this debate, that there is hard and unjust discrimination against the colored man and in favor of the white.

In the State of Virginia by the last school report, for I take it from the official school report of Virginia, of the school population between the ages of five and twenty-one the white children were 253,411, the colored, 170,-696, making 424,107 school children. The proportion of colored to the number of school children therefore is 402, 40 per cent. in round statement. Now, of the number of schools established for these children, there are 2,787 white schools and only 909 colored schools, making a total of 3,696, being only 24 per cent. in round statement—it is .243 exactly—but 24 per cent. of school facilities furnished to the colored population; only a little more than one-half of the proportion of schools that the number of scholars of that race require. . . .

In North Carolina, according to the last school report, of children of the school age between six and twenty-one, the white children were 233,751, the colored children 114,852, making a total of 348,603. The proportion of colored children to the total number therefore is .329, or in round numbers 33 per cent. Now, of the public schools there are white 2,565, colored 746, making 3,311 schools. The proportion of colored schools to white schools therefore is .225; or 22 per cent. of schools and 33 per cent. of children who ought to be entitled to the advantage of them.

When you come to the State of Georgia, the school report for 1873–, 74, the very last one made, shows that of the school population between the ages of six and eighteen, the white children are 198,516, the colored children 150,198, making a total of 348,714. The proportion of colored children to white children is therefore .427, or 43 per cent., in round statement. Of the schools, there are 1,379 white schools and 356 colored schools, making 1,735 schools. The proportion of colored schools to white is .127, or 13 per cent., there being 43 per cent. of colored children and 13 per cent. of colored schools; and in the State of Georgia the bulk of the current income derived from annual taxation is derived from the polls of the people of that State. The colored people in ratio to the population pay five-elevenths of it, almost one-half; and as a fact I believe that the law of Georgia, which requires the payment of this poll tax before one can vote, is enforced rigidly against the colored man and is not enforced rigidly against the white man. But it is not necessary to go into that question to see who pays for these schools, because I hold that the property of every State should pay for the education of all its children, for the sake of property, to put it upon no higher ground.

I refer to these figures from the official reports from these three States to show you that the danger is not by this act of right that you are to overthrow systems or schools; the danger is by not acting that under a pretense of what is called equality of the system it is intended to grind out every means of education that the colored man can have, and to feed the white at the expense of the black, in order that the ancient order of things, the aristocracy of races, may again be restored. That is my belief. Therefore, as a practical question. I say let us run the risk in doing this right thing of some momentary distrubance, in order that the great practical fact of a great wrong that now exists in these States may be redressed as well as that the inherent right which the Constitution gives may be protected and defended. . . .

MR. SARGENT. . . .

Now, sir, one single remark in reply to that only which can be considered as argument in reply to my positions, and that it, that the amendment which I propose, by providing that there may be separate schools, is a violation of the fourteenth amendment, upon the same principle that a denial of the right of a colored man to ride in the same car, or to have identical accommodations in the same hotel, would be a violation of the fourteenth amendment. I do not believe either of those cases cited as illustrations would be a denial of any right guaranteed by the fourteenth amendment. The fourteenth amendment was not intended merely to say that black men should have rights, but that black and white men and women should have rights. It was a guarantee of equality of right to every person within the jurisdiction of the United States, be he black or white. It is a very common thing for me and for every Senator here, and every white man in the country, when he goes to a railroad train without his wife on his arm or some female friend, to be assigned to a car separate from some other car more privileged than the one he takes, by its female society, though not perhaps better in its fittings, which is assigned to ladies or to gentlemen who have ladies with them. Is that a violation of the fourteenth amendment? Suppose the man who is thus required to take the second car on the train instead of the first should be black instead of white, would the difference in color make a violation of the fourteenth amendment?

I do not believe these things are of enough importance for us to legislate upon them here. They regulate themselves. I doubt if any white man ever felt outraged because he was told to take one car rather than another, on account of a discrimination in the car he should take. Why, then, should the black man?

So with reference to the hotel table. In most of the hotels, in all of them I believe in New York and in the larger cities, the tables are small, circular tables where families sit, or two or three persons who happen to be friends, and the guests are assigned by the landlord to the places they take. A person entering the dining-room does not take a seat at any table he sees fit; he is put here or there, wherever the landlord pleases. And in assigning rooms at a hotel, the landlord may put him in the fourth story or the first; and if he does not like his accommodation he can go to some other hotel. He has no direction in the matter, and certainly no right to demand under the fourteenth amendment that he shall be put in the third story instead of the fourth, or the second instead of the third. These hotel illustrations fail for that very reason. The fourteenth amendment does not apply to them at all. They are simply incidents of business which have existed for years, and will exist for years whether the fourteenth amendment exists or not.

If the car to which a white man without a lady is assigned, or the black man is assigned, is just as good as any other of the train, drawn by the same engine, at an equal rate of speed, where is the harm done by that regulation? And why should we interfere with the business of railroad companies and hotel-keepers in this inquisitive way, putting our noses into the smallest details of business?

The old maxim was that that was the best government which governed the least. Here you propose to govern down to the very lowest item, the smallest account of business. You are going to have your laws so scarching that by and by you will inquire into the quality of a man's dinner. You now want to inquire into the quality of the bedroom in which he sleeps at a hotel; you want to inquire as to the upholstering of the seat on which he sits in a railroad car; and I should like to know where the investigation will stop.

I say these things are not required by the fourteenth amendment, and consequently the amendment which I offer to this bill is not a violation of the fourteenth amendment. I say this while believing, and thoroughly believing, in the equal rights of all men, white or black; I say it from a republican stand-point; I say it because I believe as a republican that I have no right to lay a rude hand upon the system of public education; I have no right to do anything which will overthrow it into the dust; I have no right to re-enforce the forces which are now operating against it and while it is struggling with difficulty in many places in the country for its life. . . .

THE PRESIDENT PRO TEMPORE. The question now is on concurring in the amendment made as in Committee of the Whole, as amended.

The amendment was concurred in; being to strike out all of the original bill after the enacting clause and to insert as a substitute:

That all citizens and other persons within the jurisdiction of the United States shall be entitled to the full and equal enjoyment of the accommodations, advantages, facilities, and privileges of inns, public conveyances on land or water, theaters, and other places of public amusement; and also of common schools and public institutions of learning or benevolence supported, in whole or in part, by general taxation, and of cemeteries so supported, and also the institutions known as agricultural colleges endowed by the United States, subject only to the conditions and limitations established by law, and applicable alike to citizens of every race and color, regardless of any previous condition of servitude.

SEC. 2. That any person who shall violate the foregoing section by denying to any person entitled to its benefits, except for reasons by law applicable to citizens of every race and color, and regardless of any previous condition of servitude, the full enjoyment of any of the accommodations, advantages, facilities, or privileges in said section enumerated, or by aiding or inciting such denial, shall, for every such offense, forfeit and pay the sum of $500 to the person aggrieved thereby, to be recovered in an action on the case, with full costs; and shall also, for every such offense, be deemed guilty of a misdemeanor, and, upon conviction thereof, shall be fined not more than $1,000, or shall be imprisoned not more than one year: Provided, That the party aggrieved shall not recover more than one penalty and when the offense is a refusal of burial, the penalty may be recovered by the heirs at law of the person whose body has been refused burial: And provided further, That all persons may elect to sue for the penalty aforesaid or to proceed under their rights at common law and by State statutues; and having so elected to proceed in the one mode or the other, their right to proceed in the other jurisdiction shall be barred. But this proviso shall not apply to criminal proceedings, either under this act or the criminal law of any State.

SEC. 3. That the district and circuit courts of the United States shall have, exclusively of the courts of the several States, cognizance of all crimes and offenses against, and violations of the provisions of this act; and actions for the penalty given by the preceding section may be prosecuted in the territorial, district, or circuit courts of the United States wherever the defendant may be found, without regard to the other party. And the district attorneys, marshals, and deputy marshals of the United States, and commissioners appointed by the circuit and territorial courts of the United States, with powers of arresting and imprisoning or bailing offender against the laws of the United States, are hereby specially authorized and required to institute proceedings against every person who shall violate the provisions of this act, and cause him to be arrested and imprisoned or bailed, as the case may be, for trial before such court of the United States or territorial court as by law has cognizance of the offense, except in respect of the right of action accruing to the person aggrieved; and such district attorneys shall cause such proceedings to be prosecuted to their termination as in other cases: Provided, That nothing contained in this section shall be construed to deny or defeat any right of civil action accruing to any person, whether by reason of this act or otherwise.

SEC. 4. That no citizen possessing all other qualifications which are or may be prescribed by law shall be disqualified for service as grand or petit juror in any court of the United States, or of any State, on account of race, color, or previous condition of servitude; and any officer or other person charged with any duty in the selection or summoning of jurors who shall exclude or fail to summon any citizen for the cause aforesaid shall, on conviction thereof, be deemed guilty of a misdemeanor, and be fined not more than $1,000.

SEC. 5. That all cases arising under the provisions of this act in the courts of the United States shall be reviewable by the Supreme Court of the United States without regard to the sum in controversy, under the same provisions and regulations as are now provided by law for the review of other causes in said court. . . .

The question being taken by yeas and nays, resulted—yeas 29, nays 16 . . . So the bill was passed.

House of Representatives-43d Congress, 2nd Session
February 3-4, 1875

BENJAMIN BUTLER [R., MASS]. . . .

I desire to state to the House first the course which I propose this bill shall take. As instructed by the Committee on the Judiciary, I propose to yield for a motion to substitute for this bill the provisions of the Senate bill on the same subject. I am instructed by the committee then to yield to an amendment to be moved by the gentleman from Alabama, [Mr. White.] I will then yield to a motion to amend the bill by striking out all relating to schools. I do this in order that all shades of republican opinion may be voted upon. . . .

STEPHEN KELLOGG [R., CONN.]. I move to amend the bill reported from the Judiciary Committee by striking out all of the first section after the word "amusement." This amendment in effect strikes out all in reference to public schools.

THE SPEAKER [JAMES BLAINE, R., ME.]. The Clerk will read the amendment The Clerk read as follows:

Strike out all after the word "amusement," in the seventh line, as follows:
And also all common schools and public institutions of learning or benevolence supported in whole or in part by general taxation, subject only to the conditions and limitations established by law and applicable alike to citizens of every race and color regardless of any previous condition of servitude: Provided, If any State or the proper authorities in any city, having the control of common schools or other public institutions of learning aforesaid, shall establish and maintain separate schools and institutions giving equal educational advantages in all respects for different classes of persons entitled to attend such schools and institutions, that shall be a sufficient compliance with the provisions of this section so far as they relate to schools and institutions of learning. . . .

JOHN LYNCH [R., MISS.]. Mr. Speaker, I was not particularly anxious to take part in this debate, and would not have done so but for the fact that this bill has created a great deal of discussion both in and outside of the halls of Congress. In order to answer successfully the arguments that have been made against the bill, I deem it necessary, if my time will allow me to do so, to discuss the question from three standpoints—legal, social, and political. I confess, Mr. Speaker, that it is with hesitancy that I shall attempt to make a few remarks upon the legal question involved; not that I entertain any doubts as to the constitutionality of the pending bill, but because that branch of the subject has been so ably, successfully, and satisfactorily discussed by other gentlemen who have spoken in the affirmative of the question. The importance of the subject, however, is my apology to the House for submitting a few remarks upon this point in addition to what has already been said.

It is a fact well known by those who are at all familiar with the history of our Government that the great question of State rights—absolute State sovereignty as understood by the Calhoun school of politicians—has been a continuous source of political agitation for a great many years. In fact, for a number of years anterior to the rebellion this was the chief topic of political discussion. It continued to agitate the public mind from year to year and from time to time until the question was finally settled upon the field of battle. The war, however, did not result in the recognition of what may be called a centralized government, nor did it result in the destruction of the independent functions of the several States, except in certain particulars. But it did result in the recognition, and I hope the acceptance, of what may be called a medium between these two extremes; and this medium position or liberal policy has been incorporated in the Federal Constitution through the recent amendments to that instrument. But many of our constitutional lawyers of to-day are men who received their legal and political training during the discussion of the great question of State rights and under the tutorship of those who were identified with the Calhoun school of impracticable State rights theorists; they having been taught to believe that the Constitution as it was justified the construction they placed upon it, and this impression having been so indelibly and unalterably fixed upon their minds that recent changes, alterations and amendments have failed to bring about a corresponding change in their construction of the Constitution. In fact, they seem to forget that the Constitution as it is is not in every respect the Constitution as it was.

We have a practical illustration of the correctness of this assertion in the person of the distinguished gentleman from Georgia [Mr. Stephens] and I believe my colleague who sits near me [Mr. Lamar] and others who agree with them in their construction of the Constitution. But believing as I do that the Constitution as a whole should be so construed as to carry out the intention of the framers of the recent amendments, it will not be surprising to the House and to the country when I assert that it is impossible for me to agree with those who so construe the Constitution as to arrive at the erroneous conclusion that the pending bill is in violation of that instrument. It is not my purpose, however, to give the House simply the benefit of my own opinion upon the question, but to endeavor to show to your satisfaction, if possible, that the construction which I place upon the Constitution is precisely in accordance with that placed upon it by the highest judicial tribunal in the land, the Supreme Court of the United States. And this brings us to the celebrated Slaughter-house cases. But before referring to the decision of the court in detail, I will take this occasion to remark that, for the purposes of this debate at least, I accept as correct the theory that Congress cannot constitutionally pass any law unless it has expressed constitutional grant of power to do so; that the constitutional right of Congress to pass a law must not be implied, but expressed; and that in the absence of such expressed constitutional grant of power the right does not exist. In other words

The powers not delegated to the United States by the Constitution, nor prohibited by it to the States, are reserved to the States respectively, or to the people.

I repeat, that for the purposes of this debate at least, I accept as correct this theory. After having read over the decision of the court in these Slaughter-house cases several times very carefully, I have been brought very forcibly to this conclusion: that so far as this decision refers to the question of civil rights—the kind of civil rights referred to in this bill—it means this and nothing more: that whatever right or power a State may have had prior to the ratification of the fourteenth amendment it still has, except in certain particulars. In other words, the fourteenth amendment was not intended, in the opinion of the court, to confer upon the Federal Government additional powers in general terms, but only in certain particulars. What are those particulars wherein the fourteenth amendment confers upon the Federal Government powers which it did not have before? The right to prevent distinctions and discriminations between the citizens of the United States and of the several States whenever such distinctions and discriminations are made on account of race, color, or previous condition of servitude; and that distinctions and discriminations made upon any other ground than these are not prohibited by the fourteenth amendment. As the discrimination referred to in the Slaughter-house cases was not made upon either of these grounds, it did not come within the constitutional prohibition. As the pending bill refers only to such discriminations as are made on account of race, color, or previous condition of servitude, it necessarily follows that the bill is in harmony with the Constitution as construed by the Supreme Court. . . .

I will now endeavor to answer the arguments of those who have been contending that the passage of this bill is an effort to bring about social equality between the races. That the passage of this bill can in any manner affect the social status of any one seems to me to be absurd and ridiculous. I have never believed for a moment that social equality could be brought about even between persons of the same race. I have always believed that social distinctions existed among white people the same as among colored people. But those who contend that the passage of this bill will have a tendency to bring about social equality between the races virtually and substantially admit that there are no social distinctions among white people whatever, but that all white persons, regardless of their moral character, are the social equals of each other; for if by conferring upon colored people the same rights and privileges that are now exercised and enjoyed by whites indiscriminately will result in bringing about social equality between the races, then the same process of reasoning must necessarily bring us to the conclusion that there are no social distinctions among whites, because all white persons, regardless of their social standing, are permitted to enjoy these rights. See then how unreasonable, unjust, and false is the assertion that social equality is involved in this legislation. I cannot believe that gentlemen on the other side of the House mean what they say when they admit as they do, that the immoral, the ignorants and the degraded of their own race are the social equals of themselve, and their families. If they do, then I can only assure them that they do not put as high an estimate upon their own social standing as respectable and intelligent colored people place upon theirs; for there are hundreds and thousands of white people of both sexes whom I know to be the social inferiors of respectable and intelligent colored people. I can then assure that portion of my democratic friends on the other side of the House whom I regard as my social inferiors that if at any time I should meet any one of you at a hotel and occupy a seat at the same table with you, or the same seat in a car with you, do not think that I have thereby accepted you as my social equal. Not at all. But if any one should attempt to discriminate against you for no other reason than because you are identified with a particular race or religious sect, I would regard it as an outrage; as a violation of the principles of republicanism; and I would be in favor of protecting you in the exercise and enjoyment of your rights by suitable and appropriate legislation.

No, Mr. Speaker, it is not social rights that we desire. We have enough of that already. What we ask is protection in the enjoyment of public rights. Rights which are or should be accorded to every citizen alike. Under our present system of race distinctions a white woman of a questionable social standing, yea, I may say, of an admitted immoral character, can go to any public place or upon any public conveyance and be the recipient of the same treatment, the same courtesy, and the same respect that is usually accorded to the most refined and virtuous; but let an intelligent, modes, refined colored lady present herself and ask that the same privileges be accorded to her that have just been accorded to her social inferior of the white race, and in nine cases out of ten, except in certain portions of the country, she will not only be refused, but insulted for making the request.

Mr. Speaker, I ask the members of this House in all candor, is this right? I appeal to your sensitive feelings as husbands, fathers, and brothers, is this just? You who have affectionate companions, attractive daughters, and loving sisters, is this just? . . .

The enemies of this bill have been trying very hard to create the impression that it is the object of its advocates to bring about a compulsory system of mixed schools. It is not my intention at this time to enter into a discussion of the question as to the propriety or impropriety of mixed schools; as to whether or not such a system is essential to destroy race distinctions and break down race prejudices. I will leave these questions to be discussed by those who have given the subject a more thorough consideration. The question that now presents itself to our minds is, what will be the effect of this legislation on the public-school system of the country, and more especially in the South? It is to this question that I now propose to speak. I regard this school clause as the most harmless provision in the bill. If it were true that the passage of this bill with the school clause in it would tolerate the existence of none but a system of mixed free schools, then I would question very seriously the propriety of retaining such a clause; but such is not the case. If I understand the bill correctly, (and I think I do,) it simply confers upon all citizens, or rather recognizes the right which has already been conferred upon all citizens, to send their children to any public free school that is supported in whole or in part by taxation, the exercise of the right to remain a matter of option as it now is—nothing compulsory about it. That the passage of this bill can result in breaking up the public-school system in any State is absurd. The men who make these reckless assertions are very well aware of the fact, or else they are guilty of unpardonable ignorance, that every right and privilege that is enumerated in this bill has already been conferred upon all citizens alike in at least one-half of the States of this Union by State legislation. In every Southern State where the republican party is in power a civil-rights bill is in force that is more severe in its penalties than are the penalties in this bill. We find mixed-school clauses in some of their State constitutions. If, then, the passage of this bill, which does not confer upon the colored people of such States any rights that they do not possess already, will result in breaking up the public-school system in their respective States, why is it that State legislation has not broken them up? This proves very conclusively, I think, that there is nothing in the argument whatever, and that the school clause is the most harmless provision in the bill. My opinion is that the passage of this bill just as it passed the Senate will bring about mixed schools practically only in localities where one or the other of the two races is small in numbers, and that in localities where both races are large in numbers separate schools and separate institutions of learning will continue to exist, for a number of years at least. . . .

The question may be asked, however, if the colored people in a majority of the States are entitled by State legislation to all of the rights and privileges enumerated in this bill, and if they will not insist upon mixing the children in the public schools in all localities, what is the necessity of retaining this clause? The reasons are numerous, but I will only mention a few of them. In the first place, it is contrary to our system of government to discriminate by law between persons on account of their race, their color, their religion, or the place of their birth. It is just as wrong and just as contrary to republican-ism to provide by law for the education of children who may be identified with a certain race in separate schools to themselves, as to provide by law for the education of children who may be identified with a certain religious denomination in separate schools to themselves. The duty of the law-maker is to know no race, no color, no religion, no nationality, except to prevent distinctions on any of these grounds, so far as the law is concerned.

The colored people in asking the passage of this bill just as it passed the Senate do not thereby admit that their children can be better educated in white than in colored schools; nor that white teachers because they are white are better qualified to teach than colored ones. But they recognize the fact that the distinction when made and tolerated by law is an unjust and odious proscription; that you make their color a ground of objection, and consequently a crime. This is what we most earnestly protest against. Let us confer upon all citizens, then, the rights to which they are entitled under the Constitution; and then if they choose to have their children educated in separate schools, as they do in my own State, then both races will be satisfied, because they will know that the separation is their own voluntary act and not legislative compulsion.

Another reason why the school clause ought to be retained is because the negro question ought to be removed from the politics of the country. It has been a disturbing element in the country ever since the Declaration of Independence, and it will continue to be so long as the colored man is denied any right or privilege that is enjoyed by the white man. Pass this bill as it passed the Senate, and there will be nothing more for the colored people to ask or expect in the way of civil rights. Equal rights having been made an accomplished fact, opposition to the exercise thereof will gradually pass away, and the everlasting negro question will then be removed from the politics of the country for the first time since the existence of the Government. Let us, then, be just as well as generous. Let us confer upon the colored citizens equal rights, and, my word for it, they will exercise their rights with moderation and with wise discretion. . . .

JOHN STORM [DEM., PA.]. Mr. Speaker, I did not expect to address the House this evening; indeed, I have not come here for the purpose of making a set speech; neither am I prepared to do it. I voted against an evening session because I believed that this subject had been talked threadbare both before the House and the country. Since 1870 it has been discussed in all its various phases, so that it is impossible for the ingenuity of man to say anything either new or original upon it. . . .

Sir, nothing could have surprised me more than that the republican party of this House should at last have been dragooned into supporting this measure by the gentleman from Massachusetts, [Mr. Butler.] I thought, sir, that if there was one thing more than another which sent a thrill of joy through the hearts of the people without regard to parties of the last election, it was the fact that the gentleman from Massachusetts was not returned to the next Congress. It was not, sir, that the gentleman was not an able man, bold and candid in the utterance of his political convictions; but he was a man who did not represent any longer the moral and political sentiments of the American people. On the contrary he was a man who by his course had outraged the sentiments of the American people more than any other who has been in Congress during the last four years. And yet we have the novel spectacle of that gentleman by force of party discipline dragooning into the support of his measures gentlemen on the other side who were supposed to be at least conservative upon this question and opposed to this bill. In one week he has succeeded in unifying that side of the House until I believe there is not a gentleman there who dares to raise his voice in opposition to the measure, which will probably be brought to an issue to-marrow. The gentleman from Massachusetts [Mr. Butler] must enjoy his triumph with fiendish glee.

And this is the more strange to me when I consider the fact that in the recent elections the republican party was condemned on account of three measures. If gentlemen will take time to look at the editorials of the leading organ of the republican party in this country—the New York Times— published immediately after that election, they will see that the defeat of that party was said to have been caused by the Louisiana outrages, the civil-rights bill, and the "third term." What have we seen here in this House? The other day, when my friend from New York [Mr. Potter] reported a constitutional amendment, we gave our friends on the other side an opportunity to express themselves on the third-term question. Yet so far as we got an expression from the leading men on that side of the House, we find that they have come back here and in the face of the verdict of the people have put themselves again upon the record as either being afraid to denounce the third-term question or as really supporting it. Very few men on that side of the House either by word or vote dared to say that they condemned General Grant's aspirations for a third term.

And the republicans of this House instead of taking a moderate course on the Louisiana question they have gone still further in their system of oppression and wrong. And with regard to the question of civil rights, a question which we had supposed was settled by the recent elections, they come in here now and propose to pass the bill in the form in which it was introduced in the Senate in 1870; a bill which was twice reported against by the Judiciary Committee of the Senate, and which did not then have the support of leading republicans on this floor.

I presume that nothing that can be said or done on this side of the House can make any difference in the conclusions reached in the minds of our friends on the other side. They are deaf to the voice of the people they now misrepresent. In our parliamentary opposition to this bill during the last week, we believed we were representing the wishes of the great majority of the American people upon this question. I had hoped that this kind of legislation would cease; that at last we had reached the extreme limit to which the party on the other side would go in setting aside the Constitution and in trampling upon the laws of the country. It seems that such is not the case.

I wish here to call the attention of the House to the very anomalous position taken by some of our friends on the other side. I understand that the gentleman from Alabama [Mr. White] who has reported one of the substitutes for this bill, and my colleague from Pennsylvania [Mr. Cessna] by his amendment propose to leave out of this bill all provisions relating to the common schools of the country—not to have this bill apply to them. Now, if I believed that in order to enjoy his equal rights with the white man the colored man must enjoy those rights in the same railroad car, in the same theater, and at the same table in the hotel or public inn, I should certainly insist upon his enjoying the right to an education in the same school-room with the white children.

I regard the right to an education the most sacred one which the colored man can enjoy, and yet gentlemen on the other side who expect to pass this bill intend, as I understand, to strike out the provision with regard to schools. If they are consistent I cannot see how they can do this, because if the right of the colored people to an education can be enjoyed equally with the whites, by having the schools for colored persons in separate buildings, as gentlemen who are in favor of this bill will I suppose contend, why cannot the equal rights of the colored people in public conveyances, railroad cars, etc., be subsubserved by providing separate accommodations for them? If I could bring my mind to the conclusion that the colored people can enjoy their rights to education by having separate schools, then I could just as readily conclude that the colored man can enjoy his rights in a public conveyance if a separate railroad car or carriage is provided for him. I would like to know how my friends on the other side propose to amend this bill. For when they concede that the colored people can enjoy their rights to a common-school education in separate schools, they concede the whole argument. If it is not a deprivation of equal rights to say that white children shall go into one public-school building and the colored into another building, then it is no deprivation of equal rights when a railroad company makes provision for carrying white passengers in one car and black in another. There is no escape from this conclusion.

Now I say again, Mr. Speaker, that I believe this bill is thrust upon us for no other purpose than mischief. It will lead to mischief, and mischief continually. Our friends upon the other side will have to take the responsibility for thus thrusting upon the country this measure, to the exclusion of legitimate public business, and again exciting strife and hatred and disturbance in the Southern States, where peace and quiet ought to prevail.

The gentleman from Massachusetts [Mr. Butler] said to-day, in answer to a question put to him by the gentleman from Indiana, that the State courts could not be trusted to decide upon these great questions of the rights of the colored people in certain States of the Union. Well, Mr. Speaker, will the rights of those people be any safer in the Federal courts? I do not want to characterize the Federal courts in the same manner in which the gentleman spoke to-day of the State courts, but it is a well-known fact that within the last two years out of fifty-two United States district judges three have been driven into resignation by threatened articles of impeachment, and many more ought to be in the penitentiary. It is well known that if you wish to subserve the interests of the people of the country upon all these great questions, the Federal courts, in many of the Southern States, are the last places in the world where an honest man would expect a vindication of his rights. In many of these States the judges are notoriously venal and partisan; the district attorneys and marshals are no better; and the juries are packed to subserve their wicked purposes.

I believe, as I said before, that the colored people are now in the substantial enjoyment of their full rights and privileges granted by the recent amendments to the Constitution; and this bill is thrust upon us for no other purpose than exciting bad feelings and leading to disturbance and strife where there ought to be tranquillity and harmony.

But the great and conclusive objection to this measure is that its passage would be a gross and palpable violation of the Constitution. To my mind it is clear that if this measure is constitutional, then there is absolutely no limitation to the authority of the General Government, and we are not living under a Constitution of defined and limited powers, as understood by Jefferson and Madison and the early fathers.

If Congress can go into the States and regulate the minute affairs of social and domestic life, and can take from the State courts jurisdiction of question, growing out of the management of a public school, a theater, a hotel, a railroad, a stage-coach, or a cemetery, I am unable to see how that vast residuum of power which the States reserved to themselves will not soon be absorbed and the General Government become supreme and absolute in the exercise of every right heretofore belonging to the States. . . .

THOMAS WHITEHEAD [CONS., VA.]. Mr. Speaker, I should have preferred to have a larger number of the jury who are to sit on this case to whom I might address my remarks rather than the full galleries facetiously alluded to by my friend from New York and the gentleman from Massachusetts, as they have no part in this matter. This is to some extent, so far as a good many members of this House are concerned and so far as a good many of the spectators are concerned, very much like the case of the boys and the frogs. To some of these gentlemen from States north of the Potomac, perhaps to the largest part of the audience here, it may be fun, but to us who are to be affected by this law, who are to reap its bitter fruits and bear whatever of evil there is in this pernicious legislation, it is not a matter of fun, but a matter of death.

Now, sir, this House presents this singular spectacle. A radical change has been made by the majority in the rules of the House which have existed for a number of years, and it has been done for the express purpose of passing this civil-rights bill, which has been already condemned by the votes of the people in the last fall elections. Men who were condemned for giving a vote in favor of the civil-rights bill have pushed through this radical change of the rules in order that they might gratify feeling which I do not know how exactly to describe. The very father of this bill—I take that back, because the father of this bill, God rest his soul, is not here, (Charles Sumner,) — has all the credit of being the father of the bill, and I have always understood that in his last will and testament he committed it to Mr. Hoar, of Massachusetts. But, sir, another gentleman from Massachusetts [Mr. Butler] has made himself executor *"de son tort,"* and violently laid hold of the chattel. We had this bill up last winter, and speech after speech on the subject, wrangle after wrangle in this House—indeed a large portion of the time was occupied with the debate in regard to it. We adjourned without passing it, and went back to the people, and members now sitting in this House who took an active part in that debate were condemned by the people and not returned to their seats in this Hall. Yet those very men now in this House, in hot and fiery haste, force through a measure which will result in no good to the colored man, but do gross wrong to the white man in those States where this civil-rights bill is at all operative.

What matters it in Massachusetts or New York whether this civil-rights bill passes or not? Why, sir, it is almost as hard to find a real genuine black man in those States as a needle in a hay-stack. I took a trip in the year 1863 through the State of Pennsylvania on a somewhat speculative and electioneering expedition, and I did not see two negroes in one hundred and fifty miles. Yet it is by the votes of these men not at all interested in this question that it is to be put as a law upon the statute-book to affect those who are deeply interested in it.

I am not going into the Slaughter-house case. I am not going to examine particularly the constitutionality of the proposed law. We have already had a speech in favor of the constitutionality of this bill. If that satisfied anybody on that side of the House that it is constitutional, I have nothing else to say on the subject. That discussion is not necessary even if it were constitutional. The men who vote and speak here should carefully look into its expediency. If it were constitutional, it is not expedient. . . .

But, as I have said, I shall not go into the constitutionality of this matter. I shall not read the Slaughter-house case. I am perfectly satisfied on that subject from a common-sense stand-point. Congress proposes to legislate here in regard to the municipal laws of a State. We are asked to legislate in regard to the license laws of my own State. We are asked to legislate in regard to municipal laws which govern common carriers in the several States. If Congress may say who shall go into a hotel licensed by the State of Virginia and who shall have what you call equal rights, then if the landlord should give my friend General Hunton turkey, and the colored man beef, under this law proposed to be passed by the Congress of the United States you would have that man arrested for making a difference between the two, discriminating against the food of the colored man. So then the gentleman from Massachusetts who has taken charge of this bill and thereby has defied the voice of the people uttered in the last November election, where he was himself defeated for re-election, would have this House legislate for the purpose of arranging bills of fare for hotels in all the States. If you are to discriminate in regard to the rooms they are to occupy, clearly you can discriminate in regard to what they shall eat and drink. Then if you so discriminate are you not interfering with the license laws of the State? Do you not interfere with the business of those who are licensed to keep hotels? If there were no other view than this it would satisfy me as to its unconstitutionality. There is not a lawyer on that side of the House who is not as well satisfied as I am, were it not that in the last three weeks they have had a whip cracking about their ears and upon their backs making them fly into these Halls to pass this measure. I will except the gentleman from Virginia, [Mr. Sener,] who had the back-bone, despite the republican press and despite his party, to stand for what he thought to be right and just, and vote against the change of rules for a party purpose. If the voice of the people uttered last fall were to be heard in these Halls this measure could not be passed. Many of those who are pressing its passage have been before the people and have been defeated for Congress.

Well, now, what does the whole of this thing amount to, so far as its constitutionality as a law is concerned, when you come to pull it to pieces? As regards a common carrier and what a man shall carry, a wagoner is a common carrier if he hauls for pay; and whether he believes his team is strong enough or not, he has not a right under this law to choose for whom he may haul. You are to control him in this matter. You are to control the hotel-keeper in the management of his hotel. You are to control the manager in the management of his theater. And one of the bills before us says you are to control the grave-yard.

Well, sir, I say simply and plainly, and speaking as I trust to common-sense people, that this is absolute nonsense. There is not a lawyer in the United States who does not know that. . . .

BENJAMIN HARRIS [R., MASS.]. Will the gentleman allow me to interrupt him a moment?

MR. WHITEHEAD. It has been said on this floor to-day—and I call the gentleman's attention to it, and ask him to state whether it be so or not—that a Representative from a Southern State, occupying a seat upon this floor, representing a large and wealthy constituency, could not on his passage from this Capitol to his home in the South either sleep in a railway sleeping-car, get a meal of victuals in a respectable Virginia hotel, or get a bed in any southern hotel on his way home; I mean in a hotel to which the gentleman himself would feel at liberty to go. Is that true or false?

MR. WHITEHEAD. Well, I take very great pleasure in answering that question. The gentleman appears to have mistaken the words used by the gentleman from Mississippi, [Mr. Lynch.] He was referring to the States of Kentucky and Tennessee. I traveled here about two weeks ago from my home and I sat in a seat in the rear of a colored gentleman and his wife, very genteel persons and well behaved, and I never saw anybody interfere with them during the whole journey.

MR. HARRIS. That is not an answer to my question.

MR. WHITEHEAD. So far as I know, a colored man can get just as good eating at hotels as I can. I do not know that they would put the gentleman from Massachusetts at the same table with a colored man, not knowing him, if he were alone. I do not know that they would put him in the same room, but I never heard of there being any difficulty in this matter at all in my State. Since I have been a member of Congress I have ridden backward and forward between my home and Washington in the cars and I cannot recollect a single instance in which there was not a colored man or a colored woman in the cars.

MR. HARRIS. Will the gentleman say if he ever knew a colored man to occupy a place in the sleeping-car with him?

MR. WHITEHEAD. I do not sleep in the sleeping-cars, and therefore I do not know.

MR. HARRIS. Then let me ask the gentleman whether he is prepared to state that the declaration made by Mr. Lynch on the floor to-day is not actually and strictly true?

MR. WHITEHEAD. As I do not represent either the State of Kentucky or Tennessee I cannot say. I am answering for Virginia now. Is the gentleman prepared to say that when he uses the words "the Southern States" he excepts Virginia?

MR. HARRIS. No; I do not.

MR. WHITEHEAD. Then I undertake to say that all the charges on this subject made against Virginia are unfounded.

JOSEPH RAINEY [R., S.C.]. Will the gentleman from Virginia allow me to ask him a question?

MR. WHITEHEAD. Yes; several.

MR. RAINEY. I would ask the gentleman whether I would be permitted to ride in the street cars in the city of Richmond, Virginia; at least in any car not specifically designated as for colored persons?

MR. WHITEHEAD. Well, I will tell you what I think about it. I have not been there for two years, but my opinion is that you would.

MR. RAINEY. Well, the last time I was there I could not.

MR. WHITEHEAD. Did any one object to your riding in street cars in Richmond?

MR. RAINEY. O, yes.

MR. WHITEHEAD. When was that? How long ago?

MR. RAINEY. About a year ago or a little more.

MR. WHITEHEAD. Did you tell them who you were?

MR. RAINEY. I did not tell them who I was. It is not necessary for me to do so in order to ride in the street cars of New York or Boston.

MR. WHITEHEAD. Well, it may be so; I do not know. The gentleman says that he was not allowed to ride in the cars, and I presume it is so. I have only this to say, that street-car conductors and conductors on railroads are not always polite, prudent, and well-behaved; but I saw, and I assert it for the benefit of the gentleman from Massachusetts, in the ladies' car passing from here to Lynchburgh, a black man and his wife, who was a little whiter than he was, sitting in the car in front of me and I saw nobody disturb them, and I have seen the same thing a dozen of times in the State of Virginia.

Now, that is all I know on that subject. I will tell the gentleman further, and I appeal to lawyers from Virginia here to sustain me, that if a colored man were sold a ticket on a railroad in Virginia and ejected from the cars he would recover the full extent of damages from a white Virginia jury with a white circuit judge presiding over the court.

MR. HARRIS. Does the gentleman know whether a colored man can buy a ticket, first class, on a Virginia railroad?

MR. WHITEHEAD. So far as I know he can. I do not know that he cannot.

MR. HARRIS. Will the gentleman state if it is possible for a black man to buy a first-class ticket on any railroad in Virginia?

MR. WHITEHEAD. I will say that so far as I know he can.

MR. RAINEY. Will the gentleman say that in going to Lynchburgh from this city I could buy a first-class ticket?

MR. WHITEHEAD. You can go to Alexandria, and on the Orange and Alexandria Railroad you can buy the same ticket I can. I supposed you were asking questions for information, but it does not seem so. It seems that your object in asking is for the purpose of showing that somebody does not know what you do. I have been handed a paper by a gentleman from Tennessee, which says that a member of Congress and a white man on this floor from the State of Alabama could not get a berth in the sleeping-car in Tennessee because it was filled with colored people. How does that fit you in Tennessee? That is not my fight, but that is the Tennesseean's answer.

A MEMBER. Sleeping-cars are controlled by Pullman, a northern man.

MR. WHITEHEAD. That is a fact; they are controlled by a northern man who may be, so far as I know, a civil-rights man—by Mr. Pullman, of Chicago, who I understand is a great republican. Why do you not have him turned out of the party? . . .

RICHARD CAIN [R., S.C.]. . . .

The civil-rights bill simply declares this: that there shall be no discriminations between citizens of this land so far as the laws of the land are concerned. I can find no fault with that. . . .

The gentleman said that the slaves lived better than their masters. That is susceptible of grave doubt. I think there is a great difference between hog and hominy in the log cabin and all the luxuries of life in the richly-carpeted mansion. It seems to me there is a great difference when one class bear all the labor and produce all the crops, while the other class ride in their carriages, do all the buying and selling, and pocket all the money.

The gentleman says he wishes to defend "old Virginny." Now, I do not think that Virginia is any better than the rest of the States in this respect. My colleague has already stated that they do not allow colored people to ride in the cars except in cars labeled "Colored people allowed in this car." "Old Virginny never tires!" In this connection let me bring another fact to the gentleman's notice. Eight or ten months ago a lady acquaintance of mine was traveling from South Carolina to Washington; she had ridden in a first-class car through North Carolina, having paid a first-class fare; but when she got to the gentleman's noble State of "Old Virginny," she was rudely taken and pushed out of the first-class car into the smoking-car, where she was obliged to remain until she passed out of "old Virginny." It is in this way that they give colored people all their rights and privileges in "old Virginny." It seems to me that such things as this must make "bad blood" for somebody. . . .

MR. WHITEHEAD. I do not know whether I understand you correctly or whether we understand each other. Do I understand that you are in favor of forcing white and black persons to sit at the same table in a hotel?

MR. HARRIS. If the gentleman will be kind enough to allow me to do so, I will answer his question.

MR. WHITEHEAD. I just want to know whether you are in favor of a hotel-keeper being forced by law to make white and black people sit at the same table?

MR. HARRIS. Now, if the gentleman will allow me to answer him, I will tell him what the Massachusetts doctrine is. It is that when any man, white or black, respectable and well-behaved, comes into any hotel in our Commonwealth and asks to have a comfortable apartment assigned him and proper food furnished him, he has a right to it, without regard to his color. But, sir, there is nothing proposed here that would authorize any colored man to force himself on the gentleman from Virginia. This law merely provides that white and black shall be alike entitled to a common hospitality.

MR. WHITEHEAD. That does not answer my question at all. Do you wish hotel-keepers to be bound to place white and black at the same table?

MR. HARRIS. We require hotel-keepers to receive and entertain with propriety and kindness every guest that may come to them, be he white or black.

MR. WHITEHEAD. O, that does not answer my question!

MR. HARRIS. Well; I decline to be further interrupted by a gentleman who declined to answer the question I put to him. I will tell the gentleman, however, that in Massachusetts we do not make all classes of white men sit at the same table or sleep in the same bed. But every man in Massachusetts, be he white or black, can have entertainment at one of our hotels, and a black man can get entertainment there equal to that afforded to any white man, if he is respectable and pays his bill. . . .

MR. RAINEY. Mr. Speaker, it was my original intention to have submitted some remarks to-night upon this bill. But upon further reflection I had made up my mind to wait until to-morrow morning, when I hoped to have an opportunity to speak at some length and to my better satisfaction; yet I cannot permit this opportunity to pass without a few words in reply to the gentleman from Virginia, [Mr. Whitehead.] I regret that some others on that side of the House have not seen fit to participate in the debate to-night, for it looks a little uncharitable to direct all our arguments from this side against a single honorable opponent. But it so happens that he is the only one who has said anything in regard to the bill at this time. I did not come in the Hall this evening early enough to hear all the gentleman had to say. I wish I had heard his entire speech, for I might have been able then to form a better judgment of the course of his argument.

I must say, judging from what I have heard, that the gentleman has made no argument that, in my opinion, can do the civil-rights bill any harm. He has attempted to ridicule the same; he has attempted to ridicule the people whom it is designed to benefit; but he has not adduced any strong argument, logical nor legal, why the bill should not pass and become a law; why the class of people against whom he has raised his opposing voice to-night should not have their constitutional rights. His premises are erroneous altogether, consequently his conclusions are fallacious and void of force. He said the common law now provides all of the remedies this bill is intended to afford; therefore he could not see the necessity for its passage. He further adds that it was intended to create strife and not benefit the colored people. I want to say to the member from Virginia that so far as the common law is concerned, although I am not a lawyer, I am aware, however, that it contains remedial provisions; but they are so general in their character as frequently to lose specific application and force unless wrought into statutory enactment. Hence the necessity for this bill, which sets forth specifically the offenses and the means of redress. That I believe to be why, among other reasons, we enact statutory law; otherwise we would appeal to the common law and obtain our ends independent of the statutes.

The fact of the determined and earnest opposition to which this measure has been subjected is an additional argument in favor of its passage in order that we may have the constitutional rights guaranteed us, being citizens. The time has come under this Government when we must no longer be looked upon and judged by the color of our skins. Yes, the time is at hand when you must cease to take us for cringing slaves. We may have been such in the past, but you should not fail to remember that we are freemen now, and citizens of this great country in common with yourselves; therefore entitled to the full enjoyment of all the privileges and immunities incidental to that condition. . . .

It was declared, sir, that if we were enfranchised it would provoke conflict and create strife; that if we were placed in the jury-box it would create a similar result. We have been in the jury-box; we have sat upon cases involving the interests of our fellow-citizens, and have rendered verdicts, and I can say with confidence and pride that as regards my own State our action in this respect has been recognized and accepted even by the democratic lawyers, who frequently select colored jurors. We have also had the pleasure of voting; and the only trouble to-day is that the colored man is so loyal to the Government and true to the party that has given him such rights as he has, that he cannot be prevailed upon to enter the ranks of the opposition. That is the reason why gentlemen on the other side are fighting so strenuously against our advancement. But I will say to them that we intend to continue to vote so long as the Government gives us the right and the necessary protection; and I know that right accorded to us now will never be withheld in the future if left to the republican party. The sooner those opposed to us will understand and concede the fact the better it will be for the tranquillity, prosperity, and happiness of the whole country. . . .

We do not intend to be driven to the frontier as you have driven the Indian. Our purpose is to remain in your midst an integral part of the body-politic. We are training our children to take our places when we are gone. We desire this bill that we may train them intelligently and respectably, that they may thus be qualified to be useful citizens in their day and time. We ask you, then, to give us every facility, that we may educate our sons and our daughters as they should be. Deprive us of no rights belonging to us as citizens; give us an equal opportunity in life, then if we fail we will be content if driven to the wall.

But, Mr. Speaker, the subject under consideration is one in which I naturally feel a deep and almost inexpressible interest, not on account of any personal aggrandizement or exclusive individual benefit which I hope to enjoy, but for reasons far more patriotic, lofty, and disinterested in their conception. I speak in behalf of my race and people, who have long endured hardship, degradation, and proscription to subserve the pernicious and diabolical ends of slavery. . . .

Much apprehension and fear have been exhibited on account of the social aspect of this subject. A few words on that point will not be out of place. This fear and apprehension are unwarranted; there is no social precedent for this alarm. It is merely conjectural, or, in other words, it is nothing more than the result engendered by a diseased and prejudiced mind. Every impartial thinker is aware that no law is supposed possible to regulate the social customs of any people. What is social equality? Is it the undisturbed right to enter public places of amusement, and receive the same accommodations as are offered others at like cost? Surely that cannot be, for it is obvious that suspicious characters are frequently the occupants of firstclass seats among the spectators; so if this settles the question we may well tremble for the purity and reputation of good society. It is the unrestricted right to be entertained at public inns or restaurants and be respectfully treated? That cannot be, for we have daily instances before us where thieves and others of questionable repute enjoy these advantages without, I hope, being considered social equals of other guests. Is it the right of franchise, of being accommodated by common carriers, whether by land or water, and treated as other first-class passengers are? I think not. It is therefore a waste of argument to insist upon it. Social equality consists in congeniality of feeling, a reciprocity of sentiment, and mutual, social recognition among men, which is graded according to desire and taste, and not by any known or possible law. Men as a rule are always careful never to introduce into the sancity of their family circles those who would abuse the privilege, or who are not recognized as social equals. This is a right that cannot be disputed, neither can it be invaded by any law or statutory enactment.

Reference has been made, for the purpose of arousing public opposition and resentment upon the ground that it would signalize the overthrow of opposing barriers, to unrestrained association between the races and thus inaugurate intermarriage of whites and blacks. Such argument shows the weakness of this supposed salient point adduced by the opposition. It is a mere subterfuge, and unworthy of those who announce it. If their arguments are of any value and force, it reflects unfavorably upon those whose cause they are supposed to defend. Need I say it is unknown to the spirit of our Constitutions Federal or State; the possible enactment of any compulsory law forcing alliance between parties having no affinities whatever? . . .

I venture to assert to my white fellow-citizens that we, the colored people, are not in quest of social equality. For one I do not ask to be introduced into your family circles if you are not disposed to receive me there. Among my own race we have as much respectability, intelligence, virtue, and refinement possible to expect from any class circumstanced as we have been. This being so, why should I cast imputation upon my people by saying to them, "I do not want your society; I prefer to associate with the whites." Why should I be ashamed of them with their blood flowing in my veins? . . .

Much has been said about the Constitution and its bearing upon the passage of this bill, and the ultimate result of such an event. Time will not permit me to refer to them all. I will say, by way of general reply, that those who read the Constitution with partial and selfish motives in view fail to see the interests of the colored race apart from what is implied in the three last amendments thereto, and frequently with a narrow conception of those. We claim equal rights and interests with other citizens who are embraced within the limits of all its provisions. If this should not be admitted, the people would soon lose appreciation for that instrument, and clamor for a change that would afford them more general and better protection. Believing it to be adequate for the ample security of all, the people are content with it.

Article 4, section 2, of the Constitution reads thus:

The citizens of each State shall be entitled to all privileges and immunities of citizens in the several States.

According to this provision it is unconstitutional to deny any privilege or immunity to colored citizens in either Virginia, Georgia, Kentucky, or any other State that is guaranteed to other citizens. It must be remembered that we are not dealing with the past, but with the immediate present and for the future.

In this connection reference may be properly made to the public schools. All the objections that have been urged against the general commingling of white and colored children in these schools have been stated and successfully refuted in the past. There was great dissatisfaction shown at the inauguration of this system in those States where it has been in successful operation for years. It is gratifying to state that the satisfactory results of its workings has dispelled all doubts in regard to its practicability, quieted apprehension, and contributed largely to remove fears and annihilate that prejudice which has been declared upon this floor should be fostered and respected. It is with the aim of making more complete the destruction of this uncharitable sentiment and proscription that the opening of the public schools to all is so much to be desired. Surely the children are not better than their parents, who now sit with us in the jury box, the legislative hall, and are daily to be seen in the same public conveyances. Therefore I can see no reason why the white and colored children cannot attend the same public school.

What we desire, Mr. Speaker, is to have the cloud of proscription removed from our horizon, that we may clearly see our way to intellectual and moral advancement. This is nothing more than what all good citizens desire to enjoy and ought to have. I therefore favor the passage of the Senate bill now on your table. . . .

ELLIS ROBERTS [R., N.Y.]. Mr. Speaker is, not the whole of this debate an anachronism? Is it not strange that we should be called upon to inquire whether American citizens have their rights in the several States of this Union? Is it not strange that it should be a matter of debate whether there should be actual legislation guaranteeing to a certain class of our citizens their common-law rights in the several States? Gentlemen may deny that laws exist in any State refusing these rights, as the gentleman from Mississippi [Mr. Lamar] has just denied, but they cannot deny that in certain States of the Union there are no laws guaranteeing those rights to the several classes of our citizens. What do we behold? There are gentlemen sitting upon this floor who have given no offense to this body. And as the gentleman from Mississippi [Mr. Lynch] testified the other day on his way to his seat in this body through two of the States of this Union he was compelled to submit to indignities. Not only was he compelled to submit to indignities, but females, the wives and mothers of members sitting on this floor, are also compelled to submit to indignities on their way hither. Mr. Speaker, is there any trouble to-day when colored men and colored women sit in these galleries and colored men sit upon the floor of this House and are eligible to the floor of the other House? Now, bear in mind, Mr. Speaker, that opposition to this bill is not put simply on the ground of the question of our constitutional power to legislate, although my colleague from New York [Mr. Hale] has well answered that point. But gentlemen on the other side of the House tell us, as the gentleman from Virginia [Mr. Sener] told us this morning, that this sort of legislation is calculated to produce trouble in the South. Why? If these rights are already conceded, what trouble will it make to have Congress guarantee those rights? No, Mr. Speaker, the trouble is that these rights are denied, whatever may be the language of the statutes, practically, and colored men and women cannot travel in all the States as white men can travel in all the States. And besides, sir, why is it that we have seen, not for a day only but for a long week, a great party upon this floor preventing the American Congress from considering this question? If these rights are already conceded, what trouble would it make to discuss the subject? We could have considered the constitutional question without passion and without prejudice. But there are practical questions connected with this subject. These rights are denied, and because they are denied, insisting, as I do, upon the constitutional right to legislate upon the subject, I can do no less than insist that a national guarantee of these rights shall be secured to all men and women in all parts of the Republic.

But, Mr. Speaker, I rose principally to speak with reference to the school clause. I greatly fear that we may err on the one side or the other. Three propositions are before the House in reference to that subject, one insisting, as the Senate bill does, upon the same schools for both races at the South; another in most distinct antagonism to that is the proposition of the gentleman from Connecticut, [Mr. Kellogg,] who proposes to exclude entirely from the bill all reference to schools. Then there is the report of the Committee on the Judiciary of the House bill providing that the schools shall be equal in their privileges for the two races. For one, sir, I am not willing to legislate that colored men shall have their rights in the theater and to refuse to legislate that they shall have their rights in the schools. If we have erred at all in the great work of reconstruction, it has been because we have not made enough of education. If we had insisted upon making education a condition of the reconstruction of the States we would have been better off to-day.

MR. KELLOGG. As the gentleman has alluded to me, allow me one word. I moved to strike out that provision because I thought it was worse than none at all for the interests of education.

MR. ROBERTS. I understood the gentleman to move to strike out all provisions relating to schools.

MR. KELLOGG. I moved to strike out that provision in the House bill because it is worse than nothing for them and for us. . . .

CHARLES ELDREDGE [DEM., WIS.]. . . .

The law has done all it can accomplish for them. So far as the law is concerned, the black man is in all respects the equal of the white. He stands and may make the race of life upon terms of perfect equality with the most favored citizen. There is no right, privilege, or immunity secured to *any* citizen of the Republic that is not confirmed to the colored. There is no court, no tribunal, no judicial jurisdiction, no remedy, no means of any sort in the land, provided by law for the redress of wrongs or the protection of the rights of life, liberty, or property of the white man that is not equally open and available to the black man. The broad panoply of the Constitution and the whole body of laws, civil and criminal, and every means provided for their enforcement, cover and extend to every American citizen without regard to color or previous condition. The white man may with no more legal impunity, trench upon or invade the dominion of the black man's rights than the black man may the white man's. The barriers of laws surrounding and protecting them are the same. There is no distinction, no exception, no immunity in favor of the white race. And let it never be forgotten that voluntarily, in the pride and majesty of its power, the white race has thus far *done it all*. With sublime indifference and disregard of all natural and conventional differences, if not with *sublime wisdom and discretion* the LIBERATOR, the white race, decreed and proclaimed to the world that his *former slave, the negro race,* whatever he may have been or may become, is henceforth and forever shall be under the law of the Republic a co-citizen and an equal. He may compete for any office; he may contest any citizen; he may aspire to any position; he is eligible to the most exalted place in the Republic.

And, sir, what would gentlemen, what would the greatest patriot, the greatest philanthropist, have more? What would the intelligent negro, the man best capable of comprehending the wants, the necessities, the highest good of his own race, ask for more? The common-law rights of both are the same. Both are equal in its protection. White and black may alike invoke its interposition for the protection of rights and the redress of wrongs. If equality, exact and impartial equality, of legal rights and legal remedies is desired, it is now enjoyed alike by both. If you would not place one race above the other; if you would make no distinction "on account of race or color or previous condition;" if you would have the recent amendments to the Constitution impartially administered; if you would have the laws of the land throughout its length and breadth, in their application to the citizen, take no note of the color of his skin or the race from which he sprang, let the "common law" remain unchanged; let there not be one law for the white man and another for the black man. No change, no distinction in favor of the one or the other can fail to injure both.

To make the colored citizen feel that he is the pet, the especial favorite of the law, will only feed and pander to that conceit and self-consequence which is now his weakest and perhaps most offensive characteristic. If he be made to feel that extraordinary provisions of law are enacted in his favor because of his weakness or feebleness as a man, the very fact weakens and enfeebles him. The consciousness that there is necessity for such legislation and protection for him must necessarily humiliate and degrade him. Such laws, too, are a constant reminder to him that he is inferior to the white race. They not only remind him of his inferiority and the superiority of the white race in its not requiring these special enactments, but they naturally and necessarily awaken in him a feeling of bitterness and unfriendliness toward the white race. It is impossible that the negro race should live upon terms of mutual confidence and friendship with a race from whom it requires to be protected by a special code—against whose wrongs and oppressions he is not safe except those wrongs are denounced by extraordinary laws and penalties. There can be no peace, no harmony, no confidence, no mutual respect, no feeling of equality between two races living together and protected from the infringement of each other's rights by different laws and different penalties. It is useless to deprecate or deplore the natural or acquired prejudice of the races so long as the laws enacted for their government in their very nature necessarily awaken, keep alive, and foster them And whether the prejudice be the plant of the Almighty or the growth of slavery, it cannot be removed by legislative enactments. It may be, as in my judgment it most certainly will be, increased and aggravated by such legislation as this, but it cannot be lessened. If the southern man believes, correctly or erroneously, that the negro race is an inferior race, this kind of legislation is certainly not calculated to remove that belief. This bill and all such bills go upon the ground that the colored race is inferior, feebler, and less capable of taking care of itself than the weakest and most inferior white man. This is the very predicate of this legislation. And whether he claims the natural equality of the races or not, it is an insult to every colored man in the Republic. It is an unnecessary exaggeration and parading of the distinction between them. . . .

MR. KELLOGG. Mr. Speaker, I do not desire to say anything upon this bill, except in regard to the amendment I have offered. I think too much time has been consumed already and this delay has been forced upon us by the action of the other side of the House last week. The amendment I have proposed is to strike out of the House bill reported by the Committee on the Judiciary all that part which relates to schools; and I do it, Mr. Speaker, in the interest of education, and especially in the interest of the education of the colored children of the Southern States. As the bill is now drawn, we recognize a distinction in color which we ought not to recognize by any legislation of the Congress of the United States. Sir, in the legislation of this country I recognize no distinction of color, race, or birthplace. All ought to be equal before the law; and the children of all should have an equal right to the best education they can have in the public schools of the country. But this bill proposes to make a distinction by a national law. The proviso to the first section is one that makes a discrimination as to classes of persons attending public schools; and I do not wish to make any such provision in an act of Congress.

But upon this school question we should be careful that we do not inflict upon the several States of the Union an injury that we ought to avoid. A school system in most of the Southern States has been established since the war of the rebellion, by which the colored children of the South have the advantages of an education that they never could have before that time. I believe, from all the information I can obtain, that you will destroy the schools in many of the Southern States if you insist upon this provision of the bill. You will destroy the work of the past ten years and leave them to the mercy of the unfriendly legislation of the States where the party opposed to this bill is in power. And besides, this matter of schools is one of the subjects that must be recognized and controlled by State legislation. The States establish schools, raise taxes for that purpose, and they are also aided by private benefactions; and they have a right to expend the money, so raised, in their own way. So far as agricultural schools are concerned which are endowed by Congress, it may be proper to make this provision. But, sir, when I see all that has been done for the education of the colored children of the South since the war, all that has been accomplished in that direction, I could not in good conscience vote for any measure which would destroy the whole of the good work that has already been accomplished, and destroy the system of schools already established in those States. I believe the colored people of the South as well as the colored people of the North, when they understand this question, will wish that no such provision shall be made in this or any other bill. The gentleman from South Carolina, [Mr. Cain,] an illustrious example of what the education of his race can do, told us yesterday that they did not ask this provision from us. . . .

My friend from New York [Mr. Roberts] was entirely wrong in his idea yesterday when he said the effect of my amendment was that colored children should not have equal rights in the public schools of the States. Sir, does he not know that there are a few things left that State legislation can take care of and should take care of without interference by the legislation of the General Government? The States raise the taxes for the public schools; the General Government has nothing to do with it, and any interference by national law will be productive of mischief, and mischief only. I do not yield to him or any man on this floor in an earnest desire for the best educational facilities for all the children of this country, without regard to race, color, or nationality. But my friend had evidently failed to study the condition of the schools in the Southern States when he made that allusion to my amendment. He has been too much occupied with the great questions of statesmanship, to which he seems to devote himself, to give much attention to the practical effect of such a provision as this upon the schools in the several States; and he has even gone beyond that and got into the great reform of revising and correcting the Gregorian year, and has gone back some centuries to do his work of reform. If he will come down to us out of the clouds of his high statesmanship and the ages of antiquity and see what the people of this country have been doing the last ten years for the education of the colored children since the end of the war, he will not have made the point he has made upon my amendment. If he will come down to the practical question, he will find that my amendment is for the benefit of the colored children of the South especially; and in the North we have no trouble on this score, for all children are welcomed to our public schools, without regard to race or color.

Sir, though I was not born in Connecticut, like my friend from New York who spoke yesterday, yet I have lived there for many years; and I will say to the gentleman from New York [Mr. Chittenden] that there is not a church, a public school, or place of amusement where we do not welcome our colored population, our foreign-born population, and all our population, without regard to race, color, or condition. All are equal before the law, and all should be equal in the enjoyment of their rights. We believe that all men have the same privileges under the law, without distinction of race, color, or anything except as their own character or conduct in life shall make for them. But by the provisions of this bill you ask us to destroy the school system of the Southern States by an enactment which is not asked for by the colored people of the South and which they do not want, for they know it will be used to deprive them of the educational advantages that have been secured to them since their emancipation and since they became entitled to all the rights of citizens under the law of the land. . . .

WILLIAM PHELPS [R., N.J.]. I am not in the habit of making mountains out of mole-hills, nor of looking at any subject exclusively on the dark side. And yet it is impossible for me to divest myself of the feeling that this is really a solemn occasion, or that the actors here are assuming a responsibility from which they might well shrink. Among the actors in this drama, none deservedly will hold a more conspicuous position than the honorable gentleman in whose charge this bill now rests. Yet not of him exclusively will the people of this Union think to-day. But with him they will bear in mind the memory of another son of Massachusetts who is no longer with us. Nearly one year ago he died, and when he died the heart of this great people stood still for a moment under the crusing weight of its grief. It was that son of Massachusetts who created and led the republican party through the wilderness and into the land of promise; and yet then and there cruelly was he deposed and driven from the ranks by men whom he had called into them, by the lieutenants into whose hands he himself had put their commissions.

I believe that Charles Sumner died, and I believe that history will record that he died as a good man should die, free from animosity, free from revenge. But had it been otherwise, had he died full of animosity, had that great heart been steeped as was Satan's with an "unconquerable will and study of revenge," he could not have left to this country which he so loved, to the party which he created and led, a legacy so full of the seeds of disintegration and decay as the measure which the majority will this day pass.

And yet in order to pass this bill we have altered the rules of procedure under which for fifty years this House has transacted its business. We have altered the rules under which the minority has during this period enjoyed peace and security. More than this, to pass this bill we defy the opinion of the people of these United States recently and emphatically declared; for if there was any one issue on which we went to the country it was this. Said my friends on the other side, members of the democratic party all of them, "We will oppose this measure of civil rights." Said nearly all my friends on this side, members of the republican party, "We will give you civil rights." And upon the issue the two great parties went to judgment. And the people last fall declared their judgment, and with a thunder that shook one hundred members out of these seats.

When this bill was introduced one year ago, that Representative who believed it his duty to please his constituency, whether they were right or whether they were wrong, might have found a pretext for voting for it; but now this pretext is torn to shreds by the gales which swept the country in November.

Equally flimsy is the pretext that this is a different measure. It makes no difference how you amend, how you alter, how you reform; you can reform it only if you "reform it altogether." Pass the Senate bill, and you pass an unmitigated evil. Pass the House bill, and you pass a mitigated evil. But in either and all cases it is evil and evil altogether. Of course I cannot traverse the whole of this dark record. I would that my time would let me do so; to go through the various provisions that I might indicate the especial objection to each. But my hands are tied. Take a single provision. Enact your school clause, and what do you do? You close your schools! Look at the South, desolated and distracted; deluged with a flood of misery. There is but one spot on which the dove of peace might rest. There is a school system, young and tender and full of promise, full of hope. Enact this clause, and you destroy its budding promise; enact this clause, and you shut the door of every public school. Let one more autumn come, and there will not be a State in the South whose Legislature shall vote one single dollar for their creation and support. This is one thing you will have accomplished by your civil-rights bill; and what have you gained? To give to our colored fellow-citizena mere sentimental privilege—that the colored man when he dies may lie in Hollywood; that while he lives he may eat at the Saint Nicholas; that when he plays he may sit in a box at the National. To give him these sentimental advantages, which he will never use, you have slain his teachers, you have sacrificed substance to shadow. You have tickled his fancy and starved his mind.

Nor can you repair the damage. You have striven to control what you cannot construct. You have sought to regulate the schools; and the Southern States will checkmate you by giving you no schools to regulate.

Mr. Speaker, while the Federal power may accomplish some things, there are others which it can never accomplish. It may take its bayonets into the halls of these Legislatures and by them may drive out the members, but it can never, with or without bayonets, force them to vote. The white men will provide for the education of their own children at their own expense—they still have the means; but they will make no appropriation for the mixed schools, the freedman's only chance for education. The colored man has no means to pay for his own school-teacher, and he can thank the republican party that he is again relegated to a state of primal ignorance and gloom. . . .

I was speaking of inn-keepers. I say with reference to them, the reason of the law that used to govern them failing, the law itself fails. We no longer give to inn-keepers especial privileges—any monopoly in the business; we cannot therefore burden their business with any restrictions. Therefore I claim that an enlightened court will refuse to enforce the provision; and against unenlightened courts the people of the South have still this refuge, that to their process they can tender despair. They will close their inns, and the traveler from the North who may visit that country and find it necessary for his entertainment to throw himself upon the hospitality of the southerner, when he would prefer the independence of the inn, will doubtless return to the North determined to vote for the legislation of the republican party.

I cannot go through all these provisions. I pass over all special objections. I hasten to those general objections which apply to every provision of the bill. You are trying to do what it seems to me this House everlastingly tries in one form or another to do—to legislate against human nature. You are trying to legislate against human prejudice, and you cannot do it. No enactment will root out prejudice, no bayonet will prick it. You can only educate away prejudice; and to endeavor by a law to change the constitution of human nature is as idle as to send your cavalry to charge a mountain mist. . . .

MR. BUTLER. I rise now to close debate. Before I move the previous question I propose to withdraw the motion to recommit in order to allow a vote upon the preamble offered by the gentleman from Indiana, [Mr. Shanks.] It was a good old custom of our fathers to put a preamble before all laws in order that it may be understood what was meant by the law. I propose to renew that custom in this case. I now call the previous question. . . .

THE SPEAKER. The Chair will state the question. The gentleman from Massachusetts [Mr. Butler] withdraws the motion to recommit, and yields to the gentleman from Indiana, [Mr. Shanks,], who moves as a preamble to the bill that which will be read by the Clerk.

The Clerk read as follows:

Whereas it is essential to just government we recognize the equality of men before the law, and hold that it is the duty of government in its dealings with the people to mete out equal and exact justice to all, of whatever nativity, race, color, or persuasion, religious or political; and it being the proper object of legislation to enact great fundamental principles into laws: Therefore . . .

MR. BUTLER. I had hoped when this bill was first brought before the House that in all kindness of heart, in all singleness of purpose, with all propriety of tone and thought, we should discuss one of the most momentous questions of civil liberty that can be raised; a question the solution of which, for good or for evil, will affect our country longer, much longer, than we shall remain on the earth; but I have been disappointed.

It is a question of equal civil rights to all citizens—a doctrine in which I was brought up from my earliest boyhood. I have always been taught that the foundation of all democracy was equality of right, equality of burden, equality of power in all men under the law. And when a few years ago a religious and partisan furore shook the land and it was attempted to disfranchise from some of their rights in many of the States a portion of our citizens because of their foreign birth and because of their religion, when the cry went out "put no one but Americans on guard," I stood in my State in almost a hopeless minority, indeed almost alone, in saying that the privilege of American citizenship once granted was like the privilege of the Roman citizen—to be to him the same in *Latium* and at Athens. And I stood firmly to that until all that prejudice was rolled away from the foreign-born citizen by his standing shoulder to shoulder with our brothers and sons in the red track of battle.

Now comes another question of prejudice in which I was educated in my youth differently, the rights of the colored man. He has been made, by right or by wrong, but under the forms and with the force of constitutional law, a citizen of the United States. And were he as black as the black diamond, he has an equal right to every privilege with any citizen who is white as an angel. And upon that ground alone can a democratic republic stand. Upon that ground alone is civil and constitutional liberty on this continent to be preserved. And, therefore, I wonder with amazement when I hear it here stated that this bill is intended as a stab to constitutional liberty. Why, sir, this bill is the very essence of constitutional liberty. What does it do? It simply provides that there shall be an equality of law all over the Union.

My friend from Mississippi [Mr. Lamar] says that in Mississippi the white man and the colored man have equal privileges. Be it so. Good for Mississippi. This was so made by a republican Legislature in which was a colored majority. But where is the like law in Kentucky, the "dark and bloody ground?" Where is that law in Tennessee? Where is that law—without stopping to enumerate—in a majority of the Southern States? But if it is a good law in Mississippi, why should it not be extended over all the Southern States? If it is a good law, and my friend from Mississippi agrees it is a good law and works well there, why should it not be enforced by proper and sufficient penalties to restrain bad men from violating it? And that is all the bill does.

I do not here and now mean to deal with the question of schools, for this reason: There are two kinds of opinion in the republican party on this question. I myself would legislate equal privileges to white and black in the schools, if I had the power, first, to legislate, and, secondly, to enforce the legislation. But the difficulty I find in that is, that there is such a degree of prejudice in the South that I am afraid that the public-school system, which has never yet obtained any special hold in the South, will be broken up if we put that provision into the bill. Then comes the provision of the committee that there shall be separate schools wherever schools are supported by taxation. There are some difficulties with an unwilling people in carrying out that provision, and there is an objection to it on the part of the colored people, because they say they desire no legislation which shall extablish any class distinction.

Then comes the proposition of my friend from Connecticut [Mr. Kellogg] to strike out all relating to schools. I should very much rather have all relating to schools struck out than have even the committee's provision for mixed schools. I leave this provision with these observations. . . .

Now, then, what are the objections here made to this bill? The first objection stated on the other side is that this bill establishes social equality. By no means; by no means. I undertook to show, when up before, how by this law social equality is not touched by the bill. It allows men and women of different colors only to come together in public, in theaters, in stage-coaches and cars, in public houses. I am inclined to think that the only equality the blacks ever have in the South is social equality; for I understand the highest exhibition of social equality is communication between the sexes, and I have here a statute of the State of Mississippi, which I propose to have read, which will show the extent to which social equality had place in that State before the war, and how a republican Legislature had to provide for the consequences of that social equality since the war. I ask the Clerk to read the extract from the statute which I send up.

The Clerk read as follows:

Whereas James Anderson has, by petition to the Legislature of the State of Mississippi, prayed for the removal of all illegitimacy from certain of his children, and given reasons therefor in said petition, which are just and humane in their character: Therefore,

SEC. 1. *Be it enacted by the Legislature of the State of Mississippi,* That Sheppard Anderson, born August 31, 1854, and begotten of Catherine Lee; Richard Anderson, born March 5, 1859, and begotten of Jane Anderson; Lewis Anderson, born May 1, 1860, and begotten of Nellie Ellis; Benjamin Anderson, born August 9, 1862, and begotten of Nellie Ellis; Caleb Anderson, born September 12, 1863, begotten of Jensey Hunnicutt; Edward Anderson, born July 8, 1864, and begotten of Alice Courtney; and Jane Anderson, born October 7, 1858, begotten by Margaret Fisher; and all of which said children are the illegitimate issue of said women, by said James Anderson, citizen residing in Holmes County, State of Mississippi, be, and the same are hereby, declared and made the legitimate children of the said James Anderson, for all purposes in law or otherwise.

WILLIAM NIBLACK [DEM., IND.]. I desire to know if I did not do right in keeping ladies from the floor during this discussion?

MR. BUTLER. When was that law passed?

THE CLERK. On the 11th of June, 1870.

MR. BUTLER. Now, sir, if there is any greater social equality than that, to have one man become the father of seven children by six different colored women, I do not know what an exhibition of social equality is.

But more than that, sir. I hold in my hand the cry of a southern mother sent to me on the 19th of December last from Richmond, Virginia—a cry for another and different civil-rights bill—and I propose to have an extract from it read as a part of my remarks, that the mothers of this country may know the need of a civil-rights-bill in the South to correct an evil; and while this letter is written by an unlearned woman, is illy spelled, and some portions of which I will not have read, yet I propose to have an extract read for the instruction of American women, American mothers, and American fathers. Will the Clerk read the extract I have marked?

The Clerk read as follows:

I have long wanted to address a few lines to you in regard to your civil-rights bill, but could not overcome my timmidity, knowing as I do my incapacity to write as I ought to such a lurned person as yourself; but fearing I shall not do my duty to my race if I remain silent, I shall trust these lines to your genirosity for the forgiveness of all mistakes.

Dear sir, there is one important point which has escaped your notice. Nothing can ever make us equal with the white race while our daughters are forced to commit adultery by every white man and boy that chose to treat them as dogs; and if we attempt to apply to court one or more white boys will get up in court and say, I know her to be a bad woman or girl long ago; and the police justice calls us all a parcle of worthless prostitutes, and drives us out of court; and they won't even let the newspapers notice the outrage, just because we are colored people. Now, dear sir, you know no people can ever be great without their women are virtuous, and I know (because I live South) that we can never raise virtuous daughters unless there is some law made to protect us from the power of the white man to outrage our little daughters before they reach the age of twelve, and some of them are even outraged at eight, nine, and ten.

Do all that is in your power for us in this case, for on this refformation among our females depends our future wellfare. Would it not be best to have this bill by itself. Then they surely could not say aught against that. . . .

Now, my attention has been called to a speech of the gentleman from New Jersey, [Mr. Phelps,] wherein he told us that it would do no good to pass this bill, because prejudice is strong in the South. And when I compare his rose-colored report of the relations of the colored people and the state of affairs down in Louisiana with this statement, I was utterly astonished to find him stating that that prejudice is so strong there, when no mention of it crept into that report. I have shown, sir, that this bill does not touch the most terrible, the most awful question of social equality which grew up under a system where men traded in the results of their lust.

Now, sir, the next question we have to encounter is that this bill is born of malignity. Sir, I have a good authority on this point. It is generally supposed and believed that this bill was originated by Charles Sumner, of Massachusetts. . . .

When Mr. Sumner came to contemplate death, his great regret was that he had not time to finish this work, that of passing the civil-rights bill which lies upon your table now. . . .

Now I was about to say, when interrupted, that the reason why we desired to have this bill passed was the very fact that has been so often put before us, that we are about passing out of power. We are to surrender power, in one branch of this Government at least, into the hands of gentlemen who entertain the sentiments toward Union men and Union soldiers, and who avowed them on the stump and have not retracted them to my knowledge, that are contained in the report I have had read. And if I am claimed to have been wrong the other day in saying that there was a minority of murders in the South, here is my justification, the House of Representatives having solemnly said it by adopting that report—have declared that there were not only murderers in the South but *assassins*, and therefore I was right in saying it.

MR. ELDREDGE. I ask that the last words of the gentleman from Massachusetts be taken down and read at the Clerk's desk.

THE SPEAKER. They will be written out.

The notes having been written out by the reporter, the Clerk read as follows:

And if I was wrong the other day in saying that there was a minority of murderers in the South, here is my justification, the House of Representatives having solemnly said it by adopting that report—not only murderers, but assassins; and therefore I was right in saying it.

THE SPEAKER. What is the point of order that the gentleman from Wisconsin makes upon that language?

MR. ELDREDGE. The language to which I object preceded that. As I apprehended the remarks of the gentleman from Massachusetts, they were that the Government was about to be surrendered into the hands of murderers and assassins.

MANY MEMBERS. O, no! O, no!

THE SPEAKER. The Chair rules that the remarks of the gentleman from Massachusetts come within the rules of the House. There is nothing in the language read that transcends the rules of debate. The Chair of course cannot be a censor on the propriety of the language used her. . . .

MR. BUTLER. Another argument; we are told that if we pass this bill we shall not come back to Congress, and we are reminded by the gentleman from New Jersey [Mr. Phelps] that this bill was the great issue in the last election. I will not stop to make a personal application of that to the gentleman from New Jersey, [Mr. Phelps,] for he is an example quite to the contrary, if you please, as he voted against this bill and has not come back.

But I say in the face of the country that it is my deliberate conviction that the reason why some here have not been sent back is because we did not pass this bill a year ago. The people turned from us because we were a do-nothing party, afraid of our shadows; because we were aptly described by that portion of Scripture which relates how it was written to the angel of the church of the Laodiceans:

> I know thy works, that thou art neither cold nor hot: I would thou wert cold or hot. So then because thou art lukewarm, and neither cold nor hot, I will spew thee out of my mouth.

The republican party being neither hot nor cold, the country rightly spewed us out of its mouth. When I am met in the argument by the assertion "You do not represent the people; you were beaten in your election," my answer is that my successor—a very estimable gentleman he is in every sense—could no more have come here than he could have been translated to heaven as Elijah was if he had not agreed to stand upon the doctrine of equality of races and of men before the law, and so declared on every stump in my district. Nor could one democrat have been elected from Massachusetts, not even my old friend who is to represent the district of my colleague, [Mr. Dawes,] and who voted with me fifty-seven times for Jeff Davis, unless it was understood that he stood with me for the equal rights of all men.

I say again, and I want it to go forth as a thing which I stand upon, as you on the other side were compelled in your platform of 1872 to declare for equality of rights of all men before the law, so every republican was bound to stand by that. And where we were beaten it was because we had neglected to do the thing we had promised, and it was not made an accomplished fact. When we passed the thirteenth amendment to the Constitution of the United States we lost Ohio the first year; but we regained it the next. So now if the republican party will finish their great work, pass the civil-rights bill. If then, we will by bayonet or otherwise bring peace, prosperity, law and good order in the South, and put down those that ride by night there to murder and burn, which the South ought to do for itself, you will find that we will come back here sustained by voices of the loyal Union loving men of the country.

[Here the hammer fell.] . . .

THE SPEAKER. The question is on the amendment of the gentleman from Connecticut, [Mr. Kellogg,] which is to strike out from the bill reported by the Judiciary Committee the words which will be read by the Clerk.

The Clerk read as follows:

> Strike out the following:
> And also all common schools and public institutions of learning or benevolence supported in whole or in part by general taxation, and also the institutions known as agricultural colleges endowed by the United States.
> Strike out also the following:
> *Provided,* That if any State or the proper authorities in any State, having the control of common schools or other public institutions of learning aforesaid, shall establish and maintain separate

schools and institutions, giving equal educational advantages in all respects for different classes of persons entitled to attend such schools and institutions, such schools and institutions shall be a sufficient compliance with the provisions of this section so far as they relate to schools and institutions of learning.

The question being taken on the amendment of Mr. Kellogg, there were— ayes 128, noes 48. . . .

So the amendment of Mr. Kellogg was agreed to. . . .

THE SPEAKER. The question now recurs on the motion of the gentleman from Pennsylvania, [Mr. Cessna,] to substitute the test of the Senate bill for the bill of the Judiciary Committee as amended by the House.

Mr. Cessna and Mr. Speer called for the yeas and nays.

The yeas and nays were ordered. . . .

The question was taken; and it was decided in the negative—yeas 114, nays 148, not voting 27; as follows:

So the substitute was rejected. . . .

The question then recurred on the adoption of Mr. Shank's preamble, as follows:

Whereas it is essential to just government we recognize the equality of all men before the law and hold it is the duty of government in its dealings with the people to mete out equal and exact justice to all, of whatever nativity, race, color, or persuasion, religious or political; and it being the proper object of legislation to enact fundamental principles into law: Therefore, etc.,

Mr. Shanks demanded the yeas and nays on the preamble.

The yeas and nays were ordered.

The question was taken; and it was decided in the affirmative—yeas 218, nays 26, not voting 45. . . .

So the preamble was adopted. . . .

MR. BUTLER. I now call for the previous question on the passage of the bill.

The previous question was seconded and the main question ordered.

The question was on the passage of the bill.

MR. ELDREDGE. I call for the yeas and nays.

The yeas and nays were ordered.

The question was taken; and there were—yeas 162, nays 99, not voting 28. . . .

So the bill was passed.

Senate-43d Congress, 2nd Session
February 26-7, 1875

THE PRESIDING OFFICER [MATTHEW CARPENTER R., WIS.]. The Senator from Ohio demands the regular order, which is the bill (H. R. No. 796) to protect all citizens in their civil and legal rights.

JOHN LEWIS [R., VA.]. I should like to call up House bill No. 2747.

ALLEN THURMAN [DEM., OHIO]. No; I cannot give way for anything.

Mr. President, the pending question is on the motion submitted by me to strike out of the fourth section of the bill the words "or of any State." Of course no vote is to be taken on the motion until the hour of two o'clock to-morrow, but I have seen fit to make the motion now in order that it may receive that consideration which it cannot receive under a rule limiting debate to five minutes.

Mr. President, the question presented by this amendment to the Senate is whether, apart from any question of policy, it is competent for the Congress of the United States to regulate the qualifications of jurors in a State court. The section as it now stands provides—

That no citizen possessing all other qualifications which are or may be prescribed by law shall be disqualified for service as grand or petit juror in any court of the United States, or of any State, on account of race, color, or previous condition of servitude; and any officer or other person charged with any duty in the selection or summoning of jurors who shall exclude or fail to summon any citizen for the causes aforesaid shall, on conviction thereof, be deemed guilty of a misdemeanor, and be fined not more than $5,000.

When this bill was under consideration in the Senate at the last session, or a bill similar to this, I listened in vain for one word showing the constitutionality of that provision. I listened in vain for any word of argument to show that it is in the power of the Congress of the United States to regulate by law who shall be jurors in the State courts. No argument was made within my hearing to maintain any such proposition; but it was very distinctly and clearly demonstrated by you, Mr. President, (Mr. Carpenter in the chair,) as well as by others, that no such power can be deduced from any provision in the Constitution. No one will pretend that before the adoption of the fourteenth amendment such a provision as this would have been constitutional, and no one will pretend that there is anything in the fourteenth amendment to give the slightest color to such a position unless it be the first section of that amendment. Before considering that, allow me to say that neither the thirteenth nor the fifteenth amendment has anything whatever to do with this question. It all turns upon section 1 of the fourteenth amendment, which is in these words:

All persons born or naturalized in the United States, and subject to the jurisdiction thereof, are citizens of the United States and of the State wherein they reside. No State shall make or enforce any law which shall abridge the privileges or immunities of citizens of the United States; nor shall any State deprive any person of life, liberty, or property, without due process of law; nor deny to any person within its jurisdiction the equal protection of the laws.

I propose to take up this section sentence by sentence and see whether by any fair reasoning whatever the power asserted in this bill to prescribe the qualifications of jurors in a State court can be logically or reasonably deduced. The first sentence is:

All persons born or naturalized in the United States, and subject to the jurisdiction thereof, are citizens of the United States and of the State wherein they reside.

Manifestly that confers upon them no right to sit as jurors; and if it did it would confer upon every woman a right to be a juror; it would confer upon every minor a right to be a juror. The mere fact that persons born within the United States or here naturalized become citizens of the United States and of the State wherein they reside, confers no right to be selected or to act as jurors.

Let me illustrate that. Take the case of a person naturalized who cannot speak or understand one word of the English language. May not the State say that he shall not be a juror? Does not State after State declare that such persons shall not be jurors? Does not State after State as a qualification to sit upon a jury that a person shall understand the English language— I do not mean read it; I do not mean write it; but at least that he shall read and write the English language. But if the interpretation asserted in this bill were given to this sentence in the article, then it would be unlawful to deprive any citizen of the right to sit upon juries. Let us see the next sentence:

No State shall make or enforce any law which shall abridge the privileges or immunities of citizens of the United States.

Is it one of the privileges or immunities of a citizen of the United States that he shall be a juror in a State court? Who ever heard of such a proposition as that? The Supreme Court has expressly decided in the Slaughter-house cases that the sentence which I have just read only relates to the immunities and privileges of an individual as a citizen of the United States and not to any privilege or any immunity possessed by him in virtue of his State citizenship. No decision can be clearer than that. In fact it required no decision to establish that, for the language is as plain as it could possibly be. The language is—I must repeat it—"No State shall make or enforce any law which shall abridge the privileges and immunities of citizens of the United States;" not of citizens of the State but "of citizens of the United States;" and when, pray, was it ever a privilege or an immunity of a citizen of the United States that he should be entitled to sit upon a jury in a State court? When was it that the bare fact of citizenship of the United States deprived a State of the right to provide what should be the qualification of an individual to entitle him to sit as a juror in its own courts?

The next clause is:

Nor shall any State deprive any person of life, liberty, or property without due process of law.

It is not depriving any individual of life or liberty or property to refuse to seat him in the jury-box. The sentence then concludes, and this concludes the section:

Nor deny to any person within its jurisdiction the equal protection of the law.

She does not deny to any individual within the jurisdiction of the State the equal protection of her laws when she provides what shall be the qualification of the jurors in that State. No one can by any fair reasoning whatever strain that provision to cover such a case as this and to authorize Congress to set aside the State laws, to abrogate them or to modify them in any particular in relation to the qualification of jurors in the State courts. Why, Mr. President, are not the State courts the creatures of the State constitution? Are they not created by the State and do they not derive their whole authority from the State? How, then, can it be that a tribunal thus constituted can be thus regulated in its essential composition by an act of the Congress of the United States? If you can do this in respect to jurors you can do it in respect to judges; you may overthrow the constitution of the State in respect to her judges just precisely as much as you can overthrow her constitution and her laws in respect to her jurors.

There is no fair reasoning, there is no fair logic, there is no deduction admitted by any principle of legal interpretation or of any treatise on logic that admits a stretch of these words so as to justify this provision in this bill. If you can do that, then I say that every constitution of a State and every right of a State is at the absolute mercy of Congress. If you can indulge in a latitude of interpretation in respect to this section which I have read, and which is the only section that bears on the subject or that can be supposed to bear upon it which would admit the constitutionality of this provision in the bill, then I repeat there is not one single right of a State, not one single privilege of a State, not one single safeguard of a State that is not in the absolute discretion of Congress to destroy. Have we come to that? Are the States mere counties and all sovereignty in the Government of the United States? Are the States simply sovereign in name in respect to their reserved rights if Congress, by any such interpretation of this amendment as that by which this bill is sought to be sustained, can declare that they have no reserved rights at all?

I confess that I am amazed that in the face of the plain language of this section, in the face of the solemn decision of the Supreme Court of the United States adverse to this proposition, it yet is pressed upon the Congress of the United States, and we are asked to do what the language of the Constitution does not authorize us to do, and what the solemn decision of our Supreme Court declares we have no power whatever to do. Why, sir, what respect can there be for government when the Congress of the United States sets this decision of its Supreme Court thus at defiance, sets common sense and reason at defiance, and in plain, flagrant, inexcusable violation of our Federal system, of the rights of the States and of the language of our fundamental law, usurps a power that no sane man can believe exists? Sir, this language may be strong, but it is no stronger than is warranted. I say that no sane man can believe that this power exists, and when I say "sane" I mean it. I say that no man unbiased by his prejudices, unbiased by party, unbiased by his desire to carry a party triumph, no matter what may be the fundamental law of the land, can ever in his sane moments come to the conclusion that this power is within the Federal Constitution.

Now, Mr. President, I have very little hope that anything I can say will arrest this measure or even procure the adoption of this amendment. I know that all reverence for the rights of the States has been fading out of the minds of Senators here ever since I have held a seat in this body and for years before. I know that that which was most sacred with our forefathers, that feeling without which this Constitution never would have been adopted, that sacred regard for the rights of the States and the people, that belief that it was only by a Federal system that those rights could be preserved and this Union preserved—I know that those ideas have been fading away under the influences produced by civil war, under the influences of mammon and of greed and under the dictates of the narrowest fanaticism that ever distorted a human mind. I have very little hope of making any impression upon that prevailing tendency now; but I do yet believe—at least I will not give up the hope—that the American people will ere long arouse to a sense of the danger which menaces the whole system founded by our fathers, under which we have achieved unparalleled prosperity, and whose destruction will be the death-knell of liberty and the death-knell of the existence of the Republic.

GEORGE BOUTWELL [R., MASS.]. Mr. President, the remarks made by the honorable Senator from Ohio lead me to make an observation upon the meaning of the fourteenth amendment. If I differ in opinion from the honorable Senator from Ohio, it is not strange. I do not partake of the view he expresses as to the change going on even in the Senate. He says that respect for the rights of the States has been gradually fading out in the minds of Senators since he has had a seat in this body. What inference we are to draw from that remark, as to the influence he may have had upon the Senate, I cannot say. I have not observed that effect, and I doubt the existence of the fact. Nor is there in the country a disposition to interfere with the rights of the States, nor is there any change in opinion as to the power of States, except as the power of the States may have been limited by the amendments that have been made by the Constitution. I feel that this change which has taken place is due to the respect for the Constitution in those particulars wherein the powers of the States have been limited, and not from any disposition to deprive any State of its constitutional powers.

The thirteenth, fourteenth, and fifteenth amendments did limit the power of the States; they did extend the power of the General Government; and the question we are considering almost continually is the extent to which the power of the States has been limited by these amendments and the extent to which the power of the General Government has been carried by these several amendments.

I am not disposed to discuss the Slaughter-house decision, as it is called. It will stand legally and politically for what it is worth. It related to a particular case. In that case and in every other case like that, if there shall be another case like that, it is law; but it is not law beyond the case in which the opinion was rendered, and therefore for myself I dismiss that case as a legislator when I come to consider new propositions.

WILLIAM STEWART [R., NEV.]. That was by a divided court.

MR. BOUTWELL. It was by a divided court, but nevertheless the opinion of the majority of the court is the law of the case, but it is not law beyond the case; it is not law with reference to the rights of States generally, and certainly is not law for the Senate when the Senate is engaged in considering a question which is a different question from that on which the court passed.

In the fourteenth amendment I find ample power for what is proposed in the bill under consideration. The fourth section of this bill does not propose, as was suggested by the Senator from Ohio, to decide the qualifications of jurors in the States. The illustration which he gave to the Senate was not an illustration in point. He says, if a State shall provide by law that a person who does not understand the English language shall not sit as a juror, is the United States to come in and by legislative authority decide or declare that such person may sit as a juror? I think no one would contend that there was any such power in the National Government, and certainly no such power is asserted in this bill.

The fourth section is:

That no citizen possessing all other qualifications which are or may be prescribed by law

That is, by the law of the State—

shall be disqualified for service as grand or petit juror in any court of the United States, or of any State, on account of race, color, or previous condition of servitude.

That is merely by the General Government a declaration of equality of rights among citizens of the several States and of each particular State in reference to service upon the juries of the State and in the State courts.

MR. THURMAN. Will it trouble the Senator if I interrupt him?

MR. BOUTWELL. Not in the least.

MR. THURMAN. Then I beg leave to call the Senator's attention to the fact that the first section of the fourteenth amendment, on which he relies of course to sustain the bill, has no reference whatsoever to "race, color, or previous condition of servitude." No such words are in the section. No allusion is made to that distinction. Therefore I ask the Senator, if there is power to say "that no citizen," in the language of this bill, "possessing all other qualifications which are or may be prescribed by law, shall be disqualified for service as grand or petit juror of any State on account of race, color, or previous condition of servitude," why have you not equal power to strike out those words "on account of race, or color, or previous condition of servitude" and insert "on account of his ignorance of the English tongue?" Why can you not do it; or why can you not add after the word "servitude" the words "or on account of his ignorance of the English tongue;" for there is not one word in the first section of the fourteenth amendment that relates to race, or color, or previous condition of servitude.

MR. BOUTWELL. That is all very true. The fourth section of this bill provides for equality in certain particulars where the equality of citizens is assailed, and not elsewhere. It is assailed or threatened in many of the States of the Union, upon the ground that certain persons are of a particular race or of a particular color or have been subject in times past to the condition of slaves. Now, in order to protect those people against discriminations for these reasons, this provision of the bill contemplates that if they are qualified in other respects as the laws of the State require for other citizens, they shall not be excluded from the jury-box for these reasons; and, although there is not in the first section of the fourteenth article of amendment any reference to these conditions, there nevertheless is a declaration which covers these conditions, and might cover and in fact does cover many other conditions:

All persons born or naturalized in the United States, and subject to the jurisdiction thereof, are citizens of the United States and of the State wherein they reside.

What does that phrase mean? It means, first and chiefly and preeminent, as the law of the land, that "all persons born or naturalized in the United States, and subject to the jurisdiction thereof, are citizens of the United States." That is the first great primal truth of the fourteenth amendment; and what is the first privilege, right, immunity under that declaration? It is that they are citizens of the several States "wherein they reside." Therefore the leading doctrine of that provision of the Constitution is that all the persons described in it are citizens of the United States, and by virtue of their citizenship they are citizens of the State wherein they reside. That is the first immunity. The chief privilege, the great right established by the fourteenth amendment to the Constitution is that citizens of the United States are citizens of the State wherein they reside. That is the immunity, that is the privilege, that is the right. Now, then, what follows?

No State shall make or enforce any law which shall abridge the privileges or immunities of citizens of the United States.

Not "of citizens of the States," but "of citizens of the United States." And what is the first privilege of citizens of the United States? That they are citizens of the State wherein they reside. And what is the chief right of the citizen of a State? That he is the equal before the law of every other citizen. By the fourteenth amendment the people of the United States, through their constituted authorities, have grasped the question of securing to citizens of the United States their rights as citizens of the several States; and the first right is the right of equality before the law. Therefore, while we cannot go into the States and say what the rights of citizens of the State in the State shall be, whenever there is a law in a State or a provision of its constitution which secures to citizens generally their rights and discriminates against other citizens, that discrimination is not only against citizens as citizens of the State, but against the fourteenth amendment to protect them as citizens of the United States, we pass the boundaries of the several States by authority of the Constitution and secure to our citizens, the citizens of the United States, their rights under the laws of the States as citizens of the State.

MR. THURMAN. Now let me ask the Senator a question right there. Where does he find any foundation for the position that either citizenship of the United States or citizenship of a State gives a person a right to sit upon a jury?

MR. BOUTWELL. I do not find it at all.

MR. THURMAN. No; I guess not.

MR. BOUTWELL. I do not need to look for it. As a citizen of the United States and as a part of the law-making power of the United States I only look beyond, within the jurisdiction of the State, and see what the rights and privileges and immunities of citizens of the State generally are under the laws and constitution of the State. Then I say if there be a citizen of the United States within that jurisdiction who is deprived in any particular of his rights as a citizen of the State, under the laws of the State, I can, under the Constitution of the United States and as a part of the law-making power, invoke the authority of the United States, legislative, judicial, and executive, for the protection of that citizen in his just rights as a citizen of the State. The Government of the United States can take the humblest citizen in the State of Ohio who by the constitution or the laws of that State may be deprived of any right, privilege, or immunity that is conceded to the citizens of that State generally, and lift him to the dignity of equality as a citizen of that State; and all that is claimed under the fourth section of this bill is that you shall not, in the State of Ohio or in Massachusetts or in Maryland, say that a man shall not sit upon a jury because he is a black man or because he is of the German race or because he has been held in slavery, and I might say for other reasons. If for other reasons discriminations were made by the law of any of these States, we might under the fourteenth amendment protect men from such discriminations.

Therefore I do not yield to the Senator from Ohio in my respect for the constitution or the sovereign power of any State. What they have, that I will assert. What they are entitled to, that I will defend. What by the Constitution of the United States they can invoke, that I will help to protect; but I will at the same time invoke the power of the Government of the United States, under the Constitution of the United States, to protect the citizens of the United States in the several States in their equal rights under the laws and constitutions of the several States wherein they may reside.

OLIVER MORTON [R., IND.]. Mr. President, the fourth section of this bill does not establish any qualifications for jurors in the State courts. It makes no pretense of that kind. It leaves the States to fix those qualifications as they see proper. A State may provide that no man shall sit upon a jury who is not thirty years old, or if you please fifty years old. The State may provide that no man shall sit upon a jury who cannot read or write; that no man shall sit upon a jury who is not worth $500 or $5,000. The State is left perfectly free to fix the qualifications of jurors as she sees proper; but by this bill she is restrained from prohibiting any man from sitting upon a jury simply because of his race or color if he has all the other qualifications required by law. If the State requires a juror to be able to read and write, to have been a citizen of the State for two years, to be worth $1,000 in money, this bill would prevent that State from excluding a colored man from sitting upon a jury if he possessed all the other qualifications. That is the point. It does not assume to say who shall be a juror or what shall be his qualifications, but it does assume to say that if the colored man has all the qualifications to set upon a jury required of a white man, he shall not be excluded on account of his color.

Now, Mr. President, I want to call the attention of the Senator from Ohio to the fourteenth amendment, upon which he has commented. I will call his attention to the first section of that amendment and to the concluding clause of the first section.

Nor shall any State deprive any person of life, liberty, or property, without due process of law; nor deny to any person within its jurisdiction the equal protection of the laws.

I should like the distinguished Senator from Ohio to tell the Senate what is meant by the equal protection of the laws. No State shall deny to any person the equal protection of the laws. Does that simply mean that each man shall be equally protected or have an equal right to be protected from an assault and battery, from assassination? Is it confined to that? Not at all. It means in its broadest sense, it means in its true sense, that no State shall deny to any man the equal advantage of the law, the equal benefit of the law, the equal protection of the law. It means that all men shall be equals before the law, and that no man shall be denied on account of his race or color the equal advantage and benefit of the law. That is what it means. It cannot mean anything else.

Now I would like to submit to the judgment of this Senate and of the country this proposition: Whether the colored man enjoys the equal protection of the law, the equal benefit of the law, if colored men are not permitted to sit upon juries? Will any man pretend that where the right to sit upon juries is given exclusively to white men, the colored men of that State have the equal protection of the laws?. . .

MR. MORTON. Reverse the proposition and we should soon hear an outcry on the other side. There is the State of South Carolina with a large majority of colored men. Suppose that State should pass a law that no man should sit on a jury but a colored-man; that wherever a white man is arraigned for a crime or whose rights of property are undergoing investigation, that right shall be determined alone by a colored jury. Then we should find the white men of South Carolina coming up here and claiming the benefit of the fourteenth amendment. They would say they were denied the equal protection of the laws in the broadest sense; that they were to be tried by a race against whom they had prejudices and who had prejudices against them. They would claim that they could not be effectually protected by a colored jury. We know they would. They are crying out now even because colored men there are allowed equal rights. They are now crying aloud that they are not enjoying equal protection against colored men. But if white men were excluded from the jury in South Carolina, just as colored men are excluded from the juries in many Southern States, we know very well they would at once claim the benefit of the fourteenth amendment and say they were denied the equal protection of the laws.

Now, sir, here I put this bill upon a ground that is impregnable. No sophistry can answer it. The Senator from Ohio [Mr. Thurman] smiles. Let him tell the Senate first what is meant by "the equal protection of the laws." Let him then answer this question directly whether the colored race in any State would have the equal protection of the laws if they are to be tried exclusively for crime or to have their rights of property adjudicated by white men. Or reverse the case. Would the white race have the equal protection of the laws if all their rights were to be determined in courts of justice by colored men?

Mr. President, the trouble is that the rights of the colored men are not recognized by those who make this argument. They do not comprehend the spirit of these amendments. The fourteenth amendment was intended to place, and does place, men on an equality before the law. That is all. Whatever is the law for the white man must be the law for the colored man. Whatever is the law for the colored man must be equally the law for the white man. We do not say what that law shall be. The State may make the law as it seems proper; but whatever shall be the character of that law it must apply equally to all races upon the same precise conditions. . . .

MR. THURMAN. Mr. President, the Senator from Indiana had very truly said that his argument cannot be answered by sophistry. But it can be answered by reason, and answered so conclusively that even he must be compelled to admit that there is no soundness in it. If he will do me the honor to listen to me for a few minutes, I will convince even him that there is not one particle of foundation for the argument he has just made. He places his defense of this provision upon the last sentence of the first section of article 14, which says:

Nor shall any State . . . deny to any person within its jurisdiction the equal protection of the laws.

The Senator says that no class of persons receive equal protection of the laws if they are excluded from the jury-box. Now, the first thing that I have to say to that Senator is that not one woman in all the United States or the Territories thereof, outside of Wyoming Territory, is qualified to sit in a jury-box. Are they not equally protected? Do they not receive the protection of the laws? When did it come that our mothers and wives and sisters were deprived of the equal protection of the laws? But that is not all. Do not our children under the age of twenty-one years receive the equal protection of the law? Yet not one of them is qualified to sit in a jury-box. Again, this clause upon which the Senator relies covers other persons than citizens. It covers every person, alien as well as citizen. Let us see what it is:

No State shall . . . deny to any person within its jurisdiction the equal protection of the laws.

You shall not deny it to the alien; you shall not deny it to the Chinaman; you shall not deny it even to the Indian, though he be not taxed. You shall not deny it to any person within your jurisdiction, be he sane or be he insane, be he old or be he young, be he innocent or be he criminal, be he learned or be he ignorant. Every human being within the jurisdiction of the State shall be entitled to the equal protection of the laws; but is every human being in that State entitled to sit upon a jury? Do you deprive the minor of the equal protection of the law when you try his case by men of mature age? Do you deprive women of the equal protection of the laws when you try their cases by their brothers or husbands or fathers? Do you deprive the China-man of the equal protection of the laws when you try his case by citizens of the United States? Do you deprive the alien here in the District of Columbia of the equal protection of the laws when you try his case by the citizens of the United States and residents of this District? Does Ohio deprive anybody of the equal protection of the laws when she declares, as her statute does, that no man shall be a juryman unless he possesses the qualifications of an elector? Does that deprive all persons who are not electors of the equal protection of the laws? The idea which the Senator says no sane man can contest is simply, with great respect to him, without the slightest foundation. "The equal protection of the laws" is one thing; political privileges are another thing; and privileges to administer the laws of the land as judges, jurors, or in any other character are another and quite a different thing. "The equal protection of the laws" covers those laws which are designed for the protection of life, liberty, and property.

MR. MORTON. If the Senator—

MR. THURMAN. But now let me finish. I will convince the Senator out of his own mouth. The Senator says that it is perfectly competent for the States to require a property qualification for the jury-box. He says they may require a qualification of $5,000 of property; that they may require, as was formerly required in many of the States and in England, a freehold qualification. But I take the Senator's own illustration: they may require a property qualification of $5,000 in order to entitle a man to be a juror. If they can do that, what becomes of the Senator's argument? Are all men who do not own $5,000 worth of property deprived of the equal protection of the laws? I want the Senator to answer that question when he comes to reply. He says that any State, Louisiana, Mississippi, may establish a property qualification for jurors and put it as high as they please to put it, say to $5,000. That would exclude ninety-nine out of every hundred negro men there, or more than that; it would in effect exclude almost the whole colored race; it would make your provision in this bill not worth the paper upon which it is printed. But the Senator says that can be done. Then I ask him if all persons not owning $5,000 worth of property would be deprived of the equal protection of the laws?

Sir, it cannot be necessary to pursue this subject further. As I said before, the clause of the amendment which he reads has no relation to citizenship. It covers every human being within the jurisdiction of a State. It was intended to shield the foreigner, to shield the wayfarer, to shield the Indian, the Chinaman, every human being within the jurisdiction of a State from any deprivation of an equal protection of the laws; and the very fact that it embraces aliens, the very fact that it embraces the traveler passing through, shows that it has no relation whatsoever to qualifications for political office or to qualifications for the administration of justice in the courts. . . .

But my friend, chivalrous and bold as he is in defending the doctrine of inequality, falls back under the protection of the women. [Laughter.] He gets behind the ladies. That has always been the tactics. When they propose to deny a whole race, men and women, all civil and political rights, they will go and get behind a woman, and say "do women vote; do women sit on juries?" His proposition is that because the law denies to women of all races, black and white, the right to sit on the juries, therefore you have the right to deny both men and women of the colored race any right to participate in the courts of justice; and he makes that argument. It only requires that proposition to be stated in order that it may be decided. I am one of those who believe in the right of women to vote, and I have always believed in that; but because that right has been withheld from them, no argument can be made on that ground. But leaving that entirely out of view, if women are not allowed to sit upon juries, the men of their own race and color and of their own condition of life are allowed to sit upon juries and decide upon their rights of life, of liberty, and of property; but in this case that right is to be taken away from a whole race. White women are tried by white men, but colored women are to be tried by white men also and not by colored men. Is there any equality there, I ask the Senator? O, no. Mr. President, the time has come to put away all this jargon; it belongs to the past. My friend talks like a Rip Van Winkle who had been asleep twenty years. He talks the talk of twenty or thirty years ago, when the great body of the colored men in this country were slaves and were bought and sold like cattle in the market, and when the prejudices of slavery extended all through the North even, and took from the colored men there in most of the States their civil rights. We have gone past that period; thank God we have outlived it; and now there is no slave to walk the soil of this whole country. We have a constitutional amendment that makes all men equal before the law. It does not make them all equal in point of intellect, in point of property, in point of education, but they have equal rights before the law. They have the same right to struggle, they have the same right to get rich, and they have the same right to hold office; they have the same right to become the rulers of the land, provided they have the talent, the industry, and the character to obtain these things. That is what we mean by equality before the law. I do not know of a greater oppression than that here aimed. Why, how important is it in the Southern States, how important is it in those States where slavery recently existed and where its traces still remain and where the education and the feelings and the passions of slavery still remain, to establish this great right, that no man shall be excluded from the jury because of his color if he is otherwise qualified. If he has the qualifications the law requires of white men, then give him the right to sit upon the jury the same as white men.

But my friend from Ohio thought his protection in getting behind the women was not sufficient, and so he got behind the children. [Laughter.] Why he says you do not allow children to vote; you do not allow these pages to vote, and therefore you should exclude a whole race. Because you do not allow a boy ten years old to vote you ought to exclude a colored man fifty years old from voting. That is the argument. That is the force of his logic. Because you exclude infants from the right to go to the polls or sit in the jury-box therefore you must exclude a whole race of adults, of men who have arrived at mature age, from the enjoyment of the plainest common rights. That is the kind of logic which defends their great wrongs and these inequalities. It is the logic of prejudice. . . .

MR. THURMAN. Mr. President, when I was a boy at school we had an old Scotch professor of logic who was very exigent in his rule that we should reason fairly and logically, and very severe upon any one who departed from true logical reasoning in the consideration of any subject. He was asked one day by one of the students who had found himself pinned by his adversary in a corner by the inexorable logic of the argument, "Professor, what must I do in this strait in which I find myself?" Said he, "My son, I do not know anything you can do but to declaim." [Laughter.] Now, I think that my friend from Indiana must have taken lessons from that same old professor, for when he found himself driven in a corner by inexorable logic, his answer is to make a stump speech. I submit to the Senator whether he has answered my reply at all.

What was his argument, his great discovery, that which superseded all that the Senator from Massachusetts [Mr. Boutwell] had said? It was that the last sentence of the first section of the fourteenth article of amendment declared that no State should deny to any person within its jurisdiction the equal protection of the laws. Obviously that relates not simply to classes, but to every individual. And then he asserted that if any individual was deprived of the right to sit in the jury-box, that deprived him of the equal protection of the laws. I asked him, "Are women deprived of the equal protection of the laws?" What was his answer to that question? Why, that the Senator from Ohio gets behind the women. That is the logical answer of the able Senator from Indiana! That is the logical answer of the leader of the republican party on this floor! That is a specimen of his ability to reason and to reason logically! I have only to remark upon that that I am in favor of giving the white women of this country as much protection of the laws as I give the colored man, and I am not in favor of giving him any more protection of the laws than I give to my wife, my sister, and my daughter. If the Senator calls that getting behind the women, then God grant that I may always have such an array before me.

But further, I showed to the Senator that this clause on which he relies applies to every human being within the jurisdiction of a State, to the alien, to the mere transitory traveler; and I asked him if they were not entitled and did not receive the equal protection of the laws although they could not sit in a jury-box. What answer does he make to that? He makes a speech against know-nothingism; and that is the answer of the distinguished Senator from Indiana.

Again, the Senator has admitted that a State might require a property qualification for a juror, and fixed the amount himself at $5,000. Then I asked him, if that could be lawfully done, where was the equal protection of the laws for the poor men of the country who have not $5,000 of property; and the Senator does not see fit to take any notice at all of that category in which he has placed himself; but he goes on and answers by making a great speech in favor of liberty to the colored race and a speech glorifying the results of the civil war in freeing the negro from the slavery under which he formerly groaned! That is the logical answer upon a constitutional question! That is the logical answer in interpreting the Constitution of the United States, and interpreting too a provision of the Constitution which makes not the slightest allusion to "race, color, or previous condition of servitude!"

There is not one word in this first section of the fourteenth amendment that has any relation to race, color, or previous condition of servitude; but the Senator goes out of the way, clear outside of that, and finding some evil as he supposes existing in the country, undertakes by the exhibition of that evil to change the fundamental law of the land. If we were to argue in that way, where would the Constitution of the United States be? Sir, there are other evils in this country beside those that he depicts. There are other people who suffer in this country beside the colored race; there is want, destitution, almost starvation, at many a hearth-stone beside those of the colored people. There are people without hearth-stones, without homes, literally like the birds of the air and the beasts of the field, without anything to shelter their heads or their naked forms, beside the people who are of the colored race. And if we are to interpret the Constitution by pictures of suffering, of destitution, or even of wrong, and change its plain letter and extend it to meet every want or necessity that may exist in the country, then, sir, you had better abolish it at once; then, sir, the limitations of a written constitution are not worth the paper upon which they are written. . . .

AUGUSTUS MERRIMON [DEM., N.C.]. Mr. President, the question involved in the present discussion is not one that can be settled by declamation or patriotic generalities. It is a dry question of constitutional law. It is not a question of political policy. The question is not whether negroes ought to be allowed to sit upon juries, or whether white men ought to be allowed exclusively to sit upon juries, or whether any class of people ought to be excluded from juries. The question is, has the Government of the United States any power to regulate the right and authority of the States to determine who shall sit upon juries in the State courts. That is the question.

In my opinion Congress has no power to pass such a law as that provided here, and I maintain that the considerations submitted by the Senator from Indiana [Mr. Morton] do not even tend to establish the right of the Federal Government to exercise such a power. The substance, the gist of the argument he submits is, that there is a prejudice in the minds of the white people of the South and indeed of the whole country against the black people, and if a State shall undertake to exclude the black people from sitting upon juries, therefore the black man cannot have the equal protection of the laws, he is not a citizen under the Constitution of the United States, nor is he a citizen under the constitutions of the several States. He maintains that in order to have full and free citizenship a negro must have the right to sit upon juries in the courts of the several States. That I deny.

To sit upon a jury is not a civil right, in a technical sense, any more than to hold an office is a civil right. It is not a civil right of all men under the Constitution of the United States or of the several States to hold office. The rights of life, liberty, and property, and to have these protected by law and all lawful authorities, are civil rights.

But then the Senator asks, will it be pretended if juries are composed exclusively of white men that the colored people of the South have the equal protection of the laws? I answer without hesitation, "yes." What is meant by "the equal protection of the laws" is this: That whoever administers the law through the courts or anywhere else must administer it to all people without distinction for any case, according to the constitution and laws of the State where he does administer it. It is no matter whether the officer is a white man or a black man, he is bound to administer it fairly to every man, woman, and child, of every race and color, of every condition in life; and when the law is so administered by the judge or by the jury or by the other officer, whatever kind of officer he may be, that the persons to whom he administers have the equal protection of the law in the sense of the Constitution.

The Senator puts this case: He says suppose in South Carolina, where the colored race have the majority and can control, the Legislature should see fit to pass a law providing that none but negroes should sit on the juries, would there not be a great outcry on the part of the white people? I admit that there would be a great outcry in that case, and there ought to be. I think it would be a great outrage, because the white people are the more intelligent race and they are better qualified to administer the law or power. But if the Senator asks me whether they have power to do so, I answer yes, they have such power. They have the constitutional power to do it. They have not probably the moral right to do it; but they have the constitutional power to do it. Why? Because the right to sit in the jury-box is a political right; it is of that class of rights deemed political, it is in aid of the general administration of the Government. . . .

I maintain that Congress has no power to abridge this right of the States, and I do it because there is no limitation imposed upon the power of a State in this regard in the fourteenth or fifteenth articles of amendment or any other article of the Constitution. The substance and effect of the fourteenth article is that every citizen, and not only every citizen but every human being within the Union, within a State of the Union, shall have the equal protection of the laws. That I admit; that is true. But it is not meant by that that he shall necessarily be a juror, that he shall necessarily be a governor, that he shall be a member of the Legislature, that he shall be a member of Congress, or that he shall be President. It means that whoever administers the laws through the political instrumentalities of the Government, in administering the laws shall give him that equal protection for his life, his liberty, and property which every man is entitled to; and if the judge is a negro, he is bound because he is a judge—not because he is a negro—if I should be brought before him to be tried in the matter of my life, liberty, or property, to administer the law to me just as he would to one of his own color or any other color. That is the right view of it and no other view of it can be taken and maintained in law and reason. This, it seems to me, is the plain meaning of the Constitution upon its face. I may add that every judicial exposition of that instrument sustains this reasonable view.

THE PRESIDENT PRO TEMPORE. Mr. President, at the last session of Congress I voted against a bill similar to the civil-rights bill now under consideration. After thoroughly reconsidering the subject I am compelled to vote against this bill also; and, considering its importance, politically and otherwise, I am not willing at this time, just as I am to leave the Senate, to record my vote against a bill which is supported by so many of my political associates, without also putting upon the record the reasons that compel me to give that vote. I shall do this very briefly and rather in the form of an opinion than an argument. I shall make no attempt to inflame passions or antagonize anybody's arguments beyond a statement, as clear and brief as I can make it, of the reasons which compel me to vote against this bill.

I entertain, as strongly as any Senator, the sentiments which have inspired this bill; and in the present unhappy condition of the South, I would go to the extreme limit of our constitutional power to support any bill calculated to protect the colored people of the South or to restore order in that distracted section. But I cannot go beyond the limits of the Constitution. . . .

The pervading philosophy of our institutions is that liberty can only be protected against the tendency of Government to encroach upon the rights of the people by a distribution of powers. Therefore certain powers are conferred upon the United States, and all others are reserved to the States; and the powers of the Union and of the States are subdivided and distributed among the several departments of which the respective governments are composed. A citizen of the Union residing in a State owes a double allegiance and is entitled to the protection of both governments. As a citizen of the United States he owes them certain duties, and is entitled to claim from them protection of the rights and privileges which pertain to him in his character as a citizen of the Union. He also owes duties to the State, and is entitled to its protection as regards the rights and privileges which pertain to him as a citizen of the State. For instance, a citizen of the United States engaged in foreign commerce, or in commerce among the several States, or with the Indian tribes, is entitled, as respects that business, to the protection and subject to the control of the United States; while a citizen engaged in commerce between two places in a State is in that behalf entirely beyond the power of Congress, but is subject to the power of the State and entitled to its protection.

One provision of this bill declares that certain persons shall be entitled to equal accommodations and facilities of public conveyance on land or water. This might be sustained as a regulation of commerce if confined to that commerce over which Congress possesses the power of regulation—commerce with foreign nations, among the several States, or with the Indian tribes. But the bill does not purport to be a regulation of the particular branches of commerce over which Congress has control. It applies to every person or corporation engaged in transportation from point to point within a State as well as to those engaged in transportation among the several States.

It is well settled that no act of Congress can be valid under the Constitution unless it can fairly be referred to some head of Federal jurisdiction. For instance, in regulating commerce among the States, Congress might provide that every person engaged in such commerce should be entitled to the accommodation of inns in the several States through which he might pass in the prosecution of his business; and perhaps, upon the theory that a cheerful mind is favorable to enterprise, might provide that he should be admitted to theaters and other places of public amusement in the States wherein he might be temporarily sojourning during the transaction of his business. Such provision in regard to theaters would be somewhat fantastic as a regulation of commerce; and yet, if Congress saw fit so to provide, such provision might be sustained as relating to a subject over which Congress has jurisdiction.

But the bill under consideration does not rest upon this ground, because its provisions are not confined to persons engaged in such commerce.

It becomes necessary, therefore, in order to maintain the constitutionality of this bill, to select some other head of Federal jurisdiction to which it may fairly be referred. And I understand that its constitutionality is maintained upon the ground that it is within the powers conferred upon Congress by the fourteenth amendment of the Constitution.

This amendment provides:

1. All persons born or naturalized in the United States, and subject to the jurisdiction thereof, are citizens of the United States and of the State wherein they reside.
2. No State shall make or enforce any law which shall abridge the privileges or immunities of citizens of the United States.
3. Nor shall any State deprive any person of life, liberty, or property without due process of law.
4. Nor deny to any person within its jurisdiction the equal protection of the laws.

These are the only provisions of the fourteenth amendment which are claimed by any one to justify this bill.

It is manifest that the fourth clause, that "no State shall deny to any person within its jurisdiction the equal protection of the laws," has no application to this subject, especially to the jury clause of this bill. It is equally evident that the third clause, "not shall any State deprive any person of life, liberty, or property without due process of law," has no such application.

This is evident from the fact that women and infants are citizens of the United States, and the fact that they are excluded from serving as jurors in every State in the Union, and the fact that no one pretends or claims that, in consequence of such ineligibility, they are deprived of life, liberty, or property, or of the equal protection of the laws. If the ground maintained yesterday by the Senator from Indiana [Mr. Morton] that these provisions of the fourteenth amendment require that colored persons should be eligible to serve as jurors in State courts is correct, then this bill ought to be so amended as to provide that women and babes at the breast should be so eligible; because they are *persons* equally with colored citizens entitled under these two clauses of the amendment to everything secured to colored citizens.

If this bill can be maintained at all, it must be under the second clause:

No state shall make or enforce any law which shall abridge the privileges or immunities of citizens of the United States.

The phraseology of this section of the amendment merits critical examination. It provides that:

All persons born or naturalized in the United States, and subject to the jurisdiction thereof, are citizens of the United States *and of the State wherein they reside.*

The phraseology of the next clause is essentially different:

No State shall make or enforce any law which shall abridge the privileges or immunities of *citizens of the United States.*

It will be seen that this amendment does not, in words, forbid States to abridge the privileges or immunities of citizens of the State. To make the two clauses equally comprehensive, the latter should read thus: No State shall make or enforce any law which shall abridge the privileges or immunities of citizens of the United States, *or of such State.* But the words "or of such State" are not found in the second clause, and the variation in phraseology is so material that it must be considered intentional. Therefore it has been declared that the privileges and immunities which a State may not abridge are those which pertain to citizens of the United States *as such.*

In 16 Wallace's Reports, page 74, the Supreme Court of the United States declare that the distinction between citizenship of the United States and citizenship of a State is clearly recognized and established by this amendment; and that the rights which belong to a citizen of the United States, as such, are protected by this amendment; while the rights of the same person, which pertain to him in virtue of his State citizenship, are not protected by the amendment, but remain under the protection and control of the State government only. The language of the court is:

Of the privileges and immunities of the citizen of the United States, and of the privileges and immunities of the citizen of the State, and what they respectively are, we will presently consider; but we wish to state here that it is only the former which are placed by this clause under the protection of the Federal Constitution, and that the latter, whatever they may be, are not intended to have any additional protection by this paragraph of the amendment. If, then, there is a difference between the privileges and immunities belonging to a citizen of the United States as such, and those belonging to the citizen of the State as such, the latter must rest for their security and protection where they have heretofore rested; for they are not embraced by this paragraph of the amendment.

The court also say that with a few exceptions, such, for instance, as the prohibition against *ex post facto* laws, bills of attainder, and laws impairing the obligation of contracts, "the *entire domain* of the privileges and immunities of citizens of the States, as above defined, lies within the constitutional and legislative powers of the States, and *without* that of the Federal Government;" and the court hold that the fourteenth amendment makes no alteration in this particular.

Whether the opinion of the Supreme Court construing the Constitution be binding upon the other departments of the Government, is a question which has been much discussed. On one side it has been claimed that the Supreme Court is the authoritative expounder of the Constitution; and that what they hold it to be it is. On the other side it has been said that Congress and the Executive are equally entitled to construe the Constitution in regard to matters falling within their respective jurisdictions; and that the three departments being co-ordinate the court can no more bind Congress or the Executive, than Congress or the Executive can bind the court. But it is admitted on all hands that the Supreme Court, acting upon matters within its jurisdiction, that is, when determining causes, is supreme, and that all inferior courts of the Union are bound to observe its decisions.

I need not remark upon this difference in theory, because, conceding that Congress may pass a law and provide for its execution without the aid of the courts—where it can be so executed—which law the courts would hold to be unconstitutional; as for instance if the Supreme Court should decide that Congress had no power to appropriate money to carry on internal improvements, Congress might appropriate money and appoint the agents for administering the funds; yet this bill looks to the courts for its enforcement, and in the nature of things could provide no other instrumentality for its execution. Therefore this bill, should it pass through all the forms of enactment, would be a dead letter unless the rights it is intended to vindicate pertain to Federal citizenship as distinguished from those which pertain to citizenship of a State.

Let us examine this bill with reference to this principle established by the highest judicial tribunal of the Union.

This bill is entitled

An act to protect all *citizens* in their civil and legal rights.

But the first section provides, not that all *citizens*, but ——

That *all persons within the jurisdiction of the United States* shall be entitled to the full and equal enjoyment of the accommodations, advantages, facilities, and privileges of inns, public conveyances on land or water, theaters, and other places of public amusement; subject only to the conditions and limitations established by law, and applicable alike to citizens of every race and color, regardless of any previous condition of servitude.

If the phrase "*within* the jurisdiction of the United States" means the same thing as "*subject* to the jurisdiction of the United States," then the bill does not provide for Indians living in tribal relations with the United States, but does provide for stray bands of savages, not living in tribal relations, Chinamen, and all unnaturalized foreigners found within the United States.

Now, if it were admitted that Congress might provide that all citizens of the United States should be entertained at inns and amused at theaters, upon what ground can Congress justify entering within the lines of a State to provide for the entertainment and recreation of persons who are neither citizens of the United States nor of the State? And still more difficult must it be to maintain that the right which this act is intended to protect is a right which pertains to citizenship of the United States, when the person whose right is protected is not a citizen of the United States. But, according to the decision of the Supreme Court, no right can be protected by act of Congress except a right which pertains to a citizen of the United States *as such citizen*. And hence it follows that an attempt on the part of Congress to make such a provision on behalf of stray bands of savages and unnaturalized foreigners, as this bill attempts, is without any constitutional warrant whatever.

But, passing the objection as to the persons intended to be benefited, let the rights which are intended to be secured by this bill be examined with a view to determine whether they are rights belonging to the individual in his character as citizen of the United States as distinguished from his rights as a citizen of a State.

The first provision relates to inns, and includes every case in which any citizen of New York, for instance, shall apply for accommodations at an inn in that State. As before remarked, it may be that under the power to regulate commerce among the several States Congress might provide that a citizen going from one State into another, in the prosecution of commerce, should, while so engaged, be entertained in the inns of the latter State. But suppose a citizen of New York, residing in Albany, goes to New York city to buy goods to be shipped to him at Albany. In doing so he is engaged in commerce wholly within that State. Can it be said that he is so engaged in virtue of his citizenship of the United States? Over such commerce Congress has no control; and in prosecuting such commerce it would seem that such person would be exercising no right other than pertains to citizens of that State.

Take the case of theaters; and suppose a citizen of the State of New York, residing in the city of New York, applies for admission into a theater of that city. In doing so is he exercising a right which pertains to him as a citizen of the United States, as contradistinguished from his rights as a citizen of the State of New York?

As to common carriers, as I have before said, the provisions of this bill might be sustained, if confined to persons engaged in such commerce as is subject to the jurisdiction of Congress. But it is manifest that the provisions of the bill are not so restricted. The bill covers a case of transportation between New York and Albany as well as a case of transportation between New Orleans and New York. And the bill is clearly void as to all interstate transportation of persons and freight.

The fourth section of the bill is as follows:

SEC. 4. That no citizen possessing all other qualifications which are or may be prescribed by law shall be disqualified for service as grand or petit juror in any court of the United States, *or of any State,* on account of race, color, or previous condition of servitude; and any officer or other person charged with any duty in the selection or summoning of jurors who shall exclude or fail to summon any citizen for the causes aforesaid shall, on conviction thereof, be deemed guilty of a misdemeanor, and be fined not more than $5,000.

There is no doubt of the power of Congress to provide who shall be eligible to serve as jurors in a Federal court, and it has already declared that colored men shall be so eligible. But has Congress power to provide who shall be eligible to serve as jurors in a State court? Let it be borne in mind that it is not the object of this provision to secure to citizens of the United States a right of trial before a jury constituted in a particular way; but to secure to citizens of the United States the right to serve as jurors in a *State* court in the trial of citizens or inhabitants of a State. The Supreme Court of the United States, in 16 Wallace's Reports, page 138, decided that a citizen of the United States, as such, was not entitled to practice as an attorney in courts of a State. And speaking of the fourteenth amendment as affecting this question, the court say:

> In regard to that amendment, counsel for the plaintiff in this court truly says that there are certain privileges and immunities which belong to a citizen of the United States as such; otherwise it would be nonsense for the fourteenth amendment to prohibit a State from abridging them; and he proceeds to argue that admission to the bar of a State of a person who possesses the requisite learning and character is one of those rights which a State may not deny. In this latter proposition we are not able to concur with counsel. We agree with him that there are privileges and immunities belonging to citizens of the United States in that relation and character, and that it is these and these alone which a State is forbidden to abridge. But the right to admission to practice in *the courts of a State* is not one of these. This right in no sense depends upon citizenship of the United States.
>
> But on whatever basis this right may be placed, so far as it can have any relation to citizenship at all, it would seem that, as to the courts of a State, it would relate to *citizenship of the State,* and as to Federal courts it would relate to citizenship of the United States.

If it be not a right of a citizen of the United States as such to be admitted to practice law in a State court, which is a mere profession and occupation practiced for his own personal profit, involving no official connection with the Government beyond subordination to the orders and discipline of the court, upon what ground can it be maintained that it is the right of a citizen of the United States as such to sit in a *jury of a State court*? Juries in State courts perform a most important function in the administration of justice by the State government.

It will be seen that the decision to which I have referred goes far beyond what I am claiming here, because this was the case of a person applying merely to practice law, that is, to exercise and practice his vocation and calling. I argued that case for the applicant, and I attempted to establish the proposition that the Constitution of the United States guaranteed to them the right to practice all lawful professions, and therefore an attorney being a citizen of the United States might claim that privilege as a citizen of the United States everywhere; but the court, as courts sometimes do, rejected the argument which I urged upon them.

If the right to serve as juror in the courts of the State of Massachusetts, for instance, were a right which pertained to a citizen of the United States, as such, then it would follow that a citizen of the United States residing in the State of New York or California would have as much right to serve as a juror in the courts of Massachusetts as a citizen of the United States residing in that State.

Whatever right is inherent in the citizen of the United States as such he carries with him, without regard to State lines; he has the same right in California and in New York. Every right which pertains to citizenship of the Union may be exercised throughout the Union; and yet it would not be pretended that a citizen residing in California had any right to serve in a jury in the State of Massachusetts. And the fact that Massachusetts has a right to require that her jurors shall be of her own citizens shows that such service pertains to citizenship of that State, and not to citizenship of the United States. I presume no one will pretend that Congress could pass a law requiring the State of Massachusetts to select her jurymen from the whole body of citizens of the United States. And yet such law would be valid if the right to serve as a juror in Massachusetts were a right pertaining to a citizen of the United States as such.

The Senator from Indiana [Mr. Morton] maintains that a person would be denied the equal protection of the laws if he were denied the right to serve on a jury. If excluding a person from the administration of justice be a denial to him of the equal protection of the laws, as that Senator claims, would not the same consequence follow from his exclusion from the Legislature which makes the laws and from the bench which construes them? It must be "every person," because the clause which he refers to is not confined to "citizens." It relates to any person. A roaming vagabond Indian, John Chinaman in his wooden shoes, an unnaturalized foreigner just landed on the dock in Boston, is "a person" protected by that provision in the Constitution to which the Senator referred; and the Senator from Ohio [Mr. Thurman] suggests convicts in the penitentiary are also persons; but they are pretty well protected as a general thing. [Laughter.]

And if the Senator's argument establishes the right of every person in the State to serve as a juror, is it not manifest that it also establishes his right to participate in making and construing the laws? And yet it is well known that in proposing the fifteenth amendment, which secures to every citizen the right to vote, Congress purposely excluded the right to hold office. The Senator from Indiana maintains that no man enjoys the protection of the laws unless he be allowed to serve as a juror.

MR. MORTON. The Senator will allow me to say I made no such statement—

THE PRESIDENT PRO TEMPORE. Will the Senator wait until I get through, and then I will answer any question.

MR. MORTON. Very well.

THE PRESIDENT PRO TEMPORE. I can conceive of no argument based upon the fourteenth amendment establishing the right to serve as a juror which does not also establish the right to serve in the Legislature and hold any State office. And this, in view of the fifteenth amendment, must be regarded as a perfect *reductio ad absurdum*.

If the States do not possess the power of determining who shall and who shall not participate in the exercise of this important State function, then it must be admitted that the States may be interfered with in an important particular in the exercise of their conceded powers.

No one will deny that to-day, after all the amendments, a State has a right to administer justice, according to her own constitution and laws, in obedience to the Constitution of the United States, in her own courts. This is her prerogative. The States cannot interfere with the exercise of Federal functions, by taxing the instrumentalities or officers of the General Government without its consent or in any other manner; and hence it follows that the United States cannot interfere with the States in the exercise of *their* functions. In accordance with this principle it was decided by the Supreme Court, in 11 Wallace's Reports, page 113, that Congress could not impose a tax upon the salary of a judicial officer of a State.

It seems to be clear from the decision of the Supreme Court in 16 Wallace's Reports, page 138, that the right of any person to serve as a juror in a State court is a right which pertains to him in his character of State citizenship, and does not belong to him as a citizen of the United States.

It results, therefore, that all of the provisions of this bill are in conflict with the Constitution of the United States as expounded by the Supreme Court. It may be said that these decisions are incorrect. If this were conceded, still it must be admitted that the decisions exist, and that they prescribe for the judicial department of the Government a rule which must be applied to this bill, and under which the courts must hold it to be invalid and void. And of what advantage can it be to the colored citizen to declare that he may bring a suit in which it is certain that he cannot recover; a suit which must be attended with vexation and expense, and result in defeat and disappointment?

Several years ago some humorous papers were published in this city, describing among other things the country residence of a gentleman of wealth and leisure. They described his magnificent mansion and floral garden on the banks of the Hudson, and the incident of his neighbor's hogs breaking into his garden and destroying everything. Intending to ridicule the technicalities of an old barrister, the writer relates that he consulted him in regard to this injury. He says:

I asked him if I could not maintain an action of replevin for the hogs in the circuit court of the United States. He replied, with great solemnity, that under the Constitution of the United States and the practice of the courts such an action could be commenced. I asked him if I could recover. He said I could not.

This bill is framed according to the advice thus given. The colored citizen is authorized to bring a suit in which everybody knows he cannot recover. The Supreme Court of the United States, in two well-considered decisions, have settled principles upon which the validity of this bill must be denied; and every circuit court in which a suit may be commenced under its provisions will be compelled in proper judicial subordination to rule against a recovery. Its only effect, therefore, will be to involve the colored man in litigation in which he is certain to be defeated; "keeping the promise to his ear, and breaking it to his hope."

From the consideration which I have briefly stated, I am compelled to vote against the bill. I can understand how an orator like the Senator from Indiana could inflame the passions of a popular assembly, and rally it to support the provisions of this bill; but I confess my astonishment and my sorrow that he can carry along with him the highest court of the land—the Senate of the United States—and pass this bill through all the forms of enactment. I am consoled, however, by the confidence that, if it shall become a law, the judicial courts will intervene to vindicate the Constitution.

MR. MORTON. I understood my friend to say that I took the position yesterday that under the fourteenth amendment every man was entitled to sit upon a jury, or, if not, he was denied the equal protection of the laws. I did not say that, nor did I intend to say it. What I said and that which I maintain is, that so far as the fourteenth amendment is concerned the States may prescribe whatever qualifications they choose for the right to sit upon a jury; they may require such qualifications as their constitutions may allow them to do; but they cannot require qualifications of one man which they deny to another; that if they say a man twenty-one years old, a voter, who has been a resident of the State for one year is qualified to sit upon a jury if he is a white man, they cannot deny that to a colored man having those qualifications. In other words, I say that whatever qualifications or restrictions are applicable to the one must be applicable to the other; that to give the exclusive right to white men to sit upon juries and to adjudicate upon the rights of colored men is denying to colored men the equal protection of the laws, because it is placing the adjudication of their rights exclusively in the hands of another race, filled with a prejudice and passion in many States that would prevent them from doing justice. . . . I understood my friend to say that I contended that to deny a man the right to sit upon a jury was a violation of the fourteenth amendment. I said no such thing. What I meant was that there must be an equality in that right; that if I was allowed to sit upon a jury, being of age, having lived in the State the requisite length of time, to deny that also to a colored man of the same age and having lived in the State the same length of time was to make an inequality before the law and was denying to him the equal protection of the laws. . . .

JOHN GORDON [DEM., GA.]. I wish to ask the Senator from Indiana a question. His argument, as I understand him, is based upon the supposition, or at least his argument is calculated to make the impression upon the country, that this discrimination against which he inveighs actually exists by law. I want to ask that Senator or any other what State in the South has passed such laws? Let him point to one law in any southern State which violates any provision of the fourteenth amendment. There is no law—and I say it without fear of successful contradiction—which denies any race the right to sit on juries or any other right that is accorded to any other race. So that even upon the supposition that the Congress could exercise this extraordinary supervision over juries of State courts, the Senator's argument is groundless.

JOHN PATTERSON [R., S.C.]. Will the Senator from Georgia allow me to ask him a question?

MR. GORDON. Certainly.

MR. PATTERSON. I should like to ask the Senator from Georgia if any colored men sit on juries in Georgia?

MR. GORDON. I will answer the Senator by saying that any colored man can sit upon a jury in Georgia who has the requisite intelligence and is upright. These are the only qualifications requisite for jurors under the laws of Georgia. If the Congress of the United States is to undertake to alter the customs of drawing jurors, then we are to discuss another proposition entirely. I am speaking now of the laws; and if I understand the provisions of the fourteenth amendment, that amendment inhibits any State from passing laws denying to any citizens of the United States the immunities and privileges which belong to other citizens of the United States. Whenever a State passes such laws—laws denying to one class of citizens rights which are guaranteed by the Constitution to any other class of citizens, and I do not now stop to inquire what rights and immunities are granted or guaranteed by the Constitution—then I admit that under the fifth section of the fourteenth amendment Congress may proceed by appropriate legislation to protect that class of citizens so denied against such discrimination. Until that law is passed, however—until by statute a State denies some right which belongs to all citizens of the United States as citizens, not of a State but of the United States—until this is done, I maintain that Congress has no power under the fourteenth amendment to interfere. A State must not only have denied immunities, but such immunities as belong to citizens of the United States as such. . . .

THOMAS TIPTON [DEM., NEB.]. In the sixth line of the first section I move to strike out "theaters" and insert "churches."

Mr. President, this bill proceeds upon the assumption that the public will demands this legislation; and will the honorable Senator who has charge of the bill, or any other Senator, say to the country that there is a public opinion demanding that if a man is refused on account of color the accommodations, whatever they may be, that they have at a theater, or the advantages that may result from going to a theater, or the facilities for doing things that they have at a theater, or the privileges of a theater, it is a damage of $500? Do his constituents put such an estimate as that upon the advantages and accommodations that are furnished at theaters that they call upon him to impose a fine of $500 upon any man who deprives another of the privileges and accommodations of a theater? The honorable Senator goes to his constituents and to the country upon the basis that there is a public clamor among the virtuous people of this country that there must be a penalty of $500 imposed in order to secure to the African the accommodations that are said to belong to a theater. That is all the sheerest bosh. No man can vote for that honestly on this floor or anywhere else.

I therefore move that the word "theaters" be stricken out and that the word "churches" be substituted, in order that the penalty of $500 shall fall upon the man who is driven away from a church, where it is supposed that all men stand equal before the divine law; and of course such a body as this intelligent, devoted Christian legislators will vote out the "theater" and vote in the "church."

RICHARD OGLESBY [R., ILL.]. I ask the Clerk to read the bill as it will stand if it shall be amended as proposed by the Senator from Nebraska.

THE VICE PRESIDENT, HENRY WILSON, [R., MASS.]. The section will be reported as it would look if amended.

THE SECRETARY. It is proposed in line 6 of section 1 to strike out the word "theaters" and insert "churches;" so that when amended that part of the section will read:

That all persons within the jurisdiction of the United States shall be entitled to the full and equal enjoyment of the accommodations, advantages, facilities, and privileges of inns, public conveyances on land or water, churches, and other places of public amusement. [Laughter.]

THE VICE PRESIDENT. The question is on the amendment of the Senator from Nebraska.

The amendment was rejected.

GEORGE EDMUNDS [R., VT.]. We shall have the yeas and nays of course.

I avail myself, Mr. President, of this opportunity to say a few words—of course I cannot go into the argument *in extenso*—in support of this measure. It has seemed to me, in listening to the debate upon this and other measures which have become necessary from the course of events since 1860, that a very extraordinary consistency of attitude has been maintained by our friends on the other side of the Chamber and their predecessors. There has been no measure either for repressing rebellion, carrying on the war, securing the fruits of the war, that has found any favor with that party; and so I am not surprised that when we come now in some measure—not a large measure I am sorry to say, not a full measure I am sorry to say—but in some measure to protect the fundamental rights of citizens of the United States under its Constitution, we find the same party occupying its same old attitude. . . .

There is no one thing which has been proposed, or which, I venture to say, can be proposed, to enforce these provisions of the Constitution that the Senators will not, with a solidarity that is absolutely perfect, say "the Constitution gives no warrant for that." There is no law that can be proposed to enforce these provisions in the Congress of the United States, although the Constitution itself says that Congress shall have power to enforce them, that meets with their approval, be it broad or narrow. Let it touch race or religion or sect or whatever, we shall be told when it is proposed, as we have been told when it has been proposed, "We cannot find anything in the Constitution that warrants our doing so, and we are careful not to say that there is any other interpretation or any other measure which Congress can pass to enforce the fundamental rights which have become a part of the Constitution of our country." No, Mr. President, and I say it with pain, the meaning of this, as I believe, is that there is intended to be what a democratic platform not many years ago said it was then designed to be, a period of reaction, and that we are to have, if they can accomplish it, the Union and the Constitution as they were, not as they are; and either by absence of legislation or in some other way there shall be no effectual life in any of these three amendments. . . .

Now, what does this bill propose to do. This bill that we have under consideration only proposes that if there are any fundamental rights in this Constitution they shall be secured by that power which the Constitution says shall take the measures to secure them, and that the Congress of the United States by legislation appropriate shall secure to every citizen in this land the rights which the Constitution gives him; and yet Senators say this is invading State rights; this is tryannical! Why, Mr. President, State rights justly considered, the real and the true rights of States can only be secured under and by the Constitution of the United States; and therefore, in my opinion, it is an invasion of State rights instead of an attack upon them to say that you will turn every State adrift and all its citizens be subject to the turmoil and the disturbance and the passion and the prejudice which may happen from time to time to exist in any particular State. There is no security for a State that is not found under this bond of union which the Constitution of the United States secures; there is no security to any citizen or a State, either under the State or under any other provision, that is not found fundamentally and in the first place in the fact that the whole family of these States have a common interest in his protection and in the protection of his State; and it was so in the first Constitution as it is in this.

The Constitution of the United States, as was stated in an opinion of the Supreme Court once by an eminent democratic judge, is a bill of rights for the people of all the States, and no State has a right to say you invade her rights when under this Constitution and according to it you have protected a right of her citizens against class prejudice, against caste prejudice, against sectarian prejudice, against the ten thousand things which in special communities may from time to time arise to disturb the peace and good order of the community. That is all this bill undertakes to do. Now let us see what this bill is.

That first section of it simply provides that all persons shall be entitled to certain common rights in public places, in the streets, if they were in—they are not in, but that illustrates it—that no State shall have a right and no person shall have a right to interrupt the common use by citizens of the United States of the streets of a town or city. Where is the authority for that, Senators ask; where is the authority for saying that a State shall not have a right to pass a law which shall declare that all citizens of the German race shall go upon the right-hand side of the streets and all citizens of French descent shall go upon the left, and so on, and that all people of a particular religion shall only occupy a particular quarter of the town, and all the people of another religion another side? Is it possible, with a national Constitution which creates fundamentally a national citizenship, that anybody can say a State has a right to make laws of that kind? I should be amazed to hear it stated. If that can be stated, then I should be glad to know what there is in being a citizen of the United States that is worth a man's time to devote himself to defend for a single instant.

What is it to be a citizen of the United States if being that the citizen cannot be protected in those fundamental privileges and immunities which inhere in the very nature of citizenship? And there is the fault into which my honorable friends on the other side have fallen in arguing this constitutional question. The question is not whether citizens of a particular character, either as to color or religion or race, shall exercise certain functions; but the question is the other way. It is that no citizen shall be deprived of whatever belongs to him in his character as a citizen; and what belongs to a man in his character as a citizen has been long in a great many respects well understood. There was the old Constitution, the fourth article, you remember, which said that citizens of each State should be entitled to the privileges and immunities of citizens of the several States. What did that mean? That has received judicial interpretation.

By common consent of all parties, before this gravest question arising out of the rebellion and the war has been forced upon us, the courts had held with universal acceptance, I believe, that there did belong to citizens certain inherent rights which could not be denied to them and that you could not, under the Constitution of the United States, either through State or other authority, set up distinctions which interfered with these fundamental privileges. Perfectly consistent with that, as everybody knows, you may say that in order to fulfill a certain function in the State or to hold a certain office all citizens alike must conform to certain qualifications. Your courts may say—a case which seems to have troubled my honorable friend from Wisconsin [Mr. Carpenter] very much—your courts may say, be they Federal or be they State, that in order to practice law every citizen must possess certain qualifications of sex, of age, of learning, or experience, or whatever; but what has that to do with the question? Unless you can say that it is a fundamental right of a citizen to be a lawyer, you do not get ahead in the argument at all; but yet every one who is acquainted with constitutional history knows that it never has been contended that a fundamental right of a citizen was to be a lawyer or a schoolmaster or a judge or a Senator. The only thing that the Constitution says is that there shall never be a distinction in respect to the rights which belong to a citizen in his inherent character as such. Now, what are those rights? Common rights as the common lawyers used to say, common rights as the courts of the United States have said under the fourth article. Among those may be enumerated—it may be that you cannot make a precise definition, but you can always tell, when you name an instance, whether it falls within it or without it—the right to go peaceably in the public streets, the right to enjoy the same privileges and immunities, without qualification and distinction upon arbitrary reasons, that exist in favor of all others. That is what it is. Then apply it to this bill, and what have you? You say it shall not be competent for any person, either under the authority of a State or without it, to exclude from modes of public travel persons on the ground that they have come from Germany, like my distinguished friend behind me, [Mr. Schurtz,] or that they have come from Ireland, as some other Senators here may have come, or that their descent is traced from Ham or Shem or Japhet. And yet Senators seem to be greatly alarmed when this simple proposition of common right inherent in everybody is put into a statute-book, which carries out a constitution which declares that every privilege and every immunity of an American citizen shall be scared and protected by the power of the nation. That is all there is to it; and those, therefore, who go fishing and talking dialectics about attorneys and about slaughter-house cases and police regulations find themselves entirely wide of the mark. The real thing, Mr. President, is that there lies in this Constitution, just as in *Magna Charta* and as in the bills of rights of all the States, a series of declarations that the rights of citizens shall not be invaded. These bills of rights do not say that A or B or C or any class shall hold an office or be a witness or a juryman or walk the streets. They only say that these common rights, which belong necessarily to all men alike in the reason of things, shall not be invaded on the pretense that a man is of a particular race or a particular religion. . . .

THE VICE PRESIDENT. The yeas and nays have been asked for on the passage of the bill.

The yeas and nays were ordered and taken. . . .

The result was announced—yeas 38, nays 26. . . .

So the bill was passed.

THE DECISIONS

Commentary

What the Congress giveth, the Supreme Court often taketh away. In the 1875 Civil Rights Act, Congress enacted a broad prohibition against racial discrimination in inns, public conveyances, theaters and other places of public amusement. In the 1883 *Civil Rights Cases,* the highest Court ruled that such prohibition was unconstitutional. The 1875 statute was based upon Section 5 of the Fourteenth Amendment, giving Congress power to enforce, by appropriate legislation, the amendment's provisions. The Court held that the enforcement section of the amendment, like the substantive provisions of the amendment itself, was limited to "state action" alone. Hence Congress could not, as it sought to do in the 1875 act, reach discriminatory action that was purely private in character and consequently not otherwise within the scope of the amendment. In the key words of Justice Joseph Bradley, "Individual invasion of individual rights is not the subject matter of the amendment."

The holding of the *Civil Rights Cases* is of fundamental importance. Taken together with the decision in the *Slaughter-House* cases (*supra* p. 335), it has significantly limited the reach of the Fourteenth Amendment. Under *Slaughter-House,* the privileges and immunities clause of the amendment's first section was held limited in its operation to rights derived from national citizenship alone; it did not cover the ordinary civil rights of the individual, which, as rights of state citizenship, were left to the states for protection. Under the *Civil Rights Cases*, the scope of the amendment's first section (and particularly its crucial equal protection clause) was limited to "state action"; neither that section nor congressional action taken under the enforcement power given by section five could validly reach discriminatory action by private individuals, such as the inn, carrier, and theater owners covered by the 1875 Civil Rights Act.

As already pointed out (*supra* p. 659), the decision in the *Civil Rights Cases* has given rise to a chorus of criticism which has grown sharply in intensity in recent years. The high bench has been severely condemned for "narrow, debilitating construction," which has all but read the Fourteenth Amendment out of the Constitution—at least when compared to the broadly beneficent intent of its framers. Such criticism is, however, unfair in its assumption that the interpretation of the amendment by the *Civil Rights Cases* was utterly unwarranted. On the contrary, even if one may not fully agree with the result reached by the Supreme Court decision, he should recognize that the Court's construction is one which, at the least, has a rational basis in the language of the Fourteenth Amendment. The key provisions of the amendment's first section provide that "No State" shall abridge the privileges and immunities of United States citizens; "nor shall any State" deprive any person of due process, nor deny equal protection. On its face, such language appears directed only to state, not individual, action— i.e., the very interpretation taken by the *Civil Rights Cases.*

Even more important is the fact that contemporary observers did not consider the *Civil Rights Cases* decision nearly as unwarranted as more recent critics. The legislative history of the 1875 Civil Rights Act, already given, shows clearly that a substantial number of legislators considered the statute unconstitutional for the very reason stated a decade later in the *Civil Rights Cases.* In addition, the Supreme Court decision itself was met with widespread approval by most of the country. Of course, the few abolitionists still alive protested. But the general consensus was expressed by as liberal a journal as the *Nation*, which declared that the country's approval of the decision showed "how completely the extravagant expectations as well as the fierce passions of the war have died out."

CIVIL RIGHTS CASES
109 U.S. 3 (1881)

MR. JUSTICE BRADLEY delivered the opinion of the Court. . . .

It is obvious that the primary and important question in all the cases is the constitutionality of the law: for if the law is unconstitutional none of the prosecutions can stand.

The sections of the law referred to provide as follows:

SEC. 1. That all persons within the jurisdiction of the United States shall be entitled to the full and equal enjoyment of the accommodations, advantages, facilities, and privileges of inns, public conveyances on land or water, theaters, and other places of public amusement; subject only to the conditions and limitations established by law, and applicable alike to citizens of every race and color, regardless of any previous condition of servitude.

SEC. 2. That any person who shall violate the foregoing section by denying to any citizen, except for reasons by law applicable to citizens of every race and color, and regardless of any previous condition of servitude, the full enjoyment of any of the accommodations, advantages, facilities, or privileges in said section enumerated, or by aiding or inciting such denial, shall for every such offence forfeit and pay the sum of five hundred dollars to the person aggrieved thereby, to be recovered in an action of debt, with full costs; and shall also, for every such offence, be deemed guilty of a misdemeanor, and, upon conviction thereof, shall be fined not less than five hundred nor more than one thousand dollars, or shall be imprisoned not less than thirty days nor more than one year: Provided, That all persons may elect to sue for the penalty aforesaid, or to proceed under their rights at common law and by State statutes; and having so elected to proceed in the one mode or the other, their right to proceed in the other jurisdiction shall be barred. But this provision shall not apply to criminal proceedings, either under this act or the criminal law of any State: And provided further, That a judgment for the penalty in favor of the party aggrieved, or a judgment upon an indictment, shall be a bar to either prosecution respectively.

Are these sections constitutional? The first section, which is the principal one, cannot be fairly understood without attending to the last clause, which qualifies the preceding part.

The essence of the law is, not to declare broadly that all persons shall be entitled to the full and equal enjoyment of the accommodations, advantages, facilities, and privileges of inns, public conveyances, and theatres; but that such enjoyment shall not be subject to any conditions applicable only to citizens of a particular race or color, or who had been in a previous condition of servitude. In other words, it is the purpose of the law to declare that, in the enjoyment of the accommodations and privileges of inns, public conveyances, theatres, and other places of public amusement, no distinction shall be made between citizens of different race or color, or between those who have, and those who have not, been slaves. Its effect is to declare, that in all inns, public conveyances, and places of amusement, colored citizens, whether formerly slaves or not, and citizens of other races, shall have the same accommodations and privileges in all inns, public conveyances, and places of amusement as are enjoyed by white citizens; and *vice versa*. The second section makes it a penal offence in any person to deny to any citizen of any race or color, regardless of previous servitude, any of the accommodations or privileges mentioned in the first section.

Has Congress constitutional power to make such a law? Of course, no one will contend that the power to pass it was contained in the Constitution before the adoption of the last three amendments. The power is sought, first, in the Fourteenth Amendment, and the views and arguments of distinguished Senators, advanced whilst the law was under consideration, claiming authority to pass it by virtue of that amendment, are the principal arguments adduced in favor of the power. We have carefully considered those arguments, as was due to the eminent ability of those who put them forward, and have felt, in all its force, the weight of authority which always invests a law that Congress deems itself competent to pass. But the responsibility of an independent judgment is now thrown upon this court; and we are bound to exercise it according to the best lights we have.

The first section of the Fourteenth Amendment (which is the one relied on), after declaring who shall be citizens of the United States, and of the several States, is prohibitory in its character, and prohibitory upon the States. It declares that:

No State shall make or enforce any law which shall abridge the privileges or immunities of citizens of the United States; nor shall any State deprive any person of life, liberty, or property without due process of law; nor deny to any person within its jurisdiction the equal protection of the laws.

It is State action of a particular character that is prohibited. Individual invasion of individual rights is not the subject-matter of the amendment. It has a deeper and broader scope. It nullifies and makes void all State legislation, and State action of every kind, which impairs the privileges and immunities of citizens of the United States, or which injures them in life, liberty or property without due process of law, or which denies to any of them the equal protection of the laws. It not only does this, but, in order that the national will, thus declared, may not be a mere *brutum fulmen*, the last section of the amendment invests Congress with power to enforce it by appropriate legislation. To enforce what? To enforce the prohibition. To adopt appropriate legislation for correcting the effects of such prohibited State laws and State acts, and thus to render them effectually null, void, and innocuous. This is the legislative power conferred upon Congress, and this is the whole of it. It does not invest Congress with power to legislate upon subjects which are within the domain of State legislation; but to provide modes of relief against State legislation, or State action, of the kind referred to. It does not authorize Congress to create a code of municipal law for the regulation of private rights; but to provide modes of redress against the operation of State laws, and the action of State officers executive or judicial, when these are subversive of the fundamental rights specified in the amendment. Positive rights and privileges are undoubtedly secured by the Fourteenth Amendment; but they are secured by way of prohibition against State laws and State proceedings affecting those rights and privileges, and by power given to Congress to legislate for the purpose of carrying such prohibition into effect: and such legislation must necessarily be predicated upon such supposed State laws or State proceedings, and be directed to the correction of their operation and effect. . . .

Until some State law has been passed, or some State action through its officers or agents has been taken, adverse to the rights of citizens sought to be protected by the Fourteenth Amendment, no legislation of the United States under said amendment, nor any proceeding under such legislation, can be called into activity: for the prohibitions of the amendment are against State laws and acts done under State authority. Of course, legislation may, and should be, provided in advance to meet the exigency when it arises; but it should be adapted to the mischief and wrong which the amendment was intended to provide against; and that is, State laws, or State action of some kind, adverse to the rights of the citizen secured by the amendment. Such legislation cannot properly cover the whole domain of rights appertaining to life, liberty and property, defining them and providing for their vindication. That would be to establish a code of municipal law regulative of all private rights between man and man in society. It would be to make Congress take the place of the State legislatures and to supersede them. It is absurd to affirm that, because the rights of life, liberty and property (which include all civil rights that men have), are by the amendment sought to be protected against invasion on the part of the State without due process of law, Congress may therefore provide due process of law for their vindication in every case; and that, because the denial by a State to any persons, of the equal protection of the laws, is prohibited by the amendment, therefore Congress may establish laws for their equal protection. In fine, the legislation which Congress is authorized to adopt in this behalf is not general legislation upon the rights of the citizen, but corrective legislation, that is, such as may be necessary and proper for counteracting such laws as the States may adopt or enforce, and which, by the amendment, they are prohibited from making or enforcing, or such acts and proceedings as the States may commit or take, and which, by the amendment, they are prohibited from committing or taking. It is not necessary for us to state, if we could, what legislation would be proper for Congress to adopt. It is sufficient for us to examine whether the law in question is of that character.

An inspection of the law shows that it makes no reference whatever to any supposed or apprehended violation of the Fourteenth Amendment on the part of the States. It is not predicated on any such view. It proceeds *ex directo* to declare that certain acts committed by individuals shall be deemed offences, and shall be prosecuted and punished by proceedings in the courts of the United States. It does not profess to be corrective of any constitutional wrong committed by the States; it does not make its operation to depend upon any such wrong committed. It applies equally to cases arising in States which have the justest laws respecting the personal rights of citizens, and whose authorities are ever ready to enforce such laws, as to those which arise in States that may have violated the prohibition of the amendment. In other words, it steps into the domain of local jurisprudence, and lays down rules for the conduct of individuals in society towards each other, and imposes sanctions for the enforcement of those rules, without referring in any manner to any supposed action of the State or its authorities.

If this legislation is appropriate for enforcing the prohibitions of the amendment, it is difficult to see where it is to stop. Why may not Congress with equal show of authority enact a code of laws for the enforcement and vindication of all rights of life, liberty, and property? If it is supposable that the States may deprive persons of life, liberty, and property without due process of law (and the amendment itself does suppose this), why should not Congress proceed at once to prescribe due process of law for the protection of every one of these fundamental rights, in every possible case, as well as to prescribe equal privileges in inns, public conveyances, and theatres? The truth is, that the implication of a power to legislate in this manner is based upon the assumption that if the States are forbidden to legislate or act in a particular way on a particular subject, and power is conferred upon Congress to enforce the prohibition, this gives Congress power to legislate generally upon that subject, and not merely power to provide modes of redress against such State legislation or action. The assumption is certainly unsound. It is repugnant to the Tenth Amendment of the Constitution, which declares that powers not delegated to the United States by the Constitution, nor prohibited by it to the States, are reserved to the States respectively or to the people. . . .

In this connection it is proper to state that civil rights, such as are guaranteed by the Constitution against State aggression, cannot be impaired by the wrongful acts of individuals, unsupported by State authority in the shape of laws, customs, or judicial or executive proceedings. The wrongful act of an individual, unsupported by any such authority, is simply a private wrong, or a crime of that individual; an invasion of the rights of the injured party, it is true, whether they affect his person, his property, or his reputation; but if not sanctioned in some way by the State, or not done under State authority, his rights remain in full force, and may presumably be vindicated by resort to the laws of the State for redress. An individual cannot deprive a man of his right to vote, to hold property, to buy and sell, to sue in the courts, or to be a witness or a juror; he may, by force or fraud, interfere with the enjoyment of the right in a particular case; he may commit an assault against the person, or commit murder, or use ruffian violence at the polls, or slander the good name of a fellow citizen; but, unless protected in these wrongful acts by some shield of State law or State authority, he cannot destroy or injure the right; he will only render himself amenable to satisfaction or punishment; and amenable therefor to the laws of the State where the wrongful acts are committed. Hence, in all those cases where the Constitution seeks to protect the rights of the citizen against discriminative and unjust laws of the State by prohibiting such laws, it is not individual offences, but abrogation and denial of rights, which it denounces, and for which it clothes the Congress with power to provide a remedy. This abrogation and denial of rights, for which the States alone were or could be responsible, was the great seminal and fundamental wrong which was intended to be remedied. And the remedy to be provided must necessarily be predicated upon that wrong. It must assume that in the cases provided for, the evil or wrong actually committed rests upon some State law or State authority for its excuse and perpetration.

Of course, these remarks do not apply to those cases in which Congress is clothed with direct and plenary powers of legislation over the whole subject, accompanied with an express or implied denial of such power to the States, as in the regulation of commerce with foreign nations, among the several States, and with the Indian tribes, the coining of money, the establishment of post offices and post roads, the declaring of war, etc. In these cases Congress has power to pass laws for regulating the subjects specified in every detail, and the conduct and transactions of individuals in respect thereof. But where a subject is not submitted to the general legislative power of Congress, but is only submitted thereto for the purpose of rendering effective some prohibition against particular State legislation or State action in reference to that subject, the power given is limited by its object, and any legislation by Congress in the matter must necessarily be corrective in its character, adapted to counteract and redress the operation of such prohibited State laws or proceedings of State officers.

If the principles of interpretation which we have laid down are correct, as we deem them to be (and they are in accord with the principles laid down in the cases before referred to, as well as in the recent case of *United States* v. *Harris,* 106 U.S. 629), it is clear that the law in question cannot be sustained by any grant of legislative power made to Congress by the Fourteenth Amendment. That amendment prohibits the States from denying to any person the equal protection of the laws, and declares that Congress shall have power to enforce, by appropriate legislation, the provisions of the amendment. The law in question, without any reference to adverse State legislation on the subject, declares that all persons shall be entitled to equal accommodations and privileges of inns, public conveyances, and places of public amusement, and imposes a penalty upon any individual who shall deny to any citizen such equal accommodations and privileges. This is not corrective legislation; it is primary and direct; it takes immediate and absolute possession of the subject of the right of admission to inns, public conveyances, and places of amusement. It supersedes and displaces State legislation on the same subject, or only allows it permissive force. It ignores such legislation, and assumes that the matter is one that belongs to the domain of national regulation. Whether it would not have been a more effective protection of the rights of citizens to have clothed Congress with plenary power over the whole subject, is not now the question. What we have to decide is, whether such plenary power has been conferred upon Congress by the Fourteenth Amendment; and, in our judgment, it has not. . . .

But the power of Congress to adopt direct and primary, as distinguished from corrective legislation, on the subject in hand, is sought, in the second place, from the Thirteenth Amendment, which abolishes slavery. This amendment declares "that neither slavery, nor involuntary servitude, except as a punishment for crime, whereof the party shall have been duly convicted, shall exist within the United States, or any place subject to their jurisdiction;" and it gives Congress power to enforce the amendment by appropriate legislation.

This amendment, as well as the Fourteenth, is undoubtedly self-executing without any ancillary legislation, so far as its terms are applicable to any existing state of circumstances. By its own unaided force and effect it abolished slavery, and established universal freedom. Still, legislation may be necessary and proper to meet all the various cases and circumstances to be affected by it, and to prescribe proper modes of redress for its violation in letter or spirit. And such legislation may be primary and direct in its character; for the amendment is not a mere prohibition of State laws establishing or upholding slavery, but an absolute declaration that slavery or involuntary servitude shall not exist in any part of the United States.

It is true, that slavery cannot exist without law, any more than property in lands and goods can exist without law: and, therefore, the Thirteenth Amendment may be regarded as nullifying all State laws which establish or uphold slavery. But it has a reflex character also, establishing and decreeing universal civil and political freedom throughout the United States; and it is assumed, that the power vested in Congress to enforce the article by appropriate legislation, clothes Congress with power to pass all laws necessary and proper for abolishing all badges and incidents of slavery in the United States: and upon this assumption it is claimed, that this is sufficient authority for declaring by law that all persons shall have equal accommodations and privileges in all inns, public conveyances, and places of amusement; the argument being, that the denial of such equal accommodations and privileges is, in itself, a subjection to a species of servitude within the meaning of the amendment. Conceding the major proposition to be true, that Congress has a right to enact all necessary and proper laws for the obliteration and prevention of slavery with all its badges and incidents, is the minor proposition also true, that the denial to any person of admission to the accommodations and privileges of an inn, a public conveyance, or a theatre, does subject that person to any form of servitude, or tend to fasten upon him any badge of slavery? If it does not, then power to pass the law is not found in the Thirteenth Amendment. . . .

We must not forget that the province and scope of the Thirteenth and

Fourteenth amendments are different; the former simply abolished slavery: the latter prohibited the States from abridging the privileges or immunities of citizens of the United States; from depriving them of life, liberty, or property without due process of law, and from denying to any the equal protection of the laws. The amendments are different, and the powers of Congress under them are different. What Congress has power to do under one, it may not have power to do under the other. Under the Thirteenth Amendment, it has only to do with slavery and its incidents. Under the Fourteenth Amendment, it has power to counteract and render nugatory all State laws and proceedings which have the effect to abridge any of the privileges or immunities of citizens of the United States, or to deprive them of life, liberty or property without due process of law, or to deny to any of them the equal protection of the laws. Under the Thirteenth Amendment, the legislation, so far as necessary or proper to eradicate all forms and incidents of slavery and involuntary servitude, may be direct and primary, operating upon the acts of individuals, whether sanctioned by State legislation or not; under the Fourteenth, as we have already shown, it must necessarily be, and can only be, corrective in its character, addressed to counteract and afford relief against State regulations or proceedings.

The only question under the present head, therefore, is, whether the refusal to any persons of the accommodations of an inn, or a public conveyance, or a place of public amusement, by an individual, and without any sanction or support from any State law or regulation, does inflict upon such persons any manner of servitude, or form of slavery, as those terms are understood in this country? Many wrongs may be obnoxious to the prohibitions of the Fourteenth Amendment which are not, in any just sense, incidents or elements of slavery. Such, for example, would be the taking of private property without due process of law; or allowing persons who have committed certain crimes (horse stealing, for example) to be seized and hung by the *posse comitatus* without regular trial; or denying to any person, or class of persons, the right to pursue any peaceful avocations allowed to others. What is called class legislation would belong to this category, and would be obnoxious to the prohibitions of the Fourteenth Amendment, but would not necessarily be so to the Thirteenth, when not involving the idea of any subjection of one man to another. The Thirteenth Amendment has respect, not to distinctions of race, or class, or color, but to slavery. The Fourteenth Amendment extends its protection to races and classes, and prohibits any State legislation which has the effect of denying to any race or class, or to any individual, the equal protection of the laws.

Now, conceding, for the sake of the argument, that the admission to an inn, a public conveyance, or a place of public amusement, on equal terms with all other citizens, is the right of every man and all classes of men, is it any more than one of those rights which the states by the Fourteenth Amendment are forbidden to deny to any person? And is the Constitution violated until the denial of the right has some State sanction or authority? Can the act of a mere individual, the owner of the inn, the public conveyance or place of amusement, refusing the accommodation, be justly regarded as imposing any badge of slavery or servitude upon the applicant, or only as inflicting an ordinary civil injury, properly cognizable by the laws of the State, and presumably subject to redress by those laws until the contrary appears?

After giving to these questions all the consideration which their importance demands, we are forced to the conclusion that such an act of refusal has nothing to do with slavery or involuntary servitude, and that if it is violative of any right of the party, his redress is to be sought under the laws of the State; or if those laws are adverse to his rights and do not protect him, his remedy will be found in the corrective legislation which Congress has adopted, or may adopt, for counteracting the effect of State laws, or State action, prohibited by the Fourteenth Amendment. It would be running the slavery argument into the ground to make it apply to every act of discrimination which a person may see fit to make as to the guests he will entertain, or as to the people he will take into his coach or cab or car, or admit to his concert or theatre, or deal with in other matters of intercourse or business. Innkeepers and public carriers, by the laws of all the States, so far as we are aware, are bound, to the extent of their facilities, to furnish proper accommodation to all unobjectionable persons who in good faith apply for them. If the laws themselves make any unjust discrimination, amenable to the prohibitions of the Fourteenth Amendment, Congress has full power to afford a remedy under that amendment and in accordance with it.

When a man has emerged from slavery, and by the aid of beneficent legislation has shaken off the inseparable concomitants of that state, there must be some stage in the progress of his elevation when he takes the rank of a mere citizen, and ceases to be the special favorite of the laws, and when his rights as a citizen, or a man, are to be protected in the ordinary modes by which other men's rights are protected. There were thousands of free colored people in this country before the abolition of slavery, enjoying all the essential rights of life, liberty and property the same as white citizens; yet no one, at that time, thought that it was any invasion of his personal status as a freeman because he was not admitted to all the privileges enjoyed by white citizens, or because he was subjected to discriminations in the enjoyment of accommodations in inns, public conveyances and places of amusement. Mere discriminations on account of race or color were not regarded as badges of slavery. If, since that time, the enjoyment of equal rights in all these respects has become established by constitutional enactment, it is not by force of the Thirteenth Amendment (which merely abolishes slavery), but by force of the Thirteenth and Fifteenth Amendments.

On the whole we are of opinion, that no countenance of authority for the passage of the law in question can be found in either the Thirteenth or

Fourteenth Amendment of the Constitution; and no other ground of authority for its passage being suggested, it must necessarily be declared void, at least so far as its operation in the several States is concerned. . . .

The first and second sections of the act of Congress of March 1st, 1875, entitled "An Act to protect all citizens in their civil and legal rights," are unconstitutional and void, and that judgment should be rendered upon the several indictments in those cases accordingly.

And It Is So Ordered.

United States v. *Guest* is, strictly speaking, only a decision on Sections 5 and 6 of the Enforcement Act of 1870. It is, however, presented here (rather than just after that statute) because the decision and the opinions rendered therein are most relevant to the constitutional reach of all the post bellum civil rights legislation and the scope of the Fourteenth and Fifteenth Amendments upon which they were based. In particular, the *Guest* case makes for a fundamental change in the requirement of "state action" upon which much of the post-Civil War legislation had foundered. Such change is best spelled out in Justice William Brennan's opinion (*infra* p. 794).

It will be recalled that, in the *Civil Rights Cases,* the Supreme Court had laid down the broad principle that the Congress might not, under the enforcement clause of the Fourteenth Amendment, attempt to reach purely private action where no state or other official action was involved in the case. The same approach was followed in other cases—notably *United States* v. *Harris*, 106 U.S. 629 (1883), decided less than a year before the *Civil Rights Cases,* where Section 2 of the Ku Klux Act of 1871 was stricken down because its scope was not limited to official action.

Today, however, we may say that, despite the *Civil Rights* and *Harris* decisions, congressional power to enforce civil rights may validly be applied to all conspiracies to abridge rights guaranteed by the federal Constitution— and that regardless of whether the particular abridgement be by public officers or private persons. That is the case, first of all, because such application may be sustained by reliance upon congressional power other than that delegated by the enforcement clause of the Fourteenth and Fifteenth Amendments. Under the approach outlined (*infra* p. 537), such application may be supported under the congressional power to define and punish crimes. Included in such power is the authority to impose criminal penalties in order to prevent action that would violate rights, such as that to equal protection, guaranteed to citizens under the Constitution. Thus, the Supreme Court has said, "While it may be true that acts which are mere invasions of private rights, which acts have no sanction in the statutes of a state, or which are not committed by any one exercising its authority, are not within the scope of that amendment, it is quite a different matter when Congress undertakes to protect the citizen in the exercise of rights conferred by the Constitution of the United States essential to the healthy organization of the government itself." [*Ex parte Yarborough,* 110 U.S. 651 (1884)]

Even more important is the fact that a majority of the Supreme Court indicated in *United States* v. *Guest* that the enforcement clause of the Fourteenth Amendment empowers the Congress to punish all conspiracies— with or without state action—that interfere with the rights guaranteed by the Fourteenth Amendment: "A majority of the members of the Court express the view today that Section 5 empowers Congress to enact laws punishing *all* conspiracies which interfere with the exercise of Fourteenth Amendment rights, whether or not state officers or others acting under the color of state law are implicated in the conspiracy."

The view thus expressed in *United States* v. *Guest* rejects the *Civil Rights Cases* interpretation of congressional power to enforce the Fourteenth Amendment. The legislative power under the enforcement clause is not restricted by the reach of the Fourteenth Amendment itself. Though the amendment alone speaks only to state action, says Justice Brennan in *Guest*, "Legislation protecting rights created by that Amendment, such as the right to equal utilization of state facilities, need not be confined to punishing conspiracies in which state officers participate." Instead, the enforcement clause authorizes Congress to make whatever laws it deems reasonably necessary to protect any right arising under the amendment; and, Justice Brennan tells us, "Congress is thus fully empowered to determine that punishment of private conspiracies interfering with the exercise of such a right is necessary to its full protection."

UNITED STATES v. GUEST
383 U.S. 745 (1966)

MR. JUSTICE STEWART delivered the opinion of the Court.

The six defendants in this case were indicted by a United States grand jury in the Middle District of Georgia for criminal conspiracy in violation of 18 U.S.C. § 241. That section provides in relevant part:

> If two or more persons conspire to injure, oppress, threaten, or intimidate any citizen in the free exercise or enjoyment of any right or privilege secured to him by the Constitution or laws of the United States, or because of his having so exercised the same;
> They shall be fined not more than $5,000 or imprisoned not more than ten years, or both.

In five numbered paragraphs, the indictment alleged a single conspiracy by the defendants to deprive Negro citizens of the free exercise and enjoyment of several specified rights secured by the Constitution and laws of the United States. The defendants moved to dismiss the indictment on the ground that it did not charge an offense under the laws of the United States. The District Court sustained the motion and dismissed the indictment as to all defendants and all numbered paragraphs of the indictment. . . .

The second numbered paragraph of the indictment alleged that the defendants conspired to injure, oppress, threaten, and intimidate Negro citizens of the United States in the free exercise and enjoyment of:

> The right to the equal utilization, without discrimination upon the basis of race, of public facilities in the vicinity of Athens, Georgia, owned, operated, or managed by or on behalf of the State of Georgia or any subdivision thereof.

Correctly characterizing this paragraph as embracing rights protected by the Equal Protection Clause of the Fourteenth Amendment, the District Court held as a matter of statutory construction that 18 U.S.C. § 241 does not encompass any Fourteenth Amendment rights, and further held as a matter of constitutional law that "any broader construction of § 241 . . . would render it void for indefiniteness." 246 F. Supp., at 486. In so holding, the District Court was in error, as our opinion in *United States* v. *Price*, 383 U.S. 787, 86 S.Ct. 1152, decided today, makes abundantly clear.

To be sure, *Price* involves rights under the Due Process Clause, whereas the present case involves rights under the Equal Protection Clause. But no possible reason suggests itself for concluding that § 241—if it protects Fourteenth Amendment rights—protects rights secured by the one Clause but not those secured by the other. We have made clear in *Price* that when § 241 speaks of "any right or privilege secured . . . by the Constitution or laws of the United States," it means precisely that.

Moreover, inclusion of Fourteenth Amendment rights within the compass of 18 U.S.C. § 241 does not render the statute unconstitutionally vague.

Since the gravamen of the offense is conspiracy, the requirement that the offender must act with a specific intent to interfere with the federal rights in question is satisfied. *Screws* v. *United States*, 325 U.S. 91, 65 S.Ct. 1031, 89 L.Ed. 1495; *Williams* v. *United States*, 341 U.S. 70, 93-95, 71 S.Ct. 581, 593-595, 95 L.Ed. 758 (dissenting opinion). And the rights under the Equal Protection Clause described by this paragraph of the indictment have been so firmly and precisely established by a consistent line of decisions in this Court, that the lack of specification of these rights in the language of § 241 itself can raise no serious constitutional question on the ground of vagueness or indefiniteness.

Unlike the indictment in *Price*, however, the indictment in the present case names no person alleged to have acted in any way under the color of state law. The argument is therefore made that, since there exist no Equal Protection Clause rights against wholly private action, the judgment of the District Court on this branch of the case must be affirmed. On its face, the argument is unexceptionable. The Equal Protection Clause speaks to the State or to those acting under the color of its authority.

In this connection, we emphasize that § 241 by its clear language incorporates no more than the Equal Protection Clause itself; the statute does not purport to give substantive, as opposed to remedial, implementation to any rights secured by that Clause. Since we therefore deal here only with the bare terms of the Equal Protection Clause itself, nothing said in this opinion goes to the question of what kinds of other and broader legislation Congress might constitutionally enact under § 5 of the Fourteenth Amendment to implement that Clause or any other provision of the Amendment.

It is a commonplace that rights under the Equal Protection Clause itself arise only where there has been involvement of the State or of one acting under the color of its authority. The Equal Protection Clause "does not . . . add any thing to the rights which one citizen has under the Constitution against another." *United States* v. *Cruikshank*, 92 U.S. 542, 554-555, 23 L.Ed. 588. As Mr. Justice Douglas more recently put it, "The Fourteenth Amendment protects the individual against *state action*, not against wrongs done by *individuals*." *United States* v. *Williams*, 341 U.S. 70, 92, 71 S.Ct. 581, 593, 95 L.Ed. 758 (dissenting opinion). This has been the view of the Court from the beginning. United States v. Cruikshank, supra; United States v. Harris, 106 U.S. 629, 1 S.Ct. 601, 27 L.Ed. 290; *Civil Rights Cases*, 109 U.S. 3, 3 S.Ct. 18, 27 L.Ed. 835; *Hodges* v. *United States*, 203 U.S. 1, 27 S.Ct. 6, 51 L.Ed. 65; *United States* v. *Powell*, 212 U.S. 564, 29 S.Ct. 690, 53 L.Ed. 653. It remains the Court's view to-day. See, e. g., *Evans* v. *Newton*, 382 U.S. 296, 86 S.Ct. 486, 15 L.Ed. 2d 373; *United States* v. *Price*, 383 U.S. 787, 86 S.Ct. 1152.

This is not to say, however, that the involvement of the State need be either exclusive or direct. In a variety of situations the Court has found state action of a nature sufficient to create rights under the Equal Protection Clause even though the participation of the State was peripheral, or its action was only one of several co-operative forces leading to the constitutional violation. See, e. g., *Shelley* v. *Kraemer*, 334 U.S. 1, 68 S.Ct. 836, 92 L.Ed. 1161; *Commonwealth of Pennsylvania* v. *Board of Directors of City Trusts of City of Philadelphia*, 353 U.S. 230, 77 S.Ct. 806, 1 L.Ed.2d 792; *Burton* v. *Wilminton Parking Authority*, 365 U.S. 715, 81 S.Ct. 856, 6 L.Ed.2d 45; *Peterson* v. *City of Greenville*, 373 U.S. 244, 83 S.Ct. 1119, 10 L.Ed.2d 323; *Lombard* v. *State of Louisiana*, 373 U.S. 267, 83 S.Ct. 1122, 10 L.Ed.2d 338; *Griffin* v. *State of Maryland*, 378 U.S. 130, 84 S.Ct. 1770, 12 L.Ed.2d 754; *Robinson* v. *State of Florida*, 378 U.S. 153, 84 S.Ct. 1693, 12 L.Ed.2d 771; *Evans* v. *Newton, supra.*

This case, however, requires no determination of the threshold level that state action must attain in order to create rights under the Equal Protection Clause. This is so because, contrary to the argument of the litigants, the indictment in fact contains an express allegation of state involvement sufficient at least to require the denial of a motion to dismiss. One of the means of accomplishing the object of the conspiracy, according to the indictment, was "By causing the arrest of Negroes by means of false reports that such Negroes had committed criminal acts."[10] In *Bell* v. *State of Maryland*, 378 U.S. 226, 84 S.Ct. 1814, 12 L.Ed.2d 822, three members of the Court expressed the view that a private businessman's invocation of state police and judicial action to carry out his own policy of racial discrimination was sufficient to create Equal Protection Clause rights in those against whom the racial discrimination was directed. Three other members of the Court strongly disagreed with that view, and three expressed no opinion on the question. The allegation of the extent of official involvement in the present case is not clear. It may charge no more than co-operative private and state action similar to that involved in *Bell*, but it may go considerably further. For example, the allegation is broad enough to cover a charge of active connivance by agents of the State in the making of the "false reports," or other conduct amounting to official discrimination clearly sufficient to constitute denial of rights protected by the Equal Protection Clause. Although it is possible that a bill of particulars, or the proofs if the case goes to trial, would disclose no co-operative action of that kind by officials of the State, the allegation is enough to prevent dismissal of this branch of the indictment. . . .

MR. JUSTICE CLARK, with whom Mr. Justice Black and Mr. Justice Fortas join, concurring.

I join the opinion of the Court in this case but believe it worthwhile to comment on its Part II in which the Court discusses that portion of the indictment charging the appellees with conspiring to injure, oppress, threaten and intimidate Negro citizens of the United States in the free exercise and enjoyment of:

The right to equal utilization, without discrimination upon the basis of race, of public facilities in the vicinity of Athens, Georgia, owned, operated, or managed by or on behalf of the State of Georgia or any subdivision thereof.

The appellees contend that the indictment is invalid since 18 U.S.C. § 241, under which it was returned, protects only against interference with the exercise of the right to equal utilization of State facilities, which is not a right "secured" by the Fourteenth Amendment in the absence of state action. With respect to this contention the Court upholds the indictment on the ground that it alleges the conspiracy was accomplished, in part, "[b]y causing the arrest of Negroes by means of false reports that such Negroes had committed criminal acts." The Court reasons that this allegation of the indictment might well cover active connivance by agents of the State in the making of these false reports or in carrying on other conduct amounting to official discrimination. By so construing the indictment, it finds the language sufficient to cover a denial of rights protected by the Equal Protection Clause. The Court thus removes from the case any necessity for a "determination of the threshold level that state action must attain in order to create rights under the Equal Protection Clause." A study of the language in the indictment clearly shows that the Court's construction is not a capricious one, and I therefore agree with that construction, as well as the conclusion that follows.

The Court carves out of its opinion the question of the power of Congress, under § 5 of the Fourteenth Amendment, to enact legislation implementing the Equal Protection Clause or any other provision of the Fourteenth Amendment. The Court's interpretation of the indictment clearly avoids the question whether Congress, by appropriate legislation, has the power to punish private conspiracies that interfere with Fourteenth Amendment rights, such as the right to utilize public facilities. My Brother Brennan, however, says that the Court's disposition constitutes an acceptance of appellees' aforesaid contention as to § 241. Some of his language further suggests that the Court indicates *sub silentio* that Congress does not have the power to outlaw such conspiracies. Although the Court specifically rejects any such connotation, ante, p. 1176, it is, I believe, both appropriate and necessary under the circumstances here to say that there now can be no doubt that the specific language of § 5 empowers the Congress to enact laws punishing all conspiracies—with or without state action—that interfere with Fourteenth Amendment rights. . . .

MR. JUSTICE BRENNAN, with whom The Chief Justice and Mr. Justice Douglas join, concurring in part and dissenting in part.

I join Part I of the Court's opinion. I reach the same result as the Court on that branch of the indictment discussed in Part III of its opinion but for other reasons. See footnote 3, infra. And I agree with so much of Part II (page 6 to the top of page 8) as construes 18 U.S.C. § 241 to encompass conspiracies to injure, oppress, threaten or intimidate citizens in the free exercise or enjoyment of Fourteenth Amendment rights and holds that, as so construed, § 241 is not void for indefiniteness. I do not agree, however, with the remainder of Part II (page 8 to the top of page 11), which holds, as I read the opinion, that a conspiracy to interfere with the exercise of the right to equal utilization of state facilities is not, within the meaning of § 241, a conspiracy to interfere with the exercise of a "right . . . secured . . . by the Constitution" unless discriminatory conduct by state officers is involved in the alleged conspiracy.

The second numbered paragraph of the indictment charges that the defendants conspired to injure, oppress, threaten, and intimidate Negro citizens in the free exercise and enjoyment of "[t]he right to equal utilization, without discrimination upon the basis of race, of public facilities . . . owned, operated or managed by or on behalf of the State of Georgia or any subdivision thereof." Appellees contend that as a matter of statutory construction § 241 does not reach such a conspiracy. They argue that a private conspiracy to interfere with the exercise of the right to equal utilization of the state facilities described in that paragraph is not, within the meaning of § 241, a conspiracy to interfere with the exercise of a right "secured" by the Fourteenth Amendment because "there exist no Equal Protection Clause rights against wholly private action."

The Court deals with this contention by seizing upon an allegation in the indictment concerning one of the means employed by the defendants to achieve the object of the conspiracy. The indictment alleges that the object of the conspiracy was to be achieved, in part, "[b]y causing the arrest of Negroes by means of false reports that such Negroes had committed criminal acts . . . ." The Court reads this allegation as "broad enough to cover a charge of active connivance by agents of the State in the making of the 'false reports,' or other conduct amounting to official discrimination clearly sufficient to constitute denial of rights protected by the Equal Protection Clause," and the Court holds that this allegation, so construed, is sufficient to "prevent dismissal of this branch of the indictment." I understand this to mean that, no matter how compelling the proofs that private conspirators murdered, assaulted, or intimidated Negroes in order to prevent their use of state facilities, the prosecution under the second numbered paragraph must fail in the absence of proofs of active connivance of law enforcement officers with the private conspirators in causing the false arrests.

Hence, while the order dismissing the second numbered paragraph of the indictment is reversed, severe limitations on the prosecution of that branch of the indictment are implicitly imposed. These limitations could only stem from an acceptance of appellees' contention that, because there exist no Equal Protection Clause rights against wholly private action, a conspiracy of private persons to interfere with the right to equal utilization of state facilities described in the second numbered paragraph is not a conspiracy to interfere with a "right . . . secured . . . by the Constitution" within the meansing of §

241. In other words, in the Court's view the only right referred to in the second numbered paragraph that is, for purposes of § 241, "secured . . . by the Constitution" is a right to be free—when seeking access to state facilities—from discriminatory conduct by state officers or by persons acting in concert with state officers.

I cannot agree with that construction of § 241. I am of the opinion that a conspiracy to interfere with the right to equal utilization of state facilities described in the second numbered paragraph of the indictment is a conspiracy to interfere with a "right . . . secured . . . by the Constitution" within the meaning of § 241—without regard to whether state officers participated in the alleged conspiracy. I believe that § 241 reaches such a private conspiracy, not because the Fourteenth Amendment of its own force prohibits such a conspiracy, but because § 241, as an exercise of congressional power under § 5 of that Amendment, prohibits *all* conspiracies to interfere with the exercise of a "right . . . secured . . . by the Constitution" and because the right to equal utilization of state facilities is a "right . . . secured . . . by the Constitution" within the meaning of that phrase as used in § 241.

My difference with the Court stems from its construction of the term "secured" as used in § 241 in the phrase "any right . . . secured . . . by the Constitution or laws of the United States." The Court tacitly construes the term "secured" so as to restrict the coverage of § 241 to those rights that are "fully protected" by the Constitution or another federal law. Unless private interferences with the exercise of the right in question are prohibited by the Constitution itself or another federal law, the right cannot, in the Court's view, be deemed "secured . . . by the Constitution or laws of the United States" so as to make § 241 applicable to a private conspiracy to interfere with the exercise of that right. The Court then premises that neither the Fourteenth Amendment nor any other federal law prohibits private interferences with the exercise of the right to equal utilization of state facilities.

In my view, however, a right can be deemed "secured . . . by the Constitution or laws of the United States," within the meaning of § 241, even though only governmental interferences with the exercise of the right are prohibited by the Constitution itself (or another federal law). The term "secured" means "created by, arising under, or dependent upon, *Logan* v. *United States*, 144 U.S. 263, 293, 12 S.Ct. 617, 626, 36 L.Ed. 429, rather than "fully protected." A right is "secured . . . by the Constitution" within the meaning of § 241 if it emanates from the Constitution, if it finds its source in the Constitution. Section 241 must thus be viewed, in this context, as an exercise of congressional power to amplify prohibitions of the Constitution addressed, as is invariably the case, to government officers; contrary to the view of the Court, I think we are dealing here with a statute that seeks to implement the Constitution, not with the "bare terms" of the Constitution. Section 241 is not confined to protecting rights against private conspiracies that the Constitution or another federal law also protects against private interferences. No such duplicative function was envisioned in its enactment. See Appendix in *United States* v. *Price, ante*. Nor has this Court construed § 241 in such a restrictive manner in other contexts. Many of the rights that have been held to be encompassed within § 241 are not additionally the subject of protection of specific federal legislation or of any provision of the Constitution addressed to private individuals. For example, the prohibitions and remedies of § 241 have been declared to apply, without regard to whether the alleged violator was a government officer, to interferences with the right to vote in a federal election, *Ex parte Yarborough*, 110 U.S. 651, 4 S.Ct. 152, 28 L.Ed. 274, or primary, *United States* v. *Classic*, 313 U.S. 299, 61 S.Ct. 1031, 85 L.Ed. 1368; the right to discuss public affairs or petition for redress of grievances, *United States* v. *Cruikshank*, 92 U.S. 542, 552, 23 L.Ed. 588, cf. *Hague* v. *CIO*, 307 U.S. 496, 512-513, 59 S.Ct. 954, 962-963, 83 L.Ed. 1423 (opinion of Roberts, J.); *Collins* v. *Hardyman*, 341 U.S. 651, 663, 71 S.Ct. 937, 942, 95 L.Ed. 1253 (dissenting opinion); the right to be protected against violence while in the lawful custody of a federal officer, *Logan* v. *United States*, 144 U.S. 263, 12 S.Ct. 617, 36 L.Ed. 429; and the right to inform of violations of federal law, *In re Quarles and Butler*, 158 U.S. 532, 15 S.Ct. 959, 39 L.Ed. 1080. The full import of our decision in *United States* v. *Price, ante*, is to treat the rights purportedly arising from the Fourteenth Amendment in parity with those rights just enumerated, arising from other constitutional provisions. The reach of § 241 should not vary with the particular constitutional provision that is the source of the right. For purposes of applying § 241 to a private conspiracy, the standard used to determine whether, for example, the right to discuss public affairs or the right to vote in a federal election is a "right . . . secured . . . by the Constitution" is the very same standard to be used to determine whether the right to equal utilization of state facilities is a "right . . . secured . . . by the Constitution."

For me, the right to use state facilities without discrimination on the basis of race is, within the meaning of § 241, a right created by, arising under and dependent upon the Fourteenth Amendment and hence is a right "secured" by that Amendment. It finds its source in that Amendment. As recognized in *Strauder* v. *West Virginia*, 100 U.S. 303, 310, 25 L.Ed. 664, "The Fourteenth Amendment makes no attempt to enumerate the rights it designed to protect. It speaks in general terms, and those are as comprehensive as possible. Its language is prohibitory; but every prohibition implies the existence of rights . . . ." The Fourteenth Amendment commands the State to provide the members of all races with equal access to the public facilities it owns or manages, and the right of a citizen to use those facilities without discrimination on the basis of race is a basic corollary of this command. Cf. *Brewer* v. *Hoxie School District No. 46, etc.*, 238 F.2d 91 (C.A.8th Cir. 1956). Whatever may be the status of the right to equal utilization of *privately owned facilities*, see generally *Bell* v. *State of Maryland*, 378 U.S.

226, 84 S.Ct. 1814, 12 L.Ed.2d 822, it must be emphasized that we are here concerned with the right to equal utilization of *public facilities owned or operated by or on behalf of the State.* To deny the existence of this right or its constitutional stature is to deny the history of the last decade, or to ignore the role of federal power, predicated on the Fourteenth Amendment, in obtaining nondiscriminatory access to such facilities. It is to do violence to the common understanding, an understanding that found expression in Titles III and IV of the Civil Rights Act of 1964, 78 Stat. 246, 42 U.S.C. §§ 2000b, 2000c (1964 ed.), dealing with state facilities. Those provisions reflect the view that the Fourteenth Amendment creates the right to equal utilization of state facilities. Congress did not preface those titles with a provision comparable to that in Title II explicitly creating the right to equal utilization of certain privately owned facilities; Congress rightly assumed that a specific legislative declaration of the right was unnecessary, that the right arose from the Fourteenth Amendment itself.

In reversing the District Court's dismissal of the second numbered paragraph, I would therefore hold that proof at the trial of the conspiracy charged to the defendants in that paragraph will establish a violation of § 241 without regard to whether there are also proofs that state law enforcement officers actively connived in causing the arrests of Negroes by means of false reports.

My view as to the scope of § 241 requires that I reach the question of constitutional power—whether § 241 or legislation indubitably designed to punish entirely private conspiracies to interfere with the exercise of Fourteenth Amendment rights constitutes a permissible exercise of the power granted to Congress by § 5 of the Fourteenth Amendment "to enforce, by appropriate legislation, the provisions of" the Amendment.

A majority of the members of the Court express the view today that § 5 empowers Congress to enact laws punishing *all* conspiracies to interfere with the exercise of Fourteenth Amendment rights, whether or not state officers or others acting under the color of state law are implicated in the conspiracy. Although the Fourteenth Amendment itself, according to established doctrine, "speaks to the State or to those acting under the color of its authority," legislation protecting rights created by that Amendment, such as the right to equal utilization of state facilities, need not be confined to punishing conspiracies in which state officers participate. Rather, § 5 authorizes Congress to make laws that it concludes are reasonably necessary to protect a right created by and arising under that Amendment; and Congress is thus fully empowered to determine that punishment of private conspiracies interfering with the exercise of such a right is necessary to its full protection. It made that determination in enacting § 241, see the Appendix in United States v. Price, ante, and, therefore § 241 is constitutional legislation as applied to reach the private conspiracy alleged in the second numbered paragraph of the indictment.

I acknowledge that some of the decisions of this Court, most notably an aspect of the *Civil Rights Cases*, 109 U.S. 3, 11, 3 S.Ct. 18, 21, 27 L.Ed. 835, have declared that Congress' power under § 5 is confined to the adoption of "appropriate legislation for correcting the effects of . . . prohibited state law and state acts, and thus to render them effectually null, void, and innocuous." I do not accept—and a majority of the Court today rejects—this interpretation of § 5. It reduces the legislative power to enforce the provisions of the Amendment to that of the judiciary; and it attributes a far too limited objective to the Amendment's sponsors. Moreover, the language of § 5 of the Fourteenth Amendment and § 2 of the Fifteenth Amendment are virtually the same, and we recently held in *State of South Carolina* v. *Katzenbach*, 383 U.S. (*Infra*, Vol. II), 86 S.Ct. 803, 817, that "the basic test to be applied in a case involving § 2 of the Fifteenth Amendment is the same as in all cases concerning the express powers of Congress with relation to the reserved powers of the States." The classic formulation of that test by Chief Justice Marshall in *McCulloch* v. *Maryland*, 4 Wheat. 316, 421, 4 L.Ed. 579, was there adopted:

> Let the end be legitimate, let it be within the scope of the constitution, and all means which are appropriate, which are plainly adapted to that end, which are not prohibited, but consistent with the letter and spirit of the constitution, are constitutional.

It seems to me that this is also the standard that defines the scope of congressional authority under § 5 of the Fourteenth Amendment. Indeed, *State of South Carolina* v. *Katzenbach* approvingly refers to *Ex parte State of Virginia*, 100 U.S. 339, 345-346, 25 L.Ed. 676, a case involving the exercise of the congressional power under § 5 of the Fourteenth Amendment, as adopting the *McCulloch* v. *Maryland* formulation for "each of the Civil War Amendments."

Viewed in its proper perspective, § 5 appears as a positive grant of legislative power, authorizing Congress to exercise its discretion in fashioning remedies to achieve civil and political equality for all citizens. No one would deny that Congress could enact legislation directing state officials to provide Negroes with equal access to state schools, parks and other facilities owned or operated by the State. Nor could it be denied that Congress has the power to punish state officers who, in excess of their authority and in violation of state law, conspire to threaten, harass and murder Negroes for attempting to use these facilities. And I can find no principle of federalism nor word of the Constitution that denies Congress power to determine that in order adequately to protect the right to equal utilization of state facilities, it is also appropriate to punish other individuals—neither state officers nor acting in concert with state officers—who engage in the same brutal conduct for the same misguided purpose. . . .

THE 1894 REPEAL OF VOTING RIGHTS LEGISLATION

Commentary

The post-Civil War amendments and statutes in the field of civil rights, from the Thirteenth Amendment, December 18, 1863, to the Civil Rights Act of 1875, had been strongly opposed by the Democratic party. Hence, it was natural that when that party first won back the Presidency and control of the two houses of Congress in 1892, its leaders should seek to undo much of the Republican civil rights program. It should be pointed out, indeed, that the civil rights laws had already been weakened in 1873, when the government was still controlled by the Republican party. At that time, all the federal statutes had been recodified and republished as the Revised Statutes. While none of the civil rights laws were substantively altered in the 1873 revision, the provisions of those laws were rearranged and separated under unrelated titles of the Revised Statutes and, in the process, lost their distinctive, unified character.

After the Democrats won the Presidency and both houses in the 1892 election, they moved in the new Congress to repeal the most important of the civil rights statutes which had not been stricken down by the Supreme Court. These were the laws protecting suffrage, namely, those provisions of the Enforcement Act of 1870 and the Force Act of 1871 (as they were now contained in the relevant titles of the Revised Statutes) which sought to enforce the equal right of all citizens to vote. In particular, the repeal bill was aimed at those statutory provisions for federal control of elections through the appointment of federal officers (chief supervisors, supervisors, and deputy marshals) to control the election process and, in so doing, virtually to supersede the relevant state election officials. Hence, the bills introduced by the new Democratic majority provided for the repeal of all statutes relating to supervisors of elections and deputy marshals, as well as federal protection of the right to vote.

The repealing bill was introduced in the House in the first session of the new Congress. It was debated in the House during September and October, 1893, and passed by 201 to 102 on October 10. It was debated in the Senate, during the next session, in January and February, 1894. The Senate passed the bill on February 7, by 39 to 28.

The extracts from the congressional debates which follow contain the statements made by Congressman Henry Tucker [Dem., Va.] and Senator John Palmer [R., Ill.], introducing the repealing bill in the two houses, as well as the remarks of other members opposing the bill (notably Representative Marriott Brosius [R., Pa.] and Senator George Hoar [R., Mass.]. The interchange between Senators Hoar and George Gray [Dem., Del.] on the last day of debate well illustrates the opposing views on the measure.

Of particular pertinence to the present-day observer interested in law are the constitutional arguments used by participants in the debates. The constitutional issue here differs from that in the case of the statutes covered in previous portions of this volume because the Supreme Court had expressly upheld the federal election laws in the *Siebold* and *Yarborough* cases (*supra* pp. 578, 538). Despite this, many of the supporters of the repealing bill continued to urge the unconstitutionality of the election laws. Some went so far as to assert that the Supreme Court decisions were not binding in the matter, declaring, in the words of Congressman Thomas Lawson [Dem., Ga.], that "these decisions, though they had been the judgment of a unanimous court, are not obligatory upon Congress." The truth is, however, that the constitutional issue was largely irrelevant to the question of whether the repealing bill should be passed. The majority party had resolved to repeal the election laws, and nothing said about the constitutional or other issues in the debates could really alter that basic fact.

THE REPEAL ACT OF 1894
FEBRUARY 8, 1894

Be it enacted by the Senate and House of Representatives of the United States of America in Congress assembled, That the following sections and parts of sections of the Revised Statutes of the United States be, and the same are hereby, repealed; that is to say of title "Elective franchise," sections twenty hundred and two, twenty hundred and five, twenty hundred and six, twenty hundred and seven, twenty hundred and eight, twenty hundred and nine, twenty hundred and ten, twenty hundred and eleven, twenty hundred and twelve, twenty hundred and thirteen, twenty hundred and fourteen, twenty hundred and fifteen, twenty hundred and sixteen, twenty hundred and seventeen, twenty hundred and eighteen, twenty hundred and nineteen, twenty hundred and twenty, relating to the appointment, qualification, power, duties, and compensation of supervisors of election; and also sections twenty hundred and twenty-one, twenty hundred and twenty-two, twenty hundred and twenty-three, twenty hundred and twenty-four, twenty hundred and twenty-five, twenty hundred and twenty-six, twenty hundred and twenty-seven, twenty hundred and twenty-eight, twenty hundred and twenty-nine, twenty hundred and thirty, twenty hundred and thirty-one of same title, relating to the appointment, qualification, power, duties, and compensation of special deputies; and also of title "Crimes," sections fifty-five hundred and six, fifty-five hundred and eleven, fifty-five hundred and twelve, fifty-five hundred and thirteen, fifty-five hundred and fourteen, fifty-five hundred and fifteen, fifty-five hundred and twenty, fifty-five hundred and twenty-one, fifty-five hundred and twenty-two, fifty-five hundred and twenty-three, but the repeal of the sections hereinbefore mentioned shall not operate so as to affect any prosecutions now pending, if any, for a violation of any of the provisions of said sections; and also part of section six hundred and forty-three, as follows:

Or is commenced against any officer of the United States or other person on account of any act done under the provisions of title twenty-six, The Elective Franchise, or on account of any right, title, or authority claimed by any officer or other person under any of said provisions.

SEC. 2. That all other statutes and parts of statutes relating in any manner to supervisors of election and special deputy marshals be, and the same are hereby repealed.

SEC. 3. That this Act shall take effect from and after its passage.

Approved, February 8, 1894.

THE DEBATE

House of Representatives-53d Congress, 1st Session
September 26-October 10, 1893

THE SPEAKER [CHARLES CRISP, DEM., GA.]. The Clerk will read the special order.

The Clerk read as follows:

Resolved, That immediately after the second morning hour, on the 26th day of September, present, or if said second morning hour shall not have sooner ended, then, at the hour of 2 o'clock p.m. on said day, the House shall proceed to the consideration of H.R. 2331, entitled "An act to repeal the statutes relating to supervisors of elections and special deputy marshals, and for other purposes." That the consideration of said bill shall be resumed immediately after the second morning hour of each legislative day thereafter, up to and including the 9th day of October next. That at the hour of adjournment on said last-named day the previous question shall be considered ordered on all pending amendments on the bill, to its engrossment and third reading, and to its final passage. That on the next legislative day, to wit, the 10th day of October next, at the hour of 1 o'clock p.m., the House shall resume consideration of said bill, and shall proceed, without further debate and without intervening motions, to vote, first, on the pending amendments, if there be any, then on the engrossment and third reading of the bill, then on the final passage thereof, and then on motions to "reconsider and lay on the table," should such motions be made. If from any cause this order shall not be fully executed on the last day mentioned herein, then this order shall continue in force and be operative each legislative day thereafter until said bill shall be fully disposed of.

THE SPEAKER. The Clerk will report the bill.

The bill (H. R. 2331) to repeal all statutes relating to supervisors of elections and special deputy marshals, and for other purposes, was read, as follows:

Be it enacted, etc., That the following sections and parts of sections of the Revised Statutes of the United States be, and the same are hereby, repealed; that is to say, of title "Elective franchise," sections 2002, 2005, 2006, 2007, 2008, 2009, 2010, 2011, 2012, 2013, 2014, 2015, 2016, 2017, 2018, 2019, 2020, relating to the appointment, qualification, power, duties, and compensation of supervisors of elections; and also sections 2021, 2022, 2023, 2024, 2025, 2026, 2027, 2028, 2029, 2030, 2031 of same title, relating to the appointment, qualification, power, duties, and compensation of special deputies; and also of title "Crimes," sections 5508, 5511, 5512, 5513, 5514, 5515, 5520, 5521, 5522, 5523; and also part of section 643, as follows:

"Or is commenced against any officer of the United States or other person on account of any act done under the provisions of Title XXVI, 'The elective franchise,' or on account of any right, title, or authority claimed by any officer or other person under any of said provisions."

SEC. 2. That all other statutes and parts of statutes relating in any manner to supervisors of election and special deputy marshals be, and the same are hereby, repealed.

SEC. 3. That this act shall take effect from and after its passage. . . .

THE SPEAKER. . . . There are two amendments recommended by the committee. One of them, the Chair understands, is merely to correct a clerical error, and the other is a provision that the proposed repeal shall not operate to affect any prosecution now pending. The Chair would suggest that those two amendments might be considered as agreed to. In that way the road would be cleared for any other amendments that gentlemen might desire to offer. That would perfect the bill as the committee desire to have it, and would leave the way open for other amendments. . . . The Clerk will report the amendments.

The Clerk read as follows:

In line 29 strike out "fifty" and insert "fifty-five;" so as to make the number read "fifty-five hundred and twenty-three."

In line 29 after the word "three" insert "but the repeal of the sections hereinbefore mentioned shall not operate so as to affect any prosecutions now pending, if any, for a violation of any of the provisions of said sections."

JULIUS BURROWS [R., MICH.]. There ought not to be any objection to that.

THE SPEAKER. Without objection these two amendments will be considered as agreed to. [A pause.] The Chair hears no objection. The amendments are agreed to, and there is now no amendment pending to the bill. . . .

HENRY TUCKER [DEM., VA.]. Mr. Speaker, the duty devolves upon me in presenting this measure to the House of explaining its provisions, so that the House may understand exactly what is contemplated by the bill. It is a repeal bill, proposing to repeal certain sections of the Revised Statutes which are collected in the report of the majority, providing for the appointment of supervisors and deputy marshals and prescribing the duties thereof. The sections are enumerated on the first page of the majority report. Section 2002 it is also proposed to repeal, because it gives to an officer of the Army the power and discretion to use the troops at the polls when, in his opinion, it may be necessary. The other sections refer chiefly to the punishment of crimes defined therein.

The first question, Mr. Speaker, to which I desire to address myself is this: What are the duties, powers, and privileges of the supervisors so appointed in these sections; and what are the duties, powers, and privileges of the deputy marshals provided for in these sections? If those powers are not granted or guaranteed to them in the Constitution of the country, it will be admitted on all sides that the statutes which have conferred them are unconstitutional in themselves; for there can be no power in any officer of the United States Government to do any act the authority for which is not prescribed or granted in the Constitution of the country. I think I can show, Mr. Speaker, that there are such powers not contemplated in the Constitution so granted in the sections which we seek to repeal.

The first proposition, therefore, to which I ask the attention of the House is this: That the *right* of suffrage emanates from the State and is not conferred in the Constitution on the citizen by the Federal Government, but is reserved to the States and so declared to be in the Constitution itself. In the second section of Article I of the Constitution we find this provision:

The House of Representatives shall be composed of members chosen every second year by the people of the several States; and the electors in each State shall have the qualifications requisite for electors of the most numerous branch of the State Legislature.

That is, whatever provision Congress may make under its powers with reference to the "manner of holding " elections, the original *right* of suffrage rests with the States of the Union. By this provision of the Constitution suffrage is conferred through the States, and it leaves in the States the determination of the right and the conditions of suffrage; and the citizen is entitled to it because he is a citizen of the State and not because of his citizenship of the United States.

Such right of suffrage and conditions of suffrage are subject to the laws of the State of the citizen, and must be prescribed and limited by such State. The State may say that no man under 21 years of age can vote, which is a condition of suffrage; or it may say that none but property-holders can vote, which is a condition of suffrage; or it may say that no man can vote until he registers, which is a condition of suffrage; or it may say that no man shall vote who can not read or write, which is a condition of suffrage. None of these conditions, confessedly, can be regulated by the Federal Government, but are left wholly to the States.

The determination, therefore, of the question of the *right* of a citizen to vote is left to the State, and the *determination* of such right ought to be exercised only by the power that gave it. To say that the State alone can give the right of suffrage and another power pass upon whether that right exists or not, may be a denial of the original right. If the condition of suffrage be registration, and the question as to whether a man is properly registered be taken from the State authorities and given to the Federal authorities, is not the power which resides in the State of determining the condition taken from it?

If the Federal Government has the power to pass upon the question of registration, as to whether a citizen is properly registered in the State, it has the power to destroy a right given to the State by the Constitution of the country. In other words, gentlemen, if suffrage be a right given to the citizen by the State, our position is that the power of determining that question must rest with the power which gives it. Any other doctrine is a denial of the original right, and puts it in the power of the Federal Government to deny a clear power given to the States under the Constitution.

GEORGE RAY [R., N.Y.]. May I ask the gentleman a question?

MR. TUCKER. Yes, sir.

MR. RAY. I desire to understand the gentleman's position. Are we to understand he is now arguing that these laws which it is proposed to repeal are unconstitutional?

MR. TUCKER. Yes, sir, I so hold; to my mind they are unconstitutional.

MR. RAY. Let me ask the gentleman another question, which he can answer, I presume, by yes or no, without any discussion, for I do not wish to interfere improperly with the course of his argument. Has it not been decided by the Supreme Court of the United States, twice at least, that this law and all its provisions are constitutional?

MR. TUCKER. The gentleman has anticipated my argument somewhat. I knew, of course, that the question was coming, and I am prepared to meet it.

MR. RAY. Has it not been so decided by the Supreme Court of the United States?

MR. TUCKER. It has been so decided as to some of these sections; and I want to say to the gentleman right here and now that if he permits the Supreme Court to hold his conscience as a legislator, I do not.

MR. RAY. Then the proposition is simply this: You ask Congress to reverse the Supreme Court of the United States on a constitutional question.

MR. TUCKER. Exactly. . . .

Now, Mr. Speaker, the first proposition I have laid down is that the right of suffrage is conferred by the State under the Constitution, and that the power of determining that right must rest within the State itself.

I hold that the power of the citizen and the right of the citizen to vote is a right given to him not by the Constitution of the United States or by the Federal Government, but is a right reserved to the State and recognized in the Constitution.

Now, if that right exists—the right of suffrage in the State—then who is to determine that right? Is the State to determine it, or is that power to be given to another? What right is worth having that may be determined by another other than the grantor? If the State gives the power to the citizen to vote, and another authority can pass upon that right and determine it, it is a useless power. In other words, we hold that the *electoral function* and the *determinant function* must go hand in hand for the safety of each power and for the protection of the rights of each. The right to vote and the power of determining that right should rest in the same hands. . . .

Now, Mr. Speaker, I come to the next step, to show that sections 2007, 2016 and 2017, 2018, 2022, and 2026 are sections which deny that the State alone can determine the right of suffrage in its citizens. I say that these sections deny the determination of the right of suffrage to the State which granted it. . . .

What I object to is that there are sections here that give rights to Federal officers which do not belong to the Federal Government, and which ought never to have been given, because not authorized by the Constitution.

Now, I say these sections that I have cited deny the right of determining the question of suffrage to the States that gave it.

Section 2007 declares that when a citizen offers to perform an act necessary to be done under any law of a State in order to vote, and is prevented, that *he shall vote*. Who determines it? The Federal officer. This law says when the citizen does a certain act, whether the State officer says he can vote or not, that *he shall vote*, and thereby takes out of the hands of the State the power to determine whether he shall vote or not.

Section 2016 gives to the supervisor the right of challenge, the right to mark names for challenge, the right to personally inspect and scrutinize registration lists, the right to affix names to original lists and copies in such manner as will in their judgment—their *determining* judgment—detect the *improper* or *wrongful* removal therefrom of any names. There the power is granted first to challenge. Why, Mr. Speaker, what does a challenge mean? A challenge means to the voter "Stop!" just as it meant to the man who attempted to pass a sentinel during the late war. "I challenge you! Not only stop, but give the countersign before you pass!"

What is the countersign of a voter going to the polls to vote? It is to give the necessary qualifications to vote. To whom? To the supervisor of elections. And if the supervisor of elections is not satisfied with it, it is true the man may attempt to vote, but there is an additional power here to send after him the swift messenger of a warrant, and have him arrested at once. The right of challenge is the right to thwart, to obstruct, to hinder, to delay, to prevent absolutely the exercise of a right. And where that is the case, the determinant power of the right of a man to cast his vote is taken from the State that gave it, and put into the hands of the Federal challenger. The power to challenge can easily be used by designing men not only to *delay* the voter, but it may be used successfully to prevent his voting at all.

And the *delay* of many may often mean the *prevention* of some for want of time to vote.

Gentlemen may say that the challenge is not a prevention of voting—that there is no reason why a man, if challenged, can not have the matter determined by the State judge of election, and that the determinant power shall be and will be with the State that gives the right of suffrage; but I ask gentlemen to tell me this: What right has the Federal Government to impose upon a State officer any duty? How can the Federal Government say to the State officer, "Determine the question whether this man has a right to vote; I challenge it"? Why, if the Federal Government has that power; it can put upon the State officer duties so onerous and so burdensome as to destroy him as a functionary of the State which he is sworn to serve. . . .

We find in addition to this that these supervisors have the power to personally inspect and scrutinize registration lists and to affix their names to registration lists, to original lists and copies, in such manner as will in their judgment detect improper and wrongful acts. Who is to determine whether an act is an *improper* or *wrongful* act? The supervisor, the man who is put there by the Federal Government to discharge the duty and the power granted by the Constitution to the State officer.

So, Mr. Speaker, I find all through the sections which I have referred to the granting to the Federal officers, the supervisors and the deputy marshals, the power of determining the right of a citizen to vote.

Section 2017 is practically the same.

In section 2018 power is given to the supervisor "to count and canvass" the result.

Now, I put it to gentlemen that if the original right of suffrage be in the State, granted by the State, and can only be granted by it, what right has the Federal Government to come in and demand by its officer that the right of counting and canvassing the vote should be put into their hands? I speak of the *right*, not of the expediency.

Section 2022 I desire especially to call attention to:

> The marshal and his general deputies, and such special deputies, shall keep the peace, and support and protect the supervisors of elections in the discharge of their duties, preserve order at such places of registration and at such polls, prevent fraudulent registration and fraudulent voting thereat, or fraudulent conduct on the part of any officer of election, and immediately, either at the place of registration or polling place or elsewhere, and either before or after the registering or voting, to arrest and take into custody, with or without process, any person who commits, or attempts or offers to commit, any of the acts or offenses herein prohibited.

There is a distinct power given to the deputy marshals to prevent, not to stop, not to challenge, and leave it to the State judge to say whether he has the right, but the absolute power of determining whether a man has the right to vote, and to prevent it. Not only that, but he must prevent fraudulent voting. Who is to determine whether it is fraudulent or not? Ah, gentlemen of the opposition, look at it. Here is the judge of the election, here is the Federal supervisor of the election. The judge of election says that this is not a fraudulent vote that is offered to be cast. The Federal supervisor says it is. And this statute gives to the Federal supervisor the power to prevent his voting, and, if the man offers to vote, the power to arrest him. So that when gentlemen talk about these laws being laws intended to supervise and merely witness the counting and canvassing of the vote and the manner of election, I want the country to know that the power rests with the Federal deputy marshals to pass upon whether a vote is fraudulent or not, and to absolutely prevent it being cast, and to arrest the man if he attempts it.

Section 2026 gives power to the supervisor to compel the voter who has been registered, to do what? To prove his right to vote. I beg to refer to it for a moment. Among the duties are this one:

> Shall cause the names of those upon any such list whose right to register and vote is honestly doubted to be verified by proper inquiry and examination at the respective places by them assigned as their residences.

Verified how? To whom? Manifestly to the supervisor, and if not satisfactory, the deputy marshal shall prevent, if necessary, by arrest. The supervisor thereby has power to pass upon that question, under this law, and determine not only the right of suffrage, but whether the condition of suffrage has been complied with by the citizen, when that right and the original right to vote is guaranteed, as I have shown, to the citizen by the State, and the State alone.

But, Mr. Speaker, gentlemen on the other side claim that the power to appoint these Federal officers arises from the fourth section of Article I of the Constitution, which prescribes:

The times, places, and manner of holding elections for Senators and Representatives shall be prescribed in each State by the Legislature thereof; but the Congress may at any time by law make or alter such regulations, except as to the places of choosing Senators.

That is the pretension of gentlemen on the other side. But I challenge gentlemen to point out where that section of the Constitution confers upon the United States Government either the power to grant suffrage to the citizen, or to determine it after it is granted by the State. Chief Justice Waite says that the right of suffrage is derived from the State. This section says that after the State has conferred the right of suffrage, after it has determined who shall vote, after it has written in its laws the conditions upon which a man can vote, then Congress may, if it wants to, change the State regulations, not of election, but "of holding" the election, at any time that it may choose. . . .

MR. RAY. May I ask the gentleman a question?

MR. TUCKER. Certainly.

MR. RAY. Does the gentleman claim that if I, being a resident of the State of New York, should go into the State of Virginia at the next election for Congressmen and should undertake to vote there, Congress would have no power to authorize supervisors of election to interfere to prevent me from voting there?

MR. TUCKER. I am glad to see that the gentleman has understood me exactly right. That is exactly what I hold. . . .

MR. RAY. Then you think that the act of preventing a man from voting illegally at an election does not relate to the manner of conducting the election.

MR. TUCKER. To the manner of *holding* the election. That is my position.

MR. RAY. Conducting it.

MR. TUCKER. I hold my friend to the constitutional word, the manner of *holding* the election.

MR. RAY. Well, "holding," then.

MR. TUCKER. Yes, holding. I *hold* my friend down to that. [Laughter.]

MR. RAY. And you think the word "holding" does not include "conducting?"

MR. TUCKER. My friend will understand that the "holding" of the election is a very different thing from the thing that is held. The holding of the polls is a mere ministerial act. That which goes into the ballot box, the ballot of the freeman, is a right given to him by the States, which the Constitution has guaranteed to him, and which the Federal Government can not interfere with. . . .

But if the words "time, place, and manner of holding" mean that Congress by law may prescribe who shall hold the election and determine who is elected, *either Congress can appoint supervisors over the election of Senators by the Legislature, or it can not do so as to Representatives*; for the power as to each as conferred by this clause is exactly the same. If the power exists as to Representatives, it exists as to Senators. If it can not apply to Senators, neither can it apply to Representatives. . . .

If the power exists at all, there is no reason why the Federal supervisors can not go to the clerk of the house of delegates of the State of Virginia and challenge his right (for that means, according to the argument of my friend from New York, the manner of holding elections), challenge his right to put on the rolls the name of any member of the State Legislature. It is his duty to make up that list. But not only that; let me carry my friend a little further with me. Under the sections of which I have been speaking, the right is given to the supervisors or marshal, not only to challenge every one who comes up to vote, but it gives him the right to challenge the voter when he goes to register. . . .

It is the right of suffrage for which I am contending. That belongs to the State, and the power that is claimed here to challenge a man at the polls is a power that you can not defend, because, if it can be used at the polls as claimed, it can be used in challenging the right of a man to vote for a United States Senator in a State Legislature. . . .

Now I come to another proposition. Sections 2009, 5506, 5511 and 5515 are sections that require the punishment of State officials for the violation of State laws. Mr. Speaker, I think of all the laws on the statute books and of all the sections that are sought to be repealed in this bill these are the most objectionable and the most obnoxious. To say that a man who is sworn as an officer of the State of Virginia to discharge his duty to her sovereignty can, if he omits to discharge that duty, be punished by any other power is a proposition so monstrous, that I take it it need hardly be discussed in a body like this.

The power to punish for the violation of a law that it has not the power to command obedience to! The Federal Government has no right to command the obedience of the State officer to the State law, and yet it claims the power here to take the State officer and punish him for a dereliction of duty to the law of his State.

How would gentlemen like that to apply in their own homes, to have some outside party punish your child for a disobedience to your own command— the establishment of a rule to control your own house, and to have it faithfully and efficiently enforced by your neighbor applying the rod to your child for a disobedience to your command? It is a monstrous proposition. It is a proposition that ought not to live until the 10th of October.

I want to call attention to the language of Judge Bradley in the Siebold case, where he seeks to meet the trouble in that case by a hop, skip, and jump. That was a case where a State officer was indicted, I think, in the State of Maryland, for the violation of a State law. Judge Bradley, in giving his decision on that question, says:

> The imposition of punishment implies a prohibition of the act punished. The State laws which Congress sees no occasion to alter, but which it allows to stand, are in effect adopted by Congress.

And the punishment of a citizen of the United States was carried out by the Supreme Court of the United States by the declaration of the great judge that, while the citizen violated no law of Congress but the law of a State, yet that Congress had in effect adopted that law of the State. Human rights taken from citizens by implication of law! Where does such construction lead to? If Congress has the power to punish State officers, it has the power to destroy the State by punishing the State officer *by removing him from office*. And I say, gentlemen, that these provisions in reference to punishment of State officers for the violation of State laws are provisions that can not be too soon wiped out by this House. . . .

MR. RAY. Why, my dear friend, you do not undertake to say that you would defy a law of Congress because it was in conflict with the law of the State of Virginia, or because you thought that the law of Congress was unconstitutional?

MR. TUCKER. Not at all. A law of Congress should be deemed constitutional until it has been declared unconstitutional by the Supreme Court. But the law of Congress declared constitutional by the action of the Supreme Court is not constitutional to me, as a Representative here, unless in my conscience I believe it to be.

MR. RAY. But you would obey them?

MR. TUCKER. As a citizen I bow to the laws of Congress; as a citizen I bow to the decision of the Supreme Court, but as a Representative from the State of Virginia I bow only to my construction of the Constitution in determining my duty. [Applause on the Democratic side.]

But, Mr. Speaker, if these laws are wrong in principle they have certainly been wrong in practice. . . .

MR. TUCKER. Mr. Speaker, there is another section to which I wish to call the attention of the House, and that is section 2002, which provides that

> No military or naval officer, or other person engaged in the civil, military, or naval service of the United States shall order, bring, keep, or have under his authority or control any troops or armed men at the place where any general or special election is held in any State, unless it be necessary to repel the armed enemies of the United States, or to keep peace at the polls.

That act was passed in February, 1865. It was passed as a war measure. We have passed from that war now nearly thirty years. That provision of the law, then, ought to be wiped out. It ought to be wiped out for this reason, that it gives to an officer of the Army the discretion of determining when troops should be called out. The Constitution prescribes, wherever domestic violence has passed beyond the control of the State, that upon application of the executive or the Legislature of the State, as the case may be, to the Government of the United States, troops shall be directed to quell the riot in such State. The Constitutional provision is clear (Article IV, section 4). This is ultra-constitutional in that it gives to an officer of the Army the discretion of determining when troops shall be used at the polls.

Now, I want to add one further word. The public press of the country has declared that this bill proposes to wipe out the fifteenth amendment to the Constitution; that the object of the bill is to do away with this amendment. It is not so. There is not a statute among those sought to be repealed that touches in the slightest degree the fifteenth amendment except one. The object of the committee was clear. We recognize this amendment as part of the organic law of this country, and we bear full allegiance to it.

But these laws which we seek to repeal have no such purpose. The only provision that bears on the fifteenth amendment is section 2010, which refers to a contest for a State office, not a Federal office, where a man has lost the office by reason of the denial of the right of suffrage on account of race, color, or previous condition. We eliminate that, because the statute gives the right of action to the Federal court instead of to the State court, whose office is sought to be recovered. Of course if the contest proceeds under the State courts, and the question arises as to whether a man has been deprived of his right under the fifteenth amendment, the appeal is had as a matter of right to the Federal court.

These laws ought to be repealed, Mr. Speaker, because they seek to take away from the State, that alone can bestow suffrage on the citizen, the power of determining the right to vote; they ought to be repealed, because they have been the subject of collisions and jealousies and unnecessary clashing of authorities since their enactment; they ought to be repealed, sir, because they are reconstruction measures, the unhappy reminders of a period in our history forever gone, except from the memory of the people; they ought to be repealed, because the States are as much interested in seeing that their Representatives are properly elected as the Federal Government can possibly be.

Sir, I want to say to our friends on the other side that there is no doubt about the repeal of these laws. They are going to be repealed. We are sorry that there should be any objection from the other side of the House. We are sorry that our friends thought it necessary to filibuster for a week before this bill could even be reported to the House; but they are going to be wiped away, because they are the lingering evidence of a past unhappy era in our history. We belong now to that generation which has gotten away from the old unpleasantness, and is looking no longer to the dead past, but to the future. We want to obliterate from the statute books every evidence of that fratricidal strife, so that the hardships which those days entailed upon us may be forgotten, that we may go forward as a band of brothers in the development of the constitutional history of our country and the constitutional development of our people. [Applause on the Democratic side.]

MARRIOTT BROSIUS [R., PA.]. Mr. Speaker, the duty of replying to my honorable friend from Virginia [Mr. Tucker] has fallen upon me unexpectedly. It is an honor I did not seek, but will not decline. Nor will I withhold the homage due to a very good speech by omitting to congratulate my distinguished friend from Virginia upon having made an able argument in support of the views he entertains.

There were some propositions advanced by him to which I shall feel required to address myself in the course of the observations I will submit to the House. I desire to emulate his example in one particular. I would be glad if I could in the remarks I shall submit discuss the bill before us from a purely non-partisan point of view. I believe that underneath the swiftly flowing and fretting streams of our politics there is patriotism. I would like to appeal to that to-day. Underneath the current of conflicting opinion on forms of government and modes of administration there is a philosophy of government which if pursued will enable us to select out of the diverse views the only true one.

Now, having made this patriotic declaration of my purpose to try to talk about this important matter from the point of view of reason and principle, without distinction of section or race or party, I hope I have conciliated the favor of the House, and will be honored by the attention of such as have a real interest in being right upon a question of the first magnitude in American legislation. But if there are those who have made up their minds that they will be partisans first and patriots afterwards; if there are those who, like many who have gone before us, feel better satisfied to be wrong with Plato than right with his adversary, I will not indulge the vain task of even soliciting their attention.

Now, Mr. Speaker, that governments derive their just powers from the consent of the governed is a proposition which expresses the only reason for the existence of our form of government. On no other hypothesis could popular forms of government have any excuse for being, and any civil polity or mode of administration which lodges power anywhere against the consent of the people gives birth to an unjust power, and to that extent is a subversion of our form of government.

Consent then, let me say, is the word in our political terminology which expresses the very substance of our system, the totality of elements which enter into the constitution of our form of government. I have heard it said that there are three ways of conferring authority—by force, by lot, and by consent; the latter is the only way that authority can be conferred under our form of government. Every officer elected, from the President to a town constable, owes his place to the consent of the people.

Every enactment passed into law in this body derives its validity from consent; and every depository of power, great or small, high or low, can show no title to his place but the consent of the people.

But, then, I would like to say to my distinguished friend from Virginia that consent, to be effective, must be expressed. We have no mode in this Government of determining questions by the weight of sentiment, ascertained by a perception of the prevailing view, as they determine questions in Quaker meetings. We determine not by weight, but by number. We do not weigh; we can only count, and the tally decides. The agency by which consent is ascertained is suffrage. Here, then, are the two pillars upon which our Federal Government was erected—"consent," the supreme determining power, and "suffrage," its constitutional mode of expression. Patriots, I have no doubt, will agree with me that any abuse or usurpation that overawes or suppresses the one or impairs the purity or efficacy of the other is equally subversive of our system of government, and equally fatal to constitutional liberty.

The legislation which it is proposed to repeal relates to suffrage. It is a body of laws whose sole object was to erect necessary defenses around this mode of expressing the people's consent in elections for Representatives in Congress. It in no way interferes with elections for State officers. It provides for the exercise of Federal control over Federal elections; national supervision of national affairs.

A glance at the history of this legislation may help us to an understanding of its character and an appreciation of its necessity. There seems never to have been occasion prior to the war to invoke Federal power to secure an honest expression of the people's will at Federal elections. The abuses, usurpations, and infractions of law which were a serious menace to honest elections and which called this interference into requisition had their birth after the war. Not that there was any opinion entertained by any portion of our people adverse to the constitutional authority of the Federal Government to exert its power and control over its own affairs anywhere in the Union, as I shall show later on, but no conditions existed which required the exercise of such power.

After the war our situation was materially altered. Our electorate was greatly enlarged. Emancipation and enfranchisement had introduced into the arena of our politics entirely new conditions, which gave birth to manifold causes of irritation, strife, and conflict between races unequal in intelligence but equal in citizenship and the right of suffrage. Out of this difficult and complex situation were evolved temptations on the part of the strong to deprive the weak of their constitutional share in the exercise of political power. Motives existed and purposes came into being that had no existence in former times, which impelled those to take who had the power and those to hold who could.

I need not pause to enlarge upon the circumstances which intensified the real difficulties of the situation and placed the new charter of liberty which guaranteed to the enfranchised race equality of rights with their white fellow-citizens in danger of being rendered entirely nugatory by the means employed by the old citizens to maintain political ascendency over and against the superior number of the new. Thus with the advent of our new Constitution, the dawn of our new era, the birth of our new liberty, which shed upon our history a glory whose luster can never fade, came a brood of troubles which required to meet them new exertions of power on the part of the Federal Government, just as new diseases require new remedies.

Under this new regime which supervened on the triumph of the Union, and which you said was essentially a political usurpation, conceived in passion and brought forth in malice against the Southern people—showing how grossly you misconceived the situation—it is easily seen that from the point of view of the Constitution and the citizen, indeed from the point of view of any standard of national duty, justice and gratitude, the obligation to enforce the guarantees of the Constitution with respect to our new citizens, was paramount. . . .

Exhilarated by this scrap of history we can advance another step and look into the character of the legislation that now remains upon our statute books and see how perfectly innoxious it is. Under existing law no officer of the Army or Navy can in any way interfere with the qualifications of electors in any State, or with the freedom of elections, or with the exercise of the free right of suffrage, under heavy penalties. No part of the Army can be used as a posse comitatus or otherwise for the purpose of executing the laws at elections. . . .

But the proponents of this measure are not content with absolute security against the possibility of any military interference with elections—an apprehension without the slightest warrant—for no case of such interference has occurred since the passage of the act of 1870. There is no record that any soldier appeared at the place of an election in any State under orders of the United States.

They desire now to deprive the civil authorities of the United States of all power to keep the peace and protect the rights of voters at Congressional elections without any pretense that the conditions which called such legislation into being have undergone modification with lapse of time, and that the reasons which induced it have ceased to exist. They proceed upon the assumption that the legislation is wrong in principle, without warrant in the Constitution, and at all events inexpedient, because of its vicious results. These assumptions open an inviting field of inquiry which it is not possible in the limit of my time to cover. To do my best I can but touch and go. . . .

Those who believe there is warrant for these assumptions belong to that portion of our people who have held from time to time—sometimes with great laxness and at others with apparent conviction, as the fluctuations of feeling and prejudice relaxed or intensified their views—a body of doctrines with which older statesmen, belonging to what we may call the "ancient political regime" in this country, are more familiar than are the younger men who are now sharing the burdens of public responsibilities.

Those doctrines may be summarized as follows:

1. There are no national elections.

2. The United States has no voters.

3. The States have the exclusive right to control all elections of members of Congress.

4. The United States has no authority anywhere within the States to keep the peace at elections.

5. The United States is not a nation endowed with sovereign power, but only a confederacy of States. . . .

I beg now to set over and against this body of doctrine and put in contrast with it some more modern propositions which are so well established and so thoroughly crystallized in the minds of intelligent and patriotic citizens that it ought not to be necessary even to allude to them, and I recall them now to refresh the recollection of those who seem to have forgotten them.

1. The Federal Constitution is not the creature of the States, but it was ordained and established by the sovereign people of the United States.

2. The power and authority conferred by the Constitution upon the Federal Government is operative in all the States and over all the people.

3. That through the agency of the legislative, executive, and judicial arms of the Government, the nation is clothed with adequate power to enforce all the provisions of the Constitution against any and all opposition, whether from individuals or States, at all times, in all places, and under all circumstances, within the limits of the Union.

If these propositions are sound, and I doubt if any member of this House in a lucid interval will undertake to impeach their validity, it follows that no law can be obnoxious to constitutional objections which only provides the means of carrying into effect the constitutional powers of the Government. What more does this act do?

I understand there are some four or five complaints made against existing legislation on this subject. I pass over the constitutional objection, for I understand that it is not seriously urged; but there are four or five objections upon the ground of expediency, which is the other leg on which my distinguished friend's argument stands. One of those objections (the order is not important) is that there is no necessity for this kind of legislation.

Is there any prerogative of this Government, any constitutional power or authority more important, nay, more necessary to the safety and efficiency of the Government than the supervision of Federal elections, control of the agencies by which the legislative department of the Government is brought into being and maintained in effective operation? What can be more necessary to the existence of the Government, what more suitable to its character or conformable with its declared purposes, than the control of the means by which it lives and executes the objects of its creation?

To what right under the Constitution can the Government and the people of the United States establish a better and more incontestable title than the right to know how the elections of those who are to legislate for 65,000,000 of people are conducted, whether honestly or fraudulently; whether the electors in the exercise of their constitutional rights have been subjected to fear or force or fraud, or whether they enjoyed immunity from these unlawful restraints?

What principle could be more consonant with justice and constitutional liberty than that the citizens of Pennsylvania should have some guaranty that members of Congress from South Carolina, who are to enact laws affecting the former as well as the latter State, are elected conformably to the laws and Constitution of the country? When national Representatives are chosen it is in the interest of every citizen of the United States that they be lawfully chosen, for the citizens of every State are interested in the election of Representatives in every other State; and to strike down this salutary and necessary power is to inflict a wound upon the right of every State to require that elections in every other State shall be honest. . . .

Now, let me submit a few propositions which commend themselves to the justice and patriotism of every discriminating and judicious citizen of the United States.

1. It is not possible to propose an object worthier the pursuit of a free government and an honest people than the defense of the humblest citizen in the exercise of this constitutional rights.

2. In forms of government in which sovereignty resides in the people and speaks through popular elections, a free ballot and a fair count are the very breath of the nation's life; and any abuse or fraud which hinders the free expression of the sovereign will at the ballot box gags the nation while highwaymen rob it of its liberty.

3. That no darker reproach ever rested upon the fair escutcheon of the Republic than that which in the past has draped it with forbidding black, that men were suffered to climb to power and maintain political supremacy upon the ruins of the constitutional rights of American citizens, with the mightiest Republic on earth standing by consenting.

4. It is the duty of the Government to make it safe for every citizen to exercise his constitutional rights and enjoy his constitutional privileges anywhere, at any time, in any proper way, and Congress will be recreant to its duty until it exhausts every constitutional agency to guarantee that safety.

5. The humblest and feeblest citizen under the flag, whatever his color or condition, whether in New York or New Orleans, who seeks an opportunity to register his will must find as easy access to the ballot box as the strongest and the greatest. Along that way and over that box the nation must stand guard, that no terror shall overawe the citizen, no violence wrest from him his right to record his will nor fraud falsify that record.

But there can be no national sanction to any method of protection, no national resistance to any wrong, no national rectification of any mistake, no national warrant of validity, no guaranty of a free ballot and a fair count, unless there by that statutory control which it is now proposed to nullify by this repeal.

You propose to destroy the last defense which the nation has placed around its ballot box, to guard the citadel of its own life. You propose that the United States shall not employ its civil power, the ordinary and customary agencies, in preserving the public peace and protecting the rights of citizens, in conserving order and preventing crimes at the places where United States elections are being held. You propose to open the doors of the temple of constitutional liberty to every pilferer and robber that comes along. You disarm the ship and expose it to the assaults of every brigand and pirate that cruise for plunder.

You invite invasions of the rights of electors by advertising that here is an open field for plunder, unguarded, unprotected, where the lawless and the wicked can flourish like a green bay tree, with an absolute guaranty of immunity from responsibility or punishment, thus making that political equality which the Constitution guarantees "a word of promise to the ear to be broken to the hope," excepting so far as the State may mercifully intervene to protect that which the Federal Government leaves defenseless. . . .

Do I exaggerate, then, when I say that this is the most abject, ignoble, and humiliating surrender of the United States to State authority that has ever been proposed since the colossal heresy of State sovereignty was tried by the wager of battle and perished at the points of a million bayonets. Think of it, Mr. Speaker; contemplate the ignominy, the measureless mortification; sound the depths of the humiliation; compsss the baseness of the subserviency of the Government of the United States voluntarily abdicating its sovereignty over its own elections, its supervision of its own business.

Gentlemen, when this deed is done and you have retired from this Hall to enjoy the contemplation of such an ambitious achievement as your country's disgrace, and you cast your eyes toward the proud statue of America which surmounts this Capitol, you will behold that majestic figure standing with averted face, weeping Columbia's shame. Yet, gentlemen, I am not abandoned utterly to despair. "Hope springs eternal in the human breast," and I am not fully persuaded that you will let your cruelty go to the length of inflicting this wound upon your country's honor. Your justice and patriotism, which for the moment may sleep, will wake and stay the rash hand you are about to put upon the glory of this Republic. I fain hope that your better nature, rising above the mists of prejudice and the clouds of partisan passion and rancor, will point out to you the pathway to the true principles of constitutional government, and that you will have the virtue and the courage to pursue them. . . .

CHAMP CLARK [DEM., MO.]. Mr. Speaker, I am in favor of eradicating the last vestige of these Federal election laws from our political system for several reasons:

1. Because they are utterly useless.

2. Because they are unnecessary for any good purpose and are constantly prostituted for the most unworthy ends.

3. Because they are oppressively expensive and the money paid the deputy marshals and supervisors is in reality a corruption fund, used by party managers for partisan purposes and paid, not out of the party campaign fund, but out of the public treasury.

4. Because these laws contain the germs of the force bill. The agitation of that ominous measure, its passage through the House, and its strength in the Senate must have delighted Julius Caesar in his grave to think that the despotic ideas for which he died were taking root in this Western world, dedicated to the proposition that all men are created equal. [Applause.] It was enough to cause Napoleon the Great and Napoleon the Small to chuckle in their coffins to think that the theories of tyranny which they inculcated, and for which both of them were driven to perish in exile, were being adopted in what is poetically known as "the land of the free and the home of the brave."

5. I am in favor of repealing these laws because I deem them unconstitutional. I am aware that a decision of the Supreme Court sustains them in this regard. But I can never forget that while we ought to have becoming reverence for the Supreme Court of the United States, it is a matter of tradition that it was once enlarged and then packed for the purpose of securing a decision in the legal-tender cases which should be in harmony with the views of the men who then dominated the country.

It is a historic fact, known of all men, that in many instances opinions of gravest import are rendered by a divided court, five affirming and four dissenting, and that a decision good to-day may, through the death, resignation, or retirement of even one justice, be overruled to-morrow.

The results of the eight to seven commission demonstrate beyond all controversy that however just and reliable the decisions of the Supreme Court may be when only property rights are involved, when politics enters into the case at bar, the members of that high tribunal are as much blinded by partisan prejudice and are as liable to have their judgments warped by party necessities as the rest of us.

We all know that Andrew Jackson enunciated the correct, if somewhat startling, doctrine that he would construe the Constitution of his country for himself, the Supreme Court to the contrary notwithstanding; and I would just about as lief risk the opinion of Old Hickory as that of the Supreme Court of the United States. [Laughter.] He was not profoundly versed in black letter law, but he was richly endowed with common sense.

But, whether constitutional or unconstitutional, these laws ought to be repealed, because they are exasperating to the people and a standing menace to civil liberty. We have been commanded by an overwhelming majority of American freemen to repeal them, and we are eager to discharge that pleasant and patriotic duty. . . .

Senate-53d Congress, 2nd Session
January 16-February 7, 1894

JOHN PALMER [R., ILL.]. Mr. President, I have no desire to take the floor at present in the discussion of this measure. I had understood the consideration of the bill was fixed for to-day, and I had hoped that the chairman of the committee would be present in order to present the views of those who favor this measure in that elaborate and learned form in which I knew he would be likely to discharge that duty. I have no formal argument to address to the Senate. I simply approach the question as it has for years impressed itself upon my mind. I only propose to give my views as they occur to me in the course of the desultory argument which I shall offer to the Senate.

The colored people were ignorant beyond all question. In 1866 I was at Raleigh, N. C., presiding over a court-martial. The court-martial had occasion to examine a great many colored witnesses. One of them was a negro who was so lately imported, or whose ancestors were so lately imported, that he had scarcely learned the English language. After he had testified, I asked him, "If you had the right of suffrage how would you vote?" He failed to understand me. He said, "Sir?" I said "Suffrage; if you had the right to vote, how would you vote?" Said he, "Sir, I suppose I would vote according to my *intrusts*," and I think in that statement that negro from the rice fields near Wilmington stated the true philosophy of the vote, that a man should vote according to his own interests. I have no doubt that if the Union people had been in the South treated with confidence they would have perceived the unity of their interests and those of their late masters and that the conditions would have been far better than they were after the lapse of ten years.

I am gratified now to believe that these laws have exhausted their force; that the relations between the lately enfranchised and their neighbors are better and that legislation of this sort is becoming obsolete, and it will become so as those people advance in knowledge, in education. I do not mean the education of the schools, but I mean the acquisition of that practical knowledge, the means of earning a livelihood, which is true education after all. I think we may give ourselves but little trouble now in regard to the relations between the two races in the Southern States. . . .

The mistake when we passed these laws was the failure to trust those who were to be governed. The doctrine I mean to assert as being one necessarily opposed to this legislation is that the laws are based upon a distrust of the people, those for whom governments are ordained and for whom governments should be conducted. That is the radical fault of the laws, and at this moment I present that as a distinct line of objection.

I have said that possibly Congress might pass some uniform law for the regulation of the elections of members of the House of Representatives, and that possibly such a law might be framed to meet my judgment and to meet my approval, but such has not been the policy or purpose of the authors of these laws. The purpose of this legislation has been to secure party success. The purpose of this legislation has been, in my judgment, to give to the minority the right to control the majority, and those laws secure not popular government, but party government, which must have been their original purpose. . . .

It is undoubtedly true that a small number of citizens may put into operation an election machinery which is superior in authority to that of the State. To that extent it is intrusive and subversive, because to create an authority superior to another is to supersede the inferior authority. . . .

Why was this law passed? In the first place, why should such power be granted on the request of any two or ten or fifty citizens, at their own sovereign will and pleasure, without any reason, without any fact being stated?

If the Senator objects to my position that they usurp or supersede the State authorities, I suppose he will admit that they may create authorities superior to those of the States, because whatever the State officers may do in the discharge of their office these persons have an imperative, conclusive right to be present when such acts are done; they are present to watch, and these officers are under the supervision of men created at the will of ten or twenty or fifty irresponsible inhabitants of a particular district. Why is that? Why shall the free people of this country be subjected to such supervision?

With respect to the sentimental question, I have already said that the sentiment of manly self-respect is essential to the maintenance of popular liberty. The citizen must not only be secure in his rights, but his rights must be respected, and I maintain that when fifty men—I assume the highest number—obtrude upon me and upon my neighbors, men who are appointed by an irresponsible authority, it is a humiliation, a disgrace, and it leads me to undervalue my manhood and my liberty. That is sentimental. Mr. President, liberty is a sentiment, and without that manly love of liberty, which is a sentiment—a noble, grand sentiment—and which can never be insulted or degraded with impunity, liberty would be worthless. . . .

Mr. President, it is remarkable that since this law was passed there has been more corruption and more in the spirit of resistance to this despotic legislation than there ever was before. I know that it is believed by many that the American people in some sense or other need continual nursing and continual watching, and there is an idea somewhere that some person, somebody, may be intrusted with the guardianship of popular liberty, while the essential truth of our American idea is that liberty must be maintained by the people themselves, and the only apology for a despotism or for despotic legislation is that the people can no longer be trusted.

Mr. President, I have already said that the particular objection to me in the election law is that it places the government and control of the elections in the hands of a few men who may put the machinery of the law into operation. In point of fact, is it not true that the election laws in the district in which I live are whatever fifty men may determine they shall be? If any fifty men anywhere conclude that my fellow-citizens, in a district which casts many thousand votes, are incapable of acting honestly or of protecting themselves, those fifty persons have but to create the machinery by which every elector in that election district is placed under the control of those irresponsible public officers. . . .

I believe, therefore, that those who insist upon the constant supervision and watchfulness of the people are the enemies of popular liberty. They must be aware of the fact that popular liberty depends upon the people themselves, and they must be aware that this exercise of extraneous force is degrading and demoralizing, and to demoralize the citizen is to destroy that high self-respect which should characterize an American freeman.

I go back now to the point I had in view at the start. This law authorizes a limited number of persons to create the officers whom the Senator from New Hampshire defends. These officers go to an election, an election ordered by State law. They take their seats in the presence of officers created under the State law. Do I attach any significance to the fact that these laws are enacted by the States? Not in the slightest. To me their value consists in the circumstance that these laws were enacted by the people, and that the State is the mere agent of the people, the efficient means by which popular will takes the form of law. I care nothing about the source of law, and if the Federal system should be so modified as that the people themselves under the operation of Federal laws should control their own elections; the fact that the law was Federal rather than State would be no objection to me. The system exists. The one is national; it is despotic.

It is remarkable that all the officers of the Federal Government hold their offices at the will of a geographically distant authority. The marshal, the judges, the supervisors of election are appointed by the United States judges. The people are not consulted; they have no voice in the matter. Masters are named for them, and to those masters they must submit without the right of appeal, without the right of protest.

Such is the election law which I am condemning and denouncing. If the Federal election law allowed free action of the popular will, the objection would simply be that it interfered with the harmony of a system which has existed for more than a hundred years, and which I trust will be perpetual. So it is in all the arguments which are based upon any preference between Federal and State authority.

I say again that these are mere agencies for the convenient distribution of power, and the reason I prefer the State agencies is because they are popular agencies.

They are controlled by the people; and the true underlying philosophy of that control is that their interests are largely local; and this machine we call the State government lives in the popular will and it moves under the impulse of popular thought and popular preference, while this great system, which over-shadows all, is despotic in its nature; the powers of the officers are discretionary largely; and what is to me more, the officers are not subject to the popular control by means of popular elections. If the Federal Government shall ever be so reformed as that Senators here shall be elected by the people, that this horde of officers who perform the service of the Federal Government shall be chosen by the freemen, then much of the difficulty which we perceive would be obviated.

Mr. President, I had intended merely to introduce this discussion. I go back again to my original proposition. I believe the mistake of those who support this law is predicated upon a belief that some changes have taken place in the popular mind, in the popular morals, which make new and more stringent regulations necessary to maintain the purity of elections.

I notice that the war has bred these new ideas. I have alluded to the fact that our people became fond of the swift and decisive rule of the bayonet; and the poison is not there alone. We have fallen in love with arbitrary, forceful methods; we distrust ourselves; we invoke force to govern us, to control us, and we look in vain to some distant and external authority, or some authority external to ourselves, that we may find repose in its superior force and wisdom. That is the prevailing vice of the times.

My belief is that if these laws are repealed and elections are again left in the hands of the people, there will be much less ground for complaint; for, mark you, the Senator from New Hampshire himself is eloquent in his denunciation of the corruptions of elections in the large cities. These corruptions exist and have not been cured by Federal election laws. If it could be shown to me that these laws had, on the whole, been favorable to the purity of elections, they would be more tolerable in my judgment; but, according to the complaint we hear, the elections are still corrupt in the great cities, notwithstanding the law exists, and the State officers are overshadowed by those of the United States. I used the term "State officers." I desire to avoid and disclaim it at the outset. It is the people's officers who are overridden; and notwithstanding this swarm of officers and the thousands of dollars that are expended in the large cities, the same complaint exists. . . .

GEORGE HOAR [R., MASS.]. . . .

Mr. President, I am one of five persons in this Chamber who voted for the statute of 1871 when it was passed. I have been compelled ever since to discuss this question from year to year, either as chairman of some investigating committee, or as chairman of the Committee on Privileges and Elections, or for some other reason. I have never made a report upon it, or made a speech upon it which was not required by some special duty which had been assigned to me by my associates here; and while I never said anything which I did not believe, or which I do not now believe to be sound and true, I have only said what in my judgment was the opinion at the time, and is the opinion now, not only of a large majority of the Republican party, but a large majority of the American people.

It is a question of the greatest gravity. The passion for political power in free States is the one supreme passion of mankind. It surpasses as a temptation the love of money, the love of pleasure, the love of ease, the love of kindred, or the love of home. All these things are sacrificed when the supreme ambition of man for political honor at the hands of his fellow-men or to wield political power over them presents itself to the soul. And yet it is gravely urged that against this, the temptation of all temptations, the law-making power of a free country should not and ought not to be invoked.

Wherever there is a crevice in our protection of the freedom of the ballot there you will find the Democratic party trying to break through. Wherever we have left open an opportunity to get possession of an office contrary to the true and constitutional will of the majority there you will find that party pressing; there you will find that party exercising an ingenuity before which even the great inventive genius of the American people exerted in other directions fails and is insignificant in the comparison.

We leave properly and beyond question to the States the power of electing their own Legislatures. Each branch of the State Legislature determines the title to seats in its body. The act of Congress, in order that there may be no failure, provides for an election where the two houses do not agree by a joint assembly, and yet there have been many instances—there are Senators sitting on this floor now elected by Legislatures, where, in order to get that majority, one Democratic house has proceeded to turn out of their seats one after another of lawfully elected members so that the great prize of United States Senator might be so acquired, and they have trusted to the sense of constitutional duty of the Republican majority here again and again, and have been justified in the trust, to permit that to be accomplished.

In one State, Mississippi, in order to disfranchise Republicans who can not read and write and to let Democrats who can not read and write vote, there is a constitutional provision by which the Democratic election officers determine whether the understanding of the voters who can not read or write is a fit and sufficient understanding of the constitution; and, although that was denounced by able Democrats holding high public positions both in Washington and in Mississippi, the proposition finds defenders on this floor, Senators gravely comparing it to the provision of the constitution of Massachusetts.

In Delaware it is necessary that a tax should be paid a certain time beforehand, and, accordingly, unless they are much belied, the Democratic tax collector runs away when the Republicans come to pay their taxes.

GEORGE GRAY [DEM., DEL.]. No, it is the other way; it is the Republican tax collector who runs away when the Democrats come to pay their taxes.

MR. HOAR. The great inventive genius of America, which in lawful channels has relieved so much of the suffering of mankind and lightened the burdens beneath which humanity is bowed and bent, has been devoted with a devilish ingenuity to this object. . . .

When the statute of 1870-'71 was passed, the provision which is chiefly complained of, providing for the appointment of United States marshals, the only provision which gave any authority, except the mere authority of making a record of what happened, was applied only to cities of upwards of 20,000 inhabitants. At that time there were sixty-two cities of that class in this country, of which but five were in the South. It applied, in other words, to fifty-seven Northern communities and to but five Southern communities. Of those fifty-seven Northern communities, there were eleven in the Commonwealth of Massachusetts. More than twice the number of communities in Massachusetts came under the operation of the law than existed in the whole South.

But a little more than that. The South at that time was in Republican hands. With the exception of Kentucky, Maryland, Delaware, and Missouri, every Southern State had an uncontrolled Republican majority and every Southern State voted, with the exceptions I have named, for the election law of 1870. Tennessee voted for it, South Carolina voted for it, Florida voted for it, Virginia voted for it, North Carolina voted for it, and so did Louisiana, Texas, and Arkansas. When I called the attention of my honorable friend from Tennessee to that fact yesterday, he answered me that the best men of the South were at that time disfranchised. There was not a man in the South at that time deprived of the right to vote. Rebel or Union man, Democrat or Republican, secessionist or constitutionalist, every Southern citizen had the right to cast, without constraint and without interference, his ballot for the men of his choice; and the only difference between then and now is in the fact that that state of things does not exist in those States to-day.

The statute of 1870 is a Southern measure as much as a Northern measure in its origin, in the power which enacted it, and is a Southern measure twenty times as much as it is a Northern measure in the fact that it was aimed at Northern communities, and not at Southern communities. How idle to keep up this clamor that we hear, that this is a sectional question, and not a question of honest elections, as if the brave and gallant men, as brave and gallant men as ever marshaled themselves in military array, who represented the cause of the Southern Confederacy, fought and bled and died for the privilege of cheating at elections! . . .

Mr. President, this is not a question of State rights. The Senator from Illinois was arguing this matter with the zeal of a new convert, and when I heard his argument I thought of the observation of an old deacon in the neighborhood from which I came to a young convert at a camp-meeting, who reproached the deacon with the want of zeal, that he had noticed that young Christians were a good deal like young bumblebees—much the largest when they were first hatched. I think that observation is entirely applicable to the new converts to Democracy.

MR. PALMER. Will the Senator allow me to tell him a story?

MR. HOAR. Does the Senator rise to discuss the bumblebees or the bill?

MR. PALMER. I wish to tell the Senator another camp-meeting story in that line.

MR. HOAR. The Senator may do so after I get through. I do not think I shall yield for a camp-meeting story.

Mr. President, that Senator was pressed with a good deal of vigor by my honorable friend from Maine [Mr. Frye], and was asked what he thought of the admitted, unquestioned fact, proved upon the records of the Senate and certified to by a Democratic committee, that in the city of New York under Democratic management there were 60,000—I think was the number—of fraudulent naturalization papers, all purporting to have been made in two courts in the space of three or four days.

What was the Senator's answer to that proposition? He was asked whether he thought all the State processes had been quite sufficient to protect the State and the nation against that enormous fraud, by which the great State of New York was carried by a minority in 1868. His reply was that the true way was to take that out of the hands of the State courts and let nobody but the courts of the United States do the naturalization. He gave up the whole case. The State courts, under the Constitution and the laws, have been permitted to share this function with the judiciary of the United States; and if you can trust anybody anywhere you can trust the courts of this country everywhere, and yet that Senator, put forward as the leading champion of the friends of repeal, is obliged to confess that there is but one safety in this matter, and that is not to trust the State courts with the great function of naturalization.

If it would be no insult to the State of Illinois or to the State of New York to say, as that Senator would say, that the State courts are not to be trusted to pass on the judicial question of whether a man has been five years in this country and has made his preliminary declaration, what sort of an insult is it to say that the political workers about the polls are not always to be trusted with the great function of suffrage?

Mr. President, this is not a question of local control, which is the other staple and standard argument that we hear. They say you must trust the people in the localities. The Democratic party does not trust the people in the localities, and in Democratic State after Democratic State—in Virginia, in Maryland, in Delaware, in Louisiana, and in other States which I might name, within the last ten or fifteen years that party when it has got control has taken away the power of managing and ordering elections from the people who gather about the polls, which is the Massachusetts fashion, and has put it into the hands of the central power of the State, managed and wielded by the Democratic party leaders. . . .

Now, Mr. President, the Constitution and laws of the United States left to the States in the beginning the determination of the manner of elections. It was a matter of convenience, it was a matter of saving expense, so long as there were to be elections under both authorities, that the United States, reserving to itself the right to make or alter existing regulations, left it for a time to the States to enact and administer them. But complaints have arisen. Will anybody get up and say here that there is not in the length and breadth of this country, whether rightful or wrongful, a most serious complaint that the States do not provide for fair elections; that they do not have them in New York City; that they do not have them in Chicago; that they do not have them throughout almost the whole Southern country.

Mr. President, if I chose to go into that question I should be bound to say that taking all the circumstances, taking all the light, the records in the archives of this Capitol, make the history of the elections in this country since 1865 the blackest and worst history of crime since the world was created. We can only deal with that subject by silence. When those reports are read, blackening the fair fame of this land, we must "walk backwards with averted gaze and hide her shame." This is not a question of States rights, of sectional differences, of race distinctions, of local self-government. It is a question of fraud or no fraud. There is nothing else to it. It is a question whether the supreme possession and property, the pearl, the gem in the crown of American manhood, the most precious thing on the face of the earth, shall, if need be, have the strongest force on the face of the earth for its protection and defense.

Is there anything else which is a national right that the power of the United States does not accompany? You do not leave the question whether a coin or a greenback shall be counterfeited to the State law. You do not get up and say it is an insult to Virginia or Delaware when you provide that if a man in Virginia or Delaware or Massachusetts counterfeit a coin or forge a bond or a greenback he shall be punished in the courts of the United States. The letter to his son at home, which my honorable friend from Virginia [Mr. Hunton] dropped in the post-office this morning, has the sanction of the entire power of the United States, judicial, legislative, and, if need be, naval or military, for its protection and support. . . .

MR. HOAR. I have not left it yet. Why is it, if it be true that this right be precious, if it be true that citizenship of the United States is an honor and a glory and a pride and a possession to the humblest of her citizens, that it is an insult to anybody that the sanction and the protection which you throw about a 2-cent letter or a greenback worth a dollar shall be thrown about that when it is in peril?

Are these five hundred volumes of investigation reports in the archives of this body showing the crime, the menace, and the danger which under the best safeguards have attended, by reason of the greed and ambition of man, the security of the letter as there are when we come to the matter of the right to cast the ballot in honor and in safety? What is it that makes it an insult to the whole Democratic party south of Mason and Dixon's line when I wish my vote, upon which the dearest interests of the country and of mankind may depend, to have the same security that you give to a letter or to a bank bill? Now I will hear the Senator from Delaware.

MR. GRAY. I do not want to interrupt the Senator's argument; he has rather drifted away from the point he was on. I wish to ask him whether he does not think it would be quite safe to leave to the police power of the States the punishment of the crime of counterfeiting a United States greenback or United States coin, just as they punish the counterfeiting of a State bank note? Does he not think that power would be as safe in the hands of those communities as in the larger sphere of the Government?

MR. HOAR. I will answer the question by a statement which has been attributed, I have no doubt truly, to Andrew Jackson. There were some quite extensive districts in this country where at that time counterfeit money was the prevailing currency. I do not think it would. I do not think that the currency of this country would be as safe and its great commercial transactions as well conducted if you left them to the States first to establish wildcat banks, then to give as much or as little security as they chose to the currency of the Government and the banks of the United States.

Mr. President, this is a question of fraud or no fraud. They tell us that there have been some Republican invasions of the elective franchise, and it is quite possible, but where you can find one well-authenticated case of a man who has been deprived or inconvenienced in the exercise of his franchise by these United States marshals or other officers, I will pledge myself to find ten thousand well established by evidence on record here where without those securities Republicans have been deprived of their votes by Democratic practices. I incur no danger in making that challenge. If you will produce me a citizen of the United States, a Democrat, who lost his honest vote in consequence of intimidation or impediment, created by these United States marshals, I will find on record here the proof of ten thousand Republicans who have lost their votes by Democratic practices.

But I hope when I do it, when that debate comes on, you will not accuse me of waving the bloody shirt, or will not fall to abusing the New England Puritans, which are the two answers.

Mr. President, not my honorable friend from Delaware [Mr. Gray], who occasionally, when he gets out of a party question, has some wisdom in his head I admit—but the whole of the other side of the Chamber, with scarcely an exception, went beyond the Constitution, beyond the Constitution as they themselves interpret it and declare it, to protect the people of the United States from the effect on their commerce and industries of the greed of speculators in regard to the matter of dealing in options and futures. We do not hear much of its being an insult to a State not to let it regulate, wherever it please, its boards of trade, its cotton brokers, and its speculators in wheat or grain, but when it comes to casting votes for Representatives of the United States who are to determine my interest as much as yours (Delaware or Virginia elects a Representative, but when he is chosen he represents Massachusetts as much as he does Virginia), it is an insult if I say I think it is worth while that at least there should be an officer of the United States present to see fair play. . . .

Mr. President, the nation must protect its own. Every citizen whose right is imperilled if he be but one, when it is a right of national citizenship and a right conferred and enjoyed under the Constitution of the United States, has the right to demand for its protection the entire force of the United States until the Army has spent its last man and the Navy has fired its last gun. Most of us have nothing else than the right to vote. In the wealthiest nation the average man can have but little wealth. We have no titles of nobility, we have no decorations of honor, we have no superiorities of rank. We have not the luxuries or the glories which belong to foreign nations, of architecture or of art, which belong to the whole people. It is a plain, simple, arid, desert life but for this one thing which is worth all the rest, the dignity, the nobility, the honor of American citizenship. The urn in which the American casts his ballot ought to be, aye, and it shall be, as sacred as a sacramental vessel.

You are undertaking to-day to destroy the last safeguard which the power of this country places around the dignity and glory of its citizenship. You tried some years ago to destroy the glory and the sanctity of the flag itself which had no other glory and no other sanctity except as it represented this right of American citizenship. You failed then and you will fail now.

MR. GRAY. . . .

No one admires more than I do the beautiful peroration with which the Senator from Massachusetts closed his speech. I have heard it before. I admired it then. It was worth repeating. But, Mr. President, the Senator from Massachusetts must not think that because he is animated, as doubtless he is, by this nobility of thought and aspiration, those who sit on the darkened side of this Chamber have not some feeble glimmerings of light on their pathway that excites in them sometimes a desire for the glory, the honor, the perpetuity and safety of our institutions. He seems to have missed altogether the gravamen of the charge that has been made on this side against the election laws which we now propose to repeal.

Apart from the constitutional question, it is not that these laws were made to preserve the purity of elections that we want to destroy them; it is not because we believe the laws protect the weak against the strong that we want to wipe them from the statute book. It is because we believe from a bitter experience that not only are they at war with every tradition of local self-government, not only do they degrade the States of which we are citizens, but they buttress up the very fraud which you profess (and I will not say dishonestly profess) that they were intended to destroy. They have been necessarily, from the inherent vice of their structure, a mere adjunct and auxiliary to the party machine of the party in power in the Federal Government.

In every city of over 20,000 inhabitants, they have been the ready means by which in the last twenty years the Republican party has put its hands into the Treasury of the United States, in order to defray the election expenses and campaign charges of their own party. There can not be a successful denial of that statement; I have seen it, and every man who lives in a town